The Intellectual Sword

"Protesters inside University Hall during takeover at Harvard," April 9 to April 10, 1969.

Courtesy of Harvard University Archives.

The
Intellectual
Sword

HARVARD LAW SCHOOL,
THE SECOND CENTURY

Bruce A. Kimball
Daniel R. Coquillette

THE BELKNAP PRESS OF
HARVARD UNIVERSITY PRESS

Cambridge, Massachusetts
London, England
2020

First printing

Library of Congress Cataloging-in-Publication Data

Names: Kimball, Bruce A., 1951– author. | Coquillette, Daniel R., author.
Title: The intellectual sword : Harvard Law School, the second century /
Bruce A. Kimball and Daniel R. Coquillette.
Description: Cambridge, Massachusetts : The Belknap Press of Harvard
University Press, 2020. | Includes index.
Identifiers: LCCN 2019045242 | ISBN 9780674737327 (cloth)
Subjects: LCSH: Harvard Law School—History—20th century. | Law—Study
and teaching (Higher)—Massachusetts—Cambridge—History—20th century.
Classification: LCC KF292.H344 K56 2020 | DDC 340.071/17444—dc23
LC record available at https://lccn.loc.gov/2019045242

In the universe of truth, they lived by the sword: they asked
no quarter of absolutes, and they gave none.

JUDGE LEARNED HAND,
The Bill of Rights: The Oliver Wendell Holmes Lectures (1958)

One would scarcely expect to ask for quarter in the world into
which we shall so soon be thrown. Certainly none
would be given!

"A Defense of Harvard Law School by a Graduate of Yale College,"
The Student Looks at Harvard Law School (1934)

Contents

Preface

This second volume of our history of Harvard Law School, like *Battlefield of Merit,* could not have been completed without the invaluable help of many different people, to whom we are deeply grateful. Kathleen McDermott, Executive Editor for History at Harvard University Press, has been immensely helpful in guiding both volumes to publication. While this work was not authorized by Harvard Law School, the staff of the Harvard Law School Library, particularly the Historical and Special Collections Department, including former director David Warrington, current manager Karen S. Beck, and Lesley Schoenfeld of Visual Collections and Melinda Kent in Research Services, have aided us tremendously, as have the Boston College Law School librarians, particularly Mark Sullivan and Laurel Davis, Curator of Rare Books. Thompson Potter, faculty administrative assistant at Harvard Law School, has provided enthusiastic and thoughtful support for both volumes for more than two decades.

In addition, Marija Tesla, the editorial assistant to the Monan Chair at Boston College, and Sarah M. Iler, Lecturer in Educational Studies at Ohio State University, have provided truly invaluable assistance, dedication, and intelligence that mark every page. During the past twenty years, our intrepid students and dedicated research assistants—particularly Kayleigh McGlynn and Nathan Pak of Boston College Law School and Benjamin Johnson and Jeremy Luke at Ohio State University—have scoured the archives at Harvard and elsewhere on myriad topics, often finding that a document sealed in one archive was accessible in another. Overall, the students have produced some 350 research papers and memos contributing enormously to our research, and a bibliography of their works cited in this volume appears in Appendix K. Their excellent assistance is deeply appreciated. We are also grateful to Rebecca Kimball and Sarah Iler for designing Figures 2.1, 5.1, and 14.1.

At various points over the past two decades, more than a hundred individuals have contributed oral histories or interviews to our research. Nearly sixty individuals provided oral histories or conducted interviews with us or with scholars associated with our project, particularly Daniel Hamilton and Mary Beth (Basile) Chopas, to whom we are greatly indebted. In fact, an oral history was completed with most major, living administrative figures at Harvard Law School, many key members of the faculty and staff employed through the early 1990s, and some alumni and other informed persons. In the course of writing research papers, our students and research assistants conducted another forty interviews with various individuals, including, for example, early women and Latino graduates who studied at the Law School. These oral histories and interviews, which are cited throughout this volume, provide invaluable first-hand accounts of critical events in the history of the school.

A few of those interviewed sealed parts of their oral history, but even in these cases, we were permitted to draw on these recollections for background and to corroborate our interpretation of the significant controversies during the twentieth century. In addition to the oral histories and interviews, many individuals gave us their personal copies of hundreds of memos, letters, and fugitive documents. These documents, many of which are not available in institutional archives, amplified our research materials considerably.

Several scholars made helpful contributions by reading and criticizing numerous chapters of the manuscript at various stages and provided valuable feedback from different perspectives: Mary Beth (Basile) Chopas, Gail M. Hupper, J. Bruce Blain, Jackie M. Blount, and Alexander M. Wolf (J.D. 2012). We are also indebted to legal historians John H. Schlegel and Robert W. Gordon, who reviewed the entire manuscript for Harvard University Press and provided insightful feedback.

In addition, we gratefully acknowledge that the bulk of financial support for the research for this volume was provided by our respective institutions: Ohio State University and Boston College. We also wish to thank the Ames Foundation, particularly Literary Directors Charles Donahue and Mary Bilder, for their support of this research for over a decade.

This volume, like *Battlefield of Merit,* has resulted from a close collaboration between two coauthors having distinct points of view and areas of academic and administrative expertise: one a legal scholar and historian and former law school dean at Boston College and long-time visiting professor at

Harvard Law School; the other a historian of American higher education and former Liberal Arts Fellow at Harvard Law School and dean and faculty member at Yale, Houston, Rochester, and Ohio State universities. We have balanced and extended our intellectual perspectives and expertise by consulting every step of the way.

Beginning in about 1995 and lasting over twenty-five years, it has been a long, challenging, and fascinating scholarly project, and the research continues, as we discuss in the conclusion.

Abbreviations

AALS	Association of American Law Schools
ABA	American Bar Association
ACLU	American Civil Liberties Union
AES Papers	Arthur E. Sutherland Papers, 1923–1972, Harvard Law School Library Historical & Special Collections
ALL Records	Harvard Law School Dean's Office Records, Records of President A. Lawrence Lowell, 1909–1933, Harvard University Archives
Battlefield of Merit	Daniel R. Coquillette and Bruce A. Kimball, *On the Battlefield of Merit: Harvard Law School, the First Century* (Cambridge, MA, 2015)
Big Mac	Student Advisory Committee to the Michelman Committee
BLSA	Harvard Black Law Student Association
CAB	Civil Aeronautics Board
CBS	Columbia Business School
CEPD	Harvard Law School Committee on Educational Planning and Development
CLAO	Community Legal Assistance Office

CLS	Columbia Law School
CLS	Critical Legal Studies
CMS	Columbia University College of Physicians and Surgeons (Columbia Medical School)
CWE Papers	Papers and Presidential Records of Charles W. Eliot, 1807–1945, Harvard University Archives
ENG Papers	Erwin N. Griswold Papers, 1925–1994, Harvard Law School Library Historical & Special Collections
ERT Papers	Ezra Ripley Thayer Papers, 1882–1915, Harvard Law School Library Historical & Special Collections
FBI	Federal Bureau of Investigation
HBS	Harvard Graduate School of Business Administration (Harvard Business School)
HEF Records	Records of the Harvard Endowment Fund, 1916–1939, Harvard University Archives
HLR	*Harvard Law Review*
HLS	Harvard Law School
HLSB	*Harvard Law School Bulletin / Harvard Law Bulletin*
HLSF Records	Records of the Harvard Law School Fund, 1949–1976, Harvard University Archives
HLSLib	Harvard Law School Library Historical & Special Collections
HLSR	*Harvard Law School Record* (1946–1955) / *Harvard Law Record* (1956–)
HLW	Harvard Law Wives
HMS	Harvard Medical School
HUA	Harvard University Archives
HUAC	House Committee on Un-American Activities
ILS	International Legal Studies

JBC Records Harvard Law School Dean's Office Records, Records of President James B. Conant, 1933–1953, Harvard University Archives

JBT Papers James Bradley Thayer Papers, 1787–1902, Harvard Law School Library Historical & Special Collections

JML Papers James McCauley Landis Papers, 1899–1964, Harvard Law School Library Historical & Special Collections

JPJ Records John Price Jones Co. Records, 1919–1954, Harvard Business School Library Special Collections

LDF Legal Defense Fund

LSAT Law School Admission Test

LSC Law School Council

LSI Legal Services Institute

MRH Papers Marcia R. Harrison Papers, 1935–1998, Harvard Law School Library Historical & Special Collections

NLG National Lawyers Guild

NMP Records Harvard Law School Dean's Office Records, Records of President Nathan M. Pusey, 1953–1971, Harvard University Archives

NSSE National Selective Service Examination

OBU Organization for Black Unity

ROTC Reserve Officers' Training Corps

RP Papers Roscoe Pound Papers, 1888–1964, Harvard Law School Library Historical & Special Collections

SDS Students for a Democratic Society

SEC Securities and Exchange Commission

SISS Senate Internal Security Subcommittee

SSP Special Summer Program

WLA   Women's Law Association

YLS   Yale Law School

YUS Records   Yale University Secretary's Office Records, 1899–1953, ser. 3, Yale University Library Manuscripts and Archives

ZCJ Papers   Zechariah Chafee Jr. Papers, 1898–1957, Harvard Law School Library Historical & Special Collections

The Intellectual Sword

Introduction

There is "so much Harvard history I don't know about, and would really prefer not to," remarked Harvard Law School dean Elena Kagan (2003–2009) in 2008 at the fifty-fifth anniversary of the first graduation of women from the school.[1] This remark by Dean Kagan (J.D. 1986), who became a Supreme Court Justice in 2010, demonstrates one kind of challenge in writing about the history of the Law School. Another challenge stems from the myths created by the large body of contentious and dramatic literature, including novels, Hollywood movies, and celebratory and "attack" histories, as discussed in the introduction to our first volume, *On the Battlefield of Merit*. Even in the 2010s, new movies portraying Harvard Law School have obscured or skewed the historical record of events. Finally, there is the historiographical challenge. Histories of individual educational institutions have often been parochial and contributed little to scholarship beyond the particular institution.[2]

Given this background, *Battlefield of Merit* attempted to examine the first century of the school's history in light of developments in higher education and the nation, while recognizing the complexity of motivations and forces at work. We wrote what Stanford legal historian Robert W. Gordon, in a personal communication, called "an unvarnished institutional history for grownups."[3] Inevitably, some reviewers charged that the book included anachronistic, politically correct criticism of historical events, and others suggested that the book excused, or even justified, past prejudice on the very same events.[4] Nevertheless, we were gratified that a scholarly association outside of the fields of law and legal education recognized the work for its original contribution to the history of nonprofit organizations.[5] Still, the question remains: Why should one study the history of Harvard Law School?

Why Does the Study of History Matter?

More broadly, why study history at all? This question was also suggested by Justice Kagan, a history major at Princeton University, when she remarked, at the bicentennial celebration of Harvard Law School in 2017, that she turned from studying history to law because she "wanted what I did to matter."[6] Indeed, how does historical scholarship make a difference? And why does the history of *this* institution deserve attention?

Several foundations and academic and legal associations repeatedly turned down our applications to support the research for this volume. After all, they said, Harvard is studied all the time, and everything important about the history of Harvard Law School is probably known already. While granting that research on neglected institutions provides important new knowledge, we also believe that our historical inquiry into this law school has yielded significant new findings and insights.

One example appeared in the seemingly parochial controversy over the Harvard Law School shield beginning in fall 2015. Created for the tercentenary celebration of Harvard University in 1936, the shield had a faux design implying a much older pedigree. Depicting three sheaves of grain standing in a field, the shield was modeled on the family coat of arms of Isaac Royall Jr., who died in 1781 and bequeathed an endowment that, in 1817, funded the first professorship of law at Harvard University. Royall's wealth came from the family's sugar plantation in Antigua, which was worked by enslaved people under brutal conditions.[7]

The source of Royall's fortune may have been unknown or simply forgotten in 1936, or the design may be another instance of historical depictions ignoring exploited and marginalized groups. In any case, three historical facts were linked through the tercentenary celebration of Harvard University in 1936: the Harvard Law School shield was based on the Royall family coat of arms; Isaac Royall endowed the first law professorship at Harvard; and that endowment came from wealth created by enslaved people.

By fall 2015, when *Battlefield of Merit* publicized those three related facts, the shield had become the official, ubiquitous emblem of Harvard Law School. Soon thereafter, law students began to protest the school's widespread use of the shield. At the same time, similar protests erupted over the naming of John C. Calhoun College at Yale University and the Woodrow Wilson School of Public and International Affairs at Princeton University, all concurrent with the Black Lives Matter movement.[8] Spanning several months, the ensuing controversy at Harvard Law School was widely reported across the

United States and elsewhere in the world.[9] In the spring of 2016, a faculty-student-alumni committee and Dean Martha L. Minow (2009–2017) recommended, and the Harvard Corporation (the university's governing board) agreed, that the school should "retire" the shield as its "image and trademark."[10] Then, late in 2019, the Prime Minister of Antigua wrote to Harvard demanding that the university pay reparations "for the gains Harvard enjoyed at the expense" of Antiguans who were enslaved. Concurrently, Dean John F. Manning (J.D. 1985) formed a working group at the Law School to develop a new shield.[11] These developments demonstrate how knowledge of the past shapes our understanding and evaluation of the present.

But that is not the end of the story. Even the history of the seemingly narrow topic of the Harvard Law School shield is more complicated and consequential than was appreciated in 2016. The three historical facts above had been discussed separately in a few publications since 1936. But the relationship among all three, which sparked the student protest in 2015, was apparently published for the first time only in 2000 in an article written by Daniel Coquillette (J.D. 1971).[12] In the subsequent decade, Alexandra Chan, Elizabeth Papp Kamali (J.D. 2007), Janet Halley, and Coquillette contributed further research.[13] But why had knowledge of the links among those three facts been overlooked between 1936 and 2000?

One reason is that the Law School paid little attention to its new shield in 1936, likely because the Harvard Corporation did not officially sanction the shield, and merely expressed "no objection" to its "use for decorative purposes."[14] Because the Law School ignored the shield, its origin in the Royall family coat of arms was apparently forgotten following the university's tercentenary celebration in 1936. This much was known in the academic year 2015–16, but, even then, it was not recognized that the Law School had revived the shield in 1948 while assigning it a new origin and a new meaning, as discussed in Chapter 10 of this volume.[15]

During the 1950s and 1960s, the shield appeared occasionally and unofficially, with the link to Isaac Royall still forgotten. The *Harvard Law School Record* added the shield to its masthead in 1954, only to drop it in 1968.[16] Then usage of the shield as an informal logo for the school began to increase in the 1970s, when advertising exploded in higher education. Colleges and universities started employing "promotional tactics" to compete in what they began to call the "marketplace" of higher education. Often at the behest of their trustees, universities retained marketing consultants who advised them to standardize and elevate their emblems and logos in their signage, publications, decor, and so forth.[17]

In 1969 the *Harvard Law School Record* began to feature advertisements from the Harvard bookstore for ties, chairs, and shot glasses embossed with the shield, and in 1973 the *Harvard Law School Alumni Directory* started to feature the shield on its cover and title pages.[18] In 1974 the dean's office sought a "logo" for the school's stationary and students' academic transcripts, and the curator of the Harvard Law School Art Collection recommended the shield with three sheaves, while reasserting its origin in the Royall coat of arms. In 1975 Dean Albert M. Sacks (1971–1981) declared the shield "official" for the first time, and the *Harvard Law School Bulletin* announced, "The School now has an official seal. . . . It represents the coat of arms of Isaac Royall, founding father of the Law School." The registrar then began using the shield on the embossing stamp of academic transcripts.[19] The fact that Royall's wealth was acquired through the labor of brutally enslaved people remained ignored or forgotten.[20]

In the 1980s and 1990s, the shield, though still not authorized by the Harvard Corporation, rapidly became the ubiquitous emblem of the Law School, commensurate with the "branding" efforts throughout higher education, to use the term of Derek C. Bok (LL.B. 1954). In its first issue for the 1984–85 year, the *Harvard Law School Record* reinserted the shield on its masthead without explanation, and it began to appear on banners, carpets, stained glass, lecterns, and publications.[21] If not for these marketing and branding efforts between 1980 and 2000, the controversy over the shield in 2015–16 might not have gained momentum, because the ubiquity of the shield was a central complaint of those arguing to eliminate it.

The retirement of the shield in 2016 thus followed at least five stages of historical revisionism: the 1936 faux design suggesting a much older pedigree; the 1948 revival of the shield and reinterpretation of its meaning; the dean's authorization of the shield in 1975 as the school's "official seal" and the reassertion of its origin in the Royall coat of arms; the 1970–2000 marketing and branding efforts that made it ubiquitous; and the 2000 publication first linking the seal to wealth acquired from the labor of brutally enslaved people. These revisions demonstrate how historical knowledge informs and complicates present understanding, as well as the difficulty of trying to "correct" historical memorials or symbols at any particular time.[22]

Isomorphism: A University Professional School

More generally, the history of Harvard Law School matters due to the school's extensive impact on legal education, on professional education more broadly, and, therefore, on American society. The impact was recognized by historian

Robert Stevens, who observed that "Harvard set the style" of legal education in the United States at the end of the nineteenth century.[23] This influence exemplifies what social scientists have called "isomorphism": the process by which institutions in a social domain tend to replicate the organizational structures and policies of the dominant or preeminent institutions. This replication results in organizational homogeneity among institutions throughout the domain.[24]

To explain this phenomenon, social scientists have developed a theory known as "new institutionalism." The basic idea is that new or marginal institutions in a given domain need legitimacy in order to establish or advance themselves. To acquire that legitimacy, they adopt the organizational structures and practices of the premier institutions and then embrace them as their own. As a result, the great majority of institutions begin to acquire the same structure and policies over time, and the domain exhibits isomorphism.[25]

Other explanations are certainly plausible. Perhaps some replicated structures and policies have proliferated among institutions simply because they work. In other words, the structures and policies have functioned effectively to improve education, and other professional schools adopted them. This functionalist explanation has been rejected by most sociologists studying professions and professional education over the past five decades. They generally prefer instead some variant of the "new institutionalism" theory.[26] Nevertheless, we maintain that both the straightforward functionalist explanation and the subliminal drive for legitimacy or status contribute to explaining organizational homogeneity within legal education.

Whatever the theoretical explanation, *Battlefield of Merit* proposed that the institutional template of university professional education began much earlier, extended more broadly, and covered more dimensions than historians have recognized. We argued, in fact, that this template originated at Harvard Law School early in the nineteenth century and defined the contours of the American university professional school by the beginning of the twentieth century.

Our thesis that Harvard Law School pioneered the formation of the national university professional school after its founding in 1817 challenged the standard interpretation of the emergence of professional education in the United States. Scholars have long maintained that the idea of a "profession"—entailing graduate education in a university professional school—emerged in conjunction with the development of medical schools in the Progressive Era, which extended from about 1890 to 1920. This view assumed that medicine was the "prototypical" and "paradigmatic" profession, and that "the rise of medicine" and "the rise of . . . professions" were synonymous.[27] For example, in a canonical 1968 article, sociologist Talcott Parsons wrote that medicine "spearheaded . . . the marriage of the university system to the practicing professions in the United States."[28] Subsequently, even sociologists who qualified or rejected Parsons's theoretical perspective—such as Magali Larson, Paul Starr, Eliot Freidson—nevertheless presumed the "ideal-typical" or "archetypal" stature of the medical profession and medical schools.[29]

Historical scholarship assumed this, as well. For example, the leading historical analysis of university business schools by Rakesh Khurana was "directly inspired by . . . the origins and development of American medicine," as set forth by sociologist Paul Starr.[30] Such historiography cast Johns Hopkins University Medical School as the pioneering professional school, though it opened only in 1893 with four students and its leadership had already begun to wane by 1915 due to its failure to keep pace with other schools in financial resources.[31] Instead, *Battlefield of Merit* advanced the thesis that Harvard Law School initiated the organizational isomorphism of national university professional schools much earlier in the nineteenth century.

The Law School's radically new model comprised three fundamental innovations: locating the nonproprietary, degree-granting, professional school in a university; recruiting students nationally; and instituting a "new system" of professional education that measured students' professional merit in terms of their academic achievement.[32] That system included the admissions requirement of a bachelor's degree, a multiyear curriculum, tiered coursework with advanced electives requiring introductory courses, demanding written examinations, rigorous grading, and case method teaching, an inductive system of teaching through Socratic questioning about original sources.

In this volume, we argue that the widespread influence of the Law School persisted during the twentieth century, as, for example, in the proliferation of case method teaching. But in the twentieth century the Law School exerted this influence primarily within the field of legal education rather than across professional education, as it had in the nineteenth century. And, in financial terms, Harvard's impact on law schools was highly detrimental.

Financial Isomorphism

In addition to the thesis about organizational replication, *Battlefield of Merit* broke new ground by probing finances, which have generally been neglected in historical scholarship about professional education. We found that the development of university professional schools and the adoption of the "new system" of academic merit entailed four financial innovations, which were cardinal attributes of the financial isomorphism that came to prevail among national university professional schools.

First, beginning in the 1820s Harvard Law School adopted a new mode of compensating faculty. Remuneration of faculty shifted from a proprietary model—whereby students paid fees directly to the instructors—to a salaried model, whereby students remitted tuition to the institution, which paid a set annual salary to the faculty. Second, in the 1870s Dean Christopher C. Langdell (1870–1905) rejected the traditional preference for hiring experienced, successful professionals to the faculty. Instead, he sought scholarly recent graduates, believing that the faculty of a university professional school devoted to academic merit should consist predominantly of scholars. This change generated much opposition, but it saved money and strengthened the compensation model of paying set salaries.

Third, the Law School introduced a new financial model for university professional schools. Under the prevailing proprietary model, schools of law, medicine, and other professions in the nineteenth century charged relatively low tuition, admitted nearly all applicants, and required scarcely any academic work or evaluation. But Langdell and Harvard University President Charles W. Eliot (1869–1909) speculated that a high-standards, high-cost model would be financially viable because better-trained graduates would be more employable and therefore ambitious and talented students would seek to enroll. This turned out to be the case, and excellent students began flocking to Harvard Law School in the 1880s.

Fourth, the high-standards, high-cost model not only worked but led to prosperity, as the growing student body paying high tuition produced a sizable annual surplus. In the proprietary model this would have gone into the pockets of the faculty, but under the salaried model the surplus accrued to the school. Hence, by 1895 Harvard Law School had become the wealthiest university professional school in the nation, with the greatest amount of invested endowment and reserve funds.

Building on these four financial developments in university professional schools, this volume proposes that the financial homogeneity derived from Harvard Law School continued within legal education during the twentieth century. But this development was detrimental to law schools, we argue. The problems began in the first decade of the twentieth century, when wealthy Harvard Law School made a series of incredible missteps and impoverished itself.[33] Under Dean Ezra R. Thayer (1910–1915), the school fell into the debilitating syndrome of tuition dependence, which included high student enrollment, high student-faculty ratio, and relatively little external support from philanthropy, subsidies, or endowment income. These factors had yielded huge annual surpluses at the end of the nineteenth century, but concomitantly they made the school vulnerable in two respects.

On the one hand, after constructing its immense new building, Langdell Hall, Harvard Law School became heavily dependent on tuition to meet its annual expenses. On the other hand, the school's large annual revenue from tuition created the illusion of prosperity. Harvard presidents therefore did not regard the Law School's tuition dependence as a problem, though they did so for every other school and department at Harvard. Unlike all other departments and schools at the university, the Law School did not need endowment income, philanthropy, or subsidies to sustain it, the presidents believed. The syndrome of tuition dependence worsened under Dean Roscoe Pound (1916–1936) and then plagued the administration of Dean James M. Landis (1937–1946). The syndrome deepened under Dean Erwin N. Griswold (1946–1967)—even though he wished to escape it and he vastly increased the school's income—and his successor Dean Albert M. Sacks (1971–1981) struggled under the same pressures during the 1970s.[34]

Meanwhile, leading university professional schools in other major professions recognized and avoided the syndrome of tuition dependence during the first half of the twentieth century, as seen at Harvard and Columbia Universities and discussed in Chapter 9. Hence, during the twentieth century, Harvard Law School initiated a detrimental financial isomorphism in legal education, whereby law schools "must live from hand to mouth," as both Dean Pound in 1919 and Dean Griswold in 1962 lamented.[35] And if preeminent Harvard Law School depended so heavily on tuition reaped from huge classes, how could other law schools justify appeals for endowment, philanthropy, or subsidies at their universities? Law schools therefore found it much more difficult to secure external support, compared with other major professional schools. Even Harvard Law School did not run a truly successful fundraising campaign until the 1990s, under Dean Robert C. Clark (1989–2003).[36] Only a few exceptions to this syndrome existed in legal education. The leading one was Yale Law School, as explained in Chapter 15.

Flourishing, indeed surviving, while constrained by the syndrome of tuition dependence that prevailed throughout legal education, required a large and growing number of smart, well-educated, and hardworking applicants. As the number of law students and law schools rose steadily in the late twentieth century, legal education became a virtual Ponzi scheme. Law schools were vulnerable to a significant decline in the number of such applicants at some future time. Such a moment these schools could scarcely imagine throughout the twentieth century. But they were highly vulnerable just the same. The seeds of that vulnerability were planted at Harvard Law School early in the twentieth century, and cultivated in succeeding generations.

The Intellectual Sword

Beyond constraining finances, the syndrome of tuition dependence reinforced the combative and competitive culture at Harvard Law School, which, by way of metaphor, supplies the title for this volume.[37] In fact, the "ask and give no quarter" ethos at Harvard Law School arose concurrently with the realization after 1907 that prosperous Harvard Law School had impoverished itself. Only then did the infamous "Paper Chase" begin.[38] The fierce competition and aggressive pedagogy at the Law School were exacerbated by the contemporaneous "manly" culture at Harvard University.[39] In 1942, Professor Edward H. "Bull" Warren (LL.B. 1900) celebrated this cultural shift in his book *Spartan Education*.[40]

During the deanship of Ezra Thayer, the faculty started treating the attrition rate as an index of academic quality and deliberately tried to flunk students out of the school. The academic pressure abated from the time of Thayer's tragic death in 1915 until the end of World War I, due to the turmoil of the period. But during the 1920s under Dean Pound, the sword of attrition was unsheathed, and wielded again even more vigorously as the school made more financial missteps.

In the 1920s and 1930s, the academic culture and the constrained finances of the school reinforced each other. The financial pressure exerted by the syndrome of tuition dependence worsened the aggressive academic culture. The school had to admit more students in order to pay the bills, and then had to fail more in order to maintain its high academic standards. By the late 1930s the detrimental interaction between the school's finances and its academic culture and policies was explicitly recognized in various studies and reports. But President James B. Conant (1933–1953) did not support alleviating either pressure, and Dean Landis was preoccupied with matters outside of the school.

After a hiatus in the tumultuous 1940s, the interaction between financial and cultural forces intensified once again during the tenure of Dean Griswold. In fact, these two forces became more deeply enmeshed, notwithstanding the school's shift toward assessing the academic quality of the student body based on admissions selectivity rather than the attrition rate. During the 1950s and 1960s, the success of an alternative model—in both finances and academic culture—presented by Yale Law School began pressuring Harvard Law School to change its academic policies. Serious financial and cultural reform commenced under Dean Derek Bok (1968–1970) but then slowed under Dean Sacks, partly because the syndrome of tuition dependence continued to limit the opportunities for reform. In fact, the syndrome strangled the school ever more tightly, as it became increasingly dependent on the revenue generated by high tuition, which rose in great leaps between 1948 and 1981.

Meanwhile, the debilitating financial syndrome and the Spartan culture also reinforced the school's resistance to demographic diversity. The "ask and give no quarter" ethos contributed to the school's failure to admit, recruit, or welcome students and faculty who were not white, Christian men. Thus, the school's reception of Jewish students and faculty early in the twentieth century—and women and people of color throughout the century—was generally dismal. This interaction between the three factors was further complicated by the social and political upheavals that buffeted the school during the twentieth century.

One such upheaval was the Red Scare hysteria that began in 1919, prompted by the specter of the Bolshevik revolution in Russia, the influx of thousands of immigrants from southern and eastern Europe, and the rise of unionism that made 1919 "the most-strife-torn year in United States history."[41] These developments led to vilifying immigrants. Urged by Senate majority leader Henry Cabot Lodge (LL.B. 1874), Congress enacted the Emergency Immigration Act (1921) and the National Origins Act (1924), which dramatically curtailed immigration.[42]

The spreading xenophobia and fear of left-wing radicalism also prompted a series of trials in the 1920s involving prominent figures at Harvard Law School, particularly Zechariah Chafee Jr. (LL.B. 1913), Felix Frankfurter (LL.B. 1906), and President A. Lawrence Lowell (1909–1933). Furthermore, President Lowell restricted the enrollment of nonwhite students at Harvard, forbade the enrollment of women, and obstructed the enrollment of Jewish students and the employment of Jewish faculty. Concurrently, the jurisprudence of aging Dean Roscoe Pound and of the entire Law School was challenged by the new movement of legal realism and the empirical study of social influences on law.

The onset of the Great Depression brought more upheaval, resulting in the landslide election of President Franklin D. Roosevelt in 1932 and his "new deal for the American people." This revolutionized not only the federal government's relationship with its citizens but also jurisprudence, by vastly expanding administrative agencies and law. Harvard Law professors Felix Frankfurter and James Landis played central roles and recruited dozens of colleagues and recent graduates from the Law School to join them, including Alger Hiss (LL.B. 1929).

Meanwhile, Dean Pound achieved a very different kind of notoriety. Through the mid-1930s he accepted honors from the Nazi regime in Germany and publicly condoned Nazi rule. At the time, the American and foreign press reported and condemned Pound's actions, and newly declassified FBI files in Washington and the German Foreign Affairs Office in Berlin reveal that the Nazi regime deliberately cultivated Pound's favor and that he socialized with leading Nazis during his visits to Austria in the mid-1930s. Furthermore, before, during, and after World War II, Pound defended and supported his pro-Nazi, German advisee and special assistant at Harvard Law School, who was incarcerated by the U.S. government during the war. All this apparently stemmed from Pound's long-standing affection for German culture, his extreme vanity exploited by the German Foreign office, and his notorious high-handed refusal to admit that he had made mistakes, as we explain in Chapter 7.

In the late 1940s the deteriorating relations between the United States and the Soviet Union prompted the second Red Scare, which spawned the demagoguery of Wisconsin senator Joseph R. McCarthy between 1950 and 1954. The widespread fear and controversy inevitably engaged those at the Law School. The crisis of McCarthyism cost at least two students their membership in the *Harvard Law School Record,* the *Harvard Law Review,* or the Legal Aid Bureau. This crisis also prompted a famous reinterpretation of the Fifth Amendment right against self-incrimination, which has been credited to Griswold. But our analysis shows that the two ostracized students actually originated the doctrinal innovation, which the dean then advanced.

Under Griswold, the Law School also radically reformed its admissions policies. In 1949 the Harvard Law School faculty voted to admit women, as they had in 1899, 1909, 1910, and 1942. But in 1949 the Harvard Corporation finally approved the change. In addition, the school shifted from a threshold approach, which entitled to admission any applicant who met a certain level of academic attainment, to a selective approach, whereby the school selected among all applicants by comparing their credentials. We analyze these admissions revolutions, as well as the courageous persistence of the newly admitted women despite the ambivalent, if not hostile, reception by the Griswold administration. We also examine the experience of the few Latino and African American students and the belated efforts to attract them to the school in the 1960s.

In fall 1967, Dean Griswold stepped down to become U.S. solicitor general, as unrest smoldered at the school, fed by dissatisfaction with the aggressive culture, discontent over the under-enrollment of women and people of color, demands for justice by the Civil Rights movement, and opposition to the Vietnam War. Soon after Griswold departed, Harvard Law School exploded, along with the rest of Harvard University, between 1968 and 1970. This period encompassed Derek Bok's tenure as dean, and his skill in managing the crises led to his elevation to the presidency of Harvard University in 1971.

During the "very difficult" decade under Dean Sacks, Harvard Law School made small, slow steps toward opening the student body and faculty to women and people of color, although the school did better in some respects than the average of ABA-accredited law schools. Meanwhile, the breadth and depth of extracurricular opportunities and clinical programs available to students greatly expanded during Sacks's administration, offering students new ways to survive and thrive within the Spartan culture of the Law School. The faculty also made an extensive study of the formal curriculum through a committee chaired by Frank I. Michelman (LL.B. 1960). However, the study ultimately yielded little substantive change, due to dissension among the faculty that boiled into "hatred" during the term of Dean James Vorenberg (1981–1989).[43]

The 1980s

This volume concludes in the 1980s, a decade when the very idea of professions was under siege in American society and higher education. This attack marked a significant turn in the broad movement of professionalization in the United States, which had been launched a century earlier.[44] By the 1890s the term "profession" in American culture had come to denote a dignified vocation pursued by persons who employed sophisticated expertise acquired through specialized study, who organized themselves into a strong association or guild, and who espoused an altruistic ethic of service to their clients or patients. Professions were then idealized during the Progressive Era, as the president of the ABA, among many others, extolled "the true professional ideal."[45]

Comprising those three fundamental attributes, professions constituted what sociologists have called "the third logic" for the nature of work in the United States during the twentieth century. The second logic is that of bureaucracy and the state, in which jobs are defined by function and organized in a hierarchical pyramid of ascending authority. The first, often most powerful, logic of work is that of the marketplace and business, in which capital and labor compete for benefits.[46] These three "logics" of work are said to balance each other in the economic and social spheres. In fact, British scholar R. H. Tawney insightfully argued in 1920 that, in modern society, professions serve as the major bulwark against the overweening power of capitalism and business.[47]

In the 1890s the preeminence of Harvard Law School, along with Johns Hopkins University Medical School, therefore coincided with the emergence and idealization of professionalism. This coincidence magnified the stature of the leading university professional schools, particularly in law and medicine, which appeared to stand at the vanguard of social, educational, and national development. Through the 1950s and early 1960s, professionalism, professions, and professional schools ascended ever higher in status and authority in American society. More and more vocations sought to claim the title of "profession," and scholars even began to anticipate "the professionalization of everyone."[48] Culminating this trend in 1968, Talcott Parsons, in his canonical article, declared professions to be "the most important single component in the structure of modern societies."[49] At that point, this "third logic" of work seemed nearly invincible.

Parsons also advanced the theory of structural functionalism to explain and justify the three fundamental attributes of a profession. According to this theory, professionals' functional scientific expertise legitimates their authority over clients and patients, and the guild organization, defined by licensure, serves as the gatekeeper, preventing those without the requisite expertise from practicing the vocation. The service ethic ensures that professionals police each other and serve the interests of the laity. Furthermore, the degree of scientific validity of the professional expertise determines and justifies the hierarchy among professions in status, authority, and social resources.[50]

This sociological theory was tailored to fit medicine because, by 1950, medicine was considered the undisputed "queen of professions," the "prototypical" and "paradigmatic" profession.[51] University medical schools eclipsed other professional schools on practically every dimension between 1900 and 1950, to the consternation of those at Harvard Law School, as described in Chapter 9.

However, the bloom of the professional ideal withered during the late 1960s and the 1970s. Commensurate with the widespread social and political upheaval and "the debunking spirit of much of American social science," praise of professions turned to disdain in these decades.[52] The authority, status, and seeming invincibility of professions made them inviting targets for critical scholarship. In fact, "the very idea of profession was attacked, implying, if not stating, that the world would be better off without professions."[53] During the 1970s, critical sociologists anathematized Talcott Parsons and derided his theory of structural functionalism for legitimating the power of elites. Indeed, "power" became the watchword of the new theorists of professions during the 1970s and 1980s. These debunkers viewed professions purely as "market organizations attempting the intellectual and organizational domination of areas of social concern," and they took aim primarily at medicine.[54]

One regiment in this widespread attack on professions, including university professional schools, comprised the adherents of Critical Legal Studies, who concurrently began to "unmask" the law, the legal profession, and Harvard Law School as the agents of elite and capitalist interests, as described in Chapter 19. But it is important to see that such attacks were occurring across the entire professional complex. As a result, all the professions seemed to be undergoing "proletarianization."[55] Some scholars anticipated the "deprofessionalization of everyone," including lawyers.[56] Indeed, after being weakened by the critical sociologists in the 1970s, the "third logic" of professionalism began to capitulate to the logic of the marketplace and business in the 1980s and 1990s.[57] Doctors' practices and lawyers' firms were increasingly corporatized and reshaped by market forces. The bulwark envisioned by R. H. Tawney crumbled.

Consequently, as this volume concludes, Harvard Law School and the entire domain of law and legal education were coming under attack amid the social, political, and economic turmoil of the 1970s and 1980s. It remained arguably the most influential professional school in American history in terms of graduating the most national leaders in politics, the judiciary, law faculties, and law firms. At the same time, Harvard Law School continued its struggle to cope with the interplay among three factors that form central themes in this volume: the sword-wielding, combative culture of academic exclusivity that had become its hallmark over the course of the twentieth century; the severe financial constraints imposed by the long-standing syndrome of tuition dependence, which intensified that culture; and the concomitant tendency to discourage, or fail to encourage, the enrollment of students and the hiring of faculty who were not white Christian men.

NOTES

1. Elena Kagan in Ruth Bader Ginsburg and Elena Kagan, "Conversation [at Celebration 55]," *Harvard Journal of Law & Gender* 32 (2009): 245.

2. This introduction draws upon Bruce A. Kimball and Daniel R. Coquillette, "History and Harvard Law School," *Fordham Law Review* 87 (2018): 883–904.

3. Robert W. Gordon to Bruce A. Kimball, email (December 23, 2017), on file with the authors.

4. Compare G. Edward White, "Looking Backward: Harvard Law School as Seen from 2016," *Weekly Standard* (February 1, 2016), retrieved from http://www.weeklystandard .com/print/looking-backward/article/2; Jeannie Suk Gerson, "The Socratic Method in the Age of Trauma," *Harvard Law Review* 130 (2017): 2328.

5. The Association for Research on Non-Profit Organizations and Voluntary Action awarded the Peter Dobkin Hall History of Philanthropy Prize for 2017 to *Battlefield of Merit.*

6. Elena Kagan quoted in Michael Levenson, "Supreme Court Justices Reminisce about Their Harvard Days," *Boston Globe* (October 27, 2017).

7. See *Battlefield of Merit,* 81–91.

8. See Noah Remnick, "Yale Will Drop John Calhoun's Name from Building," *New York Times,* February 11, 2017; Susan Svrluga, "Princeton Protestors Occupy President's Office, Demand 'Racist' Woodrow Wilson's Name Be Removed," *Washington Post* (November 18, 2015).

9. See Harriet Alexander, "Harvard Law Students Campaign for Removal of Slavery Seal," *[London] Daily Telegraph* (November 10, 2015); "Harvard Law School Drops Official Shield over Slavery Links," *[London] Guardian* (March 4, 2016); Barney Henderson, "Harvard Law School to Scrap Crest over Links to Slavery," *[London] Daily Telegraph* (March 5, 2016); Anemona Hartocollis, "Harvard Law to Abandon Crest Linked to Slavery," *New York Times* (March 4, 2016); Steve Annear, "Harvard Law School to Ditch Controversial Shield," *Boston Globe* (March 14, 2016); Sara Randazzo, "Harvard Law Drops Slaveholder's Crest; the School's Seal Depicted the Family Crest of a Benefactor and Plantation Owner," *Wall Street Journal* (March 15, 2016); Susan Svrluga, "The Harvard Law Shield Tied to Slavery Is Already Disappearing after Corporation Vote," *Washington Post* (March 15, 2016); "Harvard Agrees to Retire Law School Shield Tied to Slavery," *Associated Press Newswires* (March 14, 2016); "Harvard Law School Drops Controversial Emblem in Slavery Row," *Agence France Presse* (March 4, 2016); Marcus E. Howard, "Harvard to Scrap Law School Seal Associated with Slavery," *Reuters News* (March 14, 2016); Bamzi Banchiri, "Is Harvard Ready to Abandon Slavery-Linked Seal?," *Christian Science Monitor* (March 5, 2016).

10. Quotation is from Martha L. Minow, email to the Harvard Law School Community (March 14, 2016), on file with the authors. See Drew Gilpin Faust and William F.

Lee to Martha L. Minow (March 14, 2016), accessed at https://today.law.harvard.edu/wp
-content/uploads/2016/03/Harvard_Corp_letter_shield.pdf; Bruce H. Mann et al., "Recommendation to the President and Fellows of Harvard College on the Shield Approved
for the Law School" (March 3, 2016), accessed at https://today.law.harvard.edu/wp-content
/uploads/2016/03/Shield-Committee-Report.pdf.

11. Quotation is from Meagan Flynn, "The Harvard Law School Traces Its Origin to
an Antiguan Slave Owner: Now the Country Wants Reparations," *Washington Post*
(November 6, 2019). See John F. Manning to Members of the HLS Community, email
(November 26, 2019), on file with the authors.

12. Daniel R. Coquillette, "A History of Blacks at Harvard Law School," *HLSR* (October 20, 2000): 6–7. Our searches, including digital searches through Harvard Law School
publications, have not found any earlier source. Compare "The Named Professorships of the
Harvard Law School: *The Royall Professorship*," *HLSB* (December 1952): 5, 13; Gladys N.
Hoover, *The Elegant Royalls of New England* (New York, 1974), 49; Charles Brooks, *His-
tory of the Town of Medford*, revised by James M. Usher (Boston, 1886), 149–150; Charles
Warren, *History of the Harvard Law School and of Early Legal Conditions in America* (New
York, 1908), 1:278–281; Arthur E. Sutherland, *The Law at Harvard: A History of Ideas and
Men, 1817–1907* (Cambridge, MA, 1967), 32–42; David B. Gaspar, *Bondmen and Rebels:
A Study of Master-Slave Relations in Antigua* (Baltimore, 1985), 30–35; Mason Hammond,
"A Harvard Armory: Part I," *Harvard Library Bulletin* 29 (1981): 284–285; "A Royall Find,"
HLSB (Summer 2001): 64.

13. *Battlefield of Merit*, 76, 81–88. See Alexandra A. Chan, "The Slaves of Colonial New
England: Discourses of Colonialism and Identity at the Isaac Royall House, Medford, Mas-
sachusetts, 1735–1755" (PhD diss., Boston University, 2003); Janey Halley, "My Isaac
Royall Legacy," *Harvard Blackletter Law Journal* 24 (Spring 2008): 117–131.

14. Quotations are from Hammond, "A Harvard Armory," 265; see 284–285. Discussion in Chapter 10 below.

15. Compare the interpretation in Mann et al., "Recommendation to the President," 5.

16. "*Veritas et Legem*," *HLSR* (April 1, 1954): 2; "The New Record," *HLSR* (October 31,
1968): 8.

17. Quotations are from A. R. Krachenberg, "Bringing the Concept of Marketing to
Higher Education." *Journal of Higher Education* 43 (1972): 370, 380; Edward B. Fiske,
"The Marketing of Colleges" *The Atlantic* (October 1979): 93–98. See Bill Readings, *The
University in Ruins* (Cambridge, MA, 1997), 10–11; David L. Kirp, *Shakespeare, Einstein,
and the Bottom Line: The Marketing of Higher Education* (Cambridge, MA, 2003), 11–27;
Jennifer Washburn, *University Inc.: The Corporate Corruption of Higher Education* (New York,
2005), ix–xii.

18. "A Good Way to Remember," *HLSB* (October 1969): 44. These usages were reported by Manager Karen Beck and her staff at the Historical & Special Collections, Harvard Law School Library. Mann et al., "Recommendation to the President," 6.

19. Quotation is from [Item], *HLSB* (Winter 1975): 14. We are grateful to Lesley Schoenfeld and Karen Beck for finding this item. See Ethan Thomas to Karen Beck, email (February 17, 2016), on file with the authors; Karen Beck to Daniel Coquillette, email (February 16, 2018), on file with the authors; "Bernice Rose Segaloff Loss" [Obituary], *Boston Globe* (April 30, 2007).

20. This connection, made in 1975, may explain why Law School publications took no heed of the 1981 article in the *Harvard [University] Library Bulletin* describing the origins of the shield in the Royall coat of arms. See Hammond, "A Harvard Armory," 284–285.

21. Derek C. Bok, *Universities in the Marketplace: The Commercialization of Higher Education* (Princeton, NJ, 2003), 84. See Mann et al., "Recommendation to the President," 6; *HLSR* (September 21, 1984): 1.

22. While appreciating the reasons for retiring the shield, we also sympathized with "A Different View" expressed by Professor Annette Gordon-Reed (LL.B. 1984), who noted the problems of historical revisionism and was joined in her dissent by Annie Rittgers (J.D. 2017), both members of the dean's committee of faculty, students, and alumni. See Annette Gordon-Reed, "A Different View," *Harvard Law Today* (March 3, 2016), retrieved from https://today.law.harvard.edu/wp-content/uploads/2016/03/Shield_Committee -Different_View.pdf.

23. Robert Stevens, *Law School: Legal Education in America from the 1850s to the 1980s* (Chapel Hill, NC, 1983), 53.

24. Paul W. DiMaggio and Walter W. Powell, "The Iron Cage Revisited: Institutional Isomorphism and Collective Rationality in Organizational Fields," *American Sociological Review* 48 (1983): 147–160.

25. Walter W. Powell and Paul J. Dimaggio, eds., *The New Institutionalism in Organizational Analysis* (Chicago, 1983); Paul J. Dimaggio, "Interest and Agency in Institutional Theory," in *Institutional Patterns and Organizations: Culture and Environment,* ed. Lynne G. Zucker (Cambridge, MA, 1988), 14–15; Mary C. Brinton and Victor Nee, *The New Institutionalism in Sociology* (Palo Alto, CA, 2001); Rakesh Khurana, *From Higher Aims to Hired Hands: The Social Transformation of American Business Schools and the Unfulfilled Promise of Management as a Profession* (Princeton, NJ, 2007), 12–15, 47–48.

26. Magali Sarfatti Larson, *The Rise of Professionalism: A Sociological Analysis* (Berkeley, CA, 1977); Paul Starr, *The Social Transformation of American Medicine* (New York, 1982), 143–144. See Eliot Freidson, *Professional Powers: A Study of the Institutionalization of Formal Knowledge* (Chicago, 1986), 28–29; Andrew Abbott, *The System of Professions: An Essay on the Division of Expert Labor* (Chicago, 1988), 5.

27. Quotations are, respectively, from Eliot Freidson, *Professionalism: The Third Logic: On the Practice of Knowledge* (Chicago, 2001), 181; Starr, *The Social Transformation,* 28, 79, 453. See William J. Goode, "Theoretical Limits of Professionalization," in *The Semi-Professions and Their Organization,* ed. Amitai Etzioni (New York, 1969), 294–295;

Everett C. Hughes, "Professions" (1963), in *The Professions in America,* ed. Kenneth S. Lynn (Boston, 1967), 1; Bernard Barber, "Some Problems in the Sociology of the Professions" (1965), in Lynn, *The Professions in America,* 31; Larson, *The Rise of Professionalism,* 19–39; Eliot Freidson, *Profession of Medicine: A Study of the Sociology of Applied Knowledge* (New York, 1970), 4.

28. Talcott Parsons, "Professions," in *International Encyclopedia of the Social Sciences,* ed. David L. Sills (New York, 1968), 12:543–544. See Talcott Parsons, "The Professions and Social Structure," *Social Forces* 17 (1939): 457–467, reprinted in Parsons, *Essays in Sociological Theory, Pure and Applied* (Glencoe, IL, 1948), 185–199, 2nd. ed. (New York, 1954), 34–49.

29. Quotations are from Freidson, *Professionalism,* 181–193; Larson, *The Rise of Professionalism,* xiii, 39. See Freidson, *Profession of Medicine;* Starr, *The Social Transformation,* 17, 28–29, 79, 453. Conversely, a scholar who adopts *a priori* the "very loose definition" of professions—occupations that employ expertise in a competition to establish jurisdictional control over work—observes that "it has been easy to mistake American medicine for the paradigm." Abbott, *The System of Professions,* 8, 30, 8–20.

30. Khurana, *From Higher Aims,* 18. See Hermann Oliphant, "Parallels in the Development of Legal and Medical Education," *Annals of the American Academy of Political and Social Science* 167 (May 1933): 156, see 156–164; Richard H. Shryock, *The Unique Influence of the Johns Hopkins University on American Medicine* (Copenhagen, 1953), 27n31; Robert Wiebe, *The Search for Order, 1877–1920* (New York, 1967), 113–123; Starr, *The Social Transformation,* 17–29. "For the new educational ideals [in medicine] to be implemented, an institutional revolution was required as well: the proprietary school had to be abandoned, and in its place had to be created the modern university medical school. Between 1885 and 1925, this transition occurred." Kenneth M. Ludmerer, *Learning to Heal: The Development of American Medical Education* (Baltimore, MD, 1985), 5. See also William G. Rothstein, *American Medical Schools and the Practice of Medicine: A History* (New York, 1987), 89–116.

31. Kenneth M. Ludmerer, *Time to Heal: American Medical Education from the Turn of the Century to the Era of Managed Care* (New York, 1999), 6–7, 55. See Samuel Williston, *Life and Law: An Autobiography* (Boston, 1940), 206.

32. Quotation is from "Harvard College Law School," *Magenta* (December 4, 1874): 67, emphasis in original. See also James J. Myers, "The Harvard Law School," *Harvard Advocate* (February 5, 1875): 146–147.

33. *Battlefield of Merit,* 559–567.

34. See Chapters 14, 17, and 18 herein.

35. Roscoe Pound, *The Harvard Law School* [New York, 1919], 16. Pound's phrase was later picked up by Erwin N. Griswold, Annual Report of the Dean of Harvard Law School 1961–1962, 395.

36. Scott G. Nichols, interview with Bruce A. Kimball and Kenneth Leung (December 2010), on file with the authors.

37. "More years ago than I like now to remember I sat in this building and listened to—yes, more than that, was dissected by—men all but one of whom are now dead. What I got from them was . . . the impress of a band of devoted scholars, patient, considerate, courteous, and kindly, whom nothing could daunt and nothing could bribe. . . . Again and again they have helped me when the labor seemed heavy, the task seemed trivial, and the confusion seemed indecipherable. From them I learned that it is as craftsmen that we get our satisfactions and our pay. In the universe of truth they lived by the sword; they asked no quarter of absolutes and they gave none. Go ye and do likewise." Learned Hand, *The Bill of Rights: The Oliver Wendell Holmes Lectures, 1958* (Cambridge, MA, 1958), 77. Printed on a bronze plaque in 1959 in the Ames Courtroom, Austin Hall, Harvard Law School. "News of the School," *HLSB* (February 1959): 10.

38. Bruce A. Kimball, "Before the Paper Chase: Student Culture at Harvard Law School, 1895–1915," *Journal of Legal Education* 61 (2011): 30–66.

39. Kim Townsend, *Manhood at Harvard: William James and Others* (Cambridge, MA, 1996), 22–24.

40. Edward H. Warren, *Spartan Education* (Boston, 1942).

41. James R. Green, *The World of the Worker: Labor in Twentieth Century America* (New York, 1980), 68, 94, 120.

42. David J. Goldberg, *Discontented America: The United States in the 1920s* (Baltimore, 1999), 170, see 14, 47–50, 64, 140; Lynn Dumenil, *Modern Temper: American Culture and Society in the 1920s* (New York, 1995), 7–11; Green, *World of the Worker,* 68, 94, 120.

43. James Vorenberg, Oral History, conducted by Daniel R. Coquillette (November–December 1997), on file with the authors.

44. Starr, *The Social Transformation,* 19. See Khurana, *From Higher Aims,* 19, 23–192.

45. John F. Dillon, "The True Professional Ideal," *Reports and Transactions of the American Bar Association* (1894): 409. See Bruce A. Kimball, *The "True Professional Ideal" in America: A History* (Oxford, 1992), 301–303.

46. Parsons, "Professions," 536; Starr, *The Social Transformation,* 140; Freidson, *Professional Powers,* 27; Freidson, *Professionalism,* 1–3, 59–60; Khurana, *From Higher Aims,* 372.

47. Richard H. Tawney, *The Acquisitive Society* (New York, 1920).

48. Harold L. Wilensky, "The Professionalization of Everyone?," *American Journal of Sociology* 70 (1964): 137–158.

49. Parsons, "Professions," 545.

50. Kimball, *The "True Professional Ideal,"* 309–317; Freidson, *Professional Powers,* 28.

51. Quotations are from Hughes, "Professions," 1; Goode, "The Theoretical Limits of Professionalization," 294–295; Freidson, *Profession of Medicine,* 4.

52. Quotation is from Khurana, *From Higher Aims,* 10. See Kimball, *The "True Professional Ideal,"* 317–322.

53. Freidson, *Professional Powers,* 28.

54. Quotation is from Abbott, *The System of Professions,* 5. See Eliot Freidson, *Professional Dominance: The Social Structure of Medical Care* (New York, 1970); Freidson, *Doctoring*

Together: A Study of Professional Social Control (New York, 1975); Larson, *The Rise of Professionalism;* Freidson, *Professional Powers,* 28; Starr, *The Social Transformation,* 143–144.

55. Martin Oppenheimer, "The Proletarianization of the Professional," *Sociological Review Monograph* 20 (1973): 213–227; Freidson, *Professionalism,* 181; Abbott, *The System of Professions,* 18; Ludmerer, *Time to Heal,* xxv.

56. Marie R. Haug, "The Deprofessionalization of Everyone," *Sociological Focus* 9 (1975): 197–213; Robert A. Rothman, "Deprofessionalization: The Case of Law in America," *Work and Occupations* 11 (1984): 183–206.

57. Freidson, *Professionalism,* 197–198. See Khurana, *From Higher Aims,* 291, 317. See Brian Z. Tamanaha, *Failing Law Schools* (Chicago, 2012); Tamanaha, "Is Law School Worth the Cost?," *Journal of Legal Education* 63 (2013): 173–188; Ronald G. Ehrenberg, "American Law Schools in a Time of Transition." *Journal of Legal Education* 63 (2013): 98–112; Freidson, *Professionalism,* 189.

CHAPTER ONE

The Tragedy of Ezra Thayer, 1900–1915

Harvard Law School "is the most successful department of the entire university, and enjoys a reputation throughout the nation which is higher than that of any other department," wrote former Harvard president Charles Eliot (1869–1909) in 1913. Confident of this prevailing assessment, Dean James Barr Ames (1895–1909) had simply continued the novel policies introduced by Dean Christopher C. Langdell (1870–1895) a generation earlier. During his tenure, Ames attempted no innovations and told the alumni, "I have very little to report to you that is new." The emphasis on continuity pleased the faculty, who did not debate, or even discuss, policies at faculty meetings and complacently accepted Ames's recommendations.[1]

Meanwhile, the world around the Law School was changing faster and more profoundly than ever before, as modernity rolled across the nation. This social and cultural change was rooted in an unprecedented economic expansion in the United States commencing in the 1870s, driven by the nation's rapid industrialization and expanding international trade. In 1870 some 53 percent of the nation's workforce made their living in agriculture, and the "agrarian myth" prevailed, idealizing the yeoman farmer as "the simple, honest, independent, healthy, happy human being."[2] In subsequent decades, immigration and urbanization proceeded rapidly, and by 1910 about 56 percent of workers or their parents were born outside of the United States, including Andrew Carnegie, one of the richest citizens in the country. In response, many Americans defensively embraced nativism and ardent nationalism.

Amid the economic expansion, the Jeffersonian ideal of the yeoman farmer was eclipsed by that of the self-made man pursuing opportunity, career, and wealth in the industrial economy. Much of the labor force became specialized, driven by advances in science and technology that accelerated the pace of change. Workers needed education to succeed, and the nation's burgeoning higher education system increased human capital enormously. By the beginning of the twentieth century, the Gilded Age of the millionaire industrial capitalist with a grade school education—such as Carnegie, Cornelius Vanderbilt, and John D. Rockefeller—was passing. Instead, "investment in human capital . . . became supreme."[3]

Beginning in 1870, Harvard Law School had pioneered such investment in the field of professional education. But self-satisfaction and pride outpaced substantive achievement in the first decade of the twentieth century. The school's preeminence was inevitably threatened. During the 1908–09 academic year, Dean Ames (LL.B. 1872) began to suffer from a mysterious ailment now known as Alzheimer's disease. At a faculty luncheon in November 1909, he announced quietly, "I am very sorry to say that I must leave the Law School. It may be only a short time . . . or I may not be able to come back at all. I have been examined by three physicians, and none of them can tell me what is the matter. . . . I can't remember names. I can't recall the name of any one of you here without extraordinary effort. It has taken me three hours to prepare a lecture that I've usually prepared in half an hour. . . . I must leave you to make provision for the School."[4] He died two months later in January 1910 at his home in Wilton, New Hampshire, at age sixty-four.

Ames's successor, Dean Ezra Thayer (1910–1915), continued to follow the deep "groove" of academic policies that Dean Langdell (LL.B. 1853) had carved and Dean Ames and his faculty had followed.[5] But the culture of the school was beginning to change. Dean Thayer (LL.B. 1891) and his colleagues found gratification in wielding the intellectual sword and failing students, and they began to regard the attrition rate as an important measure of the school's academic quality. This zeal for flunking students exacerbated the competitive and combative culture that was endemic to the Socratic teaching at the school and to the adversarial model of Anglo-American law. Nor did Thayer spare himself. His unrelenting self-criticism and fear of failure ultimately led to the end of his deanship and his tragic demise.

A New President and a New Dean

Dean Ames's death signaled not only the end of Langdell's generation on the faculty, but also the vulnerability of the Law School. The student-faculty ratio was rising sharply, as the student body grew from 475 to 765 between 1895 and 1909 and the number of professorial appointments remained at nine. Three new assistant professors were hired between 1899 and 1904—Jens I. Westengard (LL.B. 1898), Bruce Wyman (LL.B. 1900), and Edward Warren (LL.B. 1900)—but these new arrivals were offset by the departures of five senior professors between 1900 and 1913: Langdell, Ames, James B. Thayer (LL.B. 1856), Jeremiah Smith (LL.B. 1861), and John C. Gray (LL.B. 1861).[6] By 1913 the school could not afford to increase the size of the faculty, having become heavily dependent on tuition due to the debacle of financing Langdell Hall in 1906.[7]

In 1909 Harvard president Eliot retired after a tenure of forty years, leaving to his successor the obligation and opportunity to appoint a new dean who could address the school's financial vulnerability. Yet, the new president, A. Lawrence Lowell (1909–1933)—a consummate Boston Brahmin who had graduated from Harvard College in 1877 and from the Law School in 1880—believed that Eliot had overemphasized graduate and professional education at the expense of collegiate culture and undergraduate education.[8] Lowell therefore had no particular plans to strengthen the Law School or alter its course.

The decanal search was the first at the Law School since Eliot had selected the iconoclast Langdell as the school's first dean in 1869. In 1909, few of the school's faculty appeared to be likely candidates. Samuel Williston (LL.B. 1888), the interim dean, had health problems. Professor Joseph H. Beale (LL.B. 1887) had the most experience because he had helped Williston with the decanal duties during Ames's illness and had also served, on leave, as founding dean of the University of Chicago Law School from 1902 to 1904.[9] But Beale had little interest, so Lowell began to look outside the faculty. He received nominations of professors and deans at other law schools, including John H. Wigmore (LL.B. 1887) of Northwestern University, William A. Keener (LL.B. 1877) of Columbia University, and Charles N. Gregory of the University of Iowa.

Also, Lowell and other members of the university's governing board, the Harvard Corporation, wanted to appoint a dean from the practicing bar who was "in touch with the active life of his profession." Langdell had practiced law successfully on Wall Street for fifteen years, but he always had the air of a monastic scholar, and Ames had never practiced law at all. Although their scholarly inclination was an asset, "a faculty composed exclusively of such men would not command the respect of the profession, or accomplish the best for its students," stated the university's Secretary, who sat on the Corporation.[10]

Lowell agreed, but some observers warned that recruiting a distinguished lawyer would be difficult, as had been the case during the search for Langdell in 1869.[11]

Nevertheless, several prominent lawyers were nominated, and by February 1910 the academic candidates were no longer under consideration. Instead, attention focused on two young lawyers, Joseph P. Cotton and Ezra Thayer. The former had graduated from Harvard College in 1896 and the Law School in 1900 and eventually served as U.S. undersecretary of state. The latter was the son of revered Professor James Thayer, who had served on the Law School faculty from 1874 to 1902. Having graduated first in his class both from Harvard College in 1888 and from Harvard Law School in 1891, Ezra was considered "one of the most brilliant students in the history of the School."[12] The Law School had offered him a faculty appointment in 1891 and then again in 1902, but he declined both offers, electing instead to serve as legal secretary to U.S. Supreme Court Justice Horace Gray (LL.B. 1849) and then to work at law firms in Boston. But he continued some academic pursuits by joining the committee that drafted the first ABA Code of Legal Ethics and lecturing at Harvard Law School on Massachusetts practice and at Harvard Medical School on medical jurisprudence.[13]

Early in 1910 both Cotton and Thayer rejected initial overtures about the deanship, citing sacrifices to their family, income, and living arrangements. University representatives accepted Cotton's decision, but sensed that Thayer was "wobbling" and "tempted."[14] They persisted, promising Thayer that he could teach his father's courses in Evidence and Constitutional Law and remain living in his new house in the Boston Back Bay, overlooking the Charles River. After struggling with the decision through February and March and consulting senior mentors, Thayer accepted the deanship with misgivings.[15]

Thayer's reservation was more profound than financial or familial considerations. His acceptance letter of March 20, 1910, to Lowell, expressed doubts about "my fitness for so large a place." Thayer's responses to letters of congratulations likewise intimated his deep insecurity about leading the Law School. Despite his sterling success as a student and a lawyer, Ezra's correspondence reveals his extraordinary dependence on his father, extreme fear of failure, and intense perfectionism. These attributes resulted in harsh self-criticism that would eventually lead to tragedy.[16]

This nearly debilitating complex appeared in his approach to legal scholarship. Having published a few scholarly essays as a practicing attorney, Thayer maintained that each member of the faculty should publish one piece of schol-

Ezra R. Thayer, LL.B. 1891. Faculty and Dean 1910–1915.
Courtesy of Harvard Law School Library, Historical & Special Collections.

arship per year. But he fell short of his own goal, and produced only two brief essays during his deanship. Though burdened with administrative work, he was held back primarily by fear that his publications would be flawed. This perfectionism nearly prevented him from completing the minor revisions to those two essays, and his "delinquency" in doing so made him "ashamed."[17] He also wished to publish a casebook on evidence, but became paralyzed by doubt that it would have any merit. Thayer's colleagues recognized his deep fear of imperfection and failure: "He was almost morbidly anxious to be absolutely accurate and to present nothing that was not well matured. He was severely critical and . . . made repeated redrafts of everything that he wrote."[18]

This severe self-criticism, though ultimately destructive, did sensitize Thayer to the dangerous complacency and self-satisfaction that pervaded Harvard Law School when he took office in 1910. The faculty and alumni were accustomed to hearing knowledgeable outsiders declare that the school had reached "the climax of success in professional education."[19] It had no rival among law schools, and scarcely any rival among university professional schools, except Johns Hopkins University Medical School.[20] Yet, that self-satisfaction blinded all those associated with the Law School—the faculty, the alumni association, the university's leadership—to its vulnerability early in the twentieth century.

Thayer insightfully cautioned against self-congratulation shortly after his selection and even before assuming office. In his first address to the Harvard Law School [alumni] Association, he stated, "We cannot afford, however strong may be the professional temptation, to rejoice in past triumphs, to give much time to . . . congratulating ourselves on what has been done in the past. Our faces would then be turned in the wrong direction."[21]

Raising Academic Standards

Driven by perfectionism, Thayer was a purist in most academic matters. He favored confining the curriculum to the subject of law, narrowly defined and distinct from policy. He objected to law faculty teaching outside the Law School or working in private practice. Similarly, he opposed anything that would distract students from their studies. When the university proposed lengthening Christmas vacation to two weeks, Thayer objected that the academic term was already too short, and he quashed a proposal to hold a debate competition between the students of Harvard, Yale, and Columbia law schools. Nor should students' work be distracted by earning money during the academic year. Those needing income should instead work for an additional year before entering law school, he argued. In particular, the offers made to law students to teach in Harvard's Government Department infuriated Thayer, and he urged students to turn them down (though he had taught in the English Department as a law student).[22]

Above all, Thayer manifested perfectionism in his efforts to raise ever higher the admission and graduation requirements at the Law School. The infamous "Paper Chase" at Harvard Law School began with the shift in culture and policies during Dean Thayer's administration.[23]

By 1913 the four senior professors who had long sustained a gentlemanly paternal ethos at the school—James Thayer, Ames, Smith, and Gray—were gone. The next generation of senior faculty followed a different, harsh ethic. They included Joseph Beale, who, observed one student, "is rather sarcastic and points out in no gentle terms the absurdity of the answers given [by students]."[24] Another member of the new generation was Edward Warren, who, another student wrote, was "aggressive and keeps the whole class on alert— oftentimes by sheer fright. If one does not know an answer well, he is likely to make a sarcastic remark and show his 'victim' off to the ridicule of the class."[25] Nicknamed "Bull," Warren reveled in his aggressive approach, which he rationalized in his book entitled *Spartan Education.* Ironically, Warren gratefully acknowledged in this book that, during his time as a student at the Law School from 1897 to 1900, the faculty "overflowed with the milk of human kindness."[26] But the Bull did not nurse students.

Students' decreasing access to the faculty contributed to the shift away from gentlemanly paternalism, as the student-faculty ratio doubled from about 36:1 in 1901 to about 72:1 in 1916. In response, the faculty created a paid Board of Student Advisors in 1910, shortly before Thayer arrived as dean. The nine upperclassmen on the Board were charged with keeping office hours to advise the first-year students on conducting legal research, citing sources, and writing briefs. This practice was justified as providing mentoring opportunities to the advisors, although this mentoring essentially supplanted the advising of the faculty. Possibly because the Board relieved the faculty of their responsibility and distracted the advisors from their own studies, Thayer took little interest in the new Board.[27]

The new, unforgiving ethos also appeared in Dean Thayer brandishing the sword of attrition. He encouraged the faculty to eliminate the "large batch" of "halfwitted" and "utterly neglectful" students "who have the practice of sliding through on 55s or other Ds." To that end, he strictly enforced the admission standards, refusing to make an exception for a Harvard College senior who had not finished all his undergraduate work.[28] He also prodded the faculty to raise the standard of admission to the school.

Since its founding in 1817, the Law School had determined admission by relying on an academic threshold. All male applicants who met the threshold were entitled to admission, except in rare cases.[29] This approach was conventional throughout higher education during the nineteenth century, although the threshold varied across colleges, universities, and professional schools. For some institutions, the academic standard was merely English literacy; for others, a secondary school diploma; for very few, a classical education. This approach underlay Langdell's radically new threshold announced in the school's catalog in 1875: "The course of instruction in the School is designed for persons who have received a college education."[30] Even this high standard constituted an admission threshold that made selection among applicants unnecessary.

Instead of selectivity, growing enrollment was considered a measure of quality in the late nineteenth and early twentieth centuries, as higher education expanded throughout the nation. More students meant that an institution was more desirable. Even leading colleges and universities wished to enroll as many qualified students as they could get. In 1885 and again in 1897, President Eliot wrote to Johns Hopkins University president Daniel C. Gilman: "Of course you want the University to grow. . . . I am not content unless Harvard grows each year in size. . . . Our gain this year will be more than three percent."[31] Merely twenty-five years later, prominent colleges and universities would adopt a dramatically different approach.

Even as they continued to rely on academic thresholds, colleges and universities—especially the prominent private institutions—began to raise the admissions bar in the 1890s due to the expanding pool of qualified applicants. This development was driven by the rising level of educational attainment across the country, particularly the growing number of students attending secondary school. At the same time, improvements in transportation and communication facilitated college attendance. All these factors stemmed, fundamentally, from expansion of the U.S. economy and its increasing reliance on the expertise and education of the middle class.[32]

Commensurately, the Law School raised its academic threshold for admission to a standard unprecedented at professional schools in the United States. In 1893 the faculty voted that, as of 1896, only those holding "respectable" undergraduate degrees would be entitled to admission as "regular students," eligible to become candidates to earn the LL.B. The annual catalog listed the 66 undergraduate institutions deemed to be offering "respectable" degrees. By 1903 the list had been expanded to about 127 institutions, ranging from the University of Georgia to the University of Oregon. Despite this breadth, the list included few Catholic colleges and no historically black colleges or colleges exclusively for women, who were barred from admission.[33]

During the 1910s the academic thresholds for admission continued to rise throughout higher education. At the Law School, Dean Thayer elevated the threshold, prompted by a Harvard University study that found "the higher a man's rank in college the better he is likely to stand in his professional studies."[34] In 1913, the Law School divided the nation's 950 degree-granting colleges, universities, and independent professional schools into three strata. The "high grade" or "first list" institutions numbered around 250, and all their graduates were entitled to admission as degree candidates. Graduates of the some 200 "approved" or "second list" could enter only if "they ranked in the first third of the class" during the senior year. Graduates of the other 500 colleges, universities, and independent professional schools that did not appear on either list were advised to contact the secretary of the Law School about admission.[35]

In this fashion, the Law School for the first time began to discriminate on the basis of not only the quality of undergraduate institutions, but also the performance of applicants at those institutions. As Thayer foresaw, these changes would have far-reaching consequences, because the academic intensity of the Law School would no longer be diluted by the ill-prepared or the carefree devotees to "college life."[36] Yet even these higher standards constituted a threshold that entitled one to admission. The approach did not entail culling the applicants at the point of admission. Selectivity occurred through attrition by failing those already admitted, primarily during their first year of study. And because the threshold was higher and the faculty's commitment to weeding out was stronger, competition among the students intensified.

"Not Willing to Consent to the Matriculation of Women"

While Thayer focused on raising the threshold, women continued to press for admission to Harvard's professional schools. In 1899 the entire Law School faculty, save one, had voted in support of admitting women. The dissent came from Dean Langdell who wrote a memorandum itemizing eight reasons against doing so. The Corporation concurred, and decided not to admit women.[37]

In 1905 eight female physicians—all members of the Massachusetts Medical Society and affiliated with the New England Hospital for Women and Children—petitioned Harvard University to admit women to the Medical School. They observed that 103 of the 166 medical schools in the United States were coeducational. "This shows," they wrote, "that the experiment is not a new one, since it has been tried deliberately and continuously by universities of repute in this country and by all the Continental universities except those of Spain." But the medical faculty voted down the petition on the grounds that "it is impracticable, at present," to admit women to the regular curriculum. The Corporation agreed with the faculty vote.[38]

Then, in September 1909, a woman wrote to Dean Ames requesting admission to the Law School. After graduating from Vassar College, Inez Milholland had tried unsuccessfully to gain admittance to the law schools of Oxford and Cambridge Universities, and then applied to the law schools at both Harvard and Columbia. In her three-page, single-spaced letter, Milholland asked the faculty to reject "the rose-colored world of sentimentality" associated with women and to embrace instead a "more rational" approach to the question of admitting women. Appealing to social scientific research, she argued that her admission would enable Harvard to test experimentally the suitability of coeducation in its graduate schools. She also argued that she needed "the best training in the country" to help her overcome the sexual discrimination that she would encounter as a woman in the legal profession. Furthermore, she affirmed that she was not asking for any special treatment "because women too must conform" to the Law School's high academic standards.[39]

Early in October 1909 the faculty voted to recommend to the Corporation the admission of Milholland, with Professors Wyman, Bull Warren, and Eugene Wambaugh (LL.B. 1880) dissenting.[40] A few days later, Milholland visited Henry Lee Higginson, a member of the Harvard Corporation, and convinced him to support her candidacy as well. Greatly impressed with Milholland, Higginson wrote to President Lowell, "If we are to begin at all with women, we certainly can do no better than this young lady." But Higginson also cautioned, "Men are gradually being displaced by women . . . and if they are all like this young lady, it would merely hasten banishment." Similarly, Ames warned that if the Law School admitted Milholland, it would have to admit all qualified women who applied.[41] Many at Harvard thus worried that talented women presented a grave threat to mediocre men.

President Lowell added the points that women could attend other law schools, and that admitting them to Harvard posed the risk of weakening "the peculiar efficiency of our law school." But fundamentally, it was simply a truism for him that Harvard University did not confer Harvard degrees on women.[42] A week after the faculty vote, the Corporation informed the law faculty that "this Board is not willing to consent to the matriculation of women in the Law School."[43] An editorial in *Law Notes*, a New York law magazine, applauded Harvard's decision and suggested that legal education "seems to be a secondary consideration" for Milholland, who merely desired "the notoriety of forcing herself into an institution where no woman has ever been before."[44]

The question arose again soon after 1910, when Ezra Thayer became dean and Roscoe Pound (1889–90) joined the faculty. A female college graduate applied to enter the school. In the faculty discussion Bull Warren objected, "If women are admitted to the School, I will have to revise all my lectures." To this, Dean Thayer quipped, "Are there any other arguments in favor of the proposal?"[45] The faculty then voted five to four, with the dean in the majority, to recommend that the Corporation grant the application. This time, the faculty suggested to the Corporation "that the young woman might enter Radcliffe College, receive her instruction at the Law School and be granted the degree by Radcliffe." Again the Corporation refused.[46]

In 1914 the proponents tried once more when Joseph Beale attempted to organize law courses for a group of interested young women who would be taught by himself, Austin W. Scott (LL.B. 1909), Felix Frankfurter (LL.B. 1906), and some alumni and advanced law students. The plan soon fell apart, however, because the women wanted to receive law degrees and neither Radcliffe nor the Law School was willing to award them. In addition, Dean Thayer opposed diverting faculty resources to the project, and Lowell simply objected to coeducation at Harvard under any circumstances.[47] Then, in March 1915, a group of Radcliffe students and other young women, one of whom was Beale's daughter, applied for admission to the Law School. Warned by experience, the faculty asked whether the Corporation desired their opinion on the merits of the petition. The Corporation declined, stating that the school had plenty of students, that coeducation had no advantages, and that instruction of women at Harvard belonged to Radcliffe.[48]

By this point, Harvard's resistance to coeducation was attracting public attention. Walter Lippmann, founding editor of *The New Republic,* wrote to Lowell, "We are very much interested here in the petition presented by the fifteen graduates of various girls' colleges asking for admission to the Harvard Law School on the same terms as men. We are anxious to comment on that petition and to give it our support, but we do not wish to do so without finding out . . . your views and those of the authorities at Harvard."[49] Lowell replied to Lippmann the following day: "Harvard is one of the very few institutions for men alone, and in our opinion had better remain so, for the present at least. Moreover, the Law School has made a great success as it stands. No one suggests that, as a place for training young men for the bar, it would be improved by the admission of women. . . . On the other hand, the admission of women might affect it injuriously."[50]

After the Corporation refused to admit his daughter and other young women, Beale opened the independent Cambridge Law School for Women with support from other law faculty, including Roscoe Pound. Nine women enrolled and were taught by Harvard law professors and lecturers in rooms provided by Radcliffe. But the school closed after just two years due to a lack of applicants.[51] Nevertheless, Thayer welcomed the initiative, because it helped him navigate between the proponents and opponents of coeducation. As he wrote to Dean Harlan F. Stone at Columbia University Law School in 1915, "I should find it difficult to vote against" admitting women in principle. On practical grounds, however, Thayer saw no benefits and some disadvantages to admitting women, since he believed that some men preferred all-male law schools. Yet Thayer also implied that if competing schools started admitting women, he would support their enrollment at Harvard.[52] Ultimately his position was guided by expediency, and he was not unhappy to see the women's petitions denied by the Corporation. By the same token, he was pleased that the Cambridge Law School for Women seemed to provide an alternative that alleviated the pressure of the contentious issue.[53]

Led by Lowell, the Corporation continued to resist coeducation anywhere at Harvard. In August 1917 the Corporation did vote to allow women to study at Harvard Medical School, but not with men or eligible for a degree. Harvard then made this unattractive arrangement even less feasible by announcing it only a few weeks before the start of fall semester. Consequently, only twenty women were able to apply in time, and only four were found qualified, three of whom had already been accepted by other medical schools. The university therefore announced that the number of qualified women was insufficient and canceled the program. Lowell wrote disingenuously to President Ellen Pendleton of Wellesley College that women had been offered a "fair chance" to enter Harvard Medical School, and it was clear that few women had the necessary credentials. The entire arrangement was a fraud, and Pendleton, along with other prominent educators, signed a petition urging Lowell to reconsider the decision. But he refused, and the plan was abandoned. Meanwhile, Columbia, Yale, Pennsylvania, and other universities nearly doubled their numbers of female medical students eligible to earn a degree.[54]

Though later than medical schools, other law schools at prominent private universities also began to admit women while Harvard resisted. In 1918 a Yale law professor taught Isabelle Bridge in a western law school where she was enrolled. He then encouraged her to apply and recommended her to his colleagues at Yale Law School, which admitted her in 1918. In the words of Dean Thomas W. Swan, the Yale Corporation took "a progressive step in voting the admission to the Law School of women students who are graduates of approved colleges."[55]

It was also true that Yale Law School needed students, because most had left to fight in World War I. When Bridge enrolled, Yale Law School had only thirteen LL.B. students plus five B.A. students taking law courses. But Swan cited a different justification than low enrollment for the policy change: "Since so many states now admit women to the practice of law, no sound argument can be made against giving them an opportunity to acquire the best of legal education. . . . We expect several women students during the coming year, but the number of women studying law is likely never to be large."[56] After vehemently rejecting female applicants in the past, Columbia University Law School followed suit in 1927.[57]

Meanwhile, at Harvard the pattern of rejecting coeducation under the Lowell administration was firmly set. The Law School referred inquiries on the matter to the Corporation, which replied tautologically in order to discourage appeals: "The reason that women are not admitted to the law school . . . is simply that Harvard University is not a coeducational institution."[58]

"An Elimination Tournament"

After hurdling the higher admission threshold instituted by Ezra Thayer and the faculty, entering students encountered stiffer graduation requirements also championed by the dean. Prior to the Civil War, written examinations and grading did not exist at Harvard Law School or at virtually any other professional schools, including medical schools. In 1871 Dean Langdell had introduced written examinations and grades, the whetstone of the intellectual sword. For nearly a century after that point, a few grading policies remained consistent at the Law School. Professors assigned numerical grades to written examinations, and the dean (later the secretary or registrar) recorded that numerical grade for each student in each course. The numerical grade determined whether a student passed a course or achieved academic honors, such as Latin honors, entrance to the "honor course" in Langdell's time, or membership in the three honors organizations discussed below.[59]

The precise cutoffs for passing a course or earning various honors naturally changed over time. More significantly, three policies also changed: informing students about their grades, converting the numerical grades to letter grades, and ranking students. Until 1892, grades were only numerical and were kept confidential by the dean. In 1892 the faculty voted to have the dean convert the numerical grades to letter grades and then to inform the students of only the number of various letters grades that they received in their courses: how many Cs, how many Bs, and so forth, but not their grades in specific courses. Also, students were not ranked, although grades did determine qualification for the honors course of study and for the honor of competing to speak at graduation.[60]

In 1910, after Ames retired, Ezra Thayer and the faculty voted to raise the standards for the second-year students who had survived the arduous first year, when attrition was highest. The faculty increased the number of credit hours required of second-year students from ten to twelve and raised the minimum passing grade for students in all three years from fifty-five to sixty. These policies made "a high standard of capacity and diligence" even more "a condition of remaining in the school," wrote Thayer in his annual report.[61]

Next, in 1911, the faculty voted to tell students the overall numerical average of their course grades. For the first time, students could compare their own averages with each other and with the announced standards for passing and for honors. Hence, the new policy directed students' attention to minute grade distinctions and doubtlessly increased their feelings of competition and anxiety. The change thus comported with the shift from the gentlemanly culture of Ames's administration to the "ask and give no quarter" ethos under Dean Thayer.[62]

Attrition also increased, even while the admission threshold rose. The attrition rate during the first year for the classes of 1898 to 1909 in Ames's administration averaged about 17 percent and generally held at under 20 percent. During Thayer's administration, the attrition rate in the first year edged up to an average of 25 percent and sometimes jumped over 30 percent.[63] When President Lowell expressed concern about the high attrition, Thayer described it as necessary, arguing that the school needed to eliminate low achievers in order to teach large classes effectively.[64] Furthermore, the attrition was salutary because "the increased stringency with which we have excluded the poorer men . . . bespeaks a healthy condition of affairs in the law school."[65] These justifications did not satisfy the father of one student, who assailed Dean Thayer in 1915 for his "complacent tone" and "freedom of any thought of responsibility" for the "faulty system of instruction," which, the father believed, victimized his son.[66]

Having addressed the lower half of the class, the dean and faculty then turned to the top and tried to stoke competition by discriminating finely and parsimoniously in academic honors. Above the LL.B., the faculty established a fourth year of study leading to the degree of *Scientiae Juridicae Doctor* (S.J.D.), designed for "the production of jurists who will advance legal thought, and . . .

will always be few," given that "quality, not numbers, is the criterion of the value of the course."[67] In addition, the faculty reduced the percentage of LL.B. students receiving honors, and adopted the model of "an elimination tournament" when setting up the moot court competition in honor of James Barr Ames in 1910.[68]

The faculty also commenced employing grades to determine membership in the three official student organizations: *Harvard Law Review,* the Board of Student Advisors, and the Legal Aid Bureau. This innovation could have been applied in several different ways. For example, the top seventy students could have been identified and allowed to choose their organization, or the organizations could have chosen their members from the top seventy students. But, characteristically, the faculty decided to sort and rank the students hierarchically: the Law Review for students with the highest grades, the Board of Student Advisors for those with the next-highest grades, and the Legal Aid Bureau for the third-highest group.[69] Subsequently, this innovative arrangement came to appear commonsensical. But how did it originate?

The reliance on deceptively precise quantitative measures to sort people into categories was characteristic of the Progressive Era in America that extended from 1890 to 1920, and this reinforced the law faculty's belief that the final exam grade validly measured a student's intellectual and academic merit. Furthermore, the extraordinarily high student-faculty ratio, approaching 60:1, burdened the faculty, who certainly wanted an expeditious means to determine membership in these three honorary organizations. They were scarcely going to spend time holding an essay competition or conducting individual interviews, and they did not trust the students to do it.

The rank-order apparently stemmed from the seniority of the organizations and the interests of the faculty involved in the 1910s. The *Law Review* had priority because it was the oldest, founded in 1887 by a group of third-year students who had formed "the Langdell Society for the serious discussion of legal topics." After about fifteen years of publication, the student editors realized "that they were no longer editing a 'college paper,' but a periodical for legal scholars and practicing lawyers."[70] By that point, two men who as third-year students had participated in founding the *Review*—Samuel Williston and Joseph Beale—were now senior members of the faculty and surely took pride in their offspring. Annual black-tie dinners at fancy Boston hotels, like those held by the law clubs, had already established the social pedigree of the *Review* membership, and the academic pedigree secured its elite status henceforth.[71] The Board of Student Advisors was ranked second because it was founded next, in 1910, and the Board served as a bulwark between the faculty and the novice students. Therefore, it was in the interest of the faculty to ensure that the advisors were as academically competent as possible.

Ranking third was the Legal Aid Bureau because it was founded last, in 1913, and the faculty at the time did not care about its mission to provide legal services to those without means. In fact, the faculty opposed creating the Bureau, and it was Dean Thayer who responded positively to student requests to establish the organization. Initially his support was qualified and somewhat pragmatic. The project "was rather interesting," he wrote, "and as the students were bent on it, I thought it was better to give them their head rather than to take on the characteristically legal attitude of perceiving in advance why it would not work." Within a year, the Bureau began to succeed, and Thayer's feelings warmed. "Most of the faculty are tolerating [the Bureau] as a necessary evil," he wrote to Dean Stone at Columbia "[but I] am rather encouraging it."[72] Consequently, the faculty attitude explains ranking the Bureau third.

Due to all these new policies concerning grading, attrition, and honors, the informal cultural restraints on academic anxiety during Ames's administration eroded under Dean Thayer. Even if students had bachelor's degrees from reputable colleges, those who were not well prepared or highly committed began to find it harder to survive the first year and harder to make it through the second year. High-achieving students found it more difficult to make honors, and the faculty introduced several ranking mechanisms to convey distinctions among those who did well. Led by Thayer, the faculty seemed increasingly intent on stratifying the student body in thin slices.[73]

These trends slowed when Thayer's administration ended in 1915 and enrollment declined precipitously during World War I. But as enrollment began to rebound in 1919, students found that Thayer's direction and policies persevered in the succeeding regime of Dean Roscoe Pound (1916–1936). Meanwhile, the rosy employment prospects for Law School students, which buffered the anxiety of academic competition, eroded significantly after the founding of the Harvard Graduate School of Business Administration in 1908. As the Business School began to flourish, its graduates took jobs that had formerly gone to law graduates.

Also, the legal profession became more competitive in the 1920s "because a law degree had become the normal requirement for practice" and "men lacking a degree were no longer employable," noted the *New York Times*. Unlike in the past, students who flunked out of Harvard Law School in the first year were now "unable to enter other law schools and . . . their potential careers have been ruined."[74] Thus, the law students at Harvard, squeezed in Thayer's academic vice from above and below, could no longer escape into the job market, confident of success. Competition, anxiety, and resentment began to intensify.

"Exclude without Mercy": Thayer and His Students

While expecting more of students, Dean Thayer struggled as a teacher. Prior to becoming dean, he had lectured at the Law School on Massachusetts legal practice, but these practical talks did not prepare him for the year-long, case method courses in Torts and Evidence that he was to teach to first-year students in the 1910–11 school year. In addition, closing his law practice proved onerous and ate into his course preparation in the spring of 1910. Nevertheless, he worked hard at preparing his courses and borrowed the teaching notes on Evidence from John C. Gray at the Law School and professors Wesley N. Hohfeld (LL.B. 1904) at Stanford and Clarke B. Whittier at the University of Chicago. Above all, he consulted Roscoe Pound, who shared his Evidence outline, discussed the course, and reviewed Thayer's proposed syllabus.[75] During the summer, Thayer composed elaborate teaching notes for his two classes.

Even so, his first year in the classroom was a disaster. Students reported that he "was confusing and gave them no clear idea to hold on to."[76] Diligent as ever, he made daily notes on his teaching, revised his syllabus each year, and consulted with other professors, especially Pound. In fact, Thayer wrote to Pound that his notes were "invaluable to me," and "I am getting so used to sponging on you that I am gradually losing my sense of shame."[77]

Thayer's pedagogical struggles were evident to his colleagues. According to Williston, Thayer was "too quick" in his explanations and "lumped exceptions and caveats onto rules that students were still trying to understand." According to *The Centennial History of the Harvard Law School,* he was "too smart" and so thorough that he left his students "in a whirl." For example, Thayer would often "deliver a commentary on an undelivered lecture," by assigning a difficult reading to his students, assuming that they had mastered it, and then devoting class to complicated shadings on the issues.[78]

Thayer believed that his experience at the bar made teaching more difficult, undermining a major rationale for his appointment. In a 1913 address to a joint meeting of the ABA Section on Legal Education and the Association of American Law Schools, he publicly set forth this view.[79] Whatever the reason, his pedagogical failures dismayed Thayer and his teaching notes are harshly self-critical and bereft of positive comments. At one point he observed that his teaching during 1911–12 "may have been better than the year before only because nothing could have been worse."[80]

Despite his own shortcomings, Thayer did not relent on the students. Though not a bully in the classroom like Warren, Thayer was equally caustic when recording in private notebooks his evaluation of the intellectual capacities of the students in his classes. The majority of these judgments about students are extremely critical ("very weak," "hopelessly dull," "occasionally says perfectly absurd and irrelevant things"), and any laudatory comments are qualified ("strong, but brittle"). Thayer thus made sweeping judgments about students' intellectual shortcomings based on their occasional remarks in class and their performance on the final exam.[81]

Meanwhile, the dean took it upon himself to set an example for the faculty by becoming one of the most brutal graders in the school. In his first year of teaching, 1910–11, he failed twenty-five of forty-one students in his Evidence class. Justifying this on moral and expedient grounds, he wrote:

> It is absolutely essential to the welfare of the School that we shall rigidly adhere to the standards necessary for admission to the school, and still more for remaining in it, and that we shall exclude without mercy all men who fall short of that standard. . . . If you knew what I had to go through [grading exams] every summer of my life, you would see the pressure that comes to relax unless one steels his heart against the whole human race. This pressure of good nature and of wondering what difference a little more or less makes after all, is hard enough to resist at best. No faculty can avoid yielding to it more or less. The fact that we have yielded so little—so much less than is done elsewhere—is the chief thing that has kept the school up to the mark.[82]

Beyond these justifications, Thayer, along with newly hired Roscoe Pound, seemed to relish wielding the intellectual sword when grading. Each summer Thayer and Pound exchanged letters that discussed exams, analyzed grading disparities among the faculty, and gloated over the "dead" or "scalps," as they called the students who had flunked out. "Let me give you some gems from the books of the fallen. . . . Surely these deserve to die!" wrote Pound in July 1911. "Your extracts from the sayings of the fallen are genius indeed," replied Thayer, "I got [that student's] scalp too, and I am delighted to see that we shall not have him with us next year."[83] Memorialists of Thayer wrote that he eventually became a fine teacher.[84] However, the record appears mixed at best, notwithstanding his painstaking preparation.

Despite his pedagogical struggles, many students liked Thayer. Taking a personal interest in their legal education, he remained in the classroom after every lecture for as long as any student wished to discuss a question or problem. He thoroughly considered questions posed by his students in class or informal discussions and reflected on them long afterward. Thayer often composed extensive responses expounding on or correcting his initial answers and had them delivered to the student before the next class meeting.[85] Even his caustic private notes on the personalities and abilities of his students reflected his interest in their work.

Outside the Classroom

Thayer also supported the extracurricular academic activities of students. In this era before professional ethics courses, the Law School Society of Phillips Brooks House held well-attended Sunday evening lectures to address the ethical obligations of attorneys. Thayer's talk before the society in 1912 attracted a record-setting crowd of students, and he enlisted a number of practicing lawyers to give lectures. In addition, during his second year as dean, Thayer helped launch a moot court competition funded by a bequest from Dean Ames.[86]

Rooted in the English Inns of Court centuries earlier, moot court at Harvard—arguing often hypothetical law cases in adversarial teams—dates back to the beginning of the school in 1817. By 1825, Harvard Professor Asahel Stearns was organizing and conducting an extensive program of weekly moot courts and "disputations," or debates, on current topics. In 1825–26 Stearns reported thirty-seven moots, and in 1826–27, thirty-five, plus thirty-four "disputations." This for a student body not much larger than twenty! But during the 1870s the number of moot courts supervised by the faculty decreased steadily from thirty-two in 1870–71 to sixteen in 1877–78. In the 1879–80 academic year, the faculty voted to suspend its moot courts altogether.[87]

The faculty's supervision over moot courts declined because their teaching load rose in the 1870s due to the extension of the formal curriculum to three years, which Dean Langdell had championed. In response to that decline, student-run law clubs multiplied and organized their own moot courts. Such clubs had long existed, extending back to the Marshall Club, which dated its origin to 1825. But in the last quarter of the nineteenth century, law clubs became highly selective, organized, and demanding. Students drafted extensive briefs, often printed, and argued cases before moot courts staffed by upperclassmen. During the semester, clubs required work equal to that of another course, even more.[88]

The most selective of the law clubs was Pow Wow, which required excellent grades, academic commitment, and, generally, an Ivy League undergraduate degree. When Louis D. Brandeis (LL.B. 1877) was admitted in 1876, it was as noteworthy that he did not have a bachelor's degree as that he was Jewish. Until the beginning of the twentieth century, the prestige of Pow Wow exceeded that of the *Harvard Law Review*.[89] Future Harvard president A. Lawrence Lowell was a member of Pow Wow, and the club deputized him to ask Professor James Thayer to postpone his lecture on the Friday after Thanksgiving so they could have an extended weekend. Unlike the *Law Review* editors in the twentieth century, the members of Pow Wow and other leading clubs did not cut classes, and faculty expected them to attend every class and excel. Due to the academic commitment and stature of Pow Wow, Thayer agreed to their request for a postponement.[90]

In 1910, after a three-decade hiatus, the faculty reinstated formal moot courts and organized them as an "elimination tournament" that became known as the Ames Competition in honor of Dean Ames. First-year students were required to participate, under the supervision of the newly established Board of Student Advisors.[91] Dean Thayer assisted and remained involved, frequently attending arguments between the dueling law club teams and serving as judge. He also helped to find judges for the competition from among the leaders of the Boston legal community.[92]

The dean also took a personal interest in students outside of academics. He requested that the infirmary send him a daily report of admitted law students, and he set aside one afternoon a week to visit them there. Thayer wrote to parents informing them of their sons' conditions and promising to force the students to follow the doctors' instructions for recovery. When one student wanted a second opinion on his condition, Thayer summoned his personal physician to make the evaluation.[93] He also helped students with personal crises and career planning, and aided them financially, following Ames's example of supplementing the insufficient student loan fund with his own money. Known for his open hand, Thayer discreetly loaned money to students for school expenses and to young graduates for office expenses. Upon the debtor's graduation, the dean often relaxed repayment terms, and many student debts stood unpaid at the time of Thayer's death.[94]

These personal interactions reflected Thayer's belief that the law faculty should assume greater responsibility for the moral education of students, particularly given the inclination of graduates to enter large corporate firms rather than old-fashioned, small law offices where experienced attorneys would mentor young lawyers. Although the rising student-faculty ratio in the Law School prevented moral education on a broad scale, Thayer took mentoring seriously. He frequently talked with students in his office, invited them to his home every Sunday afternoon, and corresponded with his former students for years after they had left Cambridge.[95]

His informal interactions included attending "smokers" at which the students roasted the faculty with humorous songs and skits. In a notable incident in 1913, he responded to one student's performance with a characteristically brutal academic assessment: "I want to tell you something that may injure your self-esteem, but I think it best for you. Frankly, . . . your marks are abominable. You will never be a lawyer. But your music is very good, indeed. I suggest that you switch over to the excellent music school we have here and say nothing about it to anyone. Thus, they will be gaining a talented student, and we will be losing a wretched one." Following this advice, the student—Cole Porter—dropped out of Harvard Law School at the end of the term. Porter later said that if Thayer had not been so firm in denying "that I could ever become a lawyer, I might never have become a song writer."[96]

Administrative Duties and Controversies

Given his brief tenure and the school's entrenched customs, Thayer's administrative work was largely confined to the grind of routine matters, such as fighting with an uncooperative janitor, getting classroom clocks to operate on time, stopping correspondence law schools from using Harvard's name, and defending the record of the school's graduates against disparaging comments made by the dean of New York University Law School.[97] Thayer also took up the cudgels in a long-standing controversy over the alleged bias of New York State bar examiners against law students trained outside of New York State.[98]

In addition, the dean cooperated during 1913 and 1914 when Alfred Z. Reed of the Carnegie Foundation for the Advancement of Teaching asked Thayer to host "an unprejudiced European critic" in studying case method teaching at "a number of representative law schools." The prospect of this study, to be conducted by Austrian legal scholar Josef Redlich, raised some consternation among deans of other law schools. For example, Dean Stone at Columbia wrote that "Redlich came to this country several years ago and spent some time at Harvard Law School," and expressed views "extremely derogatory to the case system of instruction as it was employed at Harvard," which "would have been equally applicable to the instruction here, which we consider our best." Thus, Redlich's "opinion seemed to be based upon some misunderstanding. . . . as to the character of work carried on in our best law schools." Stone suggested that "representatives of the leading law schools [ought] to express to the Carnegie Foundation our distrust of [this] investigation."[99]

In reply, Thayer wrote that he agreed with Stone's "doubts about learned foreigners as the best persons to investigate American law schools. But I gather that the Carnegie people are bent upon having this done, and I do not see anything for the rest of us to do but submit and look pleasant." When Redlich's draft in German arrived, Reed, who would later conduct his own famous study of law schools, permitted Thayer to review it and suggest revisions.[100]

Apart from teaching method, the dean and faculty made two modest revisions in the curriculum. They created a new course on "causation" to be taken with Torts, Criminal Law, and Agency, and, responding to first-year students' difficulty in Civil Procedure, expanded its subject matter beyond pleading to include nearly all rules of procedure other than Evidence. With this broad perspective, students obtained a comprehensive and comprehensible view of an action from the beginning to the end. Professors reported that both of these changes were effective.[101]

In faculty affairs, the dean rapidly found himself drawn into controversies concerning the role and work of law professors. Thayer had been appointed on the principle that a law school should strive to hire experienced, practicing lawyers, and debate over this controversial question at the law school extended back forty years.[102] Soon after arriving as dean, Thayer ironically concluded that the principle was erroneous, and, looking back, he lauded the appointment of inexperienced James Barr Ames as an assistant professor in 1873. Thayer's view gained some notoriety, as is evident in correspondence with the secretary of the ABA Section on Legal Education.[103]

First, as a practical matter, Thayer argued that it is difficult to recruit a prominent and successful lawyer because "you cannot get him away from the prizes of practice to the rather ascetic salary of the teacher." Hence, seeking professors from the active bar likely leads to "the choice of a first-rate man without experience, or of a second-rate man with it." Second, it is better to hire faculty at a young age so "that they have not become too old to learn new tricks, and teaching [is] a new trick, as I know to my sorrow. Changing your profession in middle life is no joke."[104] Third, more substantively, Thayer concluded from his own experience in the classroom that "a long stretch of practice tends to disqualify a lawyer as a teacher by causing him to forget the mental habits and desires of beginners, and so making it harder for him to get into contact with them helpfully."[105]

On the opposite side of this issue stood John C. Gray, who had joined the law faculty from full-time practice in 1875. To Gray, the best professor was "one who can stir up an interesting colloquy" with students, a skill best learned from the dialogue that a practicing lawyer has with colleagues, judges, and opposing counsel. Attributing Thayer's opinion to an "excess of modesty" regarding his teaching skills, Gray assured Thayer that he was a better teacher than he believed and that he would not be a better teacher if he had spent his whole career at the Law School.[106]

Thayer's fourth and most contentious objection to hiring practicing lawyers concerned their working in private practice while on the faculty. Thayer's strenuous objection to this outside work ran counter to the school's long-standing informal policy and to the justification that legal practice was a valuable asset for at least some of the faculty, so long as it did not exceed about one day per week. Gray had practiced for one day weekly for more than thirty-five years, and Edward "Bull" Warren also practiced law on the side. Yet the young new dean firmly believed it was "impossible that any man should do full teaching work in the right way and carry on active practice at the same time," as he explained to the secretary of Yale University.[107]

Thayer therefore wrote a passionate letter to Warren at his office detailing why maintaining his practice was unwise. For one thing, legal practice would lead to a deterioration of the high standards of scholarship at the Law School. "Any man who is worthy of a chair in the law school must aim to become a master of his subjects; and for the scholarly mastery even of a single subject there can hardly be too much time in a long life," wrote Thayer. In addition, a professor's practice detracted from teaching. Whatever spare time Warren thought he had for practice should be used to "develop and fertilize the teacher" so that his classes do not become "dry and inferior," and Warren's maintenance of an office in the city reduced his vital, informal interactions with students on campus. Finally, practice was bad for the professor himself, who "is likely to find either that his work has fallen far short of what it should have been, or that he has so drawn down his physical reserves that both he and his work must pay for it at an inordinate price."[108]

Warren evidently shared the letter with Gray, who wrote back to Thayer that, in particular, Warren had abundant energy for both teaching and practice, and that, in general, the practicing attorney's cases can increase his standing with his students. Gray further suggested that Thayer, a novice teacher, did not yet know that after several years a professor does not have to spend as much time preparing for class, and therefore has more free time.[109]

An additional concern of Thayer's was that controversial work by a professor's law firm might reflect poorly on the Law School.[110] However, his position here was somewhat inconsistent, as it was on the issue of outside employment altogether. Thayer did not object to external consulting, as Bruce Wyman had done for the railroads. In fact, Thayer even refrained from criticizing Wyman when his consulting ensnared him in controversy. In 1913 it came to light that, while on the faculty, Wyman had made public speeches in favor of railroad companies without disclosing that he was on the payroll of one. Wyman argued that he had never actively concealed his position with the railroad and had simply put his academic study into practice. But it turned out that, in addition to compensating Wyman, the railroad paid questionable sums to his father, his siblings, and their family business. Hence, Wyman resigned to save the Law School embarrassment. Thayer not only refused to criticize Wyman's consulting, or such consulting in general, but he even suggested privately that Wyman had not been treated evenhandedly.[111] This position did not square with his remonstrating senior faculty for practicing law on the side, particularly because it might embarrass the school.

New Faculty

Thayer's ironic, inconsistent, and perhaps defensive opposition to practicing lawyers serving on the faculty was outweighed by his accomplishment in bringing four influential and long-serving professors to the faculty: Roscoe Pound, Joseph Warren (LL.B. 1900), Felix Frankfurter, and Austin Scott. The first was Pound, who had attended the Law School for one year, 1889–90, during Ezra Thayer's second year in the LL.B. program. In 1909, having read and admired Pound's pathbreaking article "Liberty of Contract," Thayer recruited Pound to fill the vacancy created by the resignation of Jeremiah Smith, and Pound joined the faculty less than two months after Thayer's appointment as dean. Thus began a close working and personal relationship between the two men that continued to deepen until Thayer's death in 1915. In fact, the young dean, age forty-four, came to treat the younger professor, age forty, not only as a colleague, but almost as a mentor.[112]

Thayer respected Pound's scholarship immensely, referring to him as a "wonderful creature" and expecting "great results" from his work. The dean even declined an honorary fellowship in the *Societé Internationale des Intellectuels* and recommended Pound instead.[113] Beyond seeking Pound's advice about teaching, as discussed above, Thayer asked him to assist in administering the school, because Pound had served as dean of the law school at the University of Nebraska. For example, Thayer sought Pound's help to raise money to hire Felix Frankfurter, to persuade Austin Scott to join the faculty, and to mentor assistant professors.[114] Thayer also sought Pound's counsel on faculty assignments, grades, admissions, and the controversy over the New York bar examiners. When Thayer became ill near the end of his life, he chose Pound to substitute for him at meetings and to reply to his mail.[115] Ultimately, Thayer wrote that he came "to count on [Pound's] judgment almost without going further" and consulting anyone else.[116] Occasionally the dean even told others that he would consult the entire faculty about a matter, but then told Pound that "I shall think whatever you do."[117]

On three particular issues, Thayer gave Pound exceptional freedom and responsibility. First, the dean handed him the reins to the school's new fourth-year S.J.D. program, which the Harvard Corporation had approved in 1909 and the faculty sketched out in 1910. But few students had enrolled, and no further plans were developed, so Thayer conferred on Pound, even before he arrived, the freedom and authority to build the doctoral program "pretty much as you please." In addition, Thayer encouraged Pound's interest in teaching graduate courses in Roman Law and Theory of Law.[118] Second, although the dean strongly objected to professors doing outside legal work, he supported Pound's periodic, and somewhat controversial, absences from the Law School in order to lecture elsewhere. In Thayer's view, "an exhibition of you is the best advertisement we get." Third, while the dean was opposed to law professors teaching courses in other departments at Harvard, he did not interfere when Pound agreed to teach in the Department of Social Ethics.[119]

The two men thus grew close. "I wish I had words to make the truth about you half as clear as I see it," Thayer wrote to Pound, "to the law school and to me personally, you are worth more than I like to think—I have really not the least idea how either could get along without you." During the summer recess, Pound was the only member of the faculty who corresponded with Thayer, and the dean frequently expressed concern that Pound was working too hard and implored him to take vacations in the summer. At the end of each summer, Thayer wrote how much he looked forward to reuniting with his colleague. Their closeness is also revealed in the tone of Thayer's letters. Normally reserved in his correspondence,

Thayer vented his criticism of other faculty in communications with Pound, particularly later in his tenure. The dean wrote to Pound in July 1914, "Please tell them jointly and severally to go to the Devil." In 1915 he exploded to Pound, "Damn our colleague! Such things as this make me blazing angry." Again, in 1915, "I wish you would tell them to go to Hell."[120]

One therefore wonders how other faculty reacted. Though documentary evidence is lacking, some professors likely felt that the young dean had bonded too closely with the new colleague, particularly because the relationship was unbalanced. Lavish praise and dependence flowed only from Thayer to Pound, very little in the other direction. Thayer's wife, Ethel, later commented to Pound that the dean "never thought how highly you held him."[121] All these points suggest that Thayer may have felt overwhelmed and threatened upon entering the deanship and sought to forge an alliance with the renowned newcomer whom he brought in from the outside.

The second senior faculty appointment made by Thayer was the promotion in 1913 of Joseph Warren, who had graduated in 1900 and been named an instructor at the school to teach the courses opened by Ames's departure in 1909. Thayer and Joseph Warren (not related to Edward "Bull" Warren) did not have a close relationship, but the dean confided to Pound that he thought highly of Warren. Arriving with Warren in 1909 was the third person to join the faculty: Austin Scott. Unlike Warren, Scott accepted the appointment ambivalently, telling Beale that he reserved the right to practice law during the academic year and to leave Harvard at the end of any academic year to practice in New York.[122]

At the end of the academic year 1910–11, Scott left to become dean of the law school at the University of Iowa, giving Thayer little notice. In January 1912, only five months after Scott's departure, Thayer arranged to meet him at a conference in Oregon, likely prompted by the Harvard faculty, who held Scott in high regard. Thayer told Scott that there were greater "opportunities for usefulness" at Harvard and invited him to name the terms that would bring him back.[123] Encouraged by Pound, Scott soon responded that he would return if he were named a full professor. Thayer was "delighted" and assured Scott that there was "no doubt" about the promotion, because he and Lowell supported it.[124] But President Lowell, in fact, was startled by the demand, and some senior faculty protested that Scott was not sufficiently seasoned. Bull Warren wrote directly to Scott to say that appointing someone two years out of law school was "hardly consistent with the dignity that ought to attach to a Harvard Law School professorship."[125]

Still early in his deanship, Thayer thus faced the dilemma of retracting the offer to Scott or battling senior faculty, some of whom he had already alienated. President Lowell had also expressed reservations about the senior appointment. Thayer sagely wrote back to Scott that he would stand by his offer to make Scott the youngest professor ever appointed at the law school, but suggested that "it might be a question from your standpoint how much . . . to ask." Would it be best to join the faculty shouldering that distinction? "On the question of what is *your* wisest attitude, I shall accept and respect your judgment." Scott reconsidered, and they reached a compromise that saved face all around. Scott returned to the Law School to teach in 1912–13 as an assistant professor with a full professorship to come in two years.[126] He later served as acting dean in 1915–16.

The fourth and most challenging appointment during Thayer's administration was that of Felix Frankfurter, who would serve on the law faculty, with intermittent breaks for public service, until 1939, when he was appointed to the U.S. Supreme Court. Thayer did not play a direct role in recruiting Frankfurter, though he supported the appointment strongly. How the idea originated is not clear, but in the summer of 1913 certain members of the faculty learned that Frankfurter, a stellar graduate in the class of 1906, might be recruited to join them from his work as an attorney in the U.S. Bureau of Insular Affairs. Although the entire faculty immediately endorsed Frankfurter, no vacancy was available or anticipated. But the professors naively assumed that the Law School could easily raise an endowment to support a professorship for Frankfurter and dispatched Edward Warren to offer him a position. Sending an emissary from the faculty was highly significant because Frankfurter was Jewish, and the Corporation, particularly President Lowell, remained strongly anti-Semitic. A recommendation sent to the dean would have gone to Lowell and then, likely, no further.[127]

Then came what the faculty considered the easy part: raising an endowment to support the additional professorship. This task they left to the dean, and he enlisted three alumni to lead the effort: Henry L. Stimson (1888–1890), Louis Brandeis, and Walter Meyer (LL.B. 1904). These reluctant conscripts made little progress through the fall of 1913, despite Thayer's persistent entreaties. Meanwhile, the dean's personal efforts to raise money in Boston did not bear fruit. As the end of the year approached, Frankfurter needed to know whether the school could afford to hire him, so Thayer abandoned the search for endowment and tried to scrape together enough smaller annual pledges to cover Frankfurter's salary for five years until a vacancy opened on the faculty. With Pound's help, this approach succeeded in just a few weeks as Brandeis,

Oliver W. Holmes Jr. (LL.B. 1866), and Learned Hand (LL.B. 1896), among others, made the necessary commitments.

But the entire effort proved unnecessary when Wyman suddenly resigned in December amid the railroad consulting controversy, creating a vacancy on the faculty. In January 1914 Thayer proposed the appointment of Frankfurter to the Harvard Corporation and—in an act likely never repeated in American higher education—returned the donated money without asking to keep it.[128] Frankfurter then joined the faculty for the 1914–15 academic year, and soon began to exasperate the dean with his "wild and erratic" grading.[129] This seemed to confirm Thayer's belief that teaching was a difficult "new trick" for a young practicing lawyer to learn.

Academic Imperium

Despite the many challenges and problems facing Thayer in Cambridge, the reach of Harvard Law School's academic imperium continued to expand across the country, as shown by the proliferation of case method teaching which had come to represent the anomalous *"new system"* of legal education that Dean Langdell had developed at the school.[130] When law schools adopted case method, they borrowed other aspects of the system as well. In 1890 only Harvard Law School employed case teaching, since law professors and jurists across the country considered it an "abomination."[131] In the subsequent twenty-five years between 1890 and 1915, the controversial case method spread rapidly to 40 percent of American law schools, and the rest of the Harvard system advanced commensurately. Legal education in the United States therefore grew progressively isomorphic based on the template established by Harvard Law School.[132]

Table 1.1 lists the forty-seven schools that converted to case method between 1890 and 1915. Conversion proceeded slowly during the first five years and accelerated after 1895. In geographical terms, law schools in the southeastern states adopted case method and the concomitant Harvard "system" of legal education more slowly and less extensively. Schools in the Great Lakes Region were particularly receptive, a factor likely explained by the high concentration of Harvard Law School alumni in Chicago.[133]

Conversion often occurred because the president of the university encouraged the law school to adopt case method, or certain "missionaries"—Harvard LL.B.s hired onto the faculty of other schools—encouraged those schools to convert. Other law schools chose to emulate Harvard without any direct in-

Table 1.1   Chronological Distribution of Forty-Seven Law Schools Adopting Case Method Teaching, 1890–1915

Time Period and Number	School and date of adoption	State	Mode of Adoption[b]
1890–1894: 4			
	Columbia U. 1892	New York	President
	Cornell U. 1892	New York	Indirect
	[a]Stanford U. 1894	California	Indirect
	[a]Northwestern U. 1890s	Illinois	President
1895–1899: 9			
	[a]U. Cincinnati 1896	Ohio	Missionaries
	New York U. 1896	New York	Indirect
	U. Pennsylvania 1896	Pennsylvania	Indirect
	[a]U. Illinois 1897	Illinois	President
	[a]Western Reserve U. 1898	Ohio	President
	U. Iowa 1898	Iowa	Missionaries
	[a]U. Maine 1898	Maine	Indirect
	U. Denver 1899	Colorado	Indirect
	[a]U. North Dakota 1899	North Dakota	Missionaries
1900–1904: 10			
	Boston U. 1900	Massachusetts	Indirect
	[a]U. California 1900	California	President
	Hastings C. 1901	California	Indirect
	[a]U. Chicago 1902	Illinois	President
	[a]Dickinson C. 1902	Pennsylvania	Missionaries
	U. Wisconsin 1903	Wisconsin	Missionaries
	U. Nebraska 1903	Nebraska	Missionaries
	U. Missouri 1904	Missouri	Missionaries
	U. Richmond 1904	Virginia	Missionaries
	Tulane U. 1904	Louisiana	Missionaries
1905–1909: 10			
	Indiana U. 1905	Indiana	Indirect
	U. Notre Dame 1905	Indiana	Indirect
	[a]U. Utah 1905	Utah	Indirect
	[a]Duke U. 1905	North Carolina	Indirect
	New York Law School 1906	New York	Indirect
	[a]Fordham U. 1907	New York	Missionaries
	[a]U. Kentucky 1909	Kentucky	Indirect
	[a]U. Oklahoma 1909	Oklahoma	Indirect
	DePaul U. 1909	Illinois	Indirect
	Indiana U. Indianapolis 1909	Indiana	Indirect

(continued)

Table 1.1   (Continued)

Time Period and Number	School and date of adoption	State	Mode of Adoption[b]
1910–1915: 14			
	U. Louisville 1910	Kentucky	Missionaries
	U. Colorado 1910	Colorado	Indirect
	George Washington U. 1910	Washington, D.C.	Indirect
	[a]U. Idaho 1910	Idaho	Indirect
	[a]U. Montana 1911	Montana	President
	U. Minnesota 1912	Minnesota	President
	[a]U. Detroit 1912	Michigan	Indirect
	U. Alabama 1913	Alabama	President
	Southern California U. 1915	California	Missionaries
	[a]Southwestern U. 1915	California	Indirect
	[a]U. Arizona 1915	Arizona	Indirect
	Valparaiso U. 1915	Indiana	Indirect
	U. Oregon 1915	Oregon	Indirect
	U. West Virginia 1915	West Virginia	Indirect

Source: Reformatted from Bruce A. Kimball, "The Proliferation of Case Method Teaching in American Law Schools: Mr. Langdell's Emblematic 'Abomination,' 1890–1915," *History of Education Quarterly* 46 (2006): 192–247, Table 1.

a. Indicates that the law school was recently established or reopened and reorganized shortly before adopting case method.

b. The three modes of adoption are: initiative of the university president, advocacy of "missionaries" who had graduated from Harvard Law School and were hired onto the faculty of the law school in question, or decision by a law school to adopt the Harvard model without any direct intervention and usually in order to appear up-to-date.

fluence by individuals associated with the Law School.[134] Several reasons led law schools to adopt case method.

Two reasons fit the "new institutionalism" explanation for the emerging homogeneity in legal education, as described in the Introduction to this volume. First, many schools desired to elevate their status or enhance their legitimacy. Dean Ames testified to this motivation when he reported that the president of Cornell University was "evidently much pleased at having secured a good Harvard man for their law school."[135] Conversely, graduates of Harvard Law School and of the associated law schools at Columbia University and the University of Chicago wished to extend the reach of their alma mater. Harvard alumni had great influence because, in 1890, the Harvard Law School Association—the oldest and most extensive alumni network of any university professional school in the country—comprised 1,390 alumni distributed over forty-three U.S. states and territories, three Canadian provinces, and four foreign countries.[136] In addition, Deans Ames and Thayer both sought to arrange "missionary" appointments to the faculty of other law schools. By 1917, sixty-seven American law schools had hired Harvard LL.B.s onto their faculty.[137]

The second "new institutionalism" reason was that case method viewed law "as an inductive science," analogous to the biological sciences. In the preface to the very first casebook in 1871, Dean Langdell had made this analogy, which endowed case method with the legitimacy of the preeminent, nineteenth-century natural sciences.[138] Josef Redlich in his Carnegie Foundation report of 1914 considered this legitimation to be one of the primary reasons for the proliferation of case method in American legal education.[139]

In addition, two functional pedagogical benefits contributed to the widespread adoption of case method. Teaching inductively from cases engaged students far better than lectures or recitations. Charged with the responsibility for interpreting original sources, students became active participants, rather than passive vessels, in the classroom. Thus, case method was "a powerful means of stimulating the interest of the student," observed both President Eliot and George Kirchwey at Columbia University.[140] Also, case method prepared law students to read and analyze cases and to discipline their minds suitably for the Anglo-American case-law system, as Redlich observed.[141]

Several practical developments also contributed to the spread of Harvard's case method across the nation. The practice of citing precedents in legal arguments increased, and more courts and jurisdictions began reporting their cases and publishing their reports. Hence, the expertise of reading and analyzing cases became more valuable.[142] Law professors therefore began publishing more casebooks after 1890, and these served as "the thin edge of the wedge" for advancing case method, in the words of Eugene Wambaugh.[143]

The casebooks of Ames and of William Keener purportedly exercised the greatest influence in this regard.[144] But far more influential were the two casebooks by Professor James Thayer, who published one on evidence in 1892 and another on Constitutional law in 1894–95.[145] His influence stemmed not from the number of his casebooks, but from his novel strategy of accommodating his readers. Approaching the casebooks as work, in his words, "that will bring in money," James Thayer was apparently the first Harvard author of casebooks who explicitly "kept in mind the fact that they might be assigned at other schools."[146]

This attention to his audience appeared in Thayer's express desire to limit the size of his casebooks to one volume. Reflecting his background as a literary figure and reviewer, James Thayer also attended to his readers by expanding the explanatory comments in order to help the student understand the cases. Whereas his colleagues on the Harvard Law School faculty confined their notes and explanatory prefaces to less than 3 percent of their casebooks, Thayer increased his explanatory commentary to nearly 20 percent of his casebooks. Additionally, whereas his colleagues cited old, classical authorities in their few notes, Thayer included mostly current authorities—largely his own articles, in fact—in order to inform the reader about the cases.[147]

Finally, James Thayer made an unprecedented effort to market his casebooks. He drew up a list of interested or influential law professors regarding his topic, and had his publisher send them a free copy of his casebooks. The strategy bore fruit among law professors in England and Australia and undergraduate instructors at American institutions, including Knox College, Dartmouth College, and the Massachusetts Institute of Technology.[148] As a result, Thayer's casebooks became "the most successful" of those published by Harvard professors through the beginning of the twentieth century.[149]

Despite all these reasons and developments contributing to the spread of case instruction, forty-two schools—about 36 percent of the total—refused adoption before 1915, as listed in Appendix A. One group of four aspiring university schools—Yale, Virginia, Michigan, and North Carolina—envied Harvard's status and often attributed its leadership to the obsequiousness of its followers, alleging that the proliferation of case method "is due not so much to any merit in the system as to the fact that it is a system adopted by Harvard University," as one Carolingian said disgustedly.[150]

Another group rejecting case method consisted of eleven local, independent, largely proprietary schools that subscribed to didactic lecturing. Their faculties comprised part-time members of the local bench and bar, and their students had relatively little academic preparation, worked full-time, and aspired to be local practitioners. These schools did not have national pretensions and proudly aimed to train "not profound jurists" but "second lieutenants in the legal profession . . . to prepare them to receive their commissions as junior officers in the great forensic army."[151] The largest group of schools rejecting case method included twenty-seven university and collegiate schools that operated with the policies and norms of local, proprietary schools. Some of these universities even leased their law schools or medical schools to local practitioners to operate autonomously for a profit. In 1875 Vanderbilt University, for example, established a twenty-five-year "lease" arrangement with three local attorneys to manage its law school.[152]

This kind of arrangement elevated the profile of the law school and attracted additional students both to that school and to the rest of the university. Even where such "leases" did not exist, universities often followed the practice of filling their law faculties with part-time, local members of the bench and bar, many of whom had neither an undergraduate degree nor a law degree, though they might have built up a respectable practice. Commensurately, the admission standards were low, the term of study brief, and the academic requirements undemanding. Among these twenty-seven university law schools with proprietary policies, the largest subgroup comprised fourteen schools in the Southeast. James Thayer's efforts to solicit interest in his casebooks therefore did not bear fruit in this region.[153]

Case Method Spreads to Other Fields

By 1915 case method teaching predominated among university law schools and began making inroads in other domains of professional education. For example, between 1900 and 1915 certain medical educators began to borrow case method from law schools. Medicine, of course, had long had "cases," and one might therefore expect case method teaching to be easily and rapidly adopted there, if not even to precede law in this regard. But no formally defined case method in medicine existed through the late nineteenth century. Among the leaders of American medical education up to that point, the watchword was "clinical instruction"—practice in relating medical science and experience through bedside instruction in the hospital. Such "clinical instruction" was clearly different from teaching with written casebooks, as the early advocate of medical case method, Walter B. Cannon, observed.[154]

In the late 1890s Cannon was a student at Harvard Medical School and happened to room with a student from Harvard Law School, who told him about the Law School's method of teaching and studying through written cases. Greatly impressed, Cannon, who went on to become a renowned medical scientist, published a noted article in January 1900, proposing "the case method of teaching systematic medicine." Cannon explicitly modeled this new method of instruction upon that used at Harvard Law School, and argued, in part, that written casebooks provided a more efficient and orderly presentation of issues than did the somewhat random cases encountered through clinical instruction in a hospital.[155]

In May 1900 the Boston Society for Medical Improvement considered Cannon's proposal at a meeting attended by President Eliot, Dean Ames, and several medical professors, all of whom spoke on behalf of "the inductive method applied to medicine."[156] Cannon's suggestion was soon put into practice by a number of medical professors at Harvard, as well as a few at the University of Pennsylvania and the University of Minnesota. In addition, these individuals published several medical casebooks in the first decade of the twentieth century.[157]

Among the notable converts was Professor Richard C. Cabot, whose 1911 medical casebook followed "the method of *case-teaching* which I have used for eight years at the Harvard Medical School, applying there a method long employed at the Harvard Law School."[158] By 1915, therefore, leading medical educators were borrowing case method directly from Harvard Law School. In fact, Cabot's case reports were the direct antecedent of the famous "case records" that later appeared weekly in the *New England Journal of Medicine,* which succeeded the *Boston Medical and Surgical Journal.*[159]

Meanwhile, colleges and universities had begun to found degree-granting business schools. In the 1890s three such business schools were founded, followed by nine in the 1900s, and nearly ninety more during the 1910s and 1920s.[160] Among these, the Harvard Graduate School of Business Administration, founded in 1908, grew to be the most influential and led the movement to borrow case method from Harvard Law School, as was announced in its very first course catalogue. Harvard Business School's explicit purpose in adopting case method was to acquire "esteem" and attract students, as the first dean, Edwin F. Gay, stated.[161]

Strongly supporting Gay in this decision was President Eliot and, especially, his successor, President Lowell. The latter wanted to elevate the status and quality of business education, and believed that adopting case method was the best means to legitimate the fledgling collegiate business schools.[162] Though Gay did not persuade the business faculty to employ case method, he announced the goal, and in 1919 Lowell appointed a Harvard Law School graduate, Wallace B. Donham (LL.B. 1910), to be dean of the business school. Under Donham, case method flourished at the business school despite the resistance from traditional faculty who preferred lectures and textbooks.[163]

These initiatives in business education, like those in medical education, therefore involved both the new institutionalist and the pedagogical explanations for the replication of Harvard Law School's case method. In the early 1910s the influence of Harvard Law School in professional education was proliferating across the nation, even as the physical and mental health of Dean Thayer rapidly deteriorated.

Thayer's Illness: "Infinitely Ashamed and Disgusted"

Though Dean Thayer did not have a history of illness and had remained active, he began to suffer from physical and psychological ailments. In March 1915 Thayer asserted that he had "disgraced [himself] by falling sick" with what his physician called "bladder disease."[164] He was forced to slow his work significantly for six weeks but managed to return with full force in mid-May. Frankfurter wrote to him, "Since you have assigned Public Service as my official subject, you will let me say that [your] complete recovery is both public duty and economy."[165] Thus began a six-month roller-coaster ride of excruciating attacks and temporary recoveries.

In June, Thayer regressed and was unable to attend local events or to travel to Salt Lake City to deliver the report of the Committee on Professional Ethics at the annual meeting of the ABA.[166] Nonetheless, he pressed on and undertook the herculean task over the summer of grading 552 exams in Evidence and Torts, the two courses that he had taught during the spring semester. In early July, however, Thayer suffered a devastating relapse. "I am infinitely ashamed and disgusted to report that things have been going rather badly with me," he wrote to Richard Ames (LL.B. 1909), secretary of the Law School. After completing the 244 exams for Evidence, Thayer delayed grading the 308 papers for Torts. Characteristically, he rejected solutions of either leaving the papers ungraded permanently or having another professor read the examinations for him. Thayer ultimately graded all the Torts examinations on his own.[167]

At the end of August, Thayer felt healthy enough to write to Pound that he was "much ashamed to have been whining about [my health] as I have in the past." Then he suffered another relapse in early September. Thayer's physician believed that he could have been cured with an operation, but that would have required a long convalescence and Thayer apparently was unwilling to take the time to heal himself.[168] His physical ailments continued to cause him tremendous pain and prevent him from working.

Meanwhile, Thayer began to suffer from what the newspapers later called "mental derangement," and his primary physician was treating him for a problem with "nerves."[169] His pain made him "despondent," and he "sometimes said he did not find life worth the living and would be glad when it all ended."[170] In July, Thayer wrote to Pound, "I am having a pretty rotten time, but I suppose it will end somehow." Writing for her husband, Ethel observed that "he is very miserable and has little or no interest in life at present, but

I am hoping for better things some day."[171] But the deep and long-term sources of his "nervous depression" lay in the continuing interaction between his personality and the work at the Law School.[172] His intense perfectionism combined with harsh self-criticism left him frequently "ashamed" or "disgusted" at his shortcomings or failures in minor events or affairs, whether personal or professional. These feelings inevitably roiled as he started working as a scholar and, particularly, as a teacher. But his responsibilities as dean intensified the feelings.

The difficulty was threefold. To Thayer, anything less than perfection was demeaning failure, and he assumed the deanship with personal doubt, if not trepidation, about his fitness for the position. Second, the school's long ascendance to preeminence and record of academic success veiled serious financial problems, which its constituents and the university administration failed to recognize, as discussed in the next chapter. Finally, the customary duties of the dean and Thayer's disposition did not allow him to address these financial problems.

Under Dean Ames, the school had operated virtually on autopilot. Continuing in Langdell's "groove," Ames did not undertake any initiatives or, really, exercise any leadership. Instead he devoted the bulk of his time to teaching. During his last full academic year, 1908–09, Ames taught five courses with enrollments of 268, 231, 145, 6, and 2 students, a staggering load for any professor, quite apart from decanal duties.[173] Arriving as a novice and outsider, Thayer was expected to shoulder the same teaching load and keep the school on its same trajectory, while addressing the unacknowledged financial problems. And any stumble was shameful failure in Thayer's mind. The predicament was intractable.

He tried desperately to manage the situation, keeping long hours, arriving at his office early in the day, and often working through the night to see dawn break from the windows of the library on the top floor of his Boston home. Thayer's doctors advised him to be "cheerful" and take the work "less seriously."[174] But he was far too dutiful and committed to perfection to take the deanship lightly.

In December 1913 he was offered a dignified escape when the governor of Massachusetts nominated him to fill a vacancy on the state Supreme Judicial Court. This position on the court was "the highest ambition of his life" and probably better suited to his personality, but he turned it down out of a sense of obligation to the school. In addition, Ezra Thayer recalled that his father, James Thayer, had recruited Oliver W. Holmes Jr. to the Law School faculty in 1881 and felt betrayed when Holmes left the professorship after merely six months for the same judicial appointment. Ezra remarked, "I know how my father would have felt about it," so he remained as dean.[175]

A leave of absence may have helped Thayer gain perspective and recover, but he would not indulge himself. He may have wished to live up to the example set by Ames, who, Thayer noted, never took a leave in thirty-seven years at the Law School. Thayer also believed that taking a leave would be irresponsible because it would throw the whole Law School "out of gear."[176] The relentless pace and anxiety were driving Thayer—insecure, sick, and exhausted—to the brink of mental collapse. The escalating tension reached a climax in early September 1915 when he returned from a summer break to resume his duties at the Law School.

The Final Tragic Days

On September 1, 1915, the Thayers closed their summer home in Hingham, Massachusetts, and traveled to Pomfret, Connecticut, to spend time with Ethel's family. The new academic year was fast approaching, so Thayer returned to Boston alone on the afternoon of Monday, September 13, to attend to school business in Cambridge. He spent Monday night in his Boston home.[177]

On the heartbreaking day of Tuesday, September 14, Thayer's mental state worsened dramatically. In the morning he went to work in his Langdell Hall office and spent some time with the school's secretary, Richard Ames. In the afternoon he returned to his Boston house, and chatted briefly with his housepainter, who was surprised that Thayer did not show his usual interest in the work. At about 3:30 p.m. Thayer went to his study on the top floor of the house, where he wrote and made telephone calls. At 4:30 p.m. he called Ethel in Connecticut, and sounded despondent and apprehensive, saying he was anxious to return to his family immediately. He promised his wife that he would take the 7:00 p.m. train that evening from Boston's South Station back to Pomfret.

Arriving at South Station about two hours later, he found that the train schedules had changed and that the last train to Pomfret had left at 5:30 p.m. A gateman at South Station said Thayer seemed "disappointed" and "taken aback" by this news but did not appear unusual in any other way. The gateman was the last person known to see Thayer alive. When Thayer did not arrive in Pomfret by train that evening, his family became alarmed. Ethel, her son James, and her sister sped to Boston by car, arriving at midnight. They broke into the family's Boston home, but found no sign of Thayer. Then they searched the Fenway neighborhood near the house, before finally giving up. Exhausted and upset, they checked into the Copley Plaza Hotel for the night.

The following morning, Wednesday September 15, the family informed the Boston Police Department that Thayer was missing. After piecing together the events of the previous day, the police began dragging the Charles River that afternoon. Ethel, distraught and near collapse, was put under a doctor's care, and moved to the quietest suite at the Hotel Vendome. Their worst fears were confirmed the following day. A Boston policeman spotted Thayer's body in the Charles River just before noon on Thursday, September 16, about 500 feet from his home. The medical examiner concluded that the cause of death was drowning and pronounced it a suicide because the body's facial expression was peaceful and there were no signs of violence.

The Thayer family accepted the coroner's determination and attributed the suicide to depression.[178] They also told the newspapers that if the 7:00 p.m. train to Pomfret had been running to take Thayer to his family, his "mental depression" would have "vanished" as it had on previous occasions. But the dean's family also attributed the depression to the burden of Thayer's work at the Law School.[179] Like many of Thayer's former colleagues at the bar, Roscoe Pound believed that the pressure of the deanship killed Thayer because the duties of the office had not been adjusted in light of the expanding student body and increasing demands of the school.[180] But even this assessment did not consider the psychological burden of Thayer's perfectionism, his difficult transition from legal practice to the faculty, and the serious financial problems of the school, thought to be flush with money. This last, unrecognized, and intractable problem surely contributed to his depression and tragic death.

NOTES

1. Quotation are from Charles W. Eliot to Albert V. Dicey (May 2, 1913), Papers and Presidential Records of Charles W. Eliot, 1807–1945, Harvard University Archives (hereafter cited as CWE Papers); James Barr Ames, "Address," in Harvard Law School Association, *Report of the Eighteenth Annual Meeting* (Boston, 1904), 71. See Samuel Williston, *Life and Law: An Autobiography* (Boston, 1941), 187, 206.

2. Quotations are from Richard Hofstadter, *The Age of Reform; from Bryan to F.D.R* (New York, 1955), 24, 116. See Morton Keller, *Regulating a New Economy: Public Policy and Economic Change in America, 1900–33* (Cambridge, MA, 1990), 1; Robert J. Gordon,

The Rise and Fall of American Growth: The U.S. Standard of Living since the Civil War (Princeton, NJ, 2016), 1, 3–4.

3. Claudia Goldin and Lawrence F. Katz, *The Race between Education and Technology* (Cambridge, MA, 2008), 11. See Gordon, *The Rise and Fall*, 3–4, 16; Sean D. Cashman, *America in the Gilded Age,* 3rd ed. (New York, 1993), 84; Glenn Porter, "Industrialization and the Rise of Big Business," in *The Gilded Age: Essays on the Origins of Modern America,* ed. Charles C. Calhoun (Wilmington, DE, 1996), 1–17.

4. Quoted in *The Centennial History of the Harvard Law School: 1817–1917* (Cambridge, MA, 1918), 188. See A. Lawrence Lowell, Annual Report of the President of Harvard University, 1908–09, 6.

5. Quotation is from Samuel Williston, *Life and Law: An Autobiography* (Boston, 1941), 187. Likely the term is based upon the usage in Alfred N. Whitehead, *Science and the Modern World: Lowell Lectures, 1925* (New York, 1925), 78, 275–276.

6. Jens Westengard joined the faculty in 1899, left in 1906 for several years to work in southeast Asia, and returned to the school in 1915 to become Bemis Professor of International Law. Bruce Wyman became a lecturer right after graduation, served for three years, and was appointed assistant professor in 1903, and then professor in 1908. Edward Warren was appointed assistant professor in 1904, and professor in 1908.

7. See Daniel R. Coquillette and Bruce A. Kimball, *On the Battlefield of Merit: Harvard Law School, the First Century* (Cambridge, MA, 2015) (hereafter cited as *Battlefield of Merit*), 559–571.

8. Lowell, Annual Report of the President, 1909–10, 16; Henry A. Yeomans, *Abbott Lawrence Lowell, 1856–1943* (Cambridge, MA, 1948), 253; Hugh Hawkins, *Between Harvard and America: The Educational Leadership of Charles W. Eliot* (Cambridge, MA, 1972), 269, 273, 282–284, 290.

9. Samuel Williston, Annual Report of the Dean of Harvard Law School, 1908–09, 164–168; Williston, *Life and Law,* 187–193; Charles W. Eliot, Annual Report of the President of Harvard University, 1901–02, 44; Frank L. Ellsworth, *Law on the Midway: The Founding of the University of Chicago Law School* (Chicago, 1977), 70–74.

10. Quotations are from Jerome D. Greene to Joseph P. Cotton (February 19, 1910), Records of President A. Lawrence Lowell, 1909–1933, Harvard University Archives (hereafter cited as ALL Records).

11. Bruce A. Kimball, *The Inception of Modern Professional Education, C. C. Langdell, 1826–1906* (Chapel Hill, NC, 2009), 85–87, 167–192.

12. "Harvard Likely to Elect Prof. Thayer. Indications That He Will Soon Become Dean of the University Law School," *Boston Journal* (March 25, 1910).

13. "Thayer Elected Dean of Harvard Law School," *Boston Herald* (April 14, 1910); Samuel Williston, "Ezra Ripley Thayer: A Fellow Worker's Appreciation," *Boston Transcript* (September 15, 1915).

14. William Rand Jr. to A. Lawrence Lowell (February 24, 1910), ALL Records.

15. Joseph P. Cotton to Jerome D. Greene (February 26, 1910), ALL Records; Ezra R. Thayer to Charles M. Storey (March 20, 1910), Ezra Ripley Thayer Papers, 1882–1915, Harvard Law School Library Historical & Special Collections (HLSLib) (hereafter cited as ERT Papers).

16. Quotation is from Ezra R. Thayer to A. Lawrence Lowell (March 20, 1910), ALL Records. See Ezra R. Thayer to Agnes Lee (April 7, 1910) and Ezra R. Thayer to Weld A. Rollins (June 13, 1910), ERT Papers; letters from Ezra R. Thayer to James B. Thayer (1889–1891), James Bradley Thayer Papers, 1787–1902, HLSLib (hereafter cited as JBT Papers).

17. Ezra R. Thayer to Evans Holbrook (March 8, 1915), ALL Records. See Ezra R. Thayer, "Public Wrong and Private Action," *Harvard Law Review* 27 (1914): 317; Ezra R. Thayer, "Observations on the Law of Evidence," *Michigan Law Review* 13 (1915): 355. In 1916 Pound stitched together Thayer's last work from drafts and notes that Thayer left behind: Ezra R. Thayer, "Liability without Fault," *Harvard Law Review* 28 (1916): 801.

18. *Centennial History,* 272. See Ezra R. Thayer to Lauriz Vold (January 8, 1915), ALL Records.

19. Charles W. Eliot, "Address," in Harvard Law School Association, *Report of the Eighteenth Annual Meeting* (Boston, 1904), 68.

20. See the discussion in Chapter 9.

21. Ezra R. Thayer, "Address," in Harvard Law School Association, *Report of the Sixth Celebration and Dinner* (Boston, 1910), 39.

22. Ezra R. Thayer, Annual Report of the Dean of Harvard Law School, 1911–12, 136–137; Ezra R. Thayer to Oscar W. Haussemann (June 28, 1913), Ezra R. Thayer to Henry Yeomans (June 13, 1913), and Ezra R. Thayer to B. J. Hurlbut (November 25, 1914), ALL Records; Ezra R. Thayer to Harlan F. Stone (October 15, 1914), ERT Papers.

23. See Bruce A. Kimball, "Before the Paper Chase: Student Culture at Harvard Law School, 1895–1915," *Journal of Legal Education* 61 (2011): 30–66.

24. Austin W. Scott to his family (October 2, 1906), *Letters from a Law Student to His Family, 1906–1908* (Cambridge, MA, 1974).

25. Albert F. Veenfliet to Papa and Mamma (October 7, [1906]), Albert F. Veenfliet, Letters to his Family and Harvard Memorabilia, 1902–1909, Harvard University Archives (HUA).

26. Edward H. Warren, *Spartan Education* (Boston, 1942), 6, 1–19.

27. Harvard Law School Faculty Meeting Minutes (March 8, 1910); Katherine M. Porter, "Learning by Doing: A History of the Board of Student Advisors, 1910–2000" (student research paper, Harvard Law School, 2001), on file with the authors; Roscoe Pound to A. Lawrence Lowell (December 11, 1916), ALL Records. On the later history of the Board of Student Advisors, see Chapter 17.

28. Ezra R. Thayer quoted in John Sheeseley, "Ezra Ripley Thayer: Dean of the Harvard Law School 1910–15" (student research paper, Harvard Law School, 2002), on file with the authors, sect. III B 2.

29. For admissions policy and procedures prior to 1910, see *Battlefield of Merit*, 406–411, 437–438, 452–455, 473–475, 499, 518n122.

30. Harvard University Catalog, 1875–76, 94. For the controversy on Langdell's move, see *Battlefield of Merit*, 406–411.

31. Quotations are from, respectively: Charles W. Eliot to Daniel C. Gilman (October 13, 1885), Daniel Coit Gilman Papers, 1773–1925, Milton S. Eisenhower Library Special Collections, Johns Hopkins University; Charles W. Eliot to Daniel C. Gilman (October 20, 1897), CWE Papers.

32. Gordon, *The Rise and Fall*, 16; Burton J. Bledstein, *The Culture of Professionalism: The Middle Class and the Development of Higher Education in America* (New York, 1976).

33. Quotations are from Eliot, Annual Report of the President, 1892–93, 30–31; Harvard Law School Catalog, 1893–94, 10–12. See Harvard Law School Catalog, 1903–04, 4–7, 11; *Battlefield of Merit*, 437–438.

34. Lowell, Annual Report of the President, 1909–10, 10.

35. Harvard Law School Faculty Meeting Minutes (November 5, 1913); Harvard Law School Catalog, 1914–15, 4–5; U.S. Commissioner of Education, *Biennial Survey of Higher Education, 1924–1926* (Washington, DC, 1928), 803.

36. Helen L. Horowitz, *Campus Life: Undergraduate Cultures from the End of the Eighteenth Century to the Present* (New York, 1987), 11–14, 41–55.

37. See *Battlefield of Merit*, 478–499.

38. Quotations are from Harvard University Corporation Records (October 30, 1905, and January 29, 1906), HUA. See Nora N. Nercessian, *Worthy of the Honor: A Brief History of Women at Harvard Medical School* (Cambridge, MA, 1995), 50.

39. Quotations are from Inez Milholland to the Dean and Faculty of Harvard Law School ([September] 1909), Inez Milholland Papers, 1906–1916, Arthur and Elizabeth Schlesinger Library Special Collections, Harvard University. See Virginia G. Drachman, *Sisters-in-Law: Women Lawyers in Modern American History* (Cambridge, MA, 1998), 141–142.

40. Harvard Law School Faculty Meeting Minutes (October 4, 1909); James Barr Ames to A. Lawrence Lowell (October 9, 1909), ALL Records.

41. Henry L. Higginson to A. Lawrence Lowell (October 8, 1909), ALL Records. See "Women in Law School," *Law Notes* 13 (December 1909): 165.

42. A. Lawrence Lowell to George A. O. Ernst (October 9, 1909), ALL Records.

43. Harvard University Corporation Records (October 11, 1909).

44. "Women in Law School," 165.

45. This incident has been reported as having occurred at different times and in different situations. Compare Nancy Waring, "A Cause to Celebrate, Women at Harvard Law School: The First 35 Years," *HLSB* (Summer 1988): 5; Erwin N. Griswold, *Ould Fields, New Corne: The Personal Memoirs of a Twentieth Century Lawyer* (St. Paul, MN, 1992), 170; David McIntosh, "A Minor Matter: The Admission of Women to the Harvard Law School" (student research paper, Harvard Law School, 1998), on file with the authors, 11.

46. [Joseph H. Beale,] untitled draft of narrative history of Harvard Law School since 1870, [1916], Zechariah Chafee Jr. Papers, 1898–1957, HLSLib.

47. See Dean Ezra R. Thayer Correspondence and Subject Files, ALL Records; Harvard Law School Faculty Meeting Minutes (February 23, 1915).

48. Harvard Law School Faculty Meeting Minutes (February 22, 1915); Petition (March 8, 1915) and Francis W. Hunnewell II to Richard Ames (March 11, 1915), ALL Records.

49. Walter Lippmann to A. Lawrence Lowell (March 19, 1915), ALL Records.

50. A. Lawrence Lowell to Walter Lippmann (April 20, 1915), ALL Records.

51. Nina A. Kohn, "Cambridge Law School for Women: The Evolution and Legacy of the Nation's First Graduate Law School Exclusively for Women," *Michigan Journal of Gender & Law* 12 (2005): 119–161. This excellent article draws upon Nina Kohn, "Cambridge Law School for Women: The Tangled Legacy of the First Graduate School Exclusively for Women" (student research paper, Harvard Law School, 2002), on file with the authors.

52. Ezra R. Thayer to Harlan F. Stone (February 1 and March 3, 1915), ERT Papers.

53. Ezra R. Thayer to Roscoe Pound (June 15, 1915), Roscoe Pound Papers, 1888–1964, HLSLib (hereafter cited as RP Papers).

54. Nercessian, *Worthy of the Honor,* 51–52.

55. Thomas W. Swan, Annual Report of the Dean of Yale Law School, 1918–19, 265, 271–272.

56. Swan, Annual Report of the Dean, 1918–19, 265, 271–272.

57. Julius Goebel Jr., *A History of the School of Law: Columbia University* (New York, 1955), 291.

58. [Francis W. Hunnewell II] to Daniel Vaughan (April 9, 1917), ALL Records. See Daniel Vaughan to [Francis W. Hunnewell II] (April 6, 1917), ALL Records.

59. Kimball, *Inception,* 160–164, 210–215. The numerical grades for each student in each course, beginning in 1871, are listed in gradebooks held in HUA.

60. Louis A. Toepfer, "Marks and the Man," *HLSB* (April 1958): 4.

61. Thayer, Annual Report of the Dean, 1910–11, 134. See Harvard Law School Faculty Meeting Minutes (June 25, 1910); Toepfer, "Marks and the Man," 4–5.

62. Toepfer, "Marks and the Man," 4; Kimball, "Before the Paper Chase," 30–66.

63. The attrition rate of first-year students varied as follows: 1908–09, 23 percent; 1909–10, 28 percent; 1910–11, 36 percent; 1911–12, 31 percent; 1912–13, 24 percent; 1913–14, 28 percent. Because students left and reentered and also moved in and out of the categories of "regular student" and "special student," the attrition rates are subject to interpretation and not easily calculated. Eric F. Fox, "Attrition Rates at Harvard Law School, 1900–1915" (student research paper, Boston College Law School, 2010), on file with the authors. By 1937 the average attrition rate for first-year students had risen to more than 30 percent. "Law Requirements Raised at Harvard," *New York Times* (January 15, 1937).

64. Thayer, Annual Report of the Dean, 1911–12, 135.

65. Ezra R. Thayer to A. Lawrence Lowell (October 5, 1912), ALL Records.

66. Rome G. Brown to Ezra R. Thayer (July 8, 1915), ERT Papers.

67. Lowell, Annual Report of the President, 1910–11, 15. See Gail J. Hupper, "The Rise of an Academic Doctorate in Law: Origins through World War II," *American Journal of Legal History* 49 (2007): 17–18.

68. *Centennial History,* 148.

69. See Kimberly Isbell, "Grade Reform at Harvard, 1968–1972" (student research paper, Harvard Law School, 2000), on file with the authors, 4n4; Porter, "Learning by Doing," 13; Thiru Vignarajah, "President's Perspectives: A History of Student Writing on the *Harvard Law Review,* 1887–1952" (student research paper, Harvard Law School, 2005), on file with the authors, 5–9.

70. Quotations are from *Centennial History,* 139–140. See Vignarajah, "President's Perspectives," 5–9; Deborah Pearlstein, "The Origins and Modern Purpose of the *Harvard Law Review*: Clinging to Community" (student research paper, Harvard Law School, 1997), on file with the authors.

71. See the Harvard Law Review black-tie dinner at the Lenox Hotel in 1908, depicted in *Battlefield of Merit,* 575.

72. Ezra R. Thayer to Harlan F. Stone (December 11, 1913), ERT Papers. See Pound to Lowell (December 11, 1916); Harry Sandick and John A. Freedman, *The Harvard Legal Aid Bureau* (Cambridge, MA, 1996), 2–3; Tilford E. Dudley, *The Harvard Legal Aid Bureau: A Brief History, April 1913—November 1930* (Cambridge, MA, 1930), 1–7; Paul Serritella, "HLAB Celebrates Ninetieth Year," *Legal Aid Bureau Newsletter* (December 2, 2004), 1.

73. Kimball, "Before the Paper Chase," 30–66.

74. "Law Requirements Raised at Harvard." See Roscoe Pound, Annual Report of the Dean of Harvard Law School, 1917–18, 118–123; oral interviews conducted with two individuals who served as assistant deans of Harvard Business School in the 1920s: John C. Baker, Oral History conducted by Bruce A. Kimball (October 1995), and Deane W. Malott, Oral History, conducted by Bruce A. Kimball (December 1995), both on file with the authors.

75. Ezra R. Thayer to Joanna Rotch (April 16, 1910), and Ezra R. Thayer to John C. Gray (July 11, 1910), ERT Papers; Ezra R. Thayer to Roscoe Pound (July 10, August 26, September 11, 1910), RP Papers. The following draws upon Sheeseley, "Ezra Ripley Thayer," sects. III B, IV.

76. Ezra R. Thayer, Notes (June 27, 1911), ERT Papers.

77. Ezra R. Thayer to Roscoe Pound ([1913 or 1914]), RP Papers.

78. Williston, "Ezra Ripley Thayer"; *Centennial History,* 28, 273.

79. Ezra R. Thayer, "Law Schools and Bar Examinations," *American Law School Review* 3 (November 1913): 374–381.

80. Ezra R. Thayer to Roscoe Pound (August 27, 1912), ERT Papers.

81. See Ezra R. Thayer, First-Year Class 1911–12, First-Year Class Torts 1912–13, Evidence 1913–14, First-Year Class 1913–14, First-Year Class 1914–15, HLSLib.

82. Ezra R. Thayer to Mark A. DeWolfe Howe (March 28, 1914), ALL Records.

83. Roscoe Pound to Ezra R. Thayer (July 28, 1911), ALL Records; Ezra R. Thayer to Roscoe Pound (August 17, [1911]), RP Papers.

84. *Centennial History,* 272–273; William G. Thompson, "Ezra Ripley Thayer," *Harvard Alumni Bulletin* (September 29, 1915); I. Maurice Wormser, "A Tribute to the Late Prof. Ezra Thayer," *New York Post* (September 27, 1915).

85. William H. Dunbar, "A Sketch of Thayer's Life," *Harvard Law Review* 16 (1916): 4; Ezra R. Thayer to [?] Gardner (May 24, 1912), ERT Papers.

86. Joseph H. Beale to A. Lawrence Lowell (February 12, 1910), ALL Records; Harvard Law School Faculty Meeting Minutes (May 2, 1911).

87. *Battlefield of Merit,* 26–27, 44–45, 45n23, 107–108, 223, 440, 472.

88. *Battlefield of Merit,* 440–461.

89. *Battlefield of Merit,* 445–446, 472. See Allon Gal, *Brandeis of Boston* (Cambridge, MA, 1980), 40–41.

90. Kimball, *Inception,* 249.

91. Quotation is from *Centennial History,* 148. See Harvard Law School Faculty Meeting Minutes (March 8, 1910).

92. Beale to Lowell (February 12, 1910); Harvard Law School Faculty Meeting Minutes (May 2, 1911).

93. Ezra R. Thayer to A. Lawrence Lowell (October 11, 1911), ALL Records; *Centennial History,* 275; Ezra R. Thayer to D. N. Wilds (March 18, 1915), ERT Papers; Ezra R. Thayer to Flora B. Miles (March 1, 1913), ALL Records.

94. Ezra R. Thayer to H. N. Curwen (January 13, 1915), and Ezra R. Thayer to Alden Ames (May 13, 1914), ERT Papers; "Student and Debtor" Galbraith to Ezra R. Thayer (June 14, 1912), ALL Records; Thayer to Vold (January 8, 1915).

95. Thayer, "Law Schools and Bar Examinations;" A. Lawrence Lowell to Jesse W. Lilienthal (December 14, 1916), ALL Records; Moorfield Storey et al., Memorial Address to the Court, in *Proceedings at the Meeting of the Bar in the Supreme Judicial Court of Massachusetts in Memory of Ezra Ripley Thayer* (Cambridge, MA, 1916), 11; *Centennial History,* 60, 273–275.

96. Richard G. Hubler, *The Cole Porter Story* (Cleveland, 1965), 12–13; William McBrien, *Cole Porter: A Biography* (New York, 1998), 50–51. See Ezra R. Thayer to Andrew R. Sheriff (June 26, 1914), ALL Records.

97. Ezra R. Thayer to W. S. Burke (November 3, 1911), ALL Records; Ezra R. Thayer to W. S. Burke (December 3, 1914), and Ezra R. Thayer to Henry B. Wenzell (December 19, 1913), ERT Papers.

98. See letters to and from Ezra R. Thayer (February 1913, June 1915), ERT Papers.

99. Quotations are from Alfred Z. Reed to Ezra R. Thayer (October 2, 1913) and Harlan F. Stone to Ezra R. Thayer (October 7, 1913), ERT Papers.

100. Quotations are from Ezra R. Thayer to Charles Noble Gregory (October 8, 1913), ERT Papers. See Ezra R. Thayer to Henry M. Bates (October 17, 1913) and Alfred Z.

Reed to Ezra R. Thayer (November 5, 1914), ERT Papers; Josef Redlich, *The Common Law and the Case Method in American University Law Schools* (New York, 1914).

101. Thayer, Annual Report of the Dean, 1913–14 and 1914–15.

102. Bruce A. Kimball, "The Principle, Politics, and Finances of Establishing Academic Merit as the Standard of Hiring for the Teaching of Law as a Career, 1870–1900," *Law & Social Inquiry* 31 (2006): 617–648.

103. Charles M. Hepburn to Ezra R. Thayer (March 5, 1912), ALL Records.

104. Quotations are from Ezra R. Thayer to Henry M. Ballantine (May 19, 1913), ALL Records; and Ezra R. Thayer to W. R. Thayer (January 21, 1914), ERT Papers.

105. Ezra R. Thayer to John C. Gray (May 18, 1913), ALL Records.

106. John C. Gray to Ezra R. Thayer (March 12, 1913), ALL Records.

107. Ezra R. Thayer to Anson P. Stokes (January 29 and February 3, 1915), ERT Papers.

108. Ezra R. Thayer to Edward Warren (January 4, 1911), ALL Records. See Sheeseley, "Ezra Ripley Thayer," sect. III B 1.

109. John C. Gray to Ezra R. Thayer (February 1, 1911), ALL Records; Gray to Thayer (March 12, 1913).

110. Thayer to Warren (January 4, 1911).

111. Bruce Wyman to A. Lawrence Lowell (December 21, 1913), Howard Elliott to A. Lawrence Lowell (November 1, 1913), A. Lawrence Lowell to Howard Elliott (November 7, 1913), and Ezra R. Thayer to Robert Wolcott (November 22, 1913), ALL Records.

112. The following draws upon Sheeseley, "Ezra Ripley Thayer," sect III A 1. See Chapter 3 below on Roscoe Pound.

113. Quotation is from Ezra R. Thayer to Henry L. Stimson (June 24, 1913), ALL Records. See Ezra R. Thayer to Thot Laszlo (December 2, 1912), ALL Records; Roscoe Pound, "Liberty of Contract," *Yale Law Journal* 18 (1909): 454–487.

114. Thayer to Stimson (June 24, 1913), Ezra R. Thayer to Julian Mack (September 26, 1913), Ezra R. Thayer to Walter E. Meyer (December 3, 1913), Roscoe Pound to Ezra R. Thayer (June 30, 1913), Austin W. Scott to Ezra R. Thayer (February 2, 1912), ALL Records; Roscoe Pound to Ezra R. Thayer (August 26, 1915), RP Papers.

115. Ezra R. Thayer to William Rand Jr. (March 30, 1915) and Roscoe Pound to A. C. Estes (July 10, 1915), ERT Papers.

116. Ezra R. Thayer to Roscoe Pound (July 26, [1914]), RP Papers.

117. Compare Ezra R. Thayer to B. H. Knollenberg (July 15, 1915), and Ezra R. Thayer to Roscoe Pound (July 15, 1915), RP Papers.

118. Quotation is from Ezra R. Thayer to Roscoe Pound (April 11, 1910), ERT Papers. See Harvard Law School Faculty Meeting Minutes (March 8, 1910); Thayer, Annual Report of the Dean, 1910–11, 140–141; Ezra R. Thayer to Roscoe Pound (August 2, 1912), RP Papers; Hupper, "The Rise of an Academic Doctorate in Law," 17–23.

119. Quotation is from Ezra R. Thayer to Roscoe Pound (May 6, [1915]), RP Papers. See Ezra R. Thayer to Robert Foerster (March 18, 1914), ALL Records.

120. Quotations are from Ezra R. Thayer to Roscoe Pound (July 26, [1914], August 2, [1914 or 1915], and undated [1915], RP Papers.

121. Ethel Thayer to Roscoe Pound (October 19, 1916), RP Papers.

122. Thayer to Pound (August 2, 1912); Austin W. Scott to Joseph H. Beale (March 14, 1910), ALL Records.

123. Austin W. Scott to Ezra R. Thayer (January 7, 1912) and Ezra R. Thayer to Austin W. Scott (January 25, 1912), ALL Records; Thayer to Pound (August 17, [1911]).

124. Ezra R. Thayer to Austin W. Scott (January 11, 1912), ALL Records. See Scott to Thayer (January 7, 1912).

125. Edward H. Warren to Austin W. Scott (January 28, 1912), ALL Records.

126. Quotations are from Thayer to Scott (January 25, 1912), emphasis in original. See Austin W. Scott to Ezra R. Thayer (February 16, 1912), ALL Records.

127. Thayer to Stimson (June 24, 1913); Edward H. Warren to Ezra R. Thayer (June 26, 1913), Felix Frankfurter to Edward H. Warren (June 25, 1913), and Felix Frankfurter to Ezra R. Thayer (July 30, 1913), ALL Records. See Thayer to Thayer (January 21, 1914).

128. Ezra R. Thayer to Louis D. Brandeis (October 30, 1913), Ezra R. Thayer to Henry L. Stimson (July 31, November 4, 1913), Ezra R. Thayer to Walter Meyer (August 1, October 30, November 18, 1913), Ezra R. Thayer to A. Lawrence Lowell (January 8, 1914), Ezra R. Thayer to Felix Warburg (January 31, 1914), ALL Records.

129. Ezra R. Thayer to Roscoe Pound (August 24, 1915), RP Papers.

130. Quotation is from "Harvard College Law School," *Magenta* (December 4, 1874), 67, emphasis in original. See also James J. Myers, "The Harvard Law School," *Harvard Advocate* (February 5, 1875), 146–147.

131. Quotation is from *Centennial History*, 35; Bruce A. Kimball, "Professor Langdell, the Case of an 'Abomination' in Teaching," *Thought & Action* 20 (2004): 23–38.

132. The following discussion draws upon Bruce A. Kimball, "The Proliferation of Case Method Teaching in American Law Schools: Mr. Langdell's Emblematic 'Abomination,' 1890–1915," *History of Education Quarterly* 46 (2006): 190–244.

133. Louis D. Brandeis, "Harvard Law School Association," pamphlet (June 12, 1890) (Cambridge, MA, 1890), 1.

134. Quotation is from Daniel R. Ernst, *The First 125 Years: 1870–1995, An Illustrated History of The Georgetown University Law Center* (Washington, DC, 1995), 85. The missionary mode has long been considered the primary, even sole, mode of dissemination of case method. See Paul D. Carrington, "The Missionary Diocese of Chicago," *Journal of Legal Education* 44 (1994): 467–518; Charles Warren, *History of the Harvard Law School and of Early Legal Conditions in America* (New York, 1908), 2:511–512; John H. Schlegel, "Between the Harvard Founders and the American Legal Realists: The Professionalization of the American Law Professor," *Journal of Legal Education* 36 (1985): 314–315; Steve Sheppard, "An Introductory History of Law in the Lecture Hall," in *The History of Legal Education in the United States*, ed. Steve Sheppard (Pasadena, CA, 1999), 1:31.

135. James Barr Ames to Charles W. Eliot (August 14, 1895), CWE Papers.

136. Louis D. Brandeis, "Harvard Law School Association," 3. See James Schouler, "Cases without Treatises," *American Law Review* 23 (January 1889): 2; Warren, *History of the Harvard Law School*, 2:504; "Notes," *Harvard Law Review* 2 (1888): 144; "Notes," *Harvard Law Review* 5 (1891): 238.

137. "Memoir of James Barr Ames," in James Barr Ames, *Lectures on Legal History and Miscellaneous Legal Essays* (Cambridge, MA, 1913), 6–7; *Centennial History*, 81–82, 185–186; Mary B. MacManamon, "The History of the Civil Procedure Course: A Study in Evolving Pedagogy," *Arizona State Law Journal* 30 (1998): 412n66.

138. Christopher C. Langdell, *A Selection of Cases on the Law of Contracts with References and Citations* (Boston, 1871), preface; Christopher C. Langdell, Annual Report of the Dean of Harvard Law School, 1873–74, 67; Christopher C. Langdell, "Address," in Harvard Law School Association, *Report of the Organization and of the First General Meeting, 1886* (Boston, 1887), 49–50.

139. Redlich, *The Common Law*, 15, 16.

140. George W. Kirchwey, "Law, Education for the," in *A Cyclopedia of Education*, ed. Paul Monroe (New York, 1912), 3:662. See Eliot, Annual Report of the President, 1879–80, 15–16.

141. Redlich, *The Common Law*, 18–25, 37, 40.

142. William P. LaPiana, "Just the Facts: The Field Code and the Case Method," *New York Law School Law Review* 36 (1991): 335, see 327–335. See Bruce A. Kimball, "'The Highest Legal Ability in the Nation': Langdell on Wall Street, 1855–1870," *Law and Social Inquiry* (2004): 80–83.

143. Eugene Wambaugh to James B. Thayer (February 17, 1892), JBT Papers. See Eugene Wambaugh, *The Study of Cases* (Boston, 1891).

144. *Centennial History*, 81–82; Goebel, *A History*, 140–141; Robert Stevens, *Law School: Legal Education in America from the 1850s to the 1980s* (Chapel Hill, NC, 1983), 56.

145. James B. Thayer, *Select Cases on Evidence at the Common Law* (Cambridge, MA, 1892); James B. Thayer, *Cases on Constitutional Law, with Notes*, 2 vols. (Cambridge, MA, 1894–1895).

146. Quotation is from James B. Thayer to Sophie Thayer (June 17, 1883), Memoranda Books, vol. 6, JBT Papers. See Thayer, *Select Cases on Evidence*, iii; Thayer, *Cases on Constitutional Law*, iv.

147. See Thayer's correspondence and records in JBT Papers, box 16; Thayer, *Cases on Constitutional Law*, vi. Compare John C. Gray, *Select Cases and Other Authorities on the Law of Property*, 6 vols. (Cambridge, MA, 1888–1892).

148. James B. Thayer to Charles W. Sever (August 13, 1892), Boston Book Co. to James B. Thayer (April 18, 1901), James F. Colby to James B. Thayer (March 31, 1894), Charles F. A. Currier to James B. Thayer (March 20, 1895), Abner C. Goodell Jr. to James B. Thayer (March 26, 1895), Robert J. Sprayal to James B. Thayer (March 22, 1901), all in JBT Papers.

149. John C. Gray, "James Bradley Thayer," *Harvard Law Review* 15 (1902): 601. See Abner C. Goodell Jr. to James B. Thayer (March 26, 1895) and George E. Gardner to James B. Thayer (September 1, 1898), JBT Papers.

150. Quotation is from Albert Coates, "The Story of the Law School at the University of North Carolina," *North Carolina Law Review* 47 (October 1968): 46. See William P. LaPiana, *Logic and Experience: The Origin of Modern American Legal Education* (New York, 1994), 144; Frederick C. Hicks, *Yale Law School: 1895–1915* (New Haven, CT, 1938), 43–45; John Ritchie, *The First Hundred Years: A Short History of the School of Law of the University of Virginia for the Period 1826–1926* (Charlottesville, VA, 1978), 54–56; Elizabeth Gaspar Brown, *Legal Education at Michigan: 1859–1959* (Ann Arbor, MI, 1959), 200, 209; Coates, "Story of the Law School," 36–42; Louis R. Wilson, *The University of North Carolina, 1900–1930: The Making of a Modern University* (Chapel Hill, NC, 1957), 551–552.

151. "Grant University Law Department," *The University Echo* (January 11, 1907). See "Chattanooga Law College Ends Successful Year," *Chattanooga Times* (June 4, 1911); "Annual Sermon Today Starts Commencement for Graduates of Chattanooga College of Law," *Chattanooga Times* (June 5, 1927); "College of Law Has No Freshmen," *Chattanooga Times* (September 3, 1943); Gilbert E. Govan and James W. Livingood, *The University of Chattanooga: Sixty Years* (Chattanooga, TN, 1947), 87–89.

152. Jon W. Bruce and D. Don Welch, "Vanderbilt Law School in the Nineteenth Century: Its Creation and Formative Years," *Vanderbilt Law Review* 56 (2003): 509, 515–518. See Mark Bartholomew, "Legal Separation: The Relationship between the Law School and the Central University in the Late Nineteenth Century," *Journal of Legal Education* 56 (2003): 368–403.

153. Charles A. Graves to James B. Thayer (May 9, 1895), R. McPhail Smith to Charles W. Sever (January 27, 1896), C. A. [Graves] to James B. Thayer (September 3, 1900), JBT Papers.

154. Walter B. Cannon, "The Case Method of Teaching Systematic Medicine," *Boston Medical and Surgical Journal* 142 (January 1900): 31–36. Cannon sent a copy of this article to William Osler, then dean of clinical instruction at Johns Hopkins University Medical School and pioneering advocate of clinical instruction, who thanked Cannon but equated case method with clinical instruction, thus denying the very distinction that Cannon was trying to establish. Saul Benison et al., *Walter B. Cannon: The Life and Times of a Young Scientist* (Cambridge, MA, 1987), 66. The distinction between case method and clinical instruction in law was later emphasized by Jerome Frank, "Why Not a Clinical Lawyer-School?," *University of Pennsylvania Law Review* 81 (June 1933): 907–923; Jerome Frank, "A Plea for Lawyer-Schools," *Yale Law Journal* 56 (1947): 1303–1344.

155. Quotation is from Cannon's subsequent article "The Case System in Medicine," *Boston Medical and Surgical Journal* 142 (1900): 563.

156. Charles W. Eliot, "The Inductive Method Applied to Medicine," *Boston Medical and Surgical Journal* 142 (1900): 557–558; Walter T. Councilman, "The Course in Pathology

at the Harvard Medical School," *Boston Medical and Surgical Journal* 142 (1900): 558–563; Herbert L. Burrell, "A Personal Experience in the Teaching of Surgery," *Boston Medical and Surgical Journal* 142 (1900): 565–567; James Barr Ames, "Discussion" in "Some Advances in Medical Instruction," *Boston Medical and Surgical Journal* 142 (1900): 568.

157. Cannon, "The Case Method of Teaching Systematic Medicine," 31–36; Cannon, "The Case System in Medicine," 563–564; Walter B. Cannon, "The Use of Clinic Records in Teaching Medicine," *Bulletin of the American Academy of Medicine* 5 (1900–1902): 203–213.

158. Emphasis in original. Richard C. Cabot, *Differential Diagnosis: Presented through an Analysis of 383 Cases* (Philadelphia, 1911), 19. See Richard C. Cabot, *Case Teaching in Medicine,* 1st ed. (Boston, 1906); Richard C. Cabot, *Case Histories in Medicine,* 2nd ed. (Boston, 1912); Walter B. Cannon, "Dr. R. C. Cabot's 'Case Teaching in Medicine,'" *Harvard Graduates' Magazine* 14 (1906): 609–610.

159. Robert E. Scully, "Preface—Weekly Clinico-Pathological Exercises Founded by Richard C. Cabot," *New England Journal of Medicine* 342 (January 13, 2000): 115.

160. Robert Gordon and James Howell, *Higher Education for Business* (New York, 1959), 20.

161. Melvin T. Copeland, "The Genesis of the Case Method in Business Instruction," in *The Case Method at the Harvard Business School,* ed. Malcolm P. McNair (New York, 1954), 25.

162. John C. Baker, Oral History, conducted by Bruce A. Kimball (October 1995), on file with the authors; Deane W. Malott, Oral History, conducted by Bruce A. Kimball (December 1995), on file with the authors.

163. Melvin T. Copeland, *And Mark an Era: The Story of the Harvard Business School* (Boston, 1958), 254–272.

164. Ezra R. Thayer to A. Leo Everett (May 20, 1915), ERT Papers. The following account draws upon Sheeseley, "Ezra Ripley Thayer," sect. VII.

165. Felix Frankfurter to Ezra R. Thayer (April 16, 1915), ERT Papers.

166. Robert D. Weston to Ezra R. Thayer (June 24, 1915) and Frederick E. Wadhams to Ezra R. Thayer (June 28, 1915), ERT Papers.

167. Ezra R. Thayer to Richard Ames (July 7, 1915), RP Papers. See Ezra R. Thayer to Roscoe Pound (July 7, August 24, 1915), RP Papers; Ezra R. Thayer to A. Lawrence Lowell (July 5, 1915), ALL Records.

168. Quotation is from Thayer to Pound (August 24, 1915). See Ezra R. Thayer to Roscoe Pound (September 4, 1915), RP Papers; Ezra R. Thayer to William G. Thompson (September 4, 1915), ERT Papers.

169. Here and below, see "Harvard Law Dean Thayer," *Boston Post* (September 17, 1915); "Lawyer's Body Found in Basin," *Boston Journal* (September 17, 1915); Ezra R. Thayer to William S. Thayer (May 27, 1912), ALL Records.

170. "Harvard Law Dean a Suicide," *Boston Journal* (September 17, 1915).

171. Quotations are from Thayer to Pound (July 7, 1915) and Ethel Thayer to Roscoe Pound [undated 1915], RP Papers.

172. Quotation is from *Centennial History*, 61.

173. Williston, Annual Report of the Dean, 1908–09.

174. "Dean Thayer of Harvard Ends Life in River," *Boston Herald* (September 17, 1915).

175. Quotations are from *Centennial History*, 275, 268. See "Thayer Refuses Seat on the Supreme Court," *Boston Herald* (December 18, 1913); "Thayer Chose Greater Duty," *Boston Tribune* (December 23, 1913). See *Battlefield of Merit*, 395–399.

176. Thayer, Annual Report of the Dean, 1909–10, 135–137. Thayer proposed the idea of retaining a teaching fellow at the law school to fill in the temporary absence of a faculty member on temporary leave, but nothing came of the idea of having a "pinch hitter for emergencies" until after his death when his widow donated $25,000 to endow such a position. See Roscoe Pound to Jesse W. Lilienthal (October 16, 1915), ALL Records.

177. The following draws on the thorough reconstruction from newspaper reports in Sheeseley, "Ezra Ripley Thayer," sect. IX.

178. See "Dean Thayer a Suicide," *New York Times* (September 17, 1915).

179. Ethel Thayer to Roscoe Pound (June 23, 1916), RP Papers.

180. Roscoe Pound, "Address of Acceptance of the Portrait," in Harvard Law School Association, *Ezra Ripley Thayer: An Estimate of His Work as Dean of the Harvard Law School* (Boston, 1916), 4. See Storey et al., *Proceedings*.

CHAPTER TWO

The Centennial Fundraising Fiasco, 1914–1920

"The Worst Endowed of All the Great Departments of Professional Education." That was how alumni described legal education in 1882 when Harvard Law School embarked on its first drive to raise money.[1] Even though wealthy individuals were donating immense sums to higher education for the first time in American history, the Law School's effort flagged. Nevertheless, the school grew wealthy during the 1890s by raking in tuition dollars from a large student body, running large annual surpluses due to a high student-faculty ratio, and accumulating a huge cash reserve.

Then, in 1906 and 1907, through a series of missteps under Dean James Barr Ames (1895–1909), the school spent nearly all of its reserve and became heavily dependent on tuition for its revenue, though it continued to appear flush because tuition revenue exceeded operating expenses so long as enrollment kept growing. Upon assuming office in 1910, Dean Ezra Thayer (1910–1915) discovered an excruciating predicament: the school that he and everyone else believed to be incredibly prosperous was, actually, penurious.[2]

This syndrome of tuition dependence—large and growing enrollment, high student-faculty ratio, illusion of prosperity, and expanding faculty and buildings leading to burdensome debt—worsened in subsequent decades. In order to maintain both financial solvency and academic rigor, the school began enrolling and flunking out more students. This required wielding the intellectual sword and failing those who "deserve to die!" in the words of Professor Roscoe Pound in 1911.[3] The financial malaise thus exacerbated the aggressive culture of the school and its devotion to weeding out the undeserving, which compounded the tendency to exclude those who did not fit the traditionally white, male, Protestant profile of the student body.

Escaping the tuition dependence required building the endowment, and that aim led Harvard Law School to conduct the first organized fundraising campaign in legal education. Commemorating the school's centennial in 1917, the drive was organized to address the "hazardous dependence on necessarily fluctuating tuition fees" by building "an adequate endowment," as the dean and alumni announced.[4]

Initially it appeared that "the greatest law school in the world" (if not the greatest professional school, according to President Charles Eliot) would get its deserving share of the torrent of benefactions flooding higher education.[5] But the centennial campaign coincided and competed with the first national, multiyear fundraising drive in higher education, which was conducted by Harvard University itself. While the university's campaign was generally considered a stunning success, the Law School's campaign was an utter failure. Despite the immense growth of the economy and philanthropy across the nation, Harvard Law School raised scarcely a quarter of its goal of $1 million, and merely 2 percent of its alumni donated. The centennial campaign thus failed to extricate the school from its reliance on tuition revenue.

This chapter explains the fiasco of the centennial campaign—overlapping the tenures of Deans Ezra Thayer and Roscoe Pound (1916–1936)—and the emergence of the debilitating tuition dependence syndrome between 1910 and 1920. Against this background of financial stress, Chapters 3–7 address other dimensions of Dean Pound's fraught administration during the tumultuous period spanning World War I, the first Red Scare, the Roaring Twenties, and the Great Depression.

From Prosperity to Penury

Enrollment at Harvard Law School exceeded 400 for the first time in 1892, then 500 in 1897, 600 in 1899, 700 in 1903, and 800 in 1911. Rising enrollment meant increasing tuition revenue, and the school began to accrue a surplus in the 1886–87 academic year. This surplus belonged to the school, as provided by the university's historical policy of "each tub on its own bottom," which made each unit financially self-sustaining.[6]

After twenty consecutive years of running a large surplus, Harvard Law School had accumulated cash reserves of almost $500,000 by 1906. Combined with its endowment of nearly $400,000, this reserve provided the school about $900,000 for investment, nine times its annual expenses of $99,500. The school was therefore not heavily dependent on tuition revenue, because investment income covered about 41 percent of the expenses. By comparison, Columbia University Law School, generally recognized as the nation's second-best law school at the time, lacked any significant investments, and Yale Law School had about $150,000 in invested funds.[7]

Nevertheless, the high enrollments feeding the surplus at Harvard Law School brought serious overcrowding, which threatened the quality of academic work and necessitated more space. In the late 1890s, planning commenced under Dean Ames for a new building that was to be named in honor of Dean Christopher Langdell (1870–1895), the first living professor of Harvard to be so recognized. But the distinction eluded Langdell because disagreements delayed completion until after he died in 1906. Finally opened in 1907, massive Langdell Hall remained for many years one of the largest buildings at Harvard, or in Cambridge, even though only two-thirds of the envisioned structure was erected before the money ran out. At that point the construction workers simply built a windowless brick wall at the open end of the building, dropped their trowels, and left a gravel construction pit beyond the wall.[8]

The funds ran out because no one sought any gifts, and the Law School paid for Langdell Hall, even though seeking money for a building was the easiest kind of fundraising.[9] Heeding that advice, professors, administrators, and "friends" of other schools and departments at Harvard began energetically approaching donors on behalf of their needs in the late nineteenth century. For example, in 1900 the philosophy faculty formulated a proposal for a new building for their department, commissioned the university architect to draw up a plan, publicized it in Harvard publications, and successfully solicited funds. The new philosophy building—Emerson Hall—was completed early in 1906 at no cost to the department or the university. Such efforts throughout Harvard produced "a remarkable inflowing of gifts," Eliot remarked in 1907.[10] But for Harvard Law School, "no benefactor came forward to present the new building," and "the Corporation did not think fit to provide more accommodations out of the general funds," as the *Centennial History* whimpered.[11]

Meanwhile, alumni gifts to the school were anemic. In 1910 the alumni association (the Harvard Law School Association) heartily congratulated itself for having donated about $360 annually during the previous decade. By contrast, each undergraduate class of Harvard College had been donating

$100,000 to its alma mater at its twenty-fifth reunion. Other law schools also received much larger gifts than did Harvard. At Yale, Dean Francis Wayland succeeded in raising $38,000 to complete its law building and $150,000 for endowment by the time he retired in 1903. At Columbia University between 1905 and 1910, the president and trustees tried to raise money for its law school and then appropriated $525,000 in university funds for a new building.[12] Unlike at those universities, the central administration at Harvard gave its law school no financial aid.

Spending about $400,000 of the cash reserve on the building reduced the school's income by about $18,000, or 15 percent, which had previously been earned from investing the reserve. Meanwhile, total expenses rose to about $127,000 by 1909, compared with $99,500 in 1906, due to increased costs in maintenance, faculty salaries, and a new university overhead charge. The critical ratio of expenses covered by investment income decreased from 41 percent to 18 percent over the same period. By 1909, when Ames retired, the invested cash reserves had plummeted from nearly $500,000 to merely $31,000. By 1911 the school was facing an annual deficit of over $16,000, compared to its annual surplus of about $49,000 just five years earlier. In addition, the student-faculty ratio approached 80:1, so more faculty were needed.[13] In financial terms, Ames's administration was a disaster.

Missed Opportunity

The Law School could have chosen a different path in 1905, notwithstanding the failure to raise any money for Langdell Hall. Academic institutions rarely have an opportunity to change their fundamental financial model, because they generally cannot reduce their largest, fixed costs: physical plant and tenured faculty. Remarkably, Harvard Law School had such an opportunity when Dean Ames and his faculty decided to build Langdell Hall. A prudent alternative would have been to raise the relatively low tuition and reduce enrollment.

Between 1870 and 1879, tuition had grown from $50 to $150, a dramatic increase, though Harvard Medical School was already charging $200. The Law School maintained the same tuition for forty years until 1920, at which point it was lower than the standard tuition at Harvard, which had increased to $200 in 1916.[14] Given its eminence, the Law School could justifiably have raised its tuition to at least $200 in 1905. By simultaneously capping its total enrollment at 400, the school would then have generated $80,000 in tuition revenue and $121,000 in total revenue, yielding a robust surplus of about $22,000, based on the expenses in 1905.

Several important benefits would have resulted. The student-faculty ratio would have dropped to 44:1, and the student body of 400 would have fit in Austin Hall, so there would have been no need to build Langdell Hall. The annual surplus of $22,000 would have continued to increase the cash reserve, generating investment income, which could have gradually supported additional faculty and scholarships. Subsequently, the school could still have grown, but gradually with a smaller student-faculty ratio, while maintaining the proportion of expenses covered by investment income at more than 34 percent. As future gifts arrived, the expansion of physical plant could have been funded from the accumulated surplus without reducing investment income, allowing the tuition revenue—and enrollment—to grow at a moderate pace.

For example, in 1905 the school received a bequest of $100,000 from James C. Carter (LL.B. 1853) that was used to endow a professorship. This windfall would have permitted spending $100,000 from the cash reserve to enlarge Austin Hall to accommodate 535 students, as had been contemplated, without diminishing the school's total invested assets of $900,000. At $200 tuition, those 535 students would have generated the same revenue of $107,000 that 713 students did at $150 tuition in 1905. And the proportion of expenses covered by investment income would have remained at the enviable 34 percent, while the annual surplus would have grown even faster with 535 students.

The dean and faculty may even have contemplated this prudent alternative, given that they had preferred to expand Austin Hall rather than construct a new building. But President Eliot and the Corporation insisted on a new building, and their disagreement with the faculty delayed construction between 1898 and 1905.[15] Even if the dean and faculty did contemplate this prudent path, no one seems to have made any financial projections, similar to the above simple calculations. Though dimly aware of the impending financial collapse, the dean and faculty reluctantly consented to building Langdell Hall.

Given the clear prospect of financial decline as the plans for Langdell Hall unfolded between 1897 and 1907, it is astonishing, and ironic, that Harvard University administrators continued to celebrate the prosperity of the Law School. In 1904 Eliot testified, "The Law School is the most successful of the University's professional Schools . . . in the relation of its receipts to its actual disbursements and its desirable expenditures." In view of this "great prosperity,"

Eliot raised the salaries of the Law School faculty above those of other departments.[16] As late as 1907 the Harvard Law School Association commended the "extraordinary growth" of the school in various measures, including the invested funds. In 1908 Charles Warren did the same in *History of the Harvard Law School.*[17] No one at the time apparently understood the school's vulnerability.

In 1910, Dean Ezra Thayer became the first Harvard administrator to recognize that the Law School had impoverished itself by paying for Langdell Hall and that the school's faculty-student ratio and endowment-student ratio were far lower than those of other Harvard schools. Thayer also became the first Harvard administrator to comprehend the cycle of tuition dependence that entrapped the school in the decade of the 1900s, despite President Eliot's earlier warnings.[18] This unforeseen and excruciating problem surely contributed to Thayer's anxiety and, ultimately, his suicide.

Despite the growth in the national economy, the titanic Harvard Law School was steaming toward a financial iceberg, and Dean Thayer—its self-critical, perfectionist captain—was frantically trying to steer away. His course correction amounted to launching the first national fundraising campaign in professional education in honor of the school's centennial in 1917. To understand this innovation and its stunning failure, we must examine the history of benefactions for American higher education and the rudimentary first attempt to mount a fundraising campaign in university professional education, undertaken at Harvard Law School in 1882.

Endowing Higher Education, except Law Schools

Since the founding of Harvard as the first colonial college in 1636, leaders of American higher education had sought funds for their institutions by soliciting wealthy individuals, conducting lotteries, and enlisting subscribers, among other tactics. But these were generally singular efforts responding to a specific need, such as opening an institution or rebuilding after a disaster. Nationally organized, systematic campaigns run by paid staff over several years first appeared in higher education during the 1910s. The roots of this development lay in the nation's economic growth after the Civil War.[19]

Prior to 1860 the economy of the United States did not produce enough surplus wealth to support significant benefactions, and most gifts to higher education were made for current use. Then the American economy began to diversify and grow enormously. Between 1870 and 1930, the gross national product of the United States grew sevenfold, as developments in transportation, communication, and manufacturing sparked a great economic expansion that was "unique in human history."[20] Commensurately, large industrial corporations emerged, producing an unprecedented number of millionaires and multimillionaires, who contributed to an enormous increase in philanthropy, most of which flowed into colleges and universities. By 1900, endowments in higher education totaled more than $165 million. Over the next two decades, retiring industrialists—particularly Andrew Carnegie and John D. Rockefeller—established foundations that enlarged the endowments of higher education even more.[21]

These large gifts continued the traditional pattern of benefaction in America in which the bulk of donations came primarily from wealthy merchants, businessmen, and their heirs. But in the early twentieth century there emerged a new phenomenon of "mass giving" or "people's philanthropy," which extended philanthropy beyond the wealthy by appealing broadly to the public for donations. The results were astonishing. In particular, the multimillion-dollar campaigns of the Young Men's Christian Association and the Red Cross during the 1900s and the billion-dollar campaigns for disaster relief during World War I set ever higher goals and made mass fundraising a common occurrence in the United States between 1900 and 1920.[22]

The new, high-pressure tactics of "mass giving"—short duration, widespread simultaneous solicitations, apocalyptic warnings of the consequences of failure, heart-wrenching anecdotes of beneficiaries, graphic thermometers or meters of progress—gradually infiltrated American higher education, supplementing its traditional reliance on wealthy benefactors. Between 1915 and 1925, Harvard University conducted the first multiyear, national, comprehensive campaign in higher education. The famous drive for the Harvard Endowment Fund (HEF) raised a staggering total of some $15 million, spawned the first fundraising consulting firm in higher education, and inspired hundreds of imitations over the next decade.

These developments filtered into professional education, as university professional schools slowly began to realize that financial resources determined their standing within the field. In 1882 a group of Harvard law alumni complained that at Harvard the endowment of the Law School was about $48,000, the Medical School $119,000, and the Divinity School $300,000.[23] This relative financial standing at Harvard typified the situation across the country. Theological schools continued for several decades to have the largest endowments. As of 1900 their aggregate endowment was about nine times larger than the aggregate of all medical schools and eighteen times larger than the aggregate of all law schools. By 1914 the aggregate endowment of theological schools was nearly $41 million compared to $20 million for medical schools and merely $2.3 million for law schools. Medical schools had closed the gap considerably, whereas law schools still straggled far behind, as the law deans of Harvard and Yale lamented in the mid-1910s.[24]

Law schools' relatively small endowment meant that they depended heavily on tuition and therefore needed large classes to sustain their revenue. This accommodation to exigency gradually became the norm. By the early 1900s even the best-endowed universities did not expect their law schools to obtain major gifts or to build endowment. Remarkably, the wealthiest universities adopted tuition dependence as policy for their law schools but not for their other professional schools.

At Harvard, during the first two decades after his inauguration in 1869, Eliot had consistently advocated endowing the Law School, which "is very inadequately endowed, and is therefore somewhat dependent . . . upon the number of its students. It is this deplorable dependence which debases so many of the professional schools of this country."[25] But after the Law School began accumulating an annual surplus in the late 1880s, Eliot changed his view. He ceased lamenting the tuition dependence and relatively small endowment of the Law School, and started extolling the school's "prosperity." For every other school at Harvard, however, Eliot continued the policy of seeking endowment and avoiding the "deplorable dependence" on tuition. In contrast, he thought that the Law School's annual surplus would sustain it during "any period of temporary depression."[26]

The same happened elsewhere. In his famous survey of medical education published in 1910, Abraham Flexner explicitly stated that medical education "can in no event" rely solely on fees for income. In 1914, Yale University president Arthur T. Hadley declared, "The best institutions of the United States are abandoning the practice of having professional schools supported by tuition fees alone." However, he continued, "the need for this change is felt with different intensity in different lines. *It is frequently possible to support a first-rate law school, taught by men of real eminence, from the fees of the students.*"[27] Based on this reasoning, universities early in the twentieth century began to adopt tuition dependence as policy for their law schools but not for other domains of professional education. Exemplary in many respects, Harvard Law School also provided the template for this financial vulnerability in legal education and incapacity in fundraising.

Charity versus Philanthropy

The fundamental and persistent challenge in fundraising was to explain why someone should donate to a law school. Convincing rationales had to fit the prevailing ideology—the meaning and justification—of financial benefaction in American culture and in higher education. During the late 1800s and early 1900s, that ideology shifted between two distinct and successive conceptions, which historians have termed "charity" and "philanthropy."[28]

The meaning of "charity" in America derived largely from the Protestant missionary impulse originating in the Puritanism of colonial New England. That impulse has been attributed to the altruistic motive of compassion and, alternatively, to the wish to impose upon others the benefactor's vision of the good and proper. By either motive, charitable benefaction constitutes an individual's response to personally witnessed problems of those in need. Charity means giving directly to specific individuals in order to alleviate the immediate effects of poverty, sickness, or personal distress. Thus, charitable benefactions are generally personal, small scale, empathetic, and palliative, temporarily satisfying the needs of particular individuals known to the benefactor.

Charity also implies that the recipients humble themselves and exhibit deference toward their benefactor. We cannot "be charitable to our equals," observed Progressive reformer Josephine Shaw Lowell in 1879.[29] Language describing gifts as charity often included references to financial "embarrassment" or "begging" for money. Leaders of colleges and universities had adopted this charitable discourse in the colonial period and continued to employ it, whether metaphorical or not. In 1910 the treasurer of Yale reported gratefully that the university did not need to borrow "any money to tide it over a temporary embarrassment." A few years later, the secretary of Yale warned that "constant personal begging on the part of a university is apt to be undignified."[30] Consequently, discretion, privacy, and anonymity usually characterized charitable gifts in higher education.

Charity had thus long carried a "stigma," as the *New York Times* observed, but dissatisfaction with terming benefactions as charity grew stronger in industrial

America.[31] During the late nineteenth century, the rising authority of natural science, the increasing power of business, and the drive for systemic, administrative organization transformed many aspects of American culture, including the ideology of benefaction. Concurrently there emerged a new understanding of monetary donations, which historians have termed "philanthropy."[32]

The rationale of philanthropy prescribed a more "scientific" approach to benefaction by emphasizing verification through reason and evidence, rather than the personal, emotional impulse of charity. Philanthropists thus consulted scientific research and professional expertise for an assessment of social ills and sought an "*orderly* or *systematic*" strategy to curing them. In particular, philanthropy relied on biological, sociological, psychological, and economic laws.[33]

Also, philanthropy intended to address "the root causes of social dysfunction" rather than the symptoms. And philanthropy did not foster personal relationships between donors and recipients, but established intermediary institutions, such as endowed foundations operating according to policy.[34] This philanthropic detachment—manifesting the widespread drive for order, system, and organization during the Progressive Era—was necessary for the assessment and correction of social problems. Such detachment contrasted with the direct and often intimate relationship between donors and recipients entailed in charity. Finally, dollars invested in benefaction had to realize a tangible return and do so efficiently, as in "the business world."[35] In John D. Rockefeller's famous phrase, "the business of benevolence" required effectiveness, economy, and efficiency.[36]

Although historians disagree on when "the much-heralded shift from charity to philanthropy" began in the United States, by 1910 contemporary figures observed that the prevailing ideology of benefaction in the United States had shifted from the palliative, personal ethic of charity to the broad, long-term, policy-oriented approach of philanthropy.[37] By that point, wealthy, retiring industrial capitalists had established and endowed new foundations dedicated to funding the philanthropic approach to social betterment. Commensurately, the term "charity" acquired a pejorative connotation and its use in public discussion declined.[38]

To be sure, the traditional charitable understanding of benefaction persisted in many sectors of American culture. Furthermore, the terminology was not used consistently, as when the *New York Times* addressed "Charity Old and New" in 1917 and defined "new charity" in terms of philanthropy. By that point, though, the conception of philanthropy had come to dominate in

American benefaction, especially the giving to higher education during the late nineteenth and early twentieth centuries. This was also the period when universities began competing for funding and trying to amass endowments.[39] As the preeminent and wealthiest law school in the nation, Harvard seemed perfectly positioned to thrive in that environment, having already begun to negotiate the ideological shift in the 1880s and 1890s.

1882 Drive: The Limits of Charity

In 1881 Harvard Law School received two significant gifts. One was a windfall, as would be typical of the school's major gifts over the next century. Edward Austin, an eccentric Boston merchant with no connection to the Law School, gave $135,000 for the construction and furnishing of Austin Hall. And alumnus Louis Brandeis (LL.B. 1877) and Professor James Thayer (LL.B. 1856) persuaded William F. Weld Jr. (1876–1879), a young wealthy Bostonian and recent student at the school, to donate $90,000 to endow a professorship for Oliver W. Holmes Jr. (LL.B. 1866).[40] Both gifts conformed to the charitable tradition that gifts should arise from discreet, personal negotiations between wealthy benefactors and university leaders, as was customary during this period.

Encouraged by Brandeis "to go ahead and get more," Thayer then expanded the solicitation and tried to raise about $80,000 for the library.[41] He began writing personal requests to alumni around the country, and recruited young alumni in various cities to personally approach older alumni. In January 1882, with Eliot's help, he arranged for newspapers to print stories about the school's need to endow scholarships, professorships, and the library. At the same time, Dean Langdell provided support by devoting nine pages of his published annual report to analyzing and justifying gifts to law schools. Whereas Thayer listed several purposes for the funds, Langdell's statement primarily addressed the need for scholarships. In his next annual report, Eliot summarized Langdell's reasoning and referred the reader to the dean's annual report for "full discussion of this subject and of the true conception of professional education in a university."[42]

In his 1882 statement, Langdell began by observing that in the United States, "money has seldom been given . . . for the promotion of legal or medical education."[43] The reason, he said, was the historical preference of Oxford and Cambridge Universities for "academic," or liberal arts, education and their depreciation of professional education. American colleges had blindly followed this tradition, according to Langdell, without recognizing that England provided support for legal training in other ways, such as at the Inns of Court.

Setting aside this circumstantial reason, the dean then turned to "the most plausible arguments against the claims of professional, and especially legal, education to pecuniary encouragement and support." His statement perfectly demonstrates an early phase of the ideological shift from charity to philanthropy. Langdell endorsed certain charitable points, while conceding and rebutting other charitable objections and broaching philanthropic arguments in his rebuttal.

First, although Langdell argued generally for gifts for legal education, he did not treat the institutions—the law schools—as the recipients. Instead, he analyzed support for legal education in terms of the students who would benefit from gifts in the form of scholarships. Thus, he adopted the personal terms of charity as his unit of analysis. Next, Langdell identified two charitable objections to providing scholarships. On the one hand, law students do not deserve gifts because they pay tuition "for their own advancement in life." On the other hand, law students, who are college graduates, are not really in need because "a young man who has received a good college education ought to be able to make his own way." In either case, law students do not qualify for charity because they do not incur a debt from which they need to be rescued. Payment for tuition is either an investment or a cost that law students can afford.

The former objection, Langdell effectively conceded by never replying. The latter he rebutted by arguing that Harvard's new, higher standard of legal education was more expensive and required more work, so a college graduate could not reasonably be expected to find a job to pay for it. In this fashion, he adopted, conceded, and rebutted certain points framed in the terms of charity.

In addition, Langdell attempted to invoke the inchoate philanthropic rationale by defending legal scholarships for their broad, long-term benefit to the public. First, providing scholarships would allow law schools to raise their academic standards and address the problem "that there are too many lawyers already, and that the interest of the public lies in reducing their number." Second, providing scholarships would allow law students to study longer and more intensively, and develop a more sophisticated understanding of law, which would serve "the most vital interests of the public and the State." Here Langdell took it for granted that stronger legal training and expertise provide a distinct social benefit. Third, beyond reducing the number of lawyers and increasing their expertise, scholarships would improve the quality of those entering the bar "by raising the standard of legal attainments, education, and character in the men [from] whom the profession is recruited." The public would be served if law students and lawyers were drawn from a larger pool of people and admitted on the basis of merit rather than ability to pay. The value of this meritocratic approach he knew from personal experience.

Nevertheless, Langdell did not expect these philanthropic arguments about public benefit to convince lay benefactors. "Perhaps no one but a member of the legal profession can be expected to take sufficient interest in the subject." He then concluded that lawyers can serve their self-interest, while also aiding the public, by improving their profession through endowing legal scholarships. Happily, lawyers who endow legal scholarships would enjoy both a better profession and a better society.

In the weeks following the publication of Dean Langdell's annual report, James Thayer's fundraising began auspiciously. His young recruits helped to solicit older alumni in New York, Philadelphia, Chicago, and San Francisco, who pledged a total of about $40,000 by early March. But then the pace of giving slowed to a crawl. "In fact, the whole outlook seems to me rather hopeless at present," wrote one young alumnus.[44] Undeterred, Thayer composed an appeal that was signed by seven prominent alumni, printed as a two-page circular, and sent to Law School alumni in Boston and New York City, the two major financial centers that were expected to provide most of the contributions. The circular proclaimed that the goal "should be not less than $60,000, and might . . . be increased to $80,000."[45]

Over the next few months gifts merely trickled in, and none exceeded a few hundred dollars. When Thayer relinquished the effort during the summer of 1882, the total had reached merely $47,000, and three-quarters of that came from two gifts. The vast majority of the Law School's alumni had not contributed. Several graduates earning large salaries in legal practice in New York City had contributed token amounts.

Extant testimony about the refusal to give is rare. But it appears that, on the one hand, law alumni were not persuaded by Langdell's philanthropic argument. "The benefits received [by the public] are not sufficiently apparent to the unprofessional mind to interest them in the school," wrote one alumnus from Salem, Massachusetts.[46] On the other hand, alumni most often framed their objections in terms of charity. They maintained that law students did not deserve help. Why should "the means of breadwinning . . . not be paid for by the recipient?" wrote an alumnus from Boston.[47] The financial needs of law students simply did not move them. One recent graduate reported to

James C. Carter, LL.B. 1853. Portrait by John Singer Sargent, ca. 1899. Carter's bequest in 1905 endowed the Carter Professorship of General Jurisprudence. From 1996 to 2015, this chair was held by Duncan Kennedy, whose photograph appears in Chapter 19.

Courtesy of Collection of the Harvard Club of New York City.

Thayer that "he approached several of his friends who were men of means" and their response "was positively chilling." Another recent graduate, who was rebuffed by older successful alumni in Chicago, "found . . . the hard stuff they are made of."[48]

A meeting of wealthy alumni, convened in New York City during April 1882 by lawyer John O. Sargent, proved most revealing. A graduate of Harvard College in 1830, Sargent had not attended Harvard Law School but nonetheless joined Thayer's fundraising for the Law School. Sargent invited several signees of Thayer's circular along with other prospects to a meeting, where he expected the signees to endorse the cause enthusiastically and to persuade the prospects to contribute. Instead, "to my astonishment," Sargent found that some of the signees "vehemently—not to say venomously—opposed . . . the whole plan." Foremost among the opponents was James Carter, who had attended the Law School from 1851 to 1853 and become a leading member of the bar in New York City.[49]

Carter and his fellow wealthy alumni interpreted benefaction in terms of charity, which they considered undignified. "It is against the interests of the university to go beg for money," they said, and "it has never been done before." Doing so "creates an unpleasant feeling in the community, which will be harmful" to the school in the long run. In their view, Harvard Law School was begging for charity and humbling itself before benefactors. Sargent "replied that there is no intention to beg."[50]

However, "Carter's opposition was persistent and uncompromising and exceedingly damaging to the cause," lamented Sargent. Instead of asking for donations, the Law School "should wait till the spirit moved someone to give a large sum—fifty years hence or more," Carter asserted.[51] In fact, Carter did just that in 1905, bequeathing $100,000 to endow a professorship in "general jurisprudence," the largest gift of endowment that the Law School had received to that point. In 1882, however, most legal alumni were repulsed by charitable appeals and deaf to philanthropic appeals. It seemed that the Law School would forever remain *"The Worst Endowed of All the Great Departments of Professional Education,"* as Thayer's circular had announced.

James Thayer's Justification, 1895

In subsequent decades, the relative poverty of university law schools became more alarming even as their academic standards gradually rose, demonstrated by the founding of the Association of American Law Schools in 1900. Doubtlessly reflecting on his experience in 1882, Thayer attempted to reframe what he called "charity" for law schools in the emerging understanding of "philanthropy." His most influential expression of the philanthropic rationale for benefaction to law schools came in an address to the American Bar Association in 1895.[52]

Thayer began with the premise that all "the great parts of human knowledge" are "alike beneficial" and "should be investigated with the deepest research and . . . critical study." Because law is one of those "great parts of human knowledge," Thayer reasoned, "our law must be studied and taught as other great sciences are studied and taught at the Universities." In order to foster and sustain such study, academic departments and schools teaching the great fields of knowledge ought to be supported with endowment. "If they are not, then the managers must needs consult the market, and . . . bid for numbers of students instead of excellence of work." To prevent legal education being shaped by the market place rather than academic excellence, "our law schools must be endowed as our colleges are endowed."

Thayer went on to elaborate the "beneficial" impact of legal study on society, which makes it deserving of philanthropy. Amplifying Langdell's argument on behalf of scholarships, Thayer proposed that legal education benefits the public through the efforts of its three kinds of students: "First of all, those [scholars] who, for any reason, propose to master these subjects. . . . Second, . . . the leaders in the practical application of these branches of knowledge to human affairs. Third, . . . all practitioners of these subjects . . . who wish to understand their business and to do it thoroughly well." But Thayer did not explain exactly how these individuals benefit society or how better legal education would increase that benefit. Instead, he merely stated the point and invoked an English authority, Richard Bethell, who maintained that "there is no other class or order in the community" than lawyers "on whom so much of human happiness depends, or whose pursuits and studies are so intimately connected with the progress and wellbeing of mankind."

Adding a philanthropic dimension to Langdell's argument, Thayer then addressed the "widespread skepticism among . . . practical men, in and out of our profession" about "use" and "necessity" of legal scholarship. Consider other fields, he said in reply. Such skepticism formerly prevailed about "what seemed to a majority of mankind useless and unpractical study and experiment" in chemistry, physics, physiology, geology, and other natural and technical subjects. Yet these studies yielded practical and technological benefits, such as "the steam-engine, the telegraph, the telephone, the electric railway and the electric light, the telescope, the improved lighthouse, the lucifer match, antiseptic surgery, the prophylactics against small-pox and diphtheria, aluminum the new metal, and the triumphs of modern engineering." Hence, the seeming impracticality of research does not mean that it cannot benefit the public.

Further, Thayer argued, the seeming impracticality of research arises from the inevitable obscurity of a complex subject. Like scientific and technical disciplines, jurisprudence is obscure and complex because the common law lies "in an immense mass of judicial decisions" extending over "six hundred years" of English legal history. These cases have yielded "certain inherited principles, formulas, and customs, and certain rules and maxims of good sense and of an ever-developing sense of justice." Indeed, a full understanding of legal doctrine in the cases requires tracing it back through the Middle Ages to Roman law.[53] Overall, in response to doubts about the use of legal research, Thayer seemed to reason that the complexity, obscurity, and seeming impracticality of research do not obviate its utility.

Attentive to the philanthropic demand for efficiency and economy, Thayer then addressed the objection: "'What is the use of carrying on our backs all this enormous load of the Common Law?' Let us codify, and be rid of all this by enacting what we need, and repealing the rest." To this, Thayer rejoined, "I have never seen any attempt at codification . . . which was not plainly marked by grave and disqualifying defects." According to his personal experience, the common law could not be made more efficient without sacrificing its effectiveness. Even if codification could work, he added, it would require the expertise of legal scholars and endowed law schools to support them.

Thayer's argument had significant weaknesses. He never presented a specific example of how research in common law did or might contribute to better decisions on practical legal questions. Nor did he specify or explain the precise benefit to the public that he promised from legal scholarship. He also seemed to hope that the reader would infer from his discussion about the telegraph, diphtheria, and so forth, that the very complexity and obscurity of legal research meant that it would be useful. In the end his statement offered little to change the fact that "the scientific systematic study of law" is "scorned or depreciated by many."[54]

Despite these problems, Thayer's argument advanced in philanthropic terms beyond Langdell's in at least two ways. First, Thayer justified gifts less for assisting individual students and more for contributing to law schools as institutions by increasing endowment and decreasing dependence on tuition. Thayer's emphasis on endowment was precisely that adopted by Harvard's

President Eliot in the 1870s and, later, by the Rockefeller-endowed General Education Board in the early 1910s through its explicit policy of aiming for the "concentration of gifts in the form of endowment."[55]

Second, whereas Langdell had described law as a "noble science" of equal rank with any other, Thayer tried to explain the potential benefit of legal scholarship to the public by pointing out the benefits of research in other academic fields. This approach framed benefactions to endow law schools as investments that yielded widespread social improvement, consistent with the emergent philanthropic reasoning. Due to this incipient philanthropic rationale, James Thayer's statement continued to be quoted two decades later during the administration of his son, Dean Ezra Thayer, when plans were launched for the first full-fledged fundraising campaign in legal education, organized around the Law School's centennial.[56]

Ezra Thayer Identifies the Financial Problem, 1910–1914

Soon after arriving as dean in September 1910, Ezra Thayer became the first Harvard administrator to appreciate the dire financial straits of the Law School. In his second year, Thayer charted the trends of expenses, revenue, enrollment, and tuition in the prior decade and identified the emerging tuition dependence syndrome: large and growing enrollment, high student-faculty ratio, illusion of prosperity and heavy debt resulting from expanding faculty and buildings. He also projected the coming deficits.[57] Thayer balanced the budget in his first year but started running a deficit in the 1911–12 fiscal year. Soon the university comptroller and president began pressuring him about the shortfall.[58]

Dean Thayer responded with various short-term fixes: "We are going . . . to save something on library expense," and "the present entering class is larger than the entering class was last year."[59] Other tactics seemed unpalatable. Concerned about excluding students with limited means, the dean and faculty resisted increasing the modest tuition of $150. They held the line even when the rest of the university raised tuition from $150 to $200 in 1915 and even when the governing boards and prominent alumni urged the Law School to follow suit.[60]

Nor did Thayer wish to increase enrollment, largely because he feared the temptation to relax academic standards in order to retain students. In fact, he attributed a modest decline in enrollment "to the increased stringency with which we have excluded the poorer men."[61] Overall, Dean Thayer's reasoning seemed to be that adding students increases tuition revenue, and high attrition validates academic standards.[62]

The easiest way to alleviate the tension between these two points was to admit more students to the first year and then flunk more out because first-year students, who had to enroll in enormous courses, were cheaper to support. Thus, high attrition in the first-year class was the most efficient way to generate revenue. By the early 1910s, about a quarter of the first-year class was failing or dropping out. But there was a difficulty. The total number of students would still plateau after an initial bump, and tuition revenue would not continue to grow unless even more students were admitted. If that happened additional faculty and facilities would be needed to accommodate the additional students required to sustain the revenue growth. It would be a never-ending cycle.

Exacerbating the predicament of tuition dependence was the widespread perception that the Law School was prosperous and did not need financial help. This illusion resulted from the large annual surpluses in prior decades, which had been reported annually in the Harvard treasurer's reports and trumpeted in Eliot's annual reports. Also, the school sometimes ran short-term surpluses in its operating expenses when the faculty was short-handed or the buildings were overflowing. By 1914 Thayer realized the detriment of the widespread perception that the school was wealthy, and he asked the editor of the *Harvard Alumni Bulletin* for assistance in "bringing to the public attention some facts about our financial condition."[63]

This was a big step for Thayer. Just as he had viewed asking for personal help as a sign of weakness, he regarded fundraising as appealing for charity. Financial need was not characteristic of a respectable institution, and Thayer confessed to feeling "some embarrassment about a public wail concerning the poverty of his institution." He repeatedly stated that soliciting funds was humble "begging" to be done quietly and privately. Furthermore, "the idea that the Law School needs money will no doubt surprise most people. The general impression is that the School is rolling in wealth. This is not surprising considering the record of the School." However, "the conditions which made such things possible were temporary and are now altogether changed." Thus, "the impression that we are so rich is not a healthy one."[64] Drawing on the dean's writings, the *Bulletin* published an account of the financial difficulties of the Law School, while the editor observed that "the fact that there can be any need for money . . . will be noted with some surprise."[65]

The fundamental long-term remedy, Dean Thayer realized, was "to raise an endowment." In this he was echoing his father, James Thayer. In 1913 the dean began making the case for increasing the endowment in his annual report and in speeches before alumni.[66] This took some initiative because he received no help or encouragement from President A. Lawrence Lowell (1909–1933). A Boston Brahmin, Lowell was generally averse to asking publicly for gifts and wrote to Thayer, "I know little or nothing about begging for money. I have not the knack for it."[67] Furthermore, Lowell reacted against the policies of his predecessor Charles Eliot, and deemphasized professional education.

Above all, Lowell's lack of support demonstrates the growing belief that law schools did not need or could not attract endowment. In his annual reports for 1910–11 and 1911–12, Lowell omitted the Law School from the list of university departments that "are in want."[68] Similarly, at Yale, the treasurer and the president omitted the law school from their appeals for deserving and needy professional schools at the university, including medicine, music, and forestry.[69] It is no surprise, then, that Thayer's appeals for endowment bore no fruit.

In 1914 Thayer asked each local chapter of the Harvard Law School Association to support a scholarship for a law student. All replied "that there was no prospect of raising any money."[70] Furthermore, the alumni repeatedly distinguished between "law school scholarships," which they opposed, and "college scholarships," which they strongly supported. Law students, they felt, did not deserve scholarship aid, because such professional training served the students' self-interest. Nor did they actually need help, because they could make their own way, having already earned a bachelor's degree. Even if law students were destitute, poor undergraduates in Harvard College ought to be helped first.[71] In fact, discouraging destitute law students might be beneficial, because the nation already had "too many lawyers." Remarkably, Langdell had itemized these same objections against scholarship aid for students in 1882.[72]

These failures in modest fundraising efforts certainly discouraged Thayer. The donors were reluctant, and the alumni and Lowell were unhelpful. The faculty became involved only when a project interested them. For example, in 1912 George Dunn, an Englishman who collected early law books and manuscripts, died suddenly, leaving "the finest [private] collection of early English law books" at the time. In January 1913, Harvard Law School librarian John H. Arnold learned that the Dunn library would be auctioned in the following month, and Arnold, Roscoe Pound, and Joseph Beale (LL.B. 1887) persuaded Dean Thayer that the school should attempt to purchase the collection, despite its financial straits. In one frantic month, Pound and Beale succeeded in raising the necessary sum of about $10,000, and the Dunn collection became the heart of the Law School's unrivaled collection of early English legal materials.[73] But this accomplishment did not alleviate the school's financial predicament.

In 1913 the Sixteenth Amendment to the U.S. Constitution authorizing a federal income tax was ratified, and Congress quickly enacted a flat tax on high incomes. Thayer, along with many others, feared that this tax would hurt philanthropy, but a charitable deduction was subsequently instituted and the dean was heartened in April 1914 when the New York City chapter of the Harvard Law School Association proposed that the school hold a fundraising campaign in conjunction with the centennial in 1917. Thayer immediately endorsed the proposal and wrote, "I shall be much interested to know what the . . . committee thinks is the right way to go at it."[74] Rather than taking charge, he apparently considered such a campaign to be the province of the alumni, perhaps because Harvard College alumni classes had independently organized twenty-fifth anniversary campaigns since 1900.[75]

Planning and Dithering, 1914–1916

The alumni fundraising effort began energetically. In June 1914 the Harvard Law School Association appointed a national committee and asked its chapters to name local committees across the country to lead the effort. Meanwhile, the New York City chapter, being the wealthiest and most active, appointed a Centennial Endowment Fund Committee to lead the drive.[76] Dean Thayer had been seeking such help and should have been overjoyed, but instead he expressed frustration about the details of organization and about having to specify the financial needs of the school. "The situation with me is simply and solely that we need money and need it badly," he wrote. "I do not care in the least for what purpose it is given. We need it for all purposes, and it would be as acceptable for one as for another."[77]

Lacking direction from the dean, the drive soon stalled. One reason was that even supportive alumni, such as Louis Brandeis, did not see the urgency.[78] After six months elapsed with little progress, Thayer appealed to Brandeis for help in recharging the effort. But the latter replied that "the needs of the Law School for added revenue are not urgent," and he seemed to think that the school could pass the hat in 1916 and collect all that it needed.[79] This response surely dismayed Thayer. If any graduate could and would help, it was Brandeis, an active alumnus who cared deeply about the school. But Brandeis did not appreciate the vulnerability of the Law School's dependence on tuition, and overestimated the willingness of the alumni to help, although he did recognize that the alumni association needed to be "revivified."[80]

Here was another reason for the stall: the alumni association was nearly moribund, though Thayer had been trying to invigorate it since he became dean. In May 1915 he was so hungry for alumni involvement that an invitation to speak to the local chapter in Utah made his "mouth water" because he was "most anxious" to energize the alumni association.[81] It was no surprise, then, that nearly a year passed before the New York Centennial Endowment Fund Committee and the Harvard Law School Association national committee finally met in July 1915.

By that point Dean Thayer could not work due to his depression, worsened by feeling "ashamed and disgusted" at his "incapacity."[82] Spiraling downward in the succeeding months, Thayer committed suicide in mid-September 1915. Professor Austin Scott (LL.B. 1909) then became acting dean and wistfully "hoped that eventually the friends of the School will by means of an endowment" liberate the school "from its present hazardous dependence on necessarily fluctuating tuition fees."[83]

In January 1916, Lowell appointed Roscoe Pound as the permanent dean, and Pound's annual report for 1915–16 built on the earlier statements of Langdell in 1882 and James Thayer in 1895 and shifted the rationale for the centennial campaign further toward the philanthropic justification of serving "the profession and the world." The centennial campaign then reprinted Pound's annual report and distributed it nationally, and his language and arguments were also repeated in the concluding chapter of the *Centennial History,* published in 1918.[84] The following year Pound incorporated his arguments and language in his tract *The Harvard Law School,* which was sent to all alumni after World War I in an effort to link the centennial campaign with the university's successful endowment campaign.[85] But Pound's writings came too late to save the centennial campaign. Their substance is analyzed in Chapter 4 in connection with the Law School's fundraising effort in the mid-1920s, when Pound repeated his arguments once again.

An important reason Pound could not save the centennial campaign is that he and Lowell did not agree on how the school should generate more revenue. Soon after appointing Pound, Lowell began pressing him about making "the ends meet in the law school budget. That is one of your jobs."[86] Lowell wanted the school to raise tuition, but Pound, like Thayer, did not believe that this would fix anything. Also, he argued that raising tuition would hit students from the West and South particularly hard, threatening the national reach of the Law School. Responding in his annual report, Lowell announced a tuition increase to $200 across the university, and pointedly observed two exceptions—the Divinity School, which was bound by external agreements, and the Law School, which, implicitly, had no excuse. The president and the dean continued to joust over raising tuition, and Pound did not seem to appreciate that the school's resistance to raising tuition contributed to the perception that it did not need money.[87]

At the same time, Pound seemed unwilling or unable to take charge of the centennial campaign. He provided summary statements outlining the financial needs of the school and the danger of depending on tuition. However, he offered no help in response to inquiries from Lowell and others: "What about the endowment fund? Have you any general plan? What do you think we ought to do out here? What steps, if any, have been taken in New York?"[88] As the date of the school's centennial crept closer during 1916, Pound did not actively participate in the campaign, or even mention the centennial campaign in any of his annual reports.

Meanwhile the national alumni committee continued to follow Dean Thayer's charitable rationale in its primary published statement mailed to all alumni. The Law School needed help to get back on its feet. Costs had risen, and few gifts were received. Like the deserving poor, the school merited assistance, because the problem "is not from any weakness. . . . The difficulty is due to lack of money."[89] Furthermore, the faculty and staff were trying as hard as they could, to the point of exhaustion. "The teaching force is seriously overworked." The alumni should not expect "that the officers of the school should carry burdens sufficient, as in Dean Thayer's case, to cause a complete breakdown." Moreover, the school had a close personal relationship with its alumni "for whose benefit the school exists." Alumni should affectionately bestow "an adequate endowment . . . as a birthday present at its Centennial Celebration."[90]

Still another problem was that the alumni planning the centennial campaign continued to dither. The New York committee and the national committee corresponded with each other for nine months through the spring of 1916, making no progress. One disgusted alumnus believed that both committees promptly answered each other's letters in order to appear active without actually doing anything. This disingenuousness "will go on indefinitely and nothing will be done," he wrote to Pound. The alumni "selected by the Harvard

Law School Association to raise this endowment fund are about as capable of doing it as *a dandelion is of sustaining a boulder weighing twenty tons.*"[91]

Thayer's suicide finally moved Lowell to help the Law School. The president expressed concern that "we seem to be overworking our best Professors, tiring them out. The death of Dean Thayer was a warning." Lowell worried especially about overworking the new dean, writing that Pound "feels that he is being driven very hard. He cannot reduce his teaching, and the work of begging, in addition, is likely to be more than he can support."[92]

The president then started to lobby for the Law School and to involve the Corporation.[93] At the end of 1916, Lowell wrote publicly for the first time that the Law School's "endowments are small in comparison with the work to be done, and have not grown with enlargement of the student body. . . . The one hundredth anniversary of the founding of the School . . . would seem an appropriate occasion for increasing the endowment, and providing new professorships."[94] Finally, Lowell began to serve as the main contact at Harvard for the centennial campaign. While Pound stood on the sidelines, the president corresponded with alumni organizers about strategies, timelines, and monetary goals; recruited the campaign chairman; and solicited prospective major givers.

Thayer's suicide also spurred the national committee, which asserted that Thayer had championed the Law School and the centennial campaign "at the cost of his life."[95] Hence, "there is no better advance agent than Thayer himself and no more fitting memorial to him."[96] Acknowledging the lethargy of the alumni, as well as their "general and widespread ignorance" about the condition of the school, the national committee in July 1916 issued a pamphlet memorializing Thayer and sent it to every alumnus in anticipation of the centennial.[97] In addition, the committee planned to publish a centennial history of the school, distribute it to the alumni, and host the centennial celebration in Cambridge during June 1917. Meanwhile, as Pound looked on, the national committee and Lowell tried unsuccessfully to recruit a campaign chairman. Finally, in July, James Byrne (LL.B. 1882), a lawyer from New York City, reluctantly accepted the role. From this point, everyone left it to a three-person executive committee and, primarily, to reluctant Chairman Byrne to raise $1 million in the next eleven months.[98]

During the fall of 1916, the law faculty began writing the *Centennial History,* their primary responsibility in the campaign. Intended to make the case for endowing the school, this was a composite work, overseen by Dean Pound,

Professor Beale, and alumni association president Frank W. Grinnell (LL.B. 1898). But Beale served as the guiding editor and delegated the irksome task of administering the many details of producing the volume and compiling chapter drafts to Assistant Professor Zechariah Chafee Jr. (LL.B. 1913), who had been hired in 1916.[99]

The account of finances in the *Centennial History* perfectly demonstrated the frustrating paradox faced by Dean Thayer. On the one hand, the volume stated that "from the beginning of the Langdell period, the School has been uniformly prosperous." On the other hand, the history lamented that the endowment of Harvard Medical School was nearly six times that of the Law School, and argued that, because "increase of tuition is not the remedy," the Law School needed a healthy endowment to maintain its high academic standards.[100]

The alumni association and executive committee meanwhile accomplished little during the fall of 1916, except that Chairman Byrne secured one significant gift—his own—for $150,000. Also, both he and Lowell solicited some potential benefactors.[101] These appeals revealed that, in addition to the lack of alumni interest, the centennial drive faced severe competition from outside the school.

Fundraising Competition

Within the Law School, Dean Pound and his young, like-minded colleague, Professor Felix Frankfurter (LL.B. 1906), saw an opportunity amid the centennial campaign to raise money for their favored projects, and they began seeking funds for endowed professorships aligned with their own scholarly interests, particularly a professor of criminal law. Initially this effort enthused Byrne, who thought that the dean and faculty were finally providing some help in soliciting funds. But Byrne soon became frustrated because the executive committee was told to restrain its effort in order to leave the field open for Pound and Frankfurter, who were exploiting the campaign for general endowment to fund their research interests.[102]

Some competition also arose from New Haven, where Yale administrators were tracking the financial situation at Harvard Law School and its centennial campaign. Notwithstanding the willingness of the Yale University administration, like that at Harvard, to allow its law school to rely on tuition revenue, Yale dean Henry W. Rogers had appealed for endowment in his annual reports for 1912–13 and 1913–14. Evidently annoyed by Harvard's incessant assertions of preeminence, Rogers declared at the end of 1915, "We were the first to establish such courses . . . for the study of International Law, General Jurisprudence, Roman Law and Modern Continental Law." He also proposed that Yale Law School needed endowment "to establish, what does not exist as yet in America, a School of Jurisprudence."[103]

These somewhat exaggerated claims piqued those in Cambridge, who were unaccustomed to any other law school claiming precedence about anything. Pound, who may have been particularly offended by Yale's claims, responded obliquely in his annual report for 1915–16, listing the financial needs of the Law School. Without mentioning Yale, Pound dismissed any proposal for a "school of jurisprudence" as "pretentious," ineffectual, and unworthy of "the large endowments demanded."[104]

Undaunted, Rogers's successor at Yale, Dean Thomas Swan, threw down the gauntlet in his annual report for 1916–17, announcing "the intention of this School" to address "the scientific and theoretical side" of law. In November 1916 the Yale law faculty issued a pamphlet proposing *"a School of Law and Jurisprudence,"* which would require $500,000 for a building and "at least $2,500,000, and probably more" in endowment. The *Yale Alumni Weekly* reprinted this pamphlet in March 1917.[105] Parrying that move in 1918, Pound and Beale concluded their call for funds in the *Centennial History* by dismissing any "pretentious 'school of jurisprudence' with elaborate courses in every phase of legal science and . . . 'research professors.'"[106]

But the Yale proposal did not yield any major gifts or substantively threaten the centennial campaign. The strongest competition to the Law School's centennial fundraising campaign came from the Harvard Endowment Fund (HEF) drive within Harvard University. The first of its kind in higher education, this drive, which Harvard College alumni began planning early in 1915, aimed to raise at least $10 million of unrestricted endowment for use by the university Corporation.[107]

In organizing the first national, multiyear, comprehensive campaign in higher education, Harvard University invented many policies that became customary in higher education in subsequent decades. One was to call a halt to "miscellaneous begging." According to this long-standing practice, any department could pursue fundraising at any time without coordination or approval by the central administration. Eliot had indirectly fostered this approach by encouraging all "tubs" to exercise entrepreneurial initiative in seeking gifts. The HEF organizers realized at the outset that "miscellaneous begging" created problems. Some solicitations might not fit the priorities of the university, or might lead to pestering donors with multiple solicitations, or might extract a smaller donation than a donor was capable of giving. After negotiating with units across the university, the Corporation adopted the policy that, during the HEF campaign, "the university must temporarily restrain all miscellaneous begging."[108]

The new policy seemed unfair to the Law School, which had begun planning its campaign before the HEF drive was conceived. Lowell therefore asked the HEF chairman, Thomas W. Lamont, to meet with Byrne and discuss some accommodation permitting the Law School to solicit its own graduates "and outsiders who would not be interested in the University otherwise."[109] In February 1917 Byrne and Lamont met and agreed to this arrangement.

The meeting also revealed that the centennial campaign was floundering. Chairman Byrne described himself equivocally as "the unofficial head." Further, he did not know exactly how much money the Law School hoped to raise, nor did he know the specific purposes apart from "several professorships." HEF leaders were surprised that the Law School leadership and its plan were so nebulous compared with the highly organized HEF campaign.[110] Sensing this perception, Byrne then wrote to Lowell somewhat defensively that his uncertainties had not caused the problems in the centennial campaign. Rather, "the delay so far has been caused (a) by the hope that [Pound and Frankfurter] might succeed in getting something and (b) by the general vague expressions . . . that we should not interfere" with the HEF drive.[111]

Dismal Outcome, 1917–1920

Having resolved the competition with the HEF drive, Byrne decided at the beginning of March 1917 that the centennial campaign should delay no longer for the sake of Pound's and Frankfurter's appeals. Byrne optimistically drew up a plan calling for a two-week blitz to solicit large gifts in Boston and New York City, a general canvass during April and May, and a centennial celebration in June.[112]

Given this plan, Lowell helpfully tried to find a Boston-area chairman for the centennial campaign. After several rejections, he finally convinced his cousin James A. Lowell (LL.B. 1894), the treasurer of the university's alumni association, to fill the role. Meanwhile, the executive committee composed a two-page general appeal for "an endowment of at least $1 million" for the Law School. Mailed to all law alumni on March 31, the letter explained that "the present tuition fee of $150 cannot be raised, because it would mean the loss of students who should be encouraged to come." The letter closed with a plea for "an adequate endowment" for the school.[113] A pledge card was enclosed,

along with Pound's annual report for 1915–16 discussing the school's financial needs pertaining to physical plant, faculty, library, scholarships, graduate
education, research, and general endowment. The centennial campaign was
under way at last!

One week later, on April 6, 1917, the United States entered World War I.
Even so, soliciting limped on during April and May, and notices appeared in
the newspapers, announcing the goal of $1 million.[114] Meanwhile, Lowell and
some alumni argued that the Law School should postpone the campaign in
deference to the war effort. But Pound, involving himself directly for the first
time, argued that the fundraising should continue. He needed the money. In
May, the school and alumni association made detailed plans for the centennial celebration in conjunction with the Harvard commencement in late June,
and invited U.S. Supreme Court Justices to speak.[115]

In early June the Harvard Law School Association finally canceled the centennial celebration and sent a notice to all the alumni. Hoping to scrape together some proceeds from the campaign, Pound appended to the notice his
personal appeal for subscriptions of ten dollars from recent graduates and
twenty dollars from older graduates to meet the anticipated deficit that the
Law School would face due to a loss of enrollment when students left for war.
He also arranged for the newspapers to publish the school's projected deficit
and wrote to some donors to see if they would honor their centennial pledges.[116]
Through the end of 1917, a few more pleas for endowment were published
and mailed to every alumnus.[117] Meanwhile, the HEF drive followed suit and
postponed its drive. Yale also delayed its plan to build "A School of Law and
Jurisprudence."[118]

Just as Pound feared, many law students rushed to join the legions leaving
higher education for wartime duty. In the fall of 1916, 857 students enrolled;
in the fall of 1917, only 297. As a result, the Law School suffered the greatest
loss of revenue among schools and departments at Harvard due to "the diminution in tuition fees" and "the comparatively small amount of endowment,"
said Lowell.[119] In the fall of 1918, enrollment fell to sixty-eight, and Lowell
wrote to Pound in June 1919 repeating the suggestion to increase tuition to
$200. Pound crumpled the letter into a paper ball.[120]

The school remained solvent throughout the war because expenses dropped,
especially for salaries, as faculty also departed to help the war effort. The large
enrollment in 1916–17 produced a surplus of more than $26,000, bringing
the accumulated surplus to nearly $77,000. Despite a deficit during 1917–18,
the total surplus stood at over $45,000 in June 1918. "The prospect, even if

we have but a handful of students, is not at all discouraging," Pound wrote to Lowell in August 1918. Indeed, the school broke even in 1918–19, and ran a surplus of nearly $26,000 in 1919–20.[121] Consequently, the temporary decline in operating expenses followed by a surge in enrollment resulted in a surplus that gave the illusion of prosperity.

But the malaise of tuition dependence remained, and the financial situation of the Law School actually worsened. Wartime inflation totaled nearly 80 percent from 1915 to 1920, and severely diminished the value of the reserves, endowments, and tuition throughout higher education.[122] Early in 1919, Lowell made a few private appeals on behalf of the Law School, and some alumni hoped to resume the centennial campaign as soon as the war ended. But the executive committee had dissolved. In fact, its chairman, Byrne, had become a member of the Harvard Corporation. He therefore ended his work on the centennial campaign and began soliciting instead for the HEF when it restarted in the spring of 1919.[123]

At that point, the HEF leaders made overtures to Pound for the first time, and appeared willing to include the Law School in their drive. Pound was delighted, but Lowell decided that the priorities of the HEF campaign should not include the Law School, so the school's needs were dropped from the HEF list of goals in June 1919, much to Pound's disgust.[124] The challenge to raise funds fell to the Harvard Law School Association, which published the complete *Centennial History* in 1918, and, in concert with the law faculty, planned "a great reunion of the graduates of the School" for June 1920. The event was held, highlighted by a speech from Charles E. Hughes, the Republican nominee for the presidency in 1916 and former Chief Justice of the U.S. Supreme Court, whose son, Charles E. Hughes Jr., graduated from the Law School in 1912. But little money was raised at the "great reunion," and the centennial campaign quietly expired.[125]

It is telling that no complete account exists of the amount contributed to the centennial campaign toward the goal of $1 million. No one at the Law School, including the dean, assumed responsibility for documenting or acknowledging gifts. The only semiofficial and incomplete records are scattered among the archives of the HEF, which haphazardly tracked donations to the Law School in order to distinguish them from its own. The amount received by the Law School scarcely required bookkeeping anyway.

The lone major gift was the $150,000 from Byrne to endow a professorship in administrative law. The second largest gift came from non-alumnus and non-lawyer Max Epstein, an industrialist from Chicago, who donated

$50,000 to the HEF for the purpose of providing repayable loans to law students. Epstein's gift carried a condition that the Law School raise tuition to $200, which the faculty reluctantly did in 1920.[126] The third largest donation, of $10,000, came from Arthur B. Emmons, a graduate of Harvard College in 1898 and Harvard Medical School in 1902. Hence, two of the three largest gifts came from individuals who were not alumni. All other gifts were less than $1,000, the vast majority less than $100. The fullest tally lists about 183 gifts totaling less than $250,000. The centennial campaign therefore netted less than a fourth of its goal, and received donations from about 2 percent of the school's 8,700 living former students.[127] It was far from a "fitting memorial" for Dean Thayer.[128]

A closer examination of some of the givers and nongivers makes the outcome seem even more pathetic. Many of the small donations of $100 or less came from lawyers working at prominent law firms and banks who were earning at least $20,000 annually. For example, in 1897 the Law School had offered a professorship to Mississippian Blewett Lee (LL.B. 1888), and he declined the offer, unwilling to relinquish or curtail his lucrative law practice. Not only did he reject the offer to join the faculty in preference for becoming a wealthy attorney, but Lee gave what he admitted to be only a "little contribution" of $100 to the centennial campaign.[129] This was likely one-half of 1 percent of his annual income.

Meanwhile, many law graduates made large gifts to other parts of Harvard rather than to the Law School! At least thirty individuals who had graduated from both Harvard College and the Law School gave $10,000 or more to the HEF and nothing to the Law School. Of these, ten gave between $25,000 and $85,000 unrestricted to the HEF and nothing to the Law School. Moreover, at least six individuals who had graduated from both Harvard College and the Law School gave restricted gifts of between $20,000 and $50,000 to other parts of Harvard, particularly the arboretum and the new school of education, rather than the Law School. These givers included President Lowell. Even more striking, five law alumni *whose only association with Harvard was graduating from the Law School* gave $10,000 or more to the HEF and nothing to the Law School. Fifteen such alumni who lived in New York gave between $1,000 and $25,000 to the HEF and nothing to the Law School.[130]

Furthermore, several figures closely associated with the Law School gave $10,000 or more to the HEF and nothing to the school's centennial drive. These included Joseph Cotton (LL.B. 1900), one of the three members of the executive committee of the centennial campaign! Others were the widow and the son of Professor John C. Gray (LL.B. 1861), who had taught at the Law School for nearly thirty years. Still another was the widow of Dean Ames, who had taught for forty years at the Law School and was lionized in the *Centennial History.* Virtually no one had responded to pleas that the centennial was "the time when the alumni of the school and of the entire university and the other friends of Harvard must provide a sufficient endowment for its great Law School" on the occasion of its centennial.[131] The campaign commemorating the centennial of Harvard Law School was a fiasco.

Reasons for Failure

Why did the centennial campaign fail so dismally? The tragedies of Thayer's suicide and World War I certainly interrupted and weakened the campaign. But these untimely events do not explain all of the outcome. Another possible reason is that conservative alumni refused to support the Law School due to the progressive politics of the faculty.

Three controversies might have prompted alumni ire. First, members of the faculty endorsed President Woodrow Wilson's nomination of Louis Brandeis to the U.S. Supreme Court in January 1916.[132] In addition, immediately following the war, Professor Felix Frankfurter became controversial for his left-leaning politics and Zionist views.[133] Finally, a special student at the school and instructor in the Government Department, socialist Harold J. Laski, gave a speech on behalf of the striking Boston police officers in October 1919.[134] These matters riled some alumni. But President Lowell maintained that upholding academic freedom actually attracted more contributions than any lost due to progressive political views of the faculty.[135] Furthermore, there is no evidence in the campaign records that political objections mattered much to donors.

A more significant reason for the failure was competition from other fundraising drives across the nation and at Harvard. As early as May 1916 some law alumni began warning that "all we can spare ought to go to the relief of the sufferers" in the war rather than to their alma mater. As the hostilities intensified in Europe, broad solicitations for disaster relief began to compete with other fundraising initiatives. During the same week in June planned for the Law School's centennial celebration in 1917, the reorganized and energized Red Cross raised more than $114 million in an unprecedented national fundraising effort.[136]

Competition also came from within Harvard. Although the HEF had agreed to cooperate with the centennial campaign, prominent law alumni argued that the Law School's effort could not and should not compete with the HEF drive, which was organized by Harvard College alumni. Law graduates also warned that alumni generally felt a stronger allegiance to their college than their professional school.[137]

In addition, many university policies regarding alumni favored graduates of the college above those of the professional schools. For example, graduating professional students who were not Harvard College alumni could not obtain tickets to commencement until Dean Thayer appealed to the president to change the rule in 1914. Similarly, Harvard did not recognize the graduates of professional schools as full-fledged alumni with the right to join the alumni association of the university or to vote for the Board of Overseers, the university's alumni advisory board to the Corporation, until 1916.[138] These policies reinforced the close relationship between college alumni and the university, while marginalizing graduates of the professional schools.

Given these advantages, the HEF honored the "very satisfactory arrangement" with the centennial campaign until the middle of 1917.[139] Then the wartime hiatus seemed to make the HEF impatient. When both campaigns tried to resume in 1919, the university drive surreptitiously disadvantaged the Law School in violation of their agreement. The HEF did not announce that gifts could be restricted to the Law School or inform law alumni who made a gift that this was even a possibility. By default, donations from law graduates were credited to the unrestricted HEF total. A striking example of this default occurred when HEF chairman Lamont received a letter from a wealthy graduate of Yale College and Harvard Law School who had read about the HEF and offered to help. In his reply, Lamont made no reference to the Law School campaign, contrary to the agreement that he, as the HEF chairman, had negotiated with Byrne.[140]

Even when alumni restricted their gifts to parts of Harvard, the HEF sometimes recorded them as unrestricted gifts to the university's endowment. Also, some HEF agents misrepresented the destination of contributions from law alumni by incorrectly telling them that the Law School would share proportionately from any donations made to the HEF. Consequently, Pound later wrote resentfully that "those in charge of [the HEF] used the Law School to procure money from our graduates by creating the impression that we were to share in the money. There never was the faintest intention that we should share."[141] Finally, Lamont and others began actively soliciting law graduates for the HEF even if they had no connection with any other part of Harvard. Only when the university campaign was satisfied that it could not extract anything from a law graduate would it refer that law alumnus to the centennial campaign.[142]

Another significant reason for the failure of the centennial campaign was weak leadership. President Lowell and Dean Pound were unwilling to participate until it was too late, and the alumni were lethargic. Some, like Joseph Cotton, one of the most prominent alumni organizing the centennial campaign, hoped that the recently formed Carnegie Foundation or Rockefeller Foundation would meet the goal with one large gift, thus ending the campaign and saving the work. Cotton therefore gave $20,000 to the HEF and nothing to the Law School.[143]

Similarly, the alumni organizers expected that writing and distributing circulars would induce alumni to contribute, saving the trouble of making personal solicitations. Dean Pound likewise devoted most of his effort to composing visionary statements, usually delivered to those already involved in the campaign. He rarely visited prospective donors or wrote personal letters. Nor is there any record that the alumni leaders did so. In contrast, the HEF leaders acted on the rule that in fundraising, "personal solicitation is the only satisfactory method." Writing statements "results in very few subscriptions."[144]

Even had the strategy of writing and disseminating appeals for funds been sound, the Law School publications fell short of the rhetorical standard espoused by HEF fundraisers. Harvard University's leading volunteer fundraiser, Episcopal Bishop William Lawrence, observed that "campaign literature . . . demands an English style strong, direct, and suggestive, the handling of facts in a way to stimulate the imagination and the kindling of a generous sentiment."[145]

Most of the centennial campaign appeals, particularly those written by Pound, read like legal briefs, setting forth abstract arguments with circumlocutions, passive constructions, parenthetical qualifications, double negatives, and a lack of specific facts or examples. Even in the public press, the Law School issued such Poundish statements as:

> The permanent maintenance of civil liberty depends upon the ultimate control through civil institutions of the belligerent tendency in human nature, whether of a domestic or international character, and this requires the training and scattering through the community of the most highly trained minds that the country

can produce. The training of such minds has been the great contribution, not only of the Harvard Law School, but of the other leading law schools in the country in the past, and it is essential that this work should continue at its highest practicable standards in the midst of, and as a part of, the campaign in support of civil liberty under law, the defense of which is the professed object for which this country has entered the European war. If the alumni will read this account of the School and its development and reflect on the significance of the service of scattering through the country highly trained minds for the practical study of the multitude of problems of civil liberty under law, the unique opportunity offered by this anniversary . . . will not have been wholly lost.[146]

Such prose could scarcely "kindle a generous sentiment," as Bishop Lawrence advised, particularly in contrast to the strong direct style of the HEF appeals.[147]

A final reason for the failure of the centennial campaign was the unwillingness of alumni to participate. They were certainly capable and energetic enough to lead a fundraising drive; several, such as Thomas N. Perkins (LL.B. 1894), filled key positions for the HEF.[148] Their reluctance to help the centennial campaign stemmed from two paradoxical attitudes.

On the one hand, many expected the drive to fail, leading to explicit and pervasive "pessimism."[149] "No amount of committees or effort is going to make contributing to a law school popular," stated Chairman Byrne in March 1917.[150] This feeling was rooted in the long-standing American animus toward lawyers that had originated in the colonial period, intensified in the Jacksonian era, and persisted subsequently. As the *Centennial History* observed in 1917, "dissatisfaction with law and distrust of lawyers are no less marked than a century ago."[151]

On the other hand, "apathy" also grew from self-satisfaction coupled with the belief among those around the Law School that it could not fail.[152] In his very first address to the Harvard Law School Association, Dean Thayer warned against this complacency: "The Harvard Law School cannot keep its present position by resting upon its past achievements."[153] Nevertheless, the centennial campaign publications were reluctant to confess needs and shortcomings and ask for help. The literature equivocated about the gravity of the school's situation and argued that the Law School needed funds in order to maintain its preeminence—a rationale that scarcely inspired a sense of urgency.[154] In contrast, the HEF literature was not reluctant to proclaim a crisis at Harvard, confess penury, and beg for charity.[155] Harvard University alumni responded to the plea of desperation.

The Law School's reluctance to beg for help reinforced the perception that it was wealthy and did not need gifts for endowment, as President Eliot had noted in the 1890s. Despite Ezra Thayer's efforts to extinguish it, the myth of the school's prosperity remained strong, and leaders of the competing HEF drive noted it, to their advantage.[156] For example, when the HEF leaders assembled data to demonstrate the budgetary shortfalls of various parts of Harvard, the figures revealed that only the Law School was running an annual surplus in 1919 and 1920. This temporary influx of cash resulted from the deluge of law students returning from the war that drove up tuition revenue, combined with the shortage of faculty that kept down costs. HEF leaders therefore argued that the Law School did not need money, compared to other units at Harvard. The perception was reinforced by the school's firm resistance to raising tuition, despite warnings from the school's allies that its resistance fed the illusion of prosperity.[157]

Underlying all these reasons—competition from the HEF drive, reluctant and inept leadership, and the pessimism and apathy of alumni—was the fundamental problem that the Law School's rationales were not compelling. The school could not explain to university administrators, its graduates, or lay citizens *why* someone should donate to a law school. The objections to giving charity to law students identified by Langdell in 1882 reverberated in the testimony from potential donors nearly forty years later: law students neither need nor deserve help, and gifts merely worsen the overcrowding of the bar.

No more effective was Pound's attempt at formulating a philanthropic rationale in the late 1910s. His arguments for the social benefit of legal education and research, were vague and unsubstantiated. His statements lacked illustrative examples and emotional appeal. Ironically, a school devoted to training effective advocates could not argue persuasively, on its own behalf, that giving to Harvard Law School fit the meaning and justification of financial benefaction in American higher education. As a result, the graduates' lethargy, pessimism, and apathy about donating to Harvard Law School persisted for decades.

Tuition Dependence Syndrome

Also persisting for decades was the need for endowment resulting from the entrenched tuition dependence, whose dimensions became manifest when the centennial campaign failed. Large and growing enrollment coupled with a high student-faculty ratio created both the illusion of prosperity and the need for additional faculty and physical plant. To enlarge the faculty and buildings, the school required more sustained revenue, which endowment could ensure. Consequently, the school ran a fundraising campaign. When that failed, the school faced a choice of whether to raise tuition. Refusing to do so, the school had to enroll more students to generate more tuition revenue, while maintaining a high student-faculty ratio to keep expenses low. Figure 2.1 depicts this development.

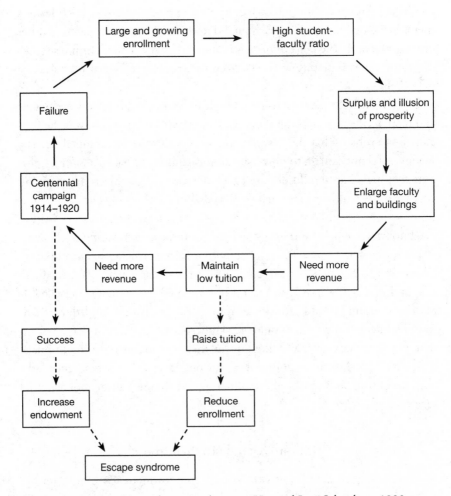

Figure 2.1. Tuition Dependence Syndrome at Harvard Law School, ca. 1920. Note: Solid arrows represent path followed from 1900 to 1920. Dotted arrows represent alternate paths available.

Increasing attrition in order to maintain academic standards complicated the financial bind, because the tactics of adding students and flunking them out worked against each other financially. But the most cost-effective way to negotiate this tension was to fail students in the first-year class, since they cost the least to educate. However, the lost first-year students would not pay tuition in their second and third years, which meant that the school had to keep enlarging the first-year class in order to make up for the loss and keep increasing its tuition revenue. It was a path of perpetual growth and deeper dependence.

The tuition dependence syndrome continued to evolve in subsequent decades. The important and lasting effect was that Harvard Law School had to "live from hand to mouth," as both Dean Pound in 1919 and Dean Erwin Griswold (1946–1967) in 1962 observed.[158] Furthermore, Harvard Law School's preeminence led other universities to apply this financial model to their law schools, contributing to the isomorphic character of legal education, as explained in the Introduction to this volume. If Harvard Law School, with the largest endowment in the nation, depended so heavily on tuition reaped from huge classes, how could other law schools justify appeals to relieve that dependence? Consequently, what President Eliot called the "deplorable" tuition dependence proliferated throughout university law schools.[159]

NOTES

1. Emphasis in original. John O. Sargent et al., *To the Friends of the Law Department of Harvard University* [printed circular] (April 1882), Harvard Law School Library Historical & Special Collections (hereafter cited as HLSLib).

2. See Daniel R. Coquillette and Bruce A. Kimball, *On the Battlefield of Merit: Harvard Law School, the First Century* (Cambridge, MA, 2015) (hereafter cited as *Battlefield of Merit*), 559–571.

3. Roscoe Pound to Ezra R. Thayer (July 28, 1911), Harvard Law School Dean's Office Records, Records of President A. Lawrence Lowell, 1909–1933, Harvard University Archives (hereafter cited as ALL Records).

4. Quotations are, respectively, from Austin W. Scott, Annual Report of the Dean of Harvard Law School, 1914–15, 149; William C. Loring, James Byrne, and William C. Osborn, *To the Graduates of the Harvard Law School* [printed circular] (Boston, March 31, 1917), 1–2, HLSLib.

5. Quotation is from William H. Taft, "Oration" in Harvard Law School Association, *Report of the Eighteenth Annual Meeting* (Boston, 1904), 15. See Charles W. Eliot, Annual

Report of the President of Harvard University, 1893–94, 23; Charles W. Eliot, "Address," in Harvard Law School Association, *Report of the Eighteenth Annual Meeting* (Boston, 1904), 68.

6. Eliot, Annual Report of the President, 1885–86, 13; Winthrop H. Wade, *Twenty Years of the Harvard Law School Association* (Boston, 1907), 8. The following account draws upon Bruce A. Kimball, "Impoverishing 'The Greatest Law School in the World:' The Financial Collapse of Harvard Law School under Dean James Barr Ames, 1895–1909," *Journal of Legal Education* 61 (2011): 4–29.

7. Annual Report of the Treasurer of Harvard University, 1905–06, 67, 102–103; Robert A. McCaughey, *Stand, Columbia: A History of Columbia University* (New York, 2003), 231; Julius Goebel Jr., *A History of the School of Law, Columbia University* (New York, 1955), 186; Annual Report of the Treasurer of Yale University, 1904–05, 38, 78.

8. *Battlefield of Merit,* 559–571.

9. Eliot, Annual Report of the President, 1882–83, 42; Christopher C. Langdell, Annual Report of the Dean of Harvard Law School, 1880–81, 75.

10. Eliot, Annual Report of the President 1905–06, 56–57.

11. *The Centennial History of the Harvard Law School: 1817–1917* (Cambridge, MA, 1918), 57, 107. See Eliot, Annual Report of the President, 1896–97, 25; 1899–1900, 17–18; 1901–02, 44.

12. Eliot, Annual Report of the President, 1902–03, 41; 1905–06, 53–54; Francis J. Swayze, "Address," in Harvard Law School Association, *Sixth Celebration and Dinner* (Boston, 1910), 29–32, 37; Frederick C. Hicks, *Yale Law School: 1895–1915* (New Haven, CT, 1938), 210–215; Brooks M. Kelley, *Yale: A History* (New Haven, CT, 1974), 276–277, 340–341; Goebel, *A History of the School of Law,* 185–186.

13. These figures count neither the windfall bequest of $100,000 received in 1906 from James C. Carter for a professorial chair in General Jurisprudence, nor the stock market collapse of 1907 because Harvard University listed its invested funds at their original book value. Current gifts account for some variation in the figures. See Kimball, "Impoverishing 'The Greatest Law School in the World.'"

14. Harvard University Catalog, 1879–1880, 132, 172; A. Lawrence Lowell, Annual Report of the President of Harvard University, 1914–15, 24; Roscoe Pound, Annual Report of the Dean of Harvard Law School, 1919–20, 158.

15. Harvard Law School Faculty Meeting Minutes (February 24 and March 17, 1898; November 6 and 13, 1899; January 28, February 1 and 18, and June 2, 1901); Charles W. Eliot to James Barr Ames (June 10, 1901), CWE Papers; Eliot, Annual Report of the President, 1901–02, 43–44.

16. Quotations are from, respectively: Eliot, "Address," 68; Eliot, Annual Report of the President 1903–04, 25.

17. Wade, *Twenty Years,* 8. See Charles Warren, *History of the Harvard Law School and of Early Legal Conditions in America* (New York, 1908), v. 2, 428.

18. Eliot, Annual Report of the President, 1871–72, 21–22; 1872–73, 17, 30–31; 1878–79, 28; 1881–82, 30; 1883–84, 34; 1885–86, 13.

19. This section draws upon Bruce A. Kimball, "The First Campaign and the Paradoxical Transformation of Fundraising in American Higher Education, 1915–1925," *Teachers College Record* 116 (2014): 1–44.

20. Robert J. Gordon, *The Rise and Fall of American Growth: The U.S. Standard of Living since the Civil War* (Princeton, NJ, 2016), 285.

21. Here and below, see Bruce A. Kimball and Benjamin A. Johnson, "The Inception of the Meaning and Significance of Endowment in American Higher Education, 1890–1930." *Teachers College Record* 114 (August 2012): 4–8.

22. Scott M. Cutlip, *Fund Raising in the United States: Its Role in America's Philanthropy* (New Brunswick, NJ, 1965), 39–47, 81–86, 110–153, 203–204; Olivier Zunz, *Philanthropy in America: A History* (Princeton, NJ, 2012), 44–75.

23. Emphasis in original. Sargent et al., *To the Friends of the Law Department.*

24. James R. Parsons Jr., *Professional Education, Monographs on Education in the United States* (New York, [1900]), 17; Henry W. Rogers, Annual Report of the Dean of Yale Law School, 1914–15, 320–321; Thomas W. Swan, Annual Report of the Dean of Yale Law School, 1916–17, 309; Roscoe Pound to A. Lawrence Lowell (December 11, 1916), ALL Records.

25. Eliot, Annual Report of the President, 1871–72, 21–22. See 1872–73, 17, 30–31; 1878–79, 28; 1881–82, 30; 1883–84, 34; 1885–86, 13.

26. Quotations are from Eliot, Annual Report of the President, 1894–95, 27. See 1904–05, 14, 39.

27. Emphasis added. Arthur T. Hadley, Annual Report of the President of Yale University, 1913–14, 13–14. See Abraham Flexner, *Medical Education in the United States and Canada* (New York, 1910), 141–142.

28. This section draws upon Bruce A. Kimball, "Charity, Philanthropy, and Law School Fundraising: The Emergence and the Failure, 1880–1930," *Journal of Legal Education* 63 (2013): 248–252.

29. Josephine Shaw Lowell, *Public Relief and Private Charity* (New York, 1884), 89.

30. Quotations are from, respectively: Annual Report of the Treasurer of Yale University, 1908–09, 11; Anson Phelps Stokes Jr., Annual Report of the Secretary of Yale University, 1912–13, 45.

31. George Gordon, "A Free University" *New York Times* (July 26, 1912).

32. See Barry D. Karl and Stanley N. Katz, "The American Private Philanthropic Foundation and the Public Sphere, 1890–1930," *Minerva* 19 (1981): 236–271; Zunz, *Philanthropy in America,* 10–18; Lawrence J. Friedman, "Philanthropy in America: Historicism and Its Discontents," in *Charity, Philanthropy, and Civility in American History,* ed. Lawrence J. Friedman and Mark D. McGarvie (Cambridge, UK, 2003), 6–10; Andrea Walton, *Women and Philanthropy in Education* (Bloomington, IN, 2005), 1–35.

33. Emphasis in original. Judith Sealander, "Curing Evils at Their Source: The Arrival of Scientific Giving," in Friedman and McGarvie, *Charity, Philanthropy, and Civility,* 218.

34. Karl and Katz, "American Private Philanthropic Foundation," 243–244. See Robert A. Gross, "Giving in America: From Charity to Philanthropy," in Friedman

and McGarvie, *Charity, Philanthropy, and Civility,* 31, 39, 44; Sealander, "Curing Evils," 220–223; Friedman, "Philanthropy in America," 7–8; Cutlip, *Fund Raising,* 3.

35. Roy Lubove, *The Professional Altruist: The Emergence of Social Work as a Career, 1880–1930* (Cambridge, MA, 1965), 6.

36. John D. Rockefeller, *Random Reminiscences of Men and Events* (New York, 1909), 184.

37. Zunz, *Philanthropy in America,* 10.

38. Carl Joslyn, "What Can a Man Afford?," *American Economic Review* 11, supp. no. 2 (December 1921), 118; Homer Folks, "Philanthropy, Educational Aspects of Modern," in *A Cyclopedia of Education,* ed. Paul Monroe, 5 vols. (New York, 1913), 4:671–674. See Cutlip, *Fund Raising,* 203–204; Karl and Katz, "American Private Philanthropic Foundation," 243–244.

39. See "Charity Old and New," *New York Times* (December 11, 1917). See Kimball and Johnson, "Inception," 1–32.

40. See *Battlefield of Merit,* 395, 420.

41. Quotation is from James B. Thayer, Memoranda Books, vol. 3, 108, HLSLib. The following draws upon Kimball, "Charity, Philanthropy," 252–257.

42. Eliot, Annual Report of the President, 1881–82, 17.

43. Here and below, the quotations are drawn from Langdell, Annual Report of the Dean, 1880–81, 78–86.

44. Victor Morawetz to James B. Thayer (March 27, 1882), James Bradley Thayer Papers, 1787–1902, HLSLib (hereafter cited as JBT Papers).

45. Sargent et al., *To the Friends of the Law Department.*

46. Arthur S. Huntington to James B. Thayer (January 24, 1882), JBT Papers.

47. Francis W. Palfrey to James B. Thayer (January 31, 1882), JBT Papers.

48. Quotations are from, respectively: Morawetz to Thayer (March 27, 1882), George F. Canfield to James B. Thayer (April 19, 1882), JBT Papers.

49. John O. Sargent to James B. Thayer (April 15, 1882), JBT Papers.

50. Quotations are from Victor Morawetz to James B. Thayer (April 15, 1882), JBT Papers.

51. Sargent to Thayer (April 15, 1882). See Eliot, Annual Report of the President, 1905–06, 52–53.

52. The following quotations are from James B. Thayer, "The Teaching of English Law at Universities," *Harvard Law Review* 9 (1895): 172–175, 178, 184.

53. Here Thayer doubtlessly had in mind his own study of English medieval courts, which he was publishing concurrently and which led to pathbreaking insights into the rules of evidence. His writings were collected in James B. Thayer, *A Preliminary Treatise on the Law of Evidence* (Boston, 1898).

54. Thayer, "The Teaching of English Law," 181, 182, quoting the English legal scholar Frederick Pollock.

55. *The General Education Board: An Account of its Activities, 1902–1914* (New York, 1915), 143; see 3–17.

56. See "News and Views," *Harvard Alumni Bulletin* (April 8, 1914), 445; Ezra R. Thayer to Mark A. D. Howe (March 28, 1914), ALL Records.

57. [Ezra R. Thayer,] untitled six-page chart, 1911, ALL Records; Ezra R. Thayer to Francis C. Huntington (March 24, 1914), Ezra Ripley Thayer Papers, 1882–1915, HLSLib (hereafter cited as ERT Papers); Thayer to Howe (March 28, 1914); Ezra R. Thayer, Annual Report of the Dean of Harvard Law School, 1912–13.

58. Annual Report of the Treasurer of Harvard University, 1911–12, 132–135; A. Lawrence Lowell to Ezra R. Thayer (September 17, 1912), A. Lawrence Lowell to Ezra R. Thayer (August 14, 1913), and Francis W. Hunnewell to Ezra R. Thayer (November 25, 1912), ALL Records.

59. Quotations are from, respectively: Ezra R. Thayer to Francis W. Hunnewell (November 27, 1912) and Ezra R. Thayer to A. Lawrence Lowell (October 5, 1912), ALL Records.

60. Thayer to Howe (March 28, 1914); Louis D. Brandeis to Ezra R. Thayer (December 22, 1914), Ezra R. Thayer to A. Lawrence Lowell (January 13, 1915), Ezra R. Thayer to Langdon P. Marvin (March 4, 1915), Richard Ames to Francis W. Hunnewell II (December 17, 1914), and A. Lawrence Lowell to Clifford Moore (March 3, 1915), ALL Records; Lowell, Annual Report of the President, 1914–15, 24; 1915–16, 5–6.

61. Thayer to Lowell (October 5, 1912). See Thayer to Howe (March 28, 1914) and Ezra R. Thayer to Cornelius W. Wickersham (April 7, 1914), ALL Records.

62. Thayer, Annual Report of the Dean, 1911–12, 135; Lowell, Annual Report of the President, 1911–12, 17–18.

63. Thayer to Howe (March 28, 1914).

64. Thayer to Howe (March 28, 1914).

65. "News and Views," 445. See "Report of the Dean of the Law School," *Harvard Alumni Bulletin* (April 8, 1914), 448.

66. Ezra R. Thayer to Henry L. Stimson (June 27, 1914), ERT Papers. See Thayer, Annual Report of the Dean, 1912–13, 127; Harvard Law School Association of New York City, Report of Committee on the Needs of the Law School [c. early June 1914], and Cornelius W. Wickersham to Ezra R. Thayer (April 6, 1914), ALL Records.

67. A. Lawrence Lowell to Ezra R. Thayer (November 16, 1914), ALL Records; Henry A. Yeomans, *Abbott Lawrence Lowell, 1856–1943* (Cambridge, MA, 1948), 230.

68. Lowell, Annual Report of the President, 1910–11, 22–24; 1911–12, 21–24. Hugh Hawkins, *Between Harvard and America: The Educational Leadership of Charles W. Eliot* (New York, 1972), 263, 275, 284–287.

69. George P. Day, Annual Report of the Treasurer of Yale University, 1909–10, 5–6; 1914–15, 8–9; Hadley, Annual Report of the President, 1913–14, 13–14.

70. Edmund K. Arnold to Ezra R. Thayer (June 20, 1914), ERT Papers.

71. Quotations are from Archibald King to Joseph Sargent (March 6, 1914), ERT Papers. See Horace F. Baker to Joseph Sargent (March 4, 1914), Alvin A. Morris to Horace F. Baker (March 5, 1914), and Justin Bowersock to Joseph Sargent (June 17, 1914), ERT Papers.

72. Quotation is from King to Sargent (March 6, 1914). See Langdell, Annual Report of the Dean, 1881–82, 82.

73. Eleanor N. Little, "The Acquisition of the Dunn Collection of Early English Law Books," *HLSB* (December 1955), 9–10.

74. Ezra R. Thayer to Cornelius W. Wickersham (April 3, 1914), ALL Records.

75. The following account draws upon Bruce A. Kimball, "The Disastrous First Fund-Raising Campaign in Legal Education: The Harvard Law School Centennial, 1914–1920," *Journal of the Gilded Age and Progressive Era* 12 (2013): 535–578.

76. Harvard Law School Association of New York City, Report.

77. Thayer to Stimson (June 27, 1914).

78. Thayer to Stimson (June 27, 1914).

79. Brandeis to Thayer (December 22, 1914).

80. Brandeis to Thayer (December 22, 1914).

81. Ezra R. Thayer to William Thomas (May 12, 1915), ERT Papers.

82. Quotation is from Ezra R. Thayer to Richard Ames (July 7, 1915), Roscoe Pound Papers, 1888–1964, HLSLib (hereafter cited as RP Papers). See Caleb Loring to Roscoe Pound (April 17, 1916), RP Papers; John Sheeseley, "Ezra Ripley Thayer: Dean of the Harvard Law School 1910–1915" (student research paper, Harvard Law School, 2002), on file with authors, sect VIII B.

83. Scott, Annual Report of the Dean, 1914–15, 149.

84. Quotation is from Loring, Byrne, and Osborn, *To the Graduates*. See Pound, Annual Report of the Dean, 1915–16, 140–150. See *Centennial History*, vi, 162–174. See Kimball, "Disastrous First Fundraising Campaign," 557–558.

85. Roscoe Pound, *The Harvard Law School* [New York, 1919], 3; Roscoe Pound to A. Lawrence Lowell (July 22, 1919), ALL Records; Edgar H. Wells to John B. Atkins (November 28, 1919), Records of the Harvard Endowment Fund, 1916–1939, Harvard University Archives (hereafter cited as HEF Records).

86. A. Lawrence Lowell to Roscoe Pound (March 20, 1916), ALL Records.

87. Lowell, Annual Report of the President, 1915–16, 5–6; Pound, Annual Report of the Dean, 1915–16, 146. See James F. Clark, "The Harvard Law School Deanship of Roscoe Pound, 1916–36" (student research paper, Harvard Law School, 1999), on file with the authors, 18–23.

88. Quotation is from Julian W. Mack to Roscoe Pound (May 18, 1916), RP Papers. See A. Lawrence Lowell to Roscoe Pound (April 28, 1916), RP Papers; Pound, Annual Report of the Dean, 1915–16, 145; Roscoe Pound to Frank W. Grinnell (April 13, 1916), RP Papers.

89. Loring, Byrne, and Osborn, *To the Graduates*.

90. Loring, Byrne, and Osborn, *To the Graduates*.

91. Emphasis in original. Loring to Pound (April 17, 1916).

92. Quotations are from, respectively: A. Lawrence Lowell to Jesse W. Lilienthal (December 14, 1916) and A. Lawrence Lowell to James Byrne (October 20, 1916), ALL Records.

93. A. Lawrence Lowell to Joseph H. Beale (November 30, 1915), ALL Records.

94. Lowell, Annual Report of the President, 1915–16, 21–22.

95. Frank W. Grinnell to Joseph P. Cotton (June 23, 1916), ALL Records. See Frank W. Grinnell to Joseph Sargent (April 26, 1916), ALL Records.

96. Frank W. Grinnell to A. Lawrence Lowell (July 19, 1916), ALL Records.

97. Quotations are from Grinnell to Cotton (June 23, 1916) and Frank W. Grinnell to Joseph Sargent (June 27, 1916), ALL Records. See Frank W. Grinnell to A. Lawrence Lowell (July 21, 1916) and Frank W. Grinnell, Joseph Sargent, and Roger Ernst to James Byrne (June 6, 1916), ALL Records; Harvard Law School Association, *Ezra Ripley Thayer: An Estimate of His Work as Dean of the Harvard Law School* (Boston, 1916).

98. Quotation is from Caleb Loring to Frank W. Grinnell (April 17, 1916), ALL Records. See Grinnell, Sargent, and Ernst to Byrne (June 6, 1916), Grinnell to Lowell (July 21, 1916), Frank W. Grinnell to Joseph P. Cotton (June 15, 1916), and Joseph P. Cotton to Frank W. Grinnell (June 21, 1916), ALL Records.

99. Kimball, "Disastrous First Fundraising Campaign," 357–358; *Centennial History*, vi.

100. *Centennial History*, 116, 118–119, 161, 170–173. See Bruce A. Kimball, "The Langdell Problem: Historicizing the Century of Historiography, 1906–2000s," *Law and History Review* 22 (2004): 290–297.

101. Lowell to Byrne (October 20, 1916); Pound, Annual Report of the Dean, 1916–17, 141.

102. Pound to Lowell (December 11, 1916), Roscoe Pound to James M. Byrne (December 22, 1916), and James Byrne to A. Lawrence Lowell (January 4 and 16, March 3, 1917), ALL Records.

103. Rogers, Annual Report of the Dean, 1914–15, 319–20; see 1912–13, 203; 1913–14, 239–241. See H. J. Ostrander to Thomas W. Swan (April 28, 1916), Yale University Treasurer Records, 1700–1973, ser. III, Yale University Archives.

104. Pound, Annual Report of the Dean, 1915–16, 141–142.

105. Quotation is from Swan, Annual Report of the Dean, 1916–17, 307. See *A Program for the Expansion of the Yale School of Law into a "School of Law and Jurisprudence"* ([New Haven, CT, 1916]), Yale University Treasurer Records, 1700–1973, ser. III, Yale University Archives, iv; Supplement to the *Yale Alumni Weekly* (Mar 23, 1917); Gaddis Smith, "Politics and the Law School: The View from Woodbridge Hall, 1921–1963," in *History of Yale Law School,* ed. Anthony T. Kronman (New Haven, CT, 2004), 138–139.

106. *Centennial History*, 168. See Roscoe Pound, *The Harvard Law School* (Cambridge, MA., 1919), 10.

107. Here and below, see Kimball, "The First Campaign."

108. Quotations are from Roger Pierce to Frederick W. Burlingham (April 16, 1918), Thomas W. Lamont Correspondence, HEF Records. See [Secretary Robert F. Duncan], Minutes of Executive Committee of the Harvard Alumni Association (January 10 and April 10, 1916), and Thomas W. Lamont to James A. Lowell (April 18, 1917), HEF Records.

109. A. Lawrence Lowell to Thomas W. Lamont (December 12, 1916), HEF Records.

110. Thomas W. Lamont to Robert F. Duncan (February 15, 1917), HEF Records.

111. Byrne to Lowell (March 3, 1917).

112. Byrne to Lowell (March 3, 1917).

113. Loring, Byrne, and Osborn, *To the Graduates.*

114. "Harvard Law School Seeks $1,000,000 Fund Endowment Needed to Carry on Work of Institution Adequately," *Boston Journal* (May 5, 1917).

115. Frank W. Grinnell to Roscoe Pound (April 24, 1917), ALL Records; A. Lawrence Lowell to Roscoe Pound (April 29, [1917]), RP Papers; "Harvard Law School Celebrates in June," *Boston Journal* (May 7, 1917).

116. "To the Graduates of the Harvard Law School Association" (June 4, 1917), ALL Records; "Harvard Law School Attendance Is Cut," *Boston Journal* (June, 16, 1917); Walter E. Meyer to Roscoe Pound (June 26, 1917), RP Papers.

117. Committee on Arrangements of the Council of the Harvard Law School Association, "Notice in Regard to the Centennial Anniversary of the Harvard Law School" (June 4, 1917), ALL Records.

118. Thomas W. Swan et al., "Report of the Committee on Plans for the School of Law" [January 1919], and Yale Law School Guaranty Fund, 1917–1920, f. 2156, Yale University Treasurer Records, ser. III, Yale University Archives.

119. Quotation is from Lowell, Annual Report of the President, 1916–17, 22. See Pound, Annual Report of the Dean, 1915–16, 146; 1916–17, 140; Harvard Law School Catalog 1917–18, 56; 1918–19, 32; Carol S. Gruber, *Mars and Minerva: World War I and the Uses of the Higher Learning in America* (Baton Rouge, LA, 1975), 95–101.

120. Lowell, Annual Report of the President, 1917–18, 22; A. Lawrence Lowell to Roscoe Pound (June 25, 1919), ALL Records. See Clark, "Harvard Law School Deanship," 24n94.

121. Quotation is from Roscoe Pound to A. Lawrence Lowell (August 16, 1918), ALL Records. See Pound, Annual Report of the Dean, 1917–18, 120. See Annual Report of the Treasurer of Harvard University, 1916–17, 149, 189–191; 1918–19, 190–192; 1919–20, 213–214.

122. Roger L. Geiger, *To Advance Knowledge: The Growth of American Research Universities, 1900–1940* (New York, 1986), 131.

123. A. Lawrence Lowell to Henry A. Yeomans (January 29, 1919) and A. Lawrence Lowell to James A. Lowell (January 12, 1918), ALL Records; H. C. Washburn to John I. Richardson (December 13, 1920), HEF Records.

124. Compare *Ten Million for Harvard, President Lowell Sets Forth the Needs of the University, Reprinted from the Harvard Alumni Bulletin, June 26, 1919* (New York, 1919); Thomas W. Lamont, "Why Harvard Needs Additional Endowment," *Harvard Advocate* (September 22, 1919); Roscoe Pound to Joseph P. Cotton (October 22, 1919) and Roscoe Pound to Edgar H. Wells (March 27, 1920), ALL Records.

125. Quotation is from Frank W. Grinnell to Zechariah Chafee Jr. (February 24, 1925), Zechariah Chafee Jr. Papers, 1898–1957, HLSLib. See Frank W. Grinnell to A. Lawrence Lowell (December 20, 1919) and *Notice of the Reunion of the Alumni of the Harvard Law School at Cambridge June 21ˢᵗ 1920* [printed circular], ALL Records; *Two Addresses Delivered before the Alumni of the Harvard Law School at Cambridge, June 21, 1920* ([Boston, 1920]), HLSLib.

126. James Byrne to Thomas W. Lamont (June 18, 1917), A. Lawrence Lowell to Thomas W. Lamont (October 30, 1919), and Max Epstein to President and Fellows of Harvard College (October 21, 1919), HEF Records; Pound, Annual Report of the Dean, 1919–20, 167–169.

127. "Restricted [Gifts] January 17, 1922 plus amendment through Aug. 1922," Lists, reports, statistics, etc., 1919–1925, HEF Records. In 1914 about 7,450 former students, including graduates, of HLS were known to be alive; in 1924 about 9,919. Interpolating and discounting for the enrollment decline during the war indicate that there were about 8,700 living graduates and former students in 1920. *Quinquennial Catalogue of the Law School of Harvard University, 1817–1914* (Cambridge, 1915), [v].

128. Grinnell to Lowell (July 19, 1916).

129. Quotation is from Blewett Lee to Joseph P. Cotton (October 18, 1919), HEF Records. See Charles W. Eliot to Blewett Lee (March 13, 1897) and Blewett Lee to Charles W. Eliot (March 15, 1897), CWE Papers.

130. See Lists, reports, statistics, etc., 1919–1925, and Correspondence with restricted subscribers, HEF Records.

131. Quotation is from Francis Rawle, "A Hundred Years of the Harvard Law School, 1817–1917," *Harvard Graduates' Magazine* (December 1917), 186. Thomas N. Perkins to Sarah R. Ames (November 26, 1920), Thomas N. Perkins to Joseph P. Cotton (December 8, 1920), and Anna L. Gray and Roland Gray to Thomas N. Perkins (November 7, 1919), HEF Records.

132. Grinnell to Cotton (June 23, 1916), Byrne to Lowell (March 3, 1917), Grinnell to Lowell (July 19, 21, 1916), Frank W. Grinnell to James Byrne (May 27, 1916), and Frank W. Grinnell to William C. Loring (May 3, 6, 1916), ALL Records.

133. Louis D. Brandeis to Roscoe Pound (May 28, 1919), in *Letters of Louis D. Brandeis,* ed. Melvin I. Urofsky and David W. Levy, 5 vols. (Albany, NY, 1971), 4:395; Melvin I. Urofsky and David W. Levy, eds., *"Half Brother, Half Son": The Letters of Louis D. Brandeis and Felix Frankfurter* (Norman, OK, 1991), 43n–44n; Thomas N. Perkins to Frederic Winthrop (October 23, 1919) and Frederic Winthrop to Thomas N. Perkins (November 17, 1919), HEF Records; John B. Trevor to Charles T. Lovering (November 24, 1920), ALL Records.

134. "Laski Scores Commissioner's Action in Walkout Crisis," *Harvard Crimson* (October 10, 1919); "Mr. Laski Gives Up University Position," *Harvard Crimson* (May 10, 1920). See letters from October 1919 concerning Laski in Thomas W. Lamont Correspondence and Thomas N. Perkins Correspondence, HEF Records.

135. Lowell to Lamont (October 30, 1919).

136. Quotation is from Joseph H. Choate to Frank W. Grinnell (May 4, 1916), ALL Records. See Cutlip, *Fund Raising*, 110–116; Zunz, *Philanthropy in America*, 56–58.

137. Quotation is from Jeremiah Smith Jr. to A. Lawrence Lowell (March 1, 1917), ALL Records. See Francis J. Swayze to Thomas W. Lamont (May 2, 1917), HEF Records.

138. Ezra R. Thayer to A. Lawrence Lowell (May 28, 1914), Law School Endowment Fund, "Harvard Law School Association [printed circular]" (April 26, 1916), and Roger Pierce to Joseph Sargent (April 26, 1916), ALL Records.

139. Quotation is from A. Lawrence Lowell to Robert F. Duncan (February 27, 1917), HEF Records.

140. Birch Helms to Thomas W. Lamont (January 30, 1917) and Thomas W. Lamont to Birch Helms (February 7, 1917), HEF Records. See Thomas N. Perkins to James J. Phelan (October 2, 1919), Thomas N. Perkins to Henry B. Endicott (October 15, 1919), and Arthur D. Hill to Thomas N. Perkins (October 10, 1919), HEF Records.

141. Roscoe Pound to Wilson M. Powell (November 24, 1926), ALL Records. See William W. Hodson to Roscoe Pound (March 3, 1920) and Pound to Wells (March 27, 1920); Ravi P. Ramchandani, "The Stalling Effort: The Harvard Law School Endowment Campaign of 1925–1927" (student research paper, Harvard Law School, 2011), on file with authors, 5–6.

142. Thomas W. Lamont to Payne Whitney (October 31, 1919), Edward Reynolds to Thomas N. Perkins (October 8, 1919), Joseph Wiggin to Thomas N. Perkin (October 25, 1919), and Edgar H. Wells to Thomas N. Perkins (March 10, 1920), HEF Records.

143. Cotton to Grinnell (June 21, 1916); Grinnell to Cotton (June 23, 1916).

144. Wells to Atkins (November 28, 1919).

145. William Lawrence, *Memories of a Happy Life* (Boston, 1926), 215.

146. "Harvard Law School Centennial Put Off," *Boston Globe* (June 8, 1917).

147. Harvard Endowment Fund, *Harvard and the Future* (Cambridge, MA, 1919), 2.

148. Thomas N. Perkins to James C. McMullin (February 21, 1920), HEF Records.

149. Grinnell to Cotton (June 23, 1916).

150. Byrne to Lowell (March 3, 1917).

151. Quotation is from *Centennial History*, 163. See Bruce A. Kimball, *The 'True Professional Ideal' in America: A History* (Oxford, 1992), 75–76, 110–112, 199; Charles Fried, "The Lawyer as Friend: The Moral Foundations of the Lawyer-Client Relation," *Yale Law Journal* 85 (1976): 1060–1089; Karl N. Llewellyn, *The Bramble Bush: On Our Law and Its Study*, 2nd ed. (New York, 1951), 171; Max Weber, *Economy and Society: An Outline of Interpretive Sociology*, ed. Guenther Roth and Claus Wittich, trans. Ephraim Fischoff et al. (New York, 1968), 2:891.

152. Charles H. Strong to Ezra R. Thayer (July 1, 1915), ERT Papers.

153. Ezra R. Thayer, "Address," in Harvard Law School Association, *Sixth Celebration and Dinner* (Boston, 1910), 39.

154. *Centennial History,* 173–174; Frank W. Grinnell to Joseph H. Choate (May 5, 1916), ALL Records; Rawle, "A Hundred Years," 186; Loring, Byrne, and Osborn, *To the Graduates.*

155. Harvard Endowment Fund, *Harvard,* 2.

156. Compare Rawle, "A Hundred Years," 186; Loring, Byrne, and Osborn, *To the Graduates; Centennial History,* 170–173, 378; Robert F. Duncan to Thomas W. Lamont (December 13, 1916), Thomas W. Lamont to Robert F. Duncan (December 20, 1916), and Edward B. Adams to Thomas W. Lamont (June 23, 1917), HEF Records.

157. Francis W. Hunnewell to Eliot Wadsworth (September 10, 1920) and Langdon P. Marvin to Ezra R. Thayer (March 3 and May 5, 1915), ALL Records.

158. Pound, *The Harvard Law School,* 16. Pound's phrase was later picked up by Erwin N. Griswold, Annual Report of the Dean of Harvard Law School, 1961–62, 395.

159. Eliot, Annual Report of the President, 1871–72, 21–22.

CHAPTER THREE

The Perilous Trials of Roscoe Pound and the Faculty, 1916–1927

Of all the Law School's leaders, Dean Roscoe Pound (1916–1936) remains the most enigmatic. Raised in Lincoln, Nebraska, far from the East Coast establishment, Pound was a brilliant student whose first love was natural science. Despite this passion, Pound's father, a prominent lawyer, persuaded him to study at Harvard Law School for the academic year 1889–90. Combined with his earlier apprenticeship and brief study in a proprietary school, that one year at the Law School qualified Pound to join the Nebraska bar and practice law. Soon his insightful, critical writings on legal practice and jurisprudence earned him appointments to the law faculty of the University of Nebraska in 1903, then Northwestern University in 1907 and the University of Chicago in 1909. By the age of forty he was one of the best-known legal scholars in America, and in 1910 he joined the faculty at Harvard Law School. This rapid ascent, however, would make his later views, particularly his denigrating "legal realism" in the 1930s, all the more controversial.

Pound's tenure as dean from 1916 to 1936 was fraught with controversy. This chapter explains the foundations and emergence of Pound's seminal jurisprudence, his views of legal education, and the trying events of his deanship during World War I and the period of the Red Scare in the early 1920s. Chapters 4–7 address students' experience and culture, the worsening syndrome of tuition dependence during the 1920s, the jurisprudential controversy over legal realism in 1930–1931, and, finally, Pound's disturbing response to the rise of Nazism during the Great Depression. By the early 1930s the faculty was in revolt, and in 1936 they forced Pound to resign. While his responses to the university's institutional prejudices, and the associated trials within and without the Law School, are still being debated, it is certain that few deans have faced such rapid change and genuine peril at Harvard.[1]

Youth and Education

In 1870, the same year that Dean Christopher Langdell (1870–1895) began reforming the Law School, Roscoe Pound was born in Lincoln, Nebraska. This may seem an unlikely hometown for someone who became an advocate of international legal study and graduate education emulating German universities. But Germans were the largest foreign-born group in the United States at the end of the nineteenth century, followed by the Irish, and many had settled in the midwestern United States.[2]

In Lincoln, Pound's parents embraced the German influence, employed a German housemaid, and sent Roscoe to a German private school, where he developed a love for German culture. Additionally, his parents, college-educated intellectuals, arranged for him to begin studying Greek and Latin at age eleven. Three years later he entered the University of Nebraska, already fluent in four languages. Pound's academic inclinations and European cosmopolitanism thus flowed from his upbringing in Nebraska, but so did his abrasive demeanor. "Pound was brilliant, but he was somewhat rough and ready from his early days in Nebraska, and he was not very sensitive," Dean Erwin Griswold (1946–1967) later wrote, who himself was not known for sensitivity.[3]

Established in 1869, the University of Nebraska was the state's land-grant university, and botanical studies were exceptionally strong there under the leadership of Charles E. Bessey. Agriculture was central to the state's economy, and Bessey brought new experimental techniques and instruments of empirical observation, including microscopes, to a subject that had previously focused on taxonomy. Pound began studying botany under Bessey, who also emphasized the importance of Darwin's theory of evolution and of the social utility of research. These two ideas later informed Pound's "sociological jurisprudence," which emphasized the evolutionary character and social consequences of the common law.[4]

Upon completing a bachelor's degree in 1888 at age eighteen, Pound decided to pursue graduate study in botany—disappointing his father, who had hoped his son would follow in his footsteps and become a lawyer. This fateful decision profoundly shaped Pound's ideas about the role of universities and research in legal education. The University of Nebraska was a dynamic, developing institution, and Pound was able to join Bessey's pioneering Botanical

Seminar. After completing his master's degree in 1889, Pound interrupted his scientific studies to attend Harvard Law School for one year at his father's behest. Returning to Nebraska, he enrolled as a Ph.D. student and undertook his earliest and, some would say, his best research.

Drawing on his work in the Botanical Seminar, Pound and his colleague Frederic Clements conducted a pioneering botanical survey of Nebraska that became the basis of his dissertation. Completed in 1897, this was the university's first Ph.D. awarded in botany and second overall. In 1898 this joint work was published as *Phytogeography of Nebraska,* the first English-language botanical study that drew on the systematic empirical techniques practiced by prominent Darwinian botanists in Germany. Hence, Pound's later inclinations to look to German research universities for an institutional template, to emphasize graduate legal studies, and to establish research institutes with a wide social agenda originated in Lincoln, Nebraska.[5]

These accomplishments in botany were entwined with legal study and practice. In the summer of 1888, after completing his bachelor's degree, Pound worked in his father's law office and also attended Robbins Law School, a small, Litchfield-type proprietary school.[6] Though Roscoe preferred botany, his father, Stephen Pound, believed that if his bright son were exposed to the best in legal education, however briefly, then his preferences would change. Roscoe Pound therefore interrupted his graduate study with Bessey to attend Harvard Law School for one year, 1889–90, primarily to please his father.

Pound's academic background easily qualified him for admission to Harvard, given that, in 1893, the Law School included Nebraska among those colleges and universities awarding "respectable" undergraduate degrees, which entitled their graduates to admission as degree candidates.[7] But the faculty sought degree candidates committed to finishing three years of study, and by 1889 they had instituted reforms discouraging exactly Pound's kind of exploratory first year. Nevertheless, though he registered as a degree candidate, Pound ignored the requirements and did not take the prescribed set of first-year courses. He was clearly not there to complete the LL.B.

In fact, Pound wished to learn Roman Law, but the subject was not offered in the curriculum, so he studied it during Christmas vacation of 1889, when he remained at Harvard because the journey home was too long. He had found *Studies in Roman Law,* written by the Scottish judge Thomas M. McKenzie, and was reading it in the library when Professor John C. Gray (LL.B. 1861) passed by. "Don't read that," said Gray, going to the stacks and returning with a copy of Rudolph Sohm's *Institutes of Roman Law,* which had recently appeared in German but not yet been translated into English. "Read that," said Gray, who continued on his way. Fluent in both German and Latin, Pound thoroughly studied Sohm's treatise and later taught Roman Law for seventeen years at Harvard, where Gray attended Pound's course.[8]

In 1889 Harvard Law School had eight professors for nearly 300 students. Everyone studied in Austin Hall—including the faculty, who worked at tables next to the students' reading room.[9] The three professors who most impressed Pound were Gray, who taught Property, William Keener (LL.B. 1877), who taught Contracts, and James Thayer (LL.B. 1856) who taught Constitutional Law, which Pound attended, though it was not normally a first-year course. Keener, the youngest of the three, was devoted to the case method, and Pound came to esteem his excellent teaching.

Keener "was, perhaps, at his best with first-year men, who began by hating him, presently admired him grudgingly, and by the middle of the year swore by him," wrote Pound. By the same token, Pound initially doubted the value of the case method, being accustomed to the clear didactic structure of botanical texts and the text-and-recitation teaching method of Robbins Law School in Nebraska. By December, however, he wrote to his father, "I must acknowledge that, after the first months, the case method seems to be better than any other."[10] In the spring of 1890, Keener announced that he was leaving for Columbia University Law School, where he became dean in 1891. Pound wrote home, "Keener, who is generally regarded as the ablest young man here has got mad or disgusted with the fogies and is going to Columbia. It seems to me a great loss."[11]

In addition to adopting Keener's fierce devotion to the case method, Pound took from Thayer a commitment to judicial restraint and respect for legislation. In fact, Pound's reasoning in "The Common Law and Legislation" (1908) closely resembles Thayer's line of argument in his classic article "The Origin and Scope of the American Doctrine of Constitutional Law" (1893).[12] But Pound was most influenced by Gray, particularly his incorporation of practical examples in teaching. In letters home, Pound called Gray "an ideal instructor," and wrote that "one can get more law and common sense (I don't know how else to express it) out of his course."[13] Gray's work, particularly his *Nature and Sources of the Law*, is repeatedly cited in Pound's legal scholarship.[14]

Despite his initial reservations, Pound might have continued his legal education at Harvard. He enjoyed his studies, and the nascent *Harvard Law Review,* founded in 1887, invited Pound to join. But his father's failing health forced him to return to Lincoln in 1890 to assist with the family law practice. Although Pound never indicated that he wished to finish the LL.B. at Harvard, his brief experience was formative, particularly in converting him to case method teaching.

Lawyer and Scholar

Soon after returning to Lincoln in 1890, Pound passed the bar (despite the examiners' skepticism about his year of esoteric study at Harvard), began practicing law, and entered the Ph.D. program in botany. Thus began a period now generally regarded as the most creative of his life. In fact, Pound's later detractors—and there have been many—have characterized these two decades as the source of all of Pound's original ideas. In their estimation, all his critical thinking occurred between the ages of twenty and thirty-nine.[15] Whether or not it ended in 1909, the creative eruption of Pound's legal scholarship beginning in 1890 seems almost beyond belief. He had minimal formal legal study, was practicing law on the side, and concurrently produced a monumental treatise on plants.

But a closer look at Pound's groundbreaking early work reveals that his botanical research and his experience at the bar, on the bench, and in legal education were all complementary. His research in botany kept him abreast of German scientific scholarship, and he studied the pioneering jurisprudence of Rudolf von Jhering, whose criticism of German legal formalists, including Friedrich Carl von Savigny, resembled debates in botany. The botanical formalists saw taxonomy as the core of botanical science, whereas the Darwinian German scientists maintained that evolution through natural selection augured for progressive and dynamic botanical science. No less did the forces of social and political evolution operate in the law, Pound concluded, echoing the insights of von Jhering.[16]

Meanwhile, he witnessed legal evolution in his frontier law practice in Nebraska in the 1890s. Everything was in flux—the judiciary, the bar, and legal education—and Pound advanced to the forefront of all three. He handled cases on any issue—real estate, wills, railroads, enforced contracts—while practicing law with his father as members of the rough-and-tumble frontier bar. Pound also represented powerful corporations, such as the Burlington and Union Pacific Railroads, and his practice grew steadily.

The Panic of 1893 struck Nebraska hard, threatening the two pillars of the Nebraskan economy: railroads and farming. But the chaos also created legal work. Pound rose rapidly in the profession. Only six years after his own admission to the bar, Pound was named to the Nebraska Supreme Court's Commission on Bar Applicants, and became instrumental in founding the modern Nebraska State Bar Association. In 1900, Pound was one of nine lawyers appointed to the Nebraska Supreme Court Commission to assist the court in clearing its hopeless backlog. At age thirty, Pound essentially became a judge in a state court, rendering decisions and writing numerous judicial opinions.[17]

Pound also began to address political issues in his writings. He consistently opposed Populism, William Jennings Bryan, and "free silver" (the unrestricted coining of silver), widely perceived by Nebraskans as the cure for plunging wheat prices and the agricultural depression of the 1890s. In the 1896 presidential election, Pound backed the Republican William McKinley, who advocated the gold standard or "sound money" and the use of high tariffs to protect America's bourgeoning industries. In his political statements, Pound appealed to empirical evidence and economic "laws," suggesting that his scientific training shaped his rhetorical style.[18]

Finally, in 1903, Pound was appointed dean of the University of Nebraska Law School, which at the time was a two-year school of fewer than 200 students, with three regular faculty. By the age of thirty-three, Pound had been a research scientist, a practicing lawyer, a judge, a political commentator, and a law dean. The only credential he really lacked was a law degree. As dean, Pound immediately instituted radical changes at the law school. He introduced the case method, extended the course of study to three years, and offered electives on Roman Law, Savigny, and von Jhering. These reforms exemplified the "missionary" efforts of Harvard Law School's graduates and former students who brought the school's model of legal education to other institutions throughout the country during the 1890s and early 1900s, as discussed in Chapter 1.

Simultaneously, Pound wrote a series of articles that would make him a nationally renowned jurist by 1910. This creative explosion was ignited by fundamental insights originating in his botanical studies and legal practice in Nebraska: that law must constantly evolve to meet the changing conditions of America in a new century, and that scientific reasoning and empirical evidence must inform this evolution.

Pound's first major essay, "The Causes of Popular Dissatisfaction with the Administration of Justice," was initially presented as a speech to the ABA in St. Paul, Minnesota, in 1906.[19] Everyone in his conservative audience knew that the U.S. Supreme Court had decided *Lochner v. New York* in the prior year. This decision culminated a series of similar cases overturning urgently needed social legislation protecting the health and safety of workers from the

Roscoe Pound, attended 1899–1900. Faculty 1913–1947, Dean 1916–1936.
Photograph by Townsend taken while Pound was the dean of the University of
Nebraska Law School, ca. 1906.

Courtesy of Harvard Law School Library, Historical & Special Collections.

exploitative practices of large corporations, such as paying wages in company
credit rather than U.S. currency. *Lochner* held that such social legislation
violated individual laborers' freedom of contract—that is, their right to negotiate the terms of their employment—while Justice Oliver W. Holmes Jr.
(LL.B. 1866) issued a landmark dissent.[20]

Following Holmes, Pound criticized the underlying assumptions of the
Lochner decision. "Justice, which is the end of law, is the ideal compromise
between the activities of all in a crowded world," Pound wrote. "The law seeks
to harmonize these activities and to adjust the relations of every man with his
fellows so as to accord with the moral sense of the community." This task can
be very difficult. "When the community is one in its ideas of justice, this is
possible. When the community is divided and diversified, and groups and
classes and interests, understanding each other none too well, have conflicting

ideas of justice, the task is extremely difficult." The inherent "individualist spirit of the common law" exacerbated the problem because it clashed with the "collectivist spirit of the present age." Furthermore, "there is a strong aversion to straightforward change of any important legal doctrine."[21]

But doctrine must evolve, and Pound argued that progressive change can legitimately come through legislation, which is preferable to judges creating novel interpretations of outdated judicial decisions and acting as though the new interpretations were consistent with the old. For judges, "to interpret an obnoxious rule out of existence rather than to meet it fairly and squarely by legislation, is a fruitful source of confusion," he wrote.[22] Add to such fictional reinterpretations an antiquated system of pleading, an outdated organization of courts, and a period of profound social change, and there is a true crisis. But Pound found hope outside the courts in reforms wrought by law schools, bar associations, and political activists.

Many of Pound's insights were not new, and historian Natalie Hull has termed his analysis "a bricolage" of "old materials."[23] In England, Henry Sumner Maine's *Ancient Law* (1861) had addressed vehicles for legal change, including fictional reinterpretations and legislation, forty-five years earlier. In Germany, Rudolph von Jhering had advanced a social interpretation of law in 1877. Pound freely admitted that "his own program of sociological jurisprudence and interest balancing . . . derived from Jhering's . . . critique of German scholars for creating a mathematical, a priori jurisprudence divorced from social realities." In the United States, Holmes expressed a similar view in "The Path of the Law" in 1897 and then from the bench after he was appointed to the U.S. Supreme Court in 1902.[24]

At the very least, Pound's innovation was to apply these insights forcefully to the dynamic but stressed American frontier and its new cities. Though relatively mild compared to his succeeding essays, "The Causes of Popular Dissatisfaction" appeared radical and stimulated passionate debate. Law reform advocates distributed 4,000 copies of the original ABA speech to bar leaders and members of Congress, while others condemned it in the proceedings of the ABA.[25] But Dean John Wigmore (LL.B. 1887) of Northwestern University Law School, saw in Pound's arguments "something really comprehensive, yet practical" and offered him a professorship.[26] For Pound, who was becoming increasingly frustrated by the lack of progress at the University of Nebraska Law School and had threatened to resign in 1905, Wigmore's offer—with a relatively light teaching load—proved irresistible in 1907. Delighted at recruiting Pound, Wigmore was moved to verse:

All hail the newest star, now fixed amidst our constellation!
A brilliant varied spectrum marks your lofty stellar station.
As sociologic jurist, may the message of your pen
Widely spread a mighty influence, from your editorial den![27]

Pound worked hard at Northwestern, editing the *Illinois Law Review* and composing several major articles, including "The Need of a Sociological Jurisprudence" (1907), "Mechanical Jurisprudence" (1908), and "Liberty of Contract" (1909). These articles anticipated the legal battles of the New Deal and the Great Depression by arguing that every form of lawmaking must consider the social consequences of law.[28] Meanwhile, Pound took a highly visible role in Chicago's legal politics and was appointed chairman of the important ABA Section on Legal Education.

Within a year, he received invitations to join the law faculties of Wisconsin, Chicago, and Yale, and to become the chancellor of the University of Nebraska. Offered a salary higher than Wigmore's own, Pound moved to the University of Chicago, where he guided a highly visible and bitterly contested program of procedural reform through the Illinois Bar Association. The Chief Justice of Illinois described Pound as "the most radical reformer . . . with a cynical determination to find some fault." Throughout, Wigmore remained Pound's loyal friend and supporter, albeit with some reservations.[29]

In 1910, Pound turned forty as the initial stage of his legal career drew to a close. He had become a national figure in jurisprudence and legal education, drawing on insights gained from his botanical studies, frontier legal practice in Nebraska, and study of legal scholars in England, Germany, and the United States. He maintained that developments in American society demanded that the law evolve, and that scientific reasoning and empirical evidence must guide that evolution in order to meet the needs of society. In 1910 this position was strongly progressive, if not radical, among law professors.

Harvard Law Professor, 1910–1916

Pound inevitably came to the attention of the faculty at Harvard Law School. His article "Liberty of Contract," published by the *Yale Law Review* in 1909, deeply impressed both his former teacher John C. Gray and Dean Ezra Thayer (1910–1915), who recommended him to President A. Lawrence Lowell (1909–1933). But Lowell moved cautiously. He was no friend of radicals, and Pound would be the first Harvard law professor not born and raised in New England, which naturally aroused suspicion.[30] Lowell made a discreet inquiry to Wigmore, a graduate of the Law School, who assured him that Pound, the supporter of McKinley and opponent of free silver, was no bomb thrower. Lowell then authorized Dean Thayer to offer Pound a professorship.

Pound had many reasons to stay in Chicago, including excellent professional ties and the chance to conduct a lucrative law practice. He had already rejected an offer from Yale in 1908 for these reasons. But Dean Thayer added inducements, offering to support Pound's emerging interest in criminal law and graduate legal education, particularly S.J.D. courses in Jurisprudence and in Roman Law. Then, too, the alma mater of Justice Holmes and Louis Brandeis (LL.B. 1877) presented a national stage for a young critic and reformer of the reigning jurisprudence. The offer proved irresistible, and Pound accepted the position, bringing with him to Harvard a vision for graduate legal education and a new "sociological" jurisprudence. In 1913 Pound succeeded Gray as the Carter Professor of General Jurisprudence, the chair that he held until his appointment as a University Professor in 1936.

After President Lowell was persuaded to support the appointment, he and Pound began to correspond regularly, particularly as Dean Thayer's health declined. Upon Thayer's tragic and unexpected death in 1915, Pound was the natural choice to become dean. But he balked. He had been a dean before, and had turned down several administrative posts since, including chancellor of the University of Nebraska. He worried that administration would distract him from his scholarly and reform ambitions. "Don't let them make you Dean," wrote University of Michigan Dean Henry M. Bates, among others.[31] Nor did Pound fit the mold of previous Harvard deans in any field. He worried that "the combination of a non-Harvard man, pro-German . . . and pro-Brandeis" might be "more than the traffic will bear."[32]

But influential figures urged Pound to accept. *The New Republic* spoke of the "opportunity" to overcome "the spirit of the Brahmin caste" at Harvard Law School.[33] Learned Hand (LL.B. 1896) wrote, "I am delighted to hear that you have been selected as Dean of the Law School, and I hope very much you will accept. Many of us look to you as the natural leader of legal education in the country today, both in equipment and in foresight; we believe that it is only through such as you that the law can hold its true place in American political life, and avoid a kind of progressive arthritis." Julian W. Mack (LL.B. 1887) and Felix Frankfurter (LL.B. 1906), both Jewish intellectuals, urged him to accept. Having joined the faculty in 1914, Frankfurter wrote, "I think I know how you feel about this community—its self-centered provincialism. But I also know . . . the indisputable need of you right here."[34]

Abbott Lawrence Lowell, LL.B. 1880. President of Harvard University 1909–1933.

Photograph ca. 1904. Courtesy of Harvard University Archives.

Negotiations with the Harvard Corporation ensued. Twice Pound declined the offer, but he finally accepted in January 1916. In the end, the deciding factor for Pound was that "things are more or less in transition in law everywhere and this School has a great opportunity."[35] The tenures of Dean Pound, the quintessential outsider, and President Lowell, the ultimate insider, would overlap for seventeen years, with Lowell's term lasting twenty-four years from 1909 to 1933 and Pound's twenty years from 1916 to 1936.

On February 1, 1916, Pound officially assumed his new duties as dean. On March 24 a German submarine torpedoed the British liner *Sussex* in direct violation of international agreements signed after the sinking of the *Lusitania* in 1915, which took 128 American lives. On July 1 fourteen British divisions attacked the German lines in the Battle of the Somme. By nightfall, 57,000 were dead.[36] War was coming to the United States and to Harvard Law School.

World War I and "Hot-Blooded Youth," 1916–1918

The horrendous war did not proceed according to anyone's plans.[37] At the outset, in 1914, both sides predicted a quick victory. Three years later, on April 2, 1917, when President Wilson asked Congress to declare war, many Americans assumed that this would be a long, monumental struggle to save civilization and "make the world safe for democracy."[38] A few days later, forces from across the British Empire launched a massive offensive at Ypres, gaining just 7,000 yards at the cost of 160,000 casualties. In spite of the horrifying conditions, often not fully reported in the press, a whole generation of "hot-blooded youth," in Pound's term, were eager to go to war. Only the firsthand experience of mustard gas and trench warfare deflated this romantic ideal about World War I.[39]

At Harvard Law School, students' rush to enlist sparked an administrative nightmare for the new dean that lasted through 1920. First, there was great uncertainty over whether the War Department was prepared to accept new enlistees.[40] Pound therefore urged students to stay until the end of the semester, because "in the majority of cases they may serve their country well by continuing their regular work to the end of the school year." He advised the faculty that "the University is making provision for thorough military training and instruction to begin . . . upon the close of the school year."[41] But many students believed that delay would hurt their chance for a commission, and some simply left.[42]

The faculty therefore had to determine the academic standing of students who were "called into service." They voted to excuse third-year students in "regular standing" from examinations and still confer on them the LL.B., and to excuse second- and first-year students, who would then be entitled to return in "regular standing" upon discharge.[43] Rumors quickly spread that those who were unprepared for exams should opt for this path, and Pound wrote to Lowell that "everyone whose record is weak is trying to find some way of getting out of our examination."[44]

For example, Nathaniel Siegel, a first-year who failed five of six courses, blamed his results on his fear for his brother, who was serving in France. He wrote to Pound, "When a man's heart is torn with apprehension for the safety of a brother, he cannot study for law examination. Your innate sense of justice must lead you to this conclusion."[45] Pound denied the request for a reprieve. Another was William M. Marston (LL.B. 1918), a graduate of Harvard College who did poorly at the Law School, received a commission to work on psychological testing in Washington, and sought a waiver for his examinations. Pound refused, and was then bombarded with letters on behalf of Marston. The controversy raged through April and May 1918, and included an attack by the *Harvard Crimson* on the Law School's "ridiculous regulation."[46] Marston ultimately received his degree, then earned a Ph.D. in psychology, and created the polygraph test and the character Wonder Woman.

But the dean gave unstinting support to the best students who wanted to leave early and assume a variety of roles. At the Federal Land Bank, Kingman Brewster Sr. (LL.B. 1911) wished to hire an excellent student, and Pound convened an emergency faculty meeting to see if this could qualify as being "called into service." He also approved appointments of top students called to Washington by faculty who had gone to the War Department, including Professors Frankfurter and Eugene Wambaugh (LL.B. 1880). Pound recommended top students for military commissions as well, noting in May 1917 that "we have found places for about ten men at Washington, and . . . a few more might be needed."[47]

The dean then had to make plans for the projected lengthy period of low enrollment and financial distress, because the departure of students was going to cost the Law School a great deal of money in tuition revenue. Some 857 students had enrolled in September 1916, and only 412 remained in June 1917. When the school opened in September 1917, merely 297 enrolled. In his annual report, President Lowell observed, "The greatest loss [in enrollment] has fallen upon the Law School," and "the diminution in tuition fees is particularly severe owing to the comparatively small amount of endowment."[48]

This was an emergency of the first order, but Pound did not seriously consider suspending operation, as did the University of Virginia Law School.[49] Harvard Law School had "succeeded in running without interruption through the Civil War even when Lee was invading Pennsylvania," noted Pound. "I do not imagine that a siege of Boston is likely, and until that happens I see no reason to suppose anything will require us to suspend."[50]

Nor did Pound stay the intellectual sword, dismissing suggestions to lower standards for admission or grading. For example, C. G. Haglund just missed completing his S.J.D. in 1918 because he received a B in Pound's course in Jurisprudence. Pound refused to wave him through and wrote to Haglund that only by "maintaining its traditional toughness" would "Harvard's continued stature . . . be assured."[51] Likewise, Pound opposed efforts to bolster enrollments during wartime by shifting one undergraduate year to the Law School and adding a fourth year to the LL.B. degree. Pound blamed Yale and Northwestern for lobbying for this plan at the Association of American Law Schools. Law schools, Pound maintained, must "resist the attempt . . . to win prospective law students away from the colleges . . . prematurely."[52] The Law School also rejected the opportunity to boost enrollments during the war by admitting women, as Yale began to do.[53] Lowell and the Corporation would have certainly vetoed this course of action in any case.

Nevertheless, as enrollment and tuition revenue declined, Pound had to respond. He rented the school's unused physical space—Austin Hall—to the Navy for its Radio School. This provided needed income, but the Radio School was under the command of a hapless Lieutenant Ayer, who constantly squabbled with Pound on mundane issues, such as building maintenance. Pound also quarreled with Lowell over costs such as heating, because "only extreme vigilance in watching every item of expense will enable us to get through this year and the next."[54] He hoped these measures—combined with a surplus of $26,000 from the 1916–17 academic year, when students who left still had to pay their tuition—would cover the deficit projected for 1917–18 and beyond.[55]

Another problem was the faculty shortage. Three of the nine full-time teachers had left for public service. Frankfurter became assistant secretary of war, Wambaugh a colonel in the War Department, and Arthur D. Hill (LL.B. 1894) a Red Cross worker in France. Compounding the problem, Professor Jens Westengard (LL.B. 1898) had died, and his replacement, Manley O. Hudson (LL.B. 1910, S.J.D. 1919), was called to diplomatic service. The war effort put nearly half the faculty out of service. Pound observed that the remaining faculty, himself included, "have been doing more than the normal quota of teaching work for several years," and he warned that "early provision must be made for an enlarged faculty."[56]

Through it all, Pound tried to maintain continuity by following Langdell's "groove" in the pedagogy and curriculum of the LL.B. program.[57] In 1918 Pound summarized his aim for continuity in a letter to Alfred Reed, who was then preparing his monumental report on legal education for the Carnegie Foundation for the Advancement of Teaching: "I feel satisfied that, when it is all over, Harvard Law School will be found to have come through the war with no deficit . . . and with no substantial impairment of its methods, its curriculum, or its morale."[58]

Given the stress during 1917 and 1918, Pound surely appreciated an anonymous letter from a student, stating that the dean "is regarded with almost unanimous approval by the law students. . . . We're thankful for your cool leadership under these trying circumstances." Perhaps mindful of Ezra Thayer, the student hoped that Pound would not take on "too great a load" or "spend too many hours with the petty legal problems of men who often are [too] lazy to think for themselves."[59]

Red Scare Begins, 1918–1920

No one at Harvard expected the fighting to end in 1918.[60] But the combatants were exhausted and withdrawing by the time the first American troops reached the Marne in May of that year. In March 1918, Russia pulled out of the war after the Bolshevik Revolution of November 1917 established a Communist regime. On November 1, 1918, the Ottoman Empire surrendered, and two days later the Austro-Hungarian Empire, economically devastated, collapsed, and the German Navy mutinied at Kiel. The Kaiser was forced to abdicate and flee to the Netherlands in an effort to avoid the fate of his cousin Nicholas II of Russia. On November 11, 1918, the armistice was signed, leaving Europe shattered and the world transformed. The devastation of war fell lighter on the United States, whose troops had fought for just nineteen months and whose territory had not been the site of battle. But many Americans died, and the walls of Harvard Law School library record the names of eighty-six fatalities.

The administrative nightmare for Pound then entered a new phase. Returning students overwhelmed the school, and the five remaining regular faculty held a "special session" from February through August 1919 for over 300 students. There was also a shortage of classroom space because Lieutenant Ayer and the Naval Radio School refused to vacate Austin Hall. The session placed additional burdens on everyone, and classes ran expanded hours throughout the week and also on Saturdays.[61] Four more professors returned for the frenetic academic year of 1919–20, when the faculty of nine taught 63 two-hour semester courses, averaging 7 courses per professor. Pound himself taught ten.[62] Finally, a steep postwar recession hit the national economy in 1920. All this was compounded by anxiety about the school's evident syndrome of tuition dependence.

Pound's desperate efforts to add and hold permanent faculty, or even short-term lecturers, ran into constant obstacles. Nathan Isaacs (S.J.D. 1920) initially refused an offer to come from the law faculty at the University of Cincinnati to be a teaching fellow, due to the small stipend of $1,000 and higher teaching load.[63] Edward S. Thurston (LL.B. 1901) refused an offer and went to Yale, later coming to Harvard in 1930. Zechariah Chafee Jr. (LL.B. 1913), frustrated by the Corporation's delay in appointing him to full professor, threatened to return to practice, despite Pound's plea that "his loyalty to his work and his willingness to work are conspicuous in a time when both virtues are rare."[64]

Finally, Manley Hudson, the indispensable replacement of Jens Westengard as the school's international jurist, was now under suspicion of disloyalty to the United States, the first ominous sign of Pound's next crisis, the Red Scare.[65] In April 1919 Pound wrote to Frankfurter, who was still on government duty in Paris, that he was "very much worried about the whole situation here. Thus far, although the Faculty have recommended Hudson twice, the authorities have balked about appointing him. . . . All over the country a vigorous attempt is being made to push out from our universities everybody suspected of liberal ideas, and to see to it that no appointments are made except of men 'against whom nothing can be said.'"[66]

Under the weight of all these pressures, Pound was becoming physically and emotionally exhausted. His stress became obvious to President Lowell and jeopardized Pound's continuing as dean. Having already lost Dean Thayer in 1915, Lowell suggested in the summer of 1918 that Pound drop some of his teaching responsibilities. By 1919 Lowell apparently considered putting Pound on leave, and in the spring of 1919, Pound contemplated resigning.[67]

At this early stage in his deanship, Pound had strong allies among the faculty, who suspected Lowell's motives for suggesting that Pound go on leave and worried whom the President might appoint in Pound's stead. Frankfurter wrote to Pound, "Please, don't let Lowell jockey you into the position which he wants you in. Don't go for any proposals about a leave of absence and stand firm. Remember that the students are with you, that the alumni can be rallied. . . . Lowell's move won't stand the light of day—not when it comes to publicity."[68] Hudson wrote, "The schools of the country will continue to look to your leadership at Harvard, and to me the only hope of our tiding over this critical period in legal education is that the work of Harvard Law School should be uninterrupted and unimpaired."[69]

Moved by this encouragement, Pound remained at the helm. His supporters, including Supreme Court Justices Brandeis and Holmes, pushed for an honorary LL.D. for Pound to demonstrate Harvard's appreciation for his work. The degree was granted at the end of the 1919–20 academic year, when 883 students were enrolled and their tuition generated a small surplus due to the high student-faculty ratio of about 68:1.[70] This surplus created, once again, the illusion of prosperity. The school finally seemed to be recovering from the war.

But international politics were still tumultuous. Germany's collapse and the Russian Revolution changed the political landscape almost beyond recognition. President Wilson urgently began work on creating a new world order through the League of Nations.[71] Meanwhile, emergency measures curtailing civil liberties during the war created new precedents for the use of presidential and administrative powers, leading to the controversies of the New Deal that emerged a decade later.

Palmerism and Fear Mongering

"The world broke in two in 1922 or thereabouts," wrote novelist Willa Cather, a close friend of Pound's sister, Olivia, referring to the political and social upheaval at home and abroad following the war.[72] These disturbances tested the legal order and Pound's deanship. Two significant events were the extraordinary "trial" of Professor Chafee at the Harvard Club of Boston on May 22, 1921, and the infamous Sacco and Vanzetti trial, particularly during the year 1927, when Professor Frankfurter publicly defended them in the press. Understanding these trials, bizarre in retrospect, requires entering the world of American politics and examining the actions of Attorney General A. Mitchell Palmer during the Red Scare of 1919–1920.[73]

The prewar era had seen some important progressive advances in American society. These included the Clayton Anti-Trust Act and the creation of the Federal Trade Commission in 1914, followed by the appointment of Louis Brandeis as the first Jewish Justice of the U.S. Supreme Court in 1916, despite opposition from the legal establishment. Perhaps the most significant advance was the extension of suffrage to women with the ratification of the Nineteenth Amendment in 1920. But the Great War and the Russian Revolution transformed the American political landscape by fomenting a surge of nativism, jingoism, and political conservatism.

In June 1917 the U.S. Espionage Act became law. Together with its 1918 amendments (collectively called the "Sedition Act"), this legislation went far beyond "espionage" and limited any speech that brought the U.S. government or its policies into disrepute. Under the authority of these acts, the Justice Department harassed many labor organizers and organizations, particularly the Industrial Workers of the World (the "Wobblies"), and convicted over 1,000 persons, including Eugene V. Debs, the Socialist labor organizer and presidential candidate. Outside of these official actions by the federal government, the notorious National Security League, the Committee on Public Information, and the Council of Defense conducted even more ruthless campaigns against pacifists, unions, and the free press.

In 1919 President Woodrow Wilson selected A. Mitchell Palmer as attorney general. Palmer then named twenty-four-year-old J. Edgar Hoover as head of a new "General Intelligence Unit," the forerunner of the FBI, within the Department of Justice. Following two serious attempts on his life by anarchists, which he initially met with restraint, Palmer began to pursue "radical" groups. His targets included moderate African American leaders, whose calls for racial equality, labor rights, and self-defense amid the violent race riots in the summer of 1919 seemed, to Palmer, to resemble the political rhetoric of socialists and communists.[74]

Between November 1919 and January 1920, Palmer orchestrated an unprecedented campaign of raids, arrests, and searches, mostly without warrants or probable cause. Thousands were detained, and deportation proceedings were brought against some 1,600 persons. The primary criterion for arrest and search was not any overt action, but merely membership in particular organizations, mostly labor groups. Immigrant aliens, subject to the Anarchist Exclusion Act of 1918, were especially targeted.[75]

President Wilson evidently did not know about the "Palmer Raids" until after the fact. Public reaction to the raids was initially positive, but the courageous resistance of Assistant Secretary of Labor Louis F. Post, who dismissed 71 percent of Palmer's 1,600 deportation cases, turned the tide. Palmer then foolishly predicted that there would be mass bombings during a "Nation-wide Uprising" on May 1, 1920. The threat was taken very seriously, with New York City deploying thousands of police and the city of Boston posting machine guns. When nothing happened, the newspapers dubbed the event the "May Day Scare" and turned against Palmer's hysteria. He resigned in disgrace in March 1921, his reputation ruined, notwithstanding a subsequent career of public service.[76]

The importance of "Palmerism" to Roscoe Pound and Harvard Law School soon became apparent. Frankfurter, by his own account, was "a Jew of alien origin." He had immigrated from Vienna, lived in the ethnic enclaves of New York City, and earned his undergraduate degree at City College of New York (CCNY).[77] In an Armistice Day speech in 1919, Frankfurter charged that, according to Palmer's ilk, his background demonstrated "that the Bolshevik Revolution had come to America."[78] The number of alumni complaints about

Frankfurter so alarmed Pound that he sought the counsel of Justice Brandeis in Washington.[79] Also under scrutiny were the internationalist Manley Hudson, whom Pound had recruited in 1918, and Francis B. Sayre (LL.B. 1912, S.J.D. 1918), who was appointed in 1917 to conduct research in criminal law and resigned in 1934 to become Franklin Roosevelt's assistant secretary of state. Finally, there was the most improbable target of all, Zechariah Chafee, a descendent of one of New England's oldest Brahmin families, appointed in 1916 to teach equity, negotiable instruments, and business practice.[80]

By 1919 Pound was thoroughly alarmed by the fear mongering directed toward his faculty, and warned that American higher education was being "governed by fourteen-dollar-a-week reporters."[81] He wrote to Justice Holmes that "many zealous alumni think that all of my writing is a cover for socialism," due to his advocacy for "sociological jurisprudence." But Pound and his colleagues did not cower. In March 1920, Pound, Frankfurter, Sayre, Chafee, and librarian Edward B. Adams (LL.B. 1897) all signed a petition to the president of the United States requesting that he pardon Jacob Abrams and two others convicted under the 1918 Sedition Act for distributing leaflets. Two months later, in May, Pound joined eleven other distinguished lawyers, including Frankfurter and Chafee, in authoring a pamphlet attacking the Palmer raids.[82]

The pamphlet was an instant success that came at a shocking cost. A powerful group of conservative Harvard Law School alumni decided that the faculty needed to be taught a lesson. While condemning all, including Pound, they chose to focus their attack on Chafee, thus presenting Pound with a major, deeply personal crisis.

Chafee's Trial, 1919–1921

Targeting Chafee was surprising. He was an impeccable blue blood, the descendent of wealthy businessmen, and his teaching interests focused on the corporate world, including negotiable instruments and unfair business competition. He was far more of an insider than Pound, the midwesterner, or Frankfurter, the Jewish immigrant. During his defense, Chafee said as much himself. "I come of a family that has been in America from the beginning of time. My people have been business people for generations. My people have been people of substance. They have made money. I believe in property, and I believe in making money." But Chafee's insistence that "my crowd . . . fight fair" was infuriating to his accusers, perhaps because he was

Zechariah Chafee Jr., LL.B. 1913. Faculty 1916–1956.

Photograph early 1930s. Courtesy of Harvard Law School Library, Historical & Special Collections.

"one of them."[83] In effect, Chafee was on trial because he was a traitor to his social group and class.

The origin of Chafee's trial lay in the case of *Abrams v. United States,* decided by the Supreme Court on November 10, 1919. Jacob Abrams and four others were convicted under the 1918 Sedition Act of distributing leaflets, some in Yiddish, that opposed sending U.S. troops to Russia and urged the cessation of the production of weapons to be used against Russian revolutionaries. They were convicted of impeding the war effort and given severe sentences of ten to twenty years' imprisonment. The Supreme Court upheld the convictions, seven to two, over a powerful dissent by Holmes, joined by Brandeis, arguing that there was no "clear and imminent danger" that justified curtailing the defendants' First Amendment rights.[84]

In June 1919 Chafee published the first of two articles in the *Harvard Law Review* attacking the decision in *Abrams.* "Freedom of Speech in War Time" was followed in April 1920 by "A Contemporary State Trial," specifically targeting the *Abrams* prosecution. According to Chafee, "the trial judge ignored the fundamental issues of fact, took charge of the cross-examination of the prisoners, and allowed the jury to convict them for their Russian sympathies and their anarchistic views." Then the judge issued "the maximum sentence available against a formidable pro-German plot" to "five obscure and isolated youngsters, misguided by their loyalty to their endangered country and ideals," for handing out circulars.[85] Chafee compiled the articles in his famous book *Freedom of Speech,* published the same year.[86]

After Chafee's first article appeared, Robert P. Stephenson (LL.B. 1905), a former editor of the *Harvard Law Review* and former U.S. assistant attorney, wrote to the *Law Review* attacking the accuracy of Chafee's article and stating that much of it had "the object of bringing about political results." Stephenson also noted that he had learned that the *Law Review* was about to publish Chafee's second article, and that a counsel "for parties on one side of this litigation" (Harry Weinberger, counsel for the defendants) had received a page proof in advance of publication.[87] Stephenson clearly intended to intimidate the *Law Review* editors and prevent the publication of Chafee's second article.

Nonetheless, the editors published the second article and forwarded the letter to Chafee. In April 1920 Chafee courteously wrote to Stephenson that the "final page proof" was sent "to Mr. Weinberger for his use in obtaining an amnesty from the President."[88] Stephenson then replied to Chafee in a long letter listing a series of enumerated questions in the format of legal interrogatories.[89] Again Stephenson intended to intimidate, but Chafee's detailed reply was still remarkably courteous: "The next time you are in Boston do come out and have tea with Frankfurter and myself." But Chafee was also guarded, noting that Stephenson seemed to "enjoy conducting a correspondence in the manner of taking a deposition," and describing his questions to Stephenson as "cross-interrogatories."[90] Chafee later came to realize that Stephenson was serving as an informal "liaison" between the U.S. Attorney's Office and Austen G. Fox (LL.B. 1871), a prominent conservative New York attorney.[91]

Fox and twenty other conservative alumni were angered that Chafee and his faculty colleagues had, in March 1920, signed the petition asking the president to pardon Abrams and his friends. In retaliation, they hatched a plan to prod the U.S. Attorney's Office that had prosecuted the *Abrams* case into punishing Chafee for his articles. After preparing for a year and employing Stephenson as their liaison, Fox and the collaborating alumni were ready to act.

In May 1921 the group sent to President Lowell and the Harvard Board of Overseers a personal statement written by Fox in response to Chafee's articles. The group had no standing to lodge an official complaint, and said they were informally conveying Fox's own statement, which deserved "careful consideration."[92] But Fox addressed his statement directly to the Harvard Corporation, indicating that the group sought to prompt official action by the university.[93] Moreover, the statement was printed like a court document and formatted like a formal legal complaint. It included a memorandum from U.S. Assistant Attorney John M. Ryan (LL.B. 1896), who had led the *Abrams* prosecution, as well as copies of correspondence between Chafee and Francis G. Caffey (LL.B. 1894), the U.S. attorney who supervised the *Abrams* prosecution.[94]

Further, these ominous documents leveled serious charges against Chafee. In one letter, Caffey observed that he, Ryan, and seven of his assistants in the U.S. Attorney's Office "are Harvard Law School men," and were shocked to "have a teacher of law—particularly in the School we love so well—exercise so little care in ascertaining the truth."[95] Lying to federal prosecutors was a crime, and the documents accused Chafee of doing this in his articles and of bringing the federal justice system into disrepute.

The Overseers referred the matter to its own subgroup responsible for evaluating the Law School: the Committee to Visit the Law School, which comprised fourteen members, including seven judges and only one academic, John Wigmore, the dean of Northwestern University Law School. The Visiting Committee could, and should, have dismissed Fox's "statement" as a clear attempt to threaten academic freedom, prevent publication, and intimidate faculty. Instead, apparently wishing to mollify the influential cadre of legal alumni amid the Red Scare, the Overseers Visiting Committee and President Lowell decided to hold a "hearing" in a private room of the Harvard Club of Boston on May 21, 1921.

The hearing was to consider a "charge of impropriety" against Pound, Frankfurter, Sayre, Chafee, and Adams for signing the amnesty petition. Chafee was also charged with making "consciously erroneous" and "culpably negligent" statements in his academic writing. The event was a trial in all but name. All five defendants attended, along with eleven Visiting Committee members (not including Wigmore, who was absent). The process was adversarial, with the accusers represented by Fox. The counsel for the Harvard Corporation, Thomas Perkins (LL.B. 1894), attended, along with Stephenson, who had "no defined capacity," but "acted as if he had some claim to ask questions of me," Chafee later observed.[96]

At the hearing, the "charge of impropriety" for signing the amnesty petition "was not sustained and was abandoned," apparently by a majority vote of the Committee. So was the charge against Chafee for making "consciously erroneous" statements in his articles. Finally, the charge against Chafee for making "culpably negligent" statements was dismissed by a bare six-to-five majority, with the deciding vote reportedly cast by Benjamin N. Cardozo.[97]

What if Chafee had been found guilty? In 1937 Lowell wrote to Chafee, "I wonder what would have happened if they had succeeded in getting a majority of the committee?—Probably nothing at all; for I suspect the Overseers would have laid it on the table, or otherwise refused to confirm it. If they had censured you, I suspect the whole, or a large part, of the Faculty of the Law School, including the Chair, might have gone overboard."[98] But Lowell's view was hindsight, sixteen years after Palmerism had been discredited. A vote to censure Chafee in 1921 would have been a crisis for Harvard Law School of the first order and, as Lowell suggested, would likely have led Pound and many, if not most, of the faculty to resign.[99]

Lowell later justified the hearing by claiming that he wanted to head off the alumni from forming a cabal with conservatives on the law faculty. Further, he said that the hearing afforded "an excellent chance to do some fighting in the cause of free speech." In other words, it was an opportunity to show up the accusers.[100] But these justifications ring hollow. Lowell could have quashed the Fox statement when he received it. The risk to academic freedom was far too great to have allowed "the case" to be "tried" at all, as Upton Sinclair argued in "The Goose-Step: A Study of American Education."[101]

Later Chafee generously recalled, "With Lowell's energetic support, we threw the Wall Street invaders back with heavy losses."[102] But Chafee's roseate judgment may have been influenced by Lowell's conduct in the earlier "trial" of the British socialist Harold Laski before the Overseers at the Harvard Club. Laski, a special student at the Law School and instructor in Government, delivered a speech during the Boston police strike of 1919 in support of the police union. He argued that everyone had a right to affiliate with any labor organization or union. Meanwhile, some 400 Harvard faculty members, alumni, and students had answered the Police Commissioner's call for "volunteers to uphold law and order," coordinated by a "volunteer" office established by Lowell in University Hall itself.[103] When the Overseers conducted a similar "trial" for Laski, Lowell had come to his defense, and Laski, like Chafee, was grateful, writing to Holmes that "Lowell was magnificent."[104] But Lowell's support was equivocal, for he warned Chafee in 1920 that it would be "a mistake" to have dinner with Harold Laski, if "publicly noticed in the press."[105] Furthermore, Laski soon left Harvard for a distinguished career at the London School of Economics.[106]

In any case, Lowell's conduct during these events, like his record on equal opportunity, is reprehensible, even considered in light of the time. The "trial" on May 21, 1921, in which even the dean was charged with "impropriety," was a disgrace. Lowell also firmly opposed racial integration of the freshman residence halls and the admission of women to Harvard. He held secret courts to try alleged homosexual students, and instituted a 15 percent quota on enrolling Jewish students.[107]

It is harder to assess Pound's conduct in these events. His correspondence reveals his private support and personal concern for Chafee. Unlike Lowell, Pound saw clearly that Chafee's accusers sought to intimidate anyone championing Progressive causes or challenging the Red Scare tactics, regardless of the outcome of the trial.[108] In 1921 Pound "stood at the pinnacle of his profession," having "achieved the status of foremost American academic jurisprudent of his day," notes historian Natalie Hull.[109] Even so, Pound made no effort in 1921 to challenge Chafee's intimidation and face down the Harvard Overseers directly. It would have been a courageous act, and Pound avoided it.

Frankfurter and the Sacco and Vanzetti Trial

Roscoe Pound and Felix Frankfurter may have come from very different backgrounds, but they did share certain attributes. Neither belonged to the Brahmin establishment in New England that had dominated the Law School for nearly a century and Harvard University for nearly three centuries. That establishment was personified by President Lowell and the Fellows of the Corporation. Also, Pound and Frankfurter shared a faith in social science and a progressive legal system. This faith made them early allies when Dean Thayer appointed Frankfurter in 1914, with Pound's enthusiastic support. Finally, both experienced bias and painful attacks on their loyalty in the postwar years. But their responses to these attacks differed, and that divergence ultimately sundered their personal alliance and destroyed their friendship.

Frankfurter had originally intended to study at Columbia University Law School. While that may have been a more congenial choice for a brilliant immigrant New Yorker from CCNY, Harvard Law School offered him a slot first. His extraordinary performance at Harvard, where he ranked first in his class every year, brought him to the attention of the faculty, particularly John C. Gray, who hired Frankfurter as his research assistant in 1903. Through Gray, Frankfurter first encountered the progressive legal realism of Holmes and Brandeis. Frankfurter was a student in the audience when Brandeis, then a leading Boston lawyer, delivered his famous address in 1905 on the legal profession's obligation to engage in public service.[110] Upon graduation, Frankfurter worked briefly for a traditional, white-shoe law firm in New York that had never before hired a Jew (a partner suggested that Frankfurter "anglicize" his name). Then, heeding Brandeis's call to be a "people's lawyer," Frankfurter joined the U.S. Attorney's Office in New York City under Henry Stimson (1888–1890), beginning a government and academic career that continued until his death in 1965.[111]

Indeed, Frankfurter rarely left government service. When Harvard offered him a faculty position in 1913, most of Frankfurter's advisors, including Stimson, Holmes, Theodore Roosevelt, and Learned Hand urged him to decline. Holmes observed, "Academic life is but half-life—it is withdrawal from the fight in order to utter smart things that cost you nothing."[112] But from the outset, Frankfurter saw the Law School as a place for political and social action, an attitude that landed him in hot water with Lowell in the early 1920s.

In 1917 Frankfurter returned to government work where he was reassigned to the President's Mediation Commission. President Wilson had charged this task force with ascertaining the "real causes" of the alarming labor violence and industrial stoppages occurring on the Pacific Coast and in the Rocky Mountain mining areas.[113] Consisting of the secretary of labor and two representatives each from labor and management, the Commission had real power, and Frankfurter was named its secretary and counsel—effectively, the "neutral" member. The Commission investigated some of the most violent and politically charged events of the day, including the "Tom Mooney Trial," in which a labor organizer in California was sentenced to death for allegedly planting a bomb in the summer of 1916, a charge Frankfurter believed to be based on perjured testimony.[114]

Felix Frankfurter, LL.B. 1906. Faculty 1914–1939. Photograph January 17, 1939, when leaving Harvard to become Associate Justice of the U.S. Supreme Court.

Thus, upon returning to Cambridge in 1919, Frankfurter already had a reputation as a leftist, which was amplified by a public exchange of letters with Theodore Roosevelt. For example, the *Boston Herald* published a letter from Roosevelt to Frankfurter stating that the latter had "an attitude which seems to be fundamentally that of Trotsky and the other Bolshevik leaders in Russia."[115] At Harvard, Frankfurter's reputation created difficulties for Pound. The Corporation denied a Law School appointment for Frankfurter's former student, Gerard Henderson (LL.B. 1916), allegedly for "Bolshevism." And Brandeis reported, after a meeting with Pound, that the Harvard establishment is "gunning hard for Felix. Old Boston is unregenerate. . . . F.F. is evidently considered by the elect to be as 'dangerous' as I was."[116]

Matters hardly improved when Frankfurter reluctantly opened a Faneuil Hall rally on Armistice Day in 1919 and urged the Wilson administration to recognize the Soviet Union. Shortly thereafter, a prominent, wealthy Harvard graduate wrote to the university administration threatening that he was coming "after Laski . . . and the rest of you." In response, Thomas Perkins, the university counsel, advised Frankfurter that "at the present time, . . . it is important not to rock the boat," noting the possible damage to the Harvard Endowment Fund campaign that was in full swing.[117]

Nevertheless, in 1920 Frankfurter assisted Sidney Hillman, a labor union leader in Rochester, New York, in fighting a permanent injunction against a textile workers' strike.[118] Later that year Frankfurter submitted an *amicus curiae* brief in *Colyer v. Skeffington* on behalf of twenty aliens arrested during the Palmer raids and threatened with deportation.[119] Frankfurter also became involved in the controversy surrounding the dismissal of Alexander Meiklejohn as president of Amherst College, reportedly for his support for free speech and progressive causes. In 1923 Frankfurter attempted to use his position as a trustee of the *New Republic* to support Meiklejohn. The following year Frankfurter, with Pound, prepared a report attacking U.S. Attorney General Harry M. Daugherty's politically motivated prosecution of Burton K. Wheeler, a progressive senator. "Wheeler means nothing to me," Frankfurter observed. "But the courageous and disinterested administration of the law means, outside of my personal life, pretty much everything to me."[120]

Frankfurter thus already had an extensive record of legal and political activism by 1925, when controversy erupted over the trial of Nicola Sacco and Bartolomeo Vanzetti, two Italian immigrants and self-described anarchists. In 1921 the two were tried and convicted of murdering a paymaster and a guard during a robbery of a payroll truck in Braintree, Massachusetts, in 1920. At the time of their arrest, both men were armed with revolvers, and Vanzetti had shotgun shells in his pocket, potentially linking him to an earlier payroll truck robbery with a shotgun in 1919.[121]

There certainly was evidence against them. Both men lied about key relationships and activities, and there were eyewitnesses who identified both Sacco and Vanzetti as among the gunmen at Braintree. At least one ballistics expert linked Sacco's gun to a bullet recovered from the bodies, and another suggested the gun found on Vanzetti was the one stolen from the guard's body. But they also had an incompetent counsel, Fred H. Moore, a political radical described by Frankfurter as a "blatherskite from the west." The jury deliberated only a few hours before convicting the pair and sentencing them to death.[122]

In addition, the trial judge, Webster Thayer, appeared blatantly biased. He and the prosecution clearly overstepped their designated roles in emphasizing that the defendants were Italian immigrants and anarchists. Alibis offered by a dozen other Italian witnesses were not deemed credible. Almost immediately after the conviction, a committee was formed to assist with the appeals, seeking a new trial at the very least. The effort was strengthened when one of the ballistics witnesses, a captain of the state police, affirmed that his five conclusions were not presented accurately to the jury. Finally, in 1925, Celestino Madeiros, a convicted murderer under sentence of death, confessed to having been part of the Braintree robbery, and stated that neither Sacco nor Vanzetti was there.[123]

By 1926 the defendants had a competent lawyer, the distinguished Bostonian William G. Thompson (LL.B. 1891), and the travesty of their trial had become a cause célèbre, not only in New England but across the world. The original trial judge had already denied motions for retrial in 1923, and the Supreme Judicial Court of Massachusetts, ruling only on contested points of law, found "no error" in May 1926.[124] Two weeks later the defense filed another motion for a new trial based on the Madeiros confession, with sixty-four supporting affidavits. That, too, was denied by the trial judge, and a second appeal was planned to the Supreme Judicial Court of Massachusetts.[125] The case was now an international affair, with demonstrations held all over the world in support of the defendants. Yet, it was still unclear whether the defendants were wrongfully convicted. But Frankfurter, drawn to the case by his passion for due process, became increasingly outraged.

In March 1927 Frankfurter published his famous "The Case of Sacco and Vanzetti" in *The Atlantic Monthly*, explaining the miscarriage of justice. It preceded the final opinion of the Supreme Judicial Court and was a clear attempt to influence the court's decision. The article was an immediate success, and Frankfurter expanded it into a book later that year, while the *Boston Herald*, in a Pulitzer Prize–winning article, took up Frankfurter's arguments. On April 4, 1927, the Supreme Judicial Court again found "no error," however. Execution seemed imminent, and Frankfurter was the talk of the nation.[126]

Pound was horrified. Writing confidentially to Lowell, he supported Frankfurter on the merits of the case, but expressed grave concerns about the effect on fundraising, given that the school was in the midst of a major campaign. Lowell did not share Pound's concerns about fundraising, but he had become disgusted with Frankfurter's forays into public affairs.[127] To Lowell's great credit, he nevertheless backed Frankfurter's right to publish the article, without agreeing with him on any of the issues. Meanwhile, prominent figures harshly criticized Frankfurter. In a private letter in May 1927, William H. Taft, the U.S. Supreme Court Chief Justice and former U.S. president, called Frankfurter "an expert in attempting to save murderous anarchists from the gallows or the electric chair."[128] Pound complained that his days were wasted by "all sorts of people complaining about Frankfurter's article."[129]

Both Pound and Perkins told Frankfurter that he had rushed into print too soon and was hurting fundraising. Frankfurter responded angrily that, after the article appeared, John D. Rockefeller had donated $100,000 to the Law School.[130] No less a figure than John Wigmore, a friend of Pound's and former Northwestern dean, attacked Frankfurter in the *Boston Transcript* for circulating inaccuracies and "disrupting the administration of justice." After Frankfurter's "crushing reply," Louis Brandeis wrote that "those responsible for his [Wigmore's] intercessions should feel humiliated." Lowell observed, "Wigmore is a fool. He should have known that Frankfurter would be shrewd enough to be accurate."[131]

By that point the drawn out legal proceedings had kept Sacco and Vanzetti alive for seven years. The defense now pinned their hopes on a pardon from Governor Alvan T. Fuller. On June 1, 1927, Fuller named a "Special Advisory Committee," consisting of Samuel W. Stratton, president of MIT; Robert Grant (LL.B. 1879), a retired judge and an Overseer of Harvard; and Harvard University president A. Lawrence Lowell, who served as chair.

It was unclear whether Frankfurter's involvement was a help or hindrance to the defendants at that point. Progressive reformer Gardner Jackson believed that "the intensity of Lowell's animosity to Felix was a very large factor in what happened."[132] In any event, the Committee did not recommend clemency, and Sacco and Vanzetti were executed at midnight on August 22, 1927. The following day, violent demonstrations swept through Europe, South America, and even Japan. Fifty years later, Michael Dukakis (LL.B. 1960), the governor of Massachusetts, issued not a pardon that would presume guilt but a proclamation that the two men had been executed for crimes they did not commit and "that any stigma and disgrace should be forever removed from the names of Nicola Sacco and Bartolomeo Vanzetti, from the names of their families and descendants."[133]

Verdict of the Red Scare Trials

The events surrounding the trial of Sacco and Vanzetti embittered Frankfurter. He wrote to Pound that Lowell was "part and parcel of the social forces which help to explain the conviction and forthcoming execution of two innocent men."[134] The depth of his disappointment began to poison his faith in the Law School itself. Over the next few years, Frankfurter's hopes for the school faded, due to "what he perceived to be the vindictiveness of Lowell, the sterile leadership of Pound, and the rude materialism that gripped the legal profession," according to one of Frankfurter's biographers.[135] He soon returned to Washington, a move that led to even more disaffection from Pound and Lowell.

By contrast, Zechariah Chafee remained positive about Harvard and its administration. Even before the Palmer Raids had been officially discredited, Chafee wrote hopefully to Pound that "Palmer himself is negligible and the whole affair has been a warning against repetitions of his course of action in the future which ought to deter other officials from imitating him."[136] Chafee also viewed his "trial" as a success, and praised both Pound and Lowell. In August 1921 he wrote to Pound "[to] thank you heartily for the unfailing support you have given me. . . . I am very glad that the rumpus is over, at least this stage of it—for the matters which were ruled out on May 22 will doubtless come up sooner or later, and I think of myself as just a sentry whom they hoped to pick off before assaulting the main positions." Chafee cheerfully dedicated his book *Freedom of Speech* (1920) to Lowell.[137]

Pound certainly did not share Chafee's positive view. "There *are* further developments," he replied. "Just what I don't clearly understand. Some sort of attack on me is in progress, and the President, in his sanguine fashion, thinks it will blow over and all will come out well. Meanwhile all my plans are hung up."[138] Pound had planned to study and teach in Paris through a faculty exchange, but his critics in America "have gone so far as to induce the Paris authorities to withdraw their invitation. . . . Lowell is trying to patch the thing up. But I won't have anything more to do with it. I don't care a damn about lecturing there. . . . What L[owell] ought to do is take a real stand against the sneaks at home, not lobby at Paris. Sooner or later they'll fire us all . . . if he doesn't."[139]

Frankfurter certainly agreed with Pound's dark assessment. It probably would not have surprised Frankfurter to learn that, during his efforts for Sacco and Vanzetti, his phones were tapped by the Massachusetts police (who were frustrated that Frankfurter and his mother always conversed in German). What

Frankfurter could not comprehend about Pound was the same sort of "pussy-footing" that Pound saw in Lowell.[140] Pound did not confront the danger to himself or others on the faculty who were under attack. "Pound was a scare cat," Frankfurter observed later. "He was afraid to stand up to people. He wanted to be thought well of by everybody."[141]

In the mid-1920s the gulf between the former allies widened, especially as Lowell became openly anti-Semitic, promoting policies that he hoped would maintain Harvard's traditional Brahmin culture. Lowell aimed to cultivate gentleman leaders at Harvard, and this aim reinforced his anti-Semitism. In contrast, Pound and Frankfurter wanted to train an academic elite by ruthlessly culling the student body. Meanwhile, the relative homogeneity of the faculty and student body deepened Frankfurter's disaffection from Pound and Harvard.

NOTES

1. This chapter draws upon David Wigdor, *Roscoe Pound: Philosopher of Law* (Westport, CT, 1974); N. E. H. Hull, *Roscoe Pound and Karl Llewellyn: Searching for an American Jurisprudence* (Chicago, 1997); and the most thorough study of Pound's administration at Harvard Law School: James F. Clark, "The Harvard Law School Deanship of Roscoe Pound, 1916–1936" (student research paper, Harvard Law School, 1999), on file with the authors. A loyal biography was published sixteen years before Pound's death in 1964 by one of his students: Paul Sayre, *Life of Roscoe Pound* (Iowa City, IA, 1948).

2. James R. Green, *The World of the Worker: Labor in Twentieth Century America* (New York, 1980), 4.

3. Erwin N. Griswold, *Ould Fields, New Corne: The Personal Memoirs of a Twentieth Century Lawyer* (St. Paul, MN, 1992), 119. See Wigdor, *Roscoe Pound*, 14–16.

4. Wigdor, *Roscoe Pound*, 22–27; Hull, *Roscoe Pound*, 36–75.

5. Roscoe Pound and Frederic E. Clements, *Phytogeography of Nebraska* (Lincoln, NE, 1898); Roscoe Pound, "Frederic E. Clements as I Knew Him," *Ecology* 35 (April 1954): 113–116.

6. On Litchfield Law School and proprietary law schools, see Daniel R. Coquillette and Bruce A. Kimball, *On the Battlefield of Merit: Harvard Law School, the First Century* (Cambridge, MA, 2015) (hereafter cited as *Battlefield of Merit*), 53–61.

7. Quotation is from Charles W. Eliot, Annual Report of the President of Harvard University, 1892–93, 31. See Harvard Law School Faculty Meeting Minutes (March 23, March 31, and April 18, 1893). The formation of this list is discussed in *Battlefield of Merit*, 499–501.

8. *The Centennial History of the Harvard Law School: 1817–1917* (Cambridge, MA, 1918), 212. See Thomas M. McKenzie, *Studies in Roman Law with Comparative Views of the Laws of France, England, and Scotland*, 2nd ed. (Edinburgh, 1815); Rudolf Sohm, *The Institutes of Roman Law*, trans. James Crawford Ledlie (Oxford, 1892).

9. See the account and floor plan of Austin Hall in *Battlefield of Merit*, 420–422.

10. Quotations are from Roscoe Pound to Laura B. Pound (September 29, 1889), Roscoe Pound to Stephen B. Pound (December 22, 1889), and Roscoe Pound to Laura B. Pound (March 10, 1890), quoted in Wigdor, *Roscoe Pound*, 36. On the text-and-recitation method, see *Battlefield of Merit*, 166–168.

11. Roscoe Pound to Laura B. Pound (March 10, 1890) quoted in Wigdor, *Roscoe Pound*, 44. See the account of Keener in *Battlefield of Merit*, 396–398.

12. Roscoe Pound, "The Common Law and Legislation," *Harvard Law Review* 21 (1908): 383–407; James B. Thayer, "The Origin and Scope of the American Doctrine of Constitutional Law," *Harvard Law Review* 7 (1893): 129–156; Wigdor, *Roscoe Pound*, 46. Hull, *Roscoe Pound*, does not attribute influence to Thayer.

13. Roscoe Pound to Stephen B. Pound (November 10, 1889) and Pound to Pound (March 10, 1890) quoted in Wigdor, *Roscoe Pound*, 41.

14. Wigdor, *Roscoe Pound*, 47; Hull, *Roscoe Pound*, 39, 45. For other examples of references to Gray in Pound's later work, see Roscoe Pound, *Interpretation of Legal History* (Cambridge, MA, 1923), 44, 131; Pound, *The Formative Era of American Law* (Boston, 1938), 26, 37, 162–163.

15. See Morton Horwitz, *The Transformation of American Law, 1870–1960: The Crisis of Legal Orthodoxy* (Oxford, 1992), 217–220. Compare Edward B. McClean, *Law and Civilization: The Legal Thought of Roscoe Pound* (Lanham, MD, 1992), xvii.

16. Rudolph von Jhering, *The Struggle for Law*, trans. John J. Lalor (1877; Chicago, 1915).

17. Sayre, *Life of Roscoe Pound*, 87–88; John N. Drydale, "Address," *Proceedings of the Nebraska State Bar Association* 9 (1916): 21–36; Wigdor, *Roscoe Pound*, 303n19.

18. Pound's empirical and ideological style appears in Roscoe Pound, "The Price of Wheat," *Nebraska State Journal* (August 2, 1856). See Wigdor, *Roscoe Pound*, 71–75, 302n10.

19. Roscoe Pound, "The Causes of Popular Dissatisfaction with the Administration of Justice," *Report of the Annual Meeting of the ABA* 29 (1906): 395–417; Sayre, *Life of Roscoe Pound*, 147–152.

20. *Lochner v. New York*, 198 U.S. 45 (1905). See Holmes's dissent at 74–76.

21. Pound, "Causes of Popular Dissatisfaction," 397, 400, 403.

22. Pound, "Causes of Popular Dissatisfaction," 400.

23. Hull, *Roscoe Pound*, 44; see 78–79.

24. Quotation is from David M. Rabban, *Law's History: American Legal Thought and the Transatlantic Turn to History* (Cambridge, UK, 2014), 107–108. See Henry Sumner Maine, *Ancient Law* (London, 1861); von Jhering, *Struggle for Law*; Oliver W. Holmes Jr.,

"The Path of the Law," *Harvard Law Review* 10 (1897): 457–478. Pound's relationship with Holmes is discussed in Chapter 6.

25. Wigdor, *Roscoe Pound*, 126–127.

26. John H. Wigmore, "Roscoe Pound's St. Paul Address of 1906: The Spark That Kindled the White Flame of Progress," *Journal of the American Judicature Society* 20 (February 1937): 178.

27. John H. Wigmore to Roscoe Pound (December 21, 1907), Roscoe Pound Papers, 1888–1964, Harvard Law School Library Historical & Special Collections (HLSLib) (hereafter cited as RP Papers). Compare Wigdor, *Roscoe Pound*, 135, 311n8.

28. Paul D. Carrington, *Stewards of Democracy: Law as a Public Profession* (Boulder, CO, 1999), 89–90.

29. See *Proceedings of the Illinois State Bar Association* (1910), 158–161; Wigdor, *Roscoe Pound*, 157, 315n69. On Wigmore's relationship to early modernist jurisprudence, see Andrew Porwancher, *John Henry Wigmore and the Rules of Evidence: The Hidden Origins of Modern Law* (Columbia, MO, 2016).

30. Carrington, *Stewards of Democracy*, 12.

31. Henry M. Bates to Roscoe Pound (September 25, 1915), RP Papers.

32. Roscoe Pound to Olivia Pound (January 20, 1916), quoted in Wigdor, *Roscoe Pound*, 203–204, 324, 345. See Clark, "Harvard Law School Deanship," 18–20.

33. "Opportunity of a Law School," *New Republic* (November 13, 1915): 33.

34. Felix Frankfurter to Roscoe Pound (late 1916) and Learned Hand to Roscoe Pound (January 4, 1916), RP Papers. See Clark, "Harvard Law School Deanship," 20.

35. Roscoe Pound to Laura B. Pound (January 20, 1916), quoted in Wigdor, *Roscoe Pound*, 204, 324n62.

36. J. M. Bourne, *Britain and the Great War, 1914–1918* (London, 1985), 55–59.

37. The following draws on Clark, "Harvard Law School Deanship," 24–30; Brandi Pugh, "Anomaly: Harvard Law School during World War I" (student research paper, Boston College Law School, 2014), on file with the authors; Jay Winter and Antoine Prost, *The Great War in History: Debates and Controversies, 1914 to the Present* (New York, 2005), 192–213; Niall Ferguson, *The Pity of War* (London, 1998), 367–462; Trevor Wilson, *The Myriad Faces of War: Britain and the Great War, 1914–1918* (Oxford, 1986), 751–798.

38. Woodrow Wilson, Address Delivered at Joint Session of the Two Houses of Congress (April 2, 1917), U.S. 65th Congress, 1st Session, Senate Document 5.

39. Quotations are from, respectively, Roscoe Pound to H. H. Kennedy (April 23, 1917); Records of President A. Lawrence Lowell, 1909–1933, Harvard University Archives (hereafter cited as ALL Records).

40. Roscoe Pound to A. Lawrence Lowell (April 3, 1917), ALL Records; Pound to Kennedy (April 23, 1917).

41. Roscoe Pound, Memorandum to Faculty (April 11, 1917), ALL Records. See Clark, "Harvard Law School Deanship," 27n15.

42. William Berman to Roscoe Pound (June 2, 1917), ALL Records.

43. Resolutions of the Harvard Law School Faculty (April 24 and May 3, 1917), ALL Records.

44. Roscoe Pound to A. Lawrence Lowell (May 2, 1918), ALL Records. See Clark, "Harvard Law School Deanship," 29n110.

45. Nathaniel Siegel to Roscoe Pound (July 20, 1917), ALL Records.

46. "The Law School and the Fourth Camp," *Harvard Crimson* (May 1, 1918). See Roscoe Pound to John Henry Wigmore (May 2, 1918) and Pound to Lowell (May 2, 1918), ALL Records.

47. Roscoe Pound to Earle C. Bailie (May 16, 1917), ALL Records. See Roscoe Pound to Kingman Brewster Sr. (May 14, 1917), ALL Records.

48. A. Lawrence Lowell, Annual Report of the President of Harvard University, 1916–17, 22. See Roscoe Pound, Annual Report of the Dean of Harvard Law School, 1915–16, 146; 1916–17, 140; Harvard Law School Catalog, 1917–18, 56; 1918–19, 32.

49. See the correspondence between Dean William Lile of the University of Virginia Law School and Roscoe Pound (April 21, 1917, and November 25, 1918), ALL Records. Clark, "Harvard Law School Deanship," 36n144, 145.

50. Roscoe Pound to Paul Clayston (July 31, 1917), ALL Records. See Clark, "Harvard Law School Deanship," 33n132.

51. Roscoe Pound to C. G. Haglund (June 24, 1918), ALL Records. See Clark, "Harvard Law School Deanship," 34n135.

52. Roscoe Pound to A. Lawrence Lowell (November 30, 1917), ALL Records. See Clark, "Harvard Law School Deanship," 34n137.

53. Thomas W. Swan, Annual Report of the Dean of Yale Law School, 1918–19, 265, 271–272.

54. Roscoe Pound to A. Lawrence Lowell (April 13, 1918), ALL Records. See Roscoe Pound to Lieutenant Ayer (September 26, 1917), ALL Records.

55. See Annual Report of the Treasurer of Harvard University, 1916–17, 149, 189–191.

56. Pound, Annual Report of the Dean, 1917–18, 119–120.

57. Quotation is from Samuel Williston, *Life and Law: An Autobiography* (Boston, 1940), 187.

58. Roscoe Pound to Alfred Z. Reed (December 16, 1918), ALL Records. See Alfred Z. Reed, *Training for the Public Profession of Law* (New York, 1921); Clark, "Harvard Law School Deanship," 25–26n100.

59. Anonymous to Roscoe Pound (April 1917), ALL Records. See Clark, "Harvard Law School Deanship," 25n115.

60. Pound, Annual Report of the Dean, 1918–19, 122.

61. Harvard Law School, *Announcement of a Special Session February–August 1919* (Cambridge, MA, 1918).

62. Harvard Law School Catalog, 1919–20.

63. Roscoe Pound to Nathan Isaacs (December 20, 1918), ALL Records. Nathan Isaacs went on to teach business law at the Harvard Graduate School of Business Administration from 1923 to 1941.

64. Roscoe Pound to A. Lawrence Lowell (June 23, 1918), ALL Records.

65. Roscoe Pound to Henry L. Stimson (June 12, 1919), and Henry Stimson to Roscoe Pound (June 13, 1917), ALL Records. See Myliefer Shaikh, "Manley O. Hudson, as Professor and Lawyer-Statesman" (student research paper, Harvard Law School, 2001), on file with the authors.

66. Roscoe Pound to Felix Frankfurter (April 28, 1919), ALL Records.

67. See Roscoe Pound to Felix Frankfurter (May 17, 1919), RP Papers; Manley O. Hudson to Roscoe Pound (September 27, 1918), ALL Records.

68. Felix Frankfurter to Roscoe Pound (June 3, 1919), RP Papers.

69. Hudson to Pound (September 27, 1918).

70. Harvard Law School Catalog, 1920–21, 59; Wigdor, *Roscoe Pound,* 237.

71. Margaret MacMillan, *Paris 1919: Six Months That Changed the World* (New York, 2001), 83–97.

72. Willa Cather, *Not Under Forty* (New York, 1936), prefatory note. See Hull, *Roscoe Pound,* 47–48.

73. The following draws upon Stanley Coben, *A. Mitchell Palmer: Politician* (New York, 1963); Green, *World of the Worker,* 101–134; David M. Kennedy, *Over Here: The First World War and American Society* (New York, 1980), 26–27; David J. Goldberg, *Discontented America: The United States in the 1920s* (Baltimore, 1999).

74. See Kenneth D. Ackerman, *J. Edgar Hoover, the Red Scare, and the Assault on Civil Liberties* (New York, 2007); Cameron McWhirter, *Red Summer: The Summer of 1919 and the Awakening of Black America* (New York, 2011). See also Robert K. Murray, *Red Scare: A Study in National Hysteria* (Minneapolis, 1955).

75. *An Act to Exclude and Expel from the United States Aliens Who Are Members of the Anarchistic and Similar Classes,* Public Law 221, *Statutes at Large of the United States of America,* 65th Congress (1917–1919), chap. 186, 40 Stat. 1012–1013 (October 16, 1918).

76. Coben, *A. Mitchell Palmer,* 234.

77. H. N. Hirsch, *The Enigma of Felix Frankfurter* (New York, 1981), 72; Michael E. Parrish, *Felix Frankfurter and His Times: The Reform Years* (New York, 1982), 1–22.

78. Quoted in Parrish, *Felix Frankfurter,* 121n6.

79. Felix Frankfurter, *Felix Frankfurter Reminisces, Recorded in Talks with Dr. Harlan B. Phillips* (New York, 1960), 168–170.

80. Donald L. Smith, *Zechariah Chafee, Jr.: Defender of Liberty and Law* (Cambridge, MA, 1986), 36–57.

81. Roscoe Pound to Louise Pound (April 27, 1918), RP Papers.

82. Roscoe Pound to Oliver W. Holmes Jr. (July 24, 1919), RP Papers. See National Popular Government League, *To the American People: Report on the Illegal Practices of the United States Department of Justice* (Washington, DC, 1920).

83. Frankfurter, *Felix Frankfurter Reminisces,* 177. "Frankfurter, when he was nearing the end of his life, said this was one of the most impressive sentences he had ever heard." Arthur E. Sutherland, *The Law at Harvard: A History of Ideas and Men, 1817–1907* (Cambridge, MA, 1967), 236.

84. *Abrams v. United States,* 250 U.S. 616, 627–28 (1919) (Holmes, J., dissenting). The more familiar phrase "clear and present danger" originates in Holmes's opinion in *Schenck v. United States,* 249 U.S. 47, 52 (1919). Holmes's dissent in *Abrams* is often said to have introduced the term "marketplace of ideas." But Holmes actually wrote, "The best test of truth is the power of the thought to get itself accepted in the competition of the market." *Abrams,* 250 U.S. 616, Holmes dissenting at 630. The phrase "market place of ideas" was apparently first used by Justice William O. Douglas in *United States v. Rumely,* 345 U.S. 41, 56 (1953) (Douglas, J., concurring).

85. Zechariah Chafee Jr., "A Contemporary State Trial—The United States versus Jacob Abrams et al.," *Harvard Law Review* 33 (1920): 773. See Zechariah Chafee Jr., "Freedom of Speech in War-Time," *Harvard Law Review* 32 (1919): 932–973.

86. Zechariah Chafee Jr., *Freedom of Speech* (New York, 1920). The book was updated in 1941 in *Free Speech in the United States* (Cambridge, MA, 1941).

87. Quotations are from Robert Stephenson to the Editors, Harvard Law Review (c. April 1920), Zechariah Chafee Jr. Papers, 1898–1957, HLSLib (hereafter cited as ZCJ Papers). See John H. Ryan, "Statement for the Information of the President and Fellows of Harvard College and the Board of Overseers of Harvard College with Respect to Certain Teachers in the Harvard Law School" (March 1, 1921), 4, RP Papers.

88. Zechariah Chafee Jr., to Robert Stephenson (April 27, 1920), ZCJ Papers.

89. Robert Stephenson to Zechariah Chafee Jr. (May 6, 1920), ZCJ Papers.

90. Zechariah Chafee Jr. to Robert Stephenson (May 21, 1920), ZCJ Papers.

91. See "Typewritten Statement of Z.C. Jr., Prepared after the Hearing," ZCJ Papers.

92. Austen G. Fox, "Statement for the Information of the President and Fellows of Harvard College with Respect to Certain Teachers in the Harvard Law School" (May 3, 1921), RP Papers.

93. In 1642 the Massachusetts legislature established the large Board of Overseers to oversee all important affairs at the young college. The Harvard Charter of 1650 then created the Corporation, composed of the president, treasurer, and five fellows, and transferred the Overseers' direct responsibilities and authority to this smaller entity. From 1650 onward, the Board of Overseers served as an advisory body that could sanction decisions by the Corporation but had few direct managerial responsibilities. The Corporation became responsible for appointing and removing administrators, faculty, and staff; creating orders and by-laws for the college; and managing college finances and property. In 2011 the membership of the Harvard Corporation was increased from seven to thirteen, and a key committee was established to address financial, capital planning, and other important issues. See *Battlefield of Merit,* 120n47.

94. Ryan, "Statement" (March 1, 1921).

95. Francis G. Caffey to Zechariah Chafee Jr. (June 10, 1920) in ibid. Caffey is listed in the class of 1895 at the Law School, but he did not graduate with the LL.B. Harvard Law School, *Quinquennial Catalog of the Law School of Harvard University, 1939* (Cambridge, MA, 1939), 37.

96. See "Typewritten Statement of Z.C. Jr." For Frankfurter's detailed account of the meeting, see Frankfurter, *Felix Frankfurter Reminisces*, 176–177.

97. See Francis J. Swayze, *Report of the Committee to Visit the Law School* (May 21, 1921), quoted in Sutherland, *The Law at Harvard*, 256–257. Cardozo's vote is discussed in Yeomans, *Abbott Lawrence Lowell*, 323; Smith, *Zechariah Chafee, Jr.*, 55; Andrew L. Kaufman, *Cardozo* (Cambridge, MA, 1998), 172.

98. A. Lawrence Lowell to Zechariah Chafee (c. November 1937), quoted in Yeomans, *Abbott Lawrence Lowell*, 323.

99. Yeomans, *Abbott Lawrence Lowell*, 323. Ever loyal to Lowell, Yeomans suggests that by "Chair," Lowell was referring to himself! It is much more likely the reference was to Pound, who was one of the accused.

100. Yeomans, *Abbott Lawrence Lowell*, 323.

101. Upton Sinclair, "The Goose-Step: A Study of American Education," *Appeal to Reason* (September 16, 1922), 2. See Upton Sinclair, *The Goose-Step: A Study of American Education* (Girard, KS, 1923).

102. Chafee quoted in Joel Seligman, *The High Citadel: The Influence of Harvard Law School* (Boston, 1978), 59.

103. "Laski Scores Commissioner's Action in Walkout Crisis," *Harvard Crimson* (October 10, 1919). The satirical *Harvard Lampoon* parodied Laski as "Professor Moses Smartelickoff" and wrote, "From the firstski to the Laski he's a Red!," *Harvard Lampoon* (January 16, 1920), 401, 408, 410, 413.

104. Quoted in John T. Bethell, *Harvard Observed: An Illustrated History of the University in the Twentieth Century* (Cambridge, MA, 1998), 93. Laski is listed as a nongraduate in the Law School class of 1919, but he does not appear in the school's annual catalogs. Harvard Law School, *Quinquennial Catalog . . . 1939*, 184.

105. A. Lawrence Lowell to Zechariah Chafee (February 2, 1920), ZCJ Papers.

106. "Mr. Laski Gives Up University Position," *Harvard Crimson* (May 10, 1920).

107. Morton Keller and Phyllis Keller, *Making Harvard Modern: The Rise of America's University* (New York, 2001), 14; William Wright, *Harvard's Secret Court: The Savage 1920 Purge of Campus Homosexuals* (New York, 2005); Bethell, *Harvard Observed*, 94–96.

108. See Zechariah Chafee Jr. to Roscoe Pound (n.d. 1920; August 22, 25, 1921; April 28, 1932), RP Papers; Roscoe Pound to Zechariah Chafee (August 22, 1921), ZCJ Papers.

109. Hull, *Roscoe Pound*, 125–126.

110. Louis D. Brandeis, "The Opportunity in the Law," Address before the Harvard Ethical Society (May 4, 1905).

111. See Melvin I. Urofsky, *Felix Frankfurter: Judicial Restraint and Individual Liberties* (Boston, 1991), 2.

112. Quotation is from Urofsky, *Felix Frankfurter*, 7. See Ezra R. Thayer to Henry L. Stimson (June 24, 1913), ALL Records; Ezra R. Thayer to W. R. Thayer (January 21, 1914), Ezra Ripley Thayer Papers, 1882–1915, HLSLib; Edward Warren to Ezra R. Thayer (June 26, 1913), Felix Frankfurter to Edward Warren (June 25, 1913), Felix Frankfurter to Ezra R. Thayer (July 30, 1913), ALL Records.

113. Quoted in Sanford H. Kadish, "Labor and the Law," in *Felix Frankfurter: The Judge* (New York, 1964), 158–159, 264n19.

114. Hirsch, *Enigma of Felix Frankfurter*, 55–56.

115. Hirsch, *Enigma of Felix Frankfurter*, 57.

116. Parrish, *Felix Frankfurter*, 120.

117. Parrish, *Felix Frankfurter*, 122. Perkins was a leader of the Harvard Endowment Fund campaign during all these events.

118. *Michaels v. Hillman*, 183 New York Supplement 195 (1920).

119. *Colyer v. Skeffington*, 265 Federal Reporter 17 (1st Circuit 1920).

120. Quoted in Hirsch, *Enigma of Felix Frankfurter*, 81.

121. Parrish, *Felix Frankfurter*, 178. The following discussion draws upon Steven Van Dyke, "The Trial of Sacco and Vanzetti at Harvard Law School" (student research paper, Boston College Law School, 2008), on file with the authors.

122. Quotations from Parrish, *Felix Frankfurter*, 181. See also Frankfurter, *Felix Frankfurter Reminisces*, 211.

123. Quotations from the so-called Holt Record, in *The Sacco-Vanzetti Case: The Transcript of the Record of the Trial of Nicola Sacco and Bartolomeo Vanzetti in the Court of Massachusetts and Subsequent Proceedings, 1920–27*, 5 vols. (New York, 1928–1929), 4:3579, 4416–4418; 5:5253; Parrish, *Felix Frankfurter*, 179–184. See Herbert B. Ehrmann, *The Case That Will Not Die: Commonwealth v. Sacco and Vanzetti* (Boston, 1969), 404–432.

124. *Commonwealth v. Nicola Sacco & another*, 255 Massachusetts 369 (1926).

125. Parrish, *Felix Frankfurter*, 184. See "Holt Record," 5:4726–4777.

126. Felix Frankfurter, "The Case of Sacco and Vanzetti," *Atlantic Monthly* 139 (March 1927), 409–432; Felix Frankfurter, *The Case of Sacco and Vanzetti* (Boston, 1927); *Commonwealth v. Nicola Sacco & another*, 259 Massachusetts 128 (1927).

127. Helen Shirley Thomas, *Felix Frankfurter: Scholar on the Bench* (Baltimore, 1960), 20; Hull, *Roscoe Pound*, 149–150.

128. Quoted in Parrish, *Felix Frankfurter*, 177.

129. Roscoe Pound, Diary (February 28, 1927), RP Papers.

130. Parrish, *Felix Frankfurter*, 186. Thomas Perkins to Felix Frankfurter (April 27 and May 9, 1927) and Felix Frankfurter to Thomas Perkins (April 27 and May 11, 1927), Felix Frankfurter Papers, 1900–1965, HLSLib.

131. Wigmore's first letter to the *Boston Evening Transcript* appeared on April 25, 1927. Frankfurter replied on April 26; Wigmore rejoined on May 10; and on May 11, Frankfurter

replied again. Quotations are from Parrish, *Felix Frankfurter,* 186–187, 306n54–55; Louis D. Brandeis to Felix Frankfurter (April 29, 1927), in *Letters of Louis D. Brandeis,* ed. Melvin I. Urofsky and David W. Levy, 5 vols. (Albany, NY, 1971), 5:283. See Louis Joughin and Edmund Morgan, *The Legacy of Sacco and Vanzetti* (Princeton, NJ, 2015), 260; Francis Russell, *Tragedy in Dedham: The Story of the Sacco and Vanzetti Case* (New York, 1962), 371.

132. Quoted in Parrish, *Felix Frankfurter,* 190. Gardner Jackson was a conspicuous advocate for liberal and labor causes in the 1930s and 1940s.

133. Proclamation by Governor Michael S. Dukakis of Nicola Sacco and Bartolomeo Vanzetti Memorial Day (August 23, 1977), http://saccoandvanzetti.org/sn_display1.php?row_ID=12.

134. Felix Frankfurter to Roscoe Pound (August 22–23, 1927), RP Papers.

135. Parrish, *Felix Frankfurter,* 197.

136. Zechariah Chafee Jr. to Roscoe Pound (August 17, 1921), RP Papers.

137. Chafee, Jr. to Pound (August 17, 1921). See Smith, *Zechariah Chafee,* 41–57; Chafee, *Freedom of Speech.*

138. Roscoe Pound to Zechariah Chafee Jr. (August 22, 1925) ZCJ Papers.

139. Roscoe Pound to Zechariah Chafee Jr. (August 27, 1921), ZCJ Papers.

140. Pound to Chafee Jr. (August 22, 1925). See Parrish, *Felix Frankfurter,* 197.

141. Quoted in Seligman, *The High Citadel,* 58.

CHAPTER FOUR

Desirable and "Undesirable" Students, 1916–1936

Based on the German university and its pursuit of research, the vision of Dean Roscoe Pound (1916–1936) for higher education could not have been farther from the Brahmin ideal of President A. Lawrence Lowell (1909–1933), who sought to emulate Oxford and Cambridge and make Harvard a congenial school for gentleman leaders. Aiming to prepare the "complete man" by shaping both the character and the intellect of students, Lowell (LL.B. 1880) promoted the orientation and advising of college freshmen, created the Harvard house system for undergraduates, and instituted the Society of Fellows for graduate students.[1]

Pound also cared about students' well-being. Though "the busiest man" on the faculty, he was the "most approachable" and never limited students' access to him, according to Paul Sayre (S.J.D. 1925), a witness at the time and sympathetic biographer of the dean.[2] Like Deans James Barr Ames (1895–1909) and Ezra Thayer (1910–1915), Pound loaned money to students in need, rescued delinquents at the Cambridge Police Station, and visited the sick in the infirmary. He faithfully attended moot courts and the subsequent student dinners of the moot court societies, where he joined in the singing.[3] Nevertheless, Pound, like Dean Thayer, did not consider Harvard Law School a seminary for gentleman leaders. Instead of nursing first-year students, the best law school in the world must uphold academic standards by mercilessly wielding the intellectual sword. This ruthlessness was accentuated by Pound's abusive tone and "apoplectic" behavior, which worsened progressively during the 1920s and 1930s, as students observed.[4]

Meanwhile, a new approach to undergraduate admissions—selecting from the pool of qualified applicants before admission and rejecting the rest—swept through leading colleges during the 1920s. But Pound and the law faculty would have none of it, preferring to exercise selectivity by culling first-year students.[5] The Law School's preference for attrition over selective admissions reinforced the Spartan culture while improving the bottom line because increasing first-year enrollment added tuition revenue with little expense. Nevertheless, the new selectivity in undergraduate admissions impacted the Law School, because that new approach reduced colleges' reliance on traditional feeder schools, and thus increased the socioeconomic and geographic diversity of college graduates, who then enrolled in law school. In addition, Harvard Law School began drawing students from a broader range of colleges than ever before, which enhanced the socioeconomic and geographic diversity of its students.

Yet the new approach to undergraduate admissions also facilitated the exclusion of Jewish students, because colleges paid more attention to personal background in selecting students. At the same time, President Lowell promulgated explicitly anti-Semitic policies. While the Law School under Pound did not cooperate, the dean and acting deans did not directly challenge the president's anti-Semitism. Nor did they question Lowell's prohibition on admitting women, and the Law School made no effort to recruit or welcome students from racial or ethnic minorities, who remained scarcely 1 percent of the student body. The vast majority of Harvard Law students continued to be white Christian men.

Academic Standards and the Sword of Attrition

In a letter to a first-year student dated November 1926, Dean Pound clearly expressed both his high-handed demeanor and his commitment to exile those deemed unfit. The student, Paul B. Sargent, had graduated from Yale College in June 1926 and matriculated at Harvard Law School the following September. On one Saturday morning in November, Sargent skipped class, like many of his fellow students, in order to socialize before the Harvard-Yale football game. The following week, Pound wrote to him:

My Dear Sir:

You have been reported to me as one of the one hundred or more first-year men who saw fit to drop their work last Saturday by staying away from one of the most difficult courses in the School. Until very recently such things have never happened in the history of the School. . . . This new attitude of first-year men toward their work is shown by the circumstances that 37 percent of last year's first-year class is out of the School. This year I do not intend to wait until June to weed out those who have no place in a serious professional school. You are now listed as prima facie an undesirable student. . . . If you are not in a law club, or you are reported to me as defaulting in or neglecting your law club work, or as not in your seat at lectures, or as being unprepared when called on, I shall bring your name before the Faculty with a recommendation that you be required to withdraw.

Yours very truly,

Roscoe Pound.[6]

One week later, Sargent withdrew from Harvard Law School and subsequently matriculated at Yale Law School, graduating in 1930.

Nor did the most diligent students escape Pound's harsh reprimands. In 1927 Pound submitted an essay to the *Harvard Law Review,* and the student president of the journal, future dean Erwin Griswold (1946–1967), assumed the customary duty of cite-checking the essay. "Dean Pound discovered me in this process," Griswold wrote, "and berated me in a loud voice in the main reading room of the library, with many students present. He said that he was paid by the University to be dean of the Law School, and that any effort by me to do anything about his footnotes showed not only great disrespect, but a lack of confidence by me in his qualifications to be dean." Griswold did not protest or try to explain. Then an hour or two later, Pound "summoned me to his office and apologized" in private, recalled Griswold, who, in fact, did find several citation errors. Griswold made the corrections, but did not tell the dean. Later, "the proofs were submitted to [Pound], and promptly returned, with no comment."[7]

Pound's abrasive attitude and behavior were reinforced by the fiercely competitive, "manly" ethos of the Law School and of the university more generally.[8] Those norms suited the social Darwinism of the era, as expressed by President Lowell in his inaugural address in 1909. Lowell called on the faculty to "increase the intellectual ambition" of students, who should engage in the "struggle for marks" following "a principle of selection . . . of the fittest." Serious study required "strenuous effort . . . ferocious energy, [and] an insubordinate resistance to the authority of the teacher," while it developed "enterprise," "aggressiveness, and "self-reliance."[9]

Lowell believed that Harvard Law School exemplified this ethic. In 1910 he described the Law School as the one among all of Harvard's schools "that most attracts ambitious and self-reliant young men," and "the one that offers them the least amount of aid."[10] Deprivation made the students and the school stronger. Professor Edward "Bull" Warren (LL.B. 1900) later named this approach "Spartan Education." The metaphor was apt. "Throughout my service on the Law Faculty I have sought to discipline the minds, pens, and tongues of the students. I have never suffered fools gladly, and regard such sufferance as mischievous," Warren wrote. "There are today ten thousand men who are leading more useful and successful lives than they would be leading, if my Spartan training had not played a substantial part in the molding of their minds; and . . . most, if not all, of them recognize that to be the fact, and are grateful."[11]

The combative, academic competition contributed to student attrition. During Thayer's deanship, the fraction of first-year students failing or dropping out rose from about one-sixth in the 1900s to about one-quarter in the early 1910s. Under Pound, the fraction grew to one-third or more, as indicated by his letter to Sargent above. At orientation, new students were told: "Look to your right, look to your left, one of you will not be back next year."[12] Even more than Thayer, Pound likely felt that this attrition demonstrated the quality of the Law School, because he surely knew the adage repeated in American universities about "students of German universities"—"of those who enter the university doors, one-third breaks down, one-third goes to the devil, but the remaining third governs Europe."[13]

Meanwhile, the Law School raised the academic threshold for admission. In the fall of 1913 the faculty designated two tiers of colleges whose graduates were entitled to admission. All graduates in first-tier colleges could enter, but graduates of second-tier colleges could do so only if "they ranked in the first third of the class."[14] Then, in the mid-1920s a study of the academic performance of Harvard College graduates over the prior twenty-five years revealed that those in the bottom quarter of the class often failed in their studies at the Law School. The faculty therefore voted to apply that standard to students from all first-tier colleges seeking to enter in September 1927. Graduates of first-tier colleges had to rank in the upper three-quarters of their class to be entitled to admission to the Law School.[15]

In 1928 the faculty raised the threshold rank for graduates of second-tier colleges from the top third to the top quarter of their graduating class.[16] In this way, the school made ever finer discriminations among the academic performance of individual applicants, as well the academic rigor of the colleges. The faculty had expected that raising the admissions threshold would cause enrollment to level off, but it rose to 1,535 in the fall of 1927. Consequently, the first-year class was broken into four sections of about 150 students each, and that became the capacity of each classroom in Langdell Hall when it was expanded in 1929.[17]

Meanwhile, the LL.B. program during Dean Pound's tenure still followed the well-worn path blazed by Dean Christopher Langdell (1870–1895).[18] Teaching aimed to generate "a dueling of intellects, on which the 'case system' is predicated," the students observed.[19] The first-year curriculum comprised the "Big Five" courses in private law that first appeared in the catalog of 1873–74 and persisted through most of the twentieth century: Contracts, Torts, Property, Civil Procedure, and Criminal Law and Liability. Second-year students were required to take Agency, Bills and Notes, Equity, Evidence, Property II, and Sales. Third-year students chose six courses out of seven: Conflict of Laws, Constitutional Law, Corporations, Equity II, Public Utilities, Suretyship, and Trusts.[20] Large classes, high attrition, fixed curriculum, and a high student-faculty ratio reinforced both the professional orientation and the ask-and-give-no-quarter ethos of the school.

Broader Collegiate Origins

During Pound's tenure, one small but significant change in the composition of the student body was the enrollment of "graduate" students, who were pursuing law degrees after the LL.B. As we have seen, the dean was committed to advancing graduate legal study, partly due to his admiration of German universities. In Pound's view, the "sociological" study of economic and scientific disciplines at the graduate level perfectly complemented the core private-law subjects of the LL.B. curriculum. Hence, all the courses on Jurisprudence and on Comparative Law (largely Roman Law) were taught in the graduate program. In 1916–17 there were 10 post-LL.B. graduate students. In 1925–26, the number tripled to 31, and then grew to 44 in 1930–31. Even so, they comprised less than 3 percent of the total enrollment, making the graduate program marginal within the school, despite its importance to Pound's "sociological" vision.[21]

Meanwhile, the total number of students grew sharply under Pound, driven partly by the need for tuition revenue. Total enrollment rose from 791 in 1915–16 to 1,201 in 1924–25 and 1,641 in 1929–30, before tailing off during the Depression to 1,458 in 1934–35. Because Pound added to the faculty, the student-faculty ratio dropped from the astronomical 72:1 in September 1916 to the still formidable 57:1 in 1929–30, although some of the new professors taught courses outside the Law School.[22] At the same time, the composition of the student body began to change. The predominantly white, male students came from a broader and more diverse range of undergraduate colleges.

During the 1916–17 academic year, Pound's first full year as dean, the school had a total of 857 students. One-half had graduated from Ivy League institutions, and fully one-half of that contingent, or one-quarter of the total, came from Harvard College. Yale sent 81 students, Princeton 55, Dartmouth 34, and Brown 26. Cornell graduates numbered 11, the University of Pennsylvania 5, and Columbia 3, likely because those universities had their own excellent law schools. In geographic terms, 54 percent of the 857 students graduated from colleges in the Northeast, and 33 percent from New England. Only three other institutions outside of the Northeast sent more than 10 students: the University of California 14, University of Michigan 11, and University of Missouri 13.[23]

During the 1920s, the students began to come from a wider range of undergraduate colleges—in number and geography, as shown in Table 4.1. The sectarian background of students also expanded. For example, the Law School first enrolled more than 10 students from a Catholic college in 1924–25, when 17 graduates of Boston College and 21 from Holy Cross matriculated. In 1929–30, Georgetown sent 21 students, Holy Cross 30, and Boston College 21. In that year, the total from these three Jesuit institutions also surpassed for

Table 4.1 Diversification of Collegiate Origins of Students Enrolled in Harvard Law School between 1916–17 and 1930–31

Collegiate Origins	1916–17	1930–31
Total enrollment at Harvard Law School	857	1,600
Total colleges represented in student body	154	220
Percentage of students who graduated from:		
Ivy League colleges (including Harvard)	50%	40%
Harvard College	25%	16%
Percentage of students who graduated from colleges by region:		
New England colleges	33%	25%
Colleges in mid-Atlantic states	22%	40%
Midwestern colleges	17%	15%
Southern colleges[a]	19%	11%
Western Colleges[a]	9%	9%

Data source: Harvard Law School Catalog, 1917–18, 56–58; 1931–32, 95–97.

a. Though the percentage did not increase in these regions, the absolute number of students rose significantly.

the first time that of the three New England little Ivy, feeder colleges—Williams, Amherst, and Wesleyan—as feeder colleges: 72 students to 71.[24]

Notwithstanding this broadening in number, geography, and sectarian affiliation of their collegiate origins, the vast majority of students during Pound's tenure were relatively homogeneous by today's standards. Almost all were white, Christian men. Yet their experience varied considerably, even among those who excelled, as revealed in the following stories of three individuals.

A Midwesterner from Oberlin

Born in Cleveland, Ohio, in 1904, Erwin Griswold (LL.B. 1928, S.J.D. 1929) came to the Law School in September 1925 from Oberlin College. Like Pound, he had seriously considered becoming a scientist, but his father, a lawyer, wished him to attend Harvard Law School. In addition, Griswold's Oberlin professors spoke highly of Pound, Felix Frankfurter (LL.B. 1906), and Zechariah Chafee Jr. (LL.B. 1913). So in 1925 Griswold traveled to Cambridge, presented his first-tier college diploma, and matriculated into the first-year class of 530 students.[25]

Though considering himself an outsider, Griswold was not among the financially pinched. His parents paid all his expenses, amounting to about $1,100 per year, as compared to about $950 per year at Oberlin. The cost of attending these institutions nearly equaled the average annual income in the United States at the time—about $1,400 for all industries, $1,150 for government workers, and $1,020 for public school teachers.[26] In addition to the first-year courses of Civil Procedure, Contracts, Criminal Law, and Torts, Griswold enrolled in Property with Bull Warren, whose "very harsh" attitude had begun to offend students. Warren's customary behavior included shouting "Take that woman out!" if a student brought a female guest to sit in the back of the class, as Griswold himself witnessed.

"I worked hard, thoroughly and conscientiously," recalled Griswold, spurred by "a sort of inferiority complex. I was sure that I had not had as good an education at Oberlin as all those Harvard, Yale, and Princeton graduates, and that I could not compete equally with them. But I was determined to do the best I could." In the final examinations at the end of the first year, "I was quite sure that there were many points that I had overlooked"—a conclusion reinforced "by post-examination discussions with fellow students who pointed out issues which I had not seen." Leaving immediately for a summer trip to Europe,

Erwin N. Griswold, LL.B. 1928, S.J.D. 1929, and his roommates, Bradley B. Gilman, LL.B. 1928, and H. Brian Holland, LL.B. 1928, standing, right to left, outside their dormitory on the new campus of the Harvard Business School. Photograph ca. 1925.

Reproduced from Erwin N. Griswold, "Ould Fields, New Corne" (St. Paul, MN: West), 1992.

Griswold wrote to his parents "that, in all likelihood, I had failed at the Harvard Law School, but . . . that I had tried very hard and done my very best." When his grade report arrived at his home in late July, his father traveled ten miles to telegraph the results to Europe. Griswold had received an A in every course and ranked second in his class.

That achievement resulted in his election to the editorial board of the *Harvard Law Review* at the beginning of his second year, when he rented an unoccupied room in the newly built campus of Harvard Business School across the Charles River. At that time and subsequently, "many of the students on the *Law Review* neglected their class work, and . . . worked until the wee hours of the morning, and sometimes all night." Instead, Griswold resolved "to attend classes regularly, to do extensive *Law Review* work, and also to be back in my room no later than midnight."

He broke his pledge for one special night in February 1927. At 2:00 a.m., after a long meeting of the editorial board, he was elected president of the *Law Review*. He recalled,

> I had not allowed myself to think that it would happen. . . . I am rather reserved, not a very good mixer, and assuredly not a person of charisma. I had also encountered at Harvard something that had not been a problem at Oberlin or in my previous life. This was the era of Prohibition, a cause for which my grandparents and parents had labored . . . I believed deeply in the cause. . . . I had seen people impaired, and lives badly affected [by alcohol]. . . . I early came to the conclusion that there was no gain from the use of alcohol which was adequate to offset the dangers to many of the people who used it. I also came to the conclusion . . . that the only sound solution was to be completely abstemious. . . . Though I always kept these thoughts to myself and tried to be unobtrusive or gracious in declining drinks, this . . . made me seem stiff and odd to some people I knew, including many members of the *Law Review*, a number of whom came from the east and from eastern universities.

As president of the *Law Review* in his third year, 1927–28, Griswold became acquainted with Professor Felix Frankfurter and "his sometimes mercurial disposition" when Frankfurter republished his articles from the *Review* in a book on the history and jurisdiction of the U.S. Supreme Court.[27] It was well known that Frankfurter unofficially nominated the clerks for Justices Oliver W. Holmes Jr. (LL.B. 1866) and Louis Brandeis (LL.B. 1877) on the U.S. Supreme Court. Griswold hoped for one of the nominations. "I did not expect to get the Holmes appointment," he recalled, "because I was not the 'polished gentleman' who was usually chosen for the post. . . . However, I would have liked the appointment with Justice Brandeis, where Henry J. Friendly [LL.B. 1927], . . . Dean Acheson [LL.B. 1918], and James Landis [LL.B. 1924, S.J.D. 1925], among others, had served in earlier years. One day,

I was invited to lunch at the Frankfurters, and I knew that I was being looked over. I tried to perform properly." But Frankfurter chose another.

Having lost out on a clerkship, Pound encouraged Griswold to enter the graduate program in September 1928, as the Law School was transforming the S.J.D. into a research degree. Griswold worked with Professor Austin Scott (LL.B. 1909) on the Restatement of Trusts project for the American Law Institute and received his S.J.D. in June 1929. Scott then recommended him to U.S. Solicitor General Charles Hughes Jr. (LL.B. 1912), and Griswold joined Hughes's legal staff in Washington in December 1929, soon after the stock market crash on Black Tuesday, October 29.[28]

A Southerner from Princeton

Born in 1907 in the northeast corner of Louisiana, Ernest J. Brown (LL.B. 1931) grew up in a small town on the Mississippi River located halfway between Vicksburg and Greenville, Mississippi. "It was farming country, cotton country at that time, almost exclusively," he recalled. "Transportation to the relative metropolis of Greenville to the north was all by river." His father, originally from southern Louisiana, was a doctor and owned one of the few automobiles in town. "It had an open top and gaslights in the front. He often made calls into the country to see a remote patient. If it was in the afternoon, he sometimes took me."[29]

Brown graduated from the local high school, and his father urged him to go north for his education, but not too far. "If someone from the South—Birmingham, New Orleans, Atlanta—were going to what later came to be known as the Ivy League, it would be to Princeton, a few maybe to Yale, very few to Harvard." After spending a year at Lawrenceville Academy in New Jersey to strengthen his secondary education, Brown enrolled at Princeton, where he found that the contingent of southern students was "substantial" but not large.

In 1927 Brown graduated from Princeton, having studied European medieval history, and spent one unhappy year working at a bank in New York City. He then decided to go to law school and applied only to Harvard, where "all you needed for admission was a diploma from a recognized college. . . . There was no screening at the beginning of the first year." In September 1928 he matriculated with 672 other new students. Professor Warren A. Seavey (LL.B. 1904) "addressed our first-year class, and stated, 'Look to your right, look to your left, one of you will not be back next year.'" Hence, the first year "was really the selection process." Only a couple of students left during the year;

the weeding out occurred after the first-year exams were graded in June. In the fall of 1929, 430 students—65 percent of Brown's class—returned to start the second year.[30]

Dean Pound was frequently away in Washington, and Edmund M. Morgan (LL.B. 1905) served as acting dean for most of Brown's time as a student. Consequently, "Dean Pound was a very remote presence except when one of his temper explosions came about. One of them I remember vividly." It happened in Brown's third year, when he was a member of the *Harvard Law Review.* The assistant to Acting Dean Morgan had told Paul A. Freund (LL.B. 1931, S.J.D. 1932), a third-year student and president of the *Law Review,* that the editors could use a seminar room in the basement of Langdell Library. "It was very convenient. The sectional reporters were outside, so we used that seminar room to work on the *Review,*" said Brown. "A number of the foreign graduate students also worked in the room, which had two doors leading into the stacks. . . . One afternoon in the springtime, I was working with two or three other people from the *Law Review* at one end of the table. At the far end of the table was a group of foreign graduate students."

Suddenly, one of the doors flew open, and "there stood Dean Pound, flanked on one side by Professor Frankfurter. . . . His face got red, and he shrieked, 'WHAT ARE YOU DOING HERE? WHAT ARE YOU DOING HERE?' I was the target. I just happened to be right in the direct line of fire facing the door. I said, 'We're doing *Law Review* work. Mr. [] said we could use this room.' Pound asked rhetorically, 'MR. [] THINKS HE IS THE DEAN OF THE SCHOOL?' I said, 'No, Dean Pound, I'm sure he doesn't think he is, but I assume he had authority from Mr. Morgan.' . . . I was taking Felix's course in Corporate [Law], and . . . he was standing there grinning at my embarrassment with Pound. . . . The foreign students were quietly moving out of the other door. So I gathered my things and tried to take on a holy look. . . . Later, I told Paul Freund that I might have gotten him in trouble. . . . It turned out this was the room Pound used for his graduate seminars. It was *his* seminar room. . . . This incident was characteristic. . . . He was very fearsome and very remote. . . . Pound looked on those occasions as though he might have apoplexy."

Of the faculty, Brown considered Frankfurter "the greatest teacher I have known," one who worked "transforming magic" in the classroom. Early in the course Public Utilities, Frankfurter called on one student to explain the second case, who responded "unprepared." Then he called on Brown. "I had read this case previously and written an abstract of it, and . . . I started reading from my abstract. . . . But Frankfurter asked, 'if you read your briefs before the Court of Appeals—what do you think the court would do?' . . . I said, 'I am not sure,' and he called on someone else.'" But soon, Frankfurter began calling on Brown every class. "If you were one of his favorites, Frankfurter called on you regularly. . . . There were a few other people whom Felix would bring into the conversation almost every day. And if you were unprepared, he would make it uncomfortable. . . . He could be sarcastic."

In Constitutional Law with Thomas Reed Powell (LL.B. 1904), "a case came up, and he called around the room. . . . Many people would say, 'unprepared.' . . . They were afraid of him. They didn't want to be the targets of his sarcasm." Eventually "he called on me. I said something which he found unacceptable. He then cut me off and called on somebody else. He went around the room . . . and came back to me." When Brown stated his argument, "Powell asked, 'why didn't you say that before?' I said, 'You didn't give me a chance.' . . . This was the only time I saw him somewhat embarrassed."

Both Powell and Frankfurter emphasized the humanity of judges. They spoke "about *the men* who were the Judges, but they treated them very differently. I never heard Frankfurter speak sarcastically of any judge. But Powell did, with this biting wit. Powell could be rather friendly sarcastic about Felix. It never went the other way, though. . . . Then later on [after 1939], when I was on the faculty and Felix was on the Supreme Court, Powell threw a few darts at Felix. He was not amused. But they were very good friends."

At the end of his first year, Brown's grades qualified him to join the Legal Aid Bureau, and, at the end of his second year, the *Law Review.* Soon thereafter, in October 1929, the stock market crashed. "Lots of students did not come back. They or their parents lost their money." Although jobs were scarce, Brown found a position in a large firm in Buffalo upon graduation in 1931. Meanwhile, the Depression had hit farmers long before the stock market crashed, and the agricultural South was more depressed at that point than the industrial North. In the spring of 1932 Brown's father died, leaving heavily mortgaged property that was dependent on cotton sharecropping. His mother and grandmother could not manage the farm, so Brown returned to help with the cotton production.

In March 1933 he received a telegram from a classmate and colleague on the *Law Review,* Milton Katz (LL.B. 1931), who was working in Washington for the Reconstruction Finance Corporation (RFC). But Katz was also assisting Frankfurter, who was advising President Franklin Roosevelt on appointments for New Deal agencies while still teaching at Harvard. Katz recommended Ernest Brown to serve on the staff of Jerome Frank, "one of the great saints of Legal Realism at Yale" and general counsel of the new Agricultural Adjustment Administration.

In those heady and fast-moving days in Washington, Brown joined Frank's staff, along with another recent graduate from Harvard Law School, Alger Hiss (LL.B. 1928), who had been a clerk to Justice Holmes. Also working in the office was "another very quiet gentleman, appreciably older than we were, and his name was Adlai Stevenson." In addition, Paul Freund had finished clerking for Justice Brandeis and joined Katz at the RFC. Freund and Brown shared a house in Washington with other "brain trusters" and "theorists," who were feared by older alumni, such as Harold S. Davis (LL.B. 1904), a leading member of the bar in Boston.[31] All these figures would play prominent roles in the future of national politics and Harvard Law School.

A Northeasterner from Harvard

The plurality of students at the Law School during the 1920s and 1930s came from distinguished northeastern families. Some had sent their sons to Harvard for generations, and these students did not find the Law School as remote or intimidating as did midwesterners like Griswold or southerners like Brown. But this group of insiders also had to face challenges and find their way. Their perspective is conveyed by the experience of Archibald Cox (LL.B. 1937).[32]

Cox's forebears included numerous Harvard Law graduates on both sides of his family, among them U.S. Attorney General and U.S. Secretary of State William M. Evarts (1839–1840), as well as Cox's father and grandfather.[33] In fact, his father, also named Archibald Cox, received both the B.A. from Harvard College in 1896 and the LL.B. from the Law School in 1899. "It was clear my whole life that I would be a lawyer and would go to the Harvard Law School," he recalled. "It's hard to think of a day when I didn't so intend."

Born and raised in New Jersey, Cox attended St. Paul's School in New Hampshire like his father and grandfather, and then entered Harvard College in 1931, when any graduate in the top three-quarters of the class was automatically admitted to Harvard Law School if he desired. Consequently, Cox did little work as an undergraduate, observing later that "it was partly father's influence. He had always said, 'You go to college to grow up. When you go to law school, you've begun your career.'"

Archibald Cox, LL.B. 1937. Faculty 1946–1984.

Harvard Law School Yearbook, 1945–1946. Courtesy of Harvard Yearbook Publications.

After earning gentleman Cs and graduating with a B.A. in 1934, he presented his diploma to the Law School and matriculated with the first-year class of 588 in the fall. Three decades later, applicants with Cox's undergraduate record would not be admitted. Despite his pedigree, Cox's family was not well off financially because his father died during his freshman year, leaving the family with little money. In order to obtain a free room as a law student, Cox served as a proctor in an undergraduate dormitory.

He enrolled in the standard first-year courses, having sections of about 150 students, and one of his teachers was "scary" Bull Warren. At the start of class "the door was closed. And if you opened it and walked in, you were kicked out." During one class, "the door opened, [and] somebody crawled in on his hands and knees. Bull went up the aisle, and [the student] scooted right onto the other aisle. And there was sort of a back and forth." Cox also witnessed students playing "the game of trying to sneak a woman in [class] on Saturday morning, which was unsuccessfully played. 'Take that woman out of here,' he'd say. . . . I heard it a number of times."

Unlike at college, Cox decided to work, and to his "complete surprise," he ranked first in his class at the end of the first year, when all grading was done anonymously. But he did not entirely abandon gentlemanly collegiate pursuits. Having played varsity squash, Cox competed in A-league squash for Lincoln's Inn, an exclusive social club at the Law School. Cox ate lunch at Lincoln's Inn or at the Delphic, a select final club to which he had belonged as a Harvard undergraduate. Saturday afternoons and all Sundays were "given over to something other than working."

Cox recalled the social divisions in Pound's Law School during the 1930s. "Those of us who had been at one of the Ivy League colleges—if Harvard, and belonged to a final club; if Yale, and belonged to one of the secret societies; if Princeton, and belonged to one of the eating clubs—really saw nothing of the very bright, dedicated students who came from CCNY during the first year, and nor thereafter if they didn't make the *Law Review.*" The social divisions were also manifested in the extracurricular law clubs, in which students prepared moot court cases. These law clubs required "much more work" and were "much more important" than later in the twentieth century.

Cox was elected to the Kent Club, one of the elite law clubs that were older and "continuing," meaning that they had a history and a pedigree.[34] This continuity conferred two great advantages. "One, there was likely to be some faculty member who had been a member of the club and . . . would have members of the club to tea, and took more interest, and was more likely . . . to sit as a judge on intra-club arguments. The other was that the members of the club from the second and third years took some interest and offered guidance. And the judges at your initial arguments . . . were likely to be younger lawyers in town, who had been members of the club when they were students."

"If you came from CCNY, you might not be invited into a 'continuing' club," Cox added. The clubs newly formed by students not invited to join a "continuing" club were called the "bastard clubs," meaning those which had no previous history. The "bastard clubs" usually ended when their members graduated. Years later, Cox received "a very moving letter from one of the very able young men in my class who was in that group and still carried some feeling of resentment."

All the same, the intense academic competition, particularly election to the three, academic honor organizations—the *Law Review,* the Board of Student Advisors, and the Legal Aid Bureau—could weaken social barriers. For Cox, it was on the *Law Review* that he got to know *them*—the best students from CCNY and other public universities. "Those barriers disappeared for someone who was on the Law Review. And I got to know them well, and worked with them sometimes surprisingly well." For example, Cox was assigned to edit the case write-up of a fellow student on the *Law Review,* who "purported to be a believer in Communism . . . and my edit made his left-wing points a good deal clearer and perhaps pressed them somewhat farther than they had been before. He had been totally expecting something different. . . . For me, it was easier because I, among my friends, had been one of the few Democrats. . . . So I was sympathetic to the New Deal and to most of the ideas."

During his second year Cox became engaged to the granddaughter of James Barr Ames, who was also the granddaughter of Nathan Abbott, the first head of the law department at Stanford University. Due to problems with his eyesight, Cox resigned from the *Law Review,* but did take Frankfurter's course, Public Utilities, in which Frankfurter addressed most of his questions to Cox. In his third year Cox was nominated by Frankfurter to be the law clerk for Judge Learned Hand (LL.B. 1896) of the U.S. Court of Appeals for the Second Circuit. It also happened that Judge Hand had known Cox's father and become close friends with his mother. After graduating with the LL.B. in 1937, Cox assumed this clerkship.

Griswold, Brown, and Cox later became distinguished professors at the Law School. Subsequently, Griswold served as dean of the school and as U.S. solicitor general. Cox also served as U.S. solicitor general, as well as special prosecutor in the Watergate scandal, and, for a crucial period, *de facto* president of Harvard University, taking the place of Nathan M. Pusey (1953–1971). Throughout their illustrious careers, Griswold and Cox remained closely involved with the school. Brown, however, left the school abruptly due to the student unrest in 1971 and went to the University of Pennsylvania Law School. He then returned to work in Washington at the U.S. Department of Justice, which awarded him its Distinguished Service Award in 1981. President George H. W. Bush awarded Brown the Distinguished Presidential Rank Award in 1991.

Notwithstanding their different backgrounds, the experience of Griswold, Brown, and Cox as students during the 1920s and 1930s reveals the predominant homogeneity in the student body by today's standards. Women, Latinos, African Americans, Asian Americans, Native Americans—together constituting a clear majority of the American population—were virtually, if not entirely, excluded. But these groups were not the primary focus of Harvard's discrimination in this era. Rather, the explicit target of President Lowell's prejudice was a group that constituted about 15 percent of the student population at the Law School during Pound's deanship: Jewish students.

Anti-Semitism and Faculty Appointments

Harvard, Yale, Princeton, and Columbia, along with many other leading colleges and universities, sought to curtail the Jewish presence on their campuses after World War I, as the number of Jewish applicants soared. President Lowell tried to make this a priority throughout Harvard University.[35] At the Law School, therefore, the Sacco and Vanzetti affair was not the only wedge that drove Frankfurter and Pound apart. How to respond to Lowell's anti-Semitism, typical of his circle at the time, was another. Lowell's invidious effort took three forms: blocking Jewish appointments to the faculty, establishing a Jewish quota for admission throughout the university, and trying to discredit Jewish students by demonstrating that they behaved poorly compared to their classmates.

As under Charles Eliot (1869–1909), the president and the Corporation had final authority over faculty appointments, and exercised that prerogative even over initial, probationary appointments.[36] In 1921, probably due to Frankfurter's Zionist activities, the Corporation had voted to reject Pound's nomination of Frankfurter to the Byrne Chair, which Pound described to Brandeis as a "monstrous outrage."[37] In 1924 Lowell, on political grounds, opposed the appointments of Francis Sayre (LL.B. 1912, S.J.D. 1918), James A. MacLachlan (LL.B. 1916), and Thomas Powell to tenured positions. But Pound stood firm in these cases, and Lowell backed down. In MacLachlan's case, Lowell acquiesced after learning that he was related to Yale president James R. Angell.[38]

While fighting Lowell over faculty appointments, Pound also found himself at odds with Frankfurter. Like Brandeis, Frankfurter preferred a small faculty that focused its efforts on cultivating the intellect of elite students. Pound disagreed, arguing that modern standards of academic productivity required more faculty, each with an academic specialty. In 1925 this disagreement came to a head when Pound advanced three new faculty candidates over strong opposition from Frankfurter, who described the three as "unrelieved sterility." In response, Pound complained that Frankfurter "opposed everything."[39]

By 1927 their positions were reversed. Frankfurter strongly urged appointing one of his favorite students, Nathan R. Margold (LL.B. 1923), to the faculty. Frankfurter had been largely responsible for bringing Margold, also a Jewish graduate of CCNY, to Harvard. Having graduated fifth in his class at the Law School, Margold was strongly supported by a number of influential judges and graduates, including Learned Hand, Augustus Hand (LL.B. 1894), and Julian Mack (LL.B. 1887), the sole Jewish member of Harvard's Board of Overseers. After graduation, Margold taught at the Law School as an instructor during the academic year 1927–28, to great student acclaim.[40]

Frankfurter naturally wanted Margold treated fairly. In addition, Frankfurter, having been the only Jewish member of the faculty for some time, wondered if appointments of more Jews were barred. In 1926 he wrote to Pound, "The issue . . . is whether or not [Margold] is to be considered on his merits . . . or whether the fact that he is a Jew is also to be taken into account."[41] Early in January 1927, Frankfurter again wrote to Pound, "I am told that you are influenced by fear lest the Corporation would reject Margold because he is a Jew. . . . I know no one who is more free of racial or religious prejudice than you. But there is no surer way of introducing the ugly atmosphere of anti-Semitism into the Law School than for you to yield to, or acquiesce in, the anti-Semitism of others, if such there be."[42]

Furthermore, Frankfurter suggested that Pound feared that the addition of Margold "would make too many Jews on the Faculty," given that Pound had other Jewish candidates whom he wished to appoint.[43] Indeed, according to Powell, Pound thought "we should not get a Jew at this time in view of . . . our desire to get other Jews later."[44] Pound thus effectively conceded a quota of Jewish professors. When the Faculty voted in late January 1928 to appoint Margold as an assistant professor, Lowell promptly rejected the appointment.

Frankfurter was furious and viewed this as the litmus test for Pound. Would the dean press Lowell for reconsideration? At a faculty meeting, Pound did argue against Lowell's decision, and asked the faculty whether to challenge it. But only eight out of twenty-five faculty voted in favor of challenging, and Pound gave up. He wrote to Lowell, "The motion to challenge the decision was overwhelmingly defeated. It was voted to make another recommendation, and I hope to be able to submit one to you in a short time."[45]

The Margold affair became even more troubling in light of two subsequent battles between Lowell and the law faculty. In March 1928, James Landis came up for promotion to the newly created position Professor of Legislation. Though not Jewish, Landis was also a Frankfurter protégé, and Lowell was doubtless suspicious of his politics. Lowell's preferred candidate was Henry L. Shattuck (LL.B. 1904), a Harvard scion and prominent Boston politician and attorney, far more Lowell's type. Frankfurter was again furious with Pound and his colleagues. Only when Shattuck dropped out did Lowell approve Landis.[46]

In 1930 the faculty recommended Wilbur G. Katz (LL.B. 1926), another Jew, for a one-year instructorship to teach Criminal Law. This time Pound never strongly supported the appointment, and left the Appointments Committee to make the case for Katz.[47] The correspondence relating to Katz reveals the prejudice of the time. Edmund Morgan, a faculty supporter of Katz, wrote to Elihu Root Jr., a partner of Katz's former law firm, "There are two objections which have been interposed. First, he is a Jew. It is true that he may be only 25 percent or 50 percent, but his name and his features are pretty certain to work against him in some quarters. Second, there is a rumor . . . that your office is not entirely sorry to lose him." The memorandum goes on to point out that "Mr. Katz's father is a Jew, but is a vestryman at the Episcopal Church in Milwaukee. His mother is a Gentile."[48]

Ultimately Pound undermined Katz's appointment. He told Lowell that the school did not need the appointment and that he could teach Katz's section of Criminal Law himself.[49] The Katz matter was the final straw for Frankfurter and marked the end of his cordial relations with Pound. In February 1930 Frankfurter wrote, "The faculty [almost] unanimously urged Katz's appointment. You were hostile and urged your hostility on the President. Naturally enough, your hostility has been effective. Thereby, you have done the School a considerable disservice, for you have deprived it of a much needed able teacher and scholar."[50] Frankfurter believed that, as in the Margold case, Pound had again deferred to Lowell's anti-Semitism.

The Rise of Selective Admissions

Limiting the enrollment of Jewish students was facilitated by two related factors that changed the nature of admissions in leading colleges and universities during the 1920s. The number of students throughout higher education grew enormously, and the undergraduate institutions adopted selective admissions.

Across the nation, enrollment in higher education rose more than 350 percent between 1900 and 1926: from 168,000 to more than 767,000 students. During the 1920s the number of college students increased annually by nearly 51,000.[51] This enrollment explosion across the nation was fueled by the rising need for professional expertise, growth of public school systems, improved means of transportation and communication, and enhanced efficiency and standardization of admission evaluations fostered particularly by the College Entrance Examination Board, formed in 1899.[52] The enrollment growth also coincided with a massive increase in immigrants from Southern and Eastern Europe, many of them Jewish.

The increasing number of students soon overwhelmed the capacity of many colleges and universities. Some prominent institutions started to cap the size of the entering class, as did Columbia in 1919, Cornell in 1920, Stanford in 1921, Princeton and Yale in 1922, and Harvard in 1923.[53] In addition, these universities, like prominent colleges, tried to stem the influx of students by raising their academic thresholds for admission. This approach did not involve selecting among the qualified applicants. In general, only those qualified and expecting to be welcomed applied, so virtually all who applied were admitted. In 1920 a survey of the forty most prominent colleges in the country found that only thirteen rejected anyone. Yale College, for example, accepted every applicant.[54] At the same time, most colleges effectively barred many qualified students who could not or would not apply due to their gender, race, ethnicity, religion, or socioeconomic class, even though official policies of exclusion were rarely announced.

The explosion of applications and need to cap enrollment compelled colleges to introduce selective admissions—that is, selecting from the pool of qualified applicants before admission instead of failing weaker students later. This novel approach then required colleges to establish selection criteria and deliberately determine the composition of their student body. Dartmouth College faced these issues acutely because it was "perhaps the nation's most popular school in the 1920s," and turned away more students than any other college in the country in 1920. Dartmouth therefore pioneered the solution.[55] Rather than expand, the college eliminated its admissions threshold in 1921, capped the number of students to be admitted, and introduced discretionary evaluation of applicants based on a range of criteria, including academic standards.

In September 1921 Dartmouth president Ernest M. Hopkins famously proclaimed the meritocratic justification for this radical shift away from accepting all qualified applicants, which was considered the "democratic" approach at the time. He argued that the traditional reliance on academic thresholds favored certain "top tier" preparatory schools that fed certain "top tier" colleges. In 1921, graduation from Phillips Exeter Academy virtually guaranteed admission to Harvard College, which virtually guaranteed admission to Harvard Law School. This would still be true in the 1950s, according to James Vorenberg (LL.B. 1951), who attended all three and became dean of Harvard Law School (1981–1989).[56]

Instead, Hopkins proposed to establish "an aristocracy of brains" via a discretionary system of admissions that selected among academically qualified applicants while considering different kinds of talent and backgrounds of applicants from schools across the United States. This new approach exercised selection *before* admission, rather than through attrition over the course of the undergraduate years. Nearly 200 newspapers throughout North America and the United Kingdom editorialized on Hopkins's speech. Most argued that his emphasis upon cultivating a meritorious elite was "un-American, undemocratic, snobbish, and elitist," amounting to "a denial of the equal chance to which American youth was entitled."[57]

Nevertheless, selective admissions for undergraduates swept across the country and became the new standard approach at leading colleges and universities. A central rationale was to reduce the "excessive rate of freshman mortality" and save everyone the wasted time, expense, and effort of flunking out first-year students.[58] In 1926 a study of "several hundred institutions" found the national rate of "freshman mortality" to be 31 percent.[59] In 1928 an article in the *New York Times* projected that about 200,000 freshmen would enter higher education that year, and about 60,000 would drop out, with the "resultant economic, social, and educational loss."[60] Public and private institutions, even land-grant universities, began raising their undergraduate admissions standards in order to reduce attrition.[61]

At the graduate level, selective admissions advanced more slowly. Medical schools led the way in the first two decades of the twentieth century. By the 1910s, Harvard Medical School was accepting only one-third of the applicants who had graduated from Harvard, Yale, Stanford, Amherst, or Williams and about one-seventh of applicants from other colleges. Other fields of graduate education did not follow until about 1930.[62] Harvard Law School also lagged behind and did not adopt the new admissions selectivity that was sweeping through elite undergraduate colleges. Instead of capping the size of its entering class, adopting discretionary evaluation, and reducing attrition, the Law School held to its academic threshold in admission. Harvard Law School would continue to cull students during their first year, while maintaining that the academic threshold was more meritocratic because it gave every qualified student a chance to enroll and then compete to earn the degree.[63]

The "Jewish Problem"

In the spring of 1918, the association of deans of New England colleges met to discuss what they called the "Jewish problem": the fact that the enrollment of Jewish students far exceeded their proportion in the general population. These colleges recognized that the Jewish applicants were generally stronger academically than most in the general pool, but they feared that admitting large numbers of Jewish students would threaten their WASPish norms and culture. Hence, the colleges tried to balance their desire for better students and their resistance to change by designing quotas to limit the proportion of Jews in the student body.[64]

In 1918 the fraction of Jewish students among undergraduates was nearly 40 percent at Columbia University, which made a sustained effort to reduce the proportion to 22 percent by 1921. Meanwhile, the Jewish fraction in the freshman class at Harvard College was about 20 percent, three times larger than at Yale College and six times larger than at Princeton. Based on his view of the required "character" or social background of Harvard students and faculty, President Lowell sought to reduce the proportion of Jewish students to 15 percent or less, and he directed Harvard College to apply an explicit quota to the admission of Jewish students during the 1920s.[65]

Harvard's exclusionary policy, like that at other colleges, coincided with the adoption of selective admissions.[66] In 1922 Harvard College introduced new application forms that included "questions as to the race and color of the applicant, his religious preference, and what changes have been made since birth in his own name or that of his father." Observers therefore suggested "that Harvard is trying to bar Jews and other races from its classes," as newspapers and journals reported.[67] Then, in 1926, Harvard College's Special Committee Appointed to Consider the Limitation of Numbers adopted the new, discretionary approach to undergraduate admissions. The Special Committee capped the entering class at 1,000 students, abolished the academic threshold of ranking in the top seventh of a secondary school's graduating class, and replaced it with a discretionary evaluation based on a range of criteria. One intent and effect of this shift to discretionary criteria was to reduce the number of Jewish students, who predominated among the academically qualified.

This shift also meant that a college no longer needed to explain to academically qualified applicants why they were denied admission. Eliminating the academic threshold negated the presumption of, or entitlement to, admission. As the Yale College dean observed in December 1926, Harvard College was "going to discontinue . . . the 'first seventh' arrangement which is bringing in as high as 40 percent Jews. They are also going to reduce their 25 percent Hebrew total to 15 percent or less by simply rejecting without detailed explanation. They are giving no details to any [rejected] candidate any longer."[68]

Lowell justified Harvard's quotas by referring not only to the supposed behavior or character of Jewish students, but also to the expected response of non-Jews to their number. His goal was not simply to eliminate "undesirable Jews," but to prevent what he feared would be an exodus of "Gentiles" that would ruin the college.[69] Writing to Julian Mack, the Jewish member of the Board of Overseers, about limiting the number of Jewish students, Lowell was completely candid: "It is the duty of Harvard to receive just as many [Jewish] boys who have come, or whose parents have come, to this country without our background as it can effectively educate; including in education the imparting, not only of book knowledge, but of the ideas and traditions of our people. Experience seems to place that proportion at around 15 percent."[70]

But Harvard Law School held back. Just as it did not adopt selective admissions, the school refused to institute Lowell's quota. While Pound was on leave during the 1921–22 academic year, Bull Warren served as acting dean, and in the spring Lowell asked to know "the number of Jews in the first-year class at various dates." In a shocking reply to Lowell in May 1922, Warren conveyed a table, compiled by Richard Ames (LL.B. 1909), secretary of the Law School, showing the number and percentages of supposed Jewish students at various dates between 1899–1900 and 1921–22. Over that period, the percentage in the first-year class had risen from about 6 percent to about 13 percent. Warren also wrote, "I am not unmindful of how residential sections and private schools have frequently been seriously harmed through a large increase in Jews," but then said that the Law School could not discriminate because "we have always welcomed all who conformed to our intellectual and moral standards."[71]

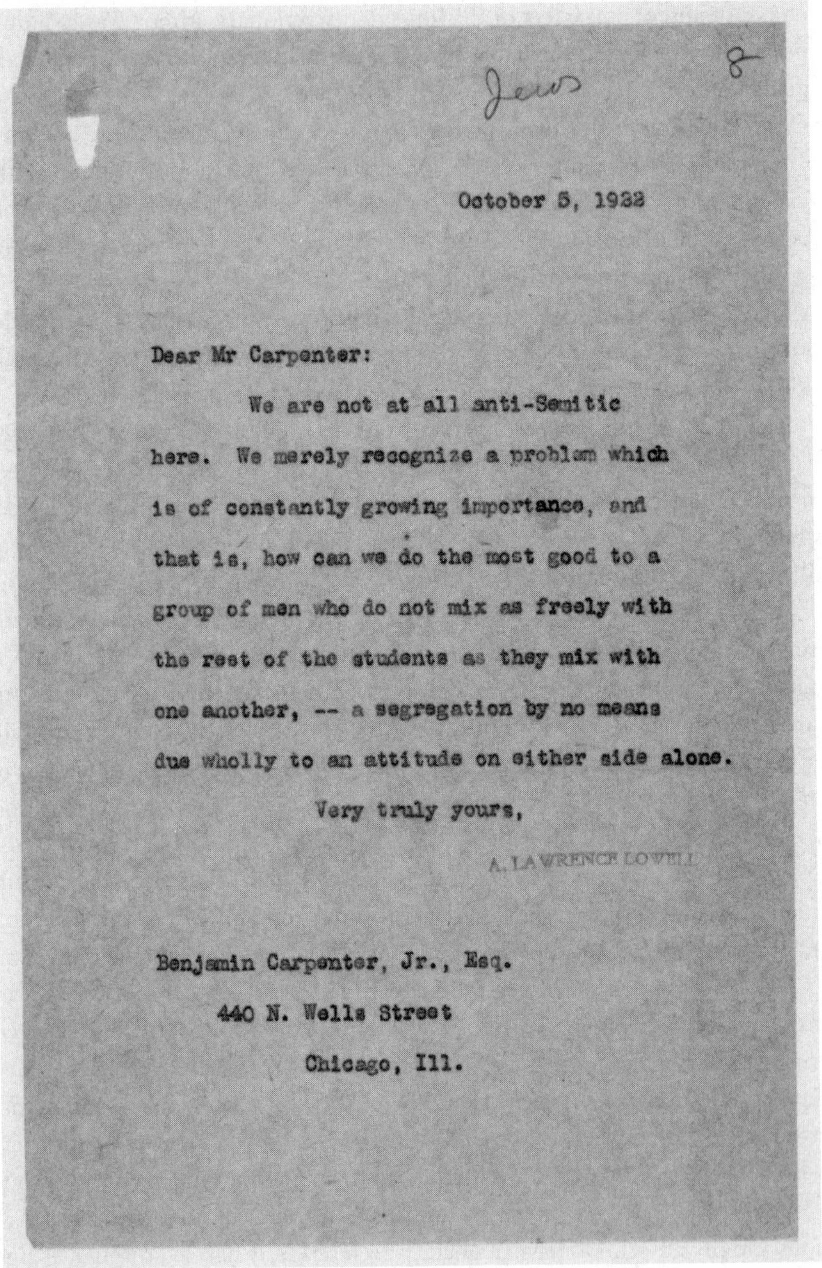

Jews   8

October 5, 1922

Dear Mr Carpenter:

We are not at all anti-Semitic

here. We merely recognize a problem which

is of constantly growing importance, and

that is, how can we do the most good to a

group of men who do not mix as freely with

the rest of the students as they mix with

one another, -- a segregation by no means

due wholly to an attitude on either side alone.

Very truly yours,

A. LAWRENCE LOWELL

Benjamin Carpenter, Jr., Esq.

440 N. Wells Street

Chicago, Ill.

Letter from Abbott Lawrence Lowell to Benjamin Carpenter Jr., October 5, 1922.

Courtesy of Harvard University Archives.

But the underlying reason for the Law School's unwillingness to discriminate was that the school's published academic threshold for admission made it impossible to impose the quota, since an undergraduate degree of the appropriate rank from the colleges in the first or second tiers entitled one to admission. Furthermore, there was no need for action by the Law School to restrict Jewish students, because the quotas on Jewish students at many of the school's feeder colleges tended to restrict their number at the Law School. Finally, the percentage of Jewish students in the Law School overall was just under 13 percent and therefore below Lowell's cap of 15 percent. In fact, Julian Mack, who became aware of the correspondence, described the Law School's figures as inflated because Warren and Ames had simply inferred ethnicity from the family names of students, and Mack observed that "good Pennsylvania Dutch names were not differentiated from Jewish names."[72]

To his credit, Pound, upon returning, was furious to learn of the school's cooperation with Lowell's investigation. Pound became further incensed to learn that Lowell intended to compare the lists of Jewish students with known disciplinary cases in order to demonstrate that Jews, as a group, were less honest than other students. Pound wrote in protest, but did not express outrage at Lowell's presumption. Instead the dean tried to show that Jewish students, in fact, were as honest as the rest of the student body. He even adjusted the data a bit to make the case more strongly. In reply to a troubled inquiry by Julian Mack, Pound stated that during his tenure, "the conduct of our Jewish students has been in every respect as good as that of the non-Jewish students, if not actually better in view of relevant numbers."[73]

Finally, another aspect "of a general movement to exclude certain persons from the University," according to Pound, was Lowell's scheme to impose dormitory housing on law students in 1922. At that time, Harvard dorms were racially and ethnically segregated, and Lowell was planning a special dormitory for Jewish students. Pound complained privately to Mack, who assisted the dean in blocking Lowell's imposition on the Law School.[74]

All these discriminatory policies persisted through the 1920s and beyond. When he retired in 1933, Lowell wrote to his successor, hoping to persuade him that "any educational institution that admits an unlimited number of Jews will soon have no one else."[75] But the incoming president, James Conant (1933–1953), brought an end to official efforts to enforce quotas on Jewish students.

Excluded and Marginalized Students

In addition to Jews, other groups experienced prejudice that violated the school's professed commitment to meritocracy. Women would not be admitted for decades, despite their acceptance at the law schools of Yale, Columbia, Cornell, Michigan, Stanford, and many others.[76] Very few Hispanic students enrolled.[77] People of Asian descent were almost completely absent, partly because they faced a series of legal barriers. For example, the Chinese Exclusion Act (1882) prohibiting Chinese immigration was not repealed until 1943. In 1890 the California decision of *In re Hong Yeo Chang* held that "a person of Mongolian nativity is not entitled to naturalization, [and] thus may not practice law." In 1902 *In re Yamashita* denied a Japanese graduate in the first class of the University of Washington Law School, who had passed the Washington State bar examination, admission to the bar "because he was not a member of any branch of the white or whitish race."[78]

Only in 1917 did Harvard Law School graduate a Chinese student, Fu-yun Chang, who came from Shanghai and later served as chairman of the National Tariff Commission of the Republic of China from 1927 to 1932. In this role, Chang negotiated tariff autonomy on behalf of China and helped to end extraterritorial rights of foreign nations and to regain control of Chinese maritime customs. No Asian Americans graduated from Harvard Law School until Hiram L. Fong (LL.B. 1935), who became the first U.S. senator of Asian ancestry and one of the first two U.S. senators from the new state of Hawaii. Fong served in the Senate from 1959 to 1977 and led a small but increasing number of Asian Americans from Hawaii over the legal and prejudicial barriers to the bench and bar, including Edward Y. C. Chun (LL.B. 1956), who became director of the Hawaii State Bar Association.[79]

There were no openly gay students. Lowell, a vehement homophobe, convened a "secret court" in 1920 to purge Harvard College of homosexuals, and was ever vigilant to counter homosexuality elsewhere in the university. One of the accused, Joseph E. Lumbard (LL.B. 1925), was expelled from Harvard College in 1920 but admitted to the Law School in 1922. After founding a law firm, Lumbard was appointed to the U.S. Court of Appeals, Second Circuit, in 1955, becoming Chief Judge in 1959. He had a heterosexual marriage, with children and grandchildren, but was stigmatized for the rest of his life. In 1953, as part of Harvard's "arrangement" with the FBI, discussed in Chapter 11, the Harvard College Registrar filed a report with

Hiram Fong, LL.B. 1935, the first Asian-American U.S. senator.

United States Senate Historical Office.

the FBI stating that Lumbard was expelled because of his "association" with homosexuals. During the 1950s the first organized "clubs" of gay students at the Law School were founded, and the membership in these groups was strictly secret.[80]

There were a few African American students, all with strong academic records, in accordance with the pattern established after the Civil War.[81] With only one or two African American students in a class during the 1920s and 1930s, forming organizations or group consciousness was impossible, and these heroic individuals focused on their academic work and excelled, despite the racism that they encountered. These included Charles Hamilton Houston (LL.B. 1922, S.J.D. 1923), William H. Hastie Jr., (LL.B. 1930, S.J.D. 1933), and Benjamin Jefferson Davis Jr. (LL.B. 1929).

Charles Hamilton Houston

Born in 1895, Charles Houston was raised in Washington, D.C., where his father had earned the LL.B. at Howard University and then worked as a lawyer.[82] After graduating as valedictorian from Dunbar High School, Houston attended Amherst College, where he graduated in 1915 both first in his class and the only African American. Despite his high academic achievements and election to Phi Beta Kappa, no fraternities would accept him.

Drafted into the army at age twenty-one, Houston had a bitter experience in the American armed forces. Required to attend all-black segregated training camps, his talent was recognized, and he was promoted to first lieutenant. Then he and a few other African American officers were moved to Camp Meade, an all-white camp in Pennsylvania. There he endured persistent racial slurs and attacks that eventually forced the African American officers to be moved to Camp Dix in the District of Columbia, where Houston again encountered rampant prejudice and also witnessed the race riots in Washington during June 1919. These experiences made him determined to fight segregation and Jim Crow when he returned to civilian life and entered Harvard Law School.

Matriculating in the fall of 1919, Houston earned A's in nearly all of his subjects during the first year, when grading was anonymous. Despite his high grades and Amherst pedigree, Houston was never invited to join any of the white extracurricular law clubs or social clubs. Instead, with the help of a Jewish lawyer in Boston, Houston and classmate Raymond P. Alexander III created their own law club, the "Dunbar Club," named after Houston's old high school. The membership comprised fourteen Jewish and African American students. It was one of the "bastard clubs" serving those outside the white Protestant elite, who belonged to the "continuing" clubs.

Houston excelled academically in his second and third year, when he was chosen for the *Law Review* purely on grades, and he established close relationships with professors Frankfurter, Pound, and Beale. But the racial discrimination at the school was a constant part of Houston's life. Southern members of the *Law Review* would leave the room when he walked in. "The editors of the *Review* don't want me," he wrote, "but I still go on my way alone. They know I am just independent and a little more so than they. My stock is pretty high around these parts, but God help me against one false move." This comment conveys the close scrutiny and double standard to which minority students were often subjected throughout higher education. Many low-performing white men were admitted to and graduated from Harvard Law School, whereas

Charles Hamilton Houston, LL.B. 1922, S.J.D. 1923.
Library of Congress, Prints and Photographs Division.

most of the few minority students performed better than most of the white students in the early twentieth century, as had been the case in the nineteenth century.[83]

After graduating with the LL.B. in 1922, Houston remained at Harvard for an additional year to earn the S.J.D. in 1923 and then joined his father's law firm in Washington. He also taught philosophy and jurisprudence at Howard University Law School, where he served as vice dean in 1929, securing its full accreditation in 1931. In 1932 he argued *Nixon v. Condon* (1932), "one of the most important voting rights cases argued before the Supreme Court," according to a young staffer to the U.S. Solicitor General who witnessed the arguments that day. This was Erwin Griswold, who later wrote that Houston "is surely entitled to be included in any list of truly great American lawyers. It was his vision, energy, and skill which underlay the great legal developments in race relations around the middle of the twentieth century."[84] As a close confidant of Thurgood Marshall, Houston helped design the legal strategy that led to *Brown v. Board of Education* (1954) and *Bolling v. Sharpe* (1954), and he represented clients on behalf of the NAACP until his untimely death in 1950 at age fifty-four.

William H. Hastie Jr.

A childhood friend of Houston, William Hastie was born in 1904 in Knoxville, Tennessee.[85] After moving to Washington, his family became close to the Houstons, and William followed in Charles's footsteps. Hastie also attended Dunbar High School in Washington, D.C., and entered Amherst College in the fall of 1921. Hastie was excluded from the evening socials hosted by the president of Amherst, but he did not passively accept such treatment. When the word "nigger" was printed in the student publication, *The Amherst Writing*, Hastie wrote to the president in protest. Like Houston, Hastie ranked first in his class at Amherst and was elected to Phi Beta Kappa.

In 1927 Hastie entered Harvard Law School, where he achieved academic distinction. He became a member of the editorial board of the *Harvard Law Review* and worked night and day, earning the respect of all of his colleagues. But he still could not escape discrimination. In April 1929 some members of the editorial board objected to Hastie's attendance at the annual black-tie dinner until a number of other student and alumni editors, including Griswold, said they would not attend unless Hastie came, so the objections were dropped.[86] Hastie fought not only racism, but also anti-Semitism. At a meeting held in 1929 to choose the next year's president of the *Review,* one of the editors remarked that the selection of a particular candidate would "place a Jew in the top post." Hastie calmly replied, "If that's a relevant factor, I'm going to leave the room immediately." No one voiced the objection again.

Despite these encounters with racial prejudice, Hastie maintained an enduring and warm appreciation for Harvard Law School. Professor Derrick A. Bell Jr. was astonished by Hastie's loyalty. Attending a ceremony when Hastie's portrait was hung at the Law School, Bell recalled, "I sat there in wonder and admiration that a black man who had attended Harvard in its pre-liberal days could speak with such warmth and affection about what must have been a very hostile place."[87]

After completing the S.J.D. in 1933, Hastie went to work with Charles Houston at the latter's firm. Together with Thurgood Marshall, Hastie and Houston selected and prepared the major cases during the 1940s that would transform civil rights and race relations in the United States. While actively engaged at the NAACP, Hastie also taught at Howard University Law School. In 1937 President Roosevelt appointed him the first African American federal judge. He became, in 1949, the first African American appointed to a U.S. Court of Appeals and, in 1968, the Chief Judge of the Third Circuit.

Benjamin Jefferson Davis Jr.

A contemporary of Houston and Hastie, Benjamin Davis had a heroic and tragic career.[88] Born in southwestern Georgia in 1903, Davis grew up in Atlanta, where his father founded the African American newspaper *Atlanta Independent*. After attending Morehouse College for one year, Davis transferred to Amherst College, where he joined the varsity football and tennis teams, played violin in the orchestra, sang in the choir, and captained the intercollegiate debate team. He graduated with William Hastie in the class of 1925.

Entering Harvard Law School in 1926, Davis overlapped with Erwin Griswold and graduated with the LL.B. in 1929.[89] Returning home, he struggled to find a job, and finally obtained a position with a law firm in Atlanta. "But he was subject to considerable discrimination," Griswold later observed, "including the fact that he was not allowed to enter the building and proceed to his office except by way of the freight elevator."[90] In 1932 Davis opened his own law practice in Atlanta.

The following year he served as the defense attorney for Angelo Herndon, an eighteen-year-old African American who had organized industrial workers and was charged with inciting insurrection under an old Georgia statute of 1866. Herndon was convicted and sentenced to twenty years on the Georgia chain gang, but later freed by a close vote of the U.S. Supreme Court.[91] The racist opposition during the original trial changed the course of Davis's life and led him to join the Communist Party, as he later explained.

I grew up in a typical Negro Republican home in the deep South. It was primarily my life as an American Negro in my country that prepared me for this political choice. The occasion was my serving as trial counsel in the Angelo

Herndon case. . . . I was so outraged as a Negro, and partly by my Harvard idealism, that I volunteered my services in the case. The basis of the indictment was primarily his membership in the Communist Party and possession of Marxist literature, including copies of *The Daily Worker*. In the course of defending Herndon, I had to familiarize myself with these Marxist books. Their political philosophy, in terms of my own status as a second-class citizen in my own country, made more sense to me than anything I'd heard from the Republican and Democratic Parties. So I joined the Communist Party. First credit for recruiting me goes not to the Communists but to the savage white supremacy assaults of the trial judge, Lee B. Wyatt, against all Negroes. Only secondarily does the credit go to the Communist Party which provided a rational, effective, and principled path of activity and struggle through which the hideous Jim Crow system could be abolished forever in the U.S.[92]

In 1935 Davis moved to Harlem to serve as editor of the Communist Party's African American newspaper, *The Negro Liberator.* He then became editor of *The Daily Worker,* the official publication of the Communist Party of the United States. In 1943 Davis was elected to the New York City Council, representing Harlem, and there he advocated for his constituency so strongly that he became known as "Fighting Ben." He 1948 he lost his bid for a third term, reportedly due to his Communist rhetoric. In the ensuing years of McCarthyism, Davis paid a heavy price for his beliefs and efforts on behalf of fair treatment for disadvantaged Americans. In 1949, he was convicted under the Alien Registration (Smith) Act of 1940 and sentenced to five years in federal prison, as discussed in Chapter 11.

Each in their own way—Houston, Hastie and Davis, along with others in their generation, such as Jesse S. Heslip (LL.B. 1922), who was elected president of the National Bar Association, the African American equivalent of the all-white ABA, and Raymond P. Alexander III (LL.B. 1923), who became the first African American judge appointed to the Court of Common Pleas in Philadelphia—made remarkable achievements in the face of daunting and persistent discrimination. But they were few in number and the Law School would not enroll a critical mass of African American students for fifty years.

In contrast to President Lowell's vision for Harvard, the Law School under Roscoe Pound did not aim to mold gentleman leaders for society, and the composition of the student body began to change. White male graduates from a broader range of undergraduate colleges—in number, geography, and sectarian affiliation—entered the Law School, as shown by the experience of Ernest Brown and Erwin Griswold. Northeastern Ivy Leaguers, such as Archibald Cox, were still a plurality, though no longer the majority of the student body.

But no women were admitted, and no effort was made to effort to recruit or welcome students of color. The numbers of those who enrolled remained minuscule, but they excelled and had remarkable careers, as did Fu-yun Chang, Hiram Fong, Charles Houston, James Hastie, and Benjamin Davis. Dean Pound refused to cooperate with the anti-Semitism directed against either students or faculty, but he failed to directly challenge the bigotry of President Lowell. This failure severed his alliance with Felix Frankfurter, who had been one of Pound's strongest advocates.

Meanwhile, the dean and faculty rejected the new selective admissions policy widely adopted in higher education during the 1920s, and they recommitted the school to weeding out the first-year students who met the admissions threshold. In contrast to the practice at medical schools, this approach treated first-year attrition as a substitute for selective admissions, though Harvard Law School's threshold remained the highest of any law school in the nation. Coupled with large classes, this threshold approach reinforced the competition among students in the coming decades at the Law School. Ruthlessness in wielding the intellectual sword was exacerbated by Pound's high-handed behavior and overbearing demeanor, which worsened during the 1920s and 1930s. In addition, financial pressures intensified the combative and exclusionary ethos of the school.

NOTES

1. William R. Castle, "The Freshman," *Outlook* (October 21, 1911); Kim Townsend, *Manhood at Harvard: William James and Others* (Cambridge, MA, 1996), 282.

2. Paul Sayre, *The Life of Roscoe Pound* (Iowa City, IA, 1948), 214.

3. Arthur E. Sutherland, *The Law at Harvard: A History of Ideas and Men, 1817–1907* (Cambridge, MA, 1967), 244.

4. Quotation is from Ernest J. Brown, Oral History, conducted by Daniel Hamilton (August 1997), on file with the authors.

5. Brown, Oral History (August 1997); Erwin N. Griswold, *Ould Fields, New Corne: The Personal Memoirs of a Twentieth Century Lawyer* (St. Paul, MN, 1992), 161.

6. This letter from Roscoe Pound to Paul B. Sargent (November 9, 1926) was sent by Sargent to Dean James Vorenberg with a note (May 11, 1983), James Vorenberg Papers, 1961–2000, Harvard Law School Library Historical & Special Collections (HLSLib).

7. Griswold, *Ould Fields,* 74.

8. Townsend, *Manhood at Harvard,* 22–24.

9. A. Lawrence Lowell, "Inaugural Address," *Harvard Graduates Magazine* (1909), 211–223. See A. Lawrence Lowell, *At War with Academic Traditions in America* (Cambridge, MA, 1934), 38, 45, 7, 69, 110.

10. A. Lawrence Lowell, Annual Report of the President of Harvard University, 1908–09, 21.

11. Quotations are from Edward H. Warren, *Spartan Education* (Cambridge, MA 1942), ix.

12. Brown, Oral History (August 1997). See Archibald Cox, Oral History, conducted by Daniel R. Coquillette and Daniel Hamilton (November 1998), on file with the authors; John Grant Haviland, The Student Looks at Harvard Law School [Observations of the School by Students in 1934] (unpublished typescript, revised spring 1934), on file with the authors, 111–112; Bruce A. Kimball, "Before the Paper Chase: Student Culture at Harvard Law School, 1895–1915," *Journal of Legal Education* 61 (2011): 66.

13. Annie W. Sabine Siebert, "Presidential Report 1900–1901," Proceedings of the Ohio State University Alumni Association, 1900, Ohio State University Archives.

14. Harvard Law School Catalog, 1914–15, 4–5.

15. Harvard Law School Catalog, 1927–28, 5; James M. Landis, Annual Report of the Dean of Harvard Law School, 1937–38, 194.

16. Harvard Law School Catalog, 1928–29, 6.

17. Roscoe Pound, Annual Report of the Dean of Harvard Law School, 1926–27, 188.

18. Quotation is from Samuel Williston, *Life and Law: An Autobiography* (Boston, 1940), 187.

19. Carl E. Newton to Sidney P. Simpson (April 30, 1935), in *Comments on Harvard Law School, 1935,* Records of Faculty Committee on Curriculum 1934–, Harvard Law School Dean's Office Records, JBC Records. See also Report of the Student Advisory Group to the Committee on Curriculum, *Comments on Harvard Law School, 1935,* Records of Faculty Committee on Curriculum 1934–, Harvard Law School Dean's Office Records, JBC Records.

20. Harvard Law School Catalog, 1919–1920. See Bruce A. Kimball, *The Inception of Modern Professional Education: C. C. Langdell, 1826–1906* (Chapel Hill, NC, 2009), 208–209.

21. See Gail J. Hupper, "The Rise of an Academic Doctorate in Law: Origins through World War II," *American Journal of Legal History* 49 (2007): 1–60.

22. Harvard Law School Catalog, 1916–17, 53; 1924–25, 3–4; 1925–26, 77; 1929–30, 3–4; 1930–31, 97; 1934–35, 3–4; 1935–36, 91.

23. Harvard Law School Catalog, 1917–18, 56–58.

24. Harvard Law School Catalog, 1930–31, 97–99. Brandi Pugh, "Anomaly: Harvard Law School during World War I" (student research paper, Boston College Law School, 2014). See Daniel R. Coquillette and Bruce A. Kimball, *On the Battlefield of Merit: Harvard Law School, the First Century* (Cambridge, MA, 2015) (hereafter cited as *Battlefield of Merit*), 499–508.

25. The following account and quotations are dawn from Griswold, *Ould Fields,* 61–77.

26. Harvard Law School Catalog, 1925–26, 21; *Historical Statistics of the United States, Millennial Edition On-line* (Cambridge, UK, 2000), part B, series Ba4361–4366.

27. Felix Frankfurter and James M. Landis, *The Business of the Supreme Court: A Study in the Federal Judicial System* (New York, 1928).

28. Austin W. Scott, *The Law of Trusts* (Boston, 1939), 4 vols.; Hupper, "The Rise," 27.

29. Here and below, we rely upon Brown, Oral History (August 1997).

30. Harvard Law School Catalog, 1929–30, 94; 1930–31, 96.

31. Letter from Harold S. Davis [December 1934?], in *Comments on Harvard Law School, 1935,* Records of Faculty Committee on Curriculum 1934–, Harvard Law School Dean's Office Records, JBC Records. See Christopher W. Schmidt, "The Failure of Reform: Legal Education at Harvard Law School, 1934–1946" (student research paper, Harvard Law School, 2006), on file with the authors, 37.

32. The following draws upon Cox, Oral History (November 1998). See "Obituary of Archibald Cox," *New York Times* (May 30, 2004); Ken Gormley, *Archibald Cox: Conscience of a Nation* (Reading, MA, 1997), 26–34.

33. On William M. Evarts, see *Battlefield of Merit,* 175.

34. On the oldest law clubs, see *Battlefield of Merit,* 445–461.

35. See David O. Levine, *The American College and the Culture of Aspiration, 1915–1940* (Ithaca, NY, 1986), 146–161; Jerome Karabel, *The Chosen: The Hidden History of Admission and Exclusion at Harvard, Yale, and Princeton* (Boston, 2005), 86–136.

36. See the discussion of faculty appointments in *Battlefield of Merit,* 385–402.

37. Roscoe Pound to Louis D. Brandeis (April 24, 1920), Harvard Law School Dean's Office Records, Records of President A. Lawrence Lowell, 1909–1933, Harvard University Archives (hereafter cited as ALL Records).

38. See A. Lawrence Lowell to Roscoe Pound (January 23, 1924), ALL Records. See James F. Clark, "The Harvard Law School Deanship of Roscoe Pound, 1916–1936" (student research paper, Harvard Law School, 1999), on file with the authors, 112.

39. Felix Frankfurter to Roscoe Pound (December 9, 1925), Roscoe Pound Papers, 1888–1964, HLSLib (hereafter cited as RP Papers). The following account of Pound and faculty appointments relies heavily on Clark, "The Harvard Law School Deanship," 106–144.

40. Learned Hand to Felix Frankfurter (December 7, 1926) and Augustus Hand to Felix Frankfurter (January 7, 1927), Felix Frankfurter Papers, 1900–1965, HLSLib. See Clark, "The Harvard Law School Deanship," 129–130.

41. Felix Frankfurter to Roscoe Pound (December 8, 1926), RP Papers.

42. Felix Frankfurter to Roscoe Pound (January 2, 1928), ALL Records. See Clark, "The Harvard Law School Deanship," 114–115.

43. Frankfurter to Pound (January 2, 1928).

44. Thomas Reed Powell, "The Harvard Law School" (ca. 1928), Thomas Reed Powell Papers, 1905–1955, HLSLib. See Clark, "The Harvard Law School Deanship," 114n511.

45. Roscoe Pound to A. Lawrence Lowell (February 21, 1928), ALL Records. See Clark, "The Harvard Law School Deanship," 118.

46. See Donald A. Ritchie, *James M. Landis: Dean of the Regulators* (Cambridge, MA, 1980), 35.

47. Clark, "The Harvard Law School Deanship," 122.

48. Edmund M. Morgan to Elihu Root Jr. (January 30, 1930), quoted in Harvard Law School Faculty Appointments Committee to A. Lawrence Lowell, Memorandum (February 13, 1930), ALL Records. The "memorandum" was for the Faculty Appointments Committee supporting Katz. Because Jewish identity is passed through the mother, Morgan may have been suggesting that Katz was not "really" or "fully" Jewish, not only because both parents were not Jewish but also because his mother, in particular, was not Jewish.

49. Roscoe Pound to Edmund M. Morgan (March 2, 1930), ALL Records.

50. Felix Frankfurter to Roscoe Pound (February 27, 1930), ALL Records. See Laura Kalman, *Legal Realism at Yale: 1927–1960* (Chapel Hill, NC, 1986), 58.

51. U.S. Commissioner of Education, *Biennial Survey of Education, 1924–26* (Washington, DC, 1928), 805.

52. See Seth Low, Annual Report of the President of Columbia University, 1899–1900, 9–13; 1900–01, 10–11; Nicholas Murray Butler, Annual Report of the President of Columbia University, 1901–02, 22–30.

53. Roger L. Geiger, *To Advance Knowledge: The Growth of American Research Universities, 1900–1940* (New York, 1986), 130–131.

54. Here and below, see Levine, *The American College,* 137–142; Scott M. Gelber, *Courtrooms and Classrooms: A Legal History of College Access, 1860–1960* (Baltimore, MD, 2015).

55. Quotation is from Levine, *The American College,* 137.

56. Ernest M. Hopkins, "An Aristocracy of Brains," Address at the Opening of Dartmouth College (September 21, 1922). See "Too Many Men in College?," *School and Society* 16 (1922): 379; James Vorenberg, Oral History, conducted by Daniel R. Coquillette (November–December 1997), on file with the authors.

57. Quotations are from Charles E. Widmayer, *Hopkins of Dartmouth: The Story of Ernest Martin Hopkins and His Presidency of Dartmouth College* (Hanover, NH, 1977), 75–76. See Hopkins, "An Aristocracy of Brains."

58. James C. Miller, "The Induction and Adaptation of College Freshmen" (Ph.D. diss., University of Missouri, 1930), 9.

59. Ernest B. Harper, "Educational Personnel Work," *Social Science* 1 (1926): 317.

60. William M. Lewis, "Student Failure Rate Alarms the Colleges," *New York Times* (September 9, 1928).

61. Christopher Jencks and David Riesman, *The Academic Revolution* (New York, 1968), 281–283; Gelber, *Courtrooms and Classroom,* 55–56.

62. Kenneth M. Ludmerer, *Time to Heal: American Medical Education from the Turn of the Century to the Era of Managed Care* (New York, 1999), 62; Roger L. Geiger, *The His-*

tory of American Higher Education: Learning and Culture from the Founding to World War II (Princeton, NJ, 2014), 493.

63. Pound, Annual Report of the Dean, 1920–21, 202; 1925–26, 185; [Edward H. Warren] to A. Lawrence Lowell (May 12, 1922), ALL Records. See Clark, "The Harvard Law School Deanship," 73.

64. See Levine, *The American College,* 146–161; Karabel, *The Chosen,* 86–136.

65. Karabel, *The Chosen,* 77, 86.

66. Levine, *The American College,* 146–161; Karabel, *The Chosen,* 86–136; Geiger, *To Advance Knowledge,* 193–196, 218.

67. "Harvard Asks Race and Color of Candidates for Admission," *School and Society* 16 (September 30, 1922): 380.

68. Quoted in Karabel, *The Chosen,* 108.

69. A. Lawrence Lowell to William Earnest Hocking (May 19, 1922), quoted in Karabel, *The Chosen,* 88. See Marcia Graham Synnott, *The Half-Opened Door: Discrimination and Admissions at Harvard, Yale, and Princeton, 1900–1970* (Westport, CT, 1979), 44–70.

70. A. Lawrence Lowell to Julian Mack (March 29, 1922), quoted in Karabel, *The Chosen,* 578n80.

71. [Warren] to Lowell (May 12, 1922). See Pound, Annual Report of the Dean, 1921–22, 157; Clark, "The Harvard Law School Deanship," 73. See Warren's letter transcribed in Appendix B of this volume.

72. Julian W. Mack to Edward H. Warren (November 6, 1922), ALL Records. See Clark, "The Harvard Law School Deanship," 73.

73. Quotations are from two letters from Roscoe Pound to Julian W. Mack (both dated October 6, 1922), ALL Records.

74. Quotation is from Roscoe Pound to Julian W. Mack (November 18, 1922), ALL Records. See William Wright, *Harvard's Secret Court: The Savage 1920 Purge of Campus Homosexuals* (New York, 2005), 26.

75. A. Lawrence Lowell to James B. Conant (December 6, 1933), quoted in Morton Keller and Phyllis Keller, *Making Harvard Modern: The Rise of America's University* (New York, 2001), 49.

76. *Battlefield of Merit,* 492, 608; Karen Berger Marello, *The Invisible Box: The Woman Lawyer in America, 1638 to the Present* (New York, 1986), 46.

77. Felipe D. Mendoza, "Hispanic [LL.B.] Graduates of Harvard Law School: A First Step toward Uncovering the Lives and Experiences of the First Graduate and the First Generation" (student research paper, Harvard Law School, 2006), on file with the authors.

78. *In re Hong Yeo Chang,* 154 California 163 (1890); *In re Yamashita,* 30 Washington 234 (1902). See Lucy E. Sayers, *Laws Harsh as Tigers: Chinese Immigrants and the Shaping of Modern Immigration Law* (Chapel Hill, NC, 1995).

79. Andrew Cheng, "Untold Stories: Asian Pacific Americans at Harvard Law School" (student research paper, Harvard Law School, 2000), on file with the authors; Li Chen,

"Pioneers in the Fight for the Inclusion of Chinese Students in American Legal Education and Legal Profession" (student research paper, Harvard Law School, 2014), on file with the authors.

80. Geoffrey Upton, "Unwise Restraints: An Oral History of Gay, Lesbian and Bisexual Student Experience at Harvard Law School" (student research paper, Harvard Law School, 2003), on file with the authors but sealed; Thomas Gagne, "Boston College Law School: Gay and Lesbian Civil Rights Incubator" (student research paper, Boston College Law School, 2000), on file with the authors, but sealed; Wright, *Harvard's Secret Court*, 178–182.

81. See *Battlefield of Merit*, 521–547.

82. The following account relies upon Erwin N. Griswold, "Charles Hamilton Houston," *Negro History Bulletin* 13 (1950): 210–216; Daniel R. Coquillette, "A Celebration of Black Alumni," Presentation to the Reunion of Black Alumni of Harvard Law School (September 22, 2000), on file with the authors.

83. See *Battlefield of Merit*, 521–547.

84. Griswold, *Ould Fields*, 182–183. See *Nixon v. Condon*, 286 U.S. 73 (1932).

85. For the following account, see Coquillette, "A Celebration of Black Alumni."

86. See the account in Griswold, *Ould Fields*, 182.

87. Coquillette, "A Celebration of Black Alumni."

88. This account draws upon: "Amherst College Class of 1925," *Amherst College Biographical Record, Centennial Edition* (Amherst, MA, 1925); William L. Patterson, *Ben Davis: Crusader for Negro Freedom and Socialism* (New York, 1967); Benjamin J. Davis, *Communist Councilman from Harlem* (New York, 1969); Gerald Horne. *Black Liberation / Red Scare: Ben Davis and the Communist Party* (Newark, NJ, 1994); Benjamin J. Davis Papers, 1949–1964, Schomburg Center for Research in Black Culture, New York Public Library, retrieved from http://archives.nypl.org/scm/20651.

89. *The Harvard Law School Quinquennial Catalog, 1939* (Cambridge, MA, 1939) lists Davis in Griswold's class of 1928, but the Harvard Law School Catalog, 1928–29, lists Davis as a third-year student.

90. Griswold, *Ould Fields*, 233–234. Griswold mistakenly identifies him as Benjamin O. Davis, which was the name of a father and a son who were heroic African American military leaders.

91. See *Herndon v. Lowry*, 301 U.S. 242 (1937). Davis served as counsel for Herndon in one of the appeals at the state level. *Herndon v. State of Georgia*, 178 Georgia 832 (May 24, 1934).

92. Excerpted as "The Making of a Communist by Benjamin J. Davis," in William L. Patterson, *Ben Davis: Crusader for Negro Freedom and Socialism* (New York, 1967), appendix.

CHAPTER FIVE

"The School Must Live from Hand to Mouth," 1919–1930s

Dean Ezra Thayer (1910–1915) was the first to sound the alarm about Harvard Law School's debilitating syndrome of tuition dependence: large and growing enrollment, high student-faculty ratio, illusion of prosperity, and expanding faculty and buildings resulting in heavy debt. As the Law School's enrollment and expenses increased, the proportion paid by the income from endowment fell and the dependence on tuition grew. This cycle, entailing perpetual growth, is well known in higher education today. At the time, however, Thayer's predecessor, Dean James Barr Ames (1895–1909), and his faculty had not recognized the difficulty because universities viewed expanding enrollment as a sign of academic quality.

Escaping from the syndrome required an equally novel effort in legal education: building "an adequate endowment" through a massive fundraising campaign.[1] But it failed. In 1882 the school had informally attempted to raise as much as $80,000 but received less than 60 percent of the goal, three-quarters of which came from just two gifts. In the late 1910s the campaign to commemorate the Law School's 1917 centennial aimed to raise $1 million, but reached scarcely a quarter of the goal and attracted donations from merely 2 percent of the alumni.

When he became dean, Roscoe Pound (1916–1936) lamented that "the school must live from hand to mouth."[2] Yet in his very first annual report, for 1915–16, Pound announced plans that were certain to exacerbate the financial problem. First, he wished to expand legal research and "graduate" legal education at the school, which would require funding drawn from the tuition of "undergraduates," the LL.B. students, and thereby worsen the overall tuition dependence. Second, Pound declared that the buildings were at full capacity and proposed to expand the physical plant. Thus, while warning against the dependence on tuition revenue, Pound's plans would aggravate it.[3]

Recognizing this, the dean launched another fundraising campaign in the mid-1920s. But this third effort at the Law School fared little better than the first two, and it is important to recognize that the school's failure was totally anomalous in the 1920s. Across the country, colleges and universities ran hundreds of successful fundraising drives that engorged their endowments. Given the Law School's preeminence, the meager result of its campaign in the 1920s was probably the greatest flop in higher education fundraising during the decade, perhaps ever.

Pound's campaign aimed to raise $5 million but received only about 30 percent of the goal in gifts and another 15 percent as a foundation grant. Still, it was by far the most that any law school had raised for endowment. Combined with a judicious enrollment strategy, it was enough to escape the financial maelstrom. But in 1927 Pound undertook his building expansion that recommitted the school to the "deplorable" tuition dependence that "debases so many of the professional schools of this country," in the words of Harvard president Charles Eliot (1869–1909).[4]

This chapter examines the Law School's third failed fundraising campaign and Pound's disastrous response in the late 1920s, and explains how both compounded the financial malaise. The Great Depression followed immediately, making recovery impossible until after World War II. Chapters 6 and 7 address Pound's jurisprudential swordplay over legal realism in the early 1930s, his inadequate response to the Depression, and his dismaying association with Nazi Germany, all of which contributed to revolt among the faculty and his resignation in 1936.

Pound's Shift to a Philanthropic Rationale, 1916–1920

Late in the nineteenth century, the meaning and justification of financial benefaction in American culture began to shift from charity to philanthropy, as described in Chapter 2. But Dean Thayer and the centennial campaign in the mid-1910s still appealed to donors in terms of the waning rationale of charity. Then, in the late 1910s, three documents moved the campaign toward the philanthropic rationale for giving to a university law school. First, Dean Pound's annual report for 1915–16 argued that the Law School served "the profession and the world."[5] Next, he elaborated the language and arguments in the concluding chapter of *The Centennial History of the Harvard Law School*

(1918) and in his pamphlet *The Harvard Law School* (1919), which was mailed to all alumni after World War I.

The philanthropic rationale, aligned with philosophical pragmatism and social progressivism, two movements that resonated with Pound's early thinking and that accompanied the rise of philanthropy in American culture. Early in his career, Pound had condemned any form of lawmaking that ignored the social circumstances and consequences of law. He advocated "sociological jurisprudence," which he defined as "a movement for pragmatism as a philosophy of law; for the adjustment of principles and doctrines to the human conditions they are to govern rather than to assumed first principles."[6] Pound's jurisprudence thus pointed him toward a philanthropic rationale for benefaction, emphasizing broad, long-term, social utility. Moreover, as the author of the renowned ABA address "The Causes of Popular Dissatisfaction with the Administration of Justice" (1906), as well as an urgent call for reform in "Law in Books and Law in Action" (1909), Pound seemed perfectly prepared to provide the requisite philanthropic rationale for funding legal education and research.[7]

In his three documents of 1916, 1918, and 1919 related to the centennial campaign, Pound's central thesis was that gifts to the Law School support scholarship that is "useful socially" and results in "solving social problems" and "securing . . . social interests."[8] Appealing to donors also in terms that John D. Rockefeller called the "business of benevolence," Pound argued that endowing legal education "gives greater promise of results . . . than any other form of investment in educational enterprises . . . at present."[9] Hence, giving to a law school is the most effective and efficient vehicle for benefactions to education, he maintained.

Elaborating the analogy of James Thayer (LL.B. 1856) between jurisprudence and advances in medical and technical fields, Pound attempted to explain the return on the investment in legal education. Legal research and graduate instruction would benefit society, according to Pound, by reconciling received legal doctrine with new social conditions and legal developments in the twentieth century, thus turning "the [common] law of the nineteenth century . . . to intelligent account as an agency of justice in the twentieth century." For examples, Pound cited law school professors advising on new legislation: "the work of Professor Samuel Williston [LL.B. 1888], as one of the Commissioners on Uniform State Laws, on the Sales Act, the Warehouse Receipts Act, the Bill of Lading Act, and the Certificates of Stock Act [is] especially noteworthy."[10] But the much larger need arises in "the body of law which is growing up outside of courts" in "administrative boards and commissions" in the early twentieth century, such as the "Interstate Commerce Commission . . . Public Service Commissions of one sort or another . . . Federal Trade Commission . . . Boards of Probation or parole."[11]

This new body of administrative law requires more than the layman's "unfettered common sense" or training "merely in the political and social sciences." Research and graduate instruction in the law are needed because "in the end, the lawyer will be called upon to formulate in legal principles the results of administrative experience."[12] For example, "reconciliation of the new principles behind our Workmen's Compensation Acts with the general law of torts is a pressing problem."[13] Conversely, the new administrative boards and commissions and their associated rules create inconsistencies with "the older fields" of law. Legal scholarship must address these as well.[14]

In Pound's view, the need for jurisprudential refinement of new legislation and administrative rules, as well as the inconsistency between older legal doctrine and twentieth-century law and rules, were fundamental problems. Legal scholarship and research were the means to solve these problems by reconciling and harmonizing the old with the new. The social benefit lay in continuity, which serves "general peace and good order" and "the paramount social interest in the general security," stated Pound. These aims demonstrate that "the study of the common law, as carried on at Harvard, is conservative in the best sense of that word. We are now concerned to conserve American institutions. . . . To teach the experience of English-speaking peoples in the administration of justice scientifically and sympathetically, as an achievement of social engineering, is one of the surest ways of perpetuating American institutions, dispelling plausible political crudities, and insuring a sane and orderly legal and political development."[15]

These fundraising appeals between 1916 and 1920 seemed to express yet another political shift for Pound. In the 1890s his representation of the Burlington and Union Pacific Railroads and his opposition to Populism, William Jennings Bryan, and "free silver" positioned him against legal reform. In the 1900s his reformist writings had urged reconciliation and harmonization among individuals and the community, in line with "the collectivist spirit of the present age." Now, in the late 1910s, Dean Pound's fundraising appeals emphasized harmonizing the old and the new, not the individual and the collective. Furthermore, his new emphasis on "general peace and good order" and "the general security" supplanted a focus on "the moral sense of the community" and "justice."[16] Thus, "throughout his life, Pound had no hesitation about reinventing himself to suit his audience," as historian Natalie Hull and other scholars have observed.[17] In any case, in the late 1910s, Pound adopted a philanthropic rationale for the centennial campaign.

Pound's Ineffective Appeals

Pound's new appeal did not move either of his two primary audiences. On the one hand, he belied the progressive jurisprudence associated with the Law School, through the writings and opinions of Zechariah Chafee Jr. (LL.B. 1913), Felix Frankfurter (LL.B. 1906), Justice Oliver W. Holmes Jr. (LL.B. 1866), Justice Louis Brandeis (LL.B. 1877), and himself. Instead, Pound's aim to ensure "sane and orderly legal and political development" reinforced the popular complaint reported by Theodore Roosevelt at a Harvard fund-raising dinner in 1905:

> Many of the most influential and most highly remunerated members of the bar . . . work out bold and ingenious schemes by which their very wealthy clients, individual or corporate, can evade the laws which . . . regulate, in the interest of the public, the use of great wealth. Now, the great lawyer who employs his talent and his learning [in this way] . . . encourage[s] the growth in this country of a spirit of dumb anger against all laws and of disbelief in their efficacy.[18]

On the other hand, Pound did not convince wealthy elites to see the law as their ally. Even if Pound tailored the law's "solving social problems" to "conservative" interests, those interests doubted the law's efficacy.[19] Businessmen did not see law or lawyers as constructive allies, and Pound's philanthropic rationale could scarcely persuade wealthy business interests to donate to a law school.

Above all, the dean's three documents of 1916, 1918, and 1919 relied on the doubtful premise that readers credited the social benefit that law provided in the past. Pound presumed that the Law School's "effectiveness in handling the law of the nineteenth century is a guarantee of ability to turn this law to . . . an agency of justice in the twentieth century."[20] However, in the opinion of both progressive and conservative donors, "dissatisfaction with law and distrust of lawyers are no less marked than a century ago," the *Centennial History* acknowledged in 1918. "Social conditions and industrial conflicts have made more than one tenet of our legal system unpopular and have roused strong opposition to . . . the supremacy of law."[21] Given this dissatisfaction and distrust, how could continuity in law and the legal profession be a desirable aim?

Even if the dissatisfaction and distrust could be overcome, how could legal research compete with medical research for funding? The new philanthropic foundations were potential sources of bountiful grants, and alumni leaders of the centennial campaign in 1917 wistfully hoped for a windfall.[22] Pound made inquiries to foundations, but discovered that their staff expected funded projects to produce direct, specific, tangible benefits like medical improvements in "individual hygiene."[23] Pound's documents did not explain, or even identify, the direct, specific, tangible benefits of individual legal research projects, though he alluded to them in references to the Sales Act, the Warehouse Receipts Act, the Bill of Lading Act, the Certificates of Stock Act, Workmen's Compensation Act, and so forth. But what were the beneficial outcomes to be achieved?

The fundamental difficulty here was that legal scholarship did not fit the methods of natural science that had come to predominate in American academe by the 1910s. In the early twentieth century, the emerging social sciences bowed to the increasing authority of natural science in American social thought, and sought to adopt a "positivist self-description as objective science."[24] Some scholars have even argued that sociological jurisprudence and legal realism arose in legal thought due to this same influence.[25] But, Pound did not model his jurisprudence on social science, perhaps due to his own appreciation of natural science from his graduate training in botany. In any event, he did not associate jurisprudence with the efforts of social scientists, who attempted to develop a "policy science" and founded the Social Science Research Council in 1923.[26] Instead, Pound took it for granted that legal expertise was autonomous and distinct from expertise in "the political and social sciences."[27]

Pound did believe that jurisprudence and social science could collaborate closely, and that criminal law provided a ripe opportunity for collaboration. Hence, his 1919 fundraising pamphlet argued that "the criminal law is our main reliance for the securing of social interests." In keeping with his "sociological" perspective, Pound had long devoted attention to problems in criminal law. In 1919 he affirmed, "No subject calls more urgently" than criminal law for research. But in this domain as well, Pound supported his proposal merely by citing the "study which the Harvard Law School has . . . devote[d] to legal problems in the past."[28] He offered no evidence of success and no explanation of how criminal law would be improved.

The general public could immediately understand the improvement resulting from James Thayer's examples in other fields: "the steam-engine, the telegraph, the telephone, . . . the prophylactics against small pox and diphtheria."[29] But how did the legal research of Professor Williston improve the Warehouse Receipts Act beyond what "unfettered common sense" could have done? What did reconciling "our Workmen's Compensation Acts with the general law of torts" actually mean and how would that solve social problems? Precisely how did "legal principles" improve the findings of those trained "merely in the political and social sciences"? Whether in regard to legislation, administrative law, or criminal law, Pound did not identify, explain, or validate the direct, specific benefits of legal research. Some observers doubted that he ever could. "The question whether . . . a school of law can appeal for a large endowment is primarily determined by . . . its teaching," opined Yale President Arthur Hadley.[30]

Preparing a New Campaign, 1920–1925

Following the centennial fiasco, three developments in the early 1920s shaped the Law School's effort to undertake a new fundraising campaign.[31] First, Pound reached "the pinnacle of his profession." He became the "foremost American academic jurisprudent of his day," and prominent legal scholars adopted his emphasis on the "sociological" factors influencing legal doctrine. In 1923 Pound turned down the presidency of the University of Wisconsin, and thereafter his leadership of the Law School grew ever more authoritarian.[32] Commensurately, Pound indulged the pride of those associated with the school by omitting mention of its shortcomings or weaknesses. For example, his historical account of the school published in 1930 makes no reference to any financial problems of the school or the failed centennial campaign, which he knew well.[33]

Second, rigorous empirical research into crime and criminal justice began to emerge. In January 1920 the Eighteenth Amendment prohibiting the manufacture, sale, or transport of "intoxicating liquors" took effect, and the ensuing attempts to evade Prohibition contributed to a national "crime wave" that attracted increasing publicity and concern during the 1920s.[34] In response, a number of public entities sponsored surveys of crime and criminal justice in order to understand the growing problem. The pioneer was the Cleveland Foundation, which in 1920 invited Pound to devise such a survey. He and Frankfurter assembled a team of social scientists with legal training, including

Sheldon and Eleanor Glueck, who produced the noted Cleveland Crime Survey in 1922. The summary of the study, *Criminal Justice in Cleveland*, written largely by Frankfurter with Pound's assistance, emphasized that criminal activity stems from sociological and psychological factors and cannot be attributed to an individual's intent alone.[35] This prominent study and its findings heightened Pound's interest in the study of criminal law while at the same time challenging his earlier distinction between expertise in the law and expertise "merely in the political and social sciences."

Third, fundraising campaigns proliferated throughout higher education, prompted by the national publicity given to the Harvard Endowment Fund (HEF) drive. While that campaign was winding down in 1920, the *New York Times* reported that "nearly seventy-five colleges throughout the country are conducting campaigns for endowment funds" totaling more than $200 million. The president of Princeton wrote to President Lowell (1909–1933) at Harvard, "We are following in your wake."[36] Various Harvard departments also began clamoring to raise money. The Corporation therefore ranked them in order of priority and slotted the Law School, having already had its chance, at the bottom. Pound was furious, but could only fume as he waited for permission to try again.

In 1923 the university decided to conduct another campaign on behalf of departments and schools that had been neglected by the HEF drive. These surely included the Law School, maintained Pound, who believed that the HEF had smothered the Law School's centennial campaign. Instead, President Lowell and the Corporation decided that Harvard's three most pressing needs lay in the business school, the chemistry department, and the fine arts department. Once again, the Law School was sidelined. Pound's frustration and anger grew when, apart from the new appeal, he was told not to approach Henry Ford for a gift because another Harvard department was planning to do so.[37]

This 1923 campaign run by the university was conducted, not in the new national public style, but in the traditional discreet style favored by Lowell, who personally chaired it. He believed that large sums "were best obtained from a few people rather than from many," so the new drive had no paid staff, operated quietly, and targeted only wealthy individuals. Lowell often told the Harvard deans—paraphrasing Jean-Baptist Colbert, the finance minister of French King Louis XIV—that a widespread appeal to alumni "brings the minimum of feathers with the maximum of squawking." By June 1924, Lowell's quiet campaign had raised nearly $10 million from wealthy donors whom the HEF had obligingly left in reserve.[38]

Meanwhile, Pound continued to lament the cycle of large and growing enrollment, high student-faculty ratio, overcrowding in the existing buildings, and excessive reliance on the tuition of LL.B. students. His pleas finally moved Lowell, who began to announce the needs of the Law School in his annual reports.[39] In late 1924 the Corporation at last gave its approval. "The embargo has now been lifted," Pound exulted, and he rapidly moved to organize a fundraising campaign.[40] But he made some serious miscalculations.

The three developments above—his preeminent stature in jurisprudence, new empirical research on crime, and widespread fundraising in higher education—inflated Pound's confidence about how much and how fast money could be raised, and this overconfidence was compounded by undue pride in his philanthropic appeals. He thus proposed raising $5 million in two years. University officials advised that no more than $3 million in total was achievable, and a prominent law alumnus and member of the Corporation warned that the university's series of campaigns conducted between 1914 and 1924 had exhausted the capacity or inclination of many alumni to give. Pound not only ignored the advice but added to the wish list another $400,000 for current operations. Six months later, enthused by the magnificent new buildings erected for the University of Michigan Law School, Pound even suggested that an additional million dollars could be raised for another building beyond that already projected.[41]

In the spring of 1925 Pound therefore envisioned raising nearly $6.4 million. This absurd goal induced the Corporation to compromise on Pound's original goal of $5 million, including $3 million for endowment and $2 million for a new building. Lowell assured Pound that the Corporation was "heartily behind the drive for the Law School, and ready to urge it with all its might."[42]

"How Badly a Campaign Can Be Organized," 1925–1927

Drawing on his three statements of 1916, 1918, and 1919 related to the centennial drive, Pound immediately began drafting a thirty-page manifesto for the new campaign, preciously titled *A Projet*.[43] In March 1925 Wilson M. Powell (LL.B. 1898), vice president of the New York City Bar Association, agreed to chair the campaign. By June, Powell had formed an executive committee of twenty-eight members and hired an executive secretary and a prominent publicity consultant in New York City. Relying on this group, he hoped to collect almost all the money from a small number of wealthy donors and foundations in September 1925, thereby avoiding a public drive. "If that does not succeed," Powell wrote to Pound, "then [we will] start a drive, making all preparations for it now, so that we will waste no time in the fall."[44]

But the campaign soon bogged down in tactical problems, arising, particularly, from Pound's behavior. He rapidly lost patience with the process of gaining consensus on plans for the campaign among prominent alumni, the law faculty, the Corporation, and the Overseers Visiting Committee to the Law School. In addition, he grew impatient with the editorial critiques from Powell and other prominent alumni on successive drafts of his *Projet* during the spring of 1925.[45] Furthermore, as in the centennial drive, Pound ignored the advice from HEF organizers and staff that "personal solicitation is the only satisfactory method" in fundraising and that writing statements "results in very few subscriptions."[46] He continued devoting most of his effort to composing visionary pronouncements for distribution.

In addition, the dean made himself unavailable at critical points in the campaign. During the early fall of 1925, the period when Powell had intended to raise most of the money, Pound took a leave from the school to serve on the American-British Claims Arbitration Tribunal in Washington, D.C. Upon returning from this leave in November, he told the executive committee that he could provide little assistance due to a backlog of administrative work and teaching.[47] Nevertheless, dozens of law alumni wrote to Pound volunteering to help after a blizzard of announcements appeared in newspapers, and the dean worked with the executive committee to form eighteen regional committees. Then, in April 1926, Pound informed Powell that he would be occupied between May and July giving nine lectures at various universities.[48]

Furthermore, Pound spent little time visiting prospective donors, although he did successfully solicit one major contribution that suited his research interest. Beginning in November 1925, he made a concerted effort to interest the General Education Board (GEB) in "research and graduate instruction in law," and succeeded in obtaining a commitment for a conditional grant of $750,000, contingent upon securing a two-to-one match of $1.5 million in order to build an endowment of $2.25 million. Officially announced in March 1926, this GEB grant was, in fact, the only yield from the quiet appeal to major donors during all of 1925.[49]

No donor made a major gift in 1925 primarily because the dean and the executive committee were too busy to work on the campaign and engage alumni. It was the centennial drive all over again. In the early months of 1926, Wilson Powell and the executive committee had no choice but to plan the public drive that they had wanted to avoid. Given the lack of staff support provided by Harvard University, the executive committee retained John Price Jones, Inc. (JPJ), the leading consulting firm for fundraising in higher education, which had been founded by staff from the HEF drive.[50]

Beginning work in late June 1926, JPJ guided the law campaign over the next twelve months. There was a great deal to do, and JPJ advised the executive committee to develop a "Survey and Plan" proposing how the $5 million could be raised. This document projected that $2 million would come from the 9,400 living alumni and former students, as much as $1.75 million from foundations, including the GEB grant of $750,000, and another $2 million from the general public and wealthy lawyers.[51] The Plan provided a healthy margin for error, and confidence soared.

But the familiar problems persisted. In September 1926 the JPJ consultant reported "that the Law School Campaign is at least a month behind" because the executive secretary made decisions too slowly and relied on the executive committee, whose members were frequently unavailable. In addition, the consultant suspected "that the field organization [of eighteen regional committees] is largely a paper one and cannot be expected to function rapidly and efficiently when the bell rings." At the end of October he observed that the Law School drive was exemplary in demonstrating just "how badly a campaign can be organized. . . . [T]he patient is doing as well as can be expected," but "an enterprise with less prestige than the Harvard Law School would have [been] killed . . . off long ago."[52]

In November 1926 the public campaign officially commenced with a series of dinners in Boston, New York, Philadelphia, and St. Louis.[53] Subscriptions began to flow in steadily and reached $1,114,067 in January 1927. The drive then stalled until it seemed "to be standing almost still," in Powell's words. Pound boldly asked the Corporation for an advance of $200,000 in order to cover expenses for a third phase appealing to the general public to reach the $5 million goal. But the Corporation doubted its success and refused. Pound offered to sink $100,000 from the Law School surplus into the venture, but he and Powell finally decided against going forward with the third phase.[54]

A critical problem remained. In order to secure the two-for-one matching grant of $750,000 from the GEB, the drive had to raise $1.5 million in gifts by June 1927. In February it was still $323,000 short. Over a million dollars hung in the balance, and Powell worked through March and April to obtain commitments for $323,000. When it became clear that this effort would not succeed, both the Law School and the GEB faced a very embarrassing situation.

Then John D. Rockefeller, who had created and endowed the GEB, stepped in and personally offered $100,000 to the Law School contingent on the school obtaining the remaining $223,000 to satisfy the terms of the GEB.[55] With Rockefeller's face-saving conditional gift, the campaign made the matching goal just before the commencement deadline in June 1927.

Final Results of the 1925–1927 Campaign

Harvard extolled the outcome. Lowell viewed the campaign with "satisfaction," and Pound considered it "fully subscribed."[56] Various Harvard historians have declared it "a great success."[57] But this assessment is disingenuous. The final total of about $2.25 million was merely 45 percent of the publicly announced goal of $5 million, let alone the $6.4 million that Pound had grandiosely "projeted." Furthermore, this sum included the GEB grant of $750,000 and Rockefeller's $100,000. Apart from those funds, some $200,000 came from 125 non-alumni and about $1.2 million from 3,492 alumni.[58] Hence, non-contingent gifts from individuals amounted to only about $1.4 million, 28 percent of the official goal of $5 million.

However, in its final report in July 1927, JPJ announced a summative tally of $3,508,180 raised. This inflated, face-saving figure counted a *loan* of $1,250,000 from the university for the building fund, a loan that eventually swelled to over $1,463,000. Pound not only avoided mentioning the loan, but implied deceptively that the construction cost was covered by "the new endowment provided in 1926 by alumni, friends of the school, and the General Education Board, together with accumulated surplus." He also neglected to mention that the university required the school to hike tuition from $200 to the university norm of $400 by 1929 as a condition of the loan.[59]

At the same time that Pound inflated the campaign's success, he avoided blame for its shortcomings. He complained that the entire amount for the building fund could have been raised if the Corporation had supported the third phase of the campaign in 1927, and he speculated that the Corporation had refused to do so as a favor to other departments that wanted to launch their own drives immediately.[60] The Corporation's lack of support halted the campaign, in the exculpatory view of Pound, who neglected the fact that he had proposed a much higher goal and then insisted on seeking $5 million, against everyone's advice.

In any case, the final tally was not inconsequential. Due primarily to the campaign, the endowment of the Law School increased from about $1.2 million to more than $4.2 million between 1925 and 1930 in nominal dollars (not adjusted for inflation). Over the longer period from 1915 to 1930, the endowment grew from about $730,000 to $4.2 million, an increase that included the proceeds from the disappointing centennial campaign as well as significant stock market growth and inflation over these periods.[61]

The increases compare favorably to the endowment growth of Columbia and Yale Law Schools over the same period. Both of those law schools took note of Harvard's 1925–1927 drive and responded with their own initiatives. Columbia launched a "mammoth study of the potential for reorganizing the curriculum along functional lines," and Yale proposed "to begin empirical research" in various legal fields.[62] Meanwhile, despite all the dithering, delaying, and tactical problems, the growth of Harvard Law School's endowment outpaced that of either Columbia Law School or Yale Law School between 1910 and 1930. In proportional terms, Columbia's endowment fell from 57 percent to 13 percent of Harvard's endowment, and Yale's endowment dropped from 63 percent to 50 percent of Harvard's endowment, as seen in Appendix C.

Even so, the failure of Harvard's 1925–1927 campaign to reach its goal by more than half was a significant lost opportunity. Given that fundraising consultants usually crowed about their campaigns, the ambivalent tone of the final JPJ report, which references "a chronic state of inertia," is striking. By 1927 the JPJ firm, founded eight years earlier, had consulted on several hundred drives, raising nearly $125 million. John Price Jones himself later regarded the 1920s as "the golden age of fundraising" and Harvard University as the premier fundraiser.[63] In light of this background and the Law School's potential, its campaign of 1925–1927 was probably one of the least successful in higher education during the 1920s. Indeed, the only drive more disappointing in the brief history of higher education fundraising to that point may have been the school's centennial campaign.

Failure of Pound's Philanthropic Rationale, 1925–1926

Some have attributed the shortfall of the campaign to the contemporaneous controversy over the Sacco-Vanzetti case, which involved Pound, Frankfurter, and Lowell. Supposedly the controversy alienated alumni on both sides of the issue and detracted from giving to the campaign.[64] But little evidence supports this interpretation. John D. Rockefeller made his contingent gift of $100,000 in the middle of the controversy, as Felix Frankfurter observed; and one member of the executive committee estimated that no more than $3,000 of pledges were canceled due to Frankfurter's outspoken defense of the defendants. Though unhappy with Frankfurter's advocacy, Lowell himself believed that principled stands on social and political issues by Harvard faculty probably attracted more contributions than they cost.[65]

The central problem, according to the JPJ firm, was not external circumstances, but that, among the Law School alumni, "every one indulges in a lot of discussion about the campaign but scarcely anyone does any work." Thus, the JPJ staff was "unable to get any effective personal solicitation in New York or in Boston, and . . . in the various cities around the country."[66] Regarding the executive committee and dean, the JPJ supervisor observed that "unless this leadership is much more positive or vigorous than it has been in the last six months, there is no chance of completing the fund." In the end the JPJ staff reported that "a chronic state of inertia . . . has settled over everyone in our campaign organization."[67]

The tactical problems of the campaign thus stemmed from volunteers' lethargy and apathy, which was rooted in the inability to explain to alumni and others why they should donate to Harvard Law School or, indeed, to any law school. Pound's explanation in his precious *Projet* of 1925 failed, as had his three earlier statements between 1916 and 1920.

The waning ideology of charity certainly could not provide the justification for donating to the Law School in the mid-1920s any better than it had in 1882, and neither Pound nor the executive committee invoked the plea to subsidize poor law students. In fact, the GEB prohibited it. When awarding its grant of $750,000 to the Law School, the GEB stipulated that none of its grant should support professional training for LL.B. students. The potential for raising money for legal education depended on how well the appeal could be justified in terms of philanthropy, which by that point had become the prevailing rationale for benefaction for higher education. Pound had to struggle to explain the "signal public service" that, he claimed, would issue from donations to legal research and education.[68]

Medical research and education were the exemplars, as Pound had recognized for more than a decade, and he conjured suitable analogies. "The social hygiene involved in proper investigation in a law school is quite as important as the individual hygiene investigated in the medical school," he wrote.[69] Regarding his favored field of criminal law, Pound suggested, "We may expect endowment of such a chair to be no less fruitful of results than the endowments of medical research which have been so conspicuously fruitful in recent years."[70] Lowell likewise invoked the point, as did the dean of Yale Law School: "Just as the public has been ready to give necessary financial support to the improvement of medical education, the combating of disease, and the creating of better health conditions, so, we believe, will it be ready to aid efforts to improve legal education and to promote the research essential to bettering the administration of justice."[71]

But Pound seemed wary of expansive analogies to medicine. He made them only in letters and annual reports, avoiding them in his public manifesto for the 1925–1927 campaign. Instead, his *Projet* advanced the philanthropic justification in two other, limited respects. First, he focused narrowly on the benefits of legal research and graduate legal education, omitting or deemphasizing needs arising from LL.B. instruction or the fundamental financial problems of the school. Since the arrival of Dean Thayer in 1914, the Law School had for two decades lamented its dependence on LL.B. tuition. Pound had led the chorus, repeatedly complaining about the "box office plan" whereby the school relied heavily on tuition revenue.[72]

Yet the dean dedicated 97 percent of the requested $3 million for endowment to professorships, graduate fellowships, publications, and library support associated with research. There was no provision for unrestricted endowment, to which the university's HEF campaign had been entirely devoted. Moreover, the $2 million requested for land and buildings would raise maintenance costs and require a tuition increase, as Pound conceded in his *Projet*.[73] According to Pound's plan, the 1925–1927 drive, even if fully subscribed, would have *expanded* the school's reliance on LL.B. tuition.

Pound's neglect of LL.B. students in the campaign seemed completely wrongheaded to some faculty, even apart from his failure to appeal for unrestricted endowment to support the LL.B. program. Professor Edward "Bull" Warren (LL.B. 1900) later observed that "Dean Pound thought the School should also take the lead in . . . 'higher legal education,'" and many on the faculty "did come to take a greater interest, enthusiasm, and pride in graduate courses than in undergraduate [LL.B.] courses." Warren likened this preference to that of the dog in Aesop's fable "who was carrying a large leg of mutton in his mouth and . . . crossing a bridge," when he "saw his own reflection in the water and thought he saw another dog carrying a much larger leg of mutton, and thereupon dropped his own . . . into the river in order to get the larger leg of mutton." In fact, Warren believed that Harvard Law School's "greatest asset" was "the good will of those students who have obtained here the foundation of their success" in the LL.B. program. He therefore maintained that the school should "remain *primarily* a professional school (devoted to fitting young men for the practice of the law)" and that "tuition paid by undergraduates [in the LL.B. program] . . . should be devoted to undergraduate purposes."[74]

Second, even granting the focus on legal research and graduate education, Pound's *Projet* weakened the philanthropic rationale by inadequately explaining their benefits to society. He asserted that legal scholars and lawyers must assist legislatures in writing better laws and "make law-making take account of the social facts to which it must be applied, and at the same time, fit harmoniously into the legal system of which it must be a part." He also affirmed that the "administration of criminal justice is admittedly the weakest point in American polity. No subject of research affords greater possibilities."[75] However, Pound did not provide details, examples, or evidence of social benefit beyond those general statements. The 1925 *Projet* repeated the approach, arguments, and language of Pound's earlier documents. He kept invoking the experience of the nineteenth century, and restating that vague social benefits would flow from legal research.

Above all, the dean neglected to address, or even acknowledge, the "widespread skepticism" that legal research and graduate study are socially useful, as James Thayer had written.[76] Pound recognized this skepticism, for he raged privately that the dean of Harvard Business School was giving lectures around the country criticizing the capacity of law to improve business.[77] And to add insult to injury, the Business School dean, Wallace Donham (LL.B. 1910), was a graduate of Harvard Law School.

Failure of the Consultants' Rationale, 1927

Wilson Powell and others had expressed reservations about the effectiveness of Dean Pound's *Projet* in 1925, and the JPJ staff voiced new doubts immediately upon coming aboard in June 1926. The consultants naturally endorsed the philanthropic thesis that law schools can provide "a vital public service . . . in re-making the law into an effective instrument for the orderly development of our present complex society." However, the JPJ staff doubted that Pound's writings "will catch the attention of the laymen. For them, the appeal should be developed in a less technical, and more popular style." Accordingly, "the appeal must be reduced to terms of every-day life. The man of affairs must be shown that scientific study of the law will bring results comparable with those already obtained by research workers in business and industry."[78]

Pound arrogantly dismissed all these doubts, and the JPJ consultants resigned themselves to publishing 15,000 copies of the *Projet* and distributing
it to more than 10,000 alumni and prominent judges in September 1926.
Three months later, the JPJ criticism was repeated by Anglican bishop William Lawrence, one of Harvard University's leading fundraisers, who had no
connection with the Law School but had agreed to assist its drive. In remarks
at the Law School campaign kickoff dinner in November 1926, Bishop Lawrence maintained that the campaign must "show all walks of life why Harvard Law School was needed for their welfare, safety, and happiness."[79] This
is precisely what Pound's *Projet* failed to do.

Apparently emboldened—or believing that the ship was sinking—the JPJ
staff sharpened its critique of Pound's appeals:

> It serves no purpose to keep telling the average citizen what a very fine thing
> law research is. He wants to know what law research will do. . . . He is not in-
> terested in generalities, law books, and law libraries. He is interested in crime
> and crime prevention . . . [and] in the conflict and disorder whenever legisla-
> tion is given an oppressive twist. . . . When we turn to the businessman, the
> appeal must be placed on a business basis. It is not enough to say that the sci-
> ence of law must keep pace with the science of business. . . . The question that
> concerns him is: how does it happen that so many things get passed only to tie
> up in red tape? . . . . The purpose of this publicity is . . . to state . . . *What
> Legal Research Could Accomplish.*[80]

Because Pound could not effectively answer this critical question in a way that
attracted philanthropy, the JPJ staff tried to rescue the campaign by preparing
a new manifesto and focusing all campaign publicity on "the need for scientific research in the field of law."[81]

It took until April 1927 for the nonlawyers on the JPJ staff to hash out a
new statement explaining unmistakably to the laity the social benefit of legal
research. The JPJ manifesto was titled *For the Safety of the Citizen and the Protection of Business, A plan to eliminate from the administration of justice in this
country many elements of delay, waste, friction, and uncertainty which are threatening the general security and hampering commerce and industry.*[82] However,
the campaign was expiring by the time 5,600 copies of this eighty-page pamphlet were mailed to prominent periodicals and individuals across the country.

It is doubtful that the JPJ pamphlet would have mattered, given that it offered a reductionist view of the social benefit of legal research. Law School
officials had alerted JPJ staff to the complex relationship between legal research

and public benefit, and provided a list of "Things to Remember" in preparing publicity for the campaign. The list included: "Make no rash promises that legal research is a cure-all"; "Legal research is . . . not the same as medical research"; and "Base arguments on business law and administration of justice, rather than on sensational aspects of criminal law."[83] But the JPJ consultants violated all these guidelines and tailored legal research to fit a direct causal model of social benefit in accordance with the methods of natural science.

For the Safety of the Citizen and the Protection of Business compared legal research to "the proved methods of Pasteur and Reed and Banting and Faraday" through which "many terrible scourges—hydrophobia, typhoid, diphtheria, malaria, yellow fever, diabetes—have been brought under control." According to the pamphlet, "national law schools shall function as great law laboratories, directly serving the public interest in much the same way as chemical and engineering laboratories, university hospitals and clinics, or our great scientific foundations."[84] The primary benefit of such laboratory research would be simpler, more efficient law, particularly in matters of crime and business.

Regarding crime, for example, the JPJ pamphlet's opening pages described the lamentable delay in extraditing and trying a heinous criminal, whose case demonstrated how "the modern professional criminal frequently finds a way to elude justice through the archaic technicalities of our inherited procedure." Legal research was evidently going to determine how to try, convict, and jail criminals expeditiously. No concern was given to due process, the rights of the accused, or the possibility that suspected criminals might be innocent. The pamphlet also said nothing concerning the paradox that lawyers had created the archaic technicalities that they were now volunteering to fix for a donation.

In the domain of business, the new manifesto assailed "legal uncertainties" and "legal perplexities" that undermine "those conditions of certainty and uniformity which are so important to the safe, orderly, and expeditious development of business and industry." Research in new areas of law could evidently reduce perplexity and uncertainty. But the pamphlet did not explain how professional expertise would cure the ills of technicality to which professional expertise had often contributed. Most importantly, the pamphlet did not consider whether technicality and complexity might be inevitable in a complicated modern economy.

In addition, *For the Safety of the Citizen and the Protection of Business* neglected politics and political bias, commensurate with its analogy to scientific research. While suggesting that the findings of legal research would directly yield practical improvements, the pamphlet did not discuss the nature of law-making in a democratic republic. Even when considering how legal research could improve the "ill-considered, badly drawn, experimental, first-impression legislation with which the country is flooded from year to year," no mention was made of the politics involved in enacting legislation.

In the end, neither the Law School leaders nor the JPJ consultants adequately responded to the problem that "to the layman . . . the value of legal research to American society . . . would probably seem questionable. The law was highly technical; its reform appeared unrelated to the ordinary man's daily welfare. It sometimes seemed a mass of exasperating rules, tending to retard . . . true justice."[85] The consultants knew what philanthropists wanted to hear; the legal scholars knew what they did; and the campaign failed to bridge the gap between them. A philanthropic rationale for donating to law schools remained elusive.

Another Missed Opportunity

Despite the failure of the 1925–1927 drive to reach its goal by more than half, the yield from the campaign, combined with a judicious enrollment strategy, could have rescued the school from its financial malaise. Academic institutions rarely have an opportunity to change their fundamental financial model, because they generally cannot reduce their largest, fixed costs of physical plant and tenured faculty. Remarkably, Harvard Law School had two opportunities to chart a new financial course between 1900 and 1930. The first was when Dean Ames and his faculty agreed in 1905 to build Langdell Hall. Their decision validated the truism in higher education that naming a building after a dean indicates that not enough money was raised to pay for it.

A second rare opportunity to chart a new financial course came in 1927. The goal of $2 million for land and buildings in the 1925–1927 campaign included a request for $1.25 million to expand Langdell Hall, since only two-thirds of the original plan for the building had been completed in 1906–1907. During the academic year 1923–24, the enrollment rose to 1,099 students and the teaching faculty to about seventeen, bringing the student-faculty ratio to about 65:1. But Pound did not consider limiting the size of the student body, arguing that "the real difficulties [of the school] are not involved in numbers," because, "even with the much smaller numbers," the school would have to face "all the unhappy phenomena which just now it is fashionable to attribute wholly to increased attendance."[86]

Here Pound was being disingenuous, for the large size of the student body coupled with low tuition had been recognized as a source of the school's problems since 1910. In truth, the dean wanted to add research capacity and graduate students, and the prospect for doing so was virtually nil if he cut the enrollment of LL.B. students, whose tuition was needed to support the endeavor. Consequently, he began calling loudly to expand Langdell Hall.

But not a single dollar was given for the building during the 1925–1927 campaign. This was actually good news, because the school was therefore under no obligation to proceed with construction. Nevertheless, without any reconsideration in light of the shortfall of the campaign, Pound plunged ahead with expanding Langdell Hall. If the fundraising adage in higher education about naming a building after a dean is correct, then it applies even more to constructing an unnamed expansion to a building named for a dean. Pound's actions proved the point.

To pay for the construction, the school borrowed the entire cost from the university. The terms were not favorable, indicating that Lowell had little interest in subsidizing the school so long as Pound refused to raise tuition. The Corporation therefore charged 4 percent interest on the loan, which was higher than the rate of return the Corporation paid on the school's endowment invested with the university. In fact, the latter rate of return fell to only 1 percent during the Depression, so the university profited handsomely from the loan to the Law School.[87] Also, to ensure that the Law School could make the payments, the Corporation required the school to raise its tuition to $300 in 1927 and $400 by 1929.[88]

Even more imprudently, Pound elected to expand the expansion to Langdell Hall in order to accommodate the enrollment that had ballooned to 1,443 during 1926–27. Completing the final third of Langdell Hall according to the original plan would have increased its capacity by 50 percent. Instead Pound added a rear extension to the building (now known as Areeda Hall), which increased its capacity by nearly 100 percent. The construction cost and the loan therefore swelled to over $1.46 million—more than all the noncontingent gifts received from individuals in the 1925–1927 campaign.[89] Pound's decision worsened the predicament of living "hand to mouth" from tuition, which he had always bemoaned.

Opening in the fall of 1929, the Langdell Hall expansion seriously burdened the school's finances for the next two decades. In 1924–25, the Law School had revenue of about $304,000 and expenses of $273,000, including $21,000 to operate the buildings, so the school netted a surplus of about $22,000.[90] In 1929–30—after the fundraising campaign, the expansion of

Completed Langdell Hall. Photograph ca. 1960.

Courtesy of Harvard Law School Library, Historical & Special Collections.

Langdell Hall, the loan from the university, and the tuition increase to $400—the Law School had revenue of about $787,000 and expenses of $663,000, including $55,000 to operate the buildings. These figures appear highly favorable, showing a potential surplus of $124,000. But the school had to pay $150,000 toward the principal and interest of the construction loan, and was saved from a deficit of $26,000 only by current gifts and sundry sources.[91]

Although the invested receipts of the fundraising campaign had increased investment income by $121,000 (from $67,000 to $188,000) between 1925 and 1930, constructing the expansion to Langdell Hall raised the annual expenses by $184,000, including $34,000 in higher operating expenses and $150,000 in the loan payment. Consequently, the construction and borrowing consumed all the income gains from the endowment received in the 1925–1927 campaign and 50 percent more! Pound's expansion of Langdell Hall left the school worse off financially than before the 1925–1927 campaign, even after doubling the tuition.

For two decades the school groaned under the burden of paying off the loan to expand Langdell Hall. During the eight years from 1928–29 to 1936–37, the school annually paid an average of $120,000 in principal and interest. This rapid repayment schedule was driven not by the Corporation but by Pound's desire to retire the loan as rapidly as possible, suggesting that he regarded it as a detriment on his record. In any case, the average payment equaled the return on an endowment of about $3 million. Hence, the figure of $4.2 million for the endowment of the Law School in 1930 is deceptive, because much of its revenue was needed to pay off the debt.

After Pound stepped down in 1936, Acting Dean Edmund Morgan (LL.B. 1905) wrote to President James Conant (1933–1953), "The enlargement of Langdell Hall has been a curse to the school by shifting emphasis from education to finance. . . . I have no doubt that the need for enlarged income to meet these payments has, consciously and unconsciously, influenced the policy as to admissions" by making it more lenient.[92] Similarly, Bull Warren wrote to Conant that the "swollen" enrollment of the school "has had three very bad results: 1) the effect on the quality of the students, 2) the dilution of the Faculty, . . . 3) an expansion of plant which went much beyond our means."[93]

Thus, in the view of several senior faculty, financial constraints forced the school to admit too many students and then ruthlessly wield the sword of attrition. Straitened finances directly reinforced the Spartan ethos. In 1937 Acting Dean Morgan and President Conant agreed to extend the repayment schedule, and the loan was finally paid off in 1948.[94] For twenty years, the school literally lived "from hand to mouth."

Expanding Langdell Hall between 1927 and 1929 was the second critical point at which the school chose not to alter its financial model and instead reinforced the syndrome of tuition dependence, presented in Figure 5.1, as it had developed by 1930. Instead of expanding Langdell Hall in 1927, Pound could have followed a different path leading to prosperity that would have provided abundant resources for research and graduate legal education. If he had raised tuition in 1927 to the Harvard University norm of $400 and capped the student body at 600, tuition revenue would have equaled the $240,000 received in 1925.

This two-pronged approach would have beneficially lowered the student-faculty ratio to about 30:1 and opened a great deal of space in Austin and Langdell Halls, which accommodated 750 to 800 students before the expansion. The opened space could have housed the graduate students and research professors that Pound envisioned in the 1925–1927 campaign. Money

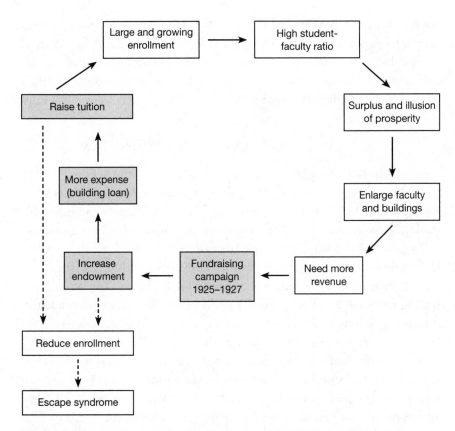

Figure 5.1. Tuition Dependence Syndrome, ca. 1930. Note: Solid arrows represent path followed during 1920s. Dotted arrows represent alternate paths available. The shaded boxes convey new developments since 1920 (Figure 2.1).

to support this initiative would have come from the resulting, immense annual surplus of about $155,000 generated by the additional investment income from the gifts received in the 1925–1927 campaign. Apart from paying for the dean's initiative, a significant cash reserve would have rapidly accumulated and supported a sustainable, debt-free rate of growth in the student body and faculty with a lower student-faculty ratio.

In 1927 no one considered this alternative of raising tuition, cutting enrollment, and foregoing expansion of the buildings. Instead the school headed into the Depression facing significant problems. Ever more dependent on high enrollment, the school had more buildings, expenses, and debt, while enrollment and endowment income began to fall due to the depressed economy.

Some faculty even proposed admitting more students in order to increase tuition income. In 1938 James Landis (1937–1946) became the first dean to oppose that course, and even suggested that the school should reduce its enrollment to a thousand students.[95] Landis's suggestion, if pursued in 1927, would have made the school prosperous once again.

"A Working Bibliography" of Ancient Greek Law

Dean Landis had the right idea, but not the opportunities that came in 1905 and 1927. Though lamenting the school's poverty throughout the 1920s, Roscoe Pound locked the school into its financial syndrome for another generation: large enrollment, high student-faculty ratio, large fixed costs, and heavy tuition dependence. Harvard's financial model then provided a template for the financing of law schools at other universities, reinforcing the detrimental financial isomorphism in legal education. If Harvard Law School, the leading law school with the largest endowment in the nation, depended so heavily on tuition reaped from huge classes, why should other universities relieve their law schools of that dependence?

Pound's stubbornness and vanity steered him toward the path of imprudence, while he seemed to take it for granted that the value of legal research was self-evident and needed no clear and practical justification. In 1927 his annual report announced triumphantly that the research supported by "the newly raised endowment . . . begins to yield fruit" in the form of "a working bibliography" of ancient Greek law.[96] Surely this scholarship convinced few philanthropists that legal research solves current social problems.

Leaders of the successful HEF campaign had maintained "that the two great lines of publicity are the appeal to the intellect and the appeal to the heart. If you can get both of these, you can hardly fail."[97] Through the late 1920s, Harvard Law School could get neither. Donors resisted giving charity to law students and law schools, and law professors and deans could not explain and justify their work in philanthropic terms, particularly in light of public skepticism about the social benefit of the legal profession.

Ironically, the Depression, the rise of fascism, and the chill of McCarthyism soon demonstrated what the Law School fundraising documents could not: the critical need for training in law and governance, particularly for Harvard Law School graduates and faculty. Even before those developments began to unfold, a simmering jurisprudential controversy came to a boil concerning the significance of "sociological jurisprudence" and "legal realism." Intensifying the controversy were the alignments and institutional interests of Harvard, Columbia, and Yale, the nation's three leading law schools in 1930.

NOTES

1. William C. Loring, James Byrne, and William C. Osborn, *To the Graduates of the Harvard Law School* [printed circular] (Boston, March 31, 1917), 1–2, Harvard Law School Library Historical & Special Collections (HLSLib). See "Report of the Dean of the Law School," *Harvard Alumni Bulletin* (April 8, 1914), 448; Roscoe Pound, Annual Report of the Dean of Harvard Law School, 1915–16, 145.

2. Roscoe Pound, *The Harvard Law School* [New York, 1919], 16. Pound's phrase was later picked up by Erwin N. Griswold, Annual Report of the Dean of Harvard Law School, 1961–62, 395.

3. Pound, Annual Report of the Dean, 1915–16, 145.

4. Quotations are from Charles W. Eliot, Annual Report of the President of Harvard University, 1871–72, 21–22. This chapter draws upon Bruce A. Kimball, "Charity, Philanthropy, and Law School Fundraising: The Emergence and the Failure, 1880–1930," *Journal of Legal Education* 63 (2013): 247–281.

5. Pound, Annual Report of the Dean, 1915–16, 140–150.

6. Roscoe Pound, "Mechanical Jurisprudence," *Columbia Law Review* 8 (1908): 609–610. See David Wigdor, *Roscoe Pound: Philosopher of Law* (Westport, CT, 1974), 161–205; N. E. H. Hull, *Roscoe Pound and Karl Llewellyn: Searching for an American Jurisprudence* (Chicago, 1997), 76–96.

7. Roscoe Pound, "The Causes of Popular Dissatisfaction with the Administration of Justice," *Report of the Annual Meeting of the ABA* 29 (1906): 395–417; Roscoe Pound, "Law in Books and Law in Action," *American Law Review* 44 (1910): 12–36.

8. Quotations are from, respectively: Pound, Annual Report of the Dean, 1915–16, 140; *The Centennial History of the Harvard Law School: 1817–1917* (Cambridge, MA, 1918), 167; Pound, *The Harvard Law School*, 18.

9. Roscoe Pound to A. Lawrence Lowell (December 11, 1916), Harvard Law School Dean's Office Records, Records of President A. Lawrence Lowell, 1909–1933, Harvard University Archives (hereafter cited as ALL Records). See John D. Rockefeller, *Random Reminiscences of Men and Events* (New York, 1909), 184.

10. Quotations are from, respectively: *Centennial History*, 168; Pound, *The Harvard Law School*, 9.

11. Pound, Annual Report of the Dean, 1915–16, 140. See *Centennial History*, 166; Pound, *The Harvard Law School*, 13–15.

12. Pound, Annual Report of the Dean, 1915–16, 141. See *Centennial History*, 166–167; Pound, *The Harvard Law School*, 14–15.

13. *Centennial History,* 167–168. See Pound, *The Harvard Law School,* 9.

14. Pound, Annual Report of the Dean, 1915–16, 141. See *Centennial History,* 167.

15. Quotations are from Pound, *The Harvard Law School,* 14–15, 24. See Pound, Annual Report of the Dean, 1915–16, 141; *Centennial History,* 166–167; Roscoe Pound, "The Law School and the Common Law," in *Two Addresses Delivered before the Alumni of the Harvard Law School at Cambridge, June 21, 1920* ([Boston, 1920]), 1.

16. Pound, "Causes of Popular Dissatisfaction," 397–398, 402–403.

17. Hull, *Roscoe Pound and Karl Llewellyn,* 39. See William Twining, "Review of N. E. H. Hull, *Roscoe Pound and Karl Llewellyn: Searching for an American Jurisprudence* (University of Chicago Press, Chicago, 1997)," *Law Quarterly Review* 115 (1998): 155.

18. "High Ideals Urged on All," *Boston Globe* (June 29, 1905). See James R. Green, *The World of the Worker: Labor in Twentieth Century America* (New York, 1980), 133–135.

19. Quotations are from, respectively: Pound, Annual Report of the Dean, 1915–16, 140; *Centennial History,* 167; Pound, *The Harvard Law School,* 18.

20. *Centennial History,* 167–168.

21. Quotations are from *Centennial History,* 167–168, 163. See Pound, *The Harvard Law School,* 9.

22. Frank W. Grinnell to Joseph P. Cotton (June 23, 1916), ALL Records. See Joseph P. Cotton to Frank W. Grinnell (June 21, 1916), ALL Records.

23. Pound to Lowell (December 11, 1916). See A. Lawrence Lowell to Roscoe Pound (May 9, 1916) and A. Lawrence Lowell to H. P. Walcott (December 26, 1916), ALL Records; Walter E. Meyer to Roscoe Pound (June 2, 1911), Roscoe Pound Papers, 1888–1964, HLSLib (hereafter cited as RP Papers); Ernest V. Hollis, *Philanthropic Foundations and Higher Education* (New York, 1938), 274–276.

24. Dorothy Ross, *The Origins of American Social Science* (Cambridge, UK, 1991), 471. See John C. Burnham, *How Superstition Won and Science Lost: Popularizing Science and Health in the United States* (New Brunswick, NJ, 1987), 7; Charles Rosenberg, *No Other Gods: On Science and American Social Thought* (Baltimore, 1976), xi.

25. Edward A. Purcell Jr., *The Crisis of Democratic Theory: Scientific Naturalism and the Problem of Value* (Lexington, KY, 1973), 159. Compare John Henry Schlegel, *American Legal Realism and Empirical Social Science* (Chapel Hill, NC, 1995).

26. Olivier Zunz, *Why the American Century?* (Chicago, 1998), 25–45.

27. Pound, Annual Report of the Dean, 1915–16, 141. See *Centennial History,* 166–167; Pound, *The Harvard Law School,* 14–15.

28. Pound, *The Harvard Law School,* 18. See Pound, Annual Report of the Dean, 1915–16, 141; Wigdor, *Roscoe Pound,* 241; Hull, *Roscoe Pound,* 151.

29. James B. Thayer, "The Teaching of English Law at Universities," *Harvard Law Review* 9 (1895): 174.

30. Arthur T. Hadley, Annual Report of the President of Yale University, 1912–13, 24.

31. The following account draws upon Ravi P. Ramchandani, "The Stalling Effort: The Harvard Law School Endowment Campaign of 1925–1927" (student research paper, Harvard Law School, 2012), on file with the authors; Kimball, "Charity, Philanthropy."

32. Quotation is from Hull, *Roscoe Pound,* 125–126. See Wigdor, *Roscoe Pound,* 233, 239–240; James F. Clark, "The Harvard Law School Deanship of Roscoe Pound, 1916–1936" (student research paper, Harvard Law School, 1999), on file with the authors, sect. IV B.

33. Roscoe Pound, "The Law School, 1817–1929," in *The Development of Harvard University since the Inauguration of President Eliot, 1869–1929,* ed. Samuel E. Morison (Cambridge, MA, 1930), 506.

34. Henry Ruth and Kevin R. Reitz, *The Challenge of Crime: Rethinking Our Responses* (Cambridge, MA, 2003), 15.

35. The typescript draft of the report, written by Frankfurter and submitted to Pound, is in RP Papers. See Wigdor, *Roscoe Pound,* 241–245; Hull, *Roscoe Pound,* 154; Palma Paciocco, "*A Sound Recommendation,* Sheldon and Eleanor Glueck and the Project to Educate Correctional Administrators at Harvard Law School" (student research paper, Harvard Law School, 2012), on file with the authors, 4–14. The extraordinary contribution of Eleanor T. Glueck to legal scholarship is discussed in Chapter 16.

36. John G. Hibben to A. Lawrence Lowell (September 24, 1919), ALL Records. See "Universities Ask over $200,000,000," *New York Times* (February 8, 1920).

37. A. Lawrence Lowell to Roscoe Pound (July 20, 1925), Roscoe Pound to A. Lawrence Lowell (July 22, 1925), and Roscoe Pound to Wilson M. Powell (November 24, 1926, January 11, 1927), ALL Records.

38. Quotations are from Ezra R. Thayer to Cornelius W. Wickersham (April 7, 1914), ALL Records. A. Lawrence Lowell, Annual Report of the President of Harvard University, 1922–23, 26–29; 1923–24, 27–29; "Commencement Gifts," *New York Times* (June 20, 1924); William Lawrence, *Memories of a Happy Life* (Boston, 1926), 417–420; Henry A. Yeomans, *Abbott Lawrence Lowell, 1856–1943* (Cambridge, MA, 1948), 252.

39. Pound, Annual Report of the Dean, 1923–24, 181–185; Lowell, Annual Report of the President, 1923–24, 15–16; 1924–25, 21–22; 1925–26, 23–24; Roscoe Pound to A. Lawrence Lowell (January 14, 1925) and Roscoe Pound to Charles H. Strong (December 13, 1925), ALL Records.

40. Roscoe Pound to Charles M. Hough (November 28, 1924), ALL Records. See Roscoe Pound to Julian W. Mack (November 26, 1924) and Roscoe Pound to John P. [Nields?] (November 28, 1924), ALL Records.

41. Roscoe Pound to Julian Mack (January 13, 1925), Roscoe Pound to Wilson M. Powell (June 19, 1925), and Jeremiah Smith Jr. to Roscoe Pound (August 15, 1925), ALL Records; Roscoe Pound, *The Harvard Law School: Its History, Its Development, Its Needs: A Projet* (New York, 1925).

42. A. Lawrence Lowell to Roscoe Pound (July 24, 1925), ALL Records.

43. Pound, *The Harvard Law School . . . A Projet,* 29. Another brief pamphlet gained some notoriety, but Pound's carried more weight. See "Memorandum concerning Plan for the Development of Harvard Law School" (March 30, 1926), John Price Jones Co. Records, 1919–1954, Harvard Business School Library Historical & Special Collections (hereafter cited as JPJ Records); "Socializing Legal Education," *New Republic* (April 14, 1926), 211–213; Mary Ann Dzuback, *Robert M. Hutchins: Portrait of an Educator* (Chicago, 1991), 50–51.

44. Wilson M. Powell to Roscoe Pound (June 1, 1925), ALL Records. See Wilson M. Powell to Roscoe Pound (March 7, 1925), Joseph P. Cotton to Roscoe Pound (March 2, 1925), and Wilson M. Powell to Roscoe Pound (March 18, 1925), ALL Records; Ramchandani, "The Stalling Effort," 19–22.

45. Roscoe Pound to James F. Byrne (May [5?], 1925) and Roscoe Pound to Wilson M. Powell (May 5, 1925), ALL Records. See Ramchandani, "The Stalling Effort," 13–16.

46. Edgar H. Wells to John B. Atkins (November 28, 1919), Records of the Harvard Endowment Fund, 1916–1939, Harvard University Archives (hereafter cited as HEF Records). See William Lawrence, "An Invigorating Avocation," *Atlantic Monthly* 132 (September 1923): 322, reprinted as "Way to Get Money Is to Go Out and Get It," *Boston Globe* (September 9, 1923).

47. Joseph Warren to H. J. Thorkelson (November 14, 1925) and Roscoe Pound to Edgar V. Frothingham (April 5, 1926), ALL Records.

48. Roscoe Pound to Wilson M. Powell (April 15, 1926), ALL Records. See "Harvard Asks $5,000,000 for Law Research," *New York Herald Tribune* (April 1, 1926); "Law Reform Fund Urged by Harvard," *New York World* (April 1, 1926); "$5,000,000 Law Fund Asked," *New York City Post* (April 1, 1926); "Dean Pound Outlines Law's Weaknesses and Its Needs," *Christian Science Monitor* (April 3, 1926); "As a Science," *Boston Daily Globe* (April 2, 1926); "Harvard Fund Committee: Leaders Are Named for Law School Endowment Campaign," *New York Times* (April 3, 1926).

49. H. J. Thorkelson to Roscoe Pound (March 5, 1926), ALL Records.

50. See Ramchandani, "The Stalling Effort," 23–31; Kimball, "Charity, Philanthropy," 270–273.

51. "Survey and Plan of Fund-Raising for Harvard University Law School Endowment Fund" (June 24, 1926), 2–7, and "Daily Reports" and "Weekly Reports," JPJ Records.

52. Quotations are from Robert F. Duncan, "Situation Reports" (September 17 and October 30, 1926), JPJ Records.

53. "Harvard Law School Fund Drive Opened," *Boston Globe* (November 2, 1926). See "Opening of the Campaign to Raise Five Million Dollars for the Harvard Law School. Addresses Made at Dinners in Boston and New York," *Harvard Alumni Bulletin* (November 25, 1926), supplement; Law School Endowment Funds, Leaflets, Processed Material, etc., 1926, Harvard University Archives; Harvard University Law School Endowment Fund Dinners, Speakers Sources, JPJ Records. Sutherland suggests that a public controversy arising at the New York dinner on November 9 detracted from the campaign. The brochure for the dinner quoted Chief Justice William H. Taft, an honored guest,

saying "the administration of criminal law in the United States is a disgrace to civilization." Taft said that attributing the quotation to him as Chief Justice was "most unfair." Arthur E. Sutherland, *The Law at Harvard: A History of Ideas and Men, 1817–1967* (Cambridge, MA, 1967), 265–269. But there is no evidence demonstrating any impact.

54. Quotation is from Wilson M. Powell to Roscoe Pound (January 31, 1927), ALL Records. See Subscription Register, HEF Records; "Many Graduates Give $1000 or More," *Boston Globe* (December 18, 1926); Ramchandani, "The Stalling Effort," 40–41.

55. Wilson M. Powell, to A. Lawrence Lowell (March 2 and April 25, 1927), ALL Records. This was the $100,000 gift from Rockefeller to which Frankfurter referred, as described in Chapter 2.

56. Lowell, Annual Report of the President, 1926–27, 5–6, 22–23; Pound, Annual Report of the Dean, 1926–27, 185.

57. Sutherland, *The Law at Harvard*, 270. See Yeomans, *Abbott Lawrence Lowell*, 238.

58. Letter to Harvard Law School community by Wilson M. Powell (n.d.), JPJ Records; "Harvard University Law School Endowment Fund Final Report, as of July 10, 1927," JPJ Records.

59. Quotation is from Pound, "The Law School, 1817–1929," 506. See "Harvard University Law School Endowment Fund Final Report," 1–4; Roscoe Pound to Wilson M. Powell (April 27, 1927), ALL Records; Lowell, Annual Report of the President, 1924–25, 7–8; 1926–27, 6.

60. Roscoe Pound to Edgar H. Wells (August 13, 1927), ALL Records.

61. Annual Report of the Treasurer of Harvard University, 1914–15, 104–132; 1924–25, 240–278; 1929–30, 267–311. The endowment for the Law School is computed by summing separate sections for the school, library funds, and scholarship funds. The 1930 figure includes a 10 percent write-up in the book value of Endowment Funds as of June 30, 1930, which was reversed in 1939. Annual Report of the Treasurer of Harvard University, 1938–39, 333.

62. Schlegel, *American Legal Realism*, 16–17. In the mid and late 1920s Yale Law School received a number of significant gifts, a large share of the bequest to the university from John W. Sterling, and a portion of the $20 million endowment fund drive that the university conducted. Thomas W. Swan, Annual Report of the Dean of Yale Law School, 1923–24, 105; 1925–26, 113; "798 Degrees granted by Yale University," *New York Times* (June 19, 1924); George P. Day, Annual Report of the Treasurer of Yale University, 1925–26, 21; 1926–27, 24; 1927–28, 31; Robert M. Hutchins, Annual Report of the Dean of Yale Law School, 1926–27, 116; 1928–29, 118; Charles E. Clark, Annual Report of the Dean of Yale Law School, 1929–30, 153.

63. Quotation is from [Robert F. Duncan,] "A New Force in American Society, Fifty Years of Dynamic Philanthropy, Final Master Copy" (October 9, 1969), 24, JPJ Records. See "Harvard University Law School Endowment Fund Final Report," 1–4.

64. Sutherland, *The Law at Harvard*, 261; Yeomans, *Abbott Lawrence Lowell*, 252–253; Seymour Harris, *Economics of Harvard* (New York, 1970), 278; Hull, *Roscoe Pound*, 149–150,

156, 161; Erwin N. Griswold, *Ould Fields, New Corne: The Personal Memoirs of a Twentieth Century Lawyer* (St. Paul, MN, 1992), 158.

65. Felix Frankfurter to Thomas N. Perkins (April 27 and May 11, 1927), Felix Frankfurter Papers, 1900–1965, HLSLib; Julian W. Mack to Roscoe Pound (September 28, 1927), ALL Records; A. Lawrence Lowell to Thomas W. Lamont (October 30, 1919), ALL Records. See Ramchandani, "The Stalling Effort," 47.

66. Quotations are from W. R. Hauslaib to Robert F. Duncan (March 15, 1927), JPJ Records. See Powell to Pound (January 31, 1927); *Harvard University Law School Endowment Fund Committee, Bulletin No. VII to Regional and Local Chairmen* (December 11, 1926), 3, Records of the Harvard Law Endowment Fund, 1926–1938, Harvard University Archives.

67. Quotations are from Duncan "Situation Reports" (February 1 and April 1, 1927).

68. Pound, Annual Report of the Dean, 1923–24, 186. See Yeomans, *Abbott Lawrence Lowell*, 252–253.

69. Pound to Lowell (December 11, 1916).

70. Pound, Annual Report of the Dean, 1926–27, 185–186.

71. Swan, Annual Report of the Dean, 1923–24, 124. See Lowell, Annual Report of the President, 1925–26, 23–24.

72. Quotations are from Roscoe Pound to Frank W. Grinnell (April 13, 1916); Pound, *The Harvard Law School*, 16. See Pound, Annual Report of the Dean, 1915–16, 145; 1923–24, 185; 1924–25, 180; Pound to Lowell (December 11, 1916); Pound, *The Harvard Law School . . . A Projet*, 23; *Centennial History*, 173; Lowell, Annual Report of the President, 1923–24, 15–16.

73. Pound, *The Harvard Law School . . . A Projet*, 20, 23, 29.

74. Edward H. Warren, "Harvard Law School Outlook in November, 1941," in *Spartan Education* (Boston, 1911), 56, 58–59.

75. Pound, *The Harvard Law School . . . A Projet*, 21–22.

76. Thayer, "The Teaching of English Law," 174.

77. See Pound to Powell (January 11, 1927); Roscoe Pound to Julian Mack (January 11, 1927), ALL Records.

78. "Survey and Plan of Fund-Raising," 21, 7.

79. "Harvard Law School Fund Drive Opened."

80. Emphasis in original. Mr. Lohrke, "Memorandum Report on Developing the Human Angle of the Harvard Law School Endowment Fund" [November 1926], JPJ Records.

81. See Harvard University Law School Endowment Fund News Releases and Magazine Articles, vol. 51, JPJ Records.

82. *For the Safety of the Citizen and the Protection of Business: A plan to eliminate from the administration of justice in this country many elements of delay, waste, friction, and uncertainty which are threatening the general security and hampering commerce and industry.* (New York, [April] 1927]), JPJ Records. The final pamphlet conflated nine separate publications that had originally been planned.

83. "Standard Practice for Harvard Law Account" (December 29, 1926), JPJ Records.

84. Here and below, the quotations are drawn from *For the Safety of the Citizen,* 9–11, 13–15, 21, 24.

85. Sutherland, *The Law at Harvard,* 264. See similar language in "Survey and Plan of Fund-Raising," 7.

86. Pound, Annual Report of the Dean, 1925–26, 185.

87. Annual Report of the Treasurer of Harvard University, 1939–40, 68–71.

88. Lowell, Annual Report of the President, 1924–25, 7–8; 1926–27, 6; Pound, Annual Report of the Dean, 1923–24, 181–5; 1925–26, 186; Griswold, Annual Report of the Dean, 1947–1948, 390.

89. Harvard Law School Catalog, 1927–28, 87; Lowell, Annual Report of the President, 1927–28, 21; Griswold, Annual Report of the Dean, 1947–48, 390.

90. Annual Report of the Treasurer of Harvard University, 1924–25, 57–59. These figures exclude current gifts and sundry sources of $9,000.

91. Annual Report of the Treasurer of Harvard University, 1929–30, 59–61. These figures exclude current gifts and sundry sources of $63,000.

92. Edmund Morgan to James B. Conant, "Memorandum for President Conant regarding the Admissions Policy of the Harvard Law School, 1936–37," quoted in Duncan Farthing-Nichol, "A Desirable Discontent: Dean James M. Landis at Harvard Law School" (student research paper, Harvard Law School, 2012), on file with the authors, 33.

93. Edward H. Warren to James B. Conant (November 24, 1941), quoted in Farthing-Nichol, "A Desirable Discontent," 37.

94. Griswold, Annual Report of the Dean, 1947–48, 390.

95. James M. Landis, Annual Report of the Dean of Harvard Law School, 1937–38, 197. See Pound, Annual Report of the Dean, 1931–32, 205; 1932–33, 215; Farthing-Nichol, "A Desirable Discontent," 29.

96. Pound, Annual Report of the Dean, 1926–27, 192; George M. Calhoun and Catherine Delamere, *A Working Bibliography of Greek Law* (Cambridge, MA, 1927).

97. Guy Emerson to Thomas W. Lamont (January 9, 1919), HEF Records.

CHAPTER SIX

Legal Realism and Pound's Decline, 1928–1931

The Great Depression overturned long-standing and fundamental economic, legal, and political assumptions in America. At the same time, the popular image of Harvard Law School shifted from being a hotbed of jurisprudential and political radicalism to a bastion of conservatism. Often citing Ralph Nader (LL.B. 1958), later criticism of the Law School's supposed conservatism generally overlooked this historical shift and the complicated reasons behind it.[1] In fact, the school had, since its founding in 1817, oscillated between conservatism and radicalism in politics, pedagogy, and jurisprudence: Cotton Whigs, Conscience Whigs, and abolitionists; didactic and Socratic teaching; hiring based on professional experience or academic merit; and then "logical" versus "sociological" jurisprudence.

To understand the shift in perception that occurred in the early 1930s, it is necessary to address legal theory, because jurisprudential swordplay, often involving Dean Roscoe Pound (1916–1936), began to define the school. The specific issue was the relationship between "sociological jurisprudence" and "legal realism." The two views were essentially alike in emphasizing that social and economic factors influence judicial decisions, and that legislation deserves as much deference as judicial precedent in deciding cases. Yet the relationship between the two became the subject of heated controversy in the second quarter of the twentieth century—largely because the former was identified with Harvard, and the latter with its rivals, Columbia and Yale. Defining and distinguishing these two views eventually became a parlor game for scholars in the last quarter of the twentieth century. Consequently, this chapter discusses both the historical controversy and its subsequent interpretation.

In 1930 and 1931 the historical controversy culminated in an acrimonious, intellectual duel between Pound and Karl Llewellyn, the "young Turk" of legal realism on the Columbia law faculty. Their sparring ended with Llewellyn's final thrust in his famous article "Some Realism about Realism."[2] At stake in the joust was not merely honor, though both Pound and Llewellyn relished intellectual combat. The fundamental question was whether and how the American legal system could contribute to solving modern social and economic inequalities, rather than reinforcing them.[3]

Roots of Realism at Harvard

Scholars have marveled that Roscoe Pound—who had earned a Ph.D. in botany, studied just one year at Harvard Law School, and held such unorthodox views—could be appointed to the Law School faculty so quickly after his emergence on the national stage. Just four years separated his signal ABA address in 1906 and his appointment as Story Professor of Law in 1910. The speed of the appointment revealed as much about the intellectual milieu at Harvard as it did about Pound's talent.

That milieu has often been misunderstood. Many scholars have claimed that Harvard Law School was the citadel of "Langdellian formalism," and that legal realism arose from an independent intellectual tradition at other law schools, particularly Columbia and Yale.[4] The former jurisprudence, known more generally as "classical formalism" or "classical legal thought," predominated in the late nineteenth century. Classical formalism neglected policy and the social consequences of legal decisions and focused narrowly on logical inferences based on hierarchically ordered, binary categories derived from received legal doctrine and decisions of cases.[5] For example, this thinking underlay a series of decisions in which the U.S. Supreme Court viewed a worker at a large industrial corporation essentially like an individual craftsman negotiating the price of a job with an individual homeowner, and the court overturned legislation protecting such workers' health and safety on the grounds that it violated their freedom of contract. Justice Oliver W. Holmes Jr. (LL.B. 1866) issued a landmark dissent to this reasoning in *Lochner v. New York* (1905).[6]

But later study of exemplary nineteenth-century Harvard "formalists" revealed that their thinking was often more nuanced and did not quite fit this category.[7] While that fact might suggest Harvard's receptivity to Pound's sociological jurisprudence, it also appeared that prominent faculty in the *next* generation at Harvard Law School—Joseph Beale (LL.B. 1887), Edward "Bull"

Roscoe Pound, Faculty 1913–1947, Dean 1916–1936. Photographed at his round desk, 1934.

Courtesy of Louis Fabian Bachrach.

Warren (LL.B. 1900), Warren Seavey (LL.B. 1904), and Austin Scott (LL.B. 1909)—subscribed to a thoroughly formalistic and mechanical jurisprudence. Hence, Harvard's commitment to classical formalism was actually stronger in the early twentieth century than it had been under Dean Christopher Langdell (1870–1895). The questions therefore remain why the Law School enthusiastically recruited Pound and why he chose to go to Cambridge in 1910 despite having received competing offers from other institutions. The answer is that leading jurisprudents from Harvard had already endorsed central ideas of legal realism.

To begin, there was Oliver W. Holmes Jr. Though an early critic of the Law School in the 1860s, he maintained a close affiliation with the school throughout his career. He taught as a lecturer on Jurisprudence from 1871 to 1873 and as Weld Professor in 1882, and in 1886 and 1895, delivered addresses at important convocations of the Harvard Law School Association, for which he served as vice president or president during the 1900s.[8] Throughout his tenure on the U.S. Supreme Court, beginning in 1902, he recruited his law clerks from the Law School.

Most historians of legal realism, no matter how they define it, attribute its American origins to Holmes's treatise *The Common Law* (1881), particularly its famous opening lines:

> The life of the law has not been logic: it has been experience. The felt necessities of the time, the prevalent moral and political theories, intuitions of public policy, avowed or unconscious, even the prejudices which judges share with their fellow man, have had a good deal more to do than the syllogism in determining the rules by which men should be governed.[9]

In 1897 Holmes elaborated this view in a speech entitled "The Path of the Law" delivered at Boston University School of Law. Holmes asserted that "judges themselves have failed adequately to recognize their duty of weighing considerations of social advantage" enjoyed by "the comfortable classes of the community . . . who no longer hope to control the legislatures [and] look to the courts as expounders of the Constitutions."[10] In 1905 he applied this approach in his famous dissent in *Lochner v. New York,* arguing that the Constitution "is made for people of fundamentally differing views, and the accident of our finding certain opinions natural and familiar or novel and even shocking ought not to conclude our judgment upon the question whether statutes embodying them conflict with the Constitution."[11]

Holmes was not the only prominent figure associated with Harvard Law School whose thinking informed that of Pound and, eventually, legal realism. Professor James Thayer (LL.B. 1856), who taught Constitutional Law, profoundly influenced Pound during his year of study at the school in 1889–90. Three years after Pound left the school, Thayer published "The Origin and Scope of the American Doctrine of Constitutional Law," a landmark article arguing that the judiciary must defer to the legislature if social reform is to be achieved. In Thayer's view, "a pedantic and academic treatment of the texts of the constitution and the laws" threatened what was really necessary to make progress—namely, a "combination of a lawyer's rigor with a statesman's breadth of view."[12] Not only did Thayer's 1893 article attack what Pound later derogated as "mechanical jurisprudence," it anticipated Holmes's "Path of the Law" in 1897 and his dissent in *Lochner.* Holmes's writings and Pound's ABA address of 1906 and his "Liberty of Contract" (1909) were more radical, but the seeds were planted by Thayer in 1893.

Another, perhaps surprising, proto-realist influence on Pound was his favorite professor during 1889–90: John C. Gray (LL.B. 1861). Scholars have traditionally associated Gray "with a rigid view of the law" and "legal formalism," while pointing to his *Rule against Perpetuities* (1886).[13] But it has recently been shown that this treatise "connects the law to public policy" and makes "a policy-driven analysis of law cabined by a respect for precedent."[14] In 1909 Gray published his most famous "sociological" work, *The Nature and Sources of the Law.* This treatise rejects the traditional view of William Blackstone's *Commentaries on the Laws of England* that judicial decisions are based on natural law, "general custom," or supposedly original and permanent meanings of written texts. Instead, Gray declared, rulings reflect "the free action of the judicial mind, affected by ideas of public policy, by popular custom, and by professional opinion."[15] These words clearly anticipate Pound's views, as well as legal realism.

While Gray was preparing *The Nature and Sources of the Law* in 1908, Louis Brandeis (LL.B. 1877) was writing his famous brief in the U.S. Supreme Court case *Muller v. Oregon* (1908), which resonated with the views of Holmes and Pound. Relying on voluminous sociological and economic data and emphasizing the socioeconomic position of the parties and the social consequences of the decision, this "Brandeis Brief" exemplified the approach to deciding cases that Pound advocated in his early writing. Their shared perspective reflected their similar backgrounds: both came from the Midwest, knew German scholarship, and learned from a great natural scientist (in Brandeis's case, the geologist Nathaniel S. Shaler). Each had also been a successful lawyer while also involved in state politics.[16]

Moreover, Brandeis maintained a close association with Harvard Law School. Throughout his career as an attorney and U.S. Supreme Court Justice, he, like Holmes, recruited his law clerks from the school. In addition, Brandeis consistently provided advice and aid to successive deans between his graduation in 1877 and his death in 1941.[17] Brandeis was thus another proto-realist associated with the Law School who embraced Pound's jurisprudence. After Pound joined the faculty, he and Brandeis rapidly became close, mutual supporters. Pound rallied to Brandeis's defense in the latter's confirmation battle for the U.S. Supreme Court in 1916, and Brandeis supported Pound when serving on the Harvard Board of Overseers.

Soon after Brandeis wrote the *Muller* brief, Gray *The Nature and Sources of the Law,* and Pound "Liberty of Contract," Ezra Thayer, the son of James Thayer, became dean of the Law School in 1910. Dean Thayer had extolled

Holmes's "Path of the Law" in 1897 and his dissent in *Lochner*, and praised Pound's "Liberty of Contract" in 1909.[18] Encouraged by Gray, Dean Thayer urged President A. Lawrence Lowell (1909–1933) to offer Pound a professorship. It is not surprising, then, that Pound left Chicago for Cambridge—the purported citadel of classical formalism—rather than for New Haven, New York, or elsewhere. Pound recognized Holmes, Gray, Brandeis, and James and Ezra Thayer as progenitors and allies at Harvard for the broad movement that he termed "sociological jurisprudence." But how exactly was that view related to legal realism?

Sociological Jurisprudence

Examining the relationship between sociological jurisprudence and legal realism begins with the simple fact that the former was personally associated with Pound, who named it. He first expressed his sociological views publicly in his bold 1906 address "The Causes of Popular Dissatisfaction with the Administration of Justice," delivered to the conservative ABA when he was the little-known dean of the University of Nebraska law school. In that provocative address, Pound announced that "comprehensive reform is needed" in the bench and bar, and he drew on the model of his graduate study in botany in applying scientific theory to legal practice.

In practical terms, the problem was that the American courts and lawyers were under a "yoke of commercialism." They served monied interests in order to help the wealthy win in "the modern American race to beat the law." But the problem was equally one of theory. Common-law jurisprudence assumed that legal principles favored no social class and that courts inferred their decisions logically from autonomous principles and precedents. This fictional neutrality of "common law dogmas . . . put [courts] in a false position of doing nothing and obstructing everything." In his home state of Nebraska, Pound observed that the judges were "organized on an antiquated system and their time is frittered away on mere points of legal etiquette." Obviously responding to the Supreme Court's decision in *Lochner*, issued the year before, Pound maintained that the courts presumed a theory of individual freedom and rights that ignored the scale and power of industrial and financial entities in modern society. Pound's solution was to undertake social scientific research addressing the urgent practical issues facing the American legal system, a page right from the manual on how botany could help the midwestern farmer.[19]

The 1906 ABA address was met with vehement criticism and called "an attack upon the entire remedial jurisprudence of America" by leaders of the bar. This response fundamentally misunderstood Pound's address, which rejected not the common law, but its perversion. Far from calling to eliminate appellate courts and codify the common law, as his critics alleged, Pound argued that judges can adapt past legal doctrine to present conditions, with the crucial help of law schools and the bar. By relying on the "scientific study of the law" and taking account of the social and economic situation of parties in cases, "our courts will be swift and certain agents of justice, whose decisions will be acquiesced in and respected by all."[20] Hence, the address also attracted support, even applause, from some legal scholars, particularly Dean John Wigmore (LL.B. 1887) of Northwestern University Law School, who lured Pound to Chicago and launched his national legal career.[21]

In the two years following his call for "comprehensive reform" of the law in 1906, Pound wrote an article analyzing the problematic, "mechanical" nature of the regnant jurisprudence and another article on "the need of sociological jurisprudence" to respond to the problem. In 1909 Pound published "Liberty of Contract," which aligned with Holmes's dissent in the *Lochner* decision and criticized the teaching in American law schools that contributed to such decisions. Throughout, Pound attacked Blackstone's *Commentaries* and its theory of law that ignored social and economic forces. This attack was later repeated by both legal realists and Critical Legal scholars.[22]

"Mechanical jurisprudence" regarded common-law doctrines as universal, eternal, and authoritative, and statutes as less legitimate, particularly those "growing out of new conditions in business and industry." In fact, even in Constitutional challenges to statutes, this "mechanical" view led "judges to try statutes by the measure of common law doctrines rather than by the Constitution."[23] "Mechanical" jurisprudence ignored the "new conditions," retarded social progress, and blinded judges to unjust outcomes. As Pound elsewhere wrote, "We have developed so minute a jurisprudence of rules, we have interposed such a cloud of minute deductions between principles and concrete cases, that our case-law has become ultra-mechanical, and is no longer an effective instrument of justice if applied with technical accuracy."[24]

To address these problems, Pound proposed a "sociological jurisprudence," which he defined succinctly in 1909:

The sociological movement in jurisprudence [is] the movement for pragmatism as a philosophy of law, the movement for the adjustment of principles and doctrines to the human conditions they are to govern rather than to assumed first principles, the movement for putting the human factor in the central place and relegating logic to its true position as an instrument.[25]

Relating sociological jurisprudence to the *Lochner* decision, Pound presented social and economic data about the terrible and coercive working conditions of laborers in contemporary American industries. Employing a "mechanical" mode of reasoning, the majority opinion struck down legislation to remediate those conditions. Such "mechanical" reasoning neglected those real-world conditions by assuming that each worker had individual autonomy and, therefore, the liberty to choose to engage in an employment contract in principle. This traditional, common-law reasoning was deeply embedded in American legal education and legal history. "More than anything else, [judges'] ignorance of the actual situations of fact for which legislation was provided and [judges'] supposed lack of legal warrant for knowing them, have been responsible for the judicial overthrowing of so much social legislation," he concluded.[26] In Pound's view, the "best exposition" of sociological jurisprudence to that point was found in Holmes's "Path of the Law" in 1897 and his dissent in *Lochner*.[27]

In 1909 Pound elaborated sociological jurisprudence in another article, "Law in Books and Law in Action." Like his 1906 address to the ABA, this essay argued that the reasoning of the *Lochner* decision was merely a symptom of an American justice system based on "social, economic, and political thinking" that was hopelessly outdated. That system was still wedded to notions of individualism and personal autonomy that may have been valid in a prior century, but could not accommodate the conditions and problems associated with industrialization and a complex economy. Pound believed that judges and lawyers could solve this problem "not by futile thunderings against popular lawlessness, nor eloquent exhortations to obedience of the written law, but by making the law in the books such that the law in action can conform to it, and providing a speedy, cheap and efficient legal mode of applying it."[28]

In his concluding paragraph, the high point of his early judicial insights and—many would argue—his entire legal writing, Pound pointed the way to a progressive legal future, when lawyers and law professors would no longer be "legal monks" studying only the common law. Instead, they would recognize the need to wed legal doctrine with the social sciences and to reject "the notion that the common law is the beginning of wisdom and the eternal jural order." Pound urged, "Let us not be afraid of legislation, and let us welcome new principles, introduced by legislation, which express . . . the facts of human conduct in the face. Let us look to economics and sociology and philosophy, and cease to assume that [common-law] jurisprudence is self-sufficient."[29]

Roscoe Pound and Legal Realism

While sociological jurisprudence was closely associated with Roscoe Pound, legal realism was a broad jurisprudential movement that emerged in the 1920s and 1930s. Since that time, scholars have debated the meaning of "legal realism."[30] Some have defined it in explicitly "narrow" terms, as engaging in "empirical legal research" on "the workings of the legal system."[31] Others have adopted a "generous" definition: "The heart of the movement was an effort to define and discredit classical legal theory and practice and to offer in their place a more philosophically and politically enlightened jurisprudence. All of the lawyers, judges, and legal scholars who contributed to that project should . . . be considered Realists."[32]

This "generous" definition certainly comprehends the writing of Holmes and Pound. Even when defined in "narrow" terms, legal realists' pursuit of empirical research was clearly anticipated by Pound's sociological jurisprudence and by the work of Holmes, Thayer, Gray, and Brandeis, who argued that legal doctrine was shaped by extralegal forces that judges and lawyers pretended to ignore. These proto-realists attracted Pound to Cambridge in 1910.

But various scholars have devalued Pound's contribution. Their view is that "legal realism" originated at Columbia and Yale, not at Harvard with all its "Langdellian formalists." These scholars have leveled three charges discounting Pound's sociological jurisprudence and distinguishing it from legal realism. The first is that Pound "was more an advocate than a practitioner of sociological jurisprudence." Despite "urging examination of the interaction between law and society through empirical studies grounded in the social sciences, he did not undertake such studies himself."[33] Paradoxically, "like the legal scholars he frequently criticized, Pound . . . remained a 'legal monk.'"[34]

But this first gambit misses the mark in several respects. For one thing, many self-described realists did not conduct empirical studies, so this charge does not actually distinguish them from Pound.[35] In addition, Pound carried a much heavier workload than nearly all realist scholars. While administering Harvard Law School during World War I and two major fundraising drives, defending his faculty against attacks from within and without the university, and teaching more courses than any of the regular faculty, Dean Pound had little time for empirical research. Even so, he did serve on the Wickersham Commission, which Congress authorized in 1929 to gather evidence and investigate the social effect of the statutes implementing Prohibition. This responsibility amounted to putting sociological jurisprudence into practice.[36]

Also, this first charge overlooks Pound's support for, organization of, and collaboration in empirical studies. The initial such study was the famous Cleveland crime survey. Sheldon and Eleanor Glueck and Felix Frankfurter (LL.B. 1906) did the bulk of the research and writing between 1920 and 1922, but Pound was instrumental, because his reputation and interest prompted the Cleveland Foundation to commission the Law School to do the study. The Cleveland study then led to an even more ambitious project in 1926, the "Survey of Crime and Criminal Justice in Greater Boston," supported by the Rockefeller Foundation and the Harvard Corporation through the auspices of Pound. Initially directed by Frankfurter, this huge project was overseen by Pound's appointee, Sheldon Glueck, while his wife, Eleanor, did much of the research.[37]

The Gluecks' first major report, *Five Hundred Criminal Careers,* was based on a study of former inmates of the Massachusetts Reformatory for Men, whose recidivism rate shattered the conventional belief that imprisonment deterred criminals from future wrongdoing. In 1934 the Boston survey issued three more groundbreaking volumes: *One Thousand Juvenile Delinquents, Crime and Criminal Statistics in Boston,* and *Police Administration in Boston.*[38] Though never completed, the mammoth project was truly sociological jurisprudence in action, and demonstrated "the responsibility of universities for research into these problems of human conduct and social policy," as Frankfurter remarked.[39]

In addition, Pound supported other empirical, legal studies, such as the pioneering research in international law conducted by Professor Manley Hudson (LL.B. 1910, S.J.D. 1919). Hudson's work assisted the League of Nations, though the United States was not a member, by providing both the empirical background and legal expertise for drafting conventions on everything from territorial waters to diplomatic privileges, piracy, and nationality law. Consequently, Pound was not cloistered, like a legal monk, from empirical research between 1920 and 1934. Indeed, this record of involvement in and support for completed empirical research overshadows that of the deans at Columbia or Yale law schools during this period.

The second charge discounting Pound's sociological jurisprudence and distinguishing it from legal realism is that Pound was so deeply committed to

the school's traditional pedagogy and curriculum that he did nothing to reform legal education in line with a sociological or realist agenda during his
twenty years as dean.[40] But this claim misunderstands Pound's strategy for reforming legal education. Because Pound's academic training occurred in the
collegial, research-oriented world of the arts-and-sciences Ph.D., he saw
graduate programs as the best means to invigorate "undergraduate" LL.B. education, to prompt empirical "sociological" research by the faculty, and to
train such scholars and teachers for the future.

Pound's approach already prevailed in leading American medical schools at
Johns Hopkins, Columbia, Harvard, Cornell, and Michigan, which had instituted a rigorous fundamental curriculum of terminology and basic concepts
followed by residency and research. As old as Francis Bacon's *scala studiorum,*
this approach does not value doctrine more than practical experience, but instead sequences the academic foundation before clinical training. Furthermore, the clinical residency that emerged in medical education between 1910
and 1930 incorporated research and advanced graduate education beyond the
M.D., just as Pound envisioned in law.[41]

Given Pound's strategy of reforming LL.B. studies by instituting graduate
education, he was naturally attracted to Dean Thayer's offer to shape the
school's new S.J.D. program.[42] This opportunity perfectly suited Pound's approach to reforming legal education based on sociological jurisprudence. He
believed that reform must begin at the top, with advanced, graduate education open only to those with a strong B.A. and an LL.B. from a university law
school. For twenty years Dean Pound's annual reports emphasized the importance of graduate work and the need to allocate resources for graduate legal
study. The goal was to cross-pollinate the traditional curriculum with faculty
who had completed graduate study in economics, sociology, and political science. Without such faculty, redesigning the LL.B. course of study, as Columbia
attempted to do in the 1920s, would accomplish nothing. But with proper
faculty, reform of LL.B. education was inevitable. By the same token, Pound
rejected the creation of a separate "School of Jurisprudence" for the graduate
program—as Yale envisioned in the 1910s and then Columbia in the 1920s—
precisely because "such a school [would be] divorced from the living law
taught in the professional curriculum."[43]

The original graduate subjects included three of Pound's favorites—Roman
Law, jurisprudence, and legislation—plus administrative law, history of the
common law, statutory interpretation, patent law, and international law. In
1912 Pound's program graduated the first S.J.D.: Eldon R. James, who became

librarian and substantially built the library of the school. In 1923 Harvard's graduate program was divided into two degrees, the LL.M., designed for practitioners, and the S.J.D., for future law professors.[44]

In Pound's view, these degree programs provided the vehicle for assisting in real "research," as opposed to the "searches" done in legal sources at the LL.B. level. By 1924, students in the graduate program, who later became distinguished professors, were assisting Felix Frankfurter in his research for *Harvard Studies in Administrative Law*, including James Landis (LL.B. 1924, S.J.D. 1925), Henry M. Hart (LL.B. 1929, S.J.D. 1931), and Paul Freund (LL.B. 1931, S.J.D. 1932), as well as Edwin W. Patterson (S.J.D. 1920), who later directed the graduate program at Columbia. In 1928 the LL.M. and S.J.D. requirements were enhanced again, focusing even more sharply on research to improve the legal system. Admission to the S.J.D. required an LL.M. or three years' teaching experience, and the doctoral degree required a thesis presenting original research.[45]

As Gail Hupper has shown, these were radical changes in legal education at Harvard, even though the LL.B. curriculum remained the same until 1936, when Pound stepped down.[46] Guided by his own experience with German research and scholarship, and his training in that model as a Ph.D. student in botany, Pound believed that graduate students were the key to making the faculty an effective force for empirical, "sociological" research, and for training future scholars. One could argue that "Pound was an elitist, a top-down reformer" or misguided in his "graduate" strategy for infusing sociological jurisprudence in legal education.[47] But he had a clear vision for reforming legal education, which he vigorously pursued for twenty years as dean.

Llewellyn and Pound, 1930–1931

The third charge discounting sociological jurisprudence and distinguishing it from legal realism maintains that in the 1920s Dean Pound gradually abandoned sociological jurisprudence and its progressive, empirical approach, and that he instead became a defender of the conservative status quo. By this view, Pound's written exchange with Karl Llewellyn in 1930 and 1931 marked the clear turning point away from his earlier radicalism.

Pound's disaffection with realism evidently began in the early 1920s, when Pound visited Italy, according to Guido Calabresi, a later dean of Yale Law School whose relatives hosted Pound. During those visits to Italy, Pound "found that most of the serious scholars were pure formalists . . . because this was a defense against fascism: if the law could not change, you could fight fascist attempts to change the law," stated Calabresi in 2018. "Pound was shocked because he was at that time a legal sociologist, and the legal sociologists in Italy were fascist hacks. And Pound was scholar enough to recognize that and didn't like that."[48]

Pound's disaffection culminated in 1938 when he made "an abrupt about-face on the uses of administrative justice," in the words of historian Morton J. Horwitz (LL.B. 1967). Judge Jerome Frank asked at the time, "Can this be the same man" who wrote the radical treatises between 1906 and 1910?[49] Consequently, this third gambit—that Pound betrayed his realist roots—is substantially true, but does not negate the contribution of Pound or Harvard Law School to the intellectual foundation of realism.

The exchange between Pound and Llewellyn began in 1930 when an article appeared in the *Columbia Law Review* entitled "A Realistic Jurisprudence— The Next Step," hurling a number of barbs at Pound. The author was a thirty-seven-year-old Columbia law professor named Karl N. Llewellyn, one of the most remarkable figures in American legal academia.[50] Born to a puritanical family in Seattle in 1893, Llewellyn, whose parents were not German, learned German in high school after his family moved to Brooklyn, despite growing national resistance to teaching German. He then attended a *Realgymnasium* in Germany, becoming fluent in the language and learning to love the culture, like Pound.[51]

Returning to the United States, Llewellyn earned a B.A. at Yale College, and then went back to Europe in 1914 to study Latin, French, and law at the Sorbonne. When World War I began, he traveled to Germany, enlisted in the Prussian army, fought in the Battle of Ypres in November 1914, was wounded, and spent three months in a German military hospital. Awarded the Iron Cross (second class) upon his discharge from the army in 1915, he is thought to be the only American citizen ever to receive this honor. Llewellyn then returned to Yale, where he entered the law school in 1915.

As a veteran of the German army, he was ineligible to serve in the American army when the United States joined the war, and he found himself in a tiny, depleted law school class with excellent opportunities to engage some of Yale's brilliant young faculty, particularly Arthur L. Corbin and Wesley Hohfeld (LL.B. 1904). Graduating in 1918 at the top of his class, Llewellyn practiced law in New York until Yale Law School called him back to join the faculty in 1923. But his wife at the time was a graduate student at Columbia University, so he moved in 1924 to the law faculty there. In 1948–49, he taught as a visiting professor at Harvard Law School, which made the great mistake of not offering him a permanent position. In 1951 he moved to the University of Chicago Law School, where he spent the remainder of his career.

Llewellyn was sharp-witted, hard-drinking, and attractive, including to the brilliant Soia Mentschikoff, who later became his third wife and, in 1946, the first woman to teach at Harvard Law School. The young and combative Llewellyn loved intellectual swordplay. When "A Realistic Jurisprudence" appeared in 1930, many legal scholars considered Llewellyn the leading "young Turk" of legal realism, while discreetly overlooking his "drinking, sex life, and clashes with colleagues."[52]

In contrast, Roscoe Pound was at the height of his influence, regarded as the leading jurisprudent in America.[53] But he was also growing old, autocratic, and pompous, alienating former allies on the faculty. More than two decades had passed since his early radical articles, and he was increasingly perceived as moderating his views and accommodating powerful interests. Privately he remained committed to sociological jurisprudence, but this stance only raised questions about his integrity, because his public positions often contradicted his private views.[54]

Pound therefore fell into the trap set for him by Llewellyn's 1930 article. No matter how he responded, Pound was Goliath to Llewellyn's David.[55] The prudent course was to not respond, and there was no reason for Pound to do so. The article obviously reflected Llewellyn's experience at Yale and Columbia: he had no Harvard connection at that point and accepted many of Pound's views, including Pound's reductionist summary of the nineteenth-century schools of jurisprudence.[56] Much of Llewellyn's article actually echoed Pound's early radical writings.[57]

Moreover, the few barbed references to Pound were incidental. Llewellyn said that Pound was "a man partially caught in a traditional precept—thinking of an age that is passing." Here Llewellyn revealed his youth and lack of historical perspective, given that Pound had launched his own radical critique twenty-four years earlier, when Llewellyn was just thirteen years old. Also, in a footnote, Llewellyn observed that Pound's work had a "constant indeterminacy"—perhaps a fair observation of Pound's shifting positions, but unappreciative of Pound's decanal responsibilities and preeminent position in jurisprudence, which entailed some prudence and caution in public pronouncements.[58] The dean of American jurisprudence could have ignored the challenge. If he had, scarcely anyone would have read, or remembered, Llewellyn's largely derivative essay.

But, in Felix Frankfurter's words, the "pathetically vain" Pound always took umbrage at being corrected or challenged, especially by his juniors, and that "weakness" prompted Pound to respond forcefully.[59] This time, however, his loud rebuke did not fade away, as it had when he berated Erwin Griswold (LL.B. 1928, S.J.D. 1929) in the reading room of Langdell Hall in 1927 or Ernest Brown (LL.B. 1931) in the basement seminar room in 1931. Instead, Pound published his response in 1931 as "The Call for a Realist Jurisprudence" in the *Harvard Law Review,* a prominent and lasting forum for all to see.[60]

It was, almost explicitly, an old man's article, referring to "the call for a realist jurisprudence insistent on the part of our young teachers of law." Pound made a series of generalizations unsupported by evidence, unsound in analysis, and simply off-target. First, he accused "realists" of challenging the integrity of well-intentioned courts and lawmakers, who "by and large . . . are trying to do what they ought to do."[61] Ironically, this erroneous charge closely resembled the criticisms of his own 1906 ABA address, which had so offended Pound.

Next, he propounded a number of methodological accusations. Realists believed "in masses of figures as having significance in and of themselves" and "in the exclusive significance . . . of some one method," while they overemphasized modern schools of psychology. But Pound supplied no proof to support these charges. Finally, the "realist" analysis of legal doctrine, he said, myopically focuses "on the unique single case rather than on the . . . course of judicial behavior," and conceives "of law as a body of devices for the purposes of business instead of as a body of means toward general social ends."[62] This point was paradoxical. While accusing the realists of holding a reductionist view of law, Pound offered a reductionist version of their critique. Here and subsequently, he maintained that the realists viewed law as "simply a pious fraud to cover up decisions of cases according to personal inclinations" or "simply a pulling and hauling of interests with a camouflage of authoritative precepts" because, realists maintained, "there is nothing in the way of reason [in] back of the legal order."[63]

Pound concluded his response to Llewellyn on a conciliatory note: "Perhaps it is asking too much of any school of jurists to call upon them for so broad an outlook. But in the house of jurisprudence there are many mansions. There is more than enough room for all of us and more than enough work. If the time and energy expended on polemics were devoted to that work, jurisprudence would be more nearly abreast of its tasks."[64] But the damage was done. Pound's response was a hack job: unsupported, unsound, and misguided. Further, the tone was defensive and doubtful about legal realism, despite its origins in his own thinking and that of his Harvard forebears, as we have seen. The leading legal scholar in the nation disowned his offspring. It seemed that one jab by young Llewellyn had exploded Pound's *Hindenburg.*

The immediate result was a direct attack by Llewellyn in "Some Realism about Realism: Responding to Dean Pound," which the *Harvard Law Review* published in 1931, despite some reluctance by the editors until Pound, to his credit, urged them to do so. Llewellyn made mincemeat of Pound's generalizations. Creating his now-famous list of twenty "Real Realists," Llewellyn defined legal realism as "a movement in thought and work," and not "a group philosophy or program" or a "group credo of social welfare."[65] From that point, Pound's reputation as a legal scholar and intellectual started to decline.[66]

At the same time, Harvard Law School was recast as an opponent of legal realism and, by extension, a citadel of conservatism. Due to his role as dean and his unrivaled stature in American jurisprudence at the time, Pound personified the school, which, like him, lost its reputation as a hotbed of jurisprudential and political radicalism. In this way Pound ceded the field of progressive, theoretical innovation to Harvard's rivals, Columbia and Yale, which eagerly assumed leadership of the movement and claimed the mantle of its true and faithful originators. Hence, the third charge is substantially true: Pound did betray his own and Harvard's realist roots. But this accusation is beside the point because Pound's wayward shift does not negate the fact that the intellectual roots of realism are to be found at Harvard.

Realism at Columbia and Yale

Situated amid "the largest body of legal talent in the world," Columbia University Law School was "the frontier of legal scholarship during the 1920s" and the progenitor of legal realism.[67] In contrast to Pound's policy of reserving sociological jurisprudence for the graduate program, a group of self-styled "legal realists" at Columbia sought to infuse the LL.B. curriculum with policy and social sciences while organizing it along functional lines. This effort commenced in 1921 and 1922 with the appointments of Herman Oliphant, Noel T. Dowling, and Edwin Patterson, who had completed the S.J.D. at Harvard in 1920. Together with Columbia professor Underhill Moore, they began offering three new courses to third-year students in 1922: Trade Regulation, Industrial Relations, and Commercial Law. These courses "organized material according to social and economic problems instead of doctrine," and assigned a great deal of nonlegal and statutory materials.[68]

Columbia president Nicholas M. Butler initially supported the realists, mostly because he took every opportunity to depreciate Harvard University. In 1923 he explicitly took aim at Harvard Law School's imperium in legal education, charging that American law schools had "slavishly initiated the program of instruction and the methods of teaching followed in one or two of the older and more influential law schools." Reform "should no longer be delayed and Columbia University may render a distinct service by undertaking it."[69] In the same year, President Butler edged out the distinguished law school dean Harlan Stone, who later became Chief Justice of the U.S. Supreme Court. The legal realists then began to develop a new design for the Columbia curriculum organized around four functional relations of modern life: business relations, familial relations, communal-political relations, and law administration, which included legal procedure.[70]

By 1927 the Columbia realists had attracted more allies, including William O. Douglas, Karl Llewellyn, Leon Marshall—a nonlawyer and a scholar of political economy from the University of Chicago—and Hessel Yntema, who had completed the S.J.D. at Harvard in 1921. In 1928, after several years of discussion, the realists produced the *Summary of Studies in Legal Education by the Faculty of Law of Columbia University*, founded on two radical ideas. First, Columbia Law School should become a "community for scholars" and a genuine research institution, not merely a professional school. Second, "law could only be taught as an integral part of the social sciences." Accordingly, Columbia Law School should be divided into a "research school" and a "training school," the latter supported by LL.B. tuition.[71] This bifurcation contradicted Pound's belief in cross-pollination by creating a separate "School of Jurisprudence" within the law school.

But 1928 turned out to be the zenith of realism at Columbia. Though sympathetic to realism, Dean Huger W. Jervey became fed up with the extended faculty debates over the configuration and role of research and resigned, culminating five years of turnover in that office.[72] The realists naively believed that they had a firm ally in President Butler and that he would follow their counsel and appoint Oliphant as dean. But Butler was interested far more in maintaining his authority than in promoting legal realism. He also worried about the finances of the law school if Columbia deemphasized training lawyers for the New York bar. Butler therefore appointed a relative conservative, Young B. Smith, as dean.

This appointment "created an immediate uproar," according to Columbia historian Julius Goebel. The realists felt that "Butler's action was autocratic and in flagrant disregard of what they conceived to be the faculty's traditional prerogative." After a contentious meeting lasting all day and far into the night, many faculty were bitter, and most of the realist contingent defected. Yntema, Marshall, and Oliphant went to the newly founded Institute of Law at Johns Hopkins, designed by Walter Wheeler Cook to be a true research institution that did not train lawyers. Douglas left for Yale in 1928, followed two years later by Underhill Moore.[73]

Realism at Columbia Law School, along with the dream of a research School of Jurisprudence, faded after 1928. Only a few realists, most notably Llewellyn and Patterson, remained. The "extreme experimentalists" had left, and the remaining faculty and Dean Smith adopted a moderate view, believing that "the utility of social sciences [in legal studies] had been exaggerated."[74] Ironically, the Columbia realists scattered shortly before their own Llewellyn grabbed the scepter of progressive jurisprudence away from Roscoe Pound, the founder of sociological jurisprudence, in 1930. Yale then wrested it away from Columbia.

In New Haven, Arthur Corbin had paved the way when he joined the Yale law faculty in 1913. Corbin campaigned to raise academic standards and adopt case method teaching, which the Yale faculty had resisted, owing partly to envy of Harvard's reputation. In the 1910s, Dean Thomas Swan and Llewellyn's teachers—Hohfeld and Corbin—strengthened the interest in legal scholarship, although Hohfeld died in 1918. In the 1920s, Yale Law School hired some distinguished scholars but had difficulty retaining them. Walter Wheeler Cook, Karl Llewellyn, Edmund Morgan, and Leon Green, among others, taught at Yale briefly and then left for other law schools.[75]

Yale's emergence as a leading realist school commenced in 1927 when Robert M. Hutchins was appointed acting dean at the age of twenty-seven and helped to found and fund the Yale Institute of Human Relations. Named dean in 1929, Hutchins departed that same year to become president of the University of Chicago, and his departure cost Yale Law School some momentum, as the Institute of Human Relations shifted its focus from the law school to the medical school.[76] Even so, Dean Hutchins boosted legal realism during his brief tenure by supporting social scientific study, particularly the work of Professor Charles E. Clark.

In 1929 Yale Law School started to change its curriculum, and forged a joint program with Harvard Business School (after Pound had refused to collaborate with the latter). But the joint program withered in 1931, when an assistant professor at the business school refused a professorship at Yale Law School.[77] Nevertheless, Yale continued its curricular reform during the 1930s, while the stodgy Harvard faculty rebuffed significant reform.

Starting in their first year, Yale LL.B. students were exposed to a broader range of topics than those at Harvard or Columbia. By 1938 a first-year Yale law student had courses in contracts, procedure, torts, property, commercial bank credit, constitutional law, public control of business, agency, and introduction to law and the profession, as well as moot court and a seminar. Sometimes students studied the same subject with two different professors having different perspectives.[78] Yale also sought to develop legal research, following the lead of Dean Hutchins and his successor, Clark, who served until 1939 and supported both curricular reform and research. Though hampered by a number of factors, this effort produced "the high tide of exuberant legal realism," which crested at Yale Law School under Dean Clark in the late 1930s. The institutional relationship between Harvard and Yale Law Schools, and its subsequent history, are examined in Chapter 15. [79]

The Decline of Roscoe Pound

The controversial relationship between legal realism and sociological jurisprudence arising in the 1930s had therefore developed out of this background between 1906 and 1909. Building on the views of Holmes, Thayer, Gray, and Brandeis, Roscoe Pound produced radical, widely circulated writings on the "sociological movement in jurisprudence." These writings launched what Llewellyn called in 1931 the "movement in thought and work" of legal realism.[80] But Pound retreated during the 1920s, allowing first Columbia and then Yale to seize the initiative during the turbulent decade when legal realism began shaping American legal education.

These points were acknowledged in 1955 by Yale law dean Eugene V. Rostow, who recognized that "members of our faculty did not first formulate these ideas," which have "been variously labeled . . . 'legal realism,' 'the functional approach,' or a form of 'sociological' jurisprudence."[81] Likewise, Harvard law dean Erwin Griswold (1946–1967) wrote in 1987, "Dean Pound and his sociological jurisprudence . . . provided the foundations for legal realism and more recent developments in the area of legal thought."[82]

Due to Pound's retreat, Harvard Law School was depicted as conservative, even reactionary, after 1930, despite its emerging reputation as a seminary for New Dealers. In fact, the jurisprudence and teaching of the Harvard law faculty became sharply polarized by 1931. The division among faculty at the Law School "was *very* clear and *very* marked" even to students, as Professor Ernest Brown recalled. Dean Pound and Felix Frankfurter stood at either pole, and faculty members remarked openly on their feud. Out of some thirty regular faculty members, only four senior professors were loyal to Pound: Joseph Beale and Samuel Williston (LL.B. 1888), both over seventy, as well as Warren Seavey and Austin Scott. Those four anchored the "formalists" on the faculty. The "anti-formalists" numbered five: Frankfurter, Landis, Thomas Powell (LL.B. 1904), Edmund Morgan (LL.B. 1905), and George K. Gardner (LL.B. 1914).[83]

Students recognized the distinctive thinking of the latter five, and some sought out their courses, as did Ernest Brown, who attended the Law School from 1928 to 1931. At the time Brown did not associate these five teachers with "legal realism," a term that was still novel to students, he recalled. Nevertheless, their distinctive approach at Harvard was clear. Courses taught by the "formalists" reminded Brown of the medieval "scholasticism" that he had studied in the history department at Princeton. For example, many students "were very enthusiastic about Mr. Seavey's course in Torts. . . . As far as I was concerned, it was just word games." To pose a hypothetical starting with "'He was walking down the street with a tiger on a leash,' and so forth . . . just dismissed any question of reality. . . . Torts seemed to me a word game . . . it was almost purely doctrinal. . . . No concern with the social use of law."[84]

Acting Dean Morgan therefore advised Brown into courses with a different approach. One was Gardner's first-year Contracts. "I remember Gardner saying that . . . in Boston when World War I broke out, one of the great German liners was in Boston Harbor and remained there during the war" protected by law. "I found in Gardner's class . . . a concern about the structure of the community that lived by these laws." And Frankfurter "carried that to greater depths," said Brown.

Each day, students walked by the large collection of portraits of Supreme Court Justices hung on the walls of Langdell South. In his Public Utilities course, Frankfurter spent the first two weeks talking "about the people in the portraits. These were men who did significant things in the world." His approach reminded Brown positively of his history courses at Princeton "because this was melding . . . history with the law. These men in the Supreme Court were really people. They were not encyclopedias, and you couldn't just press a button and get this rule or that rule. There were dissents . . . Frankfurter developed the historical background and . . . the political situation at the time. . . . He was *the most* important teacher. He made the law what I ultimately understood it to be. He and Thomas Reed Powell."

Powell taught Constitutional Law and focused upon "the recent leading cases," particularly concerning "the Commerce Clause and the Fourteenth Amendment Due Process Clause," according to Brown. "Powell's classes were marked with his complete disrespect for the Supreme Court and most of its members, and he was highly critical of their opinions. . . . He was not speaking so much about a result, because, he said, when you get nine people together, . . . the answers tend to be something reasonable. His classes were devoted to tearing the opinions apart. . . . It was highly analytical but not just empty analysis of the legal problems . . . but very realistic" in analyzing the disputes.

The jurisprudential polarization of the faculty contributed to the loss of confidence in Dean Pound's judgment and courage in the face of pressure from President Lowell and the Corporation. The Katz and Margold affairs, the failure to take a public stance on Sacco and Vanzetti and on Chafee's trial at the Harvard Club, all damaged Pound's reputation among his own faculty. In addition, there was Pound's stubborn determination to isolate his genuinely radical ideas about sociological jurisprudence in a graduate curriculum, leaving the LL.B. program in the mold of Langdell and Ames.

In the early 1930s some of his colleagues began to consider him "irrational and strangely conservative."[85] Always controlling, Pound now "clung to every administrative detail, down to allocating toilet paper to the washrooms."[86] Neither the faculty at the time nor subsequent historians appreciated that the school was facing enormous financial problems that Pound himself had exacerbated, but refused to acknowledge publicly, and was trying to solve by pinching every penny and paying down the school's debt at an accelerated rate. In 1933, when President Lowell resigned at age seventy-eight to be replaced by James Conant (1933–1953), Pound's days as dean were numbered. His opposition to the New Deal and his flirtations with Nazi Germany further damaged his reputation, and he lost control of the school.

NOTES

1. See, for example, Ralph Nader, "Introduction," in Joel Seligman, *The High Citadel: The Influence of Harvard Law School* (Boston, 1978), xxiv; Marina N. Bolotnika, "The Purpose of Harvard Law School," *Harvard Magazine* (August 17, 2016), at http://harvardmagazine.com/2016/08/the-purpose-of-harvard-law-school.

2. Karl N. Llewellyn, "Some Realism about Realism—Responding to Dean Pound," *Harvard Law Review* 44 (1931): 1222–1264.

3. The literature on legal realism and these jurisprudential issues is voluminous. We are especially indebted to David Wigdor, *Roscoe Pound: Philosopher of Law* (Westport, CT, 1974); Laura Kalman, *Legal Realism at Yale, 1927–1960* (Chapel Hill, NC, 1986); William W. Fisher III, Morton J. Horwitz, and Thomas A. Reed, eds., *American Legal Realism* (New York, 1993); John Henry Schlegel, *American Legal Realism and Empirical Social Science* (Chapel Hill, NC, 1995); N. E. H. Hull, *Roscoe Pound and Karl Llewellyn: Searching for an American Jurisprudence* (Chicago, 1997).

4. Kalman, *Legal Realism at Yale,* 67–97.

5. Schlegel, *American Legal Realism,* 31.

6. *Lochner v. New York,* 198 U.S. 45 (1905). See Holmes's dissent, *Lochner,* 198 U.S. 45, at 74–76.

7. Stephen A. Siegel, "The Three Tenors of Classical Legal Thought: Joel Bishop, Francis Wharton, and John Chipman Gray," paper presented to the American Society for Legal History (October 2000); Bruce A. Kimball, "Langdell on Contracts and Legal Reasoning: Revising the Holmesian Caricature" *Law and History Review* 25 (2007): 345–399; Brian Z. Tamanaha, *Beyond the Formalist-Realist Divide: The Role of Politics in Judging* (Princeton, NJ, 2010).

8. Oliver W. Holmes Jr., "Oration," in *Report of the Organization and of the First General Meeting, 1886, Harvard Law School Association* (Boston, 1887), 29–42; Oliver W. Holmes Jr., "Oration," in *Report of the Ninth Annual Meeting at Cambridge, June 25, 1895, in Especial Honor of Christopher Columbus Langdell, Harvard Law School Association* (Boston, 1895), 60–61.

9. Oliver W. Holmes Jr., *The Common Law* (Boston, 1881), 1. See Daniel R. Coquillette and Bruce A. Kimball, *On the Battlefield of Merit: Harvard Law School, the First Century* (Cambridge, MA, 2015) (hereafter cited as *Battlefield of Merit*), 322, 323, 328, 394.

10. Oliver W. Holmes Jr., "The Path of the Law," *Harvard Law Review* 10 (1897): 467–468.

11. See *Lochner v. New York,* 198 U.S. 45 (1905), 76 (J. Holmes dissenting).

12. James B. Thayer, "The Origin and Scope of the American Doctrine of Constitutional Law," *Harvard Law Review* 7 (1893): 138, 156.

13. William P. LaPiana, *Logic and Experience: The Origin of Modern American Legal Education* (New York, 1994), 125. See Stephen A. Siegel, "John Chipman Gray: Legal

Formalism and the Transformation of Perpetuities Law," *University Miami Law Review* 36 (1982): 439–464.

14. Siegel, "Three Tenors of Classical Legal Thought," 40, 65; see n206. See Stephen A. Siegel, "Joel Bishop's Orthodoxy," *Law and History Review* 13 (1995): 223; Stephen A. Siegel, "John Chipman Gray and the Moral Basis of Classical Legal Thought," *Iowa Law Review* 86 (2001): 1513–1599; Lewis A. Grossman, "James Coolidge Carter and Mugwump Jurisprudence," *Law and History Review* 20 (2002): 577–629.

15. Quotations are from John Chipman Gray, *The Nature and Sources of the Law* (New York, 1909), 209, 220–222. During the nineteenth century, the standard beginning textbook for American law students was William Blackstone, *Commentaries on the Laws of England* (Oxford, 1765–1769), 4 vols. See *Battlefield of Merit*, chap. 2.

16. See Wigdor, *Roscoe Pound,* 193–194; *Muller v. Oregon,* 208 U.S. 412 (1908).

17. See *Battlefield of Merit,* 421, 445–448.

18. Roscoe Pound, "Liberty of Contract," *Yale Law Journal* 18 (1909): 464.

19. Quotations are from Roscoe Pound, "The Causes of Popular Dissatisfaction with the Administration of Justice," *Report of the Annual Meeting of the ABA* 29 (1906): 403–404, 414. See *Lochner v. New York,* 198 U.S. 45 (1905).

20. Pound, "Causes of Popular Dissatisfaction," 417. See Wigdor, *Roscoe Pound,* 127, 309.

21. Listening to Pound, Wigmore "had begun to feel a thrill of intent, a prognostication of praise. Here was something really comprehensive, yet practical." See John H. Wigmore, "Roscoe Pound's St. Paul Address of 1906: The Spark That Kindled the White Flame of Progress," *Journal of the American Judicature Society* 20 (February 1937): 178.

22. Roscoe Pound, "The Need of a Sociological Jurisprudence," *Green Bag* 19 (1907): 607–615; Pound, "Mechanical Jurisprudence," *Columbia Law Review* 8 (1908): 605–623; Pound, "Liberty of Contract." See Duncan Kennedy, "The Structure of Blackstone's Commentaries," *Buffalo Law Review* 28 (1979): 209–211, 381–382.

23. Quotations are from Pound, "Liberty of Contract," 465–466. This "ultra legal" approach to Constitutional challenge was, paradoxically, adopted by Holmes himself in his first dissent written as a Justice on the U.S. Supreme Court in the case of *Northern Securities Company v. United States,* 193 U.S. 197 (1904). See Bruce A. Kimball and R. Blake Brown, "When Holmes Borrowed from Langdell: The "Ultra Legal" Formalism and Public Policy of *Northern Securities* (1904)," *American Journal of Legal History* 45 (2001): 278–321.

24. Roscoe Pound, "Law in Books and Law in Action," *American Law Review* 44 (1910): 20.

25. Pound, "Liberty of Contract," 464. On Pound's relation to "sociological jurisprudence," see David M. Rabban, *Law's History: American Legal Thought and the Transatlantic Turn to History* (Cambridge, UK, 2013), 423–469.

26. Pound, "Liberty of Contract," 470.

27. Pound, "Liberty of Contract," 464. See Roscoe Pound, "Justice Holmes's Contributions to the Science of the Law," *Harvard Law Review* 34 (1921): 449–453.

28. Pound, "Law in Books," 36.

29. Pound, "Law in Books," 35–36. See Rabban, *Law's History,* 445.

30. William Twining, *Karl Llewellyn and the Realist Movement,* 2nd ed. (Cambridge, UK, 2012), 426n101; Schlegel, *American Legal Realism,* 2–7.

31. Schlegel, *American Legal Realism,* 8, 11, 21, 25.

32. Fisher, Horwitz, and Reed, "Introduction," *American Legal Realism,* xiii–xiv.

33. Quotations are from Thomas A. Green, "Freedom and Responsibility in the Age of Pound: An Essay on Criminal Justice," *Michigan Law Review* 93 (1995): 2012.

34. Rabban, *Law's History,* 469, quoting Pound's own terminology from "The Need of a Sociological Jurisprudence," 611–612.

35. See Schlegel, *American Legal Realism,* 1–8.

36. Arthur Sutherland, *The Law at Harvard: A History of Ideas and Men, 1817–1907* (Cambridge, 1967), 276–277.

37. Mary Beth Basile, "False Starts: Harvard Law School's Efforts toward Integrating Women into the Faculty, 1928–1981," *Harvard Journal of Law and Gender* 28 (2005), 145–147. Despite her central contribution, Eleanor Glueck remained in a subordinate position at the Law School, and she appeared in the index of the Roscoe Pound Papers only indirectly as "Glueck, Sheldon (*et ux*[ore])." The extensive contribution of Eleanor Glueck to legal scholarship is discussed in Chapter 16.

38. Sam Bass Warner Jr., *Crime and Criminal Statistics in Boston* (Cambridge, MA, 1934); Leonard V. Harrison, *Police Administration in Boston* (Cambridge, MA, 1934); Henry Ruth and Kevin R. Reitz, *The Challenge of Crime: Rethinking Our Responses* (Cambridge, MA, 2003), 15; Wigdor, *Roscoe Pound,* 241–245; Hull, *Roscoe Pound,* 154; Palma Paciocco, "*A Sound Recommendation,* Sheldon and Eleanor Glueck and the Project to Educate Correctional Administrators at Harvard Law School" (student research paper, Harvard Law School, 2012), on file with the authors, 4–14.

39. Felix Frankfurter, "Introduction," in Sheldon Glueck and Eleanor Glueck, *One Thousand Juvenile Delinquents* (Cambridge, MA, 1934), xii.

40. Rabban, *Law's History,* 469; Hull, *Roscoe Pound,* 37–39.

41. Kenneth M. Ludmerer, *Learning to Heal: The Development of American Medical Education* (Baltimore, 1985), 166–218; Ludmerer, *Let Me Heal: The Opportunity to Preserve Excellence in American Medicine* (New York, 2015), 17–116; Daniel R. Coquillette, "'The Purer Fountains': Bacon and Legal Education," in *Francis Bacon and the Refiguring of Early Modern Thought,* ed. J. R. Solomon and C. G. Martin (Aldershot, UK, 2005), 145–172.

42. Ezra R. Thayer to Roscoe Pound (April 11, 1910), Ezra Ripley Thayer Papers, 1882–1915, Harvard Law School Library Historical & Special Collections (HLSLib). See Harvard Law School Faculty Meeting Minutes (March 8, 1910); Ezra R. Thayer to Roscoe Pound (August 2, 1912), Roscoe Pound Papers, 1888–1964, HLSLib.

43. Roscoe Pound, Annual Report of the Dean, 1915–16, 141–142.

44. Gail J. Hupper, "The Rise of the Academic Doctorate in Law: Origins through World War II," *American Journal of Legal History* 49 (2007): 17–42.

45. Hupper, "Rise of the Academic Doctorate in Law," 43–46.

46. See Hupper, "Rise of the Academic Doctorate in Law," 17–42.

47. Quotation is from Hull, *Roscoe Pound,* 94.

48. Guido Calabresi, "Appendix: Transcript," in "Symposium: Legal Education in Twentieth-Century America," *Fordham Law Review* 87 (2018): 904.

49. Quotations are from Morton J. Horwitz, *The Transformation of American Law, 1870–1960: The Crisis of Legal Orthodoxy* (Oxford, 1992), 217, 219. See Jerome Frank, *If Men Were Angels* (New York, 1942), 338.

50. Karl N. Llewellyn, "A Realistic Jurisprudence—The Next Step," *Columbia Law Review* 30 (1930): 431–465. The following account draws upon Twining, *Karl Llewellyn and the Realist Movement,* 87–91.

51. The *Realgymnasium* was a secondary education institution that taught modern languages and the natural sciences, in contrast to the classical *Gymnasium* that taught Greek, Latin, and usually Hebrew.

52. Quotations are from William Twining, "Review, N. E. H. Hull, *Roscoe Pound and Karl Llewellyn: Searching for an American Jurisprudence," Law Quarterly Review* 115 (1999): 154; Hull, *Roscoe Pound,* 109. Soia Mentschikoff's later work at Harvard Law School is discussed in Chapter 13.

53. Fisher, Horwitz, and Reed, *American Legal Realism,* 50. See Hull, *Roscoe Pound,* 125–126.

54. Felix Frankfurter to Thomas Reed Powell (November 19, 1933), Thomas Reed Powell Papers, 1905–1955, HLSLib; Hull, *Roscoe Pound,* 39; Kalman, *Legal Realism at Yale,* 58; Wigdor, *Roscoe Pound,* 233, 239–240; James F. Clark, "The Harvard Law School Deanship of Roscoe Pound, 1916–1936" (student research paper, Harvard Law School, 1999), on file with the authors, sect. IV B.

55. Twining, "Review, N. E. H. Hull," 155.

56. Rabban, *Law's History,* 442–451.

57. Llewellyn, "A Realistic Jurisprudence," 434. The similarity to Pound's early work is striking.

58. Quotations are from Llewellyn, "A Realistic Jurisprudence," 435.

59. Quotations are from Frankfurter to Powell (November 19, 1933).

60. Roscoe Pound, "The Call for a Realist Jurisprudence," *Harvard Law Review* 44 (1931): 697–711.

61. Quotations are from Pound, "Call for a Realist Jurisprudence," 697, 700–702.

62. Quotations are from Pound, "Call for a Realist Jurisprudence," 700–702, 707–708.

63. Quoted in Kalman, *Legal Realism at Yale,* 57.

64. Pound, "Call for a Realist Jurisprudence," 711.

65. Karl N. Llewellyn, "Some Realism about Realism—Responding to Dean Pound," *Harvard Law Review* 44 (1931): 1234, 1256.

66. See Kalman, *Legal Realism at Yale,* 57; Rabban, *Law's History,* 470.

67. Quotations are from, respectively, Julius Goebel Jr., *A History of the School of Law: Columbia University* (New York, 1955), 339; Robert Stevens, *Law School: Legal Education in America from the 1850s to the 1980s* (Chapel Hill, NC, 1983), 137.

68. Kalman, *Legal Realism at Yale,* 67–69. See Goebel, *History of the School of Law,* 249–252, 265–273.

69. Nicholas M. Butler, Annual Report of the President of Columbia University, 1921–22, 27.

70. Goebel, *A History of the School of Law,* 249–252, 265–273; Kalman, *Legal Realism at Yale,* 70–71.

71. Herman Oliphant, "A Return to Stare Decisis," *ABA Journal* 14 (1928): 23. See Stevens, *Law School,* 138.

72. Harlan Stone announced his resignation in 1922, effective 1924. Acting dean Thomas I. Parkinson filed annual reports for 1923–24 and 1924–25, and no annual reports were filed for 1925–26 and 1926–27. About this turbulent period, loyal Columbia historian Goebel maintains that "the work of the Law School proceeded smoothly and effectively." Goebel, *A History of the School of Law,* 274.

73. Quotations are from Goebel, *A History of the School of Law,* 304, 305. See 302–304.

74. Quotations are from Goebel, *A History of the School of Law,* 312–313; Kalman, *Legal Realism at Yale,* 74–75.

75. Robert W. Gordon, "Professors and Policymakers: Yale Law School Faculty in the New Deal and After," in *History of the Yale Law School: The Tercentennial Lectures,* ed. Anthony T. Kronman (New Haven, CT, 2004), 81.

76. Gaddis Smith, "Politics and the Law School: The View from Woodbridge Hall, 1921–1963," in *History of the Yale Law School: The Tercentennial Lectures,* ed. Anthony T. Kronman (New Haven, CT, 2004), 139–140; Mary Ann Dzuback, *Robert M. Hutchins: Portrait of an Educator* (Chicago, 1991), 43–66; Roger L. Geiger, *To Advance Knowledge: The Growth of American Research Universities, 1900–1940* (New York, 1986), 149, 155–157.

77. Kalman, *Legal Realism at Yale,* 75–77, 256n37; Rakesh Khurana, *From Higher Aims to Hired Hands: The Social Transformation of American Business Schools and the Unfulfilled Promise of Management as a Profession* (Princeton, NJ, 2007), 113, 173; Jeffrey L. Cruikshank, *A Delicate Experiment: The Harvard Business School, 1908–1945* (Boston, 1987), 34, 54, 70–75, 136–143, 192.

78. Kalman, *Legal Realism at Yale,* 77.

79. Smith, "Politics and the Law School," 138, 140–141.

80. Quotations are from Pound, "Liberty of Contract," 464; Llewellyn, "Some Realism about Realism," 1234.

81. Eugene V. Rostow, Annual Report of the Dean of Yale Law School, 1954–1955, 8–9.

82. Erwin N. Griswold, "Essays Commemorating the One Hundredth Anniversary of the *Harvard Law Review:* Introduction," *Harvard Law Review* 100 (1987): 730.

83. Kalman, *Legal Realism at Yale,* 49, 61; Ernest J. Brown, Oral History, conducted by Daniel Hamilton (August 1997), on file with the authors.

84. Quotations here and below from Brown, Oral History (August 1997).

85. Kalman, *Legal Realism at Yale,* 60. See Samuel Williston, *Life and Law: An Autobiography* (Boston, 1941), 193; W. Barton Leach, "The Law at Harvard: A Quasi-Review with Personalia," *HLSB* (March 1968), 7–8; Horwitz, *Transformation of American Law,* 217.

86. Donald A. Ritchie, *James M. Landis: Dean of the Regulators* (Cambridge, MA, 1980), 80. See James Landis, *Reminisces of James McCauley Landis: Oral History, 1964* [interview conducted for the Columbia University Oral History Research Program by Neil Gold in 1964] (Westport, CT, 1975), 1510.

CHAPTER SEVEN

New Deal, Nazis, and Faculty Revolt, 1931–1936

Shortly after Dean Roscoe Pound (1916–1936) debated and dismissed legal realism, three more controversies erupted between 1931 and 1936. The first concerned the government's response to the Depression, which drew many of the Law School faculty and graduates to public service in Washington. Their work on the New Deal advanced the kind of instrumental social legislation that the young, radical Pound praised and the older, conservative Pound now condemned.

The second controversy arose when Dean Pound made public statements implicitly condoning Nazi rule during visits to Germany and Austria in the mid-1930s. The ensuing criticism intensified when Pound accepted an honorary doctorate from the University of Berlin in 1934 after Adolf Hitler had become Chancellor of Nazi Germany. In addition, new research reveals that, during his visits, Pound met and socialized with high-ranking Nazi officials who were later tried and executed for war crimes. Furthermore, Pound's special assistant at Harvard was an ardent Nazi sympathizer, who was arrested and detained by the United States during World War II, despite Pound's strenuous defense and lobbying on his behalf.

Lastly, Pound's decanal leadership itself became controversial. Most of the students were unhappy, and the faculty lost patience with the entrenched LL.B. pedagogy and curriculum, as well as the dean's increasingly eccentric and autocratic administration. The country was changing profoundly due to the Depression and political upheaval in Europe, and if the aging Pound refused to embrace reform, the faculty would force it upon him. In 1933, when President A. Lawrence Lowell (1909–1933) resigned to be replaced by James

Conant (1933–1953), Pound's days as dean were numbered. He finally resigned in 1936 at age sixty-six and was named a University Professor.[1]

Depression and New Deal

In October 1929 the stock market crashed, and the United States entered the deepest and longest economic recession in its history. Initial signs of improvement appeared in 1931, but most economists agree, in retrospect, that the Federal Reserve and President Herbert Hoover failed to act strongly enough to increase the money supply and stimulate consumer demand. This led to a second phase of decline starting with a vicious deflationary cycle in 1932 that left Hoover's cautious remedies, such as the Reconstruction Finance Corporation, in disarray. Overall, between 1929 and 1932, U.S. industrial production dropped 46 percent, wholesale prices 32 percent, and international trade 70 percent, while 20 percent of banks failed. Unemployment rose sixfold, the worst increase in the Western world. These conditions led to the overwhelming victory of President Franklin Roosevelt, Democratic control of the Congress, and the announcement of a "new deal for the American people."[2]

Higher education, including Harvard Law School, fared relatively well as the Depression deepened between 1929 and 1933. High unemployment often results in growing enrollment in postsecondary education, therefore, "colleges and universities weathered the Depression far better than most other institutions."[3] At Harvard Law School, the enrollment declined only by one tenth, and the student-faculty ratio, a matter of concern before the Depression, improved commensurately, as shown in Table 7.1.[4]

Table 7.1 Student-Faculty Ratio at Harvard Law School from 1910–11 to 1934–35

Academic Year	Total Enrollment	Full Professors	Assistant Professors	Student-Faculty Ratio
1910–11	810	8	2	81:1
1915–16	791	10	0	79:1
1920–21	946	9	2	86:1
1924–25	1,201	14	3	71:1
1929–30	1,641	23	6	57:1
1934–35	1,458	27	5	46:1

Data sources: Harvard Law School Catalog, 1911–12, 3, 51; 1915–16, 3; 1916–17, 53; 1920–21, 3–4; 1921–22, 62; 1924–25, 3–4; 1925–26, 77; 1929–30, 3–4; 1930–31, 97; 1934–35, 3–4; 1935–36, 91.
Note: Number of professors excludes the president and the librarian.

Nevertheless, covering a full curriculum for some 1,500 students with about thirty professors was difficult even in the best of times. Teaching loads of seven two-hour courses each semester were common, and Pound himself taught ten two-hour courses per semester, amounting to twenty class hours a week. Partly due to this burden, Pound's teaching style deteriorated late in his career. Students began to call him "Racing Roscoe," recalled Arthur von Mehren (LL.B. 1945). His classes primarily required that students take notes on "what he was regurgitating of his previous voluminous writings.... The man was very learned, but there was nothing very exciting or stimulating about his teaching."[5]

The burden on Pound increased as faculty were drawn into government service. Roosevelt's New Deal created whole legal worlds in new or expanded agencies: the Federal Deposit Insurance Corporation (FDIC) and the Federal Emergency Relief Administration (FERA) in 1933, the Securities and Exchange Commission (SEC) and the National Labor Relations Board (NLRB) in 1934, and the Works Progress Administration (WPA) in 1935. These so-called "alphabet" agencies required experts to lead them, and Roosevelt looked to the faculty at Harvard, particularly the Law School, for help, much to the consternation of both Dean Pound and President A. Lawrence Lowell. It was said that "the most direct route to Washington was to go to Harvard Law School and turn left."[6] A remarkable paradox arose as Harvard developed a reputation as a bastion of both conservative jurisprudents and liberal reformers who supported the New Deal.

Felix Frankfurter (LL.B. 1906) began commuting to Washington and serving as an advisor to President Roosevelt. James Landis went to the Federal Trade Commission (FTC) and the SEC, Francis Sayre (LL.B. 1912, S.J.D. 1918) became assistant secretary of state, and Calvert Magruder (LL.B. 1916) went to the NLRB. Frankfurter also began recruiting the best law students, and between 1930 and 1932, twenty-eight of the forty-two editors of the *Harvard Law Review* went to Washington. In effect, Frankfurter acted as "the personnel director, staffing all of these agencies," recalled Ernest Brown (LL.B. 1931), who left the struggling family farm in Louisiana to join the new Agricultural Adjustment Administration (AAA) in 1933.[7]

In addition to draining the faculty, the New Deal kindled ideological tensions within the school. After the 1934 midterm election, the Democrats extended their congressional majorities and passed massive amounts of legislation in what became called the Second New Deal, which changed the nature of the American social contract. The Social Security Act and the National Labor Relations Act, both passed in 1935, created vast new entitlements, as well as administrative agencies and courts to run them. Conservatives on the faculty, such as Pound, had misgivings. He distrusted Roosevelt and objected to the burgeoning bureaucracies with their "administrative justice." By 1938 he was attacking "the tendency of administrative bureaus to extend the scope of their operations indefinitely even to the extent of supplanting our traditional judicial regime by an administrative regime," and he occasionally identified legal realists with Marxists, attributing to both the ethic of "Thrasymachus, that 'the just is nothing else than the interests of the stronger.'"[8]

In the 1938 report of the ABA Special Committee on Administrative Law, Pound condemned "administrative absolutism," as revealed in "ten tendencies" of the administrative process.[9] In fact, these "tendencies" were unfair and unsupported generalizations—fulminations, really—and exceeded even his distorted characterization of realism in the debate with Karl Llewellyn six years before. Pound also endorsed the notorious Walter-Logan Act, which aimed "to cripple the administrative progress with exaggerated requirements of notice, judicial review, and an incredible one-year limitation on an agency's power to develop regulations."[10]

By the late 1930s Pound had clearly succumbed to his fear of social unrest, economic disruption, and international disarray. His early radical writing of 1906–1910 had urged a new social progressivism to save America, and portrayed the individualism of the historical common-law tradition as dangerous and unsuited to modern conditions. At that time, the fierce critic of the *Lochner* decision would have denounced the Supreme Court decisions in *United States v. Butler* (1936), striking down large parts of the Agricultural Adjustment Act, and *Schlechter v. United States* (1935), destroying the National Recovery Administration.[11] After Roosevelt's overwhelming victory in 1936, the older Pound fearfully anticipated Roosevelt's expansion of executive power, culminating in the infamous Judiciary Reorganization ("court packing") Bill of 1937. But Pound's views in 1938 were not so much a change in judicial philosophy as a visceral reaction to the changing world around him.[12]

He voiced this reaction when addressing bar associations, heading commissions, issuing American Law Institute Restatements, and advising Judicial Councils during the mid- and late-1930s. Unmoved by the vast human suffering during one of the greatest social and economic crises in American history, he conceived the New Deal's administrative law as "involving the common-law judges in a conflict quite analogous to that which they waged with the Stuart kings in the seventeenth century." Thus, he fatuously cast himself as his century's Chief Justice Edward Coke (1552–1634), confronting the imperial power of King James I.[13] Viewing himself as a lone heroic figure, Pound "complained privately that the administrative absolutism dominating law schools made law reviews unsympathetic to his ideas."[14] Pound, for so long the leading theorist in American law, had become an embarrassment to many at the school, as well as to his liberal colleagues working for the New Deal in Washington.

Nazis and Harvard, 1933–1934

Amid the turbulence of the Depression, Pound visited Germany and Austria in the summer of 1934 and again in 1936 and 1937, as the dark night of fascism was falling. His motivation for these controversial trips may have originated in his youth, when he learned to love German culture and venerate German scholarship and jurisprudence. Given this, he was likely dismayed by the anti-German sentiment arising in the United States between 1915 and 1920.[15] Whether or not this contributed to his failure to resist Lowell's anti-Semitism during the 1920s is unclear. But it is certain that by 1933 American intellectuals and academics recognized and condemned the growing anti-Semitism in Nazi Germany. On March 27, 1933, a rally against anti-Semitism in Germany filled New York City's Madison Square Garden. Pound's subsequent trips and comments, implicitly condoning Nazi rule, were not made out of ignorance or naiveté.[16]

On April 7, 1933, the Nazi government enacted a law prohibiting Jews from civil service, and on April 24 the *New York Times* warned that "Jews in Germany were facing an impending catastrophe." By that point the Nazis had arrested some 45,000 political opponents and Jews and transported them to newly established concentration camps. At the same time, the *Sturmabteilung* (SA), or Brownshirts, were terrorizing Jewish shopkeepers. In October 1933, the year when James Conant succeeded A. Lawrence Lowell as president of Harvard, German scholars fleeing the Nazis established the University in Exile at the New School for Social Research in New York.[17]

By the beginning of 1934, events in Nazi Germany and the rise of Chancellor Adolf Hitler were widely discussed at Harvard Law School, as Archibald Cox (LL.B. 1937), then a student, later observed. For example, in the spring of 1934, a group of students raised objections to the dean and faculty over favorable comparisons to the "German system" of legal education made in a Law School document. Noting "recent developments in Germany," the students stated, the document "describes conditions before the advent of Hitler."[18]

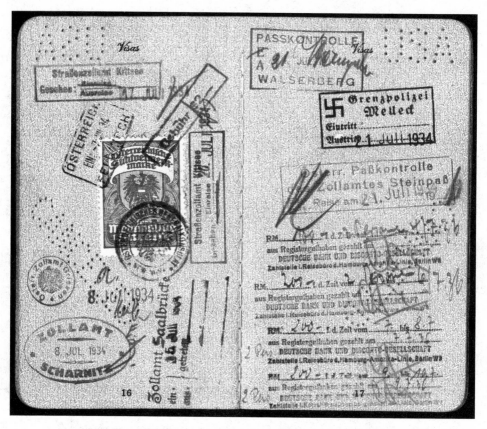

Roscoe Pound's Passport, issued June 6, 1933, stamped July 1934.
Courtesy of Harvard Law School Library, Historical & Special Collections.

Concurrently, the German government embarked on a systematic effort in the United States to legitimize and dignify Nazi rule.

One important target was Harvard. In May 1934, as Pound was wrapping up the semester and preparing to depart for Germany, the Nazi battle cruiser *Karlsruhe* visited Boston on a "good will" mission. On board was the Nazi ambassador to the United States, Hans Luther, who played a central role in the legitimation strategy. Despite widespread protests, Massachusetts governor Joseph Ely and Boston mayor Frederick Mansfield sponsored a reception for Luther and his staff. For its part, Harvard University gave the ambassador an official tour of the Germanic Museum and the Widener Library, hosted *Karlsruhe* cadets at Lowell House, and entertained them at the Harvard Military and Naval Ball. Luther reciprocated by hosting a lavish reception at the

Copley Plaza Hotel. The German consul-general in Boston, Kurt von Tippelskirch, hosted another in neighboring Newton, and many Harvard faculty members attended. When the *Karlsruhe* returned to Germany in June 1934, the Nazi defense minister concluded that the ship had "made friends for the Third Reich in all places where she dropped anchor."[19]

Another Nazi effort to make friends at Harvard occurred just before Pound's departure for Germany in June 1934, at the twenty-fifth reunion of the Harvard College class of 1909. One member of that class planning to attend was Ernst Hanfstaengl, foreign press chief of the Nazi Party and a close friend of Hitler. When Jewish leaders in Boston protested Hanfstaengl's attendance, Conant's administration declared that "Ernst Hanfstaengl is a Harvard man" who would "be warmly welcomed." In his memoirs published thirty-five years later, Conant still affirmed, "Whatever one might think of Hitler or Hanfstaengl, . . . it was perfectly plain [that] an alumnus had every right to take part in a twenty-fifth reunion."[20]

But Harvard did more than allow Hanfstaengl to take part. High-ranking administrators met with him, including Presidents Lowell and Conant. On June 17, Hanfstaengl stated publicly that "everything would soon be settled for the Jews in Germany." This statement prompted a confrontation in Harvard Yard, witnessed by Boston journalists. Rabbi Joseph Solomon Shubow challenged Hanfstaengl, asking what his statement meant: "My people want to know . . . does it mean extermination?" Rescuing Hanfstaengl from the confrontation, the Harvard police whisked him off to President Conant's house for tea. When anti-Hanfstaengl demonstrators in Harvard Square were arrested and given severe sentences of six months in jail, Conant refused to intervene, stating, even in 1970, that the demonstrations "seemed to me very ridiculous."[21] Upon his return to Germany, Hanfstaengl was given the honor of opening the sixth convention of the Nazi Party in Nuremberg in September 1934.

Pound visits Nazi Germany, 1934

Shortly after the Hanfstaengl controversy, Pound and his wife left for a summer trip to Germany and Austria, carrying a special letter from Consul Tippelskirch to ease their crossing of the German borders. During their trip, two significant events magnified the Nazi threat. While Pound was visiting Austria, the country's chancellor, Engelbert Dollfuss, was assassinated in a Nazi coup on July 25, 1934. A week later, while Pound was touring Bavaria, Hitler was named Führer on August 2, 1934. On August 4, Pound implicitly condoned

Hitler's ascendance and fascist rule in comments widely quoted by European and American newspapers, such as the *Paris Herald.* According to Pound, "The rise of Hitler is an old phenomenon in the history of man. As in Mussolini's case in 1921, Hitler rolled in on the wave of public sentiment against politics. All those countries—Austria, Germany, Hungary, Italy and the rest—are tired of internal bickering and will back up a man who can bring them freedom from agitating 'movements.'"[22]

Furthermore, Pound told the *Paris Herald* that Hitler's rule had widespread peaceful support: "In Bavaria I never saw any indication of tension or fear of the future. People discussed Hitler and everything else openly, just as we talk of Roosevelt in the United States. Once in a while, you ran across a swastika painted on a barn."[23]

In Austria, shortly after the Nazi coup, Pound told the *Paris Herald* that he "saw only a beautiful countryside inhabited by people who seemed totally unaware of startling reports involving the border. . . . 'The great bulk of the population,' he said, . . . 'isn't bothering about anything except its own private affairs. . . . We had much less trouble passing the [Austrian] border than a person meets getting from Canada into the United States.'" Pound even seemed to approve the new Nazi regime in Austria: "I see no reason why it should fail if it continues to attract the confidence of the people, as it seems to have done since Dollfuss's death."[24] In the United States, *The New Republic* reprinted Pound's statements accompanied by a warning from the prominent political scientist and historian Charles A. Beard, who warned that "citizens of the United States . . . [should] not be used by foreign governments and agents for the purposes of their propaganda."[25]

In contrast to Pound's favorable assessment, which he also expressed in his diary, the famous British travel writer Patrick Fermor described his travels in Austria in 1933 and 1934 in far different terms: "Appalling things had happened since Hitler had come into power ten months earlier; but the range of horror was not yet fully unfolded. . . . It was a desperate time for Austria . . . the country had been shaken by disturbances organized by the Nazis and their Austrian sympathizers."[26]

After traveling on to Germany, Pound returned from Europe in late August 1934 for the new academic year, and the *New York Herald Tribune* quoted Pound's report "that the average German was sincerely in favor of the Hitler regime" partly because "the Germans believe that Hitler has stopped the wholesale grafting. As to whether the powers he now holds were obtained through violations of constitutional laws of Germany, that is difficult to say. . . .

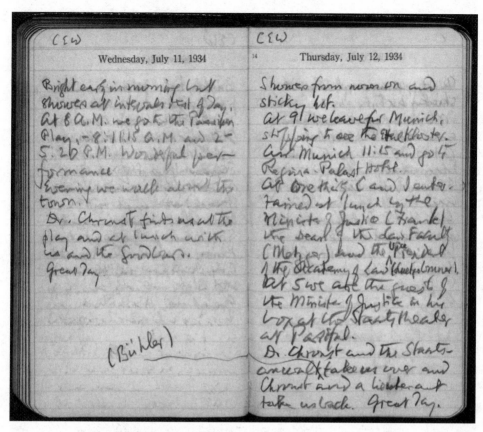

Roscoe Pound's Travel Diary, entries for July 11 and July 12, 1934.

Anything gets by under certain foreign systems of constitutions as being legal."[27] *The New Republic* also quoted this exculpatory account of Pound, who thus became one of the most prominent and respected American apologists for the Nazi regime.[28]

Not reported in the press at the time, and only discovered recently by researcher Peter Rees, was that Pound also visited prominent Nazis throughout his trip.[29] For example, Pound's diary records that on July 11, 1934—just ten days after the assassinations of opponents and rivals to the Nazi Party during the "Blood Purge," or "Night of the Long Knives," between June 30 and July 2, 1934—Pound visited the south Bavarian town of Oberammergau. There he was joined by his special assistant at Harvard Law School, Anton Hermann Chroust (S.J.D. 1933), discussed below. Pound and Chroust attended a performance of

Roscoe Pound with Anton Lang. Photograph by J. E. Goodbar, at Oberammergau, Bavaria, July 10, 1934.
Courtesy of Harvard Law School Library, Historical & Special Collections.

the *Passionspiel* ("Passion Play"), a highly anti-Semitic depiction of the life and death of Jesus Christ. Anton Lang, famous for regularly playing the role of Christus early in the century, delivered the prologue that day, and Pound was photographed with Lang. Joseph E. Goodbar (LL.M. 1931, S.J.D. 1933), one of Pound's former graduate students who was studying the German financial system, took the photograph and joined Chroust and Pound at lunch. Pound wrote in his diary: "Wonderful performance. . . . Great Day."[30]

On the following day, July 12, 1934, Pound had lunch with Hans Frank, the Bavarian minister of justice and personal legal advisor to Hitler; Edmund Mezger, dean of the law faculty in Munich and later member of the infamous Criminal Law Commission; and the vice-president of the Akademie für Deutsches Recht (Academy for German Law) Walter Luetgebrune, who until 1934 was chief legal advisor to the *Schutzstaffel* (SS). In the afternoon, Frank hosted Pound in his box at the Staätstheater to view Wagner's opera *Parsifal*. Pound was driven to the Staätstheater by Josef Bühler and Anton Chroust. After the opera, Chroust and a Nazi lieutenant drove Pound home.[31]

Four of these men were prominent Nazis, and three were eventually convicted of war crimes. Frank later became Hitler's personal lawyer and the

Photograph of Joseph Bühler (right) with Julius Dorpmüller, Reich Minister for Transport, 1942.

National Archives of Poland.

governor-general of occupied Poland. In 1946 he was convicted at Nurem-berg for the mass murder of Polish citizens and executed. Mezger worked for Heinrich Himmler, who organized and managed the concentration camps in Germany. He was sentenced to imprisonment by the Nuremberg Tribunal for lesser crimes. Bühler attended the infamous Wannsee Conference on Jan-uary 20, 1942, as the representative from the Bavarian Governor General's Office, where he supported the "Final Solution of the Jewish Question in the German Sphere of Influence in Europe." He later became deputy governor of occupied Poland. In 1946 the Supreme National Tribunal of Poland convicted Bühler of crimes against humanity, and executed him in 1948. Pound recorded no questions or reservations about his Nazi hosts, and concluded the diary entry for July 12, 1934, with "Great day."[32]

This Nazi socializing with Pound did not happen by chance, according to new research in the "Files regarding German Tributes for Foreigners" held in the Political Archive of the German Foreign Office in Berlin. In the begin-ning of June 1934, German ambassador Luther had written from Washington to the German Foreign Office in Berlin:

Dean Roscoe Pound, leader of the famous Harvard law school, . . . is recog-nized not only in the United States, but also in Great Britain, as one of the leading, if not the leading scholar in the field of Anglo-Saxon law. . . . He has always displayed positive sentiments towards Germany and expressed this several times during [World War I] in a most bold manner. It is therefore important from both a scholastic and a personal perspective to honor Dean Pound in the grandest of forms. . . . I should add that the sixty-five year-old Dean . . . is extremely receptive towards recognitions and honors. . . . I would like a commitment for Dean Pound to be welcomed in Oberammergau by an appropriate person, in order to look after him, and also to ensure that he has a successful visit to Munich. . . . In the event that Dean Pound comes to Berlin, I think a reception by the German President would be a particularly worthwhile gesture. It would also be of benefit to invite Dean Pound to deliver a guest lecture at the University of Berlin, perhaps also in Munich or Heidelberg.[33]

Through 1934, it appears therefore that Pound's involvement with the Nazis can be explained, at least in part, by his long-standing affection for German culture; his infamous vanity, which was exploited by the German Foreign Office in orchestrating events; and his notorious high-handed refusal to admit that he made mistakes. The last factor subsequently grew stronger, as he defended his protégé Chroust.

Berlin Honorary Degree and More Visits, 1934–1937

When Pound returned to the United States in August 1934, the published accounts of his trip and favorable assessment of Nazi rule bewildered and embarrassed many faculty and administrators at Harvard and other universities across the United States.[34] The furor intensified when, in September 1934, the University of Berlin offered, and Pound accepted, an honorary doctorate of laws. This, too, was orchestrated by the Nazi regime after Ambassador Luther wrote to Berlin from Washington:

I was again asked by individuals friendly to the German cause whether Dean Roscoe Pound . . . might be awarded an honorary German degree, thereby strengthening his friendly disposition towards Germany, in particular German philosophy and jurisprudence. I am convinced . . . that an award of this kind cannot be conferred quickly enough. I need not comment on the importance of Harvard Law School. It should also not be necessary to report on the scholarly achievements of Dean Pound. . . . I would like to add that Dean Pound was asked to give an opinion about the Jewish boycott in the United States, and that he voluntarily found in favor of Germany.[35]

On behalf of the University of Berlin, Ambassador Luther and Consul Tippelskirch conferred the degree in the entrance lobby of Langdell Hall on September 17, 1934, as Pound recorded in his diary. Afterward Tippelskirch hosted a lavish luncheon at the Ritz Carlton Hotel for Pound and other guests.[36]

Each member of the faculty received a personal invitation to attend the degree presentation and the luncheon. "Pound undoubtedly . . . didn't think of this as having political implications," Archibald Cox later stated.[37] But many faculty saw those implications, and did not attend. Replying to Pound's invitation, Frankfurter wrote:

> Of course, I cannot attend any function in honor of a representative of a government which Mr. Justice Holmes has accurately characterized as 'a challenge to civilization.' And it would be cowardly for me to suppress my sense of humiliation that, while other leading law schools have offered hospitality to distinguished juristic victims of German oppression, my beloved Law School, the centre of Anglo-American law, should even by indirection confer special distinction upon an official representative of enthroned lawlessness.[38]

Some faculty found a middle ground. "Accepting a medal from the German government at that time did not seem right," wrote then Assistant Professor Erwin Griswold sixty years later. "On the other hand, I was a brand new young faculty member and did not want to insult the dean. I could have stayed away from the presentation, and it is clear to me now that I should have done so." Instead, Griswold found a way "to compromise. I did not go to the entrance lobby where the presentation was made. I did not shake hands with the German Consul, nor did I speak to him. But I did go to the balcony above the entrance lobby, where I could hear and see the presentation."[39]

Harvard president Conant attended the presentation, another instance of failing to condemn Nazism publicly, for which historians have severely criticized him.[40] In private Conant echoed Frankfurter's disgust with Pound and termed the dean a "pathological case," but Conant said that he could not halt the degree-granting ceremony in Langdell Hall without Pound's consent.[41] Conant also maintained later that he expressed his disapproval of Pound's

Roscoe Pound receiving an honorary degree from the University of Berlin delivered by Dr. Hans Luther, German ambassador to the United States, at Harvard Law School, on September 17, 1934.

Courtesy of Boston Public Library, Print Department.

acceptance of the degree by refusing to be photographed with Luther, Tippelskirch, and Pound for the newspapers.[42] But this refusal seems more like Conant guarding his public image than expressing disapproval, and Harvard's hosting the degree ceremony was widely reported in the press.

A month after Pound accepted the honorary degree, Ernst Hanfstaengl, in October 1934, followed up his Harvard visit by publicly offering a scholarship of $1,000 to permit a Harvard student to study in Germany for a year. The Harvard Corporation officially rejected it, and Conant stated to the press, "We are unwilling to accept a gift from one who has been so closely associated with the leadership of a political party which has inflicted damage on the universities of Germany" and "struck at principles . . . fundamental to universities throughout the world."[43]

These events in September and October received widespread publicity. *The New Republic* sharply criticized Pound's acceptance of the honorary degree, which "will be interpreted by German propagandists around the world as an answer to Nazi critics."[44] Thus, the significance of Pound's actions in 1934 was well understood at the time, including privately by Conant. Nevertheless, Pound made additional trips to Germany, even after the Nazi Reichstag enacted the Nuremberg Laws in September 1935, including the infamous "Law for the Protection of German Blood and German Honor," which criminalized sexual relations between Jewish and non-Jewish Germans and stripped Jews of their German citizenship.

In the summer of 1936 Pound spent nineteen days traveling through Germany, starting in Berlin and gradually making his way down to Munich, where the Olympics were to be held on August 1–16. En route, he stopped at the Bayreuth Wagner Festival and, on July 21,1936, he attended the Jubilee performance of Wagner's *Lohengrin*, which was also attended by Hitler, Hermann Goering, and Josef Goebbels, although there is no record that Pound met with any of these Nazi leaders. In the summer of 1937, Pound again returned to Germany and spent eight days visiting Berlin, Dresden, Karlsbad, Nuremberg, and Frankfurt.[45]

The details of these trips are obscure because many entries in his diary are illegible. Among his papers in the Law School library, there is only one photo of Pound's trips to Germany in the mid-1930s, which seems extraordinary given the number and length of his trips, the meetings with prominent Nazis, and the plenitude of photos from Pound's trips to China.[46]

Anton Hermann Chroust

Having earned the J.D. from the University of Erlangen, Anton Chroust matriculated into the S.J.D. program at Harvard Law School in September 1932. This talented, twenty-five-year-old, German graduate student doubtlessly caught Pound's attention during the ensuing year, and Chroust completed the S.J.D. in June 1933. From that point until his arrest by the FBI at the end of 1941, Chroust served as a special assistant to Pound, as revealed in new research by Peter Rees.[47]

The nature of Chroust's position at Harvard Law School was never clear. There is no record of an official appointment of Chroust to any faculty or administrative position at the Law School. But according to archival records at the FBI, the German Foreign Office in Berlin, and the Law School, Chroust had an office, conducted research, taught a weekly seminar as part of one of Pound's classes, and assisted him in various other ways. Chroust also met or accompanied Pound in Germany during each of his three trips between 1934 and 1937. In fact, the German ambassador Luther wrote to Berlin that Chroust "may be helpful in the arranging of the necessary steps" to host Pound at Oberammergau and Munich.[48]

Over this period, between 1934 and 1937, according to the voluminous but heavily redacted and recently declassified FBI records, Chroust boasted to neighbors and acquaintances in Massachusetts that he held offices in the Nazi Party, visited Texas, Mexico, Cuba, and Belgium on missions for the Nazi Party, and had personal relationships with Hitler, Goering, Rudolph Hess, Hermann Schultz, and members of the German Ministry for Propaganda. In addition, Chroust bragged of his membership in the SS and involvement in the political assassinations of opponents and rivals to the Nazi Party during the "Blood Purge," or "Night of the Long Knives," between June 30 and July 2, 1934.[49] Roscoe Pound himself testified in 1942 that Chroust "boasted of his acquaintance with Hans Frank," later convicted at Nuremberg and executed in 1946.[50] Consequently, while working for Pound, Chroust remained "a wholehearted Nazi . . . entrusted by the Nazi government with an important mission in this country," according to U.S. Attorney General Thomas C. Clark in 1945.[51]

Concurrently, the FBI was watching Chroust. Beginning in about 1935 and continuing over the next six years, agents interviewed at least fourteen individuals, including Harvard Law School faculty, about Chroust, while Pound unofficially employed him as his assistant. On December 7, 1941, the Japanese attacked Pearl Harbor. On December 8, the United States declared war on Japan and Germany. On December 9 at 2 a.m., the FBI arrested Chroust at his rooming house on Irving Street in Cambridge. He was charged "with being a dangerous enemy alien" and detained. Over the next two years, Pound campaigned vigorously for Chroust's release, including serving as Chroust's "main witness" before the Alien Enemy Hearing Board (AEHB) on January 5, 1942.[52]

Sitting on the five-member AEHB was professor and future Harvard Law School dean Erwin Griswold (1946–1967). Persuaded by Pound's testimony, Griswold was the only board member to recommend parole, rather than detention, for Chroust, and stated to other board members that Chroust ended his "active sympathy with the Nazi government" in 1935 and opposed the Nazis thereafter.[53] However, the AEHB repatriation hearing for Chroust in 1946 found "a very great preponderance of evidence . . . that up to 1936 the subject [Chroust] was an admitted and outspoken Nazi Party member." Furthermore, the German national archives identify Chroust as a member of the Nazi Party on September 12, 1939.[54]

Anton-Hermann Chroust, S.J.D. 1933. Identification photograph for the Nazi Party (the National Socialist German Workers' Party) as of July 15, 1939.

Bundesarchiv (Germany), BArch, R 9361-VIII Kartei / 5141541.

The end date of Chroust's allegiance to the Nazis did not matter to Pound, who testified at the AEHB hearing "that, whether [Chroust] was a Nazi or not, he would still keep him under his wing as a student."[55] Pound may have been reciprocating Chroust's loyalty to him, for evidence was presented at the hearing that Chroust had helped secure the honorary degree for Pound from the University of Berlin in 1934, a time when everyone agrees that Chroust was actively working for the Nazis.[56]

After the AEHB voted in 1942 to detain Chroust, Pound initiated an extensive letter-writing campaign on his behalf. His correspondents included Massachusetts senator David Walsh, Massachusetts congressman Christian Herter, who would later become U.S. secretary of state, and Edward J. Ennis, director of the Alien Enemy Control Unit at the U.S. Department of Justice, who later became president of the American Civil Liberties Union. In March 1943, Chroust was released on parole with Pound as his official parole sponsor. Pound then continued writing letters urging that Chroust not be deported as an enemy parolee and be permitted to remain permanently in the United States. But in 1945 Chroust was again detained.[57]

In July 1945, at the urging of Pound, Senator Walsh contacted the newly appointed U.S. attorney general, Thomas Clark, who ordered that the entire file be reviewed "once more with some care." After that review, Clark decided that he would not change Chroust's status as an "enemy alien parolee" because "during the years that Dr. Chroust was in Cambridge prior to 1937, he was not only frank but boastful about his allegiance to the Nazis and about his Nazi connections . . . and had been entrusted by the Nazi government with an important mission in this country."[58] Pound responded with a seven-page reply that rebutted Clark's assertions point-by-point but that also contained a serious omission and an important falsehood.

First, Pound did not disclose the fact, recorded in his diary, that Chroust was present on July 12, 1934, when Pound and his wife met with Hans Frank, Edmund Mezger, Walter Luetgebrune, and Josef Bühler, who were all subsequently convicted of war crimes. More important, Pound asserted that Chroust could not possibly have participated in the Nazi Blood Purge because he was with Pound and his wife at the time in Germany. This alibi was clearly false. The Blood Purge ended on July 2, 1934, and Pound did not arrive in Europe until July 4, and did not meet Chroust until July 10, according to Pound's diary. Because the Blood Purge was highly publicized and dominated German politics and society over the summer of 1934, it seems incredible that Pound mistakenly believed that the Blood Purge took place after he arrived and met Chroust—a week after the purge ended.[59] Pound's omission and falsehood appear to constitute serious ethical and professional transgressions and even a criminal offense because they were written to a federal official, the U.S. attorney general.[60]

In summarizing the repatriation hearing held for Chroust in January 1946, hearing officer Edward Ennis wrote that according to Pound's sworn testimony, Chroust "was an exceptionally fine scholar and . . . a man of complete truthfulness, honor, and kindness to other people." But Ennis found that "the record overwhelmingly establishes that [Chroust] has been entirely untruthful with the Government throughout the proceeding." Ennis concluded by quoting a letter from Jerome D. Green, secretary of Harvard University, who wrote that "Chroust frequently boasted of his friendship with Pound and used it to bolster his prestige with others" and that Professor Pound "has been somewhat blinded by his partiality."[61]

When Pound continued to press the case to exonerate Chroust, Ennis wrote to the attorney general in February 20, 1946: "When Professor Pound, in the teeth of the evidence, clings to the extreme position that Chroust is one of the most honorable men he has known, his extreme bias and partisanship is clear and . . . gives further support to the view that both his work and his emotional stability have suffered a marked decline with advancing age." Nevertheless, Chroust was released on parole for the second time in February 23, 1946.[62]

Meanwhile Pound was writing letters to American law schools recommending Chroust for a faculty position "without reservation." In fact, Pound implied that Chroust had not cooperated with the Nazis, writing that "his father . . . was removed from his Professorship under the Hitler regime. Dr. Chroust . . . studied under some of the most important jurists in the German Universities as they were before the Hitler regime." Given such recommendations, the University of Notre Dame Law School hired Chroust as an associate professor in July 1946.[63]

Chroust taught at Notre Dame until 1972, and published several scholarly books, including a history of the legal profession in America.[64] Meanwhile, Pound continued trying to clear Chroust's name. In 1956, at Pound's insistence, the FBI made yet another investigation, and concluded, "Pound is still embittered over the experience of his close friend and protégé, and has seized an opportunity, perhaps by distortion of the facts, to prove that an injustice was done." The inquiry was then closed.[65]

In 1969 the Law School built a new faculty office building and subsequently named it for Roscoe Pound. In 1996 the *Harvard Law Record* published a column asserting that Pound "openly supported Adolf Hitler," "accepted an honorary degree from the University of Berlin," and "fiercely fought the appointment of three Jewish tenure candidates."[66] In response, a small group of students went to Daniel Coquillette's office at the Law School and asked "whether it was right that a building should be named for Roscoe Pound?" They also wrote to Dean Robert Clark (1989–2003) "respectfully requesting that the Law School act to change the name of Pound Hall."[67] The controversy continued in the pages of the *Harvard Law Record,* and some Jewish alumni defended Pound and, like Felix Frankfurter, maintained that Pound was not anti-Semitic.[68] In the end, no action was taken concerning the name of Pound Hall.

In 2018, at a symposium on the history of American law schools held in Florence, Italy, Guido Calabresi, who served as dean of Yale Law School from 1985 to 1994, noted that in the early 1920s Pound visited Italy, where he stayed with members of Calabresi's family, who were eminent Jewish scholars. Based on this background, Calabresi remarked,

> I knew Pound, and in my judgment, he was always a fascist, but he was not a racist any more than many Americans of that era were. He went to Italy in the early 1920s and . . . said again and again that fascism is good enough for these people. I think what happened with Germany was simply an extension of that. Pound thought Nazism was fine. You've got to put that in the context in which the presidents of Harvard, Yale, and Columbia at that time were racists of the worst sort. President Angell of Yale [1922–1937] actually wrote that if we could have something like what happened in Armenia in New Haven . . . we might be able to save our Nordic race. In other words, kill off all the Italians, Blacks, Jews, and so on.[69]

Faculty Revolt: The Curriculum Study, 1934–1936

Also contributing to the unraveling of Pound's deanship, a third contemporaneous controversy arose over his eccentric and autocratic administration, particularly regarding the entrenched LL.B. pedagogy and curriculum. By 1931 the old alliance between Pound and Frankfurter had completely broken down. Beyond the realist controversy, Frankfurter had lost confidence in Pound's independence and integrity. For his part, Pound lamented disingenuously, "During the last two or three years, whenever I have tried to get anything through the faculty, I have found an atmosphere of obstruction and objection, although I have always told the faculty everything I know and put all my cards on the table."[70] Despite his protests, the dean had lost the trust and respect of Frankfurter's circle and most of the faculty.[71]

The resignation of President Lowell and installation of President Conant in 1933 presented an opportunity for change. Pound's acceptance of the German honorary degree in 1934 infuriated Frankfurter and alienated Julian Mack (LL.B. 1887), the only Jewish member of the Harvard governing boards, who had supported Pound to that point. Frankfurter began suggesting decanal replacements for Pound to President Conant. But Pound and the Law School had key roles in the university tercentenary celebration in 1936, so Conant was not going to act immediately, even though he repeatedly described Pound as virtually "pathological."[72]

Instead, in light of growing complaints about Pound's temper and irrational micromanaging—outbursts about windows left open and personally assigning parking spaces for faculty—Conant chose to preside over Law School faculty meetings himself. This prompted his famous observation that the Law School faculty was "the most quarrelsome group of men I ever encountered."[73] But the faculty agreed on one point. As Thomas Powell (LL.B. 1931) put it, "the greater part of the dissatisfaction . . . among members of the faculty is produced by the dean."[74] Even Joseph Beale, a longtime ally, believed that Pound was "growing nuttier and nuttier."[75] Increasingly autocratic, cantankerous, and isolated, Pound prompted a faculty revolt.

The precipitating issue was curriculum reform. To the great frustration of the faculty, Pound had relentlessly opposed any change in the regular LL.B. program during his tenure as dean. In 1932, Professors Edwin M. Dodd (LL.B. 1913) and Sidney P. Simpson (LL.B. 1922) coauthored a faculty committee report recommending updates to the LL.B. curriculum, following reforms made at Columbia and Yale. But little changed, except at the graduate level.[76]

In May 1934 the faculty voted to establish a Committee on Curriculum and, in a remarkable slight to Pound, asked Conant, not the dean, to appoint its members. Conant complied, appointing five members: Warren Seavey as chairman, plus Samuel Williston, Edmund Morgan, George Gardner, and Sidney Simpson.[77] Just as he presided over faculty meetings, Conant personally attended some meetings of the Curriculum Committee meetings, which interpreted its mandate broadly. Continuing through June 1936, the two-year study became one of the most thorough self-examinations in the history of the school, taking into consideration "the size of the School, the admission of students, examination methods and requirements, teaching personnel, student activities and organizations, and methods of administration." Equally important, the Committee sought extensive input, holding sixty formal faculty meetings devoted to the study, soliciting detailed reports from each faculty member about every course taught, and consulting faculty across the university, the catalogs of other law schools, and the literature on legal education.[78]

In its boldest move, practically unheard of in the 1930s, the faculty Committee consulted the students and compiled their feedback in three documents.[79] One was the account of a six-hour discussion among third-year students that Frankfurter had organized in May 1932. This group reported that, by the end of the second year, "men [are sick] of reading cases merely as a method of training or as a means of finding out doctrines." Furthermore, "the third year is fundamentally the same old stuff and largely a bore, because the faculties of men are not actively brought into play" due to "the limited seminar opportunities," except "for *Law Review* men and . . . those who work on Ames Competition or help some of the instructors."[80]

In addition—and this point greatly impressed Frankfurter—the students felt separated from the faculty and isolated from each other. "The dominant note of the place is impersonal," students said. "The professors are comfortably separated from the life of the students and are rarely seen going to and fro as [students] used to see Ames and Gray and Williston and Beale go to and fro in old Austin [Hall]."[81] In addition, the students noted "the vastness of the reading room, the great mass of students who are necessarily total strangers to each other, the lack of any common life not only of the School as a whole but of individual classes." As a result, "men are overwhelmed by the size and impersonality of the place and are thereby prevented from finding themselves."[82] It was telling that this group—top students and favorites of Frankfurter, who should have felt engaged and included in the school—observed the widespread feelings of separation and isolation.

The second document conveying student testimony was prepared independently over the spring and summer of 1934 by members of the graduating class, under the leadership of John G. Haviland (LL.B. 1934) and John N. Hazard (LL.B. 1934). Entitled "The Student Looks at Harvard Law School," this 165-page document conveyed opinions from "some eighty men of all types and classes, including at least two graduates each from Harvard, Yale, Princeton, Williams, Amherst, Wesleyan and Dartmouth, as well as from colleges and universities in all parts of the nation."[83] Their fundamental point was that the school focused on the top students and did little for the "average" student, particularly in the third year. As a result, there was no opportunity for "individual work for the great majority of men in the School," who also felt that they were unprepared "to practice law and fill [their] larger place as a citizen."[84] The appended "Spontaneous Memoranda" offered many examples of students' discontent.[85]

A Williams College graduate stated that "the faculty should strive to make their courses more interesting." A "second year man" described his first-year experience as "terrorism." A "ninth-generation Harvard man" regretted learning nothing about "New Dealism" or anything else about the "social and legal change now taking place." There was also a "Pioneer . . . born in Russia of Jewish parents, who lived in Europe . . . [and] during the World War, was wounded twice." Paying tuition through part-time work, scholarships, and loans, he identified with the "many here who have literally fought their way through college in order to get here, or are struggling bitterly to stay here in spite of financial obstacles." He regretted that there was less mentoring at Harvard Law School than at his alma mater, Pennsylvania State University, and wished for the opportunity to take courses outside of the Law School. Another student, who had graduated from the College of the City of New York and was planning to drop out, stated, "My father lost his job just at the right time: now I have a good excuse for ending a most harrowing experience. . . . A system of teaching defeats its own ends when students refrain from asking questions or making suggestions for fear of being jeered at by the oracle behind the desk."

A third document was prepared by "a Student Advisory Group," organized by the faculty Committee. Composed of nine third-year students, this group distributed an extensive questionnaire to all 1,500 students, received 471 responses, and wrote its own report at the end of the 1934–35 academic year.[86] This document criticized the large size of classes, the high student-faculty ratio (about 44:1), the high failure rate of about 34 percent in the first year, and the stultifying third year of study. Some students proposed radical reforms, such as dividing the student body into sections according to ability. One student, who described himself as "at the extreme lower end of the class," observed of the better students that *we hold them up and they rush us.*"[87]

Some of the best students, including David Riesman (LL.B. 1934), who clerked for Justice Louis Brandeis (LL.B. 1877) on the Supreme Court and became a professor of social science at Harvard, complained that the students received "very little understanding of the development of the law."[88] Hirsh Freed (LL.B. 1935), who became a friend and campaign aid for John F. Kennedy during the 1950s, stated:

> there is no organized effort on the part of the faculty to instill in the student body that dignity and respect for the law and for the social duties of the lawyer which are so important. Instead, . . . they acquire an increasing contempt for the law, and lose any interest they might have had formerly in social reform and the law as a means to that end. . . . The law as a game is emphasized to the exclusion of the notion of the law as a means to justice.[89]

Ironically, Freed was virtually repeating the criticism of the "sporting theory of justice . . . the modern American race to beat the law" that Pound had made three decades earlier in 1906."[90]

In regard to teaching, the Student Advisory Group summarized student evaluations of certain instructors, and suggested a mandatory retirement age of seventy-two for all faculty.[91] More generally, students said that the case method had become "in practice, an inefficient and time-wasteful lecture system." Instructors' attempts to generate student discussion often failed. "In the first year . . . a large amount of time is consumed by students asking unnecessary questions or volunteering worthless information. By the second year, most students realize that verbal participation does little to develop the subject under consideration. They are content to maintain a studied silence while a few, unwilling to be discouraged, become the spokesmen for the class. . . . The result is a discussion that is meager, constrained, and indulged in by only a few."[92]

To maintain the fiction of a discussion, the professor often "turns to one of the dozen or two 'bright boys' who sit in the front rows and whose aim it is to make an impression on the professor with the idea of getting good marks, and who are pretty glib on evidencing their study of the assigned cases without being conscientiously thoughtful and, much of the time, being parrot-like rather than thoughtful at all." After all this, having "failed to elicit his point," the professor "in the last ten minutes of the period . . . sums up the subject-matter of the discussion (via the lecture system)," and the students "write furiously." As a result, "a fifty-minute period has become a ten-minute lecture, for the preceding discussion has failed to serve as a dueling of intellects, on which the 'case system' is predicated."[93]

All three student groups fundamentally blamed Pound for the problems. They complained about his micromanagement, because "everything, every last detail, goes through the Dean's office, from the purchase of a new portrait to the appropriation of toilet paper."[94] The dean's picayune control created a "factory-like atmosphere" and put the Law School in a "coma." But nothing would change because the school was regarded as the best in the country.[95] Its imperium remained absolute. All three student groups therefore doubted the possibility of significant reform since "suggestions . . . of all sorts have always been met with a freezing reception from the Dean."[96]

Alumni and Conant Oppose Reform

The students were right, but the fault lay not only with Pound. The faculty Curriculum Committee also consulted prominent alumni and other legal professionals, most of whom disagreed sharply with the students. This feedback accounts for some of Pound's ambivalence on reform and the Law School's resistance to legal realism. Most senior and distinguished lawyers and jurists were hostile to any significant reforms and opposed incorporating the study of social sciences, which they disparaged.

T. Hovey Gage had graduated from Harvard College in 1886 and the Law School in 1889, and then served as assistant to U.S. Senator George F. Hoar (LL.B. 1849) while he was coauthoring the Sherman Anti-Trust Act of 1890. Despite that exposure to economic and social policy, Gage maintained that the "social sciences, so called . . . change so rapidly . . . that instruction in them today seems to me of little value to a lawyer fifteen years hence."[97] U.S. District Court Judge Robert P. Patterson (LL.B. 1915), appointed U.S. secretary of war in 1945, stated, "The study of law requires a precision of reasoning that might well be blunted if taken up along with [social] studies where greater laxity is the ruling trend."[98]

Patterson's future colleague on the U.S. Court of Appeals, Judge Learned Hand (LL.B. 1896), wrote, "I doubt if it is desirable or practicable to enlarge the field beyond what inevitably creeps in the modern courses of administration and constitutional law."[99] Former U.S. attorney general George W. Wickersham, not an alumnus, added, "The business of the Law School is to teach law. Once you open the door to . . . fields [of social science], there is no limit to the amount of time that may be spent in futile and speculative efforts."[100]

By the same token, the alumni were profoundly conservative as to mission and pedagogical reform. "I believe thoroughly in the School as it was twenty years ago and as it is today," Patterson continued, "and I should not relish seeing the School respond to whims and passing tendencies in legal education the value of which remains unproved."[101] Likewise, Cornelius W. Wickersham (LL.B. 1905), a prominent lawyer in New York City, wrote, "Many of . . . my generation, feel that teaching should be confined to the subject of law and that the subject of so-called social justice has no place in the teaching at the Harvard Law School."[102]

Harold Davis (LL.B. 1904), a leading member of the bar in Boston, recommended "that any reference to Brandeis, Cardozo, or Holmes result in expulsion." The Law School should produce lawyers, not "brain trusters" or "theorists," Davis maintained, and "I cannot believe . . . that the way to become a lawyer is to spend three years burning incense at the shrines of individual jurists."[103] Despite some dissenting voices, primarily from recent graduates, most alumni opposed any significant reform.

Dismissing social science as "lax," "futile," and "speculative" thus went hand-in-hand with discounting "social justice" as a direct jurisprudential goal, with defining law and legal study narrowly in doctrinal terms, and with denigrating illustrious jurisprudents who had challenged that definition and supported progressive legal interpretations. These early twentieth-century views were deeply rooted at Harvard Law School and persisted throughout the century. In the 1980s they would spark renewed debate in the controversy over Critical Legal Studies. And in the twenty-first century, Harvard graduates on the U.S. Supreme Court would echo them in discounting political scientists' statistical analysis demonstrating the political impact of highly gerrymandered electoral districts.[104] Devaluing social science in defence of judicial reasoning is precisely what Holmes, Pound, and Brandeis had opposed.

Meanwhile, President Conant, though expressing doubts about Pound's leadership, disappointed all those eager for radical change. Conant rejected the key student recommendations for reduced enrollment, smaller classes, and more individualized attention.[105] The president feared that such reforms would result in "an undesirable relaxation" of academic pressure on students, which was "one of the most important factors in the School's success in the past."[106] Conant objected even more strenuously on financial grounds. The student recommendations would cost money, and the school needed to run an operational surplus in order to make payments to the university toward the mortgage on the Langdell Hall expansion.[107] Indeed, Conant seems to have been more concerned about the school's debt than its academic mores.

In 1934 the faculty Committee created a subcommittee charged to examine "Admissions and Admissions Policy" with the central goal of reducing the attrition rate and its attendant problems.[108] In 1935 the Admissions Sub-Committee proposed radically raising the academic threshold that entitled applicants to admission and reducing the size of the first-year class. Under the existing system, 1,000 students were admitted to a class with total attrition of 35 percent by graduation. Under the proposed reform, 703 would be admitted with total attrition of 18 percent.[109] By raising the admission standard before admission in order to reduce attrition in the first two years, this proposal moved closer to the new selective admissions model that had proliferated in higher education since emerging in 1921.

Overall, the Committee projected that total LL.B. enrollment would decrease by about 17 percent, from about 1,450 to about 1,200. The Admissions Sub-Committee did not propose raising tuition, and acknowledged that the reform would lead to "a considerable reduction in receipts from tuition," which the subcommittee did not bother to calculate, believing that they should consider issues only "from an educational standpoint."[110] Whatever the amount, this proposal to reduce tuition revenue was out of the question, in Conant's view. "The school's practice of admitting a large first-year class and then failing out a third of them brought in more funding than the proposed reform of admitting fewer students and allowing a smaller percentage to fail out after the first year," he said.[111] Like the Committee, Conant gave no thought to raising tuition, especially during the Depression.

Finances dominated the president's thinking because the university held the school's mortgage. Conant did not want to have to bail out an impoverished Law School in the middle of the Depression, particularly because he disliked fundraising and the university was planning a campaign for its three-hundredth anniversary in 1936. Hence, Conant would not approve changes that weakened academic competition and cost money, or changes that strengthened academic standards and cost money. He simply would not approve any changes that cost money.

As a result, the intellectual sword would not be sheathed, and the high rate of attrition continued. The Spartan ethos and straitened finances reinforced each other, as Conant effectively endorsed the school's tuition dependence syndrome in 1935: large and growing enrollment, high student-faculty ratio, and high attrition, while living "hand-to-mouth" in order to pay its debt to the university on its large physical plant. By the same token, Harvard's detrimental template for the financial isomorphism in legal education persisted.

Conservative Outcome, 1936

In June 1936 the Curriculum Committee issued a printed *Report,* as conservative in its recommendations as the process had been radical in scope, methodology, and aims. Regarding the curriculum itself, the *Report* acknowledged "the growth of the body of law since 1877" because "whole new fields have opened up." But the Committee was "satisfied that the growth of the [Harvard] curriculum has kept pace—approximately—with the growth of the law." Suggestions for major changes in the LL.B. program were rejected. Yes, some revision was required by "the growing volume of legal instruction," by "the growing demand that lawyers be trained . . . in cognate subjects," and by "a lack of coordination in the curriculum as it now stands." But the proposed changes were minor.[112]

The *Report* emphatically rejected the students' recommendations. Nearly 87 percent of the students surveyed thought that class size should be limited to 100 students. This limit, though hardly low, was rejected by the Committee, which maintained that a larger class has more "first-rate students," and "develops self-reliance while very small classes tend to 'spoon feeding.'" Further, "the mere presence of a large class acts as an inspiration to some teachers, just as a packed theater may inspire an actor or a well-filled church a clergyman."[113] As for small third-year seminars or more individualized instruction, the *Report* concluded, "In view of the School's size, the necessary limitations upon the numbers of the Faculty, and the School's tradition which insists that every student learn his law directly from the best teachers . . . the case method with classes of probably not less than 100 must remain the backbone of the system of instruction at the School." Besides, "not all members of the Faculty are temperamentally adopted to tutorial work."[114]

Absolutely no changes were to be permitted in the first year: not the courses, class size, examination format, or the case method. It was during the first year that a student learned to wield his own intellectual sword. "One of the glories of the School has been its hardy intellectual atmosphere—the tradition of 'standing on your own feet,' the autonomous student discussions outside the classroom, the independence and self-reliance of its students. . . . The budding lawyer <u>must</u> learn to stand on his own feet. . . . No system of individual assistance which detracted from this atmosphere would be worth the price. Moreover, the Law School is preparing for practice in a hard world."[115] The existing first-year course of study was therefore praised for "the stimulating effect of an immediate introduction to the School in full blast" and for "its unique and vital quality."[116]

During the fall of 1936, the faculty read and debated the report. Reform-minded members of the faculty were deeply disappointed. Zechariah Chafee Jr. (LL.B. 1913) wrote a response, stating, "I find only the present elements of the life of the school differently arranged and somewhat differently stressed."[117] Thomas Powell also responded that the *Report* "contained little of fundamental importance and practically nothing to reject."[118] In March 1937 the faculty adopted a slightly modified version of the *Report*.

Subsequent assessments of this outcome have varied. In his history of the Law School, Arthur E. Sutherland (LL.B. 1925) approved the result and considered the student complaints as typical of every generation, remarking "*Plus ça change*."[119] Others have seen simply a "rationalization of the status quo at Harvard Law School."[120] Still others interpret it as evidence of Spartan manliness: "A fear of being perceived as 'soft'" prompted the school's "emphasis on legal principles, its defenses of large classes, and its rejection of realism."[121] Though all having a measure of truth, these interpretations tend to overlook the financial constraints that guided President Conant.

"A Great Disappointment"

Over the course of the two-year study by the faculty Curriculum Committee between 1934 and 1936, Pound's personal domination of the school ebbed. His input was neither solicited nor heeded when offered. In September 1936, at the age of sixty-six, he finally stepped down as dean. Conant rewarded Pound for his service with one of Harvard's new University Professorships, a prominent role in the tercentenary ceremonies, and an initiative to endow a professorship in his name.[122]

After resigning in 1936, Pound lived another twenty-eight years in a hotel on the Cambridge common, walking daily to his office in the Law School. He wrote a monumental, but pedestrian, five-volume summary of Western jurisprudence, worked devotedly for Chiang Kai-shek and Taiwan, and stridently denounced Communism. Reversing the path of his youth, he retreated deeper into such right-wing causes as requiring loyalty oaths, supporting the Council Against Communist Aggression, and attacking the United Nations. He died in 1964, at the age of ninety-three.[123]

In their overall assessment of Pound's tenure, even critics such as Joel Seligman maintain that "by conventional criteria, Pound was a successful dean," pointing to the school's quantitative growth in enrollment, faculty, physical plant, books in the library, and endowment during his term.[124] But the school's expansion under Pound actually worsened its fundamental financial predicament. Furthermore, during the 1920s Pound donned his own "intellectual straightjacket."[125] His tenure lasted "too long," and he "really outlived his own work," according to Professor Arthur von Mehren. "The things that he had done, that had been so imaginative and creative earlier in the century, were now commonplace and people no longer credited him with his really important contributions, and he was not in position to do new things."[126]

J. Willard Hurst attended Harvard Law School from 1932 to 1935 at the very end of Pound's term. Graduating first in his class, Hurst served as a research fellow for one year with Felix Frankfurter, who then recommended him to clerk for Brandeis. In 1937 Hurst joined the faculty of the University of Wisconsin Law School, where he remained for forty-four years and became the nation's leading legal historian. In a private letter in 1957, Hurst expressed

> my feeling that the Harvard of Roscoe Pound represented a great disappointment. It was an excellent trade school, by and large, when I attended. . . . Except for T. R. Powell, Felix Frankfurter, Henry Hart, and a couple of others in

isolated courses, it was an intellectually stodgy place, content largely to teach and research law as a self-contained system, and as a largely "private" system, and as simply a logician's system. One could do well in three years at the Harvard Law School and get little or no sense of (1) legislative or executive law, (2) the dynamic role of law in mediating sizable and dangerous clashes of social interest, (3) the relation of law to the functioning of non-legal institutions.[127]

Pound's resignation therefore released a surge of excitement at the Law School. As Chafee wrote to the faculty in October 1936, there was "a spirit of adventure, of a brave new world ahead of us, of a better school and a better law, as glowing possibilities in the near future."[128] The mass of data assembled by the Committee on Curriculum could "frame a plan upon which a leader could begin to act," Gardner wrote to future dean James Landis (1937–1946), then on leave in Washington, serving as chairman of the SEC.[129] Following the "great disappointment" of Pound's tenure, the school's next leader would face "a brave new world" and a future clouded by financial challenges, the combative Spartan culture, the continuing Depression, and ominous troubles once again brewing in Europe.

NOTES

1. This chapter draws upon David Wigdor, *Roscoe Pound: Philosopher of Law* (Westport, CT, 1974); N. E. H. Hull, *Roscoe Pound and Karl Llewellyn: Searching for an American Jurisprudence* (Chicago, 1997); James F. Clark, "The Harvard Law School Deanship of Roscoe Pound, 1916–1936" (student research paper, Harvard Law School, 1999), on file with the authors.

2. See Anthony J. Badger, *The New Deal: The Depression Years, 1933–1940* (New York, 1989); Robert S. McElvaine, *The Great Depression, 1929–1941,* rev. ed. (New York, 2009); David M. Kennedy, *Freedom from Fear: The American People in Depression and War, 1929–1945* (New York, 1999).

3. Roger L. Geiger. *The History of American Higher Education: Learning and Culture from the Founding to World War II* (Princeton, NJ, 2014), 507–508.

4. For enrollment statistics in this chapter, we are indebted to research reports by Jamie M. Brown (Harvard Law School, J.D. 2015), Brandi Pugh (Boston College Law School, J.D. 2016), and Jeremy B. Luke (Ohio State University, Ph.D. 2018), on file with the authors.

5. Arthur von Mehren, Oral History, conducted by Daniel R. Coquillette and Mary Beth Basile (July–December 2000), on file with the authors.

6. Joel Seligman, *The High Citadel: The Influence of Harvard Law School* (Boston, 1978), 34.

7. Ernest J. Brown, Oral History, conducted by Daniel Hamilton (August 1997), on file with the authors. See Seligman, *High Citadel,* 64.

8. Wigdor, *Roscoe Pound,* 264, quoting Pound's correspondence with Morris Cohen. See also Morris Cohen to Roscoe Pound (July 9 and September 23, 1938), in Leonora C. Rosenfield, *Portrait of a Philosopher: Morris Cohen in Life and Letters* (New York, 1962), 307, 310.

9. Roscoe Pound, "Report of the Special Committee on Administrative Law," *Reports of the ABA* 62 (1938): 343.

10. Quotations are from Wigdor, *Roscoe Pound,* 264, 268. See David M. Rabban, *Law's History: American Legal Thought and the Transatlantic Turn to History* (Cambridge, UK, 2014), 423.

11. See *A.L.A. Schechter Poultry Corp. v. United States,* 295 U.S. 495 (1935); *United States v. Butler,* 297 U.S. 1 (1936).

12. Wigdor, *Roscoe Pound,* 271. Morton J. Horwitz, *The Transformation of American Law, 1870–1960: The Crisis of Legal Orthodoxy* (Oxford, 1992), 219–220.

13. Quotation is from Roscoe Pound, "The Future of the Common Law," *University of Cincinnati Law Review* 7 (1933): 358. See Daniel R. Coquillette, *The Anglo-American Legal Heritage,* 2nd ed. (Durham, NC, 2004), 311–361.

14. Wigdor, *Roscoe Pound,* 271, referencing Roscoe Pound to Henry M. Butler (December 22, 1942), Roscoe Pound Papers, 1888–1964, Harvard Law School Library Historical & Special Collections (HLSLib) (hereafter cited as RP Papers).

15. Hull, *Roscoe Pound,* 116.

16. Here and below, we draw upon James G. Hershberg, *James B. Conant: Harvard to Hiroshima and the Making of the Nuclear Age* (Stanford, CA, 1993); Stephen H. Norwood, *The Third Reich in the Ivory Tower: Complicity and Conflict on American Campuses* (Cambridge, UK, 2009).

17. Norwood, *The Third Reich in the Ivory Tower,* 5, 57.

18. John Grant Haviland, The Student Looks at Harvard Law School [Observations of the school by students in 1934] (unpublished typescript, revised Spring 1934), on file with the authors, 46. See Archibald Cox, Oral History, conducted by Daniel R. Coquillette and Daniel Hamilton (November 1998), on file with the authors.

19. Quotations are from Norwood, *The Third Reich in the Ivory Tower,* 42–46. See Charles A. Beard, "Germany up to Her Old Tricks," *New Republic* (October 24, 1934): 299–300.

20. Quotations are from, respectively, Norwood, *The Third Reich in the Ivory Tower,* 49–50; James B. Conant, *My Several Lives: Memoirs of a Social Inventor* (New York, 1970), 141.

21. Quotations are from Norwood, *The Third Reich in the Ivory Tower,* 53–55. See also Carol Sicherman, *Rude Awakenings: An American Historian's Encounters with Nazism,*

Communism, and McCarthyism (Washington, DC, 2011), 202–203; Conant, *My Several Lives,* 141–142.

22. "Austro-Reich Border Quiet, Dean Pound Says after Tour," *Paris Herald* (August 4, 1934), quoted in Beard, "Germany up to Her Old Tricks," 299.

23. "Austro-Reich Border Quiet, Dean Pound Says After Tour," *Paris Herald* (August 4, 1934), quoted in Beard, "Germany Up to Her Old Tricks," 299.

24. "Austro-Reich Border Quiet, Dean Pound Says After Tour," *Paris Herald* (August 4, 1934), quoted in Beard, "Germany Up to Her Old Tricks," 299.

25. "Dean Pound left Paris with Mrs. Pound for Innsbruck, July 6, and motored to Salzburg and Bad-Ischl en route to Vienna and Budapest. In Bavaria they stopped at Oberammergau and passed several days in Munich, where Dean Pound discussed the current situation as well as the new movement in German law with German teachers of the University of Munich." "Austro-Reich Border Quiet, Dean Pound Says After Tour," *Paris Herald* (August 4, 1934), quoted in Beard, "Germany Up to Her Old Tricks," 299.

26. Patrick Leigh Fermor, *A Time of Gifts: On Foot to Constantinople; From the Hook of Holland to the Middle Danube* (New York, 1977), 132, 195.

27. "Dean Pound Finds Germans Content," *New York Herald Tribune* (August 25, 1934).

28. Beard, "Germany up to Her Old Tricks," 299–300.

29. The following account of Pound's trips to Germany is indebted to the excellent research of Peter Rees, a student of Daniel Coquillette at Boston College Law School and contributor to the Harvard Law School History Project since 2014. Fuller documentation on the following points is available in Peter Rees, "Dean Roscoe Pound and the Nazis" (student research paper, Boston College Law School, 2014), on file with the authors; Peter Rees, "Nathan Roscoe Pound and the Nazis," *Boston College Law Review* 60 (May 2019): 1313–1347. The latter article explicitly attributes to Pound sympathy for Hitler and Nazism, whereas our interpretation here suggests that events can in large part be explained by Pound's long-standing affection for German culture, his infamous vanity, which was exploited by the German Foreign Office in orchestrating events, and Pound's notorious high-handed refusal to admit that he made mistakes, as in defending Chroust subsequently.

30. Pound, Diary (July 11, 1934). See Rees, "Nathan Roscoe Pound and the Nazis," 1317–1323; Harvard Law School Catalog, 1931–32, 28, 1932–33, 29; Joseph E. Goodbar, "Dollar Bond Indentures of French and German Corporations," *Boston University Law Review* 13 (1933): 22–49; Joseph E. Goodbar, "Muddling Through Monetary and Economic Law," *Boston University Law Review* 20 (1940): 298–315.

31. Roscoe Pound, Diary (July 12, 1934), RP Papers. See Rees, "Nathan Roscoe Pound and the Nazis," 1317–1323.

32. Roscoe Pound, Diary (July 12, 1934), RP Papers. See Rees, "Nathan Roscoe Pound and the Nazis," 1317–1323.

33. [Hans Luther], Memorandum to the Foreign Office: "Recognition and Award of an Honorary Degree to Dean Roscoe Pound" (June 4, 1934), Files regarding German Trib-

utes for Foreigners, vol. 9, Political Archive of the Foreign Office, Archives of the [Federal] Department of Foreign Affairs, Berlin, Germany, translated by Peter Rees.

34. Beard, "Germany up to Her Old Tricks," 299–300.

35. [Luther], Memorandum.

36. Roscoe Pound, Diary (September 17, 1934), RP Papers. See "Pound Gets Reich Honor," *New York Times* (September 18, 1934).

37. Cox, Oral History (November 1998). See "Pound Gets Reich Honor."

38. Felix Frankfurter to Roscoe Pound (September 14, 1934), Harvard Law School Dean's Office Records, Records of President James B. Conant, 1933–1953, Harvard University Archives (HUA) (hereafter cited as JBC Records).

39. Erwin N. Griswold, *Ould Fields, New Corne: The Personal Memoirs of a Twentieth Century Lawyer* (St. Paul, MN, 1992), 119.

40. The following draws upon Hershberg, *James B. Conant*, 87–88; Morton Keller and Phyllis Keller, *Making Harvard Modern: The Rise of America's University* (New York, 2001), 49; Norwood, *The Third Reich in the Ivory Tower*, 37.

41. Felix Frankfurter, "Memorandum of Conversation with Pound and President Conant regarding an Invitation from Pound" (September 14, 1934), Felix Frankfurter Papers, 1900–1965, HLSLib. See Clark, "The Harvard Law School Deanship," 136. The most explicit charges that Pound supported the Nazi cause appear in Frankfurter's private memorandum, which is quoted extensively in Rees, "Nathan Roscoe Pound," 1329–1332. It is difficult to know how much to credit this account, particularly regarding Frankfurter's conversations with Conant, whose own positions regarding the Nazis were equivocal during the 1930s.

42. "Pound Gets Reich Honor"; Conant, *My Several Lives,* 143.

43. "Harvard Refuses Hanfstaengl Gift: Scholarship Offer by Hitler Is Rejected and Conant Writes a Sharp Note," *New York Times* (October 4, 1934). See "Harvard Rebuffs Dr. Hanfstaengl," *Boston Globe* (October 4, 1934).

44. Beard, "Germany up to Her Old Tricks," 299–300.

45. Roscoe Pound, Diary (July 20–21, 1936; July–August, 1937), RP Papers. See Rees, "Nathan Roscoe Pound and the Nazis," 1317–1318; Lucy S. Dawidowicz, *The War against the Jews, 1933–1945* (New York, 1975).

46. Our research assistants believe that at some point Pound's files may have been scrubbed of photos from his trips to Nazi Germany.

47. Harvard Law School Catalog, 1933–34, 29; Harvard Law School, *Quinquennial Catalogue of the Law School of Harvard University* (Cambridge, 1939), 371.

48. [Luther], Memorandum. See Rees, "Nathan Roscoe Pound," 1326, 1333–1338.

49. FBI files cited in Rees, "Nathan Roscoe Pound," 1333–1338.

50. Edward J. Ennis, "Anton Hermann Chroust, Excerpt of Hearing, Alien Enemy Repatriation Hearing Board" (January 24, 1946), FBI files, National Archives and Records Administration, Washington, DC.

51. Quoted in David I. Walsh to Roscoe Pound (July 25, 1945), RP Papers. See Rees, "Nathan Roscoe Pound," 1340–1343.

52. Quotations are from R. W. Deitchler, Report on Hearing of Anton Hermann Chroust before Alien Enemy Hearing Board (January 8, 1942), FBI files, National Archives and Records Administration, Washington, DC; A. H. Belmont to L. V. Boardman [office memorandum] (November 30, 1956), FBI Files, National Archives and Records Administration. See Rees, "Nathan Roscoe Pound," 1334–1338.

53. Statement by Mr. Griswold to Alien Enemy Hearing Board for Massachusetts, Case of Anton-Hermann Chroust (January 6, 1942), quoted in Mary Beth Basile Chopas, *Searching for Subversives: The Story of Italian Internment in Wartime America* (Chapel Hill, NC, 2017), 84–85.

54. Ennis, "Anton Hermann Chroust," 14. See Anton-Hermann Chroust, Identification card for the National Socialist German Workers' Party (September 12, 1939), Bundesarchiv (Germany), BArch, R 9361-VIII Kartei / 5141541.

55. Deitchler, Report on Hearing of Anton Hermann Chroust (January 8, 1942); Belmont to Boardman (November 30, 1956).

56. Deitchler, Report on Hearing of Anton Hermann Chroust (January 8, 1942).

57. Chroust's second detention is reported in Kayleigh E. McGlynn, "Anton-Hermann Chroust: Did the University of Notre Dame Knowingly Appoint an Alleged Nazi Spy to a Tenure-Track Faculty Position?," (student research paper, Boston College Law School, 2019), on file with the authors, 19, 57.

58. The Attorney General is quoted in Walsh to Pound (July 25, 1945), as reported in Rees, "Nathan Roscoe Pound," 1341.

59. Rees, "Nathan Roscoe Pound," 1338–1346.

60. Making a "materially false, fictitious or fraudulent statement" can lead to "not more than five years" in prison. Title 18 U.S. Code, sec. 1011 (a) (2). It is a crime to "conceal" a "material fact." Title 18 U.S. Code, sec. 1001 (a) (2).

61. Ennis, "Anton Hermann Chroust," 14–15.

62. Edward J. Ennis, "Memorandum for the Attorney General re. Anton Hermann Chroust, Conduct of Repatriation Hearing (February 20, 1946)," FBI Files, National Archives and Records Administration, 6.

63. Quotations are from Roscoe Pound to James F. Price (April 17, 1946), RP Papers. See McGlynn, "Anton-Hermann Chroust," 28, 57.

64. Anton-Hermann Chroust, *The Rise of the Legal Profession in America,* 2 vols. (Norman, OK, 1965).

65. Belmont to Boardman (November 30, 1956).

66. Rafael Mares, "Everything Dean Clark Doesn't Want You to Know about Diversity and Student Activism at HLS," *HLSR* (December 6, 1996): 7. See "Faculty Office Building and Classroom and Administration Building for Harvard Law School . . . ," *Architectural Record* 151 (January 1972): 124–132.

67. Jacob M. Appel to Dean Robert C. Clark (December 23, 1996), on file with the authors.

68. Leon C. Baker (LL.B. 1945) wrote, "I do have personal knowledge of one fact, however, which demonstrates that Dean Pound was not anti-Semitic. In my last year of law school, another Jewish student and I lived in Pound's home." Baker, "Letter," *HLSR* (February 7, 1997): 13. T. S. L. Perlman (LL.B. 1943) pointed out that his father, Sol Phillips Perlman (LL.B. 1920), had succeeded in practice "upon recommendation of Dean Pound." Perlman, Letter, *HLSR* (March 14, 1997): 6.

69. Guido Calabresi, "Appendix: Transcript," in "Symposium: Legal Education in Twentieth-Century America," *Fordham Law Review* 87 (2018): 904–905.

70. Quoted in Felix Frankfurter, Diary (December 21, 1931), Frankfurter Papers. See Felix Frankfurter to Thomas Reed Powell (December 18, 1933), Thomas Reed Powell Papers, 1905–1955, HLSLib.

71. Clark, "The Harvard Law School Deanship," 134–137; Kalman, *Legal Realism at Yale,* 60–61; Brown, Oral History (August 1997).

72. Keller and Keller, *Making Harvard,* 113; Hershberg, *James B. Conant,* 87–88; Wigdor, *Roscoe Pound,* 251.

73. Conant, *My Several Lives,* 110.

74. Thomas Reed Powell, "Memorandum, the Harvard Law School" (February 20, 1928), Harvard Law School Dean's Office Records, Records of President A. Lawrence Lowell, 1909–1933, HUA. See Clark, "The Harvard Law School Deanship," 138.

75. Quoted in Wigdor, *Roscoe Pound,* 251.

76. Williston, *Life and Law,* 187.

77. Harvard Law School Faculty Meeting Minutes (May 15, 1934).

78. Harvard Law School Faculty Committee on Curriculum, Report (June 15, 1936), JBC Records, 1–2. The Committee's data was compiled in two immense, loose-leaf notebooks entitled "Harvard Law School Faculty Committee on Curriculum, Survey of the Harvard Law School Curriculum, 1934–35" (February 1, 1935), vols. 1–2, JBC Records.

79. Harvard Law School Faculty Committee on Curriculum, Report (June 15, 1936), 2. Here and below, we draw upon Christopher W. Schmidt, "The Failure of Reform: Legal Education at Harvard Law School, 1934–1946" (student research paper, Harvard Law School, 2006), on file with the authors; John J. Liolos, "Erecting the High Citadel's Walls: The Development of Formal Admissions Standards at Harvard Law School, 1817–1955" (student research paper, Harvard Law School, 2013), on file with the authors.

80. Quotations are from Felix Frankfurter, "Some Observations on Third Year Work," in Harvard Law School Faculty Committee on Curriculum, Survey of the Harvard Law School Curriculum, 1934–1935 (February 1, 1935), JBC Records, vol. 2, 254–258.

81. Frankfurter, "Some Observations on Third Year Work."

82. Frankfurter, "Some Observations on Third Year Work."

83. Haviland, "The Student Looks," 6.

84. Haviland, "The Student Looks," 6, 12, 14.

85. The following quotations are from Haviland, "The Student Looks," 48–95.

86. [Student Advisory Group,] " Comments on the Harvard Law School 1935," in Harvard Law School Faculty Committee on Curriculum, Survey of the Harvard Law School Curriculum, 1934–35 (February 1, 1935), JBC Records.

87. Letter from unidentified second-year student to John A. Maguire (March 18, 1935), in Records of Faculty Committee on Curriculum, 1934–, JBC Records.

88. David Riesman Jr. to Sidney P. Simpson (January 21, 1935), in Harvard Law School Faculty Committee on Curriculum, Survey of the Harvard Law School Curriculum, 1934–35 (February 1, 1935), JBC Records, 124.

89. Hirsh Freed to Roscoe Pound (July 16, 1935) [addendum to Committee minutes of September 25, 1935], Records of Faculty Committee on Curriculum, 1934–, JBC Records.

90. Roscoe Pound, "The Causes of Popular Dissatisfaction with the Administration of Justice," *American Law Review* 40 (1906): 747.

91. *Supplemental Report of Student Opinion on Members of the Faculty and Their Teaching Methods* [addendum to Committee minutes of June 17, 1935], 226–238, Records of Faculty Committee on Curriculum, 1934–, JBC Records.

92. [Student Advisory Group,] "Comments on the Harvard Law School 1935," 145.

93. Carl E. Newton to Sidney P. Simpson (April 30, 1935), in [Student Advisory Group,] "Comments," 85.

94. *Supplemental Report of Student Opinion, 1935,* np. See Ritchie, *James M. Landis,* 80; Kalman, *Legal Realism at Yale,* 60.

95. Richard H. Domuts to Sidney P. Simpson (November 26, 1934), in [Student Advisory Group,] "Comments" 118.

96. *Supplemental Report of Student Opinion, 1935,* np. Yet, Pound did express personal appreciation to the students for their feedback, as he did to the faculty concurrently. Haviland, "The Student Looks," 159.

97. T. Hovey Gage to Warren A. Seavey (February 18, 1935), in [Student Advisory Group,] "Comments," 6.

98. Robert P. Patterson to Warren A. Seavey (February 16, 1935), in [Student Advisory Group,] "Comments," 17–18.

99. Learned Hand to Warren A. Seavey (February 13, 1935), in [Student Advisory Group,] "Comments," 8.

100. George W. Wickersham to Warren A. Seavey (March 12, 1935, in [Student Advisory Group,] "Comments," 29.

101. Patterson to Seavey (February 16, 1935).

102. Cornelius W. Wickersham to Samuel Williston (December 28, 1934), in [Student Advisory Group,] "Comments," 62. Cornelius Wickersham was the son of George W. Wickersham.

103. Harold S. Davis, [letter ca. 1934] in [Student Advisory Group,] "Comments," 44.

104. See comments by Chief Justice John G. Roberts Jr. (J.D. 1979) and Justice Stephen G. Breyer (LL.B. 1964) in the oral arguments before the Supreme Court on October 3, 2017, in the case of *Gill v. Whitford,* 138 U.S. 1916 (2018).

105. Faculty Committee on Curriculum, Minutes (October 29, 1935), Records of Faculty Committee on Curriculum, 1934–, JBC Records, 295–297.

106. Faculty Committee on Curriculum, Minutes (October 29, 1935).

107. Schmidt, "The Failure of Reform," 39.

108. James M. Landis, Annual Report of the Dean of Harvard Law School, 1938–39, 195; "Law Requirements Raised at Harvard," *New York Times* (January 15, 1937).

109. *Report of the Committee on Curriculum,* 10. See Liolos, "Erecting the High Citadel's Walls," 50–61.

110. Sub-Committee on Admissions and Admission Policy, Report (May 15, 1935), Records of Faculty Committee on Curriculum, 1934–, JBC Records.

111. Schmidt, "The Failure of Reform," 42. See Sub-Committee on Admissions and Admission Policy, Report (May 15, 1935); Faculty Committee on Curriculum, Minutes (February 18, March 1, and October 29, 1935).

112. Quotations are from *Report of the Committee on Curriculum,* 5, 9. This section draws on Schmidt, "The Failure of Reform."

113. *Report of the Committee on Curriculum,* 51–52.

114. *Report of the Committee on Curriculum,* 52, 56.

115. *Report of the Committee on Curriculum,* 56–57.

116. *Report of the Committee on Curriculum,* 60, 62.

117. Zechariah Chafee Jr., "An Echo to the Report" [circa October 1936], Records of Faculty Committee on Curriculum, 1934–, JBC Records.

118. Thomas Reed Powell to George K. Gardner (August 13, 1936) in Records of Faculty Committee on Curriculum, 1934–, JBC Records.

119. Arthur E. Sutherland, *The Law at Harvard: A History of Ideas and Men, 1817–1907* (Cambridge, MA, 1967), 285.

120. Schmidt, "The Failure of Reform," 49.

121. See Kalman, *Legal Realism at Yale,* 66. See Edward H. Warren, *Spartan Education* (Cambridge, MA, 1942).

122. The professorship was fully funded only in 1950. The first holder of the Chair, from 1950 to 1963, was Sheldon Glueck, whose sociological studies of crime had been consistently encouraged by Pound. See Sutherland, *Law at Harvard,* 272–273, 279–281. Glueck's brilliant wife, Eleanor, who did much of the research, was overlooked.

123. See Wigdor, *Roscoe Pound,* 275–281; Sutherland, *Law at Harvard,* 297–299; Angela Ann-Hwey Wu, "Contextualizing 'Sociological Jurisprudence': Dean Roscoe Pound in the Republic of China 1946–1948" (student research paper, Harvard Law School, 2006), on file with the authors.

124. Seligman, *High Citadel,* 60.

125. Wigdor, *Roscoe Pound*, 255.

126. von Mehren, Oral History (July–December 2000).

127. J. Willard Hurst to Joseph H. Willits (March 20, 1957), J. Willard Hurst Collection 1932–1997, University of Wisconsin Law Library Special Collections.

128. Zechariah Chafee Jr. to Harvard Law School Faculty (October 1936), JBC Records. See Clark, "The Harvard Law School Deanship," 144.

129. George K. Gardner to James M. Landis (June 24, 1936), JBC Records.

CHAPTER EIGHT

The "Meteoric" Rise and Fall of James Landis, 1937–1946

In September 1936 Harvard University commemorated its tercentenary, holding dozens of panels and capstone lectures and conferring no less than eighty-six honorary degrees over a two-week period. To mark the event, Samuel Eliot Morison published *Three Centuries of Harvard* which served bid farewell to the Brahmin tradition of President A. Lawrence Lowell (1909–1933) and to welcome his modern successor, the chemist James Conant (1933–1953). Even so, the university scheduled the peak events during the High Holiday of Rosh Hashanah, and Jewish faculty and alumni protested. University secretary Jerome Greene, who coordinated the tercentenary celebration, conceded that "there has unquestionably been a lag in Harvard's recognition of the growing number and importance of its Jewish members." But the university did not reschedule any events.[1] The tercentenary was also a send-off for Dean Roscoe Pound (1916–1936), who participated prominently just before relinquishing his office at the end of September 1936.

Having presided at the Law School faculty meetings and appointed Edmund Morgan (LL.B. 1905) as acting dean, Conant was already seeking Pound's successor. In general, Conant preferred deans who, like himself, relied upon scientific management. In 1935 he replaced the savvy and successful dean of the medical school, David L. Edsall, with the researcher C. Sidney Burwell, who slowed that school's momentum.[2] The president would later also edge out the skillful, entrepreneurial dean of Harvard Business School, Wallace Donham (LL.B. 1910).

Part of Conant's motivation was to chart a new course for the university, just as Lowell had steered Harvard away from the focus of his predecessor, President Charles Eliot (1869–1909), on graduate and professional schools and toward the Oxbridge tradition of holistic, residential, liberal education.

Conant wanted to appoint a Law School dean who had risen purely by talent, rather than pedigree, and could "inject ideas gleaned from real life into the dreary business of academic leadership."[3] The president selected James Landis (1937–1946), whose "meteoric" career rapidly soared and shone brightly, but just as quickly plummeted and flamed out.[4] Even so, Landis left a profound legacy to Harvard Law School of justifying and teaching public law, legislation, rulemaking, and administrative process.

From Japan to Harvard: "The Strongest Man"

President Conant saw himself as utterly different from his predecessor. He did share Lowell's Boston roots and Harvard pedigree, having earned a B.A. in 1913 and a Ph.D. in 1916, both in physical chemistry, from the university. In 1919 he joined the faculty at Harvard, where he remained for the rest of his academic career, rising through the academic ranks. In contrast to Lowell, Conant considered the university to be a center of scholarship and research and a vehicle of social mobility based on academic performance. This meritocratic commitment explains his interest in expanding Harvard's enrollment of students outside of northeastern private preparatory schools. Instead, Conant wanted Harvard College to recruit from public high schools, small towns, and the South and West, and he established a famous National Scholarship Program to effect this.[5] But this commitment did not extend to women or to certain ethnic and racial minorities or to challenging anti-Semitism within the university, even as World War II approached and the Nazis' persecution of the Jews became evident.[6]

Also in contrast to Lowell, Conant saw the inevitability and necessity of social engineering and a powerful central government as the Depression deepened and war loomed in Europe. Lowell's deep dislike for and distrust of Roosevelt, shared by Pound, was replaced by Conant's belief in public policy and social mobility. In the Law School, Conant wanted a leader who viewed law and legal research as tools of social progress.[7]

Conant was well aware of James Landis, who became chairman of the Securities and Exchange Commission (SEC) on the same day in 1935 that Pound submitted his resignation. But Conant, like others, had doubts. Felix Frankfurter (LL.B. 1906) believed that Landis, his protégé, had the wrong temperament, and would not devote himself fully to the school. Mercurial as ever, Frankfurter preferred the older traditionalists on the faculty, such as Edmund Morgan, Austin Scott (LL.B. 1909), or W. Barton Leach (LL.B. 1924). Conant,

James B. Conant, President of Harvard University 1933–1953.

Courtesy of Harvard University Archives.

for his part, was concerned about the deterioration in alumni relations—partly due to Frankfurter's radical reputation—and wanted "a distinguished dean, one who would soothe tempers while staying out of the headlines."[8]

Given these varied and somewhat inconsistent aims, Conant first selected a complete outsider, Henry W. Biklé, a graduate and professor of the University of Pennsylvania Law School. Biklé was a balanced choice, being a liberal Democrat and the general counsel of the Pennsylvania Railroad. But Biklé had reservations about his health, and sensed that the Harvard Law School faculty disdained legal practice. In fact, he compared them to a military staff composed of West Point graduates who had never served in the field. He therefore declined Conant's offer in March 1936.[9]

Conant also considered U.S. District Court Judge Robert Patterson (LL.B. 1915), who opposed broadening the school's curriculum with social sciences. But Patterson had practically no academic experience, and, perhaps wisely, withdrew from consideration. Conant now needed to act quickly, given that the school had languished in Pound's closing years. Landis became the leading candidate due to his administrative experience and brilliant academic record, attributes that appealed to Conant.

James M. Landis, LL.B. 1924, S.J.D. 1925. Faculty 1926–1945, Dean 1937–1946.

Harvard Law School Yearbook, 1938–1939. Courtesy of Harvard Yearbook Publications.

But Landis was seen as a risky choice, partly because his personal background was even further removed from Brahmin Boston than Conant's or even Pound's.[10] Born in Japan in 1899, the son of an ardent Presbyterian missionary and his German wife, Landis was educated at the Tokyo Foreign School with other missionary children. At age thirteen he was sent to the United States to attend Mercersburg Academy in Pennsylvania, where he paid tuition by waiting tables. At age sixteen he went to work in a West Virginia coal-mining town to earn money for college, and his encounter with the arduous life of the miners awakened his social conscience. Determined to be a missionary like his father, Landis enrolled at Princeton in 1916, barely seventeen years old. He then dropped out to volunteer to aid the allied war effort in France by serving with the British YMCA. The horrors of the battlefield shattered his religious faith and ruined his health.[11]

Returning to Princeton after the war, Landis excelled academically. Tutoring his wealthy classmates and selling class notes made him popular as well as financially secure for the first time. His classmates elected him to a class office and voted him "most brilliant." At graduation in 1921, Landis ranked first in his class, read the Latin Salutatory at graduation, and won three major university prizes. The *Michigan Law Review* accepted his undergraduate thesis, "The Commerce Clause as a Restriction on State Taxation," for publication, and Harvard Law School awarded him a scholarship.[12]

The Law School turned out to be a perfect match. At the end of his first year, 1921–22, Landis was elected to the *Law Review* along with his classmate and close friend Barton Leach, who would join the faculty in 1929. Roscoe Pound wrote that Landis "was the strongest man I ever had under me."[13] Though Felix Frankfurter initially endorsed one of Landis's rivals for president of the *Harvard Law Review,* he became a major supporter of Landis by the end of his third year. The faculty considered the two of them "birds of a feather."[14] When Landis graduated first in his class, Frankfurter named him a research fellow in order to support Landis's study in the new S.J.D. program during 1924–25. Frankfurter then nominated him to clerk for Justice Louis Brandeis (LL.B. 1877).

After Landis completed the clerkship in 1926, Brandeis and Frankfurter recommended him for the faculty, and Landis was duly appointed assistant professor. When Landis expressed concern about the low salary, Brandeis secretly offered to loan the young man $2,000 to establish his new family in Cambridge. In 1928 the University of Pennsylvania tried to lure him away with a higher salary, but Frankfurter persuaded the Harvard faculty to appoint Landis to a new research professorship in legislation, which entailed a major salary increase and a teaching load of only one graduate seminar per year. He was just twenty-eight years old. It was a spectacular start to an academic career, even eclipsing that of Pound, who objected that the promotion was too soon and remarked that the start of Landis's career was "meteoric, almost unheard of."[15] Only five years later, Landis would leave the faculty for Washington, D.C., and in 1935 President Roosevelt named him Chairman of the SEC.

Landis's remarkable ascent doubtlessly appealed to Conant. He was exactly the kind of talented student from a humble background the president wished to attract to Harvard. In addition, Landis, in his scholarship and teaching, conceived of law and higher education as tools for social reform, a progressive view that resonated with Conant.

Landis's Defense of Legislation

Landis also seemed like an appealing candidate for the deanship because his jurisprudence resonated with "the sociological movement," advanced by Roscoe Pound between 1906 and 1909.[16] However, as Pound retrenched in the 1930s and began extolling incremental, judge-made, common law and attacking administrative decision-making and public policy, he directly challenged all that Landis stood for. At Harvard University's tercentenary celebration in 1936, Pound organized a conference titled "The Future of the Common Law," just after the Supreme Court had shocked the nation by vacating the National Industrial Recovery Act in 1935.[17] In his opening address to the conference, Pound glorified the case-by-case legal evolution in common law and attacked administrative decision-making as an "intruder" in the realm of the common law and the common lawyer, disparaging those who turned "to administration to get things done in a rush in advance of thorough consideration" by the courts.[18] Pound's address was a direct affront to Landis, who was chairman of the SEC at the time and would publish his pathbreaking justification of "the administrative process" in 1938.[19]

While Pound retreated from sociological jurisprudence, Landis eagerly embraced its implications in two ways. One was relatively familiar: legislative theory, which explained and justified legislation as a source of lawmaking coequal with judges and courts. The second had no precedent and was forged almost single-handedly by Landis: the theory of administrative law, which explained and justified rule-making by public regulatory agencies apart from the courts.

The justification for legislation as a source of law had been prepared by Professor James Thayer (LL.B. 1856) in the late nineteenth century. In 1884 Thayer had published "Constitutionality of Legislation: The Precise Question for a Court," in which he asked what standard the U.S. Supreme Court should apply in considering the constitutionality of a statute. That essay led directly to Thayer's renowned 1893 article "The Origin and Scope of the American Doctrine of Constitutional Law," in which he advocated a standard of judicial restraint. Supreme Court Justices ought to ask, not whether a given statute fits "their own judgment as to constitutionality," but whether it fits within "a range of . . . rational" interpretations of the Constitution because "whatever choice is rational is constitutional." Only statutes demonstrating "very clear" error by falling outside that range should be struck down as unconstitutional.[20]

In 1920, in his Princeton undergraduate thesis on the Commerce Clause, Landis followed Thayer's lead. Published before Landis completed his first year in law school, that article defended broad congressional powers of lawmaking on the grounds that "the framers of the Constitution had no conception of the growth of commerce under such corporate entities as are today created by state and federal action."[21] After completing the LL.B. in 1924, Landis elaborated this theme in his S.J.D. thesis, "Congressional Power of Investigation," which was published by the *Harvard Law Review* when he was just twenty-six. Again, Landis employed careful historical and jurisprudential analysis to justify broad congressional powers.[22] As the new research professor of legislation at Harvard Law School in 1928, Landis asserted an expansive view of the legitimate scope of legislation in his writing and his graduate seminar.

Finally, in 1931 Landis published his most famous defense of legislation, "The Study of Legislation in Law Schools." Most law professors and law schools depreciated or marginalized statutes enacted by legislatures and "insisted that law could not be made" by politicized legislatures. Law "could only be found" by judges, much as scientists discover natural laws. Given this belief, judges treated centuries-old precedents with more respect than new statutes.[23]

But in fact, judges do and should consider political, social, and economic facts and tenets in making decisions, Landis argued, consistent with both sociological jurisprudence and legal realism. Even granting that point, though, what should be the source of those facts and tenets? Should judges draw them from the past or, worse, from personal "unguided interpretation"? Landis argued that the primary source ought to be legislation, which conveys the public's view of those facts and tenets expressed through the people's elected representatives. Judicial decisions, by contrast, are shaped by "the social views, economic conceptions, even, at times, the prejudices of the judge or of his predecessors." Instead, judges "should draw these [public's views] from the output of the legislative mill rather than from those of an outmoded age or a narrower experience."[24]

Yet, even if legislation is the proper source of the public's view, the problem remained that law schools did not prepare lawyers and judges to develop or interpret legislation effectively. Law students did not study how to conduct basic research underlying successful legislation, how to negotiate in statutory construction, or how to draft such legislation once a consensus had been reached. Nor did they understand how to use incentives to ensure public compliance with legislation. Landis addressed these needs in his seminar on legislation. Students learned these skills by role-playing different stakeholders and discussing amendments as a legislative body would do. Most importantly, they were taught to respect legislation as a source of law. According to Landis, future judges must learn "a sense of respect for the legislature's conclusions." The lack of such sense "is attested to not only by popular clamor but by the multitude of statutes held unconstitutional because the Court remains unconvinced of the wisdom of the legislature's judgment."[25]

Landis's culminating work on legislation, "Statutes and the Sources of Law," was published in a collection of essays written by Harvard Law faculty in 1934. In sharp contrast to his colleagues, Landis criticized the imbalance between judges' deference for judicial decisions and case law and judges' lack of respect for statutes. When judges reverse precedents established in prior court decisions, subsequent judges accept the reversal, Landis observed. But when legislatures employ "the same sober judgment" in passing statutes that reverse judicial precedents, subsequent judges ignore or overturn the statute, giving deference to their professional colleagues and not to elected representatives.[26]

Landis's essay has remained central to modern theories of legislation, from the "liberal construction" clause of the Uniform Commercial Code to the debates surrounding Supreme Court decisions such as *Griswold v. Connecticut* (1965), which affirmed the right to privacy implied by the Bill of Rights of the U.S. Constitution.[27] Even in the twenty-first century, law schools throughout the country are resurrecting Landis's ideas of teaching legislative skills, as in Harvard's currently required first-year course "Legislation and Regulation," which is, effectively, part of Landis's legacy.

The Administrative Process

Landis's resonance with sociological jurisprudence and legal realism extended beyond his pathbreaking work on legislation. Even more significantly, he formulated and justified an entirely new vehicle for progressive lawmaking: the administrative, regulatory agency. This was born not in the ivory towers of Cambridge, Massachusetts, but in the cauldron of political and economic crises in Washington, D.C. In April 1933 Frankfurter begged Landis to accompany him on an emergency mission to Washington, at the special request of President Roosevelt, to save the president's legislation on financial securities. Landis agreed, expecting that he would return by the following Monday to teach his classes.[28] But he did not resume his academic career at Harvard until four years later, when he was named dean of the Law School in 1937.

In the intervening years, Landis worked in Washington as a core member of Frankfurter's team, and developed a personal relationship with Roosevelt. This led to Landis's key role in establishing both the Federal Trade Commission (FTC) and the SEC and his serving as a member of each between 1934 and 1937. In 1935 Roosevelt nominated him to become chairman of the SEC, succeeding Joseph P. Kennedy, the father of future U.S. president John Kennedy and future attorney general Robert Kennedy, all of whom became Landis's allies and friends. During these years, both behind the scenes and in direct controversies with the courts and Congress, Landis carved out the powers, procedures, and justification of the new agencies. He literally created a new body of law derived, not from the courts or legislatures, but from a new source of legal authority, conceived in economic and social crisis and located in the executive branch. This new source of legal authority was more focused, more flexible, and more capable of exercising governmental authority than anything seen before.[29]

In 1935 Yale University invited Landis to give its most prestigious lecture series, the Storrs Lectures. Landis declined because at that time he was a high-ranking government official and would not have been able to speak freely. But after becoming dean at Harvard Law School, Landis delivered the lectures in January 1938. Published as a book dedicated to Speaker of the House Samuel T. Rayburn, the great practical politician from Texas, these lectures became "the outstanding theoretical elaboration of administrative regulation" and of the proper relationship between the new agencies, the legislature, and the courts.[30] Entitled *The Administrative Process,* the revolutionary book argued that these new regulatory bodies were the only adequate answer to the challenges presented by a complex economy far beyond anything the nation's Founders could have imagined.

Pointing to the example of the Interstate Commerce Commission, created in 1887 as the first administrative agency, Landis stated the fundamental principle that governance "had to be provided to direct and control an industry, and governance . . . implied not merely legislative power or simple executive power, but whatever power might be required to achieve the desired results."[31] Here Landis identified a new source of legal authority within the executive branch, and his view was anathema to the conservative Pound of the 1930s and even to many legal realists at the time. It was the conceptual cornerstone of New Deal liberalism and has remained deeply controversial.

Landis saw regulation, not as "an enemy of industry," but as "its partner and benevolent guide." The judiciary, like the legislature, was incapable of playing this role due to "its inability to maintain a long-time, uninterrupted interest in a relatively narrow and carefully defined area of economics and social activity." Furthermore, judges and legislators lacked the specialized expertise required to exercise informed discretion. "Incredible areas of fact may be involved in the disposition of a business problem that calls not only for legal intelligence but also wisdom in the ways of industrial operation."[32] Combining legislative, executive, and judicial functions, the new regulatory agencies could protect the nation's economic health and the public security better than any of the three established branches of government. Landis's research was bold, analytically sharp, and based in practical experience.

Further, Landis believed in the power of government to achieve social fairness through regulation. Landis's critics regarded him as disloyal to capitalism, citing his trip to study the economy of the Soviet Union after he graduated from the Law School as evidence of Communist or Socialist leanings. But it was Landis's youth as a missionary in Japan and his work in the coal fields of West Virginia that forged his belief in the necessity of government regulation to advance economic justice. This, he also believed, was consistent with and supportive of capitalist enterprise and the free market, which could flourish only when affording opportunity fairly to all.

Dean Landis Arrives

At the height of the Depression, with storm clouds of war gathering in Europe, Landis was an attractive candidate to be the next dean of Harvard Law School. Coming from a humble background, he had risen through the ranks based on academic merit, acquired administrative experience leading government agencies, and shared Conant's vision for Harvard. But Conant's advisors had strong misgivings about Landis's New Deal advocacy, which were soon reinforced by his support for Roosevelt's Judiciary Reorganization ("court packing") Bill, enacted in 1937. Nevertheless, President Conant decided to take a chance on Landis and in December 1936 offered him the deanship. Perhaps Landis was one of "the very few" who could run a great law school, in the words of Acting Dean Morgan.[33]

The timing was opportune. Though deeply engaged in Washington and his work, Landis was exhausted. Throughout 1936 he repeatedly became sick with the flu, and he once fainted at an important dinner. Roosevelt was heaping more responsibilities on him by the day. In 1926 Landis had married Stella McGehee, and she had remained in Cambridge with their two daughters. By

1934 the family had not lived together for a total of six months, so Stella and the girls moved to Washington. But the move did not seem to strengthen the family. As she wrote, "Sometimes I think in my low moments he'd be better off if we were not here to bother him."[34] Perhaps the return to Cambridge would restore Landis's health and family life. Faculty support also made the moment auspicious. The Harvard Corporation "made the best selection that could have been made," wrote Austin Scott. "I think that that feeling is universal among the members of the faculty, no matter how far they differ in their views on other matters." Furthermore, the faculty was eager to head in a new direction after Pound's administration.[35]

Landis accepted the offer in January 1937 and assumed the office of dean in September. At thirty-seven years old, he became the youngest-ever dean of the school. In the following July, Supreme Court Justice Benjamin Cardozo died, and President Roosevelt nominated Frankfurter to take his place. With Frankfurter departing, Landis became the undisputed leader of the school. Though his official tenure lasted until 1946, the productive period of his deanship lasted less than four years, until the middle of 1941. During that brief period, Landis launched important initiatives to revise the admissions policy and improve students' academic experience. But his personal life simultaneously began to disintegrate.

The first problem facing Landis concerned the admissions "deadlines," the name that the faculty gave to the admissions thresholds. By this, they did not mean time limits, but the cutoffs distinguishing those who were admitted and "lived," from those who were rejected and "died."[36] That "mortality" came either through excluding unqualified applicants or failing qualified admittees, as Professor Sidney Simpson (LL.B. 1922) stated.[37]

In the mid-1930s, just before Landis arrived as dean, the faculty had begun trying to reform the school's admissions process. Until that point, the same basic policy—radical when introduced by Langdell in 1875 and adopted by the faculty in 1893—still governed admissions at the Law School. Only applicants who met the academic threshold of graduating from "approved" colleges were entitled to admission. In 1913 the faculty had raised the threshold by creating two tiers of "approved" colleges and requiring the applicants from second-tier colleges to rank in the top third of their senior class.[38]

In 1927–28, the faculty voted to require that all graduates of first-tier colleges rank in the top three-quarters of their graduating class, and graduates of second-tier colleges in the top quarter of their graduating class. Then the faculty refined its policy by voting that a specific "deadline" should be calculated for each first-tier college, indicating when its graduates had about a 50 percent chance of completing the LL.B., based on the past performance of its graduates in the Law School. All future applicants who had graduated from first-tier colleges would have to meet the assigned threshold for their particular college.[39]

But calculating separate thresholds for some 250 first-tier colleges required gathering and analyzing an enormous amount of data, and no one on the faculty or staff had the time or responsibility for it. Also, Dean Pound did not support the revised policy. The faculty Admissions Committee therefore discovered in 1934 that the 1927 restrictions on first-tier colleges had never gone into effect. Every graduate of a first-tier college was still being admitted, as in the past. Hence, neither Ernest Brown (LL.B. 1931), who graduated from Princeton in June 1928, nor Archibald Cox (LL.B. 1937), who graduated from Harvard College in June 1934, were asked about their academic rank or record when they applied to the Law School. Merely presenting their diplomas entitled them to admission.[40]

In order to implement and refine the 1927–28 policy, the Admissions Committee in 1934 finally began reviewing the college records and first-year grades of all 4,000 students admitted between 1928 and 1934. Through this mammoth effort, the Committee determined a grade-point average for each college. For example, the two colleges with the lowest minimum grades, reflecting the toughest academic standards, were Princeton and Amherst, whose graduates needed only a C– average to have a 50 percent chance of graduating from the Law School. The average "deadline" was a C+ and climbed to a B for a few colleges. In 1936 the law faculty voted to adopt these new thresholds and apply them to the class entering in September 1937, just as Landis arrived as dean.[41] The *Harvard Alumni Bulletin* called the new policy "sensible, fair, and effective."[42]

When explaining the new policy, Dean Landis wrote that the move "means not only less personal tragedy" but also "kindness to young men who . . . lack those particular endowments . . . necessary for successful work."[43] Landis was virtually alone, though, in expressing concern for those cut down by the intellectual sword. Spartan manliness gave little regard for "the fallen," in the words of Deans Ezra Thayer (1910–1915) and Roscoe Pound.[44]

The primary aim of the revised admissions policy was to reduce student attrition to 20 percent, as noted by Landis and reported in the *New York Times*.[45] The rationale was to reduce "waste"—that is, the wasted time "of the instructor and the competent students" and, to a lesser extent, those who failed.

The faculty and the dean all spoke in these terms.[46] Another rationale was to raise "the morale" of the school. But this had nothing to do with alleviating anxiety or stress among enrolled students. Instead, the revised policy was expected to eliminate the frustration "of the instructor and the competent students" with the weak students.[47] But the biggest rationale for "tightening up the existing 'deadlines'" for admission was to "halt the tendency of the student body to increase in size, if not actually reduce its numbers," as Landis and others repeatedly stated.[48]

The revised thresholds achieved the objective. The attrition rate fell from over 30 percent for the classes entering before 1936 to 22 percent for the class entering in the fall of 1937 and 20 percent for the class entering in the fall of 1938.[49] This drop seemed significant at the Law School. But the attrition rate was still much higher than in elite private higher education generally, which, more than a decade earlier, had begun to adopt selective admissions.

In 1935 the Admissions Sub-Committee had, in fact, proposed taking a step toward selective admissions, but President Conant rejected the move largely on financial grounds.[50] Even apart from Conant's reservations, the faculty appeared unwilling to deviate from its trodden path in admissions, attrition, and size of the school. As Professor Sidney Simpson explained to a group of alumni in 1938, the revised system with new academic thresholds "does not mean . . . that we are taking only the men with very highest academic records. It means that we are excluding men with very low academic records."[51]

The faculty's persistence in following this well-worn path was apparent in setting the relatively high benchmark of 20 percent for the attrition rate.[52] Moreover, the faculty concurrently raised the minimum grade average required of first-year students for promotion to the second year. This move caused more students to fail at the end of the first year, thus offsetting the reduction in attrition and "waste" intended by the elevated admission thresholds! Indeed, if the faculty had not raised the minimum first-year grade average, the attrition rate would have fallen to 19 percent (rather than 22 percent) for the class entering in the fall of 1937 and to 17 percent (rather than 20 percent) for the class entering in the fall of 1938.[53] The faculty continued to measure academic rigor by the attrition rate, as had Deans Thayer and Pound, rather than by the proportion of applicants denied admission, as the new mode of selective admissions prescribed.

Thus, the will to reduce the size of the school was weak. Because both the higher admissions threshold and the higher first-year grade requirement improved retention during the second and third years, the overall enrollment of the school grew from 1,389 in the fall of 1937 to 1,423 in the fall of 1938. Dean Landis lamented that the new admissions policy failed in "bringing about a significant reduction in the numbers of the School." A major question, the dean said, was whether "the School should now set as its definite aim reduction in numbers by say one-third, thereby giving it a total enrollment of a thousand students."[54]

"More Scientific Methods" of Admissions

The failure of the admissions policy to reduce enrollment stemmed from the continued reliance on thresholds and attrition. Throughout private higher education, the selective admissions process started by setting an enrollment cap and adjusted the discretionary criteria for selecting applicants to meet that cap. Hence, at Harvard College, the aptly named Special Committee Appointed to Consider the Limitation of Numbers had formulated flexible admissions criteria that could be adjusted to limit enrollment firmly to 1,000 entering students. But Harvard Law School and President Conant could not agree on a firm cap for the entering Law School class. Hence, Landis called for developing "more scientific methods" to identify a threshold that would keep the attrition rate at about 20 percent.[55]

The faculty continued refining the academic "deadlines" in the late 1930s. Led by Professor James MacLachlan (LL.B. 1916), a team of research assistants examined past law students' performance in individual courses at their alma mater. On long rolls of butcher paper, MacLachlan and his team tried to identify the grades of past law students in certain courses at their colleges that would predict a 50 percent chance of that student graduating from the Law School.[56] What grade of University of California graduates in Beginning Economics was correlated with graduating at the Law School? What about Ancient Philosophy at the University of Chicago? At Georgetown, was the grade in Calculus or Greek a better predictor? The task was beyond Herculean.

In 1939 the faculty authorized the Admissions Committee to reject any applicant whose undergraduate grades did not meet the "deadline" in courses for his college that predicted a 50 percent chance of completing the LL.B. at Harvard. Through this policy, the faculty intended to limit the entering class to 550 students.[57] As Landis wrote, "the Faculty began to use the admissions standards to control the class size, which the 1937–38 standards had failed to limit."[58] This shift in aim was radical. But the "control" failed as well because the correlation between those "deadlines" and the enrollment limit was speculative. The school still did not start by setting a firm cap on its enrollment and then filling the vacant seats by selecting the strongest applicants.

Meanwhile, to complement college grades and pursue "more scientific methods," Landis also wished to create a standardized "aptitude test" for applicants.[59] Many in higher education had expressed interest in such tests. Conant had endorsed it in order to expand the opportunity to attend Harvard College for students enrolled in secondary schools outside the traditional feeder schools. In the previous decade, the law schools at Yale, Columbia, and North Carolina had begun to employ aptitude tests.[60]

Consequently, a month after Landis's arrival as dean in 1937, the faculty voted to study the accuracy of aptitude tests as predictors of first-year success.[61] Landis himself joined the Admissions Committee, which, in 1940, began to consider the results of aptitude tests taken by applicants just above and below the grade "deadline" for their college. The Committee then adjusted acceptances and rejections of those few applicants accordingly. Aptitude tests thus began to influence the admission decisions on the small number of applicants near their grade-point deadline. But the Admissions Committee also concluded in 1940 that aptitude tests were no more valid than the grade deadlines in predicting academic survival at the Law School, and the faculty remained divided on the validity of such tests.[62]

In this fashion, the school began to introduce components of the selective admissions process during the late 1930s. But selecting among academically qualified applicants still lay in the future, and applications from graduates of the some 250 first-tier colleges still received little scrutiny. In 1940, after graduating from Beloit College, Louis A. Toepfer (LL.B. 1947) found that the application process at the Law School merely "entailed showing up with your diploma on the first day of class [and] signing the registration book."[63] Having graduated from Harvard College, Arthur von Mehren (LL.B. 1945) found in June 1942 "absolutely no difficulty getting admitted. . . . Nothing more than filling out the application and getting the recommendations that were required."[64]

During World War II, as the pool of applicants shrank, the school naturally did not raise the academic thresholds for admission and even relaxed them in some respects, accepting three years of college, rather than four, in some cases.[65] After graduating from Tufts University in 1944, Haig der Manuelian (LL.B. 1947) "applied to Harvard Law School on a Monday and was admitted the following Friday."[66] Hence, the admissions process "was not very significant" throughout the 1940s, according to Detlev Vagts (LL.B. 1951). "There was no point to breaking your butt in college because law school admissions standards were such that, if you were not in the bottom quarter, you were pretty sure of getting into Harvard Law School. If you wanted to go to a good medical school you had to do some grinding."[67] The attrition rate at the Law School therefore continued to be very high—20 percent or more—compared to other domains of elite higher education. In 1940, a significant number of failures "was expected," recalled Toepfer.[68]

As the 1940s progressed, wartime departures and the postwar flood of returning G.I.s complicated what the faculty called the students' "mortality" rate. But it remained true that the first year "was really the selection process. . . . the weeding out occurred after the first-year exams were graded," remarked Professor Ernest Brown, who sat on the Admissions Committee.[69] The admissions revisions of the late 1930s therefore had little influence on the size of the school. Rather than establishing a firm enrollment cap and adjusting discretionary criteria to meet that cap, the dean and faculty introduced "more scientific methods" intended to limit the enrollment and reduce the attrition rate. President Conant did not object to the effort because the methods did not really work and continuing high enrollment provided the needed tuition revenue.

Dean Landis recognized the problem and hoped to fix it. But the United States' entry into World War II turned everything upside down, as concern shifted from culling applicants and students to attracting and retaining them. Then Landis departed again for Washington, and turmoil ensued upon his return, followed by the deluge of G.I.s enrolling after the war. Reform of the admissions policy and process did not resume until 1950.

Vote to Admit Women, 1942

Dean Landis's support for admissions reform was driven by his commitment to academic meritocracy, which was deeply embedded in the Law School. By the same token, Landis wanted to use scientifically verifiable predictions—the same techniques he championed in Washington—to test and achieve policy goals. What counted was a candidate's empirically measurable chance of success. Why, then, were women still excluded from Harvard Law School during his tenure from 1937 to 1946?

Yale Law School had begun admitting women in 1918, and Columbia in 1927. As early as 1938, Landis asserted that he was making progress on reversing gender discrimination. "We are breaking . . . the old tradition already inasmuch as we awarded one research scholarship this year to a woman . . . , and we are putting another woman on our general staff as a research assistant," he wrote to an advocate of coeducation, Charles Burlingham (LL.B. 1908). With self-deprecating irony, Landis continued, "You don't want us to go completely New Deal revolutionary! Surely, as you once proclaimed yourself, the 'packing' should be subtly done and not in a brash way that offends traditions of long standing."[70]

The earlier objections had been that women did not have the aptitude to succeed at legal study, that the Law School would be accused of caving to financial pressure, or that male students would be displaced. But none of those applied now, and few women had enrolled in rival schools, such as Yale, Columbia, Cornell, and Pennsylvania.[71] The biggest barriers now were the cultural commitment of some faculty to Spartan manliness and, above all, the opposition of the president and the Corporation, who justified their position with the tautology that Harvard did not admit women because the university was not coeducational, save for Radcliffe College.

In 1925 two Radcliffe students petitioned to attend a seminar at the Law School. The faculty approved the petition of these "especially qualified" women, but the Corporation vetoed the decision.[72] Meanwhile, it was reported that when someone insistently suggested to President Lowell that women should be admitted to the Law School, he kicked his office door, stating, "I should like to make it plain, this isn't going to happen while I am president of this university."[73] During the 1930s the faculty did not petition for the admission of women because they "knew the Corporation would only turn them down," according to Toepfer, who in 1947 was appointed the first director of admissions at the Law School.[74]

In 1942, when the school began running a deficit due to low enrollment, faculty leaders such as Zechariah Chafee Jr. (LL.B. 1913) urged Landis to admit women out of concern for fairness and to avoid debt. The law schools at Yale and Columbia meanwhile were accepting more women to offset the loss in tuition from the declining male enrollment during wartime.[75] But President Conant rejected the idea out of hand. Asked by an alumnus about the state of the Law School during the war, Conant remarked that the situation was "not as bad as we thought. We have seventy-five students, and we haven't had to admit any women."[76]

Finally, on December 5, 1942, the faculty voted fifteen to eleven to admit women. Dean Landis, then on leave working in Washington, voted affirmatively by mail. Future dean Erwin Griswold (1946–1967), Thomas Powell (LL.B. 1904), Warren Seavey (LL.B. 1904), Austin Scott, and sociologist Sheldon Glueck, among others, concurred. Those voting against included Acting Dean Morgan, Edward "Bull" Warren (LL.B. 1900), MacLachlan, and Pound, who was still on the faculty.[77] The school did not forward the recommendation to the Corporation, because the vote was regarded as too close on "so fundamental a question."[78]

In addition, in the same month President Roosevelt issued an executive order lowering the minimum age for the draft from twenty-one to eighteen, and the War Manpower Commission estimated that this would increase the fraction of conscripts in the male population from about 11 percent to 20 percent, even though the great majority of American soldiers were volunteers. Morgan and the faculty feared that the school would appear compromised because admitting women at that point would seem to be "trying to fill up the places that would be made vacant by the draft," according to Brown.[79] But Landis later declared this fear "utterly irrelevant and extraneous" to the principle involved.[80]

Dean Landis had one last chance to make gender history at the Law School when the Corporation permitted Harvard Medical School to admit women in 1945.[81] In addition, Radcliffe and Harvard had combined classes during the war, so coeducation appeared less exotic to the university administration. As a result, "it became reasonably apparent" that the Corporation would approve a recommendation from the Law School to admit women, as Dean Griswold later wrote.[82] Furthermore, the influx of returning soldiers meant that the decision could no longer be dismissed as simply an economic necessity. But the Law School still held off because the faculty "had to accommodate . . . the flood of veterans" and "we didn't want a woman . . . keeping out a veteran," who might have forgone the opportunity to attend the Law School due to military service, according to Brown.[83]

Hence, a reason to bar women could always be found, although Landis saw the decision as inevitable. He believed that the school could not "isolate" itself forever and that eventually the faculty would "depart from tradition and open the School to women."[84] At the first faculty meeting in September 1945, however, Landis tabled the issue because he wanted to wait for the full faculty to return, and he did not want the school to appear that it was "seeking for students."[85] In December 1945 the dean wrote to four prospective female applicants that "we do not admit women to the Law School," and the issue remained on the table until his resignation in 1946.[86] In 2015 Landis's two daughters stated in an interview for this volume that they believed their father, though a dedicated social progressive, did not support women studying in professional school or working as professionals.[87]

Reforming Students' Academic Experience

When Landis attended Harvard in the early 1920s, small-group learning was available only to the top 5 percent of the class through their work in the three student academic honor organizations: *Harvard Law Review,* the Board of Student Advisors, and the Legal Aid Bureau. At the end of the first year, the other 95 percent could look forward only to plodding through the same curricular regimen of large classes concluding with a final exam. Landis wondered about the efficacy of this arrangement, and in 1938 he authorized a study of the bar passage rate of the school's graduates. Such a study was unprecedented, and the results were bad. The bottom 25 percent of the class frequently failed the bar exam in the most challenging states—California, Massachusetts, New York, and Pennsylvania.[88] This result "makes one wonder how good a legal education a man secures whose grade is 62 or below. . . . There is little to indicate that they have received a good legal education at the Harvard Law School," wrote the author of the study, Professor Sam B. Warner Jr. (LL.B. 1912, S.J.D. 1923).[89]

To improve the academic experience for the average or "low standing" student, Landis devised a four-part plan.[90] First, ensure that only prepared students entered the school by revising the academic thresholds for admission, as discussed above. Second, increase the number of third-year seminars in order to offer in the regular curriculum some of the small-group, directed learning experiences already available to the top students in the academic honor organizations.

These seminars would require that every student complete an essay based on legal research and work directly with a faculty member, something many did not do even for "fifteen minutes" in their entire law school education.[91] Furthermore, Landis believed that research and writing honed the mind and would make every student appreciate the law as a field of learning and a vehicle for social improvement. "Too many men graduate from the School, who . . . have failed to catch a glimpse of the law as a means for more effective living," Landis wrote in his annual report. "The zest that may develop from individual research, as well as the discipline . . . , may instill a desirable discontent with a mere vocational attitude toward the study of law." Written work had to be mandatory in the dean's view because the students most in need would lack confidence to undertake it voluntarily on their own and would appreciate the experience only afterward.[92] This requirement was adopted by the faculty soon after the war, and it has continued, in one form or another, to the present.[93]

Third, Landis called for extending editorial and publication opportunities to all students by establishing another student-edited journal, the *Harvard Law School Record,* which would publish student scholarship and "perhaps some School news." The *Record* began publishing in July 1946 after Landis stepped down, and eventually focused primarily on "School news."[94] Landis's idea of founding another student-edited journal was embraced and extended by his successor, Dean Griswold, and ultimately inspired the founding of many such journals at the Law School. Seventy years later, students were editing and publishing no fewer than seventeen such journals, on a broad range of legal subjects. Furthermore, just as the *Harvard Law Review,* with student editors chosen by academic merit, became part of the Law School's template for legal education throughout the world, other law schools also widely adopted Landis's innovation of creating student-edited journals that are based on students' interests rather than their grades.

The dean's fourth idea was to improve the academic environment of the school. The first year was inherently intimidating with its huge classes of nearly 150 taught by Socratic method. To alleviate that intimidation, Landis divided the first-year class into small groups and provided tutors to "help them through the treacherous first year."[95] Another problem in the academic environment was that students rarely interacted with faculty outside of class. "We were far removed. You would never see the faculty . . . there was this great gulf," recalled Toepfer concerning his studies in 1940 and 1941. "You kind of had to get permission to see a faculty member. . . . They didn't have office hours."[96]

In response, Landis organized a series of faculty lectures, open to all students and the entire Law School community. He intended the series to bring faculty and students together around topics of mutual interest, and to induce the faculty to publish more than they otherwise might.[97] Some faculty saw this as a waste of time and resisted, but the first ten lectures in 1939–40 had an average attendance of 425, including nearly a quarter of the student body. Immediately after the war, this initiative encouraged students to found the Harvard Law School Forum, which presented outside speakers, invited the public to attend, and broadcast events on radio.[98]

Also to improve the academic environment, Landis in 1938 arranged for the construction of a reading lounge in the library, the Elihu Root Room, equipped "not with law books, but books about law," as well as the latest journals and newspapers. This elegant room was funded by a gift from Henry Stimson, who had studied at the Law School in 1888–90 (without completing the degree) and served as secretary of war (1911–1913), secretary of state (1929–1933), and again secretary of war (1940–1945). Despite his own accomplishments, Stimson insisted that the room be named after Elihu Root, another former secretary of state and secretary of war, and a New York University School of Law graduate, who had won the 1912 Nobel Peace Prize.[99] Throughout his tenure, Landis continued to update the Root Room, and twenty years later he proudly described the room as "so beautiful that no one would dare to disrespect it."[100]

Scholars have observed that Landis failed to fulfill his planned reforms.[101] But this failure was largely due to the onset of World War II and his immediate departure to Washington to assist President Roosevelt with the war effort. In addition, he faced stiff resistance from powerful, conservative alumni, as well as most of the senior faculty, despite their warm feelings for Landis. Of the thirty professors on the faculty when Landis arrived in 1937, only three were not graduates of the Law School. Two had been appointed by Langdell, one by Ames, five by Ezra Thayer, and twenty-two by Pound, who remained on the faculty.[102] Apart from Frankfurter's circle of five, the great majority of the faculty saw no reason to make fundamental changes in academic policy, as the 1936 *Report of the Committee on Curriculum* demonstrated. Finally, Landis also faced severe financial constraints.

Money Problems

The impact of the syndrome of tuition dependence plagued Landis's deanship. His tenure began in the midst of the Depression in September 1937, while the school was struggling to repay the $1.4 million borrowed from the university a decade earlier to fund the expansion of Langdell Hall. Between 1928 and 1936, Pound made annual payments at the accelerated rate of about $120,000 in principal and interest, because he wanted to retire the loan as quickly as possible. After Pound stepped down, Acting Dean Edmund Morgan wrote to President Conant in 1936 that the debt "has been a curse to the school by shifting emphasis from education to finance." Other faculty members concurred.[103]

In order to ensure the solvency of the school, Conant consistently opposed reducing enrollment. But in 1937 Morgan and the president negotiated a new repayment schedule of about $42,000 annually to pay off the remaining $455,000 in fifteen years. Even with this adjustment, Landis had little room to maneuver financially. Enrollments were always precarious during the Depression, and fell about 5 percent between the fall of 1936 and the fall of 1937, when Landis assumed office. At that point the accumulated surplus had fallen to $13,000, because the school continued to live "from hand to mouth." Nevertheless, Landis perpetuated the illusion of prosperity by slashing expenses and running a surplus of nearly $26,000 in 1937–38 and $37,000 in 1938–39. In June 1939 the school's accumulated surplus reached $76,000.[104] The deeply indebted school still seemed to be saving money every year.

Then Landis made what soon appeared to be a terrible mistake. In 1939 he transferred $75,000 from the accumulated surplus toward reducing the debt. Like Pound, Landis thus chose to accelerate the repayment schedule rather than implement some of the academic reforms that he endorsed. Nevertheless, the transfer made sense because during the Depression the university was charging the Law School 4 percent interest annually on the loan, while it was paying only 1 percent on the school's surplus and endowment invested with the university.[105]

But in late 1940 it became clear that the United States would eventually enter the war, and that enrollment would fall drastically. It therefore seemed that Landis's transfer was a terrible miscalculation. In fact, enrollment plummeted from 1,393 in the fall of 1939, to 1,249 in 1940, 819 in 1941, 199 in 1942, 98 in 1943, and 48 in 1944.[106] The dean's already skeletal budget for 1940–41 had to be cut by $40,000.[107] In 1943 the faculty even suggested that "admission requirements might be lowered for a year or so," and the academic threshold was waived for some individual applicants.[108]

As Landis remarked, "decreased enrollment raises financial problems," which were exacerbated by the school's agreement to refund the tuition of those joining the military (which the school had not done in World War I). Early in 1941 Landis was therefore anticipating serious mounting deficits, having already applied almost all the school's accumulated surplus against the debt. By 1943–44 the accumulated wartime deficit amounted to $105,000 and in 1944–45 to $120,000, as there were still twelve faculty to pay and less than 100 students.[109] The school was facing disaster, falling deeper into debt after starving itself for a decade to climb out. And, among the schools at Harvard, the Law School was the most heavily reliant on tuition and therefore hurt the most financially by the wartime decline in enrollment.

Then, *mirabile dictu,* the Corporation decided to waive the payment of the deficits that Harvard's schools accrued during the war. In an instant, Landis's 1940 advance payment of the $75,000 in accumulated surplus became a stroke of genius. Had he not made the advance payment, that surplus would have been consumed by the school's $120,000 wartime deficit, rather than decreasing the $400,000 balance of the mortgage on Langdell Hall. The dean essentially shaved two years off the repayment schedule of the mortgage. In 1945 the return of soldiers bolstered enrollment, and the school ran a surplus of nearly $44,000 for 1945–46.[110]

But the influx of students once again raised the question of how many to admit. In November 1945 the faculty held a long discussion concerning "the question of public relations, as affected by refusing applicants" versus admitting and "flunking out of large numbers," along with "the placement problem which would arise" from graduating more. In the end the faculty decided, by a seven-to-six vote, to admit 500 *more* students in February 1947.[111]

By virtue of the Corporation's having waived wartime deficits and Landis's severe economies, the balance sheet of the school slowly improved during his tenure from 1937 to 1946. Nevertheless, the reliance on tuition revenue tightly constrained finances, and options to escape it were limited. Fundraising or increasing tuition were unthinkable during the Depression and World War II. And Landis's work for Roosevelt's New Deal made him deeply unpopular in corporate America and with many alumni. He also felt that it was inappropriate for him to solicit funds from corporations over which he had or might exercise jurisdiction.[112]

The "Iron Curtain" in Alumni Affairs

Landis, in fact, had no interest in asking for gifts. In 1946 Reginald H. Smith (LL.B. 1914), president of the Harvard Law School Association, believed that the dean had drawn an "'iron curtain' . . . between the School and the Association." Under Landis, Smith complained, the school did not appreciate the munificent contributions from the Association to buy books for the library, provide emergency loans to students, and pay for portraits hung in the school.[113] In reply, the next dean, Erwin Griswold, tried to cover for Landis and repair the damage, though he agreed with the complaints of alumni, based on his own observations as a faculty member.[114] "Landis was poison to the alumni.

They hated him, and he didn't care for them," Griswold later remarked. Landis "devoted little or no time to alumni relations, [and] considered them only a nuisance," an attitude that "hurt fund raising."[115]

Despite the lack of fundraising during the 1930s, unsolicited gifts, primarily in the form of bequests, came to the school and significantly aided its survival. Between 1930 and 1940, gifts for current use amounted to $231,000, which sustained operations. More importantly for the long term, additional gifts, mostly bequests, to endowment totaled over $1.4 million. Due to these legacies, the school's endowment grew 28 percent in nominal dollars over the decade—the same pace as the overall university endowment.[116] All these unsolicited gifts enabled the school to both increase its endowment and fund its operating costs during the Depression, while also paying back the burdensome loan to the university.

Nevertheless, the school's financial predicament significantly hindered Landis's capacity to modify administrative and academic policies. In particular, he wished to reduce the high student-faculty ratio, which averaged about 46:1 during the 1930s. Universities can normally reduce this ratio in two ways: by expanding the faculty or shrinking the student body. The former option requires more money to pay salaries—and cannot easily be reversed, because faculty, once tenured, cannot generally be let go. An institution therefore becomes committed to a larger faculty for a long time.

Shrinking the student body is easier and faster both to implement and to reverse, because a university can adjust the number of students simply by changing its admissions policies. Moreover, Landis, on other grounds, wished to reduce the size of the school from the average of about 1,400 students during the 1930s to about 1,000.[117] But this option would reduce tuition revenue, which the school, heavily in debt, desperately needed. Hence, this option seemed out of the question. However, a number of faculty were nearing retirement or about to depart, so the school's expenses were going to decline, and, without incurring a deficit, Landis could have ramped down the enrollment as faculty stepped down.

Landis picked the former option, however. He expanded the faculty from twenty-seven teaching professors in the fall of 1938 to thirty-one in the fall of 1940 by hiring four new tenured professors, even as the war and enrollment decline loomed on the horizon.[118] The primary reason was his desire to broaden and diversify the school's areas of expertise. The four new hires were A. James Casner, who received the LL.B. from the University of Illinois; Lon L. Fuller, whose LL.B. came from Stanford; Paul Freund (LL.B. 1931, S.J.D. 1932);

and Milton Katz (LL.B. 1931). Each of them bolstered the national and international reputation of the school: Casner in taxation; Fuller in legal philosophy; Freund, who clerked with Justice Brandeis, in Constitutional Law; and Katz, closely associated with Landis during the New Deal, in international legal study.[119] Then, just as these four arrived, enrollment began to decline.

"Staff Officer for National Defense"

Each of the nation's major wars profoundly impacted the Law School, but in very different ways. Relative to the size of the school, the Civil War was the bloodiest and the most deeply divisive, as 111 Law School students died, a number equaling two entire classes. Nevertheless, the school continued with nearly full enrollment throughout the conflict, thanks to permissive Northern draft policies.[120] In contrast, World War I caused almost no ideological divisions within the school, although student enlistments created a short-term crisis in enrollment and 86 Law School students died. Because the United States was mercifully in the war for only nineteen months, its most pernicious social and political effects, such as the xenophobia of the Red Scare, came later. During the much longer duration of World War II, 112 Law School graduates and former students died, and the school nearly closed.

Well before the Japanese attacked Pearl Harbor in December 1941, Landis was thinking of returning to Washington. In 1940 he announced that a public-spirited lawyer could serve the nation as "a staff officer for national defense."[121] During the presidential election of that year, he campaigned actively for Roosevelt, who was considering Landis for undersecretary of the Treasury. Frankfurter had predicted these distractions when he opposed the appointment of his protégé as dean in 1936, and Conant and the faculty were deeply concerned because Landis had been dean for only four years. But U.S. Senator David I. Walsh from Massachusetts, an isolationist and longtime enemy of the New Deal, blocked the Treasury appointment, so Landis remained at the school in 1941, while consulting for the War Department and serving as regional director of home defense for New England.[122]

In retrospect, a direct Nazi threat to the American homeland hardly seems credible. But at the time, the need to plan for civil defense was deadly serious. Late in 1941, Nazi submarines had begun to prowl off the East Coast, as American ships, not organized in convoys, were silhouetted by the lights of cities, which had no blackouts. Meanwhile, the division of authority and the rivalries between municipalities and states, police and fire departments, and

James M. Landis, as Director of Civilian Defense, standing behind President Franklin D. Roosevelt, awarding Air Medals.

Courtesy of AP Photo, George R. Skadding.

even military commands, made coordination impossible. Nevertheless, under Landis's direction, Massachusetts became the model state for civil defense, leading all others "in aircraft observation posts, information and education services, blackout systems, and air-raid shelters." The surprise attack against unprepared American territory in Hawaii, the German submarines prowling along the East Coast, and the "Blitz" of Nazi bombings on London made Landis's work in New England suddenly seem critical. After Norway and Denmark fell in the spring of 1940, the Nazis had Iceland in their sights. Launched from there, a Nazi air attack on the northeastern United States would require 100,000 men and women to respond, Landis estimated. In January 1942 Roosevelt appointed Landis head of the U.S. Office of Civilian Defense, and despite great political opposition, Congress appropriated $100 million to fund its operations.[123]

Landis thus went from worrying about thousands in his budget at Harvard, to distributing millions on both coasts of the nation, and this appointment

Communications officers doing signal drill in front of Langdell Hall, November 12, 1942.

Harvard University News Office photograph. Courtesy of Harvard University Archives.

effectively marked the end of his work as dean of Harvard Law School. His new salary was $4,000 less than at Harvard, but Conant agreed to pay the difference, hoping that Landis would eventually return. He never really did.

Edmund Morgan, then nearly sixty-five, stepped in as acting dean once again. Following Landis's example, most of the faculty left to become "staff officers for national defense," and the number teaching dropped from thirty-two in the 1940–41 academic year to twelve in 1943–44.[124] The student body shrank even more. Across the nation, enrollment in ABA-accredited law schools fell from 28,174 in 1938 to 4,803 by October 1943. Of those remaining, 22 percent were women, and about half were enrolled in the evening divisions of schools located in large cities. At that point, ten of the ninety-four schools belonging to the Association of American Law Schools had closed their doors. Of the eighty-four schools operating, thirty-four had fewer than twenty-five students, and seventy-one had fewer than fifty students. Only nine had more than seventy-five students.[125]

By the end of 1943, Harvard Law School was a skeleton. The faculty permitted students to complete their degrees with unprecedented speed, requiring only three years of college and seven terms in the Law School, based on a teaching schedule of three terms per year. In addition, third-year students who joined the service after midyear exams were granted degrees. Enrollment fell precipitously, as noted above.[126] Unlike during the Civil War, World War II brought a universal draft. And unlike World War I, the conflict lasted four years for the United States. But most students did not wait for the draft. Louis Toepfer enlisted halfway through his second year. Upon receiving orders to report, "I got up and left in the middle of the class. . . . No one said anything. Everyone understood," he later recalled.[127]

By 1944 nearly all the students who remained were not physically qualified for military service, but many went on to highly successful careers. For example, Henry N. Ess III (LL.B. 1944), a bibliophile and prominent lawyer in New York City, endowed a chair for the school's librarian. In 1939 Arthur von Mehren from Minnesota won one of Conant's national scholarships and came to Harvard College at age sixteen. He graduated in 1942 and might have aided the military because he was fluent in German and offered to learn Japanese. But von Mehren was legally blind, so he enrolled in the Law School in September 1942, and by the following year "class size was down to maybe twenty-five . . . some much smaller," he later said.[128] After completing the LL.B. in 1945 and the Ph.D. in government at Harvard in 1946, von Mehren was appointed to the Law School faculty in 1945. Reprising the famous nineteenth-century arrangement made for George Ticknor and Henry Adams to study in Europe before assuming their appointments as Harvard College professors, Lon Fuller and other senior faculty arranged for von Mehren to spend two years in Europe from 1946 to 1948 studying the legal systems there before assuming his position as assistant professor.[129]

Meanwhile, the tide of war was turning against the Axis nations of Germany, Italy, and Japan. The crucial victory in the Battle of Midway in June 1942 ensured the safety of America's West Coast, and Japan was permanently on the defensive thereafter. In March 1943 the Soviets destroyed the German Sixth Army at Stalingrad, with nearly 850,000 total Axis casualties. In May 1943 the German and Italian armies in North Africa collapsed, surrendering more than 200,000 prisoners. In light of these decisive Allied victories, Landis's urgent efforts in civil defense were no longer needed.

Conant wanted Landis back in Cambridge to prepare for the surge of students that everyone saw coming. But Roosevelt had other plans, because the collapse of Axis control of the Middle East left a power vacuum that was bound to cause huge problems in the future. In August 1943, Roosevelt asked Landis to become director of American Economic Operations and minister to the Middle East. He would be Roosevelt's special agent charged with protecting the diplomatic and economic welfare of American interests in the entire region. The offer was irresistible. Landis wrote to Morgan, "Forgive me for running out again, but I honestly think there is a job to do [in the Middle East] and that I may make some contribution to our general future."[130]

Landis's extraordinary career in the Middle East is beyond the scope of this book. He was in the middle of the conflicts and negotiations over the emerging Cold War "spheres of influence" in Egypt, Suez, Iraq, Iran, Palestine, Greece, and more. But from the narrow viewpoint of Harvard Law School, there was one disturbing fact: Landis was absent. By the middle of 1944, Conant was past all patience, and he set January 1, 1945, as an absolute deadline for Landis to return. Landis did come back, but, as Griswold later recounted, "his heart was not in it."[131]

Returning from War, 1945–46

The school could not afford halfhearted leadership. The trickle of students turned into a deluge after President Roosevelt signed the Servicemen's Readjustment Act into law in June 1944. This "G.I. Bill" provided generous financial benefits to support returning soldiers pursuing postsecondary education, and three times more veterans took advantage of those benefits than the highest number projected. As an additional accommodation, the Law School relaxed the admission requirement of an undergraduate degree for veterans, who could "substitute for not more than two academic years of college work the period spent in the service."[132]

Veterans flooded the Law School, which operated three terms year-round to accommodate them. In the fall of 1945, 478 men registered; in the winter of 1946, 1,163; and in the summer of 1946, 1,445. More than 90 percent were veterans. To make matters more difficult, several professors were unable to return promptly, and the school recovered use of its buildings only gradually. All the same, Landis stated in his last annual report that "it becomes the responsibility of our universities to compensate so far as they can for these [years of interruption to soldiers' studies] that have been incurred by men in the cause of freedom."[133]

Apart from the obligation to help, the end of the war in 1945 presented another significant opportunity to reduce the size of the school. Notwithstanding the new appointments made in 1940, by the fall of 1945 the faculty had shrunk to twenty-three professors, including the dean and eight on leave. The fourteen professors present and teaching included Pound, Seavey, and Scott, who had been on the faculty for nearly forty years and were nearing retirement.[134] The loan to the university had been paid down considerably, and large tuition surpluses would soon no longer be needed to repay the debt to the Corporation. The small wartime enrollment was starting to grow, but could be controlled, and the felt obligation of the school to serve returning G.I.s could be addressed through temporary faculty appointments. Within a few years the flood of veterans would ebb.

The year 1945 therefore offered another chance to escape the school's debilitating cycle of large enrollment, high student-faculty ratio, ruthless attrition, expanding faculty and buildings, and tuition dependence. Landis, the New Deal regulator, was the right leader in the perfect position to adapt the size of the school to its financial resources and academic mission, as Deans Thayer, Pound, and Landis himself had called for. In 1945 he could have designed a school based upon his expressly desired enrollment of 1,000 with low attrition, having already an endowment and buildings to achieve this.

But neither the dean nor the president gave serious thought to capping enrollment and decreasing the size of the school. Instead, Conant viewed the return of soldiers as "a golden opportunity" to recruit for the faculty "first-class men whose normal career paths had been upset by the war." To pursue this strategy, Conant established and chaired a Law School ad hoc committee whose membership was split among faculty, judges, and lawyers.[135] Landis effectively ran the ad hoc committee, which sometimes met in Washington, where he was still working.

Despite some disagreement between the faculty and the practitioners, five faculty appointments were made in 1945 and fulfilled Conant's hopes for great distinction. All five had served in different capacities during the war, from staffing a desk in Washington to flying fighter planes in Burma, and they would contribute to the national and international influence of the school in the 1960s and 1970s. David F. Cavers (LL.B. 1926) became the nation's leading authority on conflicts of laws; Mark A. DeWolfe Howe (LL.B. 1933), a prominent legal historian; Archibald Cox, an expert in Constitutional and labor law. Robert R. Bowie (LL.B. 1934) taught corporate and antitrust law at the Law School from 1946 to 1955, then left to serve as assistant secretary of state, and returned to Harvard in 1957 to teach foreign policy and international affairs in the university. Robert Braucher (LL.B. 1939), a national expert on contracts and commercial law, became a distinguished judge on the Supreme Judicial Court of Massachusetts in 1971. Diverse in their interests, which were balanced among private law, public law, philosophy, history, and international law, these appointments brought depth to the curriculum, excellent teaching to the classroom, and national stature in scholarship.

As these academic appointments were being made at the end of the war, Allied soldiers in Europe uncovered evidence of the horrors of the Holocaust, and Hitler's "final solution" to the problem of racial "impurity." By that point the Nazis had killed more than six million Jewish men, women, and children. Reports of the Nazis' systematic killing of Jews had started circulating as early as 1942. But these tales seemed beyond belief and were often doubted or dismissed as outrageous. In the mid-1940s, Hitler's persecution of the Jews was frequently met with indifference at the highest levels. Prominent figures, including those at Harvard, ignored the rumors and reports of the Nazis' incarceration and extermination of the Jews, and made little response to the terrible evidence that emerged after 1945.[136]

Indeed, many at the university and the Law School had little sympathy for Jews, and even harbored deep-seated anti-Semitism. Harold D. Katz (LL.B. 1950) had come to Harvard College from Indiana and matriculated in the Law School in September 1947. Shortly thereafter, he took a leave of absence and joined the Zionist underground in Palestine in support of founding the state of Israel. When his application to re-enter the Law School came before a faculty committee, Vice Dean Livingston Hall (LL.B. 1927) opposed Katz's readmission on the grounds that the school should not certify the character of a graduate who had violated British law by blowing up bridges. Professor Barton Leach, however, came to Harold's defense and secured his readmission.[137]

Even Jewish applicants who were decorated American veterans reportedly encountered an unofficial quota at the Law School. One such applicant, Kenneth Simon, had studied at the City College of New York before the war and then left to serve as a bombardier in the U.S. Army Air Corps. Simon flew sixty missions over Italy, earned a Purple Heart, was shot down, and spent a year in a German prisoner-of-war camp in Poland in 1944–1945. Returning home, he enrolled in Georgetown University hoping to become a U.S. foreign service officer but learned that the foreign service would not accept Jews. In 1947 he applied to Harvard Law School and, according to his daughter, received a telephone call from the Law School saying that the "Jewish quota" had been met for that admissions cycle, but that he could enter a subsequent class in the accelerated program for returning veterans. Simon graduated with the LL.B. in 1949 and worked on the defense team for Alger Hiss (LL.B. 1928) during his first appeal in 1950.[138]

Meanwhile, Landis did see progress on what he termed "the Jewish problem" in making the academic appointments in 1945. One of the candidates in 1945 was Harry Shulman (LL.B. 1926, S.J.D. 1927), a labor law expert. "He is, of course, Jewish," Landis wrote to Conant. "I raised this issue [with the ad hoc committee] in order to get the reaction of men outside the School." Landis received reassurance that "set my own fears at rest." George A. Brownell (LL.B. 1922), a leader of the corporate bar in New York City, wrote to Landis that Shulman was "a person of known capacity and known distinction and . . . the fact that [Shulman] was a Jew did not disturb him and would not disturb others, and that he, for one, would not be concerned with that aspect of the case. The other members of the [ad hoc] Committee echoed his views."[139] Shulman was offered a professorship but turned it down and later joined the faculty of Yale Law School.

Thus, "concern over the number of Jews on the faculty rapidly diminished as (or because) the number of Jews on the faculty rapidly increased," as historians Morton Keller and Phyllis Keller point out.[140] In 1946, when Milton Katz emerged as one of the two leading candidates to replace him as dean, Landis wrote to Conant that he was "delighted and very proud with the attitude of the faculty with regard to the Jewish problem. It became clear that the suggestion of a Jew like Katz for the deanship would create no internal problem whatsoever."[141] Of course, the fact that "Jewishness" was still termed a "problem" or a "concern" reflected the persistent anti-Semitism of the profession, to which the Law School was not immune. But the tone of these letters between Landis and Conant was much more positive than those between Pound and Lowell.

Prompted by the new faculty appointments, Landis prepared to improve and amplify the limited academic reforms undertaken before the war. In 1945 he appointed a Committee on Legal Education to pursue that inquiry. Landis charged the committee to examine the postwar needs of a recovering economy and society, to identify the educational requirements of lawyers with respect to those needs, and to propose revisions in the academic program of the school accordingly. Like the Curriculum Committee of 1934–1936, this committee was to base its recommendations on empirical research, and Conant provided a fund of $50,000 to survey alumni and bar leaders about what they saw to be the urgent legal needs of a postwar world.[142]

The five members of the Committee on Legal Education represented a new generation on the faculty. Two had joined near the end of Pound's tenure:

Ralph Baker in 1932 and Erwin Griswold in 1934. Three had been appointed by Landis himself: two in 1940, Paul Freund and the chair, Lon Fuller, and one in 1945, David Cavers, who had not yet arrived. Landis excused the members of the Committee from all teaching responsibilities for at least a semester, even though faculty resources were extremely tight with the surge of students. He charged them to "devote all of their time to devising a plan for the School's work for the next fifteen to twenty years."[143]

The dean hoped such a survey would move past the traditional strengths of the school, which "have proved themselves valuable no matter what an uncertain future has in store," and instead would affirm the future importance of public and administrative law—which, he believed, had saved the economy and won the war. Landis maintained that the war "has demonstrated more clearly than ever before that the lawyer's role extends far beyond that of the client caretaker. It moves into administration along broad lines, where the lawyer's special skills make him peculiarly adapted to shoulder important responsibilities as administrator, adjudicator, or protagonist of a special point of view."[144] Landis thus echoed the theme of lawyers' national service that he had set forth in 1940. He had great hopes for his Committee. But appointing it was one of his last acts as dean. Though only forty-six years old, he had run out of time.

Apogee and Descent

By all outward appearances, Landis's meteoric career was ascending and burning ever brighter in January 1946. As a former chairman of the FTC and the SEC, a distinguished confidant of President Roosevelt, a leading defense strategist during the war, a close friend of the rising Kennedy family, and a dean of Harvard Law School, he returned to Cambridge poised to begin a new professional epoch.

He was popular with the faculty and with students. "When he rose to welcome the incoming class, his jutting jaw, mannerisms, and long cigarette holder hauntingly reminded them of the late President Roosevelt," recalled Albert Sacks (LL.B. 1948). His newly appointed Committee on Legal Education would present a vision to inspire and challenge the faculty. "We have entered a period of more government management of our lives," Landis stated. "Some of the wartime controls will be liquidated; some of them won't. We must train men to handle the combination of law and government. We can't go on teaching law in the old-fashioned way."[145] And who better to lead such reforms than Landis himself? He literally invented much of the new paradigm.

True, he appeared exhausted. But so was the rest of the faculty, who had been teaching the legions of returning veterans year-round in three terms. Like many of his colleagues, the dean had to abandon his advanced courses in order to manage the huge first-year courses. Landis told Henry Hart (LL.B. 1929, S.J.D. 1931) that he was "too busy even to think."[146] Yet Landis had managed far bigger and more complicated, chaotic emergencies in the New Deal agencies, the Office of Civilian Defense, and the Middle East, and this enrollment surge under the G.I. Bill was sure to be short-lived.

His personal life, though, was a mess. Shortly before the war he had begun an adulterous affair with his secretary at the school, Dorothy P. Brown. He did not have the nerve to divorce his wife, Stella, who lived in their Washington house with their two daughters, Ann and Ellen. In January 1945, when Landis returned to Cambridge, Stella, Ann, and Ellen remained in Washington, as did his secretary, Dorothy, while the affair continued. In Cambridge, uncomfortable questions were asked. For ten months Landis lived alone in a hotel near the school. He began to drink heavily. He needed to divorce Stella. He loved Dorothy, and she was growing impatient; but Stella remained devoted to her husband and refused to file. Landis was wracked with guilt and "started to go off the deep end." In the summer of 1945 he sought psychiatric help.[147]

During that summer, Stella moved back from Washington to their vacation home in Newbury, Massachusetts, where Landis hoped she would stay. But in the fall of 1945 Stella sent Ann and Ellen to Cambridge to enroll in school. Landis saw only one way to avert complete disgrace, "and that is to move in with her to avoid open scandal, trust that the experiment will demonstrate its utter futility to Stella, and hope that somehow, when this shall have sufficiently broken all three of us, there will be enough left for Dorothy and me to build on."[148]

It was a futile plan, and to make matters worse, Dorothy saw the reestablishment of the Landis household as an opportunity to return to Cambridge without scandal and resume her job as Landis's secretary. But the dean moved her desk into his office, which "was quite unusual" and caused "a lot of talk" among students and faculty.[149] Daughters Ann and Ellen recalled both parents drinking heavily. Landis, who had saved no money, also became convinced this divorce, with child support and alimony, would ruin him financially. Nevertheless, he could not bring himself to live with his family, and in December 1945 he moved into the Harvard Club of Boston.

Stella's dignity, poise, and warmth made her extremely popular with the entire Law School community. Ann and Ellen recall vividly their mother's hospitality at their Cambridge home, and her many friends, who later rallied around her, including the families of Milton Katz, James Casner, and Edwin Dodd (LL.B. 1913). One of the groups Stella entertained was the Association of Harvard Law Wives, who read plays aloud together.[150] In addition, she had done everything possible to save her marriage. The faculty, staff, and students took her side as the highly public tragedy unfolded.

In Cambridge society of the 1940s, the scenario seemed straight from the pen of Nathaniel Hawthorne. The dean's behavior was scandalous, and "any divorce in that period was shocking," observed daughter Ellen.[151] Nevertheless, in June 1947 Stella finally filed for divorce, which was granted in October 1947, along with custody of Ann and Ellen. The outcome was "a traumatic experience for the family of the faculty," recalled Ernest Brown.[152] Now on the Supreme Court, Frankfurter—who had initially opposed Landis's decanal appointment partly because he regarded Landis as unstable—was particularly furious. In April 1946 Frankfurter wrote to Corporation fellow Grenville Clark (LL.B. 1906) that Landis "was not fit for the headship of the School."[153] Some faculty and neighbors refused to acknowledge Landis in the street. "He was in disgrace," noted Louis Toepfer.[154]

But the dean still had friends, many of whom were deeply concerned and had long believed that, though remarkably brilliant and talented, Landis was psychologically troubled and never suited to be dean.[155] During his years at Princeton, mature observers had commented "on what a tortured young man he was, even way back then."[156] His faculty colleagues considered him "a very tense person . . . his eyes were deep-set like an eagle."[157] To young faculty just arriving in the spring of 1946, the dean "made a rather poor impression," observed von Mehren. In their view, the school "was in administrative shambles. . . . Nothing had been done in terms of organization. A lot of new faculty had to be appointed. The facilities needed to be improved. Alumni relations were essentially non-existent. It was absolutely indispensable to have someone who was capable of making decisions and carrying them out and restore order."[158]

Nevertheless, the dean still commanded the respect of President Conant and many colleagues, who marveled at his capabilities. Early in 1946, when it became clear that he was going to leave, Landis convened informal sessions of a small group of the faculty to discuss possibilities for a dean and make a recommendation to the president. After one of these sessions, a senior member of the faculty remarked, "If we only could have Jim Landis all the time the way he was tonight!"[159]

Meanwhile, former classmates of Landis, as well as Washington insiders such as Thomas Corcoran (LL.B. 1926) and John L. Sullivan (LL.B. 1924), were looking for a suitable Washington job for their old friend. The chairman of the newly empowered Civil Aeronautics Board (CAB) was resigning. Landis, the quintessential regulator, had already developed a new course on aviation law. Truman was easily convinced to offer Landis the position. In April 1946 Landis accepted, effective June 1, and resigned as dean.[160] Landis declined Conant's generous offer of a professorship and a leave of absence, and left his law books behind.

A "Greek Tragedy"

Landis was entering what he hoped would be a new life, and maybe some kind of redemption. He later wrote to Stella, "You don't have to apologize to your world, I have to find a world that I don't have to apologize to."[161] There was no need to apologize for his work at Harvard. Landis could look back on his hiring of talented faculty, recovery from the war, establishment of the Committee on Legal Education for long-range strategic planning, as well as significant achievements in admissions reform and curriculum design. Nevertheless, of all the deans of Harvard Law School, it is only Landis whose portrait is missing from its walls. That is not just because of his personal demons, alcoholism, and adultery. Landis's portrait is missing because of the following events, which have overshadowed the significance of his deanship, even in an age when his pioneering work and scholarship on legislative, public, and administrative law have been vindicated.

President Truman was delighted when Landis agreed to lead the CAB. Created in 1938 by the Civil Aeronautics Act and reformed by Roosevelt in 1940, the CAB had important responsibilities overseeing the new and emerging industry of air travel. Landis replaced its only prior chairman, L. Welch Pogue, who had fought against a worldwide aviation monopoly. The challenges were huge, as newly vitalized airlines struggled for survival and control. From the beginning, Landis made it clear that he was not the industry's man. The CAB "was not for the selfish benefit of the carriers involved," but was to protect the public interest in what otherwise would be a "Wild West" of sloppy safety procedures and entrepreneurism. Inevitably, Landis became the target of major airline lobbies, particularly the powerful Pan American Airlines, which sought an overseas monopoly as a single "flag carrier." Landis also sided with the pilots on air safety, to the disgust of their employers, and fought all efforts to restrict domestic competition.[162]

But Landis was also becoming impolitic. His excessive drinking was the subject of Washington gossip, which his opponents exploited. Truman was no Roosevelt. He believed Landis had been doing "a magnificent job," but the political costs were becoming too high. Landis's term was set to expire on December 31, 1947, and the major airlines launched a "Hate Landis Campaign" both in Congress and in the press. On December 26, 1947, Truman caved to political pressure and told Landis that he would not be reappointed. It would take Truman three embarrassing months, and a major run-in with the Senate, before Landis could be replaced.[163]

Blindsided and shocked, Landis had no job, no money, and major financial obligations. But he still had some very loyal friends. Even Stella, who had been driven to alcoholism and suffered through Landis's repeated negligence over alimony and the girls' tuition, refused to turn on him. With the support of Joseph Kennedy and a vague job at "Kennedy Enterprises," Landis began to come back. In July 1948, twenty-four years after graduating from law school, the former dean took and passed his first bar exam, joining some associates from the CAB to form a law firm specializing in aviation law. His annual income grew rapidly, exceeding $100,000 a year in both 1957 and 1958, equal to nearly $1 million today.

In addition, his allies, Thomas Corcoran and Joseph Kennedy, founded a new political dynasty, and Landis soon became close with Joseph's sons John Kennedy and Robert Kennedy. Few have the chance to develop a close relationship with even one president. Landis was close to three. He loved Roosevelt, saw too much of Truman for his liking, and now would have another chance. During the 1960 presidential campaign, John Kennedy suggested that Landis lead his transition team after the election. After Kennedy's victory, Landis was appointed head of the Commission to Review Regulatory Procedure, charged to examine all of the regulatory commissions and resulting in the famous Landis Report of December 26, 1960. Then he was made special assistant to the president in the White House. Kennedy was even said to be considering Landis for the Supreme Court.[164]

Then two more misdeeds came to light. First, having married Dorothy after divorcing Stella, Landis was now named in a divorce suit by the husband of Landis's secretary in the White House. The incendiary news hit the press on

September 7, 1961.[165] Then, agents of the Internal Revenue Service (IRS) in New York, conducting a routine check of all presidential appointments in 1961, could not find Landis's tax returns after 1955. Attempting to avert scandal, they did not proceed with a regular investigation but instead contacted Joseph Kennedy.

Joseph Kennedy summoned Landis, who made a full confession, admitting that he had not filed returns since 1955. His failure in the first year apparently stemmed from the complexities due to a small inheritance from his mother. In the subsequent years Landis could not bring himself to lie by checking the "no" box on the question asking if he had filed the previous year on the 1040 form. Nevertheless, each year Landis did fill out and keep the returns, while opening a separate bank account and depositing money owed on the taxes.[166] As a result, there could be no defense of inadvertence or unintentional neglect. Nor could he invoke the IRS acknowledged defense that he voluntarily admitted his failure to file, because, Landis said, Joseph Kennedy had told him to confess. It was insane.

The Kennedy administration was backed into a corner. They desperately wanted to save Landis, but there were obvious conflicts of interest. The IRS commissioner refused to act and referred the matter to the Justice Department. Nicholas Katzenbach, the new deputy attorney general, was given the case, and he did everything possible to avoid an indictment, but it was inevitable. To the frustration of his psychoanalyst, Landis refused the obvious strategy of a psychological defense, arguing that it would embarrass the three presidents who had named him to high positions. On August 2, 1963, he appeared before the U.S. District Court in Manhattan to plead guilty to five counts of failure to file income tax returns between 1956 and 1960.

The U.S. attorney, Robert M. Morgenthau, stated that Landis had fully cooperated during the investigation and had already paid much of the back taxes owed. Both Katzenbach and Morgenthau had thought that Landis's best strategy, having elected not to adopt a psychological defense, was to plead guilty and pay the penalties. They expected, at most, a fine and a suspended sentence.[167] They even provided Landis with a schedule of sitting judges, and permitted his lawyers to select one known to be compassionate. But that judge disqualified himself, likely because of a stupid attempt by Corcoran to try to influence him, and Landis drew Judge Sylvester J. Ryan.[168]

Landis offered little explanation for his actions, except that he "would like to express regret, indeed repentance, for the folly that led me to put off filing of these returns" and that he did not "intend to deprive the government of any revenue," which seemed to be true, given that he regularly segregated the funds in a separate account. Judge Ryan, having heard that Landis had recently been a patient in a psychiatric hospital, was not sure he was competent to plead guilty.[169] But Landis and his lawyers told Ryan that he was, and the judge gave the "unprecedented" sentence of thirty days in prison, to be served immediately, and one-year probation.[170]

The judge, noting Landis's alcoholism, said that jail would "give you an opportunity to reflect and straighten yourself out." It is possible that Judge Ryan hoped Landis would "bottom out," helping him overcome the alcoholism. In any event, Landis was immediately transferred to the alcoholics' ward at the Public Health Service on Staten Island. The next day, the front pages of the *New York Times, Boston Globe, Washington Post,* and other papers blared, "Landis Is Jailed for Tax Delays."[171]

His condition deteriorated rapidly, and his psychiatrist prescribed antidepressants. He was treated as a potential suicide. Dorothy was deeply alarmed, and his lawyers requested a transfer to Columbia Presbyterian Neurological Institute. Robert Kennedy personally arranged the transfer, ignoring the potential political damage.[172] Both Kennedy and Katzenbach sent letters to the Appellate Division of the New York Supreme Court, urging that Landis not be disbarred. There had been no fraud or deceit. No client was involved. There was no intended theft. But on July 10, 1964, Landis was suspended from the New York Bar for one year "to uphold the dignity of the legal profession."[173]

Landis's friends helped him find a job. Among other overtures, Robert Kennedy generously offered Landis the position of chairman of the Review Committee to declassify the records of the John F. Kennedy Library. After much hesitation, Landis took the job. He was scheduled to attend an initial meeting at the National Archives in August 1964. Shortly before, on a hot July day, Landis went for a swim in the pool at his house in Rye, New York. Dorothy was coming home to join him, but was delayed in traffic. Before she arrived, two neighborhood teenagers, who had been invited over to use the pool, found him floating face down, drowned. It was just twenty days after Landis's disbarment.

Did Landis commit suicide, like Dean Ezra Thayer in 1915? His psychiatrist and the prison system certainly treated him as a potential suicide. But Landis was a strong swimmer, and the autopsy revealed a "ninety percent narrowing of his coronary arteries and signs of recent hemorrhage." Hence, the coroner ruled the drowning accidental and likely due to a heart attack in the pool.[174] Landis's daughters remain strongly convinced that he did not take his own life. A memorial service was held in Washington, and the funeral in Rye, where Robert Kennedy wept. Obituaries appeared in scores of newspapers, and a special dedication issue of the *Harvard Law Review* followed.[175]

Assessments of Landis have varied greatly. Some, including Judge Henry Friendly (LL.B. 1927), considered the Landis deanship a "Greek tragedy" that threatened the "continued primacy" of Harvard Law School.[176] Others, like Harvard Corporation fellow Charles Coolidge (LL.B. 1922), considered Landis mentally ill or neurotic.[177] Landis's own psychiatrist attributed his personal failings to "a longstanding personality disturbance in a man of high intelligence and moral conviction."[178] Furthermore, "the turbulence of the time" agitated "the crosscurrents and eddies in his complex and restless nature," observed Milton Katz.[179]

But Landis's foibles and tragic end should not overshadow his contributions. Dismissive accounts are unjustified.[180] As his successor, Dean Erwin Griswold said at Landis's memorial service—quoting Ben Jonson's tribute to Francis Bacon—"I have and do reverence him for the greatness that was only proper to himself . . . in his adversity I ever prayed that God would give him strength; for greatness he could not want."[181] Teaching about public law, legislation, rule making, and administrative process began with James Landis, both at Harvard Law School and other law schools throughout the nation. That accomplishment deserves recognition, and Landis a portrait among the deans of the school.[182]

NOTES

1. Quotation is from Morton Keller and Phyllis Keller, *Making Harvard Modern: The Rise of America's University* (New York, 2001), 4–5. See Samuel Eliot Morison, *Three Centuries of Harvard: 1636–1936* (Cambridge, MA, 1936).

2. Keller and Keller, *Making Harvard Modern*, 117–119, 257; Henry K. Beecher and Mark D. Altschule, *Medicine at Harvard: The First 300 Years* (Hanover, NH, 1977), 210–211.

3. Quotation is from Arthur E. Sutherland, *The Law at Harvard: A History of Ideas and Men, 1817–1967* (Cambridge, MA, 1967), 303. This chapter draws on Donald A. Ritchie, *James M. Landis: Dean of the Regulators* (Cambridge, MA, 1980); Duncan Farthing-Nichol, "A Desirable Discontent: Dean James M. Landis at Harvard Law School" (student research paper, Harvard Law School (HLS), 2012), on file with the authors; Duncan Farthing-Nichol, "Sunlight from the Shadows: Dean James M. Landis in the History of the Harvard Law School" (student research paper, HLS, 2013), on file with the authors; and Justin

O'Brien, *The Triumph, Tragedy and Lost Legacy of James M. Landis: A Life on Fire* (Oxford, UK, 2014), which focuses on Landis's legal theory and its influence.

4. "Meteoric" is the term used by Roscoe Pound, quoted in Thomas K. McGraw, *Prophets of Regulation: Charles Francis Adams, Louis D. Brandeis, James M. Landis, Alfred E. Kahn* (Cambridge, MA, 1984), 158. See "The Legend of Landis," *Fortune* (August 1934), 44–45.

5. James B. Conant, Annual Report of the President of Harvard University, 1936–37, 131. See James B. Conant, *My Several Lives: Memoirs of a Social Inventor* (New York, 1970), 131–138; Keller and Keller, *Making Harvard Modern,* 23. Daniel Coquillette's father, Robert M. Coquillette (B.S. 1939), came from Iowa to attend Harvard College solely due to Conant's national scholarship program.

6. Keller and Keller, *Making Harvard Modern,* 49.

7. Conant, *My Several Lives,* 153–156.

8. Ritchie, *James M. Landis,* 80–81. See "Law School Recommendations for Deanship," Harvard Law School Dean's Office Records, Records of President James B. Conant, 1933–1953, Harvard University Archives (hereafter cited as JBC Records).

9. John Dickinson, "Henry Wolf Biklé," *University of Pennsylvania Law Review* 90 (March, 1942): 513; W. Barton Leach, "The Law at Harvard: A Quasi Review with Personalia," *HLSB* (March 1968): 17.

10. See Conant, *My Several Lives,* 335.

11. Here and below, we draw upon Ritchie, *James M. Landis,* 9–15.

12. See James M. Landis, "The Commerce Clause as a Restriction on State Taxation," *Michigan Law Review* 20 (November 1921): 50–85.

13. Quoted in Ritchie, *James M. Landis,* 17.

14. Frank E. A. Sander, Oral History, conducted by Daniel R. Coquillette and Daniel Hamilton (September–December 1998), on file with the authors.

15. Quoted in Ritchie, *James M. Landis,* 34–35, 220n20. See "The Legend of Landis," 44–45.

16. Roscoe Pound, "Liberty of Contract," *Yale Law Journal* 18 (1909): 464.

17. *A.L.A. Schechter Poultry Corp. v. United States,* 295 U.S. 495 (1935).

18. Roscoe Pound, "The Future of the Common Law," in *The Future of the Common Law* (Cambridge, MA, 1937), 19. See Pound, "Public and Private Law," *Cornell Law Quarterly* 24 (June 1939): 480–482; David Culp, "Dean Pound and Administrative Law," *Columbia Law Review* 42 (1942): 89–103.

19. James M. Landis, *The Administrative Process* (New Haven, CT, 1938). Landis later observed that "Pound's position in connection with administrative law was an extremely conservative one." James M. Landis, *Reminiscences of James McCauley Landis: Oral History, 1964* [interview conducted for the Columbia University Oral History Research Program by Neil Gold in 1964] (Westport, CT, 1975), 152.

20. James B. Thayer, "The Origin and Scope of the American Doctrine of Constitutional Law," *HLR* 7 (1893): 144. See Thayer, "Constitutionality of Legislation: The

Precise Question for a Court," *Nation* 38 (1884): 314–315; James P. Hall, "James Bradley Thayer," in *Great American Lawyers,* ed. William D. Lewis (Philadelphia, 1909), 8:369; Jay Hook, "A Brief Life of James Bradley Thayer," *Northwestern University Law Review* 88 (1993): 1–8.

21. Landis, "The Commerce Clause," 68.

22. See James M. Landis, "Congressional Power of Investigation," *HLR* 40 (1926): 153–221.

23. James M. Landis, "The Implications of Modern Legislation to Law Teaching," *American Law School Review* 8 (1935): 159.

24. James M. Landis, "The Study of Legislation in Law Schools: An Imaginary Inaugural Lecture," *Harvard Graduates' Magazine* (1931), 437. See also John Manning and Mathew Stephenson, *Legislation and Regulation* (New York, 2010), 392–393; Farthing-Nichol, "A Desirable Discontent," 9–10.

25. Landis, "The Study of Legislation," 441. See Ritchie, *James M. Landis,* 36; Farthing-Nichol, "A Desirable Discontent," 9–10.

26. James M. Landis, "Statutes and the Sources of Law," in *Harvard Legal Essays: Written in Honor of and Presented to Joseph Henry Beale and Samuel Williston,* ed. Roscoe Pound (Cambridge, MA, 1934), 231.

27. Sutherland, *Law at Harvard,* 292. See *Griswold v. Connecticut,* 381 U.S. 479 (1965).

28. Ritchie, *James M. Landis,* 43.

29. Ritchie, *James M. Landis,* 57.

30. McGraw, *Prophets of Regulation,* 212. See George K. Gardner, "Review of *The Administrative Process* by James M. Landis," *HLR* 52 (1938): 336–342.

31. Landis, *Administrative Process,* 10. See Farthing-Nichol, "A Desirable Discontent," 12–13.

32. Landis, *Administrative Process,* 30–31. See Farthing-Nichol, "A Desirable Discontent," 14.

33. Edmund M. Morgan to James M. Landis (November 7, 1934), JBC Records. See Ritchie, *James M. Landis,* 75, 79; Keller and Keller, *Making Harvard Modern,* 114.

34. Quoted in Ritchie, *James M. Landis,* 53–54, 224–225n31.

35. Austin W. Scott to James B. Conant (January 14, 1942), JBC Records.

36. James M. Landis, Annual Report of the Dean of Harvard Law School, 1937–38, 197; Louis A. Toepfer, Oral History, conducted by Daniel Hamilton (March 1998), on file with the authors.

37. Sidney P. Simpson, Speech at the Forty-first Annual Meeting of Associated Harvard Clubs (Chicago, May 20–22, 1938), quoted in John J. Liolos, "Erecting the High Citadel's Walls: The Development of Formal Admissions Standards at Harvard Law School, 1817–1955" (student research paper, Boston College Law School, 2012), on file with the authors, 51. See also Landis and Simpson, "New Curriculum of the Harvard Law School," 966–969.

38. See Chapter 1 in this volume.

39. Graduates of the second-tier colleges were admitted only "so far as there is room for them, giving preference to graduates of first-list colleges." See Harvard Law School Catalog, 1927–28, 5; 1928–29, 6. For admissions policy and procedures prior to 1910, see Daniel R. Coquillette and Bruce A. Kimball, *On the Battlefield of Merit: Harvard Law School, the First Century* (Cambridge, MA, 2015) (hereafter cited as *Battlefield of Merit*), 406–411, 437–438, 452–455, 473–475, 518n122.

40. Landis, Annual Report of the Dean, 1937–38, 194; Archibald Cox, Oral History, conducted by Daniel R. Coquillette and Daniel Hamilton (November 1998), on file with the authors; Ernest J. Brown, Oral History, conducted by Daniel Hamilton (August 1997), on file with the authors.

41. Sub-Committee on Admissions and Admission Policy, Report (May 15, 1935), Records of Faculty Committee on Curriculum, 1934–, JBC Records. See Committee on Curriculum, *Final 1936 Curriculum Report*, Records of Faculty Committee on Curriculum, 1934–, JBC Records; Landis, Annual Report of the Dean, 1937–1938, 196–197; James M. Landis and Sidney P. Simpson, "The New Curriculum of the Harvard Law School," *HLR* 51 (1938): 966–969; Louis A. Toepfer, "Admissions," *HLSB* (April 1957): 3. Here and below, we draw upon Liolos, "Erecting the High Citadel's Walls," 49–50; Christopher W. Schmidt, "The Failure of Reform: Legal Education at Harvard Law School, 1934–1946" (student research paper, HLS, 2006), on file with the authors, 42; Farthing-Nichol, "A Desirable Discontent," 17–21.

42. "The 'Critical Grade,'" *Harvard Alumni Bulletin* 39 (1936–1937): 528.

43. Quotations are from, respectively, Landis, Annual Report of the Dean, 1938–39, 228; 1936–37, 213–214. See Landis, *Reminiscences*, 461, 472; "Law Requirements Raised at Harvard," *New York Times* (January 15, 1937).

44. Roscoe Pound to Ezra R. Thayer (July 28, 1911), JBC Records; Ezra R. Thayer to Roscoe Pound (August 17, 1911), Roscoe Pound Papers, 1888–1964, Harvard Law School Library Historical & Special Collections (HLSLib).

45. Quotations are from, respectively, Landis, Annual Report of the Dean, 1938–39, 228; 1936–37, 213–214. See Landis, *Reminiscences*, 461, 472; "Law Requirements Raised at Harvard."

46. Committee on Curriculum, *Final 1936 Curriculum Report*, 87, 90; Edward H. Warren, "Comments on Report of the Committee in the Curriculum" (October 4, 1936), Records of Faculty Committee on Curriculum, 1934–, JBC Records; Landis, Annual Report of the Dean, 1936–37, 214; 1938–39, 228.

47. Committee on Curriculum, *Final 1936 Curriculum Report*, 87, 90.

48. Landis, Annual Report of the Dean, 1937–38, 197. See Landis, Annual Report of the Dean, 1936–37, 213–214; Sub-Committee on Admissions and Admission Policy, Report (May 15, 1935); Warren, "Comments on Report of the Committee in the Curriculum" (October 4, 1936).

49. Landis, Annual Report of the Dean, 1938–39, 228.

50. See Chapter 7 in this volume.

51. Simpson, Speech at the Forty-first Annual Meeting of Associated Harvard Clubs," quoted in Liolos, "Erecting the High Citadel's Walls," 51. See Landis and Simpson, "New Curriculum," 966–969.

52. "Law Requirements Raised at Harvard"; Landis, Annual Report of the Dean, 1938–39, 195.

53. Landis, Annual Report of the Dean, 1938–39, 228; 1937–38, 197.

54. Landis, Annual Report of the Dean, 1937–38, 197. See Harvard Law School Catalog, 1938–39, 102; 1939–40, 103.

55. Quotation is from Landis, Annual Report of the Dean, 1937–38, 197.

56. Toepfer, "Admissions," 3; Toepfer, Oral History (March 1998); Brown, Oral History (August 1997). In 1948 James A. MacLachlan legally changed the spelling of his name from McLaughlin, the version of his family name created by a clerical error in Scotland much earlier.

57. Harvard Law School Faculty Meeting Minutes (March 21, 1939).

58. Landis, Annual Report of the Dean, 1937–38, 197. See "Report to Faculty by the Admissions Committee for the Year 1939," Harvard Law School Faculty Meeting Minutes (February 20, 1940).

59. Quotations are from, respectively, Landis, Annual Report of the Dean, 1936–37, 213; 1938–39, 195.

60. William P. LaPiana, "Merit and Discovery: The Origins of the Law School Admission Test," in Before the Paper Chase: The Scholarship of Law School Preparation and Admissions, ed. Tim A. Garrison and Frank Guliuzza (Durham, NC, 2012), 64, 82n11; A. G. Gulliver, "The Use of the Legal Aptitude Test in the Selection of Law School Students," American Law School Review 9 (1940): 560; Albert B. Crawford and Tom J. Gorham, "The Yale Legal Aptitude Test," Yale Law Journal 49 (1940): 1238. See also Liolos, "Erecting the High Citadel's Walls," 52.

61. Harvard Law School Faculty Meeting Minutes (October 19, 1937). See Toepfer, Oral History (March 1998).

62. Quotation is from "Report to Faculty by the Admissions Committee for the Year 1939," Harvard Law School Faculty Meeting Minutes (February 20, 1940); see February 27 and September 24, 1940. The "Report to Faculty by the Admissions Committee for the Year 1939" is full of statistical results and the members' conflicting opinions on using the tests.

63. Quotations are from Toepfer, Oral History (March 1998). See Liolos, "Erecting the High Citadel's Walls," 49.

64. Quotations are from Toepfer, Oral History (March 1998); Arthur von Mehren, Oral History, conducted by Daniel R. Coquillette and Mary Beth Basile (July–December 2000), on file with the authors.

65. See Farthing-Nichol, "A Desirable Discontent," 21; Liolos, "Erecting the High Citadel's Walls," 58. See Harvard Law School Faculty Meeting Minutes (September 15, December 20, 1941; March 2, 1943).

66. Haig der Manuelian, email to Karen S. Beck, manager, HLSLib (October 24, 2012).

67. Detlev Vagts, Oral History, conducted by Daniel Hamilton, Daniel R. Coquillette, and John Delionado (November 1999–February 2000), on file with the authors.

68. Toepfer, Oral History (March 1998).

69. Brown, Oral History (August 1997). See, too, Erwin N. Griswold, *Ould Fields, New Corne: The Personal Memoirs of a Twentieth Century Lawyer* (St. Paul, MN, 1992), 161.

70. James M. Landis to Charles C. Burlingham (July 5, 1938), James McCauley Landis Papers, 1899–1964, HLSLib (hereafter cited as JML Papers). The faculty voted to hire Maria Schoch as a research assistant in 1938, but was careful to avoid the impression that she would be a member of the faculty. Harvard Law School Faculty Meeting Minutes (April 26, 1938).

71. See the informative tables in Virginia G. Drachman, *Sisters in Law: Women Lawyers in Modern American History* (Cambridge, MA, 1998), 251–264.

72. Harvard Law School Faculty Meeting Minutes (October 6, 1925). See Liolos, "Erecting the High Citadel's Walls," 67.

73. Quoted in Richard N. Smith, *The Harvard Century: The Making of a University to a Nation* (New York, 1986), 85.

74. Louis A. Toepfer, Interview (May 4, 1998), quoted in David McIntosh, "A Minor Matter: The Admission of Women to the Harvard Law School" (student research paper, HLS, 1998), on file with the authors, 9. See Toepfer, Oral History (March 1998).

75. Zechariah Chafee Jr., Memorandum to the Faculty (December 5, 1942), Zechariah Chafee Jr. Papers, 1898–1957, HLSLib (hereafter cited as ZCJ Papers); "Women Still Barred from Law School," *Harvard Crimson* (February 16, 1942); Mary Elizabeth Basile, "Paul Murray's Campaign against Harvard Law School's 'Jane Crow' Admissions Policy," *Journal of Legal Education* 57 (2007): 77.

76. Quoted in Herma Hill Kay, "Symposium: The Voices of Women—A Symposium on Women in Legal Education; The Future of Women Law Professors," *Iowa Law Review* 77 (1991): 8.

77. Edmund M. Morgan, "Memorandum to the Faculty" (December 5, 1942), ZCJ Papers. Morgan wrote: "Memorandum to the Faculty: 1. Vote on Admission of women: FOR: Landis, Hall, Baker, Chafee, Dodd, Freund, Fuller, Glueck, Griswold, Hart, Scott, Seavey, Simpson, Powell, Warner. [15]. AGAINST: Gardner, Hudson, Katz, Leach, McCurdy, MacLachlan, Maguire, Morgan, Pound, Thayer, Warren, E. H. [11]." Quoted in Farthing-Nichol, "Sunlight from the Shadows," 68–69.

78. Harvard Law School Faculty Meeting Minutes (December 15, 1942).

79. Brown, Oral History (August 1997).

80. James M. Landis to Charles C. Burlingham (March 20, 1945), JML Papers.

81. "It may not be coincidental that women gained access to the Harvard Medical School before they were accepted at the Law School, for 'practicing law was even more incompatible with nineteenth-century ideas about women than was practicing medicine. Female doctors could claim that their careers were natural extensions of women's nurturing, healing

role in the home and that they protected female modesty by ministering to members of their own sex. By contrast, women lawyers were clearly intruding on the public domain explicitly reserved to men." Barbara J. Harris, *Beyond Her Sphere: Women and the Professions in American History* (Westport, CT, 1978), 112.

82. Griswold, *Ould Fields,* 170.

83. Brown, Oral History (August 1997). See Griswold, *Ould Fields,* 170–171.

84. Landis to Burlingham (March 20, 1945).

85. Harvard Law School Faculty Meeting Minutes (September 11, 1945). See Liolos, "Erecting the High Citadel's Walls," 67; Farthing-Nichol, "Sunlight from the Shadows, 70.

86. James M. Landis, Outgoing Correspondence (December 1945), JBC Records.

87. Both Ann Landis McLaughlin and Ellen Landis McKee agreed that their father "wouldn't be enthusiastic about professional women." Ann Landis McLaughlin and Ellen Landis McKee, Interview conducted by Emily W. Andersen (August 2015), on file with the authors.

88. James M. Landis to James B. Conant (May 4, 1938), JBC Records.

89. Quoted in Farthing-Nichol, "A Desirable Discontent," 24.

90. Quotation is from Landis to Conant (May 4, 1938). On the following, see Landis and Simpson, "New Curriculum," 965–987.

91. Harvard Law School Faculty Meeting Minutes (April 25, May 10, 1939). See Farthing-Nichol, "A Desirable Discontent," 25.

92. Landis, Annual Report of the Dean, 1938–39, 230.

93. See JD Written Work Requirement, http://hls.harvard.edu/dept/academics/writing -at-hls/written-work-requirement/?redir=1 (November 2017).

94. Quotations are from Harvard Law School Faculty Meeting Minutes (November 6, 1945).

95. Landis, *Reminiscences,* 472.

96. Toepfer, Oral History (March 1998).

97. Harvard Law School Faculty Meeting Minutes (December 6, 1938); Farthing-Nichol, "Sunlight from the Shadows," 71.

98. See Harvard Law School Catalog, 1947–48, 34; Farthing-Nichol, "Sunlight from the Shadows," 71; Jerome Rappaport, "A Letter from HLS Forum Founder Jerome Rappaport '49," in *Harvard Law School Forum,* https://orgs.law.harvard.edu/hlsforum/history/ (last accessed November 5, 2017).

99. Quotation is from James M. Landis to James B. Conant (June 7, 1938), JBC Records.

100. Landis, *Reminiscences,* 475. See James M. Landis to Elihu Root Jr. (December 20, 1945), JBC Records. The Root Room later became the home of the Law Library's Historical & Special Collections.

101. Joel Seligman, *The High Citadel: The Influence of Harvard Law School* (Boston, 1978), 69; Laura Kalman, *Legal Realism at Yale, 1927–1960* (Chapel Hill, NC, 1986),

66; Schmidt, "Failure of Reform," 35. Landis also proposed a seven-year curriculum to interweave the B.A. course in Harvard College with that of the LL.B. at the Law School. His plan was approved by the faculty in 1940, but no one enrolled in the program, which disappeared from the Law School catalog in 1952–53. See Landis, Annual Report of the Dean, 1939–40, 228; Harvard Law School Faculty Meeting Minutes (January 9, 1940); Harvard Law School Catalog, 1941–42, 25; Farthing-Nichol, "A Desirable Discontent," 29.

102. Harvard Law School Catalog, 1937–38.

103. Edmund M. Morgan to James B. Conant, Memorandum regarding the Admissions Policy of the Harvard Law School [ca. December 1936], JBC Records. See Edward H. Warren to James B. Conant (November 24, 1941), quoted in Farthing-Nichol, "A Desirable Discontent," 37. The following discussion draws upon Farthing-Nichol, "Sunlight from the Shadows," 88–97.

104. Annual Report of the Treasurer of Harvard University, 1937–38, 10, 68–71; 1938–39, 10, 68–71.

105. Annual Report of the Treasurer, 1939–40, 68–71.

106. Landis, Annual Report of the Dean, 1939–40, 235; 1940–41, 213; Edmund M. Morgan, Annual Report of the Dean of Harvard Law School, 1942–43, 131; 1943–44, 162; 1944–45, 164.

107. Landis, Annual Report of the Dean, 1939–40, 235.

108. Quotation is from Harvard Law School Faculty Meeting Minutes (March 2, 1943). See Morgan, Annual Report of the Dean, 1942–43, 131; 1943–44, 162; 1944–45, 164.

109. Quotation is from Landis, Annual Report of the Dean, 1939–1940, 235. See Harvard Law School Catalog, 1944–45, 3–4; Morgan, Annual Report of the Dean, 1943–44, 162; 1944–45, 164; Liolos, "Erecting the High Citadel's Walls," 57; Farthing-Nichol, "Sunlight from the Shadows," 96.

110. Harvard Law School Faculty Meeting Minutes (August 17, 1944); Annual Report of the Treasurer, 1945–46, 12; Farthing-Nichol, "Sunlight from the Shadows," 96.

111. Harvard Law School Faculty Meeting Minutes (November 27, 1945).

112. Ritchie, *James M. Landis,* 84; Farthing-Nichol, "Sunlight from the Shadows," 94; Paul A. Freund, "Remarks at the Presentation of a Bust of James M. Landis at the Harvard Law School" (October 19, 1980), Paul A. Freund Papers, 1918–1993, HLSLib.

113. Reginald Heber Smith to Erwin N. Griswold (June 6, 1946), Erwin N. Griswold Papers, 1925–1994, HLSLib (hereafter cited as ENG Papers). See Kenneth Leung, "Fundraising at the Harvard Law School during Erwin Griswold's Deanship" (student research paper, HLS, 2011) on file with the authors, appendix 2.

114. Erwin N. Griswold to Reginald Heber Smith (June 7, 1946), ENG Papers. See Leung, "Fundraising at the Harvard Law School," appendix 2.

115. Notes from Donald Ritchie's Interview with Erwin N. Griswold (June 3, 1975), James McCauley Landis Papers, 1916–2004, Library of Congress, quoted in Farthing-Nichol, "Sunlight from the Shadows," 96.

116. Annual Report of the Treasurer, 1930–31, 149–150, 166–167; 1931–32, 149–150, 163; 1932–33, 148–149, 162; 1933–34, 152–153, 168; 1934–35, 147–148, 163; 1935–36, 148–149, 168; 1936–37, 155, 178, 1937–38, 161, 179; 1938–39, 164, 182–183; 1939–1940, 167, 183–185.

117. Landis, Annual Report of the Dean, 1937–38, 197.

118. Harvard Law School Catalog, 1938–39, 3–4; 1939–40, 3–4, 40–41, 3–4.

119. See Keller and Keller, *Making Harvard Modern,* 114–115; Sutherland, *Law at Harvard,* 305, 311, 371–388.

120. See *Battlefield of Merit,* 259–303.

121. James M. Landis, "The Lawyer as Staff Officer for National Defense," *Vital Speeches of the Day* 6 (1940): 572.

122. Here and in the following paragraph we draw on Schmidt, "Failure of Reform," 31–32; Ritchie, *James M. Landis,* 95–101, 107–115.

123. Quotation is from Ritchie, *James M. Landis,* 104. See Winston S. Churchill, *The Second World War: The Grand Alliance* (Boston, 1950), 136–155, 604–711.

124. See Harvard Law School Yearbook, 1945–46, 1954, 1977, 1996; Sutherland, *Law at Harvard,* 308–311. Professor James B. Thayer (LL.B. 1921)—the Roman and comparative law expert, son of Dean Ezra Thayer, and grandson of nineteenth-century professor James Thayer (LL.B. 1856)—resigned from the faculty for undisclosed reasons in 1945.

125. Young B. Smith, Annual Report of the Dean of Columbia Law School, 1942–43, 3.

126. See "Law School Cut to 104 as Draft Slices 1200 Normal," *Harvard Crimson* (March 15, 1943).

127. Toepfer, Oral History (March 1998).

128. von Mehren, Oral History (July–December 2000).

129. Harvard Law School Faculty Meeting Minutes (November 27, 1945).

130. Quoted in Ritchie, *James M. Landis,* 121, 127–132.

131. Erwin N. Griswold, "James McCauley Landis, 1899–1904," *HLR* 78 (1964): 316. See also "J. M. Landis to Return to Harvard," *New York Times* (December 29, 1944).

132. Harvard Law School Faculty Meeting Minutes (August 28, 1945). See Suzanne Mettler, *Soldiers to Citizens: The G.I. Bill and the Making of the Greatest Generation* (New York, 2005); Harvard Law School Catalog, 1944–45, "Information for Veterans"; Landis, Annual Report of the Dean, 1944–45, 165. See Toepfer, Oral History (March 1998); Liolos, "Erecting the High Citadel's Walls," 59–60. This relaxation lasted until 1948.

133. Landis, Annual Report of the Dean, 1944–45, 165. See Morgan, Annual Report of the Dean, 1944–45, 164; Erwin N. Griswold, Annual Report of the Dean of Harvard Law School, 1945–46, 343.

134. Harvard Law School Catalog, 1945–46, 3–4.

135. Quotation is from Keller and Keller, *Making Harvard Modern,* 114, 115.

136. The Holocaust is not even mentioned in James G. Hershberg, *James B. Conant: Harvard to Hiroshima and the Making of the Nuclear Age* (Stanford, CA, 1993).

137. Harvard Law School Faculty Meeting Minutes (March 2, 1948); William Malone to Daniel R. Coquillette (May 8, 1997), on file with the authors.

138. Quotation is from Steven Goldberg to Daniel R. Coquillette (October 9, 2016), on file with the authors. See also Carol Reif, "Obituary: Kenneth Simon, 93, Formerly of Mamaroneck, Prisoner of War," *Mamaroneck Daily Voice* (June 18, 2016); Kenneth Simon, "A Recollection—In the Alger Hiss Story: A Search for Truth," accessed January 20, 1019, at http://algerhiss.com/alger-hiss/we-remember-alger/a-recollection-by-kenneth-simon/.

139. James M. Landis to James B. Conant (March 10, 1945), quoted in Keller and Keller, *Making Harvard Modern,* 115.

140. Keller and Keller, *Making Harvard Modern,* 115.

141. James M. Landis to James B. Conant (April 29, 1946) quoted in Keller and Keller, *Making Harvard Modern,* 115.

142. Landis, Annual Report of the Dean, 1944–45, 171–172; Harvard Law School Faculty Meeting Minutes (August 14, 1945). See Schmidt, "Failure of Reform," 48; Farthing-Nichol, "A Desirable Discontent," 41.

143. Harvard Law School Faculty Meeting Minutes (August 14, 1945). See Landis, Annual Report of the Dean, 1944–45, 173; James M Landis to Lon Fuller (December 1, 1945), JBC Records.

144. Landis, Annual Report of the Dean, 1944–45, 173.

145. Quotations are from Ritchie, *James M. Landis,* 138. See "Landis Adjusts Law School for Influx of Soldiers," *New York Times* (March 17, 1946).

146. James M. Landis to Henry M. Hart (November 19, 1945), Henry M. Hart Papers, 1927–1969, HLSLib.

147. Quotation is from Sander, Oral History (September 1998). See Ritchie, *James M. Landis,* 134–139; McLaughlin and McKee, Interview (August 2015).

148. Quoted in Ritchie, *James M. Landis,* 137.

149. Toepfer, Oral History (March 1998).

150. McLaughlin and McKee, Interview (August 2015); Ritchie, *James M. Landis,* 137.

151. McLaughlin and McKee, Interview (August 2015).

152. Brown, Oral History (August 1997). See Commonwealth of Massachusetts, Decree of Divorce, Probate Court, Cambridge, MA (October 13, 1947).

153. Felix Frankfurter to Grenville Clark (April 4, 1946), Felix Frankfurter Papers, 1900–1965, HLSLib.

154. Toepfer, Oral History (March 1998).

155. von Mehren, Oral History (July–December 2000).

156. Cox, Oral History (November 1998).

157. Brown, Oral History (August 1997).

158. Quotations are from von Mehren, Oral History (July–December 2000). See also Brown, Oral History (August 1997).

159. Cox, Oral History (November 1998).

160. Harvard Law School Faculty Meeting Minutes (April 16, 1946).

161. Quoted in Ritchie, *James M. Landis,* 139.

162. This account draws on Ritchie, *James M. Landis,* 141–154; O'Brien, *Triumph, Tragedy,* 10–11, 135–136.

163. Ritchie, *James M. Landis,* 153, 246n39.

164. Roosevelt had seriously considered Landis for the Supreme Court but, to Landis's annoyance, turned to Landis's New Deal colleague, William O. Douglas, to replace Brandeis. Ritchie, *James M. Landis,* 89. On his appointment as dean, Landis observed, "I always felt that the Deanship of a great law school . . . was a higher honor and more important position than that of a Justice of the Supreme Court." Landis, *Reminiscences,* 303; Schmidt, "Failure of Reform," 28.

165. "Landis Quits Job as Kennedy Aide: Ex-Harvard Dean Resigns—Named in Divorce Case," *New York Times* (September 8, 1961).

166. The following draws on Ritchie, *James M. Landis,* 189–190, 193–197; O'Brien, *Triumph, Tragedy,* 152–158.

167. O'Brien, *Triumph, Tragedy,* 157; See also Edward Ranzal, "Landis Is Jailed for Tax Delays," *New York Times* (August 31, 1963).

168. O'Brien, *Triumph, Tragedy,* 157–159. Victor S. Navasky, *Kennedy Justice* (Lincoln, NE, 1971), 431–435; Ritchie, *James M. Landis,* 198.

169. Quotations are from O'Brien, *Triumph, Tragedy,* 156–161.

170. Was this sentence appropriate? Compare Milton Gould, "Landis: Classic Case of Hubris," *New York Law Journal* 1 (December 14, 1981): 6–9, 25; Ritchie, *James M. Landis,* 199, 255n29; O'Brien, *Triumph, Tragedy,* 158, 188–189; Nicholas Katzenbach, *Some of It Was Fun: Working with RFK and LBJ* (New York, 2008), 102.

171. Ranzal, "Landis Is Jailed." See Milton Lewis, "Landis Jailed for 30 Days," *Boston Globe* (August 31, 1963); "Landis Gets 30 Days on Tax Charge," *Washington Post* (August 31, 1963).

172. Ritchie, *James M. Landis,* 199. See "Landis, Convicted of Tax Evasion, Serving Term in Plush Hospital" *Boston Globe* (September 29, 1963).

173. Was the suspension unduly harsh? See Gerald Nolan, *In the Matter of James Mc-Cauley Landis,* Supreme Court of the State of New York (May 5, 1964), 7–8; O'Brien, *Triumph, Tragedy,* 160; Ritchie, *James M. Landis,* 200.

174. Ritchie, *James M. Landis,* 255–256n37. Compare O'Brien, *Triumph, Tragedy,* 161n123.

175. McLaughlin and McKee, Interview (August 2015). See the articles on Landis in *HLR* 78 (December 1964). According to Landis's wishes, his ashes were spread at his beloved Rye, New York, home. Ironically, the I.R.S. eventually seized the property.

176. Henry J. Friendly, "Erwin N. Griswold—Some Fond Recollections," *HLR* 86 (June 1973): 1366. See Seligman, *High Citadel,* 71; McGraw, *Prophets of Regulation,* 208; O'Brien, *Triumph, Tragedy,* 159.

177. See Schmidt, "Failure of Reform," 33; Keller and Keller, *Making Harvard Modern,* 115; Ritchie, *James M. Landis,* 189.

178. Quoted in Ritchie, *James M. Landis,* 197, 255nn23–24.

179. See Milton Katz, "James M. Landis," *HLR* 78 (1964): 317.

180. See Kalman, *Legal Realism at Yale,* 207; Seligman, *High Citadel,* 71.

181. Erwin N. Griswold, "James McCauley Landis, 1899–1964," *HLR* 78 (1964): 316; Ben Jonson, *Dominus Verulamius,* in *English Essays from Sir Philip Sidney to Macauley,* Harvard Classics (New York, 1910), 60–61.

182. At the conclusion of a panel discussion on Landis at Harvard Law School in November 2014, Justin O'Brien, who had just completed *The Triumph, Tragedy, and Lost Legacy of James M. Landis,* made an appeal to "put up Landis' portrait at last." See O'Brien, *Triumph, Tragedy,* 161.

CHAPTER NINE

Harvard, Columbia, and the "Major Professional Schools," 1890–1945

In 1946 the new dean, Erwin Griswold (1946–1967), found that Harvard Law School was "unbelievably poor" compared to the rest of the university.[1] How things had changed in forty years! In 1903 President Charles Eliot (1869–1909) had raised faculty salaries at the Law School—already higher than any other Harvard faculty—20 percent due to "the pecuniary prosperity of the School."[2] How did the Law School fall from prosperity to "unbelievable" poverty in four decades?

This question cannot be answered by looking at the Law School in isolation. Poor and rich are relative judgments. One must consider developments at what scholars have called the "major professional schools" of the university—medicine, law, and business—during the first half of the twentieth century.[3] In addition, it is informative to compare the major professional schools at Columbia University, because Harvard and Columbia were the leading universities in professional education between 1890 and 1950. These two were the wealthiest universities in the United States for most of this period, and both had eminent schools in medicine, law, and business. No other university possessed these two attributes during these decades.

Historians have paid little attention to the finances of the major professional schools, and the historical data is elusive. Yet money shaped their development, and the first half of the twentieth century established the financial template of the major professional schools that persisted subsequently. This template had two primary features. First, the schools of medicine, law, and business dramatically increased their wealth faster than other departments and schools. Second, this period established the hierarchy of financial strength among those three domains: medicine at the top, business just below, and law at the bottom.

It was not always so. In the 1890s the endowed law schools and medical schools stood on a par in terms of financial capital. Over the next fifty years the medical schools rapidly outpaced law schools. Meanwhile, the fledgling business schools started far behind in financial capital, as well as status and influence, but soon caught up to and then pulled ahead of the law schools, though not the medical schools. By 1950 the resulting and persistent order of capital wealth within the echelon of major professional schools at Harvard, Columbia, and other leading universities was: medicine, business, and law.

Although external economic, social, and political factors certainly influenced these financial developments, there were internal factors that the schools and universities could control. Alumni giving was insignificant during the formative period. Graduates of medical schools and law schools donated relatively little to their alma maters, except for windfall bequests. Business school alumni were generally too young to contribute early in the twentieth century. Instead, three internal factors shaped the finances of the schools and determined the financial template that continued subsequently: the schools' strategies, their institutional leadership, and their response to the shifting ideology of benefaction in the United States.

In ideological terms, the schools responded differently to the shift from charity to philanthropy in Americans' understanding of benefaction, described in Chapter 2. Charity entails giving directly to specific individuals in order to alleviate the immediate effects of poverty, sickness, or personal distress, whereas philanthropy relies on scientific expertise and seeks to identify the root causes of social problems, and solve them permanently through institutional means that are effective, efficient, and economical. By about 1900 the rationale of philanthropy had eclipsed charity in Americans' understanding of benefaction. The professional schools' responses impacted the amount of gifts and grants received and, therefore, the wealth of the schools.

Another factor was institutional leadership, comprising the administrative and entrepreneurial work of the deans and the support from the university president and central administration. The fundamental questions here are whether these leaders exploited opportunities to advance their institutions in the competition for resources, prestige, and excellence. Finally, the schools adopted distinctive financial strategies that directly influenced their fortunes.

These three internal factors reciprocally influenced each other—as when institutional leaders designed their financial strategy in light of a professional school's prospects for attracting charity or philanthropy—and determined the financial template of the major professional schools, as well as the position of Harvard Law School relative to the others.[4]

The "Major Professional Schools" at Columbia and Harvard

During the first half of the twentieth century, American universities founded professional schools in many different fields. Amid this profusion, medical schools, law schools, and business schools rose in prestige and influence to become the "major professional schools" at universities.[5] The ascendance of these three kinds was not inevitable. For example, theological schools had long been the wealthiest professional schools. In 1899 their aggregate endowment was six times greater than that of all the schools of medicine, law, and business combined. And in 1920 the endowment of Harvard's new Graduate School of Education was 25 percent greater than that of Harvard Law School, and two-and-a-half times that of Harvard Business School.[6] Nevertheless, these other kinds of professional schools became what scholars have called "schools of the minor professions" or the "semi-professions."[7]

In 1890, university law schools numbered 61, medical schools 133, and business schools 1. In the following decade, the financial capital of the university law and medical schools stood on a par with each other. Within each group, about 15 percent of the schools were endowed, and the financial capital of those endowed schools in each group averaged about $100,000.[8] Thus, parity existed between the endowments of law and medical schools, and many observers hoped that the capital funds of medical and legal education would grow to match those in theology. In 1900 the annual report of the U.S. Commissioner of Education affirmed, "Professional education in this country has not yet received, with the exception of theological education, a fitting endowment." And "the great need of American life at the present time is better trained doctors and better trained lawyers. This need can be met only by the rich endowment of schools for the training of doctors and lawyers."[9]

The call to raise endowment funds resonated at the two wealthiest universities in the country. Columbia University had great ambitions and the largest endowment in the country in the 1870s and 1880s, when most observers considered Columbia "to be the richest of our Colleges," as Harvard president Eliot noted. In 1910 Edwin Slosson observed in his classic study *Great American Universities* that Columbia would likely become "the greatest of American universities" due to its wealth and its location in New York City.[10]

But Harvard, the oldest university in the country, also had ambitions. In 1884 one of the most prominent professors at Columbia, Theodore W. Burgess, argued that Boston was the only city in the nation with both the means and the disposition to support a full-fledged university. Between 1885 and 1915, Harvard and Columbia jockeyed back and forth for claim to the biggest endowment. Finally, in 1920, Harvard first attained the leading position among university endowments that it would not relinquish to the present time. In 1930 Columbia dropped into third place, slightly behind Yale.[11]

Beyond their wealth, Columbia and Harvard shared another significant attribute: leading professional schools in law, medicine, and business.[12] Opened in 1858, Columbia Law School emerged briefly as the most rigorous in the nation due to its attempt to raise the academic standards in legal education. But that effort flagged because the faculty profited directly from tuition and did not want to jeopardize enrollments by applying strict standards. After Columbia consolidated its professional schools in 1890, successive law deans revitalized the school's academic standards, and it remained "the nation's second-best law school" until nearly 1930.[13]

Meanwhile, by the end of the nineteenth century Harvard Law School was regarded both in the United States and in England as "the greatest law school in the world," in the words of Yale alumnus and future U.S. president William Taft.[14] The academic preeminence of Columbia and Harvard law schools early in the twentieth century is demonstrated by the proportion of college graduates among students at leading university law schools in 1905: Harvard 99 percent, Columbia 82, Chicago 60, Yale 35, Pennsylvania 35, Northwestern 31, and Michigan 13. This status led the law deans of Columbia and Harvard to consult each other more frequently than deans at other schools in the opening decades of the twentieth century.[15]

In medicine, the school at Johns Hopkins University, which opened in 1893, constituted the first tier all by itself, having adopted the highest academic standards among American medical schools. By 1910 the second tier of medical schools in terms of academic rigor included Michigan, Minnesota, Harvard (founded in 1783), and Columbia, which had associated with the College of Physicians and Surgeons in 1860. But the ranking was different in terms of financial resources. Harvard had the largest medical school budget, followed closely by Columbia. Johns Hopkins had dropped behind significantly by 1910.[16]

Degree-granting business schools began to emerge at universities in 1900, despite stiff resistance. At that point, four institutions had established collegiate, or degree-granting, business schools: the University of Pennsylvania, University of Chicago, University of California, and Dartmouth College. The movement accelerated after Harvard established its Graduate School of Business Administration in 1908. Apart from conferring the Harvard pedigree, this school was the first to put "business" in its name and to offer exclusively graduate-level instruction. In 1916 Columbia Business School opened and offered both undergraduate and graduate degrees, and the American Association of Business Schools was established in the same year. The number of business schools rose dramatically thereafter, commensurate with the growth in the economy and the number of managerial jobs.[17] Harvard and Columbia business schools thus belonged to the first generation of university business schools, and they grew rapidly.

By expanding rapidly into all three fields, Harvard and Columbia became the two leading universities in professional education during the period between 1890 and 1950. They had the largest endowments and eminent schools of law, medicine, and business. No other university had these attributes.

Despite those similarities, the two universities employed very different modes of financial governance. In the early 1800s, Harvard University put "each tub on its own bottom" financially. This decentralized financial governance meant that each school at Harvard balanced its own budget, paid its own expenses, and retained its own debt or surplus.[18] But the "tub" policy did not prevent the central administration from assisting selected units. The presidents and the Corporation exercised discretion over whether and how much to help a given unit, and this profoundly influenced the fortunes of the professional schools.

In contrast, Columbia centralized financial governance after President Seth Low (1890–1901) consolidated its loosely affiliated schools under new statutes in 1890. President Nicholas Butler (1902–1945) then reinforced the centralization. Under Butler, the central administration made yearly appropriations to the schools, forcing deans to plead annually to the president for money. Centralization meant that Butler could choose to tax certain units or to assume "very large financial sacrifices" for their benefit.[19] Although some deans called for autonomy, Butler held the reins tightly until he retired in 1945, even as the administration at Columbia expanded greatly.[20]

The different modes of financial governance influenced the financial reporting at the two universities. At Harvard, the decentralized governance required the university treasurer to report the financial situation of each unit, so the revenues, expenses, surpluses, deficits, and endowment funds were clearly stated. In contrast, Columbia's annual treasurer reports obscured the finances of the university and its individual units, and Columbia historians have attributed this opacity to Butler's desire to maintain his control over financial decisions.[21] In any event, the financial reports of Columbia and Harvard do reveal salient data about their respective law, medical, and business schools during the formative between 1890 and 1945, as reported in Appendix D.

This chapter first analyzes medical school finances in light of the ideological shift from charity to philanthropy, the work of the schools' institutional leaders, and the schools' distinctive financial strategies. Next, law school finances are examined and compared with those of the medical schools, followed by a comparison of business schools with law and medicine. These acronyms are employed: Harvard Law School (HLS), Harvard Medical School (HMS), Harvard Graduate School of Business Administration (HBS), Columbia Law School (CLS), Columbia Business School (CBS), and Columbia University College of Physicians and Surgeons (CMS).

Medical Schools Grow Wealthy

The postwar infusion of federal funding into medical research after 1945 is often said to have transformed American medical schools and established their leading financial position within universities.[22] However, that infusion simply extended the trajectory established before 1940. In the first three decades of the twentieth century, medical schools made their greatest financial advance relative to the other domains of professional education, rapidly displacing theological schools at the top of the financial hierarchy in professional education.[23]

Between 1890 and 1950, the combined endowment of Harvard and Columbia medical schools grew much faster than the combined endowments of the two universities, as shown by Figure 9.1. In fact, the combined endowments of HMS and CMS increased sixty-six times, whereas the total combined endowment of the two universities grew nineteen times. Even though the university endowments started with a larger base and fewer multiples of growth would be expected, this rapid financial ascent of the medical schools is remarkable, given that Harvard and Columbia were the wealthiest universities in the country and their endowments grew faster than those of most other universities.

Medical schools made this astounding leap primarily due to an avalanche of grants and gifts commencing at the start of the century. Between 1902 and 1934, nine major foundations contributed one-half of their total grants to medical education and research, amounting to about $154 million, and

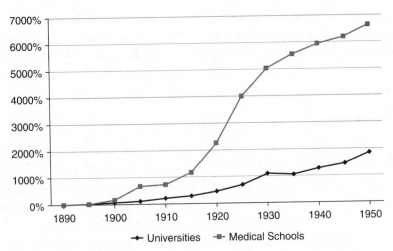

Figure 9.1. Cumulative Percentage Increase of the Combined Endowments of Harvard and Columbia Universities and Harvard and Columbia Medical Schools, 1890–1950. Data Source: Appendix E.

gifts from individuals were even greater. Thus, medicine "became the most vigorously supported of any cultural, scientific, or humanitarian activity" by 1930.[24]

At Columbia, most of the largest gifts to the university after 1891 went to CMS, and the school's sizable endowment more than tripled by 1910. Meanwhile, in the late 1890s the HMS endowment grew to twice the size of the CMS endowment, and in 1901 HMS attracted huge donations to build and endow a new medical school campus in Boston. In the following year President Eliot announced, "The Medical School now has a larger endowment than any other professional department of the University." The new medical campus opened in 1906, and new gifts swelled the HMS endowment to four times the size of the CMS endowment by 1910.[25]

In that year the Carnegie Foundation for the Advancement of Teaching published Abraham Flexner's famous survey of medical education, which inaugurated an era of medical benefaction when hundreds of millions of dollars flowed into medical schools from private donors and major foundations. The Flexner Report recommended that university medical schools model themselves after John Hopkins. HMS therefore felt slighted, but it continued to receive "large resources" whose prudent use justified "yet larger resources," stated the dean.[26] By the end of World War I, HMS was "the wealthiest and leading [medical] school in the country," according to historian Kenneth

Ludmerer.[27] Indeed, beyond medicine, HMS was the wealthiest and leading professional school in the country.

CMS had embraced the Johns Hopkins model that Flexner recommended, and in 1919 and 1920 major foundations and donors committed some $12 million to build and endow a new medical center and teaching hospital for Columbia. As a result, the CMS endowment more than doubled during the 1920s, when "medical schools enjoyed a golden age," in Ludmerer's words.[28] Meanwhile, HMS extended its lead in financial capital, as endowment income, gifts, and grants paid for its operating expenses.[29] During the 1930s, the Depression weighed heavily on all sectors of society and the economy, and most medical schools retrenched. Yet medicine remained the best-funded area of university research across the country. By the end of World War II, Columbia and Harvard were perfectly positioned to exploit the second golden age of medical research funding, launched by the federal government.[30]

Three factors propelled the enormous increase in the wealth of medical schools from 1890 to 1950. First, these schools accommodated both ideological poles of benefaction. On the one hand, medical education and research attracted massive amounts of philanthropy because they fit closely the philanthropic requirements that root causes and tangible solutions of widespread human problems be scientifically identified, and that those solutions be systematically instituted effectively, efficiently, and economically. Scholars have explained this fit in different ways, as discussed in the Introduction to this volume.

Through the 1960s, scholars studying the development of professions and professional education predominantly employed a functionalist explanation to account for that development. They argued that the strength and success of a profession are primarily determined by the validity and effectiveness of its expertise. By this view, new medical discoveries at the end of the nineteenth century dramatically increased doctors' therapeutic effectiveness, and that increase fostered confidence in medical expertise, which then prompted philanthropists to donate to medical schools in support of further medical research and the training of doctors. Some distinguished scholars still embrace this explanation.[31]

In the 1970s and 1980s, a number of critical sociologists advanced a different kind of explanation for the development of professions and professional education. According to this view, increasing therapeutic effectiveness alone does not explain the sharply rising authority, status, and wealth of doctors and medical schools and the growth of medical philanthropy. Rather, the cultural authority of natural science, the social power exercised by physicians in their relations with patients, and the competition and boundary disputes among health care providers and medical specialties together explain most of the increased authority and status of medical expertise and research, which then attracted benefactions.

The continuing scholarly debate over these two kinds of explanations and their variants cannot be resolved here.[32] In our view, each explanation fits different kinds of professional schools in different periods. In the formative period of medical education, the functionalist explanation seems most convincing. Between 1890 and 1945, scientific medicine aimed primarily at acute diseases, which were easily understood and appreciated by the public. The discovery and development of insulin, for example, directly and manifestly improved thousands of lives around the turn of the century. Furthermore, therapeutic effectiveness was the explanation most often cited by contemporaries, as President Eliot observed in 1903.[33]

To be sure, donors were not solely, or even primarily, altruistic. Desire for fame, influence, social legitimation, and, perhaps, financial gain also help to explain the gifts of various donors at various times.[34] Nevertheless, medical research and education closely fit the philanthropic rationale that had emerged in Americans' understanding of benefaction.

On the other hand, medical schools appealed successfully to wealthy donors on the traditional grounds of charity for financial support for their students. Both HMS and CMS made incessant requests for endowed scholarships to alleviate the burden of tuition on students. Such requests portrayed financially strapped, hardworking, talented medical students who were deserving of short-term funding until they could graduate and support themselves.[35] The many endowments received for medical scholarships also increased the wealth of medical schools. In this fashion, medical schools invoked traditional appeals to charity while simultaneously embracing the new philanthropic rationale.

Medical Entrepreneurs and Their Strategy

A second factor contributing to the financial ascent of CMS, HMS, and other university medical schools was their leadership: the support from the university presidents and the effectiveness of the deans. At centrally governed Columbia, the presidents had the greatest influence, and they favored the medical school in several ways. In the 1910s, Columbia University "cheerfully" covered the annual deficits of CMS, reported the medical dean.[36] During the 1920s President Butler spearheaded the fundraising for the teaching hospital, while he and the trustees borrowed $4.75 million and raised tuition by 25 percent across the university in order to make the loan payments. Hence, the rest of the university directly subsidized its wealthy medical center.[37] At Harvard, President Eliot spearheaded the drive to build the new medical campus, which raised the biggest gifts the university had received in its history.[38] Subsequently, President A. Lawrence Lowell (1909–1933) consistently encouraged the entrepreneurial efforts of HMS dean David L. Edsall, whom he appointed in 1918.

In providing such support to their medical schools, university leaders at Columbia and Harvard acted as "institutional entrepreneurs" who tried to advance their institutions in the competition among universities for resources, prestige, and excellence.[39] The deans and presidents in New York and Cambridge warned repeatedly that the university "must increase its expenditure for medical education or . . . fall behind . . . the other high grade medical schools in the country."[40] Such competitive appeals could be heard in all academic and professional fields, but they resounded most loudly in medicine after 1910 because the prestige of a university and its capacity to attract major philanthropy depended increasingly on the strength of its medical school.[41]

Institutional leadership naturally involved the entrepreneurial initiative and administrative effectiveness of the deans. Before Edsall became dean, HMS underutilized its bountiful resources, as other leading medical schools spent far more on research than did HMS. During his tenure from 1918 to 1935, Edsall became known as the most effective medical dean in the country by increasing both the productivity and the resources of HMS. In 1922 he also became dean of Harvard's new School of Public Health and then, additionally, dean of the Dental School in 1924.[42] By the time Edsall retired in 1935, both the budget and the endowment had tripled since his arrival at HMS. Thus, the dean had made the most of "academic medicine's first great bull market" and led HMS to recognized preeminence among medical schools.[43]

The endowment and expenses of CMS also nearly tripled between 1918 and 1935, largely due to the efforts of the university leadership. In the 1930s and 1940s, Dean Willard C. Rappleye (1930–1958) persuaded Butler to grant him more autonomy than any other Columbia dean, and Rappleye then navigated CMS successfully through the Depression and World War II by appealing to a broader range of corporate donors and, in the 1940s, to the National Research Council.[44] Conversely, the influence of a largely ineffective

Harvard Medical School campus, ca. 1925.

Courtesy of Harvard University Archives.

dean was demonstrated when President James Conant (1933–1953) appointed someone who, like himself, did not have an entrepreneurial bent.[45] Under Dean C. Sidney Burwell (1935–1949), a medical scientist, the HMS endowment grew merely 4 percent between 1935 and 1940, while the CMS endowment rose 10 percent, although their expenses increased at the same rate. Between 1940 and 1945, the HMS endowment rose only 6.5 percent compared to 12.5 percent for Harvard University, as shown in Appendix D. After ten years under Burwell, HMS was no longer the financial pacesetter among Harvard's professional schools.

An effective, entrepreneurial dean therefore mattered, though this factor varied with the different mode of governance at the two universities. At decentralized Harvard, the dean's effectiveness was more important, although the president determined that factor by choosing the dean, as Lowell did Edsall and Conant did Burwell. At centrally governed Columbia, Presidents Low and Butler had a stronger influence than the deans through 1930. But there were exceptions to the mode of governance at each university. Harvard president Eliot was a strong interventionist throughout his tenure. At Columbia, Dean

Rappleye successfully navigated the Depression because he persuaded President Butler to give him more autonomy. The Harvard model required a strong, effective dean, unless the president intervened. At Columbia, a strong effective dean helped, but only if the president permitted.

Strategy was the third factor contributing to the two medical schools' financial ascendance—and, remarkably, CMS and HMS adopted the same approach, despite the different governance modes at their respective universities. Each cut their enrollment nearly in half between 1895 and 1910, as donations began to arrive and admission standards increased. They allowed enrollment to rise in 1920 in order to accommodate returning veterans, but still capped it in the 400s. Thereafter, their enrollments grew merely by a third over the next twenty-five years.[46]

Columbia and Harvard were not alone in this policy. In the 1900s other leading medical schools began to reduce, or limit, enrollment as they shifted away from the proprietary model of profiting from tuition. After 1900, attracting philanthropic support for medical research and therapeutic advances became more important than tuition revenue. Hence, the leading schools resisted raising enrollments and preferred to lower them. In 1910 Flexner reinforced this trend by recommending an extremely small enrollment of 250 students for medical schools. CMS, HMS, and most of the "high grade" schools subsequently followed this policy, even in the face of strenuous opposition from their presidents.[47]

Limiting enrollment reduced tuition income, but helped raise other kinds of revenue. The policy decreased the faculty's teaching duties and increased their opportunity to pursue research that would attract gifts and grants. In addition, limiting enrollment made medical education more expensive by lowering the student-faculty ratio and raising the cost-per-student, because the school's rising expense was divided by the relatively small number of students. The effect of the policy soon became its rationale: "Medical education must necessarily be the most expensive of all forms of education," declared the dean of CMS in 1919.[48]

Between 1900 and 1945, studies by the Council on Medical Education repeatedly found that the per-student cost of medical education, excluding operating expenses for teaching hospitals, was about three times higher than in law or engineering, and five or six times higher than in business or education.[49] Part of the difference could be attributed to expensive equipment, although engineering also had such equipment. But much of the difference in per-student cost derived from the low student-faculty ratio.

The high per-student cost justified raising more revenue in several respects. It provided the rationale for increasing tuition, which both medical schools raised above the norm of their universities. In the early 1910s CMS charged $250 in tuition, and HMS $225, while the other units of Columbia University normally charged $170. In 1925 Harvard raised the university norm to $300, and HMS increased tuition to $400 a year later.[50]

High tuition then justified charitable appeals for endowed scholarships to alleviate the burden on students. CMS and HMS thus adopted a policy of low enrollment and high tuition, cushioned by scholarship funds. Furthermore, due to the low enrollment, the overall revenue from tuition paid only "a fraction of the cost" of the medical education, it was said. The shortfall then justified appeals for general endowment and "special gifts" to make up the difference.[51] During the stringent 1930s, gifts and investment income declined, and most medical schools increased enrollment, but CMS and HMS did so only modestly, and the proportion of income derived from tuition at HMS held to about 20 percent. This level persisted through 1945, as the HMS deans reported that tuition played "a minor role" in the school's revenue.[52]

Early in the twentieth century, medical schools thus made a great financial advance relative to the rest of their universities. Propelled by three factors, the combined endowments of HMS and CMS grew much faster than the combined endowment of the two universities during the formative period between 1890 and 1950. The most direct and significant cause was the great flood of grants and gifts, which came because the medical schools successfully accommodated both poles of the ideology of benefaction. Second, the university presidents strongly supported the medical schools, while the medical deans effectively nurtured and exploited that support. Finally, the medical schools adopted an effective strategy of lowering enrollment, raising tuition, and soliciting endowments to support scholarships and to subsidize the high cost of medical education that was partly driven by the low student-faculty ratio.

The Law Schools Fall Behind

Law schools at wealthy universities also significantly elevated their financial capital during the formative period. Between 1890 and 1950, the combined endowment of Harvard and Columbia law schools multiplied more than thirty-seven times, nearly twice as much as the combined endowment of the two universities, which increased almost nineteen times, as reported in Appendix E. Again, this comparison is impressive given that Harvard and

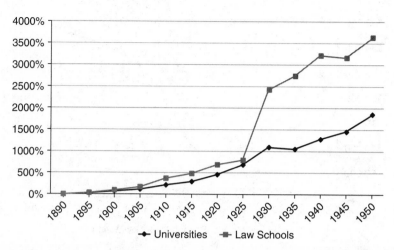

Figure 9.2. Cumulative Percentage Increase of the Combined Endowments of Harvard and Columbia Universities and Harvard and Columbia Law Schools, 1890–1950. Data Source: Appendix E.

Columbia were the wealthiest universities in the country. Figure 9.2 depicts the rapid increase of the combined endowments of HLS and CLS, as well as their faster growth compared to the combined endowment of the two universities, especially after 1925.

CLS and HLS trailed far behind the medical schools, however. At the beginning of the formative period, the average endowment of endowed law schools was on a par with that of endowed medical schools, as described above. Subsequently the law schools rapidly fell behind the medical schools in financial capital at both Columbia and Harvard. By the early 1930s the two medical schools' combined endowment was about five times larger than that of the two law schools. The difference in financial growth carried over to estimations of accomplishment and status.

The difference between law schools and medical schools in these respects grew so rapidly and so large that it seemed natural and necessary. Observers therefore projected it back in time anachronistically. In 1933 the distinguished legal scholar Herman Oliphant observed that the academic field of law had long suffered from a "lag of some three decades" behind medicine.[53] So rapidly had medicine ascended early in the twentieth century that Oliphant, like other contemporary observers, did not appreciate the parity in financial strength, status, and accomplishment that had existed between the endowed schools of the two domains in the 1890s. The changes in the combined endowments in each domain are illustrated in Figure 9.3.

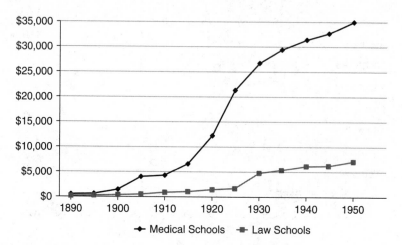

Figure 9.3. Combined Endowments of the Medical Schools and the Law Schools at Harvard and Columbia Universities, 1890–1950 (in thousands of nominal dollars). Data Source: Appendix E.

Despite growing faster than the endowments of their universities, the financial capital of CLS and HLS thus fell far behind that of CMS and HMS. The two law schools attributed their difficulty in attracting benefactions to a number of secondary causes. One was the public's long-standing "dissatisfaction with law and distrust of lawyers," as the *Centennial History of Harvard Law School* observed in 1918. At Columbia, President Butler agreed that "there is abundant criticism of the conduct and standards of many members of the Bar."[54] Yet the public also held doctors in low esteem throughout the nineteenth century, and the confusing plurality of medical sects, such as homeopathy, persisted into the early twentieth century, undermining physicians' professional status and authority.[55] In addition, law schools attributed their failure to attract benefactions to the stinginess of their alumni.[56] But the two medical schools did not rely on alumni giving. In 1917 the treasurer of the Harvard Medical Alumni Fund complained that "there are 3,000 medical alumni and only about 10 percent contribute."[57] Alumni gifts to business schools were likewise insignificant because the business schools and their graduates were so young.[58]

Three Factors Hold Law Schools Back

The financial capital of CLS and HLS fell far behind that of CMS and HMS due to three factors common to both law schools. That commonality, in fact, is more significant given that each law school operated within a different mode of university governance. First, CLS and HLS did not effectively invoke either pole of the ideology of benefaction. Donors were not persuaded that law students deserved or needed charity, nor did philanthropists see how legal research could benefit society. Both CLS and HLS received gifts and grants to improve the drafting of legislation, to "restate" the law in a clear current form, and to study social aspects of law, such as crime. But the latter kind of research often required more sociology than jurisprudence, and the sum of all these gifts and grants amounted to only a fraction of that given to medical schools.[59]

Roscoe Pound (1916–1936) was the only dean at either school to write extensive public statements attempting to explain and justify the need for gifts to support legal research. But Pound did not clearly explain how particular legal research projects would directly result in specific, tangible social benefits. Nor could fundraising consultants hired by the Law School do better. All these statements demonstrated "the inability of the law school to tap large incomes and exploit strong civic interest in law such as prevails in health problems and roads," as economist Seymour Harris later noted.[60]

The law schools' fundraising campaigns, as we have seen, therefore failed. At Columbia, in the absence of a compelling philanthropic rationale for legal research, the gifts to the law school averaged about one-tenth the size of contemporaneous gifts to the medical school over the formative period. The CLS deans found themselves gratefully acknowledging donations of a few thousand dollars, or even a few hundred. Their appeals "to do for law what generous benefaction has made it possible to do for medicine" did not move major donors.[61] In 1930, mindful of the recently completed Columbia-Presbyterian Medical Center, the CLS dean began calling for several million dollars to build "a great law center at Columbia." But over the next fifteen years, the university gave, in total, only about $15,000 and the alumni only about $10,000 for cosmetic repairs to the existing, overcrowded building.[62]

The second factor slowing the growth of law schools' capital was weak leadership. On the one hand, the deans were ineffective, as discussed above in regard to Harvard. At Columbia, the centralized governance discouraged, even prohibited, decanal initiatives. CLS deans in their annual reports therefore addressed their needs and requests, not to the public, but to President Butler, who made public and private solicitations on behalf of the school at his discretion.[63] Some deans chafed under Butler's tight rein. After a decade of negotiating fruitlessly with Butler for appropriations, Dean Harlan Stone

(1910–1923) challenged Butler's discretion over annual budgeting, and in 1923 the president edged out Stone, who later became Chief Justice of the U.S. Supreme Court.[64]

Stone's resignation precipitated a period of turmoil between 1923 and 1928, when CLS had four successive deans and the rapid turnover prevented the school from tapping into the prosperity of the 1920s. During that bountiful decade, the school received merely $75,000 in gifts to endowment, and the total of permanent funds scarcely reached $540,000 in 1930. Meanwhile, CLS was forced to share its building, Kent Hall, with other departments until 1930. By that point CLS had outgrown Kent Hall and entered the Depression needing a new building. The school avoided a financial crisis during the 1930s thanks to a few grants supporting research and a few bequests for the endowment.[65]

On the other hand, the university presidents gave little support to the law schools under either governance model. The centralization at Columbia greatly benefited whichever school had the president's enthusiastic backing. Initially, in the 1900s, President Butler helped CLS by soliciting the school's first major endowment gift and convincing the trustees to designate unrestricted gifts to fund a law building. But after 1916, Butler rarely advocated for the law school, and through 1945 the university made only a few special appropriations, amounting to merely a few thousand dollars. Furthermore, what the university provided, it could take away, and CLS was forced to share its building with other departments from 1910 to 1930.[66]

At Harvard presidential disposition also had great influence, notwithstanding the decentralized governance. The presidents and the Corporation had the discretion to help some "tubs" more than others, and the Law School was not favored during the formative era. Harvard presidents seemed to believe—as Lowell wrote in 1910—that HLS, like its students, was tougher and more resilient than other Harvard schools and required little help.[67] Soon after Dean Griswold observed in 1946 that HLS was "unbelievably poor," President Conant omitted the Law School from his public appeal on behalf of Harvard's professional schools. In 1948 Conant wrote in his annual report that "the need for adequate endowment is particularly desperate" at HMS, HBS, and the Harvard schools of education and public health.[68] Conant's omission of HLS spoke volumes. As a result, during the first half of the twentieth century, HLS was the only one of the six "major professional schools" at Columbia and Harvard that had to pay to construct its main building without any external aid.

Notwithstanding those two factors, the law schools could have competed with the medical schools financially if not for the third: their imprudent strategy of maintaining large enrollment, high student-faculty ratio, low tuition, and persistent surpluses. At Columbia, the central administration followed this path by keeping CLS tuition the lowest at the university, while the school's student-faculty ratio rose from about 30:1 in 1910 to 34:1 in 1921 and to 47:1 in 1929. At that point, enrollment had grown to 600, exceeding the capacity of Kent Hall. As a result, CLS turned a profit for the university, so the university administration likely found attractive the policy of large enrollment, high student-faculty ratio, and low tuition.[69] Apart from pocketing the surplus, the university benefited from the reputation of an eminent law school that presented little competition to other units for philanthropic dollars.

At Harvard, the deans mired the Law School in the tuition dependence syndrome, while they refused to raise the tuition of $150 out of a charitable concern about burdening their students.[70] Unlike medical deans at the time, they did not see that high tuition could justify appeals for more scholarships for needy students. Following the path of HMS by raising tuition and reducing enrollment would have avoided annual deficits, eliminated the need for building Langdell Hall, and preserved the invested cash reserves. Instead the HLS strategy fostered "the hazardous dependence on necessarily fluctuating tuition fees," which the deans succeeding Ames began to lament.[71] To escape, their only plan was to appeal for endowment in order to generate more investment income and, failing that, to enroll more students and expand the physical plant to house them.

In the 1920–21 academic year, HLS enrollment reached 946 and the student-faculty ratio was 86:1. Law School tuition rose to $200, the university tuition to $250, and the medical school tuition to $400.[72] Only when required by the terms of the loan to expand Langdell Hall did Dean Pound and the faculty raised tuition to $300 in 1927 and $400 by 1929. Notwithstanding these increases, the university's tuition remained higher and the HMS tuition even higher. After 1929 the HLS deans and faculty resisted raising tuition over the next two decades, even while paying off the burdensome mortgage on Langdell Hall.[73] Like CLS, HLS escaped a financial crisis during the Depression due to a stream of gifts and bequests for endowment.

Criticizing the HLS syndrome of tuition dependence does not require hindsight. At the time, Columbia law deans recognized the malaise and tried to follow a different course. They challenged the "obvious reasons" that legal education cost less than medical or engineering education.[74] CLS deans maintained that the cost of legal education was artificially low due to the high student-faculty ratio, and that enrollment should be capped or reduced in order to provide "greater individualized instruction," while raising tuition.[75] These moves, argued CLS Dean Smith repeatedly in the 1930s, would allow the law school to provide education "comparable to what is now done for the medical students." The fundamental question, wrote Smith, is "whether the proper education and training of lawyers is as important as that of doctors."[76]

In effect, Butler and Columbia replied negatively; as did the Harvard presidents. The CLS deans did not have the discretion to choose a different course, and the HLS deans did not exercise their discretion to do so. If not for their imprudent "box office plan" of depending primarily on tuition revenue, the law schools could have competed with the medical schools financially.[77]

Business Schools Rapidly Gain Ground

As the enrollments of the business schools increased rapidly in the early decades of the twentieth century, their financial capital rose commensurately. In the thirty-five years between 1915 and 1950, the combined endowments of HBS and CBS grew more than twenty-eight times, compared to four times for the two universities, as reported in Appendix E. The fledgling business schools also outperformed the long-standing and highly regarded law schools. Between 1915 and 1950 the financial capital of the two law schools rose by nearly six times and that of the business schools by more than twenty-eight times. The gap would have been even greater if both CLS and HLS had not received significant alumni bequests during the 1930s, which were not available to the recently founded business schools. Figure 9.4 reveals that the combined endowment of the business schools surpassed that of the law schools by 1950.

The newly founded business schools did not catch up to the medical schools, however. Both in the absolute amount and in rate of increase, the order of financial capital by 1950 was medicine, business, and law. This new financial hierarchy generally persisted in the echelon of "major professional schools" in subsequent decades.

The proliferation of university business schools stemmed directly from students' rising interest in business as a field of study and a career after 1900. When Harvard leaders began to notice that more graduates of Harvard Col-

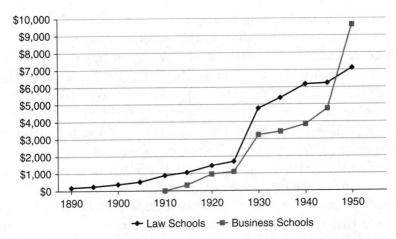

Figure 9.4. Combined Endowments of the Law Schools and the Business Schools at Columbia and Harvard Universities, 1890–1950 (in thousands of nominal dollars). Data Source: Appendix E.

lege were entering business careers. By 1916 some 55 percent of the Harvard College graduating class entered commerce or industry, more than the three long-standing "learned professions" of theology, medicine, and law combined.[78] Prior to the founding of HBS in 1908, many major corporations recruited their managers from HLS. When President Lowell appointed Wallace Donham (LL.B. 1910) as business dean (1919–1942), both believed that HBS would displace HLS as the source for the "right kind" of managers to lead major corporations. By 1920 the HBS enrollment had grown to nearly 400 students; by 1930 it was 1,000.[79]

In New York, Butler and the Columbia College faculty initially opposed the study of business. But the rising interest of undergraduates became too strong, and in 1914 Butler agreed to establish a course of study preparing students for business, though he objected to founding a business school. In 1916 Columbia finally established a separate school, though with a director and an administrative board rather than a dean and faculty like the university's other professional schools. The head of the Department of Extension Teaching, James G. Egbert (1916–1932), was named director of the new business school and served in both roles. Within a few months of opening, enrollment vastly exceeded expectations, and President Butler could resist no longer. He and Egbert began to solicit gifts for a building. By 1920 enrollment reached 269.[80]

Also in 1916, the American Association of Collegiate Schools of Business was established, and in 1922 about 122 business schools were offering undergraduate degrees. By that point, business study was the fastest growing sector in American higher education, commensurate with the increase in managerial careers. Notwithstanding the financial stringency imposed by the Depression, business school enrollments grew steadily in the 1930s. The proportion of undergraduate degrees awarded in business rose to 9 percent by 1940 and to 15 percent by 1950, the largest fraction for any discipline.[81]

The financial capital of business schools at leading universities likewise grew rapidly, though alumni giving was insignificant because the business schools and their graduates were young.[82] Instead, the same three factors shaped the outcome. First, like the medical schools, business schools accommodated the ideological shift from charity to philanthropy, but in a very different fashion. The business schools shrewdly disavowed any claim to charity for themselves or their students, and invoked the philanthropic rationale of improving business and prosperity to attract major gifts. But the donations primarily came not from foundations but from wealthy businessmen, many of whom were not alumni or even college graduates. Consequently, the institutional interest of these donors likely motivated them as much as did the philanthropic justifications.

In the 1910s at Harvard, a few industrialists and financiers who had not attended college gave nearly $300,000 to endow professorships at HBS. In the early 1920s, "financial assistance and the active cooperation of business men" helped HBS rebound after the sharp recession of 1920–21, according to Dean Donham.[83] In 1924 this kind of support culminated in a fundraising drive that netted the largest single gift Harvard University had received to that point in its history: $5 million from New York banker and non-alumnus George F. Baker to build an entire campus for the business school and increase its endowment. When the new campus was completed in 1927, two businessmen made additional endowment gifts of $1 million each.[84] As a result, the HBS endowment by 1930 had grown to half the size of the HLS endowment, the increase coming almost entirely from non-alumni.

Similarly, at Columbia, bankers and developers donated nearly $1.1 million for a building and endowment soon after CBS opened in 1916, and in 1920 the endowment of CBS drew even with that of CLS. Further appeals to "the business men of the city" boosted the endowment of CBS to $890,000 in 1930, surpassing that of CLS.[85] These gifts to business schools were framed within the rationale of philanthropy. The social problem was to expand the

Harvard Business School campus, June 1927.

Courtesy of Harvard University Archives.

local and national economy, and the solution, Egbert argued, was to "make progress in the scientific study of business and the training of . . . the business men of the future in this great metropolis."[86] CBS leaders even maintained "that philanthropy directed toward educational ends could find no more effective outlet than [business education]."[87]

Business schools' solicitations and donations were thus molded on the philanthropic rationale. But scholars explain that fit in different ways, which can be sorted into the two broad categories of functionalist and critical analyses, discussed above in regard to medical schools. On the one hand, historian Alfred Chandler argued famously that the growth of industrial corporations in the late nineteenth century created many functional roles that required new expertise. The new vocation of business manager emerged between capital and labor to fill these roles, and business schools arose to provide these managers with functional expertise. On the other hand, Rakesh Khurana has challenged the functionalist interpretation, drawing upon the theory of new institutionalism. According to Khurana, "institutional entrepreneurs," comprising both corporate and university leaders, created business schools as a way "to legitimate and institutionalize the new occupation of management," while expanding their own enterprises, status, and influence.[88]

In weighing these two explanations, one must recognize that the motivations of individual wealthy donors are complicated and vary over time, location, and many other dimensions. Nevertheless, few academic observers at the time attributed the proliferation of business schools primarily to the validity and utility of their expertise, research, and curriculum. In fact, business schools heard persistent skepticism in this regard and faced much criticism that the subject of business was unintellectual, mercenary, and therefore unsuitable to be taught at a university.[89] Nevertheless, wealthy businessmen seemed relatively credulous that the research and instruction of the young business schools would yield a return on donations, even as those businessmen carefully scrutinized claims about the benefit of medical and legal research.

During the formative era, therefore, CBS and HBS received gifts and grants far out of proportion to their academic pedigree or the perceived validity and utility of business expertise. That is the key point. Business leaders may have believed they were making philanthropic benefactions, but their institutional interest surely played a role, as Khurana has argued. This interpretation should be distinguished from the less-compelling view that wealthy donors gave primarily to advance their direct self-interest.[90]

Business School Leaders and Their Strategy

The second factor contributing to the financial rise of business schools at wealthy universities was the nature of institutional leadership. The central administration supported these schools, and the deans took initiative and acted capably. At Harvard, notwithstanding the decentralized governance, President Eliot and the Corporation helped during 1906 and 1907 to raise $125,000 to fund HBS for a trial period of five years. At the end of the trial, in 1912, President Lowell and the Corporation voted to provide the school an initial endowment of $25,000, and then, during the sharp recession of 1920 and 1921, the university covered the school's deficit.[91]

In the mid-1920s Lowell personally organized and chaired the successful campaign that netted HBS some $7 million to build its new campus and endowment. While President Conant initially doubted the academic merit of the study of business, he eventually became an advocate, appointed a confidant as dean in 1942, approved a fundraising campaign in 1945, and assigned to the business school a discretionary grant of $3 million from the Ford Foundation in 1950. At that point the HBS endowment stood at 125 percent of the HLS endowment, due in no small part to the support of the Harvard presidents.[92]

Meanwhile, at centralized Columbia, the president and trustees distinctly favored CBS by cultivating the support of businessmen and financiers in the late 1910s. In 1924 the cost of constructing a new building for CBS ran far over the projected budget of $1 million, and the university covered the unfunded balance rather than saddling the school with debt as Harvard University did to HLS three years later. In addition, Columbia annually subsidized CBS from the university during the 1920s. When the Depression began in 1929–1930, Columbia was apparently covering nearly 10 percent of the CBS expenses with transfers from the Extension Department. Meanwhile, Butler departed from his normal policy and allowed Egbert to appeal for gifts publicly. Overall, the CBS dean had good reason to express gratitude for "the active interest" of the president and trustees.[93]

The business deans also provided strong institutional leadership. At Harvard, even before the business school opened, the first dean, Edwin F. Gay (1908–1918), began appealing to businessmen and Harvard College alumni for gifts. In 1919 the next dean, Donham, began devoting as much as 80 percent of his time to fundraising, and by 1929 he had raised over $1 million from trade associations, business groups, and individual businessmen to support business research. At that point he formed a group of regular donors, whose support helped the school significantly during the Depression.[94]

During World War II, Donham's entrepreneurial initiatives paid off again. Recognizing the nation's unpreparedness for war, he offered to provide training for military officers in 1940. No other business school in the country, and no other Harvard professional school, so completely abandoned its civilian degree program and contracted with the government to conduct military training and research. As a result, HBS flourished throughout World War II "in grand style, much more so than Law or Medicine" at Harvard. By 1944–45, HBS revenues from military instruction and research contracts amounted to about 47 percent of the school's budget. Right after the war, the new dean, Donald K. David (1942–1955), successfully petitioned Conant for permission to run an endowment campaign.[95]

At Columbia, the first CBS dean, James Egbert, actively campaigned within the university to convince university leaders "that preparation for business . . . should be on the same plane as that in other professional schools." As the enrollment grew to 269 in merely four years, Egbert ceaselessly petitioned

Butler for a new building. He also appealed publicly for gifts of endowment for faculty fellowships, student scholarships, and the school in general. Though Egbert did not raise much external money, his work significantly enhanced the favor of the Columbia administration for the business school.[96]

In 1932 Roswell C. McCrea (1932–1941) became dean, and continued the entrepreneurial activity during the Depression by soliciting businessmen and appealing for grants to support research on specific subjects, such as industrial relations and actuarial science. Nevertheless, the Depression weighed on CBS, as enrollment, investment income, and expenses declined. But McCrea's fundraising stimulated the interest of businessmen, who increased their donations after CBS instituted the M.B.A. degree in 1945 and then moved entirely to the graduate level in 1948.[97]

Thirdly, the business schools successfully pursued a strategy of "conducting the School on business principles," in Donham's words. The first principle was that business students should pay all the direct instructional costs for their education, which prepared them to earn a good living. This tenet explicitly disavowed any appeal, on grounds of charity, that poor business students deserve to be subsidized. In order to provide financial aid for students of limited means, HBS offered loans "made on a strictly business basis," because the loans "lead the student to consider the business training given by the School as an investment."[98] Deans at CBS likewise appealed for gifts to endow loan funds, as well as for scholarships.[99]

The second principle was to raise tuition high enough to cover the direct instructional costs, because, again, business students did not deserve charity. Even as a young school, HBS remarkably did not hesitate to make its tuition the highest at Harvard university, raising it repeatedly to $200 in 1916, $400 in 1921, $500 in 1925, and $600 in 1930, with the full support of Lowell and interested businessmen. HBS tuition remained the highest at the university through at least 1945, while HLS tuition was among the lowest.[100] Similarly though less aggressively, CBS kept its fees above the university norm, and in 1934–35 raised them to nearly $400 in "line with comparable charges by other eastern institutions, particularly HBS."[101]

As tuition increased, HBS expected its enrollment to stop rising, but the students kept coming, and the school could have continued growing and banking more tuition revenue, as did HLS. But HBS adopted a third "business principle" of deliberately limiting enrollment, because "the quality of instruction" required "a reduction in the size of the teaching sections."[102] In

1930 HBS capped enrollment at 1,000, "the limit of students for which [the campus] was designed."[103] This tenet not only safeguarded educational quality but avoided the expense of constructing and maintaining more buildings—a tactic HLS had failed to recognize.

Fourth, having stipulated that tuition should cover direct instructional costs, the school maintained that other costs—physical plant, research, service, and other activities—should legitimately be supported by other sources, such as grants and gifts. This stipulation "met with a sympathetic response from business men" and boosted fundraising because donors and grantors did not want to subsidize business students. Hence, the fourth principle aided the dean's solicitations for donations.[104]

But this tenet, though helpful in fundraising, made HBS vulnerable to the extent that it depended on annual gifts. Donham therefore adopted a fifth "business principle" for the school: that operating costs and research "should be covered by [the income from] endowment," whenever possible.[105] The preference for endowment income suited perfectly the university's strategy formulated by President Eliot. In 1933 Donham argued that, relative to the rest of the university, the business school was underendowed, having 12.6 percent of the university's enrollment and 2 percent of the University's endowment.[106] This was the same argument that HLS was making to no avail. But Harvard presidents agreed with Donham, and Lowell and Conant supported efforts to raise endowment for the business school.

Overall, these "business principles" amounted to allocating different kinds of revenue to different kinds of expenses: students paid direct instructional costs via tuition, aided only by loans, while gifts, grants, and endowment income were allocated to noninstructional costs. This strategy justified raising tuition to meet instructional costs, while avoiding charitable requests to aid business students, instead directing solicitations for gifts toward donors' interests. At CBS the strategy was less developed, given Columbia's centralized control over finances. But the deans followed the same general approach of raising tuition, capping enrollment, and appealing for gifts to support research and endowment.

By 1930–31 the CBS endowment produced about 22 percent of its income, whereas the CLS endowment yielded merely 8 percent of its income. Impressed by the school's solvency, Columbia University trustees reorganized CBS in 1931 along the lines of Columbia's eminent law school and medical school by replacing the director and administrative board with a dean and faculty.

Merely fifteen years after it opened, CBS had reached "the same plane as that in other professional schools."[107] The strategy based on "business principles" had worked remarkably well.

Financial Template of the "Major Professional Schools"

In 1946 HLS Dean Erwin Griswold was absolutely correct in his assessment that the financial status of Harvard Law School had declined significantly between 1900 and 1945. The Law School had not kept pace with the financial norms at the medical and business schools either within Harvard or at the most closely comparable university, Columbia, during the formative era. The lag of HLS contributed to forming a new financial template of professional education over this period.

In broad terms, this template repositioned the components of the university. The wealth of the "major professional schools" of medicine, law, and business had risen above the rest of the university, including the schools of the "minor professions." In addition, the template incorporated a new financial hierarchy among those major professional schools. In the 1890s, the endowed law schools and medical schools stood on a par in financial capital with the theological schools far above them. Over the next fifty years, the financial capital of medical schools surpassed that of law schools. Meanwhile, the young business schools began with little or no financial capital, prestige, or influence, but soon outpaced the law schools, though not the medical schools. By 1950 the order of capital wealth within the echelon was: medicine, business, and law, as seen in Figure 9.5. Theological schools had generally fallen behind.

The data naturally exhibit these same trends if the figures are deflated to constant dollars, because inflation affected all the schools and universities similarly. Calculated in constant dollars, the compound annual growth rates for the combined endowments during the period from 1890 to 1950 are seen in Table 9.1. The financial standing of the "major professional schools" within the universities appears even more clearly by calculating the compound annual growth rate for the universities' endowment after subtracting the endowment totals for the schools of medicine, law, and business, also evident in Table 9.1.

Even early in the formative era, leaders in higher education began to recognize the new financial template of the "major professional schools" and the distinctions among them. In 1914 Yale president Arthur Hadley (1899–1921) reported that leading universities across the country were abandoning the view that professional schools should be "supported by tuition fees alone." But

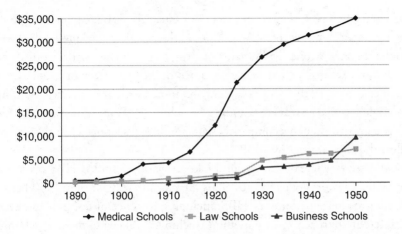

Figure 9.5. Combined Endowments of the Medical, Law, and Business Schools at Harvard and Columbia Universities, 1890–1950 (in thousands of nominal dollars). Data Source: Appendix E.

Table 9.1   Compound Annual Growth Rates (CAGR) of Endowments of Columbia and Harvard Universities and their Schools of Medicine, Law, and Business, 1890–1950 (in constant dollars, 1920 = 1)

Institution	CAGR
Universities in total	3.4%
Universities without Medical, Law, Business Schools	3.2%
Law Schools	4.6%
Medical Schools	5.5%
Business Schools (1915–1950)	7.4%

Data source: Data are calculated from Appendix E. The deflating factors are drawn from John J. McCusker. *How Much Is That in Real Money? A Historical Commodity Price Index for Use as a Deflator of Money Values in the Economy of the United States,* 2nd ed. (Worcester, MA, 2001), 58–59.

Hadley noted the one exception that "it is frequently possible to support a first-rate law school, taught by men of real eminence, from the fees of the students."[108] Hadley thus tacitly endorsed the model of large enrollment, high student-faculty ratio, and tuition dependence that he considered exceptional in professional education, but that characterized CLS and HLS and was becoming isomorphic in legal education.

Deans of the other major professional schools eventually recognized the imprudence of the distinctive financial model of the law schools. In the 1910s and 1920s, the business deans had sought to emulate law schools.[109] By the late 1930s, however, the business schools, especially HBS, began looking to medical schools, rather than law schools, as their institutional model. In 1939 Donham stated explicitly, "Quality instruction in business turns out to be much more expensive than we had assumed in the first fifteen or twenty years of our existence. In this respect it compares more nearly with medical training than it does with the work . . . in the Law School."[110] Witnessing the outcome of the competition between medical schools and law schools, HBS decided to follow the clear winner by 1939.

Conversely, whereas Dean Pound had arrogantly rebuffed HBS overtures for cooperative programs in the 1920s, Harvard Law School by 1950 began adopting various attributes of HBS, including its office of research and even its different approach to case method teaching.[111] Likewise, medical schools, which had introduced the HLS pedagogy in the 1910s, later turned to the wealthy business schools for models of professional training.[112] Law schools at leading universities—though well off compared to the "minor" professional schools—trailed behind, with their deans complaining about their "poverty" and living "from hand to mouth."[113]

The financial template of the three major professional schools exemplified at Columbia and Harvard persisted for decades. The flood of federal funding into medical research after 1945 extended the trajectory that medical schools had already established.[114] Driven by the post-1945 boom in the U.S. economy, growing corporate support did the same for business schools. In contrast, the prewar strategies and financial limitations of law schools also continued after 1945 and into the early twenty-first century, with profound implications for legal education, the legal profession, and Harvard Law School.

NOTES

1. Erwin N. Griswold to Nathan M. Pusey (September 4, 1968), Harvard Law School Dean's Office Records, Records of President Nathan M. Pusey, 1953–1971, Harvard University Archives (HUA).

2. Charles W. Eliot, Annual Report of the President of Harvard University, 1903–04, 24–25.

3. Quotation is from Morton Keller and Phyllis Keller, *Making Harvard Modern: The Rise of America's University* (New York, 2001), 114. See Amitai Etzioni, ed. *The Semi-Professions in America* (New York, 1969); Nathan Glazer, "The Schools of the Minor Professions," *Minerva* 12 (1974): 346–364.

4. This chapter draws on Bruce A. Kimball, Jeremy B. Luke, and Jamie M. Brown, "The Formative Financial Era of the 'Major Professional Schools': Medicine, Law, and Business at Columbia and Harvard, 1890–1950" in *The Economics of Higher Education in the United States*, ed. Thomas Adam and A. Burcu Bayram (Texas A&M University Press, 2019), 124–194.

5. Quotation is from Keller and Keller, *Making Harvard Modern*, 114. See Etzioni, *The Semi-Professions*; Glazer, "Schools of the Minor Professions," 346–364.

6. James R. Parsons Jr. *Professional Education* (New York, [1900]), 17; Annual Report of the Treasurer of Harvard University, 1919–20, 130–165.

7. Glazer, "Schools of the Minor Professions;" Etzioni, *The Semi-Professions*.

8. Annual Report of the Treasurer, 1898–99, 52–56; Alfred Z. Reed, *Training for the Public Profession of the Law* (New York, 1921), 443; Bruce A. Kimball, *The "True Professional Ideal" in America: A History* (Oxford, 1992), 281–282, 198–300; Kenneth Ludmerer, *Learning to Heal: The Development of American Medical Education* (Baltimore, 1985), 95.

9. U.S. Commissioner of Education, Annual Report, 1899–1900, vol. 2, 1959–60.

10. Charles W. Eliot, "What Is a Liberal Education?," *Century Magazine* (1884), 208; Edwin E. Slosson, *Great American Universities* (New York, 1910), 446. See U.S. Commissioner, Annual Report, 1874–75, 2:738–747.

11. John W. Burgess, *The American University: When Shall It Be? Where Shall It Be? What Shall It Be?* (Boston, 1884), 9; Bruce A. Kimball and Benjamin A. Johnson, "The Inception of the Meaning and Significance of Endowment in American Higher Education, 1890–1930," *Teachers College Record* 114 (2012): table 1.

12. Only the University of Pennsylvania could arguably make the same claim, but it was not among the ten wealthiest universities between 1880 and 1930. At Yale, the medical school joined the leading schools early in the twentieth century, but the law school did not do so until about 1930, and the business school was not founded until after 1970. At Stanford, founded in 1893, the three professional schools did not achieve eminence until after 1945.

13. Robert A. McCaughey, *Stand, Columbia: A History of Columbia University* (New York, 2003), 231. See Robert Stevens, *Law School: Legal Education in America from the 1850s to the 1980s* (Chapel Hill, NC, 1983), 23; William P. LaPiana, *Logic and Experience: The Origin of Modern American Legal Education* (New York, 1994), 81, 86–88; Julius Goebel Jr., *A History of the School of Law: Columbia University* (New York, 1955), 140–146, 162–165, 182–186.

14. William H. Taft, "Oration," in Harvard Law School Association, *Report of the Eighteenth Annual Meeting* (Boston, 1904), 15.

15. Eliot, Annual Report of the President, 1904–05, 39; Nicholas M. Butler, Annual Report of the President of Columbia University, 1925–26, 29; Young B. Smith, Annual Report of the Dean of Columbia Law School (CLS), 1936–37, 84–85.

16. Ludmerer, *Learning to Heal*, 4, 75, 96–97, 143. As Professor Samuel Williston (LL.B. 1888) remarked in 1940, "Harvard Law School achieved a clearer leadership in the field

of legal education than any American institution of learning has ever had in its particular department, with the possible exception *for a brief period* of Johns Hopkins Medical School." Emphasis added. Samuel Williston, *Life and Law: An Autobiography* (Boston, 1940), 206.

17. Robert Gordon and James Howell, *Higher Education for Business* (New York, 1959), 20; Steven Schlossman et al., *The Beginnings of Graduate Management Education in the United States* (Santa Monica, CA, 1994), 66–75; Rakesh Khurana, *From Higher Aims to Hired Hands: The Social Transformation of American Business Schools and the Unfulfilled Promise of Management as a Profession* (Princeton, NJ, 2007), 37, 67, 137–146; Carter A. Daniel, *M.B.A.: The First Century* (Lewisberg, PA, 1998), 15–16, 39, 49, 70–71.

18. James B. Conant, Annual Report of the President of Harvard University, 1947–48, 10–11; 1950–51, 20–21; 1951–52, 12; Seymour E. Harris, *Economics of Harvard* (New York, 1970), 226–227; George H. Williams, ed., *The Harvard Divinity School: Its Place in Harvard University and in American Culture* (Boston, 1954) 174–175, 212–213.

19. Quotation is from Butler, Annual Report of the President, 1904–05, 35–36. See James G. Egbert, Annual Report of the Dean of CBS, 1920–21, 209–10; 1928–29, 345; Horace Coon, *Columbia: Colossus on the Hudson* (New York, 1947), 93–115; McCaughey, *Stand, Columbia*, 301–310.

20. Samuel W. Lambert, Annual Report of the Dean of Columbia Medical School (CMS), 1909–10, 87–88; McCaughey, *Stand, Columbia*, 309, 351.

21. Coon, *Columbia*, 31–32. See McCaughey, *Stand, Columbia*, 302–303.

22. Roger L. Geiger, *Research and Relevant Knowledge: American Research Universities since World War II* (New York, 1993), 182.

23. Ludmerer, *Learning to Heal*, 4. See Kenneth Ludmerer, *Time to Heal: American Medical Education from the Turn of the Century to the Era of Managed Care* (New York, 1999), 21, 27; Henry W. Rogers, Annual Report of the Dean of Yale Law School, 1914–15, 320–321.

24. Quotations are from Ludmerer, *Learning to Heal*, 192. See William G. Rothstein, *American Medical Schools and the Practice of Medicine: A History* (New York, 1987), 150–151.

25. Quotation is from Eliot, Annual Report of the President, 1900–01, 49–50. See Appendix D; Thomas F. Harrington, *The Harvard Medical School: A History, Narrative and Documentary* (New York: Lewis, 1905), 3:1147, 1159, 1168.

26. Henry A. Christian, Annual Report of the Dean of Harvard Medical School (HMS), 1911–12, 145. See Abraham Flexner, *Medical Education in the United States and Canada* (New York, 1910); Henry K. Beecher and Mark D. Altschule, *Medicine at Harvard: The First 300 Years* (Hanover, NH, 1977), 168–188.

27. Ludmerer, *Time to Heal*, 57.

28. Ludmerer, *Time to Heal*, 53. See Butler, Annual Report of the President, 1919–20, 46; 1920–21, 4; 1922–23, 22; 1925–26, 45–46; McCaughey, *Stand, Columbia*, 306–307.

29. David L. Edsall, Annual Report of the Dean of HMS, 1932–33, 220.

30. Ludmerer, *Time to Heal,* 139–148; Roger L. Geiger, *To Advance Knowledge: The Growth of American Research Universities, 1900–1940* (New York, 1986), 253; Geiger, *Research and Relevant Knowledge,* 93.

31. See Ludmerer, *Learning to Heal,* 201; Ludmerer, *Time to Heal,* 134. The *locus classicus* of the structural-functionalist view is found in Talcott Parsons "Professions," in *International Encyclopedia of the Social Sciences,* ed. David L. Sills (New York, 1968), 12:536–547.

32. See the attempted resolution in Eliot Freidson, *Professionalism: The Third Logic* (Chicago, 2001).

33. Eliot, Annual Report of the President, 1902–03, 22. See Ludmerer, *Time to Heal,* 37–38.

34. See Teresa Odendahl, *Charity Begins at Home: Generosity and Self-Interest among the Philanthropic Elite* (New York, 1991).

35. Lambert, Annual Report of the Dean, 1911–12, 86; Harris, *Economics of Harvard,* 468; Harrington, *The Harvard Medical School,* 3:1147, 1159; Willard C. Rappleye, Annual Report of the Dean of CMS, 1931–32, 88; 1937–38, 87; 1940–41, 9; C. Sidney Burwell, Annual Report of the Dean of HMS, 1945–46, 355; 1946–47, 418.

36. Lambert, Annual Report of the Dean, 1914–15, 85.

37. Butler, Annual Report of the President, 1907–08, 31–32. See William Darrach, Annual Report of the Dean of CMS, 1926–27, 97; 1927–28, 119.

38. Eliot, Annual Report of the President, 1900–01, 25–26, 32–37, 49–50; Harrington, *The Harvard Medical School,* 3:1168.

39. Rakesh Khurana, *From Higher Aims,* 6, 27.

40. Lambert, Annual Report of the Dean, 1918–19, 115–16.

41. Ludmerer, *Time to Heal,* 12, 151, 191–192, 203, 205.

42. Edsall, Annual Report of the Dean, 1918–19, 137; 1920–21, 210; 1933–34, 244–245; Beecher and Altschule, *Medicine at Harvard,* 185–186, 194–195, 202–207; Rothstein, *American Medical Schools,* 235.

43. Ludmerer, *Time to Heal,* 53.

44. Rappleye, Annual Report of the Dean, 1937–38, 117; 1939–40, 165; 1940–41, 48. See Harry Atkins, *The Dean: Willard C. Rappleye and the Evolution of American Medical Education* (New York, 1975); McCaughey, *Stand, Columbia,* 309, 351.

45. Keller and Keller, *Making Harvard Modern,* 117–119, 257; Beecher and Altschule, *Medicine at Harvard,* 210–211.

46. Appendix D. See Edsall, Annual Report of the Dean, 1919–20, 172–173; Lambert, Annual Report of the Dean, 1918–19, 107–108.

47. Quotation is from Edsall, Annual Report of the Dean, 1919–20, 172–173. See Flexner, *Medical Education,* 133; Lambert, Annual Report of the Dean, 1918–19, 107–108; Ludmerer, *Learning to Heal,* 141, 207; Ludmerer, *Time to Heal,* 15, 56–58, 62.

48. Lambert, Annual Report of the Dean, 1918–19, 115–116. See Burwell, Annual Report of the Dean, 1946–47, 355.

49. Flexner, *Medical Education,* 133; Edsall, Annual Report of the Dean, 1932–33, 220; Lambert, Annual Report of the Dean, 1916–17, 90; Rothstein, *American Medical Schools,* 150–151.

50. Butler, Annual Report of the President, 1913–14, 7–8; 1914–15, 7; A. Lawrence Lowell, Annual Report of the President of Harvard University, 1914–15, 24; 1915–16, 5–6; 1920–21, 7; 1924–1925, 7–8; Edsall, Annual Report of the Dean, 1926–27, 193.

51. Quotations are from Burwell, Annual Report of the Dean, 1945–46, 355; 1946–47, 418. See Edsall, Annual Report of the Dean, 1918–19, 137; 1920–21, 210; 1933–34, 244–45.

52. Quotation is from Edsall, Annual Report of the Dean, 1932–33, 220. See Burwell, Annual Report of the Dean, 1945–46, 355; Rothstein, *American Medical Schools,* 151; Harris, *Economics of Harvard,* 468.

53. Herman Oliphant, "Parallels in the Development of Legal and Medical Education," *Annals of the American Academy of Political and Social Science* 167 (1933): 156.

54. Quotations are from, respectively, *The Centennial History of the Harvard Law School, 1817–1917* (Cambridge, MA, 1918), 163; Butler, Annual Report of the President, 1936–37, 31.

55. See Ludmerer, *Learning to Heal,* 9–138.

56. See Chapters 2 and 5 above; George W. Kirchwey, Annual Report of the Dean of CLS, 1909–10, 79–80; Goebel, *A History,* 236–7; Harlan F. Stone, Annual Report of the Dean of CLS, 1913–14, 72; 1919–20, 34–35; Smith, Annual Report of the Dean, 1937–38, 83–84.

57. Malcolm Storer to Thomas W. Lamont (January 12, 1917), Records of the Harvard Endowment Fund, 1916–1936, HUA.

58. Wallace B. Donham, Annual Report of the Dean of Harvard Business School (HBS), 1920–21, 129; Jeffrey L. Cruikshank, *A Delicate Experiment: The Harvard Business School, 1908–1945* (Boston, 1987), 200.

59. Stone, Annual Report of the Dean, 1911–12, 70–71; 1919–20, 75; Smith, Annual Report of the Dean, 1927–28, 92–93; 1933–34, 105; 1939–40, 84; 1944–45, 11; Goebel, *A History,* 273–275, 297–305.

60. Harris, *Economics of Harvard,* 19. See Chapter 5 in this volume.

61. Quotation is from Butler, Annual Report of the President, 1936–37, 30–31.

62. Quotation is from Smith, Annual Report of the Dean, 1937–38, 76–77.

63. Butler, Annual Report of the President, 1919–20, 34; 1936–37, 31, 30; Stone, Annual Report of the Dean, 1910–11, 66; 1915–16, 63; Smith, Annual Report of the Dean, 1933–34, 107–108; 1944–45, 11–13.

64. Quotation is from Stone, Annual Report of the Dean, 1921–22, 83. See McCaughey, *Stand, Columbia,* 309; Goebel, *A History,* 273–4; Laura Kalman, *Legal Realism at Yale, 1927–1960* (Chapel Hill, NC, 1986), 69.

65. Appendix D; Butler, Annual Report of the President, 1929–30, 46–47; Smith, Annual Report of the Dean, 1936–37, 89.

66. Butler, Annual Report of the President, 1901–02, 8; 1904–05, 3–4, 10; 1911–12, 1–53; 1915–16, 2–5; 1924–25, 1–5, 39; 1933–34, 55; Stone, Annual Report of the Dean, 1918–19, 104; 1920–21, 82–83; Smith, Annual Report of the Dean, 1934–35, 88; 1938–39, 76; 1939–40, 84; Goebel, *A History,* 185–186.

67. Lowell, Annual Report of the President, 1908–09, 21.

68. Conant, Annual Report of the President, 1947–48, 11–12. See 1944–45, 15–16; Bruce A. Kimball, "Charity, Philanthropy, and Law School Fundraising: The Emergence and the Failure, 1880–1930," *Journal of Legal Education* 63 (2013): 247–281.

69. This profit is difficult to validate due to the murkiness of Columbia's financial reports, but the inference is clearly warranted. Butler, Annual Report of the President, 1913–14, 7–8; 1914–15, 7; 1915–16, 4–5; 1932–33, 6; Smith, Annual Report of the Dean, 1940–41, 15; Goebel, *A History,* 233, 311, 345, 348, 473, 490.

70. Roscoe Pound, Annual Report of the Dean of Harvard Law School 1915–16, 146.

71. Quotation is from Austin W. Scott, Annual Report of the Dean of Harvard Law School, 1909–10, 149.

72. Pound, Annual Report of the Dean, 1915–16, 146; 1919–20, 58; 1925–26, 186; Lowell, Annual Report of the President, 1920–21, 7–8; Harvard Law School Catalog, 1920–21, 3–4; 1921–22, 62; Roscoe Pound, *The Harvard Law School: Its History, Its Development, Its Needs: A Projet* (New York, 1925), 23.

73. Pound, Annual Report of the Dean, 1925–26, 186; Lowell, Annual Report of the President, 1923–24, 16; 1924–25, 7–8; 1926–27, 6; Erwin N. Griswold, Annual Report of the Dean of HLS, 1947–48, 379; Edsall, Annual Report of the Dean, 1926–27, 193.

74. Quotation is from Butler, Annual Report of the President, 1915–16, 4–5.

75. Smith, Annual Report of the Dean, 1935–36, 80. See Stone, Annual Report of the Dean, 1920–21, 74.

76. Smith, Annual Report of the Dean, 1933–34, 100; see 1934–35, 79; 1935–36, 80; *Centennial History,* 170–173.

77. Quotation is from Roscoe Pound to Frank W. Grinnell (April 13, 1916), Harvard Law School Dean's Office Records, Records of President A. Lawrence Lowell, 1909–1933, HUA (hereafter cited as ALL Records).

78. Kimball, *The "True Professional Ideal,"* 99–102, 295–297, 302–303; Khurana, *From Higher Aims,* 111, 125–126.

79. Quotation is from interviews with former assistant deans of HBS John C. Baker (October 1995) and Deane W. Malott (December 1995), conducted by Bruce A. Kimball, on file with the authors.

80. Appendix D; Butler, Annual Report of the President, 1913–1914, 25; 1921–22, 6; Egbert, Annual Report of the Dean, 1917–18, 196–197; Thurman W. Van Metre, *A History of the Graduate School of Business, Columbia University* (New York, 1954), 24–25, 30, 32; Khurana, *From Higher Aims,* 125–127.

81. Daniel, *M.B.A.*, 39, 70–71, 116, 125, 144; Cruikshank, *A Delicate Experiment*, 50; Khurana, *From Higher Aims*, 67, 137–139, 144–146; Schlossman et al., *Beginnings*, 66–75.

82. Donham, Annual Report of the Dean, 1920–21, 129; Cruikshank, *A Delicate Experiment*, 200.

83. Donham, Annual Report of the Dean, 1922–23, 142.

84. Donham, Annual Report of the Dean, 1923–24, 119; Cruikshank, *A Delicate Experiment*, 99–112.

85. Quotation is from Egbert, Annual Report of the Dean, 1928–29, 345. See Appendix D.

86. Egbert, Annual Report of the Dean, 1928–29, 345.

87. Roswell C. McCrea, Annual Report of the Dean of CBS, 1933–34, 347–348.

88. Khurana, *From Higher Aims*, 1–2, 6. See Alfred D. Chandler Jr., *The Visible Hand: The Managerial Revolution in American Business* (Cambridge, MA, 1976).

89. Abraham Flexner, *Universities, American, English, German* (New York, 1930), 166–169; Daniel, *M.B.A.*, 27–29, 159; Khurana, *From Higher Aims*, 91–100, 120–176, 185; Cruikshank, *A Delicate Experiment*, 54–61.

90. See Francie Ostrower, *Why the Wealthy Give: The Culture of Elite Philanthropy* (Princeton, NJ, 1955).

91. Donham, Annual Report of the Dean, 1921–22, 84.

92. Donham, Annual Report of the Dean, 1923–24, 119; Henry A. Yeomans, *Abbott Lawrence Lowell, 1856–1943* (Cambridge, MA, 1948), 230–231; Cruikshank, *A Delicate Experiment*, 49, 93–124, 196; Keller and Keller, *Making Harvard Modern*, 119–120, 149, 197; Annual Report of the Treasurer, 1949–50, 92–93.

93. Egbert, Annual Report of the Dean, 1920–21, 209–210; 1928–29, 345; see 1917–18, 201; 1926–27, 268–269; 1929–30, 385; Van Metre, *A History*, 37, 70.

94. Edwin F. Gay, Annual Report of the Dean of HBS, 1910–11, 121; Donham, Annual Report of the Dean, 1919–20, 115–117; 1922–23, 142; 1929–30, 137; Cruikshank, *A Delicate Experiment*, 203.

95. Donald K. David, Annual Report of the Dean of HBS, 1944–45, 220–221; Cruikshank, *A Delicate Experiment*, 203–275; Keller and Keller, *Making Harvard Modern*, 120; Daniel, *M.B.A.*, 133–137.

96. Quotation is from Egbert, Annual Report of the Dean, 1917–18, 196–197. See Butler, Annual Report of the President, 1921–22, 6; Van Metre, *A History*, 37, 70, 76.

97. McCrea, Annual Report of the Dean, 1933–34, 347–348; 1934–35, 305; Steven A. Sass, *The Pragmatic Imagination: A History of the Wharton School, 1881–1981* (Philadelphia, 1982), 119–124.

98. Quotations are from Donham, Annual Report of the Dean, 1922–23, 123; 1923–24, 123; 1937–38, 228.

99. Butler, Annual Report of the President, 1921–22, 6; Egbert, Annual Report of the Dean, 1917–18, 201; 1929–30, 385; Van Metre, *A History*, 37, 70.

100. Donham, Annual Report of the Dean, 1922–23, 107, 123; 1929–30, 141; Lowell, Annual Report of the President, 1920–21, 7; 1923–24, 28–29; David, Annual Report of the Dean, 1944–45, 221.

101. McCrea, Annual Report of the Dean, 1934–35, 305.

102. Donham, Annual Report of the Dean, 1923–24, 123.

103. Lowell, Annual Report of the President, 1929–30, 21.

104. Donham, Annual Report of the Dean, 1923–24, 120.

105. Donham, Annual Report of the Dean, 1936–37, 239.

106. Donham, Annual Report of the Dean, 1932–33, 150–51.

107. Egbert, Annual Report of the Dean, 1917–18, 196–197; see 1931–32, 336; Khurana, *From Higher Aims,* 127.

108. Arthur T. Hadley, Annual Report of the President of Yale University, 1913–14, 13–14.

109. Egbert, Annual Report of the Dean, 1920–21, 211; Donham, Annual Report of the Dean, 1937–38, 226; Melvin T. Copeland, "The Genesis of the Case Method in Business Instruction," in *The Case Method at the Harvard Business School,* ed. Malcolm P. McNair (New York, 1954), 25.

110. Donham, Annual Report of the Dean, 1937–38, 226.

111. Griswold, Annual Report of the Dean, 1947–48, 381–382; 1950–51, 358–59; Erwin N. Griswold, "Opportunities for the Future," *HLSR* (December 1950): 3.

112. Daniel C. Tosteson et al., eds., *New Pathways to Medical Education: Learning to Learn at Harvard Medical School* (Cambridge, MA, 1994), 23, 88, 161–163.

113. Quotations are from, respectively, Ezra R. Thayer to Mark A. D. Howe (March 28, 1914), ALL Records; Pound, *Harvard Law School* [1919], 16; Griswold, Annual Report of the Dean, 1961–62, 395.

114. Ludmerer, *Time to Heal,* 21, 27; Geiger, *Research and Relevant Knowledge,* 182–184.

CHAPTER TEN

Griswold Brings Order to the "Madhouse," 1946–1950s

Being dean of Harvard Law School is difficult work, and "the job had, in one way or another, broken the last three persons who held it," observed Dean Erwin Griswold (1946–1967).[1] Ezra Thayer (1910–1915) and James Landis (1937–1946) broke psychologically, and Roscoe Pound (1916–1936) lost his judgment and stature. Their immediate predecessor, James Barr Ames (1895–1909), exhausted himself trying to extend the "groove" carved out by Dean Christopher Langdell (1870–1895).[2] Ames then spent the school's surplus and resigned in ill health, dying two months later due to Alzheimer's disease.

In the century since the appointment of the first dean in 1870, therefore, only Langdell and Griswold were unquestionably successful deans, at the very least in the sense that the job neither broke nor discredited them. In addition, each man left the school demonstrably stronger and stepped down on his own terms after a long tenure. It may be no coincidence, then, that both Langdell and Griswold were notoriously obtuse, blunt, and deaf to the adverse reactions of others. And their contemporaries did not consider either man a "polished gentleman."[3]

Nor was it coincidental that both Langdell and Griswold became the primary targets of progressive and critical legal scholars over the last third of the twentieth century. Perhaps attacking the broken deans of Harvard Law School seemed like piling on, save Pound to some extent, who was still an easy target. Only Langdell and Griswold deserved extensive critique because only they truly succeeded in running the decanal gauntlet.

Paradoxically, Griswold was later faulted for things he rightfully believed he had improved or advanced during his tenure at the school: student life, public service, admissions standards, enrolling women, encouraging the enrollment of minority students, raising money, promoting faculty scholarship, and reforming the LL.B. curriculum and teaching. Reading Griswold's autobiography alongside critical commentary on his deanship makes it seem at points that Griswold is facing a funhouse mirror, and it is not clear which is the image and which the man. "To my regret," he stated at one point, "I now find that these [efforts] . . . were resented."[4] The same happened to Langdell.[5]

In the next few chapters we address distinct but often overlapping developments in Griswold's administration. Focusing on the early stage of Griswold's deanship, this chapter discusses his truculent personality, his start as dean in the postwar "madhouse" of returning veterans, his funding and construction of new buildings, and his "orderly" creation of the administrative infrastructure of the modern university law school. This work during the late 1940s and the 1950s was made more difficult by the concurrent crisis wrought by the second Red Scare and McCarthyism. Chapter 11 explores this crisis, which roiled Harvard University and Harvard Law School and led Griswold to disseminate a new and expansive legal justification for invoking the Fifth Amendment right against self-incrimination.

Chapter 12 focuses on the revolution in admissions policies that also occurred in the 1950s, including the rise of selectivity, the decline of attrition, the long-delayed admission of women along with their marginalization, and, in the mid-1960s, the belated efforts to recruit African Americans. Chapter 13 examines the academic program, the work of faculty and students, and the emergence of a standard career path to the faculty. Chapter 14 addresses finances, which many have considered an indisputably great success during Griswold's administration. But the record is decidedly mixed. Griswold vastly increased the financial resources of the school, but, contrary to his reputation for pinching pennies, the dean was a big spender. And his spending worsened the fundamental financial problems of the school that he himself had identified at the outset of his deanship and aimed to address.

Overall, Dean Griswold's legacy was marked by counterpoints. Great accomplishments were interspersed with significant setbacks and shortcomings, while immense challenges and crises cascaded upon the school during his tenure. It is remarkable that the job did not break him by 1967, when he resigned to become U.S. solicitor general.

A Block of Granite

After graduating from Oberlin College in 1925, Griswold completed the LL.B. at the Law School in 1928 and the S.J.D. in 1929. In December 1929 he began working in Washington for the U.S. Solicitor General Charles Hughes (LL.B. 1912) and then joined the Harvard law faculty as an assistant professor in September 1934. Appointed full professor one year later, he remained on the faculty and began his twenty-one-year term as dean in June 1946.[6]

Griswold's legal work and scholarship, in certain respects, resembled that of his predecessor, James Landis. Each worked for the federal government before and after his deanship: Griswold in the Office of the U.S. Solicitor General and Landis in various New Deal agencies. In scholarship, each contributed to public law. Griswold pioneered the doctrinal field of federal tax law, which he taught throughout his tenure at the school.[7] Meanwhile, Landis broke new ground on the study of legislation, and Griswold said that he was "particularly impressed" by Landis's foundational essay "Statutes and the Sources of Law" (1934).[8]

Both contributed to administrative law. Having "never heard of regulations in law school" during the mid-1920s, Griswold first encountered the necessity and significance of federal regulations when he started working for the Office of the U.S. Solicitor General in 1929. He also found that there was no centralized or systematic recording of regulations issued by federal agencies. At the suggestion of Professor Felix Frankfurter (LL.B. 1906) and Justice Louis Brandeis (LL.B. 1877), Griswold wrote a pathbreaking article on the need for a uniform system of publishing federal regulations. One year later, this article prompted Congress to pass the Federal Register Act (1935) requiring regular publication of the Federal Register, beginning in 1936. Meanwhile, Landis was preparing his landmark work explaining and justifying the growth of administrative law and regulations.[9]

Despite these similarities, Griswold differed profoundly from Landis in other respects. Angular and hawklike, Landis had deep-set eyes and sported a long cigarette holder. Griswold, "a short stocky man with a stern puritanical expression," resembled "a block of granite."[10] A heavy drinker, Landis eventually became an alcoholic; Griswold, who had a Quaker grandfather, was a principled teetotaler. Landis betrayed two devoted wives with extramarital affairs. Griswold was a steadfast husband, who always supported his wife, Harriet. After she contracted polio, he visited her every day during her twenty-month hospitalization, pushing her wheelchair around the school, and carrying her up and down the stairs decades before "disability" was acknowledged, let alone accommodated.[11] Consequently, it was said that "no professors divorced while he was Dean."[12]

Landis and Griswold also differed vastly in their approach to decanal work. Even when not on leave, Dean Landis was absent for long periods, continuing the school's disarray and adrift. Griswold famously attended to every administrative detail and routinely answered letters on the day they arrived. He was a prodigious worker, highly organized, and scrupulously thorough, demanding the same of his staff.[13] In politics, Landis, the New Deal Democrat, was a personal friend of Franklin Roosevelt and the Kennedy clan. Griswold golfed with other "liberal" Republicans, and "always had reservations" about "wily" President Roosevelt and "the New Deal lawyers for the agencies," who "had unlimited self-confidence," by which he meant arrogance. Griswold publicly and prominently opposed the Judiciary Reorganization ("court packing") Bill of 1937, which Landis endorsed.[14]

Despite those differences, Griswold most often contrasted his deanship with Roscoe Pound, frequently citing Pound's failings as dean, though also extolling Pound as "a truly great scholar" and "a very great man."[15] Despite Pound's "rough" manner, impolitic conduct, ineffectual administration, and imprudent finances, he always remained "the Dean of this School" in Griswold's eyes.[16] This admiration led Griswold to emulate Pound more than he admitted or recognized. Though Griswold repeatedly distinguished his own policies, decisions, and conduct from Pound's, the intimidation felt by colleagues and students and the effect of the deans' policies were similar in significant respects.

Nevertheless, Griswold improved the school far more than Pound. Those who had known the condition of the school in the 1940s and compared it to 1967, when Griswold stepped down, considered Griswold "a very great dean."[17] It is even justified to say that Griswold "saved the school," in the words of Benjamin Kaplan (LL.B. 1929), who joined the faculty in 1947, because Griswold arrested and then reversed the previous two decades of stagnation and decline.[18] Outsiders saw this, too. In 1957 legal historian J. Willard Hurst (LL.B. 1935), who had graduated first in his class, wrote to the Educational Survey at the University of Pennsylvania that "Griswold has been working a real revolution in Harvard since he has been there."[19]

It was fitting, then, that soon after Dean Griswold stepped down in 1967, the school constructed two similar buildings and subsequently named them Pound Hall and Griswold Hall to honor the two men. In function, both structures were built to accommodate the continued expansion of the school that each dean had encouraged. And in form, both had a similar modern design: bulky, imposing blocks much like the men for whom they were named.

The "Grizz"

Griswold's demeanor was famously intimidating, rude, and contrarian. Even senior members of his staff, such as Louis Toepfer (LL.B. 1947), "lived in fear of him."[20] Harold J. Berman, who had graduated from Yale Law School, recalled that Griswold "was feared by many of the faculty," particularly those "who had studied under him."[21] When visiting classes to observe new professors, Griswold exuded "a generally threatening presence," noted Elizabeth Bartholet (LL.B. 1965), who later became the first woman appointed full professor through the regular tenure process at the school.[22]

The intimidation resulted, in part, from his "Griswoldizing": speaking gruffly, bluntly, rudely, even harshly. "He was incapable of any kind of small talk that exists between human beings. He wouldn't say, 'Good Morning.' He would walk right by you. He never wasted a moment," stated Toepfer.[23] Hence, some students called him "the Grizz," though not to his face, according to Paul D. Carrington (LL.B. 1955).[24] Exacerbating the rudeness, the dean usually made up his mind quickly and then said exactly what he thought. "He was unedited Erwin all the time," recalled Stephen Bernardi (LL.B. 1955).[25] Griswold himself recognized this.

His instinctively contrarian manner compounded this intimidating rudeness.[26] Whatever the proposal, Griswold immediately adopted the opposite position. "If you want to hear Erwin Griswold say it is raining," observed Ralph M. Andrews (LL.B. 1928), his roommate at both Oberlin and the Law School, "all you need to say is, 'what a beautiful, bright day it is.'"[27] Some faculty learned to exploit this characteristic by proposing the opposite of their purpose. Archibald Cox (LL.B. 1937) "discovered that the way to approach him was to say that I had been invited to do some [consulting], but I supposed my obligation to the School prevented it. Then he'd react, 'But that's important, isn't it? Nationwide railroad dispute? Isn't that important?'" Then he would approve it.[28]

Some have excused Griswold's tendency to intimidate as simply being "plain-spoken." "There was no guile or cunning in him, and he thought flattery or indirection unnecessary and inefficient," stated Raymond Wiacek (LL.B. 1976).[29] "This abruptness arises from his detestation of dissimulation of any kind," agreed Charles O. Porter, who completed his degree in 1947. Griswold objected to "wily" Franklin D. Roosevelt primarily because the president "acted indirectly by choice. This, to Griswold, is a major fault in any man."[30] Senior faculty "saw behind these defects of manner," maintained Cox.[31] But Griswold's manner made his subordinates—students, staff, and junior faculty—feel vulnerable and often wounded.

Cox's own experience demonstrates the point. At a tea in the faculty lounge in 1950, Cox, a new professor, was conversing with Griswold, when the dean spotted Cox's recent article in a law review on the shelves. Griswold remarked, "What have you done? Rewritten the same old article again?" The dean was trying to be funny, but Cox, the newcomer, was taken back. Four decades later, Griswold happened to meet Cox in Washington, soon after the publication of Cox's *The Court and the Constitution* (1987), issued on the two-hundredth anniversary of the U.S. Constitution. Griswold greeted him with the comment, "I see you've written a book. Not very original is it?" Griswold "thought he was being funny," Cox recalled. "But I knew him well enough at that point . . . so I didn't feel as badly as I might have felt."[32]

After commenting abruptly and negatively, Griswold often later reversed himself to correct his initial negativity and arrive at a fair, even kind and thoughtful, outcome. A few months after the encounter with Cox in Washington, Griswold sent him a long letter analyzing and praising the book.[33] Griswold routinely reversed himself in this fashion on matters large and small. After saying no, "he'd come back a week later and say, 'I've been thinking about this, and I think we can find a way to do it,'" observed Harold Berman.[34]

In the early 1950s Stephen Bernardi, a student and later an assistant dean of the school, attended a dinner hosted by the dean and Harriet in their home for the members of a student law club and their spouses. After dinner, Griswold gathered everyone in the living room, said that he rarely had the opportunity to get input from students, and invited the group to tell him any problems they were encountering. One student, whose wife was the Law School receptionist, volunteered, "Well, there is a problem with the heat in the reception area, and my wife is constantly cold." Griswold immediately responded, "Why don't you buy her a sweater?" All the students fell silent and offered no more feedback. But a day or two later, Bernardi recalled, "we heard that workmen were fixing the heating system in the reception area. So why did Erwin say that? . . . All that people remembered was 'Look to your right, look to your left. Buy your wife a sweater.' No one appreciated that he tried to help and get things done."[35]

In 1964, when classes were still held on Saturday, Alan M. Dershowitz, who is Jewish, joined the faculty. Dershowitz told Griswold that he wouldn't teach on Saturday, and the dean challenged him, asking "Are you very religious? Do you go to synagogue?" Dershowitz responded, "That's not the issue. The issue is I don't work on Saturdays, that's all." Griswold replied, "Well, I can't make an exception for you. . . . Charles Fried works on Saturday, and Paul Bator works on Saturday." Dershowitz recalled, "So we left things in kind of a tense situation. Then about a week later, a notice came around, that in the future there'd be no more classes on Saturday. So here he was. He understood that the time had come to change things. So he changed the Saturday classes for everybody."[36]

Some felt that Griswold's quick contrarian bluntness combined with a willingness to reverse himself was an effective administrative manner. "His usual reaction to suggestions of change or innovation . . . would be to point out difficulties and unforeseen problems," stated Paul Freund (LL.B. 1931, S.J.D. 1932). "The result would generally be a fuller examination of the project and an ultimate plan that could be espoused with enthusiasm."[37] Ultimately his decisions were fair, and often "very kind and thoughtful," according to many at the school who worked closely with him.[38] In particular, he would go out of his way to find ways to support faculty members in what they wanted to do."[39] By the 1970s, after his career as dean and U.S. solicitor general, Griswold had learned to apologize directly to a new female associate at his Washington law firm after unjustly criticizing her work.[40]

The explanation for this two-sided demeanor—contrarian bluntness followed by reversing himself—lies partly in Griswold's shyness and social awkwardness. But the manner was exacerbated by Griswold's "distorted, crazy sense of humor," which faculty and students noted.[41] The combination often appeared in his public introductions of outside speakers at the Law School, which were "always just mortifying," remarked Bartholet, a student at the time.[42]

For example, after U.S. Secretary of Labor Arthur J. Goldberg was appointed to the Supreme Court in 1962, W. Willard Wirtz (LL.B. 1937), Goldberg's undersecretary, was promoted to secretary of labor. When Wirtz was subsequently invited to speak at the Law School, Griswold introduced him by commenting, "How you got your job was kind of like marrying the boss's daughter, wasn't it?" The comment "just kind of fell like lead," said Bartholet. "It was supposed to be funny, but it wasn't. It was just an insult. . . .

These introductions were the main way we saw him as students. And they were usually, in my view, embarrassing. You didn't think he necessarily meant to insult these visitors, but he didn't seem very good at doing anything other than that."[43] As a result, many of his colleagues considered Griswold "an eccentric, and people expected him to do absurd things," said Kaplan.[44]

The explanation for Griswold's two-sided demeanor lies also in his conservatism and inflexible moral rectitude. "He was a loyalist and a traditionalist by nature," as he himself recognized.[45] "The fact that he didn't touch alcohol was part of the aura," remarked Detlev Vagts (LL.B. 1951).[46] And one object of Griswold's deepest loyalty was Harvard Law School. In her thank you notes to guests after his memorial service in 1995, Harriet often quoted his words: "My heart's at the Harvard Law School. It's a great institution. I want it to grow, to develop, and evolve as it needs to, so that it may continue to be the

Erwin N. Griswold. Faculty 1934–1967, Dean 1946–1967.

Harvard Law School Yearbook, 1954. Courtesy of Harvard Yearbook Publications.

greatest law school in the country and the world."[47] Even after leaving Cambridge and working in Washington, Griswold tolerated no jokes or criticism about Harvard Law School.[48]

Those thought to have betrayed the school were cast out. In June 1958 a student who cheated on an exam was expelled, had a breakdown, and was hospitalized. Paul Carrington, then completing his term as a teaching fellow, remarked to the dean that he was going to visit the student in the hospital. "I guess it's okay for you to go see him," Griswold said, "since you're leaving." What did that mean? According to Carrington, "for somebody *actually* from Harvard Law School to go visit this guy after he had been expelled and hospitalized was just inappropriate, somehow too forgiving," observed Carrington. "Erwin didn't have a whole lot of forgiveness in him. I think it had something to do with his ancestry," rooted in midwestern Quaker rectitude. "He could be very judgmental . . . He could be awful tough."[49] Under Griswold, the intellectual sword remained close at hand.

Managing the "Madhouse"

Though officially beginning his term on July 1, 1946, Dean Griswold entered his office in early June to get a head start. He found that Landis had left Cambridge on May 10, so there was no period of transition, no advice or guidance. Nor was there any activity. In fact, "the dean's office was . . . simply empty. There was no staff . . . [and] virtually no arrangements had been made for visiting faculty for the summer term, which was going to begin in about three weeks," recalled Griswold.[50] At that point, the school would become "a madhouse," in Toepfer's phrase.[51]

The immediate problem was that Griswold had no official authority to do anything until July 1. Even worse, the Corporation would not approve academic appointments until September, so Griswold had no means by which to appoint or to pay faculty for the summer. Further, both the Harvard Comptroller and President James Conant refused to make any exceptions to standard operating procedure in order to help him hire faculty and prepare for the summer term and the flood of returning G.I.s. Given the lack of preparation and cooperation at Harvard, it is surprising that Griswold did not call Stanford Law School, accept the deanship he had turned down a few months earlier, and take Harriet back to her alma mater and the pleasant climate of northern California.[52]

Whether due to loyalty or stubbornness, he dug in and began to assemble a staff and devise a backdoor procedure to hire temporary faculty. At the same time, he cajoled the permanent faculty to return immediately, as well as the five professors Landis had hired in 1945: David Cavers (LL.B. 1926), Mark Howe (LL.B. 1933), Robert Bowie (LL.B. 1934), Robert Braucher (LL.B. 1939), and Archibald Cox.[53] Enrollment jumped to 1,445 in the summer of 1946, when the school operated year-round on three semesters. Over 90 percent of the students were veterans. Toepfer, who re-enrolled in 1945 and graduated in 1947, observed that "students were finishing every seventeen weeks and starting every seventeen weeks. . . . Things weren't organized for this. There was no real plan for all these people coming back. . . . I should have had four terms, but I announced that I was going to take three. And that was all right. I got my degree." The "tiniest staff" managed the school.[54]

Arriving to teach in the fall of 1946, Ernest Brown (LL.B. 1931) found that "the school was just as full as it could be. Where the dormitories are now, there were temporary wartime structures over the tennis courts. . . . There were babies, and laundry hanging on lines outside. It was quite an atmosphere."[55] Many of the veterans had had significant responsibilities in the military. Returning from military duty in the South Pacific, Professor Braucher found his commanding officer sitting in the front row of his Contracts class as a first-year student.[56] Enrollment peaked in September 1947, when 2,131 students registered. The accelerated program continued to operate, admitting students three times a year, until 1949. The class of 1950 was overwhelmingly composed of veterans, the class of 1951 about 60 percent, and the class of 1952 less than half. Due to students' diligence and the faculty's desire to see them through, the failure rate temporarily dropped to 10 percent during these postwar years.[57]

Due to the "very chaotic time" in the late 1940s, Griswold's first annual report for the academic year 1946–47 was not issued until December 1949.[58] Only in May 1950, when the 1947–48 annual report appeared, did he identify seven priorities that would require additional resources: (1) student housing, (2) scholarship aid, (3) professorships, (4) teaching fellowships, (5) a research office, (6) the library, and (7) "the field of international law and relations."[59] He then concluded, "This is obviously an ambitious program. We should be content if we fulfill a goodly portion of it. But the School must . . . continue to function as a great center of legal education and knowledge, and a moral force in a constantly expanding community."[60]

"Orderly Evolution" of Administration

Before undertaking any of those priorities, Griswold needed to invent the administrative infrastructure of a modern law school by establishing new offices to handle additional responsibilities. Soon after starting as dean, he discovered that no one at the school knew which accounts it had, or how to pay its bills. Under Landis and Pound, the university comptroller handled everything. Griswold wanted the dean to assume control of the school's finances, so he promoted a secretary and charged her to go to the comptroller's office, learn about the school's accounts, and then teach him.[61]

The dean also discovered that relations with alumni were terrible. In fact, the treasurer of the Harvard Law School Association (HLSA), Reginald Smith (LL.B. 1914), wrote to him that an "iron curtain" stood between the school and the alumni association, and that the HLSA felt unappreciated. Griswold replied the very next day. "It will be my constant endeavor that there shall be no 'iron curtain' between the school and the Association, nor any other kind of curtain."[62]

He then learned that no one at the school knew the correct addresses of alumni, because Landis had not had the alumni directory updated since 1939. In the summer of 1946 the post office had returned truckloads of undeliverable letters from a mass mailing, which was expensive and embarrassing. Griswold promptly opened the first law school alumni office in the country and charged it with updating the school's alumni directory, the *Quinquennial Catalog*.[63] In addition, the dean established the *Harvard Law School Bulletin* to serve as the official publication of the school. The first issue of the *Bulletin* appeared on April 1, 1948, and was sent to the 11,200 living graduates of the school, including 10,780 LL.B.s, 303 LL.M.s, and 217 S.J.D.s.[64]

Yet, alumni communications and relations were tricky. In 1946 "a small group of Boston lawyers" dominated the in-bred HLSA, according to Ernest Brown.[65] Obtaining the help needed by the school required that the dean expand participation and interest without disaffecting that core group. During his first year, 1946–47, Dean Griswold went on the road and spoke before alumni groups in Kansas City, Chicago, Seattle, San Francisco, Los Angeles, New York, and Atlantic City.[66] By 1958 the new alumni office, the *Bulletin*, and Griswold's visits had paid off. The chairman of the university Overseers Visiting Committee reported that the dean had "revolutionized the relations between the Law School and its Alumni." They now had "greater knowledge, greater pride, and greater enthusiasm [about the school] than at any time of which I have knowledge."[67]

Also during his first year, Griswold realized that law firms, short-staffed during the war, would soon expand their hiring and that the wave of students attending law school on the G.I. Bill would be seeking employment. Previously, new graduates were left on their own to pass the state bar and then walk the streets looking for a position. "If you went through a whole year without a job, that was nothing extraordinary," remarked Toepfer. The dean felt it critical to facilitate the matching of employers and graduates, so in 1947 he established the first law school placement office in the country and hired Toepfer to lead it.[68]

Admissions had previously been handled solely by a faculty committee with secretarial support from the dean's office. But the postwar wave of applications made the paperwork overwhelming, so in 1948 Griswold created the position of director of admissions. He filled this post with Toepfer, who soon became de facto director of financial aid as well.[69] Gradually Toepfer became Griswold's "alter ego." The dean appointed him secretary of the school in 1956, then vice dean and member of the faculty in 1959, succeeding Livingston Hall (LL.B. 1927). From that point on, Toepfer "virtually ran the School administratively" until Griswold's departure in 1967. Toepfer subsequently became dean of Western Reserve Law School and the first president of Case Western Reserve University.[70] Meanwhile, the Admissions Office was expanded in 1963, when it dealt with nearly 60,000 items of correspondence.[71]

Griswold also began improving student life. He immediately launched the student-edited *Harvard Law School Record,* which published its first issue on July 17, 1946, with a speculative story on Landis's resignation. Today the *Record* remains the oldest law school newspaper in the United States. Its staff has included many individuals who went on to diverse and influential careers: Oregon congressman Charles Porter, social reformer and political activist Ralph Nader (LL.B. 1958), and author James A. McPherson (LL.B. 1968), who won a Pulitzer Prize and a MacArthur Fellowship.[72]

In the fall of 1946 Griswold found space in two neighboring university dormitories for the school to open and operate its first lunchroom and a nursery school employing a professional teacher, assisted by Harriet and the Harvard Law Wives association. He also opened the front doors to Langdell Hall, which had been locked thirty years earlier by Dean Pound, forcing students to use the back doors and to telephone a faculty member to gain access to the library after office hours. Griswold also landscaped the grounds to make the school look more inviting for students.[73] In 1947 he supported Jerome Rappaport (LL.B. 1949) in establishing the Harvard Law School Forum, and, in 1949, Samuel Dash (LL.B. 1950) in founding the Harvard Voluntary Defenders. The latter project collaborated and dovetailed with the Legal Aid Bureau, which helped clients in disputes with nonprofit and governmental agencies. The Voluntary Defenders assisted low-income people needing legal counsel in criminal cases.[74]

Turning to faculty, Griswold in 1951 created the position of associate dean for research and appointed David Cavers to develop a program of "legal research directed to pressing current problems."[75] Subsequently, he constituted an Administrative Board, composed of administrators and faculty, and an Appointments Committee, composed of senior faculty, to advise him.[76]

The school administration thus developed significantly in the first five years of Griswold's administration. This "orderly evolution," in the words of Detlev Vagts, continued throughout Griswold's tenure.[77] A recent study of the period 1946–47 to 1967–68 found that the number of deans and department heads grew from three to eight, the number of library professional staff from three to fourteen, and the general school staff from three to forty-two.[78] The faculty did not feel that that sevenfold growth in staff meant that the administration was ballooning unreasonably. When asked to justify the growth in 1966, Griswold remarked, "There's a lot more going on around here than there used to be!"[79]

New Buildings, More Loans

Commensurate with the growth in administration, Dean Griswold added eight buildings to the Law School, not including two more office buildings he planned before leaving. In 1946 the dean knew that the school desperately needed facilities to improve student life: dormitories, a dining hall, a commons in which to congregate, and meeting rooms for law clubs and moot court arguments. And he requested assistance from the university. Landis had identified the same need in 1945, but Conant, characteristically, refused to aid the Law School.[80]

But Griswold teamed up with the dean of Arts and Sciences, Paul H. Buck, and together they extracted a commitment from the president to provide the land for a complex of dormitories for the Law School and a commons with a dining hall and meeting rooms to serve both graduate students and law students. Conant also agreed to pay for construction of the commons building,

Harkness Graduate Center, ca. 1952.
Courtesy of Harvard University Archives.

later named the Harkness Graduate Center (popularly called the Harkness Commons), by drawing on a bequest from Yale College graduate Edward S. Harkness, who had funded the Harvard College residence houses during the 1920s. Under this arrangement, the School of Arts and Sciences would incur no cost for its graduate commons, whereas the Law School had to raise the money to construct the residence halls.[81]

Accounts of the project's funding differ. Griswold stated that he consulted a professional fundraiser who determined that the school could raise no more than $1.5 million. But Toepfer reports that, due to his conservative nature, Griswold initially priced the dormitories too low, when the school could have raised more money. By either account, the outcome was the same. Harvard enlisted the famed architect and founder of the Bauhaus movement, Walter Gropius, who had come to the university in 1937 as the first chair of the architecture department. Severely constrained by the cost limit, Gropius made a "*very* stark" design for the Harkness Commons and five connected dormitories for the Law School.[82]

Griswold commended Gropius for keeping within the budget, but later regretted that the completed structures were "too spartan."[83] Nevertheless, the buildings "generated great enthusiasm" in the architectural community, because "when erected, the complex was one of the few examples of adequately understood International style in this country," according to historian Bainbridge Bunting."[84] Some have not shared that enthusiasm, particularly some students who lived in the dormitories. But the school's subsequent attempts to renovate or replace them were blocked out of respect for the architect's oeuvre. In any case, completion of the five dormitories and Harkness Commons in September 1950 was a cause for celebration and "a great blessing," according to Arthur Sutherland (LL.B. 1925).[85] Meanwhile, the school purchased and renovated "medieval" Hastings Hall to become a Law School dormitory in 1950, dramatically increasing living space for students at that point.[86]

To pay for the dormitories, Griswold established the Harvard Law School Fund in 1948 and enlisted alumni to run the campaign. The announced goal was $2.5 million, including $1.5 million for the Gropius buildings, $150,000 for Hastings Hall, $375,000 for scholarships and teaching fellowships, $250,000 for research assistants for faculty, and $225,000 for the construction of additional stack space for the library. All of the money was to be spent within five years; none was earmarked for endowment.[87]

Led by alumnus John B. Marsh (LL.B. 1910) and focused on New York City alumni, the campaign raised $900,000 by July 1949, giving President Conant enough confidence to authorize construction of the Gropius dormitories. In July 1951 the Harvard Law School Fund announced a "grand total" of more than $1.9 million raised. But this included two windfall bequests totaling $412,000 for the school's endowment, so the amount actually raised in the campaign was $1.52 million.[88] Even so, the drive was a remarkable achievement in the postwar period and the first time in its long history that the Law School set a fundraising goal and met it—sort of.

Because all the proceeds were needed for the Gropius buildings, Griswold had to scrounge for the money to renovate Hastings Hall and forego the rest of the campaign goals, although he had already started to fund the teaching fellows out of the school's annual budget. Further, because the amount raised included pledges, the university had to advance the construction cost until the pledges were paid. Conant set "a special low rate of interest of two percent" on the advanced funds, and Griswold announced that "the University has been very generous" in making the advances, perhaps mindful of the usurious rates that the Corporation had previously charged the Law School.[89]

Even before those pledges were paid off, though, Griswold began contemplating another major construction project. In 1954 the Ford Foundation awarded the Law School a grant of $500,000 to cover half the cost of a new building for the new International Legal Studies (ILS) program. The grant was contingent upon the school securing donations to match the amount. Another fundraising campaign, headed by alumni, therefore began to solicit the $500,000 plus $150,000 to support operations and maintenance of the building. As January 1957 approached, however, appeals to alumni and other foundations had not succeeded. To save everyone embarrassment, Ford extended its deadline for an additional year, and a new campaign chairman, Henry Friendly (LL.B. 1927), then in private practice in New York city, was named to lead the renewed effort.[90]

Friendly also found that the matching funds were "comparatively modest in amount but unexpectedly difficult to get."[91] A number of American corporations in a variety of industries made contributions, which, in Griswold's view, reflected "the judgment of American business concerning the long-range needs of the American economy for the sound training and research in international legal studies."[92] But the amount of these corporate gifts was, in fact, nominal.

Nor did alumni care to donate substantively toward international legal studies, feeling that little practical benefit would result. Griswold therefore resorted to a bait and switch. He began telling alumni that the school's valuable collection of international law books occupied a great deal of space in the library, which needed more room for books on "real law." Moving the international collection to a new building would free up the needed room in the main library. This gambit "proved encouraging" to just enough alumni, and the school barely met Ford's condition in time with only 150 donors contributing.[93]

In December 1957, only six years after the Gropius dormitories and Harkness Commons opened, ground was broken for the International Legal Studies building, connected to Langdell Hall by arcades. Nevertheless, the funds fell short. The school had raised nearly $650,000 to add to the $500,000 from Ford, and this would have covered the original cost of the building plus the operations and maintenance fund. But construction costs had soared, and Griswold and Toepfer decided to add a tunnel system linking all the major Law School buildings. The total cost of construction ballooned to $1.8 million.[94]

Facing a serious shortfall, the dean scrapped the maintenance fund of $150,000, drew $250,000 from the school's surplus, and borrowed $400,000 from the university at interest, in addition to another advance on unpaid pledges. Again the school was faced with paying off a building loan, which Griswold planned to retire through gifts for current operations and annual surpluses from tuition. The whole building project in the late 1950s cost the school about $1 million out of operating funds—that is, tuition revenue. In 1960 the International Legal Studies building opened, culminating the dean's expansion of the facilities during his term.[95]

Resurrecting the Law School and Its Shield

In 1946 Griswold had walked into an empty dean's office with no orientation from his predecessor and little cooperation from the university administration. Learning the ropes and keeping the ship afloat during the postwar "madhouse" of returning veterans would have been an accomplishment for any dean, including his immediate predecessors. But Griswold did much more. He roused the sleeping giant that was Harvard Law School in 1946 and, in little more than a decade, created the administrative infrastructure that is now customary at university law schools, while also teaching a course each semester.

By the mid-1950s he had established and staffed an admissions and financial aid office, a placement office, an alumni affairs office, and an official periodical, the *Harvard Law School Bulletin.* He had personally repaired relations with alumni by speaking at their events across the country. For students, he had arranged to build the first dining commons and dormitories and acquired and renovated another dormitory. He had launched the student newspaper, the *Harvard Law School Record,* which Landis had conceived, and supported the founding of the Harvard Law School Forum and the Harvard Voluntary Defenders. In academic matters, he had created and filled the office of associate dean for research and established a functioning Administrative Board and an Appointments Committee of faculty to advise him. In addition, he had supported the postwar academic initiative of International Legal Studies, while planning and funding its new building, along with walkways and tunnels connecting all the school's facilities.

Finally, and rather incidentally, Griswold played a significant role in resurrecting the Harvard Law School shield, which would spark an intense controversy nearly seventy years later, as discussed in the Introduction to this book. The shield originated in the mid-1930s when heraldry was designed for all the various schools at Harvard in preparation for the university's tercentenary celebration in 1936. Featuring three sheaves of grain standing in a field, the Harvard Law School shield was based upon the family coat of arms of Isaac Royall Jr. (1719–1781), who had bequeathed an endowment to support the first professorship in law at Harvard University. Apparently, in the mid-1930s no one at Harvard realized (or, perhaps, cared) that Royall's wealth came from the family's sugar plantation in Antigua, which was worked by enslaved people under brutally cruel conditions.[96]

The plan for tercentenary shields came from Harvard University president and well-known Anglophile A. Lawrence Lowell (1909–1933), who wished to replicate the heraldry associated with Oxford and Cambridge Universities. After the tercentenary event, the designer of the new shields requested that the Harvard Corporation formally authorize his designs. Instead, in December 1937 the Corporation voted that it had "no objection to their use for decorative purposes," but did "not approve their use for other purposes." Thus, the Corporation did not sanction the shields for official purposes.[97]

Consequently, the Law School ignored the shield over the next decade, and the annual yearbooks featured the university's *Veritas* seal rather than the shield.[98] Then, in 1948, Harvard Law School reintroduced the shield. But the school's publications reinterpreted its meaning for coming decades by omitting the shield's link to the Royall family, even in accounts of Royall's role in the beginning of the Law School.[99]

Shortly after he started as dean in 1946, Griswold announced that the HLSA had agreed to raise funds to build a Treasure Room (now called the Caspersen Room) in the library, which would house the library's rare books and honor students and graduates of the Law School who had died in World Wars I and II.[100] The HLSA appeal succeeded, and the newly constructed Treasure Room opened in October 1948.[101] Shelved in the central, glass-walled bookcase facing the entrance was the library's prized collection of early English law books once owned by Englishman George Dunn and purchased by the Law School in 1913, as recounted in Chapter 2.

In the semicircular crown over the bookcase, there appeared a remarkable innovation. The Law School shield with its three sheaves of grain standing in a field was inscribed beside the famous phrase of English jurist Edward Coke— "out of the ould fields must spring and grow the new corne."[102] This was deemed fitting for "the Dunn Collection," wrote Eleanor N. Little, the head of the Treasure Room.[103] The phrase was also a favorite of Griswold, who used it for the title of his autobiography.[104] But how were the Dunn Collection, Coke's quotation, and the shield related?

Coke drew his quotation from a metaphor of Geoffrey Chaucer, in which "corn" meant "wheat" or "grain" and expressed how new knowledge springs from old books.[105] Hence, the Harvard Law School shield with the three sheaves of grain standing in a field illustrated the lesson of Coke's quotation

Harvard Law School shield associated with quotation from Sir Edward Coke and inscribed over the main bookcase of rare books in the Caspersen Room, Langdell Hall, Harvard Law School. Photograph 2013.

© Daniel R. Coquillette.

and Chaucer's metaphor, and suggested the potential of the Dunn Collection and other rare books in the Treasure Room.

To accentuate the connection, Coke's quotation partly framed the shield, and both were carved in wood and embossed in gold. The shield's association with Coke's words thus supplanted its origin in the Royall coat of arms, which was not mentioned in Law School publications.[106] Similarly, when the *Harvard Law Record* began featuring the shield on its masthead in April 1954, the editors associated it with Coke's phrase.[107] In the 1950s, Coke's quotation was evidently meant to explain the shield's design.

This new explanation was not intended to hide the Royall origin of the shield, which had apparently slipped from institutional memory. Meanwhile, the source of the Royall family wealth in slave labor was never mentioned and apparently unknown at the Law School. For example, in 1992 the *Harvard Law Record* described Royall as "a successful Massachusetts businessman and patron of education," suitably for the school's first benefactor.[108] Only in the year 2000 were the three points all connected by historical research and published: the Law School shield, the Royall family coat of arms, and the source of the wealth that funded the school's first endowed professorial chair.[109]

In any event, construction of the Treasure Room in 1948 was subsequently overshadowed by Griswold's other new buildings and administrative expansion. This growth in physical plant and in the school's administration was remarkable, even more so in light of its rapid pace and Griswold's awkward, gruff demeanor. Furthermore, the expansion occurred while the school faced two dramatic and concurrent challenges. One was the crisis of McCarthyism; the other was the revolution in admissions policies.

NOTES

1. Erwin N. Griswold, *Ould Fields, New Corne: The Personal Memoirs of a Twentieth Century Lawyer* (St. Paul, MN, 1992), 154.

2. Quotation is from Samuel Williston, *Life and Law: An Autobiography* (Boston, 1940), 187. See Daniel R. Coquillette and Bruce A. Kimball, *On the Battlefield of Merit: Harvard Law School, the First Century* (Cambridge, MA, 2015) (hereafter cited as *Battlefield of Merit*), 592.

3. See Griswold's account of his time as a student at Harvard Law School (HLS) in Chapter 4. On Langdell being "not a gentleman," see Bruce A. Kimball, *The Inception of Modern Professional Education: C. C. Langdell, 1826–1906* (Chapel Hill, NC, 2009), 196.

4. Griswold, *Ould Fields*, 173.

5. See Bruce A. Kimball, "The Langdell Problem: Historicizing the Century of Historiography, 1906–2000s," *Law and History Review* 22 (2004): 277–337.

6. HLS Faculty Meeting Minutes (June 5, 1946).

7. Henry J. Friendly, "Erwin N. Griswold—Some Fond Recollections," *HLR* 86 (1973): 1366; Griswold, *Ould Fields*, 80–81, 114; Kenneth W. Bergen, *Dedication of Treasury Department Library in Memory of Erwin N. Griswold* [printed pamphlet] (October 19, 1995), Elizabeth Wahlen Correspondence, 1946–1998, on file with the authors, 1–2.

8. Griswold, *Ould Fields*, 122; James M. Landis, "Statutes and the Sources of Law," in *Harvard Legal Essays: Written in Honor of and Presented to Joseph Henry Beale and Samuel Williston,* ed. Roscoe Pound (Cambridge, MA, 1934), 213–246.

9. Griswold, *Ould Fields*, 81n, 115, 113. See Erwin N. Griswold, "Government in Ignorance of the Law—A Plea for Better Publication of Executive Regulation," *HLR* 48 (1934): 198–215; James M. Landis, *The Administrative Process* (New Haven, CT, 1938).

10. Quotations are from, respectively, Judith Richards Hope, *Pinstripes & Pearls: The Women of the Harvard Law Class of '64 Who Forged an Old Girl Network and Paved the*

Way for Future Generations (New York, 2003), 104; "Griswold—Block of Granite, Man Who Sticks to His Ideals," *Boston Globe* (October 1, 1967). See Donald A. Ritchie, *James M. Landis: Dean of the Regulators* (Cambridge, MA, 1980), 138; Dennis Hevesi, "Erwin Griswold Is Dead at 90; Served as Solicitor General," *New York Times* (November 21, 1994).

11. Tom Long, "Obituary: Harriet Griswold, Librarian Who Lobbied for Disabled People," *Boston Globe* (November 30, 1999); Griswold, *Ould Fields*, 8.

12. Jane Hill, "By the Sweat of Their Fraus: The Harvard Law Wives, 1929–1972" (student research paper, HLS, 2009), on file with the authors, 12. See James Vorenberg, Oral History, conducted by Daniel R. Coquillette (November–December 1997), on file with the authors; Alan M. Dershowitz, Oral History, conducted by Daniel R. Coquillette with Andrew Klaber (October–November 2009), on file with the authors.

13. See [Elizabeth Wahlen], "Erwin N. Griswold—Some Fond Recollections," *HLR* 86 (1973): 1365–1379; Daniel M. Friedman, "In Memoriam: Erwin Nathaniel Griswold," *HLR* 108 (1995): 989–992; Linda K. Smith, "Erwin Griswold: Remembrances," unpublished memo to Bruce Kimball (January 2015), on file with the authors; Frank E. A. Sander, Oral History, conducted by Daniel R. Coquillette and Daniel Hamilton (September–December 1998), on file with the authors.

14. Quotations are from Griswold, *Ould Fields*, 106, 109, 123–125, 147. See Torry Saundra, "At 87, Erwin N. Griswold Is the Dean of Supreme Court Observers," *Washington Post* (July 15, 1991).

15. Quotations are from Griswold, *Ould Fields*, 34, 74, 113, 119, 160, 402–403. See Ellen Bernstein, "A Conversation with Erwin N. Griswold," *HLSB* (Fall 1979): 19–23; Morton Keller and Phyllis Keller, *Making Harvard Modern: The Rise of America's University* (New York, 2001), 253; Erwin N. Griswold, "Essays Commemorating the One Hundredth Anniversary of the *Harvard Law Review:* Introduction," *HLR* 100 (1987): 730.

16. Quoted in Albert M. Sacks, "Dedication of Griswold Hall: September 18, 1979," *HLSB* (Fall 1979): 30. Compare Erwin N. Griswold, Annual Report of the Dean of HLS, 1947–48, 390; Erwin N. Griswold, "The Future of Legal Education," *HLSB* (February 1953): 4; Keller and Keller, *Making Harvard Modern*, 253; Griswold, *Ould Fields*, 74, 113, 119, 160; Bernstein, "A Conversation," 19–23.

17. Quoted in "A Great Law Dean," *Harvard Crimson* (October 2, 1967); Archibald Cox, Oral History, conducted by Daniel R. Coquillette and Daniel Hamilton (November 1998), on file with the authors. See Nathan M. Pusey "A Great Dean," *HLR* 81 (1967): 291; Harold J. Berman, Oral History, conducted by Daniel Hamilton and Daniel R. Coquillette (August 1998), on file with the authors; Louis A. Toepfer, Oral History, conducted by Daniel Hamilton (March 1998), on file with the authors; Sacks, "Dedication of Griswold Hall," 28–30; Derek C. Bok, "Dedication of Griswold Hall: September 18, 1979," *HLSB* (Fall 1979): 26–27; Harry M. Blackburn, "In Memoriam: Erwin Nathaniel Griswold," *HLR* 108 (1995): 980–981; Clark Byse, "In Memoriam: Erwin Nathaniel Griswold," *HLR* 108 (1995): 981–985; Robert C. Clark, "In Memoriam:

Erwin Nathaniel Griswold," *HLR* 108 (1995): 985–987. Young faculty who arrived toward the end of Griswold's administration were less enthusiastic: "On balance, I think he was a commendable person." Dershowitz, Oral History (October–November 2009).

18. Benjamin Kaplan, Oral History, conducted by Daniel R. Coquillette (January 2006), on file with the authors. See David R. Derusha, "The Deanship of Erwin N. Griswold: A New Look" (student research paper, HLS, 2008), on file with the authors, 5.

19. J. Willard Hurst to Joseph H. Willits (March 20, 1957), J. Willard Hurst Collection, University of Wisconsin Law Library Special Collections. See Austin W. Scott, "The Dean's Decennial," *HLSB* (October 1956): 3.

20. Toepfer, Oral History (March 1998). Smith, "Erwin Griswold: Remembrances."

21. Berman, Oral History (August 1998). See Andrew L. Kaufman, Oral History, conducted by Daniel Hamilton and Daniel R. Coquillette (June 1999–April 2000), on file with the authors.

22. Elizabeth Bartholet, Oral History, conducted by Daniel Hamilton (February 1999–March 2000), on file with the authors.

23. Toepfer, Oral History (March 1998). See Sander, Oral History (September–December 1998); Vorenberg, Oral History (November–December 1997); Charles Fried, Oral History, conducted by Daniel R. Coquillette and Mary Beth Basile (August 2000–March 2001), on file with the authors.

24. Paul D. Carrington, Oral History, conducted by Daniel Hamilton (February 2003), on file with the authors.

25. Quotation is from Stephen Bernardi, Oral History, conducted by Daniel Hamilton and Daniel R. Coquillette (October 2000–April 2001), on file with the authors. See Dershowitz, Oral History (October–November 2009); Smith, "Erwin Griswold: Remembrances;" Albert M. Sacks, "Erwin N. Griswold—Some Fond Recollections," *HLR* 86 (1973): 1,369; Arthur von Mehren, Oral History, conducted by Daniel R. Coquillette and Mary Beth Basile (July–December 2000), on file with the authors; Griswold, *Ould Fields,* 154.

26. "Dean Griswold Classes Himself as Conservative in Alumni Address," *HLSR* (November 6, 1946): 3.

27. Quoted in Ernest J. Brown, Oral History, conducted by Daniel Hamilton (August 1997), on file with the authors. See Berman, Oral History (August 1998); Paul A. Freund, "Erwin N. Griswold: An Introduction," in *Remembrance: Erwin N. Griswold* [Memorial Program] (March 2, 1995), on file with authors.

28. Cox, Oral History (November 1998).

29. Raymond J. Wiacek, "In Memoriam: Erwin Nathaniel Griswold," *HLR* 108 (1995): 1001.

30. "'Griswold Looks Like Irvin Cobb, but Works Like Lord Eldon,'" says Porter," *HLSR* (October 19, 1949): 1.

31. Cox, Oral History (November 1998).

32. Cox, Oral History (November 1998).

33. Cox, Oral History (November 1998).

34. Berman, Oral History (August 1998).

35. Bernardi, Oral History (October 2000–April 2001).

36. Dershowitz, Oral History (October–November 2009).

37. Freund, "Erwin N. Griswold." See Russell A. Simpson, Oral History, conducted by Mary Beth Basile and Daniel R. Coquillette (May–September 2001), on file with the authors.

38. Quotation is from Simpson, Oral History (May–September 2001). See Toepfer, Oral History (March 1998); von Mehren, Oral History (July–December 2000); Clark Byse, Oral History, conducted by Daniel R. Coquillette and Daniel Hamilton (July–October 1997), on file with the authors.

39. Robert E. Keeton, Oral History, conducted by Daniel Hamilton and Daniel R. Coquillette (November 2000–February 2001), on file with the authors.

40. Smith, "Erwin Griswold: Remembrances."

41. Cox, Oral History (November 1998). See Griswold, *Ould Fields,* 154; Carrington, Oral History (February 2003); Simpson, Oral History (May–September 2001); Herbert P. Wilkins, Oral History, conducted by Daniel R. Coquillette (November 2014), on file with the authors.

42. Bartholet, Oral History (February 1999–March 2000).

43. Bartholet, Oral History (February 1999–March 2000).

44. Kaplan, Oral History (January 2006). See Dershowitz, Oral History (October–November 2009); Simpson, Oral History (May–September 2001). See Detlev Vagts, Oral History, conducted by Daniel R. Hamilton, Daniel Coquillette, and John Delionado (November 1999–February 2000), on file with the authors.

45. Smith, "Erwin Griswold: Remembrances." See "Dean Griswold Classes Himself as Conservative," 3; Berman, Oral History (August 1998); Hevesi, "Erwin Griswold Is Dead at 90"; "Griswold—Block of Granite"; Carrington, Oral History (February 2003); Wilkins, Oral History (November 2014).

46. Vagts, Oral History (November 1999–February 2000).

47. Harriet Griswold to Elizabeth Wahlen (ca. January 1995), Elizabeth Wahlen Correspondence, 1946–1998, on file with the authors. See Erwin N. Griswold, "Dedication of Griswold Hall: September 18, 1979," *HLSB* (Fall 1979): 40–43; Bernstein, "A Conversation," 19–23; Carrington, Oral History (February 2003).

48. Victor E. Ferrall Jr., Telephone Interview with Bruce A. Kimball (January 2015), notes on file with the authors. This may explain why, when Griswold wrote on op-ed column for the *Washington Post,* an editor, perhaps mischievously, identified him as "a Washington lawyer, a former dean of the Yale Law School and . . . solicitor general in the Nixon administration." Erwin N. Griswold, "Secrets Not Worth Keeping," *Washington Post* (February 15, 1989). His wife observed that it was "a monumental error." Harriet Griswold to Elizabeth Wahlen (February 16, 1989), Elizabeth Wahlen Correspondence, 1946–1998, on file with the authors.

49. Carrington, Oral History (February 2003).

50. Griswold, *Ould Fields,* 151.

51. Toepfer, Oral History (March 1998).

52. Griswold, *Ould Fields,* 151–154.

53. Griswold, *Ould Fields,* 159. See the account of these hires in Chapter 8.

54. Toepfer, Oral History (March 1998). See Griswold, Annual Report of the Dean, 1945–46, 343; Suzanne Mettler, *Soldiers to Citizens: The G.I. Bill and the Making of the Greatest Generation* (New York, 2005).

55. Brown, Oral History (August 1997).

56. Brown, Oral History (August 1997); Kaplan Oral History (January 2006).

57. "Dean's Report Cites Record of Veterans. Notes Exceptionally Low Failure Average of Postwar Classes," *HLSR* (January 6, 1948): 1.

58. Quotation is from Sander, Oral History (September–December 1998). See Griswold, Annual Report of the Dean, 1946–47; Scott, "The Dean's Decennial," 3; Vagts, Oral History (November 1999–February 2000).

59. Emphasis in original. Griswold, Annual Report of the Dean, 1947–48, 378–385.

60. Griswold, Annual Report of the Dean, 1947–48, 385.

61. Griswold, *Ould Fields,* 157–158.

62. Reginald Heber Smith to Erwin N. Griswold (June 6, 1946) and Erwin N. Griswold to Reginald Heber Smith (June 7, 1946), Erwin N. Griswold Papers, 1925–1994, Harvard Law School Library Historical & Special Collections (hereafter cited as ENG Papers).

63. Erwin N. Griswold, "Hopes—Past and Future," address to the Visiting Committee of Harvard Law School, Cambridge, MA (April 18, 1970), on file with the authors, 6; Griswold, *Ould Fields,* 151–157.

64. The *Harvard Law School Bulletin* changed its name to the *Harvard Law Bulletin* beginning with the Winter 1986 issue.

65. Brown, Oral History (August 1997).

66. Griswold, Annual Report of the Dean, 1946–47, 414.

67. Frederick A. O. Schwarz, "Report of the Committee to Visit the Law School" (May 12, 1958), ENG Papers. See Scott, "The Dean's Decennial," 4; Erwin N. Griswold, "Harvard Law School Bulletin," *HLSB* (April 1, 1948): 3; Griswold, Annual Report of the Dean, 1947–48, 398; 1948–49, 427; 1954–55, 643.

68. Griswold, Annual Report of the Dean, 1946–47, 409–410; Toepfer, Oral History (March 1998); Griswold, *Ould Fields,* 387.

69. HLS Faculty Meeting Minutes (September 30, 1947).

70. Quotations are from, respectively, Kaufman, Oral History (June 1999–April 2000); Simpson, Oral History (May–September 2001). See Toepfer, Oral History (March 1998).

71. "Harvard Law School Association, 77th Annual Meeting of the Council," *HLSB* (June 1963): 21.

72. "Dorr, Boston Lawyer, Offers Reasons Why Landis Resigned," *HLSR* (July 17, 1946): 1; Griswold, *Ould Fields,* 156–157; Bernstein, "A Conversation," 21; Sander, Oral History (September–December 1998). The *Harvard Law School Record* renamed itself the *Harvard Law Record* with the issue of February 2, 1956.

73. "Nursery to Open in Hastings Hall," *HLSR* (November 6, 1946): 1; Griswold, *Ould Fields,* 232–233.

74. HLS, "A Brief History of the Harvard Defenders," in *The Harvard Defenders Fiftieth Anniversary Symposium & Celebration* (Cambridge MA, 2000), 7–8. See "Harvard Voluntary Defenders," Harvard Law School Yearbook, 1952, 166–167; Harvard Law School Catalog, 1967–68 (April 5, 1967), 111. Students in the Harvard Voluntary Defenders were supervised by Wilbur G. Hollingsworth, who achieved adoption of an early student practice rule in the state of Massachusetts.

75. Erwin N. Griswold, "Professor Cavers Appointed Associate Dean," *HLSB* (April 1951): 3.

76. Kaufman, Oral History (June 1999–April 2000).

77. Vagts, Oral History (November 1999–February 2000).

78. These numbers do not include directors of special projects or, in the library, secretaries and staff on circulation desk and stack services. Alexander M. Wolf, "The Harvard Law School Faculty under the Deanship of Erwin Nathaniel Griswold" (student research paper, HLS, 2012), on file with the authors; Alexander M. Wolf, "Harvard Law School Personnel Counts, from 1946–47 through 1967–68" (research report, HLS, 2017), on file with the authors, which relies on the annual catalogs and dean's annual reports of the Law School. Compare Harvard Law School, *Governing, Teaching, and Administrative Personnel August 1, 1946* (Cambridge, MA, 1946), 6–11; "Recent Growth of Faculty and Staff—1945–1953," *HLSB* (December 1953): 9.

79. Quoted in Arthur E. Sutherland, *The Law at Harvard: A History of Ideas and Men, 1817–1907* (Cambridge, MA, 1967), 324. See Keeton, Oral History (November 2000–February 2001); Toepfer, Oral History (March 1998).

80. HLS Faculty Meeting Minutes (August 19, 1945); Griswold, Annual Report of the Dean, 1946–47, 410–11; Bernstein, "A Conversation," 19–23.

81. "Dean Griswold on the Needs of the Law School," *HLSB* (July 1948), 12; "Graduate Housing, Excerpt from President Conant's speech, June 10, to Harvard Alumni," *HLSB* (July 1948): 2; "Grad Center Commons to Be Named after Harkness, Yale Alumnus Gave Millions for Houses," *Harvard Crimson* (October 3, 1950); James B. Conant, "The Law School and Harvard University," *HLSB* (April 1949): 9; Griswold, *Ould Fields,* 165–167. In 2012, the commons was renamed the Caspersen Student Center after Finn M. W. Caspersen (LL.B. 1966), a generous donor to the school.

82. Toepfer, Oral History (March 1998). See Kersting, Brown & Co., *An Inventory of Fund Raising Resources and a Suggested Campaign Plan* (Cambridge, MA, 1948); Sutherland, *The Law at Harvard,* 349–351; Griswold, *Ould Fields,* 167. Gropius used the unex-

pended contingency fund to obtain extraordinary works of art for the dormitories, including murals by Joan Miro, Josef Albers, Jean App, and Herbert Bayer, as well as the sculpture "World Tree" by Richard Lippold.

83. Griswold, *Ould Fields,* 167. See Sutherland, *The Law at Harvard,* 349–351.

84. Bainbridge Bunting, *Harvard: An Architectural History,* ed. Margaret H. Floyd (Cambridge, MA, 1985), 223–225.

85. Sutherland, *The Law at Harvard,* 350. See Toepfer, Oral History (March 1998); Griswold, Annual Report of the Dean, 1949–50, 456; 1951–52, 520; Keller and Keller, *Making Harvard Modern,* 150.

86. "Hastings Hall Symbol of Law School Losses," *Harvard Crimson* (August 10, 1943).

87. Erwin N. Griswold, *Harvard Law School Fund: Its Objectives; A Letter from Dean Erwin N. Griswold to John B. Marsh, Esq., National Chairman* (New York, 1948); "The Harvard Law School Fund," *HLSB* (January 1949): 2–6; "Dean Griswold on the Needs of the Law School"; John B. Marsh, "Backing the Law School," *HLSB* (October 1948): 6–7.

88. Griswold, Annual Report of the Dean, 1947–48, 378; 1948–49, 424–425; Marsh, "Backing the Law School," 7; Kenneth Leung, "Fundraising at the Harvard Law School during Erwin Griswold's Deanship" (student research paper, HLS, 2011) on file with the authors, appendix 2 ; Erwin N. Griswold, "Law School Fund Reaches First Million," *HLSB* (July 1949): 1; "Final Summary—Capital Gifts Campaign Harvard Law School Fund," *HLSB* (June 1951): 14.

89. Quotations are from Griswold, Annual Report of the Dean, 1950–51, 382. See Griswold, "Law School Fund Reaches First Million," 1.

90. Griswold, Annual Report of the Dean, 1954–55, 600, 629; 1955–56, 385; 1956–57, 337. "Committee to Meet Conditional Grant of the Ford Foundation," *HLSB* (April 1955): 4. Friendly was appointed to the U.S. Court of Appeals, second circuit, in 1959.

91. Friendly, "Erwin N. Griswold," 1368.

92. Griswold, Annual Report of the Dean, 1957–58, 325.

93. Quotations are from Griswold, *Ould Fields,* 236. See Erwin N. Griswold to HLS Faculty (December 4, 1957), ENG Papers.

94. Griswold, Annual Report of the Dean, 1957–58, 323–325 327–328; brochure introducing the International Legal Studies building (1960), ENG Papers; Toepfer, Oral History (March 1998); Bernstein, "A Conversation," 19–23.

95. Griswold, Annual Report of the Dean, 1957–58, 325, 328; 1958–59, 311.

96. See *Battlefield of Merit,* 81–91. There is no evidence that those involved in the Harvard tercentenary in 1936 "were aware of or even thought to ask how the Royall family amassed its fortune." Bruce H. Mann et al. [HLS Shield Committee], "Recommendation to the President and Fellows of Harvard College on the Shield Approved for the Law School" (March 3, 2016), 6, on file with the authors. See [Law School Shield], *HLSB* (Winter 1975): 14; Mason Hammond, "A Harvard Armory: Part I," *HLSB* (July 1981):

265, 284–285; "Contents," *HLSB* (Winter 1986): 1n; "Contents," *HLSB* (Spring 1987): 1n; "Harvard Law School 175 Years Old," *HLSR* (September 18, 1992): 4.

97. Quotations are from Hammond, "A Harvard Armory: Part I," 265; see 284–285. Compare the interpretation in Mann et al., "Recommendation to the President and Fellows," 5.

98. Harvard Law School Yearbook, 1937–38, title page. In 2016 a search by the Historical & Special Collections staff of the Harvard Law School Library found no usages of the shield prior to the *HLSR* issue from April 1, 1950. Mann et al., "Recommendation to the President and Fellows," 6; Karen S. Beck to Daniel R. Coquillette, email communication (February 16, 2018), on file with the authors. But that issue actually appeared in "*Veritas et Legem*," *HLSR* (April 1, 1954): 2.

99. See, for example, "The Named Professorships of the Harvard Law School: The Royall Professorship," *HLSB* (December 1952): 5, 13; W. Barton Leach, "School's Story Told by Leach," *HLSR* (September 30, 1954): 3; "*Veritas et Legem*," 2. Frank W. Grinnell, "The Forgotten Gift of a Forgotten Man," *HLSR* (April 25, 1957): 2; Sutherland, *The Law at Harvard*, 32–42; "Decorate the Walls of the Law School," *HLSR* (February 28, 1969): 5.

100. HLS Faculty Meeting Minutes (July 23, 1946). Finn M. W. Caspersen (LL.B. 1966), a major donor to the Law School for whom the Caspersen Room was renamed, insisted that the list of Law School fatalities in World Wars I and II, which surround the doorway to the Caspersen Room, be updated with plaques of fatalities from later wars.

101. Harvard Law School Association, *Harvard Law School: The Treasure Room to Be Built in Langdell Hall* (Cambridge, MA, 1947), [1, 8]; HLS Faculty Meeting Minutes (July 23, 1946); Arthur C. Pulling, "An Appreciation," *HLSB* (October 1948): 8.

102. Edward Coke, *Reports* (London, 1600), 1, preface.

103. Eleanor N. Little, "The Acquisition of the Dunn Collection of Early English Law Books," *HLSB* (December 1955): 9–10.

104. Griswold, *Ould Fields*.

105. "For out of olde feldes . . . Cometh al this newe corn fro yeer to yere; And out of olde bokes, . . . Cometh al this newe science that men lere." Chaucer's lines thus make clear the metaphorical allusion that "olde bookes" produce "newe science," or knowledge, just as "ould fields" produce "newe corne." Geoffrey Chaucer, *Parlement of Foules* (1381), in *The Complete Works of Geoffrey Chaucer*, ed. Walter W. Skeat, 2nd ed. (Oxford, UK 1899), line 22.

106. "Law School Annals," *HLSR* (August 21, 1946): 3; "The Named Professorships," 5, 13; Little, "The Acquisition," 9–10; Leach, "School's Story," 3; "*Veritas et Legem*," 2. Grinnell, "The Forgotten Gift," 2; Sutherland, *The Law at Harvard*, 32–42; "Decorate the Walls," 5.

107. "*Veritas et Legem*," 2.

108. "Harvard Law School 175 Years Old." See Mann et al., "Recommendation to the President and Fellows," 6; [Law School Shield], *HLSB* (Winter 1975): 14; Hammond, "A

Harvard Armory: Part I," 265, 284–285; "Contents," *HLSB* (Winter 1986): 1n; "Contents," *HLSB* (Spring 1987): 1n.

109. Daniel R. Coquillette, "A History of Blacks at Harvard Law School," *HLSR* (October 20, 2000): 6–7. The current dean, John F. Manning (J.D. 1985), has a established a permanent exhibit in the Caspersen Room illustrating the history of the shield.

CHAPTER ELEVEN

McCarthyism and the Fifth Amendment, 1950s

Managing the "madhouse" of returning veterans, the "orderly evolution" of the administration, and the addition of eight new buildings was difficult enough for Dean Erwin Griswold (1946–1967). But the challenge was intensified by the concurrent Red Scare hysteria and widespread fear of Communism that gripped the nation during the late 1940s and early 1950s, culminating in the demagoguery of Wisconsin senator Joseph R. McCarthy from 1950 to 1954. "It is hard to reconstruct the atmosphere now," Griswold later wrote, "but a deep sense of fear was widespread."[1]

McCarthyism wounded all whom it touched. Two Harvard Law students, who publicly resisted, lost memberships in the Legal Aid Bureau, *Harvard Law School Record,* or *Harvard Law Review.* An African American graduate and civil rights activist, who belonged to the Communist Party, was wrongfully convicted and sentenced to federal prison for five years. The career of one of the school's first female graduates—who cooperated completely with federal investigators on the advice of Dean Griswold and her professors—was also severely damaged.

Yet the fearmongering also resulted in a fundamental reinterpretation of the Fifth Amendment right against self-incrimination. In 1954 Dean Griswold published his famous reinterpretation and became a hero for fearlessly defending the Fifth Amendment as "an old and good friend." But the origin of the doctrinal revision actually appears to be the students who defied Griswold and paid the price of resisting McCarthyism.

The Red Scare

The postwar, anti-Communist fervor rapidly entangled the Law School in controversy. In early 1947 President Harry Truman signed an executive order creating a comprehensive federal employee loyalty program and requiring a loyalty oath from all employees working in the executive branch of government. In a letter to the *New York Times,* Griswold, Zechariah Chafee Jr. (LL.B. 1913), Milton Katz (LL.B. 1931), and Austin Scott (LL.B. 1909) argued that the oath was improper.[2] Conversely, Warren Seavey (LL.B. 1904) warned that the threat of Communism must not be minimized, because "we may soon find ourselves an island of democracy in a world of communism unless we recognize and meet the issues."[3]

In November 1947 the new Harvard Law School Forum hosted a debate between Protestant theologian Reinhold Niebuhr and John A. O'Brien, S.J., on whether "Christianity and Communism" were compatible. Over 1,600 law students attended, and more were turned away.[4] Also in 1947, Griswold made "a very bold move" in appointing as assistant professor Harold Berman, a graduate of Yale Law School who was then teaching at Stanford Law School as an associate professor. Berman was hired to teach Soviet law, the first such appointment in the nation.[5]

In 1948 Whittaker Chambers, a prominent editor of *Time* magazine and former Soviet spy, testified before the House Committee on Un-American Activities (HUAC) that Alger Hiss (LL.B. 1929), a stellar graduate of the school, was a Communist agent. As a student, Hiss had been a protégé of Professor Felix Frankfurter (LL.B. 1906), who arranged for him to clerk for Justice Oliver W. Holmes Jr. (LL.B. 1866). Hiss then joined prominent law firms before moving to the legal staff of the Agricultural Adjustment Administration, where in 1934 he met Ernest Brown (LL.B. 1931), profiled in Chapter 4. In the late 1930s, Hiss and his wife, Priscilla, socialized with Brown, who felt that "Priscilla was the strong man of the family" and that she may have "inspired" Alger's "mix-up with Chambers."[6]

In response to the allegations leveled by Chambers, Hiss asked to appear before HUAC in order to clear his name. He testified under oath that he was neither a Communist nor a spy. When Chambers repeated the charge on radio, Hiss sued for defamation. In response, Chambers produced evidence that Hiss had knowingly given classified state documents to a Soviet agent. By that point, neither man could be charged with espionage. Chambers had been granted immunity as a cooperating witness for the government, and the statute of limitations had expired on Hiss's alleged activities. But in 1949 Hiss was indicted for committing perjury before HUAC.

The indictment generated "a lot of sympathy and support for Hiss" at Harvard Law School, recalled Arthur von Mehren (LL.B. 1945).[7] Several faculty "felt rather close to him and helped in putting together the defense and advising his selection of counsel and so forth," said Detlev Vagts (LL.B. 1951).[8] These included Griswold, who had served on the *Harvard Law Review* with Hiss in 1927, and the dean's support for Hiss prompted the FBI to put Griswold under surveillance. Hiss's first trial in 1949, in which Adlai Stevenson and Felix Frankfurter served as character witnesses, ended in a mistrial. After a second trial, Hiss was convicted of perjury in January 1950 and sentenced to serve two concurrent terms of five years in federal prison. He was disbarred in Massachusetts but readmitted in 1975 in a controversial decision by the Massachusetts Supreme Judicial Court.[9]

Meanwhile, in April 1949 *Life* magazine ran an article profiling the fifty most prominent Communist "Dupes and Fellow Travelers" in the United States. Nineteen of them had graduated from or worked at Harvard University at some point. One individual associated with the Law School was John Rogge, who had graduated with the LL.B. in 1925 as a member of the *Harvard Law Review* and then earned the S.J.D. in 1931. As a staff member of the U.S. Justice Department, Rogge investigated the threat of fascism to the United States after 1945. He charged that fascists were deflecting attention from their activities by claiming to be virulently anti-Communist. In 1947 the Justice Department terminated his employment, but Rogge continued to oppose the anti-Communist hysteria as a manifestation of fascism.[10]

In April 1949 the Harvard Law School Forum invited socialist Harold Laski to return from Britain and speak at the Law School. No room at the school was large enough to hold the anticipated crowd, so the Forum arranged to shift the venue to a Cambridge high school. When the Cambridge School Committee prohibited the event, Griswold arranged for the Forum to host Laski in the auditorium of the Harvard Music building, located near the Law School.[11] The Laski event went off without incident, but pressure on Harvard and other major universities to purge Communists intensified. In 1949 Maryland state legislator Frank B. Ober (LL.B. 1939) urged fellow alumni of the Law School not to donate funds for the projected dormitory complex until the university rid itself of "reds" and "pinks." In that same year the University of California Board of Regents adopted a loyalty oath and required all faculty to sign it. In 1950, thirty-one faculty members refused, and all were fired.[12]

In February 1950, speaking in West Virginia, McCarthy made his first claim to have a list of Communists working in the State Department. He then repeated the allegation on the floor of the U.S. Senate. In succeeding months, transcripts of McCarthy's speeches were "widely circulated, and he made new sweeping charges almost daily," recalled Griswold. In June, North Korea invaded South Korea, igniting the Korean War and intensifying anti-Communist fervor in the United States. Later in 1950 the ABA recommended that state bar associations require loyalty oaths of lawyers, and the Association of American Law Schools maintained that law schools should require the same of their professors.[13]

In September, Congress enacted the Internal Security (McCarran) Act, which, without criminalizing membership in the Communist Party, declared that the U.S. "Communist organization" was a "clear and present danger" to national security. The act required members of Communist-affiliated groups to register with the U.S. Attorney General's Office and stripped them of various rights and privileges of citizenship. Late in December 1950 the Senate established its own correlate of the HUAC: the Senate Internal Security Subcommittee (SISS).[14]

Meanwhile, people called before congressional and state investigative committees began refusing to answer extraneous questions intended purely to embarrass or intimidate witnesses. To shield themselves from charges of contempt, such witnesses were required to provide a legal justification for their refusal. They therefore began invoking the Fifth Amendment right against self-incrimination—"No person . . . shall be compelled in any criminal case to be a witness against himself"—when appearing before investigative committees.[15] But that invocation was unorthodox because legal doctrine supported the right against self-incrimination only in criminal cases. Against the background of these events, McCarthyism seeped into Harvard in the early 1950s.

"Kremlin on the Charles"

In 1951 the Soviet Union, at the behest of Josef Stalin, invited leading academics from all over the world to attend a large conference on global trade. At the direction of U.S. Secretary of State Dean Acheson (LL.B. 1918), the State Department advised faculty at Harvard, and elsewhere, not to attend. But assistant professor Harold Berman, who was already under surveillance by the Boston office of the FBI, decided that it would be an excellent opportunity to visit the Soviet Union for the first time. After securing an invitation,

Berman was advised to decline by Director Clark Holm of the Russian Re-search Center at Harvard, whose telephone was tapped by the FBI. Griswold initially told Berman to decide for himself, but soon thereafter reversed him-self and said to Berman, "if you decide to do it and you ever get in any trouble as a result, . . . say that I advised you to do it." The trip fell through, but Berman always appreciated Griswold's permission and offer to shield him.[16]

In 1952, congressmen on SISS and HUAC realized that they could benefit politically from investigating "radical" professors. The two committees thus began to focus their efforts on university faculty, and J. Edgar Hoover ordered the FBI to undertake broad surveillance of universities. Across the country, more than one hundred faculty members were eventually subpoenaed by the congres-sional committees, and at least thirty lost their jobs. Witnesses who refused to answer questions, and invoked the right against self-incrimination provided by the Fifth Amendment, were labeled "Fifth Amendment Communists," and most were fired. Andrew L. Kaufman (LL.B. 1954) recalled that at Harvard Law School, "people were glued to their radios" listening to the hearings.[17]

Everyone at Harvard expected that the "Kremlin on the Charles" would eventually be scrutinized.[18] Few university leaders, save University of Chicago President Robert Hutchins, publicly challenged the witch hunt. Griswold en-couraged President James Conant (1933–1953) to follow, even surpass, Hutchins's example; but historians concur that Conant's virulent anti-Communism trumped his belief in academic freedom. Caught between these two commitments, Conant, like other university presidents, adopted the par-adoxical positions "that Communists were unfit to teach but that Harvard would not investigate its faculty," and that any professor who invoked the Fifth Amendment before government investigators would be dismissed.[19]

Meanwhile, Harvard and other universities established an "arrangement" with the FBI to secretly communicate information about the activities of fac-ulty and staff. This relationship was symbiotic because both parties felt threat-ened by SISS and HUAC. The FBI wished to show that it could do its job better than the politicized congressional committees, and the universities wanted to stave off the committees' hearings. Harvard and other universities therefore provided information in exchange for protection from the FBI.[20] Needless to say, neither the FBI nor the universities publicized their "arrange-ment," which was later uncovered by historian Sigmund Diamond, who had been victimized by the "arrangement" at Harvard. In 1953, after Diamond completed his Ph.D. in history at Harvard, the university offered him a position as an assistant professor but retracted the offer when he refused to agree to inform the FBI about the activities of other faculty and staff. Diamond was then blacklisted in the academic job market until 1955, when he began a distinguished academic career at Columbia University.[21]

On January 6, 1953, the inconsistencies in President Conant's paradoxical positions on McCarthyism came to a head at a closed meeting with the Harvard Law School faculty.[22] They demanded that the president "take the offensive" against the congressional investigators, but Conant demurred. He maintained that the university had long drawn a "sharp line between activities of faculty as citizens and activities as members of the teaching staff." Consequently, Conant said, the Corporation had decided that the university would not hire or pay legal counsel for faculty members called to testify about activities not directly related to their academic duties.[23]

In the evening after his meeting at the Law School, Conant wrote in his diary that his views were "not too well received" by the law faculty. On the

Nathan M. Pusey, President of Harvard University 1953–1971, at a press conference responding to Senator Joseph McCarthy, in the fall of 1953.
Courtesy of John Loengard.

following day he stated to the Corporation, "Griswold reports that, in general, the reaction of the faculty was that I was more interested in defending the Corporation than in defending the university, that my whole attitude had been neutral and cold instead of being warm and helpful, and that I seemed to be willing to let any and all of the professors be maltreated by the congressional committees and would raise no finger to help them."[24] Conant had already decided to leave Harvard to serve as high commissioner to Germany, but the date of his departure had not yet been determined. The confrontational faculty meeting at the Law School made the prospect of a long transition appear dismal, so he resigned five days later, on January 12, 1953.[25] Nathan Pusey (1953–1971) was named his successor.

Harvard Doctrine on Pleading the Fifth

In 1952 there existed a very limited body of legal doctrine on invoking the Fifth Amendment right against self-incrimination before investigative committees, because the practice had begun only a few years earlier.[26] At Harvard, President Conant was warned about this issue by a member of the Corporation, William Marbury, who had graduated from the Law School in 1924 as a member of the *Law Review* and in 1948 served as legal counsel to his boyhood friend, Alger Hiss, in the initial libel suit against Chambers. Marbury's experience in that case led him to conclude that the university needed to discourage the growing practice of "pleading the Fifth" before congressional and investigative committees.[27]

Marbury maintained that it "makes no sense whatsoever" for anybody to invoke the Fifth Amendment and refuse to answer questions unless that individual was actually guilty of a crime. He reasoned that an innocent person did not need to avoid self-incrimination. The only reasons for an innocent person to refuse to answer were extraneous. For example, one might refuse to answer questions that would embarrass oneself or a friend or one might wish to protest the congressional investigations. But, in such cases, an innocent person who pleaded the Fifth Amendment would be committing perjury because the reason for refusing to answer was not to avoid self-incrimination. Consequently, "taking the Fifth" would only endanger an innocent individual, and only a guilty person would do it. Conant agreed with Marbury, as did the university counsel, Oscar M. Shaw (LL.B. 1929). At the end of December 1952, Marbury therefore wrote to Zechariah Chafee, the famous civil libertarian and University Professor, to speak out and discourage academics from pleading the Fifth, which damaged the university and the academic profession by creating the impression that faculty were guilty of crimes.[28]

Up to that point Chafee had deplored the anti-Communist fervor. In October 1952 he wrote in the *Harvard Law School Record* that he regarded "the present wave of loyalty oaths and subversive laws as dangerous in themselves and also as no solution to the problems they seek to meet."[29] But by the beginning of 1953 Chafee was pulling back, and he told Marbury on January 3, "I thoroughly agree with you." Chafee then consulted Arthur Sutherland (LL.B. 1925), who had joined the law faculty in 1950 and had begun to serve unofficially as the university's advisor to faculty and staff called to testify before the congressional committees. Sutherland was orthodox in his politics and jurisprudence, as in his historical writing. He drafted a statement on the Fifth Amendment "privilege" that essentially adopted the view expressed by Marbury's letter, and Chafee endorsed it.[30]

On January 13, 1953, the day after Conant resigned, Chafee and Sutherland published their famous statement as a letter to the *Harvard Crimson*. Relying on "the underlying principle" that it is "the duty of the citizen to cooperate in government," the Chafee-Sutherland statement maintained that "an individual called before a court, grand jury, or a legislative investigating committee" must "answer questions frankly and honestly." However, "to this general duty of the citizen the privilege against self-incrimination is an extraordinary exception," which is justified primarily by the rationales of barring torture and forcing police to do their job of finding sufficient evidence to convict a guilty person. By the same token, Chafee and Sutherland observed that "political protest," "mere embarrassment," or "protect[ing] one's friends" are not legal justifications for refusing to answer.

But they did note certain "special circumstances" in which "disclosure of communist association may have a tendency to incriminate," even though "'the Internal Security Act of 1950 provides 'Neither the holding of office nor membership in any Communist organization by any person shall constitute per se a violation of . . . this section or of any other criminal statute.'" In such circumstances, they maintained that "a judge must decide when the witness has gone far enough to demonstrate his peril." Finally, they warned that although "a privileged refusal to testify is not an admission of guilt for the purposes of criminal prosecution, . . . a refusal . . . inevitably casts a shadow on [one's] reputation." Therefore, "even when the legal privilege is available, there are times when it is best not exercised."[31]

This statement encouraging faculty and staff to cooperate with HUAC and SISS was endorsed by their colleagues. Robert Braucher (LL.B. 1939) expressed his support, while adding the rationale that professors should forego pleading the Fifth Amendment even when justified in doing so because doing otherwise would "cast discredit on the profession as a whole." Mark Howe (LL.B. 1933), among others, concurred with this rationale.[32] Hundreds of newspapers and university leaders also subscribed to the Chafee-Sutherland statement, relieved to find "a course of action that seemed to satisfy their Congressional critics" and that was "endorsed by Chafee, a man with impeccable civil liberty credentials," according to Sigmund Diamond. Eventually, "Chafee came to regret the letter, but Sutherland . . . never had second thoughts."[33]

The "Left-Winger" Lubells

In June 1951, twin brothers Jonathan Lubell (LL.B. 1954) and David Lubell (LL.B. 1954) graduated from Cornell University, where they had participated in a Marxist study group, distributed the Communist newspaper the *Daily Worker*, opposed the Korean War, and actively promoted civil rights. Having won full-tuition scholarships, they matriculated together at Harvard Law School in September 1951. Both excelled academically, and in the winter of 1953 the *Harvard Law School Record* elected David to be president and Jonathan to be associate editor. By that point each was known to the faculty as "a left-winger," although perhaps not a Communist, stated Berman. David enrolled in Berman's Soviet law class, but "was disgusted with Soviet law. He found out they had divorce and contracts and things like that. . . . He thought they had gotten rid of all those bourgeois things."[34]

The Lubells also joined the Harvard Law School chapter of the National Lawyers Guild (NLG). Founded in December 1936, the NLG was a national bar association for "liberal" lawyers that explicitly distanced itself from the conservative and all-white ABA. By 1940 about 3,500 lawyers had joined the NLG, including governors of two states, several U.S. senators, several prominent black attorneys, and many government lawyers from the Roosevelt administration. But Communist lawyers, though small in number, played a large role in energizing the organization. After 1945, as the anti-Communism fervor grew strong, NLG membership shrank to about 1,000. In January 1950 the NLG exposed unauthorized wiretapping, burglaries, and surveillance by the FBI, and called for President Truman to investigate the Bureau. Instead, the FBI began to investigate the NLG, causing its membership to shrink to just a few

Editorial Board of the Harvard Law School Record, 1952. David G. Lubell LL.B. 1954, second row, second from left; Jonathan W. Lubell LL.B. 1954, third row, second from left.

Harvard Law School Yearbook, 1952. Courtesy of Harvard Yearbook Publications.

hundred by 1958, though the FBI never uncovered any violations of law or professional ethics.[35]

In March 1951 an FBI wiretap revealed, ironically, that a Harvard Law School student in the NLG chapter was preparing an article on FBI wiretapping. The FBI's Boston field office was alerted, and three days later the president of the Massachusetts Bar Association, Samuel P. Sears (LL.B. 1921), publicly denounced Harvard Law School for "encouraging and playing host to the Communist party" by harboring the NLG chapter. In an open letter to Dean Griswold, Sears demanded that the dean "clean house," disband the chapter, and cancel a scheduled appearance by NLG vice president Osmond K. Fraenkel, a well-known attorney for the ACLU who had represented the nine "Scottsboro Boys" in their infamous case.[36]

Griswold received Sears's letter only after reading about it in the newspaper, and responded in kind by publishing his rejection of Sears's demand.[37] Sears continued to badger Griswold in the press, and was eventually rewarded with an appointment as special counsel to Senator McCarthy and the SISS. Though failing to disband the NLG chapter at the Law School, the FBI Boston office did recruit one member of that chapter as a "confidential informant." Code-named "BOS-627," the informant microfilmed the chapter's correspondence and membership lists for the Bureau.[38]

BOS-627 has not been publicly identified, but one member of the NLG chapter at the time, Alan F. Westin (LL.B. 1951), revealed the FBI's surveillance of the NLG in a meeting with Griswold in 1956. Westin described his involvement with the chapter, which Griswold recorded in a memo that was filed in the dean's folder labeled "Communist Students." In the fall of 1948 Westin had arrived at the Law School and joined a Communist student group, but he left in the spring of 1949, disappointed by the group's "intellectual climate." In the fall of 1949 Westin joined the NLG chapter, which had about fifteen members, including a few who had belonged to the Communist group. Eventually Westin concluded that Communists exercised too much influence in the NLG chapter and, according to Griswold, Westin went to the FBI Boston office in 1953 and "told them in detail about his experience here, including the names of associates," among whom were Jonathan and David Lubell.[39]

Consequently, in early January 1953—when Conant resigned, Chafee and Sutherland issued their statement, and the Lubells belonged to the NLG—the Harvard Law School chapter was under suspicion and close scrutiny by the FBI. At this same time, the SISS chairman, Indiana senator William E. Jenner, announced that he was bringing the committee's investigation of higher education to Boston. In mid-March 1953 the Jenner Committee subpoenaed Jonathan and David Lubell to appear on March 26–27. Some scholars suggest that the Lubells' activities at Cornell prompted the inquiry.[40] But in light of the brothers' reputation for radicalism, the subpoenas did not surprise anyone at Harvard Law School.

Upon receiving the subpoenas, the Lubells went to Dean Griswold, "who asked what we intended to do," recounted Jonathan. "We responded that, of course, we weren't going to cooperate because we believed that the committees' activities violated the First Amendment and the academic freedom that should exist at Harvard Law School. Griswold was furious and told us that others at the Law School would be talking to us. At that time, the dean expressed the position that the Fifth Amendment was available only for those who were involved in criminal activities."[41] This was essentially the position of William Marbury, President Conant, and the Sutherland-Chafee statement.

The Lubells then met with Vice Dean Livingston Hall (LL.B. 1927), who offered to enlist "the best lawyer he could find," according to Berman. One candidate was Sutherland, who now served as chairman of a Harvard committee providing legal advice to faculty members involved in congressional investigations.[42] But the Lubells "informed the vice dean that we were planning to speak with somebody at the ACLU to represent us at the hearing. Hall immediately got very upset, stating that we should not get one of those Communist lawyers. It was clear to us that the lawyers favored by the school were not going to help defend our position in any way. In fact, their role seemed to be to get us to give up our rights and change our position."[43] Ultimately, the Lubells accepted the lawyer recommended by the Law School, Lawrence R. Cohen (LL.B. 1933).

In their private meetings, both deans thus told the Lubells "to cooperate with the Committee (which meant confessing the error of their ways and identifying other students who had been in their study group and who had subscribed to the *Worker*); if they did not, they were warned, they would never be allowed to practice law," wrote Monroe H. Freedman (LL.B. 1954), a fellow student of the Lubells.[44] Dean Griswold "was the strongest advocate of their fully cooperating with the Jenner subcommittee," according to the Lubells. He "argued that taking the Fifth Amendment was widely regarded as an admission of criminal guilt and would affect their professional careers."[45] All this was consistent with the position held by Marbury, Conant, Sutherland, and Chafee.

But Griswold also proposed a work-around to the Lubells. Known as the "diminished Fifth" or "calculated contempt," this tactic involved answering all questions about oneself, refusing to answer questions about others, and not pleading the Fifth Amendment. The advantages were seeming to cooperate with the Committee in part, avoiding the social stigma and the danger of perjury from pleading the Fifth Amendment, and appearing highly moral to the public because "the sympathies of the American people do not lie with the informer," as the editors of the *Crimson* pointed out.[46] The disadvantage was that the tactic invited the charge of contempt of Congress for refusing to answer questions without a legal justification. But Griswold viewed a contempt charge as highly unlikely, given public sentiment and the Committees' reluctance to incur public disfavor. Hence, both Griswold and Hall strongly recommended this tactic to the Lubells.[47]

Indeed, the diminished Fifth or calculated contempt became the favored tactic at Harvard and other universities in the coming months. The Chafee-Sutherland statement had emphasized that the tactic was not legally defensible. But Griswold, Hall, Chafee, Mark Howe, and others began to view contempt charges as unfair and unlikely because a witness "should not be worse off for being willing to speak fully and frankly about himself" than a witness who invoked the Fifth Amendment and "would not talk at all," Griswold later wrote.[48]

Cornell University professor Philip Morrison, who was on leave and teaching at the Massachusetts Institute of Technology, successfully employed this tactic in his hearing before SISS in Boston in May 1953. His counsel, Sutherland, advised against it. But the tactic worked, as the Jenner Committee regarded him as a cooperative witness and Cornell decided not to penalize Morrison. Likewise, in January 1954, Harvard physicist Wendell Furry, having previously invoked the Fifth Amendment, adopted the tactic in his hearing before SISS without penalty.[49]

But the Lubells would not compromise. Rightly, they did not see how calculated contempt was legally valid. Nor did they see how they could answer questions about themselves and constitutionally plead the Fifth Amendment in regard to questions about others, given *Rogers v. United States* (1951). This Supreme Court decision held that a witness who testified about one incriminating fact, effectively waived the Fifth Amendment and could not plead the Fifth Amendment regarding related facts. Griswold later criticized *Rogers v. United States* for precisely the reason cited by the Lubells.[50]

Frustrated that the Lubells refused to heed their advice and compromise, Griswold and Hall maintained that the twins "were being selfish," and "going to do great harm to the School," recalled David.[51] Many faculty agreed with Griswold and Hall. "We were all sitting there waiting to be attacked" by the Jenner Committee, remarked Berman.[52]

In the week leading up to the hearing, the deans arranged for the Lubells to meet with three professors: Braucher plus John Maguire (LL.B. 1911) and Edmund Morgan (LL.B. 1905), both of whom had witnessed the First Red Scare. These three expressed fear that the Lubells' "pleading the Fifth" would invite further inquiry and subpoenas directed at the Law School.[53] "The meeting was characterized by an absence of communication," stated Jonathan. "We told the professors that we had no intention of cooperating with the Jenner Committee. When one of the professors evoked the damage that could be suffered by Harvard if we refused to cooperate, we responded that far greater would be the damage to our honor and to what we felt were the principles that the Law School should be upholding."[54]

In that same week, Robert Morris, counsel to the Jenner Committee, proposed a compromise. Morris offered to interview the Lubells in private in

Washington, D.C., and told them that "no one would know that the interview had occurred," recalled Jonathan. "Without any hesitation, both David and I had the same immediate response that 'we would know' and that the offer was unacceptable."[55] So the uncompromising Lubells persisted in their plan to invoke the Fifth Amendment.

Everyone at Harvard was anticipating the Lubells' hearing before the Jenner Committee.[56] In particular, the hearing presented a difficult dilemma to the editorial board of the *Harvard Law School Record*, which was scheduled to announce the election of its new officers—including David as president and Jonathan as associate editor—in the March 26 issue, the very day of the hearing. The editors feared that the *Record*'s reputation with many alumni subscribers would be severely damaged, if the Lubells, incoming officers, pleaded the Fifth. The *Record*'s continued existence might be jeopardized. On March 25, the day before the hearing, the editorial board of the *Record* met and decided, by one vote, to pull the announcement of the Lubells' election from the March 26 issue.[57]

Jenner Committee Hearing

According to the Lubells, the hearing in Boston on March 26–27, 1953, was a travesty for three reasons. First, the Committee never asked about patently illegal activity. There were "no questions of conspiracy to advocate the overthrow of the government by force and violence, no questions of espionage—all of which I was ready [then] and am now ready to answer at any time under oath," Jonathan wrote in his account of the hearing, published in October 1953.[58] Consequently, the Lubells were not afforded the opportunity to deny under oath that they had committed such crimes.

Second, the Committee asked about legal behavior, including questions about their political views and activities, such as "were the Lubells members of the Communist Party, had they organized for the Communist Party at Cornell University or Harvard Law School, had they distributed the *Daily Worker*, had they written briefs for the National Lawyers Guild?" as the *Harvard Crimson* reported. None of this was illegal.[59] Hence, the questioning was designed to insinuate illegal activity without allowing the opportunity to deny it.

It was in response to these questions about legal behavior that the Lubells invoked the First Amendment on the grounds that their political views and activities were protected forms of speech. However, refusing to answer solely on grounds of the First Amendment still left a witness open to a charge of contempt of Congress, according to legal doctrine at the time. Consequently, the Lubells believed that they needed to resort to the Fifth Amendment, and, further, that innocent people could rightfully invoke the Fifth Amendment not only in criminal cases but also in government inquiries. "The Fifth Amendment privilege against self-incrimination . . . in its broad scope which includes answers which might tend to incriminate one of [*sic*] a federal prosecution or which might form a link in a chain which would tend to incrimination—is available to the innocent as well as the guilty," Jonathan stated.[60] This was contrary to the Marbury-Chafee-Sutherland position.

Jonathan argued further that it was not merely a citizen's right, but a duty, to invoke the Fifth Amendment in response to questions about political activities. "Failure to use the privilege would necessitate that one give a public accounting of his political activities and ideas," he maintained. "To give such information is to aid and abet a political trend which has the characteristics of a national inquisition and which is repugnant to the spirit of the First Amendment. The practical effect of such a trend is to make freedom of speech and association subject to the approval or surveillance, at least, of a group with a narrow set of ideas."[61]

Third, the hearing's two-day schedule was designed to shame the Lubells and garner publicity for the Committee. This was the standard approach of SISS and HUAC. A closed, executive session on the first day of the hearing was followed by a public session on the next day. In the closed session, the Committee aimed primarily to determine whether and which questions would prompt the witness to plead the Fifth Amendment. In the public session on the following day, the Committee asked only those questions, intending to showcase the Lubells pleading the Fifth without gaining any new information. And most of those questions addressed a perfectly legal editorial in the *Harvard Law School Record* that attacked congressional investigations into universities and that the Lubells had helped to write.[62] The travesty worked—immediately after the hearing, the Boston newspapers and Samuel Sears demanded that the brothers be expelled.[63]

On Tuesday, March 31, four days after the Lubells' hearing, Dean Griswold distributed a long memo to the faculty arguing against expulsion, and scheduled a special faculty meeting for April 8 to consider the question. In the first week of April, memos flew back and forth among the faculty, who, three months earlier, had castigated President Conant for his unwillingness to "take the offensive" against congressional investigations of Harvard professors and to protect Harvard professors subpoenaed to testify.[64] But now the law faculty split into "an enraged minority . . . that favored ousting the Lubells, and an equally enraged majority that considered Jenner's hearings to be a witch hunt."[65]

Among the memos, that of Barton Leach (LL.B. 1924) was noteworthy for suggesting that the Lubells had refused to answer questions about "the crime of conspiring to overthrow the government of the United States." Leach thus misconstrued their testimony by inferring guilt from their Fifth Amendment plea in response to questions about legal activity. Pleading the Fifth Amendment entailed guilt, Leach argued, and therefore the Lubells had committed criminal behavior and should be expelled. This popular, mistaken reasoning was precisely what the Jenner Committee wanted to evoke.[66]

Griswold's March 31 memo sympathized with Leach's view, in part. Griswold asserted "that the Communist Party today is a criminal conspiracy against the United States" and "that no person can now be a Communist, or could have been a Communist in the recent past, without . . . engaging in unlawful conspiracy against the United States." Consequently, a student's current or recent membership in the Communist Party constituted "serious misconduct" deserving expulsion from the Law School. And "I have that suspicion" that the Lubells have "been guilty of a crime," he added.[67] Griswold here may have contradicted the Internal Security Act of 1950, and Professor Lon Fuller challenged the dean's view in a memo of April 6. Fuller argued that "it would be improper to infer from his membership in the Communist Party that a student was knowingly engaged in such a [criminal] enterprise" of conspiracy. Five of the six teaching fellows in 1952–53 concurred with Fuller in another memo of April 7.[68]

But Griswold's memo also offered a revised and nuanced view of pleading the Fifth Amendment. He asserted that "there is clearly an intermediate ground" or "a middle ground" between, pleading the Fifth when guilty and pleading the Fifth when innocent, which entailed perjury. Instead "a person may properly claim the [Fifth Amendment] privilege, even though he knows he is not guilty of any crime, if the evidence he would give would help to build up the case for a prosecution against him." Chafee and Sutherland had recognized such a middle ground, but viewed it as minuscule, and relied fundamentally on a clear distinction between guilt and innocence. Griswold expanded this "intermediate ground" between pleading when guilty and pleading when innocent, although "this middle ground . . . is not a very large one," he wrote.[69]

In the end Griswold concluded that "no evidence of any sort is available to us that proves or demonstrates that [the Lubells] have been guilty of misconduct. Their refusals to answer questions do not constitute evidence of misconduct." Moreover, the faculty must tolerate behavior by students that is unacceptable for faculty to engage in. Finally, the school is an educational institution, and this experience is educational for the Lubells and other students.[70] On April 8, the faculty followed the dean's recommendation and tabled the motion. But some dissented vigorously and Leach wrote a minority report against the decision, while Griswold wrote the press that the Law School "greatly regrets the course of conduct" followed by the Lubells.[71]

"Serious Consequences"

Pleading the Fifth Amendment had "serious consequences" as Griswold had warned in his memo.[72] After the hearing, law students would not sit next to the Lubells in class or in Harkness Commons. The Law School terminated their financial aid after newspaper stories criticized the brothers' scholarships.[73] Barton Leach wrote a letter to the Lubells' draft board in New York City calling for revocation of their student deferments so that they would be drafted to fight in the Korean War. He then published a copy of his letter in the *Harvard Crimson*. The draft board refused to revoke their deferments, and the Lubells were not drafted until their graduation in 1954. They served honorably until 1956, although the Army threatened Jonathan with a dishonorable discharge for invoking the Fifth Amendment before the Jenner Committee.[74]

Both brothers offered to resign from their yet-to-be-announced editorial positions at the *Harvard Law School Record*. The *Record* depended on its annual contract with the Harvard Law School Association to buy more than 6,000 copies each week for mailing to alumni. Members of the Association had complained about this expenditure in the past, and the *Record* editors feared that the Lubells' involvement might tip the Association against renewing the contract at its upcoming annual meeting in May. Following a close vote after more than three hours of heated debate, the editorial board decided to accept the Lubells' resignations. The board then turned down a proposal that the Lubells also be dropped from the *Record* staff, but they resigned anyway under "considerable pressure."[75] Relieved, the *Record* editors explained that this outcome assuaged any "lurking suspicion that our news is colored or . . . not the expression of attitudes we believe proper for a democracy. . . . We believe that one has a duty to testify fully and truthfully when subpoenaed to do so." Even so, the editors said that they did not approve "of all the investigative techniques used by the [congressional] Committees."[76]

Later in April, the Legal Aid Bureau considered what to do about Jonathan, who was elected a member in the summer of 1952 after his first year, and David, who qualified for membership in the summer of 1953. At that time, the three honor societies customarily selected members in this way: the *Harvard Law Review* admitted the twenty-five students with the highest grades at the end of their first year, then the Board of Student Advisors invited the next ten students, and the Legal Aid Bureau inducted the next twenty-five to thirty-five students.[77] According to some members of the Legal Aid Bureau, Boston attorneys threatened to end their cooperation with the Bureau if the Lubells were members, and Dean Griswold said that he could not ensure its continued existence if that happened. The situation was analogous to that faced by the *Record,* and the result was the same. Due to this "outside pressure," Jonathan resigned from the Bureau in May, and David was not admitted to membership.[78]

All this preceded the major controversy. In the summer of 1952, the *Harvard Law Review* had admitted twenty-five new editors from the class of 1954 based on their grades at the end of their first year, including several who went on to became eminent law professors: Andrew Kaufman, Phillip Areeda, Derek Bok, John Kaplan, and John T. Noonan. During the summer of 1953, seven or eight additional students in that class were to be added to the board of editors based on their overall grades at the end of the second year. Routinely, the school registrar sent the president of the *Review* a list of students with high grades in June. Then the president identified the top seven or eight and wrote letters to the new members informing them of their membership.[79]

But the summer of 1953 was not routine. On the one hand, during the 1952–53 academic year "there was a near revolt" among the second-year editors, according to the incoming president of the *Review,* Andrew Kaufman. "Many felt that the third-year editors had behaved in a very officious, hierarchical, high-handed way toward us," recalled Kaufman, and "as a group we decided that we didn't want the class behind us to feel the same way about us." So the second-year editors agreed to act more collegially. On the other hand, there arose the controversy surrounding the Lubells. Everyone knew that they were excellent students and might qualify for the *Review.* Anticipating this, the *Review* editors had held an advance straw vote after the Jenner Committee hearing in March 1953 on whether to admit the Lubells, and the result was sixteen in favor and eight against. President Kaufman voted with the majority.[80]

When the registrar sent the grade list to Kaufman in June, it was apparent "that Jonathan was in the group that qualified and David was not." Given all that had transpired concerning the Lubells and within the *Review* board in the prior months, Kaufman consulted the Constitution of the *Review*, which clearly stated, "Members shall be elected by the acting members of the Law Review." So Kaufman decided that the president should not make the decision unilaterally and that the board of editors should hold an election. He therefore asked all the editors to return to campus early in September in order to vote on Jonathan's membership.

Over the summer, Kaufman also consulted a few faculty who taught Constitutional Law, as well as the trustees of the *Review*, who included the dean. No one provided direct guidance or advice, because the *Review* was an independent corporation governed by the student editors, not by the Law School. Griswold, in particular, refused to give direction, though he did show Kaufman the confidential memo that he had written to the faculty. But the memo was equivocal on this point, recommending against expulsion from the school but stating that pleading the Fifth could have "serious consequences."[81]

Meanwhile, several *Review* editors said that they could not vote on membership without first hearing from Jonathan Lubell. Kaufman and a few others were delegated to meet Jonathan in New York City and put questions to him about his political views, his activities, and his reasons for pleading the Fifth Amendment. Kaufman opposed the "inquisitional" meeting. "I thought we could write him a letter and ask him to say what he wanted to say to us." Furthermore, Kaufman felt that some of the questions were "quite offensive" in asking about Jonathan's personal beliefs.[82] However, having required all the editors to return to campus early to hold an unprecedented election, Kaufman felt that he could not refuse to accommodate the editors' request that he meet with Jonathan.

As Kaufman feared, the "inquisition" in New York City—on the heels of all the negative publicity and reactions in the spring—went badly. Jonathan would not respond to questions that he felt were inappropriate. Regarding other questions, "despite the fact that I was very anxious to be on the *Review*, I didn't pretty it up," he said. At the end of the difficult meeting, the *Review* delegation asked Jonathan to write a letter so that they would have his views accurately. The resulting letter was abrasive and argumentative, similar to a letter that he later wrote to the editors of the *Harvard Crimson*.[83] Jonathan maintained that he should not have to answer questions that had never been asked of other prospective editors and that had no bearing on the customary standards for membership, which he had met. He therefore felt justified in refusing to answer. But the result was that the editors, like the Jenner Committee, regarded him as uncooperative.

Returning early to Cambridge in September, the *Review* editors held a long meeting to discuss their views before the fateful vote. Some argued that membership should be based purely on grades, and others that minimal standards of ethical character and behavior were always implicitly required. Even if so, still others maintained that Jonathan had done nothing unethical. Free-speech arguments were made on both sides. Pleading the Fifth Amendment raised thorny issues, including whether that should determine membership in a student or professional organization. In any case, there was no precedent or advance notice about its application to membership in the *Review*. When trying to justify their votes, a few editors simply seemed "confused" to Kaufman. Both Lubell brothers later maintained that the primary motivation behind negative votes was the editors' concern about jeopardizing their careers. Some editors voting for Jonathan had the same impression, as did some faculty, according to Berman.[84]

In the end, "the attitude that [Jonathan] took changed us," according to Kaufman. "People said, 'Well, you have the right to plead the Fifth Amendment, but we have the right to ask you these questions. We have the right to ask you what you did. And if you don't want to tell us, that's fine, but . . .'"[85] The vote in mid-September 1951 on whether to admit Jonathan Lubell reversed the spring poll: eight in favor and sixteen against. No record of the voting exists, and some participants have said that they forgot how they voted. President Kaufman later went on record publicly that he voted against.

In response to the editors' vote, Kaufman found that several faculty who had been noncommittal two months earlier now explicitly disagreed with the decision, including Griswold. Berman stated, "The faculty thought it was disgraceful not to take the young man on the *Law Review*."[86] On the other hand, editorials and letters supporting the editors' vote appeared in the *Harvard Crimson*, some from former *Law Review* editors.[87]

Barton Leach persisted doggedly. He wrote to the New York State Bar Examiners urging that the Lubells be denied admission to the bar for lack of the necessary character and fitness. After passing the exam in 1954, the brothers were forced to delay their application to the bar, and they ghosted work for other lawyers, acting like blacklisted Hollywood screenwriters. In 1958 the

New York State Bar finally admitted the Lubells with the support of deans Griswold and Hall.[88]

Over time, many at Harvard came to regret how the Lubells had been treated. In 1969 the Legal Aid Bureau recanted its effective ouster of Jonathan Lubell, while the *Law Review* refused to do so at that time.[89] But in February 1978, after considerable debate, the *Review* published this statement: "We the editors of Volume 91 of the *Harvard Law Review* deeply regret the injustice Mr. Lubell suffered at that time. Painfully aware that this wrong cannot be fully remedied, we nonetheless have resolved to accord Mr. Lubell the status of affiliate membership in the Harvard Law Review Association."[90] In 1978, Kaufman, Areeda, and Bok refused to comment to the *Harvard Crimson* on this matter.

Eventually David became a successful entertainment and media lawyer in New York; he died in 2012. Jonathan became a renowned libel lawyer and argued successfully before the U.S. Supreme Court. He passed away in 2016.[91] In 2006 and again in 2009, the brothers agreed to be interviewed for this book. Upon receiving the list of questions in anticipation of the interview, the Lubells did not respond to further inquiries.

"The Fifth Amendment: An Old and Good Friend"

In February 1954, about five months after the *Review* editors voted not to admit Jonathan Lubell, Dean Griswold gave a famous speech to the Massachusetts Bar Association defending the Constitutional right of innocent people to plead the Fifth Amendment and explaining its legal justification. Broadcast and rebroadcast over New England radio stations and published in the *American Bar Association Journal*, "The Fifth Amendment: An Old and Good Friend" was the first public defense of this position by a leading legal scholar.[92] After receiving a standing ovation from the Massachusetts Bar Association, Griswold expanded his view in several public forums, including the television show *See It Now*, hosted by Edward R. Murrow. The dean criticized the "corruptive investigating practices of headline-seeking congressional committees," which have "too often paid little attention to the Constitutional rights of the individuals."[93]

At the end of the year, Harvard University Press collected several of these speeches in a small book, *The Fifth Amendment Today*. The Fund for the Republic, a liberal foundation spun off from the Ford Foundation, paid to have some 35,000 free copies distributed throughout the country to libraries, judges, legislators, government officials, and other prominent individuals.[94] Many critics assailed Griswold. One wrote to him, "You are a dirty Fabian and the lowest form of humanity . . . to try and smear McCarthy who is protecting you and your job from World Marxism."[95] But hundreds voiced enthusiastic support. Yale Law professor John P. Frank wrote to Griswold, "Your statement on the Fifth Amendment is the best thing that has been done on this subject by anybody." Soon Griswold's reinterpretation became renowned and authoritative. The book has been cited by U.S. Supreme Court Justices, including Felix Frankfurter in 1956 and Ruth Bader Ginsburg in 1998.[96]

Building directly upon his March 31 memo to the Harvard Law School faculty, Griswold argued that pleading the Fifth Amendment was legally available to innocent witnesses. The Chafee-Sutherland statement had minimized the situation "where disclosure . . . may have a tendency to incriminate." Instead Griswold expanded this "intermediate ground" between guilt and innocence, where an innocent person might conclude that admissions of innocent conduct could provide the premises of inferences about criminal conduct, leading to possible prosecution and even conviction. In this situation, particularly if one were uncertain or fearful about those inferences, an innocent person would be justified in pleading the Fifth Amendment, maintained Griswold. Furthermore, admitting to facts that *appear* to incriminate one, even if one is not guilty of a crime, "at the very least . . . shift[s] the burden of proof to [the witness] so that he will have to prove his own innocence."[97] Thus, pleading the Fifth could imply something other than either guilt or perjury.

To demonstrate the point, Griswold put two cases in his first lecture: one of a college professor who innocently joined the Communist Party when it was perfectly legal and never committed any illegal acts; the other of a benefactor who innocently gave money to an organization found to be guilty of Communist conspiracy. "In both of the cases . . . , the privilege [of pleading the Fifth Amendment] may be claimed although the individual was guilty of no crime. In each case, the inference [of guilt] which would be taken from the claim of the privilege would in fact be unwarranted." In particular, "a witness lost in fear and confusion might turn to the privilege as a means of sanctuary from a situation which he feels himself incompetent to handle."[98]

Griswold subsequently added considerations expanding the middle ground, such as "the nature of the question." "The closer the question . . . gets to the area of opinion and political belief," the more the witness is justified in invoking Constitutional protection, stated Griswold, while referencing the First

Amendment right to free speech. Another consideration is "the nature of the tribunal." In legislative investigations, "nearly every safeguard which has been developed over the centuries by our courts is thrown out the window," and political motives, costs, and benefits are likely to influence the interrogation. Hence, witnesses should have no fewer protections than in judicial proceedings.[99] In this way, Griswold rebutted the "rigid and mechanical" interpretation that offered "only two" conclusions from invoking the Fifth Amendment: that one is either guilty or committing perjury.[100]

How did Griswold come to his widely applauded breakthrough? In 1979 Griswold explained that his reinterpretation was spontaneously self-generated. "When McCarthy became worse and worse, I looked for law professors all over the country to do something about it. To oppose him in some way. None of them did," he stated. "And one day . . . I decided that I would make a speech against McCarthy."[101] His 1992 autobiography repeated this point and recounted his personal breakthrough, after describing the Lubells' controversy and inserting a section break.[102] Griswold's explanation has predominated.[103]

The Lubells' Legacy

Only a few observers have noted that Griswold changed his position in the middle of the controversy over the Lubells. None have asked why he changed. Ironically, some have even suggested that the Lubells "echo[ed] Griswold's view."[104] The opposite is nearer the truth.

A catalyst for Griswold's revision has been suggested by Ellen Schrecker, the leading historian on the subject of McCarthyism and American universities. Schrecker attributed Griswold's shift away from the Chafee-Sutherland position to his encounter with the case of the Harvard physicist Wendell Furry. In the spring of 1953, amid the controversy over the Lubells, Griswold served on a Harvard ad hoc committee advising the Corporation about Furry, who appeared before HUAC in February and April 1953 and before SISS in November 1953 and January 1954. Griswold had "originally come onto the faculty advisory committee as a firm supporter of the Chafee-Sutherland position," wrote Schrecker, but "within a few months he had changed his mind, and was soon to write perhaps the most effective and authoritative defense of the Fifth Amendment."[105]

Schrecker apparently learned of Furry's putative influence in an interview with Griswold in December 1977, though Griswold made no mention of such influence in any published account. But a neglected fact supports Schrecker's account. In his February 1954 speech to the Massachusetts Bar Association, Griswold proposed a hypothetical that demonstrated the need for his revised view of the Fifth Amendment. That hypothetical closely resembled Furry's case: an innocent college professor who joined the Communist Party when it was legal and did not engage in illegal conspiracy.[106]

More startling than Griswold's omission of Furry in explaining the origin of his view is that, in 1953, 1954, 1955, 1977, 1979 and 1992, he never identified the Lubells' controversy as influencing his analysis.[107] Yet if Furry's case informed Griswold, then the Lubells' case must certainly have done so more profoundly. Unlike the Lubells, the physicist made no technical legal arguments justifying his right to plead the Fifth. Also, Furry's case was of marginal concern to the dean of Harvard Law School, compared to the public furor over his own two students. Samuel Sears and Barton Leach did not complain about Wendell Furry! Finally, the timing of Griswold's March 31 memo indicates that he began to revise his view of the Fifth Amendment shortly after meeting with the Lubells in the third week of March 1953.[108] Indeed, it appears nearly inconceivable that the Lubells did not shape Griswold's thinking. They certainly thought they did.

Certain jurisprudential points reveal the Lubells' influence. Most significantly, the brothers maintained that, when they met with the dean prior to their hearing before the Jenner Committee, Griswold had voiced the Chafee-Sutherland position that only the guilty could justifiably plead the Fifth Amendment. This is consistent with Griswold's and Schrecker's published accounts. Subsequently, "changing his position, the dean wrote that the Fifth Amendment was available to the innocent," stated Jonathan Lubell. "This was the position we had taken with Griswold when we first met with him."[109]

In addition, the Lubells proposed the fundamental reason that the Fifth Amendment was available to the innocent: the distinction between guilt and innocence is obscure in many instances. As the Lubells stated publicly on April 8 in the *Harvard Crimson*, the Fifth Amendment "may be claimed not only where it would, but also where it might, not only incriminate, but tend to incriminate one, not only of a conviction but of a prosecution."[110] Here the Lubells staked out the expansive "intermediate" or "middle" ground that Griswold began to acknowledge in his March 31 memo after meeting with the Lubells. Likewise, in October 1953 the *Harvard Crimson* published Jonathan's explanation that questions about innocent conduct could elicit "answers which might tend to incriminate one of [*sic*] a federal prosecution or which might tend to form a link in a chain which would tend to incrimination."[111] Four months later, in February 1954, Griswold expressed this view publicly for the first time.

Also, the Lubells argued, "the existing state of the law" expanded the middle ground in regard to any "question the answer to which . . . would constitute a waiver of the Fifth Amendment privilege in regard to other questions at the same hearing."[112] Answering one question would require a witness to answer all questions about related activities, according to *Rogers v. United States* (1951). In the dean's office before their hearing in March 1953, the Lubells raised this point, which Griswold echoed in February 1954 while criticizing the *Rogers* decision.[113]

Further, the Lubells argued to Griswold that the "middle ground" is expanded by the confusion arising from ambiguity in questioning. For example, the brothers told Griswold that they were uncertain how to respond to questions about whether they held Communist Party "meetings" in their rooms or did any "organizing" for the Party. Although they hosted no official meetings, Communists did gather in their rooms and discuss politics. Did such a "gathering" constitute a "meeting?" To answer "yes" was to waive the right to plead the Fifth subsequently on this subject and also to forge a link in a chain of incrimination. To say "no" exposed them to prosecution for perjury if federal prosecutors deemed a "gathering" to be a "meeting." The same ambiguity and uncertainty surrounded "organizing." Hence, they had to plead the Fifth Amendment in regard to all such questions.[114] In February 1954 Griswold likewise observed that "fear and confusion" about the interpretation and implications of questions and answers could justify invoking the Fifth Amendment.[115]

Additionally, in a letter to the *Crimson* in October 1953, Jonathan explained that the brothers responded to Jenner's questions about political views and legal activities by invoking the First Amendment on the ground that their political activities were constitutionally protected forms of speech. This is precisely what Griswold said in his speech a year later in October 1954.[116] Finally, the Lubells, in their meeting with the dean in March 1953, rejected the tactic of "calculated contempt" or "diminished Fifth" that the dean urged upon them as the prudent course. In his speech in February 1954, Griswold subordinated that tactic, which he had recommended to the Lubells a year earlier.[117]

Why would Griswold not credit the Lubells with influencing his reinterpretation? Omitting them in his statements of 1953, 1954, and 1955 makes perfect sense. At that time, associating the brothers, or Furry, with his revised view would certainly have discredited it. Also, Griswold considered the Lubells dangerous at that point. The "intermediate ground" should not shelter Communists, as he wrote in his March 31 memo. In the summer of 1953 Griswold confided privately in his office to one participant in the controversy, "If we ever get into a war with Russia and Russian ships show up in Boston Harbor, I think Jonathan and David Lubell will be down on the docks to greet them."[118]

But why not mention the Lubells in 1977, 1979, and 1992, well after the controversy? Indeed, Schrecker's interview in December 1977 took place at the very same time that the *Harvard Law Review* was considering reinstating Jonathan, and Griswold's published statement appeared in 1979 occurred shortly after the reinstatement in 1978.[119] Even though Griswold had left the Law School in 1967, he kept in close contact with the *Law Review* and must have known of its deliberations and apology.

Griswold certainly harbored some lasting resentment against the Lubells. According to Jonathan, the dean was "furious" in March 1953 when they told him that they would plead the Fifth Amendment.[120] Remarkably, Griswold's annual reports and the *Harvard Law School Bulletin* never mentioned the Lubells or the Jenner hearings. The incident was a forbidden topic. In 1992 Griswold still held the Lubells at arm's length. His autobiography introduced them not as Harvard Law School students but as "two members of the National Lawyers Guild." Their status as students must be inferred from the text and would not be immediately evident to an uninformed reader.[121]

The reason for Griswold's animus persisting through 1992 was surely his belief that the Lubells had brought disrepute on Harvard Law School and thereby betrayed and injured the school. Indeed, he told them this, as did other faculty.[122] His March 31 memo stated that allowing the Lubells to remain might have "serious consequences" for the Law School. "I regret that exceedingly . . . because, I believe, confidence in the School . . . has been at a high level. We have received extensive support from the alumni which has been important to the School's development." But his regret was also personal: "I have devoted a large part of my life to this School" and "tried . . . to merit the confidence of the faculty, students, and alumni of the school.[123]

Confirming Griswold's fears, newspapers decried the decision against expulsion, with headlines announcing "Harvard Won't Oust Lubells" and "Harvard Refuses to Expel Lubells."[124] This negative publicity damaged the school beloved by the dean and undermined his efforts to rebuild it, he believed. The Law School was therefore paying a price for the Lubells' unnecessary and indulgent dalliance with "dangerous" ideas, and bringing disrepute on Harvard Law School was a cardinal sin in Griswold's view. He must have held this belief even more strongly amid the challenges faced by the school in the late 1940s and early 1950s.

In telling words, Griswold in 1992 described the *Harvard Law Review*'s statement of 1978 as "a kind and generous act."[125] But these words subtly shifted the meaning of the statement exonerating the Lubells. The *Review* had expressed "regret" and tried to "remedy" the "wrong" and "injustice" done to Jonathan Lubell. In Griswold's construction, the *Review* had, essentially, pardoned Jonathan through "a kind and generous act." Further, Griswold discounted the *Review*'s forgiveness as made "with minimal responsibility and without full awareness of the depth of feelings" at the time.[126] In Griswold's view, the Lubells could, at best, be pardoned, but they could never be accorded any credit for doing the right thing or, even more, for contributing to revising and informing his own interpretation of the Fifth Amendment.[127] But that is surely what happened.

A "Black Man of Considerable Ability"

Dean Griswold had more sympathy for other students snared in McCarthyism. One was his classmate Benjamin Jefferson Davis (LL.B. 1928), a contemporary of Charles Houston (LL.B. 1922, S.J.D. 1923) and William Hastie (LL.B. 1930), as described in Chapter 4. Davis had joined the Communist Party of the United States (CPUSA) during the 1930s because "the Communists . . . provided a rational, effective, and principled path of activity and struggle through which the hideous Jim Crow system could be abolished forever in the U.S."[128]

In 1948, after losing an election for a third term representing Harlem on the New York City Council, Davis was indicted with eleven other leaders of the CPUSA under the Alien Registration Act (Smith) Act of 1940, at the behest of FBI director J. Edgar Hoover. The ensuing federal trial began in November 1948 and lasted nearly a year, longer than any federal trial up to that point in history. All twelve defendants were found guilty, and Davis was sentenced to five years in a federal penitentiary. He was released after three years and four months, and the U.S. Supreme Court overturned the convictions in 1957.[129]

Subsequently Davis toured the country speaking about civil rights at colleges and universities, including at the Harvard Law School Forum in March 1962. "There was a considerable amount of complaint about this," Griswold later recalled, "but I saw no reason to interfere, and I attended the

Benjamin Jefferson Davis Jr., LL.B. 1928. Testifying before the House Committee on UnAmerican Activities in February 1948.

Francis Miller / Life Magazine / Getty Images.

program." In fact, the *Harvard Law Record* announced Davis's appearance under the headline "Communist Official Invited" and reported that "appearing with him will be his classmate, Dean Erwin N. Griswold, and Professor Mark DeWolfe Howe."[130]

In his address entitled "The Communist Party and Constitutional Guarantees," Davis said, in part:

> The process through which I became a Communist was "Made in the USA," not in Moscow nor in any foreign country. Socialism and Communism cannot be exported; they grow out of the conditions native to capitalist countries. And

we Communists are ready to join with non-Communists and even anti-Communists in eliminating the very oppressive conditions under capitalism that result in people becoming Communists. Yet, with it all, I am proud to be an American, proud to be a Negro, and proud to be a Communist! And there is no contradiction between the three. I am proud to be an American because I have an abiding confidence in the creative capacity of the American people to set our country right in all respects and keep it so, and to move it to higher levels of happiness and peace.[131]

In unusually sympathetic terms, Griswold later observed that Davis "spoke very well and frankly, and quite impressively." He recalled that Davis "was a black man of considerable ability," who, "largely impelled by the discrimination to which he was subjected, . . . became a Communist."[132] Soon after appearing at the Forum in 1962, Davis was charged with violating the Internal Security (McCarran) Act, but he died in 1964 at age sixty-one before the case went to trial.

Marcia Harrison: "A Good American"

Another graduate of Harvard Law School who paid a heavy price for not fitting the social norms of the time was Marcia R. Harrison (LL.B. 1955), a single woman, much older than most other students, and reportedly somewhat eccentric. Even while she tried to conform, her personal characteristics prompted scrutiny and resistance during the McCarthy era. For twenty years Harrison endured successive federal investigations that reexamined the same evidence, including reports of her "strange" behavior given by confidential informants to the FBI. Her story has not been told.[133]

Born in 1918, Harrison was an only child who had few playmates and immersed herself in books. Enrolling in Vassar College at age sixteen, she studied economics and found companions in "the intellectual and . . . left-wing groups, which did not require social graces . . . for acceptance," according to her professors. These included the socialist American Student Union (ASU) and the Young Communist League (YCL).[134]

After graduating from Vassar in 1938, Harrison moved to Washington, D.C., hoping to pursue a career in government, and in 1939 became a cataloguer in the Library of Congress. She also attended lectures sponsored by the Washington Bookshop Association (WBA), a left-wing bookstore that offered literary and music classes and shared mailing lists with Communist-front organizations. Harrison also belonged to the Library of Congress Local of the United Federal Workers of America (UFWA). Considered by some federal investigators to be a Communist organization, the UFWA advocated federal employee rights and African American civil rights. Harrison belonged for two years and became the corresponding secretary of the local chapter.[135]

In 1941 Harrison was hired as an economist by the Office of Price Administration (OPA), which had responsibility for stabilizing prices during the war. At this point, twenty-three years old, she ended her memberships in all groups affiliated with Communism or Socialism. At the very same time the FBI began investigating her and interviewing her co-workers, neighbors, and former roommates. Some of these said that Harrison had "strange, foreign-looking friends" and held "radical" views "entirely different from those of the average American" regarding World War II and the rights of Germans.[136] In 1942 Harrison learned of the FBI investigation and gave a sworn statement to an FBI agent that she had been a member of the ASU, YCL, and WBA, but no longer belonged to these groups. In November 1942 the OPA personnel director notified Harrison that the investigation had found no subversive activity on her part and was now closed.[137]

In 1944 Harrison moved to the Foreign Economic Administration (FEA), where she analyzed and coordinated postwar economic programs in Europe. The FEA opened another investigation into Harrison and proposed to deny her security clearance. Her acquaintances and co-workers stated that she had "strange ways," could not "get along with everybody," and "was not popular among the other women," but she was cleared to work.[138] Two years later the State Department hired her to work as an economist within the Office of International Trade Policy. Prompted by the earlier investigations, the newly established security office in the State Department began another investigation into Harrison, labeling her a "definite security risk" and questioning her loyalty to the United States. But the inquiry concluded that she could not be discharged.[139]

In 1948, after President Truman issued an executive order establishing "loyalty security boards" within each executive department, the State Department's board reopened her case. J. Edgar Hoover himself arranged to send this board the FBI file on Harrison, which described the same activities that she had listed in her sworn statement of 1942. But the file also included the report of a confidential informant who claimed that in 1939 Harrison had been "one of the most active members of the Library of Congress Unit of the Communist Party . . . , associating with known members of the Washington underground Communist apparatus." For evidence, this inflammatory report merely cited Harrison's admitted affiliation with UFWA and WBA. In December 1948 the State Department's loyalty security board cleared Harrison for the fourth time.[140]

Then, early in 1950, Senator McCarthy began making speeches claiming to have a list of Communists working in the State Department. Feeling the heat of public scrutiny, the State Department loyalty security board reopened the case against Harrison yet again in October 1950, because she was a likely candidate for McCarthy's list along with other State Department employees who had already been investigated. The board set a hearing date for her case, but would not reveal the identity of the FBI's inflammatory informant. Then, in 1951, President Truman issued another executive order authorizing the loyalty security boards to dismiss federal employees if there was a reasonable doubt as to their loyalty not only in the present but at any time in the past.[141]

At the hearing, Harrison vigorously defended herself, arguing that the charges were wrong, irrelevant, or outdated. Nevertheless, in April 1951 the loyalty security board suspended her from the State Department. Harrison immediately appealed. In the ensuing months, the FBI finally revealed to her lawyer that the Bureau's chief confidential informant on Harrison had also belonged to the UFWA at the same time and was described in the file as a "neurotic, imaginative, middle-aged woman with an abnormal dependence on her mother."[142] The lawyer pleaded with Hoover to check the informant's credibility, and wrote to Harrison's senator for help.[143]

In August 1951 Harrison's case became national news when McCarthy included her on his infamous list of twenty-six State Department employees who, he said, had been officially charged with Communist activities based on FBI investigations. Harrison responded that McCarthy had "attacked a minnow with a blunderbuss," exaggerating both her importance and the nature of her activities.[144] "I am a good American and not a security risk in any way," she told the *New York Times*.[145] In the affidavit supporting her appeal, she stated that her membership in Communist-affiliated organizations during and right after college resulted from "misinformation, ignorance, and naiveté" with no disloyal activity or intent. Harrison also suggested that judgments about her personality fostered the suspicions about her political activity.[146]

Harrison at Harvard Law School

After initiating her appeal to the loyalty security board in April 1951, Harrison decided to go to law school, hoping that "somewhere, some people still cared whether or not the American system of law and government also produced a just result." Harvard's application did not ask the reasons for leaving prior employments, so she did not recount the investigations into her alleged Communist activities.[147] But after she was admitted and enrolled, Harrison told Admissions Director Louis Toepfer (LL.B. 1947) about her suspension from the State Department, fearing that McCarthy would track the twenty-six people on his list and create problems for her at Harvard. Toepfer told her that the Law School only cared whether she "could do the work," but also reported her disclosure to Griswold's new Administrative Board, which decided to take no action.[148]

Matriculating in September 1952, Harrison was an unusual student at Harvard Law School: thirty-four years old, one of thirteen women among the 520 students in the class of 1955, and publicly defamed by Joseph McCarthy after being suspended from the State Department by its loyalty security board. As she began her studies, the congressional investigative hearings and the governmental security hearings were multiplying, Benjamin Davis was serving time in a federal penitentiary, and Jonathan and David Lubell were starting their second year at the school. At the end of that fall semester, the State Department loyalty security board denied the appeal of her suspension, but noted that she could apply to the Civil Service Commission for security clearances in other agencies. Deeply disappointed, Harrison was advised by her lawyer that such an application would merely reopen old "wounds."[149]

This outcome and her anxiety did not help Harrison socially at the Law School, where most students considered her "an eccentric," according to one of her male classmates. "She came to the Law School with . . . a little bit of mystery . . . that maybe she had suffered for her political views before coming to law school. She was always accompanied by a dog, which she brought to class with her. . . . That poor little dog did not lead a good life. Imagine spending all that time in class . . . to sit through all that stuff and not earn a degree! Every now and then, as dogs do, it would stand up and would shake itself, and then various hoots and . . . whistles would go off."[150]

Marcia R. Harrison, LL.B. 1955. Application photo submitted to Harvard Law
School, ca. 1952.

Courtesy of Harvard Law School Library, Historical & Special Collections.

In the fall of 1952 Dean Griswold met Harrison at the dinner that he
and Harriet hosted each fall for all of the entering female students. Due to
her suspension from the State Department, the dean observed her "quite
carefully throughout her Law School career," along with the Lubells. He
noted that she isolated herself and did not eat meals in the law student
dining area. Though not married, she joined the Harvard University Wives
and the Harvard Law Wives associations, apparently seeking companion-
ship. Even though considered eccentric by some, she nevertheless "grew
steadily in the esteem and respect of both students and faculty," Griswold
said. By the end of her three years, Harrison had developed strong bonds
with some members of the faculty and graduated in the top quarter of her
class.[151]

One of her mentors was Arthur Sutherland, who hired her as a typist for the Committee on the Public Record on Communism in the United States, which examined the damaging effects of McCarthyism. In the fall of 1953, while controversy enveloped Jonathan Lubell and the *Harvard Law Review,* Harrison enrolled in Sutherland's Constitutional Law class. In her senior year she took his Commercial Law seminar, taught jointly with Professor Braucher. Sutherland called Harrison's work in his classes "above average and credible in every way," noting that she "spoke logically and reasonably in class."[152] Both Sutherland and Braucher, along with Griswold, helped her in analyzing the loyalty security board decision, gaining admission to the New York Bar, and obtaining employment at the Metropolitan Life Insurance Company after she graduated in June 1956.[153]

In December 1956, still hoping to pursue a career in Washington, Harrison applied for a job in the Anti-Trust Division of the Justice Department, and asked the Civil Service Commission to determine whether she was eligible for employment by a federal agency other than the State Department. Griswold, Sutherland, and Braucher provided supporting testimony for her applications, and in late 1957 the Commission ruled that a federal agency could employ Harrison if the agency found that Harrison's employment was "clearly consistent with the interests of national security."[154] This equivocal decision struck Braucher, Sutherland, and Griswold as "extraordinarily confusing," even meaningless, because a prospective agency would have to duplicate the Commission's investigation into whether Harrison was a national security risk.[155] When would the cycle of investigations end?

Griswold and Sutherland also helped her get a job at the Metropolitan Life Insurance Company, and for the next five years Harrison continued trying to find a position in the federal government. At one point the Securities and Exchange Commission (SEC) agreed to hire her; but the State Department's security board intervened, fearing that hiring Harrison would imply that the board had erred in 1951. The SEC reversed itself to avoid embarrassing the State Department. Finally, in 1962 Harrison secured a position as an economist in the Department of Interior, and in 1968 moved to the Department of Health and Human Services, where she worked until 1983 when she was discharged for unacceptable performance. Between 1984 and 1987 Harrison, then in her late sixties, unsuccessfully sued the department for age discrimination.[156]

Ruined Lives

During the Red Scare of the late 1940s and early 1950s, repressive legislation and the "corruptive investigating practices of headline-seeking congressional committees" damaged the careers and lives of many in higher education, as Dean Griswold told Edward Murrow's television audience.[157] Among those associated with Harvard Law School, the civil rights activist Benjamin Davis was driven into the Communist Party by "the savage white supremacy assaults . . . against all Negroes."[158] For his membership, Davis went to federal prison during the 1950s.

Meanwhile, Marcia Harrison followed the path of cooperation and acquiescence recommended by Griswold, Sutherland, and Braucher. She admitted Communist associations in her youth, avoided them subsequently, and cooperated fully with federal investigators. Sympathetic to her plight, Griswold, Sutherland, and Braucher assisted her over the course of a decade. But Harrison spent at least twenty years, from 1942 to 1962, in a Kafkaesque quagmire, and never really cleared herself from the stain of the political "misinformation, ignorance, and naiveté" between ages 16 and 21.[159] Hence, Harrison's life and career, like Davis's, were severely damaged by the taint of McCarthyism and ensuing investigations.

In contrast, Jonathan and David Lubell rejected the course of compliance recommended to them by Griswold, Hall, Sutherland, and Braucher, who clearly favored the cooperative Harrison. Although the brothers paid a dear price within Harvard Law School and initially in their careers, the twins ultimately found a route to rewarding work in private law firms. This route was virtually closed to women and people of color in the 1950s, when Davis was imprisoned and Harrison kept applying to the federal bureaucracy, which mired her in a series of face-saving, redundant investigations.

But the Lubells also paid a high price. They were never credited with any contribution to the enduring jurisprudential advances that resulted from the events of this tormented period, including their own ordeals. They initiated the argument that the "Old and Good Friend" of the Fifth Amendment is legally available to the innocent, uncertain, and fearful as well as to the guilty. None of their teachers affirmed these groundbreaking ideas before the twins began to do so in March 1953. In fact, every professor with whom they spoke at the time stridently objected to their position. How ironic that their argument would ultimately prevail, unattributed, through the writings of Dean Erwin Griswold himself.

NOTES

1. Erwin N. Griswold, *Ould Fields, New Corne: The Personal Memoirs of a Twentieth Century Lawyer* (St. Paul, MN, 1992), 192. See Athan G. Theoharis, ed., *Beyond the Hiss Case: The FBI, Congress and the Cold War* (Philadelphia, 1982); Ellen W. Schrecker, *No Ivory Tower: McCarthyism and the Universities* (New York, 1986); Jay S. Dushoff, "Spotlight on the Communist Problem," *HLSR* (December 15, 1955): 3. This chapter draws upon the research assistance of Sarah M. Iler concerning McCarthyism. See Sarah M. Iler, "The History of 'Multicultural' in the United States during the Twentieth Century" (Ph.D. diss., Ohio State University, 2017).

2. Zechariah Chafee Jr., Erwin N. Griswold, Milton Katz, and Austin W. Scott, "The Loyalty Order: Procedure Termed Inadequate and Defects Pointed Out," *New York Times* (April 13, 1947); Peter L. Steinberg, *The Great "Red Menace": United States Prosecution of American Communists, 1947–1952* (Westport, CT, 1984), 23–26.

3. "Seavey Asks for Capable Leaders to Save Democratic Way of Life," *HLSR* (July 2, 1947):1, 3.

4. "Forum Turns Away Crowd, Niebuhr Finds Similarity in Communism, Christianity," *HLSR* (November 18, 1947): 1.

5. Harvard Law School (HLS) Faculty Meeting Minutes (February 10, 1948; January 11, 1949); Harold J. Berman, Oral History, conducted by Daniel Hamilton and Daniel R. Coquillette (August 1998), on file with the authors.

6. Ernest J. Brown, Oral History, conducted by Daniel Hamilton (August 1997), on file with the authors.

7. Arthur von Mehren, Oral History, conducted by Daniel R. Coquillette and Mary Beth Basile (July–December 2000), on file with the authors.

8. Detlev Vagts, Oral History, conducted by Daniel Hamilton, Daniel R. Coquillette, and John Delionado (November 1999–February 2000), on file with the authors.

9. "Editorial Board," *HLR* 41 (1927): 377; Griswold, *Ould Fields,* 189–190. See *In re Alger Hiss,* 368 Massachusetts 447 (1975); Daniel R. Coquillette, *Real Ethics for Real Lawyers,* 3rd ed. (Durham, NC, 2016), 436, 450–453.

10. "Dupes and Fellow Travelers Dress Up Communist Fronts," *Life Magazine* (April 14, 1949), 42–43.

11. "Laski to Speak on Labor in Politics," *Harvard Crimson* (April 26, 1949); Griswold, *Ould Fields,* 234.

12. Jonathan Agudelo, "Requiring Good Anti-Communist Citizens: Harvard Law School and Its Experience with the Lubell Brothers" (student research paper, Boston College Law School, 2009), on file with the authors, 6–9; Roger L. Geiger, *Research and Relevant Knowledge: American Research Universities since World War II* (New York, 1993), 73. See Bob Blauner, *Resisting McCarthyism: To Sign or not to Sign California's Loyalty Oath* (Stanford, CA, 2009).

13. Quotation is from Griswold, *Ould Fields,* 192. See Senate Proceedings on Senator Joseph McCarthy's Speech Relating to Communists in the State Department, *Congressional*

Record of the 81st Congress of the United States (February 20, 1950); Percival R. Bailey, "The Case of the National Lawyers Guild," in Theoharis, *Beyond the Hiss Case,* 150; Mary Elizabeth Basile, "Loyalty Testing for Attorneys: When Is It Necessary? Who Should Decide?," *Cardozo Law Review* 30 (2009): 1856–1860.

14. Richard M. Fried, *Nightmare in Red: The McCarthy Era in Perspective* (New York, 1990), 117.

15. Schrecker, *No Ivory Tower,* 184–185; Andrew L. Kaufman, Oral History, conducted by Daniel Hamilton and Daniel R. Coquillette (June 1999–April 2000), on file with the authors; Erwin N. Griswold, "'*Per Legem Terrae,*'" *HLSR* (March 25, 1954): 2.

16. Berman, Oral History (August 1998). See Sigmund Diamond, "The Arrangement: The FBI and Harvard University in the McCarthy Period," in Theoharis, *Beyond the Hiss Case,* 351.

17. Quotation is from Kaufman, Oral History (June 1999–April 2000). See James G. Hershberg, *James B. Conant: Harvard to Hiroshima and the Making of the Nuclear Age* (Stanford, CA, 1993), 625–626; Geiger, *Research and Relevant Knowledge,* 38–39; Griswold, *Ould Fields,* 192; Sigmund Diamond, *Compromised Campus: The Collaboration of Universities with the Intelligence Community, 1945–1955* (New York, 1992), 204, 221.

18. Ben Heineman Jr., "The University in the McCarthy Era," *Harvard Crimson* (June 17, 1965); D. Dave Eesha and Jose A. DelReal, "FM Investigates: The Kremlin on the Charles," *Harvard Crimson* (February 16, 2012).

19. Quotation is from Diamond, "The Arrangement," 351. See Diamond, *Compromised Campus,* 111–137; Hershberg, *James B. Conant,* 623–626; Schrecker, *No Ivory Tower,* 111, 183.

20. Quotation is from Diamond, "The Arrangement," 365, see 361–364; Diamond, *Compromised Campus,* 24–49, 111–137.

21. A. Dunlap-Smith, "Sigmund Diamond, Sociologist, Historian and Liberal Activist, Dies at 79," *Columbia University Record* (October 29, 1999).

22. James B. Conant, *My Several Lives: Memoirs of a Social Inventor* (New York, 1970), 110.

23. Hershberg, *James B. Conant,* 629.

24. Quoted in Hershberg, *James B. Conant,* 629–630.

25. Schrecker, *No Ivory Tower,* 183.

26. Schrecker, *No Ivory Tower,* 184–185; Kaufman, Oral History (June 1999–April 2000). Griswold explicitly argued that the Fifth Amendment language "in any criminal case" must be given "comprehensive application." Erwin N. Griswold, *The Fifth Amendment Today* (Cambridge, MA, 1954), 54–55.

27. "William L. Marbury Dead at 86; Lawyer and a Fellow of Harvard," *New York Times* (March 7, 1988); Schrecker, *No Ivory Tower,* 183; Diamond, *Compromised Campus,* 123–125.

28. Quotation is from Schrecker, *No Ivory Tower,* 183–184. See Diamond, *Compromised Campus,* 123–125.

29. Quotation is from *"Civil Liberties under Attack* Features Contribution by Prof. Zechariah Chafee," *HLSR* (October 23, 1952): 1.

30. Quoted in Schrecker, *No Ivory Tower,* 184. See Simeon Botwinick, "Punished Privilege: Communism and the Fifth Amendment at Harvard Law School" (student research paper, HLS, 2016), on file with the authors, 18–29; Diamond, *Compromised Campus,* 128.

31. Zechariah Chafee Jr. and Arthur E. Sutherland, "Self-Incrimination" [Letter to the Editor], *Harvard Crimson* (January 13, 1953). See Zechariah Chafee Jr., "More on Incrimination," *Harvard Crimson* (January 20, 1953).

32. Robert Braucher, "More on Self-Incrimination," *Harvard Crimson* (January 13, 1953); "Howe Asks Called Faculty to Talk," *Harvard Crimson* (March 26, 1953).

33. Quotations are from Diamond, *Compromised Campus,* 125, 128. See Hershberg, *James B. Conant,* 629; Schrecker, *No Ivory Tower,* 184–185.

34. Berman, Oral History (August 1998). See George S. Abrams, "Lubell Twins Pressured from Top 'Record' Jobs, Twins Resign after 'Record' Staff, Alumni Turn on Squeeze; Faculty Ponders Action," *Harvard Crimson* (April 6, 1953); Alexander Cockburn, "The Lawyer's Tale: Harvard Law School's Hour of Shame," *Counterpunch* (February 20–22, 2009).

35. Bailey, "The Case of the National Lawyers Guild," 130–132.

36. Quotation is from "Bar Leader Raps Harvard for 'Encouraging' Reds," *Boston Globe* (March 5, 1951). See "Samuel P. Sears, Lawyer, 69, Dead," *New York Times* (November 18, 1964); Bailey, "The Case of the National Lawyers Guild," 147–148.

37. "Harvard Lawyers Guild to Continue, Says Dean," *Boston Globe* (March 7, 1951).

38. Quotations are from Bailey, "The Case of the National Lawyers Guild," 147–148. See "Sears Again Raps Harvard for 'Green Light' to Law Guild," *Boston Globe* (March 7, 1951); David L. Halberstam, "Sears Nomination Widely Protested," *Harvard Crimson* (April 2, 1954); Griswold, *Ould Fields,* 190–191.

39. Erwin N. Griswold, "Memorandum for the File: In re: Alan F. Westin, LL.B. 1951" (March 13, 1956), HLS Dean's Office Records, Records of President James B. Conant, 1933–1953, Harvard University Archives. In 1964 Westin completed a Ph.D. in political science at Harvard and became a national expert on privacy questions in modern society. Emily Langer, "Alan F. Westin, Scholar of Privacy in the Information Ages, Dies at 83," *Washington Post* (February 19, 2013).

40. Hershberg, *James B. Conant,* 625–626; Schrecker, *No Ivory Tower,* 183; Bailey, "The Case of the National Lawyers Guild," 170n49; Monroe H. Freedman, "John T. Noonan, Jr.: Exemplar of Ethical Conduct," *Journal of Law and Religion* 11 (1994): 232; Norman Dorsen, "John T. Noonan, Jr.: Renaissance Man in the Catholic Tradition," *Notre Dame Law Review* 76 (2001): 846–847.

41. Jonathan Lubell quoted in Cockburn, "The Lawyer's Tale."

42. Berman, Oral History (August 1998). See Freedman, "John T. Noonan, Jr.," 232; Diamond, *Compromised Campus,* 128.

43. Jonathan Lubell quoted in Cockburn, "The Lawyer's Tale."

44. Freedman, "John T. Noonan, Jr.," 232. See Monroe H. Freedman, "Legal Aid Suspension Spontaneous?," *Harvard Crimson* (May 4, 1953).

45. Quotations are from Joel Seligman, *The High Citadel: The Influence of Harvard Law School* (Boston, 1978), 85.

46. Quotations are from [Editors] William M. Beccher et al., "Education and the Fifth Amendment," *Harvard Crimson* (June 10, 1953); Schrecker, *No Ivory Tower,* 157.

47. Erwin N. Griswold, Memorandum (April 3, 1953), and Livingston Hall, "Interview with David and Jonathan Lubell" (memorandum) (April 2, 1953), cited in Kimberly Ruthsatz Stephens, "False Triumph: The Strange History behind the Supposed Vindication of the Fifth Amendment during the 1950s Communist Investigation" (student research paper, HLS, 2007), on file with the authors, 9–11, 18, 27.

48. Quotation is from Erwin N. Griswold, "The Fifth Amendment: An Old and Good Friend," *American Bar Association Journal* 40 (1954): 535. See Chafee and Sutherland, "Self-Incrimination"; Stephens, "False Triumph," 18, 27–31.

49. Schrecker, *No Ivory Tower,* 149–150, 157; Stephens, "False Triumph," 5–6.

50. *Rogers v. United States,* 340 U.S. 367 (1951). See Hall, "Interview with David and Jonathan Lubell"; Griswold, "The Fifth Amendment: An Old and Good Friend," 535; Stephens, "False Triumph," 9.

51. Quotations are from Seligman, *High Citadel,* 85.

52. Berman, Oral History (August 1998).

53. John M. Maguire to Edmund M. Morgan (April 10, 1953), John M. Maguire Papers, 1924–1973, Harvard Law School Library Historical & Special Collections (HLSLib); Agudelo, "Requiring Good Anti-Communist Citizens," 20.

54. Jonathan Lubell quoted in Cockburn, "The Lawyer's Tale."

55. Jonathan Lubell quoted in Cockburn, "The Lawyer's Tale."

56. George S. Abrams, "Law School Twins Testify at Hearing Today," *Harvard Crimson* (March 27, 1953).

57. *HLSR* (March 26, 1953); Abrams, "Lubell Twins Pressured" (April 6, 1953); Freedman, "John T. Noonan, Jr.," 233.

58. Jonathan W. Lubell, "To the Editors of the *Crimson,"* *Harvard Crimson* (October 15, 1953).

59. Quotation is from Abrams, "Lubell Twins Pressured." See Lubell, "To the Editors"; Freedman, "John T. Noonan, Jr.," 232.

60. Lubell, "To the Editors."

61. Lubell, "To the Editors."

62. Subcommittee to Investigate the Administration of the Internal Security Act and Other Internal Security Laws of the Senate Committee on the Judiciary, "Public Hearing,"

Congressional Record of the 83rd Congress of the United States (March 26–27, 1953); Agudelo, "Requiring Good Anti-Communist Citizens," 21–23; Abrams, "Lubell Twins Pressured."

63. "Sears, State Bar Chairman, Asks Griswold Fire Lubells," *Harvard Crimson* (April 7, 1953); "Lubells Defend Actions; Attack Sears' Statement," *Harvard Crimson* (April 8, 1953); Schrecker, *No Ivory Tower,* 200–201.

64. Erwin N. Griswold, "In Re: The Case of the Lubells" (March 31, 1953), on file with the authors. This critical memo has been found in the papers of various faculty, including Arthur E. Sutherland Papers, 1923–1972, HLSLib (hereafter cited as AES Papers). See Schrecker, *No Ivory Tower,* 398n15; James E. Kruzer, "Pleading the Fifth: Erwin Griswold, the Lubell Brothers, and Academic Freedom" (student research paper, Boston College Law School, 2006), on file with the authors, 14–15; Botwinick, "Punished Privilege," 20.

65. Seligman, *High Citadel,* 86.

66. W. Barton Leach, memorandum (April 3, 1953), AES Papers.

67. Quotations are from Griswold, "In Re," 2, 4.

68. Quotation is from Lon L. Fuller, memorandum (April 6, 1953), AES Papers; Agudelo, "Requiring Good Anti-Communist Citizens," 30. See Richard G. Bateson, Robert B. Fleming, Allan H. McCoi, Charles P. Schwartz Jr., and Harry H. Wellington, Memo to the HLS Faculty (April 7, 1953), Sheldon Glueck Papers, 1916–1972, HLSLib; Stephens, "False Triumph," 26.

69. Quotations are from Griswold, "In Re," 2, 4.

70. Quotation is from Griswold, "In Re," 1.

71. "Law Faculty Will Not Expel Lubells, Griswold Adds Regret of Students' Action at Jenner Probe," *Harvard Crimson* (April 9, 1953). See "Harvard Law School Won't Expel Lubells," *Boston Globe* (April 9, 1953); "Faculty Decides Not to Expel Lubells for Actions at Probe," *HLSR* (April 9, 1953): 1; "Purge without Purpose," *Harvard Crimson* (April 28, 1953); Harvey Schwed, "Harvard Will Not Expel 2 Students: Law School Dean Takes Stand against Lawyer's Demand to Oust Students," *Columbia Daily Spectator* (April 9, 1953).

72. Griswold, "In Re."

73. "Harvard Won't Oust Lubells," *Boston Post* (April 9, 1953); Seligman, *High Citadel,* 88; Cockburn, "The Lawyer's Tale."

74. "Draft Board Will Not Call Lubells This Year," *Harvard Crimson* (April 28, 1953); "Harlan Backs Army Board's Lubell Probe," *Harvard Crimson* (February 11, 1956). See Freedman, "John T. Noonan, Jr.," 233.

75. David Lubell and Jonathan Lubell, "Letter to the Editor," *HLSR* (April 2, 1953); Abrams, "Lubell Twins Pressured."

76. Mat Foner and Don Conley, "Time for Decision," *HLSR* (April 2, 1953): 2. See Lubell and Lubell, "Letter to the Editor"; Abrams, "Lubell Twins Pressured."

77. George S. Abrams, "Honor Societies Elect Law School Members," *Harvard Crimson* (September 15, 1952). See discussion about origins of this ranking by grades in Chapter 1 in this volume.

78. Quotation is from Freedman, "Legal Aid Suspension Spontaneous?" See David M. Hollander, "Law Group Rejects '53 Action," *Harvard Crimson* (February 13, 1969); James L. Tyson, "Law Review Will Revoke Old Rejection," *Harvard Crimson* (February 4, 1978).

79. Abrams, "Honor Societies Elect Law School Members." The following account relies upon Freedman, "John T. Noonan, Jr.," 233–235; Dorsen, "John T. Noonan, Jr.," 843–848; Seligman, *High Citadel*, 88; Berman, Oral History (August 1998), 7; Herbert P. Wilkins, Oral History, conducted by Daniel R. Coquillette (November 2014), on file with the authors.

80. Kaufman, Oral History (June 1999–April 2000).

81. Kaufman, Oral History (June 1999–April 2000); Wilkins, Oral History (November 2014); Griswold, *Ould Fields*, 191–192; Seligman, *High Citadel*, 88.

82. Kaufman, Oral History (June 1999–April 2000).

83. Quotation is from Seligman, *High Citadel*, 86. See Lubell, "To the Editors"; Kaufman, Oral History (June 1999–April 2000); Wilkins, Oral History (November 2014); "[Jonathan W. Lubell '54]," *HLR* 91 (1978): 1003.

84. Quotation is from Kaufman, Oral History (June 1999–April 2000). See Berman, Oral History (August 1998); Lubell, "To the Editors"; "Jonathan Lubell Attacks Law Review's Decision, Cites Exclusion as Indicative of Times," *Harvard Crimson* (October 15, 1953); Seligman, *High Citadel*, 89; Freedman, "John T. Noonan, Jr.," 234; Dorsen, "John T. Noonan, Jr.," 846–847; Wilkins, Oral History (November 2014); Dorsen, "John T. Noonan, Jr.," 846–847; Cockburn, "The Lawyer's Tale."

85. Kaufman, Oral History (June 1999–April 2000).

86. Berman, Oral History (August 1998). Likewise, see Benjamin Kaplan, Oral History, conducted by Daniel R. Coquillette (January 2006), on file with the authors.

87. "Immunizing the Lubells" (editorial), *Harvard Crimson* (September 26, 1953).

88. "Lubell Brothers Pass Bar Exam, Do Not Apply for New York Bar," *Harvard Crimson* (November 30, 1954); Freedman, "John T. Noonan, Jr.," 233; Tyson, "Law Review Will Revoke Old Rejection"; Cockburn, "The Lawyer's Tale"; Griswold, *Ould Fields*, 191–192.

89. Hollander, "Law Group Rejects '53 Action."

90. "[Jonathan W, Lubell '54.]"

91. Tyson, "Law Review Will Revoke Old Rejection"; Joel Seligman and Paul Rosenberg, "Jonathan Lubell and the Law Review: How Harvard Reclaimed Its Nerve," *The Nation* (March 18, 1978), 299–300; "David G. Lubell [death notice]," *New York Times* (May 20, 2012); "Jonathan William Lubell [death notice]," *New York Times* (December 12, 2016); Cockburn, "The Lawyer's Tale."

92. Griswold, "The Fifth Amendment: An Old and Good Friend," 502–505, 533–536. See "This Month in Harvard History," *Harvard University Gazette* (February 28, 2002); Jamie M. Brown, "Research Memo on Griswold's Doctrine of Pleading the Fifth Amendment" (student research memo, HLS, 2013), on file with the authors.

93. Quotation is from "Griswold Attacks McCarthy-Type Probes," *Harvard Crimson* (May 21, 1954). See Griswold, *"Per Legem Terrae,"* 2–3; Erwin N. Griswold, "The Fifth Amendment as a Symbol," *HLSR* (October 21, 1954), special insert; Griswold, *The Fifth Amendment Today,* v–vi; Griswold, *Ould Fields,* 193n58.

94. Griswold, *The Fifth Amendment Today;* Griswold, *Ould Fields,* 194n, 221n8; William F. Buckley Jr., "The Week: A Letter to Mr. Henry Ford," *National Review* (December 14, 1955), 5; Richard V. Carpenter, "Review . . . ," *ABA Journal* 41 (1955): 1151–1153; C. Dickerman Williams, "Problems of the Fifth Amendment," *Fordham Law Review* 24 (1955): 19–52; R. Carter Pittman, "How the Fifth Amendment was Subverted to Protect Reason," in *Selected Works of R. Carter Pittman,* ed. Joel T. LeFevre, on file with the authors.

95. The extensive correspondence is held in Erwin N. Griswold Papers, 1925–1994, HLSLib (hereafter cited as ENG Papers), box 88. See Botwinick, "Punished Privilege," 37–42.

96. Quotations is from John P. Frank to Erwin N. Griswold (February 12, 1954), ENG Papers. See Schrecker, *No Ivory Tower,* 394n50; "Record Makes Available Copies of Dean's Speech on the 5th Amendment," *HLSR* (March 4, 1954); von Mehren, Oral History (July–December 2000); Edmond Cahn "No Person Shall be Compelled," *New York Times* (January 30, 1955); Ellen Bernstein, "A Conversation with Erwin N. Griswold," *HLSB* (Fall 1979): 22; *United States v. Balsys,* 524 U.S. 666 (1998) (J. Ginsberg, dissenting). See *Ullman v. United States,* 350 U.S. 422 (1956), 426.

97. Griswold, "The Fifth Amendment: An Old and Good Friend," 504.

98. Griswold, "The Fifth Amendment: An Old and Good Friend," 534.

99. Griswold, *The Fifth Amendment Today,* 38–51.

100. Griswold, *The Fifth Amendment Today,* 56. See Mary Beth Basile Chopas, *Searching for Subversives: The Story of Italian Internment in Wartime America* (Chapel Hill, NC, 2017), 84–85; Basile, "Loyalty Testing for Attorneys," 1864–1866.

101. Bernstein, "A Conversation," 21.

102. Griswold, *Ould Fields,* 192–193.

103. See "A Great Law Dean," *HLSB* (October 1967): 3; Dennis Hevesi, "Erwin Griswold Is Dead at 90," *New York Times* (November 21, 1994); Robert C. Clark, "From the Dean," *HLSB* (Fall 1994): 2; "A Lawyer Who Spoke Up," *New York Times* (November 23, 1994); Clark Byse, "In Memoriam: Erwin Nathaniel Griswold," *HLR* 108 (1995): 984. Compare R. Carter Pittman, "How the Fifth Amendment Was Subverted to Protect Treason" (ca. 1962), in *Selected Works of R. Carter Pittman,* ed. Joel T. LeFevre, on file with the authors.

104. Stephens, "False Triumph," 3, 26. See Eleanor Kerlow, *Poisoned Ivy: How Egos, Ideology, and Power Politics Almost Ruined the Harvard Law School* (New York, 1984), 4; Seligman, *High Citadel,* 86–87; Kruzer, "Pleading the Fifth," 10.

105. Schrecker, *No Ivory Tower,* 199, 398. See George S. Abrams, "Decision on Furry May Come Today, Final Faculty Meeting Expected to Bring Corporation Disclosure," *Harvard Crimson* (May 19, 1953).

106. Schrecker, *No Ivory Tower,* 398n12; Griswold, "The Fifth Amendment: An Old and Good Friend," 534. See Stephens, "False Triumph," 4–6.

107. Schrecker discusses the Lubells separately and makes no link to Griswold's revised interpretation. Schrecker, *No Ivory Tower,* 200–201.

108. Griswold, "In Re."

109. Jonathan Lubell quoted in Cockburn, "The Lawyer's Tale."

110. "Lubells Defend Actions; Attack Sears' Statement," *Harvard Crimson* (April 8, 1953).

111. "Jonathan Lubell Attacks *Law Review*'s Decision" (October 15, 1953).

112. Lubell, "To the Editors."

113. Hall, "Interview with David and Jonathan Lubell"; Griswold, "The Fifth Amendment: An Old and Good Friend," 535.

114. Griswold, Memorandum (April 3, 1953).

115. Griswold, "The Fifth Amendment: An Old and Good Friend," 534.

116. Lubell, "To the Editors"; Griswold, "The Fifth Amendment as a Symbol."

117. Hall, "Interview with David and Jonathan Lubell"; Griswold, Memorandum (April 3, 1953); Griswold, "The Fifth Amendment: An Old and Good Friend," 535.

118. Quoted in Botwinick, "Punished Privilege," 33.

119. Tyson, "Law Review Will Revoke Old Rejection."

120. Jonathan Lubell quoted in Cockburn, "The Lawyer's Tale."

121. Griswold, *Ould Fields,* 191.

122. Jonathan Lubell quoted in Cockburn, "The Lawyer's Tale."

123. Griswold, "In Re," 5.

124. "Harvard Won't Oust Lubells"; "Harvard Refuses to Expel Lubells."

125. Griswold, *Ould Fields,* 192n57.

126. Griswold, *Ould Fields,* 192n57.

127. In 1958, Griswold suggested to Arthur Sutherland that the Lubells' case was a worthy topic for Sutherland's history of the school, published in 1967. But Sutherland did not mention the Lubells, even though Sutherland was involved and had a file of faculty memos on the Lubells' case. See Arthur E. Sutherland, *The Law at Harvard: A History of Ideas and Men, 1817–1967* (Cambridge, MA, 1967); Erwin N. Griswold to Arthur E. Sutherland (June 2, 1958) and folder of faculty memos on the Lubells' case, AES Papers.

128. Quoted from Benjamin J. Davis, "The Making of a Communist," in William L. Patterson, *Ben Davis: Crusader for Negro Freedom and Socialism* (New York, 1967), appendix. The following account draws upon "Amherst College Class of 1925," in *Amherst*

College Biographical Record, Centennial Edition (Amherst, MA, 1925); William L. Patterson, *Ben Davis: Crusader for Negro Freedom and Socialism* (New York, 1967); Benjamin J. Davis, *Communist Councilman from Harlem* (New York, 1969); Benjamin J. Davis Papers, 1949–1964, New York Public Library Manuscripts and Archives, retrieved from http://archives .nypl.org/scm/20651; Griswold, *Ould Fields,* 233.

129. *Yates v. United States,* 354 U.S. 298 (1957).

130. "Communist Official Invited," *HLSR* (March 29, 1962): 4.

131. Davis, "The Making of a Communist."

132. Griswold, *Ould Fields,* 233–234.

133. For example, Harrison is not mentioned in Judith Richards Hope, *Pinstripes & Pearls: The Women of the Harvard Law Class of '64 Who Forged an Old Girl Network and Paved the Way for Future Generations* (New York, 2003); Mona Harrington, *Women Lawyers Rewriting the Rules* (New York, 1993); Virginia G. Drachman, *Sisters-in-Law: Women Lawyers in Modern American History* (Cambridge, MA, 1998); the issues of the *Harvard Women's Law Journal,* starting in 1978; and its successor, the *Harvard Journal of Law and Gender.* This account of Marcia Harrison draws heavily upon Catherine O'Neill, "The Crimson Scare: A Harvard Law School Student's Experience Being Labeled a Communist" (student research paper, Boston College Law School, 2017), on file with the authors.

134. *Brief for Employee, Matter of Marcia R. Harrison* (typescript), Personnel Security Board, U.S. Department of State (April 27, 1948), Marcia R. Harrison Papers, 1935–1998, HLSLib (hereafter cited as MRH Papers).

135. *Brief for Employee,* 1–2, 12–15. See James M. McInerney to William E. Foley (June 16, 1950), Marcia Ruth Harrison Main File 77-14799, Special Inquiry, MRH; and Marcia R. Harrison, Statement for 1952 Appeal before U.S. Department of State Loyalty Security Board, MRH Papers, 6. See also Fried, *Nightmare in Red,* 70; Robert Cohen, *When the Old Left Was Young: Student Radicals and America's First Mass Student Movement, 1929–1941* (New York, 1993), 25, 139–142.

136. Quoted in O'Neill, "The Crimson Scare," 8. See *Brief for Employee,* 17; Andrew H. Bartels, "The Office of Price Administration and the Legacy of the New Deal, 1939–1946," *Public Historian* 5 (1983): 6.

137. Marcia Ruth Harrison Main File 77-14799, Special Inquiry; Kenneth O. Warner to Marcia Harrison (November 23, 1942), MRH Papers.

138. Quotation is from Memorandum from the Foreign Economic Administration to Kenneth O. Warner (May 31, 1944), MRH Papers. See W. D. Puleston to Kenneth O. Warner (May 24, 1944), MRH Papers; *Brief for Employee.*

139. Quotation is from Robert L. Bannerman to Mr. Lyon, Mr. Panuch, and Mr. Ryan (May 3, 1946), MRH Papers. See *Brief for Employee,* 1; Robert L. Bannerman to Mr. Neal (March 12, 1946), MRH Papers.

140. Quotation is from McInerney to Foley (June 16, 1950). See Marcia Ruth Harrison Main File 77-14799, Special Inquiry; John Edgar Hoover to the Director of Office

of Controls, Department of State (February 24, 1948), MRH Papers; O'Neill, "The Crimson Scare," 10–12; John E. Peurifoy to Marcia Harrison (December 22, 1948), MRH Papers.

141. Conrad Snow to Marcia Harrison (October 17, 1950) and Transcript of June 22, 1951, Hearing for Marcia R. Harrison Held by U.S. Department of State Loyalty Security Board, MRH Papers; Elizabeth A. Collins, "Red Baiting Public Women: Gender, Loyalty, and Red Scare Politics" (Ph.D. diss., University of Illinois at Chicago, 2008), 272–273.

142. Warner Gardner to Conrad Snow (July 5, 1951), MRH Papers. See A. E. Weatherbee to Marcia R. Harrison (April 19, 1951), MRH Papers; Harrison, Statement for 1952 Appeal, 8.

143. Warner Gardner to J. Edgar Hoover (September 20, 1951) and Warner Gardner to Herbert Lehman (January 10, 1952), MRH Papers.

144. Marcia Harrison quoted in O'Neill, "The Crimson Scare," 14. See Luther A. Huston, "M'Carthy Lists 26 in Loyalty Charge: Jessup, Davis among Group He Says Have Been under Suspicion of Board," *New York Times* (August 10, 1951); Philip Dodd, "Sen. McCarthy Lists Loyalty Probe Targets: Names 26 Employees of State Dept.," *Chicago Daily Tribune* (August 10, 1951); "Senate Given 26 Names by McCarthy: Jessup Tops Listing as 'Prize of Them All' in Loyalty Charges," *Washington Post* (August 10, 1951).

145. "M'Carthy Targets Defend Loyalty: Barnett Says Department Has Never Even Questioned Him," *New York Times* (August 10, 1951).

146. Quotation is from Harrison, Statement for 1952 Appeal, 1.

147. Quotation is from *In the Matter of the Application of Marcia Ruth Harrison under Section 9.108 Civil Service Regulations,* Civil Service Commission (October 13, 1957), MRH Papers, 5.

148. Quotation is from *In the Matter of the Application of Marcia Ruth Harrison* (October 13, 1957), 6. See O'Neill, "The Crimson Scare," 18–19; Erwin N. Griswold, *Affidavit,* Civil Service Commission (September 10, 1957), MRH Papers, 1.

149. Warner Gardner to Marcia R. Harrison (January 2, 1953), MRH Papers.

150. Stephen Bernardi, Oral History, conducted by Daniel Hamilton and Daniel R. Coquillette (October 2000–April 2001), on file with the authors. Bernardi did not identify Harrison by name, but she was the only classmate fitting his description.

151. Quotations are from Griswold, *Affidavit* (September 10, 1957). See O'Neill, "The Crimson Scare," 20–21.

152. Arthur E. Sutherland, *Affidavit,* Civil Service Commission (September 10, 1957), MRH Papers. See Jay S. Dushoff, "Spotlight on the Communist Problem," *HLSR* (December 15, 1955): 3.

153. Sutherland, *Affidavit* (September 10, 1957); O'Neill, "The Crimson Scare," 21–25.

154. Kimball Johnson to Marcia Harrison (ca. November 1957), MRH Papers; See O'Neill, "The Crimson Scare," 26–27.

155. Robert Braucher to Marcia Harrison (November 20, 1957), MRH Papers. See Marcia Harrison to Robert Braucher (November 17, 1957) and Erwin N. Griswold to Marcia Harrison (November 20, 1957), MRH Papers.

156. See O'Neill, "The Crimson Scare," 27–29.

157. "Griswold Attacks McCarthy-Type Probes."

158. Davis, "The Making of a Communist."

159. Quotation is from Harrison, Statement for 1952 Appeal, 1.

CHAPTER TWELVE

The Admissions Revolution, 1946–1967

Under Dean Erwin Griswold (1946–1967), the Law School revolutionized its admissions policy and procedures in three ways. First, it started to apply selectivity at the point of admissions and, concomitantly, to reduce attrition. By the end of Griswold's tenure, the failure rate on exams at the end of the first year had fallen below 1 percent, not including about 3 percent of first-year students who left during the year.[1] Also, in the spring of 1950 Harvard became one of the last law schools in the country to admit women as LL.B. candidates. Even then, the impact of this reform was limited during Griswold's tenure by the small number of women enrolled and the lack of institutional support they received. Finally, near the end of Griswold's tenure the school established a summer pre-law program to recruit African American students. But, like the admission of women, this initiative was both novel and belated, auspicious and disappointing.

Notwithstanding the admissions revolution, white men therefore still predominated in Dean Griswold's school. In Harvard's various published tributes to Griswold—upon his retirement as dean in 1967, his retirement as solicitor general in 1973, the dedication of Griswold Hall in 1979, and his death in 1994—a total of twenty-six individuals contributed essays. These included twenty-four white men and one white woman: Judith Richards Hope (LL.B. 1964), a member of the Harvard Corporation. The twenty-sixth was anonymous: his longtime secretary Elizabeth Wahlen.[2] The demography of those paying him tribute matched that of the school under his leadership.

Selective Admissions

Since the radical pronouncement of Dean Christopher Langdell (1870–1895) in 1875, confirmed by faculty vote in 1893, the Law School had determined admission by relying on the academic threshold of an earned bachelor's degree, which entitled the applicant to enroll as an LL.B. candidate.[3] Although the bar was far higher than at other law schools and Harvard raised it repeatedly in the early decades of the twentieth century, this approach did not amount to adopting selective admissions. The Law School continued to admit a large class of students and cull them during the first year, when "the real selection process" for admissions occurred, as both Ernest Brown (LL.B. 1931) and Erwin Griswold observed.[4] By this process, the faculty stropped a keen edge on the intellectual sword and garnered more tuition revenue for the school, mired in the syndrome of tuition dependence.

During the 1920s, elite undergraduate institutions shifted to exercising selectivity at the point of admission. This novel approach of selecting among qualified applicants implied new criteria of institutional prestige: the proportion of applicants excluded and the proportion of admittees retained and graduated.[5] Meanwhile, the school's long-standing competitive edge in admissions stringency eroded significantly during the tenure of Dean Roscoe Pound (1916–1936). The Association of American Law Schools (AALS)—the group of premier, academic university law schools—decreed that members require two years of college training for admission. Some AALS schools adopted a stricter three-year requirement, and a few began requiring a college degree for admission.[6] The academic quality of the student body in these schools edged closer to that which had distinguished Harvard since Langdell's pronouncement in 1875. Dean James Landis (1937–1946) recognized the detriments of Pound's resistance to selectivity, but did not effect any change due to his personal problems and prolonged absences, as well as the financial pressures upon the school.

Finally, Dean Griswold began addressing "our *admissions* problems" soon after he took office.[7] He correctly saw that "control of the size of our entering class . . . require[s] the development of selective admissions policies."[8] Unmentioned but surely influential was the boost in tuition revenue provided by the influx of veterans after World War II, which afforded the school the opportunity to shift its enrollment profile and admissions policy.

For two decades the faculty had searched for valid indices by which to compare applicants' undergraduate academic records and predict their probability of survival at the Law School. The school had abundant and unparalleled data on which to base these indices, and Professor James MacLachlan (LL.B. 1916) undertook this task during the 1930s, as we have seen. But the challenge was insuperable, partly because the predictive value of coursework and under-graduate grade-point average at different colleges changed continually, so the index had to be updated constantly. Nevertheless, MacLachlan did calcu-late the "deadlines"—academic admission thresholds—for many colleges, and the Law School employed these thresholds intermittently until 1941, when the thresholds were obviated by the wartime enrollment decline.[9]

Meanwhile, a number of AALS schools started developing aptitude tests for applicants that would provide a standard benchmark, given "the wide vari-ation in the meaning of college records," as historian William LaPiana has observed. In 1936 and 1937 the Harvard law faculty expressed interest in this endeavor, and in 1938 the AALS called for a national, standardized test for law school applicants.[10] Immediately after the war, Columbia University Law School and the College Entrance Examination Board enlisted the law schools at Harvard and Yale in an effort to design and employ a national, standard-ized admissions test. Twenty-two law schools rapidly joined the effort, and in 1947 Harvard Law School decided to require applicants for the class entering in the fall of 1948 to take the new Law School Admission Test (LSAT).[11]

Applicants naturally wondered what the new test would ask. Detlev Vagts (LL.B. 1951), who took the first test in 1948, recalled "some spatial questions; such as a picture of a cube, which was divided into sub-cubes and you would be asked how many were missing." In 1951 Andrew Kaufman (LL.B. 1954) encountered the question: "If you were in a sand trap on a golf course, would you use 1) a mashie, 2) a niblick, or 3) some other club?" These were "the old names, even by 1951 standards," so this was manifestly a "culturally biased question" in several respects, raising objections about the validity of the test.[12] Even so, by 1951 nearly 30,000 students nationwide had taken the LSAT, and it continued to torment applicants to Harvard Law School for nearly seventy years, until 2017 when they were first allowed to substitute scores from the Graduate Record Examination (GRE).[13]

There remained the question of how to apply the LSAT scores. After the school adopted the LSAT, the admissions committee—comprising Admissions Director Louis Toepfer (LL.B. 1947), Vice Dean Livingston Hall (LL.B. 1927), and Professor Ernest Brown—hired a statistician to develop an index that merged MacLachlan's indices of undergraduate grades with LSAT scores in order to predict an applicant's academic performance in the first year at Harvard Law School. The aim was to construct a sliding scale that put varying weight on the LSAT score and undergraduate grades, depending on the amount and validity of data the Law School had on prior graduates from the applicant's college.

For example, the grade-point average of an applicant who had graduated from the University of Colorado received less weight than the grade-point average of a graduate from Brown University, because Brown had sent many more students to the Law School for a longer period than had Colorado, so the school had more robust data on the performance of Brown graduates based on their grade-point average. Using that sliding scale, the statistician calculated a Prediction Index (PI) of academic performance at the Law School for each applicant, based on the applicant's undergraduate college, grade-point average, and LSAT score.[14]

Unlike a firm threshold, the PI was then applied flexibly on a rolling basis until the first-year enrollment reached about 540, a cap instituted for the first time.[15] Flexibility was necessary, because the weighted value of undergraduate records differed among applicants with similar LSAT scores, depending on the "occupational, income, school, and religious backgrounds" of applicants, the statistician reported in 1960. For example, among students with similar LSAT scores, those from high socioeconomic backgrounds tended to have better academic performance at the Law School than they had in college, whereas the performance of those from lower socioeconomic backgrounds tended not to improve at the Law School. Apparently the latter worked harder in college to get ahead than did the former, who presumed that their future was bright no matter what their undergraduate grades were. Hence, wealthier students entered the Law School with more untapped academic potential, according to the statistician.[16] Counter to the thinking later in the twentieth century, this finding implied that an applicant from a wealthy family might be preferred, on academic grounds, over an applicant from a poor family with the same undergraduate grades!

Apart from predicted academic performance, qualitative—or "nonintellectual"—factors were also considered in admissions decisions. These factors included geographic diversity, difficulties overcome by the applicants, and attributes suggesting future success, such as extracurricular activities, employment experience, military service, outstanding accomplishments, and even family ties, in the view of some.[17]

For example, when a Rockefeller scion who was a senior at Harvard College applied, Toepfer believed that "he ought to be admitted" even though he did not score high on the PI. Toepfer believed that "people who were much favored were going to continue to do useful and interesting things. . . . He would be a very important, successful, citizen—both in the class and later." But the Admissions Committee refused to admit.[18] So Toepfer called the faculty Master of the Harvard College house in which Rockefeller was living, and asked for any "useful" information about him. The Master replied, "Well, you admitted his roommate." Looking into his files, Toepfer found that the roommate, in fact, had a lower grade-point average and LSAT score than Rockefeller, but was a minority student who been given special consideration on qualitative grounds. "So I went back to the committee, and pulled out the two applications. And the committee was obliged to admit the Rockefeller" on "nonintellectual" grounds, as well. But Toepfer lost the same kind of argument when he favored admitting Robert Kennedy and Edward Kennedy. In the committee's view, they were too "fun-loving," and they attended the University of Virginia law school instead.[19]

But Toepfer found that qualitative reasons could also trump his preferences. In 1948 Henry Kissinger, future U.S. secretary of state and national security advisor, applied a year early in order to complete both his senior year at Harvard College and the grueling first year of Harvard Law School concurrently in the 1949–50 academic year. Other stellar Harvard College juniors had attempted this in the past, and Toepfer had always told them to wait until after their senior year, and they dutifully did so. Toepfer told Kissinger the same thing. But Kissinger "had a sense of his own importance" and went to see Dean Griswold, who directed that Kissinger be admitted. Toepfer was furious, and later commented, "It was the first time and the last time and the only time that the Dean ever interfered in an admissions decision." Toepfer omitted from his account that Kissinger was a twenty-six-year-old World War II veteran who wanted to make up for lost time in his academic career, just as Toepfer had done when he returned from World War II in 1945. In any case, Kissinger left the Law School after his first semester and went on to earn a Ph.D. in government from Harvard in 1954 and then studied as a special student at the Law School in 1954–55.[20]

Such extraordinary applications requiring attention to "nonintellectual" factors were rare. The great majority of application decisions were based solely on the PI, and attrition fell to 7 percent by June 1950. The Admissions Committee attributed many of those failures to students' personal difficulties. By 1965 the school had "virtually eliminated failure at the end of the first year," Griswold wrote.[21]

Another factor driving the shift to selective admissions was the skyrocketing number of applicants. The Law School received about 1,400 applications annually in the early 1950s, then 1,700 in 1960, 2,300 in 1963, 2,800 in 1964, and 3,100 in 1967, for some 540 seats in the entering class. In addition, the quality of the applicants improved dramatically. In 1960 there were 291 applicants with "outstanding" undergraduate academic records; in 1966 there were 597. On the LSAT, 115 applicants scored in the top 1 percent in 1960, and 552 applicants did so in 1966. In 1960 the median LSAT score (631/800) of those *admitted* was lower than the median score (636/800) of the 3,000 *applicants* in 1966. Selection among the qualified became selection among the "well-qualified" and then among "the highly-qualified."[22] The distance between the floor and the ceiling of the class shrank rapidly.

The increasing selectivity influenced the socioeconomic composition of the student body. "The inevitable result of a highly selective admission process is that only the best educated survive," Toepfer observed. "The students who succeed in the competition for admission seldom come from the bottom economic groups. They are the children of doctors and lawyers, bankers, merchants, teachers, storekeepers. Almost none of them are really poor."[23]

Inevitably, the increasing size and quality of the applicant pool intensified competition for admission. The acceptance rate fell from 49 percent in 1960 to 25 percent in 1967.[24] Throughout the 1960s the yield of enrollees from those admitted was about 70 percent, as the school accepted between 750 and 800 applicants in order to realize about 540 first-year enrollees. Where else did the admittees decide to go? About half did not go to law school after all, and headed to graduate school instead. Some went to other law schools, particularly Yale, Columbia, Chicago, or Stanford, for various reasons, including more financial aid or a better fit.[25]

Admission of Women

Following the end of World War II, private all-male colleges and universities slowly began opening their doors to women. In 1942 the Law School faculty had voted fifteen to eleven in favor of admitting women, but then decided not to forward the recommendation to the Corporation because the vote was so close. In 1945 the Corporation approved the admission of women to Harvard Medical School, and soon thereafter the law faculty began raising the issue. The first professor to do so formally at a faculty meeting was Lon Fuller in August 1947.[26]

At that point Harvard was one of only five law schools in the United States that excluded women.[27] But Griswold, who had voted for coeducation in 1942, moved cautiously on the issue for several reasons. He was a new, young dean, and the school faced serious problems, notably strained relations with alumni. Also, several of the senior faculty opposed the change. In addition, he intended to escape the tuition dependence syndrome by limiting the student body and building the endowment—after climbing out of debt. This financial strategy implied that admitting women would reduce the number of men. Finally, Griswold was a traditionalist who saw men as the natural leaders in the legal profession.

But the immediate barrier to admitting women was the obligation, felt by the whole faculty, to accommodate the returning veterans.[28] Only in January 1949, when some degree of order came to the postwar "madhouse," did Mark Howe (LL.B. 1933), a firm advocate for coeducation, ask at a faculty meeting to address "the question of admitting girls to the school." Griswold's response at the meeting was equivocal. He stated that the Corporation would likely approve the measure, but he cited objections about additional cost and about women displacing men in the school and then in the profession.[29]

Interpretations of Griswold's position vary. His own autobiographical account implies that he personally orchestrated and effected coeducation, which scholars have considered to be disingenuous revisionism.[30] A number of researchers conclude that the school admitted women "despite him, rather than because of his efforts."[31] Some faculty attending the meeting believed that Griswold's equivocal view reflected his typically contrarian manner: initially opposing what he actually supported. It is also said that, because some senior faculty disapproved of coeducation, Griswold wanted to voice their concerns in order to induce consensus around the inevitable decision to admit women. In any case, when Zechariah Chafee Jr. (LL.B. 1913) proposed that the issue be studied, Griswold supported the suggestion. The faculty then voted to establish a committee, to which Griswold appointed both opponents and proponents, including Howe as chairman.[32]

The committee evidently never met, and Howe wrote the report himself. Issued on April 15, the report forthrightly addressed objections to coeducation, particularly those that Griswold repeatedly stressed: "the probability that a relatively small proportion [of women] would make professional use of their training for a significant period of time, and that, for each woman admitted, a qualified man, somewhat more likely to use his training in his career, would have to be excluded." The latter objection stemmed from the shift to selective admissions and adoption of an enrollment limit.[33]

Nevertheless, the report finally recommended "that beginning in the fall of 1950 qualified women be admitted to the Law School," but added the caveat that "until we learn how many women will apply for admission and until we have had some experience in evaluating the records of women's colleges, we must proceed by gradual stages." Hence, "in the first years of executing the new policy admission of women should be on a separately planned selective basis," even though it may be "unworkable as a matter of administration to have one standard of qualifications for women applicants and another for men." Further, the report charged the Admissions Committee to determine the number of women to be admitted "after applications have been received and evaluated."[34]

The executive council of the alumni association was consulted and voted eight to three in favor of the proposal. The *Harvard Law School Record* invited input from alumni and received only fourteen letters, seven in favor and seven opposed. On May 10, 1949, President James Conant (1933–1953) chaired the meeting at which the faculty considered a motion to admit women as of September 1950. Griswold persisted in his equivocal warning that the admitted women would necessarily displace some highly qualified men and the women would likely not practice law for long, if at all. Among several rebuttals to Griswold, Howe emphasized that only "a limited number of specially qualified women would be accepted at first." Conant then called for the vote, and the motion "was carried by a show of hands, twenty-two Yeas and two Nos." The faculty minutes do not record the names of the dissenters, but presumably they were among those who opposed the motion in 1942. As signaled by Conant's presence, the approval of the Corporation and concurrence of the Overseers followed in the next two months.[35]

Response to the monumental change was muted and accepting. Few alumni wrote to the school, and Griswold was surprised that only one complained to him. The *New York Times* lamely defended the school against any charge of "belated action." *Life* magazine never mentioned the admission of women in its forty stories that referenced Harvard Law School in the four decades between 1935 and 1975.[36] To many, the decision therefore seemed inevitable. Professor Austin Scott (LL.B. 1909), a member of Howe's committee, stated, "I have voted in favor of admitting women three times in the past forty years and I'm glad that the majority has finally come around." The lone woman on the faculty, Visiting Professor Soia Mentschikoff, attended the May 10 meeting

Vice Dean Livingston Hall, LL.B. 1927, greeting the first class of women matriculating into Harvard Law School in the fall of 1950.

Courtesy of FayFoto Boston, Inc.

and commented charitably, "The action was inevitable under the school's tradition of liberal and realistic admissions policy."[37]

In October 1949 the dean publicly announced that the Law School was receiving applications from women. Few applications were expected, and the Admissions Committee of Ernest Brown, Livingston Hall, and Director Toepfer heavily weighted LSAT scores due to their lack of experience with women's colleges, and delegated final decisions to Toepfer.[38] Then the overall number of applications from men began rising unexpectedly, probably due to the Korean War and the prospect of conscription for military service. Toepfer, therefore, sat on the eighteen applications received from women for seven months, doubtlessly because Griswold worried about women displacing men in the student body.[39]

In March 1950 the *Crimson* and the *Harvard Law School Record* began inquiring about the lack of acceptances, so Toepfer finally admitted nine of the eighteen applicants during April.[40] Ultimately the school received about twenty-five applications from women, accepted fifteen, and enrolled fourteen in the fall of 1950. Five came from Radcliffe, three from Wellesley, and six from other colleges.[41]

A range of factors and motivations led these women to enroll in the first class. "I loved the idea of being a pioneer . . . of breaking down this male bastion of discrimination," said Sondra Markowitz Miller (LL.B. 1953).[42] Similarly, Beverly S. Coleman observed, "I heard that Harvard was going to admit women and I applied. I thought it would be fun to integrate the school."[43] Others like Helen M. Cunningham (LL.B.1953) did not "feel like pioneers," and "just plain went to law school and woke up ten years later to discover that we were supposed to have been trail blazers."[44]

Many women in the first class simply wanted greater career opportunity and believed that law might suit them. Mary-Elizabeth Jacques (LL.B. 1953) felt limited in her job as a bacteriologist, as did Frederica S. Brenneman (LL.B. 1953), who was working as an entry-level economist for the Bureau of Labor Statistics.[45] Similarly, Ruth Marshall Paven (1950–1952) recalled, "I was a senior at Radcliffe—an English major. . . . The traditional wisdom at that time was that you would take a couple of education courses and become a schoolteacher. . . . Or you took a secretarial course, and I didn't want to do that. . . . Then Harvard Law School came out and said that next fall they were admitting women. And I thought, 'what fun.'"[46]

Carolyn MacTear Anderson (LL.B. 1953) had "an interest in the law and social sciences," but "in 1950, Radcliffe seniors looking for practical career training were usually advised to go to secretarial school. I had sometimes thought of law school, but it didn't seem a practical possibility. But [Radcliffe] Dean Sherman was highly enthusiastic when I hesitantly advanced the idea. She was particularly interested . . . in having [Radcliffe] well represented when HLS first opened its doors to women."[47]

Since at least 1870, many young men, including Roscoe Pound and Erwin Griswold, had entered law and Harvard Law School because their fathers urged them to do so.[48] This factor also influenced the first class of women, including Mary M. Truschel (LL.B. 1953) and Ann Pfohl Kirby (LL.B. 1953).[49] Likewise, Sondra Miller, who later became a justice in the Appellate Division of the New York State Supreme Court, stated,

> My father was an immigrant from Romania who had a very limited education of his own. He came to this country, worked very hard and became a very

successful merchant. He always said to me "If I had been born in this country, I would want to be a lawyer . . . or, if I could, be a judge!" So I had this idea that if you were a lawyer you could change things; you could help people. . . . My father also emphasized that men were not to be trusted, so women had to be independent. . . . He really emphasized the importance of having a profes- sional career.[50]

At the end of their first year, in June 1951, the women's grade distribution on the anonymously graded final exams matched closely that of the men, ranging from high B to low C. One woman did not meet the minimum re- quirements for promotion, and the other thirteen women went on to graduate. Two became judges on high state courts, one became a lawyer in the federal government, five practiced in law firms, and five worked as professor, editor, librarian, consultant, or state bar official. Also in June 1951, the school con- ferred its first degrees on women. Barbara A. Dooling and Erlinda A. Arce Ig- nacio received LL.M. degrees with thirty men. Dooling had previously earned an A.B. from Emmanuel College and an LL.B. from Boston University. Arce Ignacio had earned two degrees in the Philippines: the B.A. from Far Eastern University and the LL.B. from Manuel L. Quezon Educational Institute.[51]

Harvard Law Wives

Between 1945 and 1970, women who aspired to higher education, especially in the major professions, had to negotiate carefully between their aspirations and the cultural norms set for them as wives and mothers. Recent discussion about the early female LL.B. students has often neglected the most promi- nent, contemporaneous association of women at the school: the Harvard Law Wives (HLW). In contrast, the history of the Law School written by Arthur Sutherland (LL.B. 1925), published in 1967, devotes three paragraphs to the admission of women and three pages to HLW and the lives of married law students after World War II.[52] Though seemingly myopic in retrospect, the proportion of Sutherland's coverage roughly corresponds to the relative atten- tion given to the two groups during Griswold's administration. When the first fourteen women enrolled in the LL.B. program in 1950, the dues-paying membership of HLW stood at 100. As the total number of female students in the student body rose to about fifty in 1960 (where it hovered through 1967), the dues-paying membership of HLW grew to 200, even as the fraction of married students in the student body declined from about 40 percent to about 30 percent.[53]

The prominence of HLW naturally reflected the cultural norms, social roles, and accommodations for women at Harvard University in the 1950s. As Ruth Bader Ginsburg (1956–1958), who entered the Law School in the fall of 1956, later described, women were not allowed to live in the regular dormitories, eat in the main dining room of the faculty club, use the athletic facilities, or visit the reading room in the undergraduate library. At the Law School, "one could invite one's father, but not one's wife or mother, to the *Law Review* banquet; . . . law firms could use the school's placement facilities though they would engage no women; and Harvard Business School enrolled only men. Textbooks imparted such wisdom as 'land, like woman, was meant to be possessed.'" Statutes in many states maintained, "The husband is head of the family. He may choose any reasonable place or mode of living, and the wife must conform thereto."[54]

These norms of the university and the broader society were sustained within the school by HLW. While Dean Griswold downplayed the presence and professional potential of female law students, the school's official publications treated HLW as a "vital part" of the Law School.[55] The *Harvard Law Bulletin* listed HLW events among "student activities," and the *Handbook for New Students Entering Harvard Law School* included a description of HLW. As late as 1961, the student-edited *Harvard Law School Record* featured the HLW president in its "Profiles of Leaders" at the school.[56]

HLW originated in about 1930 when the wives of faculty began hosting a formal tea to welcome the small number of wives of students, who then socialized occasionally. Organized by Elizabeth Beale, wife of Professor Joseph Beale (LL.B. 1887), the annual tea was held in the Harvard Faculty Club with Marion Frankfurter serving as "pourer." After 1936, Stella Landis, loyal wife of the unfaithful Dean James Landis, actively helped to organize and lead HLW. Her cheerful perseverance in the face of the dean's public infidelity exemplified the self-sacrificial outlook of HLW and the expectations for the law wife. In subsequent decades, HLW members often cited the metaphor that law is "a jealous and exacting mistress" and referred to themselves as "law widows."[57] In 1941 the *Harvard Law School Yearbook* devoted two pages to HLW and listed all ninety-four members—by the name of their husband: Mrs. James S. Armstrong, Mrs. Hugh Gregg, and so forth. The *Harvard Law School Record* followed this nomenclature through at least 1961.[58]

HLW activities ceased during World War II, but Stella Landis resuscitated the association in 1945. Then it was Harriet Griswold who invigorated HLW in 1946, when her husband became dean. Harriet resumed the welcoming teas for law wives at the start of the academic year, and became the de facto sponsor of HLW, helping to organize meetings and frequently speaking to the group. Weekly meetings presented relevant information, usually on homemaking or child-rearing. Monthly gatherings generally had a social purpose, including fashion shows, potluck suppers, and cocktail parties. HLW also operated a nursery school and lunchroom for the Law School until the Harkness Commons opened in 1952.[59]

HLW aimed fundamentally to encourage and support the wives in serving their husbands. Harriet's frequent talks promoted the self-sacrificing role of the law wife and urged the women to devote themselves to advancing their husbands' careers. Her favorite opening line was: "Husbands go through Law School by the sweat of their *fraus*." Harriet always listed her name publicly as Mrs. Erwin N. Griswold, and recommended that the women refer to themselves by their husband's name. When a guest speaker once suggested to HLW members that women should develop autonomy and independent endeavors apart from their husband's career, Harriet stood up and rebutted the speaker directly.[60]

Then, in 1960, the preponderant image and role of women at the school began to shift from wife to LL.B. student. This change manifested the broad shift in gender norms taking place in American society, fostered by the proliferation of birth control that decoupled marriage and motherhood, and the publication of Betty Friedan's *Feminine Mystique* in 1963. But the shift at the Law School was remarkably distinct, and Professor Derek Bok (LL.B. 1954) played a catalytic role.

In January 1960, Bok shocked the HLW when, at one of its meetings, he gave a presentation urging women to pursue their own careers for the good of themselves, their families, and their husbands. Many members left the meeting deeply offended and angry, feeling that Bok had demeaned their role and work as wives and mothers. Derek's wife, Sissela Bok, a distinguished ethicist, attended the talk and later observed that the many pregnant wives in the audience reacted as if Derek had declared "war on motherhood itself."[61]

Nevertheless, his presentation was a watershed. In April 1960 Harriet Griswold made the last of her numerous presentations to HLW. Also in 1960, Professor Abram Chayes (LL.B. 1949), the advisor to female law students, and his wife, Antonia, a well known lawyer, began to organize seminars for HLW in which faculty presented an overview of their area of law, and assigned one or two cases to read in advance. For the first time, HLW hosted presentations about legal issues not directly related to women. The popular seminars continued periodically in the subsequent decade with an average attendance of about one hundred.[62]

Furthermore, the nature of HLW meetings changed after Bok's presentation. From 1946 through 1960, HLW had hosted ninety-seven presentations: 58 percent related to the work of wives or mothers, 39 percent to travel or current events, and 3 percent to legal issues, primarily concerning women. From 1961 to 1970, HLW hosted fifty-four presentations: 9 percent related to the work of wives or mothers, 63 percent to current events or cultural subjects, and 28 percent to legal issues, unrelated specifically to women.[63]

Yet even after 1960 the roles of wife and LL.B. student seemed irreconcilable to many in the school. In 1963 Elizabeth Bartholet (LL.B. 1965) and her husband were enrolled in the same course, and Elizabeth did better on the final exam. This outcome "distressed" the course's professor, who feared it would be "a crisis if a woman did better than her husband," because "it could ruin her marriage." The professor confided in two other faculty members, who later relayed the incident to Bartholet. She recalled, even at "this ultimate meritocratic place, as Harvard Law School sees itself, there was a professor who . . . actually wondered what he should do . . . as if lowering my grade or raising my husband's, was a possibility."[64]

The female LL.B. students generally steered clear of HLW. For one thing, during Griswold's tenure only two women were married when they matriculated: Ginsburg and Bartholet. More importantly, HLW did not suit the interests and ambitions of the female students, although Harriet invited them to join, starting in 1950. "I was asked to join. I, of course, *was* a Harvard Law wife," said Bartholet, "but they also reached out to women who weren't wives. . . . I dimly remember withdrawing from their overture because that was definitely not the identification I was seeking for myself."[65]

Nevertheless, the gap between the two groups began to narrow, as Caroline M. Simon (LL.B. 1965) observed when she attended the HLW seminar on manufacturer's liability in 1965:

> Although many male students evidently view the Law Wives as a bevy of gossiping cookie-bakers, the women at the meeting proved to be charming and intelligent. The wives practice a brand of graciousness that is noticeably missing from most Law School gatherings. . . . The seminar itself revealed the women to be eager students. . . . Most of the 50 participants proved to be as well prepared as their husbands usually are. . . . Where were the husbands? Not present. . . . Husbands do participate in other [HLW] functions. . . . It is

unfortunate that Law School men who give females the burden of rebutting a presumption of idiocy, were not present at the meeting.[66]

Likewise, Judith Hope observed that in 1963 more HLW members than female law students were participating in the civil rights movement. "Several of the law wives volunteered for the front lines," stated Hope, "but most of the law students didn't; we were nervous about getting through the state bar committees and worried that an arrest would block our admission into the practice of law."[67]

In the mid-1960s, HLW subdivided into diverse interest groups, and the organization began to appear antiquated. Fewer students were married or had children upon matriculation, and some law wives began to resist Harriet's continuing advice to subordinate their identities to that of their husbands. In 1970 the last regular fashion show was held, and an alternative association was formed, the Women's Law Group. In 1972 HLW changed its name to the Harvard Law Community Association, and the yearbook for 1972–73 no longer featured the group as a student organization. After forty years, the HLW era ended.[68]

Women's Experience and Ladies Day

According to reports from the first female students, most of the upperclassmen in 1950 welcomed them, although a few echoed Griswold's repeated warning that women would take jobs from men. The great majority of men "were delighted to have women in our class. Most of us came from co-ed schools, and we thought it was a good idea," stated Andrew Kaufman.[69] Their small number also contributed to the welcome. Nothing seemed to have changed. Some male students did not even realize that women were in their class until late in the fall semester.[70]

The continuity felt by male students reflects the minimal accommodations that the dean and the school made for women. In logistical terms, Mark Howe's faculty committee had observed that the university would provide no housing, medical, or athletic facilities for women. Griswold opposed taking any stack space in the library to make provision for them. Harvard Medical School had spent $80,000 to provide restrooms for women, which Griswold considered "wasteful." His school spent $11,000 to install one bathroom for women in the basement of Austin Hall.[71]

In cultural terms, the school refused to compromise its Spartan manliness, which the faculty and deans viewed not as a gendered norm but as natural and necessary ethos for legal education. Most of the early women thus stated that the faculty treated them evenhandedly, except for some embarrassing or hurtful attempts at humor or paternalism.[72] But Edith Henderson (LL.B. 1953, S.J.D. 1959), who became rare books librarian and Curator of the Treasure Room, reported "innumerable horror stories about her experiences" to Stanley N. Katz, who studied at the Law School in 1959–60 as a Liberal Arts Fellow. It was therefore not surprising that some women "did not want to talk in class" and "seemed hesitant to bring up their problems, their thoughts, in respect to a matter," according to Arthur von Mehren (LL.B. 1945).[73] Likewise, Elisabeth Owens, who graduated from Yale Law School in 1951, taught at Harvard Law School as a lecturer in the 1960s, and was herself regarded as shy, recalled that the female students at Harvard seemed "meek and unassertive." Some said nothing in class, but then wrote "A" examination papers.[74]

The few women did make their presence known by participating in student organizations. In 1952 Kirby and Truschel became the first women elected to one of the three academic honor societies, the Harvard Legal Aid Bureau, and in 1954 Priscilla Holmes (LL.B. 1955) became the first woman elected to the *Harvard Law Review*.[75] Nevertheless, the women learned to keep their heads low because they were often singled out for questioning on cases related to marriage, domestic topics, or rape. According to Bartholet, the "outrage" here was both the implication that women could not address other topics and the coercion to accede to that. The easiest path "through the interrogation, for everybody, was to treat the fact that you were there, as something of a joke," said Bartholet.[76]

The epitome of this sexist behavior occurred in "Ladies Day," conducted by Professor Barton Leach (LL.B. 1921). Never calling on women on other days, Leach held this notorious event two or three times during the semester when the class was devoted to interrogating the few women in the course. Seated on the dais at the front and facing the men in the class, the women were aggressively questioned on cases assigned to them, sometimes with the male students hooting and hollering. The assigned cases often addressed topics involving women, such as divorce, marital property, or women's garments, implying that women could not handle general legal topics. Other minority groups were not singled out in this way.[77]

James Casner also held "Ladies Day," according to Frank E. A. Sander (LL.B. 1952) and Stanley Katz, although Judith Hope associates it only with Leach. But Hope agrees that questions put to the women by Casner and other professors "often seemed designed to amuse the men—and embarrass us."[78] In any case, Leach and Casner were birds of a feather. After joining the faculty in 1929, the former had recruited the latter to the faculty in 1938, and both had military experience and exuded "toughness" in their demeanor.[79] Leach, in particular, embraced the ask-and-give-no-quarter ethic of "teaching by humiliation" in all his classes.[80] Many of the female students considered him "crude," "a horror," and "a real misogynist."[81]

In the words of Mary J. Mullarkey (LL.B. 1968), "Ladies Day was a mean-spirited game that marginalized women and reinforced the view that women in the law were not to be taken seriously." But other female students recalled Ladies Day as "a good-natured form of hazing."[82] Still others rationalized it as beneficial preparation for the even more hostile professional world they were facing.[83]

In any event, Ladies Day became notorious, and many believed it was wrong, although no professors or students, female or male, officially protested Ladies Day during Griswold's administration.[84] Even "Leach knew it was wrong," observed Louis Toepfer. "I have no doubt that the dean said something to him. But he persisted. He was something of a smart-Alec. . . . He did it for the fun of it."[85] Griswold tolerated this abuse of the women not only in professors but also in deans, for he appointed Casner associate dean for administration in 1961. Casner continued in that role until 1967, when Griswold left the school and Casner became acting dean. In 1968 student protest finally brought an end to Ladies Day.[86] By that point Leach was becoming "somewhat disturbed," according to Toepfer, and committed suicide in 1971.[87]

The small, targeted group of female law students might be expected to have bonded together between 1950 and 1967. But they did not, and many later reported feeling isolated. To be sure, many male students, even those on the *Law Review,* reported similar feelings, a consequence of the combative and competitive culture.[88] But the women had absolutely no senior role models or mentors on whom they could rely.

Harvard "was so much a male world then that, when they told us we were privileged to be attending Harvard Law School, we believed them. It never occurred to us that we had a right to be there," stated Charlotte Horwood Armstrong (LL.B. 1953).[89] Mary Mullarkey observed that "the male-dominated culture of Harvard seemed to have a mean edge to it that I had not experienced before."[90] The mean edge of the intellectual sword was honed by Spartan pride.

Dinner at the Griswolds'

As with accounts of Griswold's personality, interpretations of his view of the female students range widely: from hostility to grudging acceptance to enthusiastic support for equal opportunity. Overall, it seems that Griswold—like James B. Thayer (LL.B. 1856) and John C. Gray (LL.B. 1861)—could not deny women's right to enroll "but personally [did] not want them."[91] Griswold's objection rested on three deeply conservative assumptions: that women would ultimately choose a domestic role, that women had to pursue a domestic role because the legal profession would not admit them, and that Harvard Law School had no obligation to initiate change. Those three premises led to his conclusion that women would not practice law for any significant length of time, so their legal education would be wasted. Furthermore, these women would be displacing men from the opportunity to practice law and provide for their families. He repeated these conclusions to the faculty and to the women themselves in his opening "welcome" to the entering class. And he continued to assert them throughout his decanal tenure.[92]

As a result, Griswold sublimated the presence of women at the school and rarely even mentioned them, as students and faculty noted.[93] In the 1950 yearbook, for example, he observed that the admission of women was not "either very important or very significant. . . . There seems to be no likelihood that we will have a very large proportion of women among our students."[94] Then, in 1958, when suggesting issues for Sutherland to examine in the sesquicentennial history of the school, Griswold did not mention the admission of women.[95] In his annual reports relating data on enrollment, the dean routinely listed various categories of students: the number in each class, the number of veterans, the number who were married, the number from Ceylon, and so forth. But he never noted the number of women, though he did report how many women graduated, as seen in Table 12.1.[96]

The dean's closest and most extensive interaction with female students was limited to the annual dinner that he and Harriet hosted in their home each fall to welcome the fifteen or so women in the entering class.[97] Like Ladies Day, this now "legendary" dinner was highly scripted.[98] Formal invitations were issued, and Harriet cooked the meal following the same menu every time. After eating, the women took seats in a circle of chairs in the living room around the dean, who then questioned each of them on why they had come to the Law School and why they were taking the place of a man. According to

Table 12.1   Number of Women Graduating from Harvard Law School, 1950–1967

Year	LL.B.	LL.M.
1950–51	0	2
1951–52	0	0
1952–53	11	2
1953–54	14	0
1954–55	9	4
1955–56	14	4
1956–57	4	2
1957–58	6	2
1958–59	8	1
1959–60	7	5
1960–61	6	7
1961–62	16	1
1962–63	15	2
1963–64	15	2
1964–65	20	3
1965–66	22	3
1966–67	25	2
Total	192	42

Data sources: Erwin N. Griswold, Annual Report of the Dean of Harvard Law School, 1955–56, 412; 1956–57, 340; 1957–58, 339; 1958–59, 317; 1959–60, 424; 1960–61, 340; 1961–62, 416; 1962–63, 292; 1963–64, 229–30; 1964–65, 270; 1965–66, 249; 1966–67, 283; A. James Casner, Annual Report of the Dean of Harvard Law School, 1967–68, i, 269.

many of the guests, Griswold was relentless; the questions seemed insulting, and the interrogation was an arduous ordeal.[99]

Even more than his stance on admitting women, the Griswolds' dinner gave rise to divergent interpretations.[100] To some, the dean's behavior was demeaning and sexist, virtually an attempt to intimidate the young, first-year students into leaving the school. More personal and directly confrontational than Ladies Day, the interrogation could not even be construed as a joke.[101] Others, particularly Judith Hope, remembered the questioning as a form of "tough love," meant to prepare the women for questions they would face in the legal profession.[102] Still others, including Harriet, the hostess, considered the event to be "welcoming" and encouraging to the small group of women, who were vastly outnumbered by the male students. In fact, Harriet's idea of a dinner for female students came directly from the welcoming tea for the law wives, which was still being held.[103]

Griswold's recollection was that he genuinely wanted to learn why the women had chosen the unusual path of coming to law school. At the dinners

Griswold often told the women, "I don't know what you're going to do with your legal education," reported future attorney general Janet Reno (LL.B. 1963).[104] The most likely hypothesis the dean could conjure was that women "will be able to do all the pro bono work that has so strained the energies and the time of the men, and [the men] will be able to provide better for their families," as he told the women in October 1950.[105] Thus, the Griswolds could scarcely conceive of an independent professional role for women. They did not even have a vocabulary for it, as indicated by Harriet's custom that women should name themselves publicly by adding "Mrs." to their husband's full name. How could female lawyers or doctors practice using their husband's full name? It was impossible. Harriet's naming custom implicitly denied women an independent professional identity.

The differing views of the dinners arose from several factors. One was the asymmetry of the social encounter. To the women, the dean's event was like "a state dinner at the White House: an honor and a command performance."[106] To the Griswolds, it was one of many dinners that they hosted for groups related to Harvard or the legal community. The Griswolds, who entertained major political, judicial, and international figures, had few opportunities to host events for a small group of students. Fitting a dinner for the first-year women into their busy calendar was an act of goodwill, they felt. "Our having them over each year, made them feel that we were paying attention to them," Harriet later wrote.[107]

In addition, the dean's infamous obtuseness, awkwardness, and gruffness colored his interactions with everyone, but especially the female students.[108] The new assistant professors, whom the Griswolds also invited to the women's dinners, took note of this. Alan Dershowitz and his wife came to the dinner in October 1964, and Dershowitz observed the "mixed nature" of the dean's questioning of the young women:

> On the one hand, he was welcoming them to his house; on the other hand, he was saying things which could easily be misunderstood as demeaning. For example, at the meal—at the time I was kosher—I ate the string beans and potatoes, but I didn't eat the roast beef. The next day, the dean called me into his office and said, "Harriet was upset that you did not like her food." I said, "No, I did like it, but I am kosher." And he said, "But, you know, even the Catholics have now changed their rule about eating meat on Friday. Don't you think it's really time for the Jewish people to do the same thing?" I thought he was joking, but he wasn't. That shows you the mixed nature of his interactions.[109]

Another factor complicating the interpretations was Griswold's contrarian, Socratic approach to conversations. He believed that posing a counter thesis and demanding a refutation—Why are you taking the place of a man?—was the best way to get to the heart of an issue. This habitual manner, combined with his gruffness, intimidated even senior faculty members. No wonder that the first-year female students felt demeaned.

Finally, a personal factor supports the "tough love" explanation. After Harriet contracted polio in 1939, it was fourteen months before she could get herself up out of bed and another fourteen weeks before she could try to walk with braces. To accommodate her disability, Erwin installed hand controls in their car, a ramp over the stairs to their house, a bench in the shower, and a laundry on the first floor of the house. Beyond that, "he leaves me alone and treats me as if there were absolutely nothing wrong with me," Harriet wrote in *Collier's* magazine in 1949. "He drives me up to the screened porch door, and I get out and go in the house myself while he drives down to put the car in the garage. If the children are with us, they dash past me, without even holding the door for me. I like their taking it for granted that I can look after myself. . . . If the children cry out in the night, I can't go to them immediately. It takes me eighteen minutes to put on my braces. My system is to shout and have them come to me. . . . Perhaps the children are more self-reliant than they would have been, had I not had [polio]."[110]

This "tough love" may partly explain why neither Erwin nor Harriet perceived any offensiveness at the dinners for the women, who "carried on good discussions" with the dean, Harriet said. It may also clarify, why Griswold later expressed surprise that his questions "were resented, and . . . are now recalled by some women graduates as examples of sexism on my part. . . . I was trying, if anything, to encourage the women to make full use of their legal training."[111] Nevertheless, through the end of his administration, Griswold maintained that women could not attain leading positions in the legal profession.

"A Small Number of Unusually Qualified Women"

Beyond the harassment of Ladies Day, the "mixed" welcome dinners, and the persistent charge that they were displacing men, the greatest barrier to women's progress at Harvard Law School was the small number enrolled during Griswold's administration. Official statistics on the admission or enrollment of women are not available, and the best indication is the number of graduates, presented in Table 12.1. The trend is slightly upward, but the proportion in the graduating class rose only from about 3 percent in the 1950s to about 4 percent in the 1960s. This "did not seem like much progress," Mary Mullarkey rightly observed.[112]

School officials denied the existence of a quota for women. Dean Griswold, Admissions Director Toepfer, and the members of the Admissions Committee, such as Charles Fried, maintained that the applicant pool was very small and that more female applicants "didn't exist."[113] However, over 100,000 women graduated annually with bachelor's degrees in the 1950s, and over 200,000 in the mid-1960s. The small applicant pool therefore reflects a lack of initiative and effort to recruit women.

In any event, there were always more women applying than were admitted. In 1950 there were 25 applications, 15 admitted, and 14 enrolled; in 1961, 48 applications, 27 admitted, and 20 enrolled; in 1965, 139 applications and 22 enrolled. Yet criticizing the decreasing ratio of enrollments to applications over time, as some have done, does not account for the increasing selectivity applied to admissions over the same period.[114]

The salient question concerns the degree of selectivity applied to female applicants versus male applicants. Was the intellectual sword wielded more severely against the women? Did the Admissions Committee admit "just the women that they thought would be an unbelievably safe bet?" as Bartholet asked.[115] Early on, that clearly was the case. In 1949 the faculty and dean announced the policy of admitting only "a small number of unusually qualified women students."[116] Determining how long the school pursued this policy would require a complicated analysis of data that remains sealed.

Nevertheless, Griswold certainly expressed his preference for a small enrollment of women. Faculty and students "did not get the sense that the dean was a fighter for more women here," noted Frank Sander. In contrast, Griswold clearly stated "that we did not have as many blacks as we should," according to Clark Byse, who joined the faculty in 1957.[117] This distinction between gender and race was demonstrated when the Law School initiated a special program in the summer of 1965 to recruit African American undergraduates. In reviewing the applications of African Americans, the school discriminated "heavily" in favor of the men and against the women, the *Harvard Law School Bulletin* announced publicly. After all, it said, "the law and the law schools have a relatively low proportion of women." This citing of the status quo as a justification speaks volumes about the unquestioned assumptions about gender at the school.[118]

In September 1966 Griswold expressed "puzzlement and consternation" in his welcoming speech to students that the number of women in the first-year class had jumped to thirty-seven, well above the prior norm of about twenty.[119] In the following spring, Griswold conveyed "a little disappointment" to the new Admissions Director Russell A. Simpson (LL.B. 1965) that forty-five women had been admitted to the entering class. Shortly before stepping down in June 1967, Griswold, among others on the faculty, still "believed that women were taking places away from men who would put their legal education to better use," said Simpson. "While he didn't tell me not to admit women, the message was certainly there."[120]

Even if no official quota existed and the "small number" of women resulted simply from a small applicant pool, the reasons for that deserve a closer look. Given the thousands of women receiving bachelor's degrees each year across the country, why did scarcely more than a hundred apply to Harvard Law School until shortly before Dean Griswold stepped down? Broad social factors certainly played an important role. But the school's renowned Spartan manliness, exhibited in positive discouragement through the various affronts to the female students, kept the applicant pool small.

Whether capped officially or not, the small number of women enrolled between 1950 and 1967 had a major impact. Already the influence of women with Harvard LL.B.s on the legal profession, the law, and American politics had been delayed for sixty years between 1893—when admitting them would have been a progressive, but not radical, decision—and 1950. That influence was then seriously weakened by the low enrollment of women that persisted for two decades after 1950. All this was the nation's loss.

If not for this low enrollment, the small group of such women who attended Harvard between 1950 and 1970 and attained the highest positions of influence by the 1990s—Attorney General Janet Reno, Congresswoman Patricia Scott Schroeder (LL.B. 1964), Cabinet Secretary Elizabeth Hanford Dole (LL.B. 1965), Harvard Law Professor Elizabeth Bartholet, Harvard Corporation member Judith Hope, Supreme Court Justice Ruth Bader Ginsburg, and others—would have been a legion.[121] The influence of women on the bench, the bar, and politics in the United States would have been greatly expanded. Whatever may be said about Ladies Day, the dean's welcoming dinners, and other affronts, the lost generation of Harvard Law women is surely the greatest discredit to the school's record on gender under Dean Griswold.

After Griswold stepped down, the number of women began to rise significantly under Acting Dean Casner, when the Admissions Office established "a kind of informal affirmative action program for women," given that women "were not scoring particularly well in the LSAT," according to Simpson. In 1968 the number of women in the entering class rose to forty-one, or 7.4 percent. But progress slowed during the brief deanship of Dean Derek Bok (1968–1970). The class matriculating in September 1969 had forty-eight women, or 8 percent, and the class matriculating in 1970 had forty-seven women, or 8.5 percent.[122]

"A Man's Profession"

Severe discrimination prevented the early female graduates from finding professional work, particularly during the 1950s. Though having graduated cum laude, Mary-Elizabeth Jacques received few interviews in response to her dozens of letters of inquiry. At one major Boston law firm, the interviewing attorney "told me that he was not prejudiced against women attorneys and that 'all things being equal,' he would as soon hire a woman as a man. I asked him under what circumstances he would consider all things being equal. 'Under none that I can think of,' he replied."[123]

Even the first woman elected to the *Harvard Law Review*, Priscilla Holmes, had difficulty obtaining interviews, let alone job offers. She "found many firms and often whole cities (e.g. Denver and San Francisco) unwilling even to consider hiring a woman."[124] In a 1986 study of thirty-four women who had graduated thirty years earlier in the first three classes, Nancy Young (LL.B. 1954) reported that, when employed, "women are generally expected to work in certain fields—probate, estate planning, and tax. A number of other areas are completely closed to them," including litigation. She concluded, "it is still far more difficult for a woman attorney to find a position today than it is for a young man even though he may not have as good an academic record. . . . The barriers remain highest in the city firm which is often bound by tradition, precedent, and a wary eye to the reactions of the clients with substantial retainers."[125]

In New York City, as of 1956, only about eighteen female lawyers were employed in major firms. After Ruth Bader Ginsburg graduated from Columbia at the top of her class in 1959, she found that no firm would hire her because she was a woman, a mother, and a Jew. Esther Roditti (LL.B. 1957) encountered the same prejudices and made no progress until she stopped wearing her wedding ring and ceased using her Jewish-sounding married name (Schachter). And then she had to fend off flirtatious advances and field questions about contraception.[126]

These conditions almost certainly depressed the number of applications to the Law School from women and confirmed the assumptions of the conservative faculty. It became a self-fulfilling prophecy. In 1961, when Rosemary Masters (LL.B. 1964) interviewed with Arthur Sutherland for admission at the Law School, he told her that completing secretarial school along with law school "would guarantee my landing a job with a prestige law firm as personal secretary to a senior partner. My first reaction was 'He's kidding.' My second reaction was 'Oh, my God, he's not kidding.'"[127] Several women reported receiving similar advice from other members of the Law School faculty. Through 1967 there were few prominent female lawyers throughout the country to counter this view.[128]

The placement office gave little help to the women in their job hunting, inasmuch as Placement Director Toepfer conceded that law would remain "a man's profession" beyond the school's control. Hence, the Law School permitted firms interviewing on campus to refuse to meet with women, to conduct interviews in a prejudicial manner when they did, and to refrain from making any offers to women.[129] The situation did not change until the academic year 1967–68, when Acting Dean Casner—who, paradoxically, had conducted Ladies Days—summoned "all of the hiring partners of the Boston firms and told them that, unless the third-year female students began receiving follow-up interviews and job offers, the firms could no longer use the placement services at Harvard Law School. Soon after, women began to get job offers."[130] If Griswold had done that, the hiring practices certainly would have changed much earlier.

Though a great deal has been written about the experience of the women who enrolled at the Law School during Griswold's administration, no comprehensive study has been conducted of the careers of the 192 LL.B. female graduates between 1953 and 1967.[131] Only close study of such data can begin to illuminate women's career choices during this critical period and how those changed over time and in different regions. Nevertheless, the professional accomplishments of these early women in the face of barriers are clearly remarkable. Within the field of law, at least fourteen became judges, many in federal courts and state supreme courts. Others, like Reno, Schroeder, Dole, Hope, and Bartholet, became major figures in politics, government, legal practice, and academe.[132]

Ruth Bader Ginsburg

One woman whose career exemplifies the tortuous path of early female students at the Law School and their complicated relationship with Dean Griswold did not actually receive her LL.B. from Harvard: Ruth Bader Ginsburg.[133] The daughter of Russian Jewish immigrants, Ginsburg completed her B.A. at Cornell in 1954 and married Martin D. Ginsburg (LL.B. 1958) before matriculating at the Law School in September 1956. She was one of only two married women admitted during Griswold's administration and the only mother. Her class of 1959 had 552 students, including nine women, whose "every move was closely watched," she felt.[134]

Though not subjected to Ladies Day, Ginsburg attended the Griswolds' already legendary dinner in October 1956 and found it "intimidating and unwelcoming." Griswold's question about why she was taking the place of a man prompted "one of life's most embarrassing moments," she recalled. "I stood up to answer, forgetting that I had a full ashtray in my lap. I watched in horror as butts and ashes cascaded onto the Griswolds' carpet. The dean appeared not to notice. Being married with a fourteen-month-old baby, I managed to mumble that my husband was a Harvard 2-L and it was important for a woman to understand her husband's work."[135]

An excellent student, Ginsburg, like her husband, was elected to the *Harvard Law Review,* but at the end of her second year, a serious dilemma prompted her estrangement from Griswold and the Law School. Martin had accepted a good job in New York City but then became seriously ill with cancer, and Ruth did not want to remain in Cambridge for her third year, especially as a single mother. She therefore petitioned the dean to spend the third year on leave at Columbia and then receive her degree from Harvard Law School. A generation later, such a petition would be routinely granted, but Griswold denied it. Ruth went to Columbia anyway, which credited the two years of work at Harvard and awarded her the LL.B. in 1959, tied for first in her class.

The Ginsburgs always considered Griswold's decision unreasonable and hurtful, and the events have been retold, implicitly attributing Griswold's decision to invidious sexism.[136] In 1998 Stanford law professor Gerald Gunther (LL.B. 1953) wrote that Griswold denied Ginsburg's application in 1958 "even

Ruth B. Ginsburg, attended 1956 to 1958. Faculty 1971.

Harvard Law School Yearbook, 1957. Courtesy of Harvard Yearbook Publications.

though, to my knowledge, applications by males for similar permissions were quite frequently granted."[137] Though stung by this, Griswold, who died in 1994, never publicly explained his decision, but wrote privately that he had followed the "long-established practice" that Harvard Law School did not award its LL.B. to students who left to complete work elsewhere.[138]

The past deans' handling of such petitions is obscure. But it seems highly doubtful that Deans Ezra Thayer, Roscoe Pound, or James Landis would have agreed to grant the Harvard LL.B. to any students who transferred to another law school prior to their third year. And Griswold fiercely defended the singular prestige of the Harvard LL.B. Also, Griswold seemed inflexible in responding to some petitions from men about enrolling and earning the Harvard LL.B. For example, Leonard B. Sand (LL.B. 1951), a member of the *Harvard Law Review* and later a federal judge, was drafted into the Naval Reserve in his third year during the Korean War and needed special permission from the Navy and the Law School to return and finish his degree. James Vorenberg (LL.B. 1951), president of the *Law Review* at the time, served as Sand's advocate with the deans and considered the matter an easy case. But Vorenberg found Griswold resistant because Sand had left in his third year.[139]

Nevertheless, Griswold's own revisionist account of Ginsburg's 1958 departure from Harvard Law School suggests that his decision was based, at least partly, on her gender. When Ginsburg served on the U.S. Court of Appeals for the District of Columbia Circuit during the 1980s, Griswold was also working in Washington. He would often introduce her to his colleagues by saying "that I had met my husband at the Harvard Law School, and when my husband got a good job in New York, I left Harvard and transferred to Columbia for my third year." In Griswold's account, Ginsburg had chosen to leave Harvard in order to follow her husband and support his career. In the 1980s, Griswold was still fitting Ginsburg's departure into his traditional domestic narrative, contrary to the facts, as Ginsburg gently pointed out to him.[140]

Even as the Ginsburgs' resentment about Griswold's 1958 decision lingered, Ruth forged a brilliant career during the 1970s as cofounder of the Women's Rights Project at the ACLU and then as its general counsel. During that decade, she brought six gender discrimination cases to the U.S. Supreme Court, and won five.[141] This astonishing accomplishment led to her appointment on the U.S. Court of Appeals for the District of Columbia Circuit in 1980 by President James Carter.

Then, in 1985, came Griswold's chance to redeem himself. In an address praising lawyers who had appeared before the U.S. Supreme Court, he spoke of the work of Charles Houston (LL.B. 1922, S.J.D. 1923) and Thurgood Marshall, and then observed that Judge Ginsburg had done analogous work for the rights of women. Eight years later, in 1993, New York Senator Daniel Patrick Moynihan suggested to President Bill Clinton that he appoint Judge Ginsburg to fill an opening on the U.S. Supreme Court. But Clinton demurred, observing that women's groups would not support the nomination because Ginsburg endorsed the outcome, but not the reasoning, of *Roe v. Wade* (1973). Soon thereafter, Moynihan happened to hear Griswold's analogy—frequently repeated as "Ruth Bader Ginsburg was to women's rights what Thurgood Marshall was to civil rights." Moynihan shared it with David Gergen (LL.B. 1967), a new advisor to Clinton, who related Griswold's analogy to the president. Clinton then decided to nominate Ginsburg in June 1993, and she later affirmed, "I have every assurance the Dean's words counted heavily in the President's nomination."[142]

In 2009 Justice Ginsburg opined that Griswold "was educated over the years." She began to observe this change in the early 1970s when arguing cases about women's rights before the Supreme Court. Griswold, then the solicitor general defending the government's position, acknowledged her appreciatively. Ginsburg believed that Griswold "had become sensitive to a kind of discrimination" due to his wife's prominent work in the Americans With Disabilities movement. Thus, Griswold began to change his view on women's work after leaving the deanship in 1967. He actively assisted alumnae, as well as women working with him in legal practice.[143]

Occasionally he also took some credit for women's enrollment at Harvard Law School and their career success, mixed with regret for his early view that the admission of women was not "either very important or very significant."[144] Meanwhile, Harriet never ceased writing in private letters that "Erwin got women admitted to the Law School." As to Justice Ginsburg, Griswold himself wrote privately, perhaps hopefully, in 1988, "I was the tyrant who said she could not get a Harvard degree. . . . For some time she was much annoyed with me, but that is past."[145]

Hispanic Students

While women struggled for acceptance at Harvard Law School and in the legal profession, the enrollment of minority students at the school remained minimal, as seen in Table 12.2. Several ethnic groups were represented by only one or two individuals, and even identifying them presents difficulties.

In his study "Hispanic Graduates of Harvard Law School," Felipe D. Mendoza (J.D. 2006) has made the most thorough effort to identify those who graduated from Harvard Law School prior to 1970. Before 1916, Hispanic students graduated from the Law School rarely and never more than one in any given year.[146] After 1916 the gap between graduating classes with Hispanic members diminished to four years or less, and the number of graduates in a given year increased, but never exceeded five. Why the pattern changed in 1916 is not evident, but it persisted through Griswold's administration until 1967. Over the entire period from 1916 to 1967, some seventy-seven Hispanics received the LL.B. from the school. These included thirty-two in the thirty years from 1916 to 1946, and thirty-five in the twenty-one years of Griswold's administration between 1946 and 1967. The great majority of the seventy-seven were raised in middle- or upper-middle-class families in South America, Cuba, Mexico, Spain, or Puerto Rico.[147]

Table 12.2	Number of Students, Sorted by Race, Ethnicity, and Gender, in Entering LL.B.
Classes at Harvard Law School in the Fall of 1938, 1960, and 1964

Group	1938[a]	1960[b]	1964[c]
White	548	458	482
African American	2	0	11
Hispanic	0	3	1
Asian	1	0	2
Other	1	0	3
Total Minority	4	3	16
Total Female	0	13	24

Data sources: Data compiled from review of pictures in Harvard Law School "face books" of entering students, pictures of Harvard Law School Yearbooks, and figures from Harvard Law School Admissions Office reported intermittently in *HLSR*.

a. Six students not counted because race could not be determined.

b. About thirty students not counted because race could not be identified.

c. Fifty-one students not counted because their pictures were not available.

Mendoza was able to locate and interview three who graduated during Dean Griswold's tenure: Carlos Cebollero (LL.B. 1951), Jorge Luis Cordova (LL.B. 1957), and Victor Ortega (LL.B. 1959). Cebollero was raised in a well-to-do family in Puerto Rico, where his father ran a food wholesale business. Entering the Law School in 1948 amid the influx of veterans, he found that the teaching "was Socratic" and "people were terrified about it." He did not remember any reference to ethnicity or race during his enrollment. As one of the eleven Hispanic graduates during the postwar years between 1946 and 1951, he became a lawyer in San Juan and served on the Board of Bar Examiners of Puerto Rico and as president of the Puerto Rico chapter of the Federal Bar Association.

Also raised in Puerto Rico, Jorge Luis Cordova matriculated into the Law School in 1954, after graduating from Princeton University. His father, Jorge Luis Córdova Díaz, had earned the LL.B. at the Law School in 1931 and served in the U.S. Congress as the Resident Commissioner of Puerto Rico from 1969 to 1973. Concerning the "very tough" first year at the Law School, the son recalled, "the level and quality of effort considered high at both Harvard and Princeton is essentially the same, but you were expected to reach that level of effort more often at Harvard Law School than you were at college. There was greater pressure to perform on a daily basis at Harvard . . . [even though] exams were only once a year."

Cordova reported that he felt "lost in some of my courses" and "did not do very well that first year" and "briefly considered leaving and many of our classmates did leave." But working over the summer in a law firm convinced him "that the law could be extremely interesting and fruitful," and he returned to Harvard with renewed interest. Cordova nevertheless had some bad experiences at the Law School: "Some professors really browbeat and chewed up students. There seemed to be a . . . lack of communication and contact between students and teachers, which I was not used to. At Princeton we had small classes and it was very easy to talk to the teachers, and . . . they seemed interested in making sure the students . . . were part of this educational structure. I missed that at Harvard."

Cordova also felt a cultural difference manifested in jurisprudence: "I represented a different legal system because the French and the Spanish [civil-law] legal systems, based on the Napoleonic code, are very different from the common-law education at Harvard. . . . Some of the teachers made what I would consider snide remarks about the civil law. Some professors would openly sneer at these crazy civil-law solutions for problems that [the common law] had solved in a different manner. That may be a more highly sophisticated form of discrimination, but I did certainly feel that."

Cordova's circle of friends from Princeton at the Law School "made me a bit of a WASP compared to other Hispanics," and he did not feel "discomfort or lack of recognition in terms of being Hispanic" or "personal discrimination." This contrasted with the experience of his African American classmates. "There were very few blacks," said Cordova. "I certainly did not feel as discriminated against as they did. . . . We compared experiences in college as opposed to law school, and our discrimination at that time was much worse in college than . . . at the Law School."

Lastly, Victor Ortega entered the Law School in 1956, after graduating from Harvard College in 1954 as a member of Phi Beta Kappa. His father, who had been raised in Santa Fe, New Mexico, during the Depression, was an accountant and owned a struggling bar and restaurant. Eventually he was elected county treasurer, and found work as an accountant for the U.S. Postal Service. The family was "comfortable but lived very modestly by today's standards."

Regarding his first year at the Law School, Ortega recalled that "to some degree, everybody was terrified" of the competition. Selective admissions and the LSAT requirement had begun, and "a high percentage of the members of my class came from Harvard, Princeton, or Yale" and "from all over the country, from other universities. . . . You knew you were competing with a very elite group of students." Until exams were graded at the end of the year, students did not know how well they were doing. "When the grades came out fine, I stopped worrying about it. Up to that point, it was somewhat terrifying."

According to Ortega, "nobody paid attention to the fact that I was Hispanic. In law school I can't remember that being a factor or any other nationality being a factor of any kind. Most of the time you were focused on where you stood in the class. I wasn't disadvantaged, nor was I socially any different from any of my friends who are still friends to this day, some of whom . . . might be Irish or English or whatever." But, like Cordova, Ortega found that African Americans felt discrimination acutely.

African American Students, 1940s and 1950s

Having attended Oberlin College, Griswold evidently became more sensitized to Oberlin's tradition of pioneering abolitionism and enrollment of African Americans than to its simultaneous trail-blazing in coeducation, both of which began in the 1830s. His Quaker-Presbyterian upbringing may also have contributed to his concern about discrimination against people of African descent.[148] In the 1940s he began to respond by arranging for African legal scholars and students to visit the Law School, while also contributing expertise on voting rights, legal services, and legal education in visits to South Africa.[149]

His involvement in the African American civil rights movement began while he served on the staff of the Office of the Solicitor General in 1929–1934, when he argued more than twenty cases before the Supreme Court. In 1932 he witnessed Charles Houston's argument before the Supreme Court in the voting rights case of *Nixon v. Condon* (1932), leading to Griswold's acquaintance with Houston and Thurgood Marshall. In 1942, after the Supreme Court held in *Betts v. Brady* that legal representation "is not a fundamental right, essential to a fair trial," Griswold publicly opposed the decision, jeopardizing his future at Harvard and the Solicitor General's Office. But his public opposition contributed to the reversal by Supreme Court in *Gideon v. Wainwright* (1963).[150]

In the early 1940s, after Thurgood Marshall became legal director of the National Association for the Advancement of Colored People (NAACP), he came to Harvard Law School and consulted faculty about the strategy for overturning the standard of "separate but equal" established by *Plessy v. Ferguson* (1896). In 1948, at Marshall's request, Dean Griswold traveled to North

Carolina and Oklahoma to testify as an expert witness on legal education in cases challenging the practice of states to establish substandard public law schools for African Americans in order to appear to meet the *Plessy* standard, while keeping the main public law school of the state reserved for whites. Griswold "learned later that President Conant [who resigned in 1953] was not pleased" by his involvement.[151]

The work with Marshall culminated in *Sweatt v. Painter* (1950) and led to the final assault on segregation in *Brown v. Board of Education* (1954). In 1961 Griswold was appointed to the U.S. Civil Rights Commission and served until 1967, when he became solicitor general. In 1963 he joined the Lawyers Committee for Civil Rights, which had emerged from a convention of jurists called by President John Kennedy at the White House, and Griswold served on that Committee for thirty years.[152]

Notwithstanding Griswold's involvement in civil rights legal work, the vast majority of students at Harvard Law School were white, male, Protestant, and from well-to-do families. Selective admissions reinforced their preponderance.[153] In addition, public funding to assist students enrolling in higher education, such as that provided by the G.I. Bill (1944), did not improve racial diversity during the 1950s. In order to secure the support of southern congressmen for the G.I. Bill, the authors of the bill did not prohibit racial discrimination, and allowed local officials and college administrators, rather than federal officials, to distribute the benefits. As a result, in some states little funding went to African Americans, including those wishing to attend out-of-state law schools.[154] Because of such factors and the school's lack of initiative, only one or two African American students enrolled in each class at Harvard Law School during the 1940s and 1950s.

One graduate was William T. Coleman Jr. (LL.B. 1946), who became the first African American to clerk for a Supreme Court Justice. Born in 1920 to a middle-class family in Philadelphia, Coleman attended the predominantly white Germantown high school, which disbanded its swim team rather than permit Coleman to participate. After graduating from the University of Pennsylvania in 1941, he entered Harvard Law School but interrupted his studies to serve as an officer in the U.S. Army, though he could not enter an officer's club due to his race. After the war, Coleman returned to Harvard, earned a place on the *Harvard Law Review,* and graduated first in his class in 1946.

After clerking for Judge Herbert F. Goodrich (LL.B. 1914) of the U.S. Court of Appeals, Coleman clerked for Justice Felix Frankfurter (LL.B. 1906) in 1948, when few restaurants in the nation's capital permitted Coleman to dine with the other clerks, all of whom were white. In about 1950 Coleman returned to Philadelphia and, after an arduous job search, became the first African American hired by a major law firm in that city. He also worked with Thurgood Marshall on the NAACP legal team and argued nineteen cases in front of the U.S. Supreme Court during his career. He served in many posts, advising ten presidential administrations, from Dwight D. Eisenhower to George W. Bush. President Gerald R. Ford named him secretary of transportation, making him only the second African American to hold a cabinet-level appointment.[155]

In 1920 Wade H. McCree Jr. (LL.B. 1948) was born in Iowa, but his father, a pharmacist who worked for the federal government, moved the family to Boston. After graduating from Boston Latin School, the son attended Fisk University and earned the B.A. with highest honors. In 1942 he enrolled in Harvard Law School, and soon left to join the Army during World War II, serving four years, rising to the rank of Captain, and earning a bronze star. Returning to Cambridge, he graduated in 1948, twelfth in his class. In 1961 President John Kennedy appointed him the second African American U.S. District Court judge, and in 1968 President Lyndon Johnson named him the second African American U.S. Court of Appeals judge. In 1977 he became the first African American Solicitor General, and argued the famous cases, on behalf of the government, concerning the presidential tapes of Richard Nixon, *United States v. Nixon* (1974), and "reverse discrimination" in medical school admissions, *Regents of the University of California v. Bakke* (1978). McCree died in 1987.[156]

C. Clyde Ferguson Jr. (LL.B. 1951), a future Harvard Law professor, was born in North Carolina in 1924. His family moved to Maryland, where he was barred from the public institutions of higher education because of his race. So he attended Ohio State University and served in the Army, earning a Bronze Star for his service in the Battle of Normandy. In 1948 he graduated Phi Beta Kappa and entered Harvard Law School, where he excelled as a student and nearly made the *Harvard Law Review.*

His classmate, friend, and future dean of the Law School, James Vorenberg, recalled the common affronts encountered by Ferguson and other African American students in 1950. In their third year, "Clyde was sitting next to me in accounting class when Professor Robert Amory Jr. (LL.B. 1938) used the phrase, 'Nigger in the wood pile,'" recalled Vorenberg. After class, "Clyde . . . charged up to Bob Amory and started shouting at him. . . . It was one of the moments when I recognized that there were not many black students at the

C. Clyde Ferguson Jr., LL.B. 1951. Faculty 1975–1983.

Harvard Law School Yearbook, 1976. Courtesy of Harvard Yearbook Publications.

School."[157] After graduating and working at the NAACP and on the U.S. Commission on Civil Rights, Ferguson in 1955 became the first African American law professor at Rutgers University. He served as dean of the law school at Howard University from 1963 to 1969. In 1975 he joined the faculty of Harvard Law School as a visiting professor and in 1977 was promoted to tenured professor. Ferguson continued on the faculty until his sudden death from a heart attack at age fifty-nine in 1983.[158]

Christopher F. Edley Sr. (LL.B. 1952) was born in Charleston, West Virginia, in 1928.[159] After serving in the Army in 1946 and 1947, he studied at Howard University, graduated in 1949, and then entered Harvard Law School. According to his son—Professor Christopher F. Edley Jr. (LL.B. 1978)—his father's experience at Harvard was "pretty painful," though he "mostly talked about the fine education and the teaching."

But his father did have "one extraordinarily positive story about the Law School," said Edley Jr. During his first semester in the fall of 1949, his father literally ran out of money and went in to see Vice Dean Livingston Hall, who "cross-examined him." Then, "my father pulled out his accounts showing all his expenses and so forth. Hall listened thoughtfully, pulled out . . . a checkbook, and wrote him a check. This confirmed what people at Howard University had told my father as an undergraduate in college, that if you could get in, Harvard would help you to make it through."

After a second tour of duty during the Korean War, Edley returned to the Law School in 1951. He found "only two or three black students, but he made some good friends among the white students." After graduating in 1953, he began seeking "a city or town in which a young black lawyer could make a living," and brought his family to Philadelphia. At that time, William Coleman was working there, and William Hastie (LL.B. 1930, S.J.D. 1933) was sitting on the U.S. Court of Appeals, the highest judicial position held by an African American. But major firms told Edley that they would not hire a second African American until they determined whether the first, Coleman, would survive. He therefore went to work for the district attorney, Samuel Dash (LL.B. 1950), who later became chief counsel to the U.S. Senate committee investigating the Watergate scandal in the 1970s. Edley then joined a small African American law firm that provided legal services to poor and blue-collar African American families and often struggled to make the weekly payroll.

One day sitting at the kitchen table in about 1960, Edley discussed the Emancipation Proclamation with his ten-year-old son, who later became a Harvard Law professor:

> We were talking about slavery and the Emancipation Proclamation. I was arguing to [my father] that, from the perspective of the slave owners, Lincoln was taking their property. . . . We argued back and forth. Finally he said, slamming his fist on the table, "This is my house, so long as you're in my house, the Emancipation Proclamation was a good thing, and slavery was a bad thing."

In 1963 the Ford Foundation selected Edley to be its first African American program officer. Ten years later he was named president of the United Negro College Fund, where he worked for eighteen years and raised more than $550 million to support historically black colleges and universities.

Three years after Edley graduated from the Law School, Rosa Parks refused to give up her seat on a bus to a white man in Montgomery, Alabama. As the Montgomery Bus Boycott proceeded during 1956, Lila Althea Fenwick (LL.B. 1956) became the first African American woman to graduate from Harvard Law School. Her father was a prominent businessman, and her mother had taught school in Trinidad. She had graduated from Barnard College in 1953 and enrolled at Harvard Law School in only the fourth class to admit women. After completing the LL.B., Lila studied briefly at the London School of Economics, and in 1958 joined the Human Rights Division of the United Nations. In 1971 she became a section chief and cofounded the Foundation for Research and Education in Sickle Cell Disease. In 1995 the Black Law Students Association at Harvard Law School created the Ruffin-Fenwick Trailblazer Award, named for her and George Lewis Ruffin (LL.B. 1869), the first African American man to attend the law school.[160]

Special Summer Program for Diversity

By 1960 the number of applications from African Americans, particularly southerners, had fallen considerably, and the tiny number of these students in the Law School had declined even further to merely one per class, and sometimes none. In 1961 the dearth of such law students nationally was highlighted when Attorney General Robert Kennedy wrote to forty-four law deans around the country requesting recommendations of African American law students for positions in the Department of Justice. Very few candidates could be found.[161]

In the spring of 1962 the issue became publicly embarrassing for the Law School when Dean Griswold testified in Washington at hearings on "Literacy Tests and Voter Requirements in Federal and State Elections" before the Senate Subcommittee on Constitutional Rights. Griswold asserted that voter registration statistics indicated that the proposed voting rights bill was necessary to counter discrimination. North Carolina senator Sam Ervin then observed that, by the dean's reasoning, one could infer that Harvard Law School discriminated against nonwhites because the school had "only four black students."[162]

Meanwhile, the Admissions Committee at the Law School started giving special consideration to applications from African Americans, and Toepfer began making recruiting trips to historically black colleges around the country. But he had little success. "It would be announced that I was there, and I would go to the assigned office, and I'd sit there all day and nothing would happen. . . . It was very frustrating," stated Toepfer. A major problem was that few law firms would hire African American attorneys. Nevertheless, these efforts began to yield some results. In the fall of 1963, three African Americans entered in the first-year class; in the fall of 1964 eleven came.[163]

In 1964, as the civil rights movement grew, the newly created U.S. Office of Economic Opportunity (OEO) began to fund summer programs, such as A Better Chance, at private colleges and universities to prepare and recruit young African Americans into higher education.[164] Following the template of those OEO programs and guided by input from leaders of the black colleges, Toepfer and an ad hoc faculty committee designed a Special Summer Program (SSP) to interest juniors at historically black colleges in entering the legal profession and applying to law school in their senior year. In the summer of 1965 the SSP held its first, eight-week session for forty students from twenty-eight colleges. The participants visited law firms, participated in mock trials, learned about legal problems and methods, and took mini-courses taught through the case method by regular Harvard faculty and the dean of Howard University Law School. The following October, twenty-seven of the forty students reported that law was definitely their career choice. Given this success, Harvard repeated the program in 1966, directed by Professor Frank Sander, and in 1968 it was merged into the national Council on Legal Education Opportunity, which Sander chaired until 1970.[165]

Although the point of the program was to interest college juniors generally in the legal profession, some seniors attended as well, and four entered law school right after the SSP in 1965: two went to Howard and two to Harvard. One of the latter was Reginald F. Lewis (LL.B. 1968), who had grown up in Baltimore and attended Dunbar High School like Charles Houston and William Hastie. Lewis won a football scholarship to historically black Virginia State College. Though not a distinguished student in the SSP cohort, Lewis's tenacity and drive convinced Toepfer to admit him to Harvard, and he enrolled with only a few dollars in his pocket. After graduating in 1968, Lewis worked for a corporate law firm, and in 1983 he founded a fabulously successful venture capital firm. By 1992 his wealth was estimated at $400 million and *Forbes* listed him among the 400 wealthiest Americans. That same year, he donated $3 million to the Law School, the largest gift it had received to that point, and the International Legal Studies Building was renamed in his honor. For many years the Lewis International Law Center was the only building in the Ivy League named for an African American. In 1993 Lewis died at age fifty.[166]

The other student entering the Law School right after the 1965 SSP was James McPherson (LL.B. 1968), who had graduated in June from Morris Brown College. Every SSP student was also required to take a course in Harvard Summer School, and McPherson chose a course in Shakespeare, whose

Reginald F. Lewis, LL.B. 1968.
Photograph 1991. © Gregory Heisler.

instructor told the SSP faculty that McPherson really ought to pursue a career in writing. But the faculty admitted him that summer, and McPherson decided to attend and complete the LL.B., while working as a janitor and writing short stories. After graduation, he earned an M.F.A. at the University of Iowa and became a brilliant fiction writer, winning a Pulitzer Prize and a MacArthur Fellowship.[167]

In addition to these two exemplars, an increasing number of African Americans from the SSP program applied to and matriculated at the Law School:

sixteen in 1965, twenty-one in 1966, twenty-eight in 1967, and thirty-five in 1968, when the entire first-year class was expanded by about 10 percent to 609.[168] But these efforts also demonstrated the justified resentment by students of color at the slow rate of progress. Having assisted Thurgood Marshall with the legal challenge to segregated education in the late 1940s and early 1950s, Dean Griswold felt it fitting to invite Marshall, then U.S. solicitor general, to speak at the closing dinner of the first SSP in 1965. Following Marshall's speech, the students aggressively questioned Marshall, implying that he had sold out and become part of the white power structure. This confrontation astonished and offended Griswold, although Marshall was understanding and patient with the students.[169]

"Segregated Colleges"

Over the course of Dean Griswold's tenure from 1946 to 1967, the Law School completed a three-step revolution in its admissions policy and procedures: adopting selective admissions, admitting women, and recruiting African American students. Each development was characterized by good intentions, resentment, and unanticipated outcomes that demonstrated the huge gap in understanding to be bridged.

The chasm is shown by the inaccurate references to the historically black colleges in the public literature of the Law School. In 1965 and 1966 the dean, the *Harvard Law School Bulletin,* and the faculty leading the SSP publicly described the black colleges as "segregated colleges" and the overwhelmingly white institutions as "integrated colleges," implicitly placing the onus on the black colleges for segregation.[170] But of course, it was the white colleges and universities that had adopted segregation by prohibiting, or severely limiting, enrollment of African Americans. The black colleges and universities were established in response, and virtually none of them prohibited whites from attending. They were not segregated in principle or in fact.

The language of "segregated colleges" expressed poignantly the lack of understanding about race that prevailed, just as Dean Griswold's "mixed" message in welcoming speeches and at welcoming dinners took for granted the gendered culture of Spartan manliness at the school and in the legal profession. All the misunderstanding, resentment, good intentions, and unanticipated outcomes would feed the conflict and dissension that erupted in the Law School during the two decades after Griswold departed.

NOTES

1. Arthur E. Sutherland, *The Law at Harvard: A History of Ideas and Men, 1817–1907* (Cambridge, MA, 1967), 320.

2. Nathan M. Pusey "A Great Dean," *HLR* 81 (1967): 291; "Erwin N. Griswold," *HLR* 86 (1973): 1365–1379; "Dedication of Griswold Hall: September 18, 1979," *HLSB* (Fall 1979): 26–39; *Erwin N. Griswold, 1904–1994* (printed pamphlet, March 10, 1995) (Cambridge, MA, 1995), on file with the authors; "In Memoriam: Erwin Nathaniel Griswold," *HLR* 108 (1995): 980–1002.

3. Daniel R. Coquillette and Bruce A. Kimball, *On the Battlefield of Merit: Harvard Law School, the First Century* (Cambridge, MA, 2015) (hereafter cited as *Battlefield of Merit*), 408–411, 431n104–106; 472–475, 499–501.

4. Ernest J. Brown, Oral History, conducted by Daniel Hamilton (August 1997), on file with the authors. See, too, Erwin N. Griswold, *Ould Fields, New Corne: The Personal Memoirs of a Twentieth Century Lawyer* (St. Paul, MN, 1992), 161.

5. See John J. Coss, "Introduction," *Five College Plans* (New York, 1931), 1; David O. Levine, *The American College and the Culture of Aspiration, 1915–1940* (Ithaca, NY, 1986), 137–142; Roger L. Geiger, *To Advance Knowledge: The Growth of American Research Universities, 1900–1940* (New York, 1986), 115.

6. Harvard Law School (HLS) Faculty Meeting Minutes (December 14, 1948).

7. Emphasis in original. Erwin N. Griswold, Annual Report of the Dean of HLS, 1947–48, 395–396.

8. Griswold, Annual Report of the Dean, 1949–50, 452.

9. Louis A. Toepfer, "Admissions," *HLSB* (April 1957): 3; Louis A. Toepfer, Oral History, conducted by Daniel Hamilton (March 1998), on file with the authors; Brown, Oral History (August 1997).

10. Quotation is from William P. LaPiana, "Merit and Diversity: The Origins of the Law School Admission Test," in *Before the Paper Chase: The Scholarship of Law School Preparation and Admissions*, ed. Tim A. Garrison and Frank Guliuzza (Durham, NC, 2012), 64. See HLS Faculty Meeting Minutes (December 14, 1936; October 19, 1937); Albert B. Crawford and Tom Jay Gorham, "The Yale Legal Aptitude Test," *Yale Law Journal* 49 (1940): 1238; Thomas O. White, "LSAC / LSAS: A Brief History," *Journal of Legal Education* 34 (1984): 369–370.

11. HLS Faculty Meeting Minutes (August 19, September 30, November 18, 1947); Harvard Law School Catalog, 1948–49, 11; LaPiana, "Merit and Diversity," 67–69; John J. Liolos, "Erecting the High Citadel's Walls: The Development of Formal Admissions Standards at Harvard Law School, 1817–1955" (student research paper, HLS, 2013), on file with the authors, 61–66.

12. Quotations are from Detlev Vagts, Oral History, conducted by Daniel Hamilton, Daniel R. Coquillette, and John Delionado (November 1999–February 2000), on file with the authors; Andrew L. Kaufman, Oral History, conducted by Daniel

Hamilton and Daniel R. Coquillette (June 1999–April 2000), on file with the authors. See James Vorenberg, Oral History, conducted by Daniel R. Coquillette (November–December 1997), on file with the authors; Stephen Bernardi, Oral History, conducted by Daniel Hamilton and Daniel R. Coquillette (October 2000–April 2001), on file with the authors.

13. "Law School Admission Test," *HLSB* (October 1951): 5; Michael Levenson, "Harvard Decision Could Spark Shift in How Law Schools Test Applicants," *Boston Globe* (March 21, 2017).

14. "Use of Law School Admission Test," *HLSB* (October 1948): 2; "The Entering Class of 1950," *HLSB* (October 1950): 9; Toepfer, "Admissions," 4–5; Toepfer, Oral History (March 1998); Robert R. Ramsey Jr., "The Riddle of the Non-Intellectual: A Report on the Academic Behavior of Law Students," *HLSB* (December 1960): 3.

15. Toepfer, Oral History (March 1998); Russell A. Simpson, Oral History, conducted by Mary Beth Basile and Daniel R. Coquillette (May–September 2001), on file with the authors.

16. Ramsey, "Riddle of the Non-Intellectual," 4–5.

17. Quotation is from Erwin N. Griswold, "Intellect and Spirit," *HLR* 81 (1967): 301. See Griswold, Annual Report of the Dean, 1955–56, 394; Toepfer, "Admissions," 4; Brown, Oral History (August 1997).

18. Toepfer, Oral History (March 1998).

19. Toepfer, Oral History (March 1998).

20. Toepfer, Oral History (March 1998). The published records of the Law School do not list Kissinger as enrolling in 1949.

21. Griswold, *Ould Fields,* 162. See Toepfer, Oral History (March 1998); Griswold, Annual Report of the Dean, 1949–50, 452; "The Entering Class of 1950," 9.

22. Quotations are from Griswold, Annual Report of the Dean, 1963–64, 223; Russell A. Simpson, "Admissions," *HLSB* (March 1967): 12. See "The Entering Class of 1950," 9; "The First Year Class," *HLSB* (October 1952): 3; "Harvard Law School Association, 77th Annual Meeting of the Council," *HLSB* (June 1963): 21.

23. Louis A. Toepfer, "Scholarships and Loans," *HLSB* (April 1959): 4.

24. Compare "A Change in Grading Procedures," *HLSB* (June 1961): 14; "Harvard Law School Association, 77th Annual Meeting," 21; Simpson, "Admissions," 12.

25. Toepfer, Oral History (March 1998); Simpson, Oral History (May–September 2001).

26. HLS Faculty Meeting Minutes (August 19, 1947); "Admission of Women," *HLSB* (October 1949): 4; Toepfer, Oral History (March 1998).

27. The other schools were Georgetown University Law Center, which admitted women in 1951; Notre Dame Law School, which admitted women in 1969; Washington and Lee University School of Law, which admitted women in 1972; and Brigham Young University School of Law, which admitted women in 1973. Kayleigh McGlynn, "Law Schools Enrolling the First Female Students after Harvard Law School" (student research report, Boston College Law School, 2017), on file with the authors.

28. HLS Faculty Meeting Minutes (August 19, 1947); Griswold, *Ould Fields,* 170–172. See David McIntosh, "A Minor Matter: The Admission of Women to the Harvard Law School" (student research paper, HLS, 1998), on file with the authors, 14–15.

29. HLS Faculty Meeting Minutes (January 11, 1949).

30. Griswold, *Ould Fields,* 169–171. See McIntosh, "A Minor Matter," 3; Kenneth Leung, "The Deanship of Erwin Nathaniel Griswold, 1946–1967" (student research paper, HLS, 2010), on file with the authors, 9.

31. Quotation is from McIntosh, "A Minor Matter," 5, 16. See Leung, "The Deanship of Erwin Nathaniel Griswold, 1946–1967," 12–13; Mary Beth Basile, "False Starts: Harvard Law School's Efforts toward Integrating Women into the Faculty, 1928–1981," *Harvard Journal of Law and Gender* 28 (2005), 154; Judith Richards Hope, *Pinstripes & Pearls: The Women of the Harvard Law Class of '64 Who Forged an Old Girl Network and Paved the Way for Future Generations* (New York, 2003), 16.

32. HLS Faculty Meeting Minutes (January 11, 1949); Griswold, *Ould Fields,* 169; Harold J. Berman, Oral History, conducted by Daniel Hamilton and Daniel R. Coquillette (August 1998), on file with the authors; McIntosh, "A Minor Matter," 18–20.

33. Report of the Committee on the Admission of Women (April 15, 1949), HLS Dean's Office Records, Records of President James B. Conant, 1933–1953, Harvard University Archives (HUA) (hereafter cited as JBC Records). See Hope, *Pinstripes & Pearls,* 15–17, 266; McIntosh, "A Minor Matter," 21–25, 36; Julia Chen, "The Harvard Law School Experience for Women in the 1950s" (student research paper, HLS, 2013), on file with the authors, 2–3.

34. Report of the Committee on the Admission of Women (April 15, 1949).

35. Quotations are from HLS Faculty Meeting Minutes (May 10, 1949); see January 11 and September 20, 1949; "Admission of Women," 4; Griswold, *Ould Fields,* 170–171; McIntosh, "A Minor Matter," 29–37; Hope, *Pinstripes & Pearls,* 17; Chen, "The Harvard Law School," 5–6.

36. "Women at Harvard," *New York Times* (October 11, 1949). See Morton Keller and Phyllis Keller, *Making Harvard Modern: The Rise of America's University* (New York, 2001), 58–59; McIntosh, "A Minor Matter," 35; Rebecca H. Kimball, "Literature Review of Writings by and about Ruth Bader Ginsburg" (student research paper, Ohio State University, 2013), on file with the authors.

37. Quotations are from "Comments Approve Decision to Admit Women to School," *HLSR* (October 11, 1949): 1. See "Editorials," *HLSR* (October 11, 1949): 2; McIntosh, "A Minor Matter," 36–37. Mentschikoff is discussed in Chapter 13.

38. "HLS to Admit Co-Eds," *HLSR* (October 11, 1949): 1; "The Entering Class of 1950," 9; Brown, Oral History (August 1997).

39. Brown, Oral History (August 1997).

40. "No Women Taken Yet, Says Toepfer," *HLSR* (March 8, 1950): 1; "Nine out of Eighteen Women Admitted, the Office of Admissions Announces," *HLSR* (April 5, 1950): 1.

41. "The Entering Class of 1950," 9; "Alumni News," *HLSB* (October 1953): 20. Fourteen women ultimately enrolled in the first class: Carolyn MacTear Anderson, Charlotte Horwood Armstrong, Frederica S. Brenneman, Roberta Allene Good Brundage, Beverly S. Coleman, Helen Marie O'Connor Cunningham, Wilhelmina Louise Florencourt, Edith Guild Henderson, Miriam E. Huff, Mary-Elizabeth Jacques, Ann Pfohl Kirby, Sondra Markowitz Miller, Ruth Marshall Paven, and Mary M. Truschel. Denise Villeneuve, "Women at Harvard Law School: The First Class" (student research paper, HLS, 2001), on file with the authors, 6.

42. Sondra Markowitz Miller, Interview (November 12, 2000), quoted in Villeneuve, "Women at Harvard Law School," 9–10.

43. Beverly S. Coleman, Interview (November 12, 2000), quoted in Villeneuve, "Women at Harvard Law School," 9.

44. Quotation is from Helen Marie O'Connor Cunningham, quoted in "The Women of '53, Then and Now," *HLSB* (Summer 1988): 7. See Mary M. Truschel, Interview (January 23, 2001), quoted in Villeneuve, "Women at Harvard Law School," 9; Karen Berger Morello, *The Invisible Bar: The Woman Lawyer in America 1638 to the Present* (New York, 1986), 103.

45. Mary-Elizabeth Jacques, Interview (November 12, 2000), quoted in Villeneuve, "Women at Harvard Law School," 9–10; Frederica S. Brenneman, unpublished statement (September 11, 2000), quoted in Villeneuve, "Women at Harvard Law School," 7; Frederica S. Brenneman, quoted in "The Women of '53," 6.

46. Ruth Marshall Paven, Interview (November 16, 2000), quoted in Villeneuve, "Women at Harvard Law School," 10.

47. Quotations are from, respectively, Carolyn MacTear Anderson, quoted in "The Women of '53," 6; Carolyn MacTear Anderson, email to Denise Villeneuve (January 31, 2001), quoted in Villeneuve, "Women at Harvard Law School," 7–8.

48. Bruce A. Kimball, "Before the Paper Chase: Student Culture at Harvard Law School, 1895–1915," *Journal of Legal Education* 61 (2011): 47–48.

49. Truschel, Interview (January 23, 2001); Ann Pfohl Kirby, Interview (November 22, 2000), quoted in Villeneuve, "Women at Harvard Law School," 10.

50. Miller, Interview (November 12, 2000).

51. "Women Students," *HLSB* (October 1951): 5; Chen, "The Harvard Law School," appendix.

52. Sutherland, *The Law at Harvard*, 316–319. See Linda Eisenmann, *Higher Education for Women in Postwar America, 1945–1965* (Baltimore, 2006).

53. Jane Hill, "By the Sweat of Their Fraus: The Harvard Law Wives, 1929–1972" (student research paper, HLS, 2009), on file with the authors, 8–9; "School Greets Class of 1957," *HLSR* (September 30, 1954): 1; Toepfer, "Scholarships and Loans," 4; Richard Hoffman, "The New Class: A Conglomerate Merger," *HLSR* (October 13, 1967): 7; Simpson, Oral History (May–September 2001).

54. Ruth Bader Ginsburg, "The Changing Complexion of Harvard Law School," *Harvard Women's Law Journal* 27 (2004): 307.

55. "Student Activities," *HLSB* (February 1951): 11.

56. Harvard Law School Board of Student Advisors, *Handbook for New Students Entering Harvard Law School* (Cambridge, MA, 1948), 45; 1952, 37; 1957, 40. "Profiles of Leaders," *HLSR* (February 16, 1961): 12. See Hill, "By the Sweat of Their Fraus," 9.

57. Valerie Handler, "Law's Presence Felt at Home, Discloses Law Student's Wife," *HLSR* (February 19, 1955): 3; "The Law Wife's Lot Is Not a Happy One," *HLSR* (November 6, 1958): 1. See Hill, "By the Sweat of Their Fraus," 2–5, 14–15, 21–22.

58. Harvard Law School Yearbook, 1941, 217–219; "Reorganized Law School Yearbook," *Harvard Crimson* (December 14, 1940); "Profiles of Leaders," *HLSR* (February 16, 1961): 12.

59. Hill, "By the Sweat of Their Fraus," 21–32.

60. Hill, "By the Sweat of Their Fraus," 7–8, 11–17, 40. See "Mrs. Griswold to Speak," *HLSR* (October 10, 1951): 3; "The Choice Is Always Ours," *HLSR* (March 19, 1953): 3; "Law Wives," *HLSR* (October 3, 1957): 3; Harvard Law School Yearbook, 1957, 182; 1955, 182; Mrs. Truman S. Casner, "Varied Activities Planned by Harvard Law Wives," *HLSR* (October 17, 1957): 1; Hope, *Pinstripes & Pearls,* 132.

61. Sissela Bok, *Alva Myrdal: A Daughter's Memoir* (Boston, 1991), 326. See "January Events: The Interim Report," *HLSR* (February 4, 1960): 9; Hope, *Pinstripes & Pearls,* 130–131.

62. Hill, "By the Sweat of Their Fraus," i–vii, 23–27.

63. Table of Speakers at HLW Meetings, in Hill, "By the Sweat of Their Fraus," i–vii.

64. Elizabeth Bartholet, Oral History, conducted by Daniel Hamilton (February 1999–March 2000), on file with the authors.

65. Bartholet, Oral History (February 1999–March 2000). See "Mrs. Griswold to Speak," 3; "Law Wives," 3; Hill, "By the Sweat of Their Fraus," 42n337.

66. Caroline M. Simon, "Seminar Held with Charm and Intelligence," *HLSR* (February 18, 1965): 13.

67. Hope, *Pinstripes & Pearls,* 139.

68. Simpson, Oral History (May–September 2001); "Women's Law Group Finds New Allies," *HLSR* (February 12, 1970): 13; "Law Notes," *HLSR* (April 1, 1970): 11; "Harvard Law Wives Group Changes Its Name after Forty Years," *HLSR* (December 8, 1972): 1; Randy Phillips, "Couple Workshop: Staying Together despite HLS," *HLSR* (February 4, 1977): 1, 7; Hill, "By the Sweat of Their Fraus," 26–30, 39–40.

69. Kaufman, Oral History (June 1999–April 2000). See Vorenberg, Oral History (November–December 1997); Derek C. Bok, Oral History, conducted by Daniel R. Coquillette and Daniel Hamilton (February 2002), on file with the authors; Chen, "The Harvard Law School," 20–21; Mary J. Mullarkey, "Two Harvard Women: 1965 to Today," *Harvard Women's Law Journal* 27 (2004): 368; Kirby, Interview by Denise Villeneuve

(November 22, 2000), 11–12; Edith Guild Henderson, quoted in "The Women of '53," 7; Charlotte Armstrong, Interview (January 29, 2001), quoted in Villeneuve, "Women at Harvard Law School," 10.

70. "Some Facts and a Few Figures," *HLSR* (October 4, 1950): 2, 4. McIntosh, "A Minor Matter," 43; Herbert P. Wilkins, Oral History, conducted by Daniel R. Coquillette (November 2014), on file with the authors; Brown, Oral History (August 1997); Bernardi, Oral History (October 2000–April 2001); Vagts, Oral History (November 1999–February 2000).

71. Quotation is from Chen, "The Harvard Law School," 6. See *Report of the Committee on the Admission of Women;* Hope, *Pinstripes & Pearls,* 81; Villeneuve, "Women at Harvard Law School," 17.

72. Anderson, email (January 31, 2001); Kirby, Interview (November 22, 2000), 22–23; Mullarkey, "Two Harvard Women," 371; Nancy Waring, "A Cause to Celebrate, Women at Harvard Law School: The First 35 Years," *HLSB* (Summer 1988): 7; "The Women of '53," 7; Chen, "The Harvard Law School," 16–17; Arthur von Mehren, Oral History, conducted by Daniel R. Coquillette and Mary Beth Basile (July–December 2000), on file with the authors.

73. Stanley N. Katz, email to Bruce Kimball (September 12, 2019), on file with the authors; von Mehren, Oral History (July–December 2000). See Kaufman, Oral History (June 1999–April 2000); Morello, *The Invisible Bar,* 103; Marjorie W. Burke, quoted in "Celebration 50: Harvard Law Fifty Years of Women Graduates," *Harvard Law School Alumnae Directory, 1953–2003* (Cambridge, MA, 2003), 86–87.

74. Basile, "False Starts," 154.

75. Priscilla Holmes, "Alumnae Careers through the Decades, Priscilla Holmes '55: Trying Times, Lovely Victories," *HLSB* (Summer 1988): 8; "Top Rankers Listed on Honors Groups; First Girls Named," *HLSR* (October 3, 1951): 1.

76. Bartholet, Oral History (February 1999–March 2000). See Chen, "The Harvard Law School," 17, 24; Frank E. A. Sander, Oral History, conducted by Daniel R. Coquillette and Daniel Hamilton (September–December 1998), on file with the authors.

77. Sander, Oral History (September–December 1998); Hope, *Pinstripes & Pearls,* 96–103; Katz, email (September 12, 2019).

78. Hope, *Pinstripes & Pearls,* 90. See Sander, Oral History (September–December 1998); Katz, email (September 12, 2019).

79. Quotations are from Sander, Oral History (September–December 1998).

80. Ruth I. Abrams quoted in Chen, "The Harvard Law School," 18.

81. Sondra Miller, Charlotte Armstrong, and Ruth I. Abrams, quoted in Villeneuve, "Women at Harvard Law School," 23–24.

82. Quotations are from Mullarkey, "Two Harvard Women," 370–371. See Villeneuve, "Women at Harvard Law School," 23–24; Waring, "A Cause to Celebrate," 5; Chen, "The Harvard Law School," 18. See mixed views in Julia Collins, "Celebration 45: The Alumnae

of Harvard Law Return to Cambridge," *HLSB* (Spring 1999): 24–27; Bartholet, Oral History (February 1999–March 2000); Judith Richards Hope, "The Women of 1964: Paving the Way," *Harvard Women's Law Journal* 27 (2004): 382.

83. Ruth Smith Baker-Battist quoted in "Celebration 50," 30; Frederica Brenneman, quoted in *Celebration 40: Forty Years of Women at Harvard Law School, 1953–1993* (Cambridge, MA, 2003), 55.

84. Mullarkey, "Two Harvard Women," 371; Laurence H. Tribe, Oral History, conducted by Daniel R. Coquillette and Andrew D. Klaber (September 2008), on file with the authors; Sander, Oral History (September–December 1998); Andrea Sachs, "Taking the Law in Her Hands," *Ms. Magazine* (Summer 2003).

85. Toepfer, Oral History (March 1998).

86. Waring, "A Cause to Celebrate," 5.

87. Toepfer is quoted in Hope, *Pinstripes & Pearls,* 102–103. Obituaries in newspapers at the time do not identify a cause of death. "W. Barton Leach, a Law Professor," *New York Times* (December 17, 1971); "W. Barton Leach: Story Law Professor at Harvard," *Washington Post* (December 18, 1971); "Harvard Law Professor W. B. Leach Dead at 71," *Boston Globe* (December 16, 1971). The *Harvard Crimson* was most forthcoming by stating that his death was "sudden." "W. Barton Leach Dies; on Faculty since 1929," *Harvard Crimson* (December 17, 1971).

88. Committee of the *Harvard Law Review* Board, Report to the Chairman of the Committee on Curriculum (March 22, 1935), *Survey of the Harvard Law School Curriculum, 1934–35* (February 1, 1935), JBC Records, 130–134.

89. Charlotte Armstrong quoted in Morello, *The Invisible Bar,* 203. See Jill Abramson and Barbara Franklin, *Where They Are Now: The Story of the Women of Harvard Law 1974* (Garden City, NY, 1986), 10; Holmes, "Alumnae Careers through the Decades," 8; Chen, "The Harvard Law School," 15, 21; Clark Byse, Oral History, conducted by Daniel R. Coquillette and Daniel Hamilton (July–October 1997), on file with the authors; Frederica S. Brenneman, Interview (November 11, 2000), quoted in Villeneuve, "Women at Harvard Law School," 15; Anderson, email (January 31, 2001); Armstrong, Interview (January 29, 2001); Bartholet, Oral History (February 1999–March 2000).

90. Mullarkey, "Two Harvard Women," 368.

91. [James Barr Ames], "Opinions . . . Taken in [HLS] Faculty Meeting in 1896–97," Papers and Presidential Records of Charles W. Eliot, 1807–1945, HUA.

92. "Griswold Welcomes First Year Group," *HLSR* (October 4, 1950): 8; Coleman, Interview (November 12, 2000), 10; McIntosh, "A Minor Matter," 3–4; Hope, *Pinstripes & Pearls,* 8; Mona Harrington, *Women Lawyers: Rewriting the Rules* (New York, 1994), 45; Wilkins, Oral History (November 2014); Simpson, Oral History (May–September 2001); Griswold, Annual Report of the Dean, 1957–58, 340–341.

93. Armstrong, Interview (January 29, 2001), 11. See Griswold, Annual Report of the Dean, 1950–51, 1; Erwin N. Griswold, "The School since the War," *HLSB* (December 1950): 3.

94. Erwin N. Griswold, "Developments at the Law School," Harvard Law School Yearbook, 1950, 10. See Griswold, *Ould Fields,* 169–170, 173–174; Harriet Griswold to Elizabeth Wahlen (May 2, 1993), Elizabeth Wahlen Correspondence, 1946–1998, on file with the authors; Armstrong, Interview (January 29, 2001), 11.

95. Erwin N. Griswold to Arthur E. Sutherland (June 2, 1958), Arthur E. Sutherland Papers, 1923–1972, Harvard Law School Library Historical & Special Collections.

96. Griswold, Annual Report of the Dean, 1965–66, 247–249.

97. Bartholet, Oral History (February 1999–March 2000).

98. Judith Richards Hope, "Remembrance," in *Erwin Nathaniel Griswold: 1904–1994* (memorial program) (Cambridge, MA, 1995), 16–19; Basile, "False Starts," 154.

99. Hope, *Pinstripes & Pearls,* 104–105; Bartholet, Oral History (February 1999–March 2000).

100. Hope, "Remembrance," 16–19; Basile, "False Starts," 154.

101. Wilkins, Oral History (November 2014); Bartholet, Oral History (February 1999–March 2000); Hope, *Pinstripes & Pearls,* 106–107.

102. Hope, "Remembrance," 19–20. See Hope, *Pinstripes & Pearls,* 108; Bartholet, Oral History (February 1999–March 2000).

103. Quotation is from Bartholet, Oral History (February 1999–March 2000). See Griswold to Wahlen (May 2, 1993); Mullarkey, "Two Harvard Women," 371; Hope, *Pinstripes & Pearls,* 105–108; Griswold, *Ould Fields,* 173; Mary Ellen Thomsen, "Woman in the Driver's Seat," *HLSB* (May 1965): 11; Miller, Interview (November 12, 2000), 11; Sondra M. Miller, quoted in "Celebration 50," 442.

104. Janet Reno, "Celebration 50: Keynote Address," *Harvard Women's Law Journal* 27 (2004): 309. See Kirby, Interview (November 22, 2000), 10–11; Archibald Cox, Oral History, conducted by Daniel R. Coquillette and Daniel Hamilton (November 1998), on file with the authors; Hope, *Pinstripes & Pearls,* 106; Griswold, *Ould Fields,* 173–174.

105. Miller, Interview (November 12, 2000), 11. See Griswold to Wahlen (May 2, 1993); Sondra Markowitz Miller, quoted in "Celebration 50," 442.

106. Hope, *Pinstripes & Pearls,* 104.

107. Griswold to Wahlen (May 2, 1993). See Harriet Griswold, "Justices of the Supreme Court of the United States I Have Known," *Supreme Court Historical Society Quarterly* 8 (1987): 1–5.

108. Paul D. Carrington, Oral History, conducted by Daniel Hamilton (February 2003), on file with the authors; Hope, *Pinstripes & Pearls,* 104–106; Bartholet, Oral History (February 1999–March 2000).

109. Alan M. Dershowitz, Oral History, conducted by Daniel R. Coquillette with Andrew Klaber (October–November 2009), on file with the authors. See Griswold to Wahlen (May 2, 1993).

110. Harriet F. Griswold, "I Had Polio," *Collier's* (January 29, 1949), 56–57. See Harriet Griswold to Elizabeth Wahlen (April 17 and May 22, 1994), Elizabeth Wahlen Correspondence, 1946–1998, on file with the authors.

111. Quotations are from, respectively, Harriet Griswold to Elizabeth Wahlen (February 12, 1993), Elizabeth Wahlen Correspondence, 1946–1998, on file with the authors; Griswold, *Ould Fields*, 173–174. See Griswold's account of overcoming his own "inferiority complex" upon arriving at HLS as a student, discussed in Chapter 10.

112. Mullarkey, "Two Harvard Women," 368. See Cynthia Fuchs Epstein, *Women in Law* (New York, 1981), 52.

113. Quotation is from Charles Fried, Oral History, conducted by Daniel R. Coquillette and Mary Beth Basile (August 2000–March 2001), on file with the authors. See Louis A. Toepfer, Interview (May 4, 1998), quoted in McIntosh, "A Minor Matter," 44; Griswold, *Ould Fields*, 170–171; Hope, *Pinstripes & Pearls*, 106.

114. See McIntosh, "A Minor Matter," 44; "The Entering Class of 1950," 9; Hope, *Pinstripes & Pearls*, xxiv; Epstein, *Women in Law*, 52.

115. Bartholet, Oral History (February 1999–March 2000).

116. McIntosh, "A Minor Matter," 34–35. "HLS To Admit Co-Eds."

117. Sander, Oral History (September–December 1998); Byse, Oral History (July–October 1997).

118. "Special Summer Program," *HLSB* (January 1966): 5. See Louis A. Toepfer, "Harvard's Special Summer Program," *Journal of Legal Education* 18 (1966): 444.

119. Epstein, *Women in Law*, 52.

120. Simpson, Oral History (May–September 2001).

121. A second Supreme Court Justice, Elena Kagan, received her J.D. in 1986, after the "lost generation."

122. Simpson, Oral History (May–September 2001). See Derek C. Bok, Annual Report of the Dean of HLS, 1969–1970, 281; Steven Prye, "Statistics Show Fewer Crimson in Class of '78," *HLSR* (December 5, 1975): 1, 3. There was a significant improvement entering in the fall of 1971 in the Class of 1974, admitted in the spring of 1971, which showed 64 women for a percentage of 11 percent. See Chapter 17, Table 17.2.

123. Mary-Elizabeth Jacques quoted in Chen, "The Harvard Law School," 32.

124. Priscilla Holmes quoted in Chen, "The Harvard Law School," 32.

125. Nancy Young quoted in Morello, *The Invisible Bar*, 205.

126. Esther Claire Roditti quoted in *Celebration 40*, 411; Maria Politis, "Ginsburg: Days of Token Women Over," *HLSR* (October 8, 1993): 1; Morello, *The Invisible Bar*, 205; Melissa Nasson, "The Quiet Decades: 1940 to 1960," in *Breaking Barriers: The Unfinished Story of Women Lawyers and Judges in Massachusetts*, ed. Patti B. Saris et al. (Boston, 2012), 45.

127. Quoted in Morello, *The Invisible Bar*, 105.

128. Hope, "The Women of 1964," 382; Abramson and Franklin, *Where They Are Now*, 23.

129. Quotation is from Toepfer, Oral History (March 1998). See Abramson and Franklin, *Where They Are Now*, 23; Frederica Brenneman quoted in *Celebration 40*, 55; Harrington, *Women Lawyers*, 19.

130. Mullarkey, "Two Harvard Women," 374.

131. In 2013 student Julia Chen made a valuable effort to track the careers of the earliest ninety-three female students through 1957. Chen, "The Harvard Law School," 42–44.

132. Chen, "The Harvard Law School," 42–44; Collins, "Celebration 45," 27. The judges include Frederica Brenneman (LL.B. 1953), Sondra Miller (LL.B. 1953), Raya S. Dreben (LL.B. 1954), Antoinette L. Dupont (LL.B. 1954), June Strelecki (LL.B. 1955), Ruth I. Abrams (LL.B. 1956), Sylvia A. Bacon (LL.B. 1956), Elizabeth A. Evatt (LL.M. 1956), Rya W. Zobel (LL.B. 1956), Edith Witty Fine (LL.B. 1957), Zita L. Weinshienk (LL.B. 1958), Judith W. Rogers (LL.B. 1964), Mary J. Mullarkey (LL.B. 1968), and Patricia Burgy Minzner (LL.B. 1968).

133. Many articles and a number of books have recently been published about Ginsburg, including children's books, demonstrating her influence on popular culture. Her recent book—Ginsburg, *My Own Words* (New York, 2016)—compiles many of her prior writings. See Kimball, "Literature Review of Writings by and about Ruth Bader Ginsburg."

134. Politis, "Ginsburg: Days of Token Women Over." See Herma Hill Kay, "Ruth Bader Ginsburg, Professor of Law," *Columbia Law Review* 104 (2004): 7–9; Ruth Bader Ginsburg, "Harvard Law School Celebration 45, November 14, 1998" (typescript address), on file with the authors; Gerald Gunther, "Ruth Bader Ginsburg: A Personal, Very Fond Tribute," *University of Hawaii Law Review* 20 (1998): 583.

135. Ruth Bader Ginsburg quoted in Hope, *Pinstripes & Pearls,* 105. See Ruth Bader Ginsburg, "Remarks Commemorating Celebration 55: The Women's Leadership Summit," *Harvard Journal of Law and Gender* 32 (2009): 239.

136. See Martin D. Ginsburg, "Spousal Transfers: In '58, It Was different," *HLSR* (May 6, 1977): 11; Ginsburg, "Harvard Law School Celebration 45"; Ginsburg, "The Changing Complexion of Harvard Law School," 303n; Elena Kagan, "Introduction: Remarks Commemorating Celebration 55: The Women's Leadership Summit," *Harvard Journal of Law and Gender* 32 (2009): 234.

137. Gunther, "Ruth Bader Ginsburg," 583. See Kay, "Ruth Bader Ginsburg," 8–9.

138. Erwin N. Griswold to Archibald Cox (January 12, 1988), Elizabeth Wahlen Correspondence, 1946–1998, on file with the authors.

139. Vorenberg, Oral History (November–December 1997).

140. Ginsburg, "Remarks Commemorating Celebration 55," 238–239.

141. Amy Leigh Campbell, *Raising the Bar: Ruth Bader Ginsburg and the ACLU Women's Rights Project* (Princeton, NJ, 2003); Kagan, "Introduction: Remarks Commemorating Celebration 55," 233–234.

142. Quoted in Ginsburg, "Harvard Law School Celebration 45." This account also appears in Ginsburg, "The Changing Complexion of Harvard Law School," 303; Harriet Griswold to Elizabeth Wahlen (September 15, 1993), Elizabeth Wahlen Correspondence, 1946–1998, on file with the authors; Sidney Blumenthal, "A Beautiful Friendship,"

New Yorker (July 5, 1993), 37–38; Antonin Scalia, "The 100 Most Influential People: Ruth Bader Ginsburg," *Time* (April 27, 2015): 140. Compare Jeffrey Toobin, *The Nine: Inside the Secret World of the Supreme Court* (New York, 2007), 82.

143. Quotation is from Ginsburg, "Remarks Commemorating Celebration 55," 238–239. See Hope, "Remembrance," 16–19; Reno, "Celebration 50: Keynote Address," 309; Linda K. Smith, "Erwin Griswold: Remembrances," unpublished memo (January 20, 2015), on file with the authors.

144. Griswold, "Developments at the Law School," 10. See Griswold, *Ould Fields,* 169–170, 173–174; Griswold to Wahlen (May 2, 1993); Armstrong, Interview (January 29, 2001), 11.

145. Quotations are from Griswold to Wahlen (May 2, 1993); Griswold to Cox (January 12, 1988).

146. See *Battlefield of Merit,* 522–527.

147. Here and below, the accounts and quotations are drawn from Felipe D. Mendoza, "Hispanic [LL.B.] Graduates of Harvard Law School, 1817–1973: A First Step toward Uncovering the Lives and Experiences of the First Graduate and the First Generation" (student research paper, HLS, 2006), on file with the authors. The term "Hispanic" has been officially employed by the United States government, but the term "Latino / a" is often preferred now.

148. See Griswold, *Ould Fields,* 4, 8.

149. Simpson, Oral History (May–September 2001); Erwin N. Griswold, "The 'Coloured Vote Case' in South Africa," *HLR* 65 (1952): 1361–1374; Griswold, *Ould Fields,* 201–209; James T. Kilbreth III to Harriet Griswold (September 12, 1995), Elizabeth Wahlen Correspondence, 1946–1998, on file with the authors.

150. *Betts v. Brady* 316 U.S. 455 (1942), 471. See *Nixon v. Condon* 286 U.S. 73 (1932); *Gideon v. Wainwright* 372 U.S. 335 (1963); Daniel M. Friedman, "In Memoriam: Erwin Nathaniel Griswold," *HLR* 108 (1995): 989–990; Griswold, *Ould Fields,* 142–144.

151. Quotations are from Griswold, *Ould Fields,* 184–185.

152. Theodore M. Hesburgh, "In Memoriam: Erwin Nathaniel Griswold," *HLR* 108 (1995): 992–994; Griswold, *Ould Fields,* 245–252; Robert F. Drinan, S.J. "Remembrance," *Erwin Nathaniel Griswold: 1904–1994* (Cambridge, MA, 1994), 33–36; Louis L. Jaffe, "Erwin N. Griswold—Some Fond Recollections," *HLR* 86 (June 1973): 1373; Dennis Hevesi, "Erwin Griswold Is Dead at 90; Served as Solicitor General," *New York Times* (November 21, 1994).

153. Toepfer, Oral History (March 1998); Simpson, Oral History (May–September 2001).

154. Nick K. Friedman, "When Affirmative Action Was White: Uncivil Rights," *New York Times* (August 28, 2005); Hillary Herbold, "Never a Level Playing Field: Blacks and the GI Bill," *Journal of Blacks in Higher Education* 6 (Winter 1994): 104–108.

155. "Counsel for the Situation: William T. Coleman Jr. '46 (1920–2017): Civil Rights Pioneer Was a Trusted Attorney and Public Servant for over 70 Years," *Harvard Law Today* (April 4, 2017); James R. Hagerty "William Coleman Fought Civil-Rights Battles from

the Inside," *Wall Street Journal* (April 12, 2017); Dennis Hevesi, "William T. Coleman Jr., Who Broke Racial Barriers in Court and Cabinet, Dies at 96," *New York Times* (March 31, 2017); Matt Schudel, "William T. Coleman Jr., Barrier-Breaking Civil Rights Lawyer, Cabinet Officer, Dies at 96," *Washington Post* (March 31, 2017); Stephen Breyer, "William Coleman's Legacy," *Wall Street Journal* (November 3, 2017). The first African American Cabinet secretary was Robert C. Weaver, who earned his B.A. and Ph.D. (1954) from Harvard.

156. Eric Pace, "Wade H. McCree, Jr. Dies at 67; Was Judge and Solicitor General," *New York Times* (September 1, 1987). See *United States v. Nixon* 418 US 683 (1974); *Regents of the University of California v. Bakke* 438 US 265 (1978).

157. Vorenberg, Oral History (November–December 1997). See Vagts, Oral History (November 1999–February 2000).

158. "First Year Teaching Fellows," *HLSB* (October 1951): 4; Clarence Mitchell, "In Memoriam: C. Clyde Ferguson, Jr.," *HLR* 97 (1984): 1253–1254; Charlotte Hinger, "Ferguson, Clarence Clyde Jr. (1924–1983)," BlackPast.org (2017), retrieved from http://www.blackpast.org/aah/ferguson-clarence-clyde-jr-1924-1983.

159. The following material and quotations are drawn from Christopher F. Edley Jr., Oral History, conducted by Daniel R. Coquillette and Daniel Hamilton (October 2000–September 2001); "Christopher F. Edley, 75; Former Chief of United Negro College Fund," *Los Angeles Times* (May 8, 2003). See also John L. Joy, "A Legacy of Their Own: A History of Second Generation African American Families at Harvard Law School" (student research paper, Boston College Law School, 2016), on file with the authors.

160. Barnard College, *The Mortarboard* (New York, 1953), 67; Barnard College, "U.N. Officer," *Barnard Alumnae Magazine* 53 (Spring 1964): 32; "Launch Education Program on Sickle Cell Disease Fight," *New York Amsterdam News* (March 27, 1971); Crystal Hubbard, "Harvard BLSA Seeks Solutions to Violence," *Bay State Banner* (April 27, 1995); Daniel R. Coquillette, "A History of Blacks at Harvard," *HLSR* (October 20, 2000): 7; "Lila A. Fenwick '56," *HLSB* (Summer 2003): 30. On Ruffin, see *Battlefield of Merit*, 279–281.

161. David Niven, *The Politics of Injustice: The Kennedys, the Freedom Rides, and the Electoral Consequences of a Moral Compromise* (Knoxville, TN, 2003), 220n121. See Simpson, Oral History (May–September 2001).

162. Ernest Gellhorn, "The Law Schools and the Negro," *Duke Law Journal* 17 (1968): 1082–1083n61; Walter Leonard, *Black Lawyers: Training and Results: Then and Now* (Boston, 1977), 195–197.

163. Toepfer, Oral History (March 1998). See Griswold, Annual Report of the Dean, 1964–65, 261; Fried, Oral History (August 2000–March 2001); Jack Tate, "Black Awareness and Black Unity Surging Forward at Law School," *HLSR* (September 26, 1968): 6.

164. Bruce A. Kimball, *"No Reason . . . Except Faith": Ten Years of ABC* (Hanover, NH, 1974).

165. "Summer Scene," *HLSB* (July 1965): 2; "Special Summer Program," 5, 7; Toepfer, "Harvard's Special Summer Program," 443–444; Kenneth S. Tollett, "Affirmative Action

in Law Schools: The Declining Concern for the Interest of Blacks," *Harvard Blackletter Journal* 4 (1987): 48–50; Clark Byse, "In Memoriam: Erwin Nathaniel Griswold," *HLR* 108 (1995): 982–983; Nathan Pak, "The Harvard Law School Special Summer Program of 1965 and What Happened Afterwards" (student research paper, Boston College Law School, 2017), on file with the authors.

166. "The Forbes Four Hundred," *Forbes* (October 19, 1992), 256–270; Sander, Oral History (September–December 1998); Toepfer, Oral History (March 1998). See the description of the SSP in Reginald F. Lewis and Blair S. Walker, *Why Should White Guys Have All the Fun: How Reginald Lewis Created a Billion Dollar Business Empire* (New York, 1995), 47–59.

167. Sander, Oral History (September–December 1998).

168. Tate, "Black Awareness and Black Unity," 6.

169. Hevesi, "Erwin Griswold Is Dead at 90"; Griswold, *Ould Fields,* 239–240.

170. Griswold, Annual Report of the Dean, 1964–65, 261; Sander, Oral History (September–December 1998); "Special Summer Program," 18.

CHAPTER THIRTEEN

"The School Has Not Grown Soft," 1946–1967

No sooner had the tumult of the postwar madhouse subsided in 1950 than a series of major changes and controversies rapidly unfolded at the Law School, as described above. At the same time, Dean Erwin Griswold (1946–1967) sought to strengthen the academic work of the school in several respects. He considered the faculty's scholarly productivity to be deficient and tried to encourage research and publication. In addition, he supported the growth of graduate programs and "International Legal Studies," a term that originated in his administration, and he vastly increased the number of smaller elective courses and seminars available to second- and third-year LL.B. students. Finally, in order to support the additional coursework, Griswold hired many more professors, while an unofficial career ladder to a faculty appointment became customary.

But adding faculty and seminars did not imply sheathing the intellectual sword and weakening the competitive and combative culture in the school, though attrition waned due to the new policy of selective admissions. Class rank based on minute grade distinctions and competing membership in the academic honor organizations supplanted the threat of failing grades. "The School has not grown soft," the dean announced in the *Harvard Law School Bulletin* in 1950.[1] And it would remain hard. "A law student who has to be spoon-fed, who has to be led by the hand step by step, may not succeed in developing the toughness and resiliency . . . needed when he steps out by himself into the world of practice or teaching or public affairs," Griswold insisted.[2] Despite the admission of women, Spartan manliness continued to guide academic policy.

Faculty Research

The new dean, as well as some professors, including Archibald Cox (LL.B. 1937), maintained that the faculty's production of scholarship was meager. Even those who wrote something of great significance did not feel obliged to bring it to publication, Griswold complained, citing the famous unpublished textbook on "the Legal Process" by Henry Hart (LL.B. 1929, S.J.D. 1931) and Albert Sacks (LL.B. 1948).[3] The dean therefore announced that every faculty member should publish regularly, and he encouraged faculty publication in several ways. Beginning in his annual report for 1948–49, he listed the publications produced by each faculty member during the year, implicitly shaming those professors who had only one entry, or none. Griswold always had several. But Griswold's definition of "publication" was extremely liberal. Commission reports, invited lectures, public addresses, professional bulletins, and articles in the *Harvard Law School Bulletin, Harvard Law School Record,* and *Harvard Alumni Bulletin* all counted, as did casebooks and law review articles.[4]

Griswold also fostered scholarship by reading and reviewing virtually everything that any professor published. He often read a publication on the day it appeared, and wrote to the author with comments on the following day—an astonishing and exhausting commitment that virtually no dean of any university professional school would contemplate subsequently.[5] In the 1950s he particularly commended casebooks, which "helped to fulfill [the faculty's] responsibility to legal education in the United States" and to extend the school's academic influence.[6] In 1959 the dean formed a Committee on Faculty Research and approved its suggestion to provide release time and budgetary support for faculty to pursue scholarship.[7]

Finally, in 1951 Griswold created the position of associate dean for research and charged the first appointee, David Cavers (LL.B. 1926), to develop a program of "legal research directed to pressing current problems" that "will often fall outside the direct range of the Law School curriculum" but might still involve "graduate students or even third-year men." Griswold thus envisioned applied research projects involving "the practicing bar, especially our alumni," because much legal knowledge "is found in the law offices rather than in the law reports," he maintained. Tapping "this learning" would "increase the School's service to the bar and to the administration of justice."[8]

Like his definition of faculty publications, Griswold's vision of research was therefore highly pragmatic. He discounted "abstract and academic" scholarship and encouraged research addressing "practical legal problems" facing lawyers, judges, and legislators.[9] His own scholarship and teaching on federal tax law, a field he virtually invented, served as a model. Griswold spoke of such research as working in a "laboratory." He even said that he "hesitate[d] to use the word 'research'" for such work, because "'research' sometimes connoted deep delving into ancient tomes on problems which bore very little relation to our current situation."[10]

Some professors objected to Griswold's conception of scholarship. In particular, Lon Fuller, a legal philosopher and graduate of Stanford Law School, suggested that the focus on "practical problems" might blind one to profound questions, whereas some "abstract and academic" questions might have more practical influence in the long run. In fact, "research" that aimed to solve practical problems was scarcely research at all, implied Fuller, endorsing Griswold's own reservation about his use of the term.[11]

Beyond that conceptional disagreement, Fuller objected to Griswold's prioritizing his own definition of research. The house of scholarship has many mansions, argued Fuller, who did not insist on his own "abstract and academic" view and conceded that other scholars might hold different conceptions of research. What Fuller fundamentally opposed was any particular conception of research being given priority in the school.

Nevertheless, Associate Dean Cavers followed Griswold's direction, and developed a scheme of "institutional research" or "programmatic research" modeled on that of Harvard Business School. According to this model, the Law School would acquire resources to support projects aimed at solving specific legal problems and then enlist and fund teams of faculty and research associates to address each problem.[12] In Fuller's view, this business-school approach constrained the autonomy and creativity of scholars, who would be induced to skew their academic work in order to participate in the school-supported research. Fuller maintained that unbridled freedom of inquiry was absolutely necessary for any notion of true scholarship and research.[13] Fuller and Cavers debated the nature and proper organization of legal research repeatedly and extensively at faculty meetings.[14]

Some professors sided with Cavers and Griswold, including Cox.[15] But Fuller's view of "research" may have been validated during the 1956–57 academic year, when H. L. A. Hart, professor of Jurisprudence at Oxford University, served as a visiting professor at Harvard Law School. In April 1957, Hart delivered the Oliver W. Holmes Jr., Lecture at the school and addressed an apparently "abstract and academic" question. In his lecture, Hart analyzed and defended the positivist distinction between "law and morals"—between "what is and what ought to be." Many critics of positivism reject the distinction and maintain that the two "are somehow indissolubly fused or inseparable," observed Hart. These critics allege that the positivist distinction confers legitimacy upon the law of oppressive regimes by implying, for example, that the Nazis had "law" and "a legal system," however immoral. But Hart responded that this criticism misunderstands the distinction and, further, that law is a neutral, non-normative concept. Hart's fundamental clarification of legal positivism in the Holmes Lecture became the core of his acclaimed book, *The Concept of Law* (1961).[16]

Over the course of the 1956–57 academic year, Fuller debated with Hart in a faculty discussion group, and he responded to Hart's lecture in the *Harvard Law Review*. Fuller framed the distinction between "law and morals" as one between "order and good order." Law thus entailed a "morality of order," Fuller maintained. Hence, "law" was not a neutral, non-normative concept, but incorporated an internal moral logic, which Hart had overlooked. According to Fuller, this oversight appeared in Hart's discussion of the Nazi regime, in which Hart failed to examine precisely "what 'law' itself meant under the Nazi regime." Such regimes repudiated or violated that inner "morality of order" and did not really have what could be called a "legal system," argued Fuller. Under the Nazis, law did not adhere to order, but sanctioned arbitrary will effected by brutal force. Like Hart, Fuller developed his essay into a monumental book, *The Morality of Law* (1964).[17]

This exchange did not, of course, "solve" the problem of explaining the relationship between law and morality. But it did become the starting point for future consideration of this fundamental issue due to the brilliant analyses of Hart and Fuller. Hence, their debate is considered one of the most significant exchanges in twentieth-century jurisprudence. In terms of both intellectual influence and the Law School's institutional influence, this "abstract and academic" investigation by Hart and Fuller eclipsed and outlasted the results from most of the now-forgotten "programmatic research" projects supported by Cavers's office.[18]

S.J.D. and LL.M.

Having elevated the LL.B. to the postbaccalaureate level in the 1890s, Harvard Law School in 1910 took another step that would be replicated by several leading university law schools: offering the *Scientiae Juridicae Doctor* degree. Introduced as a one-year course of study, the S.J.D. served as the vehicle to teach what were called "cultural" courses outside of the regular LL.B. curriculum, such as public law, jurisprudence, legal history, and comparative and international law. In the subsequent four decades, other law schools began to offer the S.J.D., and eight schools conferred the great majority of these degrees: Columbia, Harvard, Yale, Chicago, Georgetown, Michigan, Wisconsin, and New York University.[19]

A few of the schools responded to the rise of legal realism by incorporating more social science into their graduate curricula. Some modeled their S.J.D. on the Ph.D. by requiring a thesis, and established the LL.M. degree with fewer requirements. Until 1940 the largest S.J.D. programs aimed to prepare and qualify American LL.B.s to teach in American law schools, although the LL.M. degree had become the more common credential across the nation.

But even in the 1940s and 1950s, relatively few law schools offered the LL.M. or the S.J.D., because the degrees were largely superfluous as professional credentials in the United States. Many practicing lawyers in the nation still did not have law degrees, and most law schools did not require a B.A. or B.S. until the 1960s. An LL.B. from a leading law school remained sufficient to obtain a professorship, particularly given the growing market for legal education and the increasing number of law schools during the rapid expansion of higher education between 1945 and 1975.[20]

After 1950, several significant trends developed in graduate legal education at Harvard and other law schools.[21] The number of LL.M. candidates grew much larger than the number of S.J.D. candidates. Also, the number of foreign students rose and surpassed that of domestic students. The total number of law doctorates conferred on American LL.B.s fell from 155 in the 1950s to 65 in the 1970s, while the fraction of S.J.D. students who had graduated from foreign law schools reached two-thirds by 1970, and the enrollment of foreign LL.B.s in LL.M. programs was even higher.[22] In this fashion, over the course of the 1950s and 1960s the graduate programs at Harvard and many other schools shifted from their pre-1950 focus on training future American law professors to a post-1950 emphasis upon educating graduates of foreign law schools.

International Legal Studies

Commensurate with the shift in enrollment, the Law School inaugurated a new field of scholarship that it called International Legal Studies (ILS). In its handbook for incoming foreign law school graduates, the school explained that "the term International Legal Studies is new as a formal designation of an area of law teaching and scholarship," which "deals with the legal aspects of international transactions, whether these involve business enterprises, individual citizens, or governments." To support the new ILS programs, the Ford Foundation made large grants between 1954 and 1966 that went to Harvard ($3 million), Columbia ($1.5 million), Yale ($750,000), Michigan ($500,000), and New York University ($450,000).[23]

Harvard viewed its work in ILS as public service. Griswold and his administration have often been criticized for neglecting "public service," understood to mean alleviating inequality and injustice in America.[24] But in the postwar era, Griswold and the faculty believed international conflict to be the greatest public threat and ILS to be the school's fundamental contribution to improving the world. "My own experience in foreign travel, and . . . interest in working towards better understanding among nations, were powerful motivations," Griswold wrote. "I regarded this as a very important mission of the Harvard Law School. I looked upon these [foreign, graduate] students as future leaders in their countries, and I felt that the development of able people in various parts of the world, who had a common tie, would contribute materially to world progress and peace."[25]

Whether the effort was effective is another question, but in the 1950s many believed that World War II "had changed the world, and it was important that we now talk about one world, about the United Nations," in the words of Arthur von Mehren (LL.B. 1945). "We needed to understand more about how this fundamental form of social and political organization could operate and . . . what the fundamental differences among nations really are."[26]

Harvard Law School was well positioned to undertake this effort. By 1945 the school had assembled the world's largest collection of legal records from different countries, due to the efforts of Dean Roscoe Pound (1916–1936) and Professor Manley Hudson (LL.B. 1910, S.J.D. 1919).[27] Nevertheless, in 1945 Professor Barton Leach (LL.B. 1924) proposed "that we get rid of our foreign law collection because . . . the war was over, . . . and it was costing a lot of money to keep it up, and there was nobody to use it." Ironically, this was the very time when Dean James Landis (1937–1946) was leading American diplomacy in the Middle East, leaving the school rudderless. In the vacuum of decanal leadership in 1945 and early 1946, David Cavers and Lon Fuller countered Leach's suggestion by proposing that the valuable collection be saved, and that "we should start a program and use it," recalled Harold Berman.[28] The appointment of Arthur von Mehren and the support for his leave from 1946 to 1948 to study legal systems in postwar Europe was a critical first step, followed closely by Griswold's "very bold move" of hiring Harold Berman to teach Soviet Law in 1947.[29]

Over the next three years, a faculty Committee on International Legal Studies, led by Fuller and Cavers, drafted a proposal to establish "a World School of Law," as an adjunct to Harvard Law School, where American and foreign students would study together. To support this project, the school submitted a breathtaking request for $10 million to the Ford Foundation in 1951. The prospect seemed auspicious because Milton Katz (LL.B. 1931), who had helped oversee the Marshall Plan in Europe and was still on leave from the Law School faculty, was then serving as a vice president at the Ford Foundation.[30] But the foundation turned down the request for the World School of Law, so the Law School then proposed a series of more modest grants.

In 1952 the Ford Foundation awarded the school a grant of $200,000 to finance the first three years of a research and training program in world tax law, to be directed by Professor Stanley S. Surrey, who later became U.S. assistant secretary of the Treasury for tax policy. At the very end of 1954, the Ford Foundation approved a major proposal from the Law School to expand its ILS program and house it in a new building, and for Katz to return to the Law School faculty to direct the expanded program. Katz brought with him in 1955 the challenge grant of $500,000 to fund the new ILS building, and another grant of $1.55 million for the ILS program. The latter included $800,000 to endow two professorships and $750,000 for fellowships, research projects, and aid to the library, to be expended over ten years.[31]

These resources, which some colleagues termed Katz's "dowry," afforded the ILS program a magnificent start.[32] By 1960 Harvard was "the leading law school in the country in International Legal Studies," stated Berman. "It was absolutely head and shoulders above any other school."[33] Some sixteen faculty were teaching at least one course in the program, including von Mehren, Berman, Fuller, Cavers, Katz, Detlev Vagts (LL.B. 1951), Kingman Brewster Jr. (LL.B. 1948), and Louis B. Sohn (LL.M. 1940, S.J.D. 1958). ILS programs of research were producing series of monographs, such as the World Tax Series. By 1960, volumes had been completed on the United Kingdom, Brazil, Mexico, Australia, Sweden, and India—and others, on Germany, France, the United States, Colombia, Italy, Japan, the Netherlands, Venezuela, and Belgium, were under way, with another five volumes planned. By that point the Ford Foundation had awarded the school a new grant of $600,000 to support the International Program in Taxation and the World Tax Series over the next five years.[34]

It was a superb beginning, but after 1965, progress began to slow. One reason was that the Ford grants started to run out, so fellowship support for visiting scholars and graduate students dried up. In addition, Griswold became occupied with other issues, and the civil rights movement, Vietnam War, and student unrest began to redefine the meaning of public service at the Law School. But the major problem was that Katz lacked vision and organization, according to his colleagues. As early as 1956, Griswold wrote to Katz expressing disappointment in his performance. Katz "never had a detailed plan or program," observed von Mehren.[35] "We were very unhappy that Katz . . . didn't have a clear vision," said Berman. After Katz retired in 1978, the faculty affiliated with the program "had very little to talk about and very little in common. There was nothing that had developed under Katz that we could carry on. Each of us was going his own way," stated Berman.[36]

The fault did not lie entirely with Katz. ILS at Harvard was spread too thin across many divergent institutional responsibilities. These included offering courses for LL.B. students and for graduate students, both foreign and American; preparing scholars to become faculty at American universities (notably John H. Langbein [LL.B. 1968] who taught at Yale Law School); conducting exchange programs with institutions in other countries, particularly Japan; and bringing law faculty from other countries to teach at Harvard Law School. Furthermore, other law schools were trying to do the same things, and most were focusing on European or Commonwealth countries with little coordination or cooperation among them.[37]

Exacerbating this diffusion of effort was the fundamental conceptual problem that "international legal studies" had at least three distinct meanings. One was "traditional international law concerning relations among states," on which Sohn and Katz focused. Entirely different was "comparative law": the study of legal systems of different nations. Following this approach, von Mehren taught the French and German systems; Berman, the Russian and Soviet systems; and Jerome Cohen, Chinese law. Third was "international economic law" governing international trade and international tax, taught by Berman, Katz, and others.[38]

Given the divergent institutional responsibilities and these different meanings, ILS at Harvard operated as a consortium of academic ventures rather than a coordinated program. ILS also cost a lot of money and rapidly consumed its own abundant resources, while siphoning funds from the LL.B. side of the Law School. As director, Katz failed to rein in the diffuse efforts, identify a cohesive mission, and direct ILS toward achievable goals at Harvard. After reaching its high watermark in the 1960s, Ford Foundation support evaporated during the 1970s. In subsequent decades ILS pressed on, but "at the margins of the educational enterprise," according to scholar Gail Hupper.[39]

Nevertheless, it remained true that "no place . . . can come close to Harvard in terms of editions and collections of foreign legal materials and their availability," stated von Mehren. Furthermore, many graduates of the S.J.D. and LL.M. programs assumed significant roles on the faculties, the bench, the bar, and the government of nations outside the United States.[40] The contributions of ILS to international understanding were therefore substantial.

LL.B. Curriculum

Notwithstanding the revolutionary development of graduate programs and ILS, Griswold and the faculty have been criticized for continuing the traditional LL.B. curriculum in the groove laid down by Dean Christopher Langdell (1870–1895), with minimal changes. The required, doctrinal courses on private law and financial matters predominated, virtually excluding courses on public law, public policy, social science, social justice, clinical education, or legal ethics.[41] Griswold did not deny the importance of these other subjects, noting that "law is not a merely logical structure. The ties between law and economics, and government, and history, and sociology, and business, and anthropology must be . . . more widely understood."[42] Yet the dean opposed changing the curriculum.

In some cases he discounted the need for new coursework, such as clinical education in legal practice or human relations, even though he acknowledged the value of such training.[43] Other times he argued that the traditional courses already offered preparation in "legal ethics," "professional responsibility," and "public interest." To this, critics responded that the dean was "self-delusional, disingenuous, or . . . had a very different notion of professional responsibility" and public interest.[44] Finally, Griswold also argued that because all the traditional courses were necessary, none could be dropped, and that the school "cannot . . . cover all of the things that our students might well know."[45]

To the end of his tenure as dean, Griswold was therefore satisfied that "much of the material that we teach is the stuff of business and finance—contracts, commercial law, taxation, creditors' rights . . . the traditional areas of the law."[46] At best, the school could make accommodations on the margins, but private and commercial law must occupy the bulk of the curriculum. The traditional discounting of other legal and academic fields thus continued, and Griswold hired only a few "outsiders" and only near the end of his tenure, appointing Alan A. Stone, a psychiatrist, and Richard Musgrave, an economist, in 1965.[47] Meanwhile, Griswold defended other dimensions of the school's traditional regimen: large class size and case method teaching, which he employed vigorously.[48]

Nor did the faculty push for curricular reform. The reports of three successive faculty committees did not elicit any consensus for significant change. In 1945 Dean Landis had great hopes for major reforms when he appointed the first Committee on Legal Education, chaired by Lon Fuller. In response to its preliminary reports, the faculty held extensive discussions. But Fuller's committee ultimately recommended relatively minor changes: hiring teaching fellows to help first-year students with legal writing; adding to the second year a required course in accounting and a required "cultural" course, chosen among four options; and making most third-year courses elective while increasing the number of "seminars and relatively small classes" and requiring students to complete a "piece of written work." Adopted by the faculty in 1949, this was the extent of curricular reform through the first two-thirds of the twentieth century.[49]

In 1960 a second faculty Committee on Legal Education proposed major changes. But these encountered strong opposition, and the faculty voted "that no action on such important matters should be taken unless it was supported by a substantial majority of the Faculty."[50] In 1962 Griswold named a Special Committee on Planning and Development to examine all aspects of the school, particularly "increases in our Faculty, and related personnel" in ILS and fields related to business and finance.[51] Headed by Associate Dean James Casner, this committee issued a long report in 1964 that effectively ratified the dean's agenda for growth and expansion.[52] By 1965 the faculty had had its fill of self-examination and committee reports, observed Andrew Kaufman (LL.B. 1954), a newcomer to the faculty.[53]

Nevertheless, the growth of ILS and the graduate program greatly increased the number of courses available to LL.B. students during Dean Griswold's tenure. The first-year course of study remained uniform and prescribed. But the second-year curriculum gradually shifted from six required courses and no electives to four required courses and two openings chosen from twenty electives. In the third year, the twenty-four electives in 1946–47 more than doubled to fifty-two in 1966–67.[54] To provide the additional courses, the school needed more faculty, and Griswold began to hire them, guided by his understanding of the culture and mission of Harvard Law School.

Hiring Faculty

Although Dean Landis had made two sets of faculty appointments in 1940 and 1945, the faculty numbered only thirty-one professors when Griswold began as dean in 1946. These included five near retirement: Roscoe Pound, Warren Seavey (LL.B. 1904), Austin Scott (LL.B. 1909), Thomas Powell (LL.B. 1904), and Edmund Morgan (LL.B. 1905). By the fall of 1948 the faculty had shrunk to twenty-six professors, not counting the dean, plus about eight temporary appointments to handle the influx of veterans.[55]

At that point Griswold had the opportunity to reduce the size of the school after the wave of returning soldiers ebbed. Academic institutions rarely have such an opportunity, but the dean took no interest in it. Like large classes, courses in private law, and case method teaching, the prewar enrollment of 1,500 was "normal," he said.[56] Indeed, it was part of the school's identity. "Our predecessors decided that Harvard should be a large school," he wrote, "and it is our task to see that it continues to be, as it was under them, as good a large school as it is possible to make it."[57]

Much has been written about Griswold's conservative views regarding jurisprudence, corporate law practice, gender, and the LL.B. curriculum. Underlying these views was a conservatism about the very nature of Harvard Law School. In the late 1940s he envisioned many changes. But he also wished to recover the Harvard Law School that he knew as a student in the mid-1920s, before the G.I. Bill, before World War II, before Landis, before the Depression, before legal realism. In the 1940s Griswold brought to the school "a sense of things having to be restored . . . of bringing it back to where it was," as Detlev Vagts observed.[58] That included the size of the student body. Without apparently considering alternatives, Griswold therefore decided to return to the prewar enrollment of 1,500 or more, while doubling the size of the faculty.

The dean was proud of this plan. But he recognized that it would encounter opposition, given the discussion about reducing the size of the school under Landis. Hence, Griswold did not announce the plan and decided to proceed incrementally. Rightly anticipating that the faculty could not resist the temptation to hire a few, young, talented professors each year, he strategically spaced out the appointments, enticing the faculty to agree to hire one or two more at a time. "As a result, the size of the faculty grew slowly, year by year," Griswold remarked. "The new faculty members were fine additions, and the size of the faculty increased with a minimum of friction."[59]

In 1967 Griswold fairly crowed that "over the past twenty years we have nearly doubled the number of faculty members." Calculating the number of different kinds of faculty is complicated, and various statements have reported different totals. But a recent, thorough study confirms Griswold's conclusion. The teaching faculty at the Law School grew from thirty-four in 1946–47 to forty-seven in 1955–56, then to sixty-seven in 1967–68.[60]

The overall increase of 97 percent included professors of all ranks, whether full-time or part-time and whether on leave or not; as well as lecturers, visiting, and cross-listed faculty, and administrators with professorial appointments. By comparison, across the nation over the same period, the number of full-time law faculty rose even more steeply from 991 to 2,264—an increase of 128 percent.[61] In any event, it is noteworthy that doubling the size of the faculty did not reduce the enrollment in first-year courses, which remained at about 140 for each section, although teaching fellows had been introduced. It was primarily the enrollment in third-year seminars and graduate courses that decreased.

Commensurate with the rapid faculty growth during Griswold's deanship, a three-step professorial career ladder became conventional at the Law School. The first step for a student who aspired to be a Harvard Law professor was to attend one of a small group of elite law schools. This was necessary because faculty openings were not advertised or even announced publicly. Solicitations and invitations were made entirely through the interpersonal network of deans and faculty at the small group of elite, private, university law schools.[62] Until Pound's appointment as dean in 1916, virtually every professor at the Law School had received the LL.B. from Harvard. Over the next fifty years, recruitment expanded slightly to include LL.B.s from Yale, Columbia, and Stanford, with very few exceptions, such as James Casner (Illinois, LL.B. 1929) and Clark Byse (Wisconsin, LL.B. 1938).

The second step on the professorial career ladder was to achieve membership in one of the three academic honor organizations: the *Harvard Law Review*, Board of Student Advisors, and Legal Aid Bureau, which totaled about 12 percent of the student body. Above all, election to the editorial board of the *Review* became "a separating out and anointing you with some blessing like the Good Housekeeping Seal of Approval and slightly beyond," said Professor Frank Sander (LL.B. 1952).[63] Furthermore, "the officers of the *Law*

Review, elected by the members, were the elite within the elite and they were really quite well known to the faculty," observed Detlev Vagts.[64]

For those who aspired to the *Review* and fell short, the failure could be searing. Professor Laurence H. Tribe (LL.B. 1966) came to Harvard Law School as a brilliant student from the Harvard Ph.D. program in mathematics with great expectations. He recalled:

> At the end of the first year, I did well enough to get in the Legal Aid Bureau, but not well enough to get in the Board of Student Advisers or the *Law Review.* . . . Coming back for the second year not on the *Law Review* was like crawling into some place where you hoped no one would see you. It was horrible. In fact, I didn't want to come back. My mother and my wife . . . persuaded me it was worth a try. . . . My second year, I did very well, but not quite well enough to make the *Review.* . . . [After graduating fifth in the class,] everything sort of worked out. . . . But not making the *Law Review* was, for many years, like carrying a cross, wearing a scarlet letter![65]

Conversely, those who did make *Law Review* were delighted, and gratified that "the process was entirely dependent on grades." As a result, members "were largely happy to welcome anyone who made the cut, regardless of their background," said Andrew Kaufman. "Thus, the president of the *Law Review* in 1953 could be Jewish, even at a time when Jews were not hired at many of the biggest and most prestigious law firms." Similarly, Priscilla Holmes (LL.B. 1955) became the first woman admitted to the *Law Review* in 1953, three years after women were admitted to the law school, although major law firms would not hire women.[66]

Elizabeth Bartholet (LL.B. 1965) concurred, in part: "There was no other woman for the two years that I was on the *Review.* It was overwhelmingly Jewish. It was the first time at the law school that I felt I had my own place and friends. . . . And I think it was meritocratic. . . . But it was not likely that [a woman] would get to be the head or an officer [of the *Review*], even if you were just as good. If you were tons better, maybe. But that was not an era when you expected truly equal treatment. The best you could expect was to get the grade you earned on an exam."[67]

Given this "meritocratic" basis, members of the *Law Review*—particularly the elected officers—received various perquisites, including special lunches with the faculty, unsolicited offers to collaborate with professors, and, in general, deference from faculty and hiring partners of law firms. When Derek Bok

(1968–1970) became dean, he took stock of this preferred access and deference, and the hierarchy in the student body. "Much of this . . . was rather bad,"
he concluded, and he decided "to increase the number of law-related extracurricular activities, including law reviews."[68] But this weakening of the elite
status and perquisites of members of the *Law Review* and expanding the
number of student law reviews dismayed some faculty from the Griswold era.[69]

Apart from objections to elitism and inequitable perquisites, the meritocratic
selection based primarily on first-year grades had drawbacks. After election to
the *Law Review*, many members did not go to class or, if they did, did not prepare for class. In some years the editors divvied up their courses, and one attended each course and took careful notes, while the others did not attend
class. The nonattending editors then used the notes to prepare for the exam.[70]

Even Griswold, who had made it a point of honor to do all his coursework
while serving on the *Review* in 1927, excused *Review* members who skipped
classes that he taught as dean in the 1950s and 1960s. Consequently, "*Law
Review* editors had grades that were all over the map. They spent time on some
things and did well, but in some other courses they didn't go to class," Kaufman
stated. Even editors whose grade-point average slipped below the minimum
grade (a low B) required to stay on the *Law Review*, could obtain a waiver from
the president of the *Law Review* to remain.[71]

As a result, a number of students—such as Tribe—who did not make the
Law Review but worked harder on their courses in all three years, finished
higher in class rank than most of the "elite" *Law Review* editors, who had
done superlatively in their first-year classes. Graduating fifth in his class,
Tribe outranked almost 90 percent of the thirty-five editors on the *Harvard
Law Review* in his class, and he eventually achieved Harvard's highest faculty
honor, a university professorship. As an overall indicator of academic merit,
attaining membership in the *Harvard Law Review* therefore was not valid or
reliable in the long term. All the same, Tribe long felt stigmatized, while the
elite status of *Law Review* members perdured for life. More importantly,
members of the *Law Review* had taken the second step on the career ladder to
becoming professors, judges, and partners in major law firms.

Judicial Clerkships

The third step on the professorial career ladder was the judicial clerkship.
Chief justice of the Massachusetts Supreme Judicial Court Horace Gray (LL.B.
1849) introduced the modern judicial clerkship in 1875 when he began hiring

and paying a law clerk each year to help with his caseload. Relying on the rec-ommendations of his younger half-brother, Professor John C. Gray (LL.B. 1861), Justice Gray customarily selected an honors graduate from Harvard Law School.[72] After his appointment to the U.S. Supreme Court in 1882, Justice Gray continued the practice. By 1888 all the U.S. Supreme Court Jus-tices were hiring clerks, who were paid by the federal government.[73]

In 1902 Justice Gray died, and Oliver W. Holmes Jr. (LL.B. 1866) followed his footsteps from the position of chief justice of the Massachusetts Supreme Judicial Court to the "Massachusetts seat" on the U.S. Supreme Court. Holmes continued the practice of hiring as his clerk a Harvard Law School honors graduate recommended by John Gray, a close friend.[74] In 1913 Gray retired from the faculty, so Holmes turned to like-minded Professor Felix Frankfurter (LL.B. 1906) for recommendations of law clerks. When Louis Brandeis (LL.B. 1877) joined the Supreme Court in 1916, he also began re-lying on Frankfurter for recommendations. Frankfurter nominated only stellar students, but directed the "polished gentlemen" to the Brahmin Holmes, and the nonconformists to Brandeis, as Erwin Griswold and others recognized during the 1920s.[75]

In 1930 Congress began providing a clerk for each federal circuit judge and, in 1936, for some federal district court judges. By 1942 about half of the states had authorized clerks for the justices on their highest court. In 1947 Con-gress expanded the provision for each U.S. Supreme Court Justice to two clerks. The expectations of graduates from any law school who filled these positions generally conformed to the Harvard model: they were honors graduates who had been members, and usually officers, of the law review at their school. Through 1957, some 410 law school graduates had clerked on the U.S. Su-preme Court, and most had come from Harvard (148), Yale (45), George Washington (34), Columbia (29), and Georgetown (24).[76]

Nevertheless, this third step of clerking was still in a formative stage. In the mid-1950s, "very few students wanted to do it . . . my own firm took a dim view of clerkships," observed Stephen Bernardi (LL.B. 1955). Partners asked, "What do you want to do? Do you want to practice law?" Through 1960 only about a third of *Harvard Law Review* members pursued a judicial clerk-ship, although Dean Griswold portrayed a clerkship as the common aspira-tion of students.[77] For many *Law Review* members at the time, such as Gerald E. Frug (LL.B. 1963), a future professor and leader of the Critical Legal Studies movement, clerking was not the "obvious next thing" to do after graduation.[78]

After 1965 the attraction of judicial clerkships rose sharply nationwide, as shown by the composition of faculties ten years later at ABA-accredited law schools. In 1975 the proportion of former judicial clerks among the regular faculty who had graduated between 1966 and 1975 (22 percent) was twice as large as the proportion of those who graduated between 1946 and 1955 (11 percent). This growing interest in clerking stemmed partly from the deferments for judicial clerks granted by some draft boards during the Vietnam War.[79]

As this third step became more common at Harvard after 1965, the process of picking judicial clerks changed. It had been a small, tight "old boys network," closed even to most members of the Harvard Law School faculty.[80] Certain justices and judges had "total confidence in their pickers" on the faculty, "who not only were trying to get smart people for them, but obviously were trying to get people that they thought would be compatible with what those judges wanted," said Frank Sander.[81]

And the role of "picker" was handed down. When Felix Frankfurter ascended to the Supreme Court in 1939, he asked Professor Henry Hart to recommend his clerks. When Griswold became dean, he assumed Frankfurter's former role of recommending the clerks for the leading Circuit Court judges Learned Hand (LL.B. 1896), Augustus Hand (LL.B. 1894), and Calvert Magruder (LL.B. 1916).[82] These recommendations required no application, academic transcripts, interview, or even inquiry by the students, who generally did not even know they were being considered. One day the "picker" would simply ask about the student's interest in a clerkship, which was tantamount to offering the position. Thus, students were "passive about pursuing judicial clerkships," because "their clerkships found them."[83]

In the late 1960s the process of selecting clerks became more open and formal, as clerking became an index of accomplishment that matched, or even eclipsed, law review membership. Commensurately, more students sought clerkships, and procuring a clerkship became more competitive. Hence, "a free market application system" emerged, involving submission of credentials.[84] This more open and formal process established competition for "a blue-chip clerkship" as the third step on the professorial career ladder, in the words of Richard D. Parker (J.D. 1970). The rising importance of the clerkship corresponded inversely with the declining enrollment by American LL.B.s in S.J.D. programs, because a clerkship was a better credential than the S.J.D.[85]

"The Faculty Will Have You as a . . . Law Teacher"

By the late 1960s the three-step career ladder to the Harvard Law School faculty was firmly in place. The faculty Appointments Committee routinely relied on recommendations from the justices and judges with whom they themselves had clerked and from the former *Harvard Law Review* officers who were their friends. During Griswold's twenty-one-year deanship, the school offered tenure to forty-five professors (aside from the professors of international legal studies or legal history), of whom thirty-two had attended Harvard Law School, twenty-nine had served on the *Harvard Law Review,* and twenty-three had been officers of the *Review.* The great majority of the twenty-nine former *Law Review* members had clerked for Supreme Court Justices Frankfurter, John M. Harlan II, or William J. Brennan Jr. (LL.B. 1931) or Judges Calvert Magruder, Learned Hand, Augustus Hand, or Henry Friendly (LL.B. 1927), after being nominated by Harvard Law School professors.[86]

For aspirants who did not attain appointment to the Harvard faculty, the ladder led to faculty appointments in many other law schools. In fact, Harvard LL.B.s from Griswold's tenure predominated in law faculties nationally. This was an important mechanism of the school's isomorphic influence. As of 1975–76, eight years after Griswold resigned as dean, the Law School was the biggest producer of law professors in the country. Of regular faculty at ABA-accredited schools, 524 (13.9 percent) had graduated from Harvard, 258 (6.8 percent) from Yale, and 164 (4.3 percent) from Columbia. In this representation of its graduates, Harvard Law School was, of course, advantaged by its size. In proportional terms of students graduating between 1948 and 1975 who became full-time law faculty, Yale had the highest fraction at 4.7 percent (215 faculty), then Chicago 4.1 percent (129 faculty), and, third, Harvard at 2.9 percent (417 faculty), after which the fraction fell to 1.7 percent for a number of schools.[87]

At Harvard, the three-step professorial career ladder was widely recognized and taken for granted. The faculty gave "total deference to the faculty Appointments Committee, partly because it was a club and everybody had trust in the other members of the club," said Sander, a former Frankfurter clerk. By the same token, the Appointments Committee would not consider the former clerks of Supreme Court justices deemed heterodox, such as Hugo Black or William O. Douglas, recalled Detlev Vagts.[88] Consequently, "the faculty, as a whole, was pretty homogeneous. . . . There was sort of a mold," said Sander.[89]

Differences in background among the faculty were small. "Through 1967, there were no serious political divisions," observed Harold Berman. "It was a conservative faculty, though democrat and republican, to be sure."[90]

Dean Griswold did try to diversify the faculty somewhat, at least in terms of academic and religious background. In 1947 he hired Berman (Yale, LL.B. 1947) to teach Soviet law, and, in 1952, Louis Loss (Yale, LL.B. 1937) to teach securities law, both of whom came from Jewish backgrounds. In 1954 Griswold hired Robert E. Keeton (LL.B. Texas, S.J.D. 1956) from the faculty of Southern Methodist University Law School.

At alumni gatherings Griswold would sometimes cite these appointments and "brag about Harvard Law School becoming more open," Keeton stated. But Keeton also conceded that some Harvard professors did not approve of diversifying the faculty, and that the limited changes occurred only because "it was very clear that Erwin Griswold was absolutely behind it, and he was in control."[91] In 1962 the dean recruited James Vorenberg, who was Jewish and had practiced law for over a decade. In 1964 "Griswold felt that he was reaching out" in hiring Alan Dershowitz, a Yale graduate and "a non-conformist, who was rather aggressively Jewish in a way that previous Jewish members of the faculty hadn't been," said Vagts.[92]

Offers of a faculty position at Harvard Law School were communicated indirectly and awkwardly, as had been the case in the late nineteenth century.[93] One reason was that Harvard would not officially make an offer unless assured of its acceptance, as Keeton surmised during his year as a visiting professor in 1953–54.[94] Therefore, initial offers were often implied or made through intermediaries, creating misunderstanding and confusion.

In 1958, after agreeing to join a law firm in San Francisco, future dean Derek Bok was invited by Professor Kingman Brewster to consider teaching at the Law School. Bok came to the school for a visit and talked to a number of faculty members, then heard nothing for several weeks. "I thought . . . maybe the whole thing was just an idle exercise and would be quietly forgotten by both sides. Finally, I got a rather petulant letter from Erwin Griswold saying, 'We had expected to hear from you about whether you were interested in taking a job.' So I said, 'Gosh, I didn't know you cared.' Then I quickly received an offer and decided to go there."[95]

The second reason for faulty communication was Dean Griswold's personal awkwardness. In 1962 he solicited the interest of Vorenberg, who was practicing law at a leading Boston law firm. With the faculty's endorsement, the dean went to Vorenberg's law office to make the offer. "In his typically gracious way, Griswold said, 'The faculty will have you as a corporation law teacher.' I thought that was a funny way of putting it," recalled Vorenberg, who had neither initiated the inquiry nor thought of doing so.[96]

Equally funny was Griswold's visit to the Supreme Court on a rainy spring day in 1964 to see Dershowitz, who was clerking for Justice Arthur Goldberg. Griswold "asked me to come out to meet with him . . . in the hallway of the Supreme Court," said Dershowitz. "He leaned on me as he took off his galoshes. . . . And he says to me, 'the faculty at the Law School has decided that you can be a professor here.' . . . It was done in a way, [as if] you were anointed."[97]

Once hired, faculty were required to meet certain standards in order to be promoted and tenured. The school expected excellent teaching, cooperative service, and good scholarship, defined as having published at least one article in total, usually in a law review.[98] This standard of scholarship was not as high as in other academic fields, observed Charles Fried, who was born in Czechoslovakia and earned four degrees, at Princeton, Oxford, and Columbia Universities, before joining the Harvard law faculty in 1961. Not only was the expected quantity of publications small, but articles in student-edited law journals were not anonymously reviewed by established scholars, as is customary in other academic fields. In Fried's view, the absence of blind peer review reinforced the practice of basing hiring decisions on academic performance early in law school and on an insular "old-boys network."[99]

During Griswold's deanship, most new, young faculty were appointed as untenured assistant professors. Within three years most were promoted and tenured as full professors, since there was no intermediate rank of associate professor. Having originally fit the mold, they almost had to disprove the premise of their worthiness.[100] After all, Harvard did not make mistakes.

As dean, it fell to Griswold to communicate to assistant professors the faculty decision on their promotion and tenure, and he did so in his typically awkward fashion. In the spring of 1962, after the faculty vote on Assistant Professor Vagts, "Erwin comes into my office and starts talking about . . . things that I could do better," Vagts recalled. "At the end of it, he . . . said, 'I expect you to take care of these things next year.'" Then he left Vagts's office and walked down the hall. "If he expects me to do things better next year, . . . that must mean I'll be around as a tenured professor," Vagts concluded. "And that's how the message came to me."[101]

First (Visiting) Woman on the Faculty (for Two Years)

Like Landis, Griswold had no inclination "to go completely New Deal revolutionary" by appointing women to the faculty.[102] Even if he had, the three-step career ladder provided the means and justification to refrain from appointing women and people of color to the homogeneous faculty club. Barred from "blue chip" judicial clerkships by their gender, ethnicity, or race, they did not have credentials comparable to the white men under consideration. For example, the first female clerk in the U.S. Supreme Court was hired in 1944, likely because World War II was under way and male candidates were scarce. No Supreme Court Justice hired another female clerk until 1966. Even then, it was highly unlikely that a woman could be elected an officer of the *Harvard Law Review* "even if you were just as good," Elizabeth Bartholet observed.[103] Women could barely get to the second step, let alone the third step of the career ladder, through the end of Griswold's deanship.

Although appointing no tenure-line female professors, Griswold did hire the first woman to the faculty in 1946. Born in Moscow, Soia Mentschikoff came to New York with her family at age three, and graduated from Hunter College in 1934 and Columbia Law School in 1937. She then worked as a research assistant for one of her professors, Karl Llewellyn, whom she married in 1945. Meanwhile, Mentschikoff became a partner at a Wall Street firm, and met Harvard Law School professor Ralph J. Baker, who brought her to the attention of Dean Griswold.[104]

In the fall of 1946, Griswold proposed to the faculty hiring Mentschikoff as a visiting professor for the academic year 1947–48 in order to teach the courses of Professor William E. McCurdy (LL.B. 1921, S.J.D. 1922), who was going on leave. Since the dean could have easily found a qualified man to teach those courses, his proposal was revolutionary, and his consultation with Judge Augustus Hand and President James Conant (1933–1953) beforehand indicates some interest in breaking the gender barrier on the faculty.[105] Indeed, Judith Richards Hope (LL.B. 1964) has suggested that Mentschikoff's appointment might have been "part of [Griswold's] long-range strategy to persuade the Corporation to reverse its historical opposition to women at the Law School."[106]

Nevertheless, Griswold's interest had limits. Not only did the faculty endorse Griswold's proposal, but several maintained that Mentschikoff should be hired whether or not McCurdy took a leave of absence. Griswold quickly responded that he had contemplated appointing Mentschikoff only if McCurdy left, implying that he was not interested in breaking the gender barrier for its own sake. But the faculty voted to hire Mentschikoff with the understanding "that the motion was not tied to Mr. McCurdy's plans." The faculty were prepared to make gender history even if the dean was not, although the faculty's desire to recruit her husband Karl Llewellyn from Columbia may also have played a role.[107]

In any case, Harvard Law School appointed Mentschikoff as a visiting professor to teach sales and commercial law during the 1947–48 academic year. The newspapers made a great deal of "the fact that an attractive woman in her early thirties would be occupying the chair once held by Samuel Williston (LL.B. 1888). Reporters were struck by Mentschikoff's height as well as her deep voice, which was likened to that of Marlene Dietrich and Lauren Bacall," as historian Mary Beth Basile Chopas has written.[108] In the fall of 1948, the Law School then appointed Llewellyn as a probationary visiting professor.

Mentschikoff taught for two successive years, 1947–48 and 1948–49, and impressed the great majority of the faculty with her brilliance, academic rigor, indomitable personality, and nonconformist behavior. But some found her lack of deference shocking and unpalatable.[109] Another problem was that, in the spring of 1949, the Law School decided not to offer Llewellyn a tenured professorship, largely due to his widely recognized abrasive demeanor.[110] Indeed, when Llewellyn had done fieldwork among the Cheyenne tribe to learn about their law, his explosive personality prompted the tribe to name him "Fire-Gets-Away," as the *Harvard Law School Record* reported.[111] Thus, the equally incandescent Mentschikoff got away as well, and the Law School "made a great mistake" on both accounts, according to Berman. Llewellyn and Mentschikoff moved to the faculty of the University of Chicago Law School in 1949, and Mentschikoff eventually became dean of the University of Miami Law School in 1974.[112]

After Mentschikoff left Harvard 1949, no woman held the title of professor at Harvard Law School until Elizabeth A. Owens in 1972. Owens had studied economics and worked in several federal agencies before earning the LL.B. at Yale and graduating in 1951. She then practiced law at a prominent Boston firm until the Law School hired her in 1957 as a research assistant to Professor Stanley Surrey in the International Tax Program. In 1961 Owens published her first book, *The Foreign Tax Credit*, which was very well received. Promoted to lecturer in 1964, she began teaching International Aspects of U.S. Income Taxation regularly to classes of thirty students, as well as substituting for Griswold, when he could not teach his tax courses.[113]

Elisabeth A. Owens. Professor 1972–1981.
Harvard Law School Yearbook, 1965.
Courtesy of Harvard Yearbook Publications.

When the dean stepped down in 1967, some women in the student body suggested that Owens should fill Griswold's vacated professorship, and they were told that Owens did not have adequate teaching experience, although Harvard had hired many men with little or no experience at all. By 1971 Owens was teaching Water Rights, National Resources Law, and a course on women in the law. While men were commonly tenured after just three years of probation, Owens had been teaching for eight years when she finally received her appointment as full professor in the spring of 1972. Even then, she believed that she was appointed only due to the pressure of gender equity and that it would never have happened otherwise. There is likely some truth to this, partly because she was not a dynamic teacher by all accounts and never taught the large sections of required courses in which tenure-track junior faculty were expected to prove themselves.[114]

Dean Griswold: "Austere, Forbidding, Uncompromising"

Due to the homogeneity resulting from the hiring process, the small faculty of about thirty white men—most of whom had graduated from Harvard Law School and belonged to the *Harvard Law Review*—formed a close-knit *brüderbund* in the late 1940s. Griswold fostered their collegiality by holding a faculty tea daily at 5 p.m., which all were expected to attend. Many faculty ate lunch together daily in the faculty dining room. Even on Saturday, though only junior faculty and lecturers taught classes, the senior faculty trooped in to have lunch together with them. This collective spirit persevered nearly to the end of Griswold's administration in 1967, but weakened as the size of the faculty and the range of their disciplines and academic backgrounds expanded.[115]

Reinforcing this spirit was Griswold's "autocratic" style and micromanagement, which he had, ironically, criticized in Pound.[116] In the faculty lunchroom, the dean "would sit at the head of the table and pronounce, and often the only two dissenters at the table would be Lon Fuller and Henry Hart," recalled Alan Dershowitz.[117] The dean "epitomized the Harvard Law School as we knew it—austere, forbidding, uncompromising but ultimately commanding our grudging admiration and respect," said Derek Bok. "To us younger faculty members, he was the kind of leader one does not often find today in universities—decisive, magisterial, and rarely contradicted."[118]

In faculty meetings, "there wasn't any real give or take, except about appointments. . . . Ordinarily, what the dean said, that was it. Nobody challenged him. Nobody criticized him. Nobody faulted him," stated Louis Toepfer (LL.B. 1947).[119] For example, in the mid-1960s Paul Bator (LL.B. 1956) wrote a memo to the dean and the faculty proposing that classes no longer be held on the Friday and Saturday after Thanksgiving Day. At the next faculty meeting, "Erwin presented the issue and his own disagreement, and said, 'Does anyone want to speak in favor of Mr. Bator's proposal?'" Although most faculty agreed with Bator, the question was met with silence, and the dean moved on to the next issue. "People knew what Erwin thought, and no one was willing to speak up and spend their chips on that issue."[120]

That unwillingness stemmed in part from Griswold's approach to setting salaries. Until Landis left in 1946, the deans had determined professorial salaries according to a standard scale, which started at about $8,000 and advanced by $2,000 every fifth year until the maximum of about $12,000 was reached.[121] In 1946 Griswold began exercising discretion and adjusting salaries individually,

Table 13.1   Faculty Salaries of the Eight Highest-Paying Law Schools, 1955–56

Law School	Average Salary	Median Salary	Difference between Median and Average
Pennsylvania	14,000	16,125	2,125
Michigan	13,600	13,750	150
Yale	13,450	14,000	550
Berkeley	12,365	12,600	235
Harvard	**12,259**	**15,500**	**3,241**
UCLA	12,041	12,300	259
Illinois	11,907	12,000	93
Columbia	11,820	13,000	1,180

Data source: Erwin N. Griswold to Nathan M. Pusey (September 30, 1957), NMP Records.
Note: Data in the "difference" column was not included in Griswold's letter.

creating large discrepancies by 1957, as compared to other leading law schools at the time. Griswold inadvertently revealed the differences when sending President Nathan Pusey (1953–1971) salary data for the eight highest-paying law schools in the academic year 1955–56, as reported in Table 13.1. Griswold intended to demonstrate that Harvard was "not paying the top salaries, either on a median or average basis," and that "we are barely holding our own with our most important competition."[122]

Griswold did not mention, or perhaps realize, that the figures also showed that the median (or midpoint) of salaries at Harvard was much greater than the average salary, and this difference at Harvard was far greater than at the other law schools. This difference suggests that certain salaries at Harvard were either extremely high or extremely low. In contrast, Table 13.1 reveals that the median and average salaries at most of the law schools—especially Yale, Michigan, Berkeley, UCLA, and Illinois—were very close, so the salary range was likely small.

The range at Harvard might be explained by an unusual age distribution of faculty there, particularly a preponderance of younger, lower-paid faculty. But several younger faculty have stated that they received large raises from Griswold after he hired them. Hence, the explanation for the large difference seems to be that, in the ten years between 1946 and 1956, Griswold introduced great discrepancies in salaries by rewarding some faculty and punishing others to an unusual extreme. One of the professors targeted was Ernest Brown (LL.B. 1931), because he did not publish and devoted himself to teaching and service.[123] Many faculty recognized that "there were some members of the faculty that Erwin treated badly and consequently failed to get the best out of them," in the words of Archibald Cox.[124]

After Griswold left, Acting Dean James Casner (1967–68) renounced "Dean Griswold's reserve power to differentiate salary between different people of the same seniority," which "had served for the faculty as a symbolic authoritarianism." Instead, Casner instituted uniform increases, "and the faculty felt much relieved."[125] Upon becoming dean in 1968, Derek Bok discovered the large and "very, very arbitrary" differences in salary, which he tried to correct, by continuing Casner's approach.[126]

Consequently, by 1966, when Russell Simpson (LL.B. 1965) assumed the position of assistant dean of admissions at the Law School, "people were chafing. [Griswold] tended to be a real autocrat. He was forthright with everyone, but he liked to do things his own way."[127] In particular, the new young faculty believed that "the atmosphere of the school was stifling," as stated Charles R. Nesson (LL.B. 1963), who joined the faculty in the fall of 1967. "The status of faculty members depended upon the extent to which they had the dean's approval, and his approval could be obtained best by pursuing his image of what it meant to be a faculty member at the Harvard Law School." "Repression" suffused the school, Nesson maintained.[128]

The Students: "What a Rat Race It Is"

While some professors thought that the dean was heavy-handed, many students felt positively oppressed. Griswold had improved student life, but he seemed to have a "tough love" approach. He believed that students benefited academically from self-reliance born of salutary neglect—except for the very best, who needed and deserved extra attention. In December 1951 Griswold publicly assured alumni, the administration, and anyone else that Harvard Law School would not stay the intellectual sword, notwithstanding the relaxation of competition that some might infer from the school having admitted women or veterans on the G.I. Bill. "Lest anyone be worried, the school has not grown soft. The rigor of the classroom is unchanged," he stated. "The younger members of the faculty are not lacking in iron. The Law School remains a competitive place. Life is like that, and it is not too early for law students to learn it."[129]

Nevertheless, by the mid-1960s many students, even highly successful ones, considered the "compulsive competition" to be "terrible," according to Laurence Tribe.[130] One third-year student, Karl Bemesderfer (LL.B. 1966), wrote,

"Put law students together and before you know it, they begin to talk about what a rat race it is."[131] In 1967 a *Time* magazine story observed, "Academic competition [at Harvard Law School] is so intense that stories abound of students who hang blankets on their windows so that neighbors will not suspect extra nocturnal studying or, conversely, students who sleep with eye guards and all the lights on to panic a classmate."[132]

Student complaints were rebuffed. In the spring of 1956 some students formed a "Tensions Committee," which "aimed at reducing the 'tensions' or 'pressures' of which many students have complained," and recommended publishing an "Unofficial Guide to Law School Life" that would include "an explanation of the grading system and its importance." The deans agreed to publish the guide in the fall of 1956, but rejected the draft submitted by the committee in August. The *Harvard Law Record* then offered to publish the explanation of the grading system, but Vice Dean Livingston Hall (LL.B. 1927) objected, and it never appeared.[133]

In his next annual report, Griswold acknowledged but set aside the student "complaints." "The atmosphere of the School is largely set by the students, and they have long provided an atmosphere which is conducive to work," Griswold wrote. "There are some who assert that the School is too 'competitive.' The faculty of the School do not believe in tension or pressure or competition as ends in themselves. They do believe in maintaining high standards of legal education."[134] A number of faculty who had attended Harvard College and the Law School in the 1940s concurred with Griswold that the academic pressure was largely "self-generated" by the students.[135]

Many students did not agree that the problem was of their own making. Conditions in higher education and the legal profession were changing rapidly during the 1950s and 1960s. Gone were the days of showing up with a diploma from a "respectable" college and strolling into Harvard Law School. Career prospects at all levels of the bar, the bench, the professoriate, and government depended increasingly upon academic performance in secondary school, then in college, and finally in law school.[136] And certain policies and practices at the Law School stoked the concomitant anxiety.

The new selective admissions policy, which yielded a higher proportion of excellent enrollees who were accustomed to academic success, added to the academic pressure. This policy shifted the nature of academic rivalry—from the minimal pre-1950 worry about surviving the first year, to pressure to achieve a high class ranking in the top 12 percent (or seventy students) of the class, who could join one of the three honor organizations. Dean Griswold noted this shift in his annual report for 1961–62.[137]

The examination format also raised the pressure. Since Dean Langdell had introduced written examinations and grades at the Law School in 1871, the evaluation instrument in the all-important first-year courses, as well as most others, remained a lone written exam at the very end of the course. Such an exam, though a significant advance in the 1870s, would scarcely be recommended as a valid and reliable measure of an entire year's academic work by later experts in educational measurement or assessment. Did the lone exam actually measure a student's command of the material? Would retesting yield the same results? With so much riding on one exam—whose validity and reliability were unproven, if not suspect—tension and anxiety naturally roiled the class of high-achieving, selectively admitted students.[138]

The grading and ranking system contributed as well. In the century after 1871, the faculty assigned numerical grades to the written examinations, which the school secretary or registrar recorded as the grade for the course. That numerical grade determined whether a student passed a course or achieved academic honors. The precise point where the sword fell, determining failure or various honors, naturally changed over time, as did policies about informing students of their grades, converting the numerical grades to letter grades, and ranking students.

Grades were solely numerical and kept confidential by the dean until 1892, when the faculty voted to have the dean convert the numerical grades to letters and then inform the students of the total *number* of Cs, Bs, and so forth they received, but not their grades in specific courses. In 1911 Dean Ezra Thayer (1910–1915) and the faculty rescinded the conversion to letters, and voted to tell students the overall average of their numerical course grades. With this more precise information, students could compare their average with their fellow students as well as the announced standards for passing and for honors.[139] This change heightened academic pressure under Deans Thayer and Pound.

In 1937 the faculty voted to tell students their grades for individual courses, but only after the numerical grades were converted to letter grades. Soon after Dean Griswold arrived in 1946, the faculty decided to inform students of their numerical grades in individual courses. After professors graded the exams, the registrar therefore began posting students' names, numerical grades in each course, and overall numerical averages in rank order for the 500+ students in the class.[140] Recollections of the postings by students and faculty vary, but Lon Fuller's Committee on Legal Education reported in 1948 that students' "most deeply felt complaint relates to 'the grading system.'"[141] During the 1950s the public display of students' course grades and class rank apparently reached its apogee at the Law School, and the student Tensions Committee focused on this issue during the year 1956–57.

In 1960 the faculty and dean began to ease the pressure by preserving anonymity, as the students were assigned personal numbers, which were listed on the public rankings, rather than names. In the following year, the faculty voted to end the public listing of students' numerical averages and class rank, except for the honors students with averages of 72 or higher on a 100-point scale. But the registrar still calculated numerical averages and ranks for the entire class, which were made available to employers. Also, in communicating the numerical grades, averages, and ranks to students and employers, the registrar added the equivalent letter grade in parentheses.[142]

This modest revision accomplished little because more than half the class received grades below 69, which corresponded to a grade of C+ or worse, and saddled most of the class with relatively poor letter grades. Furthermore, all the numerical grades were bunched between 50 and 80, so the registrar averaged grades to the hundredths in order to distinguish class rank among the 500+ students in the class. In the densely packed middle range of the bell curve, a few hundredths' difference in overall grade average (as between 67.56 and 67.59) could mean a change in class rank of twenty or thirty places, or 5 to 6 percent of the class.[143]

The grading and ranking thus "became increasingly absurd" during the 1960s, as Vagts remarked, and naturally exacerbated students' anxiety and tension. Evaluation of the work of some 140 students in a section of a major course depended on one four-hour essay exam. Though based on a scale of 100 points, numerical grades on the exams normally fell in a small range, and this led to making minute distinctions of doubtful validity, as between the grades of 67 and 68 on an exam. The weight of those minute distinctions was then compounded by distinguishing even more finely in overall numerical average and class rank. Meanwhile, the numerical precision conveyed a misleading sense of precision to the distinctions.[144] Finally, these numerical grades were normally the only feedback that students received about their work; professors did not provide written comments. Faculty long recognized these problems, but the system continued, largely because it usefully sorted students for employers, said Bok and others.[145]

Before and during his deanship, Griswold recognized all these factors contributing to the academic competition and anxiety: selective admissions, public ranking of students, lone written examinations at the end of courses, and minute numerical distinctions in grading, coupled with large classes and little feedback. Though expressing some regret, he did not initiate significant reforms in response to student complaints. The dean believed that "the basic rigor of the Harvard Law School was good," and academic rigor, in his view, entailed a struggle for success.[146]

Some critics have suggested that Griswold's conservatism on these issues and on the LL.B. curriculum pushed Harvard graduates toward careers in corporate law firms.[147] But the dean repeatedly called on students to work in public service.[148] Heeding his own call, he spent almost his entire career in public service and academia, when he could have made a great deal of money practicing in commercial law. Griswold characteristically expected others to have his fortitude in choosing a career that would bring them "future success and happiness."[149]

Nevertheless, Griswold acknowledged that the school's educational program induced students to join major, well-heeled law firms. "Much of our best teaching has been in the property and business fields. Almost inevitably our students are led to feel that it is in these areas that the great work of the lawyer is to be found," he conceded. "By methods of teaching, by subtle and often unconscious innuendo, we indicate to our students that their future success and happiness will be found in the traditional areas of the law.[150]

But the most important factor drawing more students into corporate law firms was likely the changing market for young lawyers. During the 1950s and 1960s, the gap between salaries in public service and leading law firms widened significantly, as the firms' demand for young lawyers increased.[151] Consequently, the financial sacrifice for entering public service grew immensely during these decades.

In any event, Griswold did little to counterbalance students' disposition or to slow the academic "rat race." By 1966 student discontent over the educational program's destructive influence on the school's environment was becoming severe. At the suggestion of Clark Byse, Dean Griswold established a committee, composed of six students and six faculty members, to give an official conduit to express their concerns. This Joint Student-Faculty Committee, as it became known, reported in December 1966 and criticized the entire complex of academic policies.[152] The discontent and agitation under Griswold set the stage for the "the grade war" that would plague Dean Bok.

"Harvard Law School Has No Glee Club"

Dean Griswold was profoundly equivocal concerning student life in the school. On the one hand, longtime colleagues affirmed that Griswold "genuinely cared enormously about the lives" of students,[153] and he repeatedly claimed to make "a conscious effort . . . to make the School a friendly place" and "a more humane institution."[154] That effort included providing the dining commons, dormitories, additional meeting rooms, system of tunnels, placement office, first-year writing groups, many more faculty members and small classes, a tenfold increase in financial aid, and new student organizations.[155]

As of the academic year 1966–67, over 1,000 students were engaged in school clubs, organizations, and activities outside of the classroom. The number of memberships in student organizations totaled 2,755, more than three memberships for every two students.[156] Of particular note was the growth of student-edited journals beyond the *Harvard Law School Review.* "Students came to me with plans to establish new journals, and I encouraged them," stated Griswold. By 1967 these included the *Harvard International Law Journal, Harvard Legal Commentary, Harvard Journal on Legislation,* and *Harvard Civil Rights–Civil Liberties Law Review.*[157] Given all this activity, Griswold expressed frustration that some criticized student life at the school, without comparing it to that of prior generations.[158]

On the other hand, even while Griswold made this effort, his public posture contravened it, as though fearing that he would appear to encourage frivolity. In his welcoming address to new students each fall, he famously stated, "Harvard Law School has no Glee Club," warning students that they must focus on their academic work.[159] His personal interactions with students were often even more damaging, as he was frequently rude or dismissive. In 1947 one student, a talented musician and a veteran, visited the dean in his office seeking permission to take a course in musical composition. "His only words to me were 'Get the hell out of here,'" recalled the student. Another remarked, "Students now want to be chummy with the dean and show up in the dean's office to chat. . . . Showing up in Erwin Griswold's office usually meant disaster. You didn't relish that at all."[160] "Students were scared of Griswold. He was gruff. He was distant," stated Gary Bellow (LL.B. 1960). "I don't think he was trying to scare us, but he did," recalled Bernardi.[161]

Nor did the great majority of students find comfort from the faculty, who remained "very distant," although relations between professors and a relatively small number of high-achieving students grew closer and stronger, partly due

"All Hope Abandon, Ye Who Enter."

Harvard Law School Yearbook, 1951. Courtesy of Harvard Yearbook Publications.

to the declining student-faculty ratio.[162] But even then, Griswold worried that students' desire for faculty attention and time was becoming excessive.[163]

Meanwhile, the student body became more socioeconomically homogeneous. Even though the school vastly increased financial aid, "the inevitable result of a highly selective admission process is that only the best educated survive," Toepfer observed. "The students who succeed in the competition for admission seldom come from the bottom economic groups. . . . Almost none of them are really poor."[164]

Concomitantly, the degree of "class consciousness" and certain traditional customs of social exclusivity began to decline as the civil rights movement and Vietnam War protests heated up.[165] These included the "preppiness" of the graduates of Ivy League institutions and New England colleges, who wore coats and ties and carried briefcases.[166] Private eating clubs that restricted membership also fell out of favor. Founded in 1926, the Chancery Club was, by reputation, racist and anti-Semitic, and closed its doors in 1963.[167] Founded in 1908, Lincoln's Inn proudly announced that, at its clubhouse at 44 Follen Street, "all meals are served by waiters at the tables." In 1968 Lincoln's Inn abandoned "its selective membership policy and adopted a lottery system instead," apparently due to the financial pressure from declining membership.[168]

But there also existed at least one all-male, all-white, secret social club, whose members were recruited by "tapping." Formed in 1946, the existence of the Choate Club, to which both students and faculty belonged, was revealed by the *Harvard Crimson* in 1968. Proponents of such exclusive clubs argued that their purpose was innocuous and that scrutiny amounted to a "witch hunt." What mattered, in the view of others, was that members of these exclusive clubs had privileged access to faculty who had previously been members themselves. Still others fundamentally objected to the secrecy of the exclusive clubs, which amplified the sense of alienation, competition, and exclusion that pervaded the Law School and was felt particularly by those who were marginalized, such as African American students.[169]

In any event, the student culture was deeply influenced by the academic mores of the school, which were driven by the policies of the dean and the faculty. It was simply disingenuous to say that the students created the intense rivalry when the school dangled the academic sword overhead and warned about "not going soft." Yet, compared to his own experience in the 1920s, Dean Griswold had good reason to believe that he had improved student life throughout his decanal term from 1946 to 1967. But more improvement was needed, and students focused on the shortfall, causing him some frustration. Furthermore, his puritanical midwestern heritage made him fearful that reducing anxiety and tension would lead to permissiveness and indulgence.

He therefore focused on strengthening academic rigor by encouraging faculty research, supporting the growth of graduate programs, adding small courses and professors, and normalizing the three-step career ladder for faculty. Meanwhile, he remained committed to the traditional core of the LL.B. curriculum in private and commercial law, and considered International Legal Studies at the graduate level to be the most important kind of public service the Law School could provide in the postwar era. All this cost a lot of money. Dean Griswold procured it and spent it, reinforcing the syndrome of tuition dependence.

NOTES

1. Erwin N. Griswold, "The School since the War," *HLSB* (December 1951): 4.

2. Erwin N. Griswold, "Legal Education at Harvard," *HLSB* (January 1950): 1.

3. Erwin N. Griswold, *Ould Fields, New Corne: The Personal Memoirs of a Twentieth Century Lawyer* (St. Paul, MN, 1992), 155n; Archibald Cox, Memo to the Harvard Law School Faculty (January 13, 1960), on file with the authors. See Henry M. Hart and Albert M. Sacks, "The Legal Process: Basic Problems in the Making and Application of Law" (1950s), typescript, Harvard Law School Library Historical & Special Collections (HLSLib); William N. Eskridge Jr. and Philip P. Frickey, "The Making of 'The Legal Process,'" *HLR* 107 (1994): 2031–2055.

4. Charles Fried, Interview (April 2008), in David Derusha, "The Deanship of Erwin N. Griswold: A New Look" (student research paper, Harvard Law School (HLS) 2008), on file with the authors, appendix 3; Erwin N. Griswold, Annual Report of the Dean of HLS, 1948–49, 431–434; 1950–51, 370–373; 1951–52, 503. The following draws upon Alexander M. Wolf, "The Harvard Law School Faculty under the Deanship of Erwin Nathaniel Griswold" (student research paper, HLS, 2012), on file with the authors.

5. Fried, Interview (April 2008); Harold J. Berman, Oral History, conducted by Daniel Hamilton and Daniel R. Coquillette (August 1998), on file with the authors; Frank E. A. Sander, Oral History, conducted by Daniel R. Coquillette and Daniel Hamilton (September–December 1998), on file with the authors; Robert C. Clark, "Remembrance," in *Erwin Nathaniel Griswold: 1904–1994*, 5–9.

6. Griswold, Annual Report of the Dean, 1953–54, 554; see 1952–53, 476; 1955–56, 388, 390.

7. Clark, "Remembrance," 5–9; Archibald Cox, "In Memoriam," *HLR* 108 (1995): 986; Griswold, Annual Report of the Dean, 1960–61, 324.

8. Erwin N. Griswold, "Professor Cavers Appointed Associate Dean," *HLSB* (April 1951): 3.

9. Griswold, Annual Report of the Dean, 1947–48, 381–382.

10. Griswold, Annual Report of the Dean, 1951–52, 491. See Erwin N. Griswold, "The Future of Legal Education," *HLSB* (February 1953): 5; Henry J. Friendly, "Erwin N. Griswold—Some Fond Recollections," *HLR* 86 (1973): 1366; Griswold, *Ould Fields*, 80–81, 114, 224; Kenneth W. Bergen, *Dedication of Treasury Department Library in*

Memory of Erwin N. Griswold (printed pamphlet) (October 19, 1995), Elizabeth Wahlen Correspondence, 1946–1998, on file with the authors, 1–2.

11. Berman, Oral History (August 1998); Clark Byse, Oral History, conducted by Daniel R. Coquillette and Daniel Hamilton (July–October 1997), on file with the authors; Andrew L. Kaufman, Oral History, conducted by Daniel Hamilton and Daniel R. Coquillette (June 1999–April 2000), on file with the authors.

12. Griswold, Annual Report of the Dean, 1947–48, 381–382; 1950–51, 356–360; 1951–52, 507–509, 511–512; 1953–54, 559; Griswold, "Professor Cavers Appointed Associate Dean," 3; Robert E. Keeton, Oral History, conducted by Daniel Hamilton and Daniel R. Coquillette (November 2000–February 2001), on file with the authors.

13. Lon L. Fuller, Memo to the Faculty: "Our Appointment Policy" (January 6, 1960), on file with the authors.

14. Berman, Oral History (August 1998); Byse, Oral History (July–October 1997); Kaufman, Oral History (June 1999–April 2000); Keeton, Oral History (November 2000–February 2001).

15. Cox, Memo (January 13, 1960).

16. H. L. A. Hart, "Positivism and the Separation of Law and Morals," *HLR* 71 (1958): 594. See "Fifty Years Later" (editorial), *New York University Law Review* 83 (October 2008): 993–999; H. L. A. Hart, *The Concept of Law* (Oxford, UK, 1961).

17. Lon L. Fuller, "Positivism and Fidelity to Law—A Reply to Professor Hart," *HLR* 71 (February 1958): 630–672. See Fuller, *The Morality of Law* (New Haven, CT, 1964).

18. Nicola Lacey, "Philosophy, Political Morality, and History: Explaining the Enduring Resonance of the Hart-Fuller Debate," *New York University Law Review* 83 (2008): 1059–1087; Daniel R. Coquillette, R. Michael Cassidy, and Judith A. McMorrow, *Lawyers and Fundamental Moral Responsibility,* 2nd ed. (Durham, NC, 2010), 136, 162.

19. The following draws upon Gail J. Hupper, "The Rise of an Academic Doctorate in Law: Origins through World War II," *American Journal of Legal History* 49 (2007): 1–60; Arthur von Mehren, Oral History, conducted by Daniel R. Coquillette and Mary Beth Basile (July–December 2000), on file with the authors.

20. Robert Stevens, *Law School: Legal Education in America from the 1850s to the 1980s* (Chapel Hill, NC, 1983), 209; Donna Fossum, "Law Professors: A Profile of the Teaching Branch of the Legal Profession," *American Bar Foundation Research Journal* (1980): 501, 505. See Richard M. Freeland, *Academia's Golden Age: Universities in Massachusetts, 1945–1975* (New York, 1992); Louis Menand, *The Marketplace of Ideas: Reform and Resistance in the American University* (New York, 2010), 63–73.

21. See the snapshot of Harvard's graduate programs in 1950: Erwin N. Griswold, "Graduate Study in Law," *Journal of Legal Education* 2 (1950): 272–286.

22. Hupper, "The Rise of an Academic Doctorate," 1–60; Gail J. Hupper, "Educational Ambivalence: The Rise of a Foreign-Student Doctorate of Law," *New England Law Review* 49 (2015): 319–339, 368–380; von Mehren, Oral History (July–December 2000).

23. Quotation is from Harvard Law School, *Program for Students and Lawyers from Abroad* (Cambridge, MA, 1966), 13. See also Harvard Law School Catalog, 1967–68, 90; Hupper, "Educational Ambivalence," 319–399; von Mehren, Oral History (July–December 2000); Fossum, "Law Professors," 509. Compare Eugene V. Rostow, Annual Report of the Dean of Yale Law School, 1954–55, 16; Arthur E. Sutherland, *The Law at Harvard: A History of Ideas and Men, 1817–1907* (Cambridge, MA, 1967), 336–337.

24. Ralph Nader, "Introduction," xxiv, in Joel Seligman, *The High Citadel: The Influence of Harvard Law School* (Boston, 1978); Seligman, *The High Citadel,* 71; Marina N. Bolotnika, "The Purpose of Harvard Law School," *Harvard Magazine* (August 17, 2016), 5.

25. Griswold, *Ould Fields,* 234–235. See Griswold, Annual Report of the Dean, 1946–47, 405; 1947–48, 384–385; 1949–50, 457; 1954–55, 602–603; Griswold, "The Future," 6; Erwin N. Griswold, "Some Thoughts about Legal Education Today," *HLSB* (December 1959): 3.

26. von Mehren, Oral History (July–December 2000).

27. "Dean Griswold on the Needs of the School," *HLSB* (July 1948): 12; Berman, Oral History (August 1998); Myliefer Shaikh, "Manley O. Hudson, as Professor and Lawyer-Statesman" (student research paper, HLS, 2001), on file with the authors.

28. Berman, Oral History (August 1998).

29. Quotation is from Berman, Oral History (August 1998). See "Arthur T. von Mehren, 83, Scholar of International Law, Is Dead," *New York Times* (January 29, 2006); "In Memoriam: Arthur T. von Mehren," *HLR* 119 (2006): 1949–1973.

30. HLS Faculty Meeting Minutes (November 25 and December 16, 1947; September 28, 1948); "A Project for a 'World School of Law,'" *HLSB* (April 1949): 6; Griswold, Annual Report of the Dean, 1947–48, 384; David F. Cavers, "The Enlarged Curriculum in International Legal Studies," *HLSB* (June 1951): 5–6; Erwin N. Griswold, *A Project for a World School of Law* (Cambridge, MA, 1948). The figure of $10 million was provided by Berman, Oral History (August 1998).

31. David Cavers, "Research Progress," *HLSB* (October 1952): 2; "A Project for a Program in International Legal Studies Submitted by the Harvard Law School to the Ford Foundation" (August 28, 1953), Louis B. Sohn Papers, 1936–1979, HLSLib; Griswold, Annual Report of the Dean, 1954–55, 600, 607, 629; Edward S. Godfrey, "Advanced Study for Law Teachers—Ford Foundation Fellowships," *HLSB* (June 1958): 6.

32. Quotation is from von Mehren, Oral History (July–December 2000).

33. Berman, Oral History (August 1998).

34. Stanley S. Surrey to Erwin N. Griswold and Milton Katz, "International Program in Taxation, Status of Work as of October 1960" (September 27, 1960), typescript, HLS Dean's Office Records, Records of President Nathan M. Pusey, 1953–1971, Harvard University Archives (hereafter cited as NMP Records).

35. Quotation is from von Mehren, Oral History (July–December 2000). See Erwin N. Griswold to Milton Katz (June 20, 1956) and Milton Katz to Erwin N. Griswold, Memorandum (September 19, 1956), NMP Records.

36. Berman, Oral History (August 1998).

37. Erwin N. Griswold, "Intellect and Spirit," *HLR* 81 (1967): 297–298; Griswold, Annual Report of the Dean, 1954–55, 603; von Mehren, Oral History (July–December 2000); Griswold, Memorandum to the Faculty [on International Legal Studies] (March 25, 1958), NMP Records.

38. Berman, Oral History (August 1998). See the three divisions in Harvard Law School Catalog, 1966–67, 84–95.

39. Hupper, "Educational Ambivalence," 440; see 319–395. See von Mehren, Oral History (July–December 2000); Berman, Oral History (August 1998); Fossum, "Law Professors," 509.

40. Quotations are from von Mehren, Oral History (July–December 2000).

41. J. Willard Hurst to Joseph H. Willits (March 20, 1957), J. Willard Hurst Collection, University of Wisconsin Law Library Special Collections; Alan A. Stone, "Legal Education on the Couch," *HLR* 85 (December 1971): 428; Seligman, *The High Citadel*, 74, 81; Elizabeth Bartholet, Oral History, conducted by Daniel Hamilton (February 1999–March 2000), on file with the authors; James Vorenberg, Oral History, conducted by Daniel R. Coquillette (November–December 1997), on file with the authors; Seligman, *The High Citadel*, 74–75.

42. Griswold, "The Future," 4. See Griswold, Annual Report of the Dean, 1947–48, 382; 1951–52, 490–491, 496–497; Griswold, "Introduction," *HLR* 100 (February 1987): 729–730.

43. Erwin N. Griswold, "Law Schools and Human Relations," *Chicago Bar Record* 37 (1956): 199; Griswold, Annual Report of the Dean, 1965–66, 259–260; 1966–67, 261, 268–269; Griswold, "The Future," 4; Griswold, "Intellect and Spirit," 304; Stone, "Legal Education," 428, 431; von Mehren, Oral History (July–December 2000).

44. Quotations are from Kaufman, Oral History (June 1999–April 2000); Bartholet, Oral History (February 1999–March 2000). See Griswold, Annual Report of the Dean, 1951–52, 493, 496–497.

45. Griswold, "Some Thoughts," 4. See Griswold, Annual Report of the Dean, 1951–52, 496–497.

46. Griswold, "Intellect and Spirit," 301.

47. Seligman, *The High Citadel*, 126.

48. Griswold, "Some Thoughts," 6; Griswold, "Intellect and Spirit," 298–299; Griswold, *Ould Fields*, 114.

49. Griswold, Annual Report of the Dean, 1948–49, 420–422; Lon L. Fuller, "Work on the Curriculum," *HLSB* (July 1948): 4; HLS Faculty Meeting Minutes (October 19, November 5, November 23, December 7, 1948).

50. Griswold, Annual Report of the Dean, 1960–61, 322. See A. James Casner, "Faculty Decisions on the Report of the Committee on Legal Education," *HLSB* (October 1961): 10–13. Griswold observed that "two major goods" resulted from the Committee's report: "the debate itself" and the establishment of "a Continuing Committee on Legal Educa-

tion." Griswold, Annual Report of the Dean, 1960–61, 323. See HLS Committee on Legal Education, Report to the Faculty (June 10, 1960), on file with the authors.

51. Griswold, Annual Report of the Dean, 1961–62, 395–396.

52. Griswold, Annual Report of the Dean, 1963–64, 219–220. HLS Committee on Planning and Development, Final Report (September 1964), on file with the authors.

53. Kaufman, Oral History (June 1999–April 2000).

54. Alexander M. Wolf, "Harvard Law School Courses during Dean Erwin Griswold's Administration, 1946–47–1966–67" (research report, HLS, 2017), on file with the authors.

55. Harvard Law School Catalog, 1946–47, 3–4.

56. Quotation is from "Meeting of the Visiting Committee," *HLSB* (April 1948): 2.

57. Griswold, "Legal Education at Harvard," 1.

58. Detlev Vagts, Oral History, conducted by Daniel Hamilton, Daniel R. Coquillette, and John Delionado (November 1999–February 2000), on file with the authors.

59. Griswold, *Ould Fields,* 163. See Griswold, Annual Report of the Dean, 1966–67, 272; Berman, Oral History (August 1998).

60. Quotation is from Griswold, Annual Report of the Dean, 1966–67, 272. See Alexander M. Wolf, "Harvard Law School Personnel Counts, from 1946–47 through 1967–68" (research report, HLS, 2017), on file with the authors; Wolf, "The Harvard Law School Faculty." Compare "Recent Growth of Faculty and Staff, 1945–1953," *HLSB* (December 1953): 9; Austin W. Scott, "The Dean's Decennial," *HLSB* (October 1956): 4; Morton Keller and Phyllis Keller, *Making Harvard Modern: The Rise of America's University* (New York, 2001), 253.

61. Fossum, "Law Professors," 501, 505.

62. Alan M. Dershowitz, Oral History, conducted by Daniel R. Coquillette with Andrew Klaber (October–November 2009), on file with the authors; Vagts, Oral History (November 1999–February 2000); Byse, Oral History (July–October 1997); Louis A. Toepfer, Oral History, conducted by Daniel Hamilton (March 1998), on file with the authors. See, for example, Erwin N. Griswold to Eugene V. Rostow (November 9, 1956), Yale University Secretary's Office Records, 1899–1953, ser. 3, Yale University Library Manuscripts and Archives.

63. Sander, Oral History (September–December 1998).

64. Vagts, Oral History (November 1999–February 2000). See Vorenberg, Oral History (November–December 1997).

65. Laurence H. Tribe, Oral History, conducted by Daniel R. Coquillette and Andrew D. Klaber (September 2008), on file with the authors.

66. Kaufman, Oral History (June 1999–April 2000).

67. Bartholet, Oral History (February 1999–March 2000).

68. Derek C. Bok, Oral History, conducted by Daniel R. Coquillette and Daniel Hamilton (February 2002), on file with the authors.

69. Byse, Oral History (July–October 1997); Vagts, Oral History (November 1999–February 2000); Sander, Oral History (September–December 1998); Kaufman, Oral History (June 1999–April 2000); Stephen Bernardi, Oral History, conducted by Daniel Hamilton (October 2000–April 2001), on file with the authors; Bok, Oral History (February 2002); Caroline Daniels, "The *Harvard Law Review* and the Legacy of the Meritocracy" (student research paper, HLS, 2000), on file with the authors.

70. Kaufman, Oral History (June 1999–April 2000); Archibald Cox, Oral History, conducted by Daniel R. Coquillette and Daniel Hamilton (November 1998), on file with the authors; Sander, Oral History (September–December 1998); Richard D. Parker, Oral History, conducted by Daniel R. Coquillette and Daniel Pincus (June 2010), on file with the authors; Griswold, *Ould Fields*, 67.

71. Quotations are from Kaufman, Oral History (June 1999–April 2000). See Cox, Oral History (November 1998); Sander, Oral History (September–December 1998); Parker, Oral History (June 2010); Griswold, *Ould Fields*, 67.

72. Quotation is from Franklin G. Fessenden, "Rebirth of the Harvard Law School," *HLR* 33 (1920): 508.

73. Jenny Ellickson, "'The Next Brass Ring': The Increase in Law Students' Interest in Clerkships since 1940" (student research paper, HLS, 2002), on file with the authors, 4–5.

74. Mark DeWolfe Howe, *Justice Oliver Wendell Holmes*, vol. 1: *The Shaping Years, 1840–1870* (Cambridge, MA, 1957), 251–252.

75. Quotation is from Griswold, *Ould Fields*, 75. See Ellickson, "'The Next Brass Ring,'" 4–5.

76. Ellickson, "'The Next Brass Ring,'" 6–7, 9.

77. Bernardi, Oral History (October 2000). See Griswold, Annual Report of the Dean, 1960–61, 335–336. See Detlev Vagts, Interview (April 12, 2002), and Andrew L. Kaufman, Interview (April 8, 2002), quoted in Ellickson, "'The Next Brass Ring,'" 13, 15.

78. Gerald E. Frug, Interview (April 22, 2002), quoted in Ellickson, "'The Next Brass Ring,'" 17.

79. Hupper, "Educational Ambivalence," 373–374; Ellickson, "'The Next Brass Ring,'" 16.

80. Vagts, Oral History (November 1999–February 2000).

81. Sander, Oral History (September–December 1998); Vorenberg, Oral History (November–December 1997).

82. Sander, Oral History (September–December 1998); Vorenberg, Oral History (November–December 1997); Vagts, Oral History (November 1999–February 2000); Kaufman, Oral History (June 1999–April 2000); Cox, Oral History (November 1998).

83. Ellickson, "'The Next Brass Ring,'" 10. See Vorenberg, Oral History (November–December 1997); Vagts, Oral History (November 1999–February 2000); Kaufman, Oral History (June 1999–April 2000); Cox, Oral History (November 1998).

84. Ellickson, "'The Next Brass Ring,'" 19.

85. Quotation is from Parker, Oral History (June 2010). See Hupper, "Educational Ambivalence," 373–374.

86. Seligman, *The High Citadel,* 80, 122. See Ellickson, "'The Next Brass Ring,'" 18; Sander, Oral History (September–December 1998); Bernardi, Oral History (October 2000); Kaufman, Oral History (June 1999–April 2000); Vagts, Oral History (November 1999–February 2000).

87. Fossum, "Law Professors," 505–508.

88. Vagts, Oral History (November 1999–February 2000).

89. Sander, Oral History (September–December 1998).

90. Berman, Oral History (August 1998).

91. Keeton, Oral History (November 2000–February 2001).

92. Vagts, Oral History (November 1999–February 2000). See Vorenberg, Oral History (November–December 1997).

93. See Daniel R. Coquillette and Bruce A. Kimball, *On the Battlefield of Merit: Harvard Law School, the First Century* (Cambridge, MA, 2015), 386–397.

94. Keeton, Oral History (November 2000–February 2001).

95. Bok, Oral History (February 2002).

96. Vorenberg, Oral History (November–December 1997).

97. Dershowitz, Oral History (October–November 2009).

98. Byse, Oral History (July–October 1997); Toepfer, Oral History (March 1998); Keeton, Oral History (November 2000–February 2001); Sander, Oral History (September–December 1998); Charles Fried, Oral History, conducted by Daniel R. Coquillette and Mary Beth Basile (August 2000–March 2001), on file with the authors.

99. Fried, Oral History (August 2000–March 2001); Fried, Interview (April 2008).

100. Byse, Oral History (July–October 1997); Fried, Oral History (August 2000–March 2001); Toepfer, Oral History (March 1998); Keeton, Oral History (November 2000–February 2001); Sander, Oral History (September–December 1998).

101. Vagts, Oral History (November 1999–February 2000).

102. James M. Landis to Charles C. Burlingham (July 5, 1938), James McCauley Landis Papers, 1899–1964, HLSLib.

103. Quotations are from Vagts, Oral History (November 1999–February 2000); Bartholet, Oral History (February 1999–March 2000). See Ellickson, "'The Next Brass Ring,'" 38.

104. Mary Beth Basile, "False Starts: Harvard Law School's Efforts toward Integrating Women into the Faculty, 1928–1981," *Harvard Journal of Law and Gender* 28 (2005): 148–149.

105. HLS Faculty Meeting Minutes (October 1, 1946).

106. Judith Richards Hope, *Pinstripes & Pearls: The Women of the Harvard Law Class of '64 Who Forged an Old Girl Network and Paved the Way for Future Generations* (New York, 2003), 15.

107. Quotation is from HLS Faculty Meeting Minutes (October 1, 1946). See Basile, "False Starts," 149.

108. Basile, "False Starts,"148–149. See HLS Faculty Meeting Minutes (January 6, 1948).

109. HLS Faculty Meeting Minutes (January 6, 1948).

110. Berman, Oral History (August 1998). See von Mehren, Oral History (July–December 2000); Basile, "False Starts," 150; Keeton, Oral History (November 2000–February 2001); Hope, *Pinstripes & Pearls,* 15.

111. Jerome Shestack, "Gallery: Karl Nickerson Llewellyn," *HLSR* (April 27, 1949): 2.

112. Berman, Oral History (August 1998). See von Mehren, Oral History (July–December 2000); Basile, "False Starts," 151.

113. Basile, "False Starts," 165–166. See Elizabeth A. Owens, *The Foreign Tax Credit: A Study of the Credit for Foreign Taxes under the United States Income Tax Law* (Cambridge, MA, 1961); Herma Hill Kay, "In Memoriam: Elizabeth A. Owens," *HLR* 112 (May 1999): 1403, 1406; Mary J. Mullarkey, "Two Harvard Women: 1965 to Today," *Harvard Women's Law Journal* 27 (2004): 369n3.

114. Basile, "False Starts," 164–167. See Owens, *The Foreign Tax Credit;* Kay, "In Memoriam"; Mullarkey, "Two Harvard Women," 369n3. Views are decidedly mixed on why Owens's appointment took so long.

115. Berman, Oral History (August 1998); Vagts, Oral History (November 1999–February 2000); Kaufman, Oral History (June 1999–April 2000); Vorenberg, Oral History (November–December 1997).

116. Quotation is from Vorenberg, Oral History (November–December 1997). See Berman, Oral History (August 1998); Kaufman, Oral History (June 1999–April 2000); von Mehren, Oral History (July–December 2000); Russell A. Simpson, Oral History, conducted by Mary Beth Basile and Daniel R. Coquillette (May–September 2001), on file with the authors; Keller and Keller, *Making Harvard Modern,* 253.

117. Dershowitz, Oral History (October–November 2009).

118. Derek C. Bok, "Remembrance," in *Erwin Nathaniel Griswold: 1904–1994,* 23–26.

119. Toepfer, Oral History (March 1998).

120. Kaufman, Oral History (June 1999–April 2000).

121. James M. Landis to Edwin D. Dickinson (January 3, 1946), NMP Records; HLS Faculty Meeting Minutes (November 19, 1946).

122. Erwin N. Griswold to Nathan M. Pusey (September 30, 1957), NMP Records.

123. Bok, Oral History (February 2002). See Kaufman, Oral History (June 1999–April 2000); Berman, Oral History (August 1998); Byse, Oral History (July–October 1997).

124. Cox, Oral History (November 1998). See Keeton, Oral History (November 2000–February 2001); Toepfer, Oral History (March 1998); Vorenberg, Oral History (November–December 1997).

125. Vagts, Oral History (November 1999–February 2000).

126. Bok, Oral History (February 2002).

127. Simpson, Oral History (May–September 2001).

128. Quoted in David Margolick, "Legal Notes: Those against Bequest to Attack P.L.O. Aims," *New York Times* (May 23, 1982).

129. Griswold, "The School since the War," 4.

130. Tribe, Oral History (September 2008).

131. Karl Bemesderfer, "On Being a Law Student," *HLSB* (November 1965): 19. See Parker, Oral History (June 2010); Seligman, *The High Citadel*, 90.

132. "The Law: Law Schools: Harvard at 150," *Time* (October 6, 1967), 75.

133. "Student Guide Put Off," *HLSR* (October 11, 1956): 1, 3.

134. Griswold, Annual Report of the Dean, 1957–58, 321–322.

135. Vorenberg, Oral History (November–December 1997); Sander, Oral History (September–December 1998); Griswold, Annual Report of the Dean, 1961–62, 405. Compare Bok, Oral History (February 2002).

136. Lon L. Fuller, "Survey of Student Opinion," *HLSB* (October 1948): 4–5; Louis A. Toepfer, "Marks and the Man," *HLSB* (April 1958): 4; Griswold, Annual Report of the Dean, 1961–62, 405; Ezekiel Solomon, "Postgraduate Study at Harvard Law School: An Australian Tells Australians about Legal Studies at Harvard Law School," *HLSB* (December 1962): 6; Bok, Oral History (February 2002); Tribe, Oral History (September 2008); R. W. Schmidt, "Grades Related to Potential Earning Power," *HLSR* (October 1968): 2; Christopher Jencks and David Riesman, *The Academic Revolution* (New York, 1968), 281–283.

137. Griswold, Annual Report of the Dean, 1961–62, 405.

138. Bruce A. Kimball, *The Inception of Modern Professional Education: C. C. Langdell, 1826–1906* (Chapel Hill, NC, 2009), 160–164; Hope, *Pinstripes & Pearls*, 122; Griswold, *Ould Fields*, 161. As of 2016 the American Bar Association–Association of American Law Students accreditation guidelines mandated student assessment outside of a single exam at the end of the semester.

139. Toepfer, "Marks and the Man," 4.

140. Toepfer, "Marks and the Man," 4; "All Marks Now to be Numerical," *HLSR* (September 5, 1946): 1.

141. Fuller, "Survey of Student Opinion," 4–5. Compare Byse, Oral History (July–October 1997); Kaufman, Oral History (June-November 1999, April 2000); Bok, Oral History (February 2002); Cox, Oral History (November 1998); Vagts, Oral History (November 1999–February 2000); Bernardi, Oral History (October 2000–April 2001); Herbert P. Wilkins, Oral History, conducted by Daniel R. Coquillette (November 2014), on file with the authors; Vorenberg, Oral History (November–December 1997); Sander, Oral History (September–December 1998).

142. "A Change in Grading Procedures," *HLSB* (June 1961): 14.

143. David L. Shapiro and Daniel A. Taylor, "Change at the Law School: The Grading System," *HLSB* (July 1968): 3–4. See Sander, Oral History (September–December 1998); Tribe, Oral History (September 2008); Wilkins, Oral History (November 2014); Vorenberg, Oral History (November–December 1997).

144. Quotation is from Vagts, Oral History (November 1999–February 2000). See John Tepaske, "Marking System Examined at Open Meeting: Student Opinion Varies Widely on Reforming Grades," *HLSR* (February 24, 1966): 1, 12–14; Shapiro and Taylor, "Change at the Law School: The Grading System," 3–4; Seligman, *The High Citadel*, 13–14.

145. Bok, Oral History (February 2002); Bartholet, Oral History (February 1999–March 2000); Schmidt, "Grades Related to Potential Earning Power," 2.

146. Griswold, *Ould Fields*, 161.

147. Seligman, *The High Citadel*, 77, 90–92; Bolotnika, "The Purpose of Harvard Law School," 5.

148. Griswold, "Intellect and Spirit," 301, 306; Griswold, "The Future," 5; Griswold, Annual Report of the Dean, 1959–60, 408–409; 1960–61, 335–337.

149. Griswold, "Intellect and Spirit," 301.

150. Griswold, "Intellect and Spirit," 301.

151. Bernardi, Oral History (October 2000); Detlev F. Vagts, Interview (April 6, 2010), quoted in Kenneth Leung, "The Deanship of Erwin Nathaniel Griswold, 1946–1967" (student research paper, HLS, 2010) on file with the authors, 28; Marc Galanter and Thomas Palay, *Tournament of Lawyers: The Transformation of the Big Law Firm* (Chicago, 1991), 24; Eleanor A. Appel, "The Interview Season at the Placement Office," *HLSB* (May 1965): 6.

152. Keith Watson, "Student-Faculty Unit Studies Law School," *HLSR* (November, 10, 1966): 1; "A Modest Beginning" (unsigned editorial), *HLSR* (November 17, 1966): 8; Steven Goddard, "Student Group Urges Law Reforms," *HLSR* (December 8, 1966): 1; Byse, Oral History (July–October 1997).

153. Cox, Oral History (November 1998); Toepfer, Oral History (March 1998).

154. Griswold, Annual Report of the Dean, 1953–54, 553. See Griswold, Annual Report of the Dean, 1961–62, 405; Ellen Bernstein, "A Conversation with Erwin N. Griswold," *HLSB* (Fall 1979): 19–23; Griswold, *Ould Field*, 161–162.

155. Griswold, Annual Report of the Dean, 1957–58, 322; 1961–62, 405; Cox, "In Memoriam," 987–989.

156. Griswold, Annual Report of the Dean, 1966–67, 264–265.

157. Quotation is from Griswold, *Ould Fields*, 232. See Michael H. P. Belknap, "The *Harvard International Law Journal* Comes of Age," *HLSB* (January 1967): 8–9.

158. Griswold, Annual Report of the Dean, 1953–54, 553; Bernstein, "A Conversation," 19–23; Griswold, *Ould Fields*, 161–162.

159. Vagts, Oral History (November 1999–February 2000); Griswold, *Ould Fields*, 162; Nader, "Introduction," xiv; Judith Richards Hope, "Remembrance," in *Erwin Nathaniel Griswold: 1904–1994*, 16–19.

160. Quotations are from, respectively, Haig der Manuelian, email to Karen S. Beck (October 24, 2012), on file with the authors; Kaufman, Oral History (June 1999–April 2000).

161. Quotations are from, respectively, Gary Bellow, Oral History, conducted by Daniel R. Coquillette (January 1997), on file with the authors; Bernardi, Oral History (October 2000–April 2001). See Kaufman, Oral History (June 1999–April 2000); Sander, Oral History (September–December 1998); Vagts, Oral History (November 1999–February 2000); Bok, Oral History (February 2002).

162. Bernardi, Oral History (October 2000–April 2001). See David L. Ratner, "Classroom Strategy—A Student's View," *HLSB* (February 1954): 7; Tribe, Oral History (September 2008); Bartholet, Oral History (February 1999–March 2000); Ernest J. Brown, Oral History, conducted by Daniel Hamilton (August 1997), on file with the authors; Kaufman, Oral History (June 1999–April 2000); Byse, Oral History (July–October 1997); Paul D. Carrington, Oral History, conducted by Daniel Hamilton (February 2003), on file with the authors; Hope, *Pinstripes & Pearls,* 138.

163. Griswold, Annual Report of the Dean, 1966–67, 272.

164. Louis A. Toepfer, "Scholarships and Loans," *HLSB* (April 1959): 4. See Cox, Oral History (November 1998).

165. Cox, Oral History (November 1998).

166. Wilkins, Oral History (November 2014); Bartholet, Oral History (February 1999–March 2000); Parker, Oral History (June 2010); Bok, Oral History (February 2002); Fried, Oral History (August 2000–March 2001); Mullarkey, "Two Harvard Women," 369; Sander, Oral History (September–December 1998); Kaufman, Oral History (June 1999–April 2000); Simpson, Oral History (May–September 2001).

167. Founded in 1926, the Chancery Club had its own premises, at 1557 Massachusetts Avenue. The photograph in the 1953 Yearbook shows an all-male, all-white membership. Harvard Law School Yearbook 1953, 168–169; Robert A. Grayson, "Chancery Club Shuts Its Doors," *HLSR* (December 19, 1963): 1, 7.

168. Quotations are from Harvard Law School, *Handbook 1970,* 63–64; Harvard Law School Yearbook, 1971, 216–217. Bernardi, Oral History (October 2000–April 2001); Vagts, Oral History (November 1999–February 2000); Bartholet, Oral History (February 1999–March 2000); Wilkins, Oral History (November 2014); Cale Keable, "A History of the Lincoln's Inn Society" (student research paper, HLS, 2001), on file with the authors.

169. Henry Hammond, "Choate Exposé Called a Witch Hunt," *HLSR* (October 24, 1968): 12. See Cox, Oral History (November 1998); Vagts, Oral History (November 1999–February 2000); Peter D. Hutcheon, "Choate and Choate Are Two Many," *Harvard Crimson* (September 26, 1968); Paul M. Bator, letter to the editor, *HLSR* (September 26, 1968): 11, 13; "The Secret Social Club" (editorial), *HLSR* (September 12, 1968): 8; Roger Lowenstein, letter to the editor, *Harvard Crimson* (April 30, 1968); "The

Secret Social Club," 12; Bernardi, Oral History (October 2000–April 2001). Professor Richard Parker later recalled that, in 1968–69, the Choate Club comprised "people who had gone to all the right prep schools and colleges and they had . . . black-tie dinners with faculty who had been members of Choate. . . . Richard Cooper, then president of *Harvard Law Review,* to his great credit, said you could not be a member of the *Law Review* if you were a member of the Choate Club." Parker, Oral History (June 2010).

CHAPTER FOURTEEN

"A Vast Expansion" in Spending, 1946–1967

Harvard Law School's financial difficulties held back its academic develop-ment—for example, by delaying the adoption of selective admissions—and also damaged its academic culture by deepening the commitments to attri-tion, huge classes, and cutthroat competition, even though these commitments were rationalized by principled arguments. Dean Griswold (1946–1967) rec-ognized that the school had imprudently adopted tuition dependence early in the twentieth century and that Dean Roscoe Pound (1916–1936) had ex-acerbated the situation during the 1920s by enrolling more and more students, while burdening the school with heavy debt.[1] Beginning his decanal tenure in 1946, Griswold complained that the Law School was "unbelievably poor" compared to the rest of Harvard University.[2]

Griswold had an opportunity to change course because he vastly expanded the revenue of the school, and many have applauded this accomplishment and the growth of the programs, services, and facilities of the school.[3] He could have concurrently pioneered a new model for financing legal education. In-stead, he spent all the money and sharply increased operating expenses, which he paid with tuition hikes and proceeds from a new annual fund. These ac-tions worsened the Law School's tuition dependence, which "debases so many of the professional schools of this country," as President Charles Eliot (1869–1909) had warned a century earlier.[4]

Their impact on all of legal education was equally significant. During the twentieth century, Harvard Law School "set the style" not only for academic policies in legal education, as historian Robert Stevens observed, but also for the financial isomorphism in the field.[5] Thus, "law schools have traditionally supported themselves largely out of tuition" and have "long been the stepchildren of education," Griswold observed regretfully.[6]

The "Golden Age" of Higher Education, 1945–1970

Following World War II, two new sources of federal funding launched American higher education to global leadership and produced what scholars have called a "golden age," especially for research universities, extending from 1945 to 1970. On the one hand, large federal research grants became available, mostly for scientific and medical fields. On the other hand, colleges and universities began filling their coffers with tuition dollars subvented by federal financial aid programs. The first windfall came via the Servicemen's Readjustment Act (G.I. Bill) of 1944, which supported some 2 million returning veterans to enroll in postsecondary education.[7]

Colleges and universities naturally jumped at the chance to draw on federally subsidized financial aid. Scurrilous for-profit institutions relied on the G.I. Bill to increase their student enrollments and profits, while offering insubstantial programs. The nonprofit institutions increased their enrollments far less proportionally but received a larger share of the money, because they were more numerous. Within the nonprofit domain, the public and private sectors were about equal in size during the 1940s, and near the end of that decade the G.I. Bill paid about 56 percent of student fees in private colleges and universities and 67 percent in public ones. The private institutions generally had higher fees, but the Veteran's Administration paid the out-of-state tuition rate for all students on the G.I. Bill, swelling tuition revenue at public institutions, as well.[8]

Meanwhile, the influx of students raised the student-faculty ratio at virtually all colleges and universities in the late 1940s, so the average cost-per-student across the nation, adjusted for inflation, was lower in 1948 than in 1940.[9] With enrollments and tuition revenue increasing and per-student cost falling, the overcrowded colleges and universities prospered. In Cambridge, Harvard University enjoyed "the most favorable situation in our history in regard to student aid," stated President James Conant (1933–1953), because "approximately three quarters of the students in the University were receiving financial assistance, primarily in the form of allowances under the G.I. Bill."[10]

By 1950 the party seemed to be ending. At Harvard, for example, President Conant reported that the proportion of students supported by the G.I. Bill had fallen from about 75 percent in 1947 to about 10 percent in 1950.

At that point the average per-student cost began to climb across higher education. But the wave of returning Korean War veterans in 1951–1953 then provided another, smaller surge of enrollment, which briefly arrested the increase in the per-student cost.[11]

Despite the evident success of the G.I. Bill, a political stalemate in Washington blocked general funding of higher education through the mid-1950s. Then, in 1957, the Soviet Union launched the first Sputnik. Congress responded in 1958 by passing the National Defense Education Act (NDEA), which provided generous financial aid for students in higher education, including those in professional and graduate studies. The NDEA was followed in 1963 by the Higher Education Facilities Act, supporting construction and renovation of buildings at nonprofit colleges and universities. Next came the Higher Education Act (HEA) of 1965, authorizing federally insured low-interest loans for professional and graduate students, along with other aid designed to strengthen the financial resources of colleges and universities. The value of these increasing revenues was somewhat diminished by inflation, which drove up commodity prices by about 49 percent between 1946 and 1967. Still, the major research universities flourished because the increase of federal grants significantly outpaced inflation.[12]

But few federal grants aimed to support legal scholarship, so law schools received little of this bounty and were relatively pinched within universities. During the 1966–67 academic year, "severe pressures" on the budget forced Harvard Law School to cut $100,000 from its financial aid, and in 1969 Yale Law School drastically reduced its first-year scholarship awards. At that point the deans of the law schools at Harvard, Yale, Chicago, Pennsylvania, and New York University convened to discuss how to cooperate in order "to reduce costs and increase efficiency in the admissions and financial aid process," a meeting that might raise antitrust issues today.[13]

Two Financial Problems

In his first annual report, Griswold identified the two fundamental problems, which he continued to lament throughout his tenure. The first was "the School's heavy dependence on tuition income," amounting to 75 percent of the school's revenue in 1946. Even worse, the Harvard Corporation considered this a natural and necessary condition for the Law School.[14] Griswold challenged this assumption, while employing Roscoe Pound's language and metaphors (though criticizing Pound for worsening this dependence). Griswold lamented "the box office theory of legal education" that linked the school's welfare to the market of paying students.[15]

The second problem was that, even though the school had a larger endowment than any other law school in the country, it was relatively small by Harvard's standard. In 1946 the Law School enrolled about 12 percent of the students at Harvard, but had only 3.5 percent of the university's total endowment. These proportions had changed little in the prior thirty years, and Griswold was determined to bring the school's endowment more in line with the size of the student body by Harvard's standard.[16]

The two problems of tuition dependence and relatively low endowment were opposite sides of the same coin. One solution was to greatly increase the endowment, which would yield more income and allow the school to reduce its reliance on tuition revenue, if expenses did not increase. Conversely, another solution was to cut enrollment and expenses, which would increase the proportion of revenue from endowment income and decrease the reliance on tuition. The latter option would have the added benefit of reducing the student-faculty ratio, and the optimal time to follow this route was when the faculty was short-staffed because cutting enrollment would not require laying off faculty.

To choose his path, Griswold had four huge advantages in the late 1940s. First, due to a series of retirements, the faculty shrank to about twenty-six regular professors by 1948, not counting the dean, plus about eight temporary appointments to handle the enrollment bulge.[17] Reducing the number of professors is normally difficult because faculty positions are hard to eliminate once they are filled with tenured professors. But Griswold began with a small tenured faculty, so he had the flexibility to limit the expense of faculty salaries, the largest cost to the school.

Second, the G.I. Bill was an enormous windfall boon to a tuition-dependent school. Already in the fiscal year 1946–47, the Law School "received the largest income in its history" due to the influx of veterans, said the dean. This happened even though Griswold initially resisted raising tuition so the school would not appear to be exploiting the government funding. Nevertheless, tuition income supported by the G.I. Bill income enabled the Law School to accumulate a large surplus because the expense for faculty salaries was small. In 1947 the accumulated surplus rose to nearly $117,000, or 10 percent of annual expenses.[18]

Third, in 1948 the school made its final annual payment on the mortgage on Langdell Hall, retiring the debt, which "removes a heavy burden," the dean remarked. Indeed, this liberated about $50,000 annually, or 4 percent of the annual expenses, which could cover the salaries of about four full professors or six assistant professors, according to the salary scale at the time.[19] Finally, the school had not raised tuition in almost twenty years, so Griswold easily justified a 50 percent tuition increase to $600 beginning in September 1948. This increase compounded the additional income from the G.I. Bill.[20]

Dean Griswold mentioned these four significant advantages—small tenured faculty, G.I. Bill surplus, paid-off mortgage, tuition increase—only occasionally and separately. Taken together, they contributed to a vastly stronger financial situation by 1950 than the laments in his annual reports conveyed. In fact, he had the opportunity, rare in higher education, to avoid or escape the heavy dependence on tuition. Remarkably, he was the school's third dean presented with this opportunity, following James Barr Ames (1895–1909) in 1905 and Roscoe Pound in 1928.

In 1950, as the wave of returning veterans ebbed, the 50 percent tuition increase afforded Dean Griswold the opportunity to cap the enrollment at 1,000 and receive the same tuition revenue that had previously come from 1,500 students. Dean James Landis (1937–1946) had recommended this course. Doing so would have lowered the student-faculty ratio and prevented the need to add expense by immediately hiring more tenure-line faculty. With the mortgage paid off, the continually expanding surplus could have been allocated to the school's invested reserves and treated as quasi-endowment, as in the 1880s and 1890s.[21] The income from the invested reserves would have slowly grown, allowing the dean to gradually address the seven priorities he had identified in 1950. Meanwhile, the fraction of annual revenue coming from endowment income would have risen and the fraction from tuition declined.

Instead, Griswold chose a different course, and he later asserted that the school could not have afforded to lower its enrollment after World War II. Arthur Sutherland (LL.B. 1925) concurred, maintaining that Dean Landis's idea of limiting the school's enrollment to a thousand, was "beyond the imaginable possibilities."[22] But, by 1950, the school was banking a large surplus every year that belied the assertions of Griswold and Sutherland. Both simply felt bound by the patriarchs' commandment that Harvard Law School should enroll about 1,500 students. "Our predecessors decided that Harvard should be a large school," Dean Griswold declared.[23]

Griswold even suggested in 1965 that Harvard Law School was heroically and virtuously bearing "a heavy burden" by enrolling so many students. Due to the growth of legal doctrine and of the population, more lawyers were needed, he said. "We have many [law] schools with 200 students, 300 students, or 400 students. This has been a cozy, fine, friendly, and comfortable number, and many schools have liked this small size." But "a considerable number of other law schools should increase their size," he argued. "Such changes would involve capital costs, for buildings, for libraries, for additions to faculty. . . . There is no sound reason why so much of the pressure, and so much of the need for capital costs, should be focused on a few law schools." Like Atlas, Harvard Law School was burdened with holding up the orb of legal education, and Sutherland sympathetically repeated Griswold's point.[24]

However, neither heroism nor virtue required Griswold to increase the LL.B. enrollment of Harvard Law School by 10 percent from 1,459 in 1950–51, when the influx of veterans ended, to 1,604 in 1966–67.[25] Nor did necessity. The national capacity of law schools expanded significantly during the "golden age" in higher education. Between 1947 and 1967, the number of accredited law schools rose 12 percent from 111 to 136, their full-time faculty rose 128 percent from 991 to 2,264, and their enrollment grew 41 percent from 45,719 to 64,406 students.[26] Harvard Law School could have decreased enrollment, or at least stabilized it, and the rest of legal education would have supplied the need. In fact, the 10 percent growth in the school's enrollment about equaled the proportion devoted to women and students of color over the period, so the net result was to maintain the enrollment of white men, as much as to increase the supply of lawyers.

An "Incredible" Rise in Revenue

Building on the four financial advantages, Dean Griswold greatly increased the school's revenue through two conduits: tuition revenue and the annual alumni fund. When he took office in June 1946, tuition had not risen since 1929, and it trailed that of the medical and business schools during the first half of the twentieth century. The dean therefore heard no objection to raising tuition from $400 to $600 in 1948. Four more tuition hikes followed, driving up the annual tuition fee to $1,500 by 1966–67. Due to these hikes and the 10 percent rise in enrollment, the total tuition revenue from LL.B. students grew 354 percent in nominal dollars, and 138 percent in constant dollars (adjusted for inflation) during Griswold's twenty-one-year tenure.[27]

How did the dean keep the students from rebelling against the repeated tuition increases, particularly during the 1960s era of student protest? In order to cushion the impact of the rising tuition on students, he provided more financial aid.[28] Prior to 1938 the school had no comprehensive program or policy in this regard. The 1,500 students were eligible for about thirty-five full-tuition scholarships. A few were awarded to entering students who had excelled in college; the rest were based upon the results of a special examination in January. As of 1946 the school had about $50,000 available each year to fund some 120 full-tuition scholarships. About forty-four scholarships were awarded to first-year students based on exam results at the Law School. The rest went to second-year or third-year students who demonstrated need and had a grade-point average of 70 or above, putting them in the top 10 percent of the student body.[29] Financial aid, therefore, had little role in recruiting students prior to Griswold's deanship.

Beginning in 1947 and continuing over the next twenty years, Griswold's administration effected a "mammoth rise in Law School financial assistance to its students," as evident in Table 14.1.[30] By 1967 the school had largely eliminated minimal academic requirements for financial aid, and distributed nearly all the aid according to financial need, while meeting all the demonstrated need of LL.B. students, half in grants and half in loans.[31]

The growth in scholarships came primarily from Griswold's second major new source of revenue: the annual alumni fund. This was an innovation for the school and for legal education. To prepare the way, the dean had to repair and nurture relations with alumni. In the fall of 1946 he began traveling around the country, speaking at alumni events and personally replying to any letter from an alumnus on the very next day, if not the same day. At the same time, Griswold had to cultivate the "small group of Boston lawyers" who dominated the insular Harvard Law School Association (HLSA).[32]

Some critics have considered Griswold's efforts sinister or mercenary.[33] But the chairman of the Harvard Overseers Visiting Committee maintained that, already in 1958, Griswold had "revolutionized" alumni affairs and instilled in the school's graduates "greater knowledge, greater pride, and greater enthusiasm" than in the prior three decades.[34] During his decanal tenure, membership in the HLSA climbed from 3,500 to over 12,000.[35]

Meanwhile, Griswold initiated the annual solicitation of the Law School's alumni. The practice is so widespread today that it is difficult to imagine a time when universities did not annually solicit their alumni for a donation. Yet the annual alumni fund was an innovation introduced by Yale College alumni in the 1890s. Harvard University adopted the practice in the 1920s, and the Corporation permitted only one central campaign at the university,

Table 14.1   Growth of Financial Aid for LL.B. Students at Harvard Law School from
1946–47 to 1966–67 (rounded to thousands of dollars)

Type of Financial Aid	1946–47	1966–67	Increase in multiples
SCHOLARSHIPS[b]			
nominal dollars	$30,000	$527,000	17.6
constant dollars[a]	$30,000	$316,000	10.5
number awarded	103	550	5.3
LOANS[b]			
nominal dollars	$14,000	$1,077,000	77
constant dollars[a]	$14,000	$647,000	46.2
number awarded	ca. 50	ca. 900	18
TOTAL AID			
nominal dollars	$44,000	$1,604,000	36.4
constant dollars[a]	$44,000	$963,000	21.9

Data sources: [Andrew L. Kaufman, Chair], Memorandum to the Faculty from the Financial Aids Committee [Cambridge, MA, ca. March 1970], typescript on file with the authors, 5–6, appendix 2; John J. McCusker, *How Much Is That in Real Money? A Historical Commodity Price Index for Use as a Deflator of Money Values in the Economy of the United States,* 2nd ed. (Worcester, MA, 2001), 58–59.

a. 1946 = 1. Amounts indexed as of the beginning of the academic year.

b. These amounts include funding from the Law School and Harvard University, or administered through them, as well as from federally subsidized and insured loans and from other agencies, such as the ABA. The amounts do not include the G.I. Bill or various external awards and loans obtained by students on their own.

which prioritized the undergraduate college.[36] Under this arrangement, "if a donor had gone to Harvard College, his gift was credited to the College, even though he had also gone to the Law School—or to the Medical School or to the Business School," observed Griswold. "The only amounts . . . made available to the Law School, unless otherwise requested by the donor, were gifts received from Law School graduates who had not gone to Harvard College." During 1946–47, Griswold's first year as dean, the Law School received merely about $7,700 through the Harvard Annual Fund.[37]

That arrangement seemed both unfair and unproductive, and Griswold, together with Dean Donald David of the business school, requested President Conant's permission to create separate annual funds appealing directly to their alumni. Conant "stoutly resisted," believing that those efforts would siphon gifts away from Harvard College. Ultimately, the two deans persuaded him by arguing that the whole university would receive more donations if the professional schools conducted separate campaigns.[38]

To establish the new annual fund, Griswold turned to the fundraising campaign that had been formed in 1948 to raise the money for the Gropius dormitories and was scheduled to end in 1950. The dean simply authorized this short-term building campaign, named the Harvard Law School Fund, to continue as an annual solicitation. To explain this extension to the alumni, the school announced early in 1950 that the building campaign "will probably fall short of its goal," so "new annual giving will be needed to help fill the gap in the current campaign."[39] Hence, annual giving was initially introduced to compensate for that shortfall. But the "gap" would never be filled.

Officially chaired by an alumnus, the annual fund was directed, within the school administration, by Wesley E. Bevins Jr. (LL.B. 1948), who continued in this role for the next thirty-two years, although some considered him less than effective.[40] Indeed, the giving by Harvard Law School's alumni did not match the record for higher education generally between 1955 and 1966, as reported by the Council for Financial Aid to Education and the leading consulting firm on fundraising in higher education.[41]

Nevertheless, the annual fund exceeded all expectations at the Law School, given its dismal record of fundraising up to that point. In its first full year of operation, 1951–52, the annual appeal exceeded Griswold's wildest expectations, yielding about $158,500.[42] Overall, from 1950 to 1967, the number of annual donors grew from 1,781 to 9,783, and the annual receipts rose from $64,056 to $806,719.[43] Consequently, Griswold was applauded for this bountiful new stream of revenue. "Its success has been almost incredible," wrote Sutherland.[44]

Where did the money go? The initial aim was to compensate for the shortfall of the 1948 building campaign. In 1950 Griswold announced a second purpose for the annual fund: to support scholarships. This aim remained the primary declared goal for the annual fund through the rest of his tenure as dean.[45]

By 1967 the aggregate receipts of the annual fund were $8.7 million, of which the donors had designated some $4.1 million for scholarships, including some $2.9 million to endow scholarships. In Griswold's last year, 1966–67, the annual fund supported directly, or indirectly through its endowments, 72 percent of the $527,000 in scholarships granted to LL.B. students. In addition, the annual fund supported a continuing loan fund, which provided 6 percent of the $1.1 million loaned to LL.B. students in 1966–67, while federally subsidized or insured loans contributed 54 percent. All together, the annual fund and federally subsidized or insured loans provided 64 percent of the school's $1.6 million in financial aid in 1966–67.[46] Hence, the annual fund coupled with federally subsidized or insured loans provided "the backbone of our Financial Aid Program," the dean wrote.[47]

In the very same breath, Griswold also noted that the annual fund "helps to make possible many other activities at the School."[48] This aim, in fact, became the third, less publicized purpose of the annual appeal. Of the aggregate total raised between 1950 and 1967, 43 percent, or $3.8 million, was completely unrestricted. The dean had complete discretion over disbursing it.[49]

Griswold could have directed that surplus income into an invested cash reserve, or quasi-endowment. This approach in the 1880s and 1890s made the school rich. Even better, Griswold could have declared that the third goal of the annual fund was to enlarge the school's permanent endowment and then added the $3.8 million directly to the permanent endowment. This amount, compounded by appreciation during the booming 1950s and 1960s, would have grown to the $5 million gift for endowment that Griswold repeatedly said would solve the school's problems for the future.[50]

Instead Griswold spent it, by adding the unrestricted annual fund receipts to operating income. This third aim—"to provide funds . . . for current expenditure"—was announced by the *Harvard Law School Bulletin* and the campaign chairman as soon as it became clear that the annual fund was vastly exceeding expectations.[51] In his annual reports Griswold stated various justifications for directing this windfall into current income: saving the school from a deficit, allowing the school to run a surplus, or preventing a tuition increase.[52] But the dean had complete discretion over the growth of expenses and the uses of this new stream of unrestricted revenue. By 1954 Griswold was building the projected annual fund receipts into his annual budget for the subsequent year, and predicting a deficit at the same time![53] Alumni now had to give each year to keep the school afloat. But the more that came in, the more expenses rose.

Meanwhile, the annual fund literature justified the appeal on the grounds that a beneficent wind had not yet inflated the endowment to its rightful size: "If the Law School's endowment funds were substantially increased, . . . the School might continue its program of educational development without the need to ask for alumni assistance. However, substantial increases in endowment have not been received, and costs continue to rise."[54] But Dean Griswold had such "substantial increases" within his grasp and was spending them instead.

Griswold, the Spender

Griswold poured virtually all the new income into current operating expenses. Not only the unrestricted $3.8 million from the annual fund, but also the additional tuition revenue that grew by 138 percent in constant dollars. Furthermore, because only 5 percent of the scholarship funds came from the school's operating funds, the rising tuition revenue was not discounted by returning tuition to students in the form of scholarships. Hence, virtually all the rising tuition revenue was new income for the school. As seen in Table 14.2, the school's annual expenses rose by nearly 390 percent in nominal dollars and more than 250 percent in constant dollars between the start of the annual fund in 1950 and the end of Griswold's tenure in 1967.

By massively increasing spending, Dean Griswold missed the opportunity to strengthen the school financially in the long term by adding to its endowment, while he also mired the school more deeply in the tuition dependence syndrome, which he had identified in 1946 and said that he wished to escape. One possible explanation is that the dean naively neglected to make a financial plan. But examples of such plans were readily available from Landis, Harvard Medical School, and Harvard Business School, which Griswold admired.[55] In addition, in May 1946, just as Griswold was taking the reins at Harvard, a faculty committee at Yale Law School undertook such planning.[56] But "it wasn't like [Griswold] to plan in detail," noted Berman, who observed him through his tenure as dean.[57]

It seems more likely that Griswold had a general, imprudent strategy that he did not want to disclose. The dean denied requests to form a faculty budget

Table 14.2 Growth in Annual Expenses of Harvard Law School, 1946–67 (rounded to thousands)

Academic Year	Total Expense (nominal dollars)	Total Expense (constant dollars[a])
1946–47	1,205,000	1,205,000
1949–50	1,207,000	1,119,000
1955–56	2,439,000	2,074,000
1962–63	4,237,000	3,091,000
1966–67	5,918,000	3,960,000

Data source: Jeremy B. Luke, "Harvard Law School Endowment, Expense, Income, Enrollment Totals, 1895–1970" (student research report, Ohio State University, 2016), on file with the authors.

a. 1947 = 1. Amounts indexed as of the end of the academic year. Due to significant and variable inflation over the period 1946–1967, the absolute value of constant dollars can vary considerably, depending on the base year used for calculation.

advisory committee, and deflected inquiries about the budget by granting requests from individual faculty for resources (though he often initially denied such requests).[58] Griswold even kept Louis Toepfer (LL.B. 1947)—his "alter ego" who "virtually ran the School administratively" from 1959 until 1967—ignorant about but satisfied with the school's finances.[59] "I didn't have to worry much where the money was coming from . . . because there would always be enough money. Where he got it? How he got it? [I don't know.] The school was very prosperous in many ways," said Toepfer.[60]

Griswold explicitly admitted to concealing his financial strategy. Faculty salaries and benefits were the biggest component of the school's expenses and grew much faster than nonpersonnel costs.[61] Despite the great financial impact, Griswold kept secret his intent to double the size of the faculty. "I deliberately refrained from advising the faculty that this was my objective," he later wrote, "for I knew that, if I told them that I wanted to double the size of the faculty, there would be substantial opposition." Instead, Griswold expanded the faculty incrementally and stealthily, relying on professors' typical inability to resist the temptation of adding to their ranks one-by-one.[62]

Early on, an outsider challenged the dean's approach. Harold Berman joined the Harvard faculty as an assistant professor in 1947, and soon thereafter Griswold announced plans to hire five more professors, expanding the faculty by 20 percent. Having graduated from and taught at relatively small law schools (Yale and Stanford, respectively), Berman asked the dean at a faculty meeting, "What is the policy of the Appointments Committee with respect to the size of the faculty?" Griswold, who chaired the committee, replied that there was no policy.[63] Berman then argued that the new hires might cause "great difficulties because five people were being added to this faculty of twenty-five. . . . What does this mean for the ultimate nature of the faculty? . . . We ought to consider what the consequences will be if the faculty is suddenly increased to a very large size." In typical Griswoldizing fashion, the dean responded, "Well, if we had taken that attitude, we never would have appointed you." Berman then rejoined, "I hereby . . . offer my resignation in deference to the principle."[64]

None of the other faculty echoed Berman's concern, and Griswold simply continued the meeting. But Berman was left troubled by the impending hires, and what he correctly suspected was Griswold's hidden agenda, as well as his apparent failure to consider the consequences of that agenda. The dean "claimed at that time—and I don't believe it—that he had no policy with respect to the size of the faculty," recalled Berman. "I think he must have envisioned a vast expansion. . . . And I don't think that he wanted to think about what it meant."[65]

In June 1962, after his planned expansion was well under way and the new revenue was flowing in, Griswold finally appointed a Committee on Planning and Development for the Law School with future dean Albert Sacks (1971–1981) as chairman. Anticipating the school's 150th anniversary in 1967, Griswold charged this committee to project future needs of the school, and its final report in 1964 ratified Griswold's agenda for future growth without reservations.[66] It is noteworthy that Sacks, after he became dean in 1971, also was criticized for failing to create a prudent plan for the school.

Three Spending Myths

How did Griswold sustain the contradiction between his persistent complaints about the school's poverty and the massive growth in spending? Three prominent myths diverted attention from the inconsistency: that Griswold was notoriously frugal, that he did not enlarge the school, and that he prioritized and significantly expanded the endowment.

"Griswold was by all accounts a very frugal man," stated Toepfer and many other colleagues.[67] Indeed, Griswold hated waste, and his frugality became legendary.[68] Regarding office supplies for faculty, "his policy was to furnish letterhead and envelopes. The rest you bought yourself. In this way the faculty didn't waste a whole lot of supplies," said Clark Byse.[69] Griswold was famous for slamming shut open windows in the winter, and turning off the lights in the Law School buildings. When the great blackout enveloped the northeastern United States in November 1965, Robert Braucher (LL.B. 1939) was heard to remark, "Erwin, you've gone too far this time!"[70] Griswold's personal frugality made it unthinkable that he would make imprudent decisions for the school.

On some large issues, the dean's instinctive frugality backfired. In 1947, when President Conant invited the Harvard deans to submit the development needs of their schools, Griswold asked for only $2 million, while the medical school dean requested $19 million and the business school dean $18 million. Upon learning this, Griswold tried to revise his request to $17 million, but Conant, as was typical, refused to accept this revision from the Law School, even as he endorsed the stated needs of the medical and business schools.[71] Similarly, in 1948 Toepfer believed that the school could have raised more money to make the Gropius dormitories commodious, but Griswold "priced the project at the very lowest level." That price then set the expectations for the fundraising, and the school was saddled with the Spartan dormitories for eternity because they became architectural landmarks.[72] While his personal frugality was not a myth, it disguised his institutional profligacy. Griswold tended to be penny wise and pound foolish, and, because he veiled the finances, no one could evaluate or question the trade-offs or long-term implications.

A second, ironic myth Griswold touted himself. He said repeatedly, "I would like to see engraved on my tombstone: 'He kept the Harvard Law School from getting any bigger.'"[73] Here, too, it seems that the dean was "self-delusional, disingenuous, or . . . had a very different notion" of the issue.[74] Griswold's yardstick was the number of students, and even by this measure the total enrollment rose 10 percent from 1950–51 to 1966–67, a significant expansion.[75] In any event, the student body is not the best measure of size. Enrollment in higher education is relatively easy to limit or reduce, compared to the size of the physical plant and the faculty, which involve long-term fixed costs and require decades to shrink. Griswold added eight buildings and committed the school to build two more as he was departing, while doubling the size of the faculty.[76] According to these more salient measures, Dean Griswold vastly expanded the school, notwithstanding his assertions to the contrary, including his proposed epitaph.

A third, paradoxical myth was that he prioritized the endowment and fostered a large increase, of which, he said, 73 percent came from "gifts received for endowment" during his administration.[77] In fact, the endowment grew appreciably between 1946 and 1967, but Griswold contributed little to it. This key paradox requires some explanation, because many observers have subsequently credited Griswold for the endowment growth.[78]

During his deanship, the Law School endowment grew 310 percent, as did the Medical School endowment, while the Business School endowment rose 470 percent, as seen in Table 14.3. The university's endowment grew 290 percent during this period. The Law School's endowment therefore kept pace with that in medicine but lost ground compared to the business endowment, and all three did somewhat better than the university endowment during that period. When Griswold assumed office in 1946, he noted that the Law School's endowment had long been about 3.5 percent of the university's endowment, and he wanted to significantly increase that small fraction. At the end of his term, however, the percentage was virtually unchanged, as seen in Table 14.4.

Table 14.3   Endowments of Harvard Law, Medical, and Business Schools, 1946–1967 (nominal dollars in millions)

Year (as of June 30)	Law School	Medical School	Business School
1946	5.4	19.3	3.8
1952	6.3	21.3	9.2
1958	9.3	32.7	12.7
1964	13.9	60.5	16.1
1967	22.4	79.1	21.7

Data sources: Jessica Meylor, "The Harvard Law School Endowment: What Is the Rest of the Story?" (student research report, Boston College Law School, 2010), on file with the authors; Jamie M. Brown, "Harvard University Endowment, Expense, Enrollment Totals, 1900–70 (in current dollars)" (student research paper, Harvard Law School, 2014).

Table 14.4   Harvard Law, Medical, and Business School Endowments as Percentages of the Harvard University Endowment, 1950–70

Year[a]	Law School	Medical School	Business School	University Total (millions of nominal dollars)
1950	3.1%	10.3%	3.9%	$196
1960	2.9%	10.8%	3.8%	$371
1967	3.6%	12.7%	3.5%	$622
1970	3.6%	12.4%	4.2%	$733

Data source: Computed from Jamie M. Brown, "Harvard University Endowment, Expense, Enrollment Totals, 1900–70 (in current dollars)" (student research paper, Harvard Law School, 2014), on file with the authors.
a. As of June 30.

One reason was that Griswold did not actually focus on that goal and mount a campaign to raise endowment until he was about to depart. Another reason was that he received little encouragement or help from President Conant, who pushed the Law School to the back of the line for endowment fund-raising. According to Conant, the Law School was not one of the departments that regularly ran deficits and therefore needed endowment, such as the schools of public health, business, medicine, and education.[79]

Conant came to this conclusion because Griswold kept generating more revenue and a surplus, which he spent, creating the illusion of prosperity and perpetuating the myth that the Law School did not need more endowment. Griswold, like his predecessors, thus supplied the president with the justification to withhold assistance. By virtue of the policy "each tub on its own bottom" at Harvard, "one faculty may depend primarily on tuition fees, as does the Law School; another primarily on endowment and current gifts, as does the Faculty of Medicine," Conant observed.[80]

Succeeding Conant as president in 1953, Nathan Pusey (1953–1971) was a more successful fundraiser than Conant.[81] But Griswold's persistent pleas of poverty and need for a capital campaign still did not persuade the Corporation.[82] The dean resorted to wishing for the intercession of a spontaneous benefactor in his annual report: "If an endowment of, say, $5 million was made available to the Law School . . . *without a campaign* . . . the results produced within ten years would greatly exceed those . . . from a succession of *ad hoc* grants."[83]

Those at the Law School had longed for such an intercession since the beginning of the twentieth century. But their wistful calls went unanswered. At the very end of his administration Griswold wrote, "The Law School has never received a truly large gift. No one has ever given us $5 million, or $1 million, or even $500,000."[84] How then did the school's endowment grow during his tenure?

Three Sources of Endowment Growth

In 1966 Griswold asserted that the "gifts received for endowment" during his administration amounted to nearly $10.6 million, or 73 percent of the $14.7 million increase during that period.[85] The dean did not identify the "gifts," and the university treasurer's reports reveal that about $10.9 million, or 74 percent, of the endowment growth actually came from three other kinds of sources.

First, $2.8 million of what Griswold described as "gifts" came as two, earmarked grants from the Ford Foundation. In 1955 Milton Katz (LL.B. 1931) brought a large grant to endow two professorships in International Legal Studies as part of his "dowry" from the Ford Foundation, as we have seen. The other large grant came through a national program of faculty salary endowment grants that the Ford Foundation offered to only seventeen, private universities beginning in the late 1950s. Harvard was virtually guaranteed to get its fair share of the $250 million available, and a number of Harvard departments and schools received these grants, along with the Law School.[86]

Second, about $2.6 million of Griswold's "gifts received for endowment" came as bequests.[87] These continued the pre-1940 pattern of bequests significantly contributing to the school's endowment during a time when fundraising was not possible. Bequests might be considered "gifts," and modern development offices usually take credit for them. But bequests are generally windfalls that are not attributable to the efforts of the administration that receives them. Some of those arriving during Griswold's deanship were decades-old residuary bequests, which came to the Law School after the life beneficiary had died.[88]

Third, about $5.5 million of the endowment growth under Griswold consisted of distributions of capital gains from the university, compounded by further stock appreciation during the period. This development is somewhat technical but highly revealing about the relationship between the university administration and Harvard's professional schools, including the Law School.[89]

Well before the founding of the Law School in 1817, Harvard University began pooling endowment funds held by its various departments and schools and investing the total pool together. This approach required that the university treasurer keep track of the value and income of the separate endowment funds within the total pool. To do so, the treasurer listed the endowment funds by their "book value"—the value of the funds when they were acquired. As departments and schools received new endowment funds, the treasurer added them to the pool and listed them at their book value. Long standard throughout higher education, this policy of listing by book value was followed by Harvard and most other colleges and universities until 1970.[90]

For example, in 1882 William Weld gave $90,000 to endow the Weld Professorship at the Law School.[91] According to Harvard policy, this Weld endowment continued to be listed at its book value of $90,000, as decades passed. Over time, however, the Harvard treasurer credited some capital growth to very old endowments, so the Weld professorship was listed at an adjusted book value of $106,294 as of 1941.[92]

Income was then credited to the separate endowment funds within the total pool according to their listed book value. Each year, the treasurer typically received into his income account a return of 6 to 8 percent on the total investment pool. After reinvesting about 2 to 3 percent to preserve the value of the pool, the treasurer typically had net income of 4 to 5 percent. The treasurer then returned that net income to the departments and schools based on the listed book value of their endowment funds within the total pool. For example, in 1941 the net income on the university's pooled investments was 4.1 percent, so the treasurer credited to the Law School 4.1 percent income based on the value of the Weld endowment.

Here arose the problem. In 1941 the Weld endowment had an adjusted book value of $106,294, so the treasurer credited the Law School with income of 4.1 percent of that figure, or $4,385.[93] That return might seem generous, because, according to the strict policy, the Law School should have received income of about $3,700, or 4.1 percent of the original book value of $90,000 of the Weld endowment.

In fact the return was meager. The entire investment pool generated income based on the market value of its investments—that is, their worth in the marketplace in 1941. Over time the market value grew much larger than the book value of the endowments. This growth came both from inflation and from substantive appreciation of the investments. For example, inflation alone drove up the market value of the Weld endowment to almost $129,000 in 1941 dollars.[94] Substantive appreciation—based on a very modest growth rate of 1 percent—would have raised the market value of the Weld endowment to nearly $232,000 in 1941.[95] At that market value, the Weld endowment would have yielded to the treasurer's account an income of some $9,512 at the 4.1 percent net income for the invested pool in 1941.

Confirmation of these calculations may be found by comparing a full professor's salary over time. In 1881 each professor in the Law School received a salary of about $4,250. This amount equaled a reasonable 4.75 percent net income from the Weld endowment of $90,000. In 1941 each full professor in the Law School received a salary of about $9,500.[96] This amount was very close to the 1941 net income of $9,512 calculated above for the market value of the Weld endowment, as shown in Table 14.5.

But the treasurer credited the Law School with a net income of only $4,385, based on the adjusted book value of the Weld endowment. What happened

Table 14.5 Valuation and Income of the William F. Weld Endowment of Harvard Law School, 1882–1967 (in nominal dollars of the year indicated)

Kinds of Valuation	1882	1941	1967
Book Value	$90,000	—	—
Adjusted book value	—	$106,294	$155,624
Income paid to Law School based on (adjusted) book value[a]	$4,275	$4,385	$8,092
Market Value	$90,000	ca. $232,000[b]	ca. $680,000[b]
Income due to Law School based on market value[a]	$4,275	ca. $9,512	ca. $34,680
Average annual salary of a full professor in the Law School	$4,250	ca. $9,500	ca. $31,300

Data source: See discussion and notes in surrounding text.

a. Rate of return was 4.75% in 1882, 4.1% in 1941, and 5.2% in 1967.

b. Assuming inflation plus 1 percent annual appreciation.

to the difference of $5,119 between that figure and the $9,504 net income based on the market value of the Weld endowment in 1941? The balance of $5,119 was retained in the treasurer's income account and ultimately credited to the general funds of the university. The Corporation and the central administration then either spent the difference or reinvested it as part of the unrestricted quasi-endowment of the university.[97]

This happened every year, and the difference became larger over time because the market value of the investments grew inexorably and the book value did not. If the market value dropped sharply during a recession, then the Corporation dramatically reduced the net return on the book value to compensate. During the Depression, for example, the net income that the treasurer returned to the departments and schools on their endowments fell to 1 percent.[98] Consequently, the short-term effect of the investment-pool policy was to create a slush fund that the Corporation could allocate at its discretion. The long-term effect was to slowly depreciate the historical endowments of the departments and schools and to transfer their value to the unrestricted quasi-endowment of the university controlled by the Corporation.[99]

The transfer had been occurring for more than a century and it surely worried the Corporation throughout that period. In 1842, 1866, 1876, and 1908, the president and the treasurer of the university earnestly discussed how to solve it. But no one could figure out a solution, so the worrying continued, as did the transferring.[100] After the stock market ran up during the 1920s, the Corporation finally tried to correct the problem in 1930. The treasurer was directed to write up the book value of all the university's endowed funds by 10 percent in a weak attempt to approximate their market value. Due to the Great Depression, this turned out to be terrible timing. The market value of the investment pool plummeted, so the Corporation reversed itself in 1938 and wrote down the value of all the endowed funds by 10 percent.[101]

After World War II the stock market rose spectacularly in value. Between 1950 and 1965 Harvard's common stock portfolio rose 473 percent, while a general index of common stock prices rose 380 percent. This growth immensely increased the difference between the book value and the market value of the various endowments in the investment pool. In response, the Corporation made a series of capital gains distributions to the endowed funds of the departments and schools, boosting their value. Between 1957 and 1965, these distributions to the Law School amounted to about $4.5 million, and the earlier distributions were compounded by the rising stock market.[102] The total distribution to the Law School's endowment amounted to about $5.5 million of the $14.7 million growth during Griswold's administration.

Yet even these distributions fell considerably short of correcting the depreciation in value of the older endowment funds. In 1967, after the distributions, the treasurer listed the Weld endowment at a value of $155,624, which returned net income to the Law School of $8,092 at the rate of 5.2 percent. But since 1882, inflation alone had driven up the value of the Weld endowment to nearly $292,000 in 1967 dollars. Substantive appreciation, based on a very modest annual rate of 1 percent, would have further raised the Weld endowment to about $680,000 within the investment pool in 1967 dollars.[103]

At that value, the Weld endowment would have yielded net income of some $34,680 to the Law School in 1967 at the rate of 5.2 percent. Again, this projected value comports with the average salary of a full professor at that time. In 1965 a survey of members of the Association of American Law Schools found that the range of "high" salaries of senior law professors in private universities averaged between $27,501 and $30,000. This benchmark suggests that, in 1967, the average salary of full professors at Harvard Law School was about $31,300.[104] That figure is close to the projected yield from the Weld Endowment of $34,680. All these comparisons for the Weld professorship endowment are summarized in Table 14.5.

Consequently, in 1882 the Law School received income from the Weld endowment sufficient to pay the full salary of a professor. By 1941 the income from the Weld endowment received by the Law School had fallen to one-half of a professor's salary. By 1967 the income had fallen to about one-quarter. In 1967 the value of $155,624 listed by the treasurer for the Weld endowment was less than a quarter of its value when William Weld endowed the professorship in 1882—even after the capital gains distributions of the 1950s and 1960s! The other three-quarters in value did not evaporate. It had been spent by the university or transferred to the university's unrestricted quasi-endowment under the control of the Corporation. Griswold apparently did not explore this depreciation issue, if he was aware of it.[105]

In sum, about $10.9 million, or 74 percent, of the Law School's $14.7 million endowment growth actually came from the Ford Foundation grants, older bequests, capital gains distributions, and stock appreciation during Griswold's tenure.[106] The other $3.8 million can legitimately be called "gifts for endowment" received during Griswold's administration. But $2.9 million of that amount came from alumni directing their annual fund contributions to endow scholarships. Consequently, less than $1 million could be considered "gifts to endowment" that Griswold secured outside of the annual fund contributions that alumni designated for endowment. And if the alumni had not made these designations, it is likely that Griswold would have spent the gifts on current operating expenses, as happened to other unrestricted gifts.

Consequently, Dean Griswold had little to do with the growth of the school's endowment during his administration. Though he complained about its deficiency in nearly every annual report and other official publications over the same two decades, he elected to spend nearly all the unrestricted new revenue, rather than to invest it in the endowment. As a result—despite his reputation for frugality and claim not to have enlarged the school—expenses increased dramatically during his administration. Then in 1966 he suggested that the endowment grew primarily by dint of "gifts received for endowment" during his administration.[107]

Tuition Dependence Syndrome, 1967

Between 1950 and 1967, Dean Griswold increased annual expenses by more than 250 percent in constant dollars. Apart from funding eight new buildings the additional spending had many benefits. It funded smaller classes for students and many additional course offerings. It provided new journals and organizations for students, such as the Harvard Law School Forum and Harvard Voluntary Defenders. It supported additional faculty and teaching fellows, who offered more instruction and expertise. In particular, it advanced the graduate programs, including International Legal Studies (ILS).

This last development leads to an interesting academic and financial question. Although criticized for neglecting public service, Griswold's administration viewed the formation of ILS following World War II as the school's fundamental contribution to building international understanding, a global community, and world peace. The dean invested substantial resources in the effort. He repeatedly stated, "We need increases . . . in the fields of comparative law, including Russian Law, Moslem Law, African Law, and Japanese Law. We need similar increases in the fields of International Legal Studies on the commercial, financial, and tax sides."[108]

By 1960 some sixteen faculty were teaching at least one graduate or international course. These faculty also taught LL.B. courses, and many graduate courses were open to LL.B. students, so it is difficult to quantify the number of faculty committed to the graduate program. But it appears that the equivalent of about six full-time, regular faculty slots were devoted to the graduate

Table 14.6   Distribution of Financial Aid at Harvard Law School, 1959–60 and 1965–66 (in nominal dollars)

Academic Year	1959–60		1965–66	
Degree program	LL.B.	LL.M. and S.J.D.	LL.B.	LL.M. and S.J.D.
Number of students enrolled	1,488	80	1,573	90
Scholarship amount available per enrolled student	$155	$1,938	$313	$3,067
Loan amount allocated per enrolled student	$142	$88	$401	$35
Total aid awarded per enrolled student	$297	$2,026	$714	$3,102
Tuition charged by School	$1,000	$1,000	$1,500	$1,500

Data sources: Erwin N. Griswold, Annual Report of the Dean of Harvard Law School, 1959–60, 423–426; 1965–66, 248–254; Harvard Law School Catalog, 1960–61, 1966–67.

programs, including ILS, during the 1960s. That would amount to about 9 or 10 percent of the teaching faculty by 1967—a considerable investment, given that the cost of personnel constituted most of the school's expenses and rose faster than nonpersonnel costs.[109]

Similarly, the financial aid went disproportionately to graduate students in the LL.M. and S.J.D. programs, as shown in Table 14.6. That allocation between the two populations can be justified on several grounds, including the costs, resources, and prospective income of the graduate students. In any case, the funding of faculty and students in the graduate programs was heavily subsidized by the rise in tuition revenue and proceeds from the annual fund, which came almost entirely from LL.B. students or LL.B. alumni. Hence, the school's LL.B. program heavily subsidized the graduate programs, faculty, and students, notwithstanding the grants received from the Ford Foundation and other sources. This subsidy is implied but not stated explicitly in the school's publications. Later decades would see the pattern reversed, as the LL.M. program began to subsidize the LL.B. students.[110]

Whatever the extent of these subsidies, the fundamental point is that Dean Griswold exacerbated the tuition dependence syndrome, as seen in Figure 14.1. If he had reduced enrollment while raising tuition, the need for more hiring and facilities would have decreased, along with the student-faculty ratio. Instead, by spending the new revenue and doubling the size of the faculty, he locked the school into more expense and exhausted the important option of raising tuition in the future in order to generate more revenue. The enormous growth of the school's physical plant, enrollment, and student-faculty ratio

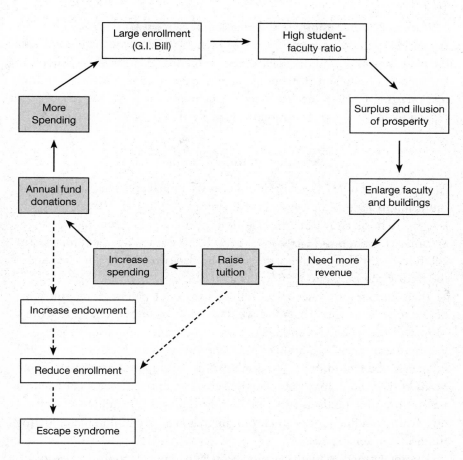

Figure 14.1. Tuition Dependence Syndrome, 1946–1967. Note: Solid arrows represent the path followed after 1930. Dotted arrows represent alternate paths available. The shaded boxes convey new developments since 1930.

began with Deans James Barr Ames, Ezra Thayer, and Roscoe Pound. While continuing those policies, the compounding factors of raising tuition and escalating operating expenses began with Dean Griswold.

The worsening malaise of tuition dependence was evident to everyone by the end of Griswold's deanship, even granting that the school had "a lot more going on around here than there used to be!" as he exclaimed in 1966.[111] For the academic year 1965–66, Harvard economist Seymour Harris calculated that tuition contributed about 19 percent of all income for the whole university, as compared to 7 percent for the school of medicine, 15 percent for education, 27 percent for arts and sciences, 38 percent for design, 43 percent for business, and 57 percent for the law school.[112] The Law School was still the poor stepchild. And the malaise beset more than Harvard Law School, as law schools throughout the country sharply raised tuition. Griswold's tuition hikes starting in 1948 inevitably set a benchmark for other law schools, inducing them to raise their tuition while neglecting to raise endowment.

Sesquicentennial Campaign

At the very end of his administration, Griswold finally planned a fundraising campaign to address the need for endowment. At long last, "Dean Griswold is trying to break away from the historical experience of depending excessively on tuition," economist Harris observed.[113] But it was too little and too late. In addition, Griswold figured that the school needed two more buildings to house the faculty and programs that he had added.

The planning for the school's 150th anniversary began in 1958, nine years before the event, when Dean Griswold invited Arthur Sutherland to write a history of the school. In 1963, again well in advance, the dean appointed a Committee on the Celebration of the 150th Anniversary. Meanwhile, in 1962 he named the Committee on Planning and Development to project future needs of the school. In September 1964 this committee issued a confidential report proposing needs of $29.4 million, including $22.5 million in new endowment, $6 million for two new buildings, and $6.74 million in liquidating funds for current expenses.[114]

This total proposed by the faculty seemed unattainable to the university administration. Considering how to pare it down, Dean Griswold and President Pusey noted that Yale Law School had raised over $5 million in the early 1960s. Being three times as large as Yale, Harvard leaders felt their law school should raise three times as much, and so the goal was set at $15 million.[115] Although this amount was unprecedented in legal education, no one appeared to noticed that it was about equal in constant dollars to the $2.25 million that the Law School had actually raised in the 1925–1927 campaign.

Reducing the total of $29.4 million to $15 million forced Griswold to reapportion the subgoals. This created a difficult problem. The school needed a new faculty office building and another new building for classrooms and program offices. The need resulted from Griswold's expansion of the faculty by 97 percent, the total student body by 10 percent, and the course offerings by 255 percent.[116] Since the cost of these buildings had to come out of the Sesquicentennial Fund, that $6 million consumed 40 percent of the $15 million goal. Only 60 percent, or $9 million, would go to endowment.[117]

Griswold's additional spending therefore consumed not only the unrestricted annual fund revenue that could have raised the endowment, but also the proceeds of the capital campaign designated for the endowment. Furthermore, the reduced plan eliminated the $6.74 million in the original proposal that would have contributed to maintenance of the new buildings for the near future. Even if it succeeded, the Sesquicentennial Campaign ultimately would increase the operating expenses of the school due to the two new buildings. This additional cost would come back to strangle the school under Dean Sacks.

Begun in 1966, the Sesquicentennial drive "was not an easy campaign," as Assistant Director Stephen Bernardi (LL.B. 1955) later stated. The alumni chairmen, Robert Amory Jr. (LL.B. 1938) and Stuart N. Scott (LL.B. 1930), worked more effectively than had alumni chairmen earlier in the century. But Wesley Bevins, the director of the campaign, never developed a prospect list or solicited donations systematically and nationally. Instead, Bevins, his staff, and the deans focused solely on the white-shoe law firms in Boston, New York, and Washington.[118]

The proceeds trickled in. As in the past, the campaign leaders—including Bevins—wished for an angel to appear and save all the work of asking for money. Griswold's departure in the middle of the campaign in 1967 dampened enthusiasm because he was popular with the alumni. But more problematic was alumni disapproval of the student upheaval and cancellation of classes and exams upon the assassinations of Martin Luther King Jr. and Robert Kennedy in 1968.[119]

In April 1970 the campaign officially ended with a grand total of $15,101,250, reaching the goal with only a bit of "creative bookkeeping," in Bernardi's words.[120] The profile of giving also resembled the campaign of 1925–1927. No alumnus made a major gift. The largest donations were a federal HEA grant of $500,000 toward the buildings and a Ford Foundation grant of $1 million, which was not for capital, so the amount realized for endowment was proportionately reduced.[121]

Before the campaign ended, ground was broken for a "Faculty Office Building" and a "Classroom and Administration Building," evidently relying on funds advanced by the university at interest. Both were finished by 1970; the former was named for Griswold in 1979 and the latter for Pound, again confirming the truism in higher education about naming nondonated buildings for deans.[122] Though both were praised as "the most adroit example of design for a given environment produced at Harvard since World War II," half of Pound

Erwin N. Griswold speaking at the Sesquicentennial Celebration, 1967. Massachusetts Governor John A. Volpe is on the lower right.

Courtesy of Harvard Law School Library, Historical & Special Collections.

Hall was demolished in 2011 to improve the siting for the new Wasserstein-Caspersen Hall.[123] The Sesquicentennial Campaign was the school's most successful fundraising drive up to that point, but the outcome was modest and alumni support tepid.

Griswold's Departure

In the mid-1960s, the social and political turmoil in the United States surrounding civil rights, urban upheaval, the Vietnam War, and the feminist movement began buffeting the Law School. It was "a moment of institutional disintegration," in the words of Professor Richard Parker (LL.B. 1970).[124] New students and young faculty chafed under the norms of Griswold's school.

The dinner parties that the dean and Harriet hosted annually for the faculty became even more strained. Alcohol was never served, and his house became known as "Dry Hill." Many faculty stopped on the way for a drink at the Casners, who lived a block from the Griswolds. The dean later said this customary detour hurt his feelings, because it reminded him that he had never fit in socially at Harvard Law School, even as a student in the 1920s.[125] The Grizz was not as unfeeling as many believed. But he made little effort to improve his sociability. When he felt that the party was over, Griswold would go over to the mantel and wind up the clock in "a not-so-subtle suggestion to leave," recalled Detlev Vagts (LL.B. 1951).[126]

In September 1967, U.S. Attorney General Ramsey Clark telephoned Griswold and asked if he would like to be considered for the position of solicitor general by President Lyndon B. Johnson. "I took fifteen agonizing seconds and said yes," Griswold later observed. He resigned as dean on October 1, and the U.S. Senate confirmed him as solicitor general later that month.[127] Griswold was surprised that President Richard Nixon kept him in office after 1968, because Griswold considered himself "one of those leftist Republicans that Senator [Strom] Thurmond is worried about."[128] After he stepped down as solicitor general in 1973, Griswold joined a prominent law firm in Washington, D.C. Upon his death in 1994, he was one of three lawyers who had argued more than a hundred cases before the Supreme Court during the twentieth century. Some say that he had argued the most.[129]

His accomplishments at Harvard Law School were no less noteworthy. In 1946 he had walked into an empty dean's office and steered the school through the postwar "madhouse" of returning veterans. Over the next decade Griswold built the administrative infrastructure that is now customary in a university law school. He also added eight buildings and planned two more as he departed. He personally repaired relations with alumni and doubled the size of the faculty, while raising the expectations for scholarship. He greatly expanded the number of course offerings, and taught a course each semester. He supported and in many ways sponsored the postwar academic initiative of International Legal Studies.

In addition, Griswold weathered McCarthyism and championed a new and authoritative defense of pleading the Fifth Amendment, though he did not originate it. He instituted selective admissions and the admission of women, but did not appreciate their professional role and potential, leaving the impression that he did not favor increasing the small number of women at the school. He also encouraged faculty to establish a summer recruitment program for African American students, though it should have been done much earlier.

To improve student life, he built the first dining commons and dormitories, and greatly expanded opportunities in extracurricular programs and student law journals. But he also embraced the combative and competitive Spartan manliness, lest the school appear to be going "soft." He vastly expanded the revenue of the school, but did not employ it prudently. Throughout his tenure, as Derek Bok observed, Dean Griswold appeared "austere, forbidding, uncompromising . . . the kind of leader one does not often find today in universities—decisive, magisterial, and rarely contradicted."[130]

Such a formidable figure and profoundly mixed record naturally prompted conflicting assessments. Many, like Benjamin Kaplan (LL.B. 1929) and Archibald Cox (LL.B. 1937), both of whom joined the faculty in 1946, believed that Griswold "saved the school," and considered him "a very great dean."[131] Such assessments come mainly from those who witnessed the difficulties Griswold faced in the 1940s and 1950s and who successfully climbed the career ladder. Those who studied at Harvard Law School in the 1960s or who faced great obstacles in pursuing their careers were much less approving, if not thoroughly critical. "I didn't experience him as a great dean," particularly "when all this civil rights stuff happened in the 1960s," stated Elizabeth Bartholet (LL.B. 1965).[132]

One outsider, Alan Dershowitz, who did not study at Harvard Law School under Griswold and came to the faculty in 1964 after graduating from Yale, viewed the dean with equanimity. In his eyes, Griswold "probably came with lots of biases and bigotries which he overcame, or he didn't act on. He was a better person than what his background may have given him. On balance . . . I think he did a very good job."[133]

Whatever the judgment on an absolute scale, it is certainly true that the job did not break Erwin Griswold. Moreover, he improved and strengthened Harvard Law School far more than did any of his predecessors in the twentieth century. But he failed to fix the school's financial model, even though he considered it to be the fundamental weakness and had the means and opportunity to correct it. Was he, therefore, a seemingly frugal spendthrift who actually weakened the school's core finances? We turn next to the surprising justification for Dean Griswold's imprudent strategy.

NOTES

1. Erwin N. Griswold, *Ould Fields, New Corne: The Personal Memoirs of a Twentieth Century Lawyer* (St. Paul, MN, 1992), 160.

2. Erwin N. Griswold to Nathan M. Pusey (September 4, 1968), HLS Dean's Office Records, Records of President Nathan M. Pusey, 1953–1971, Harvard University Archives (HUA) (hereafter cited as NMP Records).

3. Austin W. Scott, "The Dean's Decennial," *HLSB* (October 1956): 4; "News of the School," *HLSB* (February 1959): 2; Arthur E. Sutherland, *The Law at Harvard: A History of Ideas and Men, 1817–1907* (Cambridge, MA, 1967), 355–336; Albert M. Sacks, "Dean Erwin N. Griswold—Some Fond Recollections," *HLR* 86 (1973): 1370–1371; Joel Seligman, *The High Citadel: The Influence of Harvard Law School* (Boston, 1978), 75–77; Laura Kalman, *Legal Realism at Yale, 1927–1960* (Chapel Hill, NC, 1986), 208–209; Keller and Keller, *Making Harvard Modern,* 253; Nathan M. Pusey "A Great Dean," *HLR* 81 (1967): 291.

4. Charles W. Eliot, Annual Report of the President of Harvard University, 1871–72, 21–22.

5. Robert Stevens, *Law School: Legal Education in America from the 1850s to the 1980s* (Chapel Hill, NC, 1983), 51–72.

6. Quotations are from Erwin N. Griswold, "The School and the Fund," *HLSB* (April 1949): 7; Griswold, Annual Report of the Dean of Harvard Law School (HLS), 1949–50, 455.

7. Roger L. Geiger, *Research and Relevant Knowledge: American Research Universities since World War II* (New York, 1993), 13–15, 40–41, 195–196; Richard M. Freeland, *Academia's Golden Age: Universities in Massachusetts, 1945–1975.* (New York, 1992).

8. A. J. Angulo, *Diploma Mills: How For-Profit Colleges Stiffed Students, Taxpayers, and the American Dream* (Baltimore, 2016), 59; Geiger, *Research and Relevant Knowledge,* 41.

9. William G. Bowen, *The Economics of the Major Private Research Universities* (Berkeley, 1968), 19.

10. Conant, Annual Report of the President, 1948–49, 18–19.

11. Conant, Annual Report of the President, 1948–49, 18–19; Bowen, *The Economics,* 19.

12. John J. McCusker, *How Much Is That in Real Money? A Historical Commodity Price Index for Use as a Deflator of Money Values in the Economy of the United States,* 2nd ed. (Worcester, MA, 2001), 58; Geiger, *Research and Relevant Knowledge,* 41–42, 162–163.

13. [Andrew L. Kaufman, Chair], Memorandum to the Faculty from the Financial Aids Committee [HLS, ca. March 1970], typescript, on file with the authors, 12, 21, 22. See Morton Keller and Phyllis Keller, *Making Harvard Modern: The Rise of America's University* (New York, 2001), 144–145,185; Seymour Harris, *Economics of Harvard* (New York, 1970), 23, 336, 344.

14. Quotation is from Erwin N. Griswold, "Annual Giving: The Need for Increased Funds," *HLSB* (February 1951): 8. See Griswold, Annual Report of the Dean, 1946–47, 410; 1949–50, 455–456; 1951–52, 490; 1961–62, 395; Griswold, "The School and the Fund," 7; Griswold, "Some Thoughts about Legal Education Today," *HLSB* (December 1959): 6; Conant, Annual Report of the President, 1947–48, 10–11; Harris, *Economics,* 496; Keller and Keller, *Making Harvard Modern,* 184.

15. Erwin N. Griswold, "The Future of Legal Education," *HLSB* (February 1953): 4; Griswold, "Some Thoughts," 6; Griswold, Annual Report of the Dean, 1961–62, 395. See Griswold, *Ould Fields,* 160.

16. Griswold, Annual Report of the Dean, 1957–58, 335; see 1949–50, 455–456; 1946–47, 410; 1959–60, 430; 1961–62, 395; Griswold, "The School since the War," *HLSB* (December 1951): 4; Griswold, "The School and the Fund," 7; Griswold, "Annual Giving," 8; Harris, *Economics,* 496.

17. Harvard Law School Catalog, 1946–47, 3–4.

18. Griswold, Annual Report of the Dean, 1946–47, 410. See Annual Report of the Treasurer of Harvard University, 1946–47, 16.

19. Griswold, Annual Report of the Dean, 1947–48, 390. See James M. Landis to Edwin D. Dickinson (January 3, 1946), HLS Dean's Office Records, Records of President James B. Conant, 1933–1953, HUA (hereafter cited as JBC Records).

20. Griswold, Annual Report of the Dean, 1947–48, 379.

21. James M. Landis, Annual Report of the Dean of HLS, 1937–38, 197; Daniel R. Coquillette and Bruce A. Kimball, *On the Battlefield of Merit: Harvard Law School, the First Century* (Cambridge, MA, 2015) (hereafter cited as *Battlefield of Merit*), 559–560.

22. Sutherland, *The Law at Harvard,* 361. See Griswold, *Ould Fields,* 163.

23. Erwin N. Griswold, "Legal Education at Harvard," *HLSB* (January 1950): 1.

24. Erwin N. Griswold quoted in Sutherland, *The Law at Harvard,* 362–363. See Griswold, "Memorandum for the Faculty, Harvard Men in Law Teaching" (March 5, 1948), JBC Records; Griswold, "Legal Education," 1.

25. Harvard Law School Catalog, 1950–51, 106; 1967–68, 190. Total enrollment rose 13 percent from 1,524 in the academic year 1950–51 to 1,716 in 1966–67.

26. Donna Fossum, "Law Professors: A Profile of the Teaching Branch of the Legal Profession," *American Bar Foundation Research Journal* (1980): 501, 505.

27. In 1946–47, at the $400 tuition fee, 1,701 LL.B. students paid $680,400; in 1966–67, at $1,500 tuition fee, 1,614 students paid $2,421,000. HLS Faculty Meeting Minutes (December 9, 1947); [Kaufman], Memorandum, appendix 2; McCusker, *How Much Is That,* 58–59.

28. HLS Faculty Meeting Minutes (January 14, 1947); Griswold, Annual Report of the Dean, 1947–48, 379; 1953–54, 580. See Louis A. Toepfer, Oral History, conducted by Daniel Hamilton (March 1998), on file with the authors.

29. [Kaufman], Memorandum, 1–2; John Grant Haviland, "The Student Looks at Harvard Law School" (observations of the school by students in 1934) (unpublished type-

script, revised spring 1934), on file with the authors, 13; Ellen Bernstein, "A Conversation with Erwin N. Griswold," *HLSB* (Fall 1979): 19–23.

30. Quotation is from [Kaufman], Memorandum, 5. See HLS Faculty Meeting Minutes (January 14, 1947).

31. Louis A. Toepfer, "Admissions," *HLSB* (April 1957): 4. See Griswold, Annual Report of the Dean, 1952–53, 481–482; [Kaufman], Memorandum, 6–7, 74, appendix 2; Bernstein, "A Conversation," 19–23; Toepfer, Oral History (March 1998); Sacks, "Dean Erwin N. Griswold," 1370; Russell A. Simpson, Oral History, conducted by Mary Beth Basile and Daniel R. Coquillette (May–September 2001), on file with the authors.

32. Ernest J. Brown, Oral History, conducted by Daniel Hamilton (August 1997), on file with the authors. See Toepfer, Oral History (March 1998); Griswold, Annual Report of the Dean, 1946–47, 414; 1948–49, 427; Reginald Heber Smith, "The Harvard Law School Association and Its 'Committee of Five,'" *HLSB* (April 1950): 10; Scott, "The Dean's Decennial," 4.

33. Seligman, *The High Citadel,* 76–77; Marina N. Bolotnika, "The Purpose of Harvard Law School," *Harvard Magazine* (August 17, 2016).

34. Frederick A. O. Schwarz, "Report of the Committee to Visit the Law School" (May 12, 1958), Erwin N. Griswold Papers, 1925–1994, Harvard Law School Library Historical & Special Collections (HLSLib) (hereafter cited as ENG Papers).

35. Smith, "The Harvard Law School Association," 10; "News of the School," 2; "78th Annual Meeting of the Council of the Harvard Law School Association," *HLSB* (June 1964): 14; "81st Annual Meeting of the Council of the Harvard Law School Association," *HLSB* (July 1967): 17, 19.

36. Bruce A. Kimball, "'Democratizing' Giving at Yale and Harvard: The Discursive Legitimation of Mass Fundraising at Elite Universities, 1890–1920," *History of Education Quarterly* 55 (2015): 164–189.

37. Erwin N. Griswold, "Grateful Thanks," *HLSB* (October 1967): 2.

38. Quotation is from Griswold, *Ould Fields,* 167–168. See Griswold, Annual Report of the Dean, 1949–50, 455–56; Griswold, "Grateful Thanks," 2; Conant, Annual Report of the President, 1949–50, 15–16; Wesley E. Bevins Jr. "The Harvard Law School Fund—A Review of Its Origins and Progress," *HLSB* (October 1960): 7.

39. Committee on the Harvard Law School Fund, "Report to the Executive Committee and Council [of the Harvard Law School Association] (March 27, 1950), Records of the Harvard Law School Fund, 1949–1976, HUA (hereafter cited as HLSF Records). See Griswold, Annual Report of the Dean, 1949–50, 459; Griswold, "Annual Giving," 8. The deficit on the dormitories was actually paid off in 1952. Griswold, Annual Report of the Dean, 1952–53, 505–506.

40. Scott G. Nichols, Interview with Bruce A. Kimball and Kenneth Leung (December 2010), on file with the authors; Scott G. Nichols, Interview (February 2011), quoted in Kenneth Leung, "Fundraising at the Harvard Law School during Erwin

Griswold's Deanship" (student research paper, HLS, 2011), on file with the authors; Stephen Bernardi, Oral History, conducted by Daniel Hamilton and Daniel R. Coquillette (October 2000–April 2001), on file with the authors; Griswold, *Ould Fields,* 167; Frank E. A. Sander, Oral History, conducted by Daniel Coquillette and Daniel Hamilton (September–December 1998), on file with the authors. Compare Griswold, Annual Report of the Dean, 1951–52, 525; Griswold, "Grateful Thanks," 2; Brad Hudson, "Bevins Steps Down as Head of Fund," *HLSR* (March 19, 1982): 8.

41. Bowen, *The Economics,* 42–43, 45; John Price Jones Company, Inc., *American Philanthropy for Higher Education: Gifts and Bequests to Fifty Selected Colleges and Universities, A Report for 1965–66* (New York, 1966).

42. Griswold, *Ould Fields,* 168. See Sutherland, *The Law at Harvard,* 349; Griswold, Annual Report of the Dean, 1952–53, 482–483; 1957–58, 324; 1959–60, 429; 1965–66, 241; [Kaufman], Memorandum, 5.

43. J. Bruce Blain, "Harvard Law School Fund, 1950–1968" (research report, HLS, 2012), on file with the authors.

44. Sutherland, *The Law at Harvard,* 349. See Keller and Keller, *Making Harvard Modern,* 183.

45. Griswold, Annual Report of the Dean, 1952–53, 482–483; 1957–58, 324; 1959–60, 429; 1965–66, 241; [Kaufman], Memorandum, 5; Griswold, *Ould Fields,* 168. See Sutherland, *The Law at Harvard,* 349.

46. Another 27 percent came from the school's own continuing loan fund, 5 percent from university scholarships and foundation grants, and 5 percent from the school's operating funds. All these figures are interpolations based on Griswold, Annual Report of the Dean, 1966–67, 285–287; Annual Report of the Treasurer, 1966–67, 130; [Kaufman], Memorandum, 4–6, appendix 2; Blain, "Harvard Law School Fund, 1950–1968." In these sources, the reporting year varies, and the distinction between funds for graduate students and for LL.B. students is not always clear or consistent.

47. Griswold, Annual Report of the Dean, 1965–66, 241.

48. Griswold, Annual Report of the Dean, 1965–66, 241.

49. Blain, "Harvard Law School Fund, 1950–1968."

50. Griswold, Annual Report of the Dean, 1957–58, 335; Harris, *Economics,* 487; Wesley E. Bevins Jr. to Erwin N. Griswold (March 8, 1968, and February 21, 1969), ENG Papers.

51. Quotation is from John B. Marsh, "Final Report of the Capital Fund," *HLSB* (April 1951): 10. "New Plan for Annual Giving to the Law School," *HLSB* (December 1950): 14.

52. Griswold, Annual Report of the Dean, 1952–53, 506; 1953–54, 579, 583; 1954–55, 628; 1956–57, 341; 1960–61, 341; 1965–66, 241, 252; 1966–67, 284; 1964–65, 271; Wesley E. Bevins Jr., "Harvard Law School Fund Sixteenth Annual Giving Year Progress Report," *HLSB* (May 1966): 12; A. James Casner, Annual Report of the Dean of HLS, 1967–68, 272–273.

53. Erwin N. Griswold, "In Appreciation," *HLSB* (February 1954): 16.

54. HLS Fund Pamphlet for the Third Year of Annual Giving (1952–53), HLSF Records, 1, 4.

55. Griswold, Annual Report of the Dean, 1947–48, 381–382; 1950–51, 356–360; 1951–52, 507–509, 511–512; 1953–54, 559.

56. Gail J. Hupper, "Educational Ambivalence: The Rise of a Foreign-Student Doctorate in Law," *New England Journal of Law* 49 (2014): 334–335.

57. Harold J. Berman, Oral History, conducted by Daniel Hamilton and Daniel R. Coquillette (August 1998), on file with the authors.

58. Clark Byse, Oral History, conducted by Daniel R. Coquillette and Daniel Hamilton (July–October 1997), on file with the authors.

59. Quotations are from, respectively, Andrew L. Kaufman, Oral History, conducted by Daniel Hamilton and Daniel R. Coquillette (June 1999–April 2000), on file with the authors; Simpson, Oral History (May–September 2001). See Toepfer, Oral History (March 1998).

60. Toepfer, Oral History (March 1998).

61. Annual Report of the Treasurer, 1946–47, 14; 1949–50, 14; 1952–53, 14; 1955–56, 14; 1959–60, 14; 1962–63, 14; 1964–65, 14; 1966–67, 16.

62. Quotations are from Griswold, *Ould Fields,* 163.

63. Berman, Oral History (August 1998).

64. Berman, Oral History (August 1998).

65. Berman, Oral History (August 1998).

66. HLS Committee on Planning and Development, "Report, Confidential," typescript (September 1964), on file with the authors, appendix B.

67. Louis A. Toepfer, Interview (May 4, 1998), quoted in David McIntosh, "A Minor Matter: The Admission of Women to the Harvard Law School" (student research paper, HLS, 1998), on file with the authors, 20–21. See Paul A. Freund, "Erwin N. Griswold: An Introduction," in *In Remembrance: Erwin N. Griswold* (memorial program) (Washington, DC, 1995).

68. Griswold, "Annual Giving," 8; Griswold, Annual Report of the Dean, 1952–53, 506.

69. Byse, Oral History (July–October 1997).

70. Arthur von Mehren, Oral History, conducted by Daniel R. Coquillette and Mary Beth Basile (July–December 2000), on file with the authors. See Detlev Vagts, Oral History, conducted by Daniel Hamilton, Daniel R. Coquillette, and John Delionado (November 1999–February 2000), on file with the authors; Erwin N. Griswold, Statement about terms of renting 36 Kenmore Road, Belmont, MA (typescript 1992), Elizabeth Wahlen Correspondence, 1946–1998, on file with the authors; Victor E. Ferrall Jr., Telephone interview with Bruce A. Kimball (January 2015), notes on file with the authors; Bernardi, Oral History (October 2000–April 2001); Judith Richards Hope, "Remembrance," 16–19, and Derek C. Bok, "Remembrance," 23–26, in *Erwin Nathaniel Griswold: 1904–1994* (memorial program) (Cambridge, MA, 1995).

71. Keller and Keller, *Making Harvard Modern,* 116–117.

72. Toepfer, Oral History (March 1998).

73. "A Meeting of Two Deans" (Dean Clark Interviews Dean Griswold), *HLSB* (Fall 1994): 5. See Griswold, Annual Report of the Dean, 1963–64, 224; Griswold, *Ould Fields,* 163.

74. Quotations are from Kaufman, Oral History (June 1999–April 2000); Elizabeth Bartholet, Oral History, conducted by Daniel Hamilton (February 1999–March 2000), on file with the authors.

75. Harvard Law School Catalog, 1950–51, 106; 1967–68, 190.

76. "A Meeting of Two Deans," 5. See Griswold, *Ould Fields,* 160.

77. Griswold, Annual Report of the Dean, 1965–66, 258.

78. Sacks, "Dean Erwin N. Griswold," 1370–1371; Sutherland, *The Law at Harvard,* 255–256; Scott, "The Dean's Decennial," 4; "News of the School," 2; Pusey, "A Great Dean," 291; Kalman, *Legal Realism,* 208–209; Seligman, *The High Citadel,* 75–77; Nichols, Interview (December 2010); Nichols, Interview (February 2011); Harris, *Economics,* 477–480.

79. Conant, Annual Report of the President, 1947–48, 11–12; see 1944–45, 15–16; Harris, *Economics,* 487; Nichols, Interview (December 2010); Nichols, Interview (February 2011).

80. Conant, Annual Report of the President, 1947–48, 10–11.

81. Harris, *Economics,* 351; Keller and Keller, *Making Harvard Modern,* 147–151, 178–183.

82. Griswold, Annual Report of the Dean, 1946–47, 410; Griswold, "The School and the Fund," 7; Griswold, "The School since the War," 4; Griswold, Annual Report of the Dean, 1949–50, 455–456; 1961–62, 395; 1959–60, 430; Griswold to Pusey (September 4, 1968).

83. Griswold, Annual Report of the Dean, 1957–58, 335, emphasis added; see 1959–60, 411–412; 1961–62, 396; Erwin N. Griswold, "Intellect and Spirit," *HLR* 81 (1967): 298; Griswold, *Ould Fields,* 228.

84. Quoted in Harris, *Economics,* 487. See Griswold, Annual Report of the Dean, 1957–58, 335; Bevins to Griswold (March 8, 1968, and February 21, 1969).

85. Griswold, Annual Report of the Dean, 1965–66, 258.

86. Annual Report of the Treasurer, 1954–55, 66–67; 1964–65, 57, 75; Bowen, *The Economics,* 43; Roger Geiger, "Southern Higher Education in the Twentieth Century," *History of Higher Education Annual* (1999): 108.

87. Annual Report of the Treasurer, 1948–49, 246; 1963–64, 57; 1965–66, 74–78. See "Bequests," *HLSB* (October 1964): 5; (October 1965): 3; (October 1966): 5.

88. Nichols, Interview (December 2010); Nichols, Interview (February 2011). Compare Wesley E. Bevins Jr. to Erwin N. Griswold (December 6, 1972), and Wesley E. Bevins Jr. to Erwin N. Griswold (June 21, 1968), ENG Papers.

89. The following account draws upon Harris, *Economics,* 350–360.

90. Annual Report of the Treasurer, 1969–70, 5.

91. See *Battlefield of Merit,* 395.

92. Annual Report of the Treasurer, 1940–41, 315.

93. Annual Report of the Treasurer, 1940–41, 315.

94. $90,000 × 176 / 123 = $128,780. See McCusker, *How Much Is That*, 58.

95. 1941$ = $128,780 × (1 + .01)^{[1941–1882 = 59]} = $128,780 × 1.799 = $231,804.

96. *Battlefield of Merit*, 387–389; Bruce A. Kimball, *The Inception of Modern Professional Education: C. C. Langdell, 1826–1906* (Chapel Hill, NC, 2009), 172–173; Landis to Dickinson (January 3, 1946); HLS Faculty Meeting Minutes (November 19, 1946).

97. Harris, *Economics*, 512.

98. Annual Report of the Treasurer, 1939–40, 68–71.

99. Harris, *Economics*, 350, 353, 357.

100. Harris, *Economics*, 356–360, 374.

101. Annual Report of the Treasurer, 1938–1939, 333.

102. Griswold, Annual Report of the Dean, 1965–66, 258; Harris, *Economics*, 351, 359, 370.

103. Annual Report of the Treasurer, 1966–67, 249; McCusker, *How Much Is That*, 58.

104. This accounts for inflation and assumes a 1.0 percent growth in substantive appreciation. See William D. Ferguson, "Economics of Law Teaching," *Journal of Legal Education* 19 (1967): 440; McCusker, *How Much Is That*, 58.

105. Griswold alludes to this issue in Erwin N. Griswold to Wesley A. Sturges (November 2, 1949), Yale University Secretary's Office Records, 1899–1953, ser. 3, Yale University Library Manuscripts and Archives.

106. 10,900,000 = 2,600,000 in bequests + 2,800,000 in Ford Foundation endowment grants + 4,500,000 in capital gains transfers + 1,000,000 in appreciation.

107. Griswold, Annual Report of the Dean, 1965–66, 258.

108. Griswold, Annual Report of the Dean, 1961–62, 395–96.

109. See Alexander M. Wolf, "Harvard Law School Personnel Counts, from 1946–47 through 1967–68" (research report, HLS, 2017), on file with the authors; Wolf, "Harvard Law School Courses during Dean Erwin Griswold's Administration, 1946–47–1966–67" (research report, HLS, 2017), on file with the authors.

110. Hupper, "Educational Ambivalence," 395–447.

111. Quoted in Sutherland, *The Law at Harvard*, 324. See Robert E. Keeton, Oral History, conducted by Daniel Hamilton and Daniel R. Coquillette (November 2000–February 2001), on file with the authors; Toepfer, Oral History (March 1998).

112. Harris, *Economics*, 496.

113. Harris, *Economics*, 487.

114. Harvard Law School Committee on Planning and Development, "Report," appendix B; Erwin N. Griswold to Arthur E. Sutherland (June 2, 1958), Arthur E. Sutherland Papers, 1923–1972, HLSLib (hereafter cited as AES Papers); Griswold, Annual Report of the Dean, 1963–64, 219–221.

115. Erwin N. Griswold to Nathan M. Pusey (November 1, 1960), NMP Records. See "79th Annual Meeting of the Council of the Harvard Law School Association," *HLSB* (July 1965): 20; Keller and Keller, *Making Harvard Modern*, 254.

116. Griswold, Annual Report of the Dean, 1965–66, 256; Wolf, "Harvard Law School Courses;" Cory Wishengrad, "Changing Harvard Law School, 1966–1974" (student research paper, HLS, 1999), on file with the authors, 3–4; Griswold, *Ould Fields,* 163; Sutherland, *The Law at Harvard,* 360.

117. Griswold, Annual Report of the Dean, 1965–66, 242. See Robert Armory Jr., "Sesquicentennial Fund of the Harvard Law School," *HLSB* (November 1966): 36. The Law School's internal financial records for the period are sealed. But the records of the architect, Benjamin Thompson Associates, indicate that the cost for the faculty office building was $1,724,000, and for the classroom building, $3,722,137, making a total of $5,446,132. Kayleigh McGlynn, "Costs of Griswold Hall and Pound Hall" (student research memo, Boston College Law School, 2017), on file with the authors.

118. Bernardi, Oral History (October 2000–April 2001); Nichols, Interview (December 2010); Nichols, Interview (February 2011); Griswold, Annual Report of the Dean, 1965–66, 241.

119. Bernardi, Oral History (October 2000–April 2001); Nichols, Interview (December 2010); Nichols, Interview (February 2011); Griswold, Annual Report of the Dean, 1965–66, 241; Erwin N. Griswold to Wesley E. Bevins Jr. (June 25, 1968; February 26, 1969), ENG Papers; Bevins to Griswold (March 8, 1968, and February 21, 1969); Bevins to Griswold (June 21, 1968).

120. Bernardi, Oral History (October 2000–April 2001). See "Law School Reaches Its $15 million Mark in 4-Year Fund Drive," *Harvard Crimson* (April 21, 1970); List of donors, HLS Sesquicentennial Fund Leaflet (Summer 1970), HLSF Records; Jessica Meylor, "Harvard Law School Fundraising and Endowment Materials in Harvard University Archives" (research Report, Boston College Law School, 2010), on file with the authors.

121. Bernardi, Oral History (October 2000–April 2001); Casner, Annual Report of the Dean, 1967–68, 261; Bevins to Griswold (March 8, 1968, and February 21, 1969); Harris, *Economics,* 487.

122. "Faculty Office Building and Classroom and Administration Building for Harvard Law School," *Architectural Record* 151 (January 1972): 124–132; "Dedication of Griswold Hall: September 18, 1979," *HLSB* (Fall 1979): 23.

123. Quotation is from Bainbridge Bunting, *Harvard: An Architectural History,* ed. Margaret H. Floyd (Cambridge, MA, 1985), 246. Robert Keeton exercised great influence in chairing the Building Committee.

124. Richard D. Parker, Oral History, conducted by Daniel Coquillette and Daniel Pincus (June 2010), on file with the authors. See Kaufman, Oral History (June 1999–April 2000); Simpson, Oral History (May–September 2001); von Mehren, Oral History (July–December 2000); Brown, Oral History (August 1997); Sander, Oral History (September–December 1998); Keeton, Oral History (November 2000–February 2001); Bernstein, "A Conversation," 19–23.

125. Quotation is from Judith Richards Hope, *Pinstripes & Pearls: The Women of the Harvard Law Class of '64 Who Forged an Old Girl Network and Paved the Way for Future*

Generations (New York, 2003), 104. See Griswold, *Ould Fields,* 61–77; Toepfer, Oral History (March 1998); Vagts, Oral History (November 1999–February 2000); "Dedication of Griswold Hall: September 18, 1979," *HLSB* (Fall 1979): 45.

126. Vagts, Oral History (November 1999–February 2000).

127. John A. Harfort, "Dean Griswold Appointed Solicitor General," *Harvard Crimson* (October 2, 1967); Bernstein, "A Conversation," 19–23; Griswold, *Ould Fields,* 255–256.

128. Erwin N. Griswold to Elizabeth Wahlen (July 18, 1970), Elizabeth Wahlen Correspondence, 1946–1998, on file with the authors. See Saundra Torrey, "At 87, Erwin N. Griswold Is the Dean of Supreme Court Observers," *Washington Post* (July 5, 1991); "A Lawyer Who Spoke Up," *New York Times* (November 23, 1994).

129. "Erwin Nathaniel Griswold, 1904–1994," *HLSB* (Winter 1995): 2. Compare Torry, "At 87, Erwin N. Griswold" (July 5, 1991).

130. Bok, "Remembrance," 23–26.

131. Quotations are from, respectively, Benjamin Kaplan, Oral History, conducted by Daniel R. Coquillette (January 2006), on file with the authors; Archibald Cox, Oral History, conducted by Daniel R. Coquillette and Daniel Hamilton (November 1998), on file with the authors. See "A Great Law Dean," *Harvard Crimson* (October 2, 1967); Pusey "A Great Dean," 291; Berman, Oral History (August 1998); Toepfer, Oral History (March 1998); Albert M. Sacks, "Dedication of Griswold Hall: September 18, 1979," *HLSB* (Fall 1979): 28–30; Derek C. Bok, "Dedication of Griswold Hall: September 18, 1979," *HLSB* (Fall 1979): 26–27; Harry M. Blackburn, "In Memoriam: Erwin Nathaniel Griswold," *HLR* 108 (1995): 980–981; Clark Byse, "In Memoriam: Erwin Nathaniel Griswold," *HLR* 108 (1995): 981–985; Robert C. Clark, "In Memoriam: Erwin Nathaniel Griswold," *HLR* 108 (1995): 985–987; David R. Derusha, "The Deanship of Erwin N. Griswold: A New Look" (student research paper, HLS, 2008), on file with the authors, 5; von Mehren, Oral History (July–December 2000); Phanor Eder to Arthur Sutherland (July 20, 1967), AES Papers.

132. Bartholet, Oral History (February 1999–March 2000). See Parker, Oral History (June 2010); Laurence H. Tribe, Oral History, conducted by Daniel R. Coquillette and Andrew D. Klaber (September 2008), on file with the authors; Charles R. Nesson, quoted in David Margolick, "Legal Notes: Those against Bequest to Attack P.L.O. Aims," *New York Times* (May 23, 1982); Paul D. Carrington, Oral History, conducted by Daniel Hamilton (February 2003), on file with the authors; Mary J. Mullarkey, "Two Harvard Women: 1965 to Today," *Harvard Women's Law Journal* 27 (2004): 370–371.

133. Alan M. Dershowitz, Oral History, conducted by Daniel R. Coquillette with Andrew Klaber (October–November 2009), on file with the authors.

CHAPTER FIFTEEN

The Harvard-Yale Game, 1900–1970

Since the 1930s, comparing Harvard Law School (HLS) and Yale Law School (YLS) has become a popular pastime for alumni and legal scholars alike. According to the predominant David-and-Goliath account, giant Harvard, along with Columbia, had a seemingly insurmountable lead in prestige, influence, and wealth in 1900, while Yale straggled behind. Then, in one amazing decade between 1925 and 1935, heroic Yale slew first Columbia and then Harvard to become the premier law school in the nation. Whether and how Yale triumphed in this way have been debated extensively.

The significance of this comparison transcends the parochial competition between two law schools. Their complex relationship illuminates the strengths and vulnerabilities of two dramatically different models for university professional education. This chapter emphasizes the internal factors under the control of the schools and the universities, and focuses on the five critical decades between 1920 and the end of Erwin Griswold's deanship (1946–1967)—the period when Yale made its astonishing advance among law schools in the United States.

The analysis is divided into three parts. First, the factors commonly cited for the rise of YLS—jurisprudence, politics, size, educational policy, and admissions selectivity—are examined, primarily in the second quarter of the twentieth century. The second part explains the actual discontinuity in the relative prominence and strength of the two law schools between 1920 and 1970. Lastly, the neglected influence of finances is analyzed. Beginning in the 1890s the Yale University administration heavily subsidized YLS, in contrast to Harvard University's persistent squeezing of HLS. By 1970 the cumulative value of those subsidies to YLS reached about $27.7 million, exceeding the

$26.2 million endowment of HLS, the largest of any law school in the world.

Then YLS tacked in the opposite direction when Yale University ran into severe budget problems during the 1980s. YLS ironically invoked Harvard University's policy of "each tub on its own bottom" and persuaded the Yale University administration to grant the law school financial autonomy rather than siphon funding away from it. Hence, YLS was not dragged down by the university's financial problems in the 1980s. The rise of YLS in the twentieth century therefore relied heavily on its shrewd manipulation of Yale University's financial resources. Conversely, the difficulties of HLS largely resulted from its failure to manage its money judiciously and from Harvard University's unwillingness to support its law school financially. Yet, each university acted similarly as an institutional entrepreneur.

Jurisprudence: The Predominant Explanation for Yale's Rise

In 1904 Yale alumnus and future U.S. president William Taft and Harvard University president Charles Eliot (1869–1909) agreed that HLS had "reached the climax of success in professional education."[1] At that point YLS lagged behind other law schools at leading universities because it refused to adopt several of Harvard's key reforms: employing full-time faculty, teaching via case method, and requiring a college degree for admission. Both the YLS faculty and Yale president Arthur Hadley (1899–1921) believed that Harvard's progressive policies did not suit YLS, even though Hadley admitted "the brilliant success of the Johns Hopkins Medical School and the Harvard Law School."[2]

YLS resisted HLS policies partly out of fear that adopting them would cause Yale's enrollment to plummet, and partly due to jealousy. The leading and most resistant YLS professor in the late nineteenth and early twentieth centuries, Simeon E. Baldwin, continually "fulminated against Harvard's reputation" in his diary, as historian William LaPiana has noted.[3] Only in 1909 did YLS start requiring a college degree for admission, after which enrollment dropped by two-thirds. Case method teaching did not gain full acceptance at Yale until 1916, when Dean Thomas Swan (1916–1927) was appointed. Despite this and other changes inaugurated by Swan, Yale remained a local law school, struggled to maintain sufficient enrollment, and was forced to enroll students without a bachelor's degree until late in the 1920s.[4]

According to the predominant historical explanation, Yale's ascendance began when the school embraced legal realism and wrested leadership of that jurisprudential movement away from Columbia in the mid-1920s. Led by Professor Arthur Corbin and Dean Swan, YLS attracted such brilliant scholars as Karl Llewellyn, Leon Green, Thurman Arnold, Underhill Moore, Walter W. Cook, and William Douglas. In 1927 Robert Hutchins was appointed acting dean and then dean in 1929. Young, charismatic, and supremely self-confident, Hutchins left Yale in 1929 to become president of the University of Chicago. Although his departure cost YLS some momentum, Hutchins had led the faculty to incorporate social sciences and extralegal disciplines into the curriculum, to pursue empirical and interdisciplinary research, and to become an "honors school."[5]

Soon recognized as the jurisprudential hallmark of YLS, legal realism evolved under Dean Charles E. Clark (1929–1939) and was also called "the functional approach" and "a form of 'sociological' jurisprudence" by subsequent deans.[6] This "Yale approach" to legal study attracted talented students and powered the school's institutional ascent, it is said.[7] During the late 1920s, YLS "almost overnight . . . emerged as the most exciting and controversial law school in the country" and thus "completed its rise to pre-eminence," wrote Yale historian George Pierson.[8] "Indeed, "the Yale experiment stands out as arguably the most significant development in American legal education in the century following 1870," according to historian Laura Kalman.[9] YLS deans Hutchins, Clark, and Eugene Rostow (1955–1965) endorsed this interpretation.[10]

Yale faculty not only applauded their own school but fired off mortars at HLS, which supposedly enshrined outmoded "conceptualism"—the view that judges decide cases by relying solely on legal concepts and logical analysis, without considering social or economic forces.[11] "Harvard was the enemy," noted Kalman, and the Yale realists took "delight in mocking Harvard's stodginess in prose and verse." Felix Frankfurter (LL.B. 1906) attributed this behavior to "their inferiority complex about Harvard," in Kalman's words.[12] In any event, YLS graduates did begin to describe themselves as academically superior, as Ernest Brown (LL.B. 1931) found when working for the Agricultural Adjustment Administration (AAA) in the early 1930s.[13]

At the AAA, Brown's supervisor was YLS professor Jerome Frank, a legal realist who embraced psychological functionalism whereas most other realists emphasized the social and economic functions of law. Frank maintained that judges' decisions are shaped primarily by their own psychological purposes and traits, and therefore entitled his classic work *Law and the Modern Mind* (1930).[14] Frank's writings also became the *locus classicus* of YLS literature that condemned HLS by way of caricaturing Dean Christopher Langdell (1870–1895) as the personification of conceptualist error in jurisprudence and in legal education.[15] Relying on the authority of Frank's writings, other scholars subsequently presented the Langdellian caricature as the source of Harvard's misguided jurisprudence and educational practices. The Goliath-slaying view also found its way into the popular literature, such as the *Time* magazine issue in 1967 commemorating the 150th anniversary of the founding of HLS.[16]

Amid the social and political movements of the 1960s and 1970s, this mode of attacking HLS by associating it with the Langdellian caricature intensified. The attacks culminated in the writings of Grant Gilmore, who taught at YLS from 1946 to 1965 and again from 1973 to 1978. During his second stint on the Yale faculty, Gilmore published two noted works that skewered Langdell. Like Jerome Frank, Gilmore cited secondary sources quoting snippets of Langdell and never apparently did any original research or read a complete text written by Langdell. During the 1980s, Critical Legal scholars at HLS often assigned Gilmore's two books to their students to explain the origins of the misguided jurisprudence and educational theory of their own law school.[17]

This predominant explanation for the rise of YLS involves several doubtful points. First, it credits a particular development in legal scholarship with effecting institutional change. But such change in higher education rarely results from one factor or from one development in scholarship, even if scholars may wish it so. Second, the posited status shift was remarkably rapid and sharp, as the two law schools apparently reversed their positions within a decade. But such a status shift generally occurs over a considerable period of time. Third, the trajectories of the schools were fairly smooth and constant, with YLS continuing to rise while HLS lumbered along behind. Yet, significant institutional change usually proceeds discontinuously, not smoothly, because it depends on several factors. Finally, the interpretation is an ideational or "conceptualist" explanation for Yale's ascent, which is said to result from embracing legal realism. But it is contradictory to posit a conceptualist explanation for the triumph of an anticonceptualist critique of law and legal development. After all, Yale's own realism maintains that logical doctrine and "isms" do not shape law as much as social and economic (and psychological) forces do. Consequently, additional explanations must be considered.

Politics, Size, Educational Policy, Selectivity

The ascent of YLS has also been attributed to four additional factors: its reputation for liberal politics, its small size, its progressive educational policies, and its selective admissions process. Already in the early 1930s, Yale Law School's liberal politics were contributing to its "increase of prestige," stated President James Angell (1921–1937), because the New Deal opened opportunities "for lawyers to assist in drafting the great masses of new legislation" and interpreting "this legislation before the courts and the innumerable commissions which have been created."[18] Four years later, Yale president Charles Seymour (1937–1950) observed that public commentary sometimes "labels the Yale Law School faculty as 'radical' and implies that they, like Socrates, are corrupting the youth."[19]

For example, a series of articles in the *Chicago Tribune* in 1939 condemned the YLS faculty because "a leftist element . . . dominates the teaching of the 394 students there." Further, the *Tribune* reporter wrote, most of the faculty support "the socialistic experimentation of the Roosevelt administration" and Dean Charles Clark "has led the parade of a dozen or more members of the Yale law faculty to Washington." After reading the *Tribune*'s articles, a number of Yale alumni wrote to President Seymour to complain.[20] Nevertheless, in 1949 Dean Wesley A. Sturges (1946–1954) maintained that the continuing emphasis "on the socio-economic background of the law, together with a willingness to defend this emphasis against conservatism and virulent criticism," was a main attraction of YLS.[21]

Yale's left-wing reputation and claim to academic superiority were so well known by the early 1950s that HLS dean Erwin Griswold and YLS Law dean Sturges joked about them amid the crisis of McCarthyism and the controversy over Jonathan and David Lubell. Only a day or two after the *Harvard Law Review* board of editors voted against admitting Jonathan Lubell, Griswold wrote to Sturges, "I am arranging for the transfer of David and Jonathan Lubell to the Yale Law School. It is obvious that that is the place where they should be, and that they will find things more congenial there than they are here. Under these circumstances, I am sure that you would not stand in the way."[22] Sturges replied, "Yale might . . . have taken a genuine interest in the enrollees in the Harvard Law School to whom you refer and scouted them seriously. As I get the report, however, it would not be probable that they would qualify for admission to Yale much beyond the sophomore year in college. Accordingly, it will be necessary for us . . . to leave them *in nubibus* until you have given them your LL.B."[23]

Joking aside, the controversy over the Lubells is a reminder that HLS also came under attack during the two Red Scares, in the 1920s and the 1950s. In between, the leading roles of Frankfurter, Landis, and their associates in the New Deal gave HLS a left-wing reputation.[24] When the *Chicago Tribune* attacked YLS in 1939, the newspaper included HLS among "the American Marxists" and ran the cautionary headline "Radical Doctrine Taught In Law Schools . . . Harvard, Yale." In fact, Yale alumni wrote

"Another Color on the Campus," Chicago Daily Tribune, January 21, 1939.

to President Seymour in 1939, complaining that YLS was drifting leftward—toward HLS.[25]

It was during Dean Griswold's tenure at HLS, especially in the 1960s, that Yale's reputation for social and political activism made it distinctive and more attractive than Harvard to sympathetic applicants. As Elizabeth Bartholet (LL.B. 1965) recalled, "In the 1960s, Yale was thought of as . . . a nurturing environment for lawyers" who were "particularly interested in public policy, social justice, . . . Harvard didn't take it seriously."[26] YLS dean Anthony T. Kronman (1994–2004) maintained that the school's "commitment to public service and the strong activist streak . . . more often than not . . . in left liberal causes" is one of the "characteristics of the school that make it special."[27]

Another factor said to elevate YLS over both Columbia and Harvard was its small size. During the late 1920s and 1930s, Dean Clark reported that students preferred Yale's small enrollment, which ranged between 290 and 350.[28] In 1949 Dean Sturges considered the small size and low student-faculty ratio to be "the basic difference between Harvard and Yale."[29] After visiting YLS in 1947, editors of the *Harvard Law School Record* agreed, and this difference continued to attract students in subsequent decades.[30]

In addition, Yale's educational policies were said to propel the law school's ascent. Small enrollment does not necessarily entail small classes or a low student-faculty ratio. But YLS adopted those attributes because they provide "a much closer contact and relationship between the student and [the] faculty," said Sturges.[31] "Through small informal classes . . . Yale is on the way to doing more for its students than Harvard," commented a neutral observer at Princeton in 1934.[32] Other "new ideas of legal education" were also cited by many students in the early 1930s as their reason for applying to Yale, according to Dean Clark.[33] These included the freedom to select courses during the first year and the broad range of courses both on legal and extralegal subjects, such as economics, history, psychiatry, statistics, business, and "interdisciplinary work."[34] YLS also had "new ideas" about grading, and by 1955 was employing "a four-category grading system—excellent, good, satisfactory, and failure."[35]

Finally, the ascent of YLS was attributed to its adoption of selective admissions, the new approach to college admissions arising early in the 1920s. In a news release in June 1926, President Angell announced the law school's "adoption of a policy of limiting numbers and confining its efforts to training superior students," with the intention of "giving its entire attention to the intensive training of a few men of the highest quality."[36] YLS thus aimed "toward becoming a place for a small and highly selected group of students," remarked

Dean Hutchins in 1927.[37] While HLS clung to the traditional approach of establishing a threshold that entitled qualified applicants to admission and then flunking out those who failed, Yale became the first law school in the country to adopt highly selective admissions.[38]

In the 1880s HLS dean Langdell and Harvard president Eliot had worried that if HLS raised its academic standards, the school might not attract enough strong students to fill its classrooms. Yale leaders in the late 1920s had the same concern, as President Angell noted in the 1926 news release.[39] But by 1930 the gamble was paying off, and YLS deans began highlighting the number of applicants refused admission and claiming, therefore, that their students were the best. In 1930 Dean Clark affirmed that "Yale is now dedicated to the better training of the few," and in 1935 "that a number of applicants who would have been welcomed two years ago were refused admission."[40] President Angell then inferred that "its rigid selective system of admission" meant that YLS "has been able to choose from among an unusually choice group of candidates." YLS professor Arthur Corbin went further, claiming that "for ability and intellectual quality, our student body cannot be matched in the United States," and President Seymour quoted that assertion in 1939.[41]

In 1950 Dean Sturges implied in the opening lines of his annual report that the key measure of quality was the proportion of applicants a law school denied, and Yale's rejection rate was "the highest of any law school."[42] In 1965 Dean Rostow likewise maintained in his annual report, "By all the usual criteria of judgment . . . the class which entered the School in the fall of 1964 was noticeably superior to any previous class, and to the entering class in any other School."[43]

Weak Validation of "Superior" Students

The new policy of selective admissions thus helped to advance Yale's reputation beginning in the late 1920s, as YLS deans cited two kinds of evidence to prove the superior quality of their student body. On the one hand, "the improvement of the student body under the selective process" was referenced by Hutchins in 1929 and Clark in 1935.[44] But such reports showed the strengthening of Yale's own student body over time, not that it was "noticeably superior to . . . any other School." On the other hand, YLS deans emphasized the growing number and proportion of rejected applicants, and reasoned that because they were excluding a higher proportion of their applicants than "any other school," their entering class had the best students. Later historians accepted that reasoning as validation of Yale's "rise to pre-eminence."[45] But did the highest proportion of rejected applicants necessarily mean the highest quality of admittees?

Yale's new selective standard of admission in 1926 approximated the admissions threshold Harvard had instituted in 1913.[46] Of the approximately 950 colleges, universities, and independent professional schools in the nation at the time, HLS and YLS each maintained a list of about 250 institutions that they considered the top tier. Harvard admitted all graduates of colleges on that list. Yale required that such graduates have a C average in order to be admitted, so Yale had a higher standard in this respect. Applicants who had graduated from the 700 institutions not in the top tier needed to rank in the upper third of their class to be admitted to YLS. HLS applied this same standard only if an applicant's college appeared on a second list of about 200 second-tier colleges. If an applicant had graduated from one of the other 500 colleges, universities, or independent professional schools that did not appear on the two lists, then the applicant had to write to HLS for special consideration. Thus, Harvard apparently had a higher standard than Yale with respect to these 500 institutions.[47]

Furthermore, after Yale announced its selectivity standard in 1926, the Harvard faculty in 1927 revised the admissions threshold for applicants from the 250 first-tier colleges, who were then required to rank in the upper three-quarters of the class. This was roughly equivalent to Yale's C-average standard at the time. In 1928 Harvard raised its admission threshold for second-tier colleges from ranking in the top third to ranking in the top quarter of the class.[48] Consequently, Harvard's overall announced threshold in 1928 was actually higher than Yale's selective standard of 1926.

In addition, though employing a threshold rather than selectivity, Harvard still rejected applicants in two additional ways. First, it stopped admitting applicants when it reached its enrollment capacity, notwithstanding the wishes of Dean Roscoe Pound (1916–1936) to accept all of the applicants. Indeed, Pound virtually apologized for rejecting qualified applicants, at the same time that Yale was touting its rejections.[49] Thus, the two schools were operating on different admissions systems with different rationales.

But the outcome was similar at both schools. For example, according to its Faculty Committee on Curriculum, HLS in 1927 and 1932 received some 1,000 applications and had to reject nearly 30 percent to limit its entering class to about 700, since almost every admitted applicant enrolled. Furthermore, about 40 percent, or 280, of those initial enrollees never graduated. Consequently, in 1927 and in 1932, about 420, or 42 percent, of the original HLS applicant pool of 1,000 graduated. By comparison, the Harvard Committee reported that, in 1932, YLS admitted about 34 percent of its applicants while limiting its entering class to about 100, almost of all whom graduated.[50]

Moreover, Harvard effectively denied admission by discouraging applicants through its announced policy barring admission to those who did not meet the threshold. An institution employing selective admissions, like YLS, determined admissions through a somewhat variable and opaque process, which encouraged students to apply. In fact, selective institutions like to encourage applications, so they can reject more and extoll their selectivity, as did YLS.

In sum, neither Yale deans nor later historians provided salient data comparing the academic quality of the students enrolling at YLS and HLS in the early 1930s, even while affirming that, in the early 1930s, "the common view was that Yale was getting the best students" and that, over the next two decades, "more than a third of Harvard Law School's best admittees did not accept, and . . . for the most part, they went to New Haven." But this "common view" relied heavily on the public pronouncements of YLS leaders about the proportion of applicants that their law school rejected.[51]

Furthermore, the judgment about "best students" in the 1930s is anachronistic because it presumes both competition among undergraduates for admission to law school and standardized measures of academic quality, such as the LSAT. Both the academic competition and the standardized measures started only in the 1950s. For example, Archibald Cox (LL.B. 1937) entered HLS in 1934 after a relaxed tour through Harvard College, where he played squash and received "Gentleman C's." Cox might not even have made the YLS admissions cutoff, although YLS was eager to enroll as many Harvard College graduates as it could. But Cox, future solicitor general and distinguished professor, had a brilliant legal mind and career. Conversely, Kingman Brewster Jr. graduated from Yale College in 1941. During the period when YLS was claiming to be most selective, Brewster chose to attend HLS, earned the LL.B. in 1948, and became president of Yale University in 1963. The preferences of the "best" undergraduates prior to 1950 are therefore difficult to ascertain because competition for admission to a leading law school through 1950 did not resemble what it became in the 1960s.[52]

Graduates of Eleven Selective Colleges

Enrollment data of the graduates of eleven selective colleges—Harvard, Yale, Brown, Columbia, Cornell, Dartmouth, Pennsylvania, Princeton, Amherst, Williams, and Wesleyan—offers insight into the preferences of stronger students for HLS or YLS. No one disputes that HLS was preferred over other law schools in 1926, so the enrollment patterns of these graduates who attended either HLS or YLS during the subsequent decade indicate whether and how their preferences changed during the critical period between 1926 and 1935.

The alumni of Harvard and Yale must be analyzed separately from those of the other nine colleges, because the choices of these students were naturally skewed by their ties to their alma mater. One would expect a high proportion of Harvard undergraduates to enroll at HLS and a high proportion of Yale undergraduates to go to YLS. Furthermore, both law schools regarded the enrollment of alumni of their own universities as an important index of their appeal, so each law school encouraged graduates of its university to remain at their alma mater for legal study.[53] Hence, the proportion of Harvard and Yale B.A.s who left their alma mater to enroll at the law school of the other university indicates the relative attraction of each law school

Between 1926 and 1935, only about 2 percent of Harvard University graduates who enrolled in either law school went to YLS, as shown in Figure 15.1. Conversely, at least 32 percent of Yale graduates who enrolled in either law school attended HLS. That percentage actually rose to 42 percent by 1932–33, while YLS deans were proclaiming their greater attractiveness and selectivity. Overall, at least one- third of Yale alumni left New Haven to attend law school in Cambridge, whereas only 2 percent of Harvard alumni made the opposite move. This pattern did not result from differences in selectivity, because the admission standards of HLS and YLS were very similar. Furthermore, both law schools were eager to enroll as many Harvard and Yale alumni as possible, and almost never denied them admission, so far as extant records reveal.

Similarly, a significant comparison can be made by calculating the enrollment of graduates from the nine other selective colleges—Brown, Columbia, Cornell, Dartmouth, Pennsylvania, Princeton, Amherst, Williams, and Wesleyan—whose choice of either HLS or YLS was not influenced by ties with their alma mater. Out of the population of those graduates who attended either of these two law schools, how many went to HLS, and how many to YLS? Here again, both law schools wished to maximize their enrollment of gradu-

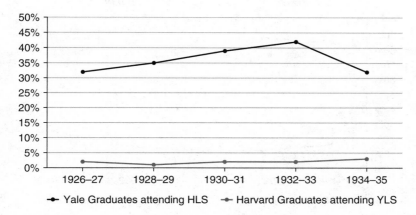

Figure 15.1. Percentage of Harvard Graduates enrolling in Yale Law School (YLS) and Yale Graduates enrolling in Harvard Law School (HLS) out of those enrolling at either law school, 1926–1935. Note: Graduates are categorized by their most recent degree received prior to enrolling in law school. Data Source: Appendix F.

ates from these institutions, so differences in selectivity and size are not germane to this analysis.[54]

Between 1926 and 1935, those graduates of these nine colleges predominantly enrolled in HLS (see Figure 15.2). Between 1926–27 and 1932–33 the proportion going to Cambridge for law school held fairly steady at about 85 percent. The fraction then fell to 75 percent in 1934–35, and the number going to New Haven rose commensurately. This small shift may be significant because it corresponds with a number of other developments indicating that Yale's exuberant statements about its selectivity were shaping the perception of leaders at these nine colleges.

In June 1934, President James Conant (1933–1953) told the HLS Committee on Curriculum that Yale and Columbia Law Schools had adopted selective admission standards, to their apparent advantage. The HLS committee then solicited information from Yale and Columbia about their admissions process, and at the same time discovered that Dean Pound had permitted exceptions to the 1928 HLS admissions policy, allowing applicants with records below the threshold to enroll.[55] Later in 1934, Conant wrote to Princeton president Harold W. Dodds, asking for a confidential, third-party comparison of HLS with other leading law schools.[56] Dodds responded by sending to Conant the evaluation of William S. Carpenter, the head of Princeton's Department of Politics.

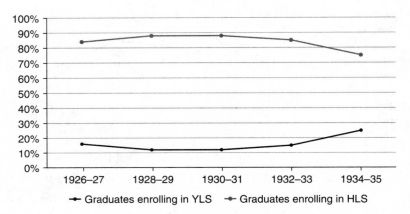

Figure 15.2. Percentage of Graduates of Nine Selective Colleges enrolling in Yale Law School (YLS) or Harvard Law School (HLS) out of those enrolling at either law school, 1926–1935. Note: Graduates are categorized by their most recent degree received prior to enrolling in law school. The nine selective colleges are Princeton, Dartmouth, Brown, Columbia, Cornell, Pennsylvania, Amherst, Williams, and Wesleyan. Data Source: Appendix F.

Carpenter wrote that as of 1930 there was "no question of the superiority of the Harvard Law School over the schools at Yale and Columbia. At that time the Yale Law School graduates were not doing so well in the bar exam." But since 1930, "there has been a great improvement in the Yale Law School," Carter stated. "The enormous prestige of the Harvard Law School continues to attract our best students. . . . Most of our students prefer Harvard to Yale but an increasing number are going to the latter place."[57]

Also in 1934, a group of HLS students issued an evaluation of their school, which compiled the opinions of "some eighty men of all types and classes." A number of these students recommended that HLS follow YLS and admit a "smaller and more selected group of men . . . by means of entrance requirements or / and aptitude tests." At HLS, "not enough care has been exercised in selecting the right students from the outset—the policy of letting everyone come, and let only the fit survive is a cumbersome, inefficient, and inhumane one."[58]

Finally, in the fall of 1936, HLS Acting Dean Edmund Morgan (LL.B. 1905) wrote to President Conant that academic leaders at Amherst, Dartmouth, "and other New England colleges" were starting to recommend "the Yale Law School to [their] best men, and the Harvard Law School to the mediocre."[59] During the 1920s, after these colleges adopted selective admissions, their leaders began to view the number of excluded applicants as a significant new standard of academic quality. When Yale deans and presidents asserted that YLS was excluding more applicants than any other law school and therefore had the best students, this reasoning made perfect sense to the leaders of selective colleges, even without data comparing the academic quality of the student bodies.

All this testimony is consistent with the 1934–35 shift in enrollment of graduates of the nine selective northeastern colleges, exhibited in Figure 15.1 above. That decline from 85 to 75 percent attending HLS apparently indicated that "the enormous prestige of the Harvard Law School" was beginning to lose its luster by the year 1934–35. Even so, the trend was mixed. In September 1935, YLS Dean Clark reported internally that his school had "328 formal applications this year as compared with 322 last year, 344 in 1933, and 289 in 1932. . . . The colleges represented in the entering class are: Yale sixty-eight . . . ; Dartmouth twelve; Princeton eleven; Amherst four; Harvard three."[60]

In any event, the mounting challenge of YLS was clear. Due to the failure to adopt selective admissions, "the reputation of [HLS] as the leader in its class is in danger," wrote Acting Dean Morgan to President Conant. "By far the most important question confronting the Law School at present is that of raising the standards of admission."[61] Furthermore, Morgan believed that the YLS publicity was key. "The remedy . . . lies in the adoption and publication of advanced standards of admission," he wrote. "Let it be known that our men are a selected group, chosen from those who have made good records in college," and "the question of numbers and smaller classes will, I believe, become of much less importance."[62] Yet even while appreciating the tactical importance of publicity, Morgan was unaware of the expediency that led YLS to adopt selective admissions in the first place.

Small Size and Admissions Selectivity

To Dean Erwin Griswold, large enrollment was part of the identity of HLS. He cited educational rationales for the school's big size, but those justifications were really *ex post facto* (though he denied it).[63] HLS expanded haphazardly and then out of expedience—not due to a deliberate analysis of educational benefits. Size also became part of the identity of YLS. Starting in 1925, Yale leaders described their preference for a small school as the result of deliberately weighing educational benefits. "The School definitely set its face toward becoming a place for a small and highly selected group of students.

We must make sure that our selection is based on intellectual and not on financial considerations," wrote Dean Hutchins in 1927.[64] But Yale's decision to remain small was no less expedient, though shrewder and more deliberate, than Harvard's process of growing large.

In about 1910 YLS began to adopt the academic reforms of Harvard and Columbia, including requiring a college degree for admission starting in 1909 and adopting case method teaching in 1916. Yale then began to consider how to match Harvard and Columbia in quality, prestige, and influence. The problem was that YLS was small and local, and situated in New Haven with a population of about 130,000, about halfway between two major financial centers—Boston, with nearly 800,000 residents, and New York City, with 5.5 million residents—each with its own eminent university.[65]

This location hindered the development of Yale University, as Yale historian Brooks Kelley noted. But the problem for YLS was magnified because the school was "not in a position to compete effectively with the great law schools to the east and the west," Dean Kronman later remarked. Harvard and Columbia "were much larger and stronger than us. How could Yale effectively compete with them?" Yale could not simply replicate those schools and expect to draw away talented students.[66]

The challenge, then, was to identify a singular quality that would attract strong students to Yale. To this end, the university treasurer extolled New Haven's ambience as early as 1913. He reported that Yale alumni cite "the advantages possessed by Yale over Harvard and Columbia because of the greater temptations in Boston and New York."[67] But fewer temptations was not a promising enticement for law students. Quite the opposite. Over the next sixty years, many students considering whether to attend Harvard or Yale would maintain, with Elizabeth Bartholet and Arthur von Mehren (LL.B. 1945), that Cambridge "is a better place to live."[68]

Instead, size emerged as a salutary distinction when the number of Yale's entering class suddenly jumped from 78 to 131 between September 1923 and September 1924. YLS could no longer fit into its building, Hendrie Hall, and was forced to seek new accommodations.[69] Fortunately, construction funds were available because Yale University had received an enormous gift of some $15 million in 1918, so YLS dean Swan and his colleagues drew up a proposal for a new law building during the academic year 1924–25. This proposal required that they determine "the size of the student body" and weigh "the chief arguments for a large school" and "a small school." Such deliberations never occurred under Deans Pound or Griswold in Cambridge. On

July 1, 1925, Swan and his colleagues submitted their proposal to the Yale University administration for a new complex of buildings for YLS.[70]

The proposal sided with "a small school," and stated that "the chief arguments" were educational in nature. But strategic and financial considerations carried great weight, as the document stated:

> In 1924–25 Harvard Law School had a registration of 1202, Columbia 655, and Yale 404. . . . At the present time our faculty will be disposed to limit our school to 500 students . . . for two reasons. . . . *Our school should be materially smaller than Columbia if we are to get the advertising value of a limited school.* Further, if the second-year class is substantially larger than 150 it should be divided into sections. We wish to keep the numbers small enough to avoid this necessity.[71]

Thus, Swan and his colleagues sought to make YLS distinctive by virtue of its small enrollment. "The law school learned very early on to make a virtue out of necessity and, beginning at a competitive disadvantage, found a way of turning it into a competitive advantage," Dean Kronman later observed.[72]

Significantly, the original proposal did not envision selective admissions or low attrition. As of July 1925, YLS was projecting an enrollment capped at 500. But it was also planning to follow the attrition strategy of HLS because the proposal envisioned enrollment of 225 in the first year, then 33 percent attrition resulting in enrollment of 150 in the second year, and then 17 percent attrition for an enrollment of 125 in the third year.[73] The overall enrollment would be 500, but only 56 percent of the entering class would graduate. This was attrition that even Spartan HLS could not match. As of July 1925, YLS was evidently planning to distinguish itself from HLS by enrolling only 500 students and wielding the intellectual sword even more ruthlessly!

Yale leaders subsequently maintained that YLS adopted small size and selective admissions concurrently as a package of reforms justified by educational benefits and principles.[74] But the documentary record indicates that the decision unfolded like this: first, the recognition that Yale must distinguish itself from Harvard and Columbia in order to compete for students; second, the decision to cap enrollment in order to fit within the smaller market of New Haven and accrue "the advertising value of a limited school"; and third, the adoption of selective admissions to garner prestige by excluding a high number of applicants and to enhance collegiality by nearly eliminating attrition.

This third step occurred during discussions with the university administration in 1926, and surely stemmed from the example of selective admissions that undergraduate colleges, including Yale College, had initiated in 1920. Selective admissions would make YLS even more distinctive. This policy was under consideration when President Angell announced publicly on June 1926 the law school's "adoption of a policy of limiting numbers and confining its efforts to training superior students." But it was not until the faculty voted in December 1926 to cap first-year enrollment at about 100 that the fateful step was taken to institute selective admissions and virtually eliminate attrition.[75]

At that point Dean Swan observed the novelty and formative nature of the new policy: "So far as is known no American law school has limited its numbers, and the technique of selecting a limited number so that the best of the applicants shall be accepted has yet to be developed. Some experiments along this line are to be made next year."[76] In 1927 YLS began developing its selection procedures to admit a small select class, a step that would make the school distinctive and competitive with Columbia and Harvard.

Yale's strategy was remarkably shrewd and timely, hitting HLS at its weakest points. By 1934 it was widely acknowledged that YLS had surpassed Columbia in stature, and Figure 15.1 suggests that YLS was beginning to attract a larger fraction of graduates from selective northeastern colleges, with the exception of Harvard College and Yale College. YLS certainly denied admission to a higher proportion of applicants than any other law school in the country and claimed greater selectivity due to that. But evidence as to where the "best" students went, and even what "best" meant in this pre-LSAT era of the Gentleman C, was not presented.

Strictures at Yale University, 1910–1960

Having addressed the factors commonly cited for Yale's ascension, the discussion now turns to the actual ebb and flow of the relative prominence and strength of HLS and YLS between 1920 and 1967. During the first two-thirds of the twentieth century, Harvard University often beggared its law school. Meanwhile, YLS was impeded by the difficulties experienced by its university. As a result, the fortunes of the two schools were discontinuous.

After trailing behind through 1925, YLS made a breathtaking advance between 1925 and 1935. Meanwhile, HLS stagnated between 1929 and 1946 during the last years of Pound's deanship and the roller coaster of the Landis deanship. In the mid-1930s, YLS thus had the opportunity to eclipse

HLS, but was impeded by financial and academic strictures at Yale University, described below. Those impediments persisted through the late 1950s, whereas HLS awoke in 1946 and made enormous progress under Griswold through the mid-1960s. Meanwhile, in 1955 YLS began advancing under Dean Rostow and continued to do so through 1965, at which point HLS began slowing down once again. The following sections explain the difficulties at Yale University that impeded YLS, and the detriments and benefits that obtained at HLS.

In the early 1910s YLS began trying to catch Columbia and Harvard law schools, but was held back because Yale University lagged behind its peers due to its disaggregated structure. Prior to 1919 the university was divided into four different units and faculties—one each for the freshman year, Yale College, Sheffield Scientific School, and the graduate school—all with different loyalties, statutes, and, in some cases, trustees. In 1919–20, Yale University was entirely reorganized and consolidated, and in 1921 a non-alumnus (James Angell) was appointed as president for the first time in order to carry out the unifying reforms and to recruit active scholars to strengthen the Yale faculty. Only at that point did Yale University start competing intensively with the other leading research universities of Harvard, Columbia, and Chicago.[77]

Then during the 1920s, extraordinary good fortune befell Yale University. Over that decade, Yale received more financial support in gifts and grants than any other university in the nation, and by 1930 Yale's endowment had surpassed Columbia's to become the second largest in the country, behind only Harvard's.[78] This beneficence stemmed primarily from three sources. One was a fundraising drive in 1927 and 1928 that netted over $21 million. Another was a pledge from Edward S. Harkness of nearly $16 million in 1929 to build eight residential quadrangles for Yale College. The third was bequeathed in 1918 by John W. Sterling, who left his entire fortune of $15 million to Yale. At the time, it may have been "the largest, single gift ever made to a university," reported the *New York Times*. Fortunately, spending Sterling's gift was delayed during the 1920s, so it grew in value to some $39 million by 1930. Unfortunately, the delay resulted from strictures of the bequest, which directly impacted YLS.[79]

Sterling made his bequest not directly to Yale University, but to a separate trust, and his will gave the small group of trustees complete authority and freedom to dispense the money for the benefit of Yale. Also, the trustees felt bound by Sterling's stated preference for beautiful buildings, but the bequest did not provide for the purchase of land or for the expenses of operating or maintaining the new buildings, and the Sterling trustees refused to subsidize those expenses. Notwithstanding its relatively large endowment, Yale was already facing financial problems in 1918, and simply planning for new buildings stretched its resources even thinner. Yale balked at accepting any more buildings, and the university administrators spent the 1920s delicately negotiating with the Sterling trustees as to how the bequest could best be used. Ultimately, nearly two-thirds of the entire gift was spent on buildings, and the university was forced to run annual deficits to support the construction.[80]

The overall result was that Yale University lost an important opportunity to increase its endowment significantly, even to become the national leader. Yale's endowment grew by a smaller amount ($58.9 million) than did Harvard's endowment ($63.5 million) during the 1920s, even though Yale University received more voluntary support ($91 million) than did Harvard University ($83 million) during the same period. Then, in the early 1930s, the new Harkness residential quadrangles and various Sterling buildings burdened Yale with operating and maintenance costs that weakened it financially as the Depression deepened. The university therefore began to struggle financially. Endowment income declined more than 20 percent, and gifts to the Yale alumni fund fell by 85 percent. The university started cutting expenses in 1931, and enrollment dropped by almost 1,000 in four years. In 1933, pressed for tuition revenue, Yale College admitted over 100 applicants with inferior qualifications, and more than one-third of those soon flunked out.[81]

These problems affected YLS, which lost a major opportunity to vastly increase its endowment. In response to Dean Swan's 1925 proposal, the Yale University administration recommended and the Sterling trust approved a grant of $5 million to the law school. But difficulties quickly arose. Dean Hutchins and President Angell wanted to locate the YLS complex near the medical school and to direct nearly half of the grant into the YLS endowment. Instead, the Sterling trustees required YLS to build an expensive, ornate Gothic structure far from the medical school, and the construction cost ballooned to $4 million.[82]

As the prospect of the Sterling trust making a major grant to the endowment ebbed in the late 1920s, YLS pursued another path to solicit gifts. In conjunction with the university endowment drive of 1927–28, YLS ran a campaign to celebrate its centennial. But it netted only about $456,000—merely 2 percent of the university's total receipts and one-sixth of the medical school's total. Fortunately, this amount was supplemented in 1928 by a bequest from Simeon Baldwin of more than $500,000, and, in 1929, another grant from the Sterling trustees of $500,000 to endow fellowships and a professorship.

Sterling Law Building, Yale Law School. Jack Devlin.
Courtesy of Yale University.

These donations therefore added considerably to the endowment of YLS in the early 1930s.[83]

But the university's financial problems began to weigh down YLS just as it started seriously challenging Harvard's preeminence. In 1932 Dean Clark reported that the university's depression-driven stringency had forced him to make cuts throughout the budget. In addition, President Angell and the Yale Corporation wanted to maintain a uniform salary scale across the university. Due to the combined stringency and uniformity, YLS began to lose its leading realist faculty to other schools that paid higher salaries, and the YLS intellectual signature faded between 1933 and 1939.[84]

Beyond Yale University's lost opportunity to increase its academic resources from the abundant philanthropy in the 1920s and then its budgetary cutbacks during the Depression, YLS was hampered by the university's academic strictures. Yale held back from participating in the new research economy of higher education that emerged in the first quarter of the twentieth century. In 1924 the first authoritative ranking of academic departments appeared in American higher education. Of the top two departments in the twenty fields examined, thirty-four of the forty spots were occupied by Harvard, Chicago, and Columbia.

Yale then continued to lag behind in the second quarter of the twentieth century. Through 1950, the highest ranks of the most powerful departments "were almost monopolized by Harvard, Chicago, and Columbia."[85]

Thus, the issue was not only raising money, but also what a university did with it. The Sterling trust forced Yale University to spend a great deal on the construction and maintenance of expensive buildings. Also, entrenched traditionalists on the Yale College faculty stymied President Angell's efforts to advance research. His successor, Charles Seymour, was a noted historian and proponent of research. But the natural sciences at Yale languished under both Angell and Seymour in the 1920s, 1930s, and 1940s—a time when those fields became the engine of research universities. Yale advanced in the social sciences, but it was harder to validate new findings in those areas or to attract as much financial support.[86]

By 1946, Yale had developed many top-ranked departments, according to a survey conducted by the Association of American Universities. But these were generally small and minor participants in the postwar research economy: anthropology, art, geology, history, German, linguistics, Oriental Studies, philosophy, and physiology. Yale's four lowest-ranked departments were chemistry, physics, economics, and sociology. The former two natural sciences would be the biggest recipients of postwar government research dollars (outside of medicine), while the latter two social sciences would receive the most support from the Ford Foundation, the largest funder of university research outside of the natural sciences.[87]

Nevertheless, in 1950 Yale still possessed the second largest university endowment in the nation, so it had the reputation and resources to advance itself significantly as a research university. But the next president, A. Whitney Griswold (1950–1963), did not exploit the opportunity and also held back YLS.[88] He believed "that all Yale faculty should concentrate on 'pure' scholarship and teaching uncontaminated by contact with living issues in society," in the words of Yale historian Gaddis Smith. By the same token, President Griswold opposed "organized research"—conducted by teams of scholars—or "programmed research," which addressed subjects and questions specified by funders. Instead, he esteemed the solitary scholar working on a subject of personal interest without regard for application.[89] This approach was virtually incompatible with empirical social scientific research that nourished the "Yale Approach" at YLS.

During the 1950s, President Griswold did build up Yale's scientific facilities, but his conception of research led many of Yale's natural scientists to leave and discouraged others from coming to New Haven. Also, due to his resistance, the university failed to advance in the social sciences or even "to keep pace with Chicago and Columbia, which, given Yale's resources, would have been a reasonable expectation," according to historian Roger Geiger.[90] President Griswold also opposed nontraditional and applied academic fields. He closed the Education Department at Yale and refused to found a business school, both of which would have provided sites and opportunities for funded social scientific research.[91]

The progress of YLS therefore continued to slow under President Griswold because his approach to research did not resonate with the law school's academic commitments. Certainly, some legal scholars embraced President Griswold's view of research, including HLS professor Lon Fuller, as discussed in Chapter 13. But the realist perspective of YLS was informed by "organized," "programmed," applied research that President Griswold did not value.

In addition, President Griswold held YLS back by refusing to make faculty salaries competitive with its peer institutions. "Neither the average salary at the Yale Law School, nor the highest salary paid to its outstanding men, is . . . near the top for law schools in this age of rapid and competitive progress among American universities," stated Dean Rostow in 1962 at the end of President Griswold's tenure. "Yale ranks no higher than seventh among the reporting law schools."[92] Change did not begin until 1961, when Kingman Brewster was recruited from the HLS faculty to serve as provost at Yale and then to succeed Griswold as president in 1963.[93]

HLS Awakens, 1946–1955

In the 1940s the collapse of enrollment during World War II, followed by the influx of veterans under the G.I. Bill, made standardizing and raising admissions standards impossible. YLS deans continued to tout its "tight admissions policy," and in 1950 Dean Sturges announced that its "ratio of roughly six applicants for each place is . . . the highest of any law school."[94] But such data still did not prove that the "best students" attended or preferred YLS. Graduating from Beloit College in 1940, Louis Toepfer (LL.B. 1947) was admitted to both YLS and HLS and chose the latter, and in 1942 Arthur von Mehren found "there was absolutely no difficulty getting admitted" to any top law school for a graduate from a selective college.[95] After graduating from the University of Texas in 1952, Paul Carrington (LL.B. 1955) selected HLS, though he was also admitted to Yale, Columbia, and Michigan.[96]

Meanwhile, YLS was struggling to remain small. The influx of veterans on the G.I. Bill inflated the LL.B. enrollment to about 500, up from 350 before the war. Alumni began to complain, and Sturges noted regretfully "our lack of progress" in cutting back to the prewar enrollment.[97] The problem was "financial considerations," said Sturges. YLS could not afford to lose tuition revenue by lowering enrollment or to raise costs by resuming the prewar faculty-student ratio. "Inflation, our high rate of tuition, and the exhaustion of the G.I. funds explain in most part our increasing need," Sturges wrote in 1951.[98] As the financial vise tightened, YLS lost a third of its faculty in the mid 1950s. The total number dropped to seventeen, and the student-faculty ratio rose sharply. The illness and death of Dean Sturges and the interim status in 1954–55 of Dean Harry Shulman (Harvard LL.B. 1926, S.J.D. 1927) contributed to the regression. Through it all, some YLS faculty, such as Jerome Frank and Fred Rodell, continued to lob grenades at Langdell and HLS, causing some resentment there.[99]

In Cambridge, Dean Griswold's new policy of selective admissions was beginning to pay off. In the fall of 1955, Toepfer, the new admissions director, prepared a confidential report on admissions selectivity at Harvard, Yale, and Columbia. Toepfer's data was so rare and revealing that Griswold forwarded the report to President Nathan Pusey and asked him to keep it confidential. The data is conveyed in Table 15.1, which sorts the applicant pools of the three schools according to their LSAT scores. In each category, Harvard's entering class in 1955 was distinctly stronger in terms of LSAT scores than the entering classes of either Yale or Columbia. This was true on both an aggregate and a proportional basis.

About 6 percent of all those taking the LSAT nationally scored above 650. Of that group, most of those who applied to either YLS or HLS likely applied to both schools. Therefore, Dean Griswold maintained, the higher percentage yield of those applicants at HLS likely indicated that YLS lost more top students to HLS than vice versa.[100] Stated another way, Harvard had four times as many first-year students who scored 650 or higher than did Yale, while Harvard's class was about three times as large as Yale's. On either an aggregate or a proportional basis, Harvard had more of the highest-scoring first-year students in 1955, even though Yale was turning down "roughly six applicants for each place."[101]

Griswold therefore concluded, "Despite the attractiveness of Yale because of its smaller size and supposed closer relations between faculty and students, a much higher proportion of the top students admitted here actually come and study here than is true at Yale. . . . Although we do lose some students to

Table 15.1 Admissions Selectivity in Terms of LSAT Scores for the Classes Entering September 1955 at Harvard, Yale, and Columbia Law Schools (perfect score was 800)

Applicants	Harvard	Yale	Columbia
Applicants with LSAT scores at or above 700			
Number of applicants	44	17	ca. 16
Number who enrolled	28	5	4
Percent who enrolled	64%	29%	ca. 25%
Percent of entering class	6%	3%	1%
Applicants with LSAT scores at or above 650[a]			
Number of applicants	183	67	85
Number who enrolled	114	28	28
Percent who enrolled	62%	42%	33%
Percent of entering class	25%	18%	9%
Enrollees with LSAT scores below 500			
Number in entering class	19	8	39
Percent of entering class	4%	5%	13%

Data source: Erwin N. Griswold to Nathan M. Pusey (December 1, 1955), NMP Records.

Note: All three schools accepted virtually all applicants with LSAT scores above 650, leaving only the question of whether the applicants chose to enroll.

a. This category includes the above numbers of "Applicants with LSAT scores at or above 700."

Yale, it is clear that they lose not only more students to us, but also a much higher proportion of those with higher bracket scores on the LSAT." Conversely, among those who scored lowest on the LSAT (below 500), HLS had a lower percentage (4 percent) than either Yale (5 percent) or Columbia (13 percent). With respect to the total number of admitted applicants, Harvard had a higher yield of enrollees (61 percent) than either Yale (42 percent) or Columbia (45 percent).[102] Whether one looked across the entering class or at the top or the bottom, in terms of LSAT scores, HLS had a significantly stronger enrollment than Yale or Columbia in September 1955. By way of confirmation, two years later University of Wisconsin legal historian J. Willard Hurst (LL.B. 1935) was asked to rate "the ten best law schools in the United States." Without having seen this confidential data, Hurst wrote that HLS is "over-all, without question, . . . the Number One law school."[103]

In 1960 the inauguration of President John F. Kennedy boosted the national profile and influence of Harvard University and, concomitantly, HLS, because Kennedy, who had graduated from Harvard College in 1940, actively recruited Harvard faculty and graduates to serve in his administration. This development contributed to the stronger applicant pool and admissions selectivity that Griswold fostered through the 1960s. The HLS applicant pool grew from

1,700 in 1960 to nearly 3,000 in 1965, and then to 5,100 in 1970, while the median LSAT score of applicants rose from 630 to 665 and then 695 over the same decade.[104]

YLS Resurgence and a "Community of Feeling," 1955–1967

The beginning of Yale's resurgence came with the appointment of Eugene Rostow as dean in 1955. Already in 1957 Dean Griswold himself acknowledged the new "life and vitality at the Yale Law School," as did subsequent YLS deans and historians.[105] Rostow was not shy about asserting the distinctiveness and significance of YLS, but did so in a measured way that Griswold seemed to appreciate. Rostow's first annual report was a veritable call to arms that nevertheless accorded Harvard and Columbia their due.[106]

Rostow also broached the question of Yale's size in that annual report. Should it, could it, shrink to the prewar dimensions? Should it grow larger? The answers "will of course alter the broad financial picture," because "we shall need substantial new endowment funds . . . , even if the student body is kept rigidly to its present size," he wrote.[107] In 1959, urged by Rostow, the Yale Corporation voted that YLS should "continue to be a small school," with the necessary support from the university. But there was no prospect of returning to the LL.B. student body of some 325 for which the Sterling building had been planned. An enrollment of about 550 and a faculty of about thirty-five were envisioned as the new norm.[108]

In addition to resolving the enrollment question and garnering resources from the university administration, Rostow successfully raised money from donors. He also rebuilt the faculty, and in 1960 YLS "seemed poised for greatness," in Laura Kalman's words.[109] YLS then ratcheted up its admissions selectivity. The underlying cause was the national increase in the quantity and quality of applicants to law school, which commensurately boosted Harvard's selectivity. But the growing political activism of students and their desire for more student-centered pedagogy during the 1960s also expanded the appeal of liberal YLS, as compared with HLS.[110] In 1965 Dean Rostow stated, "The School's reputation has continued to attract an embarrassing number of highly qualified applicants for admission. By all the usual criteria of judgment . . . the class which entered the School in the fall of 1964 was noticeably superior to any previous class, and to the entering class in any other School."[111]

Rostow did not present comparative data, apart from the proportion rejected, to support this claim, but anecdotal evidence confirms that YLS was starting once again to erode Harvard's edge in admissions selectivity and attracting top students. In all the oral histories conducted for this volume, the earliest point at which any interviewees reported that YLS was equally or more appealing than HLS to them or their contemporaries was 1961, and the reports multiply after that date.

For example, in 1961 Alan Dershowitz turned down HLS and enrolled at YLS. In that same year Dean Griswold displayed sensitivity about this issue. At his welcoming dinner held in the fall of 1961 for new female students, Ann Dudley (LL.B. 1964) became irritated at Griswold's interrogation about why the women had come to study law. When the dean asked Dudley, she replied that she came to Harvard because Yale had turned her down. Griswold "got furious: 'I remember him just going crazy, flaming crazy,'" recalled Dudley. Griswold raged, "'That's not true, Yale always lets more women in than we do,' and so forth, the implication being that Yale had much lower standards than Harvard." In 1962 Elizabeth Bartholet felt that she might also have preferred YLS if her husband was not already enrolled at HLS.[112] In 1966 Judith C. Areen, later the dean of Georgetown University Law Center, chose to matriculate at YLS over HLS because one of her undergraduate professors at Cornell told her that "in many ways, it's like going to graduate school."[113]

Notwithstanding such occasional assertions of superiority both by YLS deans and by Dean Griswold, a new sense of parity and cooperation between the schools—and of their leadership of legal education—emerged between these deans in the 1950s and 1960s. In making comparisons to other law schools, Griswold sometimes observed that "of course, the most important ones, from our point of view, are Yale, Columbia, and Chicago."[114] But he encouraged the view that "among national law schools in the United States, Harvard and Yale are at the top of the profession," as the *Harvard Crimson* asserted.[115]

YLS and HLS deans expressed the growing sense of parity and cooperation by minimizing the jurisprudential differences and the asserted superiority that had often been stridently expressed in the late 1920s and 1930s. Dean Sturges and his successor, Acting Dean Shulman, described Yale's academic commitment as an "emphasis."[116] Rostow called it an "approach," and wrote to Griswold, "The differences between Yale and Harvard? I don't quite smell those famous differences manifested here." Griswold concurred.[117] By the same token, Kalman identified a jurisprudential "convergence" between the schools during the 1950s. HLS "moved toward the legal realism from which Yale was retreating."[118]

Hence, the deans seemed eager to call a truce between the schools. "With you, I see no sense in pulling and hauling between the Yale and Harvard Law Schools," wrote Griswold to Rostow in 1957. "There is plenty for both of us to do, and we will do it better . . . if we work together with 'a community of feeling,' as you say in your letter." Rostow wrote a year later, "The Yale-Harvard theme is one of the silliest things in the world to have a row about, or even a joke. In the immortal words of the French song, *Vive la difference.*"[119] Due to this cooperative spirit, Griswold and Rostow refused an invitation to appear at a law school forum that Amherst College tried to organize for its students. "Such meetings . . . are inevitably so 'competitive' in nature that we have concluded that it would be best for us not to join in them," wrote Griswold to Amherst.[120]

Moreover, Griswold and the YLS deans began consulting on matters large and small, including faculty salaries, secretarial support, office supplies, tuition rates, and financial aid, while they exchanged financial reports as well.[121] This went so far as to present anti-trust issues today.[122] In any case, Rostow and Griswold developed a close professional relationship. The two deans commiserated on the poverty of law schools, advised each other on financial problems and their annual funds, and strategized about approaching the Ford Foundation for major grants.[123] After Rostow stepped down in 1965, the "community of feeling" dissipated, as YLS became embroiled in social and political turmoil earlier than HLS.[124]

Detriments and Benefits of HLS's "Rugged Individualism," 1927–1967

Aside from its realist jurisprudence, liberal politics, small size, selective admissions, and progressive education policies, YLS began to lure students away from HLS between 1927 and 1967 simply because HLS did not respond to student discontent.[125] In October 1928 presidential candidate Herbert Hoover, in a speech in New York City heard by millions on the radio, famously contrasted the "American system of rugged individualism" with European "paternalism" and warned against the dangers of "state socialism."[126] Echoing Hoover, HLS students explicitly observed that the school followed a policy of "rugged individualism" or the "laissez-faire principle."[127]

But many of these students considered that policy outmoded or detrimental, even while conceding the justification of weeding out weak students and fostering self-reliance in the survivors. One graduate of Dartmouth College suggested that "rugged individualism was not so important as a sympathetic idealistic socialism." Another student, a Jewish immigrant from Russia, maintained, "in these days of 'New Deals' we are coming more and more to realize the necessity of coordinated cooperation. All such ideas . . . are in contrast to 'rugged individualism.'"[128] Subsequently, despite Griswold's attempts to improve conditions for HLS students, many still considered their LL.B. studies "a rat race" and felt they were subjected to "terrorism."[129]

The detriments of HLS and the contrast with YLS were widely publicized. In 1947 the editors of the *Harvard Law School Record* visited New Haven and published a report that made YLS appear absolutely enticing:

> Because of the high ratio of faculty members to students, there is inevitably a great deal of faculty student cooperation in extra-curricular activities. Many students are engaged with the faculty in writing new books, planning new courses, or throwing beer parties. . . . the general tone at Yale made it seem that student and faculty were all members of a friendly drinking society. In myriad instances there was a first-name relationship between student and teacher. The individual, man-to-man relations resulted in a relaxed attitude; recitation in class was a genial matching of wits. . . . It is difficult to assess the educational value of this camaraderie, but to the Harvard observers it seemed to create a happier group of students than one finds north of the Charles.[130]

The *Yale Law School Association Newsletter* reported this favorable assessment to its readers.[131]

In 1950 a group of undergraduate editors from the *Harvard Crimson* visited YLS and came to the same conclusion. "The mere size of the Harvard Law School precludes the sort of friendly community spirit evident at Yale. . . . There is no doubt that the grind [at Harvard] is more demanding, and that the atmosphere of the place is less leisurely." HLS students "usually must carry a heavier work load, putting in over 20 hours a week outside of class, as compared to over ten hours for his New Haven brother-in-law. And, of course, there is always the possibility of flunking out of Harvard, while Yale seldom fails a student. At Harvard, also, examinations do not come until the end of the year, while Yale has mid-year finals which provide a more regular progress check. . . . Grades are more important at Harvard too, since only a small percentage of top men are eligible for the *Law Review,* the Board of Student Advisors, and the Legal Aid Bureau."[132] In the late 1950s Victor E. Ferrall Jr., who studied as an LL.B. candidate at both HLS and YLS, observed the same contrast.[133]

Given the attraction and benefits of Yale's educational atmosphere, why did Harvard not follow suit? For that matter, why did any student admitted to YLS choose to come to HLS? And why did most of the strongest students verifiably still choose Harvard as late as 1955?

Some students preferred Harvard because the "manly" culture suited them. As the head of Princeton's Department of Politics explained the point to President Dodds, who relayed it to President Conant: "Harvard was undoubtedly the place . . . to go" for "a brilliant and aggressive chap," eager to wield the intellectual sword. Paul Carrington chose HLS over YLS in 1952 because "it was hard, and I wanted to show that I can do this. . . . It was kind of a macho thing in a way."[134] Thus, Harvard's "rugged individualism" had certain benefits, said its proponents. One was the freedom "that, if a man has the capacity and the willingness for creative work, he may exercise them . . . without interference." Another benefit of leaving students to struggle on their own was fostering self-reliance, which both the report "The Student Looks at Harvard Law School" in 1934 and, later, Dean Griswold extolled, while criticizing "spoon-feeding."[135]

Above all, the school's "ask and give no quarter" ethos was said to instill rigor, resilience, and discipline in studying and arguing legal issues. "Many of us . . . develop a fighting spirit we never thought possible before," wrote an HLS student who had graduated from Yale College. Under "the whip of student competition, . . . the industrious, intelligent student learns much good law," stated another student. By the same token, students did not want to "appear soft" or to "lack guts."[136]

Like President A. Lawrence Lowell (1909–1933), Conant endorsed this competitive ethos at HLS, which Dean Griswold considered one of the defining and beneficial characteristics of HLS.[137] The benefit becomes fully evident after graduation, Griswold stated, because "law is not a pipe and slippers occupation." A law student must develop "the toughness and resiliency . . . needed when he steps . . . into the world of practice or teaching or public affairs."[138]

Many HLS students endorsed this justification for the competitive, academic dueling. "One would scarcely expect to ask for quarter in the world into which we shall so soon be thrown. Certainly none would be given!" observed a Yale College graduate in "A Defense of Harvard Law School." "It is a cruel process, but it is no other than the process of selection at work in every day American society."[139] Likewise, Princeton's President Dodds wrote to President Conant:

The [HLS] training involves the principle of the survival of the fittest and undoubtedly puts guts in a man who will go through with it. A Harvard man will
find, I think, that the conditions in the law school more nearly approximate
the sort of competition he will face after graduation than will the Yale man. . . .
While Yale tries to do more for its students than Harvard, there may be a question as to whether a law school ought to do too much for its men. Men have
got to stand on their own feet after they get into the profession.[140]

Discussion about the putative benefits and detriments of "rugged individualism" inevitably addressed the different sizes of HLS and YLS. All the deans
agreed that at times "there are clearly advantages" for either, and that there
exists "both need and room for the best possible small schools and the best
possible large schools."[141] Nevertheless each dean believed that the size of his
own school was superior.[142]

Dean Griswold suggested that the advantages of Yale's small size "can be
easily overrated."[143] He pointed out that large enrollment affords a larger library and facilities, a larger and more diverse faculty, more student organizations in kind and number, and permits a "very cosmopolitan student
body," which "brings great intellectual stimulus." Griswold even saw merits
in large classes, which have value "in putting both students and instructor on
their toes." Furthermore, "it is better for a considerable number of men to
study with a great teacher than it is for a smaller group to study with a teacher
of lesser stature," a proposition assuming that Harvard employed only great
teachers, who were few in number.[144]

Though Griswold rarely mentioned this in his public statements, he surely
realized that larger enrollment also resulted in greater professional influence
for HLS—in the bar, on the bench, and on the faculties of law schools. Indeed, Yale's 1925 proposal to cap its enrollment identified this impact as one
of "the chief arguments" for a large school.[145] And studies repeatedly found that
HLS produced about twice as many law faculty as the next-largest producer,
which was YLS after 1930.[146] In 1967 *Time* magazine announced that HLS
"has prepared fully one-fourth of all U.S. law professors, and its 21,000 living
graduates constitute one-sixth of the lawyers in the country."[147] HLS graduates also predominated in the state and federal judiciary and in many of the
most powerful law firms in the country. This alumni network benefited HLS
directly, and also supplied alumni with "professional contacts," as Griswold
noted.[148] In addition, the professional network of HLS graduates reinforced
the school's isomorphic influence in legal education. Bigness had benefits.

Financial Aid Competition

In several ways, money also played a critical role in the relationship between the two law schools. First, they competed in awarding scholarships and discounting tuition during the decades after World War II. Both denied that they were buying students, and there is no evidence that they bid on individuals.[149] But each school did reshape its policies during the 1950s and 1960s in line with what economist Gordon Winston has called "the positional arms race in higher education." In this contest, institutions aggressively raise tuition and allocate some of the additional revenue to financial aid, intending, at least in part, to recruit excellent students and maintain or advance their position in institutional rankings.[150] The allocating of tuition revenue into financial aid is often called "tuition discounting," and this practice became widespread in higher education in the late twentieth century. HLS and YLS were among the earliest tuition discounters and entrants into this "positional arms race."

The early steps in their competition over financial aid are obscure. Data on student preferences was incomplete and informal, and is now sealed at Harvard in any case. Even in the late 1960s the HLS Financial Aids Committee, chaired by Andrew Kaufman (LL.B. 1954), could obtain only limited data and had to estimate the overlap between applicants, admittees, and acceptances of students entering HLS and YLS. Nevertheless, in 1970 that Committee prepared the most thorough retrospective analysis of financial aid at HLS during the previous decades.[151] Apart from these kinds of data gaps and barriers, explaining the twists and turns in financial aid policies is complicated by many external factors, including institutional resources, the national economy, and the social and political climate of the 1960s.

But it is clear that prior to 1940 the fluctuating and inchoate financial aid policies at both schools were not designed to recruit students. Fewer than 10 percent of students generally received aid, and the schools awarded most of their limited scholarships and loans on the basis of financial need and academic achievement, as determined by first-year exam results. Consequently, very few students received offers of financial aid before they matriculated, so that factor did not generally influence where they chose to attend.[152]

In the late 1940s the G.I. Bill elevated financial aid to a previously unimagined level by supporting some 2 million returning veterans pursuing higher education. As the number of funded veterans ebbed in 1950, HLS began to raise its tuition dramatically. Other law schools did too, so Harvard's tuition was not the highest. In 1967–68, Harvard charged $1,750, Yale $1,900, and

Chicago $1,980. This rise in tuition increased students' financial need, but also provided more resources, via tuition discounting, to meet that need. The result was "the mammoth rise in [Harvard] Law School financial assistance to its students."[153]

During the 1950s and 1960s, the growth of financial aid dollars and number of students requesting aid forced leading law schools to revise their financial aid policies at the same time that selectivity in admissions was intensifying. The "positional arms race" thus commenced in legal education. Between 1948 and 1956, HLS shifted the target population and the timing of its scholarship grants toward first-year students before they matriculated, moves suggesting that the school was responding to competition from YLS.[154] It is possible that this shift contributed to the decided preference of excellent students to enroll at HLS that Griswold identified in 1955, although we have found no testimony that indicates this.

In any case, Rostow observed that by the late 1950s, "the two law schools which have been the most direct alternatives to Yale in the minds of most prospective students—Harvard and Columbia—have made far greater strides than Yale in student-aid programs."[155] YLS soon responded. Anecdotal evidence of its influence can be found in the testimony of Alan Dershowitz. In 1961 he was attracted to Yale's interdisciplinary curriculum and small size, but "the deciding factor" for him to decline HLS was that YLS offered him "a small scholarship and a loan."[156] The race was on.

By 1964 administrators and faculty in Cambridge suspected that HLS was losing an increasing number of admitted applicants to YLS (although comprehensive overlap data was not available). In that year Harvard's Faculty Committee on Planning and Development therefore recommended awarding more full-tuition scholarships to entering students having need and excellent academic records, in order "to increase the attractiveness" of HLS. Nevertheless, in the spring and summer of 1966, when seventy scholarship offers were made under the initiative, only thirty-six, or 51 percent, were accepted by students entering in fall—a disappointing outcome.[157]

Not all the students who rejected HLS went to YLS. In the fall of 1962, of the 820 students admitted to Harvard, 34 percent (281) declined admission. Of those declining, 47 percent (132) decided not to go to law school at all. Of the 149 who turned down Harvard to go to another law school, 54 percent gave as their reason that they had received a larger scholarship elsewhere. Of the 149 who went to another law school, 54 went to Yale, 18 to Columbia, 17 to Chicago, 12 to Michigan, 10 to Stanford, 9 to New York University, 6 to Virginia, 5 to Pennsylvania, and a few each to other schools.[158] Assistant Admissions Director Russell Simpson (LL.B. 1965) later asserted about the mid-1960s, "Many times other schools offered a lot more than the student needed just to attract them. We never did that . . . But most of the students that we lost for that reason went to Yale."[159] In any event, in the fall of 1962, of the total HLS admittees who declined to enroll, 19 percent went to YLS

Despite the disappointing outcome of the expanded scholarship program for the fall of 1966, HLS could not immediately intensify the effort. Severe budgetary pressures forced a cut of 20 percent ($100,000) in the scholarship grants for 1967–68. Consequently, the HLS financial aid offers, adjusted for tuition differences, were generally below those of Columbia, Chicago, Stanford, and Yale. In particular, the HLS Admissions Office noted that Yale's financial aid offers exceeded Harvard's because YLS had higher tuition than HLS (so YLS could discount tuition more) and also because YLS was offering financial aid that exceeded the need gap. The financial aid relationship between the two schools thus reversed from that of the early 1950s, and applicants were following the money. Meanwhile, the number of admitted applicants who did not receive financial aid and chose HLS over YLS held steady in the late 1960s.[160]

These points suggested two conclusions to the HLS Financial Aids Committee. First, the students without financial need may have been attracted by Harvard's traditional emphasis upon "business and finance—contracts, commercial law, taxation, creditors' rights," in Griswold's words.[161] Second, the competition with YLS for students centered on financial aid applicants, who showed "a growing tendency . . . to choose Yale over Harvard." Apparently, "the financial aid student was more taken with the 'Yale image' than the non-financial aid student," the committee concluded. In other words, students having financial need were more attracted to the social and political activism and public policy interest at Yale.[162] Conversely, students who did not need financial aid generally came from families with greater means, and these students were likely more interested in business and finance and therefore more inclined to choose HLS.

In any case, Acting Dean James Casner (1967–68) named a faculty committee to study financial aid and then a student committee, which soon merged into one of the school's first joint student-faculty committees. By the time this joint committee reported in 1970, the percentage of financial aid students choosing HLS over YLS had risen significantly, for the first time in several years. In the fall of 1968, out of Harvard's top twenty-five admittees offered financial aid, fifteen, or 60 percent, came to Cambridge. In the fall of 1969, financial stringency forced Yale to cut its scholarship awards drastically. By March 1970 the "tendency of common financial aids applicants to choose Yale over Harvard . . . has become less acute," observed the joint committee.[163] The positions in the "arms race" had shifted once again, heavily influenced by the financial resources of the two schools.

Yale University's Generous Support

Underlying the financial aid competition, distinctive policies shaped the finances of HLS and YLS.[164] We have seen the constraints on Harvard due to its syndrome of tuition dependence. Yet, early in the twentieth century, Yale presidents also endorsed tuition dependence as policy for law schools.[165] The deans of both HLS and YLS therefore complained that they—like other law schools—deserved more endowment, gifts, and grants, particularly in comparison to medical schools.[166] These financial concerns made Yale's decision in 1926 to cap enrollment at 500 "a courageous move," in Dean Clark's view.[167] Likewise, in the early 1950s, YLS struggled to cut its enrollment back to the prewar level due principally to "financial considerations."[168] The academic policies of YLS, like HLS, were thus persistently shaped by "financial considerations," notwithstanding assertions to the contrary.[169]

Nevertheless, YLS achieved and maintained its elite character as "an honors school" because "the President and Corporation of Yale University . . . generously supported the School in all the changes which have been made."[170] This financial support took three forms. The Yale president and Corporation backed YLS fundraising campaigns, arranged funding for YLS buildings, and subsidized YLS with large annual appropriations.

The support for fundraising began in the late 1920s when YLS ran its centennial fundraising drive concurrently with an endowment campaign held by the university. These circumstances closely replicated those at Harvard ten years earlier. But in Cambridge, President Lowell had allowed the university's campaign to establish primary access to the major potential donors of HLS. In contrast, the YLS centennial campaign received the full-fledged endorsement and assistance of the Yale administration.[171] This assistance continued into the 1940s when Yale president Seymour wrote directly to all YLS graduates in support of YLS's fundraising goal of $1 million. Then in 1959 the Yale Corporation voted that raising $5 million for YLS was "among Yale's most urgent needs" and that the university development office would aid YLS in planning a campaign. Furthermore, the Corporation agreed to add "a total of $12 million . . . for the Yale Law School in official University lists of future capital needs."[172]

These endorsements and promotions contrasted sharply with the neglect and even obstruction by Presidents Lowell and Conant, who repeatedly omitted HLS from their published lists of schools at Harvard in need of endowment. This difference between the fundraising assistance provided by each university for its law school mattered greatly. In the early 1960s, soon after the Yale Corporation endorsed and promoted its "urgent needs," YLS ran a capital campaign that exceeded its $5 million goal by 20 percent.[173]

Second, Yale University supported construction funding so that YLS did not have to pay or borrow money for its own buildings. In the late 1890s the Yale Corporation made a series of donations to the school's building fund, amounting to $127,000.[174] Contemporaneously, Harvard University made no financial contribution to HLS for building and furnishing Langdell Hall in 1906 and 1907. As a result, between 1904 and 1909, the ratio of total invested funds to expenses of HLS fell from 9:1 to 5:1, while those of YLS rose from 4:1 to 5:1. Harvard's huge proportional advantage in financial capital had evaporated.[175]

In the late 1920s the endorsement of the Yale Corporation persuaded the Sterling trustees to grant $5 million to build a new complex of buildings for YLS, although the terms of the Sterling trust did not stipulate any funds for the law school.[176] Contemporaneously, Harvard University would not contribute funds for the expansion of Langdell Hall, and HLS had to borrow the entire cost from the Corporation at interest. Despite the plea of Acting Dean Morgan to President Conant that "the future of the Harvard Law School depends on its effectiveness as an educational institution, and not as a commercially profitable investment," HLS ultimately paid to the university nearly $2 million in principal and interest.[177] In 1970 dollars, the subsidy to YLS for its building was worth about $9.3 million, while the cost to HLS for its contemporaneous building expansion was about $4.7 million.

Finally, and most significantly, Yale University subsidized YLS with annual appropriations. In 1911 the enrollment of YLS dropped sharply after the school began requiring a bachelor's degree for admission, and Dean Henry Rogers (1903–1916) requested a temporary subvention, while observing that since 1900, YLS "has made a profit" that went to the university, and now was the time for the university to reciprocate.[178] In contrast to Harvard's "each tub on its own bottom" policy, Rogers thus believed that Yale University had a symbiotic financial model. Any surplus from YLS would go to help the university, and the university would support YLS when it faced a deficit. In 1912–13, the university accommodated Rogers's request by making what the university treasurer termed a "donation" of $5,600, constituting about 13 percent of the school's expenses.[179] Beginning with this contribution, the subsidizing of YLS continued annually for at least the next six decades, as seen in Appendix G.

The subsidies not only continued, but started growing during the sharp recession that followed World War I. In 1919–20, while HLS was operating year-round in order to accommodate the great influx of students, YLS enrolled only 130 students, and the Yale Corporation supplied 10 percent of the school's budget, to cover a shortfall. In 1921–22 the Yale administration gave YLS a total subsidy of more than 35 percent of the school's expenses.[180] In 1925 the YLS proposal to cap its enrollment at 500 students called for regularizing the ad hoc subsidy "so that limiting numbers would not result in curtailing educational policies." The proposal projected an annual deficit of about $75,000, and equated that to 5 percent return on new endowment of $1.5 million.[181]

In 1926–27, after the fateful decision to establish the enrollment cap, the envisioned deficit loomed large until Yale University increased its annual subsidy to YLS to $75,000, nearly 19 percent of the school's expenses. Over the next decade the subventions continued at this level, and Dean Clark observed that the Corporation was effectively allocating to YLS the income from $1.5 million of the general university endowment to supplement the law school's own endowment of $2 million. Both Sturges and Rostow subsequently affirmed the necessity of the annual appropriations.[182]

The original rationale for the subvention in the 1910s was simply to cover a temporary deficit.[183] Following the decision to cap the enrollment of YLS, the justification for the regular subsidy became compensating for small enrollment, because "a school of 500 cannot be run . . . more cheaply than a school of 800 so far as instructional expenses are concerned." By the same token, Yale leaders in both the law school and the university administration maintained that the primary reason for a large enrollment (as at HLS) was merely to make money and "avoid a deficit."[184]

Yale leaders, such as Dean Hutchins and President Angell, thus maintained that YLS based its academic and enrollment policies "on intellectual and not on financial considerations."[185] Meanwhile, Columbia Law School deans chided HLS for expanding its enrollment, which Columbia deans virtually attributed to gluttony.[186] Subsequently, Yale deans echoed the principle that YLS enrollment should not and would not expand due to financial induce-ments, even when, in fact, it was doing so under the G.I. Bill.[187]

Inconsistencies of the "Tub" Policy at Yale

The implication of all these statements was that giant HLS was gorging itself, whereas YLS provided better education while exercising prudence and fol-lowing principle. But HLS had to live within its means, and YLS did not. Through correspondence with the Yale deans, Erwin Griswold became the first HLS dean to understand this, and therefore found it difficult to sympathize when YLS deans complained that "our financing could be more satisfactory." Their dissatisfaction stemmed primarily from the fact that any surplus gener-ated by YLS "is absorbed by the University at the end of the year." The Yale deans did not acknowledge that such a surplus came only by virtue of the uni-versity's subsidy.[188]

Indeed, it is remarkable that, after Yale University made its annual "dona-tion" to YLS in order to cover the school's deficit, there was sometimes a re-sidual balance, or surplus, which the Yale treasurer added to the surplus ac-count of YLS. Given this arrangement, it is not surprising that the Yale Corporation in the 1950s wished "to cut off this appropriation" in order "to make us live off our own funds," in the words of Dean Sturges. To this, Sturges observed, "I am agreeable if we are relieved from certain charges made against us by the University."[189]

In Griswold's view, Sturges's stipulation simply meant that YLS was un-willing to pay its own expenses and live within its means. In 1949 Griswold explained to Sturges the "tub" policy at Harvard.

> Under this arrangement, each major part of the University . . . operates with financial independence and responsibility. . . . Each school makes its own budget. . . . The University does not make any appropriation to the Law School for any purpose. . . . Our surplus and departmental balance is never taken into the general funds of the University.[190]

The only major exception to the "tub" policy, Griswold noted pointedly, was the university's custom of paying the deficit of Harvard's wealthiest school: the medical school.[191] This observation came just after Griswold made the last annual payment of $50,000 to the university for the mortgage on Langdell Hall in 1948. Notwithstanding the announced policy of "each tub on its own bottom," the Harvard Corporation had, in effect, been siphoning money from HLS to subsidize Harvard Medical School!

Here may lie Griswold's justification for his massive growth in spending. Griswold was trying not only to make up for past deficiencies at HLS, but also to match the YLS programs, which were heavily subsidized by its university. In 1960, hoping for a more sympathetic hearing than President Conant had given the Law School, Griswold wrote to President Pusey that Harvard's "tub" policy disadvantaged HLS because other law schools enjoyed "the active support of their university administrations." Griswold then cited a new building for Columbia University Law School, a new building and $6 million contribution to the University of Chicago Law School, and an annual subvention of "$500,000 or more per year" for YLS. In contrast, HLS, "does not have, and never has had, adequate funds for capital improvement, developments, and endowment," Griswold wrote.[192]

In the early 1960s the hugely successful YLS fundraising campaign under Dean Rostow must have reinforced the disadvantage in Dean Griswold's mind.[193] Even as the campaign receipts came in, Yale University continued to bestow its annual appropriation on YLS! This subsidy grew to $445,500—over 20 percent of the law school's budget—in 1964–65. Thus, Dean Rostow's "creative financing enabled the law school to thrive by bleeding the central administration," as historian Laura Kalman stated.[194] In Cambridge, Dean Griswold likely felt that HLS was hemorrhaging money, as he kept spending to keep pace with Yale.

Nevertheless, by 1970 Yale University began to experience financial problems, which deepened in the late 1970s as "stagflation" gripped the national economy: a combination of high inflation, rising unemployment, declining consumer demand, and stagnant business activity, all of which buffeted higher education.[195] The Yale Corporation could no longer afford to subsidize YLS, and began to tax units to support central functions of the university, following the symbiosis envisioned by Dean Rogers in 1911. After sixty years of running deficits covered by the university, YLS would finally have an opportunity to help the university once again.[196]

But YLS resisted cutting its spending to live within its own revenue. And YLS alumni protested that their gifts would, in effect, be subsidizing the university. Just at this point, YLS Dean Guido Calabresi (1985–1994) opened an escape hatch for the school. Invoking the "tub" policy at Harvard, Calabresi argued to Yale's provost that YLS should have "financial autonomy." Otherwise, Calabresi maintained, HLS would have a great advantage over YLS, because any financial problems experienced by Harvard University could not drag down HLS, as was happening at Yale. Dean Calabresi thus succeeded in "winning . . . financial independence from the central administration," in Kalman's words. Alumni donations skyrocketed, and YLS was able "to really nail down its current preeminence," in Calabresi's words.[197] Indeed, his successor, Dean Kronman, suggested that it was Calabresi's leadership in the late 1980s that "catapulted Yale out of [Harvard's] shadow" and finally enabled YLS to "throw a long shadow of its own."[198] Also applauding Calabresi's accomplishment, Kalman observed that prior YLS deans "had known [Harvard's advantage] too, but could not win . . . financial autonomy."[199] A longer view suggests a different interpretation, however.

In the early twentieth century, both universities wanted their law schools to "live off our own funds." But Yale University subsidized YLS through the 1970s. Then, in the 1980s, when it benefited YLS to stop "bleeding" the university and assert its financial independence, YLS did so. In contrast, the Harvard presidents and Corporation applied the "tub" policy ruthlessly to HLS, treating the law school just like it treated most of its students throughout much of the twentieth century—demanding "rugged individualism" and self-reliant "toughness and resiliency."[200]

The inconsistent application of the "tub" policies at the two universities produced a huge financial advantage for YLS over HLS between 1890 and 1970. The amount is difficult to calculate precisely, but a partial account of Yale's gains and Harvard's losses can be computed by tallying YLS receipts from its university's contributions toward buildings and annual expenses, and HLS payments for its buildings from its own annual income. This account is presented in Appendix H, which converts the sums into 1970 dollars. Accruing over the period between 1894 and 1970, the YLS financial advantage was enormous—about $27.7 million in 1970 dollars—according to this calculation of only part of Yale University's support. This amount exceeded the entire HLS endowment of about $26.2 million in 1970, the largest of any law school in the world at the time. The second largest, some $11.1 million, belonged to YLS. Hence, those contributions from Yale University effectively totaled two and a half times the amount of the YLS endowment by 1970.

The parity between the HLS endowment and this rough calculation of Yale's financial advantage suggests a justification for Dean Griswold's unwillingness to direct new revenue into endowment between 1946 and 1967. Even though YLS was much smaller, its subsidy was on a scale that required Griswold to spend all of his new revenue on developing HLS programs in order to keep pace with Yale. In particular, the income from the new, successful, annual fund of HLS was needed to offset the huge annual subsidy that YLS received from its university.

At the same time, the luxury of the subsidy allowed YLS to direct the great bulk of the receipts from its highly successful fundraising campaign in the early 1960s into its endowment. This point deserves emphasis. YLS banked the proceeds of a major fundraising campaign at the very same time that Yale University was steeply increasing its large subsidy for the school. As a result, the YLS endowment doubled in size during the campaign from about $4.6 million in 1960 to $9.2 million in 1965.[201] In contrast, HLS was forced to direct over 40 percent of its Sesquicentennial Fund into buildings and operations, reducing the amount that could go to endowment.

The relationship between HLS and YLS took several turns between 1900 and 1967. After straggling in the 1900s and 1910s, Yale's jurisprudential embrace of realism in the late 1920s gave YLS an aura of intellectual excitement, particularly in contrast to reputedly tradition-minded and stodgy HLS. Of equal importance was Yale's tactical decision in 1925 to remain small. In addition, YLS wisely provided small classes, a low student-faculty ratio, close student-faculty relationships, and extralegal studies, all of which strengthened the school's distinct market niche. In 1926 YLS adopted selective admissions, and, as the number and proportion of rejected applicants rose, Yale leaders inferred that YLS was the most selective school in the nation and had the best students. But comparative data to support that inference is lacking until at least 1934–35.

At that point YLS was poised to continue its spectacular advance, while HLS was stagnating between 1929 and 1946. But financial and academic strictures at Yale University impeded YLS from exploiting that opportunity and caused the school to lose its leading realist faculty by 1939. Then, in 1946, HLS began a resurgence under Dean Griswold that continued into the 1960s. Meanwhile, in 1955 Dean Rostow began to reinvigorate YLS and to foster a spirit of parity and cooperation between the two law schools. Nevertheless, in the early 1960s Rostow claimed, once again, that YLS enrolled the best law students, based largely upon its necessarily small fraction of admitted applicants.

Yale's claim to attract the best law students was subsequently strengthened during the 1960s by its reputation for social and political activism, for a broad curriculum including extralegal studies, and for becoming "the most theoretical and academically oriented law school in America," in Kalman's words.[202] In contrast, its main competitors—Harvard and Columbia law schools— emphasized "the stuff of business and finance."[203] Focusing on other "stuff" reinforced Yale's distinctiveness and suited its location outside of a major commercial center.

Although Yale's undisputed ascent from 1900 to 1970 is generally attributed to its jurisprudence, politics, size, selectivity, and educational policies, some students also began to prefer it because the HLS commitment to "rugged individualism" made legal education at Harvard grueling, competitive, and combative, with an intellectual sword hanging over every student's head. But this sword cut both ways. Some of the most talented students wanted that kind of legal education because "law is not a pipe and slippers occupation," in Griswold's words.[204]

Finally, YLS ascended by virtue of major financial assistance provided by its university, surely unmatched by any other law school. Embracing the vision of a small, honors law school, the Yale presidents and Corporation backed fundraising campaigns, arranged funding for law school buildings, and subsidized the school with annual appropriations. All three kinds of assistance contrasted sharply with Harvard University's stringent treatment of HLS. By 1970 YLS had enjoyed a cumulative financial advantage amounting to about $27.7 million over HLS. Dean Griswold had to spend every penny of revenue trying to keep up.

Notwithstanding the very great differences in their approaches, the Yale Corporation and the Harvard Corporation were playing similar roles as "institutional entrepreneurs."[205] A university benefits from the preeminence of a leading school in a major domain of professional education, and Yale University certainly benefited from the ascent of YLS during the mid-twentieth century, so the subsidizing of YLS was a shrewd investment for Yale University.

Why would that strategy not apply to Harvard? First, the heavy subsidizing of a small school was cost effective; commensurate subsidizing of HLS would have required three times as much money, a prohibitive sum. Second, the graduate and professional school sector at Harvard was three to four times as large as that at Yale during this period, forcing the Harvard Corporation to decide which professional school could do the most with the least external support. By design or default, the Harvard Corporation consistently chose the "rugged individual" among the professional schools, and HLS continued to lead in its domain, without support. This approach by the Harvard Corporation was therefore shrewd as well, whether or not contemplated.

While both the Yale Corporation and the Harvard Corporation thus acted, in effect, as "institutional entrepreneurs" trying to maximize the prestige of their universities, HLS and YLS differed in their potential to serve as exemplars that "set the style" of legal education in the United States, in the words of Robert Stevens.[206] HLS has long exercised this isomorphic influence, but YLS has not served as a model to replicate precisely because of its cultivated iconoclasm. The school "is a boutique: it is small. It is considered special, the 'best'" and has a "liberating reputation for quirkiness," according to Laura Kalman.[207] In Dean Kronman's words, the school "takes every question of law with a boundless intellectual seriousness, indeed to the point where we seem to those who would caricature us like a bunch of otherworldly speculatists with our head in the clouds, completely out of touch with the hard realities of the law."[208]

This "otherworldly" character virtually precludes YLS from serving as an exemplar. Furthermore, if schools began to replicate the "quirky alternative," that very attribute would lose its meaning.[209] And such "intellectual extravagance" is expensive.[210] YLS succeeded magnificently because Yale University heavily subsidized its formative development for eighty years far beyond what is imaginable for any other law school—even for the law school with the largest endowment in the world, which has lived within its means. That would be Harvard.

NOTES

1. Charles W. Eliot, Address, in Harvard Law School Association, *Report of the Eighteenth Annual Meeting* (Boston, 1904), 68. See William H. Taft, "Oration," in Harvard Law School Association, *Report of the Eighteenth Annual Meeting* (Boston, 1904), 15.

2. Arthur T. Hadley, Annual Report of the President of Yale University, 1901–02, 14. See William P. LaPiana, *Logic and Experience: The Origin of Modern American Legal Education* (New York, 1994), 122–147; Henry W. Rogers, Annual Report of the Dean of Yale Law School, 1904–05, 155; 1908–09, 200–01; Frederick C. Hicks, *Yale Law School:*

1895–1915 (New Haven, CT, 1938), 43–45; Laura Kalman, *Legal Realism at Yale, 1927–1960* (Chapel Hill, NC, 1986), 99–100; Daniel R. Coquillette and Bruce A. Kimball, *On the Battlefield of Merit: Harvard Law School, the First Century* (Cambridge, MA, 2015) (hereafter cited as *Battlefield of Merit*), 384–435.

3. Quotation is from LaPiana, *Logic and Experience,* 144. See Simeon E. Baldwin, Diaries, Baldwin Family Papers, 1854–1977, ser. 6, Yale University Library Manuscripts and Archives, vols. 7, 8, 9.

4. Charles E. Clark, Annual Report of the Dean of Yale Law School, 1929–30, 144–145; Robert W. Gordon, "Professors and Policymakers: Yale Law School Faculty in the New Deal and After," in *History of the Yale Law School: The Tercentennial Lectures,* ed. Anthony T. Kronman (New Haven, CT, 2004), 81; Robert Stevens, *Law School: Legal Education in America from the 1850s to the 1980s* (Chapel Hill, NC, 1983), 136–141; Jeremy B. Luke, "Academic Origins of Harvard Law School and Yale Law School LL.B. Students, 1921–1935" (research report, Ohio State University, 2017), on file with the authors.

5. Quotation is from "News Release . . . Yale Law School to Train Only Superior Students" (June 1, 1926), Yale University Secretary's Office Records 1899–1953, ser. 3, Yale University Library Manuscripts and Archives. See Gordon, "Professors and Policymakers," 81; Julius Goebel Jr., *A History of the School of Law: Columbia University* (New York, 1955), 302–304; John H. Schlegel, *American Realism and Empirical Social Science* (Chapel Hill, NC, 1995),17; Mary Ann Dzuback, *Robert M. Hutchins: Portrait of an Educator* (Chicago, 1991), 43–66. See also discussion in Chapter 6, this volume.

6. Quotations are from Eugene V. Rostow, Annual Report of the Dean of Yale Law School, 1954–55, 8. See Rostow, Annual Report of the Dean, 1959–1962, 39; "Harry Shulman, Dean, Yale Law School," *HLSR* (February 17, 1955): 2; "Dean Sturges Compares Harvard Methods with Those in Use at Yale," *HLSR* (October 26, 1949): 1, 4; Kalman, *Legal Realism,* 3–10.

7. Maxwell E. Foster and William M. Simmons, "In Re: Harvard, Yale Law Schools . . . Yale Uses Sociological Method; Harvard Emphasizes Rigor," *Harvard Crimson* (May 4, 1950).

8. George W. Pierson, *Yale: The University College, 1921–1937* (New Haven, CT, 1955), 259. See Morton Keller and Phyllis Keller, *Making Harvard Modern: The Rise of America's University* (New York, 2001), 112; Christopher W. Schmidt, "The Failure of Reform: Legal Education at Harvard Law School, 1934–1946" (student research paper, HLS, 2006), on file with the authors, 15.

9. Laura Kalman, "The Dark Ages," in Kronman, *History of the Yale Law School,* 155. See Kalman, *Legal Realism,* 11–20.

10. Robert M. Hutchins, Annual Report of the Dean of Yale Law School, 1928–29, 117; Clark, Annual Report of the Dean, 1929–30, 144; Rostow, Annual Report of the Dean, 1959–1962, 39; James R. Angell, Annual Report of the President of Yale University, 1933–34, 35–36.

11. Karl Klare, "Contracts Jurisprudence and the First-Year Casebook Book Review" (book review), *New York University Law Review* 54 (1979): 876–878; Morton J. Horwitz, *The Transformation of American Law, 1870–1960: The Crisis of Legal Orthodoxy* (Oxford, 1992), 129; Albert W. Alschuler, *Law without Values: The Life, Work, and Legacy of Justice Holmes* (Chicago, 2000), 89, 113.

12. Kalman, *Legal Realism,* 22, 120.

13. Ernest J. Brown, Oral History, conducted by Daniel Hamilton (August 1997), on file with the authors.

14. Jerome Frank, *Law and the Modern Mind* (New York, 1930).

15. Jerome Frank, "Why Not a Clinical Lawyer-School?," *University of Pennsylvania Law Review* 81 (1933): 907–908, 911, 921; Jerome Frank, "A Plea for Lawyer-Schools," *Yale Law Journal* 56 (1947): 1303–1304. See Anthony Chase, "The Birth of the Modern Law School," *American Journal of Legal History* 23 (1979): 330–331; Bruce A. Kimball, "The Langdell Problem: Historicizing the Century of Historiography, 1906–2000s," *Law & History Review* 22 (2004): 305–306; Laura Kalman, *Yale Law School and the Sixties* (Chapel Hill, NC, 2005), 19.

16. "The Law: Law Schools—Harvard at 150," *Time* (October 6, 1967): 75. See Preble Stolz, "Clinical Experience in American Legal Education: Why Has It Failed?," in *Clinical Education and the Law School of the Future,* ed. Edmund W. Kitch (Chicago, 1969), 72; Bernard Schwartz, *Main Currents in American Legal Thought* (Durham, NC, 1993), 346nn518–519.

17. Grant Gilmore, *The Death of Contract* (Columbus, OH, 1974), 6, 11–13, 97–98; Grant Gilmore, *The Ages of American Law* (New Haven, CT, 1977), 42. As a Liberal Arts fellow at HLS between 1984 and 1986, Bruce Kimball first learned about Langdell through these assignments of Gilmore's books. Compare Kimball, "The Langdell Problem," 308–311.

18. Angell, Annual Report of the President, 1933–34, 36.

19. Charles Seymour, Annual Report of the President of Yale University, 1937–38, 28.

20. Quotation is from William Fulton, "New Deal Ideas Influence Yale School of Law," *Chicago Daily Tribune* (January 17, 1939). See "The American Marxists," *Chicago Daily Tribune* (January 17, 1939); Fulton, "Reveal Radical Doctrin[e] Taught in Law Schools: Propaganda Sown by Harvard, Yale," *Chicago Daily Tribune* (January 15, 1939); Charles Seymour to Ralph H. Pierce (January 25, 1939), and Comrades Clow, Scribner, Blair, F. Hannaford, Preston and Albert Farwell to Comrade Charles Seymour (January 21, 1939), Yale University Secretary's Office Records, 1899–1953, ser. 3, Yale University Library Manuscripts and Archives (hereafter cited as YUS Records).

21. "Dean Sturges Compares."

22. Erwin N. Griswold to Wesley A. Sturges (September 18, 1953), YUS Records.

23. Wesley A. Sturges to Erwin N. Griswold (September 22, 1953), YUS Records. *In nubibus* literally means "in the clouds," or in a suspended state.

24. Fulton, "Reveal Radical Doctrin[e]." On the association of HLS with left-wing politics in the 1920s and 1950s, see the discussion in Chapters 3 and 11, this volume.

25. Quotations are from "The American Marxists"; Fulton, "Reveal Radical Doctrin[e]." See Comrades Clow et al. to Comrade Charles Seymour (January 21, 1939).

26. Elizabeth Bartholet, Oral History, conducted by Daniel Hamilton (February 1999–March 2000), on file with the authors.

27. Anthony T. Kronman, Interview with Daniel Hamilton and Daniel R. Coquillette (January 2003), on file with the authors. See Kalman, *Yale Law School,* 68–192.

28. Clark, Annual Report of the Dean, 1930–31, 160. See Luke, "Academic Origins."

29. "Dean Sturges Compares," 1.

30. "Yale Admission Procedure Screens Applicants for Varied Capabilities," *HLSR* (October 29, 1947): 1, 4. See Alan M. Dershowitz, Oral History, conducted by Daniel R. Coquillette with Andrew Klaber (October–November 2009), on file with the authors; Richard D. Parker, Oral History, conducted by Daniel R. Coquillette and Daniel Pincus (June 2010), on file with the authors.

31. "Dean Sturges Compares," 1.

32. Quotation is from William S. Carpenter to President Harold W. Dodds (October 1934) [conveyed to Harvard President James B. Conant], HLS Dean's Office Records, Records of President James B. Conant, 1933–1953, Harvard University Archives (HUA) (hereafter cited as JBC Records). See Clark, Annual Report of the Dean, 1929–30, 146; 1930–31, 160; "Dean Sturges Compares," 1; Wesley A. Sturges, Annual Report of the Dean of Yale Law School, 1949–50, 40.

33. Clark, Annual Report of the Dean, 1929–30, 146; see 1930–31, 160.

34. Quotation is from Dershowitz, Oral History (October–November 2009). See Sturges, Annual Report of the Dean, 1949–1950, 40; "Dean Sturges Compares,"1; Foster and Simmons, "In Re: Harvard."

35. "Harry Shulman, Dean."

36. "News Release," 1–2.

37. Hutchins, Annual Report of the Dean, 1926–27, 119. See Clark, Annual Report of the Dean, 1929–30, 152–53; Charles E. Clark to Carl A. Lohmann (September 30, 1935), YUS Records; Sturges, Annual Report of the Dean, 1949–50, 3.

38. Thomas W. Swan, Annual Report of the Dean of Yale Law School, 1925–26, 109–110.

39. "News Release"; *Battlefield of Merit,* 413–416.

40. Quotations are from, respectively, Clark, Annual Report of the Dean, 1929–30, 144–145; Clark to Lohmann (September 30, 1935).

41. Quotations are from, respectively, Angell, Annual Report of the President, 1933–34, 35–36; Seymour to Pierce (January 25, 1939).

42. Sturges, Annual Report of the Dean, 1949–50, 4.

43. Rostow, Annual Report of the Dean, 1963–1965, 41.

44. Quotations are from, respectively, Hutchins, Annual Report of the Dean, 1928–29, 119; Clark to Lohmann (September 30, 1935). See Clark, Annual Report of the Dean, 1929–30, 153.

45. Quotations are from, respectively, Pierson, *Yale: The University College,* 259; Kalman, "The Dark Ages," 157; Keller and Keller, *Making Harvard Modern,* 112–113, 253.

46. See the discussion in Chapter 1.

47. HLS Faculty Meeting Minutes (November 5, 1913); HLS Catalog, 1914–15, 4–5; "News Release"; U.S. Commissioner of Education, *Biennial Survey of Higher Education, 1924–1926* (Washington, DC, 1928), 803.

48. HLS Catalog, 1927–28, 5; 1928–29, 6; "Law Requirements Raised at Harvard," *New York Times* (January 15, 1937).

49. Roscoe Pound, Annual Report of the Dean of HLS, 1926–27, 188.

50. Pound, Annual Report of the Dean, 1926–27, 188; HLS Faculty Committee on Curriculum, "Report on Certain Tendencies in Law School Teaching" (1934), HLS Dean's Office Records, Records of President A. Lawrence Lowell, 1909–1933, HUA.

51. Keller and Keller, *Making Harvard Modern,* 113, 253–254, 539n5. Keller and Keller cite "Law—3 Centuries," William Bent[in]ck-Smith manuscripts, HUA, which Harvard archivists could not locate. They also cite this letter discussed below: Erwin N. Griswold to Nathan M. Pusey (December 1, 1955), HLS Dean's Office Records, Records of President Nathan M. Pusey, 1953–1971, HUA (hereafter cited as NMP Records).

52. Archibald Cox, Oral History, conducted by Daniel R. Coquillette and Daniel Hamilton (November 1998), on file with the authors. See Detlev Vagts, Oral History, conducted by Daniel Hamilton, Daniel R. Coquillette, and John Delionado (November 1999–February 2000), on file with the authors. On the increasing competition for admission to leading law schools, see Chapter 12, this volume.

53. Swan, Annual Report of the Dean, 1921–22, 255; 1922–23, 294; Clark, Annual Report of the Dean, 1930–31, 148; *Battlefield of Merit,* 578–582.

54. See Clark to Lohmann (September 30, 1935); Edmund M. Morgan to James B. Conant, Memorandum regarding the Admissions Policy of the Harvard Law School [ca. December 1936], JBC Records.

55. HLS Faculty Committee on Curriculum, Meeting minutes (June 14, 1934; January 30, 1935), JBC Records.

56. James B. Conant to President Harold W. Dodds (October 23, 1934), JBC Records.

57. Carpenter to Dodds (October 23, 1934).

58. John Grant Haviland, "The Student Looks at Harvard Law School" (observations of the school by students in 1934) (unpublished typescript, revised spring of 1934), on file with the authors, 3, 44–45, 64–67.

59. Morgan to Conant, Memorandum [ca. December 1936].

60. Clark to Lohmann (September 30, 1935).

61. Morgan to Conant, Memorandum [ca. December 1936].

62. Morgan to Conant, Memorandum [ca. December 1936].

63. Erwin N. Griswold, "Legal Education at Harvard," *HLSB* (January 1950): 1. See Chapter 13, this volume.

64. Hutchins, Annual Report of the Dean, 1926–27, 119. See "Draft of a Program for Yale Law School Buildings" (July 1, 1925), YUS Records.

65. Swan, Annual Report of the Dean, 1923–24, 121–122; Clark, Annual Report of the Dean, 1929–30, 144–145; Rogers, Annual Report of the Dean, 1905–06, 153–154; 1908–09, 200–201; 1909–10, 193–194; 1910–11, 220–221.

66. Kronman, Interview (January 2003). See Brooks M. Kelley, *Yale: A History* (New Haven, CT, 1974), 276–277, 285; Kalman, *Legal Realism,* 104; Kalman, "The Dark Ages," 155.

67. George P. Day to Andrew S. Taylor (February 4, 1913), YUS Records.

68. Quotation is from Bartholet, Oral History (February 1999–March 2000). See Arthur von Mehren, Oral History, conducted by Daniel R. Coquillette and Mary Beth Basile (July–December 2000), on file with the authors.

69. Swan, Annual Report of the Dean, 1924–25, 88.

70. "Draft of a Program." This anonymous document was apparently written by Dean Swan and some of his colleagues. Here and below, this interpretation differs from that in subsequent accounts about Yale Law School, including Kalman's excellent works *Legal Realism,* 104–106, and *Yale Law School,* 33.

71. Emphasis added. "Draft of a Program," 3–4.

72. Kronman, Interview (January 2003).

73. "Draft of a Program," 4.

74. Hutchins, Annual Report of the Dean, 1926–27, 119; Clark, Annual Report of the Dean, 1930–31, 148; 1929–30, 144–145.

75. "News Release"; Swan, Annual Report of the Dean, 1925–26, 109–110. See Kalman, *Legal Realism,* 106, 263n44.

76. Swan, Annual Report of the Dean, 1925–26, 109–110.

77. Roger L. Geiger, *To Advance Knowledge: The Growth of American Research Universities, 1900–1940* (New York, 1986), 203–205.

78. *Battlefield of Merit,* appendix F; Roger Geiger, "After the Emergence: Voluntary Support and the Building of American Research Universities," *History of Education Quarterly* (Fall 1985): 375. See Geiger, *To Advance Knowledge,* 205–207.

79. "$15,000,000 Sterling Bequest to Yale," *New York Times* (July 17, 1918), 11. See Angell, Annual Report of the President, 1927–28, 3; 1926–27, 3; George W. Pierson, *Yale College: An Educational History, 1871–1921* (New Haven, CT, 1952), 371n; Pierson, *Yale: The University College,* 597–601; Kelley, *Yale,* 374–376.

80. Anson P. Stokes, Annual Report of the Secretary of Yale University, 1918–19, 42–46; Hadley, Annual Report of the President, 1918–19, 25–26; Pierson, *Yale College,* 535–538; Pierson, *Yale: The University College,* 254, 597–598; Kelley, *Yale,* 373.

81. *Battlefield of Merit,* appendix F; Geiger, "After the Emergence," 375; Gaddis Smith, "Life at Yale during the Great Depression," *Yale Alumni Magazine* (November–December, 2009), Retrieved from https://yalealumnimagazine.com/articles/2644/life-at-yale-during -the-great-depression.

82. Swan, Annual Report of the Dean, 1925–26, 109; "News Release"; Angell, Annual Report of the President, 1925–26, 21; Hutchins, Annual Report of the Dean, 1926–27, 116; Clark, Annual Report of the Dean, 1929–30, 153–156; Gaddis Smith, "Politics and the Law School: The View from Woodbridge Hall, 1921–1963," in Kronman, *History of Yale Law School,* 140–141; Kalman, *Legal Realism,* 114–115, 121–122.

83. See Appendix G; Hutchins, Annual Report of the Dean, 1926–27, 119; 1928–29, 118; Annual Report of the Treasurer of Yale University, 1927–28, 13, 31.

84. Quotation is from Clark, Annual Report of the Dean, 1931–32, 123; see 1929– 30, 163; 1930–31, 178; Kalman, *Legal Realism,* 115–130; Smith, "Politics," 138, 140– 141; Robert Stevens, "History of the Yale Law School: Provenance and Perspective," in Kronman, *History of the Yale Law School,* 13; Gordon, "Professors," 81.

85. Geiger, *To Advance Knowledge,* 207–208. See Roger L. Geiger, *The History of American Higher Education: Learning and Culture from the Founding to World War II* (Princeton, NJ, 2014), 495.

86. Geiger, *The History,* 496; Roger L. Geiger, *Research and Relevant Knowledge: American Research Universities since World War II* (New York, 1993), 97, 116–118; Geiger, *To Advance Knowledge,* 203–207.

87. John T. Wilson, *Academic Science, Higher Education, and the Federal Government, 1950–1983* (Chicago, 1983), 1–42; Geiger, *Research and Relevant Knowledge,* 82–83, 99– 100, 105, 107.

88. Erwin Griswold was a distant cousin of Whitney Griswold. Harriet Griswold to Charles Renfrew (May 27, 1991), Elizabeth Wahlen Correspondence, 1946–1998, on file with the authors.

89. Smith, "Politics," 138. See Geiger, *Research and Relevant Knowledge,* 87–90.

90. Geiger, *Research and Relevant Knowledge,* 108, see 89–90.

91. John S. Brubacher et al., *The Department of Education at Yale University, 1891–1958* (New Haven, CT, 1960); Rakesh Khurana, *From Higher Aims to Hired Hands: The Social Transformation of American Business Schools and the Unfulfilled Promise of Management as a Profession* (Princeton, NJ, 2007).

92. Rostow, Annual Report of the Dean, 1959–62, 50. See Smith, "Politics," 138.

93. Kalman, *Yale Law School,* 234.

94. Sturges, Annual Report of the Dean, 1949–50, 4–5, 9.

95. Louis A. Toepfer, Oral History, conducted by Daniel Hamilton (March 1998), on file with the authors; von Mehren, Oral History (July–December 2000). See John J. Liolos, "Erecting the High Citadel's Walls: The Development of Formal Admissions Standards at Harvard Law School, 1817–1955" (student research paper, HLS, 2013), on file with the authors, 49.

96. Paul D. Carrington, Oral History, conducted by Daniel Hamilton (February 2003), on file with the authors. See Stephen Bernardi, Oral History, conducted by Daniel Hamilton and Daniel R. Coquillette (October 2000–April 2001), on file with the authors.

97. Sturges, Annual Report of the Dean, 1949–50, 4–5, 9.

98. Sturges, Annual Report of the Dean, 1950–51, 24; see 1949–50, 9; 1951–52, 11–12; 1952–53, 9.

99. Kalman, *Yale Law School,* 47; Kalman, *Legal Realism,* 145–176. See Frank, "A Plea for Lawyer-Schools," 1303–1304; Fred Rodell, "Review of 'Zechariah Chafee, Jr., and John M. Maguire, *A List of Books for Prospective Law Students Now in Service Prepared by a Committee of the Faculty of Harvard Law School,'" Yale Law Journal* 54 (September 1945): 897–901.

100. Griswold's percentages have been rounded off. Griswold to Pusey (December 1, 1955). Keller and Keller, *Making Harvard Modern,* 539n5, cite this source as evidence that "more than a third of HLS's best admittees did not accept, and it appeared that for the most part they went to New Haven" (253–254).

101. Sturges, Annual Report of the Dean, 1949–50, 4.

102. Griswold to Pusey (December 1, 1955).

103. J. Willard Hurst to Joseph H. Willits (March 20, 1957), J. Willard Hurst Collection, 1932–1997, University of Wisconsin Law Library Special Collections.

104. Derek Bok, Annual Report of the Dean of HLS, 1969–70, 281; Keller and Keller, *Making Harvard Modern,* 209.

105. Erwin N. Griswold to Eugene V. Rostow (May 13, 1957), YUS Records; Kalman, *Yale Law School,* 57; Stevens, "History of the Yale Law School," 14.

106. Rostow, Annual Report of the Dean, 1954–55, 8–9.

107. Rostow, Annual Report of the Dean, 1954–55, 48–49.

108. Rostow, Annual Report of the Dean, 1957–1959, 34–36.

109. Kalman, *Yale Law School,* xi; see 47, 57.

110. Kalman, *Yale Law School,* 68–139.

111. Rostow, Annual Report of the Dean, 1963–65, 41; see 1957–1959, 21–22.

112. Quoted in Judith Richards Hope, *Pinstripes & Pearls: The Women of the Harvard Law Class of '64 Who Forged an Old Girl Network and Paved the Way for Future Generations* (New York, 2003), 107. See Dershowitz, Oral History (October–November 2009); Russell A. Simpson, Oral History, conducted by Mary Beth Basile and Daniel R. Coquillette (May–September 2001), on file with the authors; Bartholet, Oral History (February 1999–March 2000).

113. Judith C. Areen, Interview with Mary Beth Basile and Daniel R. Coquillette (July 2002), on file with the authors.

114. Erwin N. Griswold to Nathan M. Pusey (July 1, 1960), NMP Records.

115. Foster and Simmons, "In Re: Harvard."

116. "Dean Sturges Compares"; "Harry Shulman, Dean."

117. Quotations are from, respectively, Rostow, Annual Report of the Dean, 1963–65, 41; Eugene V. Rostow to Erwin N. Griswold (February 7, 1961), YUS Records. See Erwin N. Griswold to Eugene V. Rostow (February 2, 1961), YUS Records.

118. Kalman, *Legal Realism,* 228.

119. Quotations are from, respectively, Erwin N. Griswold to Eugene V. Rostow (January 11, 1957) and Eugene V. Rostow to Erwin N. Griswold (February 3, 1958), YUS Records.

120. Erwin N. Griswold to Benjamin M. Ziegler (October 9, 1956), YUS Records. See Erwin N. Griswold to Eugene V. Rostow (October 9, 1956), YUS Records.

121. Wesley A. Sturges to Erwin N. Griswold (April 23, 1948; November 3, 1949; June 5, 1952), Erwin N. Griswold to Wesley A. Sturges (November 26, 1947), Eugene V. Rostow to Erwin N. Griswold (December 14, 1956; June 19, 1959), Erwin N. Griswold to Eugene V. Rostow (March 19, 1958), and Louis A. Toepfer to Elsa E. Wolf (May 8, 1950), YUS Records.

122. See *Massachusetts School of Law at Andover, Inc. v. American Bar Association* 107 F. 3d 1026 (Third Circuit, 1997).

123. Eugene V. Rostow to Erwin N. Griswold (May 2, 1988), Erwin N. Griswold Papers, 1925–1994, Harvard Law School Library Historical & Special Collections; Erwin N. Griswold to Eugene V. Rostow (January 7, 22, October 28, 1958), Eugene V. Rostow to Erwin N. Griswold (October 15, 1956; January 13, 20, 27, 29, November 3, 1958), YUS Records.

124. Kalman, *Yale Law School,* 61, 98–192.

125. Haviland, "The Student," 45–48, 81, 105; Griswold, "Legal Education," 1; Kalman, *Legal Realism,* 66.

126. Herbert Hoover, "Principles and Ideals of the United States Government," presidential campaign speech given at Madison Square Garden, New York City (October 22, 1928). See David J. Goldberg, *Discontented America: The United States in the 1920s* (Baltimore, 1999), 177.

127. Haviland, "The Student," 44, 71.

128. Haviland, "The Student," 71–72, 82–83.

129. Quotations are from, respectively, Karl Bemesderfer, "On Being a Law Student," *HLSB* (November 1965): 19; Haviland, "The Student," 92. See Joel Seligman, *The High Citadel: The Influence of Harvard Law School* (Boston, 1978), 90.

130. "Yale Admission Procedure Screens."

131. "Harvard Law Record Reports on Yale Law School," *Yale Law School Association Newsletter* (January 1948).

132. Foster and Simmons, "In Re: Harvard."

133. Victor E. Ferrall Jr., Telephone interview with Bruce A. Kimball (January 2015), notes on file with the authors.

134. Quotations are from, respectively, Carpenter to Dodds (October 1934); Carrington, Oral History (February 2003).

135. Quotations are from, respectively, Haviland, "The Student," 45–48, 71–73, 81, 105; Griswold, "Legal Education," 1.

136. Quotations are from Haviland, "The Student," 54–55, 76, 94, 105. See Foster and Simmons, "In Re: Harvard."

137. Quotation is from HLS Faculty Committee on Curriculum, Meeting minutes (October 29, 1935). See Schmidt, "The Failure of Reform," 4.

138. Griswold, "Legal Education," 1. See also Erwin N. Griswold, "The School since the War," *Harvard Law School Bulletin* (December 1951): 4.

139. The Compilers of the Class of 1934, "A Defense of Harvard Law School by a Graduate of Yale College," in *The Student Looks at Harvard Law School* (unpublished typescript, revised spring of 1934), on file with the authors, 77; see 48, 77.

140. Carpenter to Dodds (October 1934).

141. Quotations are from Griswold, "Legal Education," 1. See "Dean Sturges Compares," 1.

142. Griswold, "Legal Education," 1.

143. Griswold, "Legal Education," 1.

144. Quotations are from Griswold, "Legal Education," 1. See Foster and Simmons, "In Re: Harvard"; Ellen Bernstein, "A Conversation with Erwin N. Griswold," *HLSB* (Fall 1979): 19–23; Frank E. A. Sander, Oral History, conducted by Daniel R. Coquillette and Daniel Hamilton (September–December 1998), on file with the authors.

145. "Draft of a Program," 3.

146. Erwin N. Griswold, Memorandum for the Faculty, Harvard Men in Law Teaching (March 5, 1948), JBC Records; David F. Cavers, "Harvard Law School's Contribution to the Education of Law Teachers in the United States" (December 19, 1960), NMP Records; Donna Fossum, "Law Professors: A Profile of the Teaching Branch of the Legal Profession," *American Bar Foundation Research Journal* (Summer 1980): 501–505.

147. "The Law: Law Schools: Harvard at 150," *Time* (October 6, 1967): 75.

148. Griswold, "Legal Education," 1.

149. [Andrew L. Kaufman, Chair], Memorandum to the Faculty from the Financial Aids Committee [Cambridge, MA, ca. March 1970], typescript on file with the authors, 21–22.

150. Gordon C. Winston, "The Positional Arms Race in Higher Education: Discussion Paper," Education Resources Information Center Document (Washington, DC, April 2000).

151. [Kaufman], Memorandum, 17.

152. Sturges, Annual Report of the Dean, 1949–50, 21; [Kaufman], Memorandum, 2, appendix 2.

153. Quotation is from [Kaufman], Memorandum, 5. See Rostow, Annual Report of the Dean, 1957–1959, 36; University of Chicago Law School Announcement, 1967–68, 49; HLS Catalog, 1967–68, 120; George W. Pierson, *A Yale Book of Numbers: Historical*

Statistics of the College and University, 1701–1976 (New Haven, CT, 1983), 594; discussion in Chapter 14, this volume.

154. [Kaufman], Memorandum, 2.

155. Rostow, Annual Report of the Dean, 1959–1962, 45.

156. Emphasis added. Dershowitz, Oral History (October–November 2009).

157. Quotation is from [Kaufman], Memorandum, 20; see 3, 18.

158. Donald W. Kramer, "Why Some Turn Us Down," *HLSR* (January 31, 1963): 3–4.

159. Simpson, Oral History (July 24, 2001), 49.

160. [Kaufman], Memorandum, 12–15, 116–121.

161. Erwin N. Griswold, "Intellect and Spirit," *HLR* 81 (December 1967): 301.

162. Quotations are from [Kaufman], Memorandum, 16–17.

163. [Kaufman], Memorandum, 16; see i, 8, 17–18, 21.

164. The following analysis draws on data presented in Appendix G.

165. Hadley, Annual Report of the Dean, 1913–14, 13–14; Annual Report of the Treasurer of Yale University, 1909–10, 5; 1914–15, 8–9.

166. Quotation is from Rostow, Annual Report of the Dean, 1959–1962, 42. See Rostow, Annual Report of the Dean, 1954–55, 47–48; Rogers, Annual Report of the Dean, 1914–15, 320–321; 1915–16, 302; Swan, Annual Report of the Dean, 1925–26, 110; 1916–17, 309; 1923–24, 124; Hutchins, Annual Report of the Dean, 1926–27, 119; Clark, Annual Report of the Dean, 1929–30, 164; 1930–31, 175–176; Wesley A. Sturges to Erwin N. Griswold (October 21, 1949), YUS Records.

167. Clark, Annual Report of the Dean, 1929–30, 144–145. See Rogers, Annual Report of the Dean, 1910–11, 217–220.

168. Quotations are from, respectively, Sturges, Annual Report of the Dean, 1949–50, 9; 1952–53, 9. See 1950–51, 11, 24; 1951–52, 11–12.

169. Quotation is from Hutchins, Annual Report of the Dean, 1926–27, 119. See Rogers, Annual Report of the Dean, 1910–11, 220–221; Rostow, Annual Report of the Dean, 1957–1959, 34–35.

170. Quotation is from Clark, Annual Report of the Dean, 1929–30, 162–163. See Hutchins, Annual Report of the Dean, 1928–29, 118; Rostow, Annual Report of the Dean, 1954–55, 47–48; 1957–59, 34–35.

171. Swan, Annual Report of the Dean, 1923–24, 121–122.

172. Quotations are, respectively, from Charles Seymour, "Why the Yale Law Library Needs Additional Endowment Funds: A Communication from President Seymour to All Yale Men in Law" (April 10, 1940), printed broadside, YUS Records; Rostow, Annual Report of the Dean, 1957–1959, 34–35.

173. Rostow, Annual Report of the Dean, 1963–1965, 47.

174. Annual Report of the Treasurer of Yale University, 1894–95, 38; 1896–97, 42; 1897–98, 43; 1899–1900, 69–70; Francis Wayland, Annual Report of the Dean of Yale Law School, 1899–1900, 66–67; 1900–01, 92–94; Rogers, Annual Report of the Dean,

1903–04, 151; Hicks, *Yale Law School: 1895–1915*, 43–45; Kelley, *Yale*, 210–215, 276–277, 340–341.

175. *Battlefield of Merit*, 567–570. These ratios differ from those derived from Appendix G, which considers only the formal endowment, not quasi-endowment or invested surplus. See Annual Report of the Treasurer of Harvard University, 1904–05, 35, 65–70; 1905–06, 67, 102–103; 1908–09, 12, 71–72, 154; Annual Report of the Treasurer of Yale University, 1904–05, 38–39, 78–79; 1908–09, 78, 123.

176. Griswold to Conant (December 3, 1947).

177. Morgan to Conant, Memorandum [ca. December 1936]. See Griswold, Annual Report of the Dean, 1947–48, 390.

178. Rogers, Annual Report of the Dean, 1910–11, 220–221.

179. Annual Report of the Treasurer of Yale University, 1912–13, 120.

180. Annual Report of the Treasurer of Yale University, 1919–1920, 155; 1921–22, 160.

181. "Draft of a Program," 3–4.

182. Clark, Annual Report of the Dean, 1930–31, 178; Annual Report of the Treasurer of Yale University, 1926–27, 176; 1929–30, 16; 1934–35, 12; Sturges to Griswold (October 21, 1949); Rostow, Annual Report of the Dean, 1957–1959, 36.

183. Rogers, Annual Report of the Dean, 1910–11, 220–221; Annual Report of the Treasurer of Yale University, 1934–35, 12.

184. Quotations are from "Draft of a Program," 3–4.

185. Quotation is from Hutchins, Annual Report of the Dean, 1926–27, 119. See also Rogers, Annual Report of the Dean, 1910–11, 221; Angell, Annual Report of the President, 1931–32, 22.

186. Stone, Annual Report of the Dean, 1920–21, 74; Smith, Annual Report of the Dean, 1935–36, 80.

187. Sturges, Annual Report of the Dean, 1949–50, 9; 1950–51, 24; 1951–52, 11–12; 1952–53, 9; Rostow, Annual Report of the Dean, 1957–1959, 34–36; 1959–1962, 42–43.

188. Quotations are from Sturges to Griswold (October 21, 1949). See Griswold to Rostow (January 7, 22, October 28, 1958); Rostow to Griswold (January 13, 20, 27, 29, and November 3, 1958).

189. Sturges to Griswold (October 21, 1949).

190. Erwin N. Griswold to Wesley A. Sturges (November 2, 1949), YUS Records.

191. Griswold to Sturges (November 2, 1949).

192. Griswold to Pusey (July 1, 1960).

193. Rostow, Annual Report of the Dean, 1959–1962, 38–39, 42–43; 1963–1965, 47.

194. Kalman, *Yale Law School*, 57.

195. Liudvika Leisyte and Jay R. Dee, "Understanding Academic Work in a Changing Institutional Environment," in *Higher Education: Handbook of Theory and Research*, ed. John C. Smart and Michael B. Paulsen (London, 2012), 137.

196. Rogers, Annual Report of the Dean, 1910–11, 220–221.

197. Quotations are from Kalman, *Yale Law School,* 8, 322; see 319–323.

198. Kronman, Interview (January 2003).

199. Kalman, *Yale Law School,* 321–322.

200. Quotation is from Griswold, "Legal Education at Harvard," 1. See Lowell, Annual Report of the President, 1908–09, 21.

201. See Appendix G.

202. Quotation is from Kalman, *Yale Law School,* 273.

203. Quote is from Griswold, "Intellect and Spirit," 301.

204. Griswold, "Legal Education," 1.

205. Khurana, *From Higher Aims,* 6. See 18, 26–32, 44–49, 100–102, 127, 133, 150, 173.

206. Stevens, *Law School,* 35–84.

207. Kalman, *Yale Law School,* 363.

208. Kronman, Interview (January 2003).

209. Quotation is from Kalman, *Yale Law School,* 312.

210. Quotation is from Kronman, Interview (January 2003).

CHAPTER SIXTEEN

Derek Bok's Tumultuous Interlude, 1968–1970

After Dean Erwin Griswold (1946–1967) left for Washington, Harvard president Nathan Pusey (1953–1971) appointed Associate Dean James Casner as acting dean for 1967–68, and "everybody sort of breathed a huge sigh," recalled Professor Harold Berman. "All of a sudden faculty meetings became very different. With Erwin, you always said, 'Mr. Dean.'"[1] Pent-up complaints and suggestions could suddenly be voiced, and individual faculty responded to the president's invitation for thoughts about the school's needs with ninety-three, single-spaced, typed pages of recommendations.[2]

In January 1968, Pusey appointed Derek Bok (1968–1970) to be dean, and Bok led the Law School through the ensuing student unrest and protests concerning the civil rights movement and the Vietnam War. In April 1969, protestors against the war occupied University Hall in Harvard Yard. Four hundred riot police were called to clear the building, and they arrested 145 Harvard and Radcliffe students. In December 1969, members of the newly formed Organization for Black Unity (OBU), including five law students, occupied University Hall, precipitating disciplinary hearings before the Harvard law faculty. As those hearings were reaching a crisis stage in April 1970, an antiwar demonstration in Harvard Square erupted into a riot that left scores of people injured, buildings trashed, and police cars burning amid widespread looting that 2,000 riot police could barely control.

In subsequent weeks, law students boycotted classes and the library, and the faculty postponed exams. President Pusey observed that the "shameful events" challenged "reason, fairness and decency," but he had already lost control of the campus and been secretly sidelined by the Harvard Corporation, which called on Professor Archibald Cox (LL.B. 1937) to preside unofficially over the university. Cox's insight and skill allowed Harvard to avoid a tragedy that could have surpassed the killings at Kent State University in May 1970.[3]

The protests against racial injustice and the Vietnam War differed in significant respects, but both issues contributed to fostering "distrust of authority" among students, as Dean Bok stated in April 1969.[4] Though the gender inequity pervading the Law School was not yet targeted, this general distrust also ignited a revolt against the Law School's grading system, the whetstone of the intellectual sword. Instead of competing with each other for grades, students sought to abolish grades altogether.

Dean Derek Bok

Derek Bok (LL.B. 1954) was well suited by disposition and training to lead a law school buffeted by change and turmoil, much of it beyond the school's actual control. He was born into a prominent Pennsylvania family in which dignified reserve and confidence were assumed. His father, Curtis Bok, was an author and a justice of the Pennsylvania Supreme Court; his mother, Margaret Plummer Bok, founded the progressive school that Derek attended as a boy.[5] Bok eventually enrolled at Stanford University, where he became interested in foreign affairs and diplomacy and earned a B.A. in political science. Upon graduation in 1951, he narrowly chose Harvard Law School over enlisting in the Foreign Service.

At Harvard, Bok's interest in human relations and conflict resolution led him to study labor law with Archibald Cox and Kingman Brewster Jr. (LL.B. 1948). He excelled academically and was elected to the *Harvard Law Review,* but rather than pursuing a judicial clerkship, he traveled to Paris on a Fulbright Scholarship to study political science. Between 1955 and 1958, Bok completed a master's degree in economics and psychology at George Washington University while serving in the U.S. Army at the Office of the General Counsel in Washington, D.C.[6]

This was not the standard path to the Harvard Law School faculty that had been established in the mid-twentieth century. In fact, election to the *Harvard Law Review* was just about the only conventional step in Bok's law school academic career. But his training in diplomacy, psychology, economics, and political science were exactly what he would later need. Practically everyone who experienced Bok's administration shared their admiration of the man's incredible external restraint under provocation and his uncanny ability to convince even his worst adversaries that he was listening to them.

In 1958 Cox, Brewster, and David Cavers (LL.B. 1926) recruited Bok to the faculty. Cox, in particular, mentored his young colleague, and they co-authored the leading casebook on labor law. In 1961, at age thirty-one, Bok was promoted to tenured professor.[7] He kept a fairly low profile, living in Belmont close to the Griswolds, with his daughters and his wife, Sissela, a brilliant ethicist whose parents, Gunnar Myrdal and Alva Myrdal, were both Nobel laureates. His most noteworthy role on the faculty was chairing the Continuing Committee on Legal Education from 1965 to 1968. This committee proposed a policy to strengthen student relationships with the faculty by encouraging regular mentoring meetings between students and faculty members. Bok noted that the policy would "give every student the feeling that there is at least one member of the faculty with whom he may meet, if he wishes, and whose advice he might even seek on other questions."[8] In light of the alienation between faculty and students in the early 1970s, the policy was prescient.

Having appointed Associate Dean Casner to be acting dean in September 1967, President Pusey appointed Bok as the next dean in January 1968. Bok was just thirty-seven, but he had widespread faculty support—a tribute to his low-key style and collegiality. Pusey reported to the Corporation that "one of the more vocal younger members of the Faculty mentioned Mr. Bok's thoughtful skepticism and caution as a possible sign that he might not be a bold and vigorous leader in matters of public concern." But Pusey felt just the opposite. "Skepticism and caution," he thought, were "virtues in a dean."[9]

No one could have predicted how quickly, dramatically, and even violently these virtues would be tested. Two of the initial challenges intruded forcefully from the outside: the civil rights movement and the Vietnam War. Another came from within: the "Grade Wars." Although these developments caused "much unrest among students" during his first year, "it is a credit to Dean Bok that his administration has been very responsive to student needs and complaints," observed the *Harvard Law School Yearbook 1970*.[10] Indeed, in February 1968, immediately after he was named dean, Bok emphasized in the student newspaper that the Continuing Committee on Legal Education and the Joint Student-Faculty Committee offered two major advantages to the Law School and its students: "that the School obtained the benefit of ideas from the students, who see things from a different vantage point," and that "students have a forum to discuss their ideas and overcome any feeling that they are dealing with an impersonal institution."[11]

Derek C. Bok, LL.B. 1954. Faculty 1958 to present, Dean 1968–70, President of Harvard University 1971–1991, Interim President 2006–2007.

Harvard Law School Yearbook, 1978. Courtesy of Harvard Yearbook Publications.

The Civil Rights Movement, 1960–1970

African Americans had been fighting for their civil rights in the United States since the founding of the republic, but even after the Civil War, the nation and Harvard Law School did not adequately begin to appreciate their struggle until the 1960s. Legal foundations of the civil rights movement were laid prior to World War II by Charles Houston (LL.B. 1922, S.J.D. 1923), William Hastie (LL.B. 1930, S.J.D. 1933), Thurgood Marshall, and other renowned African American lawyers. In the decade after World War II, long-standing legal barriers to racial justice began to fall. In July 1948 President Truman desegregated the armed services by executive order. In May 1954 the Supreme Court declared segregated schools unconstitutional in *Brown v. Board of Education*.[12] Then, a series of events in the early 1960s—including the Montgomery Bus Boycott, the horrific burning of the Birmingham Seventeenth Street Baptist Church, and the murder of three civil rights workers in Mississippi—focused public attention on the injustice facing African Americans and galvanized students on campuses throughout the country.

At Harvard Law School, a small number of students and recent graduates, particularly William L. Higgs (LL.B. 1955), Elizabeth Holtzman (LL.B. 1965), Michael O. Finkelstein (LL.B. 1958), and Fred Wallace (LL.B. 1964), joined the wave of Harvard students traveling south to participate in the civil rights protests. Wallace, an African American graduate, even faced trumped-up charges while representing civil rights demonstrators in Virginia. These courageous students received support from the *Harvard Law Record* and from certain faculty—particularly Clark Byse, Paul Freund (LL.B. 1931, S.J.D. 1932), John H. Mansfield (LL.B. 1956), Charles Nesson (LL.B. 1963), and Albert Sacks (LL.B. 1948).[13]

Within the Law School, the civil rights movement inspired a number of initiatives, including the opening of the Harvard Civil Rights–Civil Liberties Research Service (1960) and the hosting of debates on civil rights topics at the Harvard Law School Forum, where Martin Luther King Jr., Malcolm X, Governor Ross Barnett of Mississippi, and U.S. Senator Strom Thurmond of South Carolina spoke. In 1963 the Law School began offering a course on civil rights and discrimination, and a seminar on civil rights taught by Sacks.[14]

In the mid-1960s the unrest and protests expanded beyond the south. Race riots in the Watts neighborhood of Los Angeles in August 1965, the founding of the Black Panthers in October 1966, and the riots in Newark and Detroit in July 1967 alienated many sympathetic white northerners. In April 1968, shortly after Bok's appointment as dean, Martin Luther King Jr. was assassinated, and two months later, in June 1968, Robert Kennedy, the Democratic presidential candidate, was also shot down.

At the Law School, a number of students joined the effort to desegregate the Boston school system. Within the Law School itself, the low enrollment of African American students became increasingly troubling and embarrassing.

Martin Luther King with students at the Harvard Law School Forum, 1963.

Harvard Law School Yearbook, 1963. Courtesy of Harvard Yearbook Publications.

In 1963 only 3 African American students had entered in the class of 550. There were 28 in the fall of 1967, and then 35 in Bok's first year as dean. Yet the total in the school was only 82, merely 5 percent of the student body.[15] In September 1968 the African American students at the school rightfully complained that the student body was only part of the problem, as all the faculty were white along with almost all the school staff. Also, the curriculum failed to address the "social conditions of our time."[16]

Bok then appointed Walter J. Leonard, a graduate of Morehouse College and Howard University Law School, as assistant director of admissions and financial aid—the first senior African American administrator in the school's history. Leonard's term from 1969 to 1971 was full of challenges, but led to a more effective effort to "attract, recruit, and develop black legal talent," in his words.[17] By 1970 the number of African American students had risen to 110 out of 1,666, or nearly 7 percent.[18] Due to this appointment and progress, many African American students held Dean Bok in high regard, according to Weldon J. Rougeau (J.D. 1972), who became a prominent civil rights leader.[19]

Bok also appointed African Americans to the faculty, though none were tenure-track, which would have required assent by the faculty. In 1969 Bok appointed as a lecturer David S. Nelson, a graduate of Boston College Law School, who later became one of the nation's early African American federal judges. During the academic years 1969–70 and 1970–71, Derrick Bell, a graduate of the University of Pittsburgh law school, was hired as a lecturer to teach a course on "Race, Racism and American Law." Also, Charles H. Jones Jr., a graduate of the University of Chicago Law School, was appointed as a teaching fellow.[20]

Occupation of University Hall

These actions failed to prevent a major civil rights crisis during Bok's deanship. On November 14, 1969, the Harvard-Radcliffe Association of African and Afro-American Students, whose members included both undergraduate and graduate students (as well as law students), presented fourteen demands to the university administration, including that it hire dramatically more minority employees. The following day, November 15, these students entered the office of Harvard College dean Ernest May to confront him about the university's hiring practices.[21] By this point the Harvard Corporation had already taken responsibility for daily operation of the university away from President Pusey and entrusted it, unofficially, to Professor Archibald Cox.

Cox negotiated with the students, who had created a new umbrella organization, the OBU, and they reached a deal committing the university to specific actions to promote minority hiring. But on December 11 the OBU accused the university of stalling, and about seventy-five members occupied a series of Harvard properties, including University Hall. This time Cox obtained a restraining order from the court and persuaded the occupying students, on being served, to leave the building.[22] The university then filed disciplinary charges against more than half of the undergraduates involved. Seeking to avoid a confrontation, Cox announced that the university would drop the charges against seven students, issue warnings to twenty, and suspend discipline for nine. None would be forced to leave Harvard, and the undergraduate controversy then died down.[23]

Five of the student occupiers were enrolled at Harvard Law School. When law students participate in such protests, a special consideration arises. Should they be subject to stricter discipline than other students, given that they aspire to be admitted to the bar as "officers of the court" and take oaths to uphold the legal system? Most Boards of Bar Examiners, including Massachusetts, require both the applicant and the law school dean to disclose disciplinary proceedings involving law students. For example, in Massachusetts today, law school deans must report to the Board "anything which appears to me to be adverse in respect of moral character or fitness to practice law of the applicant."[24] In short, when law students engage in illegal acts, even acts of nonviolent civil disobedience, they are exposed to professional risk.

The Law School chose to bring disciplinary charges against the five African American law students who participated in the OBU occupation of University Hall.[25] The reaction was swift. On February 5, 1970, fifty-two of the 110 African American students in the Law School petitioned the faculty "to receive the same punishment as the five law students facing discipline for participating in the [OBU] takeover of University Hall."[26]

In addition, one of the five students charged, Gregory K. Pilkington (J.D. 1972), who later became a name partner of a London firm, refused to attend his disciplinary hearing at the Law School because it was closed to the public. The school's Administrative Board had agreed to a public hearing, but denied Pilkington's request for a room that would "accommodate 200 to 300 people." Pilkington responded that "these hearings are designed to repress those students who ally with Campus workers and fight Harvard racism." He paid a severe price for these actions—on February 12 the Law School Administrative Board recommended "warnings or probation" for the other four students, but recommended "suspension" for Pilkington.[27]

When the faculty met on February 24 to consider the recommendation, forty students entered the meeting and refused to heed Dean Bok's repeated requests that they leave. About 150 students had gathered outside the meeting to protest both the imposition of discipline and the exclusion of students from the faculty meeting. When Pilkington was admitted to the meeting and told that he could bring in two or three "advisors," about eighty students filed into the meeting room, believing that they were allowed to do so. Confusion ensued. Bok insisted that the students leave. They refused, and the meeting was adjourned.[28]

The following day the faculty met again, with forty students waiting outside discussing "disruptive action." The faculty then convened that night at a "secret location" in the Holyoke Center, but thirty students discovered the location and gathered outside the room. The entire procedure was turning into a farce. The faculty voted to hold an open meeting for students and faculty on Friday, February 27. Nearly 700 students attended, with 200 listening in from an overflow room. Bok made an opening statement, and faculty members, including Louis Loss and Charles Fried, joined the defendants and students in a full debate. On that day and the following Monday, the law students held huge "community meetings" to protest the proposed discipline, focusing particularly on the career-threatening disciplinary action against Pilkington.[29]

On March 3 the faculty met in closed session for ten hours, but reached no decision. The most senior African American faculty member, Lecturer Derrick Bell, refused to participate, stating beforehand:

> I view the unwillingness to do justice now, but to promise to correct any future difficulties resulting from current injustice, as the typical traditional willingness of whites to treat blacks as, at the moment, it pleases them, secure in the knowledge that at some later date they can call some other white men and clear up any problems.[30]

On the following day the faculty voted to uphold the recommendation of the Administrative Board for two warnings, two probations, and one suspension. The students were furious. On March 26, 1970, the Harvard Black Law Students Association (BLSA) condemned the actions of the Law School as blatantly racist.[31] Nevertheless, Pilkington's suspension stood. This was the kind of institutional standoff that Bok had sought to avoid.

How far this might have escalated will never be known, because a little more than two weeks later, on April 15, an even more explosive event occurred. Police and antiwar protestors clashed violently in Harvard Square following a Vietnam Moratorium rally on Boston Common. Suddenly the Law School and Dean Bok faced a new set of crises that temporarily pushed the Vietnam War to the forefront.

The protests against racial injustice and the Vietnam War were interrelated and reinforced each other, due not only to their concurrence, similar tactics, and rebellious spirit. In addition, African Americans paid a particularly high price in the Vietnam War, which relied heavily on draftees, because they had less access to the deferments available to students in higher education. Hence, President Johnson's use of force in Vietnam was sometimes compared to violence against African Americans in the South. Muhammad Ali, the heavyweight boxing champion of the world, made this point in refusing to obey his induction orders, stating that "No Viet Cong ever called me a nigger." He refused to travel "10,000 miles to help murder, kill, and burn other people to simply help continue the domination of white slave masters over dark people."[32]

In April 1967 Martin Luther King Jr. remarked on the tie between the civil rights movement and resistance to the Vietnam War:

> This madness must cease. We must stop now. I speak as a child of God and brother to the suffering poor of Vietnam. I speak for those whose land is being laid waste, whose homes are being destroyed, whose culture is being subverted. I speak for the poor of America who are paying the double price of smashed hopes at home and death and corruption in Vietnam. I speak as a citizen of the world, for the world as it stands aghast at the path we have taken. I speak as an American to the leaders of my own nation. The great initiative in this war is ours. The initiative to stop it must be ours.[33]

By the late 1960s the links between the Vietnam crisis and the civil rights movement had become explicit.

Vietnam: Three Phases, 1965–1970

Between 1964 and 1973, 40 percent of the 2.7 million eligible American men were drafted, and 10 percent were sent to fight in Vietnam.[34] Initially the war seemed far removed from the everyday life of Harvard Law students. But, gradually, they had to take a position on the war and to confront the choice of whether they would participate.

Serving in the military had never been questioned by Harvard law students in prior wars. The Civil War was profoundly divisive, but the law students willingly fought for the North and the South and died in appalling numbers. In World War I, the problem for the school was that too many students wished to volunteer at once, far more than the Army could process. Over 86 died. In World War II, the classrooms of the school emptied, and 112 students and graduates died. But of the 58,307 Americans killed in action in Vietnam, only one Harvard Law School student was among them, Nelson Ramon Morales, who matriculated in September 1964, completed his first year, and withdrew in June 1965. For the first time in its history, the Law School encountered a national war that many students opposed, and many evaded.

The Vietnam crisis at Harvard Law School developed in three distinct phases during the administration of Dean Bok. Phase I, lasting from the onset of the war in 1965 through the spring of 1968, saw growing dissent about the legality of the war and increasing anxiety about the draft. But life at the school continued as usual. During this time, more enlisted men than draftees were fighting, and huge numbers were exempted from the draft.

During Phase II, lasting the 1968–69 academic year, things turned ugly at the university. Instead of orderly debates and discussion, students began to engage in active and sometimes violent protests, culminating with the student occupation of University Hall in April 1969. But the protests and strikes during Phase II occurred outside the Law School, although law students and faculty were certainly involved.

Phase III brought the upheaval inside the Law School. The unrest began quietly in the fall of 1969, but grew as opposition to the Vietnam War mounted and combined with civil rights activism, culminating in violent riots and protests in April and May 1970. The antiwar protests—coupled with the bitter internal debate about the disciplinary action taken against the five African American law students involved in the OBU takeover of University Hall— brought the Law School to a virtual standstill. All classes were suspended, and the spring 1970 examinations were deferred and rescheduled.[35] Each of these three phases requires careful analysis.

Vietnam: Phase I, 1965–1968

When Phase I began in the fall of 1965, the Vietnam crisis seemed distant from the everyday life of law students. There was conscription, requiring every male—97 percent of the Law School students—to register with his local draft board and carry a draft card. But the automatic deferment for college and graduate students, extending to age twenty-six and beyond for husbands and fathers, meant that the conflict in Southeast Asia did not affect students privileged enough to attend Harvard Law School.

Yet, when students returned to the Law School for the fall semester in 1965, the first American troops had arrived in Vietnam and begun fighting. Many students started to worry how long their deferments would continue. According to a student essay published in 1966, "roughly 80 percent of all male conversation concerns evading the draft."[36] In October 1965 a recruitment meeting for the Judge Advocate General's Corps, which had drawn only nine students the year before, attracted an overflow crowd of 380. When an Oklahoma draft board accidentally eliminated the deferments of a group of law students, a momentary panic ensued, prompting "every male student to wonder about his own status," noted the *Harvard Law Record.*[37]

In December 1965, Lieutenant General Lewis Hershey, director of the Selective Service System, spoke on campus. Some of his remarks, particularly those on the need to rein in the discretion of local draft boards, were reassuring. But other comments were not. "Hershey stated that he hoped it would not be necessary to revert to basing deferments on class standing and scores on a national exam, but claimed this might happen if colleges did not 'clean their own stables,'" reported the *Record.* This possibility was worrisome because at that time law students were treated as undergraduates and thus could lose their deferment due to low class rank.[38] At the Law School, this possibility magnified the existing anxiety about grading and class rank, which now determined not only one's professional prospects, but also whether one might have to go to war.

Hershey's warning became reality when a National Selective Service Examination (NSSE) was instituted in 1966, and young men who scored high enough could earn a deferment. The NSSE sought to limit the socioeconomic advantages of young men whose families could afford to keep them enrolled in higher education and thus ensure their student deferment until age twenty-six. Nevertheless, the NSSE still seemed to favor college-educated students and created controversy as the war casualties mounted. In addition, college students who ranked in the top quarter of their class in their senior year and went directly to law school after graduating were entitled to a deferment, which further advantaged such students whose families could afford to send them to law school.[39]

The Selective Service then eliminated that entitlement in order to nudge law students into taking the NSSE. Furthermore, the Selective Service announced that law students—originally grouped with undergraduates and requiring only a grade of 70 on the NSSE to ensure deferment—were now to be regarded as graduate students, requiring a minimum grade of 80. These changes led Harvard Law School secretary William L. Bruce (LL.B. 1951) to encourage all law students to take the NSSE to ensure their deferment, no matter how well they did in college. Suggestions that class rank in law school might also be counted intensified the anxiety, and no one was comforted by the assurances of Vice Dean Louis Toepfer (LL.B. 1947) that "under an identical system in place during the Korean War very few students were forced to leave the Law School."[40] A new kind of intellectual sword was about to fall, and pressure rose at the Law School.

During Phase I, extensive debate also commenced in the Law School about the war itself. In November 1965 a petition circulated at the Law School supporting the war "to stop the spread of Communism," and 400 students signed, including members of both the Harvard Law School Republican Club and the Harvard Law-Graduate Democratic Club. Others expressed extreme opposition. Certain members of the faculty, particularly David Cavers and Mark Howe (LL.B. 1933), publicly criticized President Lyndon Johnson's administration for intimidating critics of American foreign policy by threatening to investigate protestors. The *Harvard Law Record* ran concurring editorials.[41]

At this time, there also appeared the first student organization opposing the war, cautiously named the Vietnam Study Committee. The Harvard Law-Graduate Democratic Club began espousing opposition and resolved that, "since the Administration has disregarded valid criticisms of its Vietnamese policy, while continuing to escalate the War, we oppose the present Administration policy." The Democrats' resolution also called for an immediate halt to the bombing, unconditioned peace negotiations, and free elections in Vietnam.[42]

When the students returned to the school in the fall of 1966, opposition to the Vietnam War became entwined with students' dissatisfaction about academic issues. The possibility of basing draft deferments on class rank in law school magnified frustration with what Clark Byse called "institutional arthritis," concerning grading policy in general. In one of his last acts as dean, Griswold had established the Joint Student-Faculty Committee, chaired by Byse and comprised of six professors and six students, all chosen by the dean. Established primarily to address academic policies, this committee also started to serve as a forum to debate the war.[43]

Although discussions about Vietnam became louder and more polarized, they continued to be civil and even academic at the Law School, despite divisions and anxiety among the students. The International Law Club invited Leonard Meeker (LL.B. 1940), legal advisor to the State Department, to speak, and he defended the legality of the war before a respectful audience. The same Club invited Harvard professors Roger D. Fisher (LL.B. 1948), Stanley Hoffmann, and Adam Yarmolinsky to propose alternative ways to end American involvement in the war.[44]

During the spring of 1967, the school tried to ease students' worry about the NSSE and about the draft generally. School secretary William Bruce pointed out that no law student had yet been drafted, and that if a student deferment was revoked, students would still have a right to a temporary deferment that allowed them to finish the academic year. Thus, if a student lost his deferment and was not drafted during the summer between academic years, he could get another temporary deferment to finish the succeeding academic year. Of course, students lost their deferment upon graduation, and third-year students showed unprecedented interest in teaching positions and defense work, which brought deferments.[45]

Selective Service Changes

Everything changed when Congress passed the Military Selective Service Act in June 1967. Under the new rules, the 1967–68 school year would be the last one in which automatic deferments would be given to graduate and professional school students. Of the 539 students who entered the Law School in September 1967, 29 percent eventually enlisted, were drafted, or dodged the draft by fleeing to Canada. By 1970–71, the third-year class had only 388 students, the smallest since World War II.[46]

Consequently, debate about the war began to intensify within the Law School during the 1967–68 year. In October 1967, fifty Law School students joined the antiwar March on the Pentagon in Washington, D.C., and students organized an "Open Meeting" at the Law School in early November to discuss the war. The majority of those attending the meeting opposed the war, but many expressed alternative views, and the *Harvard Law Record* described the event as a "model" meeting, having an "impromptu, yet moderate tone."[47] At the end, 120 students and ten faculty members, led by Paul Bator (LL.B. 1956), formed an Anti-Vietnam Committee to conduct a letter-writing campaign to persuade alumni to act and provide legal services to draft resisters. It was widely agreed that law students should not engage in civil disobedience.[48] Nevertheless, in early November several law students joined a predominantly undergraduate demonstration on the main campus where a Dow Chemical recruiter was involuntarily detained in a classroom for seven hours. The incident prompted President Pusey to call for "sufficiently harsh punishment" for the activists involved.[49] Still, the atmosphere within the Law School remained calm compared to growing demonstrations elsewhere in the university and across the country.

This relative calm stemmed partly from the disagreement among the law students themselves, many of whom were in ROTC and an increasing number of whom were veterans. A student poll in December 1967 reported that 52 percent demanded an immediate halt to bombing, while 20 percent supported current troop numbers, and only 16 percent favored an immediate withdrawal. Hence, the responses were mixed and not all radical.[50] A noncredit "course" on the war was taught in the spring of 1968 by Professors Paul Freund, Abram Chayes (LL.B. 1949), Frank Michelman (LL.B. 1960), Louis L. Jaffe (LL.B. 1928), Lloyd L. Weinreb (LL.B. 1962), John Mansfield, Paul Bator, Alan Dershowitz, Charles Fried, and Albert Sacks. On February 19, 1968, some 700 students and thirty-nine faculty members signed a full-page ad in the *Wall Street Journal* calling for "military and political de-escalation" and "genuine negotiations."[51] Even this unprovocative action attracted less than half of the students.

Far from Cambridge, things were beginning to change profoundly. First, the Selective Service made a serious tactical error by sending a letter to local draft boards recommending that they revoke deferments of students engaged in "illegal activity that interferes with recruiting" on college campuses. Even law students who supported the war saw this as a threat to civil liberty, and the Harvard law faculty voted to condemn the action.[52] More significantly, the Viet Cong launched the "Tet Offensive" on January 30, 1968, after which many Americans started to realize that the war was going badly. In response, President Johnson called for thousands more additional combat troops in Vietnam, and many occupational and graduate deferments were gradually phased out. The *Harvard Law School Yearbook 1970* described Johnson's announcement as "a moment of doom for most students."[53]

Also, for the first time the Law School itself began to recognize that it could lose a substantial number of students. Professor Robert Braucher (LL.B. 1939), a distinguished World War II veteran, wrote a statement on the school's policies on readmission after military service. Braucher observed that the school had always "readmitted students who have had to withdraw because of military service," though readmission was sometimes limited by available space.[54] First-year students then sought clarification on what would happen if they refused induction. The faculty made a tentative response in April 1968 with an official readmission policy, stating, "It is expected that the [readmission] policy would be applied to a student convicted for a refusal to serve which was rooted in grounds of conscience."[55]

This tentative language meant that both students and faculty at the Law School now had to confront a fundamental issue. Law students, and the Law School itself, were dedicated to the rule of law and loyalty to the legal profession and the American justice system. Graduates would swear oaths on being admitted to the bar to support the legal system. What room was there for serious conscientious objection and civil disobedience, for such students and such a school?

These issues took on added significance as events outside the Law School turned increasingly ominous. In May 1968 the FBI launched a secret investigation into "New Left" groups on campuses. The popular jest "Just because you're paranoid, doesn't mean they aren't really out to get you" now seemed serious. On May 17, 1968, Philip F. Berrigan S.J. and his brother Daniel J. Berrigan S.J. entered a draft board office in Catonsville, Maryland, and destroyed the files in front of a crowd of press and supporters.[56] In June 1968 Robert Kennedy, the presidential candidate supported by antiwar activists, was assassinated.

Meanwhile, the Law School again tried to reassure first-year students that if they made it back to the school for the fall, they would receive a temporary deferment. The head of the Massachusetts Selective Service Appeals Board promised that students would not be drafted out of law school in the middle of the semester or, perhaps, the academic year.[57] On that equivocal note, Phase I, the period of relative calm and order within the university, ended. Phase II followed, extending through the academic year 1968–69, when strikes and protests erupted at Harvard University but still remained largely outside the Law School.

Phase II: The Gathering Storm, 1968–69

The 1968–69 academic year began quietly. The *Harvard Law Record* observed in September that both the students and the faculty "lacked the 'organization, interest, and purpose' needed to oppose the Vietnam War." Likewise, Archibald Cox did not expect that Harvard would experience the violent student unrest that he had studied as chair of the Columbia University commission investigating the disturbances there in the summer of 1968.[58]

But the war was going badly. By 1968 nearly 16,600 Americans had been killed, and far more Vietnamese. The Tet Offensive continued from January through September 1968, and in February the Johnson administration called up 48,000 more draftees. At the Law School, the quiet fall of 1968 masked the fact that 63 second-year students did not return to campus.[59] Only 4 had been drafted, but 30 others had enlisted or joined either the Peace Corps or Vista. Sixty-five more had dropped out by November 1968, largely for draft-related issues. A total of 128 out of the class of 550 were gone by December. More sobering still, Walter A. Reiser Jr. (LL.M. 1967), the Law School's advisor on draft issues, predicted another 200 would be drafted by June 1969.[60]

Still, the law students took no radical action during the fall of 1968. On December 13, 1968, a small group picketed recruiters from a law firm for the first time when they protested Milbank Tweed's recruiters at the Placement Office. But this action protested Milbank's involvement in South Africa. Meanwhile, Dean Bok directed student demands for reform into constructive channels. He arranged to include students on school committees, and asked the Joint Student-Faculty Committee to recommend student members. Also, the students would be chosen by petition and lottery, not handpicked by the dean. Bok urged the students to get involved, and a student-organized Ad Hoc Committee on Student Participation recommended that the chosen students attend faculty meetings, a genuinely radical step that Bok neither opposed nor supported, but promised to present to the faculty for consideration.[61] Despite the ominous developments in Vietnam, the Law School was quiet.

Again, the shock that upset this equilibrium came from the outside, prompted by Pusey's unwillingness to compromise and inability to calm student unrest. By the fall of 1968 some students had organized a Harvard chapter of the Students for a Democratic Society (SDS) and begun to protest the presence of ROTC programs at Harvard, which, they believed, directly contributed to the war's continuation. Unlike Bok, who had always maintained that the Law School was neutral in discussions about Vietnam, Pusey gave unconditional support to ROTC. When SDS members staged a sit-in at a meeting of the Faculty of Arts and Sciences in Paine Hall on December 12, 1968, Pusey sought discipline, and on March 20, 1969, Harvard College announced that scholarships would be reduced for some of the students involved. Furthermore, Pusey rejected a request, voted by the Faculty of Arts and Sciences in February 1969, to make ROTC "a regular extracurricular activity without special privileges." In fact, a month later Pusey announced his full support for the continued existence of the ROTC at Harvard.[62]

Pusey's unwillingness to compromise on ROTC played directly into the hands of SDS, which on April 6, 1969, issued a pamphlet entitled "The Time to Fight Is Now" listing six demands, including the abolition of ROTC.[63] After some debate, the SDS leaders then decided on the immediate, illegal action of seizing University Hall, the seat of Harvard's administration. On April 9, SDS members stormed the building, forcibly removing university officers, including the college's dean for students, Archie C. Epps III, who was carried out on his chair.[64]

Pusey believed that militant leaders of SDS had led the occupation against the wishes of most of their followers as well as the larger community. In any event, his immediate and high-handed response ensured broad support for the occupiers among university groups who would normally have been unsympathetic or directly opposed. At dawn on April 10, 1969, nearly 400 riot police forced their way into University Hall, arresting 145 Harvard and Radcliffe students and seriously injuring 48. Two thousand more moderate students immediately gathered in Memorial Hall to protest the president's action.[65] Meeting secretly, the members of the Harvard Corporation agreed it was a botched operation. They quietly began easing Pusey out of the daily operations, and sought counsel from Archibald Cox.[66]

Following Pusey's disastrous decision to forcibly clear University Hall, over 10,000 students from across the University declared a three-day strike. On April 11, the Faculty of Arts and Sciences condemned in equally harsh terms both the student occupation and Pusey's reaction. But the Law School remained relatively calm, with law students assisting arrested demonstrators at the East Cambridge Courthouse. The same day, students at the Law School adopted a resolution in support of the university-wide strike (but not SDS), and only a third of the 1,500 law students signed. "Teach-ins" were organized in the law library. Nearly forty faculty members and 500 students participated, and everything was orderly.[67]

As to ROTC, the law faculty believed that the issue fell within the jurisdiction of the Faculty of Arts and Sciences. and many law students did not believe that eliminating ROTC would "have a serious effect on the Vietnam War by dramatically reducing the supply of officers."[68] Meanwhile, President Richard M. Nixon had been inaugurated in January 1969 and begun negotiations with the North Vietnamese to end U.S. involvement. Attempting to gain an advantage in the talks, Nixon sought to attain military superiority, and in 1970 he expanded the war into Cambodia. This was a great political blunder by an otherwise savvy politician, who failed to see that domestic politics was determining the end of the war.[69]

By June 1969, ominous events were brewing at Harvard. At commencement, two-thirds of the Harvard College graduating class turned their backs on Henry Kissinger, the invited commencement speaker, who, after matriculating at Harvard Law School in September 1949, earned the B.A. in 1950 and the PhD in 1954, both from Harvard, as described in Chapter 12. In his speech at the Law School commencement in the afternoon, graduating student Meldon Levine (J.D. 1969) asserted that "universities, like society in general, refused to take student concerns seriously. . . . Thus, students were left with no means other than violence to achieve their ideals."[70] Fulfilling this ominous warning, Phase III brought the upheaval inside the Law School.

Phase III: Protest within the Law School, 1969–70

At the beginning of fall semester 1969, the "protests" at the Law School were mild, even frivolous. There was a basketball "dribble-in" to protest hours at the Hemenway Gym, and a boycott of Harkness Cafeteria by "Students for Less Overpricing" (SLOP).[71] But the third-year class of 1970 had 200 fewer students than the first-year class. Only ten students had failed; the rest had been drafted or dodged the draft. The second-year class had lost eighty-one students.[72]

In October 1969 the entire Law School community debated whether to participate in the nationwide "Moratorium on the Vietnam War." The students requested that classes be canceled, but the faculty, under Bok's leadership, adhered to the principle that the school should not be committed to a political position. Many students agreed with this decision, although the leaders of the HLS Moratorium Day Steering Committee argued that "the War is not a partisan political issue." When the Faculty of Arts and Sciences voted officially to oppose the war, even more law students wished the Law School would do the same. But Bok diplomatically argued that "more harm than good will be done by attempting to take an institutional stand on matters of this sort." Simultaneously, he ignored the cancellation or rescheduling of classes by many faculty and the absence of over 550 law students during the Moratorium.[73]

In November some Harvard law professors, including Laurence Tribe (LL.B. 1966) and Alan Dershowitz, conducted a "Harvard Law Mini-Forum" on the war. Soon after, Dershowitz and Professor Stephen Breyer (LL.B. 1964), a future Supreme Court Justice, planned to lead a Law School contingent to join the second moratorium march in Washington D.C. in November. At the event, the Law School representatives served as "law marshals," constituting "a large moderate buffer between police and more militant members of the peace movement," in the words of Breyer.[74]

These developments disappointed the small minority of students who organized the Harvard Radical Law Students' Group, which maintained that the moratorium was advanced by establishment leaders as a harmless outlet for discontent.[75] Yet even that "moderate buffer" attracted only a few hundred law students to the Washington, and protests against recruiters at the Law School focused on South African apartheid and racial issues and involved fewer than a hundred students, mostly members of the BLSA.[76] Thus, Dean Bok's conciliatory policies successfully maintained ordinary operations at the Law School during the fall of 1969.

Then came the dreaded draft lottery. Many law students and other Americans across the country agreed that, with dramatically rising casualty rates after the Tet Offensive in 1968, educational deferments were no longer morally justified. In an effort to be more equitable and transparent, the federal government adopted a new military draft system in which one's eligibility for the draft depended on the random selection of one's birthday. For the first time since World War II, male students at the Law School, who constituted about 95 percent of the Law School student body, would be subjected to the same probability of being drafted into military service as all other American men. On December 1, 1969, the first lottery to determine the draft order by birthday took place, as millions of Americans across the country listened on radio or watched on television. The 1970 *Yearbook* observed that the results meant "students now knew where they stood with respect to the draft and just how likely they were to be inducted."[77] But the results also brought the prospect of fighting in Southeast Asia much closer to students at elite institutions.

Concurrently, student protests arising against Harvard's racial inequities bled into those against the war. As described above, the OBU occupation of University Hall on December 5, 1969, led to the contentious proceedings at the Law School through the winter and the decision in March 1970 to discipline the five participating law students. The Vietnam crisis and the civil rights protests thus reinforced each other. Both involved occupations of University Hall, illegal protests by law students, and, by the spring of 1970, the participation of large numbers of "moderate" students.

This was the context at the Law School for the third national Vietnam Moratorium, on April 14, 1970. In recognition of the event, Professor Abram Chayes presented a petition signed by over 1,000 students and faculty at area law schools, calling for a total withdrawal of troops and an end of military aid.[78] On the following day a rally was held on Cambridge Common, followed by a march to Boston Common, involving more than 5,000 local students.

Rioting in Harvard Square, April 13, 1970.

Police Department, City of Cambridge, Massachusetts.

After that rally, roughly 3,500 people headed across Harvard Bridge toward Harvard Square. A riot ensued, with protestors pulling up bricks from the Cambridge sidewalks and hurling them at police, yelling "Peace now!" and "Kill the pigs!"[79]

More than 2,000 riot police used nightsticks and tear gas against the protestors, but they could not control the widespread looting. At least two buildings were set on fire, and three police cars were overturned and torched. The riot lasted for six hours, with over 200 people injured and thirty-five arrested, including three Harvard law students, although many more were involved. The three law students claimed that "they were among the majority of Harvard students that watched but did not take place in the demonstration," and that they had been "trapped between young people and police throwing rocks." They accused the police "of attempting to provoke some kind of response from us that would permit them to use violence."[80]

President Pusey called the riot an "inexcusable event," and claimed that "very few of the rioters were Harvard students."[81] Harvard Square was a ruin of broken glass, shuttered windows, and looted stores. But worse was coming. On April 30, 1970, President Nixon announced that the United States had been secretly bombing Cambodia. American and South Vietnamese troops had crossed the border, informing the Cambodian government only after the fact. The purpose was to strengthen the position of the South Vietnamese military in anticipation of peace negotiations.[82] The invasion was a military success, destroying Viet Cong havens and supply lines along the Ho Chi Minh Trail. But it was a violation of Cambodian sovereignty and a disaster in domestic politics in the United States.

Kent State Aftermath

Nixon's announcement about bombing Cambodia led to widespread protests on campuses across the country. On May 4, 1970, Ohio National Guardsmen shot and killed four unarmed students at Kent State, two of whom were not even protestors. Two days later, on May 6, police shot four unarmed demonstrators at the University of Buffalo. Then, on May 14, police responding to reports of student unrest fired about 400 rounds into a women's dormitory at historically black Jackson State University in Mississippi, killing two and wounding twelve others. Meanwhile, thirty ROTC buildings were burned or bombed, twenty-six campuses saw violent clashes with police, and the National Guard was mobilized on twenty-one campuses in sixteen states.[83]

It almost happened at Harvard. The Corporation relieved Pusey of day-to-day operation of the university and turned control over to Archibald Cox, who later became the special prosecutor in the Watergate investigation. On May 7, 1970, Harvard students occupied an unused university building, igniting a fire that injured four firefighters. On May 8, more than 100,000 demonstrators gathered in Washington, D.C., and 150,000 in San Francisco, protesting the invasion of Cambodia and the Kent State killings. That same day, hundreds of protestors surrounded Harvard's wooden ROTC building, which was protected by a small, vastly outnumbered contingent of university police. Mindful of the burning of ROTC buildings on other campuses, Cox arranged with local police to secretly assemble the National Guard at a nearby armory.[84]

In what he later described as "the toughest decision in my life," Cox decided not to bring the National Guard onto the Harvard campus, and to withdraw the university police, leaving the building unprotected. It was a dangerous gamble. Had the unprotected building been burned, lives might have been lost. If the National Guard had been called in, the Kent State shootings might have been replicated at Harvard. But upon seeing the police leave, the crowd dispersed.[85] Cox's judgment had been astute. A show of force would have precipitated violence. What Pusey would have done is anybody's guess.

Meanwhile, at the Law School on May 4, the same day as the shootings at Kent State, about a hundred students met in Harkness Commons, and proposed that all students be given three options to finish the semester: take exams at the regularly scheduled times, take exams at home over the summer, or receive a "pass" in each of their subjects without taking exams. They also urged Dean Bok to call an emergency faculty meeting to act on the proposal, in order to free law students to participate in a university-wide strike, which was being planned later that day by over 2,500 students, mostly undergraduates, assembled in Memorial Hall.

But on the next day, May 5, another group of some 700 law students met in the Ames Court Room to discuss the strike and to act, they claimed, on behalf of the Law School student body. This group voted to prohibit students from taking exams on the regular schedule and to ask the faculty to show support for the antiwar protest by canceling exams altogether.[86] Later that day, the law faculty held an emergency meeting and, rather than endorse either student proposal, voted to permit law students the option of taking their exams on schedule or to take them in the fall. Third-year students could delay their tests for one week. This, the faculty believed, "would be sufficient to allow students to participate in the rally and lobbying activities in Washington, D.C., the following weekend." In response, students at the Law School began boycotting classes and picketing the library. In class and section meetings throughout the school, the students gathered to debate alternative courses of action, against the backdrop of a national crisis, as over 200 colleges shut down and students struck at 400 others.[87]

At the Law School, some classes were disrupted and taken over by the students, as witnessed by Daniel Coquillette (J.D. 1971), a student at the time. Some faculty were effectively driven from the Law School. Ernest Brown (LL.B. 1931) was one tragic casualty. He had devoted his career to teaching and to service at the Law School. For decades he served as the faculty representative on the school's Admissions Committee and charted the course through great controversies involving admissions. Brown "received great sustenance from the appreciation and respect . . . he received from students," recalled Bok. "Then, suddenly, they turned bitter," and no professor "got any respect at all. . . . So Ernest left law teaching altogether. For me, to have Ernest leave the Harvard Law School because he was totally disaffected with the students, was a very sad personal event. . . . His departure was saying something about Harvard Law School and the spirit of the times."[88]

Facing this upheaval, the law faculty reconsidered its vote, and on May 21 adopted a plan proposed by the students. Third-year students could either (1) take their regularly scheduled exams, (2) pick up their exams early and take them at home, or (3) have their exams mailed to them. Within twenty-four hours, 85 percent of the third-year students had picked up their exams. All other students could sit for their regularly scheduled examinations or have exams mailed to them to be taken over the summer. An overwhelming number chose the latter option, although many failed to complete their "take-home" exams by the September deadline, and had to be given extensions.[89]

Standing left to right: Mark De Wolfe Howe (LL.B. 1933), Paul Freund (LL.B. 1931, S.J.D. 1932), Ernest J. Brown (LL.B. 1931), and Arthur Sutherland (LL.B. 1925). Photograph ca. 1954.

The main achievement of the faculty policy was to get the law students out of Cambridge. About 400 participated in the national demonstrations in Washington, D.C., over the weekend of May 8, some traveling on a bus chartered by Professors Breyer, Chayes, and Tribe. Others "used their newly created free time to raise money for antiwar organizations, canvass, work on the campaigns of peace candidates, organize discussion groups, and do war-related research," the *Harvard Law Record* reported.[90] Many students just went home and waited for their exams. Given the dangerous events of May 7 and 8 on Harvard's main campus, sending the law students home proved to be wise.[91]

By the time the students returned in September 1970, the Vietnam crisis had effectively ended at the Law School, even though casualties in the war were still mounting and protests continued apace nationwide, including massive demonstrations in April and May 1971 in Washington, D.C., and San Francisco. Calm returned to the Law School partly because it was clear that most of the faculty and Bok's administration were responsive to student concerns, and largely supportive. Even Pusey now expressed support for the protestors. In addition, the draft lottery, based on birthdays, removed uncertainty from the lives of most of the students, assuring nearly 70 percent that they could continue their studies, and giving notice to the rest to enlist or cope with the draft in other ways. Finally, the national mood had changed. Returning veterans joined in the protests, and the Law School was essentially unified in its desire to end the war and find constructive outlets for the energies and frustrations that had built up over the past five years. There was light at the end of the tunnel.[92]

But even as the antiwar protests wound down, demonstrations against racial injustice continued, as both movements had fundamentally changed the perspective of students, Dean Bok observed in 1969. "Instead of wondering whether they were cut out for law school, students were now asking, 'how can the law school be changed to more nearly accommodate my needs?'" This change reflected "the students' increasing distrust of authority stemming from race issues and the Vietnam War," he wrote.[93] With this new mind-set, students at Harvard Law School set their sights on reforming the grading system.

The First Grade War

The student effort to reform grading was described as "the Grade War," even a "Blitzkrieg attack" on the system.[94] It began in 1966 when the new Joint Student-Faculty Committee, chaired by Clark Byse, proposed, and the faculty approved, a one-week reading period before exams for first-year students, abolition of required courses in the second year, and averaging grades to the nearest whole number, rather than to the nearest hundredth of a point. In the fall of 1967, the faculty also agreed to institute a reading period before exams for second-year and third-year students.[95] Despite these reforms, the "emotional climate" at the school remained "grim." A *Harvard Law Record* poll in December 1967 found that only 22 percent of respondents supported the existing grading system. Acting Dean James Casner encouraged the Joint Committee to continue its work and not wait for a new permanent dean to arrive.[96]

Many students favored radical solutions. Thirty percent of respondents to the same poll supported a three-tier—"high-pass, pass, fail"—system, and 18 percent endorsed using pass / fail alone. Two percent polled favored no final exam at all. Seventy-three percent wanted to abolish the ranking list or limit any ranking to the top seventy-five places for the purposes of selecting members of the three honor organizations. There was much support for replacing the deceptively precise numerical averages with letter grades.[97] Meanwhile, Yale Law School, facing the threat of student boycotts in 1968, moved from an eight-tier alphabetical system to a four-tier system: "Honors, Pass, Low Pass, and Fail," while the first year had mandatory "credit / no credit," with no grades at all. Furthermore, grading curves were eliminated, so a professor was not limited in the number of high grades that could be awarded.[98]

Then, in May 1968, the Harvard law faculty approved a recommendation from the Joint Committee to abolish class rank except for internal purposes, convert the numerical grading system to a nine-tier, letter-grade system, and raise the grading curve from a mean of C to B.[99] This change is presented in Table 16.1. This was the situation facing Derek Bok when he officially became dean on June 30, 1968, and it looked encouraging. An orderly and collaborative process had resolved some serious outstanding problems and abolished some clearly outmoded practices. But the Grade War had only just begun.

The Harvard faculty believed that the Joint Committee's reforms, approved in May 1968, were substantial and adequate steps for change. Furthermore, in the fall of 1968, responding to pressure from students and alumni, the faculty entertained a proposal from a student committee, chaired by Kathleen Imholz (J.D. 1969) to change the name of the degree from *Legum Baccalaureus* (LL.B.) to *Juris Doctor* (J.D.). A faculty committee, chaired by Ernest Brown, reviewed and recommended the change, which was approved by the faculty in March 1969 and then by the Corporation. At that point, 85 percent of the nation's law schools were granting the LL.B. rather than the J.D.[100]

Table 16.1   Reform of Harvard Law School Grading System, 1968

Letter Grade	Numerical Equivalent before 1968	Numerical Equivalent after 1968
A+	NA	80 and above
A	75 and above	77–79
A–	NA	74–76
B+	NA	71–73
B	70–74	68–70
B–	NA	65–67
C+	66–69	NA
C	61–65	60–64
D	55–60	55–59
F	Below 55	Below 55

Data source: David L. Shapiro and Daniel A. Taylor, "Change at the Law School: The Grading System," *HLSB* (July 1968): 3–4.

Though generally approving that change, many students viewed the new grading system of May 1968 as inadequate. In fact, students began attacking grading itself as invalid and unreliable. "The grade is likely not to be an accurate guide to ability in the legal profession," a first-year student wrote to the *Harvard Law Record.* Instead of ranking the top seventy-five students in the class, the outgoing officers in the three honor organizations could choose new members "through an interview or writing process," the student continued, and prospective employers could rely on "confidential recommendations from members of the faculty."[101] This approach directly challenged two fundamental assumptions of the school since Dean Christopher Langdell (1870–1895) had introduced graded exams in 1870: first, that these grades measure academic ability; and second, that institutional honors and appointment to the faculty should be based primarily on these measures.[102] Harvard's meritocratic assumptions had proliferated throughout legal education since the late nineteenth century.

The debate intensified in February 1969 when the *Harvard Law Record* published the essay "An Argument for Pass / Fail," which generated much discussion. A week after its publication, more than 150 first-year students distributed a twenty-seven page proposal, "The Trouble with Grades," that denounced the 1968 reforms of the Joint Committee as inadequate. The new proposal "points up the weaknesses of the Joint Student-Faculty Committee, whose work . . . is now regarded as obsolete," observed the *Record.* In addition, the proposal "involved a large number of students, far more than took part in last year's process."[103]

But others disagreed. First-year student Richard Parker (J.D. 1970), who later become a professor at the Law School, wrote to the *Record* that "grades do test for something employers prize, if only compulsiveness or devotion to the law." Furthermore, Parker stated, reliance on "faculty contacts" or "recommendations" in a school with a terrible student-faculty ratio is an invitation to special dealing.[104] Likewise, a group of third-year students endorsed grades, warning that the first-year students "have too lightly dismissed the danger" of employment discrimination and "shown too little respect for the Law School as a meritocracy." Some alumni wrote to the *Record,* concurring.[105] An African American student wrote to the *Harvard Law Record* challenging the premise that "major law firms evaluate students solely, or primarily, on the basis of a grade" without considering other factors. Demonstrating the rapidly changing social context, he maintained that "law firms today are begging for black law students. A black law student at Harvard is deemed acceptable regardless of his grades, because it's fashionable."[106]

"Failed"

Amid the swirling unrest over civil rights and the Vietnam War, Dean Bok sensed the gravity of these complaints and sought to avoid a crisis by steering a middle course. In a memorandum to the faculty on March 6, 1969, Bok conceded "the main thrust of these criticisms" but affirmed the need for some form of assessment in order to ensure motivation and to select members of the three honor organizations.[107] To formulate a proposal, he appointed a committee, chaired by Professor Robert Keeton (S.J.D. 1956), with eight faculty members and, regrettably, no students. This so-called Keeton Committee was unimpressed with the student proposals and rejected them in an interim report at the end of March. Furious, the students returned hundreds of copies of the Keeton Report marked "Failed" across the first page, and began to formulate plans to demonstrate at upcoming faculty meetings and to boycott exams.[108] In the following week, on April 10, Vietnam War protesters occupied University Hall, resulting in the mass arrest of Harvard students. Suddenly a violent conflict over grades appeared imminent.

In view of these developments, the Keeton Committee reassessed its position, although Archibald Cox wrote a passionate dissent. He argued that further reform would "devalue all grades and all grading" and that grades "are essential to set and sustain an unreachable goal of excellence in disciplined intellectual performance in law; they make it plain that this is an institution where only performance counts." Furthermore, blind grading "opens opportunities to hundreds of young men and women who would not otherwise enjoy them."[109] Here was the meritocratic argument that the intellectual sword ensured equal opportunity.

Other Harvard University faculty, like the sociologist David Riesman (LL.B. 1934), argued that students' criticism of grading stemmed from changes in the U.S. higher education system since 1945. Students growing up in the 1950s and 1960s experienced academic pressure and competition earlier, longer, and more intensely than previous generations. The experience of these students differed greatly from that of himself, Cox, or Bok, who attended elite preparatory schools that guaranteed admission to an elite college, where Gentleman C's ensured admission to Harvard Law School. Students now matriculating into the first year at the Law School had competed intensely for grades in secondary school and college for at least eight years prior to their enrollment.[110] Such students did not need to be motivated or sorted by minute grading distinctions.

Seeking to compromise, the Keeton Committee proposed that first-year students could choose one of three options: the nine-tier, letter-grade system of 1968 shown in Table 16.1; a four-tier system (high, satisfactory, low, fail); or simply pass / fail. Small classes were exempted. Also, the *Law Review* and Board of Student Advisors would no longer determine membership solely on the basis of grades, following the lead of the Legal Aid Bureau, which now relied on a random lottery to select from among those who applied. After anguished deliberation, the faculty approved the proposal in late April 1969. In the following September, 47 percent of the first-year students selected the second or third options.[111]

But the compromise satisfied no one. Conservative faculty, led by Cox, were aghast. Many students also objected, as reported in December 1969 by the *Harvard Law Record*. These students maintained that the freedom to choose was illusory because employers would evaluate students based on the option they chose. Consequently, the grading system had to be uniform and mandatory for all courses and students. Confirming those objections, only 27 percent of the first-year class chose the second or third options in the fall of 1970.[112] The Keeton Committee also proposed that employers simply refrain from requesting the grades of first-year students, but this proposal was widely derided as disingenuous.[113]

In the spring of 1971 Dean Bok tried again and appointed a third committee to address the grading issue. This new Committee on Legal Education, chaired by Professor David L. Shapiro (LL.B. 1957), included three professors, three students, Assistant Dean Stephen Bernardi (LL.B. 1955), and Associate Dean Albert Sacks. Meanwhile, another student group issued a report, "A Short Critique of the Grading System," based on a survey of first-year students, of whom 69 percent endorsed mandatory pass / fail. In fact, even more endorsed mandatory pass / fail if more than 75 percent of their peers did so.[114] The support for mandatory pass / fail had thus risen significantly in the fifteen months since the *Harvard Law Record* poll in December 1969, when barely half of the first-year students favored it.[115] Over that period, more students had become willing to embrace unorthodox grading policies, likely fueled by their "increasing distrust of authority stemming from race issues and the Vietnam War," as Bok had written.[116]

Nevertheless, the faculty expressed deep reservations about extending the pass / fail system.[117] The Committee on Legal Education therefore voted against taking any further action on grades, leaving the nine-tier, letter-grade system in place. All three students dissented. The faculty on the committee reasoned that the Joint Student-Faculty Committee had made an "exhaustive" study in 1968 and that the school had already made a substantial reform when it adopted the nine-tier system. They also maintained that the student report, "The Trouble with Grades," was "highly politicized and . . . a source of emotional tension and division throughout the Law School community."[118] After blaming the students for making grades a bone of contention, the faculty charged that "A Short Critique of the Grading System" contained "many questionable assumptions and overstated premises."[119]

The faculty on the committee then asserted that "adoption of an unqualified, mandatory pass / fail system is unacceptable on its merits," contrary to the express view of more than two-thirds of the first-year class. In addition, the faculty on the committee maintained that studying the issue of grades any further would be a "very substantial drain on our resources." Finally, they observed that "the substantial number of students who want . . . grades should not have their interests thwarted because a larger number of students want everyone's performance to be ungraded."[120]

The three dissenting student members—David R. Riemer (J.D. 1975), Andrew Shepard (J.D. 1972), and Mary L. Frampton (J.D. 1971)—were unpersuaded. They argued that "emotional tension and division" in the school and the "very substantial drain" on the faculty "are outweighed by the need to respond to the professional concern of the present first-year class."[121] Nevertheless, in April 1971 the faculty voted to accept the committee's recommendation of no action.[122] The Grade War was far from over, and students renewed the "Blitzkrieg attack" with a vengeance the following academic year.[123] But that would be a problem for Dean Bok's successor.

No Gender Progress

In his brief tenure, Bok was unable to increase women's presence at the school—in the student body, the faculty, or the administration—despite his expressed concern and his catalytic presentation at the Harvard Law Wives meeting in 1960, urging women to pursue their own careers. Bok later recalled that, during his decanal tenure, he felt "completely embroiled in student activism" concerning civil rights, the Vietnam War, and grades.[124] The small number of women also meant there were few to protest for their cause.

In June 1967, at the end of Griswold's term, the number of female LL.B. graduates reached twenty-five in a class of 550, less than 5 percent, as seen in Table 12.1. Acting Dean Casner made a greater effort to encourage women to apply, and in September 1968 the number of women in the entering class rose to forty-one, over 7 percent, the same as at ABA-accredited law schools nationwide. This fraction improved little during Bok's deanship. The class matriculating in September 1970 had forty-seven women, nearly 9 percent, as compared to the 10 percent at ABA-accredited law schools nationwide. Admissions officers Louis Toepfer and Russell Simpson maintained that efforts were made to recruit women, and they attributed the slow progress to a small and reluctant applicant pool.[125]

The absence of role models and exemplars also discouraged female applicants, however. There were no women on the regular faculty and only a few in administrative positions. The most prominent was Eleanor Roberts Appel, the placement director, who lacked a graduate degree and had started her career as secretary for Vice Dean Louis Toepfer when he first established the Placement Office.[126] Other women were limited to staff roles. The best known were Mary Conlan and Elizabeth Whalen, the dean's secretaries.[127] It was not an encouraging picture.

It is difficult to assess the very brief Bok administration. Tumultuous events made it an achievement just to keep the school operating. Even this failed when examinations in the spring of 1970 were canceled, followed by the departure of long-serving faculty, notably Ernest Brown. But the school could have suffered much greater damage if not for Bok, an astute student of human nature and a skilled diplomat, who tended to bring out the best in faculty and students.

Bok's decanal term of two and a half years was the shortest in the school's history, but his coolness in difficult situations led the Harvard Corporation to appoint him to succeed Pusey as president. Bok then served for twenty years, from 1971 to 1991, and as acting president, from 2006 to 2007. During his presidential tenure, he appointed the next three deans of Harvard Law School: Albert Sacks (1971–1981), James Vorenberg (1981–1989), and Robert Clark (1989–2003). The paradox of Bok's leadership, then, is that he exerted a long and profound influence on the school despite his short time as dean.

The crises that emerged during this brief but dramatic deanship—the civil rights movement, the Vietnam War protests, the Grade War—scarred the Law School and forced it to reexamine what it meant to be an elite university in modern America. This challenge immediately confronted President Bok's first appointment of a dean, Albert Sacks, while disagreements among the faculty intensified and an economic downturn began to strangle higher education in the late 1970s.

NOTES

1. Harold J. Berman, Oral History, conducted by Daniel Hamilton and Daniel R. Coquillette (August 1998), on file with the authors. See Stephen Bernardi, Oral History, conducted by Daniel Hamilton and Daniel R. Coquillette (October 2000–April 2001), on file with the authors; Detlev Vagts, Oral History, conducted by Daniel Hamilton, Daniel R. Coquillette, and John Delionado (November 1999–February 2000), on file with the authors.

2. Harvard Law School (HLS) Faculty, "Comments to President Pusey by Members of the Faculty concerning Legal Education and the Harvard Law School, 1967" (typescript, 1967), on file with the authors.

3. Quotation is from "A Year of Anxiety," *HLSB* (February 8, 1971): 18–19. See Morton Keller and Phyllis Keller, *Making Harvard Modern: The Rise of America's University* (New York, 2001), 314–329.

4. Derek C. Bok, "A Different Way of Looking at the World," *HLSB* (March–April, 1969): 2.

5. See Craig Lambert, "DB: The Public Figure and the Private Man," *Harvard Magazine* (June—August, 1991), 26–34, 105–107; J.P., "No Shock It's Bok," *Harvard Bulletin* (February 8, 1971): 11–18; "The Complete Bok," *Harvard Bulletin* (February 8, 1971):

22–30. See also Thomas Geisler, "Law at Harvard, Rainy Bombay, and Professor Derek Curtis Bok," *HLSR* (February 8, 1968): 4–5, 12, 14–15; Joel Seligman, *The High Citadel: The Influence of Harvard Law School* (Boston, 1978), 126–127.

6. Geisler, "Law at Harvard," 5. See HLS Yearbook, 1970, 19.

7. Derek C. Bok, Oral History, conducted by Daniel R. Coquillette and Daniel Hamilton (February 2002), on file with the authors. Archibald Cox and Derek C. Bok, *Cases and Materials on Labor Law* (Brooklyn, NY, 1962).

8. Quotation is from Seligman, *The High Citadel,* 134. See HLS Yearbook, 1970, 19; Geisler, "Law at Harvard," 4–5.

9. Quoted in Keller and Keller, *Making Harvard Modern,* 254. See "Casner Vows to Keep Firm Hand on Reins," *HLSR* (October 13, 1967): 1, 10.

10. HLS Yearbook, 1970, 19.

11. Quoted in Geisler, "Law at Harvard," 15.

12. *Brown v. Board of Education* 347 U.S. 483 (1954).

13. Jason Kreag, "Reciprocal Impact: An Examination of Harvard Law School and the Civil Rights Movement" (student research paper, HLS, 2003), on file with the authors, 3–15, 45; Charles M. Hamann, "Higgs Hits Obstructionists in South Fights for Integration," *HLSR* (October 25, 1962): 5. The following draws upon the research of Kreag, who conducted interviews with Elizabeth Bartholet, Andrew Kaufman, Frank Sander, Alan Dershowitz, Frank Michelman, and Archibald Cox during the academic year 2002–03.

14. Ken Gormley, *Archibald Cox: Conscience of a Nation* (Reading, MA, 1997), 191; Kreag, "Reciprocal Impact," 45.

15. Louis A. Toepfer, Oral History, conducted by Daniel Hamilton (March 1998), on file with the authors; Nathan Pak, "The Harvard Law School Special Summer Program of 1965 and What Happened Afterwards" (student research paper, Boston College Law School, 2017), on file with the authors, 1.

16. Jack Tate, "Black Awareness and Black Unity Surging Forward at Law School," *HLSR* (September 26, 1968): 1, 6, 7. See "600 New 1L's Flock to Law School," *HLSR* (September 12, 1968): 4; Tate, "Black Awareness and Black Unity," 6.

17. See HLS Yearbook, 1970, 68. See also Oliver Henry, "Black Dean Plows Tough Row," *HLSR* (October 9, 1969): 4–5, 13. When Bok became president, Leonard became his special assistant and fashioned an affirmative action program for the Law School that became a national model. In 1977 Leonard left Harvard to become president of Fisk University. Leonard received the Law School's "Medal of Freedom" in 2011. His illness and then death in 2015 prevented an oral history for this volume. See Brando S. Starkey, "Two Steps Forward Then Two Steps Back: The Black Story of Harvard Law School" (student research paper, HLS, 2008), on file with the authors, 49–50; Sam Roberts, "Walter J. Leonard, Pioneer of Affirmative Action in Harvard Admissions, Dies at 86," *New York Times* (December 16, 2015).

18. Carol Plumb and John York, "HLS Geographic and Ethnic Profile," *HLSR* (December 3, 1970): 2–4. Under Leonard, the Law School began to outperform the national

average for enrollment of African American law students, which climbed from 2 percent in 1967 to 4.5 percent in 1975. Harry T. Edwards, "The Journey from *Brown v. Board of Education* to *Grutter v. Bollinger:* From Racial Assimilation to Diversity," *Michigan Law Review* 102 (2004), 954; William G. Bowen and Derek C. Bok, *The Shape of the River: Long-Term Consequences of Considering Race in College and University Admissions* (Princeton, NJ, 1998), 5.

19. Weldon J. Rougeau, Oral History (April 2015), conducted by John L. Joy, on file with the authors. See John L. Joy, "A Legacy of Their Own: A History of Second Generation African American Families at Harvard Law School" (student research paper, Boston College Law School, 2016), on file with the authors, 8.

20. Kreag, "Reciprocal Impact," 3–45.

21. Laura A. Murray, "From Debate to Demonstration: Harvard Law School in Vietnam Era" (student research paper, HLS, 2002), on file with authors, 46. See "Harvard's OBU—A Review, from November to January," *HLSB* (February 1970): 4.

22. "Harvard's OBU," 4–5; "From Debate to Demonstration," 47; "Spring-1970; Issues and Events," HLS Yearbook, 1971, 14; Gormley, *Archibald Cox,* 212–213; Murray, "From Debate to Demonstration," 46–48.

23. Murray, "From Debate to Demonstration," 50–52; "Harvard's OBU," 9.

24. See Daniel R. Coquillette, *Real Ethics for Real Lawyers,* 3rd ed. (Durham, NC, 2016), 473, 660–661.

25. "Black Law Students Face Disciplinary Decision," *HLSR* (January 29, 1970): 1. See "Harvard's OBU," 9; Murray, "From Debate to Demonstration," 49–51.

26. "Ask Equal Disciplinary Actions; Fifty-Two Blacks Send Petition," *HLSR* (February 5, 1970): 1, 6.

27. "Black Law Students Face Disciplinary Decision"; Murray, "From Debate to Demonstration," 50.

28. Murray, "From Debate to Demonstration," 50; "Harvard OBU," 9; Michael Lurey, "Refuse to Leave Meeting: Protestors Confront Faculty," *HLSR* (February 26, 1970): 1; Laurence Gartner, "Almost 700 Attend; Discipline Debate Packs Ames," *HLSR* (March 5, 1970): 5; Michelle Scott, "Law School Discusses Discipline Issues," *HLSR* (March 5, 1970): 3.

29. Laurence Gortus, "Almost 700 Attend, Discipline Debate Packs Ames," *HLSR* (March 5, 1970): 1, 10.

30. Quoted in "Bell Walks Out in Protest: Law Faculty Disciplines Blacks," *HLSR* (March 12, 1970): 1.

31. See "HBLSA Finds Discipline Decision Racist and Hypocritical Process," *HLSR* (March 26, 1970): 3. Pilkington returned to the Law School and graduated in 1972.

32. Bob Orkland, "I Ain't Got No Quarrel with Them Vietcong," *New York Times* (June 27, 2017); Allyson Hobbs, "Muhammad Ali and His Audience," *New Yorker* (June 10, 2016), retrieved from https://www.newyorker.com/news/news-desk/ali-and-his-audience.

33. Martin Luther King Jr., "Beyond Vietnam: A Time to Break Silence," Speech (April 4, 1967), retrieved from https://kinginstitute.stanford.edu/king-papers/documents/beyond-vietnam.

34. Richard Lee Howell, *Harvard University and the Indochina War* (Ann Arbor, MI, 1987), 23; Murray, "From Debate to Demonstration," 16.

35. Murray, "From Debate to Demonstration," 1–2.

36. William Resnick, "Makings," *Opinions: A Collection of Essays by Harvard Law Students on the Vietnam War,* ed. James Conahan and Joseph P. Maissner (Cambridge, MA, 1966), 35.

37. Brian Sweeney, "Oklahoma Students Lose Draft Deferment," *HLSR* (October 28, 1965): 15.

38. Murray, "From Debate to Demonstration," 3; Paul M. Branzburg, "Selective Service Director Defends System and Vouches for Local Board Autonomy," *HLSR* (December 2, 1965): 1; "The Murky Depths" (unsigned editorial), *HLSR* (December 2, 1965): 8.

39. Murray, "From Debate to Demonstration," 4–5. See Martin Robins, "Law Students Can Expect Undergrad's Draft Criteria," *HLSR* (February 24, 1966): 7; "Hazy Mandate Reclassifies Law Students Much Discretion Retained: 80 is Minimum Score," *HLSR* (April 14, 1966): 1, 4.

40. Murray, "From Debate to Demonstration," 4. See Roggins, "Law Students," 7; "Hazy Draft Mandate," 1.

41. Keith S. Watson, "Profs and Dems Hit LBJs Intimidation," *HLSR* (November 4, 1965): 1–2; Murray, "From Debate to Demonstration," 5n15; Keith S. Watson, "Students Wage Petition Duel over Vietnam," *HLSR* (December 2, 1965): 2; Theodore Curtis and Brian Sweeney, "Bay State Senators Boost Vietnam Policy," *HLSR* (December 2, 1965): 5; Murray S. Levin, "Gruening Sees Vietnam Policy as 'Nonsense,'" *HLSR* (December 16, 1965): 5; Paul M. Branzburg, "Reuss Urges U.N. Act to Resolve Viet War," *HLSR* (February 3, 1966): 1; John Spitzer, "Cong. Tunney Sees War Frustrations to Continue," *HLSR* (February 10, 1966): 1; "Frelinghuysen Complains of Inadequate Viet Facts; Reluctantly Backs Johnson," *HLSR* (February 24, 1966): 1; Lowell R. Wedemeyer, "Rep. Laird Warns GOP to Gain—or Else; Cites Inflation, Lengthy War as '66 Issues," *HLSR* (March 10, 1966): 5. See Conahan and Maissner, *Opinions.*

42. Frank R. Parker, "New HLS Group to Study Vietnam Policy," *HLSR* (December 16, 1965): 12; Harvard Law Graduate School Democratic Club, "Vietnam Resolution," in Conahan and Maissner *Opinions,* 44.

43. Clark Byse, Oral History, conducted by Daniel R. Coquillette and Daniel Hamilton (July–October 1997), on file with the authors.

44. "War Policy Held Legal," *HLSR* (December 1, 1966): 1, 13; "'Viet Settlement' Discussed by Profs," *HLSR* (March 16, 1967): 1.

45. Jay Becker, "Draft Chills Student Interest in Clerkships," *HLSR* (April 13, 1967): 7. See also "Selective Service Examination to Be Administered in March," *HLSR* (February 9, 1967): 6.

46. Murray, "From Debate to Demonstration," 15. See "Draft Rules Confuse Many," *HLSR* (November 9, 1967): 1, 10; HLS Yearbook, 1970, 232.

47. "A Model Meeting" (unsigned editorial), *HLSR* (November 9, 1967): 8.

48. Ira Finkelstein and Steve Goddard, "Vietnam Concern Grows at Law School; Meeting Explores Methods of Expressing Opposition to War," *HLSR* (November 9, 1967): 1.

49. Murray, "From Debate to Demonstration," 13. See Nathan M. Pusey, Annual Report of the President of Harvard University, 1968–69, 6; Roger Lowenstein, "Aftermath of Dow Incident: Greater 'Due Process' for Students Urged," *HLSR* (November 16, 1967): 7.

50. "Students Favor Halt in Bombing, Split on Other Vietnam Issues," *HLSR* (December 14, 1967): 6–7.

51. Roger Lowenstein, "Offer Course on Vietnam War," *HLSR* (February 1, 1968): 11–12; Lowenstein, "Course Examines Viet Policy," *HLSR* (February 23, 1968): 1; Murray, "From Debate to Demonstration," 14–15.

52. Murray, "From Debate to Demonstration," 16. See "Selective Servitude," *HLSR* (November 16, 1967): 8; "Selective Service," *HLSR* (February 1, 1968): 14.

53. Guy M. Blynn, "Class of 1970—A Brief History," HLS Yearbook, 1970, 84. See Howell, *Harvard University,* 23.

54. Robert Lowenstein, "Faculty Readmission Statement Prepared," *HLSR* (March 28, 1968): 1. See "Readmission Statement: Students Refusing Induction May Return," *HLSR* (April 11, 1968): 3.

55. "Readmission Statement," 3.

56. Blynn, "Class of 1970," 84–86. See generally, Stanley Karnow, *Vietnam: A History* (New York, 1997), 9–59.

57. Murray, "From Debate to Demonstration," 17–18, 22; "Draft Official Tells It Like It Is—Not Good," *HLSR* (April 25, 1968): 9.

58. Gormley, *Archibald Cox,* 206; Archibald Cox, Oral History, conducted by Daniel R. Coquillette and Daniel Hamilton (November 1998), on file with the authors; Lawrence E. Eichel et al., *The Harvard Strike* (Boston, 1970), 131; Murray, "From Debate to Demonstration," 35. See Epps, "The Harvard Student Rebellions," 1–15.

59. "63 2Ls Have Departed: Draft's Damoclean Drop Delayed," *HLSR* (September 12, 1968): 6.

60. "Eighty Students Gone," *HLSR* (October 10, 1968): 1; Kevin Kane, "Draft Loss: 125 Gone, 325 by June," *HLSR* (November 21, 1968): 1, 10.

61. Murray, "From Debate to Demonstration," 22, 73. See Laurence Gartner, "Radical Group Started," *HLSR* (September 26, 1968): 1–12; Laurence Gartner, "Radicals Argue Student Power," *HLSR* (October 24, 1968): 2, 7; "Students Picket Milbank Tweed," *HLSR* (January 30, 1969): 2; "Dean Bok's Statement Calls for Students to Decide Whether to Work on Committees," *HLSR* (February 18, 1969): 14; Richard Hoffman, "Open Faculty Meetings Asked," *HLSR* (March 6, 1969): 1; "Student Participation Ad Hoc," *HLSB* (March–April, 1969): 19.

62. Eichel et al., *The Harvard Strike,* 353–355. See Howell, *Harvard University,* 55.

63. Quoted in Eichel et al., *The Harvard Strike,* 354. See Howell, *Harvard University,* 55.

64. Eichel et al., *The Harvard Strike,* 83–85. See Archie C. Epps III, "The Harvard Student Rebellions of 1969: Through Change and through Storm," *Proceedings of the Massachusetts Historical Society* 107 (1995): 1–2.

65. Murray, "From Debate to Demonstration," 34–35; Gormley, *Archibald Cox,* 209; Howell, *Harvard University,* 66.

66. Archibald Cox, Oral History (November 1998); Eichel et al., *The Harvard Strike,* 131; Murray, "From Debate to Demonstration," 35. See Epps, "The Harvard Student Rebellions," 1–15.

67. Murray, "From Debate to Demonstration," 36; Epps, "The Harvard Student Rebellions," 6, 11–13.

68. Quotation is from Richard Hoffman, "Harvard Sit-in Stirs Students," *HLSR* (April 24, 1969): 1, 3. See Howell, *Harvard University,* 67–69; Murray, "From Debate to Demonstration," 29; "Law School ROTC Program to Continue," *HLSB* (June 1969): 16.

69. Karnow, *Vietnam,* 592–684. See Robert S. McNamara with Brian VanDeMark, *In Retrospect: The Tragedy and Lesson of Vietnam* (New York, 1993), 273–317.

70. Meldon Levine, "A Conflict of Conscience: Our Practice of Your Principles," *HLSB* (July 1969): 2–4.

71. Murray, 40. See Blynn, "Class of 1970," 87; Richard Hoffman, "Blowing the Whistle on a Crisis," *HLSR* (March 5, 1970): 15.

72. "3Ls Have High Rate of Attrition," *HLSR* (September 25, 1969): 1.

73. Quotations are from "October Moratorium Day," *HLSB* (December, 1969): 21. See Bob Hernandez, "Students March, Canvass, Listen; Moratorium Comes to HLS," *HLSR* (October 23, 1969): 3; "Vietnam Moratorium," *HLSR* (October 2, 1969): 14; Michal Lurey, "Cancelling Classes up to Each Prof.: No Moratorium Action Taken," *HLR* (October 9, 1969): 1–2, 6.

74. "Moratorium Enters Phase Two," *HLSR* (November 14, 1969): 1; "Profs. Urge Students to Join March," *HLSR* (November 14, 1969), 2. See Pusey, Annual Report of the President, 1969–70, 10.

75. Murray, "From Debate to Demonstration," 44.

76. See Olin Henry, "Radicals Continue Fight against Firms," *HLSR* (October 30, 1969): 4; Bob Hernandez, "Pickets Confront Ropes & Gray then Press Deans on Placement," *HLSR* (November 14, 1969): 1; Blynn, "Class of 1970," 88. Approximately twenty law students picketed the on-campus interviews of Ropes & Gray on October 5, 1969 (focused on "black lung" issues), and about forty student "members of the Harvard Black Law Students Association, the Harvard Student Bar Association, and the Radical Law Students Group" picketed the on-campus interviews of Cravath, Swain and Moore (focused on clients supporting South Africa). Murray, "From Debate to Demonstration," 45–46.

77. Blynn, "Class of 1970," 88; Murray, "From Debate to Demonstration," 41; Howell, *Harvard University,* 141.

78. "Boston Lawyers Protest Vietnam," *HLSR* (April 23, 1970): 7.

79. Murray, "From Debate to Demonstration," 56; Will Kredlik, "Militant Mood Pervades Peace," *HLSR* (April 24, 1970): 4.

80. Ray L. Fuller and Stephen J. Hausman, "Arrested Students Statements," *HLSR* (April 24, 1970): 4, 10.

81. Robert L. Turner "200 Hurt in Harvard Square Riot," *Boston Globe* (April 16, 1970). See Donald Janson, "Damage Estimated at $100,000 after Harvard Square Riot," *New York Times* (April 17, 1970); Garrett Epps, "Rioting Devastates Harvard Square; Windows Smashed, Scores Injured," *Harvard Crimson* (April 16, 1970). Pusey, Annual Report of the President, 1969–70, 6.

82. McNamara, *In Retrospect*, 273–315; Karnow, *Vietnam*, 27; 595–663, 698; Howell, *Harvard University*, 154.

83. Karnow, *Vietnam*, 698; Howell, *Harvard University*, 172.

84. Cox, Oral History (November 1998). See Gormley, *Archibald Cox*, 211–217; Murray, "From Debate to Demonstration," 61; "May Days," *HLSB* (June 1970): 9; Keller and Keller, *Making Harvard Modern*, 314–329.

85. Cox, Oral History (November 1998). See Gormley, *Archibald Cox*, 211–217; Murray, "From Debate to Demonstration," 61; "May Days," 9; Keller and Keller, *Making Harvard Modern*, 314–329.

86. Murray, "From Debate to Demonstration," 59–60. See "May Days," 8; Michael Lurey, "Law Students Vote to Join Strike," *HLSR* (May 21, 1970): 1, 3.

87. Quotation is from Lurey, "Law Students Vote," 3, 18. See Bob Hernandez, "Faculty Alters Final Exams," *HLSR* (May 21, 1970): 1; Howell, *Harvard University*, 161.

88. Bok, Oral History (February 2002). Professor Richard Parker, who attended the Law School from 1967 to 1970, enrolled in Tax with Ernest Brown in the spring of 1969. "I went to the first class and Brown said, as I remember it, he had practiced tax in Buffalo, and therefore he was going to use the Code section numbers that had been in place years before when he was in Buffalo. This was incredible. He was not given to joking. But I was so horrified . . . that I never went to his class again until the last class. Now at the last class . . . Brown wound up something or other, and suddenly, as if a tornado was coming, the whole class roared with hisses. Everyone was hissing. It really was like a storm. And the man, of course, must have been shocked. He turned and left. And, as everyone knows, he left Harvard Law School after that year." Richard D. Parker, Oral History, conducted by Daniel R. Coquillette and Daniel Pincus (June 2010), on file with the authors.

89. Murray, "From Debate to Demonstration," 61. See "May Days," 9; Hernandez, "Faculty Alters Final Exams," 6.

90. Michelle Scott, "HLS Groups Begin Peace Activities," *HLSR* (May 21, 1970): 3.

91. Gormley, *Archibald Cox*, 215–217; Murray, "From Debate to Demonstration," 61; "May Days," 9.

92. "Statement by President Nathan M. Pusey" (press release) (May 5, 1970); Murray, "From Debate to Demonstration," 66; Keller and Keller, *Making Harvard Modern*, 326–327.

93. Bok, "A Different Way of Looking."

94. "The Grade War–1969," HLS Yearbook, 1970, 227–231; David L. Shapiro and Daniel A. Taylor, "Change at the Law School: The Grading System," *HLSB* (July 1968): 3–4; Ned Hines, "A Matter of Course," *HLSR* (October 13, 1967): 1. See October 14, 1966, and November 10, 1966, issues of *HLSR;* Clark Byse, "Memorandum to the Faculty and Students of Harvard Law School on the Activities of the Joint Student-Faculty Committee on the Harvard Law School, November–December 1966" (January 6, 1967), on file with the authors, 1; Byse, Oral History (July–October 1997).

95. The following discussion draws upon Louis A. Toepfer, "Marks and the Man," *HLSB* (April 1958): 4–5, 17; Kimberly Isbell, "Grade Reform at Harvard, 1968–1972" (student research paper, HLS, 2000), on file with the authors.

96. Fenno, "Tongue 'n' Cheek," *HLSR* (December 7, 1967): 8. See Jack Tate, "Students Ask Changes in Evaluation of Their Ability," *HLSR* (December 14, 1967): 1; "Joint Student-Faculty Committee Forms Units to Study Problems," *HLSR* (December 7, 1967): 6.

97. Shapiro and Taylor, "Change at the Law School," 3–4. See Isbell, "Grade Reform," 12; Richard Hoffman, "Ask Grading Change," *HLSR* (April 11, 1968): 1, 5, 6.

98. Laura Kalman, "The Dark Ages," *History of the Yale Law School: The Tercentennial Lectures,* ed. Anthony T. Kronman (New Haven, CT, 2004), 163; Laura Kalman, *Yale Law School in the Sixties: Revolt and Reverberations* (Chapel Hill, NC, 2005), 84, 96; Seth S. Goldschlager, "Revolution at Yale: Credit / No Credit Replaces Traditional Grades," *HLSR* (January 30, 1969): 5; Emily Anderson and Elise Medley, "Grading System at HLS and Peer Law Schools" (student research report, HLS, 2015); Phoebe Kimmelman, "YLS Alters Grading Policies," *Yale Daily News* (February 27, 2015).

99. Shapiro and Taylor, "Change at the Law School," 3–4. See Isbell, "Grade Reform," 12; Hoffman, "Ask Grading Change."

100. R. W. S. Schmidt, "Faculty Approves J.D.," *HLSR* (March 13, 1968), 1.

101. Jonathan Brant, "Letter to the Editor: 1Ls Modest Proposal to Abolish Grades," *HLSR* (November 21, 1968): 9. See Gordon D. Miller, "Letter to the Editor," *HLSR* (September 26, 1968): 14.

102. This challenge was at the heart of Duncan Kennedy's later critique: *Legal Education and the Production of Hierarchy: A Polemic against the System* (Cambridge, MA, 1983).

103. Roland Berenbern, "An Argument for Pass / Fail," *HLSR* (February 18, 1969): 8, 16; "Grading Revisited," *HLSR* (February 28, 1969): 8.

104. Richard D. Parker, "Letter to the Editor: Eliminating Grades Not the Answer," *HLSR* (February 28, 1969): 9–10.

105. Kenneth R. Schild, Lester Lovier, and Allan Grossman, "Letter to the Editor: Comment on Pass/Fail," *HLSR* (March 13, 1969): 9–10. See Charles Lennhoff, "Letter to the Editor: Pressure Desirable at Law School," *HLSR* (April 10, 1969): 16.

106. Harold Wade Jr., "Disinterested Cynic Views Pass/Fail," *HLSR* (April 10, 1969): 9.

107. "Dean's Memo Agrees with Grading Criticisms," *HLSR* (March 6, 1969): 1; Bok, Oral History (February 2002).

108. Harvard Law School Special Committee on Examinations, Grading and Related Matters, Memorandum to Faculty and Students (March 27, 1969), on file with the authors; Richard Hoffman, "Pass/Fail Rejected for Now," *HLSR* (April 10, 1969): 1.

109. Quoted in Seligman, *The High Citadel,* 14.

110. Christopher Jencks and David Riesman, *The Academic Revolution* (Garden City, NY, 1968), 61–154.

111. Seligman, *The High Citadel,* 14; John York, "Legal Aid Ends Grade Standard," *HLSR* (May 1, 1969): 1; "Few Pick Up Grades; Pass/Fail Less Popular with Class of '72," *HLSR* (October 15, 1970): 2.

112. Bob Hernandez, "First-Year Poll Rates Pass/Fail," *HLSR* (January 29, 1970): 3; "Few Pick Up Grades," 2.

113. Robert L. Stern, "Letter to the Editor: Undisclosed Grades Hamper Job Hunters," *HLSR* (December 3, 1970): 11; Richard Hoffman, "The Backbencher: Can't Win as Proponent of Grading," *HLSR* (December 3, 1970): 14–15; Verne M. Laing, "Letter to the Editor: Aren't Grades HLS Entrée?," *HLSR* (February 4, 1971): 11. See Isbell, "Grade Reform at Harvard, 1968–1972," 24.

114. Isbell, "Grade Reform at Harvard, 1968–1972," 25.

115. Hernandez, "First-Year Poll," 3.

116. Bok, "A Different Way of Looking."

117. Richard McManus, "1L Small Courses Go Pass/Fail," *HLSR* (March 11, 1971): 1–2; Alan M. Dershowitz, "Letter to the Editor: Dershowitz Corrects Pass/Fail Position," *HLSR* (March 18, 1971): 11.

118. HLS Committee on Legal Education, Memorandum (March 30, 1971), on file with the authors, 2–3.

119. HLS Committee on Legal Education, Memorandum (March 30, 1971), 3. See Isbell, "Grade Reform at Harvard, 1968–1972," 27.

120. HLS Committee on Legal Education, Memorandum (March 30, 1971), 4–5.

121. HLS Committee on Legal Education, Memorandum (March 30, 1971), 7.

122. "No Pass/Fail Review This Year," *HLSR* (April 23, 1971): 3.

123. Bert Halprin, "Freaks Fraternity," *HLSR* (October 1, 1971): 6.

124. Bok, Oral History (February 2002). See page 464 above.

125. Toepfer, Oral History (March 1998); Russell A. Simpson, Oral History, conducted by Mary Beth Basile and Daniel R. Coquillette (May–September 2001), on file with the

authors. See Derek C. Bok, Annual Report of the Dean of HLS, 1969–70, 281; Steven Prye, "Statistics Show Fewer Crimson in Class of '78," *HLSR* (December 5, 1975): 1, 3; Emily Anderson and Elise Medley, "Women at Harvard Law School" (student research report, Boston College Law School, 2016), on file with the authors.

126. HLS Yearbook, 1968, 82.

127. See Erwin N. Griswold, *Ould Fields, New Corne: The Personal Memoirs of a Twentieth Century Lawyer* (St. Paul, MN, 1992), 152; *Alumni Directory of the Harvard Law School* (Cambridge, MA, 2001), 24.

CHAPTER SEVENTEEN

"An Especially Difficult Period": Albert Sacks, 1971–1981

On becoming the president of Harvard in January 1971, Derek Bok named his associate dean, Albert Sacks, as acting dean, and then as permanent dean of the Law School as of July 1, 1971. Though not surprising, the appointment of Dean Sacks (1971–1981) was a significant departure from the school norm. His predecessors had been WASPs, if not blue bloods, and Sacks's first language was Yiddish. His sickly mother died when he was ten, during the depths of the Depression, and he was raised in the Bronx by his father and aunt, a recent Russian immigrant. Working at his father's candy store, Sacks nevertheless excelled at school and proceeded to that citadel of opportunity for the bright and the poor, the City College of New York (CCNY), where he graduated with distinction at age nineteen.

In 1939 Sacks wrote to Harvard Law School asking how much it would cost to attend. The estimated annual expense of $1,000 was too high, so he took a job as an accountant. Drafted into the army in 1942, he spent the war designing psychological and intelligence tests for soldiers, and in 1945, financial aid from the G.I. Bill enabled him to enroll at the Law School. There he met Warren Seavey (LL.B. 1904) who recognized Sacks's potential. Among the 2,000 students at the vastly overenrolled school, Sacks became president of the *Harvard Law Review* in 1947 and graduated *magna cum laude* in 1948.[1]

From that point, Sacks's career path to the faculty became more typical. Recommended by Henry Hart (LL.B. 1929, S.J.D. 1931), Sacks clerked for a year with Judge Augustus Hand (LL.B. 1894) and then Justice Felix Frankfurter (LL.B. 1906). Following two years in a major Washington law firm, Sacks joined the Harvard Law School faculty in 1952, and Frankfurter reportedly remarked, "Al Sacks should be Dean of Harvard Law School someday."[2]

Ever mindful of his earlier experience as a poor Jewish youth in the Bronx, Sacks remained a lifelong liberal and social activist. In 1963 he joined Martin Luther King Jr.'s March on Washington, and he and his wife were tear-gassed at Washington's Dupont Circle during a 1967 antiwar protest. In 1970 Associate Dean Sacks signed an open letter to Congress urging withdrawal from Vietnam. But the 1970s were "an especially difficult period in the life of the School," in the words of Professor David Shapiro (LL.B. 1957), and turned out to be a terrible decade for an idealistic liberal such as Sacks to serve as dean.[3]

Like President Jimmy Carter, who served only one term, 1977–1981, Al Sacks was widely regarded as a public spirited and fair-minded individual whom almost everyone liked personally. As Harvard President Bok observed, he had "a rare capacity for fairness and open-mindedness—an unfailing willingness to entertain every point of view . . . and to arrive at reasoned decisions wholly devoid of partisan feeling."[4] But Sacks has also been criticized as a weak leader. Without directly referring to him, President Bok suggested Sacks's shortcomings when explaining his choice of Sacks's successor, Dean James Vorenberg (1981–1989): "Because of all the conflicts and recriminations . . . occurring at the time, the Law School needed somebody who was tough, not

Albert M. Sacks, LL.B. 1948. Faculty 1952–1991, Dean 1971–1981.

Harvard Law School Yearbook, 1981. Courtesy of Harvard Yearbook Publications.

in the sense of being nasty, but someone who had enough self-confidence and courage, if need be, to really stand for the right thing amid very great pressure. I thought Jim [Vorenberg] was the closest that I could see on the faculty with those qualities who would be eminently fair, not play favorites, but could withstand terrible pressures on the dean."[5]

The "Very Difficult" 1970s

The Law School was assailed by a series of fundamental challenges from within and without during the 1970s. Students still objected to the grading system. The faculty and student body were overwhelmingly white and male. The painful outcome of the Vietnam War in 1973 and the humiliating fall of Saigon in 1975 cast a shadow over both military veterans and the many students who had evaded the draft. Worse still was the train wreck of President Richard Nixon's initially promising administration. Despite important domestic and foreign policy successes, the administration collapsed under the weight of the Watergate scandal, which slowly unfolded between 1972 and 1974, and led to two historic landmarks: the first appointment of a vice president under the Twenty-Fifth Amendment, Gerald Ford, and the first resignation of a sitting president, Richard Nixon. The scandal also touched the Law School through the involvement of Attorney General Eliot L. Richardson (LL.B. 1947) and Special Prosecutor Archibald Cox (LL.B. 1937).[6]

Both Nixon and his vice president, Spiro T. Agnew, who resigned in disgrace in 1973, were lawyers, and in response to the scandals the ABA added a new accreditation standard in professional ethics and responsibility. Dean Sacks also considered how legal education should respond, because this "is a serious problem for the Law School, and I find it impossible to avoid our taking responsibility for it." He thus called for a required course in professional responsibility to meet the ABA standard and help students recognize "issues which . . . posed serious problems—both moral and professional."[7]

The government upheavals in 1973 and 1974 ushered in a period of weak national political leadership that lasted for the remainder of Sacks's deanship. Neither President Gerald Ford, who was inaugurated in August 1974, nor his vice president, Nelson Rockefeller, had been elected to their position by the American people. In addition, Ford's full pardon of Nixon in September 1974 was profoundly unpopular. Despite Ford's announcement that "our long national nightmare is over," his popularity plunged. The Democrats won a majority of both the House and the Senate in the 1974 midterm elections, crippling Ford's executive power.

Then came a financial meltdown, as the national debt grew from $398 billion in 1971 to more than $1 trillion in 1981. For years the nation had been living beyond its means due to government spending on President Lyndon Johnson's Great Society programs and the Vietnam War. The inevitable result was high inflation. When Sacks entered the deanship in 1971, inflation stood at 3 percent. By 1975, inflation had grown to 9 percent and, by 1980, to over 13 percent. Meanwhile, interest rates rose to an incredible 18 percent. Concurrently, the winding down of the Vietnam wartime economy led to a rapid rise in unemployment, from 4 percent in 1970 to more than 8 percent in 1981, at the end of Sacks's deanship.

The high inflation, high unemployment, and stagnant economic growth at the national level weighed heavily on the Law School and worsened the syndrome of tuition dependence. The large physical plant required constant upkeep, and the new buildings—Pound Hall and Griswold Hall—had heavy maintenance and operating costs that were not covered by the Sesquicentennial Fund. As result, the dean had to dramatically raise tuition, which was already $2,100 for the academic year 1971–72.[8]

Even though inflation hovered near 4 percent, Sacks increased tuition by 14 percent for 1972–73. After running a deficit for 1973–74, he raised tuition more than 10 percent for 1974–75, while inflation stood at 6 percent. Thus, the school's own expenses were driving the huge increases, particularly for clinical programs, financial aid, and building operations and maintenance. In the spring of 1975, inflation soared to 11 percent, and Sacks proposed to the faculty raising tuition to match inflation and reducing financial aid. To spare the students, the faculty tabled both proposals.[9] In the spring of 1976, the dean again proposed to raise tuition, but withdrew the proposal when the faculty unanimously voted to decline salary increases for that year. Unable to delay longer, Sacks raised tuition 30 percent to $3,550 for the 1977–78 academic year.[10]

More was to come. In the spring of 1980 the Harvard Corporation approved Sack's request for a 14 percent tuition hike, largely due to rising energy costs as part of building operations. In his final year, Sacks made one more increase of 17 percent to $5,850 for the 1981–82 academic year. Overall, Sacks raised tuition 183 percent in nominal dollars, more than double the inflation rate of 85 percent over the same period.[11]

This rapid tuition growth expanded students' debt and skewed their career choices by discouraging work in government and public service and pointing the vast majority of graduates toward remunerative private practice.[12] Though identified by earlier faculty committees under Dean Griswold, this pressure on career choice had not been addressed when Sacks started his series of even steeper tuition hikes. Only in 1975 did the Law School establish a program to extend the loan repayment schedule of students in need of assistance.[13]

Given his background and liberal viewpoint, Sacks was surprisingly slow to appreciate the magnitude of the problem. His annual report written at the end of 1976 predicted that "over the next decade . . . public interest law seems likely to flourish."[14] In fact, the opposite was occurring. During the 1970s the percentage of students taking positions outside of law firms or clerkships, hovered around 9 percent, among those reporting their jobs to the school's Placement Office. In 1978 the *Harvard Law Record* reported that out of 526 graduating students in the class of 1977, only 21 had gone into positions outside of law firms or clerkships: 19 to government positions and 2 to public interest entities.[15]

In response, the faculty in March 1978 approved, in principle, what became known as the "Low Income Protection Plan" (LIPP) to compensate graduates who took positions outside of private firms.[16] But LIPP got off to a slow start due to funding limitations, and not until his last annual report did Sacks note for the first time the decrease in public service and public interest employment. He also remarked that students' response to LIPP and a loan forgiveness program was "disappointing."[17]

One obvious solution was to increase financial aid through fund-raising, and the Harvard Law School Fund set an unprecedented goal of $2 million in October 1978. Sacks announced that $800,000 would be used for financial aid to offset the impact of tuition increases, $500,000 for library expense, $300,000 to support clinical education, and $200,000 for handicap accessibility construction. Another $100,000 went to the professional responsibility program, one of Sacks's priorities, and $100,000 to career services, a priority of the students.[18]

Conspicuously missing from these annual targets were major capital gifts. None of the annual fund was allocated for endowment of any kind, though the fund had been a major source of scholarship endowment growth under Griswold. Nor were gifts solicited for building projects, though the need was certainly there. By May 1980 Sacks had spent $4.2 million on capital improvements to the library and Harkness Commons. With interest rates reaching 18 percent in April 1980, borrowing was extremely costly. In addition, the accelerated reliance on annual alumni giving likely discouraged major gifts.

In fact, during the ten years of Sacks's administration, the school received only one significant capital gift—$242,000—which covered one-third of the expense to purchase and renovate a large house to serve as the Development and Alumni Affairs Office.[19]

Whereas the dean maintained that building operations and energy costs primarily drove expense, expansion of the administrative staff contributed as well. The number of regular (tenured and tenure-track) faculty during Sacks's deanship remained at about sixty, while the number of senior administrators grew from ten to fifteen, not counting faculty with administrative responsibilities. At the outset, Sacks's administration comprised ten senior administrators for 1,600 students, mostly held over from Derek Bok: the dean, one vice dean, four assistant deans, the librarian, and three other directors. These included two African Americans—Acting Librarian George A. Strait and Assistant Dean Walter Leonard, who became special assistant to President Bok in 1971 but continued to work on Law School admissions—and two women, Eleanor Appel, placement director, and Mary Upton, registrar.[20] By 1981, four of the eight assistant deans and seven of the fifteen senior administrators were women, but none were persons of color.

This growth of 50 percent in total senior administration seems moderate, given the high student-faculty ratio and the evolving needs in clinical legal education, professional responsibility, career placement, and graduate programs. Most of the other additional costs were related to building operations and energy costs. In any event, Sacks inherited a school that was utterly dependent on frequent tuition increases, and he bequeathed an almost identical, if not worse, financial situation to his successor. This resulted, in part, because he had no "big vision or plan of what to do," future dean Robert Clark (1989–2003) remarked later.[21]

Progress Enrolling Women

The classes matriculating under Dean Bok (1968–1970) in the fall of 1968, 1969, and 1970 had less than 9 percent women, and Dean Sacks and Admissions Director Russell Simpson (LL.B. 1965) began to make significant progress in the admissions cycle during the spring of 1972. The number of female applicants increased by 17 percent, and the enrollment of women jumped to 15 percent, as Simpson proudly described in September in the *Harvard Law Record.* He also emphasized that male and female applicants had the same acceptance rate of 13 percent.[22]

Harvard Women's Law Association, 1971.

Courtesy of Martin Paul, Studio C. Inc., and Harvard Law School Library, Historical & Special Collections.

But there was a note of concern. The yield—the number of admitted women who enrolled—was a disappointing 39 percent. Given that women were such a small part of the applicant pool, only 16 percent, the poor yield meant that the proportional gain in female enrollment was still modest. The Women's Law Association (WLA), with support from the Sacks administration, began to study the reasons for "the relatively high percentage of women refusing . . . admission," while Simpson planned both to increase the applicant pool of women and, by personal contact, to increase the yield.[23]

After that initial jump, progress slowed. In the following fall of 1973, the female enrollment in the entering class increased only to 18 percent. One study placed Harvard only thirteenth out of seventeen national law schools in enrolling women, as seen in Table 17.1. In response, Simpson and his staff, assisted by the WLA, began personally contacting and recruiting admitted women. The result was an incoming class in the fall of 1974 with 120 women, or 22 percent, which still put "the Law School far down the list when compared to other U.S. law schools," noted the *Harvard Law School Record*."[24] When Simpson was promoted in 1975, Sacks bolstered the female staff in admissions by naming Patricia Lydon, a graduate of the University of Minnesota

Table 17.1   Percentage of Women Entering Various Law Schools, Fall 1973

Law School	Percentage of Women in First-Year Class
Northeastern University	50
University of California at Berkeley	33
New York University	31
Arizona State University	30
University of Southern California	30
Yale University	23
Boston University	23
Georgetown University	22
Indiana University (Bloomington)	21
Tulane University	20
University of Minnesota	20
Washington University	20
Duke University	18
Harvard University	**18**
University of Chicago	18
Vanderbilt University	17
University of Georgia	9

Data source: Jim Stewart, "Ratio of Women at HLS Ranks 13 of 17 Schools," *HLSR* (December 7, 1973): 1, 6.

Law School, as director of admissions from 1975 to 1978, and then Molly Geraghty, who served in the post from 1979 to 1989. Meanwhile, Norma Thompson worked as an admissions officer from 1969 to 1989. This greater female presence aided recruiting. "A factor encouraging women to enroll at Harvard Law School could be that there is a woman's signature on the acceptance letter," stated Lydon.[25]

By 1977 nearly 27 percent of the incoming class were women. This substantial gain was achieved while holding to "three basic principles." First, the acceptance rate of male and female applicants should remain as even as possible. Second, the admissions system should be, in Lydon's words, "as sex blind as possible," favoring neither gender. Finally, the yield—the percentage of enrollees out of admitted applicants—should be consistent with the percentage of women in the applicant pool.[26]

The efforts of WLA contributed to this progress. With the support of a travel budget from Dean Sacks, WLA members traveled to colleges in various parts of the country and urged women to apply. According to Regina Williams Tate (J.D. 1978), "many women are qualified but had never thought of applying to Harvard and many colleges had told their students not even to bother to apply." WLA members then contacted every admitted woman. Finding that "many women . . . had doubts about attending Harvard once they were accepted," the "WLA members tried to restore their confidence." And there was a feedback effect, Lydon observed: "As more women enroll, they send back information to their colleges that there are women here who are doing well, and more women consequently choose to apply."[27]

In 1978, women constituted 32 percent of applicants, and female enrollment neared 30 percent, the *Record* trumpeted. This article also underscored the "sex-blind" admissions, because the acceptance rate was almost identical for both genders at just over 10 percent.[28] But the yield remained disappointing. When the next year, 1979, showed only a marginal increase in the number of women enrolled, the WLA became openly critical of admissions policies. Referring to the 29 percent of women in the total student body as "the Law School's biggest minority," the chair of the WLA, Melissa Allain (J.D. 1980), stated that the administration had "a long way to go to the goal point—equal representation of the sexes" among students and the tenured faculty, which included only two women.[29]

Director Geraghty responded that, thanks to the WLA's own participation, including contacting each admitted woman, the Harvard "program" for recruiting women was "the most ambitious in the country" and added that each admitted woman "receives a 'special letter' from Dean Sacks."[30] Geraghty noted that Harvard was not far behind the national average of 33 percent female enrollment in all law schools, and had caught up to Yale in this regard.[31] But WLA disagreed. The refusal of the admission office to release the LSAT scores and the grade-point averages of the male and female applicant pools raised the possibility that the academic records of female applicants were stronger and that men were favored.. Nancy Wiegers (J.D. 1981), of the WLA Coordinating Committee, pointed out that "recent studies comparing men and women entering liberal arts colleges and graduate schools" had found that female applicants were "more qualified than their male counterparts." If so, the Law School's policy of "equal yield" was, in fact, "an unspoken quota system," stated Penny Marshall (J.D. 1981).[32]

The complaints and criticism were entirely understandable, even though at the end of Sacks's administration in 1981, the percentage of women in the entering class had risen to 37 percent and matched many of the school's peer institutions, as seen in Table 17.2. This increase in the number of women enrolling at Harvard Law School between 1971 and 1981, though modest, was arguably Dean Sacks's biggest achievement. In the subsequent decade under

Table 17.2 Percentage of Women Enrolled in the Law Schools at Harvard, Yale, and
Georgetown, and the ABA Total, 1974–1981

Year	Harvard (first year)	Yale (third year)	Georgetown (first year)	ABA (total enrollment)
1974	13	16	17	—
1975	15	17	18	—
1976	17	22	21	16
1977	22	21	26	20
1978	21	27	N/A	23
1979	25	23	37	26
1980	33	26	35	28
1981	37	34	37	31

Data source: Jim Stewart, "Ratio of Women at HLS Ranks 13 of 17 Schools," *HLSR* (December 7,
1973): 6. Source did not provide missing entries.

Dean Vorenberg, the enrollment of women at Harvard Law School would rise
to 45 percent, while the national enrollment average increased steadily to
46 percent in 1997–98.[33]

"Moving Backward" on Minority Enrollment

The oral histories conducted for this volume testify to Sacks's commitment to
the values and goals of the civil rights movement and to improving racial and
ethnic diversity at Harvard Law School. In the fall of 1970, Bok had laid a
foundation, enrolling 13 percent minority students, including African Americans, Hispanics, and Asian Americans,. In 1971 Sacks and Simpson then recruited Robert Williams, an African American graduate of the University of
Virginia, to collaborate with Walter Leonard, who developed an affirmative
action admissions program that became a national model while working as
special assistant to President Bok.[34] In the fall of 1971 the percentage of minority students rose to 16 percent, as seen in Table 17.3.

But progress then halted. In November 1974 the Admissions Office for the
first time publicly announced minority statistics for the entering class—a testa-
ment to Sacks's commitment to transparency on the issue. The 545 law students included 48 termed "black," 11 "Chicanos," 3 "other Spanish-surnamed"
students, 5 "Asian Americans," and 3 "Native Americans," for a total of almost
13 percent.[35] Subsequently, even as the enrollment of women steadily grew,

Table 17.3 Percentage of Students by Race and Gender in Entering LL.B. or J.D. Classes at Harvard Law School, 1964–1980

Group	1964	1970	1971	1976	1980
White	92	88	84	88	87
African American	2	10	10	8	7
Hispanic	1	2	2	2	3
Asian	1	1	3	2	3
Other	0	0	1	0	0
Total Minority	4	13	16	12	13
Total Female	4	9	13	24	29

Data sources: Data compiled from review of figures from Harvard Law School Admissions Office reported in *HLSR*, pictures in Harvard Law School "face books" of entering students, and pictures in volumes of the *Harvard Law School Yearbook*.

minority enrollment stalled—and for some groups, such as African American men, actually declined.[36] The class entering in the fall of 1976 had only 6 percent African American men and 2 percent African American women, with tiny numbers in all other categories, for a total of 12 percent minority enrollment. The last class admitted under Dean Sacks, in the fall of 1980, had the lowest African American enrollment of all, at 7 percent, and a total minority enrollment of 13 percent, as seen in Table 17.3.

Why did this happen? First, the school failed to expand the applicant pool by recruiting aggressively at historically black colleges. In addition, the school's steep tuition increases surely discouraged applicants. Also, the closure of the national Council on Legal Education Opportunity in 1973, the departure of Walter Leonard from the Law School to assist President Bok in 1971, and the resignation of Robert Williams from the Admissions Office in 1975 damaged recruitment efforts.[37] Fourth, the school was reluctant to employ criteria that would place the admission of applicants in special categories, including women and minorities, apart from the rest of the applicant pool.[38] In this regard, subsequent critics argued that narrow and highly debatable measures of "merit" assumed by the Law School stood in the way of progress.[39]

Finally, the national percentage of African Americans enrolling in ABA-accredited law schools leveled off during the 1970s at about 5 percent. Likewise, the national enrollment of all minority students improved relatively little from about 7 percent to 10 percent over the decade.[40] Compared to these benchmarks, the Sacks administration did better than law schools nationally, despite the lack of improvement over ten years, as seen in Figure 17.1.

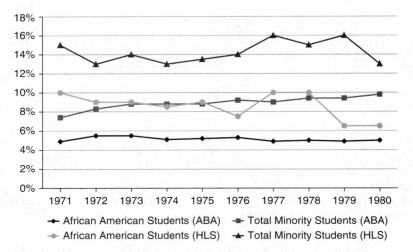

Figure 17.1. Percentage of Minority J.D. Enrollment at Harvard Law School under Dean Sacks compared to all ABA-accredited Law Schools in the United States, 1971–1980. Data sources: ABA, *Report on Minority Statistics, 1971–1980*; Harvard Law School Review; Harvard Law School "face books" of entering students; and pictures of Harvard Law School Yearbooks.

In the 1980s Dean Vorenberg had little more success, and the cumulative minority enrollment remained at 16 percent, only slightly better than during the Sacks administration. But this increase stemmed from growing enrollment of both Hispanic and Asian American students, while African American enrollment remained at 9 percent. Walter Leonard's words upon leaving Harvard in 1977 to become president of Fisk University proved correct not only retrospectively but also prospectively: "Not only have we not progressed a great deal since October 1971 (both statistically and attitudinally), but I fear we have moved backwards."[41]

Early Female Legal Scholars at Harvard

In 1962 and 1963, the University of Chicago and Yale University appointed women as tenured professors of law for the first time.[42] At Harvard, the highest-ranking appointment of a woman at the Law School until 1972 was the hiring of Soia Mentschikoff as a visiting professor for 1947–1949. A few other accomplished academic women stood outside the faculty relegated to marginal positions prior to 1972.

Helen Maud Cam, a medieval historian who had graduated from Cambridge University, was appointed the first female professor in Harvard's Faculty of Arts and Sciences in 1948. Between 1951 and 1953 she taught a cross-listed seminar in English legal history at the Law School, but then returned to England in 1954 after making gender history at Harvard College by daring to use Lamont Library, which barred women.[43]

Another accomplished scholar was Edith Guild Henderson (LL.B. 1953, S.J.D. 1959), a member of the first class of women at the Law School. She could not find a job during her third year, so she accepted an offer from Professor Louis Jaffe (LL.B. 1928) to assist his research in legal history. In 1959 she completed the S.J.D. at the Law School, and in 1963 became curator of the Treasure Room in the Law School library, serving until 1987. In that role, she inspired generations of young legal historians, and published five groundbreaking treatises, including the classic *Foundations of English Administrative Law* (1963).[44] But she was never considered for a faculty appointment and never even taught a course at the Law School.

Particularly significant was Eleanor Glueck, who conducted pioneering research on criminology with her collaborator and husband, psychologist Sheldon Glueck. Their work became internationally renowned, and Sheldon was promoted to full professor—while Eleanor was confined to various "research" appointments from 1928 until she retired in 1964. The Law School faculty never discussed elevating her academic appointment, but Harvard University did award both Gluecks honorary doctorates in 1958.[45] In 1964, their joint portrait was hung in the main reading room of Langdell Hall—the only portrait of a woman among dozens of portraits hung throughout the school.

In 1971 the Law School honored Eleanor Glueck and her husband by naming a classroom for them in newly opened Pound Hall. Their joint portrait was moved to the new Glueck Room, and individual portraits, photographs of them and their work, and plaques honoring their research were also hung around the room. Eleanor died in 1972, and Dean Sacks delivered a eulogy at her funeral acknowledging the barriers and slights that she had faced.[46] The *Harvard Law School Bulletin* observed, "From beginning to end, she was a pioneer, and now in retrospect—beyond the formalities that for so long forbade women to teach or study at Harvard Law School—there can be little doubt that Eleanor Glueck was the first lady of Harvard Law School."[47] So amends had been made, according to the *Bulletin,* and Eleanor appeared to have her rightful place in the school at last.

Sheldon Glueck, Faculty 1929–1963. Eleanor Glueck, Researcher 1928–1964, never appointed to the faculty. Sheldon and Eleanor Glueck. Portrait by Franz Lenhart, 1964.

Courtesy of Harvard Law School Library, Historical & Special Collections.

That lasted only until 2012, when the Law School renovated Pound Hall. All references to the Gluecks were removed, and their portraits, pictures, and plaques went into storage. This effacing of "the first lady of Harvard Law School"—so long marginalized and belatedly honored—was surely a disgrace. Historian Mary Beth Basile Chopas observed that the Law School "put Eleanor right back into the shadows where she existed during her entire time working there." In 2016, after inquiries were made, their joint portrait was located, dusted off, and hung in the reading room of the Historical and Special Collections department in the library.[48]

"Sex-Based Discrimination and the Law"

In addition to honoring Eleanor Glueck, the school made another effort in 1971 to extinguish "the formalities that for so long forbade women to teach or study at Harvard Law School," as the *Yearbook* noted. In the fall of 1971 the Law School finally appointed the first woman to be considered for a tenure-track position, Ruth Bader Ginsburg (1956–58). She was initially appointed lecturer for the fall semester, and Dean Sacks assured her that a tenure-track appointment would follow. Since she was still teaching at Rutgers in New Jersey, working for the ACLU, and living in New York City with her husband and two children, the arrangement was for her to come to Cambridge one day per week and teach one course, Sex-Based Discrimination and the Law, and assist students on related projects.[49]

Soon after starting to teach, Ginsburg found that, in the eyes of senior faculty, the appointment was not to introduce her as a future tenure-track assistant professor but to look her over as a possible appointee. Though feeling misled, she could not change her frenetic schedule of commuting between Cambridge, New Jersey, and New York City. Being present in Cambridge one day per week to teach her course and meet with students meant that, in the words of Professor Vorenberg, "the main faculty members had [not] gotten to know her very well. And that included me who was in the next office." In fact, some professors came to consider Ginsburg "quite standoffish."[50] In addition, although she was a popular teacher among the students, some faculty criticized her teaching. For example, Phillip Areeda (LL.B. 1954) reportedly expressed reservations after dropping in on her class without notice—the day after she pulled an "an all-nighter" to complete an ACLU brief.[51]

Though personally encouraging her, Dean Sacks did not adequately rebut these faculty reservations about collegiality and teaching, which he related to Ginsburg at the end of the semester. Ironically, Ginsburg now had the dean's appreciation and support, missing from Griswold, but not Griswold's gravity and force to challenge the faculty, which was lacking in Sacks. Nevertheless, Sacks invited her to return as a lecturer in the fall of 1972. But Ginsburg had no interest in a "second semester-long audition," particularly at Harvard Law School, and instead accepted Columbia's offer of a tenured professorship in December 1971.[52] Once again, Columbia, which had awarded Ginsburg her LL.B. after Harvard refused, benefited from Harvard's gender obtuseness.

It is noteworthy that these faculty reservations would not pass muster subsequently in American higher education. Such evaluations of collegiality would be highly suspect, particularly concerning minority candidates. Also, universities would expect teaching evaluations to be announced beforehand and documented with specific points in writing and communicated to the candidate with the opportunity to respond and improve, while student evaluations would also be considered in the appointment and promotion process.

In fact, Sacks's one-shot, up-or-down assessment conveyed at the end of the semester without specific, written feedback was remarkably similar to the school's grading system, which so upset students and would appear deficient to later experts in educational measurement and assessment. But unlike the grading of anonymous exams, the subjects of teaching evaluations were not anonymous, and this is a critical point. Impressionistic, undocumented evaluations reported privately to the dean tend to confirm and replicate the prevailing cultural norms within a faculty. In this way, the evaluation process of female faculty candidates contributed directly to their being found deficient over the next dozen years.

When Ginsburg left, the WLA was furious, and Sacks's failure to secure a tenure-track position for Ginsburg was a public embarrassment. But the pattern typified women's appointments between 1971 and 1984, when the Law School routinely hired women as lecturers or visiting professors, giving the appearance of gender equity while hiring few women to tenure-track faculty appointments. During this period, no fewer than twenty-four temporary appointments of women were made, and only eight tenure-track appointments, as reported in Appendix I. Then most of the tenure-track appointments were turned down—repeatedly because the woman's collegiality or teaching did not fit the norms of the all-male Harvard law faculty.

Almost immediately after Ginsburg left, the faculty agreed to appoint Elizabeth Owens, a long time researcher and lecturer, to a tenured professorship, as described in Chapter 13. Also in response to Ginsburg's departure, Dean Sacks focused on appointing Diane T. Lund (LL.B. 1961) directly to a tenure-track position. At the Law School, Lund had been a superlative student, graduating *magna cum laude* and ranking thirteenth in a class of 550 that was 98 percent male. Invited to join the *Law Review,* she declined, partly to spend more time with her fiancé, Erik Lund (LL.B. 1961), and partly to earn money. Coming from a family of modest means, Lund was dependent on scholarships and loans and joined the Board of Student Advisors because it paid for advising first-year students. Her decision not to join the *Law Review*

Diane Theis Lund, LL.B. 1961. Faculty 1972–1984.

Harvard Law School Yearbook, 1973. Courtesy of Harvard Yearbook Publications.

was problematic, given that the *Review* had become virtually a *sine qua non* for appointment to the faculty. Professor Barton Leach (LL.B. 1924), the well-known conservative, unsuccessfully urged her to reconsider.[53]

After practicing law for ten years, Lund was recruited by Dean Sacks and Frank Michelman (LL.B. 1960) for a tenure-track position as assistant professor. In 1972 she thus became the first woman in the school's history appointed to the regular faculty, setting aside the unique circumstances of Elizabeth Owens. To have time to care for her three children, Lund negotiated an unusual two-thirds workload and a five-year contract.[54]

The appointment started off well. The dean and faculty needed a genuinely tenured woman, and Lund wanted that too. Her husband recalled that Lund wished "to be the first tenured female professor" and "a role model for others."[55] Lund held Dean Sacks in high regard and said that he had warned her about the conservatism of the faculty and the stress of making tenure. He assigned her to teach upper-level courses in Estates and Trusts, Family Law, and the

Legal Status of Women. These were considered "appropriate" courses for women at the time, and this assignment also meant that she was not thrown in the "deep end" of the mandatory, huge first-year sections. She found a mentor and co-teacher in the Family Law course, Professor Alan Stone.[56] Lund also pioneered teaching a course in Professional Responsibility, which greatly interested Dean Sacks. By all accounts, she was an excellent teacher who was popular with her overwhelmingly male classes.

But problems arose. Lund felt "patronized" in faculty meetings and "believed her views were not valued." In fact, "it was the first time in her professional life she encountered tokenism." Also, she struggled writing the law review articles required for tenure, and "was not willing to submit them for formal review" because "she was not happy with the quality."[57] Above all, she disliked the elitism of the male faculty and found balancing family and academic responsibilities highly stressful. Mary Beth Basile Chopas points out, "Women who choose to prioritize family responsibilities at night and on weekends, and therefore have little time for research and writing, are at a severe disadvantage in meeting the significant criteria for publication for a tenured professorship."[58]

Finally, in 1976, she resigned and returned to law practice in her own firm, specializing in family law, estates and trusts, and employment discrimination. Sacks arranged for her to continue as a part-time lecturer.[59] It was another missed opportunity and an embarrassment for Harvard Law School. "Sacks was dismayed, and concerned about repercussions," wrote Lund's husband, Erik. The dean "was relieved, however, that she wanted to continue teaching both the family law course and the professional responsibility course. Her presence and her influence would continue."[60]

After teaching annually as a lecturer since 1977, Lund was informed in the spring of 1983 that the course in professional responsibility she had pioneered was now required, and therefore had to be taught by a regular member of the faculty. She wrote to Dean Vorenberg asking whether she should continue as a lecturer teaching Family Law. By this time Lund had been a member of the Massachusetts Board of Bar Overseers since 1979, and elected its chair in 1983, the first woman to be so honored. Despite this distinction and her long record teaching at the Law School, Dean Vorenberg "never acknowledged" her letter or told her that "she wouldn't be reappointed. That news came to her when the Law School's fall 1984 catalog came out and her family law course wasn't listed," wrote Erik.[61]

Glendon and Neely, 1974–1976

The pattern persisted during the visit by Mary Ann Glendon in the academic year 1974–75. A brilliant graduate of the University of Chicago Law School and protégé of Soia Mentschikoff, Glendon was a tenured professor at Boston College Law School, specializing in Property, Comparative Law, and Family Law. She had coauthored a book, *The Law of Decedents' Estates* (1971) with Max Rheinstein, and had published two major law review articles. During her year as a visiting professor, she became the first woman to teach a required first-year course (Property 1) with 135 or more students, and received excellent teaching reviews.[62] But at the end of her term as visiting professor, Glendon was not offered a tenure-track position.

The news came at the end of the year when Glendon "received a visit from Dean Sacks, who informed her that the faculty felt that they had not gotten to know her. In particular, she recalls that he said, 'You didn't have lunch in the faculty lunch room.'" This was true. Glendon, who had three small children, ate lunch at her desk so that she could get home in time to relieve her nanny of childcare.[63] Furthermore, during Glendon's visiting year, Raya S. Dreben (LL.B. 1954), a member of the second class enrolling women, served as a lecturer at the Law School and "recalls that she and Diane Lund, with whom she was very friendly, tried eating in the faculty dining room on several occasions but abandoned their efforts since the atmosphere was unpleasant and not conducive to collegiality."[64] As in the case of Lund, the all-male faculty of Harvard Law School were clueless. But they eventually realized their error, and in 1986 hired Glendon as a tenured professor, elevating her to the Learned Hand Chair in 1993.[65]

An even more painful case followed. In 1975, Sally Schultz Neely, a distinguished Stanford Law graduate who clerked for Judge Ozell M. Trask of the U.S. Court of Appeals, Ninth Circuit, was appointed as a tenure-track assistant professor. She had no teaching experience and came directly from law practice in Phoenix. Inexplicably, Sacks assigned her to teach the required, first-year Contracts course to a class of 135 students plus a seminar on limited partnerships. The combative Spartan culture had not died, and the overwhelmingly male students "badly mistreated" her. "She was challenged unmercifully and cruelly by students unwilling to give her the respect and deference automatically given to male professors, no matter how inexperienced," stated Eric Lund.[66]

Sally Schultz Neely. Faculty 1975–1979.
Harvard Law School Yearbook, 1976. Courtesy of Harvard Yearbook Publications.

"Her closest friend on the faculty," Assistant Professor Richard Parker (J.D. 1970), knew her "extremely well," and recalled,

> Right from the start, she was a fish out of water. Her manner . . . had a kind of a [kindergarten teacher] quality to it, but I liked her energy. . . . When she would finish a class and would be weeping, she came to my office, time and time again. I went to her class once, and I saw what the problem was. She struck these students—the male students, in particular—as their kindergarten teacher, and in those days . . . when Harvard Law students sensed weakness, or blood in the water, they attacked like a herd of sharks. They were throwing Frisbees in her class; it was grossly disrespectful. She was driven out, and I think gender had a lot to do with it. I don't think the faculty reached out to her, except for me. . . . But it was mainly the students who drove her out.[67]

Neely lasted two academic years, 1975–1977, and then took a leave of absence, 1977–1979, to return to law practice in Los Angeles, where she has spent the rest of her career with great distinction in bankruptcy law, eventually chairing the Committee on Legislation of the National Bankruptcy Conference from 2001 to 2013.[68] Neely declined several requests for interviews concerning her experience at Harvard Law School. By all received accounts, her experience at the Law School was traumatic, and she did not wish to revisit it.[69]

Thus, five years into Sacks's deanship, only Elizabeth Owens was promoted and tenured, and she "sort of had to back in," as Vorenberg said.[70] All four women brought in from the outside and considered for regular faculty positions—Ginsburg, Lund, Glendon, and Neely—were denied or forced out. Evaluation of teaching was sometimes given as the reason, but the data generally consisted of impressionistic and undocumented reports not shared with the candidate, and student evaluations mattered little, unless they were bad. Lund's difficulty in publishing might have been a problem, but Glendon's prolific record did not seem to help.

Collegiality and going to lunch with the faculty mattered a lot, and none of the four women, including three mothers with children, went to lunch—or liked it, if they did. Here, too, undocumented personal impressions largely determined the fate of appointees being considered for regular faculty positions, so it is not surprising that only candidates who fit the prevailing norms succeeded, as did all of the men over the same period. The senior white male faculty were replicating themselves. As of 1976 the Harvard Law School faculty's record on gender equity was terrible. And then it got worse.

Years of Rage, 1976–1981

Between 1976 and 1981, nine distinguished women "visited" for short terms, never to be offered tenure-track positions: Herma Hill Kay (J.D. Berkeley) in 1976–77, Carole Goldberg (J.D. UCLA) in 1977, Barbara Black (J.D. Yale) in 1978–79, Sally Falk Moore (J.D. UCLA) in 1978 and 1982, Linda Siberman (J.D. NYU) in 1979–80, Tamar Frankel (J.D. Boston University) in 1978–1980, Mary Luise Fellar (J.D. Illinois) in 1980–81, Margaret Berger (J.D. Brooklyn) in 1980, and Catharine MacKinnon (J.D. Yale) in 1981. Today all these women are recognized as major scholars, teachers, and civil rights leaders.[71] None stayed at Harvard, where their legacy was the illusion of diversity.

Meanwhile, two women were tenured after harrowing experiences. Elizabeth Bartholet (LL.B. 1965) was a star student at the Law School, graduating *magna cum laude*. Unlike Lund, she joined the *Harvard Law Review,* which eventually provided her with a cadre of loyal supporters. Bartholet then achieved a top federal clerkship with Judge Henry W. Edgerton (LL.B. 1914) of the U.S. Court of Appeals, D.C. Circuit, who was "one of the only federal judges at the time that would hire a woman," according to Bartholet.[72] After the clerkship, she followed one of "the few paths open to women"—government service and nonprofits—where she flourished, serving as special assistant to James Vorenberg, executive director of staff of the President's Commission on Law Enforcement, and later dean of the Law School. Bartholet then became a staff attorney with the Legal Defense Fund (LDF) of the National Association for the Advancement of Colored People (NAACP) and director of the Legal Action Center in New York.[73]

After several overtures, Sacks successfully recruited her to join the faculty in 1977. Coming from a "privileged" background, "she was self-assured to the point of being cocky, and had no doubt whatsoever that she belonged on the Harvard Faculty and would be offered tenure in due course," stated Erik Lund.[74] As an assistant professor, she successfully taught the large, required courses Civil Procedure and Constitutional Law, and established a new clinical course, Public Interest Litigation: Race and Diversity. She also published "Application of Title VII to Jobs in High Places" in the *Harvard Law Review*. At the close of the Sacks administration, she had been at the school for four and a half years, and was confident of tenure. But she felt "isolated," because the faculty had "virtually total disinterest . . . in her and what she'd accomplished."[75] She "thought of herself as highly successful, but she had no natural cohort at Harvard, no one her year, her age, or with her experience," observed Lund.[76]

Bartholet was not considered for promotion until after Sacks had left, and the nightmare that ensued was attributable to his successor, Dean Vorenberg, who told her early in 1982 that she would not be promoted due to "inadequacy in her teaching evaluations." Bartholet knew that, in the past, "women were firmly, routinely, and discretely pushed aside. They were expected to depart quietly." Instead, "she was going to fight." She asked a "shadow" committee of faculty to monitor the Appointments Committee. She also deferentially asked senior professors to attend her classes and tell her "what she should do to be a better teacher."[77]

In addition, the students rallied around her. Scores wrote to Vorenberg and the Appointments Committee on her behalf. One hundred students signed a petition to Vorenberg urging her tenure. In her words, she went through eighteen months "of hell in which I sort of bit my tongue and taught." At the end of that academic year, 1982–83, she was granted tenure. "It took me another number of years, certainly several, to recover from a year and a half of rage that I had experienced, mostly silently," she recalled.[78]

The second tenured woman appointed under Dean Sacks was Martha A. Field, who came through a lateral appointment from the University of Pennsylvania Law School. In 1968 she had graduated at the top of her class at the University of Chicago Law School, and Justice Abe Fortas appointed her as a law clerk, after two other Supreme Court justices told her that they "would not feel comfortable with a woman clerk." During the clerkship, she learned about Harvard's gender discrimination when she sought interviews for teaching positions. In 1970 the Supreme Court clerks were told that Harvard "would be glad to meet with 'all but the girl,'" and she was never invited to interview.[79] Accepting an offer from the University of Pennsylvania, Field became the first woman on the faculty there and, in 1973, the first woman there to receive tenure.[80]

In the spring of 1978 Dean Sacks asked Field if she would accept a visiting professorship to teach Constitutional Law, Sex Discrimination, and Federal Courts at Harvard, and she accepted. But knowing that Harvard had never tenured a woman coming from the outside, she made it clear that she would not consider joining the Harvard faculty except with tenure. At the end of fall semester 1978, her excellent teaching reputation and extraordinary production of six law review articles since 1972 convinced the Harvard faculty to vote unanimously to promote her to tenured professor.[81] Sacks assured her "that the decision had nothing to do with her being a woman," and that she could continue to teach Federal Courts and Constitutional Law and "would not be shuffled into courses most often taught by women, such as Trusts and Estates, Family Law, and Women and the Law."[82]

In the end, Field accepted, with reservations. She had felt "that the atmosphere at the Law School was incredibly cold and forbidding," in contrast to Pennsylvania, where she had been "welcomed into a circle of male faculty for lunch." At Harvard she too suffered the "lonely lunch syndrome."[83] And there had been a group of students in Constitutional Law "out to get her," not unlike Sally Neely in Contracts. But Field handled the male student hostility better. Though only age thirty-four, she had been teaching for nine years, and had already encountered many who "did not believe a twenty-five-year-old woman could be a real law professor."[84]

Today, both Elizabeth Bartholet and Martha Field are senior members of the Harvard faculty, who hold distinguished endowed chairs. But their hard-won successes were not the end of gender discrimination on the Harvard Law School faculty. In 1979, immediately after Field was appointed, the WLA ex-

Clare Dalton. LL.M. 1973. Faculty 1981–1988.

Harvard Law School Yearbook, 1982. Courtesy of Harvard Yearbook Publications.

pressed "dismay" to Dean Sacks that the faculty included only two tenured women, and the small number was discouraging women from enrolling at Harvard.[85] In his final year, 1980–81, Dean Sacks and Associate Dean Charles Nesson (LL.B. 1963) persuaded the Appointments Committee to appoint three women as tenure-track assistant professors: Claire Dalton, Martha Minow, and Susan Estrich (J.D. 1977).

Dalton was English and a graduate of Oxford, who earned the LL.M. from Harvard in 1973. In that same year she married Robert Reich, who later became secretary of labor under President Bill Clinton. Dalton pursued a career in Washington, teaching at American University from 1974 to 1978, and then practicing at a major law firm. Appointed to the Harvard faculty in 1981, she was assigned to teach Contracts, Antitrust, and Legal History, although the focus of her legal scholarship was domestic violence and feminist legal theory.

She also brought an international and comparativist perspective to the faculty, and early on identified with Critical Legal Studies, as discussed in Chapter 19.[86]

Susan Estrich (J.D. 1977) had all the traditional requirements to be a law professor, including a brilliant academic record at both Wellesley College and the Law School. Not only did her grades qualify her for membership on the *Harvard Law Review,* but in 1976 she was elected the first female president of the *Review* over Merrick Garland (J.D. 1977), the future U.S. Supreme Court nominee. But Estrich's road was not easy amid the manly, Spartan culture at the Law School. In addition to accolades, the *Harvard Law Record* published sexist and sexual humor upon her election as president of the *Law Review.*[87] After graduation, Estrich clerked for Judge J. Skelly Wright of the U.S. Court of Appeals, D.C. Circuit, and then Supreme Court Justice John P. Stevens. Next she became staff counsel for the Senate Judiciary Committee and deputy director and platform coordinator for Senator Edward Kennedy's presidential campaign in 1980.[88]

Martha Minow was the daughter of a distinguished lawyer and former chair of the Federal Communications Commission. After graduating from the University of Michigan, she earned the Ed.M. at Harvard Graduate School of Education and the J.D. from Yale Law School in 1979, where she was editor of the *Yale Law Journal.* She then clerked with Judge David L. Bazelon, U.S. Court of Appeals, D.C. Circuit, and Supreme Court Justice Thurgood Marshall. Unlike Dalton and Estrich, Minow, in 1981, went directly from the clerkships to the faculty at Harvard Law School in 1981, with no intervening practice experience.[89]

The careers of these three women had vastly different outcomes during the Vorenberg administration. Dalton was denied tenure in 1988 and sued Harvard for sex discrimination, prompting an acrimonious public controversy over the merits of feminist theory and Critical Legal Studies. In 1988 she moved to Northeastern University, where she founded the Domestic Violence Institute, which was awarded over $4 million of grant funding. In 2000, Dalton was named a distinguished university professor at Northeastern.[90]

After five tumultuous years at Harvard, Estrich was promoted to tenured professor in 1986 at the age of thirty-four, the first woman, along with Minow, to be promoted from the tenure-track at the Law School. Soon thereafter, in 1987 and 1988, she became the first woman to direct a presidential campaign, that of Massachusetts governor Michael Dukakis (LL.B 1960). In 1989 she left Cambridge for California, where she became a successful author, news commentator, and law professor at the University of Southern California.

Estrich declined several requests by the authors and their research assistants to provide an oral history about her time at Harvard, including an offer to visit her in California.

Martha Minow was the one great success story of Sacks's administration, in terms of advancement at Harvard Law School. In 1986, just thirty-two years old, she earned tenure along with Susan Estrich, and went on to a highly successful academic career, advancing among the chaired professorships at the school. In 2009 she became dean of the Law School, serving until 2017. In 2018 she was named a university professor, Harvard's highest faculty honor. Although her spectacular career was helped by Vorenberg's mentoring, Minow notes that Sacks recruited and appointed her.[91]

As these accounts of the women's experiences reveal, the appointment and promotion of women on the faculty was arduous and painful during the Sacks administration. Following his departure, the string of temporary and visiting appointments continued under his successor, Dean Vorenberg.[92] Out of the nineteen such appointments between 1971 and 1986, only two women— Martha Field and Mary Ann Glendon (in 1986)—were advanced to tenured professor. Out of the six women appointed tenure-track assistant professors over the time span, only two—Bartholet and Minow—were tenured and built a career at Harvard Law School. In contrast, most male appointees succeeded.

Glacial Progress in Minority Hiring

While the number of appointments of women to the faculty was small under Dean Sacks, the hiring of people of color to the faculty was worse. It amounted to only three African American men, one of whom left shortly after being appointed. During this decade, no Asian Americans, Hispanics, Native Americans, or African American women were hired. Two other African American men were appointed as lecturers at different points: David S. Nelson, later a U.S. District Court Judge, and Rudolph F. Pierce (J.D. 1970), subsequently a judge of the Massachusetts Superior Court. When Sacks left in 1981, sixty of the sixty-two regular faculty members were white.

One of the two African Americans was Derrick Bell, the first person of color appointed to the Harvard Law School faculty. Bell grew up in a working-class family that valued devotion to hard work, family, military service, and his hometown of Pittsburgh. His family lived in the Hill District, the center of the city's African American community, and Derrick, the oldest of four children, took responsibility for his siblings. An excellent student, he became the first person in his family to attend college, and remained close to home at

Derrick A. Bell. Faculty 1969–1980, 1986–1992.

Harvard Law School Yearbook, 1971. Courtesy of Harvard Yearbook Publications.

Duquesne University. He joined ROTC and, after graduation in 1951, served two years in the Air Force, including a stint in Korea. Returning home from the military, he was determined to make a difference in fighting racism and chose law as the field to do so. Enrolling at the University of Pittsburgh School of Law, he was the only African American student in his class of 140, and one of only three in the entire law school.[93]

Again Bell excelled academically. He was elected to the law review, named associate editor in chief, and graduated fourth in his class in 1957. Such a top black law graduate dedicated to public service attracted attention in the African American civil rights struggle in the 1950s, and the U.S. Department of Justice recruited Bell to its famous Honors Graduate Recruitment Program. Thus Bell began a long and active career as a prominent civil rights lawyer.[94]

Starting out, Bell was assigned to the Civil Rights Division at the Justice Department and then told to resign his $2-a-year membership in the NAACP because it was a "conflict of interest." He was furious. "I decided that I would not resign my membership, and I would wait for them to fire me—which they didn't. They simply moved me out of my office into the hall and started to give me kinds of busywork, which was a message that maybe I should leave, and that's what I did."[95] This decision became typical in Bell's life. Unwilling to accommodate a demand that violated his conscience, he left instead.

Departing Washington, Bell returned to Pittsburgh to work with the local chapter of the NAACP, where he met Thurgood Marshall, founder and head of the LDF. Having heard of Bell's principled stand at the Department of Justice, Marshall recruited him to the LDF. After working on key desegregation cases between 1960 and 1966, Bell served as deputy director of the Office for Civil Rights at the U.S. Department of Health, Education and Welfare in Washington, D.C., from 1966 to 1968. He went on to become the executive director for the Western Center on Law and Poverty at the University of Southern California School of Law.

Bell began teaching law school classes while at the same time applying for academic positions "at a half dozen law schools, including Harvard, none of which expressed an interest in hiring me," he later wrote. Then Charles Nesson, whom Bell had met at the Department of Justice, invited him to address Nesson's class in Civil Rights at Harvard. Bell was well received but was told that Harvard had no faculty position "for someone with my expertise."[96] However, by 1969 African American students had organized the Harvard Black Law Student Association (BLSA) under the leadership of its first president, Reginald E. Gilliam Jr. (LL.B. 1968).[97] Responding to BLSA demands for racial diversity on the faculty, Dean Bok hired Bell as a lecturer to teach a course entitled "Race, Racism and American Law" at the Law School, as well as a course at the Harvard Graduate School of Education. Bell remained a lecturer for two years, and was promoted to tenured professor under Sacks in 1971.[98]

It is noteworthy that Bell's academic credentials, though impressive, were unorthodox for such an appointment at the Law School, especially given that, at the same time, the school was invoking extreme orthodoxy to avoid promoting or tenuring women. The personnel records of these appointments are sealed by Harvard, but the available records clearly suggest that a triple standard obtained in hiring faculty. The normative career ladder was created in the 1950s by white men to suit the paths open to them. That standard was then applied inflexibly to women without considering the constraints on their professional advancement. Finally, a different standard was applied in the case of Bell's appointment to tenured professor.

Bell recognized this. Notwithstanding his own merit, he attributed his appointment largely to political pressure on the Law School by BLSA and the students. But Bell had no desire to be a "token" minority professor or to merely placate the BLSA, and made it clear that he would push to expand attention to racial inequities. In fact, he believed that Bok had hired him to do just that. "My effectiveness as a 'first black' depended on never letting the Law School forget the nature of my appointment and the commitment we [Bok and Bell] both made at that time," he later wrote.[99]

But Bell's efforts in the early 1970s encountered resistance from some faculty. First, he began building a coalition between himself and student groups, which disgusted some other professors, who believed that faculty should not curry favor with or respond to pressure from students. In fact, the faculty at the very same time was rebuffing student calls to reform the grading system. Second, Bell did not want to be pigeon-holed into teaching courses on "Race, Racism, and American Law" and "Slavery Law and Current Racial Issues," and wished to teach the foundational courses Constitutional Law and Criminal Law. But other faculty felt that Bell was not qualified because he, by his own admission, did not meet the orthodox criteria of graduation from a top law school and a federal clerkship, and he published solely about race issues. Nevertheless, Bell continued enlisting students to pressure the faculty.[100]

In 1973 Bell became aware that Clyde Ferguson Jr. (LL.B. 1951) was under consideration for a faculty appointment, and Bell wrote to Ferguson in July urging him to come to Harvard. Ferguson had excelled as a student at the Law School and went on to become the first African American law professor at Rutgers University and then dean of at Howard University Law School from 1963 to 1969. In 1973 Ferguson was working in the State Department.[101]

He wrote to Bell that Duke University Law School had made an "extremely attractive offer" of a tenured professorship with a high salary, tax-free stipends for his daughters while in college, and "unlimited access to funds in support of research." His only doubt was whether "my lifestyle would be completely [consistent] with the mores of Durham, NC." Nevertheless, Ferguson wrote, he was "obviously interested" in coming to Harvard, but an appointment without tenure was "out of the question."[102] Bell replied that the Appointments Committee at Harvard would offer only a visiting position initially, and that Sacks was reluctant to offer even that if Ferguson had an attractive tenure offer in hand from another law school, lest the tenured appointment at Harvard not come through.[103] The memory of Ginsburg's appointment was surely on Sacks's mind.

As these negotiations continued, Bell and Assistant Dean Walter Leonard, who was also becoming impatient with Harvard, organized in September 1974 a Conference on the Recruitment, Hiring and Advancement of Minority Group Teachers. Leonard and Bell "hoped to discuss the standards which are presently used in hiring minority faculty and ask specifically whether such standards are realistic." They wanted to focus on "immediate recruitment," rather than wait "five or ten years" for the next crop of minority students.[104]

Confronting Authority

By November 1974, Bell was fed up that no progress had been made on a regular appointment for a second African American professor since his own appointment in 1971. In his autobiography, *Confronting Authority: Reflections of an Ardent Protester*, Bell reports that he sent "a bold and . . . foolhardy" letter to Dean Sacks, copied to the entire faculty. Bell charged "that the Law School had not made significant efforts to hire minority Law School faculty." The letter demanded the hiring of "additional black faculty members" or Bell would not continue as the school's "only black law teacher."[105] The ultimatum upset President Bok, who had originally recruited Bell and did not believe his complaint to be "legitimate." Leonard, now special assistant to Bok, came to Bell's defense, and characterized Bell's letter as "well thought-out." Leonard also urged the Law School to "recognize its responsibility to seek out black professors and other minority professors that are not represented." At the time, of the fifty-four professors at the Law School, all but one was white and all but two were men.[106]

Meanwhile, Ferguson was still negotiating with Sacks, who was being pressured by Bell's brinkmanship and advocacy by the BLSA. In 1975 Dean Sacks appointed Ferguson to a two-year visiting professorship with some assurance of promotion to tenured professor, which followed in 1977. According to Bell, when Sacks told him of Ferguson's appointment, "the Dean assured me that my 'bold and . . . foolhardy' letter had nothing to do with it." Bell did not believe Sacks, but for once he "didn't question" the dean. "As with so many civil rights advances, blacks are so happy to get there that we accept without complaint or question."[107]

Similarly, Bell's confrontational advocacy accelerated Harvard's appointment of Harry T. Edwards, a tenured professor at the University of Michigan Law School. After excelling in the LL.B. program at Michigan and graduating in 1965, Edwards's application for a job in legal practice was rejected by all major Chicago law firms, until his Michigan advisor interceded on his behalf. He then obtained a position at a leading firm, where he worked from 1965 until 1970, when he joined the Michigan law faculty as the first African American professor. In 1975 Harvard appointed Edwards a visiting professor and a tenured professor in the following year. Sacks made every effort to keep Edwards, matching Michigan's high salary and benefits and subsidizing the expenses of his research. Nevertheless, Edwards, after spending only one year in his tenured position, left Cambridge and returned to Michigan in 1977. He later became Chief Justice of the U.S. Court of Appeals, D.C. Circuit.[108]

The intense and persistent advocacy by Bell and the BLSA contributed to advancing the appointments of Ferguson and Edwards. But the faculty clearly preferred these "establishment" men who, they believed, were not going to make waves, unlike the radical Bell. In the end, Bell observed that "there was little change in either the pattern of appointments or the assumptions about academic qualifications that determined those appointments," factors that clearly held back appointing faculty of color.[109]

In 1980, Bell, totally frustrated with Harvard, resigned to become dean of the University of Oregon Law School. His departure, coupled with Edwards's exit in 1977 and Ferguson's tragic early death from a heart attack in 1983, rolled back nearly all the limited progress made in the 1970s. In 1986 Bell returned to Harvard Law School after resigning angrily from Oregon when an Asian American woman was denied tenure. In 1990 he took an unpaid leave of absence, refusing to return until the Law School hired an African American woman on the faculty. In 1992 Harvard decided not to extend his leave, and Bell moved permanently to New York University School of Law as a full-time visiting professor. In 1998 Harvard Law School hired the first woman of color to its faculty, Lani Guinier.[110] Although Bell was the Law School's first tenured African American faculty member, there is still no portrait or historical memorial to him at the Law School.

Meanwhile, the lone continuing African American faculty member appointed by Dean Sacks was Christopher Edley Jr. (LL.B. 1978), who began his career as an assistant professor in 1981. Edley was one of several second-generation African American academicians who would graduate from Harvard Law School.[111] His father, Christopher Edley Sr. (LL.B. 1952), rose to become the hugely successful president of the United Negro College Fund, and the son's advantaged background seems typical for a law professor at an elite law school. Raised in a professional family in New Rochelle, New York, he attended Swarthmore College, Harvard's Kennedy School of Government, and Harvard Law School. But he never forgot what drove his father: the memory of a racism and poverty growing up in Lynchburg, Virginia.[112]

In 1974–75, Edley found his first-year courses to be "heavily Socratic," with Clarke Byse in Contracts "still trying to play the part" of Professor Charles W. Kingsfield Jr. from the movie *The Paper Chase*.[113] His most influential professor was Laurence Tribe (LL.B. 1966), for whom Edley worked as a research

Christopher F. Edley Jr., J.D. 1978. Faculty 1981–2003.
Harvard Law School Yearbook, 1982. Courtesy of Harvard Yearbook Publications.

assistant—as would Barack H. Obama (LL.B. 1991), later president of the United States. In the spring of 1975 Edley was selected for the *Harvard Law Review* by way of a writing competition, a recent innovation that applied to about ten of the twenty-five new editors. As a result, he felt less of "a sense of entitlement than if I had gotten on by grade." Edley was the first African American on the *Law Review* since William Coleman Jr. (LL.B. 1943) and John R. Wilkins (LL.B. 1943), thirty two years previously.[114]

In his second year, 1975–76, Edley was "intensely focused" on the *Law Review*, and had just gotten married, so he "became less engaged with other students," he recalled. "I think I was among the black students who felt most comfortable at the Law School, and I didn't need the close mentoring that Derrick [Bell] so critically provided to a great many students." One student Edley did get to know well was Susan Estrich, and they became close friends. After Estrich was elected president of the *Law Review*, Edley was named Supreme Court note editor. In the following August of 1976, Edley was invited to work on the Carter presidential campaign in Atlanta. Encouraged by Estrich, Edley, then twenty-three, left Cambridge to become Carter's deputy national campaign coordinator.[115]

His plan was to register for classes, go to Atlanta, then "come back right after the election [and] cram for exams." This plan comported with the long-standing practice of many *Law Review* editors to stop attending classes during the semester while working on the *Review*. But *Time* magazine happened to run a picture of Edley serving on Carter's campaign staff, and the Law School's Administrative Board suspended him.[116] As a result, Edley received his two degrees, from the Law School and the Kennedy School, a year later, in 1978. He then became assistant director of the White House Domestic Policy Staff for Carter from 1978 to 1980, working under Stuart E. Eizenstat (LL.B. 1967).

At the end of 1980 Edley was promoted to special assistant secretary of the Department of Housing and Urban Development, and it looked like his career in government was launched. But Edley decided to return to Cambridge to be a research fellow for Dean Graham Allison at the Kennedy School. Resolving then to become a law professor, he applied and interviewed at Yale, which made an offer, but Harvard also recruited him vigorously and won out.[117] Subsequently, Edley earned tenure under Dean Vorenberg, and spent twenty-four years on the faculty before becoming dean of the law school at the University of California, Berkeley.

The last efforts in the glacial progress toward diversifying the faculty at the Law School were two offers made early in 1980. These apparently originated

with Sacks, but were still pending in September 1982. One was made to Adebayo O. Ogunlesi (J.D. 1979), an Oxford-educated, Nigerian-born student
who had graduated *magna cum laude* from both the Law School and Harvard
Business School in 1979.[118] After graduation, Ogunlesi clerked for Judge J.
Skelly Wright and Justice Thurgood Marshall. In 1982 he reportedly accepted
the Law School's offer of a tenure-track appointment, but Ogunlesi never
came, and instead worked in private equity, where he was immensely successful.[119] In 2017 he became a lead donor in establishing an endowed professorship in honor of his friend Professor Charles J. Ogletree (J.D. 1978).[120]

Harvard Black Law Students' Association, ca. 1978. Charles Ogletree, J.D. 1978.
Faculty 1984 to present, is in the next to last row, far left. Odebayo O. Ogunlesi,
J.D. 1979, is in the back row, far left.

Harvard Law School Yearbook, 1978. Courtesy of Harvard Yearbook Publications.

The other offer was made to John Payton (J.D. 1977), who went to work for a major law firm after graduation. As an African American student at both Pomona College and the Law School, Payton actively lobbied on racial issues. Like Ogunlesi, he turned down Harvard's offer. But instead of pursuing finance, he practiced law and eventually became president of the LDF, where he litigated several major civil rights cases. Both Presidents Clinton and Obama honored him before his death in 2012.[121]

The cost of the departures or rejections by Bell, Edwards, Ogunlesi, and Payton between 1977 and 1982 to the diversity of the Law School's faculty can hardly be overemphasized. After Clyde Ferguson died tragically in 1983, only Edley remained. By 1981 Harvard was back to where it began in 1971, with just one faculty member of color and still no Asian Americans, Hispanics, or Native Americans. After a decade of anxiety, rage, and controversy under Dean Sacks, the Law School had made no progress on hiring faculty of color and little progress on hiring women. As of 1983, only 6 percent of the regular faculty—four of sixty-two—were not white men.

NOTES

1. Howard Raiffa, "In Memoriam: Albert M. Sacks," *HLR* 105 (November 1991): 1–3.

2. Quoted in Clark Byse, "In Memoriam: Albert M. Sacks," *HLR* 105 (November 1991): 5. See Erwin N. Griswold, "In Memoriam: Albert M. Sacks," *HLR* 105 (November 1991): 3–4.

3. David L. Shapiro, "In Memoriam: Albert M. Sacks," *HLR* 165 (November 1991): 10. See Frank I. Michelman, "In Memoriam: Albert M. Sacks," *HLR* 105 (November 1991): 18.

4. Derek C. Bok, "Albert Sacks: An Appreciation," *HLR* 94 (June 1981): 1749. See "Albert M. Sacks," Harvard Law School (HLS) Yearbook, 1972, 19; "Sacks Appointed Acting Dean," *HLSR* (January 28, 1971): 1–2; "Sacks Appointed Dean," *HLSR* (September 24, 1971): 1–2; Alfonzo A. Narvaez, "Albert M. Sacks, 70, Harvard Law Dean and Noted Teacher," *New York Times* (March 23, 1991).

5. Derek C. Bok, Oral History conducted by Daniel R. Coquillette and Daniel Hamilton (February 2002), on file with the authors. See Joel Seligman, *The High Citadel: The Influence of Harvard Law School* (Boston, 1978), 3, 18–19, 201–216.

6. The following account draws upon Charles Riordan, "General Historical Timeline: 1970–1980" (student research memo, Boston College Law School, 2015), on file with the authors; Stanley Karnow, *Vietnam: A History* (New York, 1997), 630–684; Howard Zinn, *A People's History of the United States* (New York, 2003), 493–550; Morton Keller

and Phyllis Keller, *Making Harvard Modern: The Rise of America's University* (New York, 2001), 341–382.

7. Quotation is from "Sacks, to the Law School Visiting Committee" *HLSB* (Fall 1974): 4. See "Standard 302(a)(iii)," *ABA Standards and Rules of Procedure for the Approval of Law Schools* (Chicago, 1973), 7.

8. The following draws upon Emily Anderson, "Harvard Law School Tuition Increases" (student research memo, Boston College Law School, 2016), on file with the authors; Charles Riordan, "Dean Sacks' Timeline by Subject: Finances" (student research report, Boston College Law School, 2015), on file with the authors.

9. Patrick F. Kennedy, "Tuition Increase Threatens; Writing Program Adopted," *HLSR* (February 28, 1975): 1, 2, 8.

10. "Sacks Recommends $300 Tuition Hike," *HLSR* (March 12, 1976): 1; Gary D. Hailey, "Students Profit as Professors Nix Pay Raise," *HLSR* (March 19, 1976): 1.

11. Kayleigh E. McGlynn. "Costs of Griswold Hall and Pound Hall" (student research memo, Boston College Law School, 2017), on file with the authors.

12. Tammy Jacobs, "3Ls Destined for Law Firms, Placement Office Study Shows," *HLSR* (April 14, 1978): 1, 7, 13.

13. [Andrew L. Kaufman, Chair], Memorandum to the Faculty from the Financial Aids Committee [Cambridge, MA, ca. March 1970], typescript on file with the authors, 3–4, 30. See also Jos Rubenstein, "A History of the Law Income Protection Plan at Harvard Law School" (student research paper, HLS, 2000), on file with the authors, 2–3; Harvard Law School, *Financial Aid Guide, 1975–1976* (Cambridge, MA, 1975), 15.

14. Albert M. Sacks, Annual Report of the Dean of HLS, 1975–76, 294.

15. Jacobs, "3Ls Destined for Law Firms," 1. See also Joan Shear, "Changing HLS Corporate Bias," *HLSR* (October 28, 1977): 12; *HLSR* (March 21, 1975), 2; (February 11, 1977), 1, 7; (April 14, 1978), 7. See Seligman, *The High Citadel*, 3, 18–19, 201–216.

16. Russell A. Simpson, Memorandum on New Proposals for Loan Repayment Program to HLS Dean Albert Sacks (March 1, 1978), on file with the authors, 5. See Rubenstein, "A History," 16, 18.

17. Sacks, Annual Report of the Dean, 1980–81, 273–274. See Jacobs, "3Ls Destined for Law Firms," 1, 7, 13; Rubenstein, "A History, 21–23.

18. See Sacks, Annual Report of the Dean, 1978–79.

19. The gift from Leon Baker (LL.B. 1949) permitted the Law School to purchase a large Victorian home on Massachusetts Avenue in the spring of 1981, which was renamed Baker House, home of the new Development and Alumni Affairs Office. "Dean Sacks Speaks to Alumni," *HLSR* (May 2, 1980): 1, 3, 14; "Harvard Corporation Approves the Law School's Purchase of Dow House," *HLSR* (April 17, 1981): 4; Dan Hershman, "HLS Purchase of Dow House Imminent," *HLSR* (December 5, 1980): 4. Sacks, Annual Report of the Dean, 1980–81, 280.

20. These included vice dean, William Bruce (LL.B. 1951), the executive officer of the school, and four assistant deans: Stephen Bernardi (LL.B. 1955), secretary of the Law

"An Especially Difficult Period": Albert Sacks, 1971–1981   **717**

School with special academic responsibilities; Wesley Bevins Jr. (LL.B. 1948), director of the Law School Fund; Russell Simpson (LL.B. 1965), director of Admissions. Among the faculty appointments, Gary Bellow (LL.B. 1960) directed the Legal Services Clinic; Jerome Cohen, the East Asia Legal Studies Program; Oliver Oldman, the International Tax Program; James Vorenberg, the Center for Criminal Justice; Morris Cohen, the Library; and Milton Katz (LL.B. 1931), International Legal Studies. In 1980 Sacks appointed Paul W. Upson to oversee finances; Upson would continue for more than two decades as head of finances and operations for the school.

21. Robert C. Clark, Oral History, conducted by Daniel R. Coquillette, Mary Beth Basile, and Kristy Kirkpatrick (April 2003), on file with the authors.

22. "Enrollment of 1L Women Rises: Total Applications Up Slightly," _HLSR_ (September 22, 1972): 3. See Russell A. Simpson, Oral History, conducted by Mary Beth Basile and Daniel R. Coquillette (May–September 2001), on file with the authors.

23. "Enrollment of 1L Women Rises," 3. See also "Data Released about 1L Class," _HLSR_ (October 6, 1972): 1–2.

24. Quotation is from "Admissions Report Indicates Women's Enrollment Rising," _HLSR_ (November 22, 1974): 14. See Robert A. Williams, "HLS Lags in Enrolling Women," _HLSR_ (December 7, 1973): 6.

25. Quotation is from HLS Yearbook, 1977, 5, 91. See Simpson, Oral History (May–September 2001); Louis A. Toepfer, Oral History, conducted by Daniel Hamilton (March 1998), on file with the authors.

26. Quotations are from Barbara Kritchevsky, "Enrollment's Up by 2.2 Percent for 1L Women," _HLSR_ (September 23, 1977): 1, 5.

27. Quotations are from Kritchevsky, "Enrollment's Up," 5.

28. Quotations are from Becky Wesley, "Female Enrollment Nears 30 Percent," _HLSR_ (September 22, 1978): 3.

29. Quoted in Rusty Russell, "WLA Criticizes Female Admissions," _HLSR_ (October 19, 1979): 4.

30. Quotations and data are from Russell, "WLA Criticizes Female Admissions," 4.

31. Quoted in Russell, "WLA Criticizes Female Admissions," 4–5.

32. Quoted in Russell, "WLA Criticizes Female Admissions," 4–5.

33. Quotation is from Russell, "WLA Criticizes Female Admissions," 4. See ABA, _First-Year and Total Enrollment by Gender (1947–2011)_, on file with the authors.

34. See HLS Yearbook, 1972, 68. See Brando S. Starkey, "Two Steps Forward Then Two Steps Back: The Black Story of Harvard Law School" (student research paper, HLS, 2008), on file with the authors, 49–50; Sam Roberts, "Walter J. Leonard, Pioneer of Affirmative Action in Harvard Admissions, Dies at 86," _New York Times_ (December 16, 2015).

35. "Admissions Report Indicates," 14.

36. "'78: Columbia, Wellesley Surge; Radcliffe, Cornell Lag," _HLSR_ (December 5, 1975): 3.

37. See Nathan Pak, "The Harvard Law School Special Summer Program of 1965 and What Happened Afterwards" (student research paper, Boston College Law School, 2017), on file with the authors, 5–6.

38. Simpson, Oral History (May–September 2001); Toepfer, Oral History (March 1998); Frank E. A. Sander, Oral History, conducted by Daniel R. Coquillette and Daniel Hamilton (September–December 1998), on file with the authors.

39. See Duncan Kennedy, *Legal Education and the Reproduction of Hierarchy* (Cambridge, MA, 1983), 61–93.

40. Harry T. Edwards, "The Journey from *Brown v. Board of Education* to *Grutter v. Bollinger:* From Racial Assimilation to Diversity," *Michigan Law Review* 102 (2004): 954; William G. Bowen and Derek C. Bok, *The Shape of the River: Long-Term Consequences of Considering Race in College and University Admissions* (Princeton, NJ, 1998), 5.

41. Walter J. Leonard, *Black Lawyers: Training and Results, Then and Now* (Boston, 1977), 235–237. Leonard's ill health and death in 2015 prevented the authors from obtaining an oral history about his time at Harvard.

42. Mary Beth Basile, "False Starts: Harvard Law School's Efforts toward Integrating Women into the Faculty, 1928–1981," *Harvard Journal of Law and Gender* 28 (2005): 153n95; Laura Kalman, "The Dark Ages," in *History of the Yale Law School: The Tercentennial Lectures,* ed. Anthony T. Kronman (New Haven, CT, 2004), 156.

43. Basile, "False Starts," 145–148, 151–153; Barbara Fiasco, "The First Appointments of Women to the Harvard Law School Faculty" (student research paper, HLS, 2000), on file with the authors, 5–6; W. K. Jordan et al., "Helen Maud Cam," *Harvard University Gazette* (December 7, 1968), 92.

44. Basile, "False Starts," 152–155; Fiasco, "First Appointments of Women," 6–7. See Edith G. Henderson, *Foundations of English Administrative Law: Certiorari and Mandamus in the Seventeenth Century* (Cambridge, MA, 1973). Another classic was her article, jointly authored with Louis L. Jaffe, "Judicial Review and the Rule of Law: Historical Origins," *Law Quarterly Review* 72 (1956): 345–364.

45. Edwin J. Lukas, "The Glueck Researches in Criminology," *HLSB* (April 1949): 3. See Basile, "False Starts," 145–148; Fiasco, "First Appointments of Women," 5–6. See also "Eleanor T. Glueck, 74, Pioneer in Crime and Delinquency Studies," *Washington Post* (September 26, 1972). Eleanor and Sheldon Glueck jointly received honorary degrees of Doctor of Science from Harvard in 1958, "the finest husband-wife team to be honored in this way." Basile, "False Starts," 148.

46. Basile, "False Starts," 148. Many thanks to Thompson Potter and Lesley Schoenfeld for their research on the portrait.

47. "Eleanor Glueck," *HLSB* (November 1972): 8.

48. Mary Beth Basile Chopas, email to Daniel R. Coquillette (March 22, 2018), on file with the authors.

49. HLS Yearbook, 1972, 63. This section draws upon Basile, "False Starts," as well as Barbara Fiasco, "First Appointments of Women"; Emily Anderson and Elise Medley,

"Women at Harvard Law School" (student research memo, Boston College Law School, 2016), on file with the authors.

50. James Vorenberg, Oral History, conducted by Daniel R. Coquillette (November– December 1997), on file with the authors.

51. Quoted from Ruth Bader Ginsburg, Interview (January 2004), quoted in Basile, "False Starts," 168. See Basile, "False Starts," 168–169; Ruth Bader Ginsburg, "The Changing Complexion of Harvard Law School," *Harvard Women's Law Journal* 27 (2004): 303–308; Daniel Taubman, "Owens to Be Named First Tenured Woman Professor," *HLSR* (January 28, 1972): 1.

52. Quoted from Ginsburg, Interview (January 2004); Basile, "False Starts," 168–169. See Taubman, "Owens to Be Named," 1.

53. Basile, "False Starts," 170; Fiasco, "First Appointments of Women," 14–15; Erik Lund, *Song for an Unsung Hero* (Augusta, ME, 2005), 141–175.

54. Fiasco, "First Appointments of Women," 14.

55. Lund, *Song for an Unsung Hero,* 187; Basile, "False Starts," 171n248.

56. See HLS Yearbook, 1972, 63. Lund's teaching schedule is listed in Basile, "False Starts," 171n240.

57. Quotations are from Basile, "False Starts," 171–172.

58. Basile, "False Starts," 172.

59. See HLS Yearbook, 1978, 96; 1979, 90; 1981, 91.

60. Lund, *Song for an Unsung Hero,* 183.

61. Quotations are from Lund, *Song for an Unsung Hero,* 187.

62. See Basile, "False Starts," 175–178; Fiasco, "First Appointments of Women," 18– 19. See Max Rheinstan and Mary Ann Glendon, *The Law of Decedents' Estates* (Mineola, NY, 1971).

63. Quotation is from Mary Ann Glendon, Interview (December 2003), quoted in Basile, "False Starts," 177.

64. Basile, "False Starts," 174–175; see 173–175. See Fiasco, "First Appointments of Women," 18–19. Dreben continued as a lecturer from 1974 to 1977, but did not wish to leave her law firm, Palmer and Dodge, in Boston to join the Law School faculty full time.

65. Mary Ann Glendon's departure from Boston College, where she was greatly esteemed, was a great disappointment to Daniel Coquillette, who was then dean of Boston College Law School.

66. Lund, *Song for an Unsung Hero,* 191; Fiasco, "First Appointments of Women," 19–20.

67. Richard D. Parker, Oral History, conducted by Daniel R. Coquillette and Daniel Pincus (June 2010), on file with the authors.

68. See Basile, "False Starts," 178; Lund, *Song for an Unsung Hero,* 190–191. In March 1979 there was a simple statement by the Appointments Committee that "Assistant Professor Sally Schultz Neely, who has been on leave for the last two years, is not scheduled

to teach at the Law School next year." See Michael Smith, "Appointments Difficult,"
Harvard Law Record (March 23, 1979): 1, 6–7.

69. Requests for interviews were made by the authors, their research assistants, historian Mary Beth Basile Chopas, and Erik Lund in connection with his book about his late wife, Diane.

70. Vorenberg, Oral History (November–December 1997).

71. Fiasco, "First Appointments of Women," 26–27; Basile, "False Starts," 173–178, 178–182.

72. Elizabeth Bartholet, Oral History, conducted by Daniel Hamilton (February 1999–March 2000), on file with the authors. Edgerton, who had a succession of female law clerks, served on the U.S. Court of Appeals (D.C. Circuit) from 1937 to 1963 and was Chief Judge from 1955 to 1958.

73. Lund, *Song for an Unsung Hero,* 192. See Basile, "False Starts," 186–189; Fiasco, "First Appointments of Women," 21.

74. Lund, *Song for an Unsung Hero,* 193.

75. Lund, *Song for an Unsung Hero,* 193. See Elizabeth Bartholet, "Application of Title VII to Jobs in High Places," *HLR* 95 (March 1982): 948–1026.

76. Lund, *Song for an Unsung Hero,* 193.

77. Lund, *Song for an Unsung Hero,* 193.

78. Quotations are from Bartholet, Oral History (February 1999–March 2000). See Michael Medina, "Law Students Seek Tenure for Women," *HLSR* (April 23, 1982): 2.

79. Martha A. Field, Oral History, conducted by Mary Beth Basile and Daniel R. Coquillette (November 2001–April 2002), on file with the authors.

80. Basile, "False Starts," 183.

81. Basile, "False Starts," 183.

82. Field, Oral History (November 2001–April 2002).

83. Field, Oral History (November 2001–April 2002).

84. Basile, "False Starts," 184.

85. Russell, "WLA Criticizes Female Admissions," 4. See Fiasco, "First Appointments of Women," 27; Gabe S. Vorges, "Visitors Present Varied Backgrounds," *HLSR* (September 19, 1980): 2, 13.

86. Fiasco, "First Appointments of Women," 30–31. See Newton White, "Six Women to Join Faculty for '81–'82," *HLSR* (May 1, 1981): 2; HLS Catalog, 1981–82, 9; Mary Torduno, "Dean Sacks Tells Alumni State of HLS; Cites Gains in Hiring Women Faculty," *HLSR* (May 1, 1981): 4.

87. See Beth Emery, "Woman Heads Review," *HLSR* (February 27, 1976): 7. For vicious, sexist ridicule, see Bruce Howard, "Girl Law Review Editor Gushes; Mongrel 'Streaky Goldberg' Leads CR-CL," *HLSR* (March 19, 1976): 3.

88. Fiasco, "First Appointments of Women," 29–30. See HLS Yearbook, 1981, 90; HLS Yearbook, 1982, 44; Dave Quinto, "Estrich Relates to HLS Students," *HLSR* (October 10, 1981): 4, 14.

89. See Fiasco, "First Appointments of Women," 29. See also Mary Torduno, "Paying Attention to Education," *HLSR* (October 16, 1981): 5. Minow later observed that Sacks's "incremental" approach meant there was no "critical mass" of women who could share experiences and exchange advice, and that neither she nor Elizabeth Bartholet ever met Elizabeth Owens. Martha L. Minow, Interview (April 1996), quoted in Fiasco, "First Appointments of Women," 31–32.

90. "Head of Harvard Says No to Teacher's Tenure," *New York Times* (March 11, 1988); David Lat, "From Torturing Law Students to Sticking Needles in People," *Above the Law* (June 19, 2013). After retiring from Northeastern, Dalton became an acupuncturist.

91. "Minow Named University Professor: Human Rights Expert, Former Law School Dean, Receives Harvard's Highest Honor," *Harvard University Gazette* (June 19, 2018); Martha L. Minow, Conversation with Daniel R. Coquillette (September 5, 2017), on file with the authors.

92. These included Lea Brimeyer (Chicago) 1981, Deborah Schenk (Brooklyn) 1982, Alison Anderson (UCLA) 1983, Zipporah Wiseman (Northeastern) 1983, Linda S. Greene (Oregon) 1984, Sylvia Ann Lou (NYU) 1984, and Wendy Williams (Georgetown) 1984. After Sacks's departure and the postponement of Elizabeth Bartholet's tenure decision, the students became very concerned with the gender balance. See Fiasco, "First Appointments of Women," 32–33; Melina, "Law Students Seek Tenure for Women"; John Morris, "Faculty Discusses Hiring," *HLSR* (December 3, 1982): 1.

93. The discussion here and below relies heavily on Derrick Bell's autobiography, *Confronting Authority: Reflections of an Ardent Protestor* (Boston, 1994), 10–15. See Kadesha Bagwell, "What I Am" (student research paper, HLS, 1999), on file with the authors, 7–12; Andrew C. Goodwin, "Losing the Battle; Winning the War? An Examination of the Impact of Derrick Bell and the Griswold 9 on Faculty Diversity at Harvard Law School" (student research paper, HLS, 2015), on file with the authors.

94. Bell, *Confronting Authority*, 16–20. Goodwin, "Losing the Battle," 5–6.

95. Quoted in Goodwin, "Losing the Battle," 5–6. See Bell, *Confronting Authority*, 19.

96. Quotations are from Bell, *Confronting Authority*, 29–30. See Bagwell, "What I Am," 11–12; Linda Standridge, "Bell Lectures on Racism, Law from Civil Rights Experience," *HLSR* (March 12, 1970): 7; Goodwin, "Losing the Battle," 8. Verification of Bell's accounts are not possible, as the files are sealed.

97. Goodwin, "Losing the Battle," 8. See Jack Fate, "Black Awareness and Black Unity Surging Forward at Law School," *HLSR* (September 26, 1968): 1; Reginald Gilliam's picture in the HLS Yearbook, 1968, 104.

98. Bagwell, "What I Am," 13. See Standridge, "Bell Lectures," 6, 7; Jason Kreag, "Reciprocal Impact: An Examination of Harvard Law School and the Civil Rights Movement" (student research paper, HLS, 2003), on file with the authors, 3–45.

99. Bell, *Confronting Authority*, 29, 34.

100. Bell, *Confronting Authority*, 35–47.

101. Clarence Clyde Ferguson Jr. to Derrick Bell (July 3, 1973), on file with the authors; "Clarence Clyde Ferguson," Research File (January 1, 1983), Harvard Law School Library Historical & Special Collections. Ferguson was passed over for the seat of William Hastie Jr. (LL.B. 1930, S.J.D. 1933) on the Federal Court of Appeals. Hastie commented, "It would appear that for some reason, Ferguson's selection is objectionable to the President." See Lawrence M. O'Rourke and Orrin Evans, "Hastie Retiring, Raps Nixon on Appeals Court Vacancy," *Sunday Bulletin* (December 13, 1970). For Ferguson's diplomatic career, see "Our Black Envoy in Uganda," *New York Post* (November 21, 1970). Much of Ferguson's pragmatic but progressive philosophy of racial advancement is set out in Albert P. Blaustein and Clarence Clyde Ferguson Jr., *Desegregation and the Law: The Meaning and Effect of the School Segregation Cases* (New Brunswick, NJ, 1960).

102. Clarence Clyde Ferguson Jr. to Derrick Bell (July 19, 1973), on file with the authors.

103. Ferguson to Bell (July 3, 1973).

104. Quoted in "HLS Conference Studies Minority Law Professors," *HLR* (September 20, 1974): 13. See Leonard, *Black Lawyers*, 235–237.

105. Quoted in Bell, *Confronting Authority*, 43.

106. Roger P. Evans, "Bell's Claim about Hiring Not 'Legitimate,' Bok Says," *HLSR* (December 13, 1974): 1.

107. Bell, *Confronting Authority*, 44.

108. Harry T. Edwards to Morris Cohen, Memorandum (May 15, 1976), on file with the authors; Albert M. Sacks to Harris T. Edwards (December 16, 1974; January 10, June 6, and June 26, 1975), on file with the authors; Douglas H. Ginsburg et al., "Portrait Presentation Ceremony: Harry T. Edwards" (pamphlet) (November 4, 2005); "Harry T. Edwards: Biography," *New York University Law School Faculty Catalogue* (New York, 2016), on file with the authors; Roger P. Evans, "Sacks Announces New Appointees," *HLSR* (January 31, 1975): 2; Ricardo Hnojosa, "UN Delegate Takes Teaching Post," *HLSR* (February 28, 1975): 3.

109. Bell, *Confronting Authority*, 44.

110. Fred A. Bernstein, "Derrick Bell, Law Professor and Rights Advocate, Dies at 80," *New York Times* (October 6, 2011).

111. Other distinguished African American, second-generation, academicians who graduated from Harvard Law School include Harvard Law Professor David B. Wilkins (J.D. 1980), whose father was Julius B. Wilkins (LL.B. 1949), and Boston College Law School dean Vincent D. Rougeau (J.D. 1988), whose father is the famous civil rights leader Weldon Rougeau (J.D. 1972). Wilkins's uncle, John Wilkins (LL.B. 1943), also was a Law School graduate. John L. Joy, "A Legacy of Their Own: A History of Second-Generation African American Families at Harvard Law School" (student research paper, Boston College Law School, 2016); Vincent Rougeau, Interview with John L. Joy (March 2015), on file with the authors.

112. Christopher F. Edley Jr., Oral History, conducted by Daniel R. Coquillette and Daniel Hamilton (October 2000–September 2001), on file with the authors. See Christopher Edley Jr., *Not All Black and White: Affirmative Action, Race and American Values* (New York, 1996).

113. Edley Jr., Oral History (October 2000–September 2001).

114. Susan Gillette, "2L Members Announced by *HLR,*" *HLSR* (October 24, 1975): 1, 9.

115. Edley Jr., Oral History (October 2000–September 2001). See also Emery, "Woman Heads Review," 1, 6–7, 9.

116. Edley Jr., Oral History (October 2000–September 2001); Gretchen Rule, "Edley: Juggling Academic and Political," *HLSR* (October 16, 1981): 4–5.

117. Edley Jr., Oral History (October 2000–September 2001).

118. See HLS Yearbook, 1979, 123.

119. "One Black Accepts Offer, Another Still Considering," *HLSR* (September 24, 1982): 1; Susan Young, "Adebayo O. Ogunlesi, JD / MBA 1979: 2017 Alumni Achievement Award Recipient," *Harvard Business School Alumni: Achievement Awards* (Cambridge, MA, 2017), 1–2; Adebayo Ogunlesi, "The Basic Human Needs Approach to Development" (student paper, HLS, submitted to Professor C. Clyde Ferguson, 1979); Andrew Ross Sorkin, "While Upset in Private, Many C.E.O.s Fear Inviting the Wrath of the President," *New York Times* (August 15, 2017); "Who's on (and off) Trump's Advisory Committee," *New York Times* (August 16, 2017).

120. "'Tree's Tremendous Legacy," *Harvard Law Today* (February 2018): 3.

121. Dennis Hevesi, "John Payton, Lawyer Who Fought for Civil Rights, Dies at 65," *New York Times* (March 23, 2012); "John Payton In Memoriam," NAACP Legal Defense and Education Fund Announcement (March 23, 2012), on file with the authors.

CHAPTER EIGHTEEN

The World of the Students,
1970s and 1980s

The academic facilities at Harvard Law School in the 1970s were simply inadequate for a school of 1,600 students. Most of the classrooms were meant for classes of 135 students or more: three in Austin Hall, built in 1883, and four in Langdell Hall, designed in 1905, with a few seminar rooms tucked into the corners here and there. After the completion of Langdell Hall in 1929, these two buildings remained largely untouched for the next half century. In 1958 the new International Law Center (now the Lewis Center) added five small classrooms. Completed in 1970 and 1971, Griswold Hall and Pound Hall housed offices and a few medium-size classrooms. Overall, the dozen seminar rooms and small classrooms were insufficient for the student body, and no areas existed for individual or group study. Outside of class, law students had few places to meet on campus in the 1970s, except in the crowded and cavernous Langdell reading room, the small Harkness Commons, or a meeting room of the few extracurricular organizations fortunate enough to have one.

Given these facilities, student activity within the school occurred primarily in three modes. First was the formal curriculum, whose organization still followed the template established a century earlier, but would be reviewed thoroughly by the so-called Michelman Committee at the end of Dean Albert Sacks's term (1971–1981). Then there were clinical programs, involving some faculty supervision and some student self-selection, but these could accommodate only a few students and operated largely off campus. Finally, there were extracurricular activities, including the moot court clubs, student periodicals, affinity groups, various research projects, and the historic "honorary" organizations: the *Harvard Law Review,* the Board of Student Advisors, and the Legal

Aid Bureau, though the membership criteria for these had begun to change by 1971.

Decade of Curricular Inertia

The curriculum naturally anchored the formal academic program, and its importance prompted episodic, multiyear reviews by faculty committees: a Committee on Curriculum that reported in 1936; a Committee on Legal Education in 1948; and a second Committee on Legal Education in 1960. Each committee report was publicly proclaimed and debated by the deans and faculty, but resulted in little, if any, change. Nevertheless, these curricular studies happened about every dozen years, and in 1971 it was time for another. But during this "especially difficult period," Dean Sacks delayed appointing another committee until 1979. So for the class that began with Dean Sacks in the fall of 1971, the curricular bible remained the *Harvard Law School Catalog, 1971–72* and the 1971 *Handbook for New Students Entering Harvard Law School.*[1]

Their commandments were very old and offered very little choice about anything. In the first year, the same "Big Five" courses laid down a century earlier in the 1873–74 academic year perdured: Property, Contracts, Torts, Civil Procedure, and Criminal Law.[2] Furthermore, these courses met in the very same classrooms, and were taught in the same large sections in virtually the same way. And faculty still evaluated students on the basis of one exam at the end of the year and provided virtually no feedback except for the grade.

One modest innovation in 1971 was a nongraded, fall-semester "Legal Methods" course taught by teaching assistants drawn largely from the Board of Student Advisors. The other small innovation was a nongraded, spring-semester "Small Groups" course, which was taught by regular (tenured and tenure-track) faculty. Aiming primarily to elicit a "moderate-sized" essay from each student, this course also tried to offset the colossal anonymity of the big classes by serving a "general advisory" function for the students in the Small Group. But the course met only once weekly for twelve weeks.

The second year was barely different from the first year. In theory it was "fully elective," but in practice, Corporations, Constitutional Law, and Taxation, all full-year courses, and Accounting, a half-year course, were strongly recommended as essential. Students joked that Corporations taught students "how to make money," Accounting, "how to count the money you made," and Taxation, "how to keep the government from taking your money away." As in the first year, these large courses were scheduled in coordinated sections, so the same students attended the same section across all courses. Because second-year students were limited to a range of thirteen to sixteen credits in the fall and ten to fourteen credits in the spring, they had no opportunity to take more than two electives. The second-year experience thus continued the first-year pattern of grouping students in sections of big classes that were effectively mandatory.

Even in the so-called "elective" third year, students were directed toward Antitrust Law, Estate Planning, Evidence, and Conflict of Laws, which were most frequently chosen and also taught in large classes. Third-year students were permitted to enroll in one seminar, plus a second if "special permission" was obtained. These seminars required a paper, rather than an exam, which could fulfill the other special feature of the third year, "a satisfactory piece of written work in one selected field of study." A decent variety of seminars was offered—such as "Computer and the Law," taught by Arthur R. Miller (LL.B. 1958) and "Sex-Based Discrimination and the Law," taught by Ruth Bader Ginsburg (1956–1958)—but the seminars filled up quickly, even though third-year students had priority. Overall, the course of study consisted predominantly of big, full-year courses that grouped students in sections, except for the third-year seminar with a written-work project. There was no study of professional ethics, no experiential learning, and no clinics outside of student-run organizations.

A decade later, in 1980–81, the curriculum template remained largely the same.[3] In the first year, the same five courses, taught in sections of 135 students, persisted. (Due to complaints that there was "no feedback" until the end of the first year, Criminal Law and Torts had been "semesterized" into the fall, and Property into the spring, with Civil Procedure and Contracts still a full year.) The introductory, nongraded course, now called "Problems in Legal Practice and Methods," continued; the Small Groups course had been axed. Students were, however, permitted a choice of one or two first-year electives from a short list of six two-credit courses and four five-credit courses. The second year continued emphasizing the same "essential" courses, as did the third year, and the "written work" requirement was unchanged.

But three substantive changes occurred for the students over the decade from 1971 to 1981. First, tuition almost tripled in nominal dollars from $2,100 to $5,850. Second, "Professional Responsibility" became a required course for graduation, largely in response to the scandals of the Nixon administration. Third, there arose some very limited opportunities for credit-bearing, experiential education. A full-time, third-year elective in clinical education became available, but only for about twenty-five students, who were subjected to rigorous application requirements and had to compete for slots with Northeastern University law students.[4] Those not admitted to the clinical elective could enroll in one of eleven small elective courses that offered "simulated classroom exercises and supervised field experience" in "the role and responsibilities of practicing lawyers," under the supervision of experienced litigators and judges. The majority of students therefore had no opportunity for clinical training or experiential preparation for law practice within the formal curriculum.

Finally, in 1979, responding to calls for reform, Dean Sacks established a Committee on Educational Planning and Development, which had great promise. In the *Journal of Legal Education,* outside observers called it "the most ambitious and the most exciting, and . . . the most controversial, effort in recent years to achieve educational improvements by committee."[5] Indeed, this committee ignited the fiery disputes that consumed the Harvard Law School faculty during the 1980s.

The Michelman Committee, 1979–1982

In 1979 Dean Sacks charged the Committee on Educational Planning and Development "with reporting to the Faculty its judgments and recommendations as to the future direction of the School's educational activities."[6] For chair, he selected Frank Michelman (LL.B. 1960), who was regarded as brilliant and, more importantly among an increasingly politicized faculty, strictly fair. In the words of radical critic Duncan Kennedy, Michelman was "one of the most respectable liberals at Harvard Law School."[7] The other faculty members of the committee represented pedagogical viewpoints ranging from the far-left critique of Kennedy, to centrists Charles Nesson (LL.B. 1963), Victor Brudney, and Douglas H. Ginsburg, and then to conservatives David Shapiro (LL.B. 1957) and Robert Clark (J.D. 1972), who would later become dean. Student members were Karen Falkenstein (J.D. 1981), Nancy Wiegers (J.D. 1981), Molly Burke (J.D. 1982), and Robert Mallett (J.D. 1982).[8]

At the end of its study, in the spring of 1982, the "Michelman Committee" submitted a compilation of documents to the faculty, but not a finished report. Chairman Michelman called it a "final draft" expressing the view "of the committee majorities" on various issues. More precisely, he called it a "tentative final draft," indicating that the committee had "no future changes to

Frank Michelman, LL.B. 1960. Faculty 1963–2012.

Harvard Law School Yearbook, 1971. Courtesy of Harvard Yearbook Publications.

suggest" but that the material seemed "ripe for distribution and discussion."[9] This after three years of work!

Even this "tentative final draft" was not a unified document, but issued in separately paginated sections and chapters, and released in six installments in April, May, and June 1982. In addition, two years earlier the committee had released an extensive file of memoranda written by individual committee members and groups of members. In a cover memo to this "Memoranda File," Michelman stated that the items do not necessarily represent the final or considered views" of the individuals.[10] Furthermore, the committee correctly "anticipated that . . . some members will issue separate statements, expressing either additional views or dissents."[11] In sum, the Michelman Committee "report" comprised a bundle of provisional documents that conveyed little consensus and primarily the ideological disagreements and political tensions growing within the school.

In its first installment, the committee said that it adopted an "aspirational" or "utopian" approach to planning, without regard for practical constraints of resources or physical plant. The committee therefore began by defining the school's "institutional purpose" and contribution to the "general good."[12] This "aspirational" and "utopian" vision closely resembled the traditional trinity of faculty duties in American higher education: teaching, research, and service, or, in the committee's language, "education, scholarship, and service." This "institutional purpose" was endorsed by a majority of the committee.

Among these, "education" had the "threefold" objective of serving "future clients, . . . society at large, and . . . the student herself or himself." Legal scholarship was the key "social good" of the school, given that "truth-seeking is intrinsically valuable." Service was a weak third, considered only "in conjunction with [the school's] teaching and learning activities." In addition, the definition of "institutional purpose" affirmed the school's historical emphasis on teaching legal doctrine. A majority of the committee thus endorsed the long-standing norm of faculty pursuing doctrinal scholarship and students learning doctrine, with "community service" being incidental for both groups.[13]

Turning to the curriculum, the committee then became utterly timid. They refrained from proposing any major curricular reforms, because that "might be wasteful of the faculty's energies, or even positively damaging to the School," because, in the committee's view, law teaching basically depends on individual talent. This reason seemed to imply that the curriculum did not matter, but the deeper reason was that "we lack enough insight into, or consensus about, what might be wrong for any major revisions effort to be available now." The committee simply could not agree and instead blandly suggested an incremental "multi-level approach" to curriculum revision, which would "require . . . serious and sustained discussion." Of course, this had been precisely the job of the Michelman Committee for the prior three years.[14]

Chairman Michelman was not to blame, because the committee members dissented even from this bland and inconclusive proposal in the "tentative final draft." David Shapiro, for example, believed that the enterprise was doomed from the start due to political divisions among the faculty. According to Shapiro, "Our meetings often served only to reflect in miniature the range of political disagreements in the institution around us." The "utopian" approach, though adopting only conventional norms, was also "a fundamental error," to Shapiro, who was "at heart an incrementalist."[15] Similarly, pragmatic Robert Clark had urged the committee to focus on specific, narrow projects that a divided faculty might actually adopt.[16]

On the opposite side, others accused the committee of being too cautious. Charles Nesson filed a "Separate Statement" calling the report "chicken soup," which "fails to attack the fundamental problem of the school." But Nesson also thought it pointless for the faculty to discuss the committee's "final draft," because "we are a highly politicized faculty. . . . Relationships among us are deeply affected . . . by political assumptions about each other's motivations and actions," and "friendship, respect, empathy and intellectual discourse is bounded to a significant extent by party lines."[17]

Student members on the committee, such as Molly Burke, agreed that the faculty's polarization and antipathies poisoned the entire process. The committee's "utopian" deliberations were often dystopian, she implied.

> Despite the promises . . . that the committee would be able to recommend any changes which it believed were educationally justified, limited only by some outside budgetary constraints, the actual constraints . . . were considerably greater. Our recommendations had to be palatable to the majority of the faculty and [to] proposals that individual members of the existing faculty were ready and willing to go forward with. . . . Moreover, . . . the proposals could not impose any additional burdens on the faculty as a whole.[18]

As a result, wrote Burke, "we were producing recommendations for a faculty that would treat them as political footballs." She rejected any suggestion "that this power struggle is conducted out of sincere beliefs about . . . the best interests of students." Absorbed in its own swordplay, the faculty "fails to consider the effect of [their] divisiveness on the educational experience of the students at the School."[19]

The longest and most fervent dissent to the committee's first installment came from Duncan Kennedy, who wrote a forty-page tract entitled "Utopian Proposal on Law School as a Counterhegemonic Enclave," which proposed replacing the existing curriculum with a "New Model Curriculum." Instead of the traditional first- and second-year doctrinal courses, Kennedy envisioned a first-year program of three mandatory courses: "doctrine," "theory," and "clinical." They would be "all interwoven, planned and staged so as to call upon each other for motivation and understanding," with a required clinical internship after the first year. The third year would focus on research and advanced studies.[20]

In addition, Kennedy proposed a fundamental "reform of admissions, grading, *Law Review* selection, faculty appointment practices, and Law School salary schedules . . . to reduce or reverse the School's role in promoting illegitimate hierarchies." Perhaps with Shapiro and Clark in mind, he wrote, "There are times in the life of an institution when what is needed is for moderates to put forward incremental proposals." "[But] we are at present much too divided and uncertain" to make small, practical changes. So the faculty should at least "think about more radical proposals."[21]

Allegedly, the committee dismissed Kennedy's proposals in "little more than an hour."[22] But Victor Brudney believed that "the group gave more earnest attention to Duncan than the world did." Michelman maintained that Kennedy's proposals were fully discussed, and in any case the point was not to make a decision but "to give these ideas circulations and dissemination, and to stimulate general discussion about them."[23] Even before issuing its "tentative final draft," the Michelman Committee's deliberations thus anticipated the fierce battles to come over faculty appointments and Critical Legal Studies (CLS) with Kennedy and Clark at opposite poles and moderates, like Nesson, increasingly distressed about the tone of the discourse.

Meager Outcomes

Subsequent installments from the Michelman Committee contained shorter chapters with about a dozen specific suggestions for change, but only four were adopted, and these only temporarily, partially, or indirectly.[24] The first, sponsored by Robert Clark, was to establish a "Research Program" for third-year students. Fifteen to twenty students would work on a major research project, under the supervision of a faculty member, and earn twelve credits, almost a full semester's worth. The rationale was to address third-year students' declining interest in their coursework and, incidentally, to assist faculty in pursuing research.[25] In the fall of 1981, Clark taught such a course, "Health Law and Policy," and in the spring of 1982 Professor Phillip B. Heymann (LL.B. 1960) taught another, "Federal Law Enforcement." Students responded positively to these courses, but no more were offered because faculty could not be spared from teaching the basic courses, due to the very high student-faculty ratio and the financial constraints of the early 1980s.[26]

The second proposal was to provide small courses for first-year students because the huge sections of 135 made many feel insignificant or intimidated. The related, third proposal was to offer more feedback and grades earlier in the first year. In response, the faculty agreed that every first-year student would have one class enrolling 40 instead of 135, in which the instructors would offer additional feedback and exercises "of their own choosing." This reform actually survived until 2002.[27] Nevertheless, students both on and outside the Michelman Committee regarded these responses to the first three proposals as feeble efforts to address the deep concerns of third-year and first-year students. They also recognized that the responses entailed little faculty sacrifice.[28]

The fourth proposal, for a "Program on the Legal Profession and Legal Ordering," was supported by Professor Andrew Kaufman (LL.B. 1954), a pioneering teacher on legal ethics, who also suggested establishing a "center" to "focus research and curriculum in this area."[29] This approach would advance well beyond that advocated in 1974 by Dean Sacks to integrate teaching legal ethics and professional responsibility in all courses.[30] But the faculty did not authorize either the program or the center, although by 1980 accreditation requirements of the ABA and the Association of American Law Schools led to establishing a two-credit course on "The Legal Profession," which indirectly fulfilled this proposal.[31]

None of the eight other specific proposals by the Michelman Committee were ever adopted. One was to reform the upper-class years by introducing "sequential studies," with advanced electives building on required courses.[32] Dean Christopher Langdell (1870–1895) had introduced this sequencing to American legal education in his own academic specialty of equity, but his faculty colleagues at Harvard Law School in the early 1870s did not endorse this specialization.[33] The same happened in 1982. Faculty could not agree on which subjects to sequence, and, as Brudney said, some felt that it "was too early . . . to start narrowing [students'] interests."[34]

Other proposals sought to "integrate doctrine, theory, and practice," inspired by Duncan Kennedy's "Dissent." Initially, "integration of theory was supported by people on the left and the right," observed Robert Clark.[35] But this temporary consensus apparently relied on the ambiguity of "theory." Conservatives interpreted "theory" as generic philosophizing about the law. But to those on the left, "theory" meant specifically the "critical theory" derived from the Frankfurt School of philosophy and the writings of Karl Marx, Sigmund Freud, and Max Weber. A central tenet of critical theory is that thinking and teaching are shaped by social, economic, and political forces; and that concepts of truth, justice, and other virtues are largely determined by the interests of those who espouse them.

Consequently, "the older faculty . . . who tended to be more doctrinally oriented" became "a little skeptical" of "theory" that provided "an opening for political agendas," observed Clark.[36] Professor Todd Rakoff (J.D. 1975) agreed that conservatives on the faculty thought that "politics" should be avoided and doctrine emphasized. They therefore came to believe that "theory was dangerous" and feared that the integration of theory would "teach people to be radicals." Conservatives thought "the Critical Legal Studies people were teaching essentially that 'there's no law there,' that the law doesn't matter," and that all jurisprudence is political, Rakoff maintained.[37]

One experiment at "integrating theory with doctrine" in first-year sections was made in the fall of 1983 by Professors Michelman, Rakoff, Morton Horwitz (LL.B. 1967), and Abram Chayes (LL.B. 1949). According to Rakoff, the experimental section attempted "overtly teaching across the boundaries that traditionally separate courses" and "periodically dropping the boundaries altogether." The boundary-crossing was to be achieved by occasionally holding "bridge periods" that addressed common topics, such as "remedies, in the doctrinal courses."[38] The bridge periods attempted to "deconstruct" the doctrinal subject divisions persisting at Harvard Law School since 1873–74. The experimental sections were well-received, and accounts of them were even published in the *Journal of Legal Education.* But some students thought the program was biased. The *Harvard Crimson* quoted one student as saying, "The professors—they're all Jewish, they're all slightly liberal, some more than others, and some [students] object to the liberal bent."[39]

In any event, the experiment soon ended, largely due to faculty "burn-out."[40] As Rakoff observed, the experiment "ran for a while on revolutionary fervor," and then it became impossible to recruit enough faculty, particularly because Dean James Vorenberg (1981–1989) was "lukewarm." The dean "wasn't antagonistic to it, but he wasn't putting a lot of muscle behind it either."[41] Michelman also blamed a lack of administrative support, although he had served as associate dean from 1981 to 1985. The call for integrating theory with doctrine "was right, but the only tool or method we actually had was exhortation, and that was hopeless," Michelman said.[42] In addition, the proposal was ahead of its time. Integrating theory, by any definition, with doctrine gained traction only in the 1990s, when the "Law School started hiring professors who had doctoral degrees in outside subjects," observed Clark.[43] Yet, the Michelman Committee's proposals to integrate theory with doctrine created the fertile ground for such appointments.[44]

The Michelman Committee also recommended certain innovations in legal pedagogy, including more team teaching, more opportunities to write, and more "role playing and problem exercises."[45] These recommendations did not effect change, but one other innovative proposal came very close: Computer-Aided Instruction (CAI).[46] This offered important advantages attributed to small classes: more opportunities for interaction with the professor, more frequent and timely feedback, better sequencing of subject matter by requiring a certain proficiency in the initial steps before permitting a student to advance to later steps, and greater personalization by "branching"—that is, providing special tracks depending on the students' strengths or weaknesses in answering initial questions.[47]

Faculty from across the ideological spectrum, including Kennedy, Nesson, and Clark, supported CAI, and Clark published an article on it in 1983.[48] The Michelman Committee asked that the Law School devote some money and release time to develop this form of instruction, but the issue was never brought to a vote. Thus, CAI went by the wayside, along with an excellent opportunity to foster collaboration across the different camps of the highly politicized faculty.

Conspicuously neglected by the Michelman Committee was graduate legal education. But no complaints were raised, because by the 1970s the LL.M. and S.J.D. degrees no longer served to train faculty for American law schools, as Gail Hupper has shown. By 1980 these degree programs predominantly enrolled foreign students, and the school catalog did not even describe the requirements of the two degrees, but referred applicants to a separate publication. The days when 20 percent of the Harvard law faculty, and 25 percent of the Yale law faculty, held an S.J.D were over. Consequently, the Michelman Committee gave little thought to graduate legal education.[49]

The Michelman Committee began its work with great anticipation, but in the end "only a few . . . concrete proposals have been adopted by the faculty."[50] In fact, the bundle of provisional documents issued by the Michelman Committee in 1982 yielded little more than the relatively inconsequential Committee reports of 1936, 1948, and 1960. Even worse, some feared "that the faculty has been so dissatisfied with the proposals and the ensuing discussions that it will avoid any real efforts at reform in the near future."[51]

The Second Grade War and "Big Mac"

Under Dean Derek Bok (1968–1970), the first Grade War rivaled the invasion of Cambodia and civil rights protests as a reason to shut down the school. Responding to students' criticism, the faculty in 1968 had adopted a nine-tier letter-grade system, summarized in Table 16.1. But many students were not satisfied, and demanded pass/fail options. Hence, in April 1969 the faculty approved a further modification allowing first-year students to choose one of three options: the nine-tier letter grade system of 1968, a four-tier system (high, satisfactory, low, fail), or simply pass/fail. Small classes were exempted.

Also, by 1972 the *Law Review,* the Board of Student Advisors, and the Legal Aid Bureau no longer determined their membership solely on the basis of grades.[52] Despite those changes, in the early 1980s, grades still determined one's prospects for entering the upper echelon of the legal profession, because offers for jobs at prestigious firms and judicial clerkships depended heavily on first- and second-year grades.[53]

The grading issue therefore continued to simmer, and students closely monitored the deliberations of the Michelman Committee on this subject. Some formed a "shadow" committee—the Student Advisory Committee to the Michelman Committee—which became known as "Big Mac." This advisory committee commented almost exclusively on grades, which, it said, "perpetuate a hierarchical system [that] runs counter to the long-run goals which the school should be trying to promote."[54]

Kennedy's "Dissent" also criticized the focus on grades, beginning with admissions criteria that relied primarily on indices intended to predict grades in the first year at law school: LSAT scores and undergraduate grade-point average. According to this view, the system was self-fulfilling. The admissions process was geared to emphasize grades, rather than success in practice, contribution to social welfare, political leadership, or demographic diversity, as Kennedy pointed out. Grading at Harvard Law School reinforced the professional hierarchy built upon *Law Review* membership, summer jobs at prestigious firms, judicial clerkships, and positions at big law firms and on law faculties.[55]

Kennedy and other CLS scholars also challenged the validity of grades, alleging that the best marks were given to students who did not challenge the ideological and jurisprudential premises of their teachers, thus "reproducing a hierarchy" of like-minded and unoriginal law teachers, embracing a conservative orthodoxy.[56] Likewise, they questioned the validity of the hiring criteria of faculty, which were based largely on the grades that the candidates had received in law school. Why not count "original" or new political ideology, diversity of race or gender, commitment to "public service," "character," or assessment by faculty interviews? By 1983 and the publication of Kennedy's *Legal Education and the Reproduction of Hierarchy,* grading became one of the "political footballs" in faculty contests that, students asserted, were all about which professors would win, not what was educationally sound and beneficial for the students.[57]

Meanwhile, by 1980 the students had curtailed their expectations and goals for grading reform. In 1973 the faculty rejected a proposal, supported by 80 percent of first-year students, to make pass/fail grading mandatory in first-semester, first-year courses. Worse still, the faculty reversed their concession of April 1969 by abolishing the option of choosing pass/fail or the four-tier grading instead of the nine-tier system. In addition, the faculty failed to respond when 85 percent of third-year students voted that faculty supervision of their written-work requirement was "inadequate."[58] Exhausted by this faculty intransigence, the students no longer pushed for mandatory pass/fail grading in all courses, a cause that had rallied the crowds during the first Grade War of 1969 and 1970.

In 1981 the *Harvard Law Record* reported that about half of the student body supported pass/fail grading for the first year's first-semester courses. But only about a quarter of the students supported mandatory pass/fail for all first-year courses and optional pass/fail in the second and third year.[59] Big Mac therefore focused on the first year, and proposed—given the ignorance of many incoming students about law and the lack of early feedback in first-year courses—to level the playing field by making pass/fail grading mandatory in the first year or the first semester, with a chance to retake the exam if the student failed. In an open letter to the Michelman Committee in November 1980, Big Mac argued that this reform would alleviate the "overly competitive atmosphere which is not conducive to open-minded intellectual exploration" and would acknowledge that "one three-hour examination is an insufficient basis for making the extremely fine distinctions in a nine-category grading system."[60]

After Big Mac made a presentation about grades to the Michelman Committee in January 1981, the committee in April proposed two limited reforms for faculty consideration: (1) providing "feedback" at the midpoint of first-year courses, and (2) giving pass/fail grades in first-semester, first-year courses. The committee voted 8–3 in support of these reforms. But those in favor included all four students, so the faculty voted only 4–3 in favor.[61] Despite the close faculty vote on the committee, the students were generally optimistic about the fate of the proposal, which addressed the worst problems of the first year and which many students regarded "as a compromise."[62] However, the faculty overwhelmingly rejected the committee's recommendation by a 20–7 vote in May 1981, adding an essentially meaningless platitude of their concern for "enhanced feedback." Once again the Michelman Committee had nothing to show for its three years of deliberations on the matter of greatest concern to students.[63]

The committee also considered one other grading issue: class participation. The standing rule was that class participation could not be graded, except in classes of "fewer than 50 students, and then only to adjust grades upward." In a separate statement, David Shapiro advocated grading class participation both up and down in classes of any size.[64] Neither Big Mac nor students on the committee favored Shapiro's idea. Molly Burke wrote, with deft irony, "I would not want to add the burden of making an equitable assessment of classroom performance to a faculty which is unable to provide written comments on examinations."[65] Nevertheless, the committee endorsed this grading reform, which the students opposed. In any event, the faculty did not adopt Shapiro's proposal.[66]

Several decades later, the limited changes on grading proposed by Big Mac and recommended by the Michelman Committee—to reduce the overemphasis on grades, to provide more and earlier feedback, and to introduce pass / fail grading in the first year—became widespread practice in law schools. In 2015 the ABA mandated that "a law school shall utilize both formative and summative assessment methods in the curriculum to measure and improve student learning and provide meaningful feedback to students."[67] Then, in 2018, recognizing "that all of our students should begin law school with a common baseline of knowledge, so that none of them has to feel as if everyone else 'gets it,'" the Law School introduced Zero-L. This "online pre-matriculation course . . . provides incoming students, before they arrive on campus, with a firm foundation in the key features of the U.S. legal system and the vocabulary of law school," in the words of current Dean John F. Manning (J.D. 1985).[68]

These developments resemble the reforms that Big Mac and the students on the Michelman Committee had tried to advance. But even the committee's modest proposals went nowhere. On the one hand, tradition-minded faculty seemed to fear that staying the intellectual sword would let the students off easy and make the school "soft," as Dean Griswold (1946–1967) had feared. On the other hand, faculty on the left wanted to overthrow the entire system of grading and the hierarchical regimes that it supported. Meanwhile, as Molly Burke attested, students felt that neither camp had their welfare in mind.[69]

Clinical Legal Education

Another contentious issue addressed by the Michelman Committee was clinical education, which had long-standing antecedents at Harvard Law School.[70] During the nineteenth century, most students, including Dean Langdell, completed a supervised apprenticeship either before, during, or after their time at

Gary Bellow, LL.B. 1960. Faculty 1971–2000. Photograph ca. 1972.

Courtesy of Harvard Law School Library, Historical & Special Collections.

the school, a custom encouraged by the school's policies.[71] In 1913 the students petitioned to establish the Harvard Legal Aid Bureau, the oldest student-run legal services office in the United States and, in 1949, the Harvard Voluntary Defenders. In 1966 the Harvard Student District Attorney Project commenced, and in 1967 the Law School opened the Community Legal Assistance Office (CLAO) off-campus. All these student organizations were early sources of clinical instruction.[72]

In 1970 these extracurricular clinical forerunners inspired Dean Bok to recruit Gary Bellow (LL.B. 1960) from the University of Southern California law faculty, where his clinical students worked with the United Farm Workers and the Black Panther Party. Appointed a visiting professor in 1971, Bellow was promoted and tenured in 1972, and, together with a few other law faculty, developed a fully integrated, year-long clinical program. In 1978 the Legal Services Institute (LSI) of Harvard Law School was founded in Jamaica Plain under the direction of Jeanne Charn (J.D. 1970), who had interned in CLAO and was appointed lecturer at the Law School.[73]

But LSI enrolled fewer than twenty-five students, who were split between law schools at Harvard and Northeastern University. This minimal availability of clinical education to Harvard students reflected "the School's generally non-committal attitude regarding their value and their legitimate place in the educational program," stated the Michelman Committee.[74] Fundamentally, the "noncommittal attitude" stemmed from the faculty's reservations about LSI, as run by Bellow and Charn, who were married.

According to the Michelman Committee, many faculty objected that the relatively low student-faculty ratio made LSI expensive compared to other classes in the Law School. They also felt that LSI separated clinical education from the rest of the school, in terms of both organization and physical location, because Bellow insisted that all clinical classes be held at the Jamaica Plain facility and that the "clinical students" commit to a "full-year total program." Furthermore, a number of faculty resented the openly "partisan" politics and "left wing" ideology at LSI, while others worried that the Law School would be entangled in legal problems if LSI were more closely integrated in the school.[75]

Finally, fundamental financial and pedagogical problems of LSI were identified in a separate report by Christopher Edley Jr. (J.D. 1978), an untenured assistant professor. Though supporting clinical education and legal services, Edley noted that LSI had been supported by grants from the Ford Foundation, which had ended in 1978, and subsequently by funding provided by Congress through the Higher Education Act, which was unreliable in the long run. Edley recommended an alternative approach "modeled after the teaching hospitals affiliated with major medical schools," which would be fully integrated with the Law School and financially sustainable.[76]

Responding to all these concerns, the Michelman Committee suggested establishing a "Practicing Law Center" on a model entirely different from LSI. Located near campus, this center would have a smaller staff, serve more Harvard students, and not require full-time enrollment. Finally, the associated clinics would be affiliated with "a public or quasi-public agency," thus alleviating "concerns" about partisan involvement by the school.[77] By suggesting, essentially, to displace LSI, the Michelman Committee was implicitly and harshly criticizing Bellow, Charn, and LSI, confirming their fears that the faculty, given the chance, would gut LSI, as Bellow recounted in 1997. An additional question in the controversy was the status of clinical faculty. Bellow was a tenured full professor, but the LSI faculty were not. The Michelman Committee ducked the question as to whether faculty at the Practicing Law Center would be tenure-track or continue in a second-class status.[78]

But the fate of the suggestion typified the rifts on the committee, whose members could not agree on whether to recommend establishing a Practicing Law Center. In fact, Chairman Michelman could not even discern the positions of some committee members and promised to update the committee's stance in the future.[79] But this was never done, and the committee, over the votes of a dissenting minority, recommended instead forming a new Committee on Clinical Education and Fieldwork to advise the dean and faculty, "from time to time."[80] This equivocal outcome kicked the issue further down the road, exemplifying the indecision and dissension pervading the Michelman Committee.

Nevertheless, the Michelman Committee did recommend that the school take the new step of incorporating clinical education into the formal curriculum and broadening access to it. When Dean Vorenberg officially received the Michelman Report in 1982, he singled out "the analysis of clinical legal education" as one of its most noteworthy contributions.[81]

The Extracurricular World

Generations of students have regarded extracurricular activities as central to their legal education and sometimes as even better learning experiences than the official curriculum. Nevertheless, the historical relationship between student-run organizations and the school was fraught, and the 1970s were no exception. This decade saw major debates and changes concerning all five types of extracurricular activity: (1) law clubs, moot courts, and debating societies, (2) law journals, (3) legal services, (4) student governance groups, and (5) student clubs, organizations, and affinity groups.

The oldest and, to many students, the most important of these extracurriculars—the moot courts, the law clubs, and the debating societies—developed students' advocacy skills. As we have seen, moot courts date back to the origins of the school in 1817 and the English Inns of Court centuries earlier, but in the 1870s the faculty ceased organizing and supervising moot courts. In response to that change, student-run law clubs multiplied and organized their own moot courts. In 1910 the faculty reinstated school-authorized moot courts and organized them as an "elimination tournament" named the Ames Competition, in honor of Dean James Barr Ames (1895–1909). At the same time, the faculty established the Board of Student Advisors and assigned it the responsibility of assisting law clubs in preparing for the Ames Competition.[82]

Within this framework, the law clubs continued to flourish through the middle of the twentieth century. In 1937–38, they numbered twenty-seven "established clubs" and thirty-seven "orphan" or "bastard" clubs. Into the early 1970s the law clubs survived, often proudly bragging about their antecedents. In April 1970 the elite club, the Pow Wow, launched their second century with a magnificent feast," the school *Yearbook* reported.[83]

Faculty gladly served as advisors, and some clubs took their names—such as the Dawson Club and the Kaplan Club. The elite clubs included the Learned Hand Club, the Pow Wow, and the Cardozo Club, in which membership increasingly depended on social class and collegiate background.[84] During the mid-1970s, the law clubs' exclusivism and social elitism made them less attractive, and the final entry in the school yearbook for the venerable Marshall Club, over 150 years old, appeared in 1979. Thereafter, the school's yearbooks no longer featured the law clubs, and the 1984–85 the school catalog observed that "these 'law clubs' have virtually disappeared from the Law School scene."[85]

As the stature and appeal of the law clubs changed in the 1970s, so too did that of the school-authorized moot courts. Initially, first-year students were required to participate in the Ames Competition, under the supervision of the Board of Student Advisors, while second- and third-year students had the option to compete. In the mid-twentieth century, students followed the jousts between the four-person teams like the playoffs in professional sports. In the final round of the tournament, the teams argued before a three-member bench that usually included a U.S. Supreme Court Justice, one Federal Circuit Court Judge, and one State Supreme Court Justice. Awards were given for "best briefs, best oralist, and best overall teams," and substantial monetary prizes went to the winning and losing teams in both the semifinal and final rounds.[86]

During the turbulent 1960s, voluntary participation in the Ames Competition declined rapidly, and in 1968–1970 "the downward spiral of Ames participation continued." First-year students were still required to join the Ames Competition during the fall semester as part of their Legal Methods course, but in spring semester 1970, at least one hundred first-year students opted out, along with hundreds of second- and third-year students.[87] After Sacks became dean in 1971, interest continued to decline due to what the *Yearbook* called "an anti-competitive spirit . . . currently fashionable among law students."[88]

The conflicting opinions about the Ames Competition, as about grading, were then manifested by successive faculty votes making participation voluntary in 1973, then mandatory again in 1982, then voluntary once more in 1984, even as the catalog hailed the competition as "one of the highlights of the academic year" and most first-year students still elected to participate.[89] Nevertheless, by the mid-1980s the Ames Competition was ebbing while clinical education was growing as an elemental part of the school's formal academic program.

Student Journals

If anything rivaled being an Ames finalist in the traditional prestige hierarchy of the school, it was membership in the *Harvard Law Review,* which prided itself on teaching legal research, writing, and editing skills outside the classroom. In several ways, the *Law Review* differed from the other student journals founded later at the school. First, it was the oldest by far, founded in 1887. Second, it was self-funded, and therefore financially independent, although the school provided its offices. By the same token, it was independently governed—"student-controlled and student-edited"—as a corporation separate from the Law School, as seen in the Lubell controversy of the early 1950s.[90]

The *Review*'s most significant distinction began in the 1910s, when it was decided that students with the highest grades in the first and second years would compose the membership of the *Law Review.* Given this emphasis on grades, most of the school's faculty, many eminent members of the judiciary, and numerous partners of leading law firms were drawn from members of the *Review,* so election to the editorial board was a gateway into the professional elite.

Starting in 1970 the *Law Review,* and the definition of academic merit for which it stood, began to change profoundly. The cancellation of spring exams in May 1970 delayed issuing first-year grades until October and, therefore, determining membership on the *Review,* which normally occurred over the summer. Amid the growing critique of grades as a valid measure of academic merit and the increasing concern about racial and gender equity, this delay raised the question as to whether grade-point average was an appropriate criterion for membership on the *Review.*[91] After all, until the particular historical circumstances of the early 1910s, membership had not been determined in this way and the grades-based hierarchy of the *Law Review,* Board of Student Advisors, and Legal Aid Bureau had not existed.

In 1971, "one of the most troublesome years in *Review* history," the editors adopted a new additional mode of determining membership.[92] About a third of the membership would be determined by a "writing competition" evaluating writing and research skills. The year 1972, and volume 85 of the *Review,* "marked the full maturity of the Writing Competition, as the *Review* was led by a President and six (of fifteen) other officers who had been invited to join the Review on the basis of their writing performance," reported the school's *Yearbook.*[93] In 2019 twenty students were chosen on the basis of the writing competition alone, eighteen on "all available information," and the rest on a combination of the writing competition and first-year grades. Meanwhile, in 1977 the first woman was elected president, Susan Estrich (J.D. 1977); in 1987 the first person of color, Raj Marphatia (J.D. 1988); and in 1990 the first African American, Barack Obama (J.D. 1991).[94]

Not only did the standard of academic merit for membership in the *Law Review* become more complex and, perhaps, more valid in the 1970s, but the opportunity to participate in editing law reviews continued to be extended

Editors of the Harvard Law Review, 1977. Susan Estrich, J.D. 1977 and faculty 1981–1989, the first woman to serve as president stands in the fourth row, third from the right.

Harvard Law School Yearbook, 1977. Courtesy of Harvard Yearbook Publications.

across the student body. The extension had begun under Dean James Landis (1937–1946), who conceived the *Harvard Law School Record* in 1946. Other student law journals followed, supported by Dean Griswold: the *Harvard International Law Journal* in 1959, *Harvard Journal on Legislation* in 1964, *Harvard Civil Rights–Civil Liberties Law Review* in 1966, and *Harvard Legal Commentary* in 1967.[95] In the 1970s came the *Harvard Women's Law Journal, Environmental Law Review,* and *Harvard Journal of Law and Public Policy,* among others.[96]

The extension continued in 1973 when the Second-Year Writing Program was founded under the supervision of Frank Sander (LL.B. 1952), "in order that students could benefit from the type of editing and writing experience available on the *Harvard Law Review.*" Second-year students were chosen for the program "strictly at random from applications of those interested," without grade requirements. Student work was published in the *Harvard Legal Commentary,* which the program adopted as its journal. In this way, the law review experience was formally integrated into the official curriculum for pedagogical purposes, without entailing competitive selection.[97]

By 2017 the Dean of Students Office supported fifteen student-edited law journals, which provided legal-editing experience to hundreds of students. All of these periodicals have faculty advisors and receive space from the school, and none of the editors, including those of the *Harvard Law Review,* receive academic credit for their work.[98] Meanwhile, the quasi-official and preeminent status of the *Review* began to dissipate. As of 1972 the school catalog no longer listed and described the *Review,* and after 1979 the *Yearbook* no longer featured the *Review* first among student organizations. In 1981 the Michelman Committee resolved that the school should stop furnishing grades to the *Law Review* unless the student released them.[99] Today many top students do not enter the writing competition, which is now required of all candidates for the *Review* regardless of grades. Thus, the *Review's* role as the ultimate arbiter of academic merit within the school, commencing in the 1910s, slowly began to diminish after 1972.

Legal Services Organizations

Extracurricular student groups offering legal services tended to combine clinical experience with concern for socioeconomic and political issues. Since its founding in 1913, Harvard's Legal Aid Bureau was the only extracurricular organization described in the school's catalog except for the *Law Review* and the Ames Competition. More importantly, the Bureau was the only clinical experience and legal services option available to students until the founding of the Harvard Voluntary Defenders in 1949.

Originally, membership in the Legal Aid Bureau was determined solely by academic rank in class based on grades. That approach changed radically in 1969, when members began to be selected randomly from the qualified applicants.[100] Despite that change, the operation and pedagogy of the Bureau remained the same. A broad range of nonprofit and governmental agencies referred clients to the Bureau, and a student volunteer handled each case "from the initial interview . . . to actual appearance in court" under the supervision of a practicing attorney who served as attorney of record. Into the 1980s the student members effectively ran the Bureau, while reporting to an elected Board of Delegates.[101]

Meanwhile, in 1966 the Voluntary Defenders were joined by the Harvard Student District Attorneys. This new student group provided similar experience in criminal trials but on the prosecution side, and its members made two court appearances each month under the supervision of an assistant district attorney and the project director, Professor Livingston Hall (LL.B. 1927). In 1970 the Harvard Student Bar Association was founded to work "on projects which attempt to create a legal education more concerned with rectifying the injustices in our society."[102]

But the most significant extracurricular group offering legal services and clinical education, apart from the Legal Aid Bureau, was the Community Legal Assistance (CLAO). Proposed by an informal faculty committee chaired by Frank Sander, CLAO opened in 1967 with a director, full-time staff attorneys, and a Student Steering Committee. The seventy-five second- and third-year participating students "maintain regular office hours and interview clients, investigate the facts, prepare appropriate documents, negotiate with opposing counsel or principals, and otherwise help prepare cases for trial."[103]

Students testified that they learned a great deal from the completely extracurricular experience at CLAO. John M. Ferren (LL.B. 1962), who became the first director of CLAO in 1966 and subsequently a judge of the U.S. Court of Appeals, District of Columbia, stated,

> The Harvard Legal Aid Bureau at the time was still one of the three honors organizations, and felt anxious or threatened when CLAO opened. The Bureau had been little more than a divorce mill, whereas CLAO—handling both criminal and civil matters of all sorts—offered a much better experience. We were heavily

involved in the community, drafting, for example, with the help of a community planning group, the Cambridge Model Cities Program. We also took big cases, challenging, for example, the Massachusetts civil commitment scheme and seeking receivership for the Cambridge Public Housing Authority.[104]

And the students loved it. As Mark E. Budnitz (LL.B. 1969), a student volunteer from 1967 to 1969 and a staff attorney from 1969 to 1971, recalled, "CLAO was the most rewarding learning and personal experience I had as a law student. . . . It taught me how to interview a client, how to represent that client in court, and how to interact with lawyers. Perhaps most important, I found myself in a position of greater responsibility than had ever been demanded of me. I was in a relationship where persons from backgrounds starkly different from my own had to trust me to properly represent them when they were faced with serious legal problems."[105]

In short, among all the extracurricular legal service groups, CLAO offered the most robust clinical education within a structured, supervised program. Officially, though, it was largely ignored, despite recommendations from the original faculty committee and the Michelman Committee that CLAO be incorporated into the formal curriculum in some form. In Budnitz's words, "We received no course credit or any formal recognition for the many hours we spent each week at CLAO. Most of my classmates planned to work for major law firms. If they made any detour before reaching that goal, it was to clerk for a federal court judge. None of my professors ever mentioned CLAO, much less recommended that we consider making it part of our legal education."[106]

Nevertheless, the Bok and Sacks administrations did support student legal services, whether in the Legal Aid Bureau, in CLAO, or in another new model, the "research bureau." The oldest such bureau, the Student Legislative Research Bureau, was founded in 1952 to assist "federal, state, and local legislators, state attorney general, and civic groups" in drafting and researching legislation. In the 1960s, after merging with groups concerning civil liberty and civil rights, this bureau became the Harvard Civil Rights–Civil Liberties Research Committee, which was joined by the Prison Legal Assistance Project in 1970.[107]

In 1977 the faculty made a tentative step toward integrating legal services organizations into the formal curriculum, when the Harvard Government Attorneys Project was approved as an alternative to the mandatory Ames Competition in the first year. Students selecting this alternative could choose between representing "either a criminal case or an Attorney General's action, handling the case from its initial stages to trial."[108]

However, the Michelman Committee, and most of the faculty, viewed this diverse and growing world of student-run, legal-services groups with ambivalence. On the one hand, they saw some value in the experiences and recognized that the students wanted clinical legal-services programs. On the other hand, the faculty would not legitimize such programs by incorporating them into the formal curriculum, and then, paradoxically, complained that these programs were largely unsupervised.[109] Furthermore, faculty grumbled that extracurricular groups consumed school resources and drew students' attention and energy away from the formal academic courses, thereby contributing to "the waning of classroom commitment over the three years of law school," as the Michelman Committee stated.[110] The faculty wanted the students to listen to them!

These questions of overseeing or assimilating more of these groups into the formal curriculum would be hotly debated over the next decade. Because some, like the Student Bar Association, were either covertly or openly political, direct involvement of the Law School raised problems that had to be battled out in the faculty appointments process during the 1980s. Throughout that decade these questions remained unresolved, and the clinical extracurricular groups were largely left untouched, but helped to legitimize clinical and legal services education within the school.

"Limited Success" in Governance

The oldest student governance organization, the Board of Student Advisors, was formed in 1910 in order to lighten the workload of the outnumbered faculty. The student advisors were paid to counsel first-year students on conducting legal research, citing sources, and writing briefs, while also helping the law clubs prepare for moot courts. Originally and for many decades, membership in the Board of Student Advisors was determined solely by academic class rank based on course grades. In 1971 the Board, like the *Law Review,* widened its membership criteria to include "legal and teaching experience, interviews, short essays, as well as grades."[111]

Although its original mission was strictly co-curricular, the Board soon began to influence the school's academic program. Its responsibility to assist the law clubs rapidly expanded due to the creation of the Ames Competition and the requirement that first-year students participate. In fact, the Board began organizing the Ames Competition and helping to create new law clubs, because the traditional law clubs could not and would not accommodate all the students. In 1937 the Board's role expanded even more, when Dean Landis recognized the Board "as the official medium and entity for student-faculty communication" to the school administration, and "authorized the Board to provide counseling to students for individual problems." In subsequent decades the Board's role as the official "mouth piece of student opinion" became problematic as student complaints about academic policies mounted.[112]

In the 1970s the Board's co-curricular responsibility of providing academic advice to individual students grew into a formal, curricular role. In the early 1970s, a few sections of the Legal Methods course were taught by faculty, but most were taught by graduate students serving as teaching fellows.[113] In 1975 Dean Sacks decided to increase faculty involvement in the Legal Methods course, link it more closely to the first-year major courses, and replace the graduate student teaching fellows with J.D. students working under faculty supervision.[114] David Shapiro, associate dean at the time, was charged with implementing the changes. In selecting the J.D. students, Shapiro drew heavily on the Board of Student Advisors—but not exclusively, because he felt that the Board's new selection procedure deemphasizing grades diluted academic rigor.[115]

At the same time, the Board tripled in size to forty-four members and dramatically increased the scope of its activities to include such programs as a Model Trial, Client Counseling Competition, and a Mock Appellate Argument featuring prominent attorneys. The Board also expanded its role in peer advising to include more social and recreational activities, contributing to "the humanization and the de-ivory-towerization of the Law School," according to the *Yearbook*.[116] Nevertheless, the Board of Student Advisors did not fill the vacuum of student governance because it did not really "govern" and was not elected or formally representative. The Board was a faculty organ, and direct student input into governing the school remained minimal, except during crises such as the first Grade War under Bok.

Meanwhile, one elected student governance organization had emerged by the time Sacks became dean in 1971. This was the Dormitory Council, which had very limited purview and represented only a fraction of the student body. Elected annually by dormitory residents, this council, in theory, gave voice to "student wants, complaints and ideas." But in practice it simply operated the vending machines and laundry services in the dorms and used the revenue to sponsor dorm parties, mixers, and intramural sports leagues. Even so, until 1973 the Dormitory Council's twenty members served as "the functional, if not the nominal, student government of the Law School."[117]

In 1974, responding to the faculty's "deaf ear to students" concerning grades, the Sacks administration established the Law School Council (LSC) to involve students in school governance.[118] The LSC comprised fifteen J.D. students (five elected by each class), one LL.M. or S.J.D. student, and six appointed faculty members. Eight slots were reserved for "special interest" groups, at the "discretion" of the Council.[119] The LSC had real power. It alone could select the student members of the faculty committees—the ten students who could fully participate in faculty meetings (apart from voting), and the five students who could attend faculty meetings as "observers."[120]

The LSC also established a Governance Committee to hear complaints from both students and faculty. And the LSC assumed a broad mandate to resist "overemphasis of the corporate model," deemphasis of clinical education, "racist and sexist hiring practices," "oversized first-year classes," lack of "student input into hiring and tenure decisions," and denial of "first-year students' access to Placement Office Facilities." In short, the LSC saw itself as "the hope for structural reform at the Law School."[121]

Nevertheless, in 1976 LSC president Jeffrey Reiman (J.D. 1976), in his letter to incoming first-year students, wrote that the law faculty often made "decisions that vitally affected the lives of students without any more than token efforts at facilitating or accepting student input." Perfectly validating Reiman's view, the Law School refused to publish his letter in the *Student Organization Booklet 1976*, "on the grounds it was political in nature."[122] In the following year the LSC again told incoming students that "when students have sought to affect the policies of the institution, they have met with limited success."[123] Some members of the J.D. classes of 1976 and 1977 then boycotted the school's annual alumni fund due to "the lack of student input at the Law School," Reiman told the *Harvard Crimson* in 1978.[124]

Even so, establishing the LSC was a real achievement of the Sacks administration. Its influence could be seen in the LSC's appointment of the four student members to the Michelman Committee and its creation of Big Mac. But the minimal influence of the dissents by the four student members of the Michelman Committee demonstrated that student input still mattered little, though at least it could be voiced officially by the early 1980s.

A View from the Bottom

Deeply concerned about student morale in 1932, Felix Frankfurter gathered six students whom he regarded as "unusually sagacious" for a candid, six-hour discussion. Their "core concern was the sheer size and anonymity of the institution," Frankfurter reported.[125] Sharing that deep concern almost four decades later, Professor Alan Stone and Dean Bok took the same approach of interviewing extensively a small number of selected students to determine the quality of their life at the school. They found that many students, particularly those who did not excel academically, felt isolated and regarded themselves as "second-class citizens." In addition, their peer relations were "formal and task-oriented in contrast to those among undergraduates which are more informal, intimate and socially oriented."[126] Appropriately, if ironically, the published report of these interviews was entitled *Harvard Law School: A View from the Bottom.*

A decade later, Professor Charles Nesson wrote a memorandum to the Michelman Committee concerning the "demoralization" of the students that "now plagues" the school. He argued that this problem, identified by Frankfurter, Bok, and Stone, not only persisted but had worsened due to new anxieties about the legal profession and the faculty culture. Nesson observed that as of 1979 the faculty was becoming divided into "hostile camps," willing to "engage in personal and political invective." The students could not help but be troubled and divided themselves. "This is a liberal institution. . . . We believe in intellectual discourse, academic freedom, and pluralism." The key goal, among students and faculty alike, should be "mutual respect."[127]

In this milieu, an important role in boosting student morale was played by even apparently frivolous social clubs—such as the Beckwith Circle Eating Club, the Saturday Night Poker Club, the Amused and Abused Club (with just two members, Lisa Hemmer [J.D. 1980] and Jorie Roberts [J.D. 1980], duly photographed for the yearbook), and the Committee to Save the Moose, whose motto was "The essential thing is that every obstacle should be denied, and that the irrational should be triumphant. (Albert Camus)."[128] There were also intramural sports, with teams like the Razzle Dazzle Football Champs, and cooking clubs, like The Society for the Promotion of Culinary Arts.[129]

"Dedicated to the art of inconspicuousness," the Harvard Backbenchers club sought "to achieve and maintain as low a classroom profile as possible," the 1976 *Yearbook* reported. "The only qualifications for membership are a fear of hearing one's own voice in class, a flexible grip on reality, and payment of the modest dues. This year's activities include early attendance at all Corporations and Constitutional Law classes in order to save choice backrow seats for fellow Backbenchers, the annual turkey shoot, and sponsorship of an Ames Alternative." That "alternative" project "involved fall indoctrination sessions for HLS first year students interested in acquiring backbenching skills such as finding an unassigned seat in Pound 102 and looking innocent when a pro-

"The Harvard Backbenchers."

Harvard Law School Yearbook, 1976. Courtesy of Harvard Yearbook Publications.

fessor calls on your vacant assigned seat." In 1976 the recipient of the "Most Improved Backbencher Award" was Hilary Jordan (J.D. 1977), the club president, who attended all of his second-year classes without asking or answering a single question."[130]

Some student groups exhibited remarkable continuity that boosted student morale. The Drama Society, highly popular year after year, staged elaborate parodies of the life of the school. Though sometimes cutting close to the bone, these parodies were also immensely funny, with titles like "Something L's" (Fall 1979) and "Paradise Remanded, or Replevin Can Wait" (Spring 1979).[131] The *Harvard Law School Record, Harvard Law School Yearbook,* and Harvard Law School Forum also engaged students year after year, and fostered friendships.

Law School Drama Society, 1969. Photo by Allan Grossman, LL.B. 1969.
Harvard Law School Yearbook, 1969. Courtesy of Harvard Yearbook Publications.

Affinity groups also helped boost student morale, even apart from the important missions they fulfilled, while their role and profile at the school increased dramatically. For example, the 1970 *Handbook for Entering Students* and the 1971 *Yearbook* had made no mention of the Black Law Student Association (BLSA), founded in 1967, or the Women's Law Association (WLA), founded in 1969. But in 1977 the *Handbook for Entering Students* described BLSA as "the second largest Black Law student population in the country," and nearly fifty BLSA members were photographed on the steps of Austin Hall. Together with the new *Women's Law Journal,* the WLA also got prominent billing for its role in "furthering women's interests in admissions and place-ment" and "advocating the hiring of additional female members of the fac-ulty."[132] In 1980 the *Yearbook* featured, for the first time, the Asian Law Students Association (ALSA), which was established "to promote actively the interests of Asian Americans on campus and in the community at large," al-though it would be twenty-six years before the first Asian American, Jeannie C. Suk Gersen (J.D. 2002), was appointed to the regular faculty.[133]

The development of other affinity groups and student organizations over the 1970s was also striking. In the 1970 *Handbook for Entering Students* and the 1971 *Yearbook,* the descriptions of many clubs seem, naturally, dated. The Bull and Bear Club was dedicated to "business investment and finance," and reported a "Splendor in the Grass" picnic with the Wellesley College Young Republicans. Somewhat presumptuously, the Democratic Club claimed "the membership of all politically conscious law students." The Harvard Law Wives featured "a beer party, faculty cocktail party, winter sports night, and a fashion show," and Lincoln's Inn hosted black-tie dinners, tailgate parties, dances, and a "James Bond Martini Night," among other events.[134]

Some of these groups had changed dramatically by the end of Sacks's dean-ship. For example, Lincoln's Inn admitted women in 1970, and, despite de-clining membership, hung on, with over 300 members in 1998–99. The Inn featured a Kentucky Derby party, Mardi Gras night, and "kegs 'n' eggs" parties until 2007, when it merged with HL Central, another social club, and closed its club house due to "declining membership and lack of funds."[135] The 3,200 alumni members included Supreme Court Justices Anthony Kennedy (LL.B. 1961), Stephen Breyer (LL.B. 1964), and David H. Souter (LL.B. 1966).

In the early 1970s the Harvard Law Wives simply disappeared. So did the Committee for Legal Research on the Draft. In their place, religious clubs arose, such as the Harvard Jewish Law Students Association and the Harvard Law School Christian Fellowship, as well as new ethnic and gender associa-tions, such as La Alianza and the Committee on Gay and Lesbian Legal Is-sues.[136] These new organizations evidenced an atmosphere that encouraged di-versity and tolerance, and gave confidence to those who were not openly organized, even ten years earlier. This new atmosphere exemplified the ideo-logical shift in American culture during the decade of the 1970s.[137]

For this encouragement, Dean Sacks deserves much credit. He was nothing if not a true liberal who supported "intellectual discourse, academic freedom, and pluralism" at every opportunity. In his introduction to the 1981 *Yearbook,* Sacks observed that student organizations "forced attention to problems that needed attention and would have gone unnoticed otherwise," and "played a powerful role in certain curricular reforms, as in the growth of clinical legal education." He maintained "that the student role in law school governance will continue to grow and will, on balance, be a positive contribution."[138] Given the institutional struggles ahead, foreseen by Charles Nesson in 1979, the "powerful role" and "positive contribution" of student organizations would be increasingly vital to the Law School.

NOTES

1. The following sections draw on Harvard Law School (HLS) Catalog, 1971–72; and Harvard Law School, *Handbook for Entering Students 1971* (Cambridge, MA, 1971), 51.

2. Bruce A. Kimball, *The Inception of Modern Professional Education: C. C. Langdell, 1826–1906* (Chapel Hill, NC, 2009), 208–209.

3. The following sections are derived from HLS Catalog, 1980–81, 47–110.

4. HLS Catalog, 1980–81, 45.

5. Elyce H. Zenoff and Jerome A. Barron, "So You Want to Hire a Law Professor?," *Journal of Legal Education* 33 (1983): 391.

6. Committee on Educational Planning and Development [CEPD], "The Present State and Future Direction of Legal Education at Harvard" (April 21, 1982), on file with the authors, chap. 1, 1. See Albert M. Sacks, Memorandum to HLS Faculty (February 12, 1979), on file with the authors, 1; Dan Hershman, "Faculty Committee Reviews Curriculum," *HLSR* (March 9, 1979): 1. Much of the following analysis draws on Abigail Burger Chingos, "The Michelman Committee: A History of Its Work and an Analysis of Lessons Learned about Curricular Reform" (student research paper, HLS, 2009), on file with the authors.

7. Duncan Kennedy, Remark to Daniel Coquillette (December 2012) while preparing Duncan Kennedy, Oral History, conducted by Daniel R. Coquillette and Jay Hook (July 2013), on file with the authors. Frank Michelman served as associate dean of the faculty from 1981 to 1985, and was awarded a university professorship, Harvard's highest academic honor, in 1992.

8. James Vorenberg, "To the Members of the Committee on Educational Planning and Development" (May 26, 1982), on file with the authors, 2.

9. Frank I. Michelman, Memorandum to the HLS Faculty for the Committee on Educational Planning and Development (April 21, 1982), on file with the authors, 1.

10. Frank I. Michelman, Explanatory Note to the CEPD (May 1, 1980), on file with the authors, 1–2. In addition to the memoranda file, many "Prior Reports and Recommendations" were not included in the "tentative final draft." Sometime after Abigail Burger

Chingos completed her research paper on the Michelman Committee in 2009, these "Prior Reports and Recommendations" were sealed by the HLS Dean's Office and are no longer available for review.

11. Michelman, Memorandum, 1.

12. CEPD, "The Present State, chap. 2.

13. CEPD, "The Present State," chap. 1, 3–8, 12–14.

14. CEPD, "The Present State," chap. 1, 25–31.

15. David L. Shapiro, "Separate Statement" (from the Report of the Committee on Educational Planning and Development) (February 4, 1981), on file with the authors, 1, 3.

16. Robert C. Clark, "To the Faculty: Sketch of a Sample Proposal That Would Be Carried Out in the Proposed Research Program" (November 12, 1980), on file with the authors; Clark, "A Proposal for Research Programs and Harvard Law School Research Institute" (October 21, 1980), on file with the authors. See also Jack Lange, "Committee Proposed Research Semester," *HLSR* (November 14, 1980): 4; Chingos, "The Michelman Committee," 17–18.

17. Charles R. Nesson, "Separate Statement" (from the Report of the Committee on Educational Planning and Development) (April 26, 1982), on file with the authors, 1–2.

18. Molly Burke, "Separate Statement" (from the Report of the Committee on Educational Planning and Development) (October 14, 1982), on file with the authors, 1–2. See Nancy Wieger and Karen Falkenstein, "Memorandum to Members of the Michelman Committee: The First Year Curriculum" (June 22, 1979), on file with the authors; Karen Falkenstein, "Re: A Proposal for an Alternative Method of Evaluation in the Experiential Contracts Section" (February 25, 1980), on file with the authors.

19. Burke, "Separate Statement," 2.

20. Duncan Kennedy, "Dissent from the Report of the Committee on Educational Planning and Development" (April 5, 1982), on file with the authors, 1, 8–9. On April 1, 1980, Duncan Kennedy wrote a memo to the HLS faculty entitled "Utopian Proposal on Law School as a Counterhegemonic Enclave." On April 5, 1982, in response to the first installment of the Michelman Committee, Kennedy wrote a cover memo to which he attached his "Utopian Proposal on Law School as a Counterhegemonic Enclave," and the two documents were filed together as "Dissent from the Report of the Committee on Educational Planning and Development" (April 5, 1982), on file with the authors.

21. Duncan Kennedy, Cover Memo (April 5, 1982), on file with the authors, 1.

22. Lange, "Michelman Group," 1; Chingos, "The Michelman Committee," 16.

23. Chingos, "The Michelman Committee," 1; Victor Brudney, Interview (March 2008), quoted in Chingos, "The Michelman Committee," 16.

24. CEPD, "The Present State," chap. 2.

25. See Lange, "Committee Proposed Research Semester," 4; Chingos, "The Michelman Committee," 17–18.

26. Chingos, "The Michelman Committee," 29.

27. CEPD, "The Present State," chap. 3, 15. See Chingos, "The Michelman Committee," 28.

28. Burke, "Separate Statement," 2.

29. CEPD, "The Present State," chap. 3. Andrew Kaufman's pioneering text, *Problems in Professional Responsibility for a Changing Profession* (Boston, 1976) remains a classic.

30. "Message from the Dean," *HLSB* (Fall 1974): 4. Sacks also recommended offering a purely elective course on the subject.

31. See HLS Catalog, 1980–81, 95–96, 122. Sacks's idea, in fact, was reminiscent of the "self-delusional" approach of Dean Erwin Griswold (1946–1967), discussed in Chapter 13.

32. Chingos, "The Michelman Committee," 44; CEPD, "The Present State," chap. 3.

33. Kimball, *Inception,* 131–133.

34. Brudney, Interview (March 2008). See Chingos, "The Michelman Committee," 44; John Morris, "The Fate of the Michelman Committee," *HLSR* (February 4, 1983): 6.

35. Robert C. Clark, Interview (March 2008), quoted in Chingos, "The Michelman Committee," 48–49.

36. Clark, Interview (March 2008), 48–49.

37. Todd D. Rakoff, Interview (March 2008), quoted in Chingos, "The Michelman Committee," 48.

38. Todd D. Rakoff, "The Harvard First-Year Experiment," *Journal of Legal Education* 39 (1989): 491–499. See Chingos, "The Michelman Committee," 60; CEPD, "The Present State," chap. 4, 1; Frank I. Michelman, "The Parts and the Whole: Non-Euclidean Geometry," *Journal of Legal Education* 32 (1982): 352–354; Robert F. Cunha Jr., "The Great Experiment," *Harvard Crimson* (March 6, 1985).

39. Quoted in Charles R. Kurzman, "Law School Experiment Uses 140 'Guinea Pigs,'" *Harvard Crimson* (October 8, 1983).

40. Frank I. Michelman, Interview (March 2008), quoted in Chingos, "The Michelman Committee," 63. As a Liberal Arts Fellow at the Law School from 1984 to 1986, Bruce Kimball observed that students throughout the school attended these bridge sessions.

41. Rakoff, Interview (March 2008), 63–64. See also Cunha, "The Great Experiment"; Todd D. Rakoff and Martha L. Minow, "A Case for Another Case Method," *Vanderbilt Law Review* 60 (2007): 597.

42. Michelman, Interview (March 2008), 49.

43. Clark, Interview (March 2008), 50.

44. Clark, Interview (March 2008), 50. See Michelman, Interview (March 2008), 50.

45. CEPD, "The Present State," chap. 5, 21–23.

46. CEPD, "The Present State," chap. 7; Burke, "Separate Statement," 1.

47. CEPD, "The Present State," chap. 7.

48. CEPD, "The Present State," chap. 7. See Clark, Interview (March 2008), 67; Robert C. Clark, "The Rationale for Computer-Aided Instruction," *Journal of Legal Education* 33 (1983): 459.

49. Gail J. Hupper, "The Rise of an Academic Doctorate in Law: Origins through World War II," *American Journal of Legal History* 49 (2007): 415, 419, 454. See also Gail J. Hupper, "Educational Ambivalence: The Rise of a Foreign-Student Doctorate of Law," *New England Law Review* 49 (2014): 387; Jenny Page, "The Forgotten Class: The History of the LL.M. Program at Harvard Law School, 1923–2006" (student research paper, HLS, 2000), on file with the authors; Lucia Foulkes, "Graduate Education in a New Global Area" (student research paper, Boston College Law School, 2015), on file with the authors.

50. Morris, "The Fate of the Michelman Committee," 6. See Zenoff and Barron, "So You Want to Hire a Law Professor?," 391.

51. Morris, "The Fate of the Michelman Committee," 6.

52. Joel Seligman, *The High Citadel: The Influence of Harvard Law School* (Boston, 1978), 14; John York, "Legal Aid Ends Grade Standard," *HLSR* (May 1, 1969): 1; HLS Yearbook, 1971, 199; Susan Gillette, "2L Members Announced by Harvard Law Review," *HLSR* (October 24, 1975): 1, 9.

53. The school still awarded the Sears Prizes to the two students receiving the highest averages in the first year and the two students receiving the highest averages in the second year. The Fay diploma, the school's highest academic accolade, was awarded to the student with the best average on graduation. Latin honors of *cum laude, magna cum laude,* and the very rare *summa cum laude* were made on the basis of grade-point average.

54. Student Advisory Committee to the Michelman Committee [Big Mac], "Open Letter: To the Michelman Committee and the Law School Community," *HLSR* (November 7, 1980), 5; Kimberly Isbell, "Grade Reform at Harvard, 1968–1972" (student research paper, HLS, 2000), on file with the authors, 38–41.

55. Kennedy, "Dissent," 4–6, 30–31, 37–41, 30–31.

56. Kennedy, "Dissent," 4–6, 30–31, 37–41, 30–31.

57. Burke, "Separate Statement," 2. See Duncan Kennedy, *Legal Education and the Reproduction of Hierarchy* (Cambridge, MA, 1983) 1–13, 58–97.

58. See HLS Yearbook, 1976, 218. See K. R. Kubitz, "Backbenches: Attacking Anachronism: P / Fs Failing," *HLSR* (October 5, 1973): 15; Isbell, "Grade Reform," 33–36.

59. Erich Merrill, "Pass / Fail May Survive First Hurdle," *HLSR* (February 27, 1981): 3. See also Wiegers and Falkensten, Memorandum to the Members of the Michelman Committee, 3.

60. Student Advisory Committee, "Open Letter," 5. See also Rob Woolmington, "Pass / Fail Grading Debate Reopened by Big MAC," *HLSR* (November 14, 1980): 1; "Will Pass / Fail Make the Grade?," *HLSR* (November 14, 1980): 10; Isbell, "Grade Reform," 39; Chingos, "The Michelman Committee," 17. Big Mac also recommended a pass / fail option in the upper years and alternative criteria, such as participation in the proposed third-year Research Program or the clinical programs.

61. A more ambitious proposal to extend pass / fail grading to the entire first year was voted down 6–5, with one student joining those opposed. See CEPD, "The Present State," chap. 3, 39; John Morris, "Michelman Report Favors Pass / Fail, More Feedback,"

HLSR (May 1, 1981): 1; Isbell, "Grade Reform at Harvard, 1968–1972," 40. See also John Morris, "Faculty Discusses Michelman Proposals, but No Vote Taken Yet," *HLSR* (May 1, 1981): 4.

62. "Lewis J. Liman, "Less Pressure: Law School Considers Pass / Fail," *Harvard Crimson* (April 25, 1981). "Of the students on the committee, only one, Karen Falkenstein, a third-year student, voted for the first semester pass / fail option." Chingos, "The Michelman Committee," 20. See also Morris, "Michelman Report Favors Pass / Fail," 1.

63. "No Thanks: Faculty Rejects Pass / Fail Plan," *Harvard Crimson* (May 22, 1981).

64. Quotation is from Shapiro, "Separate Statement," 2.

65. Burke, "Separate Statement," 2.

66. "No Thanks," 3.

67. ABA, "Managing Director's Guidance Memo: Standards 301, 302, 314 and 315" (June 2015), on file with the authors; Standard 314 "Assessment of Student Learning."

68. Dean John F. Manning to HLS Faculty and Staff, Email (May 21, 2019), on file with the authors. See Erick Trickey, "Common Knowledge: Harvard Law School's New Zero-L Online Course Helps Prime Incoming Students for Success," *Harvard Law Today* (April 29, 2019).

69. Burke, "Separate Statement," 2.

70. CEPD, "The Present State," chap. 6. The following section draws upon Daniel Pincus, "Dichotomy of Legal Education—Practice v. Theory: The Tale of Clinical Legal Education" (student research paper, Boston College Law School, 2010), on file with the authors; Tad Polley, "Putting the Law in Law School: The Utility of Clinical Education to Alumni of the Harvard Legal Aid Bureau" (student research paper, HLS, 2003), on file with the authors; Laura Cromer-Babycz, "Clinical Legal Education in the United States: A Brief History and a Proposal for Movement towards Further Reform" (student research paper, HLS, 2012), on file with the authors.

71. Daniel R. Coquillette and Bruce A. Kimball, *On the Battlefield of Merit: Harvard Law School, the First Century* (Cambridge, MA, 2015), 169, 207n45, 436–455; Kimball, *Inception,* 31–32, 233–234, 252–253.

72. See Chapters 1 and 10, this volume.

73. "Legal Aid Pioneer Bellow Dies," *Harvard Crimson* (April 17, 2000). Gary Bellow, Oral History, conducted by Daniel R. Coquillette (January 1997), on file with the authors. See also HLS Yearbook, 1972, 58; "About Gary Bellow," Gary Bellow Public Service Award (July 10, 2017), retrieved from https://orgs.law.harvard.edu/bellow/about-gary-bellow/.

74. CEPD, "The Present State," chap. 6, 24–26. See also CEPD, Memorandum (December 1, 1981), on file with the authors; David Rosenberg, Memorandum to Faculty (December 15, 1981), on file with the authors, 4–7; David Rosenberg, Memorandum to Daniel R. Coquillette (March 8, 2017), on file with the authors.

75. Quotations are from CEPD, "The Present State," chap. 6; Bellow, Oral History (January 1997). See Gary Bellow and Jeanne Charn, Memorandum (October 13, 1981), on file with the authors; Committee on the Legal Services Institute, Report (December 1, 1981), on file with the authors, 18–45.

76. Christopher F. Edley Jr., "Clinical Instruction in Conjunction with Coursework—An Apprenticeship Approach," Memorandum to the Michelman Committee (November 3, 1981), on file with the authors, 1–7.

77. CEPD, "The Present State," chap. 6.

78. CEPD, "The Present State," chap. 6; Bellow, Oral History (January 1997). See Bellow and Charn, Memorandum; Committee on the Legal Services Institute, Report, 18–45.

79. Frank I. Michelman, Cover memorandum to the Faculty (May 7, 1982), on file with the authors, 4.

80. CEPD, "The Present State," chap. 6.

81. Vorenberg, "To the Members" (May 26, 1982).

82. Quotation is from *The Centennial History of the Harvard Law School: 1817–1917* (Cambridge, MA, 1918), 148. See discussion in Chapter 1, this volume.

83. HLS Yearbook, 1972, 203. See Kennedy, *Legal Education,* 73–78.

84. HLS Yearbook, 1970, 208–219; 1971, 228–233. See Katherine M. Porter, "Learning by Doing: A History of the Board of Student Advisors, 1910–2000" (student research paper, HLS, 2001), on file with the authors, 8–11, 41.

85. HLS Catalog, 1984–85, 55. See HLS Yearbook, 1975, 212; 1979, 211.

86. Quotations are from HLS Catalog, 1984–85, 55–56; see 1971–72, 61–62.

87. Porter, "Learning by Doing," 57, 58–59.

88. HLS Yearbook, 1971, 231.

89. HLS Catalog, 1973–74, 108; 1982–1983, 53; 1984–1985, 55.

90. Quotation is from HLS Catalog, 1968–69, 113. See Chapter 11, this volume, on the Lubell controversy.

91. HLS Yearbook, 1971, 199; 1972, 180; Deborah Pearlstein, "The Origins and Modern Purpose of the Harvard Law Review: Clinging to Community" (student research paper, HLS, 1997), on file with the authors.

92. Quotation is from HLS Yearbook, 1971, 199. See Gillette, "2L Members Announced," 1, 9.

93. HLS Yearbook, 1972, 180.

94. Pearlstein, "The Origins," 19–21. See also Frederick G. Medick, "Barack Obama's Years at Harvard Law School" (student research paper, HLS, 2008), on file with the authors but sealed. There continues to be controversy about gender issues in *Law Review* membership. In 2010, 64 percent of the editors were male and only 36 percent were women, despite a roughly even gender split in the student body. See "Gender Gaps Persist on Law Review and in Grades," *HLSR* (April 11, 2016): 1, 3.

95. HLS Yearbook, 1971, 208, 211.

96. HLS Yearbook, 1981, 196–198. See HLS Catalog, 1971–72, 73; Harvard Law School, *Handbook for Entering Students 1977* (Cambridge, MA, 1977), 27.

97. Harvard Law School, *Handbook for Entering Students 1973* (Cambridge, MA, 1973), 51.

98. Pearlstein, "The Origins," 19–23. As of 2017 the following law journals are published at HLS: *Harvard Business Law Review; Harvard Civil Rights–Civil Liberties Law Review; Harvard Environmental Law Review; Harvard Human Rights Journal; Harvard International Law Journal; Harvard Journal of Law & Gender; Harvard Journal of Law & Public Policy; Harvard Journal of Law & Technology; Harvard Journal on Racial and Ethnic Justice; Harvard Journal of Sports and Entertainment Law; Harvard Latino Law Review; Harvard Journal on Legislation; Harvard Law and Policy Review; National Security Journal; Harvard Negotiation Law Review.*

99. HLS Catalog, 1971–72, 61; HLS Yearbook, 1980; CEPD, "The Present State," chap. 2.

100. York, "Legal Aid Ends Grade Standard," 1.

101. Mark E. Budnitz, "Reflections on My Years as a Law Student and Staff Attorney at the Community Legal Aid Office (CLAO) 1967–1971" (January 30, 2018), on file with the authors, 1–2; Mark E. Budnitz, Email to Daniel Coquillette (November 14–15, 2017), on file with the authors.

102. HLS Catalog, 1971–72, 69–70. See Harvard Law School, *Handbook 1973*, 47–48; HLS Yearbook, 1970, 183.

103. Quotations are from HLS Catalog, 1967–68, 108–109; CEPD, "The Present State," chap. 1, 24. See Budnitz, "Reflections," 6.

104. John M. Ferren to Daniel R. Coquillette (February 15, 2000), on file with the authors, 2. See John M. Ferren and A. Van C. Lanckton, "Harvard's Community Legal Assistance Office: A History, Analysis, and Proposal" (March 1970), on file with the authors, 1–3; Meldon E. Levine, "The Politics of CLAO" (student research paper, HLS, April 7, 1969), on file with the authors, 2–82.

105. Budnitz, "Reflections," 1.

106. Budnitz, "Reflections," 1.

107. HLS Yearbook, 1971, 208–211; 1970, 182. See Harvard Law School, *Handbook 1973*, 42, 44, 52–53.

108. Harvard Law School, *Handbook 1977*, 33–34.

109. HLS Committee on Clinical Education, Report (1979), on file with the authors, 16a; CEPD, "The Present State," chap. 6.

110. CEPD, "The Present State," chap. 1, 28.

111. Porter, "Learning by Doing," 61. See 58–59; Jon Lamberson, "Board of Student Advisors," *HLSR* (November 21, 2002): 1.

112. Porter, "Learning by Doing," 2–3, 44.

113. HLS Catalog, 1966–67, 41; 1970–71, 51; 1971–72, 52. See Porter, "Learning by Doing," 11–12, 63–66.

114. David L. Shapiro, Interview (November 2000), quoted in Porter, "Learning by Doing," 63.

115. Porter, "Learning by Doing," 64–65.

116. HLS Yearbook, 1977, 196. See Porter, "Learning by Doing," 65–66; HLS Yearbook, 1970, 175.

117. HLS Yearbook, 1972, 61. See Harvard Law School, *Handbook for Entering Students 1970* (Cambridge, MA, 1970), 61.

118. Quotation is from "Fenno," *HLSR* (October 5, 1973): 10.

119. HLS Yearbook, 1975, 209.

120. HLS Yearbook, 1975, 209.

121. HLS Yearbook, 1976, 218.

122. Quotations are from "Law School Council," HLS Yearbook, 1976, 218.

123. Harvard Law School, *Handbook 1977,* 35.

124. David A. Demilo, "Law School Grads Boycott Fund Drive," *Harvard Crimson* (November 10, 1978).

125. Felix Frankfurter, "Some Observations on Third Year Work," in HLS Faculty Committee on Curriculum, Survey of the Harvard Law School Curriculum, 1934–35 (February 1, 1935), HLS Dean's Office Records, Records of President James B. Conant, 1933–1953, Harvard University Archives, vol. 2, 254–258.

126. *Harvard Law School: A View from the Bottom* (Cambridge, MA, 1969), 14–15. The study was done with Professor Alan Stone, M.D., who was a member of the faculty and a psychiatrist.

127. Charles R. Nesson, Memorandum to the HLS Committee on Educational Planning and Development (December 5, 1979), on file with the authors, 3.

128. See HLS Yearbook, 1980, 203, 213, 218; 1981, 219.

129. HLS Yearbook, 1971, 234–236; 1981, 197.

130. HLS Yearbook, 1976, 179.

131. HLS Yearbook, 1971, 224–226; 1980, 222–223; 1981, 204–205.

132. Harvard Law School, *Handbook 1977,* 32.

133. HLS Yearbook, 1980, 207. This was the first yearbook appearance for the Asian Law Students Association. The first Asian American faculty member appointed to tenure track at the Law School was Jeannie C. Suk Gersen (J.D. 2002), who was appointed in 2006 and tenured in 2011. In April, 2017 a second Asian American was elected to tenure, Mark Wu.

134. Quotations are from Harvard Law School, *Handbook 1970,* 55–57, 63–64.

135. HLS Yearbook, 1971, 216–217; Lincoln's Inn, Annual Report, 1998–99, on file with the authors, 3. See Cale Keable, "A History of the Lincoln's Inn Society" (student research paper, HLS, 2001), on file with the authors. The files of Lincoln's Inn were apparently discarded by the last members.

136. Harvard Law School, *Handbook 1970*, 60; HLS Yearbook, 1982, 197, 199, 209.

137. The cultural metaphor employed is of a shift from the "melting pot" to a "salad bowl." Bruce Schulman, *The Seventies: The Great Shift in American Culture, Society, and Politics* (Cambridge, MA, 2001), 68–72. See also Sarah M. Iler, "The History of 'Multicultural' in the United States during the Twentieth Century" (Ph.D. diss., Ohio State University, 2017), 161–164.

138. HLS Yearbook, 1981, 18.

CHAPTER NINETEEN

Faculty Discord, 1970s and 1980s

The inability of the Michelman Committee to achieve significant reform, along with the struggles over gender and race, resulted from faculty discord during the term of Dean Albert Sacks (1971–1981). The Dissents and Separate Statements to the Michelman Report—from the faculty "left," centrists, and conservatives, as well as the student members—all attributed the failure of the three-year planning process to conflicts among the professors.[1] And these conflicts arose, said the Dissents and Statements, from the composition of the regular faculty, which was determined by faculty hiring.[2]

Although Sacks resigned as dean before the worst of the bitter faculty disputes during the 1980s, he has been held responsible for making these conflicts inevitable by acquiescing to politicized faculty appointments. Sacks "wasn't a fighter . . . , which you would have to be," observed Charles Fried, along with many others interviewed for this volume. President Derek Bok (1971–1991) indirectly said the same thing.[3] The implicit accusation is that Sacks allowed a partisan faculty group—particularly those aligned with Critical Legal Studies (CLS)—to gain veto power over appointments and thereby to advance their political agenda within the school by voting in a bloc along ideological, rather than meritocratic, lines. Is this borne out by the historical record?

Griswold's Departures and Bok's Arrivals

The first point to consider is the timeline of the appointment process. In early fall, the dean of the Law School usually named an Appointments Committee, which solicited or received applications for regular faculty positions, evaluated candidates during the fall, and made recommendations to the faculty in January or February. If the recommendations were approved, negotiations began with the candidate, and new appointees started teaching in the following fall or, often, a year after that. In addition, the candidate sometimes had an initial visiting appointment, permitting a review on both sides before a mutual commitment was made. Hence, there was a lag time of at least one year, and often two or three years, between consideration by the Appointments Committee and the arrival of a new regular faculty member. Because Sacks became acting dean in January 1971 and permanent dean in June, the first full hiring cycle that he oversaw began in the fall of 1971. New faculty were appointed in the spring of 1972 and joined the faculty in the following fall. If the appointment involved a "visit," the earliest possibility to begin a regular position was in the fall of 1973.

Given these lag times, four developments transformed the composition of the regular faculty while Sacks was in office from 1971 to 1981: nineteen professors retired; six others resigned, including two white women and two African American men; fourteen tenure-track professors arrived; and ten professors were appointed laterally from another law school (several after a "look see" as a "visitor").[4] In sum, twenty-five regular faculty departed, and twenty-four joined, not including five assistant professors who were appointed by Sacks and arrived after James Vorenberg (1981–1989) became dean. Thus, Sacks barely managed to keep the number of regular faculty from shrinking due to all the departures. Compared to prior deanships, the gateway to the faculty became a revolving door during Sacks's decade as dean, with as many coming out as going in.

The stream of retirees changed the politics and demography of the faculty. All nineteen retirees were somewhat "conservative" in their politics, scholarship, and teaching, and all were white men who had served under Dean Erwin Griswold (1946–1967). The only exception was Elizabeth Owens, who generally held conservative views like the others.[5] If one wished to change the composition and ideology of the Harvard law faculty, Sacks's decade was a golden opportunity.

Far from seeking or seizing this opportunity, Sacks backed into it because he inherited ten incoming appointments between 1971 and 1973 that Dean Derek Bok (1968–1970) had previously made due to the lag time described above. The ten regular faculty who departed by 1973 were conservative. None of the incoming ten appointments, negotiated and approved by Bok, belonged on that side of the aisle.

Four of the ten were centrists: Laurence Tribe (LL.B. 1966), Lance Liebman (LL.B. 1967), Richard B. Stewart (LL.B. 1966), and Victor Brudney (visitor 1970–71, tenured 1971).[6] The other six were all left-leaning, if not radical. Three of these came through lateral professorial appointments: the new librarian, Morris Cohen (tenured 1971); Derrick Bell (lecturer 1969–1971, tenured 1971); and Gary Bellow (LL.B. 1960; visitor 1971–72, tenured 1972). The other three were assistant professors: Morton Horwitz (LL.B. 1967), appointed in 1970 (teaching fellow in 1968–1970); Duncan Kennedy appointed in 1971; and Roberto M. Unger (LL.M. 1970, S.J.D. 1976) appointed in 1972. Soon to become major intellectual and political leaders of the CLS movement, these three extended Harvard's jurisprudential influence on the left in a way not seen since the early Roscoe Pound (1916–1936), Felix Frankfurter (LL.B. 1906), and Dean James Landis (1937–1946) had enraged conservative alumni.

The departure of Griswold's colleagues and the arrival of Bok's appointees set the stage for the raw politics of faculty appointments and promotions in the Sacks period. According to the long-standing process, all regular faculty voted on entry-level appointments, and only tenured professors voted on cases of promotion to tenure. Furthermore, the convention "was that, if a substantial minority were opposed to an appointment, it wouldn't be made," particularly if those opposed taught the same field of law as the candidate. And voting was done openly before the rest of the faculty. Consequently, even though the meetings were closed and the voting records confidential, it quickly became known throughout the school who opposed whom.[7]

In addition, promotion votes were technically just recommendations. The dean participated in the faculty discussion, evaluated the voted outcome, and decided whether to give his endorsement before forwarding it to the president and the Harvard Corporation. The Corporation made the final decision, but normally concurred with the recommendation of the faculty and the dean, so the tenured faculty usually held the power to determine their own composition in the future. The president and the Corporation sometimes refused to follow the faculty's preference, as in the appointment controversies of the late nineteenth century.[8] Such challenges resulted most often when the dean did not endorse the faculty's view, as happened when President A. Lawrence Lowell (1909–1933) rejected certain Jewish faculty candidates due to the lukewarm support by Dean Roscoe Pound.[9] Standing between the faculty and the president, the dean thus played a critical role in shaping and evaluating the faculty's vote.

A "Substantial Minority"

The dean's critical role was magnified by the "substantial minority" rule, because traditionally "it was left to the dean to decide what was 'a substantial minority,'" Vorenberg recalled. "That worked fine when Griswold was dean and nobody was interested in fighting with him about what was a substantial minority." Dean Griswold "would just decide how many people" made "a substantial minority."[10] But Al Sacks was universally known as a "nice guy," who wished to avoid conflict and angering anyone.[11] Amid the faculty dissension in the 1970s, Dean Sacks had to decide whether to quash an appointment or promotion because "a substantial minority" of faculty objected, and "that was not a good way to proceed in the kind of atmosphere we had," Vorenberg remarked.[12]

The school's personnel records are currently closed to researchers, so it is impossible to determine whether Sacks simply acquiesced to disputed appointments. But it is significant that every one of the fourteen assistant professors considered for promotion during his term was approved—apart from Diane Lund (LL.B. 1961) and Sally Neely, who withdrew before their consideration for tenure. Likewise, all ten lateral appointments to visiting positions and then to tenured faculty were approved, apart from Ruth Bader Ginsburg (1956–1958) and Mary Ann Glendon. Amid the great discord on the faculty between 1971 and 1981, these patterns suggest that Sacks did not exercise the "substantial minority" rule on any kind of regular faculty appointments and went along with the prevailing majority.

Richard Parker's (J.D. 1970) account of his promotion to tenured professor is an example. In the fall of 1978, the Appointments Committee evaluated Parker, who was allied with CLS at the time. The Committee agreed that he was a superb teacher, but voted 4–3 to postpone the promotion decision for a year because he had not published any scholarly work. The four voting to postpone were Dean Sacks, Richard Stewart, Paul Bator (LL.B. 1956), and Arthur Miller (LL.B. 1958), according to Parker, who agreed with their decision.[13]

In the following fall of 1979, when Parker's case was reconsidered, he still had not published an article, although the *Harvard Law Review* had accepted his essay entitled "Political Vision and Constitutional Argument." But he was dissatisfied with the long, "airy" essay and withdrew it.[14] Nevertheless, the Appointments Committee was apparently going to recommend Parker positively for tenure, when President Bok involved himself for the first time in the Law School appointments process. According to Vorenberg, who was on the Appointments Committee at that point,

> Derek came over and met with the Appointments Committee, . . . saying that he wanted some substantial writing [from a candidate] and thought the faculty was making a mistake. . . . I can visualize the meeting in which this was discussed. And my recollection is that Derek was less concerned with the Parker appointment as such, than with what was going to happen afterwards. He wanted to establish a principle that there should be some writing, and it should be evaluated by somebody other than just internally by the faculty.[15]

In any event, Parker was promoted to tenured professor in the fall of 1979, and he published his first article in 1981, on a different subject.[16]

This case suggests, in several respects, that Sacks could not bring himself to stop any appointment or promotion by exercising his decanal judgment about "a substantial minority," as Griswold did. First, Sacks would not block a candidate who had no publications, even one allied with CLS, as Parker was at that time. Second, Sacks would not do so even though the president clearly would have supported the dean. Furthermore, the fact that President Bok remarkably interjected himself into the law faculty appointment process and assumed the gatekeeping role that the dean normally played suggests that by 1979 Bok believed that Sacks was unwilling to exercise decanal oversight and was simply concurring with the faculty majority.

Finally, Parker—a young white man with all the blue-chip credentials of *Harvard Law Review* membership and a Supreme Court clerkship—was essentially excused from the conventional, though not universal, criterion of scholarly publication. Contemporaneously, women whom Sacks genuinely supported were being delayed, forced out, or rejected because their collegiality or teaching did not fit the manly, Spartan norms of the Law School. In either kind of case, Sacks did not buck the faculty majority. Rather than fight, he would, at most, postpone a decision, as he did with Parker and Ruth Bader Ginsburg, to avoid offending anyone—except the women who were let go.

Leftward Ho!

In the years following 1971–72, the law faculty continued tilting leftward during Sacks's administration. In 1972 the appointment of Diane Lund and John H. Ely, who was tenured in 1973 after a visiting appointment, added two more to the left. In 1973, due to faculty dissension, no new appointments of regular faculty were made, but in 1974 the appointments of Lewis D. Sargentich (J.D. 1970) and Richard Parker increased the CLS contingent by two. In 1975 the appointment of Sally Neely added another left-leaning vote, and conservatives Hal Scott and Douglas Ginsburg, graduates of the University of Chicago, were also appointed. Harry Edwards, a conservative African American, arrived in 1975 as a visitor, but then resigned in 1977 after one year as a tenured professor, and he is not included in the following counts.

As of 1975, these were the tallies of new appointments to the regular faculty since 1971: eleven leaning left (six named by Bok, five by Sacks), four centrists (Tribe, Brudney, Liebman, and Stewart), and two conservatives (Scott and Ginsburg). To be sure, individuals had complex ideological commitments that sometimes shifted and crossed boundaries. For example, Richard Parker identified with the left until 1987, and Charles Fried, a conservative intellectual, was a principal supporter of Morton Horwitz, a major CLS intellectual. "Many of us were very interested in making this a more intellectual place, and Morty seemed exactly the right person for that," Fried said.[17] Also, people within the same camp sharply criticized each other. Nevertheless, the distinct political orientations did exist.

In 1976 the faculty once again could not agree on any appointments of regular faculty. In 1977 the left gained one through the appointment Elizabeth Bartholet (LL.B. 1965), but lost two through the resignations of Lund and Neely. The center increased by two with the tenure-track appointment of economist A. Mitchell Polinsky and the lateral appointment of Clyde Ferguson (LL.B. 1951). In 1978 Sacks recruited future dean Robert Clark (LL.B. 1972) from Yale on a lateral appointment, giving the conservatives their leader for years to come.[18] Also, Martha Field was hired to the tenured faculty on the left, and Todd Rakoff (J.D. 1975) and David Rosenberg in the center, if not the right. The resignation of Derrick Bell also cost the left a vote.

In 1980, faculty discord prevented any regular appointments for the third year of the decade. "Everyone agrees that the appointments problem is a very serious one," stated Phillip Areeda (LL.B. 1954), and even the student newspaper, the *Harvard Law Record*, discussed the stalemate.[19] Heading into Dean Sacks's final year, the scorecard of new appointments to the regular faculty read: thirteen on the left, though three (Lund, Neely, and Bell) had stepped down, leaving eleven; eight on the center (Tribe, Liebman, Brudney, Stewart, Ferguson, Polinsky, Rakoff, and, at the time, Rosenberg); and three on the right (Scott, Ginsburg, and Clark).[20]

In 1981 the logjam broke, as five new assistant professors were hired. Four leaned left: Claire Dalton, Christopher Edley Jr. (J.D. 1978), Susan Estrich (J.D. 1977), and Martha Minow. Only one, Steven Shavell, a "law and economics" appointment, tilted to the right.[21] Given the struggles to make any appointments in the barren years of 1973, 1976, and 1980, this was an extraordinary hiring year for Sacks, particularly in adding three women and an African American man to the regular faculty. In addition, Gerald E. Frug (LL.B. 1963), a CLS supporter, was appointed laterally to tenure later in 1981, and two lecturers clearly on the left, David Kennedy (J.D. 1980) and Daniel K. Tarullo, were appointed and eventually moved to the tenure-track faculty. In the late 1980s, Kennedy and Tarullo became the focus of tenure disputes, along with Clare Dalton.

These new arrivals—part of the legacy of Sacks, who did not resign until the fall of 1981—shifted the political math of the faculty significantly, because all but one were on the left. As of 1982 the new regular appointments made during Sacks's term or by his authority tallied seventeen leaning left, eight in the center, and four conservatives. The net gain of thirteen votes on the left transformed the composition of the faculty, and these appointees, together with existing allies on the faculty, such as Charles Nesson (LL.B. 1963) and Vern Countryman, gave the left an effective veto over new appointments. This was due to two changes in the appointment process made under Dean Vorenberg.

Whereas Griswold had embraced the discretion of deciding when "a substantial minority" of the faculty opposed a faculty appointment and therefore when to stop it, Sacks hesitated to exercise that discretion. Vorenberg therefore changed the appointments process soon after he assumed the office. "I decided that in the kind of atmosphere we had . . . I didn't want to make that call" about what constituted "a substantial minority." Instead, "I said we would do with the two-thirds vote. I did that fairly earlier in my deanship." Then, "shortly after that," the faculty "went to a secret ballot."[22]

The first change meant that if a candidate received a two-thirds vote of the faculty for appointment, the dean was bound to recommend the appointment to the Corporation, regardless of how strongly the minority objected or the dean felt. Conversely, control of one-third-plus-one votes barred an appointment. The result was to encourage bloc voting and to eliminate deference to the faculty experts in the candidate's specialty. The second change, the secret ballot, also undercut individual discretion and accountability. The prior, open-vote system required that one justify one's vote before the faculty. The secret ballot meant that a particular group could decide to vote together to bar a candidate, even in advance of the faculty meeting—a tactic that also obviated genuine discussion at the faculty meetings.

Relying on their proportional increase achieved under Sacks and these procedural changes introduced under Vorenberg, those on the left effectively exercised a veto during the 1980s, while the bitter divisions among the faculty turned the school's appointment process into "grim trench warfare."[23] Confrontation with President Derek Bok and the Corporation was inevitable, and came to a head with Claire Dalton's highly controversial promotion and tenure review in 1988. CLS supporters pulled out all the stops, even paying to fly Richard Parker back from Greece, first-class, in order to vote in favor of Dalton. But she "failed by a small margin to get a two-thirds vote," according to Vorenberg. Nevertheless, given the majority vote in favor, the faculty's recommendation for promotion was forwarded to President Bok. He then appointed an external *ad hoc* committee of "fourteen outside experts" to evaluate Dalton's case, and the Corporation ultimately turned down Dalton's promotion to tenure. The president had essentially taken over the appointment process from the Law School. This "was a very unhappy time for me," said Dean Vorenberg, and he stepped down in the following year.[24]

Sacks certainly did not intend to encourage this trench warfare or confrontation. If any reasonable accusation can be made against Sacks and his record on faculty appointments, it is that he recoiled from personal acrimony and avoided imposing his judgment. According to Charles Fried, "Al was a man who understood a great deal. He was superbly intelligent, and in some respects he was much better than Jim Vorenberg. . . . He was more of an intellectual, he read more. . . . He could see [what] was pure propaganda, and he saw this in a number of situations. But he wasn't a fighter. He wasn't willing to be a son of a bitch, which you would have to be."[25] Sacks was a genuine, kindly liberal. No contemporary ever charged him with judging appointment candidates on anything but intellectual merit.

Rise of the Crits

This volume has stressed the intellectually aggressive edge to the culture at Harvard Law School, dating back to James Barr Ames's practice of the Socratic pedagogy introduced by Dean Langdell (1870–1895).[26] Ingrained in the culture, this aggressive edge made faculty disputes during the 1980s "more bitter and more public."[27] The intellectual swordfights intensified due to fundamental disagreements about the ideology and mission of the school and the composition of the faculty.

Over the decade after Griswold departed in 1967, the disagreement and divisiveness slowly heated up. On January 17, 1977, an "organizing committee" of nine professors at various law schools sent a letter to faculty at law schools around the country proposing "a gathering of colleagues who are pursuing a critical approach toward the study of law in society." Five of the nine members of the "organizing committee" taught or would teach at Harvard Law School. Three were current professors: Duncan Kennedy, Morton Horwitz, and Roberto Unger. In 1986–87 David M. Trubek joined the faculty as a visitor, and would later be denied a tenured appointment after a disputed promotion case.[28] Another signatory, Mark Tushnet, joined the faculty much later, in 2005.[29]

The gathering in 1977 gave rise to a continuing series of annual conferences and to the intellectual and political movement of CLS, whose adherents were known as "Crits." Like most emerging intellectual movements, its exact definition was elusive, particularly given that the Crits argued passionately among themselves. By 1984 "there had been nine, large, national meetings of this once tiny conference, [and] innumerable 'summer camps' and workshops where newcomers and founders alike argue obsessively," observed Mark Kelman, a leading CLS scholar at Stanford Law School. "Yet it was still a fair question whether anyone knew what 'critical legal studies' meant."[30]

Within Harvard Law School, however, the CLS movement was more firmly anchored and defined, due partly to its foundation in legal history. In 1977 Morton Horwitz published *The Transformation of American Law, 1780–1860,* which won the Bancroft Prize in American history in 1978. The following year Duncan Kennedy published a major article, "The Structure of Blackstone's Commentaries" in the *Buffalo Law Review.* Both of these studies of American legal history followed the critical approach to orthodox legal theory introduced by their Law School colleague, Roberto Unger, in his groundbreaking *Law in Modern Society: Toward a Criticism of Social Theory,* published in 1976.[31]

In brief, all three of these works drew upon legal realism and modern literary scholarship, particularly the "deconstruction" of texts. Unger argued that the widely accepted "liberal" and "scientific" tenets of fairness, objectivity, and fidelity to rules and laws were illusory or eroding. He went so far as to write that "legalism and terrorism, the commitment to rules and the seduction of violence, are rival brothers, but brothers nonetheless."[32]

According to Horwitz and Kennedy, historical legal "formalism" rested on the fiction that legal doctrines were "value neutral" and "scientific." In fact, the courts actually formulated doctrines that advanced certain economic and political goals and favored, deliberately or not, the interests of particular social classes, particularly the wealthy and those who control capital. The initial CLS call of January 17, 1977, stated, "If there is a single theme, it is that law is an instrument of social, economic, and political domination, both in . . . furthering the concrete interests of the dominators and in . . . legitimating the existing order."[33]

Viewed within the larger academic context, this CLS critique was one expression of a broad, contemporaneous, critical assault on university professional schools, professions, and the very idea of professionalism, as discussed in the Introduction to this volume. In terms of jurisprudence, some legal scholars maintained that CLS merely recapitulated the thinking of Oliver W. Holmes Jr. (LL.B. 1866) and the early Roscoe Pound.[34] Others, mostly conservative critics, protested vigorously against CLS. The dean of Duke University Law School, Paul Carrington (LL.B. 1955), asserted: "Some of our colleagues may be heard to say, 'law is a mere deception by which the powerful weaken the resistance of the powerless.' . . . The professionalism . . . of lawyers does not require rejection of Legal Realism and its lesson that who decides also matters. What it cannot abide is the embrace of nihilism and its lesson that who decides is everything, and principle nothing but cosmetic."[35]

Although these disagreements might enliven faculty workshops and summer retreats, they would not tear an institution apart. What brought the decade-long, simmering disagreements at Harvard Law School to a boil? It was precisely the deliberations of the Michelman Committee, which had been charged with formulating "judgments and recommendations as to the future direction of the School's educational activities."[36] This was the opportunity for CLS to institute concrete reforms. Even as the Michelman Committee was drafting its first installment on fundamental institutional goals, Kennedy circulated his dissent, "Utopian Proposal on Law School as a Counterhegemonic Enclave," in April 1980, and delivered a talk at the Harvard Faculty Club titled "Alternative System of Legal Education" in March 1981. He then published his provocative "little red book," *Legal Education and the Reproduction of Hierarchy*, in 1982.[37]

Following the analysis of Unger and Horwitz, Kennedy argued that, far from being neutral, most legal doctrines are tools of economic exploitation and political power. Furthermore, students who accept their teachers' views

Duncan Kennedy. Faculty 1971–2015, who was Carter Professor of General Jurisprudence, 1996–2015. See portrait of James C. Carter in Chapter 2.

get high grades, and those who challenge them are penalized. If faculty are appointed based on the "objective" criteria of class rank, *Law Review* membership, top federal clerkships, and so on, those appointments simply reproduce a hierarchy of established political and economic values.

The only course of remedial action, according to the Crits, was straightforward. Harvard Law School graduates had enormous influence. If progressives could be recruited, appointed, and promoted to tenure, then social justice would advance throughout the country. The creative minds required for such appointments might or might not have the top grades and credentials of the traditional elite. New criteria, incorporating political and ideological beliefs, were needed for faculty appointment and promotion.

At Harvard Law School, the CLS argument had three ominous implications for the existing regime. First, it undercut the traditional standards of academic merit. Second, it attacked the legitimacy of the tenured faculty's own credentials. Finally, it challenged what the orthodox faculty were teaching their students. Now the academic arguments felt like personal attacks on particular members of the faculty and long-standing policies of the school. In the words of Morton and Phyllis Keller, the Crits "laid claim to an academic purity that their more workaday colleagues found difficult to challenge. The result was an ever greater loss of community. . . . The Crits and their enemies waged aerial dogfights over legal philosophy, while grim trench warfare went on below over admissions, appointments, and curriculum."[38] Meanwhile, as Molly Burke (J.D. 1982) observed, the faculty lost sight of "the best interests of the students," who hunkered down and just tried to complete their degrees.[39]

The Right Responds

In 1981 the CLS challenge was mounting. A tired and ailing Dean Sacks was preparing to step down, the Law School faculty was gridlocked, and the Michelman Committee began wrapping up its deliberations amid a flurry of Dissents and Separate Statements. Outside of the Law School, the inauguration of President Ronald Reagan solidified the rise of the New Right in reaction to the left-leaning activism of the 1960s. That political and cultural development directly impacted the Law School, as a powerful conservative advocate, John M. Olin, came to the same basic conclusions as the Crits: first, that legal study was not inherently neutral as to policy; second, that the faculties molded the ideology at their schools; and finally, that control of the faculties at the elite law schools, particularly Harvard Law School, shaped the nature of the bench, the bar, and legal education in the United States. "The importance of Harvard Law School is difficult to overstate. At the dawn of the twenty-first century, five of the nine Supreme Court justices had attended it, along with nine senators, 28 percent of the managing partners in top-fifty law firms, and 16 percent of America's law-school professors (with an even higher percentage at first-tier law schools)."[40]

Olin was one of the wealthiest men in America, and he set out to curtail the influence of left-wing intellectuals in legal education by creating a "counter-intelligentsia." The strategy was to generously support young, right-leaning scholars, particularly those devoted to the philosophy of Milton Friedman and the conservative "law and economics" school at the University of Chicago, the no-longer-realist Yale Law School, and elsewhere. Thus the John M. Olin Foundation was born, and it funded programs primarily at Yale, Stanford, and

Harvard, contributing more than $18 million to the Law and Economics Program at Harvard alone.[41]

In 1979 Alan M. Polinksy, an economist and an assistant professor at Harvard Law, left the school to become director of the Olin Program in Law and Economics at Stanford Law School. After the Olin Foundation made an initial grant of $1 million to establish the Program of Law and Economics at Harvard, the Law School in 1981 appointed Steven Shavell, a young conservative, as assistant professor and director of the new program. Promoted and tenured in 1982, Shavell did not initially find a sympathetic audience. At Harvard, "law and economics had not penetrated the curriculum the way it had at Chicago, and the entire movement was ostracized."[42] "It was ludicrous," Shavell stated. "Almost nothing was more politically incorrect. Students would hiss in the classroom. The climate was simply unbelievable."[43] But over the next decade, graduates from Law and Economics Programs at Harvard and elsewhere joined law faculties across the country.

Meanwhile, the Olin Foundation also supported a conference of conservative students that grew into the Federalist Society, which became a leading affinity group at elite law schools and a key credential for advancement in conservative presidential administrations, including those of George W. Bush and Donald Trump.[44] At Harvard, the Federalist Society in 1985 published the volume *A Discussion on Critical Legal Studies at the Harvard Law School*, which influenced the perception of Harvard law alumni about CLS.[45]

In addition, in 1980 another conservative group, the Institute of Education Affairs, chaired by William E. Simon, a Republican businessman and secretary of the Treasury under President Richard Nixon, began a conservative student newspaper at the University of Chicago. Seeing the advantage of this venture, the Olin Foundation in March 1982 pledged $6,000 to support the *Harvard Journal of Law and Public Policy*, a right-leaning student journal founded in the summer of 1978.[46] In the very same month, that journal joined with the Federalist Societies at Chicago and Yale and the right-leaning Stanford Foundation for Law and Public Policy to sponsor a "Symposium on Federalism," aided by a subvention of $15,000 from the Institute of Education Affairs.[47]

During the 1980s the Olin effort achieved its goal of counterbalancing the 1970s leftward shift of the law faculty and students, at least at Harvard. For example, Supreme Court Justice Neil Gorsuch (J.D. 1991) and former Associate Attorney General Rachel Brand (J.D. 1998) were active with the *Harvard Journal of Law and Public Policy* and the Federalist Society when they were students at the Law School. In fact, "by 2000 the Law and Economics movement—in intellectual style and political subtext the polar opposite of CLS—could claim greater intellectual standing in academic law, much as did the rational choice approach in political science, and sociobiology and its physiological-neurological offshoots in psychology and anthropology," according to Morton and Phyllis Keller.[48]

Meanwhile, President Bok also concluded that CLS influence at the Law School had to be contained, as did others on the law faculty and elsewhere.[49] Dean Sacks may have been unwilling or unable to do this, but he certainly did not intend to leave a toxic faculty dynamic to his successor. When Sacks stepped down and returned to the faculty, President Bok appointed James Vorenberg as the next dean, believing that he was "tough" and could "withstand the terrible pressures on the dean."[50] Similarly, as successor to Vorenberg, Bok appointed conservative Robert Clark (1989–2003), who "has always been willing to play hard ball in a way that Al [Sacks] never was," stated Charles Fried.[51]

Robert C. Clark, J.D. 1972. Faculty 1978 to present, Dean 1989–2003. Photograph by John Chapin, ca. 1980.

The "Struggle Session" Begins

At the end of his term, Dean Sacks wrote a short introduction to the 1981 *Yearbook*, and began by quoting the "Chinese Curse of Doom": "May you live in an age of transition." Although this curse "stresses the insecurity and anxiety that usually accompany a period of rapid and substantial change," it "fails to invoke the sense of opportunity or achievement that may accompany such change," Sacks observed.[52] But he then acknowledged that the school's educational model had begun to "unravel" during his decade.[53] Critics, such as Joel Seligman, were harsher, stating that, under Sacks, the school experienced "dissolution and then drift."[54]

Robert Clark, later to become dean, attributed the unraveling and drift to a lack of planning and vision in the Sacks administration.

> There didn't seem to be any big vision or plan about what to do. It was all just problem-solving. As things come up, you deal with them in a wise and thoughtful way, as if being a dean was like being a judge: You wait for the problem, and then you make the best decision and reason about it and handle it properly. . . . From my point of view as the dean, it all seems very strange. Why didn't they have some set of goals for the money or the buildings or the faculty size? I don't think I ever heard them talking about . . . appointment objectives . . . in terms of numbers, subject matters, or mix. Nobody thought in terms of a total. It was all just one thing after another.[55]

In sum, although Dean Sacks was personally admired, if not beloved, by faculty, staff and students alike, his decanal record is mixed at best. Certainly Sacks faced severe financial constraints, both within and without the school. But fundraising during his administration was weak. It was a mistake to retain Wesley Bevins (LL.B. 1948) as director of the Law School Fund, and he was later retired by Vorenberg. Also, Sacks's inability to inspire major alumni donors was a critical shortcoming. To obtain only one (relatively small) major gift of less than $250,000 over a decade was a disaster.

These shortcomings contributed to the dramatic hikes in tuition, which created a significant barrier to pursuing public service employment. Sacks was slow to respond, and after the Low Income Protection Plan (LIPP) and a loan forgiveness program were finally instituted, he observed in 1981 that the students' response was "disappointing."[56] In fact, raising tuition without also establishing programs to address the impact on admissions, diversity, and career

James Vorenberg, LL.B. 1951. Faculty 1962–2000, Dean 1981–1989, and
Martha L. Minow, Faculty 1981–Present, Dean 2009–2013.
Courtesy of Harvard Law School Library, Historical & Special Collections.

choice was worse than "disappointing"—it was irresponsible. Only after Vorenberg was named dean did serious efforts begin to address the deterrent to
students entering public service.[57]

Despite the steep tuition increases, Sacks did leave a significantly more diverse student body in terms of gender, but not in other dimensions. The last
class admitted under Sacks was approximately 22 percent women, 7 percent
African American, and 4 percent other persons of color. Also, Sacks made little
progress in diversifying the regular faculty, though he did succeed in appointing
three women and one African American man as tenure-track assistant professors as he departed in 1981. In terms of the academic program, Sacks tried to
advance Bok's vision of incorporating clinical legal education into the formal
curriculum of the school.[58] His major initiative of establishing the Michelman
Committee came far too late in his deanship, and the work of that committee,
ironically, catalyzed the faculty acrimony during the 1980s.

After the Michelman Committee had submitted its various documents to
the dean and faculty in the spring of 1982, Frank Michelman sent a memo to
the faculty in mid-September announcing a series of four faculty meetings and

a retreat to be held for two days at a hotel in late October to discuss different parts of the Report.[59] On October 12, Dean Vorenberg sent out a proposed agenda for the retreat, which was followed by a flurry of faculty memos, some incorporating invective and profanity, that doomed any prospect of constructive discussion.[60]

To cite a mild example, Morton Horwitz's memo entitled "Some Pre-Retreat Observations" decried the school's history "of a homogenous faculty using illegitimate social and intellectual pressures" and stated that "success in the institution was dependent on subordination to one's seniors and nasty domination of one's juniors."[61] Two days later, in a responding memo, Paul Bator wrote that "if fraying of our social and intellectual bonds are the problem then the tone, vocabulary, and (above all) methodology of [Horwitz's] memo seem to me to constitute part of the problem, not part of the solution."[62]

It is not known whether or which faculty memos went to the student members of the Michelman Committee. But as these volleys were flying back and forth among the faculty, student Molly Burke circulated her insightful and strident "Separate Statement" maintaining that the faculty had lost sight of "the best interests of the students."[63] Meanwhile, Charles Fried, echoing Charles Nesson's "Separate Statement" of April 1982, adopted a moderate and positive tone.

> I believe a major problem in our communal life has surfaced in the last five or more years arising out of the emergence for the first time of distinct schools of thought within the faculty. The sharpness of the issues is increased because these schools of thought are pervasive, going not just to convictions about specific legal issues, but to broad philosophical differences regarding the function of law, the purpose of the law school, the nature of society, politics, the meaning of life, etc. . . . My guess is that it is a change for the better, signaling a deeper, more reflective stance towards our common enterprise. Be that as it may, it is here to stay.[64]

Despite Fried's hopeful note, the October retreat "unraveled."[65] It came to be known as the "Struggle Session," and revealed that no systematic or thoughtful discussion of the Michelman Report's recommendations was going to occur— not then, and not ever.[66]

Still in his first year as dean, Vorenberg was taken aback by "the bitterness with which people hated one another. The level of hatred hit me like a ton of bricks." The chief "protagonists" were "four or five people," who had "a willingness, which I had never seen before, to say and do things that might be damaging to the School, . . . or might be damaging to colleagues. And it really surprised me."[67] The Michelman Committee recommendations, issued after three years of deliberations, thus signaled the end of the liberal spirit of Dean Sacks's administration. The "Struggle Session," begun in October 1982, would continue through 1989, when Vorenberg stepped down, and beyond.

NOTES

1. Quotations are from, respectively, Charles Nesson, "Separate Statement" (from the Report of the Committee on Educational Planning and Development) (April 26, 1982), on file with the authors; Duncan Kennedy, "Dissent from the Report of the Committee on Educational Planning and Development" (April 5, 1982), on file with the authors, 1. See David L. Shapiro, "Separate Statement" (from the Report of the Committee on Educational Planning and Development) (February 4, 1981), on file with the authors, 1; Molly Burke, "Separate Statement" (from the Report of the Committee on Educational Planning and Development) (October 14, 1982), on file with the authors, 3.

2. See Harvard Law School Committee on Educational Planning and Development (CEPD), "The Present State and Future Direction of Legal Education at Harvard" (April 21, 1982), on file with the authors, 25–31; Kennedy, "Dissent," 37–41.

3. Quotation is from Charles Fried, Oral History, conducted by Daniel R. Coquillette and Mary Beth Basile (August 2000–March 2001), on file with the authors. See Derek C. Bok, Oral History, conducted by Daniel R. Coquillette and Daniel Hamilton (February 2002), on file with the authors; Morton Keller and Phyllis Keller, *Making Harvard Modern: The Rise of America's University* (New York, 2001), 439–440; Joel Seligman, *The High Citadel: The Influence of Harvard Law School* (Boston, 1978), 1–19.

4. The six faculty who resigned from the tenure track, rather than retired, during this period were Diane Lund (1976), Harry Edwards (1977), Sally Neely (1979), Derrick Bell (1980), Alan Polinsky (1979), and Morris Cohen (1981). Derek Bok (1971) retained his appointment while serving as university president. Resignations and appointments have been calculated by consulting the official faculty appointments list in Harvard Law School, "Officers of Instruction and Administration," *Alumni Directory* (Cambridge, MA, 2001), 18–50; and *Harvard Law School Yearbooks* and the HLS Catalogs during the Sacks administration.

5. Arthur E. Sutherland, *The Law at Harvard: A History of Ideas and Men, 1817–1967* (Cambridge, MA, 1967), 373–379.

6. Laurence H. Tribe, Oral History, conducted by Daniel R. Coquillette and Andrew D. Klaber (September 2008), on file with the authors, in which Tribe sets out his "centrist"

position. "And there were very few. I was one of the very few who sort of had a foot in each camp. I wasn't identifiably one or the other. I sometimes agreed with the Crits, sometimes didn't. I made enemies all around, very upset with me that I wasn't on their side."

7. Quotation is from James Vorenberg, Oral History, conducted by Daniel R. Coquillette (November–December 1997), on file with the authors. Due to the University's eighty-year seal on faculty minutes concerning appointments, we have had to rely on oral histories for this important procedure.

8. Daniel R. Coquillette and Bruce A. Kimball, *On the Battlefield of Merit: Harvard Law School, the First Century* (Cambridge, MA, 2015), 89, 120n47, 389–402; Kimball, "The Principle, Politics, and Finances of Establishing Academic Merit as the Standard of Hiring for the Teaching of Law as a Career, 1870–1900," *Law & Social Inquiry* 31 (2006): 617–648; Albert M. Sacks, "A Time of Ferment and Change," HLS Yearbook, 1981, 17–18.

9. See Chapter 4.

10. James Vorenberg, Oral History conducted by Daniel R. Coquillette (November–December 1997), on file with the authors.

11. Quotation is from Keller and Keller, *Making Harvard Modern*, 439–440. See Vorenberg, Oral History (November–December 1997); Charles Fried, Oral History, conducted by Daniel R. Coquillette and Mary Beth Basile (August 2000–March 2001), on file with the authors; Bok, Oral History.

12. Vorenberg, Oral History (November–December 1997).

13. Quotations are from Richard D. Parker, Oral History, conducted by Daniel R. Coquillette and Daniel Pincus (June 2010), on file with the authors.

14. Parker, Oral History (June 2010).

15. Vorenberg, Oral History (November–December 1997).

16. Parker, Oral History (June 2010).

17. Parker, Oral History (June 2010); Charles Fried, Oral History, conducted by Daniel R. Coquillette and Mary Beth Basile (August 2000–March 2001), on file with the authors.

18. Robert C. Clark, Oral History, conducted by Daniel R. Coquillette, Mary Beth Basile, and Kristy Kirkpatrick (April 2003), on file with the authors.

19. Quoted in Michael Smith, "Appointments Difficult," HLSR (March 23, 1979): 1, 6–7, at 7.

20. These faculty allegiances were identified in Fried, Oral History (August 2000–March 2001); Vorenberg, Oral History (November–December 1997); Stephen Bernardi, Oral History, conducted by Daniel Hamilton and Daniel R. Coquillette (October 2000–April 2001), on file with the authors; Parker, Oral History (June 2010); Steven Shavell, Oral History, conducted by Daniel R. Coquillette (February 2012).

21. Shavell, Oral History (February 2012).

22. Vorenberg, Oral History (November–December 1997).

23. Keller and Keller, *Making Harvard Modern*, 438.

24. Quotations are from Vorenberg, Oral History (November–December 1997). See Parker, Oral History (June 2010). On the appointment of an *ad hoc* committee, see Smith, "Appointments Difficult."

25. Fried, Oral History (August 2000–March 2001).

26. Bruce A. Kimball, "*Warn Students That I Entertain Heretical Opinions, Which They Are Not To Take as Law:* The Inception of Case Method Teaching in the Classrooms of the Early C.C. Langdell, 1870–1883," *Law & History Review* 17 (1999): 74–75.

27. David Margolick, "The Split at Harvard Law Goes Down to Its Foundation," *New York Times* (October 6, 1985).

28. Mark Kelman, *A Guide to Critical Legal Studies* (Cambridge, MA, 1987), 297n1. On Trubek, see Vorenberg, Oral History (November–December 1997). To Vorenberg's disappointment, Bok became involved in the Trubek matter as well as the Dalton promotion. "I didn't think the role he played in the Trubek one was a constructive role." Vorenberg, Oral History (November–December 1997).

29. Kelman, *A Guide,* 297n1.

30. Kelman, *A Guide,* 2. A useful "Program" of the movement and its members is provided by Kelman, whose *Guide to Critical Legal Studies* describes the intellectual leaders of the movement at length and their jurisprudence. See also Duncan Kennedy, "Critical Legal Studies," and Morton Horwitz, "Legal History," in *Legal Intellectuals in Conversation,* ed. James R. Hackney Jr. (New York, 2012), 19–45, 63–85; and Janet Halley, "Of Time and the Pedagogy of Critical Legal Studies," in *Legal Education and the Reproduction of the Hierarchy: A Polemic against the System,* ed. Duncan Kennedy (New York, 2007), 185–201; Robert W. Gordon, "Critical Legal Studies," *Legal Studies Forum* 10 (1986): 335–340. One of the best-known accounts of the movement was Calvin Trillin, "A Reporter at Large: Harvard Law School," *New Yorker* (March 26, 1984): 53–83. See also Harvard Society for Law and Public Policy and the Federalist Society, *A Discussion on Critical Legal Studies at the Harvard Law School* (Cambridge, MA, 1985), with an account of the famous debate at the Harvard Club of New York City on May 13, 1985, moderated by the Hon. Ralph K. Winter. We are also indebted to Dan Traficonte, "'Soul of This Institution': Faculty Conflict in the 1980s and the Making of Today's Harvard Law School" (student research paper, HLS, 2016), on file with the authors.

31. See Morton J. Horwitz, *The Transformation of American Law, 1870–1960: The Crisis of Legal Orthodoxy* (Oxford, 1992); Duncan Kennedy, "The Structure of Blackstone's Commentaries," *Buffalo Law Review* 28 (1979): 205–382; Roberto Unger, *Law in Modern Society: Toward a Criticism of Social Theory* (New York, 1976).

32. Roberto Unger, *Knowledge and Politics* (New York, 1975), 75.

33. Quoted in Kelman, *A Guide,* 297n. See Horwitz, *The Transformation of American Law, 1870–1960,* 17–30; Daniel R. Coquillette, *The Anglo-American Legal Heritage,* 2nd ed. (Durham, NC, 2004), 502, 562–569.

34. See Chapter 6, this volume; Coquillette, *Anglo-American Legal Heritage,* 502, 562–569.

35. Paul D. Carrington, "Of Law and the River," *Journal of Legal Education* 34 (1984): 227.

36. CEPD, "The Present State," chap. 1, 1. See Albert M. Sacks, Memorandum to HLS Faculty (February 12, 1979), on file with the authors, 1.

37. Here and below, see Duncan Kennedy, "Alternative Systems of Legal Education" (March 19, 1981), speech given at the Harvard Faculty Club, on file with the authors; Kennedy, *Legal Education;* Duncan Kennedy, "Cost-Benefit Analysis of Entitlement Programs: A Critique," *Stanford Law Review* 33 (1981): 587; Kelman, *A Guide,* 298n7; Duncan Kennedy, Oral History, conducted by Daniel R. Coquillette and Jay Hook (July 2013), on file with the authors.

38. Keller and Keller, *Making Harvard Modern,* 438.

39. Burke, "Separate Statement," 2.

40. John J. Miller, *A Gift of Freedom: How the John M. Olin Foundation Changed America* (San Francisco, 2006), 74.

41. Miller, *A Gift of Freedom,* 74–75.

42. Miller, *A Gift of Freedom,* 74–75.

43. Quoted in Miller, *A Gift of Freedom,* 75. See Shavell, Oral History (February 2012).

44. Miller, *A Gift of Freedom,* 89. See also George W. Hick, "Against the Grain: The Federalist Society and the Conservatization of the Harvard Law School Student Body" (student research paper, HLS, 2007), on file with the authors.

45. Robert Clark, Duncan Kennedy, Paul Bator, Abram Chayes, and Ralph K. Winter, *A Discussion on Critical Legal Studies at the Harvard Law School* (Cambridge, MA 1985). See also Hick, "Against the Grain" (Madison's silhouette was on the cover).

46. Miller, *A Gift of Freedom,* 88–89. By its own account, "Its distinguishing feature is that its editorial perspective is what may be generally characterized as conservative . . . to provide a forum of alternative to the liberal establishment law review perspectives." "Harvard Journal of Law and Public Policy," HLS Yearbook, 1979, 216.

47. Miller, *A Gift of Freedom,* 90. Later, conservative benefactor Irving Kristol would call this "the best money we ever spent at IEA" (90).

48. Keller and Keller, *Making Harvard Modern,* 437.

49. Bok, Oral History (February 2002). See Fried, Oral History (August 2000–March 2001); Vorenberg, Oral History (November–December 1997); Carrington, "Of Law and the River," 227.

50. Bok, Oral History (February 2002).

51. Fried, Oral History (August 2000–March 2001).

52. Sacks, "A Time of Ferment," 17.

53. Sacks, "A Time of Ferment," 18–19.

54. Seligman, *The High Citadel,* 1–19. See Fried, Oral History (August 2000–March 2001).

55. Clark, Oral History (April 2003).

56. Albert M. Sacks, Annual Report of the Dean of HLS, 1980–81, 273–274.

57. After 1982 the basic policy of LIPP was that, for students engaged in relatively low-paying public service employment, the school would cover law school debt and, eventually, even the college debt, "to enable students to imagine that they could afford the huge indebtedness that they had incurred coming to law school and to college before." Vorenberg, Oral History (November–December 1997). Vorenberg also observed that LIPP "was really a plan that was designed to promote diversity. In the process we felt we also needed more public interest at the university. We could make it possible for people to go back to small towns and the south . . . places that were not associated with big money in people's minds."

58. Sacks, "A Time of Ferment," 18–19.

59. See Frank I. Michelman, "Discussions of the COMEPD Report, September 22 and Beyond," Memorandum to the Faculty (September 15, 1982), on file with the authors, 1–2.

60. James Vorenberg, "Proposed Agenda for Faculty Retreat," Memorandum to faculty (October 12, 1982), on file with the authors.

61. See Morton J. Horwitz, "Some Pre-Retreat Observations," Memorandum to faculty (October 19, 1982), on file with the authors.

62. Paul Bator, "Horwitz Retreat Memo of 10/19/82," Memorandum to faculty (October 21, 1982), on file with the authors.

63. Burke, "Separate Statement," 1–2.

64. Charles Fried, Memorandum to the Faculty (October 15, 1982), on file with the authors, 1. See Nesson, "Separate Statement," 1–2.

65. Parker, Oral History (June 2010).

66. See Detlev Vagts, "Proposed 'Struggle Session' Tomorrow," Memorandum to faculty (October 22, 1982), on file with the authors, 1.

67. Vorenberg, Oral History (November–December 1997).

Conclusion

Some readers have considered our first volume, *On the Battlefield of Merit*, to be hypercritical and unappreciative of Harvard Law School. In fact, our thesis emphasized its influence by arguing that, in the nineteenth century, the school established the template for subsequent university professional schools in the United States. Likewise, this volume has maintained that Harvard Law School is arguably the most influential professional school in American history.

Its graduates include three U.S. presidents, ten attorneys general, twelve deputy attorneys general, eight solicitors general, twenty-three cabinet secretaries, nineteen governors, thirty-seven senators, and fifteen sitting congressmen. Seventeen justices of the Supreme Court attended the school, more than any other law school, including four of the current associate justices and the chief justice. Among its international graduates have been presidents of India, Taiwan, Ireland, Peru, and other countries.[1]

Despite its dismal record on race and gender, Harvard Law School graduated the first black judge, the first two black U.S. District Court judges, the first two black U.S. Court of Appeals judges, the second black cabinet secretary, the first black solicitor general, and the first black U.S. president. The first women to serve as attorney general, solicitor general, or secretary of two different cabinet departments also graduated from the Law School, as did the first Asian American federal judge, the first Asian American U.S. senator, and the first Jewish justice of the Supreme Court. The school has graduated the plurality of faculty at elite law schools and partners at leading law firms. Its impact on legal institutions, political life, and public policy in the United States is unrivaled among law schools or other professional schools.

Nevertheless, like *On the Battlefield of Merit*, this volume has not aimed to celebrate the school's history. Our intent has been to study that history in light of related social, economic, and political events during the twentieth century, including developments in American higher education, the professions and professional education, as well as race, gender, and ethnicity. We have therefore explained how the school's isomorphic influence continued during the twentieth century. In some respects that influence extended beyond law schools, as in the proliferation of case method teaching. But primarily the twentieth-century academic influence appeared in legal education, and this impact was widely recognized, even on very particular issues.

For example, at a Harvard Law School faculty meeting in December 1948 addressing the teaching of criminal law, David Cavers (LL.B. 1926) reported to his colleagues that Indiana University professor Jerome Hall, a graduate of the University of Chicago Law School and a distinguished expert on criminal law, had written to him on the subject. Hall had cautioned "that the Harvard Faculty's action in regard to [teaching] criminal law would have a serious impact upon the planning of other law schools," and Cavers "pointed out the faculty's broad responsibility in this regard."[2]

More generally, Harvard Law School impacted the domain of legal education through its struggle to cope with the interplay among three factors that form central themes in this volume: the sword-wielding, combative culture of academic exclusivity and elitism that became its hallmark over the course of the twentieth century; the severe financial constraints that intensified that culture; and the reluctance to admit, recruit, or welcome students and faculty who were not white, Christian men. Each of these factors had its own origins and determinants, but all three reinforced each other during the twentieth century, we have argued here.

Tuition Dependence Syndrome

During the twentieth century, the financial isomorphism derived from Harvard Law School became highly significant for legal education and fundamentally detrimental. In the first decade of the twentieth century, the Law School fell into the debilitating cycle of tuition dependence: high enrollment, high student-faculty ratio, illusion of prosperity, high fixed costs and debt, and little external support, as Dean Ezra Thayer (1910–1915) first recognized. Harvard's syndrome deepened under the subsequent deans, each of whom bemoaned the problem. Dean James Landis (1937–1946) was unable to solve it, and Deans Roscoe Pound (1916–1936) and Erwin Griswold (1946–1967) could have but did not. Skyrocketing tuition then exacerbated the syndrome under Deans Griswold and Albert Sacks (1971–1981).

The impact of this development on legal education was profound due to the size and eminence of Harvard Law School. If Harvard, the law school with the largest endowment in the world, depended so heavily on tuition reaped from huge classes, how could other law schools justify appeals for endowment, philanthropy, or subventions at their universities? Law schools therefore found it much more difficult to secure external support, compared to other major professional schools. Indeed, some universities treated their law schools as cash cows. Even Harvard Law School ran its first truly successful fund-raising campaign only in the 1990s, under the leadership of Robert Clark (1989–2003), the first Law School dean to successfully solicit major gifts, and Scott G. Nichols, head of development.[3] Due to that successful campaign, the 2000s offered a third opportunity to escape the syndrome.

Only a few exceptions to this syndrome existed in legal education. The most prominent was Yale Law School, whose very different educational and organizational model relied on large subsidies from its university over at least seventy years. It is doubtful that another law school—even small schools at well-endowed universities, such as Stanford, Chicago, or Cornell—could have enjoyed such large and long-term subsidies during the twentieth century. For most law schools, survival, while constrained by tuition dependence, required a large and ever-expanding pool of smart, well-educated, and hardworking applicants.

But what happens when the pool starts to dry up? Law schools are extremely vulnerable to a sharp decline in the number of such applicants. After the Great Recession of 2008, the market for new J.D.s sharply contracted, and the pool of talented applicants to law school shrank rapidly across the nation. In the five years following 2008, annual applications to law schools plummeted from over 100,000 to 60,000, and enrollments in law schools dropped from over 50,000 to about 37,500. Students who did enroll began taking on substantially more debt, and fewer entered the lower-paying field of legal services, while many law schools struggled to maintain their academic standards and balance their budgets. Many cut their enrollment.[4]

Precipitating this crisis in legal education was precisely the combination of high enrollment, high tuition, high student-faculty ratio, relatively low endowment, and little external support, which economist Ronald Ehrenberg described in 2013.[5] We have argued in this volume that the seeds of that vulnerability and the twenty-first century crisis were planted at Harvard Law School early in the twentieth century and cultivated in succeeding generations.

The Intellectual Sword

Beyond limiting financial resources, the tuition dependence syndrome compounded the aggressive Spartan culture of the school. The sword-wielding "rugged individualism" at the Law School has sometimes been viewed as an autonomous cultural norm, or attributed to certain academic policies and practices, such as the Socratic method of teaching. In addition, its roots have been identified in the supposed adversarial nature of Anglo-American law or the "manly" culture at Harvard University.[6]

Whatever its genesis, the combative and competitive culture of the school was reinforced by the financial malaise. In fact, the "ask and give no quarter" ethos arose concurrently with the realization after 1907 that prosperous Harvard Law School had impoverished itself. Only then did the infamous "Paper Chase" begin.[7] That culture then intensified as the school's financial problems worsened under Dean Pound and seemed to leave no other way to operate academically. The school had to "live from hand to mouth."[8] Subsequent attempts to modify academic policies in response to student complaints were explicitly stymied by the financial constraints, exemplified by the veto of reform proposals by President Conant (1933–1953).

Meanwhile, wielding the intellectual sword in grading, failing, and ranking students began to appear natural and necessary at Harvard Law School, as it did to Dean Pound. Having "GUTS" and "toughness" came to appear right and good, along with treating students as "rugged individuals" who did not need "spoon feeding."[9] Law is not a "pipe and slippers occupation," so going "soft" is the greatest threat to the Law School, in the view of Dean Griswold.[10]

Practices and policies driven by financial necessity were then rationalized as educationally advantageous. Teaching new students in huge classes enhanced learning, said the deans and faculty; and the high student-faculty ratio fostered self-reliance and should not be changed, even if the school had the money. All this rationalization diverted attention from the underlying necessity of responding to the syndrome of tuition dependence.

"A Preparation, of the Fittest"

Spartan manliness then contributed to the school's reluctance to admit, recruit, or welcome students and faculty who were not white, Christian men. This volume has chronicled the school's deplorable record of effectively cooperating with Harvard University's quota on Jewish students and faculty early in the twentieth century, as well as Dean Pound's reprehensible condoning of the Nazi regime, even as American intellectuals and academics recognized and condemned the growing danger of anti-Semitism in Nazi Germany. We have also documented the resistance of many on the law faculty and the Harvard Corporation to admitting women to the Law School before 1949, and thereafter the failure to welcome or support them as students or faculty over the next four decades.

The school's utter failure until 1965, and halting efforts thereafter, to encourage or recruit people of color—especially African Americans, Asian Americans, and Latinos—to enroll as students or to join the faculty are also evident. Relatively few such individuals came to study at the Law School, though many of those who did excelled, such as Charles Houston (LL.B. 1922, S.J.D. 1923). Even so, Houston was ever mindful that "my stock is pretty high around these parts, but God help me against one false move." These words reveal the close scrutiny and double standard to which students of color were often subjected. Many lower-performing white men were admitted to and graduated from Harvard Law School, while most of the few minority students surpassed most of the white students in academic achievement during much of the twentieth century, as had been the case in the nineteenth century.[11] A minority person had to be a super-performer in order to enroll and survive at the Law School.

This dismal record might be attributed to ignorance, self-interest, or blind prejudice that yielded, with excruciating slowness over decades, to a more enlightened view. But institutional change is rarely a matter of simply altering personal attitudes. In fact, the executing of "unfit" students and the elitist sorting of the rest into ranked tiers—on which the Law School prided itself—discouraged inclusion. All three factors therefore reinforced each other: the debilitating financial syndrome, the Spartan culture, and the resistance to diversifying the student body and faculty. Indeed, the connection among these three factors at the Law School was recognized and endorsed by the Harvard University presidents.

In his inaugural address President A. Lawrence Lowell (1909–1933) called upon the Harvard faculty to "increase the intellectual ambition" of students,

who should engage in the "struggle for marks" based on "a principle of selection, or as a preparation, of the fittest," which would develop "enterprise,"
"aggressiveness," and "self-reliance."[12] Lowell then sought to depress the enrollment and hiring of Jews, marginalize people of color, and bar women from
Harvard. He also commended the Law School as the one among all of Harvard's schools "that most attracts ambitious and self-reliant young men," and
"the one that offers them the least amount of aid."[13] By the same token, Lowell
was reluctant to help the Law School escape from its financial bind, particularly in comparison to other Harvard professional schools. President Lowell
thus endorsed all three reinforcing factors at the Law School.

President James Conant, though often considered a progressive educator,
did the same. He rejected any reforms at the Law School that would result in
"an undesirable relaxation" of academic pressure on students, which he considered "one of the most important factors in the School's success in the past."[14]
Conant also had little empathy for the plight of Jews under Nazism before
World War II, and endorsed the admission of women only after the war when
it became clear that the Law School was positively regressive in this regard.
Finally, he repeatedly pushed the Law School to the end of the queue, or left
it out altogether, when prioritizing funding needs among Harvard's professional schools. By the time President Nathan Pusey (1953–1971) assumed office, the Law School had declined considerably in financial strength compared to the other "major professional schools" at Harvard.

In the late 1960s, the 1970s, and the 1980s, the students' war on the grading
system went hand-in-hand with their protests to diversify the student body
and faculty. These were reactions against the same cultural complex, even
though the separate student groups may not have explicitly collaborated.
Meanwhile, the financial constraint on the whole complex was rarely acknowledged. Similarly, the fervent competition between Harvard and Yale
Law Schools was commonly analyzed and explained in terms of jurisprudence, politics, size, educational policy, or admissions selectivity, without giving
attention to the powerful influence of financial resources, which greatly favored Yale.

By the same token, the worsening financial difficulties during the "stagflation" of the 1970s precluded options that might have alleviated the faculty
discord under Dean Sacks and avoided the vitriolic "hatred" among the faculty that exploded under Dean Vorenberg. Duncan Kennedy's proposal for a
"New Model" curriculum in the early 1980s demonstrates this point perfectly.
Sacks authorized, and the Michelman Committee invited, "utopian" proposals.

Kennedy's forty-page proposal was the *only* such proposal put forward. It was not seriously discussed by the faculty or even, apparently, by the Michelman Committee, because it was radical—which, of course, any "utopian" proposal would have to be. But this neglect, and the absence of any alternative proposal, demonstrates that utopian reorganizing of the entire J.D. curriculum seemed wholly unfeasible and not worth considering. The fundamental reason for this assumption was the school's lack of resources and the deans' inability to acquire the resources.

In contrast, Harvard Medical School successfully handled a similar utopian proposal at the very same time, in the early 1980s. The medical dean and some faculty wished to attempt a fundamental and radical reform of the M.D. program that was opposed by traditionalists. Rather than accepting the limits of existing resources and either ditching the utopian reform or seeking compromises that would have satisfied no one, the medical dean persuaded the medical faculty to approve the creation of an alternative and optional new pathway to the M.D. so long as financial resources were not withdrawn from the traditional pathway. Then, with the help of President Derek Bok (1971–1991), the medical dean obtained external funding and created a second, parallel course of study for the M.D. by hiring additional faculty and providing facilities, while leaving the traditional course of study untouched. Entering students could choose their path, and student learning was rigorously assessed (far beyond one end-of-course exam). Over the ensuing decade, the radical reform was found to be preferred by most students and many faculty, and to be at least as educationally effective as the traditional curriculum.[15]

This strategy allowed Harvard Medical School to test a radical reform of the M.D. course of study while accommodating both traditionalists and radical reformers and forcing neither to compromise their academic commitments. At Harvard Law School, the notion of building and evaluating a utopian J.D. path, while leaving the existing program intact, was inconceivable due to the limits of resources. The Law School could not even sustain the modest, first-year "experimental sections" in the mid-1980s. As student Molly Burke (J.D. 1982) observed, the Michelman Committee was charged to consider any "educationally justified" changes that did "not impose any additional burdens on the faculty as a whole."[16]

Quite apart from the merits of Kennedy's particular proposal, the law deans and faculty presumed zero-sum resources, and their inability of think strategically—coupled with the financial constraints imposed by the school's historical, imprudent management—made radical or truly utopian reforms seem outlandish. Hence, only one utopian proposal was made and even that was not given serious consideration.

It is important to see that the Law School paid a heavy price for this inability. The radical reformers among faculty and students were left to smolder in frustration without a serious hearing or outlet for their proposals. Launching an alternative, optional, experimental pathway to the J.D. might have prevented the calamitous vituperation that poisoned the 1980s. Thus, the Law School's financial constraints intensified the dissension arising from the Michelman Committee's deliberations about educational reform. In addition, the capacity to increase the gender and racial diversity of the faculty and the student body was curtailed by the limitation of resources for financial aid and additional professorial positions. That limitation, along with the lack of strategic planning, stoked discord throughout the Law School.

In 2018, addressing the nature of elites, ethnicity, diversity and gender, Harvard College dean Rakesh Khurana stated, "I have a great deal of humility knowing that some day history will judge us. I think that's why we are

Six deans of Harvard Law School. Front row, left to right: James Casner (Acting Dean, 1967–1968); Erwin N. Griswold (1946–1967). Back row, left to right: James Vorenberg (1981–1989); Robert C. Clark (1989–2003); Derek C. Bok (1968–1970); Albert M. Sacks (1971–1981).

Reproduced from Erwin N. Griswold, "Ould Fields, New Corne" (St. Paul, MN: West), 1992.

constantly asking ourselves this question: How can we do better? How could we be better?"[17] Forthright and probing institutional histories enable us to address these questions with the necessary insight and humility, as suggested by Khurana, whose scholarship is cited repeatedly in this volume.

The need for research therefore continues.[18] There is a great deal more to examine: the vitriolic turmoil of the late 1980s; the recovery in the 1990s, culminating in the unprecedented success of a fund-raising campaign; the resulting opportunity in the 2000s for the Law School to escape tuition dependence. All this amid the highly important and growing diversity of the student body and the faculty, as well as the rightward swing of American politics and culture that made Critical Legal Studies seem, to some, not so utopian, and even prescient, after all.

Meanwhile, the Law School has made a deliberate effort to become more "friendly." In 2015 Meredith B. Osborn (J.D. 2006), daughter of John J. Osborn (LL.B. 1967), author of *The Paper Chase,* told a group of alumni, "Although Harvard Law School has always been a very challenging place, that challenge has become a much more positive challenge and less a fearful one over the years."[19] Concurrently, the applicant pool to law schools recovered. In 2018 the national pool of applicants to law schools rose by more than 8 percent from the prior year, and the applicant pool at Harvard Law School rose 32 percent.[20] Thus, as expressed in the university's bicentennial hymn of 1836, Harvard Law School continues to move "thro' change and thro' storm" from "the Age that is past to the Age that is waiting before."

NOTES

1. Counted among the U.S. presidents is Franklin Pierce, who graduated from the Northampton Law School, annexed by Harvard in 1829. See *Battlefield of Merit,* 60–61. Counted among the Supreme Court justices is Ruth Bader Ginsburg, who attended 1956–1958 and received her law degree from Columbia University Law School in 1959.

2. Harvard Law School (HLS) Faculty Meeting Minutes (December 7, 1948).

3. Scott G. Nichols, Interview with Bruce A. Kimball and Kenneth Leung (December 2010), on file with the authors; Scott G. Nichols, Interview (February 2011), quoted in Kenneth Leung, "Fundraising at the Harvard Law School during Erwin Griswold's Deanship" (student research paper, HLS, 2011) on file with the authors.

4. Daniel R. Coquillette, "American Legal Education: Where Did We Come From? Where Are We Going?," *Bar Examiner* 82 (June 2013): 45; Aaron N. Taylor et al., *How a*

Decade of Debt Changed the Law Student Experience (Law School Survey of Student Engagement, Annual Results) (Bloomington, IN, 2016).

5. Ronald G. Ehrenberg, "American Law Schools in a Time of Transition," *Journal of Legal Education* 63 (2013): 109. See Brian Z. Tamanaha, "Is Law School Worth the Cost?," *Journal of Legal Education* 63 (2013): 173–188.

6. Quotations are from, respectively, John G. Haviland, "The Student Looks at Harvard Law School" (observations of the school by students in 1934) (unpublished typescript, revised spring 1934), on file with the authors, 44, 71; Kim Townsend, *Manhood at Harvard: William James and Others* (Cambridge, MA, 1996), 22–24. See Edward H. Warren, *Spartan Education* (Boston, 1942).

7. Bruce A. Kimball, "Before the Paper Chase: Student Culture at Harvard Law School, 1895–1915," *Journal of Legal Education* 61 (2011): 30–66.

8. Roscoe Pound, *The Harvard Law School* [New York, 1919], 16.

9. Quotations are from Haviland, "The Student Looks," 76, 94, 54–55, 105.

10. Erwin N. Griswold, "The School since the War," *HLSB* (December 1951): 4.

11. See Daniel R. Coquillette and Bruce A. Kimball, *On the Battlefield of Merit: Harvard Law School, the First Century* (Cambridge, MA, 2015), 521–547.

12. A. Lawrence Lowell, "Inaugural Address," *Harvard Graduates Magazine* 18 (1909), 211–223. See A. Lawrence Lowell, *At War with Academic Traditions in America* (Cambridge, MA, 1934), 38, 45, 7, 69, 110.

13. A. Lawrence Lowell, Annual Report of the President of Harvard University, 1908–09, 21.

14. Faculty Committee on Curriculum, Minutes (October 29, 1935).

15. See the account of these developments in Daniel C. Tosteson, ed., *New Pathways to Medical Education: Learning to Learn at Harvard Medical School* (Cambridge, MA, 1994), 25, 89, 154–156.

16. Molly Burke, "Separate Statement" (from the Report of the Committee on Educational Planning and Development) (October 14, 1982), on file with the authors, 1–2.

17. Rakesh Khurana quoted in Anemona Hartocollis, Amy Harmon, and Mitch Smith, "'Lopping,' 'Tips' and the 'Z-List': Bias Lawsuit Explores Harvard's Admissions Secrets," *New York Times* (July 29, 2018).

18. See Appendix J.

19. Quoted in Andrew M. Duehren, "Harvard Law School Kicks Off $305 Million Capital Campaign," *Harvard Crimson* (October 25, 2015). See John J. Osborn, *The Paper Chase* (Boston, 1971). Furthering this goal, in fall 2019, Dean John Manning formed the HLS Student Well-Being Working Group with the purpose "to study and explore how best to foster community and to support the well-being of our students." That working group submitted its report in December 2019. John Manning, email to students, faculty, and staff of Harvard Law School (December 20, 2019), on file with the authors.

20. Aidan F. Ryan, "Harvard Law Sees Spike in Applications. Some Point to 'Trump Bump'" *Harvard Crimson* (September 10, 2018).

Law Schools Rejecting Case Method and the Harvard "System," 1890–1915

Type of Law School	Name	State
Aspiring, National University Schools (total: 4)	Yale U.	Connecticut
	U. Michigan	Michigan
	U. North Carolina	North Carolina
	U. Virginia	Virginia
Local, Independent Schools (total: 11)	San Francisco Law School	California
	San Francisco YMCA law school	California
	Bloomington Law School	Illinois
	Suffolk Law School	Massachusetts
	Detroit College of Law	Michigan
	St. Paul College of Law	Minnesota
	City College of Law and Finance	Missouri
	Kansas City School of Law	Missouri
	Wilmington Law School	North Carolina
	Cleveland Law School	Ohio
	Chattanooga College of Law	Tennessee
University Schools Operating as Local, Proprietary Schools (total: 27) In the Southeast (14)	Mercer U.	Georgia
	U. Georgia	Georgia
	U. Florida	Florida
	Louisiana State U.	Louisiana
	U. Maryland	Maryland
	Millsaps C.	Mississippi
	U. Mississippi	Mississippi
	Wake Forest U.	North Carolina
	U. South Carolina	South Carolina
	Cumberland U. Law School	Tennessee

(*continued*)

Type of Law School	Name	State
	Walden U.	Tennessee
	Vanderbilt U.	Tennessee
	U. Tennessee	Tennessee
	Washington and Lee U.	Virginia
In Ohio, Pennsylvania and Western New York (6)	Syracuse U.	New York
	Albany Law School	New York
	U. Toledo	Ohio
	Ohio Northern U.	Ohio
	Ohio State U.	Ohio
	U. Pittsburgh	Pennsylvania
Widely Distributed (7)	McKendree College	Illinois
	Tri-State U.	Indiana
	U. Kansas	Kansas
	Willamette U.	Oregon
	U. South Dakota	South Dakota
	U. Washington	Washington
	Howard U.	Washington, D.C.

Source: Reformatted from Bruce A. Kimball, "The Proliferation of Case Method Teaching in American Law Schools: Mr. Langdell's Emblematic 'Abomination,' 1890–1915," *History of Education Quarterly* 46 (2006): 192–247, Table 5.

Letter on Enrollment of Jewish Students, 1922

Dr. A. Lawrence Lowell
President, Harvard University
12th May 1922.

Dear Mr. Lowell:

Enclosed is a table indicating the number of Jews in the first-year class at various dates, and also the number in the whole School in 1900 and in the present year.

Mr. Ames and I went over together the names of all students now in the School most of whom are known to one or both of us, and I am confident that the figures for this year are close to the facts. There is more chance for error in the earlier years, but I believe that the figures for those years are not far from the facts.

The relative increase is noteworthy, and I am not unmindful of how residential sections and private schools have frequently been seriously harmed through a large increase of Jews, but I am at a loss to suggest how the relative increase may be properly checked. The Law School is a public school, and we have always welcomed all who conformed to our intellectual and moral standards.

Very truly yours,

[Acting Dean Edward H. Warren, Harvard Law School]

Year	Number of all students in first-year class	Number [of Jewish students]	Percentage [of Jewish students]
1899–1900	234	13	5.5%
1904–1905	286	19	6.6%
1909–1910	312	15	4.8%
1914–1915	288	23	8%
1916–1917	334	36	10.7%
1920–1921	360	46	12.7%
1921–1922	383	51	13.3%

Year	Number of students in whole school	Number [of Jewish students]	Percentage [of Jewish students]
1899–1900	613	27	4.4%
1921–1922	1002	127	12.7%

Source: [Edward H. Warren] to A. Lawrence Lowell (May 12, 1922), Harvard Law School Dean's Office Records, Records of President A. Lawrence Lowell, 1909–1933, Harvard University Archives.

Law School Endowments of Harvard, Yale, and Columbia Universities, 1910–1930 (in nominal dollars, rounded to hundreds)

Year[a]	Harvard Law School Endowment	Yale Law School Endowment	Percentage of Harvard Endowment	Columbia Law School Endowment	Percentage of Harvard Endowment
1910	$567,300	$358,300	63%	$321,000	57%
1920	$969,100	$500,100	52%	$488,000	50%
1930	$4,229,600	$2,126,600	50%	$538,000	13%

Data sources: Annual Report of the Treasurer of Harvard University, 1909–10, 63–70; 1919–20, 130–165; 1929–30, 267–311; George W. Pierson, *A Yale Book of Numbers: Historical Statistics of the College and University, 1701–1976* (New Haven, CT, 1983), 548. Compare Annual Report of the Treasurer of Yale University, 1909–10, 88, 132; 1919–20, 16, 96; 1930–31, 109–110, 190–191. In the reports of the Columbia University treasurer, endowments are not identified by unit, and can be calculated only by summing up over time the permanent funds listed annually in the gifts to a particular unit or department.

a. As of June 30

Enrollments, Endowments, and Annual Expenses of Medical, Law, and Business Schools of Columbia and Harvard Universities, 1890–1945 (in thousands of nominal dollars)

Year	Columbia Medical School[a]	Harvard Medical School	Columbia Law School	Harvard Law School	Harvard Business School (1908)	Columbia Business School (1916)
1890						
Enrollment[b]	215	454	212	254		
Endowment[c]	$281	$240	$0	$185		
Expenses[d]	—	$79	$35	$40		
1895						
Enrollment	799	454	288	404		
Endowment	$300	$318	$0	$248		
Expenses	$156	$120	$38	$56		
1900						
Enrollment	787	558	380	613		
Endowment	$490	$958	$12	$361		
Expenses	$134	$157	$37	$84		
1905						
Enrollment	555	307	341	758		
Endowment	$825	$3,180	$141	$370		
Expenses	$371	$155	$45	$103		
1910						
Enrollment	346	279	324	763	78	
Endowment	$861	$3,419	$321	$567	$1	
Expenses	$259	$260	$71	$117	$29	
1915						
Enrollment	374	321	453	730	166	
Endowment	$2,419	$4,197	$321	$735	$329	
Expenses	$570	$370	$101	$155	$60	

Year	Columbia Medical School[a]	Harvard Medical School	Columbia Law School	Harvard Law School	Harvard Business School (1908)	Columbia Business School (1916)
1920						
Enrollment	446	419	451	879	394	269
Endowment	$4,925	$7,325	$488	$969	$476	$481
Expenses	$540	$637	$134	$171	$149	$96
1925						
Enrollment	406	506	710	1,201	614	380
Endowment	$9,828	$11,512	$508	$1,192	$614	$482
Expenses	$868	$610	$181	$273	$495	$120
1930						
Enrollment	438	516	600	1,639	1,011	485
Endowment	$11,118	$15,610	$538	$4,230	$2,348	$890
Expenses	$2,542	$905	$303	$663	$1,053	$180
1935						
Enrollment	458	523	635	1,452	724	428
Endowment	$12,386	$17,026	$605	$4,776	$2,516	$913
Expenses	$1,623	$1,052	$295	$754	$842	$192
1940						
Enrollment	472	522	523	1,390	929	534
Endowment	$13,664	$17,737	$849	$5,424	$2,894	$958
Expenses	$2,157	$1,312	$324	$697	$906	$210
1945						
Enrollment	506	567	218	47	57	194
Endowment	$13,778	$18,901	$871	$5,365	$3,774	$979
Expenses	$2,148	$1,487	$266	$425	$1,512	$145

Data source: Bruce A. Kimball, Jeremy B. Luke, and Jamie M. Brown, "The Formative Financial Era of the 'Major Professional Schools': Medicine, Law, and Business at Columbia and Harvard, 1890–1950," in *The Economics of Higher Education in the United States,* ed. Thomas Adam and A. Burcu Bayram (Texas A&M University Press, 2019), table 5.2.

a. The annual reports of the Columbia University Treasurer vary in reporting expenses for the "Medical School" and the "College of Physicians and Surgeons." The figures here are drawn from the "Medical School" proper, which granted the M.D. degree. The medical school endowment funds do not include endowments for the teaching hospitals and clinics attached to the College of Physicians and Surgeons. Columbia assumed financial control of the College of Physicians and Surgeons in February 1891, so CMS expenses are not listed for the academic years 1889–90 or 1890–91.

b. Enrollment figures do not include extension, summer, or part-time, or cross-registered graduate students, but do include college seniors registered as law degree candidates.

c. Endowment includes income-producing funds and properties. But Harvard endowment totals do not include invested cash reserves.

d. Expenses do not include construction expenses for buildings, but do include maintenance and operations. Expense data is not presented because it cannot be calculated from the Columbia reports, as discussed above, though income is discussed at points in the text. CLS expenses in 1890 are for 1888. CBS expenses in 1920 are drawn from 1921–22, the first academic year for which the Columbia treasurer listed expenses in the annual report. CMS expenses for 1925 do not include "Teacher's College Salaries," which the Columbia treasurer listed within expenses of the "Medical School."

Increases of Combined Endowments of Columbia and Harvard Universities and Their Medical, Law, and Business Schools, 1890–1950 (in millions of nominal dollars)

	Universities		Medical Schools		Law Schools		Business Schools	
Year	Total	Cumulative Percentage Increase	Total	Cumulative Percentage Increase	Total	Cumulative Percentage Increase	Total	Cumulative Percentage Increase
1890	$15.2	NA	$.52	NA	$.19	NA	NA	—
1895	$19.1	26%	$.62	19%	$.25	32%	NA	—
1900	$25.9	70%	$1.4	169%	$.37	95%	NA	—
1905	$32.4	113%	$4.0	669%	$.51	168%	NA	—
1910	$47.8	214%	$4.3	727%	$.89	368%	NA	—
1915	$59.4	291%	$6.6	1,169%	$1.1	479%	$.33	—
1920	$84.2	454%	$12.3	2,265%	$1.5	689%	$.96	191%
1925	$119.5	686%	$21.3	3,996%	$1.7	795%	$1.1	233%
1930	$181.5	1,094%	$26.7	5,035%	$4.8	2,426%	$3.2	870%
1935	$175.0	1,051%	$29.4	5,554%	$5.4	2,742%	$3.4	930%
1940	$209.4	1,278%	$31.4	5,938%	$6.3	3,216%	$3.9	1,082%
1945	$236.0	1,453%	$32.7	6,188%	$6.2	3,163%	$4.8	1,355%
1950	$297.0	1,854%	$35.0	6,631%	$7.1	3,637%	$9.6	2809%

Data sources: Data is drawn from Appendix D; and from Bruce A. Kimball and Benjamin A. Johnson, "The Inception of the Meaning and Significance of Endowment in American Higher Education, 1890–1930," Teachers College Record 114 (2012): Table 1.

Enrollment of College Graduates in Harvard and Yale Law Schools, 1920–1935

Table 1. Number of graduates from various colleges and universities who enrolled in either Harvard Law School (HLS) or Yale Law School (YLS), 1920–1935

Academic Year	Harvard University Graduates[a]	Yale University Graduates[a]	Graduates of Northeastern Selective Colleges[b]	Graduates of Other Colleges	Non-graduates	Total LL.B. Students
1920–21						
HLS	195	61	176	391	20	843
YLS	0	65	12	85	18	180
1921–22						
HLS	185	54	175	475	11	900
YLS	0	75	12	109	14	210
1922–23						
HLS	203	44	203	459	3	912
YLS	3	86	19	111	14	233
1923–24						
HLS	212	48	220	522	0	1,002
YLS	3	103	25	142	12	285
1924–25						
HLS	237	44	249	592	0	1,122
YLS	3	102	41	166	10	322
1925–26						
HLS	257	51	283	624	0	1,215
YLS	5	123	46	174	9	357

(*Continued*)

Academic Year	Harvard University Graduates[a]	Yale University Graduates[a]	Graduates of Northeastern Selective Colleges[b]	Graduates of Other Colleges	Non-graduates	Total LL.B. Students
1926–27						
HLS	279	56	311	704	0	1,350
YLS	6	119	58	177	10	370
1927–28						
HLS	300	76	328	762	0	1,466
YLS	4	125	44	138	4	315
1928–29						
HLS	296	73	350	778	0	1,497
YLS	2	133	46	106	1	288
1929–30						
HLS	287	81	387	813	0	1,568
YLS	2	125	48	109	0	284
1930–31						
HLS	259	84	365	813	0	1,521
YLS	4	134	48	129	0	315
1931–32						
HLS	263	92	368	792	0	1,515
YLS	6	138	48	115	2	309
1932–33						
HLS	308	98	308	715	0	1,429
YLS	5	136	55	93	1	290
1933–34						
HLS	310	89	303	693	0	1,395
YLS	9	162	75	80	0	326
1934–35						
HLS	312	77	287	708	0	1,384
YLS	11	160	97	85	1	354

Data sources: Compiled from HLS and YLS catalogs in Jeremy B. Luke, "Academic Origins of Harvard Law School and Yale Law School LL.B. Students, 1921–1935" (student research report, Ohio State University, 2017), on file with the authors.

Note: Totals based upon most recent degree received by a student.

a. A few of these Harvard and Yale graduates received degrees from other parts of their universities outside of the undergraduate college.

b. Princeton, Dartmouth, Brown, Columbia, Cornell, Pennsylvania, Amherst, Williams, Wesleyan.

Table 2. Distribution by percentage of graduates from various colleges and universities who enrolled in either Harvard Law School (HLS) or Yale Law School (YLS), 1926–1935

Law School Enrolled in by Year	Harvard University Graduates	Yale University Graduates	Graduates of Nine Northeastern Selective Colleges[a]	Graduates of Other Institutions	Total LL.B. Students
1926–27					
HLS	98%	32%	84%	80%	1,350
YLS	2%	68%	16%	20%	370
1928–29					
HLS	99%	35%	88%	88%	1,497
YLS	1%	65%	12%	12%	288
1930–31					
HLS	98%	39%	88%	86%	1,521
YLS	2%	61%	12%	14%	315
1932–33					
HLS	98%	42%	85%	88%	1,429
YLS	2%	58%	15%	12%	290
1934–35					
HLS	97%	32%	75%	89%	1,384
YLS	3%	68%	25%	11%	354

Data source: Data drawn and calculated from Table 1 above.

a. Princeton, Dartmouth, Brown, Columbia, Cornell, Pennsylvania, Amherst, Williams, Wesleyan Graduates sorted by most recent degree received prior to enrolling in law school.

Endowments, Expenses, and Enrollment of Harvard Law School and Yale Law School, 1905–1970 (in nominal dollars, rounded to hundreds)

Academic Year	Endowment*	Expense†	Endowment/ Expenses	Yale University Subvention	LL.B. Students	Endowment/ Student
1904–05[a]						
HLS	$370,000	$102,800	3.6		706	$524
YLS	$151,300	$37,600	4.0	0	238	$636
1909–10[b]						
HLS	$567,300	$117,100	4.8		693	$819
YLS	$358,300	$52,800	6.8	0	284	$1,262
1914–15[c]						
HLS	$734,500	$154,900	4.7		655	$1,121
YLS	$502,500	$52,600	9.6	$1,000	116	$4,332
1919–20[d]						
HLS	$969,100	$171,100	5.7		825	$1,175
YLS	$500,100	$110,300	4.5	$11,500[e]	130	$3,847
1926–27[f]						
HLS	$1,817,800	$398,200	4.6		1,350	$1,347
YLS	$1,371,300	$218,000	6.3	$73,700[g]	353	$3,885
1929–30[h]						
HLS	$4,229,600	$663,300	6.4		1,568	$2,697
YLS	$2,126,600	$327,800	6.5	$78,100[i]	296	$7,184
1934–35[j]						
HLS	$4,776,000	$754,400	6.3		1,384	$3,451
YLS	$1,643,000	$374,700	4.4	$73,300[k]	334	$4,919

Academic Year	Endowment*	Expense[†]	Endowment/ Expenses	Yale University Subvention	LL.B. Students	Endowment/ Student
1939–40[l]						
HLS	$5,424,000	$696,600	7.8		1,337	$4,057
YLS	$1,763,000	$367,500	4.8	$64,200[m]	353	$4,994
1944–45[n]						
HLS	$5,364,800	$425,200	12.6		47	NA
YLS	$2,560,100	$301,700	8.5	$108,000[o]	67	NA
1949–50[p]						
HLS	$6,121,000	$1,206,900	5.1		1,497	$4,089
YLS	$2,873,300	$671,600	4.3	$56,000[q]	491	$5,852
1954–55[r]						
HLS	$7,770,100	$2,406,400	3.2		1,407	$5,522
YLS	$3,047,000	$746,800	4.1	$173,200[s]	415	$7,342
1959–60[t]						
HLS	$10,590,800	$3,014,400	3.5		1,488	$7,117
YLS	$4,553,600	$1,274,800	3.6	$175,600[u]	519	$8,774
1964–65[v]						
HLS	$18,669,900	$4,656,400	4.0		1,553	$12,022
YLS	$9,159,100	$2,193,900	4.2	$445,500[w]	533	$17,184
1969–70[x]						
HLS	$26,186,000	$7,073,500	3.7		1,675	$15,633
YLS	$11,144,900	$3,513,200	3.2	$305,000[y]	512	$21,767

Data source: See notes below.

* Endowment includes only permanent funds, not surplus invested by the University Treasurer on behalf of the law school.

† Expense listed by treasurer of the university.

a. For 1904–05, Harvard data is drawn from Annual Report of the Treasurer of Harvard University (hereafter ARTHU), 1904–05, 35, 65–70; Harvard Law School (HLS) Catalog, 1900–01, 41; 1905–06, 47. Yale data is drawn from Annual Report of the Treasurer of Yale University (hereafter ARTYU), 1904–05, 38–39, 78–79; Henry W. Rogers, Annual Report of the Dean of Yale Law School (YLS), 1904–05, 154.

b. For 1910–11, Harvard data is drawn from ARTHU, 1909–10, 11, 63–70; HLS Catalog, 1910–11, 50. Yale data is drawn from ARTYU, 1909–10, 88, 133; Rogers, Annual Report of the Dean, 1909–10, 193.

c. For 1914–15, Harvard data is drawn from ARTHU, 1914–15, 11, 104–132; HLS Catalog, 1915–16, 53. Yale data is drawn from ARTYU, 1914–15, 68, 123–124; Rogers, Annual Report of the Dean, 1914–15, 294.

d. For 1919–20, Harvard data is drawn from ARTHU, 1919–20, 11, 130–136, 149–151, 162, 165; Roscoe Pound, Annual Report of the Dean of HLS, 1920–21, 202–204. Yale data is drawn from ARTYU, 1919–20, 90, 155–56; Thomas W. Swan, Annual Report of the Dean of YLS, 1919–20, 388.

e. In 1919–1920, YLS had a shortfall of $55,281 on expenses of $110,293, due to its enrollment of only 130 LL.B. students. The Yale Corporation provided a subvention of $26,858, including a university appropriation of $11,500 toward salaries and a transfer of $15,358 of income from a university endowment fund. To cover the remaining deficit, the university transferred $28,423 from the law school's surplus. ARTYU, 1919–20, 155.

(*Continued*)

f. More reliable data was available for 1926–27 than for 1924–25. Annual Report of the Treasurer, 1926–27, 61–63, 256–257; HLS Catalog, 1927–28, 87. Yale data is drawn from ARTYU, 1926–27, 105, 176–177. The enrollment for YLS was computed by deducting forty Yale College seniors, ten Sterling Fellows, and fifteen graduate students from Pierson's total of 418. George W. Pierson, *A Yale Book of Numbers: Historical Statistics of the College and University 1701–1976* (New Haven, CT, 1983), 9.

g. This subvention for 1926–27 included an appropriation of $24,959 toward salaries, a transfer of $16,213 from income from a university endowment fund, and a university "donation" of $32,492. ARTYU, 1926–27, 176.

h. Growth of the Harvard endowment between 1925 and 1930 is largely due to proceeds from the 1925–1927 fundraising campaign. Growth of the Yale endowment resulted largely from various allocations made by the trustees of the Sterling bequest to Yale University. For 1929–30, Harvard data is drawn from ARTHU, 1929–30, 8, 267, 276, 279, 286–289, 306, 311; HLS Catalog, 1930–31, 97. Yale data is drawn from ARTYU, 1929–30, 16, 31; Charles E. Clark, Annual Report of the Dean of YLS, 1929–30, 152–53; Pierson, *Yale Book of Numbers*, 548.

i. This subvention for 1929–30 included an appropriation of $38,400 toward faculty salaries, an allocation of $21,844 from the university's endowments funds, and a donation of $17,833 to balance the law school's budget. ARTYU, 1929–30, 16.

j. Growth in the Harvard endowment between 1930 and 1935 reflects a 10 percent write-up in the book value of all endowment funds held by the university, as of June 30, 1930. ARTHU, 1938–39, 333. For 1934–35, Harvard data is drawn from ARTHU, 1934–35, 67, 264, 273–277, 284–286, 306; HLS Catalog, 1935–36, 91. Yale data is drawn from ARTYU, 1934–35, 12; Pierson, *Yale Book of Numbers*, 9, 548. Pierson's total enrollment figure of 359 is reduced by ten Sterling Fellows and fifteen graduate students.

k. The 1934–35 subvention of $73,329 included a university appropriation of $48,000, an allocation of $24,553 from the income of the university's endowments funds, and a donation of $775 "to balance the budget." ARTYU, 1934–35, 12.

l. For 1939–40, Harvard data is drawn from ARTHU, 1939–40, 73, 241; HLS Catalog, 1940–41, 102. Yale data is drawn from ARTYU, 1939–40, 12; Pierson, *Yale Book of Numbers*, 9, 548. Pierson's figure for total enrollment is reduced by ten Sterling Fellows and fifteen graduate students.

m. ARTYU, 1939–40, 12.

n. For 1944–45, Harvard data is drawn from ARTHU, 1944–45, 14, 78–79; HLS Catalog, 1944–45, 718. Yale data is drawn from ARTYU, 1944–45, 19; Pierson, *Yale Book of Numbers*, 9, 548. YLS enrollment includes all degree candidates.

o. ARTYU, 1944–45, 18. The subvention of 1944–45 includes the university's appropriation of $31,500 for teaching plus $76,513 to cover the remaining deficit.

p. For 1949–50, Harvard data is drawn from ARTHU, 1949–50, 14, 92–93; [Andrew L. Kaufman, Chair], Memorandum to the Faculty from the Financial Aids Committee [Cambridge, MA, ca. March 1970], typescript on file with the authors, appendix 2. Yale data is drawn from ARTYU, 1949–50, 17–18; Wesley A. Sturges, Annual Report of the Dean of YLS, 1949–50, 3; Pierson, *Yale Book of Numbers*, 548.

q. ARTYU, 1949–50, 17. Includes the university's appropriation of $33,000 for teaching and coverage of deficit of $23,100.

r. For 1954–55, Harvard data is drawn from ARTHU, 1954–55, 14, 100–101; [Kaufman], Memorandum to the Faculty from the Financial Aids Committee, appendix 2. Yale data is drawn from ARTYU, 1954–55, 17–18; Pierson, *Yale Book of Numbers*, 9, 548. Pierson's figure of 435 degree candidates is reduced by twenty graduate students.

s. ARTYU, 1954–55, 17. Includes university's appropriation of $39,200 for teaching and coverage of deficit of $134,000.

t. For 1959–60, Harvard data is drawn from ARTHU, 1959–60, 14, 120–121; [Kaufman], Memorandum to the Faculty from the Financial Aids Committee, appendix 2. Yale data is drawn from ARTYU, 1959–60, 19–20; Eugene V. Rostow, Annual Report of the Dean of YLS, 1959–1962, 55; Pierson, *Yale Book of Numbers*, 548.

u. ARTYU, 1959–60, 19. This subvention includes university's appropriation of $53,400 for teaching and coverage of deficit of $122,200.

v. The large jump in the HLS endowment between 1960 and 1965 is due to capital gains distribution by the university. For 1960–1965, Harvard data is drawn from ARTHU, 1964–65, 14, 5–6, 132–133; [Kaufman], Memorandum to the Faculty from the Financial Aids Committee, appendix 2. Yale data is drawn from ARTYU, 1964–65, 18–19; Rostow, Annual Report of the Dean, 1964–65, 43; Pierson, *Yale Book of Numbers*, 548.

w. ARTYU, 1964–65, 18.

x. As of July 1, 1970, Harvard University changed its book-value method of accounting for endowments and other funds in its General Investments Account to the market value or unit method of accounting. ARTHU, 1969–70, 5. Along with additional capital gains distributions, this accounting change contributed to increasing the endowment value. For 1965–1970, Harvard data is drawn from ARTHU, 1969–70, 16, 32–33, 138–139; Harvard University Catalog, 1969–70, 886. Yale data is drawn from ARTYU, 1969–70, 33; Pierson, *Yale Book of Numbers*, 11. Pierson's enrollment figure of 572 degree candidates is reduced by sixty graduate students.

y. ARTYU, 1969–70, 33. This figure is the deficit of the school covered by university appropriations and transfers.

Financial Advantage of Yale Law School over Harvard Law School, 1894–1970

Period	Building Cost Paid by HLS (nominal dollars)	Building Cost Paid for YLS (nominal dollars)	Sum of Annual Subsidies to YLS[a] (nominal dollars)	YLS Financial Advantage (constant dollars, 1970 = 1)
1894–1900		127,000		589,000
1906–1910	400,000			1,642,000
1912–1919			96,000	343,000
1919–1926			218,000	496,000
1930		4,000,000		9,280,000
1926–1940			1,050,000	2,833,000
1928–1948	1,995,000			4,747,000
1940–1950			860,000	1,713,000
1950–1960			1,555,000	2,255,000
1960–1970			3,050,000	3,754,000
Total	NA	NA	NA	27,652,000

Data sources: Annual Report of the Treasurer of Yale University and Annual Report of the Treasurer of Harvard University from 1894–95 through 1969–70; Erwin N. Griswold, Annual Report of the Dean of Harvard University, 1947–48, 390; John J. McCusker, *How Much Is That in Real Money? A Historical Commodity Price Index for Use as a Deflator of Money Values in the Economy of the United States,* 2nd ed. (Worcester, MA, 2001), 56–59.

a. Subsidy amounts are averaged over the period and rounded to 1000s, and include university "appropriations for teaching purposes" and the "excess of expenses over available income," as reported by the Yale University Treasurer.

Women with Teaching Appointments at Harvard Law School, 1968–1985

Dean (1981–1989) | Derek Bok (1968–1970) | Albert Sacks (1971–1981) | James Vorenberg (1981–1989)

| | 1968 | 1969 | 1970 | 1971 | 1972 | 1973 | 1974 | 1975 | 1976 | 1977 | 1978 | 1979 | 1980 | 1981 | 1982 | 1983 | 1984 | 1985 |

Regular (tenured or tenure-track) Appointments

Elizabeth Bartholet
Claire Dalton
Susan Estrich
Martha Minow
Sally Schultz Neely
Martha Field
Diane Lund
Elisabeth Owens

Visiting or term Appointments

Alison Anderson
Margaret Berger
Barbara Black
Lea Brilmeyer
Raya Dreben
Mary Louise Fellows
Tamar Frankel
Ruth Bader Ginsburg
Mary Ann Glendon
Carole E. Goldberg
Linda Sheryl Greene
Herma Hill Kay
Silvia Anne Law
Catherine Mackinnon
Sally Falk Moore
Deborah Scherk
Linda Silberman
Wendy Williams
Zipporah Wiserman

Data source: Harvard Law School Catalogs, 1968–1985

Key: Regular, tenure-line Appointment (Assistant Professor or Professor of Law)

Note on Further Research and Access
to Harvard University Records

We had originally intended to bring this volume into the twenty-first century, but several factors forced us to stop in the 1980s. First, the book was becoming quite large, and we did not want to pare back our findings in earlier chapters or to shortchange the 1990s or 2000s. Second, as the subject moves closer to the current day, the dangers of presentism and partiality become more acute, particularly given that coauthor Daniel Coquillette (J.D. 1971) began teaching at the Law School in 1979 and subsequently served on the Harvard Board of Overseers Committee to Visit the Law School.

Third, we have encountered increasing difficulty in conducting archival research in the libraries of Harvard University. In 1986 the distinguished historian Ellen Schrecker observed that "Harvard is one the few universities to keep its archives closed to scholars."[1] In fact, Harvard seals its records far longer than even the FBI or the CIA, which are now subject to the twenty-five-year stricture that the U.S. government applies to its agencies. Indeed, many universities provide greater access to historians of their law schools than we have encountered (though our history was not authorized by Harvard Law School).[2] In any event, Harvard University's administrative records are sealed for fifty years, and records pertaining to individuals who worked or studied at Harvard are sealed for eighty years.

Prior to 2012 these seals were applied with discretion at Harvard's individual libraries. Records known to be sensitive were closed, but archivists generally tried to make materials available to researchers. Hence, it was possible to conduct research on many subjects of interest while consulting more recent materials than the official seals allowed. In 2012, however, Harvard centralized and reorganized its library system.[3] This centralization was soon followed by stricter, uniform enforcement of the university's seals on archival materials. By 2014 our research assistants were being denied access to all Harvard-related files dated later than 1963, and even older files were subject to a search by archival staff to determine if the files contained materials pertaining to individuals, triggering the eighty-year seal.[4]

This shift toward strict and uniform enforcement made research on issues after the mid-1960s much more difficult than previously. In fact, we have found that sources on Harvard Law School that were previously accessed and cited by historians, such as Morton and Phyllis Keller and Justin O'Brien, are now unavailable to us and other researchers.[5] Many of the papers written by our own research assistants prior to 2012 quote sources that are now sealed.

The deans of Harvard's various schools are authorized to make sealed materials available at their discretion, but several of our requests for access since 2000 have been denied, even when we arranged to have an archivist review materials before we saw them. No less significantly, the procedure of appealing to the dean for access to a file, justifying the request, and arranging for the items in a file to be reviewed and vetted is itself prohibitively burdensome. Regular Harvard faculty are apparently extended deference in this regard, but other individual scholars cannot afford the time, energy, and funding to pursue these appeals, especially if the researcher comes from a distant university. Even with the help of research assistants who can visit Harvard daily, we have not had the time and resources to keep appealing and have virtually given up doing so. The application of the policy effectively bars outside researchers from examining the archives about Harvard's history in the last third of the twentieth century or later.

Furthermore, it appears that some of Harvard's professional schools are extending the seals beyond those mandated by the Harvard Corporation. For example, in 2013 Harvard Law School sealed all of the minutes of its faculty meetings, which begin in 1871, far beyond the seal authorized by the Harvard Corporation. The school's authority for sealing all its faculty minutes is not evident. Without those minutes, which we consulted before 2012, writing *On the Battlefield of Merit* would have been impossible.

In addition, according to one of our colleagues working on the history of Harvard Business School, the fifty-year seal is interpreted there to mean fifty years after a dean *ends* his or her tenure. Thus, the early administrative records of a dean who served twenty years are effectively sealed for seventy years. Such an embargo would have obstructed all our research about Erwin Griswold. Similarly, a collection of student records at Harvard Business School running, for example, from 1927 to 1942 is considered sealed for eighty years *after* 1942. Hence, the records from 1927 are sealed for ninety-five years. This embargo would have barred our research and findings about Roscoe Pound and Nazism.

Whether these seals and barriers are necessary to protect individuals or the university can perhaps be measured by an assessment of the merit of the research and findings of this volume. In fact, it appears that centralizing the Harvard libraries has led gradually to shifting from the traditional approach of promoting scholars' access to archives to limiting that access in service of exercising proprietary control over records. One assumes that the Harvard Corporation is unaware of the actual application and effect of the university's policy on sealing records.

NOTES

1. Ellen W. Schrecker, *No Ivory Tower: McCarthyism and the Universities* (New York, 1986), 198.

2. In writing *Fordham University School of Law: A History* (New York, 2012), Robert J. Kaczorowski observed that he had unrestricted access to all of Fordham Law School's archives. Comments at the Legal Education in Twentieth-Century America symposium, held at New York University's Villa La Pietra conference center in Florence, Italy, on July 2–4, 2018. See Scott Shane, "U.S. to Declassify Secrets at Age 25," *New York Times* (December 21, 2017).

3. The purpose of the "strategic reorganization" was to improve "a fragmented system by promoting University-wide collaboration" and "enable Harvard to invest in innovation and collections, make decisions strategically, reduce duplication of effort, and leverage the University's buying power." The "strategic reorganization" and "reduction of duplication" in 2012 were accompanied by early retirement offers to 273 of the 930 full-time employees of the Harvard libraries, many with long years of service. "University Offers Voluntary Retirement to Library Employees," *Harvard Magazine* (February 13, 2012), retrieved from https://harvardmagazine.com.

4. Jamie M. Brown, Email to Bruce A. Kimball (November 20, 2014), on file with the authors.

5. Morton Keller and Phyllis Keller, *Making Harvard Modern: The Rise of America's University,* 2nd ed. (New York, 2007); Justin O'Brien, *The Triumph, Tragedy and Lost Legacy of James M. Landis: A Life on Fire* (Oxford 2014).

Student Research Reports, Memos, and Articles Cited

Jonathan Agudelo, "Requiring Good Anti-Communist Citizens: Harvard Law School and Its Experience with the Lubell Brothers" (student research paper, Boston College Law School, 2009), on file with the authors.

Emily Anderson, "Harvard Law School Tuition Increases" (student research report, Boston College Law School, 2016), on file with the authors.

Emily Anderson and Elise Medley, "Grading System at Harvard Law School and Peer Law Schools" (student research memo, Harvard Law School, 2015), on file with the authors.

Emily Anderson and Elise Medley, "Women at Harvard Law School" (student research memo, Boston College Law School, 2016), on file with the authors.

Kadesha Bagwell, "What I Am" (student research paper, Harvard Law School, 1999), on file with the authors.

J. Bruce Blain, "Harvard Law School Fund, 1950–1968" (research assistant report, Harvard Law School, 2012), on file with the authors.

J. Bruce Blain, "Research Notes and Analysis of the Harvard Law School Bulletin" (research assistant report, Harvard Law School, 2012), on file with the authors.

J. Bruce Blain, "Research on the Griswold Deanship" (research assistant report, Harvard Law School, 2013), on file with the authors.

Simeon Botwinick, "Punished Privilege: Communism and the Fifth Amendment at Harvard Law School" (student research paper, Harvard Law School, 2016), on file with the authors.

Jamie M. Brown, "Analysis of the Annual Reports of the Deans of Yale Law School, 1899–1965" (research assistant report, Harvard Law School, 2015), on file with the authors.

Jamie M. Brown, "Analysis of Relations between Harvard and Yale Law Schools revealed in Archived Correspondence of the Deans, Presidents, and Secretaries of Yale University, 1919–1965" (research assistant report, Harvard Law School, 2015), on file with the authors.

Jamie M. Brown, "Columbia University Law School, Medical School, and Business School: Fundraising, Expenses, and Enrollment, 1890–1945" (research assistant report, Harvard Law School, 2014), on file with the authors.

Jamie M. Brown, "Comparisons Made of Harvard Law School and Yale Law School, 1900–1967" (student research paper, Harvard Law School, 2014), on file with the authors.

Jamie M. Brown, "Harvard Law School Enrollment, Expense, and Endowment Statistics" (research assistant report, Harvard Law School, 2014), on file with the authors.

Jamie M. Brown, "Research Memo on Erwin Griswold's Doctrine of Pleading the Fifth Amendment" (student research memo, Harvard Law School, 2013), on file with the authors.

Erin Carroll, "Bibliographical Review of the Members of the Harvard Law School Class of 1901" (research assistant report, Harvard Law School, 2008), on file with the authors.

Erin Carroll, "Harvard Business School and Harvard Law School" (research assistant report, Harvard Law School, 2008), on file with the authors.

Julia Chen, "The Harvard Law School Experience for Women in the 1950s" (student research paper, Harvard Law School, 2013), on file with the authors.

Li Chen, "Pioneers in the Fight for the Inclusion of Chinese Students in American Legal Education and Legal Profession" (student research paper, Harvard Law School, 2014), on file with the authors.

Andrew Cheng, "Untold Stories: Asian Pacific Americans at Harvard Law School" (student research paper, Harvard Law School, 2000), on file with the authors.

Abigail Burger Chingos, "The Michelman Committee: A History of Its Work and an Analysis of Lessons Learned about Curricular Reform" (student research paper, Harvard Law School, 2009), on file with the authors.

James F. Clark, "The Harvard Law School Deanship of Roscoe Pound, 1916–36" (student research paper, Harvard Law School, 1999), on file with the authors.

Laura Cromer-Babycz, "Clinical Legal Education in the United States: A Brief History and a Proposal for Movement towards Further Reform" (student research paper, Harvard Law School, 2012), on file with the authors.

Caroline Daniels, "The *Harvard Law Review* and the Legacy of the Meritocracy" (student research paper, Harvard Law School, 2000), on file with the authors.

David R. Derusha, "The Deanship of Erwin N. Griswold: A New Look" (student research paper, Harvard Law School, 2008), on file with the authors.

Jenny Ellickson, "'The Next Brass Ring': The Increase in Law Students' Interest in Clerkships since 1940" (student research paper, Harvard Law School, 2002), on file with the authors.

Duncan Farthing-Nichol, "A Desirable Discontent: Dean James M. Landis at Harvard Law School" (student research paper, Harvard Law School, 2012), on file with the authors.

Duncan Farthing-Nichol, "Sunlight from the Shadows: Dean James M. Landis in the History of the Harvard Law School" (student research paper, Harvard Law School, 2013), on file with the authors.

Barbara Fiasco, "The First Appointments of Women to the Harvard Law School Faculty" (student research paper, Harvard Law School, 2000), on file with the authors.

Eric F. Fox, "Attrition Rates at Harvard Law School, 1900–1915" (research assistant report, Boston College Law School, 2010), on file with the authors.

Eric F. Fox, "Harvard Law School Centennial Fundraising Campaign and the Harvard University Endowment Fund Campaign, 1914–1921" (research assistant report, Boston College Law School, 2010), on file with the authors.

Eric F. Fox, "Harvard Law School Finances and the Building of Langdell Hall 1895–1910" (research assistant report, Boston College Law School, 2009), on file with the authors.

Lucia Foulkes, "Graduate Education in a New Global Arena" (student research paper, Boston College Law School, 2015), on file with the authors.

Thomas Gagne, "Boston College Law School: Gay and Lesbian Civil Rights Incubator" (student research paper, Boston College Law School, 2000), on file with the authors.

Andrew C. Goodwin, "Losing the Battle; Winning the War? An Examination of the Impact of Derrick Bell and the Griswold 9 on Faculty Diversity at Harvard Law School" (student research paper, Harvard Law School, 2015), on file with the authors.

Ariana Green, "Analysis of the Harvard Law School Finances Made in Records of the President of Harvard University, Abbott Lawrence Lowell, 1909–1933" (research assistant report, Harvard Law School, 2010), on file with the authors.

Ariana Green, "Fundraising in the Roscoe Pound Papers, 1914–1921" (research assistant report, Harvard Law School, 2010), on file with the authors.

George W. Hick, "Against the Grain: The Federalist Society and the Conservation of the Harvard Law School Student Body" (student research paper, Harvard Law School, 2007), on file with the authors.

Jane Hill, "By the Sweat of Their Fraus: The Harvard Law Wives, 1929–1972" (student research paper, Harvard Law School, 2009), on file with the authors.

Sarah M. Iler, "The History of 'Multicultural' in the United States during the Twentieth Century" (PhD. diss., Ohio State University, 2017).

Kimberly Isbell, "Grade Reform at Harvard, 1968–1972" (student research paper, Harvard Law School, 2000), on file with the authors.

John L. Joy, "A Legacy of Their Own: A History of Second Generation African American Families at Harvard Law School" (student research paper, Boston College Law School, 2016), on file with the authors.

Cale Keable, "A History of the Lincoln's Inn Society (student research paper, Harvard Law School, 2001), on file with the authors.

Rebecca H. Kimball, "Literature Review of Writings by and about Ruth Bader Ginsburg" (research assistant report, Ohio State University, 2016), on file with the authors.

Nina Kohn, "Cambridge Law School for Women: The Tangled Legacy of the First Graduate School Exclusively for Women" (student research paper, Harvard Law School, 2002), on file with the authors.

Jason Kreag, "Reciprocal Impact: An Examination of Harvard Law School and the Civil Rights Movement" (student research paper, Harvard Law School, 2003), on file with the authors.

James E. Kruzer, "Pleading the Fifth: Erwin Griswold, the Lubell Brothers, and Academic Freedom" (student research paper, Boston College Law School, 2006), on file with the authors.

Kenneth Leung, "The Deanship of Erwin Nathaniel Griswold, 1946–1967" (student research paper, Harvard Law School, 2010), on file with the authors.

Kenneth Leung, "Fundraising at the Harvard Law School during Erwin Griswold's Deanship" (student research paper, Harvard Law School, 2011), on file with the authors.

John J. Liolos, "Erecting the High Citadel's Walls: The Development of Formal Admissions Standards at Harvard Law School, 1817–1955" (student research paper, Harvard Law School, 2013), on file with the authors.

Jeremy B. Luke, "Academic Origins of Harvard Law School and Yale Law School LL.B. Students, 1921–1935" (student research report, Ohio State University, 2017), on file with the authors.

Jeremy B. Luke, "Harvard Law School Enrollment, Expense, and Endowment Statistics" (student research report, Ohio State University, 2014), on file with the authors.

Kayleigh E. McGlynn, "Anton-Hermann Chroust: Did the University of Notre Dame Knowingly Appoint an Alleged Nazi Spy to a Tenure-Track Faculty Position?" (student research paper, Boston College Law School, 2019), on file with the authors.

Kayleigh E. McGlynn. "Costs of Griswold Hall and Pound Hall" (student research memo, Boston College Law School, 2017), on file with the authors.

Kayleigh E. McGlynn, "Law Schools Enrolling the First Female Students after Harvard Law School" (student research report, Boston College Law School, 2017), on file with the authors.

David McIntosh, "A Minor Matter: The Admission of Women to the Harvard Law School" (student research paper, Harvard Law School, 1998), on file with the authors.

Frederick G. Medick, "Barack Obama's Years at Harvard Law School" (student research paper, Harvard Law School, 2008), on file with the authors but sealed.

Felipe D. Mendoza, "Hispanic Graduates of Harvard Law School: First Graduates and First Generation" (student research paper, Harvard Law School, 2006), on file with the authors.

Felipe D. Mendoza, "Hispanic [LL.B.] Graduates of Harvard Law School, 1817–1973: A First Step toward Uncovering the Lives and Experiences of the First Graduate and the First Generation" (student research paper, Harvard Law School, 2006), on file with the authors.

Jessica Meylor, "Harvard Law School Fundraising and Endowment Materials in Harvard University Archives" (student research report, Boston College Law School, 2010), on file with the authors.

Jessica Meylor, "The Harvard Law School Endowment, 1910–2006" (student research paper, Boston College Law School, 2015), on file with the authors.

Laura A. Murray, "From Debate to Demonstration: Harvard Law School in Vietnam Era" (student research paper, Harvard Law School, 2002), on file with authors.

Catherine O'Neill, "The Crimson Scare: A Harvard Law School Student's Experience Being Labeled a Communist" (student research paper, Boston College Law School, 2017), on file with the authors.

Palma Paciocco, "*A Sound Recommendation,* Sheldon and Eleanor Glueck and the Project to Educate Correctional Administrators at Harvard Law School" (student research paper, Harvard Law School, 2012), on file with the authors.

Jenny Page, "The Forgotten Class: The History of the LL.M. Program at Harvard Law School, 1923–2006" (student research paper, Harvard Law School, 2000), on file with the authors.

Elizabeth F. Paice, "The Manifestation of McCarthyism at the Ohio State University" (student research paper, Ohio State University, 2016), on file with the authors.

Nathan Pak, "The Harvard Law School Special Summer Program of 1965 and What Happened Afterwards" (student research paper, Boston College Law School, 2017), on file with the authors.

Deborah Pearlstein, "The Origins and Modern Purpose of the Harvard Law Review: Clinging to Community" (student research paper, Harvard Law School, 1997), on file with the authors.

Gabriel A. Pell, "Academic Context of the Griswold Deanship" (research assistant report, Harvard Law School, 2012), on file with the authors.

Gabriel A. Pell, "Research Notes on Erwin N. Griswold" (research assistant report, Harvard Law School, 2012), on file with the authors.

Daniel Pincus, "Dichotomy of Legal Education—Practice v. Theory: The Tale of Clinical Legal Education" (student research paper, Boston College Law School, 2010), on file with the authors.

Tad Polley, "Putting the Law in Law School: The Utility of Clinical Education to Alumni of the Harvard Legal Aid Bureau" (student research paper, Harvard Law School, 2003), on file with the authors.

Katherine M. Porter, "Learning by Doing: A History of the Board of Student Advisors, 1910–2000" (student research paper, Harvard Law School, 2001), on file with the authors.

Brandi Pugh, "Anomaly: Harvard Law School during World War I" (student research paper, Boston College Law School, 2014), on file with authors.

Ravi P. Ramchandani, "The Stalling Effort: The Harvard Law School Endowment Campaign of 1925–1927" (student research paper, Harvard Law School, 2011), on file with authors.

Peter Rees, "Roscoe Pound and the Nazis" (student research paper, Boston College Law School, 2014), on file with the authors.

Peter Rees, "Roscoe Pound and the Nazis" (research assistant report, Boston College Law School, 2017), on file with the authors.

Charles Riordan, "Dean Sacks Timeline by Subject: Finances" (student research report, Boston College Law School, 2015), on file with the authors.

Charles Riordan, "General Historical Timeline: 1970–1980" (student research memo, Boston College Law School, 2015), on file with the authors.

Joshua Rubenstein, "A History of the Law Income Protection Plan at Harvard Law School" (student research paper, Harvard Law School, 2000), on file with the authors.

Christopher W. Schmidt, "The Failure of Reform: Legal Education at Harvard Law School, 1934–1946" (student research paper, Harvard Law School, 2006), on file with the authors.

Mark Severs, "A Look at the JD-MBA Program of Harvard Law School and Harvard Business School" (student research paper, Harvard Law School, 2011), on file with the authors.

Myliefer Shaikh, "Manley O. Hudson, as Professor and Lawyer-Statesman" (student research paper, Harvard Law School, 2001), on file with the authors.

John Sheeseley, "Ezra Ripley Thayer: Dean of the Harvard Law School 1910–1915" (student research paper, Harvard Law School, 2002), on file with the authors.

Brando S. Starkey, "Two Steps Forward Then Two Steps Back: The Black Story of Harvard Law School" (student research paper, Harvard Law School, 2008), on file with the authors.

Kimberly Ruthsatz Stephens, "False Triumph: The Strange History behind the Supposed Vindication of the Fifth Amendment during the 1950s Communist Investigation" (student research paper, Harvard Law School, 2007), on file with the authors.

Dan Traficonte, "'Soul of This Institution': Faculty Conflict in the 1980s and the Making of Today's Harvard Law School" (student research paper, Harvard Law School, 2016), on file with the authors.

Geoffrey Upton, "Unwise Restraints: An Oral History of Gay, Lesbian and Bisexual Student Experience at Harvard Law School" (student research paper, Harvard Law School, 2003), on file with the authors but sealed.

Steven Van Dyke, "The Trial of Sacco and Vanzetti at Harvard Law School" (student research paper, Boston College Law School, 2008), on file with the authors.

Thiru Vignarajah, "President's Perspectives: A History of Student Writing on the *Harvard Law Review*, 1887–1952" (student research paper, Harvard Law School, 2005), on file with the authors.

Denise Villeneuve, "Women at Harvard Law School: The First Class" (student research paper, Harvard Law School, 2001), on file with the authors.

Lance Wade, "Louis Brandeis, Julian Mack, and Felix Frankfurter: Their Lives with Abbott Lawrence Lowell" (student research paper, Boston College Law School, 2002), on file with the authors.

Cory Wishengrad, "Changing Harvard Law School, 1966–1974" (student research paper, Harvard Law School, 1999), on file with the authors.

Alexander M. Wolf, "Harvard Law School Courses during Dean Erwin Griswold's Administration, 1946–47–1966–67" (research assistant report, Harvard Law School, 2017), on file with the authors.

Alexander M. Wolf, "Harvard Law School Personnel Counts, from 1946–47 through 1967–68" (research assistant report, Harvard Law School, 2017), on file with the authors.

Alexander M. Wolf, "The Harvard Law School Faculty under the Deanship of Erwin Nathaniel Griswold" (student research paper, Harvard Law School, 2012), on file with the authors.

Angela Ann-Hwey Wu, "Contextualizing 'Sociological Jurisprudence': Dean Roscoe Pound in the Republic of China 1946–1948" (student research paper, Harvard Law School, 2006), on file with the authors.

Publications with Research Assistants, Cited

Bruce A. Kimball and Benjamin A. Johnson, "The Inception of the Meaning and Significance of Endowment in American Higher Education, 1890–1930," *Teachers College Record* 114 (2012): 1–32.

Bruce A. Kimball and Jeremy B. Luke, "Historical Dimensions of the 'Cost Disease' in US Higher Education, 1870s–2010s," *Social Science History* 42 (2018): 29–55.

Bruce A. Kimball and Jeremy B. Luke, "Measuring Cost Escalation in the Formative Era of U.S. Higher Education, 1875–1930," *Historical Methods: A Journal of Quantitative and Interdisciplinary History* 49 (2016): 198–219.

Bruce A. Kimball, Jeremy B. Luke, and Jamie M. Brown, "The Formative Financial Era of the 'Major Professional Schools': Medicine, Law, and Business at Columbia and Harvard, 1890–1950," in *The Economics of Higher Education in the United States,* ed. Thomas Adam and A. Burcu Bayram (Texas A&M University Press, 2019), 124–194.

Bruce A. Kimball and Brian R. Shull, "The Ironical Exclusion of Women from Harvard Law School, 1870–1900," *Journal of Legal Education* 58 (2008): 3–31.

Peter Rees, "Nathan Roscoe Pound and the Nazis," *Boston College Law Review* 60 (May 2019): 1313–1347.

Index

Note: end note information is denoted with an n and note number following the page number.